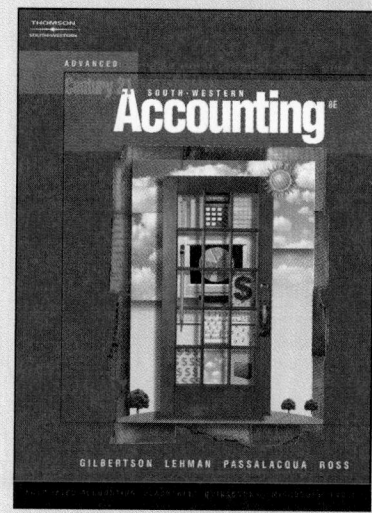

CENTURY 21 ACCOUNTING, 8E

Gilbertson, Lehman, and Ross

A Proven Century. An Innovative Century.
Discover the Century Crafted with Your Needs in Mind!

Discover the text that teachers and students have relied upon for decades! Featuring time-tested features and ground-breaking innovations that set the standard, *Century 21 Accounting* has guided countless students to accounting success.

In this edition, the trusted approach and comprehensive support that have defined this market-leading text are even stronger.

In the following pages, you'll find a wealth of enhancements and updates—a simplified organization featuring earlier coverage of corporations . . . new features and real-world examples that encourage learning . . . the latest technology, integrated to keep students involved, connected, and a step ahead of today's changing business times . . . and more!

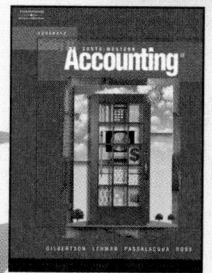

Your Century, Your Way—
Proven Choices and Solutions for Your Course

Only *Century 21 Accounting, 8e* provides you with these choices:

- *Century 21 Accounting, 8e*—Multicolumn Journal (with Student CD)

  The "Blue Text" starts with the five-column multicolumn journal, then moves into special journals in part two. (0-538-97275-0)

- *Century 21 Accounting, 8e*—General Journal (with Student CD)

  The "Green Text" begins with a two-column general journal and then introduces students to special journals in part two. (0-538-97255-6)

- *Century 21 Accounting Advanced, 8e* (with Student CD)

  The "Red Text" takes your students' corporate accounting proficiency to a new level of excellence. (0-538-97229-7)

A CENTURY OF INNOVATIONS, CHOICES, AND SOLUTIONS

For a complete list of your choices and solutions, see pages 14–15.

THE POWER OF CHOICES & SOLUTIONS 21

INNOVATIONS THAT REACH TODAY'S STUDENTS

Reorganized, Clear Approach—Based on your input, we've reorganized and streamlined this edition to simplify the presentation for students and make teaching easier for you. Using the proven teaching techniques you've trusted for years, *Century 21 Accounting, 8e:*

• starts with proprietorships organized as service businesses

• progresses to corporations organized as merchandising businesses

• concludes with special topics, partnerships, and recording international sales and electronic transactions

UNIQUE! The Student Companion CD-ROM—Packaged **FREE with New Copies of the Text**—Exclusive to *Century 21,* this CD-ROM provides the tools students need to understand and prepare for accounting success. It includes a spreadsheet tutorial, *Winning Edge* tools for competitive event preparation, *Automated Accounting* data files, electronic flash cards, important Web links, worksheets and PowerPoint presentations, portfolio assessment tools, and much more. *For complete details, see Page 8.*

Integrated Technology Tools Throughout the Text—This edition offers a perfect blend of cutting-edge software—including Peachtree, QuickBooks, Microsoft Excel, Xtra!, and *Automated Accounting*—to provide students with a solid understanding of principles. *See the details on Pages 8–9.*

STRENGTHS THAT SET *CENTURY 21* APART AND YOUR STUDENTS AHEAD

We've listened . . . This edition features a simplified organization—improving students' understanding and making it easier for you to cover all the fundamentals in a single school year. Highlights include:

- **New! Corporations are presented early in the text**—enabling you to cover this important content early in the year.
- **T accounts are always used** to analyze transactions into debit and credit parts to increase student comprehension of journalizing transactions.
- **New! Actual Source Documents are presented with each new transaction** in the text to provide objective evidence for journalizing every transaction.
- **New! Source Documents are also included in the Working Papers** for selected end-of-chapter problems.
- **Each chapter is divided into 3–4 short, accessible lessons** that cover 1–2 concepts for maximum understanding. Corresponding assessment activities, which include application problems, allow for immediate feedback.

TABLE OF CONTENTS

FOR ADVANCED STUDENTS
Century 21 Accounting Advanced, 8e
(with Student CD)
takes your students to the next level.
See page 13 for details.

A CENTURY OF PROVEN INNOVATION

3

NEW! Accounting in the Real World— Each chapter introduction spotlights an actual business familiar to students such as amazon.com, Gap, Hershey, Verizon, Tommy Hilfiger, Toyota, Walt Disney, and many more. Intriguing questions demonstrate how the chapter's content applies to business today.

Gap, Inc.

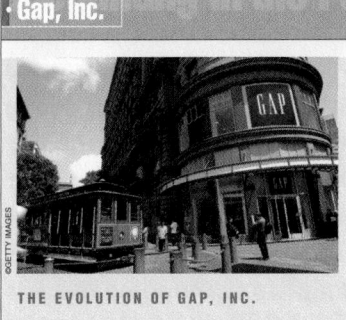

©GETTY IMAGES

THE EVOLUTION OF GAP, INC.

Many of today's most notable companies had very humble beginnings. Gap, Inc., began in 1969 when Don and Doris Fisher opened a clothing store in San Francisco. The company grew quickly, becoming a publicly traded company in just seven years.

The company expanded beyond its Gap store concept in 1983 by purchasing Banana Republic, a small safari and travel clothing company. Gap further extended its penetration into the clothing market by introducing the Old Navy brand in 1994. The rest, as they say, is history. With over 3,000 stores, Gap, Inc., is now a major force in the apparel industry.

Each of its clothing brands targets different customers. The original Gap brand targets style-conscious customers in the casual specialty market. Banana Republic targets men and women who want more sophisticated seasonal fashions, shoes, personal care products, intimate apparel, and gifts for the home. Old Navy is more value focused, providing families with great fashions at affordable prices.

ical Thinking

should a single set of financial statements be prepared for Gap Inc., or should financial statements be prepared for each brand?

ow would the chart of accounts differ among the three brands?

making ethical decisions
Integrity—Doing What's Right

What does the word *integrity* mean to you? The word is derived from a Latin word meaning "wholeness," "completeness," and "purity." Many companies include an interpretation of integrity in their code of conduct.

"We always try to do the right thing." —Procter & Gamble

"To say what we mean, to deliver what we promise, to fulfill our commitments, and to stand for what is right." —Lockheed Martin

"We do the right thing without compromise. We avoid even the appearance of impropriety." —Intel

Companies with integrity have an absolute commitment to do what is right in all business activities. Integrity is ultimately the most critical component to long-term business success. A business that fails to act with integrity will soon find it difficult to hire employees, deal with suppliers, and enjoy repeat customers.

The American Institute of Certified Public Accountants recognizes that integrity is critical for maintaining public confidence in its members' professional services. "Integrity is an element of character fundamental to professional recognition. It is the quality from which the public trust derives and the benchmark against which a member must ultimately test all decisions."

Instructions

In private, write down five qualities that you believe people of high integrity possess. Using a typical grading schedule (A+, A, A−, etc.), identify how you believe your friends, teachers, and others would rate your integrity. Do you have integrity as defined by the three companies above?

270   Chapter 10   Journalizing Sales and Cash Receipts Using Special Journals

NEW! Making Ethical Decisions— Situational ethical dilemmas appear in every chapter. These assist students with decision-making and critical thinking in light of current events, highlighting the ethical policies and business decisions of real companies.

©GETTY IMAGES/PHOTODISC

business structures
Forming a Corporation

Many businesses need amounts of capital that cannot be easily provided by a proprietorship. These businesses choose to organize using another form of business. An organization with the legal rights of a person and which many persons may own is called a **corporation**. A corporation is formed by receiving approval from a state or federal agency. Each unit of ownership in a corporation is called a **share of stock**. Total shares of ownership in a corporation are called **capital stock**. An owner of one or more shares of a corporation is called a **stockholder**.

A corporation is a business organization that has the legal rights of a person. A corporation can own property, incur liabilities, and enter into contracts in its own name. A corporation may also sell ownership in itself. A person becomes an owner of a corporation by purchasing shares of stock.

The principal difference between the accounting records of proprietorships and corporations is in the capital accounts.

Proprietorships have a single capital and drawing account for the owner. A corporation has separate capital accounts for the stock issued and for the earnings kept in the business, which will be explained in more detail in Chapter 16. As in proprietorships, information in a corporation's accounting system is kept separate from the personal records of its owners. [CONCEPT: Business Entity] Periodic financial statements must be sent to the stockholders of the corporation to report the financial activities of the business.

Critical Thinking

1. The names of many corporations include the words *Corporation, Incorporated, Corp.,* or *Inc.* in their names. Based on their names, identify several corporations in your area.

2. Why do you think many very large companies are organized as corporations?

234   Chapter 9   Journalizing Purchases and Cash Payments

NEW! Business Structures— The text discusses business structures—proprietorships, corporations, and partnerships— to focus students on the practical business and legal issues involved.

POSTING AN ENTRY TO WRITE OFF AN UNCOLLECTIBLE ACCOUNT RECEIVABLE

Illustrations are consistently placed at the top of the page with step-by-step instructions and key descriptions that get students engaged—reinforcing concepts throughout the text.

analyzing Best Buy's financial statements

Annual reports contain a report by management designed to inform potential investors and business partners about how the financial statements were prepared. The report describes, in detail, accounting and management policies that are followed to ensure that the amounts on the financial statements can be relied upon for making business decisions.

Instructions: Use the Report of Best Buy Management on Appendix B page B-17 to answer the following questions.

1. Who is responsible for the preparation of the Best Buy's financial statements?
2. What is the system of internal control designed to do?
3. What do internal auditors do?
4. What does the Audit Committee oversee?
5. What kind of assurance can the internal control system provide with respect to financial statement preparation?

NEW! Analyzing Best Buy's Financial Statements—Throughout the book, students apply what they've learned as they analyze business performance in all aspects of operations using financial statements from a real business.

Xtra!
Careers.
accountingxtra.swlearning.com

careers in accounting

Anna McNeese, Future Certified Financial Planner

When Anna McNeese started college, entering the field of accounting wasn't part of her career plan. Through high school she worked at a mental health facility and enjoyed the personal contact she had with the clients in the physical therapy department. But an interest in business (and a sudden lack of interest in biology) led her to change majors as a college sophomore.

After considering the different business degrees offered, she decided to go into accounting. Anna recalls, "I knew I was interested in business, and I thought accounting would be the most challenging. I also heard about the great job market, and since I was going through school during the height of the WorldCom/Enron scandals, any degree that could guarantee job placement was attractive."

But her desire to affect lives personally didn't seem to mix with the large corporate jobs that recruiters from the "Big Four" firms were offering. So when one of her professors told her about a part-time job working for Ernie George, a certified financial planner, Anna saw an opportunity to experience a different type of career.

By working closely with Mr. George and his assistant, Anna has been able use her accounting background to better understand the stock market and what it takes to advise people on how to invest their money. She has found that as a certified financial planner, Mr. George has a close personal relationship with his clients and is able to make the impact that she dreamed of in her early college career.

"I will finish my bachelor's of accountancy next year and immediately enroll in the Master of Taxation program," Anna explains. "Within five years of graduation, I hope to have obtained my certified public accountant (CPA) and certified financial planner (CFP) certifications and go into private practice as a certified financial planner with professional tax expertise."

Salary Range: Median annual earnings of financial planners were $56,680 in 2002, according to the *Occupational Outlook Handbook.* Over 25% of financial planners earn more than $100,000. (Source: Bureau of Labor Statistics, U.S. Department of Labor, *Occupational Outlook Handbook, 2004–05 Edition*; Financial Analysts and Personal Financial Advisors, on the Internet at www.bls.gov/oco/ocos259.htm [visited October 11, 2004].)

Qualifications: A college degree is required, and professional certification is recommended. Financial planners must have good communication skills. Because many financial planners are self-employed, they must also possess the skills necessary to manage a business.

Occupational Outlook: More and more people are choosing alternative ways to plan for retirement. The complexity of the stock market and the tax laws (which can limit how much you can save) have increased the need for professionals who can give sound advice to individuals interested in investing.

NEW! Careers in Accounting—Interviews with individuals working in accounting and related fields highlight educational requirements and future trends in accounting.

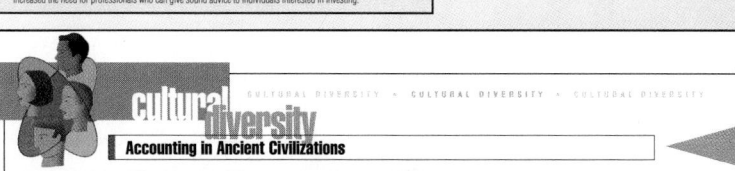

cultural diversity

Accounting in Ancient Civilizations

In the ancient civilizations of Asia Minor and northern Africa, most citizens were illiterate. The scribe, who could read and write, became a very important person in the society. Of ancient Hebrew origin, the scribe has been called the forerunner of today's accountant.

Public scribes often recorded transactions as citizens arrived to do business. Most scribes recorded transactions on moist clay tablets that were then dried in the sun. Therefore, permanent records of transactions were not possible until scribes could write them down on clay tablets.

The Greeks invented coined money around 630 B.C., which facilitated assigning values to transactions.

The Babylonians in Asia Minor used an early form of banking. They transferred funds with a system resembling our modern-day checking accounts, one of the first uses of business documents.

These early practices provided the foundation for today's financial system and recordkeeping methods.

Critical Thinking
1. Estimate how many transactions might occur in a single day in a modern grocery store with which you are familiar.
2. List the number of different methods of payments that are accepted by modern grocery stores.

Cultural Diversity—Students see how different cultures around the world and throughout history have contributed to the development of accounting.

A CENTURY OF PROVEN INNOVATION

5

■ **NEW! Enrichment Problems**—These new end-of-chapter *Graphing Workshop, Auditing for Errors,* and *Source Documents* problems give students extra accounting practice and the opportunity to hone important skills.

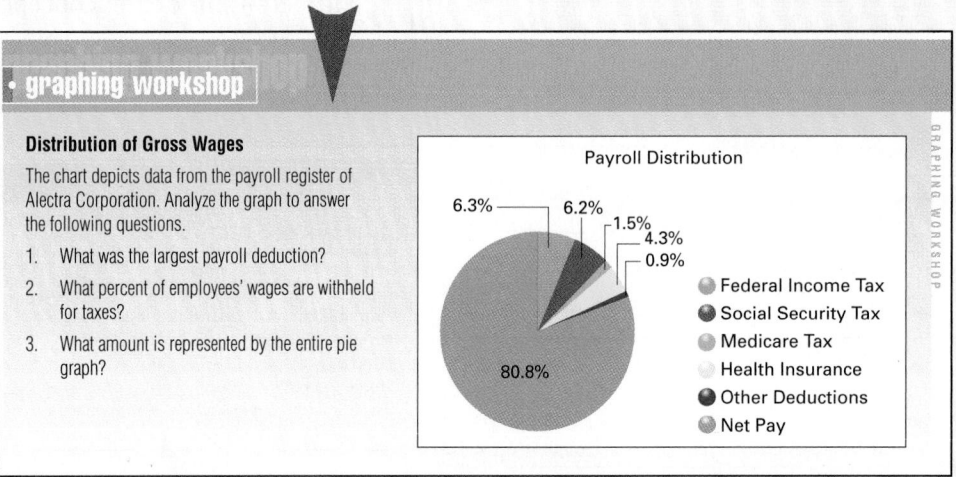

graphing workshop

Distribution of Gross Wages

The chart depicts data from the payroll register of Alectra Corporation. Analyze the graph to answer the following questions.

1. What was the largest payroll deduction?
2. What percent of employees' wages are withheld for taxes?
3. What amount is represented by the entire pie graph?

Payroll Distribution

- 6.3%
- 6.2%
- 1.5%
- 4.3%
- 0.9%
- 80.8%

- Federal Income Tax
- Social Security Tax
- Medicare Tax
- Health Insurance
- Other Deductions
- Net Pay

GRAPHING WORKSHOP

SCANS workplace competency

Basic Skill: Listening

Concept: You receive many verbal messages every day. You must attend to them, interpret them, and often respond to them. Sometimes you simply need to understand the message, as when a work task is explained. Sometimes the verbal message is intended to teach you something. Other times you need to evaluate a verbal message. In the workplace, some of your responsibilities will be communicated verbally. In school or in your personal life, you may receive verbal messages that you must interpret and then apply to meet some requirement.

Application: Describe a situation in which you were given a verbal assignment and misunderstood it in some way. Describe what you could have done to realize that you did not fully understand the requirement and how you could have clarified it.

SCANS WORKPLACE COMPETENCY

■ **NEW! SCANS Workplace Competency Activities**—Exercises prepare your students with SCANS skills at the end of each chapter, as activities reinforce the basic skills needed for a successful career.

■ **NEW!** *Winning Edge*—
http://winningedge.swlearning.com
Students can now prepare for success at FBLA and BPA competitive events with *Winning Edge* reinforcement problems at selected points within the text.

A CENTURY OF PROVEN INNOVATION

THE CHOICE FOR TECHNOLOGY

NEW! Internet Research Activities—At the beginning of every chapter, students search the Internet to answer questions related to chapter content, giving them practice in developing technology and research skills.

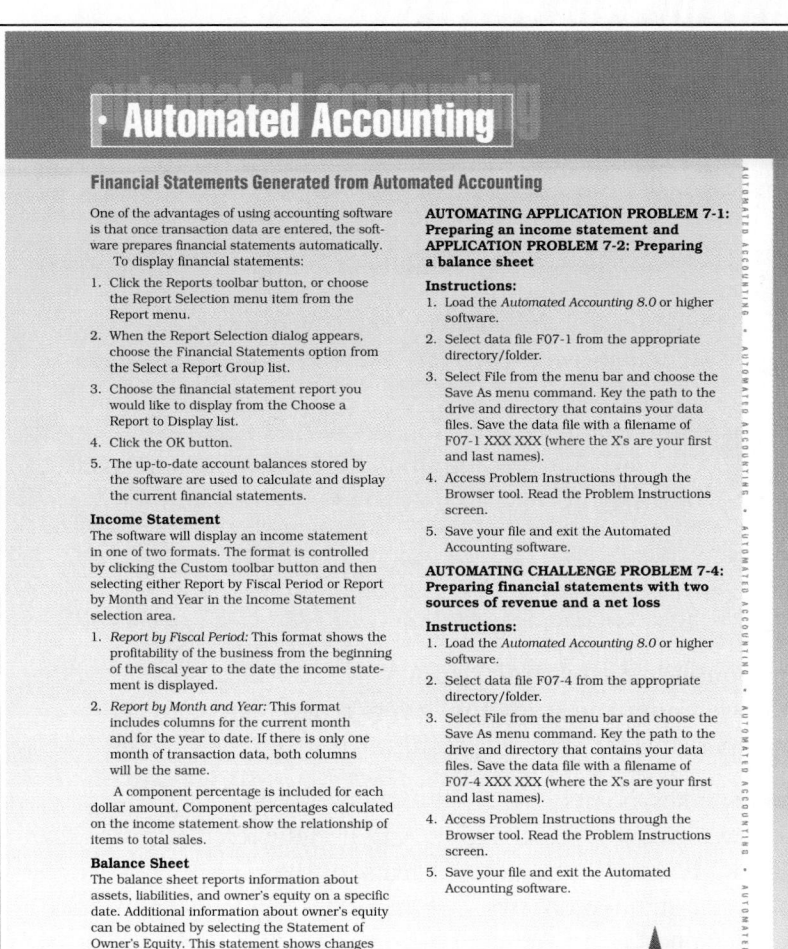

Automated Accounting

Financial Statements Generated from Automated Accounting

One of the advantages of using accounting software is that once transaction data are entered, the software prepares financial statements automatically.

To display financial statements:

1. Click the Reports toolbar button, or choose the Report Selection menu item from the Report menu.
2. When the Report Selection dialog appears, choose the Financial Statements option from the Select a Report Group list.
3. Choose the financial statement report you would like to display from the Choose a Report to Display list.
4. Click the OK button.
5. The up-to-date account balances stored by the software are used to calculate and display the current financial statements.

Income Statement
The software will display an income statement in one of two formats. The format is controlled by clicking the Custom toolbar button and then selecting either Report by Fiscal Period or Report by Month and Year in the Income Statement selection area.

1. *Report by Fiscal Period:* This format shows the profitability of the business from the beginning of the fiscal year to the date the income statement is displayed.
2. *Report by Month and Year:* This format includes columns for the current month and for the year to date. If there is only one month of transaction data, both columns will be the same.

A component percentage is included for each dollar amount. Component percentages calculated on the income statement show the relationship of items to total sales.

Balance Sheet
The balance sheet reports information about assets, liabilities, and owner's equity on a specific date. Additional information about owner's equity can be obtained by selecting the Statement of Owner's Equity. This statement shows changes to the capital account during the period.

AUTOMATING APPLICATION PROBLEM 7-1: Preparing an income statement and APPLICATION PROBLEM 7-2: Preparing a balance sheet

Instructions:
1. Load the *Automated Accounting 8.0* or higher software.
2. Select data file F07-1 from the appropriate directory/folder.
3. Select File from the menu bar and choose the Save As menu command. Key the path to the drive and directory that contains your data files. Save the data file with a filename of F07-1 XXX XXX (where the X's are your first and last names).
4. Access Problem Instructions through the Browser tool. Read the Problem Instructions screen.
5. Save your file and exit the Automated Accounting software.

AUTOMATING CHALLENGE PROBLEM 7-4: Preparing financial statements with two sources of revenue and a net loss

Instructions:
1. Load the *Automated Accounting 8.0* or higher software.
2. Select data file F07-4 from the appropriate directory/folder.
3. Select File from the menu bar and choose the Save As menu command. Key the path to the drive and directory that contains your data files. Save the data file with a filename of F07-4 XXX XXX (where the X's are your first and last names).
4. Access Problem Instructions through the Browser tool. Read the Problem Instructions screen.
5. Save your file and exit the Automated Accounting software.

EDGAR—PART 1

Go to the homepage for the Securities and Exchange Commission (SEC) (www.sec.gov). The SEC provides almost instant access to forms filed with the SEC. Investors can access these forms through a system called EDGAR. Click on "Filings and Forms (EDGAR)." Search the site to find out more about EDGAR.

Instructions

1. Each letter in "EDGAR" is an abbreviation for a word. List the word connected with each letter in EDGAR.
2. Briefly state how EDGAR helps investors.

Automated Accounting 8.0 has been seamlessly integrated into each chapter—This leading software combines the functionality of commercial software with the strength of educational support to make both teaching and learning accounting easy.

- *Automated Accounting* provides solid instruction on the foundations of accounting software without limiting instruction to a specific commercial software package.

AUTOMATED ACCOUNTING · **PEACHTREE** · **QUICKBOOKS** · **EXCEL**

NEW! QuickBooks, Peachtree, and Microsoft Excel Problems—Selected end-of-chapter problems use these popular commercial accounting software packages, familiarizing students with these programs for tomorrow's workplace.

7

DISCOVER THE BEST 21

TECHNOLOGY SOLUTIONS PERFECT FOR TODAY'S STUDENTS

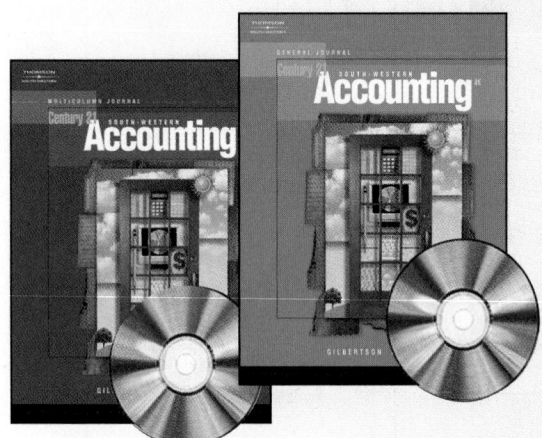

NEW! A FREE Student Companion CD-ROM packaged with every text!
This CD offers exclusive learning tools that ensure accounting understanding and confidence, featuring:

- *Winning Edge* tools for competitive event preparation
- Important Web links
- PowerPoint presentations
- Crossword puzzles

- Math worksheets
- Portfolio assessment
- Electronic flash cards of key terms
- Interactive spreadsheets
- And much more!

FREE—Xtra!
http://accountingxtra.swlearning.com
This online learning and study tool offers a truly interactive learning experience for students, featuring:

- Summary of key points
- e-lectures
- Accounting FAQs
- Interactive, game-like reviews of every lesson
- Online chapter review and test prep
- Web links
- Graphing workshop
- *NewsEdge*

- Crossword puzzles
- Additional exercises, problems, quizzes
- Spanish and English glossaries
- *Winning Edge* tools for competitive event preparation
- Workplace readiness materials
- Student portfolio activities
- And more!

Personal Trainer® 3.0
http://c21personaltrainer.swlearning.com
Personal Trainer takes the work out of homework—boosting your students' grades while reducing your own course preparation time and effort. Students can enhance their skills with practice problems, receive immediate feedback, and complete assigned homework, all from the convenience of their computer. An integrated gradebook makes it simple to track your students' progress and review their completed assignments online. Contact your sales representative to order **Personal Trainer** packaged with the *Century 21 Accounting* text of your choice.

- **Adobe eBook** *for Century 21 Accounting, 8e*—Take your traditional course to a new level with digital material that offers the same rich visuals and illustrations as the printed text! Students view **eBooks** on their computers using the free Adobe® Acrobat® Book Reader.

- **Accounting Connection Software**

  This interactive tutorial CD-ROM takes students step-by-step through accounting concepts such as T accounts, ledgers, journals, and postings.

- **Automated Accounting 8.0**

  Integrated into every chapter of *Century 21 Accounting, 8e,* this software combines the functionality of commercial software with proven educational features to make teaching and learning easier. See Page 12 for details.

- *South-Western Accounting with Peachtree Complete®*

  Students learn to journalize accounting transactions, post to ledger accounts, and prepare financial statements using Peachtree software and *Century 21 Accounting* data files. An individual version of the Peachtree software is available on the CD that accompanies this text. A site license for Peachtree Complete is available separately from South-Western.

- *South-Western Accounting for QuickBooks® Pro™*

  Students learn to use QuickBooks software and the principles of *Century 21 Accounting* as they journalize accounting transactions, post to ledger accounts, and prepare financial statements with this text and data CD. A site license is available from Intuit, Inc. or other software vendors.

TRUSTED SOLUTIONS FOR TODAY'S STUDENTS NOW EVEN BETTER

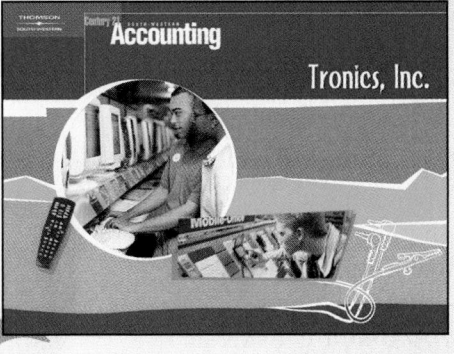

- **NEW! Automated and manual simulations** give students hands-on, real-world experience in accounting practice:

  - **Simulation 1: Eddie Ortega, DJ**—Students work with this service business organized as a proprietorship after Ch. 8.

  - **Simulation 2: Zenith Global Imports**—Students practice skills with this merchandising business organized as a corporation after Ch. 16.

  - **Simulation 3: Tronics, Inc.**—Students reinforce skills with this merchandising business organized as a corporation after Ch. 22.

- **Working Papers**—These reliable worksheets provide comprehensive forms for completing end-of-lesson, end-of-chapter, and reinforcement activities.

- **Dictionaries in Spanish and English** assist students in learning the language of accounting.

■ **Instructor's Resource CD-ROM featuring LessonView**—You'll find all the support you need for each *Century 21 Accounting* title with this all-in-one convenient tool. The CD includes:

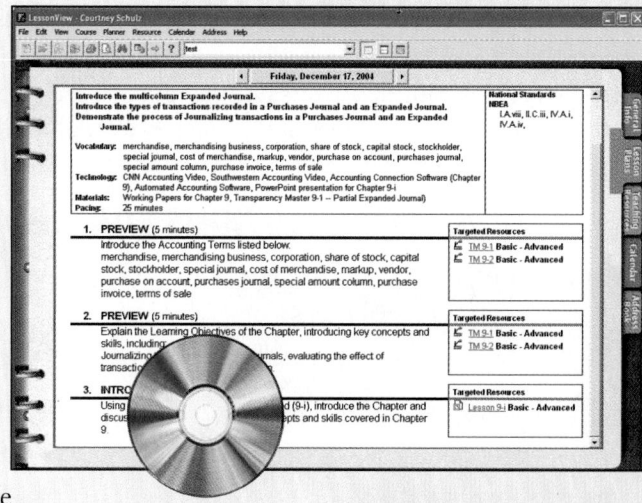

- **NEW LessonView Software**—This state-of-the-art electronic planner and resource library gives you the flexibility to use lesson plans provided in the software, customize these plans, or create plans from scratch using convenient tools. Links to a large variety of teaching resources save time. Both lesson plans and teaching resources are aligned with national as well as many state and local standards.

- Variety of lesson plans for traditional or block schedules

- Transparency and blackline masters

- PowerPoint presentations

- *Winning Edge* tools for competitive test preparation for BPA and FBLA

- Crossword puzzles and solutions

- Supplemental accounting problems and solutions—one per chapter

- Spanish and English accounting glossaries

- International business case studies

- Quizzes, correlation guides, and much more

■ **FREE—Xtra!** http://accountingxtra.swlearning.com

A password-protected Teacher Resources area includes a wealth of supplemental materials:

- Solutions

- Lesson plans

- PowerPoint presentations

- Quizzes, drills, and other teaching tools

- Block scheduling correlation with *Century 21 Accounting*

- Business ethics presentation

- Time management activities and workplace readiness skills

■ **Video News Clips from CNBC/Dow Jones-Mike Hegedus's "Outside the Box"**—provide an entertaining and enlightening view into American entrepreneurship, business structures, markets, and products. A brief introduction and series of questions and activities guide students to connect "Outside the Box" to *Century 21 Accounting* material.

SPEND MORE TIME TEACHING WITH LESS PREPARATION AND EFFORT

No one offers more teaching solutions and technology, backed by reliable service and a responsive commitment to helping you provide your students with the best in accounting education. You'll find a wealth of resources for preparation, testing, and presentation— all designed to minimize your preparation time while maximizing your impact within the classroom.

- *New!* **Wraparound Teacher's Edition** (Multicolumn: 0-538-97296-3; General Journal: 0-538-97267-X)—Reduced student pages are surrounded with comprehensive teaching tips and correlated support, including:
  - Overviews of each part and chapter within the text
  - Teaching strategies
  - Resource Integration Guide
  - Effective teaching model lesson plans
  - Check figures

- **Teacher's Resource Kit** (Multicolumn: 0-538-97301-3; General Journal: 0-538-97272-6)— This comprehensive teaching solution provides all of the resources you need in one place, such as:
  - Lesson plans
  - Solutions for all simulations, text problems and worksheets
  - Transparency samplers
  - Accounting masters (blank accounting forms)
  - Career success and assessment resources
  - Enrichment topics

- **Teacher's Editions** of working papers, recycling problems, and chapter and part tests

- **Solutions, Rulings,** and **Illustrative Transparencies**

YOUR COMPLETE ASSESSMENT SOLUTION

- **Complete Assessment Binder**—Find all the testing resources you need in one convenient location, including *ExamView,* Chapter and Part Test masters, and solutions.

- **ExamView** *ExamView* **Computerized Testing Software**—Create, customize, and deliver tests and study guides in minutes—in print, online, or over a LAN! *ExamView's* "what you see is what you get" inter- face, along with a *Quick Test Wizard* and an *Online Test Wizard,* guides you through the test creation process. Includes all the items in the printed *Test Bank*.

- **Chapter and Part Test Masters**—Two separate test masters (for every chapter and part in the text) include longer problems and objective questions.

AUTOMATED INNOVATION FOR THE NEXT CENTURY

Automated Accounting 8.0 Software

This cutting-edge software combines the functionality of commercial software with proven educational features that make teaching and learning computerized accounting easy. Students gain in-depth experience with computerized accounting problems as they use this software.

- *Automated Accounting 8.0* is seamlessly integrated into every chapter of *Century 21 Accounting* for cohesive practice.

- No prior knowledge of computers or computerized accounting is needed.

- Students learn how to apply accounting concepts using key business applications, such as spreadsheets.

- *An Electronic Auditor* function reduces your grading time by allowing you to check every problem automatically.

- *Automated Accounting 8.0* **data files** contain opening balance data for each Automated Accounting problem. These are available for use on Windows®-compatible computers.

Update Now with the *Century 21 Accounting, 8e* Teacher Plus Pack

If you are currently using *Century 21 Accounting, 6e* or *7e,* with *Automated Accounting 8.0,* you can easily update your data files, simulation data files, and Electronic Auditors for use with *Century 21 Accounting, 8e* first-year course and advanced course with the Teacher Plus Pack.

12

A CENTURY OF ADVANCED INSTRUCTION

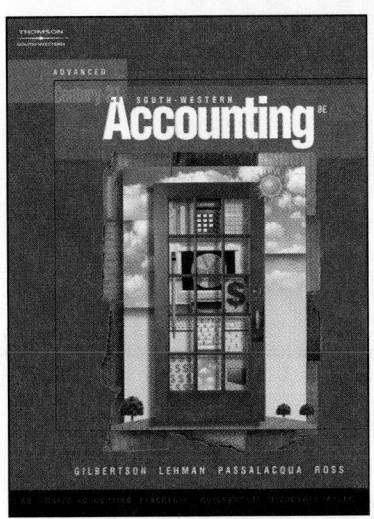

CENTURY 21 ACCOUNTING ADVANCED, 8E

Gilbertson, Lehman, Ross, and Passalaqua

Help your students take their accounting proficiency to a new level of excellence with the latest edition of this leading corporate accounting text.

Critical accounting skills and contemporary computer practices prepare students for ongoing accounting work and business success. A wealth of student and instructor tools delivers the power and progress you expect only from *Century 21.*

A TRADITION OF INNOVATION

- **NEW! A FREE Student Companion CD-ROM** is packaged with each new text. Features include:
  - *Winning Edge* competitive event preparation
  - Electronic flash cards of key terms
  - Crossword puzzles
  - Web links
  - PowerPoint presentations
  - Math worksheets
  - Portfolio assessment
  - Interactive spreadsheets

- **NEW! Technology integrated throughout this new edition** prepares students for success using the latest from *Automated Accounting 8.0,* Peachtree, QuickBooks, Microsoft Excel, and Xtra!

- **NEW! Expanded coverage of important topics** reinforces skills learned in the first-year course, while adding new topics such as management accounting, cost accounting, not-for-profit accounting, and financial analysis.

- **NEW! Real-World Businesses**—students learn how accounting concepts apply to the real world as each chapter presents actual business situations in companies familiar to students.

- **Clear organization for student understanding**—T accounts are always used to analyze transactions into debit and credit parts.

- **NEW! Automated and manual simulations** give students hands-on, real-world experience in accounting practice:
  - Simulation 1: **Sounds, Inc.**—This simulation features a departmentalized merchandising business organized as a corporation.
  - Simulation 2: **First Class ImageWear, Inc.** — Students work with a merchandising business organized as a corporation.
  - Simulation 3: **Progressive Badge Company**— This simulation features a manufacturing business organized as a corporation.

- **Short application problems**—found at the point of use, and at the end of each lesson and each chapter—ensure students understand concepts before they complete longer mastery and challenge problems.

- **Consistent placement of illustrations** with step-by-step instructions and descriptive text helps to clarify and reinforce accounting concepts throughout the text.

- **Each chapter is divided into 3–4 short, accessible lessons** that include corresponding assessment activities for immediate feedback.

- **Chart of Accounts** on part opening pages provides easy reference to key material throughout the course.

13

A CHOICE AND SOLUTION FOR EVERY ACCOUNTING COURSE

Century 21 Accounting 8E Multicolumn Journal

Item	ISBN
Text/CD (hardcover, 4-color, 784 pages) Chapters 1–24	0-538-97275-0
Introductory Text/CD (hardcover, 4-color, 528 pages) Chapters 1–16	0-538-97281-5
Adobe eBook	0-538-44216-6
Teacher Editions	
Wraparound Teacher's Edition	0-538-97296-3
Instructor's Resource CD	0-538-97295-5
Instructor's Resource Kit	0-538-97301-3
Working Papers	
Chapters 1–16	0-538-97283-1
Chapters 17–24	0-538-97284-X
Bundle Chapters 1–24	0-538-97282-3
Recycling Problems	0-538-97285-8
Teacher Editions Working Papers	
Teacher's Edition 1–16	0-538-97298-X
Teacher's Edition 17–24	0-538-97299-8
Teacher's Edition Recycling Problems	0-538-97300-5
Simulations	
Eddie Ortega, DJ, Manual Simulation	0-538-97286-6
Eddie Ortega, DJ, Automated Simulation	0-538-97287-4
Zenith Global Imports, Manual Simulation	0-538-97288-2
Zenith Global Imports, Automated Simulation	0-538-97289-0
Tronics, Inc., Manual Simulation	0-538-97290-4
Tronics, Inc., Automated Simulation	0-538-97291-2
Simulation Keys	
Teacher's Key, Eddie Ortega, DJ, Manual Simulation	0-538-97302-1
Teacher's Key, Eddie Ortega, DJ, Automated Simulation	0-538-97303-X
Teacher's Key, Zenith Global Imports, Manual Simulation	0-538-97304-8
Teacher's Key, Zenith Global Imports, Automated Simulation	0-538-97305-6
Teacher's Key, Tronics, Inc., Manual Simulation	0-538-97306-4
Teacher's Key, Tronics, Inc., Automated Simulation	0-538-97307-2
Assessment	
Assessment Binder	0-538-97277-7
ExamView	0-538-97276-9
Print Chapter Tests 1–24	0-538-97292-0
Teacher's Edition Chapter Tests	0-538-44139-9
Transparencies	
4-color Illustrations (85)	0-538-44220-4
Rulings (24)	0-538-97293-9
Solutions (512)	0-538-44221-2
Videos	
Video	0-538-97278-5
Learning Aids	
English Dictionary of Accounting Terms	0-538-97308-0
Spanish Dictionary of Accounting Terms	0-538-97309-9
Technology	
Accounting Connection Tutorial CD	0-538-97279-3
Personal Trainer	0-538-44217-4

Century 21 Accounting 8E General Journal

Item	ISBN
Text/CD (hardcover, 4-color, 784 pages) Chapters 1–24	0-538-97255-6
Introductory Text/CD (hardcover, 4-color, 528 pages) Chapters 1–16	0-538-97259-9
Adobe eBook	0-538-44211-5
Teacher Editions	
Wraparound Teacher's Edition	0-538-97267-X
Instructor's Resource CD	0-538-97295-5
Instructor's Resource Kit	0-538-97272-6
Working Papers	
Chapters 1–16	0-538-97261-0
Chapters 17–24	0-538-97262-9
Bundle Chapters 1–24	0-538-97260-2
Recycling Problems	0-538-97263-7
Teacher Editions Working Papers	
Teacher's Edition 1–16	0-538-97269-6
Teacher's Edition 17–24	0-538-97270-X
Teacher's Edition Recycling Problems	0-538-97271-8
Simulations	
Eddie Ortega, DJ, Manual Simulation	0-538-97264-5

Order Your Choices and Solutions for Accounting Success Today with *Century 21 Accounting, 8e.* Call to Order: 1-800-824-5179

Eddie Ortega, DJ, Automated Simulation	0-538-97287-4
Zenith Global Imports, Manual Simulation	0-538-97288-2
Zenith Global Imports, Automated Simulation	0-538-97289-0
Tronics, Inc., Manual Simulation	0-538-97290-4
Tronics, Inc., Automated Simulation	0-538-97291-2
Simulation Keys	
Teacher's Key, Eddie Ortega, DJ, Manual Simulation	0-538-97273-4
Teacher's Key, Eddie Ortega, DJ, Automated Simulation	0-538-97303-X
Teacher's Key, Zenith Global Imports, Manual Simulation	0-538-97304-8
Teacher's Key, Zenith Global Imports, Automated Simulation	0-538-97305-6
Teacher's Key, Tronics, Inc., Manual Simulation	0-538-97306-4
Teacher's Key, Tronics, Inc., Automated Simulation	0-538-97307-2
Assessment	
Assessment Binder	0-538-97257-2
ExamView	0-538-97256-4
Print Chapter Tests 1–24	0-538-97266-1
Teacher's Edition Chapter Tests	0-538-44136-4
Transparencies	
4-color Illustrations (85)	0-538-44214-X
Rulings (24)	0-538-97293-9
Solutions (512)	0-538-44215-8
Videos	
Video	0-538-97278-5
Learning Aids	
English Dictionary of Accounting Terms	0-538-97308-0
Spanish Dictionary of Accounting Terms	0-538-97309-9
Technology	
Accounting Connection Tutorial CD	0-538-97279-3
Personal Trainer	0-538-44212-3

Century 21 Accounting Advanced 8E

Item	ISBN
Text/CD (hardcover, 4-color, 768 pages) Chapters 1–24	0-538-97229-7
Adobe eBook	0-538-44223-9
Teacher Editions	
Wraparound Teacher's Edition	0-538-97244-0
Instructor's Resource CD	0-538-97295-5
Instructor's Resource Kit	0-538-97249-1
Working Papers	
Chapters 1–9	0-538-97234-3
Chapters 10–24	0-538-97235-1
Bundle Chapters 1–24	0-538-97233-5
Recycling Problems	0-538-97236-X
Teacher Editions Working Papers	
Teacher's Edition 1–9	0-538-97246-7
Teacher's Edition 10–24	0-538-97247-5
Teacher's Edition Recycling Problems	0-538-97248-3
Simulations	
Sounds, Inc., Manual Simulation	0-538-97237-8
Sounds, Inc., Automated Simulation	0-538-97238-6
First Class Image Wear, Manual Simulation	0-538-97239-4
First Class Image Wear, Automated Simulation	0-538-97240-8
Progressive Badge, Manual Simulation	0-538-97241-6
Simulation Keys	
Teacher's Key, Sounds, Inc., Manual Simulation	0-538-97250-5
Teacher's Key, Sounds, Inc., Automated Simulation	0-538-97251-3
Teacher's Key, First Class Image Wear, Manual Simulation	0-538-97252-1
Teacher's Key, First Class Image Wear, Automated Simulation	0-538-97253-X
Teacher's Key, Progressive Badge, Manual Simulation	0-538-97254-8
Assessment	
Assessment Binder	0-538-97231-9
ExamView	0-538-97230-0
Print Chapter Tests 1–24	0-538-97242-4
Teacher's Edition Chapter Tests	0-538-44134-8
Learning Aids	
English Dictionary of Accounting Terms	0-538-97308-0
Spanish Dictionary of Accounting Terms	0-538-97309-9
Technology	
Personal Trainer	0-538-44224-7
Automated Accounting and Century 21 8E CD (site license, Windows/Macintosh)	0-538-44228-X
Automated Accounting and Century 21 8E CD (individual license, Windows/Macintosh, no electronic auditors)	0-538-97294-7
Plus Pack for Century 21 and Automated Accounting 8.0 (site license, Windows/Macintosh)	0-538-44229-8
Web Site	accountingxtra.swlearning.com

Order Your Choices and Solutions for Accounting Success Today with *Century 21 Accounting, 8e*. Call to Order: 1-800-824-5179

DISCOVER ASSIST 21

THE ACCOUNTING SELECTION SOFTWARE FOR INSTRUCTORS

TAKE THE GUESSWORK OUT OF YOUR ORDER TODAY!

Let ASSIST 8 help you determine the textbook and support materials best for your needs. ASSIST guides you through a series of questions to pinpoint your instructional needs. Based on your choice of textbooks, ASSIST:

- Identifies the appropriate support materials

- Describes any unfamiliar terms

- Allows you to easily "shop" electronically

- Automatically identifies the instructor support materials for each of your product choices

- Prints out a complete purchase order based upon your selections, and allows you to cut and paste the information into any Microsoft Office application

SOUTH-WESTERN CENTURY 21 ACCOUNTING EIGHTH EDITION

ASSIST 8E

Accounting Selection
Software for Instructors

YOUR CHOICE. *CENTURY 21* SOLUTIONS. ACCOUNTING SUCCESS.

ASSIST—YOUR CHOICE FOR EASY ORDERING

ADVANCED · ADVANCED · ADVANCED · ADVANCED · ADVANCED · ADVANCED ·

Century 21

SOUTH-WESTERN
Accounting 8E
WRAPAROUND TEACHER'S EDITION

CLAUDIA BIENIAS GILBERTSON, CPA
Teaching Professor
North Hennepin Community College
Brooklyn Park, Minnesota

MARK W. LEHMAN, CPA
Associate Professor
School of Accountancy
Mississippi State University
Starkville, Mississippi

DAN PASSALACQUA, MA
Oak Grove High School
San Jose, California

KENTON E. ROSS, CPA
Professor Emeritus of Accounting
Texas A&M University—Commerce
Commerce, Texas

THOMSON
SOUTH-WESTERN

Australia · Brazil · Canada · Mexico · Singapore · Spain · United Kingdom · United States

THOMSON

SOUTH-WESTERN

Advanced, Wraparound Teacher's Edition, Century 21 Accounting 8E
Claudia Bienias Gilbertson, CPA; Mark W. Lehman, CPA; Dan Passalacqua, MA; Kenton E. Ross, CPA

VP/Editorial Director:
Jack W. Calhoun

VP/Editor-in-Chief:
Karen Schmohe

Acquisitions Editor:
Marilyn Hornsby

Project Manager:
Carol Sturzenberger

Consulting Editor:
Bill Lee

Verification Editors:
Howard Rankin; Juli Cook

VP/Director of Marketing:
Carol Volz

Marketing Manager:
Courtney Schulz

Marketing Coordinator:
Angela Russo

Senior Promotions Manager:
Terron Sanders

Production Editor:
Kim Kusnerak

Production Manager:
Patricia Matthews Boies

Manufacturing Buyer:
Kevin Kluck

Manager of Technology-Editorial:
Liz Prigge

Senior Technology Project Editor:
Mike Jackson

Web Coordinator:
Ed Stubenrauch

Art Director:
Tippy McIntosh

Photography/Permissions Editor:
Darren Wright

Production House:
Lachina Publishing Services

Cover/Internal Design:
Ann Small, a small design studio

Cover Illustration:
Philip Brooker

Internal Illustration:
Mark Shaver, The Wiley Group

Printer:
Courier Kendallville, Inc.
Kendallville, IN

Instructional Strategies
Table of Contents

Instructional Strategies

A CENTURY OF INNOVATION

Featuring time-tested elements and ground-breaking innovations that set the standard, *Century 21 Accounting* has guided countless students to accounting success. In the 8th edition, the trusted approach and comprehensive support that have defined this market-leading text are even stronger. You will find a wealth of enhancements and updates, such as new features and real-world examples that encourage learning; and the latest technology, integrated to keep students involved, connected, and a step ahead of today's changing business times.

A Reorganized, Clear Approach

Using the proven teaching techniques that have been trusted for years, *Century 21 Accounting* 8E, Advanced continues to extend coverage from the first-year course. Students begin the Advanced course by reviewing many of the topics learned in the first-year course. The remaining parts of the text explore various aspects of accounting, including accounting control systems, accounting adjustments, management and cost accounting, and not-for-profit accounting.

Short, Accessible Lessons

Each chapter is divided into 3–4 short, accessible lessons that cover one or two concepts each, for maximum understanding. Corresponding assessment activities, which include application problems, allow for immediate feedback. Instructors can use these end-of-lesson pages to make sure that students fully understand all concepts and procedures before moving on to the next lesson. This Wraparound Teacher's Edition contains comprehensive lesson plans for each lesson, which allows you to plan your instructional time with greater efficiency.

Consistent Placement of Illustrations

Illustrations are consistently placed directly above the corresponding text. Steps and call-outs are completely integrated into the illustrations. This makes it easy to understand and then apply the procedure being taught. Listed below an illustration are clear, concise, step-by-step instructions that are directly linked to the specific part of the illustration where the work is recorded.

Problems, Problems, Problems

Century 21 Accounting 8E gives students many short problems. Students can easily find and fix mistakes. Many of the problems can be completed using *Auto-*mated Accounting, *South-Western Accounting with Peachtree* and/or *South-Western Accounting for Quick-Books* software.

INNOVATIONS THAT REACH TODAY'S STUDENTS

The *Century 21 Accounting* 8E package offers a wealth of materials that feature both time-tested methods and ground-breaking innovations.

The Student Companion CD-ROM

Packaged with the textbook, this CD-ROM provides the tools students need in order to understand and prepare for accounting success. It includes a spreadsheet tutorial, *Winning Edge* tools for competitive event preparation, electronic flash cards, important Web links, crossword puzzles, worksheets and PowerPoint presentations, and portfolio assessment tools.

Integrated Technology Tools

Century 21 Accounting 8E offers a perfect blend of cutting-edge technology to engage and assist students.

- *Personal Trainer* takes the work out of homework—boosting students' grades while reducing instructors' course preparation time and effort. Students can enhance their skills with practice problems, receive immediate feedback, and complete assigned homework, all from the convenience of their computers.
- The *Adobe eBook* contains digital material that offers the same rich visuals and illustrations as the printed text.
- *Automated Accounting 8.0* is integrated into every chapter of the textbook and combines the functionality of commercial software with proven educational features to make teaching and learning easier.
- A Peachtree symbol in the textbook denotes end-of-chapter problems that can be worked with *South-Western Accounting with Peachtree*.
- A QuickBooks symbol in the textbook denotes end-of-chapter problems that can be worked with *South-Western Accounting for QuickBooks*.
- The *Accounting Xtra! Web Site* offers a variety of resources and activities for students to explore. Xtra! Web Site icons within the textbook alert students to these opportunities for enrichment and assessment.

Special Features and Activities

Exciting special features and activities in the text-book enhance the accounting instruction to add interest to the course.

- *Accounting in the Real World* features a photo and description of a real company with questions linked to the chapter's content.
- *Internet Research Activity* sends students to the Internet to locate information to answer questions related to the chapter's subject matter.
- *Careers in Accounting* introduces students to people working in accounting or in positions where accounting knowledge is useful. This feature includes entry-level job requirements, career tracks, and projected trends for the future.
- *Cultural Diversity, Technology for Business, Business Structures, Global Perspective,* and *Small Business Spotlight* features provide additional information on a variety of subjects.
- *Making Ethical Decisions* requires students to read a scenario and determine whether the actions described are ethical or not.
- End-of-lesson activities and problems provide reinforcement. *Terms Review* lists new accounting terms introduced in the lesson. *Audit Your Understanding* questions provide an informal review of comprehension. *Work Together* problems offer the opportunity for the instructor and the students to work as a group to complete a problem based on the lesson before proceeding to independent work. *On Your Own* problems provide the student's first opportunity to work a short problem, based on the content covered in the lesson. On Your Own is designed to mirror the concepts and procedures covered in Work Together.
- End-of-chapter problems are linked to the content of the lessons. *Application Problems* are provided so that students can apply their learning to extended problems. *Mastery Problems* integrate the learning from all the lessons into one problem and demonstrate mastery of the chapter content. *Challenge Problems* stretch students to apply their learning to slightly different applications.
- *Explore Accounting* includes opportunities for higher-level learning.
- *Applied Communication* offers exercises for strengthening students' communication skills—a must for future employment!
- *Cases for Critical Thinking* ask students to consider questions based on accounting scenarios.

- *SCANS Workplace Competency* helps students learn about skills they'll need in the business world.
- *Graphing Workshop* and *Auditing for Errors* provide students with specific situations in which they can analyze and investigate accounting tools.
- *Analyzing Costco's Financial Statements* allows students to examine a real business's annual report and financial documents and put their knowledge to work.
- *Automated Accounting* features, within each chapter, describe the procedures necessary to use *Automated Accounting* to complete selected end-of-chapter problems.

STUDENT SUPPORT MATERIALS

Major student supplements aid student understanding and reinforcement of skills.

Working Papers

Using the Working Papers is the most efficient method of assuring that students complete problems accurately and in the least time necessary. Each workbook provides sufficient ruled paper for completing the Work Together problems, On Your Own problems, Application Problems, Mastery Problems, Challenge Problems, and Reinforcement Activities 1, 2, and 3. In addition, Study Guides present objective questions and matching exercises for terminology that cover the presentation of each chapter.

All Working Papers volumes have accompanying Teacher's Editions.

Recycling Problem Working Papers

For each chapter, Recycling Problems provide an additional problem for students who need more reinforcement after completing the Application and Mastery Problems. The narrative of the recycling problems is in Appendix D of the student text. The Recycling Problem Working Papers provide ruled paper for completing these problems.

The Recycling Problem Working Papers workbook has an accompanying Teacher's Edition.

Simulations

Manual and automated simulations give students hands-on, real-world experience in accounting practice. The simulations available are as follows:

Sounds, Inc., a departmentalized merchandising business organized as a corporation, is recommended for use after Part 1.

First Class Image Wear, Inc., a merchandising business organized as a corporation, is recommended for use after Part 4.

Progressive Badge Company, a manufacturing business organized as a corporation, is recommended for use after Part 6.

All simulations have accompanying Teacher's Keys.

ORGANIZATION OF THE TEXT

The student text is organized in a logical manner. Learning progresses from the simple to the complex both within a given Part and across Parts as similar topics are treated in progressively more detail in each succeeding Part.

- The **Part Opener Page** lists the chapter titles in the Part.
- The **Chart of Accounts** at the beginning of each Part provides a point of reference for account titles and numbers.
- The **Chapter Opener Page** shows a list of the learning objectives and a preview of the terms to be defined.
- **Accounting vocabulary terms** are carefully defined in complete sentences and highlighted in color.
- The chapters feature many **illustrations**, most of which include steps indicated within the illustrations.
- **End-of-Lesson Activities** include Terms Review, Audit Your Understanding, Work Together, and On Your Own.
- **End-of-Chapter Activities** include Explore Accounting; Application, Mastery, and Challenge Problems; Applied Communication; Cases for Critical Thinking; SCANS Workplace Comptency; Graphing Workshop, or Auditing for Errors; and Analyzing Costco's Financial Statements.
- An **Automated Accounting** feature at the end of each chapter describes how accounting activities are automated.
- **Reinforcement Activities** at the end of various Parts synthesize all learning from the Part. These activities can be used by students to prepare for success at FBLA and BPA competitive events. The *Winning Edge* logo directs students to the *Winning Edge* Web Site for additional information.
- **Appendices** present Accounting Concepts; Costco's Financial Statements; Using a Calculator and Computer Keypad; Recycling Problems; and Answers to Audit Your Understanding.
- A **Glossary** lists and defines the vocabulary terms from the text.

- A detailed **Index** directs the reader to the appropriate pages covered in each entry.

USING SOFTWARE AND TECHNOLOGY

After manual accounting procedures are mastered, computer software may be used as an enrichment activity to facilitate the processing of accounting data and the use of computers in accounting.

Several technology-related products are available to use with *Century 21 Accounting* 8E to augment teacher instruction: the Student Companion CD-ROM; Personal Trainer; Automated Accounting and its accompanying data files; Peachtree and its accompanying data files; QuickBooks and its accompanying data files; and the Accounting Xtra! Web Site. Software applicable to individual chapters is noted in lesson plans and interleaf pages. An Automated Accounting icon in the student textbook denotes end-of-chapter problems that can be worked with Automated Accounting. A Peachtree icon in the textbook denotes end-of-chapter problems that can be worked with *South-Western Accounting with Peachtree.* A QuickBooks icon in the textbook denotes end-of-chapter problems that can be worked with *South-Western Accounting for QuickBooks.*

Student Companion CD-ROM

Packaged with the textbook, this CD-ROM includes a spreadsheet tutorial, *Winning Edge* tools for competitive event preparation, electronic flash cards, important Web links, crossword puzzles, worksheets and PowerPoint presentations, and portfolio assessment tools.

Personal Trainer

This homework software helps students to enhance their skills with practice problems and to complete assigned homework while receiving immediate feedback. An integrated gradebook allows the instructor to track students' progress and review their completed assignments online.

Automated Accounting

Automated Accounting may be used to complete selected end-of-chapter problems, several Reinforcement Activities, and several simulations.

End-of-chapter problems with corresponding data files are marked with an icon. Instructions for using the data files are included in the Automated Accounting features at the end of relevant chapters. Students should be careful to open the filename given in those instructions.

Instructors may choose to demonstrate the operation of Automated Accounting. A good method would be to open a data file provided for the chapter being covered. The instructor can then enter sample transactions from the end-of-chapter problem corresponding to the data file.

It is suggested that the Automated Accounting textbook be used as a reference for students who need complete information about the operation of the software. Students can also access Problem Instructions through the Automated Accounting Browser Tool.

The Electronic Auditor helps check students' work. The software will compare student data files (stored on data disks or a hard disk) with solution data files. In addition, a summary report of the results will be provided. There are certain data files that do not have a corresponding solution provided for Electronic Auditor. These data files are simply exercises in which students generate relevant reports using Automated Accounting.

Solutions may be added to the Electronic Auditor for problems created by instructors. Once added, these solutions will appear in the solutions directory and can be used to check students' solutions. A full explanation of how to use the Electronic Auditor is provided in the instructor's manual that accompanies Automated Accounting.

South-Western Accounting with Peachtree

Various end-of-chapter and Reinforcement Activity problems in *Century 21 Accounting* are marked with a Peachtree symbol, which indicates that the problems can be worked with *South-Western Accounting with Peachtree.*

South-Western Accounting for QuickBooks

Various end-of-chapter and Reinforcement Activity problems in *Century 21 Accounting* are marked with a QuickBooks symbol, which indicates that the problems can be worked with *South-Western Accounting for QuickBooks.*

Accounting Xtra! Web Site

This online learning and study tool offers a truly interactive learning experience for students. Xtra! Web Site icons within the textbook alert students to online opportunities for enrichment and assessment, such as the following:

- Summary of key points in each chapter
- E-lectures
- Accounting FAQs
- Interactive, game-like reviews of every lesson
- Online chapter review and test prep
- Web links
- Graphing Workshop

- NewsEdge
- Crossword puzzles
- Additional exercises, problems, and quizzes
- Spanish and English glossaries
- *Winning Edge* tools for competitive event preparation
- Workplace readiness materials
- Student portfolio activities

USING THE WRAPAROUND TEACHER'S EDITION

The Wraparound Teacher's Edition has margin notes next to reduced student pages that contain lesson plans for each lesson of each chapter; teaching suggestion boxes that address relevant topics; answers to features; and check figures for end-of-chapter problems.

Chapter Interleaf Pages

Preceding each chapter, interleaf pages contain grids to assist the instructor in planning the presentation of the chapter.

Lesson Plans

A complete lesson plan is printed in the margins of the Wraparound Teacher's Edition for each lesson in each chapter. In addition, modified lesson plans are provided for the beginning of each Part and chapter, as well as for the end-of-chapter pages. A typical plan for each chapter is as follows:

Introductory Pages

- **Overview.** The opener page for each of the Parts describes the chapter content of all the chapters in that Part.
- **Chart of Accounts.** The chart of accounts page has a list of important points about the chart of accounts for that Part.
- **Introduce the Chapter.** There are two sections in the Introduce the Chapter notes: (1) Preview Chapter Objectives and (2) Preview Accounting Terms.
- **Software Focus.** A Software Focus box details the software that is available for use with the chapter and the problems to be used with the software.
- **Accounting in the Real World** and **Internet Research Activity.** These features always appear on the second page of each chapter. This section of the teaching suggestions lists ways to present the features and suggested answers to the questions asked of the students.

Lesson Plan for Each Lesson

Every lesson in every chapter has its own lesson plan. The following elements are included in each lesson plan:

- **Objectives.** The chapter learning objectives that apply to the lesson are listed.
- **Motivate.** The Motivate section suggests questions, examples, or group discussion topics. A **Preview** subheading suggests ways to encourage students to preview the lesson using good study habits.
- **Materials.** A list shows the transparencies, software, working papers, and other materials needed.
- **Explain.** Items detailed are the points that should be emphasized in the presentation of the lesson.
- **Demonstrate.** This section describes how to demonstrate accounting procedures. Instructors may wish to vary the order of presentation of the Explain and Demonstrate sections to fit the needs of the classroom.
- **Ongoing Assessment.** The instructor notes facial expressions, responds to student questions, and re-presents concepts. A Troubleshooting section describes problems students typically have with the content of the lesson.
- **Reteach.** The Reteach suggestions give specific means of reteaching the lesson.
- **Guided Practice.** The Terms Review, Audit Your Understanding questions, and Work Together problems are the means for providing guided practice. The instructor and students do the suggested guided practice activities together. The instructor's role is to demonstrate, monitor, observe, and answer questions.
- **Independent Practice.** Students perform suggested independent practice activities by themselves. The On Your Own and Application Problems are the means for providing independent practice for the lesson.
- **Enrich.** Suggestions for extension and enrichment activities take students beyond the traditional assignments.
- **Close.** Closure suggestions describe ways to review and reinforce the lesson.

End-of-Chapter

The end-of-chapter pages also contain a lesson plan. Different activities are suggested for completing the chapter.

- **Putting It All Together.** This section suggests a summarizing activity, such as using a summary transparency.

- **Independent Practice.** Mastery and Challenge Problems bring together all lessons of the chapter. In addition, this section specifies ancillary products (such as Study Guides, Personal Trainer, the Xtra! Web Site, and the Student Companion CD) that are appropriate for independent practice.
- **Ongoing Assessment.** Solutions are reviewed and reteaching is conducted as needed.
- **Reteach.** Recycling Problems are available for reteaching purposes.
- **Enrich.** Included in this section are suggestions for activities to extend the chapter presentation.
- **Formal Evaluation.** Formal assessment instruments (tests) are suggested. In addition, the final page of each chapter suggests how portfolio assessment can be used in an accounting program.
- **Automated Accounting.** The Automated Accounting pages also have lesson plan suggestions.

Teaching Suggestions

In addition to the lesson plans, boxes in the side and bottom margins of the Wraparound Teacher's Edition describe various teaching strategies or tips. These can be categorized in three general areas:

1. *Suggestions Related to Building Student Skills*: These boxes describe actions the instructor can take to build applied skills in the following areas:
   - Communications
   - Mathematics
   - Building Study Skills
   - Language Arts
   - Writing Across the Curriculum

2. *Suggestions Related to Other Teaching Methodology*: These boxes describe actions the instructor can take to reinforce concepts developed in the chapter. They can be categorized in the following areas:
   - Assessment by Portfolio
   - Different Learning Abilities
   - Different Learning Styles
   - Cooperative Learning
   - Expanding Beyond the Classroom

3. *Suggestions Related to Student Features*: These boxes highlight special student features and their benefits and/or solutions:
   - Accounting in the Real World
   - Internet Research Activity
   - Software Focus
   - Making Ethical Decisions
   - Cultural Diversity
   - Technology for Business
   - Small Business Spotlight

- Careers in Accounting
- Business Structures
- Global Perspective
- Explore Accounting

Check Figures

Check figures are given for end-of-chapter activities and reinforcement activities. When student solutions match these check figures, it can be assumed that the student's solutions are significantly correct.

OTHER RESOURCES FOR INSTRUCTORS

In addition to this Wraparound Teacher's Edition, the *Century 21 Accounting* 8E package contains a host of instructor resources for preparation, presentation, and testing—all designed to minimize instructors' time while maximizing their impact within the classroom.

- The *Instructor's Resource CD-ROM* is an all-in-one convenient tool, offering Lesson Plans; PowerPoint teaching presentations; *Winning Edge* tools for competitive test preparation; Spanish and English accounting glossaries; and numerous supplemental materials to support the instructor.
- The *Teacher's Resource Kit* contains lesson plans, accounting ruling masters, career success and assessment resources, enrichment resources, and solutions to Working Papers and simulations.
- *Teacher's Editions of Working Papers, Recycling Problems,* and *Tests* show all the student editions with answers in place, for easy use by instructors.
- The *Assessment Binder* contains ExamView computerized testing software, test masters, and solutions.

STRATEGIES FOR OPTIMIZING INDIVIDUAL LEARNING

The student population not only reflects the cultural diversity in American society as a whole, but it also consists of students with different abilities and styles of learning. Many of these individual student differences require an adjustment in teaching style or presentation. This section describes teaching strategies for students with different learning abilities and styles, and cooperative learning.

Teaching Strategies for Students with Different Learning Abilities

Classrooms typically contain students with a wide variation of ability, intelligence, and motivation. Although the instructor must direct a majority of the instruction to the "average" student, optimal learning will occur only when the curriculum is modified to meet the needs of each individual student.

The first and greatest challenge facing the instructor is identifying the special abilities of each student. Learning disabilities can be very difficult to detect and categorize. Classifying students solely on examination scores and prior classroom performance may be misleading and should be avoided. For example, poor subject examination scores and short attention spans may be the symptoms of either a student with a specific learning disability or a gifted student who is bored.

The correct assessment of students should be a combined effort of the instructor, the school counselor or special education instructor, and the student. Together, this team can design an individualized program that will challenge the student while providing adequate opportunity to achieve attainable goals.

Gifted Students

One objective of programs for gifted students should be the development of leadership skills. Current literature suggests that four skill areas are involved in the development of effective leadership.

1. *Cognition*—The ability to identify, research, and learn factual knowledge.
2. *Problem Solving*—The ability to identify problems and develop creative solutions.
3. *Interpersonal Communication*—The ability to work with other people.
4. *Decision Making*—The ability to develop and implement realistic goals and evaluate performance of the goals.

Different hemispheres of the brain control these functions. Cognition and problem solving are typically associated with left-brain functions; interpersonal communication and decision making are associated with right-brain functions. Therefore, effective leadership training must target development of both hemispheres. Most students will enter the classroom with stronger development in some skill areas than in others. Thus, a student lacking interpersonal communication skills should undertake projects to develop those skills.

The Making Ethical Decisions and Applied Communication activities in the student textbook provide opportunities for gifted students to develop these leadership skills. Encourage gifted students to extend these activities by developing related activities.

Gifted students may need to move through the accounting program at an accelerated pace. It may not be appropriate for gifted students to work every problem provided. For example, after a chapter has been reviewed, gifted students may demonstrate mastery by working only the Mastery or Recycling Problem. Others may need to work one or more of the Application Problems. The Challenge Problem should always be assigned to gifted students to provide the "stretch" for exploring alternatives to the chapter content.

Additional activities might include the following:

1. Gifted students should master transaction analysis quickly; therefore, challenge them to identify a special research project that interests them. The students should be encouraged to identify a project that requires interaction with a businessperson. For example, a student could contact a bank loan officer to learn how a proprietor would apply for a loan, research formats for a business plan, and develop a business plan for a hypothetical business. Finally, the student could invite the bank loan officer to class and use role-playing to demonstrate how communication skills can enhance an individual's chance of getting the loan.

2. Partnerships require effective communication and cooperation among partners. Gifted students can best learn about the opportunities, problems, and challenges of a partnership by forming a real partnership. Encourage gifted students to form a partnership to sell a service or product of their selection. The students should prepare the partnership agreement, operate the business, and report the results of operations. Suggest that the students consult businesspersons, such as lawyers and accountants, for assistance.

3. Using gifted students as tutors for other students can be an effective way of teaching the topics students find most difficult. Allow the gifted student to complete one of these chapters while the class completes the first chapters of a Part. The gifted students can then assist you in presenting the concepts and procedures on their chapter to the class. Encourage the students to use visual aids and develop methods to assess student learning.

Limited English Proficiency Students

Limited English Proficiency (LEP) students are individuals whose native or dominant language is a language other than English. Although these students may be involved in special English-as-a-Second-Language (ESL) classes, the instructor can significantly improve learning by adopting several strategies.

1. Provide students with translations of key terms prior to presenting each chapter. Encourage students to use dictionaries.

2. Create visual instructional methods, such as posters and bulletin boards, that reinforce accounting concepts in both English and the other dominant language(s).

3. At early levels, LEP students have limited comprehension of English and can respond with one- or two-word answers. Assess understanding by having students match, choose, move, draw, or point. Students at this level can respond to directions that require them to name, list, categorize, label, or reply with one or two words.

4. Allow for longer pauses when you ask questions. Non-native speakers need more time to formulate their answers.

5. Speak directly. Avoid negative constructions and passive verbs, such as "Don't forget that Cash is not debited in this transaction." Instead say, "Remember to credit Cash in this transaction."

6. Rather than asking students whether they understand what you have said, ask them to restate what you have said in their own words.

7. Adjust the length of time allotted to complete assignments and tests. Remember that the primary objective is to assess knowledge of accounting rather than the ability to translate and comprehend the question or problem.

8. Be cautious if there are no interruptions or questions. It may mean that very little has been understood.

Additional activities might include the following:

1. Recruit businesspersons willing to act as mentors for LEP students. These mentors should be invited to speak to the class and periodically meet with LEP students to assist with assignments. The instructor should be actively involved in any meetings with LEP students to show support for both the mentor and the students.

2. Although LEP students may feel handicapped in the classroom, their knowledge of two languages provides them with excellent career opportunities in today's international business environment. LEP students should identify what unique career opportunities exist for them in various types of organizations, such as international businesses and government. Students could create a bulletin board to inform other students of these opportunities. Successful bulletin boards could also be used in the classrooms of younger students, or in elementary schools.

Specific Learning Disability (SLD) Students

Instructors need not be reminded that adolescence is a period of turmoil and adjustment. What many instructors often view as adolescent behavior may, however, be caused by a student's specific learning disability (SLD). The correct assessment of SLD students is difficult because adolescent behavior is similar to the typical characteristics of SLD students.

- **Passive Learners.** When faced with making a decision, SLD students avoid making a decision in favor of waiting for a teacher to provide specific direction.
- **Poor Self-Concept.** Years of failure cause SLD students to have low self-esteem, thus reducing their confidence that they can achieve academic success.
- **Inept Social Skills.** SLD students often have difficulty making and keeping friends.
- **Attention Deficits.** SLD students often lack the ability to concentrate on one topic for an extended period.
- **Lack of Motivation.** Years of failure have conditioned SLD students to doubt their abilities and therefore view their efforts as being futile.

Once an SLD student is correctly assessed, the instructor should work with the student to develop an individualized program. The basic objective of the program should be the development of functional (life) skills. The student should be counseled to establish challenging yet attainable goals and provide frequent feedback as to the attainment of these goals. The student's academic success should be measured on the demonstrated ability to learn as much as the mastery of a defined body of knowledge.

Several general instructional strategies are effective in teaching SLD students:

1. When asking questions during class, ask SLD students questions that they can likely answer successfully. Save more difficult or unstructured questions for better students.
2. Rotate instructional materials rather than trying to complete a single text. Supplemental instructional materials may include additional texts, business magazines, government publications, etc.
3. Encourage students to maintain a daily log or journal that describes their academic progress. Students can share this log, if they desire, with the instructor when updating their individual program.
4. When feasible, SLD students should become involved in work-study programs that are consistent with course content. When work-study opportunities are unavailable, simulations can be used to provide a simulated work environ-

ment. Field trips are an excellent method to expose students to the business world.

Additional activities might include the following:

1. The popular board game Monopoly is well known as an enjoyable way to practice mathematical skills. The game also provides students the opportunity to analyze and record their transactions. Playing Monopoly enables students to see how transaction analysis and the accounting equation provide information for business decisions. Students should use T accounts until they have completed the first Part. The instructor may need to assist students with identifying accounts, such as plant assets, that are not presented in the first Part.
2. Many students will ultimately work in inventory-related jobs. Simulating the inventory of a business will enable students to actively participate in the accounting for inventory. For example, students could establish a classroom store carrying school supplies, snacks, or other low-cost items. The students would record the purchase and sales transactions and update the perpetual inventory. Students would periodically take inventory and reconcile the periodic and perpetual inventory quantities.

At-Risk Students

Many environmental factors may negatively affect a student's ability and motivation to succeed academically. Any student who is a potential dropout may be classified as an at-risk student. At-risk students typically are deficient in mathematics, reading, and language skills. These students provide a unique challenge to the accounting instructor because the instructor has little, if any, power to correct problems in the home environment.

Effective instructional strategies for at-risk students should be based on the premise that all individuals have a need for achievement and social acceptance. Within the accounting classroom, these needs can be fulfilled by developing a curriculum that promotes academic success and acceptance by the instructor. Techniques for working with at-risk students include the following:

1. Develop a personal profile of the student. Avoid placing too much significance on past academic performance as this may represent a symptom rather than the underlying problem.
2. Together with the student, develop an individualized program that allows the student to attain both short-term and long-term goals. When

identifying goals, consider the student's anticipated career goals.

3. Modify presentation strategies to include more visual displays, and supplement explanations with current, realistic examples.

4. Organize field trips and mentor programs to expose students to the business environment.

Additional activities might include the following:

1. Assist students to understand how accounting is a useful skill in careers that interest them. This could be accomplished in many ways. For example, a student who shows interest in auto mechanics could be introduced to the owner of a local auto repair business. The student could then report his/her observations to the instructor in oral or written form. If no mentor is available, trade magazines often present articles to assist their readers in managing their businesses.

2. Many at-risk students can become motivated to begin self-improvement only when they recognize that they have a need to improve. One method of promoting self-evaluation is to have students identify the qualities they would require of another individual. Have students imagine that they are partners in a business that is consider-ing hiring employees for both service and office positions. Require the student to prepare a job description that includes both skill and personal characteristics that applicants should possess. This activity should enable students to compare their qualifications with the job descriptions they have developed.

Visually-Impaired Students

Students with mild visual impairments are typically mainstreamed and may elect to enroll in accounting. The nature and degree of students' visual impair-ments will vary. A student's visual impairment may include a difficulty in reading print, an inability to distinguish colors, a sensitivity to light, and a limited field of vision. The instructor must identify each stu-dent's exact impairment and adapt teaching strate-gies appropriately.

Many sources exist for providing alternative teaching materials. Most states have schools for the blind and rehabilitation service agencies that can enlarge the textbook and working papers. Consult these organizations to identify the latest technologies available for assisting the students.

The instructor and student should develop an individualized program that establishes a time frame for achieving specific learning objectives. The learn-ing objectives should be consistent with the student's

anticipated career goals. The time frame should con-sider the student's impairment and the availability of technical assistance, such as enlarged materials and closed circuit television. The use of software should not be overlooked for visually-impaired students, particularly if oversized monitors with larger displays are available.

Additional activities might include the following:

1. It is important for visually-impaired students to have confidence in their ability to participate fully within the business world. Require students to pre-pare an oral or written report that profiles a suc-cessful visually-impaired business professional.

2. New technologies are continually being developed that assist visually-impaired students to partici-pate fully in both school and business. Students must be aware of these technologies and know how to continually learn of new technologies. Using government agencies as a resource, assist the students in preparing a report concerning anticipated technologies.

Teaching Strategies for Students with Different Learning Styles

There are many different learning styles. Some peo-ple learn best from reading material. Others need to see a demonstration or learn by feeling. Still others may learn best from auditory cues. It is important to remember, however, that no matter what learning style works best for any individual, learning style is not an indicator of intelligence. Two people of similar levels of intelligence may learn best in two different styles of learning. Learning style is also not necessar-ily a rigid behavior. Many individuals may have a dominant learning style; however, most also have the flexibility to adapt their learning styles to the demands of the material to be learned. Different learning styles include print, visual, auditory, tactile, and kinesthetic learning.

Print Learners

The print learner prefers to see the data in print—preferably printed in words.

1. When introducing the T account, a print learner would prefer to study the illustration in the text-book which shows a T account, labeled with the words *DEBIT* and *CREDIT*.

2. When covering journal entries, the instructor should discuss the entries, using the textbook examples and referring to the textbook. The print learner can later go back and study the entries.

3. When learning how to post, the print learner would prefer to see the process in print. This can

be done by distributing a handout that explains the steps in the posting process. Allow the student to study the handout.

Visual Learners

The visual learner needs to *see* the concept. One way for the learner to see the concept is mental visualization. Illustrations and visual aids are important to the visual learner.

1. Ask the student (with eyes closed) to picture a T account. The student should be able to see both sides of the account. Next, the student should visualize the word *DEBIT* on the left side of the account. Finally, the student should visualize the word *CREDIT* on the right side of the account. Once this concept takes on a visual form, the student will be able to access it when needed.
2. When covering journal entries, the instructor should discuss the entries, using a transparency or the chalkboard to record the entry. In addition, the student should be asked to mentally picture each part of the entry before the instructor actually writes it on the transparency or chalkboard.
3. To teach posting, the instructor could use a transparency to assist in the lecture. The transparency could be (1) a blank transparency that the instructor completes or (2) a prepared transparency that uses arrows to trace the steps involved in posting.

Auditory Learners

The auditory learner will best learn by hearing. Auditory learners who read a textbook chapter benefit from hearing reinforcement of key concepts spoken out loud.

1. When introducing the T account, have the student say out loud that "the left side is the debit side of the account." Repeating this statement a few times will increase the chances of its being reinforced. Repeat the process with the statement "the right side is the credit side of the account."
2. To reinforce the learning of journal entries, the auditory learner should verbally repeat the analysis of the transaction. The student should also verbally list the steps involved in making the entry.
3. When learning how to post, the auditory learner would prefer to hear the steps involved in posting. This can be done via a live lecture or a taped tutorial. To reinforce learning, the student could recite the posting steps to another student or group of students.

Tactile Learners

The tactile learner learns best by touching or handling objects.

1. Using play money, have the student touch the right side of the desk and place an amount of money on it to reinforce an amount in the right side or credit side of an account. Repeat the process for the left/debit side.
2. Tactile learners may benefit from using the computer to key journal entries and then print reports. The student should be encouraged to place a finger on each account title in the journal entries report and trace it over to the amount in the amount column of the report to check it for accuracy. Tactile learners should also be given the opportunity to journalize transactions from at least one simulation that contains source documents, which must be handled to analyze, journalize, and file.
3. The tactile learner can use a group of index cards to represent the general ledger. Each card should represent an account and should have three vertical lines to distinguish between the debit and credit columns, and balance columns. Have the tactile learner post each example of a journal entry to the appropriate cards (accounts).

Kinesthetic Learners

The kinesthetic learner learns best by taking an active part in the instruction. Motion is an important part of kinesthetic learning.

1. Have the student draw a T account in the air or use a finger to draw a T account on the back of the hand or arm. Next, have the student label the left side with the word *DEBIT* and the right side with the word *CREDIT.*
2. The kinesthetic learner would prefer to participate in the posting process. Use a transparency of the ledger account and have each student complete one or more steps of the posting process at the overhead projector. Other students can be completing the posting process individually on printed ledger accounts.
3. Provide the opportunity to perform the calculations to solve formulas. Calculators or computerized spreadsheet programs may be used.

COOPERATIVE LEARNING

Cooperative learning activities should be an integral part of accounting pedagogical strategies. Cooperative learning involves small heterogeneous groups of students who work together to share the responsibility for learning. Cooperative learning activities should be designed with the following goals in mind:

1. All students should be able to participate.
2. Groups should be heterogeneous.
3. Each student needs to be held accountable for his or her contribution to the group.

Cooperative learning is more successful with heterogeneous rather than homogeneous groups. Research further supports cooperative learning as a teaching strategy to increase students' motivation, achievement, and behavior. The teacher should select team members for a cooperative learning activity. Group composition should include a mixture of gender, ability level, cultural or ethnic background, and learning style. For example, placing a visual learner with an auditory learner enhances and strengthens the group's performance. Group members should be rotated frequently.

The time needed to complete an activity will vary among groups. Therefore, the teacher needs to provide additional activities to be completed by groups as they finish. These activities might include, for example, specific questions about the activity. These additional activities are often referred to as debriefing.

Cooperative learning promotes the development of higher-order thinking skills where brighter students explain concepts or principles to slower students. Using higher-order thinking skills to articulate ideas in accounting will normally result in the material being learned more effectively with improved retention rates.

To be successful, each student must be held accountable for his/her contribution to the cooperative learning activity. A variety of evaluation methods may be employed. These methods may include (1) a short quiz taken individually, (2) instructor observation of individual contributions to a group activity, or (3) bonus points assigned to individuals only if all group members do well individually. Performance on cooperative learning activities in accounting should range from no more than 5 to 10 percent of the final grade.

One of the goals of cooperative learning is to have students work out the roles of the group members themselves. Some groups will assign a role to an individual, such as when a representative of the group will need to record results and present them to the class, and sometimes individuals within a group will assume roles within the group without being asked to do so.

Some cooperative learning activities are as follows:

1. *Research project:* Assign students to groups of two. Each group researches the financial statements (through the annual report) of a company in which they are interested, perhaps because they are familiar with the product. Students look for a list of specific items such as what kinds of stock is the corporation authorized to issue, what categories of assets are listed on the balance sheet, what is the total of current liabilities, did net income increase/decrease from the previous period, and so on. The group must then plan and deliver a presentation of the data to the entire class. Additional time outside class is needed to complete research and prepare the presentation. Time frame: 45 minutes.

2. *Explain what component percentages measure.* Assign students to groups of three. Each group is to plan, prepare, and deliver a presentation to *non-accountants.* The presentation should explain what component percentages are and how they are used to analyze financial statements. Time frame: 30 minutes over several class periods.

3. *Divide the class into groups of two or three students each.* Have each group discuss and prepare a list of service businesses found in the local community. Each group should appoint a leader who will present the list of businesses and services to the class. Time frame: 20 minutes.

4. *Divide the class into two groups.* Each group stands and faces each other. The instructor or a student moderator states an accounting term. The first student to raise a hand has the opportunity to give the correct definition. The group with the most correctly defined terms is declared the winner. As an alternative to this game, the instructor or moderator may read the definition of a term, such as "Anything of value that is owned," while the groups must identify the term. If you wish to imitate a popular television show, the answer should be given in a question format, such as "What is an asset?"

5. *Reinforcement Activities:* Assign reinforcement activities as homework. Divide the class into groups of two students each. Each pair of students exchange and evaluate each other's work in class. Students are permitted to correct their work, based on their partner's evaluation. Time frame: 15 minutes.

6. *Divide the class into groups of four or five students each.* Using Cases for Critical Thinking, each group analyzes the cases and arrives at agreed-upon solutions. One member of each group is

appointed the recorder and presents the group's analysis to the class. Time frame: 20 minutes.

7. *Divide the class into groups of two or three students each.* Each group will discuss and prepare a list of merchandising businesses found in the local community. The group-appointed leader presents to the class the list and merchandise being sold. Time frame: 25 minutes.

8. *Divide the class into auditing groups of three or four students per group.* Each auditing group is responsible for assisting other class members as well as correcting homework assignments. A lead auditor is appointed by the group and is responsible for turning in completed homework assignments for each group member to the instructor.

SUGGESTIONS FOR TEACHING BUSINESS ETHICS

Businesses have recently become aware of the severe implications of unethical behavior on the part of employees. In response, many businesses have begun training their employees to make ethical decisions and establishing company codes of conduct. The message from businesses today is clear—employees must be capable of making ethical decisions to protect the business from legal liability and to maximize long-term profits.

Most students' principles of right and wrong are well established prior to their enrolling in high school accounting. Thus, the presentation of business ethics does not involve the teaching of right and wrong. Instead, students need to learn how to apply their principles of right and wrong to business situations.

Making Ethical Decisions

The Making Ethical Decisions features in this text give instructors an opportunity to teach ethics in the accounting class.

Steps for Analyzing Ethical Situations

In Chapter 2, a four-step checklist is presented to help students analyze the ethics of an action. This approach encourages students to collect pertinent information that will provide a basis for their decision. Ultimately, students' decisions are based on their personal ethics applied to the facts of the situation.

Assessment

Correct solutions are generally obvious if the action is either illegal or violates a business or professional standard. For example, most students will agree that it is unethical to dispose of hazardous waste into the water supply. However, students may challenge compliance with other laws and standards. A class dis-cussion of whether the truck drivers of a business should be required to drive the speed limit and wear safety belts may demonstrate many students' willingness to disregard selected laws.

Many of the situations in the Making Ethical Decisions activities involve circumstances where the line between right and wrong is unclear. As a result, students will likely differ in their decisions as to whether the action is ethical. Assessment of Making Ethical Decisions activities should be based on the students' analysis of the facts and the objective support for their decisions.

Teachers can adopt several strategies to cover a Making Ethical Decisions activity. The activity can be presented initially as a classroom discussion. Alternately, the activity can be assigned as an individual or group project. Whichever method is used, students should be given the opportunity to discuss the case in class. This exchange of ideas enables students to observe how other individuals make and support their decisions. When asking questions and making observations, the instructor should be careful not to reveal her or his personal bias.

Suggested Solutions for Some Making Ethical Decisions Features

Chapter 3: Insider Trading

1. *Recognize you are facing an ethical dilemma.* As a loan officer, Marcus should be aware of laws relating to insider trading.
2. *Identify the action taken.* Marcus purchased the stock of a customer of his employer. Through his relationship with the customer, he had access to confidential information.
3. *Analyze the action.*
   a. *Is the action illegal?* Yes. The SEC states that employees of banks who were given information while providing services to the corporation whose securities they traded are involved in insider trading.
   b. *Does the action violate company or professional standards?* No analysis is required because the action is illegal.
   c. *Who is affected, and how, by the action?* No analysis is required because the action is illegal.
4. *Determine if the action is ethical.* Marcus's purchase of the stock was illegal and, therefore, is unethical.

Sources: www.sec.gov/answers/insider.htm (February 1, 2004); www.citigroup.com/citigroup/corporategovernance/codeconduct.htm (February 1, 2004)

Chapter 4: Sharing Your Knowledge

Sample Solution: John followed the guidance in the Code of Professional Conduct in declining the engagement. Ethics Ruling 15, Section Rule 391.029-.030, prohibits a member from using information gained from one client to benefit another client if the prospective client would know the origin of the information. It is likely that the theatre manager knew that John worked with the competing theatre. Therefore, John can accept the engagement only with the permission of his existing theatre client.

Chapter 6: Is Someone Reading Your E-Mail?

Sample Solution:

1. *Recognize you are facing an ethical dilemma.* Managers should always evaluate a decision to dismiss an employee.
2. *Identify the action taken.* Michael dismissed Janice for sending threatening messages.
3. *Analyze the action.*
   a. *Is the action illegal?* No. It is not illegal to fire an employee for conduct that is inconsistent with corporate policies.
   b. *Does the action violate company or professional standards?* No. The company's code of conduct specifically states that e-mail communication is subject to monitoring. However, the policy does not address whether the company will hold "private" messages confidential.
   c. *Who is affected, and how, by the action?*

STAKEHOLDERS	NEGATIVE	POSITIVE
Janice Tillman	Lost her job.	
Michael Ulman		The worry that Janice's threats may become a reality is removed.
Other company employees	Some employees may feel uncomfortable with the reality that their e-mails are being monitored.	Employees have an increased feeling of security, knowing that an employee who has shown some tendency toward violence has been removed from the workplace.
Company	May have to defend itself against a discrimination lawsuit if Janice elects to sue the company.	Increased employee security should yield higher profits.
Stockholders		Increased employee security should yield higher profits.

4. *Determine if the action is ethical.* Michael's action appears to be ethical.

For more information about employee privacy issues, instruct your students to visit the Privacy Rights Clearinghouse Web Site. The organization states that selecting an e-mail "private" option is not an issue unless the company has specifically promised its employees to keep these messages confidential. Even so, at least one civil case has demonstrated that the privacy of "private" messages can be mitigated if the messages contain inappropriate or illegal statements.

Source: www.privacyrights.org/

Chapter 7: Sharing the News

Sample Solution:

1. *Recognize you are facing an ethical dilemma.* Phillip should know that disclosing significant events of his company may violate confidentiality rules.
2. *Identify the action taken.* Phillip disclosed confidential information to his wife.
3. *Analyze the action.*
   a. *Is the action illegal?* Possibly. Phillip or his wife have violated insider training laws if either shares this information with anyone who subsequently uses the information to their advantage in the purchase or sale of the company's stock.
   b. *Does the action violate company or professional standards?* Yes. The *Code of Business Conduct* states that confidential information, including business plans, should not be disclosed without a legitimate business purpose. The information should not even be shared with family members.
   c. *Who is affected, and how, by the action?* No analysis is required because the action appears to be illegal and violates company standards.
4. *Determine if the action is ethical.* Phillip's action appears to be unethical. The fact that he told only his wife is not an issue.

Chapter 8: The Land of Opportunity?

Suggested Solution: The section titled *Corporate Opportunities* contains guidance relevant to this decision. The section states that employees owe a duty to the company to advance its business interests. Business opportunities discovered by employees in the function of their position must be offered to the Company first. In addition, employees are prohibited from competing with the company.

Kelly needs to inform the company that a competing business near the proposed resort site is available for purchase. If the company elects not to purchase the restaurant and does not consider it to be a significant competitor, Kelly may be able to purchase the restaurant. However, Kelly should first consult with the company's legal staff.

Source: http://media.corporate-ir.net/media_files/
nys/hlt/corp%20gov/codeofethics_013004.pdf

Chapter 11: Just Following Orders

1. *Recognize you are facing an ethical dilemma.* Jared should be very familiar with the government contract and realize that recording picnic costs as salary expense may violate the government contract.

2. *Identify the proposed action.* Jared has been instructed to record the picnic costs as a salary expense.

3. *Analyze the proposed action or the action taken.*
   a. *Is the action illegal?* Yes. The government contract specifically states that entertainment expenses are not contract costs. Although the president's statement regarding worker productivity may be correct, the guidance provided in the government document clearly precludes entertainment expenses.
   b. *Does the action violate company or professional standards?* Because the action is illegal, no evaluation of this question is necessary.
   c. *Who is affected, and how, by the action?* Because the action is illegal, no evaluation of this question is necessary.

4. *Determine if the action is ethical.* Recording the picnic costs as salary expenses is illegal and, therefore, unethical.

Chapter 12: Exercising Stock Options

Suggested Solution:

1. *Recognize you are facing an ethical dilemma.* The corporation should recognize that any employee receiving substantially more compensation than other employees may constitute an unethical situation.

2. *Identify the action.* The corporation issued stock options as part of the CEO's compensation package.

3. *Analyze the action.*
   a. *Is the action illegal?* No. No laws limit the salary that any individual can earn in a private business.
   b. *Does the action violate company or professional standards?* Possibly. The code requires that employee compensation be consistent with that employee's contribution. Did Brent make a contribution to the corporation consistent with his salary? Further analysis is required.
   c. *Who is affected, and how, by the action?*

STAKEHOLDERS	NEGATIVE	POSITIVE
Brent McGowan		Provides a substantial increase in salary if he can improve the company's profitability.
Employees	May resent the high salary provided to the CEO.	Improved profitability results in more and better paying jobs.
Burnett Corp.		Provides CEO with incentive to improve profitability.
Stockholders	Additional shares reduce earnings per share, lowering stock market price.	Increases the wealth of stockholders only if CEO is successful in increasing profitability.

4. *Determine if the action is ethical.* Answers will vary.

Chapter 22: Impending Merger Affects Student's Employment

Sample Solution:

STAKEHOLDERS	NEGATIVE	POSITIVE
Sallie Kaplan	Limits the time she can search for another position in Columbus. May feel betrayed by John Jensen and his firm.	Prevented Sallie from having to keep the merger information confidential.
John Jensen	Lost a potentially valuable employee. May affect his ability to obtain Sallie or her future employer as a client.	Ensures that all employees and clients receive notice of the merger at the same time, ensuring everyone receives equitable treatment.
Clients of Jensen, Pearson & Marris		All clients will receive notice of the merger directly from the firm. Hearing of the merger "through the grapevine" could damage professional relationships.
Other students majoring in accounting	Delays other students from seeking and accepting the New York position.	

SUGGESTIONS FOR TEACHING APPLIED COMMUNICATION

Several accounting organizations have emphasized that successful accounting professionals must possess good oral and written communication skills. Since effective communication is a skill developed with practice, this textbook has incorporated several opportunities for students to develop their skills. There is an Applied Communication activity at the end of every chapter. Suggested solutions are printed in the margin of this Wraparound Teacher's Edition.

Students' knowledge of communication and language arts skills will vary. You may consider asking an English or communications instructor to assist you in reviewing communication skills that students have learned previously in other classes.

Whether preparing an outline for an oral presentation or a letter for a written assignment, students should be encouraged to use word processing software to prepare their messages. Word processing software is now used extensively by both public and private accountants, and proficiency in its use is essential. By using word processing to complete Applied Communication activities, you will be able to emphasize the importance of computer skills from the first week of the semester.

Assessment

Since the activities allow students to prepare unique messages, there are no "correct" answers. Your students may create excellent solutions that differ significantly from the sample solution. Thus, evaluate each student's solution on its ability to transmit the message in an efficient, effective, and professional manner. The activities should be evaluated for both content and format. Each instructor must determine the importance of errors.

Revising Written Documents

A significant amount of learning occurs when students are provided the opportunity to correct mistakes in their original written documents. Require students to revise documents and incorporate your suggestions. The revised document should be assessed and, if necessary, revised again. Teachers should consider giving students credit for successful revisions.

Cases for Critical Thinking

Most of the Cases for Critical Thinking in this textbook require students to prepare a written answer. You can adapt these cases to further reinforce students' communication skills. Rather than simply answering the questions, require students to prepare an oral or written message to an individual or business mentioned in the case. Vary the requirements of each activity by requiring different types of oral and written messages.

ASSESSMENT BY PORTFOLIO

Assessment by portfolio is a popular tool for assessing student performance. A portfolio enables the instructor to assess student goals and accomplishments while providing the student with the opportunity to collect information that will help set and accomplish current and future goals.

A portfolio should be organized across the curriculum with each discipline making a contribution. A complete portfolio should include the following:

1. A resume.
2. Copies of personal information such as social security card and driver's license.
3. A completed job application to use as a guide.
4. Copies of awards and achievements.
5. Samples of letters of application, cover memos to attach with a resume, and thank-you letters for interviews.
6. Reference letters.
7. Copies of performance in skills, communications, and any other evaluation that would contribute to success in a job.

The accounting class can contribute as many of these items to the portfolio as the instructor desires. Most instructors will want to have accounting students complete a resume (#1) and documentation of performance (#7).

Writing a resume is an Applied Communication activity in Chapter 1, which provides the opportunity for Writing Across the Curriculum. This can be a positive writing experience for students and is a good way to start off the school year.

Documenting performance in accounting should include a variety of accounting material that is produced by the student. A portfolio might include items such as problems the student has completed, a personal journal describing references and procedures the student used to complete the problem, and a summary report on what was learned from the project. The portfolio should be based on the accounting cycle to produce the most desirable results. Each documentation of performance should have an evaluation sheet that the student completes to explain what activity has been accomplished. The instructor should review and sign this evaluation. A sample Portfolio Assessment sheet is in the Teacher's Resource Guide and on the Student Companion CD.

The portfolio should be an example of the student's best work that will reflect the skills and knowledge the student has learned. Each student should have a binder or folder so that the work may be organized and presented in an attractive manner. Suggested organization of the portfolio is as follows:

1. Table of contents.
2. Personal information (resume, job applications, etc.).
3. Documentation of performance (work samples, personal journals).

SPECIAL FEATURES GRID

Century 21 Accounting, Advanced covers many contemporary special features. The following grid illustrates the features and their location.

Chapter	Accounting in the Real World	Internet Research Activity	Careers in Accounting	Making Ethical Decisions	Business Structures	Cultural Diversity	Technology for Business	Global Perspective	Explore Accounting	Automated Accounting
1	New Balance	Student Credit Cards		Researching Codes of Conduct		Professional Organizations			Accounting Professionals	Automated Entries for Purchases and Cash Payments
2	Blockbuster, Inc.	Federal Deposit Insurance Corporation (FDIC)		At What Price Safety?				International Terms of Sale	Transfer Pricing	Recording Entries for Sales and Cash Receipts Using Special Journals
3	Cisco Systems, Inc.	Payroll Tax Support		Insider Trading					Pretax Benefits	Automating Payroll Accounting Data—Payroll Procedures
4	Trek Bicycles	Accounting Firms	Part-Time Senior Accountant and Accounting Instructor	Sharing Your Knowledge	Differentiating Between Personal and Business Taxes	African American Businesses; Hispanic-Owned Firms Growing Rapidly			Exception Reports	Completing End-of-Fiscal-Period Work for a Departmental Business
5	Procter & Gamble	Accounting Firms (part 2)		Integrity in Management Accounting					Internal Control Systems	Safety Tips to Maintain Your Computer and Disks
6	Toys "R" Us	FASB Mission Statement		Is Someone Reading Your E-Mail?			Spreadsheet Activity—Valuation of Inventory		Computerized Purchasing Systems	Inventory Planning and Valuation
7	J.C. Penney	Resume Writing		Sharing the News				Business Introductions	Representative Payees for Social Security Benefits; Credit Scoring Systems	Automated Entries for Uncollectible Accounts and Write-offs
8	Sysco	Occupational Outlook Handbook		The Land of Opportunity?			Spreadsheet Activity—Depreciation Schedule		Changes in Historic Cost; Limitations of Historic Cost Concept; Tax Laws Encourage Plant Assets Purchases	Automated Depreciation and Creating Depreciation Schedules
9	The Mall of America	Service Corps of Retired Executives (SCORE)		Reporting Ethics Violations		Hispanic American Businesses			The Impact of Changes in Foreign Exchange Rates; Gains or Losses on Accounts Payable and Notes Payable; Accounting for Warranty Expenses	Calculating Notes and Interest Using Planning Tools
10	Northwest Airlines	Accounting Terms		Conflicts of Interest			The Federal Government Is Learning to Shop at Electronic Stores		The Impact of Changes in Foreign Exchange Rates on Accounts Receivable and Notes Receivable; Gains or Losses on Accounts Receivable and Notes Receivable; Factoring Accounts Receivable	Correction of Errors

Chapter	Accounting in the Real World	Internet Research Activity	Careers in Accounting	Making Ethical Decisions	Business Structures	Cultural Diversity	Technology for Business	Global Perspective	Explore Accounting	Automated Accounting
11	General Mills	New York Stock Exchange (NYSE)	Diverse Accounting Background	Just Following Orders	Advantages and Disadvantages of a Corporation	Businesses Owned by Asian Americans and Other Related Groups		International Packages and Customs Inspections	Intangible Assets; Stock Splits	Using the Loan Planner
12	Famous Dave's	Audit Letter		Exercising Stock Options					Stock Price Fluctuation in a Market Economy; Effective Interest Method; Convertible Bonds	Understanding Graphs
13	Medtronics	College Accounting Programs	Accounting Employee at CPA Firm, Accounting Student, Future CPA	Client Referrals			Electronic Backups		Contingent Liabilities; Differences Between GAAP and Tax Law; Notes to Financial Statements	End-of-Period Work for a Corporation
14	KPMG	Organizational Charts		Confidentiality		Who Owns This Small Business?	Numerical Format Options		Spreadsheet Budgeting Tools	Preparing a Performance Report
15	RC Cola	Institute of Management Accountants	Licensure Requirements for Financial Careers	Due Care			Using a Spreadsheet to Perform Breakeven Analysis	International Organizations	Differential Costs; Mixed Costs	Using Computerized Reports for Management Decisions
16	Verizon	Bankruptcy		Bribing Government Officials			Spreadsheet Functions for Present and Future Value Analysis		The Power of Compounding	Using the Retirement Planner
17	Yum! Brands, Inc.	New York Stock Exchange (NYSE)	Forensic Accountant	Could You Be a Whistle Blower?				International Mail	Detailed Information on Financial Statements	Analyzing Automated Financial Statements and Ratio Analysis
18	Hospitality Properties Trust	Software for Specific Industries	Transferable Skills	Channel Stuffing			Keeping Financial Transactions Safe		FASB Statement No. 95	Using the Savings Planner
19	Hershey	Manufacturing Inventory Accounts		Occupational Fraud					Activity-Based Costing; Equivalent Units of Production	Replacing Written Documents with Electronic Spreadsheets
20	Toyota	Dividends Paid by Corporations	Director of Accounts Payable	Fair Competition				International Banking	ISO 9000 Certification	Financial Statements for a Manufacturing Business
21	Pricewaterhouse-Coopers, LLP	Franchises Available	Group Marketing Director	Accurate Accounting Records		Minority Recruiting			Limited Liability Partnerships	Setting Up Automated Accounting Systems for Partnerships
22	Hewlett-Packard Company	CPA Designation		Impending Merger Affects Student's Employment	The FTC Franchise Rule		Spreadsheet Activity—Distribution of Partnership Earnings		Accounting for Mortgage and Lease Payments; Determining Value of Partnership	Generating Financial Reports for a Partnership
23	The United States Postal Service	CMA Designation	Financial Specialist	Evaluating Auditor Independence				International Travel	Accounting in Not-for-Profit Organizations	Using Automated Reports for Analyzing Budget to Actual Business Activity
24	San Jose	Online College Accounting Classes	Vice President of Finance and Technical Operations	Your Personal Code of Conduct					Governmental Accounting Standards Board	Using the Journal Wizard to Customize the Appearance of Journals

PLANNING THE YEAR'S WORK

A time schedule for a complete year should be planned before the year begins. Five steps for planning the year's work are given below.

1. Review what has been previous experience with the pace of work that students have maintained in past accounting classes.
2. Determine how many business simulations and reinforcement activities are to be used during the current year.
3. Decide how much allowance should be made for interruptions in the school day that occur on short notice.
4. Determine if computers will be used in the class. Learning how to use software may require additional class time. However, if computers are used to complete some problems, reinforcement activities, and simulations (rather than working them manually), time may be saved in the schedule.
5. Prepare a proposed schedule of work to be completed. Inspect the schedule to determine if typical breaks in the school year (vacations, special events, and scheduled reporting periods) come at a logical time.

A sample time schedule is given for planning the year's work.

SAMPLE TIME SCHEDULE (FOR THREE QUARTERS—180 DAYS TOTAL)			
Week	**First Quarter—12 Weeks (Chapters 1–8)**	**Second Quarter—12 Weeks (Chapters 9–16)**	**Third Quarter—12 Weeks (Chapters 17–24)**
1	Begin Chapter 1	Chapter 9	Begin Chapter 17
2	Compete Chapter 1	Chapter 10	Complete Ch. 17; Begin Ch. 18
3	Chapter 2	Chapter 11	Complete Ch. 18; Begin Ch. 19
4	Begin Chapter 3	Chapter 12	Complete Ch. 19; Begin Ch. 20
5	Complete Ch. 3; Begin Ch. 4	Begin Chapter 13	Complete Chapter 20
6	Complete Ch. 4; Begin R.A. 1	Complete Ch. 13; Begin R.A. 2	Reinf. Act. 3
7	Complete R.A. 1; Begin Sim. #1	Complete R.A. 2; Begin Sim. #2	Sim. #3
8	Complete Sim. #1	Complete Sim. #2	Chapter 21
9	Chapter 5	Begin Chapter 14	Chapter 22
10	Chapter 6	Comlete Ch. 14; Begin Ch. 15	Begin Chapter 23
11	Chapter 7	Complete Ch. 15	Complete Ch. 23; Begin Ch. 24
12	Chapter 8	Chapter 16	Complete Chapter 24

SOFTWARE CORRELATION

After manual accounting procedures are mastered, software may be used as an enrichment activity to facilitate the processing of accounting data and experience the use of computers in accounting.

Several software products are available to use with *Century 21 Accounting* 8E to augment teacher instruction: Automated Accounting and the accompanying disk files; Peachtree and the accompanying disk files; and QuickBooks and the accompanying disk files. Symbols for Automated Accounting, Peachtree, and QuickBooks within the textbook denote problems that can be worked with the software indicated.

Automated Accounting may be used to complete selected end-of-chapter problems, all three Reinforcement Activities, and all three simulations.

End-of-chapter problems with corresponding data files are marked with an icon. Instructions for using the data file are included in the Automated Accounting sections at the end of relevant chapters. Students should be careful to open the filename given in those instructions.

It is suggested that the *Automated Accounting* text be used as a reference for students who need complete information about the operation of the software. Students can also access Problem Instructions through the Automated Accounting Browser Tool.

Various end-of-chapter problems in *Century 21 Accounting* are marked with Peachtree or QuickBooks symbols, which indicate that the problems can be worked with *South-Western Accounting with Peachtree* or *South-Western Accounting for QuickBooks*.

AUTOMATED ACCOUNTING, PEACHTREE, QUICKBOOKS, AND EXCEL ACCOUNTING PROBLEMS

Text Chapter	Automated Accounting	Peachtree	QuickBooks
1	**1-3 Application Problem:** Journalizing and posting departmental cash payments **1-4 Mastery Problem:** Journalizing departmental purchases and cash payments	**1-2 Application Problem:** Journalizing and posting departmental purchases on account and purchases returns and allowances **1-4 Mastery Problem:** Journalizing departmental purchases and cash payments	**1-2 Application Problem:** Journalizing and posting departmental purchases on account and purchases returns and allowances **1-4 Mastery Problem:** Journalizing departmental purchases and cash payments
2	**2-2 Application Problem:** Journalizing and posting departmental cash receipts **2-3 Mastery Problem:** Journalizing departmental sales, sales returns and allowances, and cash receipts	**2-1 Application Problem:** Journalizing and posting departmental sales on account and sales returns and allowances **2-2 Application Problem:** Journalizing and posting departmental cash receipts **2-3 Mastery Problem:** Journalizing departmental sales, sales returns and allowances, and cash receipts	**2-2 Application Problem:** Journalizing and posting departmental cash receipts **2-3 Mastery Problem:** Journalizing departmental sales, sales returns and allowances, and cash receipts
3	**3-6 Mastery Problem:** Completing payroll records, journalizing payment of a payroll, and journalizing payroll taxes	**3-5 Application Problem:** Calculating and journalizing payment of payroll tax liabilities	**3-5 Application Problem:** Calculating and journalizing payment of payroll tax liabilities
4	**4-3 Application Problem:** Preparing a work sheet with departmental margins **4-4 Application Problem:** Preparing financial statements **4-5 Application Problem:** Journalizing adjusting and closing entries for a departmentalized business **4-6 Mastery Problem:** Completing end-of-fiscal-period work for a merchandising business using departmental margins	**4-5 Application Problem:** Journalizing adjusting and closing entries for a departmentalized business	**4-3 Application Problem:** Preparing a work sheet with departmental margins **4-6 Mastery Problem:** Completing end-of-fiscal-period work for a merchandising business using departmental margins
Reinforcement Activity 1	Processing and Reporting Departmentalized Accounting Data	Processing and Reporting Departmentalized Accounting Data	Processing and Reporting Departmentalized Accounting Data

Text Chapter	Automated Accounting	Peachtree	QuickBooks
6	**6-1 Application Problem:** Keeping perpetual inventory records **6-2 Application Problem:** Determining Inventory cost using FIFO, LIFO, weighted average, and lower of cost or market	**6-1 Application Problem:** Keeping perpetual inventory records	**6-1 Application Problem:** Keeping perpetual inventory records **6-2 Application Problem:** Determining Inventory cost using FIFO, LIFO, weighted average, and lower of cost or market
7	**7-1 Application Problem:** Journalizing entries to write off uncollectible accounts—direct write-off method **7-4 Application Problem:** Journalizing entries to write off uncollectible accounts and collect written-off accounts—allowance method **7-7 Mastery Problem:** Journalizing entries for uncollectible accounts—allowance method; calculating and journalizing the adjusting entry for uncollectible accounts expense	**7-4 Application Problem:** Journalizing entries to write off uncollectible accounts and collect written-off accounts—allowance method	
8	**8-7 Application Problem:** Calculating depreciation expense using the straight-line, declining-balance, and sum-of-the-years'-digits methods **8-11 Mastery Problem:** Recording entries for plant assets **8-12 Challenge Problem:** Recording entries for plant assets	**8-11 Mastery Problem:** Recording entries for plant assets **8-12 Challenge Problem:** Recording entries for plant assets	**8-11 Mastery Problem:** Recording entries for plant assets **8-12 Challenge Problem:** Recording entries for plant assets
9	**9-1 Application Problem:** Journalizing notes payable transactions **9-4 Mastery Problem:** Journalizing adjusting and reversing entries for prepaid expenses initially recorded as expenses and for accrued expenses	**9-1 Application Problem:** Journalizing notes payable transactions **9-4 Mastery Problem:** Journalizing adjusting and reversing entries for prepaid expenses initially recorded as expenses and for accrued expenses	**9-1 Application Problem:** Journalizing notes payable transactions **9-4 Mastery Problem:** Journalizing adjusting and reversing entries for prepaid expenses initially recorded as expenses and for accrued expenses
10	**10-1 Application Problem:** Journalizing transactions for notes receivable **10-4 Mastery Problem:** Journalizing notes receivable, unearned revenue, and accrued revenue initially recorded as revenue transactions	**10-1 Application Problem:** Journalizing transactions for notes receivable **10-4 Mastery Problem:** Journalizing notes receivable, unearned revenue, and accrued revenue initially recorded as revenue transactions	**10-1 Application Problem:** Journalizing transactions for notes receivable **10-4 Mastery Problem:** Journalizing notes receivable, unearned revenue, and accrued revenue initially recorded as revenue transactions
11		**11-4 Application Problem:** Journalizing transactions for declaring and paying dividends **11-5 Mastery Problem:** Journalizing transactions for starting a corporation, declaring and paying dividends, and preparing a balance sheet	**11-2 Application Problem:** Journalizing transactions for stock subscriptions and preparing a balance sheet **11-4 Application Problem:** Journalizing transactions for declaring and paying dividends
12		**12-1 Application Problem:** Journalizing capital stock transactions **12-4 Mastery Problem:** Journalizing stock and bond transactions	**12-1 Application Problem:** Journalizing capital stock transactions **12-4 Mastery Problem:** Journalizing stock and bond transactions
13	**13-5 Mastery Problem:** Completing end-of-fiscal-period work for a corporation	**13-5 Mastery Problem:** Completing end-of-fiscal-period work for a corporation	**13-5 Mastery Problem:** Completing end-of-fiscal-period work for a corporation
Reinforcement Activity 2	Processing and Reporting Accounting Data for a Corporation	Processing and Reporting Accounting Data for a Corporation	Processing and Reporting Accounting Data for a Corporation

Text Chapter	Automated Accounting	Peachtree	QuickBooks
14	**14-5 Challenge Problem:** Preparing a performance report		**14-5 Challenge Problem:** Preparing a performance report
17	**17-7 Mastery Problem:** Analyzing comparative financial statements		**17-1 Application Problem:** Analyzing comparative financial statements using trend analysis
18			**18-4 Application Problem:** Calculating the cash flows from financing activities and completing a statement of cash flows **18-5 Mastery Problem:** Preparing a statement of cash flows
19			**19-5 Application Problem:** Recording entries in a finished goods ledger
20		**20-1 Application Problem:** Journalizing cost accounting transactions for a manufacturing company **20-5 Challenge Problem:** Journalizing entries that summarize cost records at the end of a fiscal period; preparing financial statements	**20-1 Application Problem:** Journalizing cost accounting transactions for a manufacturing company
Reinforcement Activity 3	An Accounting Cycle for a Corporation: Journalizing and Posting Transactions	An Accounting Cycle for a Corporation: Journalizing and Posting Transactions	An Accounting Cycle for a Corporation: Journalizing and Posting Transactions
21	**21-1 Application Problem:** Forming a partnership **21-6 Mastery Problem:** Forming and expanding a partnership	**21-1 Application Problem:** Forming a partnership **21-6 Mastery Problem:** Forming and expanding a partnership	**21-1 Application Problem:** Forming a partnership **21-6 Mastery Problem:** Forming and expanding a partnership
22	**22-5 Mastery Problem:** Completing end-of-fiscal-period work for a partnership **22-6 Challenge Problem:** Completing end-of-fiscal-period work for a partnership	**22-5 Mastery Problem:** Completing end-of-fiscal-period work for a partnership **22-6 Challenge Problem:** Completing end-of-fiscal-period work for a partnership	**22-5 Mastery Problem:** Completing end-of-fiscal-period work for a partnership **22-6 Challenge Problem:** Completing end-of-fiscal-period work for a partnership
23		**23-3 Application Problem:** Journalizing governmental encumbrances, expenditures, and other transactions **23-4 Mastery Problem:** Journalizing governmental transactions	**23-3 Application Problem:** Journalizing governmental encumbrances, expenditures, and other transactions **23-4 Mastery Problem:** Journalizing governmental transactions
24		**24-3 Application Problem:** Journalizing adjusting and closing entries for a governmental organization **24-4 Mastery Problem:** Completing the end-of-fiscal-period work for a governmental organization	**24-4 Mastery Problem:** Completing the end-of-fiscal-period work for a governmental organization **24-5 Challenge Problem:** Completing end-of-fiscal-period work for a governmental organization

CURRICULUM AND INSTRUCTION THROUGH INTEGRATION OF SCANS

(The Secretary's Commission on Achieving Necessary Skills)

The Secretary's Commission on Achieving Necessary Skills (SCANS) was asked to examine the demands of the workplace and whether our young people are capable of meeting those demands.

Specifically, the commission was directed to advise the Secretary on the level of skills required to enter employment. SCANS research verifies that what we call workplace know-how defines effective job performance today. This know-how has two elements: competencies and a foundation. This report identifies five competencies (resources, interpersonal skills, information, systems, and technology) and a three-part foundation of skills and personal qualities (basic skills, thinking skills, and personal qualities) that lie at the heart of job performance. These eight requirements are essential preparation for all students, both those going directly to work and those planning further education. Thus, the competencies and the foundation should be taught and understood in an integrated fashion that reflects the workplace contexts in which they are applied.

Century 21 Accounting 8E seamlessly integrates the SCANS competencies through the text and suggested activities. The following table correlates the specific areas of the SCANS skills with the SCANS Workplace Competencies feature at the end of each chapter in the *Century 21 Accounting*, First-Year Course and Advanced Course textbooks.

Note, however, that many of these skills are also reinforced throughout *Century 21 Accounting*. For example, arithmetic/mathematic skills are used in virtually every problem. Every chapter includes an Applied Communication activity that requires the use of oral and written communications. The Making Ethical Decisions features and the Challenge Problems in every chapter expand information, decision-making, and thinking skills. Internet Research Activities and problems designed for use with Automated Accounting, Peachtree, and QuickBooks software increase information skills.

CENTURY 21 ACCOUNTING CORRELATION WITH SCANS COMPETENCIES

	First-Year Text Chapter	Advanced Text Chapter
A THREE-PART FOUNDATION		
Basic Skills: Reads, writes, performs arithmetic and mathematical operations, listens, and speaks		
A. Reading	10, 13	
B. Writing	3	11
C. Arithmetic/Mathematics	6, 22	
D. Listening	21	
E. Speaking		2
Thinking Skills: Thinks creatively, makes decisions, solves problems, visualizes, knows how to learn, and reasons		
A. Creative Thinking	9	
B. Decision Making		16
C. Problem Solving		10
D. Seeing Things in the Mind's Eye	8	
E. Knowing How to Learn	16	
F. Reasoning	15, 17	12
Personal Qualities: Displays responsibility, self-esteem, sociability, self-management, and integrity and honesty		
A. Responsibility	5	
B. Self-Esteem	7, 12	
C. Sociability	19	
D. Self-Management	18	24
E. Integrity/Honesty		21

	First-Year Text Chapter	Advanced Text Chapter
FIVE WORKPLACE COMPETENCIES		
Resources: Identifies, organizes, plans, and allocates resources		
A. Time: Selects goal-relevant activities, ranks them, allocates time, and prepares and follows schedules	1, 2	6
B. Money: Uses or prepares budgets, makes forecasts, keeps records, and makes adjustments to meet objectives		13
C. Material and Facilities: Acquires, stores, allocates, and uses materials or space efficiently		4
D. Human Resources: Assesses skills and distributes work accordingly, evaluates performance and provides feedback		18
Interpersonal: Works with others		
A. Participates as Member of a Team	11	1
B. Teaches Others New Skills		14
C. Serves Clients/Customers		15
D. Exercises Leadership		17
E. Negotiates		19
F. Works with Diversity		20
Information: Acquires and uses information		
A. Acquires and Evaluates Information	20	
B. Organizes and Maintains Information	4	8
C. Interprets and Communicates Information		9
D. Uses Computers to Process Information		3
Understands complex inter-relationships		
A. Understands Systems		5
B. Monitors and Corrects Performance	23	
C. Improves or Designs Systems		7
Works with a variety of technologies		
A. Selects Technology	24	22
B. Applies Technology to Task		23
C. Maintains and Troubleshoots Equipment	14	

NATIONAL BUSINESS EDUCATION ASSOCIATION STANDARDS FOR ACCOUNTING

The Role of Accounting in Business Education

Accounting is an essential aspect of every business institution and organization. As future workers, small business owners, and entrepreneurs, students who understand basic accounting principles will more knowledgeably manage their companies' financial resources. As citizens, future parents, and investors, these students will be better prepared to make the economic decisions that will affect their communities—such as passing a referendum to build new schools—and to make the financial decisions that will affect their own economic futures.

The introduction of computerized systems has made the mastery of technology skills an integral part of the accounting curriculum. Automated proce-dures eliminate the repetitive tasks required for manual accounting and facilitate the inclusion of individual and group activities that involve higher-level thinking skills. The Internet also offers tremendous opportunities for financial research and a wide variety of learning applications and activities.

The following attitudes and skills should be integrated and reinforced throughout the entire accounting curriculum: critical thinking, decision making, problem solving, team building, ethics, work quality, communication, and technology.

These accounting standards identify the knowledge and skills appropriate for courses at both the high school and two-year college levels. Performance expectations appropriate for the second year of high school accounting are indicated with an asterisk. These accounting standards do not address topics generally taught in intermediate, cost, tax, and other advanced accounting courses.

CENTURY 21 ACCOUNTING CORRELATION WITH NBEA ACCOUNTING STANDARDS

	Required In			Found in Chapters	
	1st Year	Advanced	College	First-Year Course 8th Edition	Advanced Course 8th Edition
I. THE ACCOUNTING CYCLE **Achievement Standard: Complete and explain the purpose of the various steps in the accounting cycle.**					
1. Define accounting and explain the purpose of the accounting system	•			1	
2. Define the concept of generally accepted accounting principles and ascertain the source of these standards	•			Concepts explained and referenced throughout. Also listed and described in Appendix A.	
3. Demonstrate an understanding of the fundamental accounting equation	•			1	
4. Classify items as assets, liabilities, or owner's equity	•			1–2	
5. Describe the purposes of the revenue, expense, and drawing accounts and illustrate their effects on owner's equity	•			2	
6. Analyze business transactions using source documents and describe the effect on the accounting equation	•			3 Source document problems in Chapters 3, 4, 9, 10, and 11; Zenith Global Imports and Tronics, Inc. simulations.	
7. Explain the double-entry system of accounting and apply debit and credit rules when analyzing business transactions	•			2–3	
8. Explain the purpose of the journal and the process of journalizing business transactions	•			3	
9. Analyze the relationship of the journal to the ledger	•			4	
10. Explain the purpose of a ledger account and post information from the journal to the ledger	•			4	
11. Prepare a trial balance and explain its uses and limitations	•			6, 14, 22	
12. Explain the purpose of adjusting entries	•			6, 14, 22	
13. Analyze the trial balance to determine the necessary adjustments (accruals and deferrals) to prepare financial statements	•			6, 14, 22	

	Required In			Found in Chapters	
	1st Year	**Advanced**	**College**	**First-Year Course 8th Edition**	**Advanced Course 8th Edition**
14. Prepare and explain the purposes of each financial statement and describe the way they articulate with each other	•			7, 15, 22	
15. Explain the purposes of the closing process and journalize and post closing entries	•			8, 16, 22	
16. Use spreadsheet and accounting software to maintain accounting records and describe the differences between manual and computerized accounting systems	•			Automated Accounting topics at the end of every chapter with problems; spreadsheet data files and Peachtree and QuickBooks problems for most chapters.	
17. Evaluate the effect of adjusting entries on financial statements		•		6, 14, 17–22	4, 6–10, 13, 20, 22

II. THE ACCOUNTING PROCESS

Achievement Standard: Apply generally accepted accounting principles to determine the value of assets, liabilities, and owner's equity.

A. Assets

	Required In			Found in Chapters	
	1st Year	**Advanced**	**College**	**First-Year Course 8th Edition**	**Advanced Course 8th Edition**
1. Define and identify current and long-term assets and explain their impact on financial statements	•			18	
2. Define cash; prepare bank reconciliations; establish, maintain, and reconcile petty cash and change accounts; identify cash control techniques; explain the benefits of electronic fund transfers, automated teller machine transactions, electronic data interchange, automated bill paying, and uses of a debit card	•			5, 9, 10	
3. Create and maintain the accounts receivable subsidiary ledger and an account for credit card sales	•			10	
4. Apply appropriate accounting techniques for uncollectible accounts	•			17, 20, 21	
5. Establish and maintain accounts for receivables and related interest	•			10, 11, 17, 20, 21	
6. Compare and evaluate inventory concepts and costing procedures and apply these concepts and procedures to merchandising and manufacturing businesses	•			19	
7. Explain the purpose of depreciation	•			14, 18	
8. Apply appropriate accounting concepts and techniques for acquisition, depreciation, and disposal of property, plant, and equipment	•			18	
9. Use spreadsheet or accounting software to maintain accounting records for short-term and long-term assets	•			18 (spreadsheet data files, Automated Accounting, Peachtree, and QuickBooks problems)	
10. Convert an amount of foreign currency into the equivalent U.S. dollar value		•		24	9, 10
11. Explain the impact of changes in foreign exchange rates on accounts receivable and notes receivable		•			10
12. Compute the gains or losses on accounts receivable and notes receivable resulting from changes in foreign exchange rates		•			10
13. Compute and compare the cost basis and fair value of assets		•			8
14. Compare and analyze various depreciation methods and their impact on financial statements		•			8
15. Use appropriate accounting concepts and techniques to analyze and record repairs and improvements of plant and equipment and exchanges of equipment		•			8

	Required In			Found in Chapters	
	1st Year	**Advanced**	**College**	**First-Year Course 8th Edition**	**Advanced Course 8th Edition**
16. Define intangible assets and account for their acquisition, amortization, and disposal		•			11
17. Define natural resources and account for their acquisition, depletion, and disposal		•			8
18. Define short-term investments and describe the accounting concepts and techniques used to analyze and record transactions involving trading, available-for-sale, and held-to-maturity securities			•		
19. Identify long-term investments that represent a significant degree of influence or controlling interest in another company			•		
B. Liabilities					
1. Define and identify current and long-term liabilities and explain their impact on financial statements	•			20–22	
2. Create and maintain the accounts payable subsidiary ledger	•			9	
3. Explain the purposes of notes payable; establish and maintain accounts for payables and related interest	•			21–22	
4. Use spreadsheet or accounting software to maintain accounting records for short-term and long-term liabilities	•			(spreadsheet data files, Automated Accounting, Peachtree, and QuickBooks problems)	
5. Explain the impact of foreign exchange rates on accounts payable and notes payable with suppliers		•			9
6. Compute the gains or losses on accounts payable and notes payable resulting from changes in foreign exchange rates		•			9
7. Use appropriate accounting concepts and techniques to analyze and record the issuance, amortization, and retirement of bonds		•			12
8. Use appropriate accounting concepts and techniques to analyze and record mortgage and lease obligations and subsequent principal and interest payments			•		
9. Compare and contrast straight-line and effective interest amortization methods for bond premiums and discounts			•		
10. Analyze a trial balance and identify any contingent liabilities			•		
C. Owner's Equity					
1. Explain the purpose of the capital and drawing accounts for a sole proprietorship and partnership	•			2, 3, 8, 15, 22, 23	
2. Explain the purpose of the capital stock and retained earnings accounts for a corporation	•			14–16, 22	
3. Apply appropriate accounting techniques to account for investments and withdrawals by owners		•			21, 22
4. Explain the purpose of the following accounts: common stock, preferred stock, paid-in capital, retained earnings, and dividends for a corporation		•			11–13
5. Apply appropriate accounting concepts and techniques to analyze and record investments by stockholders and the declaration and payment of dividends		•			11–13
6. Analyze the effect of cash dividends on financial statements			•		

III. FINANCIAL STATEMENTS

Achievement Standard: Prepare, interpret, and analyze financial statements using manual and computerized systems for service, merchandising, and manufacturing businesses.

A. Financial Statement Preparation and Analysis

	1st Year	Advanced	College	First-Year Course 8th Edition	Advanced Course 8th Edition
1. Analyze the effect of cash dividends on financial statements			•		

	Required In			Found in Chapters	
	1st Year	Advanced	College	First-Year Course 8th Edition	Advanced Course 8th Edition
2. Analyze the income statement and balance sheet of a business by comparing a vertical analysis with industry standards	•			7, 15, 22	
3. Analyze the statement of cash flows by comparing it with previous statements	•			Appendix A	
4. Use spreadsheet or accounting software to evaluate the impact of changes in operating procedures, accounting methods, and estimates on the financial statements and ratios	•			Spreadsheet data files and What-If sections.	
5. Use a spreadsheet or accounting software to prepare charts and graphs useful in analyzing the financial condition of the business	•			Spreadsheet and Automated Accounting data files; Graphing Workshop feature in Chapters 1, 5, 7, 12, 13, 15, 17, 19, 21, 24.	
6. Explain the importance of high ethical standards in the preparation of financial statements	•			Ethics feature in every chapter.	
7. Research and analyze financial statements of corporations using a variety of sources (e.g., the Internet and primary source documentation)	•			Appendix B: Best Buy's Financial Statements is referenced at the end of every chapter to analyze information in the report; Accounting in the Real World and Internet Research Activity at the beginning of each chapter require research and analysis.	
8. Identify and define the three basic types of business activities—operating, investing, and financing		•			18
9. Prepare a statement of cash flows		•			18
10. Perform horizontal and vertical analyses and compute appropriate ratios to evaluate solvency and earning power		•			4, 13, 17
11. Analyze corporate financial data using a variety of sources (e.g., the Internet and primary source documentation)		•			Appendix B: Costco's Annual Report is referenced at the end of every chapter to analyze information in the report; Accounting in the Real World and Internet Research Activity at the beginning of each chapter require research and analysis.
12. Explain the inherent limitations of the historical cost accounting model when interpreting financial statements prepared during periods of inflation or changing prices			•		8
B. Income Statements for the Three Types of Business Operations					
1. Apply the revenue realization and matching principles in the preparation of an income statement or statement of operations for service and merchandising businesses	•			7, 15, 22, 23	
2. Determine cost of goods sold and gross profit for a merchandising business	•			15, 22	
3. Apply the revenue realization and matching principles in the preparation of an income statement or statement of operations for a manufacturing business		•			20

	Required In			Found in Chapters	
	1st Year	**Advanced**	**College**	**First-Year Course 8th Edition**	**Advanced Course 8th Edition**
4. Determine cost of goods sold and gross profit for a manufacturing business		•			20
5. Define discontinued operations, extraordinary items, and earnings per share and show how they are reported on the income statement or statement of operations			•		

IV. SPECIAL APPLICATIONS

Achievement Standard: Apply appropriate accounting principles to payroll, income taxation, managerial systems, and various forms of ownership.

A. Forms of Ownership

	Required In			Found in Chapters	
	1st Year	**Advanced**	**College**	**First-Year Course 8th Edition**	**Advanced Course 8th Edition**
1. Explain the advantages and disadvantages of the three forms of business ownership—sole proprietorships, partnerships, and corporations	•			1, 9, 23	
2. Apply appropriate accounting techniques for the formation and allocation of earnings of a partnership	•			23	
3. Apply appropriate accounting principles to government and not-for-profit entities		•			23, 24
4. Apply appropriate accounting techniques for the formation and allocation of earnings of a corporation		•			4, 11–13

B. Payroll

	Required In			Found in Chapters	
	1st Year	**Advanced**	**College**	**First-Year Course 8th Edition**	**Advanced Course 8th Edition**
1. Prepare and maintain payroll records using manual and computerized systems	•			12, 13, spreadsheet data files, Automated Accounting, Peachtree, and QuickBooks problems.	
2. Calculate earnings at an hourly and piece rate and on a salary, commission, and salary/commission basis	•			12	
3. Calculate deductions including federal income tax, Social Security tax, Medicare tax, state income tax, and other deductions to determine net pay	•			12	
4. Calculate employer's payroll taxes (e.g., Social Security, Medicare, federal unemployment, and state unemployment) and employee benefits paid by the employer	•			12, 13	
5. Prepare federal, state, and local payroll reports	•			13	

C. Income Taxation

	Required In			Found in Chapters	
	1st Year	**Advanced**	**College**	**First-Year Course 8th Edition**	**Advanced Course 8th Edition**
1. Differentiate between taxation at the personal and business levels		•			4
2. Explain how income tax law is formed			•		
3. Explain the basic differences between generally accepted accounting principles and tax law			•		

D. Managerial Accounting Principles and Systems

	Required In			Found in Chapters	
	1st Year	**Advanced**	**College**	**First-Year Course 8th Edition**	**Advanced Course 8th Edition**
1. Describe the management process and the role of managerial accounting in this process		•			14–18
2. Describe and explain those costs and accounts that are unique to the manufacturing process and distinguish between product and period costs		•			19–20
3. Prepare the statement of cost of goods manufactured and explain its purpose on the income statement of a manufacturing business		•			20
4. Describe the cost flow concepts followed by a manufacturing business		•			19–20
5. Describe the types of products and manufacturing processes most appropriate for job order and process costing systems		•			19

	Required In			Found in Chapters	
	1st Year	Advanced	College	First-Year Course 8th Edition	Advanced Course 8th Edition
6. Apply appropriate accounting concepts and procedures for a job order costing system		●			19–20
7. Apply appropriate accounting concepts and procedures for a process costing system		●			19
V. INTERPRETATION AND USE OF DATA **Achievement Standard: Use planning and control principles to evaluate the performance of an organization and apply differential analysis and present-value concepts to make decisions.**					
A. Planning and Control					
1. Explain and compare the behavior of fixed, variable, and mixed costs		●			15
2. Apply cost-volume-profit and contribution margin analyses in planning operations		●			15
3. Prepare a budget for planning purposes		●			14, 23
4. Explain activity-based costing		●			19
5. Use spreadsheet or accounting software for budget analysis		●			14, Spreadsheet data files and Automated Accounting problems.
6. Apply variable and absorption costing concepts to analyze profitability			●		
7. Prepare master and flexible budgets and use them to evaluate performance			●		
8. Evaluate company performance by applying standard costing and variance analysis			●		
9. Apply responsibility accounting concepts to evaluate cost, profit, and investment centers			●		
10. Develop a plan for activity-based costing for a manufacturing business			●		
B. Decision Making					
1. Apply differential analysis to make the following types of decisions: making or buying a product; leasing or buying an asset; discontinuing a department, plant, or product; offering discounted prices on special orders; replacing or repairing equipment			●		
2. Apply present-value concepts to evaluate capital investment opportunities			●		16

LOCATION OF ANSWERS AND SOLUTIONS

Due to the abundance of teacher support material available with this course, the table below is provided to guide you in locating solutions to student activities.

Item	Found In
Accounting in the Real World	Margins of Wraparound Teacher's Edition
Internet Research Activity	Margins of Wraparound Teacher's Edition
Making Ethical Decisions	Margins of Wraparound Teacher's Edition and Instructional Strategies section in Wraparound Teacher's Edition
Business Structures, Careers in Accounting, Cultural Diversity, Technology for Business, Global Perspective features	Margins of Wraparound Teacher's Edition
Terms Review	Glossary in Student Text
Audit Your Understanding	Appendix E in Student Text
Work Together Problems	Teacher's Edition of Working Papers
On Your Own Problems	Teacher's Edition of Working Papers
Explore Accounting	Margins of Wraparound Teacher's Edition
Application Problems	Teacher's Edition of Working Papers
Mastery Problems	Teacher's Edition of Working Papers
Challenge Problems	Teacher's Edition of Working Papers
Applied Communication	Margins of Wraparound Teacher's Edition
Cases for Critical Thinking	Margins of Wraparound Teacher's Edition
SCANS Workplace Competency	Margins of Wraparound Teacher's Edition
Auditing for Errors and Graphing Workshop	Margins of Wraparound Teacher's Edition
Analyzing Costco's Financial Statements	Margins of Wraparound Teacher's Edition
Reinforcement Activities	Teacher's Edition of Working Papers
Recycling Problems	Teacher's Edition of Recycling Problem Working Papers
Automated Accounting Problems	Teacher's Resource Guide and the Electronic Auditor
Study Guides	Teacher's Edition of Working Papers
Tests	Assessment Binder
Manual Simulations	Keys for manual simulations
Automated Simulations	Keys for automated simulations
Peachtree Problems	*South-Western Accounting with Peachtree* Instructor's Manual
QuickBooks Problems	*South-Western Accounting for QuickBooks* Instructor's Manual

PROFESSIONAL REFERENCES AND RESOURCES

Periodicals

Accountancy Age, VNU Business Publications, London, UK. (international accounting)

Accounting Horizons, American Accounting Association, Sarasota, FL.

Accounting, Organizations, and Society, Elsevier, New York, NY.

Accounting Review, American Accounting Association, Sarasota, FL.

Accounting Technology, Source Media, New York, NY.

Accounting Today, Source Media, New York, NY.

American Accounting Association Newsletter, Sarasota, FL.

Black Enterprise, Earl G. Graves Ltd., New York, NY. (multicultural awareness)

Business Ethics: The Magazine of Corporate Responsibility, Business Ethics Magazine, Minneapolis, MN.

CPA Journal, New York State Society of CPAs, New York, NY.

Electronic Magazine of Multicultural Education, Eastern University Education Department, St. Davids, PA. (multicultural awareness)

Entrepreneur, Entrepreneur Media, Irvine, CA.

Forbes, Forbes Publishing, Inc., New York, NY. (business news)

Fortune, Time, Inc., New York, NY. (business news)

Hispanic Magazine, Hispanic Publishing Group, Coral Gables, FL. (multicultural awareness)

Inc. Magazine, Gruner + Jahr USA, New York, NY. (small business/entrepreneurship)

Internet Bulletin for CPAs, Kent Information Services, Inc., Kent, OH.

Journal of Accountancy, AICPA, New York, NY.

Journal of Accounting Education, Elsevier, New York, NY.

Journal of Business Ethics, Springer, Berlin, Germany.

Management Accounting Quarterly, Institute of Management Accountants, Montvale, NJ.

Multinational Business Review, University of Detroit—Mercy, Boeing Institute of International Business, Detroit, MI. (global business)

Native Peoples, Media Concepts Group, Inc., Phoenix, AZ. (multicultural awareness)

Practical Accountant, Source Media, New York, NY.

Transpacific, Transpacific Media, Inc., Malibu, CA. (multicultural awareness)

Wall Street Journal, New York, NY. (business newspaper)

Books

Adams, Dennis. *Cooperative Learning: Critical Thinking and Collaboration Across the Curriculum.* Springfield: Charles C. Thomas Publisher, Limited, 1996.

AICPA. *Accounting Trends and Techniques*, 58E.

AICPA. *FASB Accounting Standards.*

Albrecht, W. Steve, James D. Stice, Earl Kay Stice, and Monte Swain. *Accounting: Concepts and Applications*, 9E. Mason, OH: South-Western College, 2005.

Albrecht, W. Steve. *Ethical Workplace.* Menlo Park: Crisp Publications, Inc., 1998.

Baldwin, Bruce, and Clayton Hock. *Financial Reporting Project and Readings*, 3E. Mason, OH: South-Western College, 2005.

Bieg, Bernard J. *Payroll Accounting*, 15E. Mason, OH: South-Western College, 2005.

Bloom, Benjamin S., ed., et al. *Taxonomy for Learning, Teaching, and Assessing.* White Plains: Longman, 2000.

Brooks, Leonard J. *Business and Professional Ethics for Directors, Executives, and Accountants*, 3E. Mason, OH: South-Western College, 2004.

Cantlon, Teresa L. *Structuring the Classroom Successfully for Cooperative Team Learning.* Portland, OR: Prestige Publishers, 1989.

Chatfield, Michael. *The History of Accounting: An International Encyclopedia.* New York: Garland Publishing, Inc., 1996.

Elashmawi, Farid, and Philip R. Harris. *Multicultural Management 2000.* Houston: Gulf Publishing Company, 1998.

Estes, Ralph. *Dictionary of Accounting*, 2E. Cambridge: The MIT Press, 1985.

Fisher, Paul, William Taylor, and Rita Cheng. *Advanced Accounting*, 9E. Mason, OH: South-Western College, 2006.

Gelinas, Ulric J., Steve G. Sutton, and Jim Hunton. *Accounting Information Systems*, 6E. Mason, OH: South-Western College, 2005.

Gibson, Charles H. *Financial Reporting and Analysis: Using Financial Accounting Information*, 9E. Mason, OH: South-Western College, 2005.

Griseri, Paul. *Managing Values.* New York: Palgrave Macmillan, 1998.

Gronlund, Norman E. *Assessment of Student Achievement*, 7E. New York: Allyn and Bacon, 2002.

Gronlund, Norman E. *Writing Instructional Objectives for Teaching and Assessment*, 7E. New York: Prentice Hall, 2003.

Hall, James A. *Accounting Information Systems*, 4E. Mason, OH: South-Western College, 2005.

Harrell, Earl, and Cassandra Harrell. *Surviving in the Workplace.* Milwaukee: E.T. Publishing Company, 1994.

Harris, Philip R., and Robert T. Moran. *Managing Cultural Differences: Global Leadership Strategies for the 21st Century.* New York: Butterworth, 2004.

Heintz, James A., and Robert Parry. *College Accounting*, 18E. Mason, OH: South-Western College, 2005.

Ingram, Robert, Thomas Albright, Bruce Baldwin, and John Hill. *Accounting: Information for Decisions*, 3E. Mason, OH: South-Western College, 2005.

Iqbal, Zafar. *International Accounting with InfoTrac College Edition.* Mason, OH: South-Western College, 2002.

Johnson, D. *Cooperation and Competition.* Edina: Interaction Book Company, 1989.

Jones, Frederick, and Dasaratha Rama. *Accounting Information Systems: A Business Process Approach,* 2E. Mason, OH: South-Western College, 2006.

Knapp, Michael C. *Contemporary Auditing: Real Issues and Cases,* 5E. Mason, OH: South-Western College, 2004.

Knechel, W. Robert. *Auditing: Assurance and Risk,* 2E. Mason, OH: South-Western College, 2001.

Konrath, Larry F. *Auditing: A Risk-Analysis Approach,* 5E. Mason, OH: South-Western College, 2002.

LaBonty, Dennis, ed. *Integrating the Internet into the Business Curriculum.* Reston: National Business Education Association, 1998.

Lerner, Janet W. *Learning Disabilities,* 9E. Boston: Houghton Mifflin, 2002.

Mager, Robert F. *Preparing Instructional Objectives: A Critical Tool in the Development of Effective Instruction.* Atlanta: Center for Effective Performance, Inc., 1997.

Mamchur, Carolyn. *A Teacher's Guide to Cognitive Type Theory and Learning Style.* Alexandria, VA: Association for Supervision and Curriculum Development, 1996.

Marzano, Robert J. *A Different Kind of Classroom: Teaching with Dimensions of Learning.* Alexandria, VA: Association for Supervision and Curriculum Development, 1992.

National Society of Public Accountants. *Portfolio of Accounting Systems for Small and Medium-Sized Businesses.* Revised. Paramus, NJ: Prentice Hall, 1992.

Nikolai, Loren, and John Bazley. *Intermediate Accounting,* 9E. Mason, OH: South-Western College, 2004.

Palepu, Krishna G., Victor L. Bernard, and Paul M. Healy. *Business Analysis and Valuation: Using Financial Statements, Text, and Cases,* 3E. Mason, OH: South-Western College, 2004.

Perry, James, and Gary P. Schneider. *Building Accounting Systems Using Access 2003,* 3E. Mason, OH: South-Western College, 2005.

Pratt, Jamie, Krishnamoorthy Ramesh, and David Foster. *Interactive Cases in Financial Analysis CD-ROM.* Mason, OH: South-Western College, 2000.

Ricchiute, David. *Auditing,* 8E. Mason, OH: South-Western College, 2006.

Riding, Richard. *International Perspectives on Individual Differences: Cognitive Styles.* Ablex Publishing, 2000.

Schloss, Patrick J. *Career-Vocational Education for Handicapped Youth.* Gaithersburg, MD: Aspen Publishers, Inc., 1982.

Scott, John L. *Vocational Special Needs.* Homewood: American Technical Publishers, 1995.

Secretary's Commission on Achieving Necessary Skills. *What Work Requires of Schools: A SCANS Report for America 2000.* Washington, DC: U.S. Department of Labor, 1991.

Simons, George F., Carmen Vazquez, and Philip R. Harris. *Transcultural Leadership: Empowering the Diverse Work Force.* Houston: Gulf Publishing Company, 1993.

Solomon, Robert C. *Ethics and Excellence: Cooperation and Integrity in Business.* New York: Oxford, 1992.

Stice, James, Earl Kay Stice, and Fred Skousen. *Intermediate Accounting with Thomson Analytics,* 15E. Mason, OH: South-Western College, 2004.

U.S. Department of Labor. *Dictionary of Occupational Titles.*

U.S. Department of Labor. *Occupational Outlook Handbook.*

Verduin, John R., Jr. *Helping Students Develop Investigative, Problem-Solving, and Thinking Skills in a Cooperative Setting: A Handbook for Teachers, Administrators, and Curriculum Workers.* Springfield: Charles C. Thomas Publisher, Limited, 1996.

Warren, Carl S., James M. Reeve, and Philip E. Fess. *Accounting,* 21E. Mason, OH: South-Western College, 2005.

Warren, Carl S., James Reeve, and Philip E. Fess. *Financial Accounting,* 9E. Mason, OH: South-Western College, 2005.

Warren, Carl S., James Reeve, and Philip E. Fess. *Financial and Managerial Accounting,* 8E. Mason, OH: South-Western College, 2005.

Weirich, Thomas, Thomas Pearson, and Alan Reinstein. *Accounting and Tax Research,* 6E. Mason, OH: South-Western College, 2005.

Wolk, Harry, James Dodd, and Michael Tearney. *Accounting Theory,* 6E. Mason, OH: South-Western College, 2004.

ADVANCED • ADVANCED • ADVANCED • ADVANCED • ADVANCED • ADVANCED • A

Century 21

SOUTH-WESTERN
Accounting 8E

CLAUDIA BIENIAS GILBERTSON, CPA
Teaching Professor
North Hennepin Community College
Brooklyn Park, Minnesota

MARK W. LEHMAN, CPA
Associate Professor
School of Accountancy
Mississippi State University
Starkville, Mississippi

DAN PASSALACQUA, MA
Oak Grove High School
San Jose, California

KENTON E. ROSS, CPA
Professor Emeritus of Accounting
Texas A&M University—Commerce
Commerce, Texas

THOMSON
*

SOUTH-WESTERN

Australia · Brazil · Canada · Mexico · Singapore · Spain · United Kingdom · United States

THOMSON

SOUTH-WESTERN

Advanced, Century 21 Accounting 8E

Claudia Bienias Gilbertson, CPA; Mark W. Lehman, CPA; Dan Passalacqua, MA; Kenton E. Ross, CPA

VP/Editorial Director:
Jack W. Calhoun

VP/Editor-in-Chief:
Karen Schmohe

Acquisitions Editor:
Marilyn Hornsby

Project Manager:
Carol Sturzenberger

Consulting Editor:
Bill Lee

Verification Editors:
Howard Rankin; Sara Wilson

VP/Director of Marketing:
Carol Volz

Marketing Manager:
Courtney Schulz

Marketing Coordinator:
Angela Russo

Senior Promotions Manager:
Terron Sanders

Production Editor:
Kim Kusnerak

Production Manager:
Patricia Matthews Boies

Manufacturing Buyer:
Kevin Kluck

Manager of Technology-Editorial:
Liz Prigge

Senior Technology Project Editor:
Mike Jackson

Web Coordinator:
Ed Stubenrauch

Art Director:
Tippy McIntosh

Photography/Permissions Editor:
Darren Wright

Production House:
Lachina Publishing Services

Cover/Internal Design:
Ann Small, a small design studio

Cover Illustration:
Philip Brooker

Internal Illustration:
Mark Shaver, The Wiley Group

Printer:
Quebecor World
Dubuque, IA

For permission to use material from this text or product, submit a request online at www.thomsonrights.com. Any additional questions about permissions can be submitted by email to thomsonrights@thomson.com.

For more information contact Thomson Higher Education
5191 Natorp Boulevard
Mason, Ohio 45040
USA
Or you can visit our Internet site at: http://www.swlearning.com

Century 21

SOUTH-WESTERN
Accounting 8E

The Choice for Real-World Technology!

Integrate technology into your advanced accounting course with solutions only available from Thomson South-Western!

➡ **Automated Accounting**

The functionality of commercial software incorporated with educational features makes teaching and learning computerized accounting easy. *Automated Accounting 8.0* is fully integrated into every chapter of *Century 21 Accounting.*

Automated Accounting 8.0 Individual User CD (Windows)   0-538-97294-7
Automated Accounting 8.0 Site License (Windows)   0-538-44228-X

➡ **Creating the Band**

An accounting simulation for Peachtree, QuickBooks, and Microsoft Excel. This text is designed to give realistic experience in keeping accounting records for a small business. Students will work as an accountant for CTB, which is a band whose members have formed a business partnership.

Student Text and Data CD   0-538-44150-X

➡ **South-Western Accounting with Peachtree Complete 2005**

South-Western *Accounting with Peachtree Complete* is the ideal supplement for teachers who want to introduce Peachtree software. The text teaches students to work step-by-step through Century 21 problems using Peachtree. Interactive tutorials are also included on South-Western's Peachtree individual user disk and the site license.

Text/CD Package (softcover, 118 pages)   0-538-44209-3

➡ **South-Western Accounting for QuickBooks Pro**

This supplement is perfect for incorporating QuickBooks software into your *Century 21 Accounting* class. The text with data CD teaches students to journalize accounting transactions, post to ledger accounts, and prepare financial statements using QuickBooks Pro software.

Text Data/CD package (softcover, 272 pages)   0-538-44205-0

How to Use This Book

PART OPENERS focus on a particular business that you'll learn about:

- **A listing of the chapters** covered in each Part helps you focus on what you'll be learning.

- The **Chart of Accounts** used in the entire Part is provided for easy reference as you work through the chapters.

CHAPTER OPENERS introduce the subject matter you'll investigate:

- **Objectives** listed at the beginning of each chapter highlight lesson concepts and preview what you will learn.

- The **Terms Preview** displays all the key words introduced in the chapter. You can also find these terms and their definitions in the Glossary at the back of the text.

- **Accounting in the Real World** features a photo and description of a real company with questions linked to the chapter's content.

- **Internet Research Activity** sends you to the Internet to locate information to answer questions related to the chapter's subject matter.

LESSON OPENERS focus on one or two topics:

- Most **Illustrations** are placed above the text that discusses them. You can quickly find the illustrations when you're reviewing or working problems.

- **Steps and callouts** make it easy to understand and apply the procedures you learn. Clear instructions are directly linked to the part of the illustration where the work is recorded.

END-OF-LESSON PAGES help you fully understand all concepts and procedures before moving on to the next lesson:

- **Terms Review** lists all the new words learned in the lesson.

- **Audit Your Understanding** asks two or more questions about the lesson material. You can check your answers in the Appendix.

- **Work Together** gives you guided practice through hands-on application of the lesson's procedures and concepts.

- **On Your Own** challenges you to complete problems by yourself.

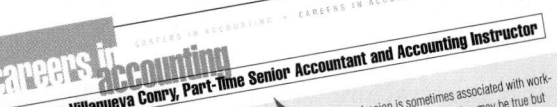

careers in accounting

CAREERS IN ACCOUNTING • CAREERS IN ACCOUNTING • CAREERS IN ACCOUNT

Dianne Villanueva Conry, Part-Time Senior Accountant and Accounting Instructor

Employment in the accounting profession is sometimes associated with work-ing long, intense hours. In many instances, this association may be true but certainly not in all. For Dianne Villanueva Conry, a career in accounting has allowed her to keep her primary focus on her family. Presently, Dianne works as a part-time senior accountant at Clinimetrics Research Associates, Inc., and teaches an evening accounting class at the University of California Santa Cruz Extension Program in Cupertino, California.

To reach her current positions, Dianne earned a Bachelor of Science degree in Business Administration with the Accountancy Option from Califor-nia State University, Fresno. Following graduation, she remained at CSUF for another year and earned a Master of Science degree in Financial Accounting. Because of her strong academic background and part-time work experience with a local CPA, she was hired by PricewaterhouseCoopers, one of the four largest accounting firms in the world. During her tenure at PWC, she acquired public accounting auditing experience and passed the certified public account-ancy exam for the state of California. After three years of employment as a public accountant, she accepted a job offer from Sony Electronics. Dianne's new position helped satisfy her expanding interest in corporate accounting and allowed her to gain a more complete understanding of private industry practices.

After starting her family, Dianne had an opportunity to work part-time for Horn Murdock Cole. Working as the internal controller, start-up services instructor, and information technology trouble-shooter, Dianne gained invaluable experience regarding all levels of consulting.

Presently, Dianne teaches an evening accounting class and works 24 to 28 hours per week at Cli metrics Research Associates, Inc., a privately held firm that performs clinical research and drug trials related to the pharmaceutical, biotechnology, and medical device industries. At Clinimetrics, she h successfully combined her experience and knowledge in auditing, private industry, and consulting. Although Dianne has recurring accounting and payroll responsibilities, she finds special projects to be the most rewarding.

Salary Range: A senior accountant could expect to earn $70,000–$150,000, depending on the industry, company, part of the country, and level of experience.

Qualifications: To qualify for entry-level employment in the accounting industry, Dianne recommends that students develop the ability to multi-task, acquire strong written and oral communication skills, build a solid knowledge of accounting basics, and obtain proficient spreadsheet and word processing skills. Dianne also encourages students to view accounting as a flexible profession that offers individu-als a variety of career options and alternatives that can assist them with the attainment of personal goals.

Occupational Outlook: For the future, Dianne envisions more analyses of variances and business activities. Accountants will be needed to assist managers in determining why revenues and expenses are fluctuating from original budget projections. This critical information will be used by managers to make sound financial decisions.

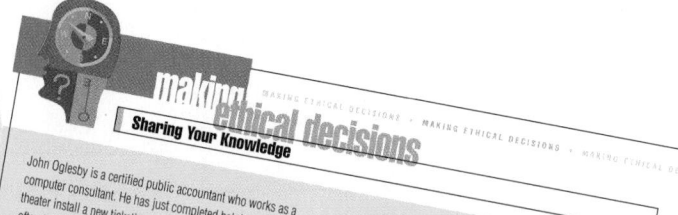

making ethical decisions

MAKING ETHICAL DECISIONS • MAKING ETHICAL DECISIONS • MAKING ETHICAL DECISIO

Sharing Your Knowledge

John Oglesby is a certified public accountant who works as a computer consultant. He has just completed helping a local movie theater install a new ticketing system that tracks when and how often individuals come to the theater. The system will enable the theater to analyze its customers and select movies that target customers having specific movie preferences.

John has just received a phone call from another theater in the same city. The theater owner asks John to evaluate its existing computer systems and suggest any recommendations. After allow-ing the theater owner to present his request, John politely declines to accept the engagement.

Instructions

Use the AICPA *Code of Professional Conduct* to determine if John's actions violate the confidentiality rule. When researching the AICPA *Code of Professional Conduct*, begin by selecting the section title that most closely relates to the issue. Read the Rule and any related Interpretations. Then scan the titles of the Ethics Rulings for any case that may be similar to the issue.

SPECIAL FEATURES provide information about real-life issues:

- **Careers in Accounting** intro-duces you to actual people working in accounting or in positions where accounting knowledge is useful. This feature includes entry-level job requirements, career tracks, and projected trends for the future.

- **Making Ethical Decisions** helps you understand compli-cated issues in the business world, such as confidentiality and integrity.

- **Business Structures** provides information on characteristics of proprietorships, corporations, and partnerships.

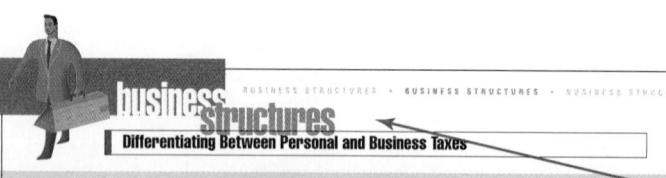

business structures

BUSINESS STRUCTURES • BUSINESS STRUCTURES • BUSINESS STRUCTURES

Differentiating Between Personal and Business Taxes

When running a business, owners must differentiate between the *personal taxes* collected from employees and customers and the *business taxes* incurred by a company as a consequence of daily operations. Each category is handled differently. For example, businesses similar to Zytech are required to withhold payroll taxes from their employees, such as federal income tax and Medicare tax, and forward the tax amounts to the appropriate government agency. Consequently, these personal payroll taxes represent a liability for Zytech until they are paid.

The sales tax collected on the sale of merchandise or services is also classified as a personal tax. Like personal payroll taxes, it is paid by individuals, collected by businesses, and later remitted to the required government agency. Until the sales tax is paid, it too represents a liability.

Like individuals, businesses also pay taxes. For example, successful businesses like Zytech must pay income tax on business profits. Zytech is also required by law to pay taxes on the earnings of its employees. Based on its payroll, Zytech must pay social secu-rity tax, Medicare tax, and unemployment taxes. Companies classify the taxes paid by a business as expenses, although they are tem-porarily recorded in liability accounts until they are paid.

global perspective
International Terms of Sale

Terms of sale for international business are very similar to those used in the United States. However, it is important to make sure that all parties understand the terms before business is complete.

Selected international terms of sale are described below:

C.I.F. (Cost, Insurance, Freight) to the named port of import. Under this method, the seller quotes a price for the goods. The price includes insurance, all transportation, and all miscellaneous charges to the point of unloading the goods from the vessel.

F.A.S. (Free AlongSide a ship at the named U.S. port of export). Under this term, the seller quotes a price for goods that includes charges for delivery of the goods alongside a vessel at the port. The seller handles the cost of the unloading and and wharf charges. All charges once goods are delivered to the vessel, including loading, ocean transportation, and insurance, are the responsibility of the buyer.

F.O.B. VESSEL (named port of export). The seller quotes a price that includes all expenses up to, and including, delivery of

goods upon an overseas vessel that is provided by or for the buyer. Once the goods are loaded "on board," all subsequent charges are the sole responsibility of the buyer.

EX ("EX" means "from" the named point of origin) such as EX FACTORY. Under this term, the price quoted applies only at the point of origin, and the seller agrees to place the goods at the disposal of the buyer at the specified place on the date or within the period fixed. All other charges are the responsibility of the buyer.

Instructions

Research the following terms of sale. Tell what the initials represent and what the actual terms involve.

1. F.O.B. (named port of exportation)
2. F.O.B. (named inland point of origin)
3. CFR (Cost and Freight)

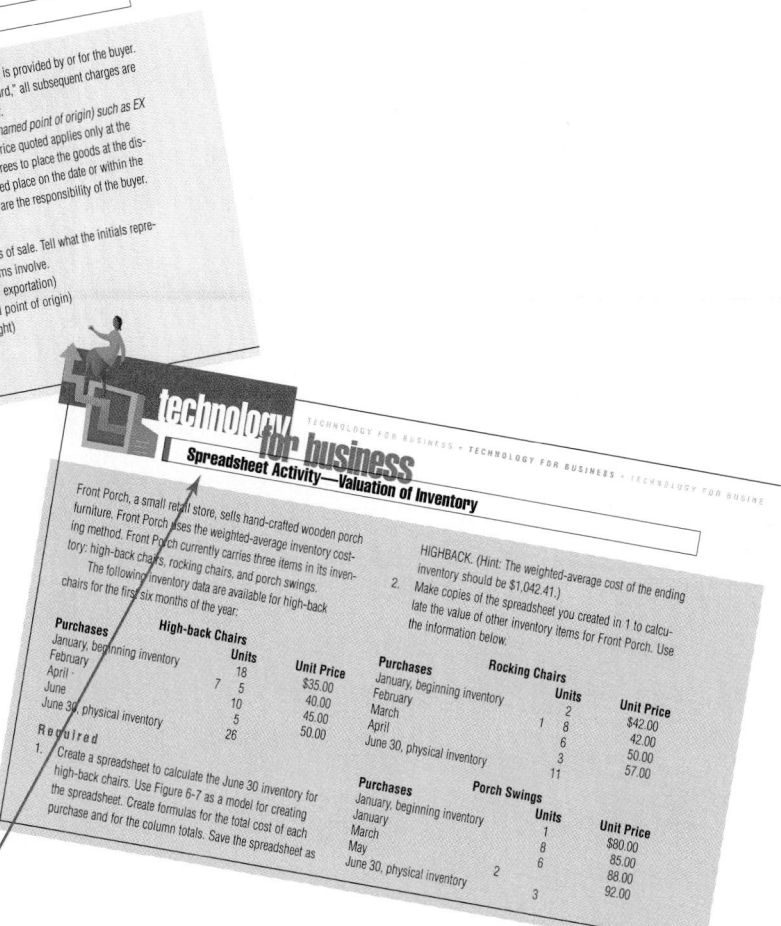

technology for business
Spreadsheet Activity—Valuation of Inventory

Front Porch, a small retail store, sells hand-crafted wooden porch furniture. Front Porch uses the weighted-average inventory costing method. Front Porch currently carries three items in its inventory: high-back chairs, rocking chairs, and porch swings.

The following inventory data are available for high-back chairs for the first six months of the year:

High-back Chairs

Purchases	Units	Unit Price
January, beginning inventory	18	
February	7 5	$35.00
April	10	40.00
June	5	45.00
June 30, physical inventory	26	50.00

Required

1. Create a spreadsheet to calculate the June 30 inventory for high-back chairs. Use Figure 6-7 as a model for creating the spreadsheet. Create formulas for the total cost of each purchase and for the column totals. Save the spreadsheet as

HIGHBACK. (Hint: The weighted-average cost of the ending inventory should be $1,042.41.)
2. Make copies of the spreadsheet you created in 1 to calculate the value of other inventory items for Front Porch. Use the information below:

Rocking Chairs

Purchases	Units	Unit Price
January, beginning inventory	2	
February	1 8	$42.00
March	6	42.00
April	3	50.00
June 30, physical inventory	11	57.00

Porch Swings

Purchases	Units	Unit Price
January, beginning inventory	1	
January	8	$80.00
March	6	85.00
May	2	88.00
June 30, physical inventory	3	92.00

- **Global Perspective** will expose you to some of the ways in which accounting and business differ in other countries.

- **Technology for Business** focuses on common business applications of technology.

- **Cultural Diversity** explains how different cultures have contributed to the field of accounting.

cultural diversity
African American Businesses

The Census Bureau's Survey of Minority-Owned Business Enterprises indicates that minority-owned enterprises are increasing in number and size. Firms owned by African Americans increased from 620,912 in 1992 to 823,000 in 1997. This represents a 32.5% increase. In 1997, these firms employed 718,300 people and generated $71.2 billion in revenue.

Six states—New York, California, Texas, Florida, Georgia, and Maryland—accounted for 47% of the nation's African American-owned businesses. The metropolitan areas of New York City, Washington, D.C., Los Angeles-Long Branch, Chicago, and Atlanta accounted for 26% of African American-owned firms.

Slightly more than half of businesses owned by African Americans operate in the service industries, such as health services, business services, and personal services. The retail trade

accounted for the next largest concentration of African American-owned firms.

Black Enterprise magazine lists the nation's 100 largest black businesses in its "B.E. 100." The list is comprised of industrial and service businesses that are at least 51% African American-owned. It maintains separate listings for the "Auto Dealer 100," which lists the largest auto dealerships that are at least 51% African American-owned. It also has lists for companies such as advertising agencies, banks, and insurance companies. From the 2004 "B.E. 100," World Wide Technology, Inc., of Maryland Heights, Missouri, was ranked in first place.

Source: U.S. Census and "Black Enterprise 100."

END-OF-CHAPTER PAGES give you opportunities to check your knowledge of the chapter content:

- **Chapter Summary** restates the chapter objectives for your reference.

- **Explore Accounting** includes opportunities for higher-level learning.

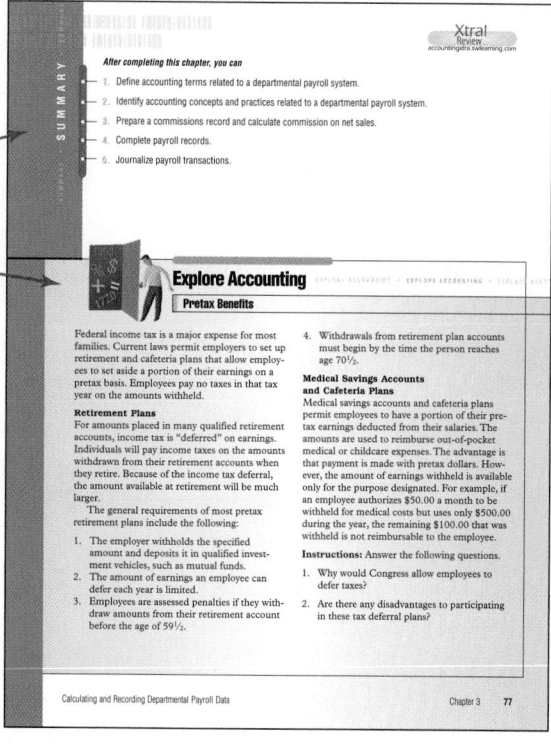

SUMMARY

Xtra!
Review
accountingxtra.swlearning.com

After completing this chapter, you can

1. Define accounting terms related to a departmental payroll system.
2. Identify accounting concepts and practices related to a departmental payroll system.
3. Prepare a commissions record and calculate commission on net sales.
4. Complete payroll records.
5. Journalize payroll transactions.

Explore Accounting

Pretax Benefits

Federal income tax is a major expense for most families. Current laws permit employers to set up retirement and cafeteria plans that allow employees to set aside a portion of their earnings on a pretax basis. Employees pay no taxes in that tax year on the amounts withheld.

Retirement Plans
For amounts placed in many qualified retirement accounts, income tax is "deferred" on earnings. Individuals will pay income taxes on the amounts withdrawn from their retirement accounts when they retire. Because of the income tax deferral, the amount available at retirement will be much larger.
The general requirements of most pretax retirement plans include the following:

1. The employer withholds the specified amount and deposits it in qualified investment vehicles, such as mutual funds.
2. The amount of earnings an employee can defer each year is limited.
3. Employees are assessed penalties if they withdraw amounts from their retirement account before the age of 59½.

4. Withdrawals from retirement plan accounts must begin by the time the person reaches age 70½.

Medical Savings Accounts and Cafeteria Plans
Medical savings accounts and cafeteria plans permit employees to have a portion of their pretax earnings deducted from their salaries. The amounts are used to reimburse out-of-pocket medical or childcare expenses. The advantage is that payment is made with pretax dollars. However, the amount of earnings withheld is available only for the purpose designated. For example, if an employee authorizes $50.00 a month to be withheld for medical costs but uses only $500.00 during the year, the remaining $100.00 that was withheld is not reimbursable to the employee.

Instructions: Answer the following questions.

1. Why would Congress allow employees to defer taxes?
2. Are there any disadvantages to participating in these tax deferral plans?

Calculating and Recording Departmental Payroll Data   Chapter 3   77

5-1 APPLICATION PROBLEM

Xtra!
Quizzing
accountingxtra.swlearning.com

Preparing a voucher and journalizing vouchers in a voucher register

TeleTronics uses a voucher register similar to the one described in this chapter.

Transactions:
Sept. 1. Purchased merchandise on account from Eastern Company, 9424 Denison Pkwy., Corning, NY, 14830, terms: 2/10, n/30, $3,100.00. V87.
1. Post Real Estate Developers sent an invoice for $1,150.00 for September's rent. V88.
5. Received merchandise on account from Supra Supply Company, $258.00. V89.
5. Bought sales supplies on account from Newport News, $87.50. V90.
11. Received invoice for advertising from Hoyer Company, $3,347.75. V91.
11. Purchased merchandise on account from Rapid Rabbit, $235.15. V92.
18. Received invoice for delivery service on account from Beggen Company, $1,315.00. V93.
19. Purchased $1,973.00 of merchandise on account from Syracuse Company, $185.00. V95.
23. Bought office equipment on account from Northside Electric Cooperative, $185.00. V95.
25. Received invoice for utilities from Northern Supply, $317.00. V96.
29. Bought administrative supplies on account from Northern Supply, $317.00. V96.
30. Manley Maintenance Company sent an invoice for $25.00. The amount was for a miscellaneous sales expense. V97.

Instructions:
1. Prepare Voucher 87 for the September 1 transaction.
2. Journalize the transactions completed during September of the current year. Use page 9 of a voucher register. The abbreviation for voucher is V.
3. Prove and rule the voucher register.

The voucher register prepared in Problem 5.1 is needed to complete Problem 5.2.

5-2 APPLICATION PROBLEM

Journalizing cash payments and deposits in a check register

TeleTronics uses a check register similar to the one described in this chapter.

Transactions:
Sept. 2. Paid cash to Post Real Estate Developers, $1,150.00, covering V88. C83.
8. Paid cash to Newport News, $87.50, covering V90. C84.
9. Paid cash to Eastern Company, $3,038.00, covering V87 for $3,100.00, less 2% discount, $62.00. C85.
13. Paid cash to Supra Supply Company, $258.00, covering V89. C86.
18. Paid cash to Rapid Rabbit, $235.15, covering V92. C87.
19. Paid cash to Hoyer Company, $3,280.79, covering V91 for $3,347.75, less 2% discount, $66.96. C88.
24. Made a deposit in the checking account, $5,684.54.
25. Paid cash to Northside Electric Cooperative, $185.00, covering V95. C89.
30. Paid cash to Manley Maintenance Company, $25.00, covering V97. C90.

Instructions:
1. Use page 9 of a check register. Record the bank balance brought forward on September 1 of the current year, $19,443...
2. Continue using page... alize the cash payments and deposits completed during Septem... ... ...d is journalized, make the appropriate notation... ...as follows: check, C; voucher. V...
3. Prove and rule the...

- Exercises contain at least one **Application Problem** for each lesson, plus one **Mastery Problem** and one **Challenge Problem** to test your understanding of the entire chapter. Many of these problems can also be worked using accounting software: **Automated Accounting, Peachtree®, and QuickBooks®!**

5-5 MASTERY PROBLEM

Journalizing transactions in a voucher system

Jameson Company uses a voucher register and a check register similar to the ones described in this chapter.

Transactions:
Nov. 1. Purchased merchandise on account from Georgia Company, $975.00. V68.
2. Bought $916.80 of administrative supplies on account from Supply World. V69.
4. Bought store equipment on account from Equipment Plus, $1,998.00. V70.
8. Purchased merchandise on account from North Heights Corporation, $1,695.15. V71.
8. Paid $955.50 to Georgia Company covering V68 for $975.00, less 2% discount, $19.50. C57.
10. Made a deposit in the checking account, $3,579.00.
14. Received invoice for delivery service from Quick Delivery, $24.10. V72.
14. Paid cash to Quick Delivery, $24.10, covering V72. C58.
14. Issued DM10 to North Heights Corporation for return of merchandise purchased, $225.00. Cancel V71. V73.
15. Paid cash to North Heights Corporation, $1,440.75, covering V73 for $1,470.15, less 2% discount, $29.40. C59.
16. Recorded voucher for semimonthly payroll for period ended November 15, $1,459.64 (total payroll: sales, $1,183.50; administrative, $789.00; less deductions: employee income tax payable—federal, $295.88; employee income tax payable—state, $59.18; social security tax payable, $128.21; Medicare tax payable, $29.59). V74.
16. Paid cash for semimonthly payroll, $1,459.64, covering V74. C60.
22. Paid cash to Supply World, $216.80, covering V69. C61.
25. Issued Voucher No. 75 to buy office equipment on account from Fischer Equipment, $2,350.00.
29. Deposited $1,170.15 in the checking account.
30. Purchased merchandise on account from Georgia Company, $2,258.50. V76.

Instructions:
1. Use page 20 of a check register. Record the bank balance brought forward on November 1 of the current year, $11,676.77.
2. Journalize the transactions completed during November of the current year. Use page 22 of a voucher register and page 20 of a check register. When a voucher is paid or canceled, make appropriate notations in the voucher register. Source documents are abbreviated as follows: check, C; debit memorandum, DM; voucher, V.
3. Prove and rule both the voucher register and the check register.

5-6 CHALLENGE PROBLEM

Journalizing purchases invoices at the net amount in a voucher system

Cayman Company uses a voucher system. All of the vendors with whom Cayman Company does business offer terms of 2/10, n/30. Cayman has a policy of paying all invoices within the discount period. The business records invoice vouchers at the net amount (invoice total less a 2% discount). Thus, a $1,000.00 invoice, allowing a 2% discount of $20.00, is recorded at the net amount, $980.00. Purchases is debited and Vouchers Payable is credited for $980.00. A purchases discount account is not used.

A Voucher System   Chapter 5   163

viii

- Enrichment materials help you take a step further into understanding accounting. **Applied Communication** offers exercises for strengthening your communication skills—a must for future employment! **Cases for Critical Thinking** asks you to consider questions based on accounting scenarios. **SCANS Workplace Competency** helps you learn about skills you'll need in the business world. **Graphing Workshop** and **Auditing for Errors** provide you with specific situations in which you can analyze and investigate accounting tools. **Analyzing Costco's Financial Statements** allows you to examine a real business's annual report and financial documents and put your knowledge to work.

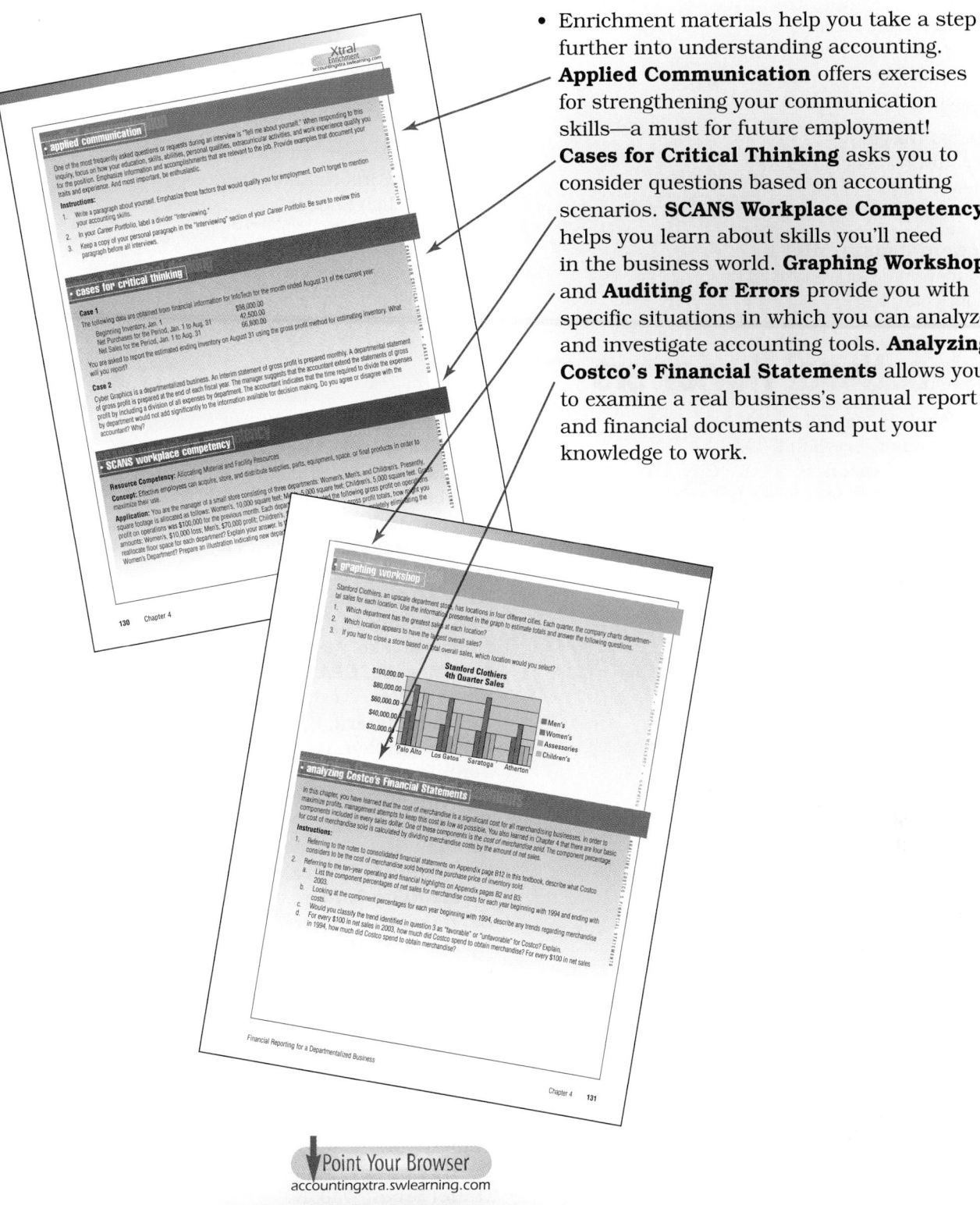

Point Your Browser
accountingxtra.swlearning.com

THE ACCOUNTING XTRA! WEB SITE offers a variety of resources and activities for you to explore. As you use this textbook, watch for the Xtra! Web Site icons that will lead you to your online accounting connection!

Educational Consultants

Carolyn Holt Balis
Computer/Business Teacher
Cuyahoga Heights High School
Cuyahoga Heights, OH

Madge Gregg
Accounting Teacher
Hoover High School
Hoover, AL

Howard Rankin, MBA
Educational Consultant
Monticello, KY

Joyce Rowe
Business Department Chair
Monterey High School
Lubbock, TX

Jennifer Wegner
Business & Information Technology
Mishicot High School
Mishicot, WI

Educational Reviewers

Jon Abel, Salem, OR
Abe Aleman, Levelland, TX
Kathy Andreason, Salt Lake City, UT
Cynthia S. Aycock, Eagle Lake, FL
Carolyn Holt Balis, Cuyahoga Heights, OH
Anne Berten, Portland, OR
Chad E. Bobb, Indianapolis, IN
Ellen Clizbe, Moreno Valley, CA
Tony Composto, Brooklyn, NY
Becky Cornacchia, Naples, FL
Alicia E. Censi Corso, Los Angeles, CA
Donna Davis, Charlotte, NC
Paula Davis, Atlanta, GA
Sylvia Davis, Lakewood, CA
Dana Dingell, Vienna, VA
Kathy Dixon, Richmond, VA
Keith Downs, Dallastown, PA
Dr. Judith A. Drager-McCoy, Lititz, PA
Ann Droptini, Gladewater, TX
Jean Eckert, Wexford, PA
Julie Eckhart, Salem, WI
Carrie English, Woodbridge, VA
Barbara Erwin, Orlando, FL
K. Skip Fabritius, Olympia, WA
Debbie Fischer, St. Petersburg, FL
Kathleen Ford, Rochester, MI
Lance B. Garvin, Indianapolis, IN
Debbie Gentene, Mason, OH
Wendy Gentry, Garden Grove, CA
Andy Gilley, Hendersonville, TN
Kathy Goos, Moreno Valley, CA
Madge Gregg, Hoover, AL
Tracy Gutierrez, Garden Grove, CA
Craig Halberstadt, Racine, WI
Jean Harms, Port Orange, FL
Cindy Hiester, Astoria, OR
Beth Hubbard, Virginia Beach, VA
Lisa Huddlestun, Kansas, IL
Steve Ingmire, Indianapolis, IN
Gladys Jackson, Woodbridge, NJ

Beverly Kaesar, Neenah, WI
Fran Loos, Salt Lake City, UT
Ann M. Ludlow, St. Louis, MO
Frances Mallard, Brentwood, TN
H. Jean Malonson, Hayward, CA
Chris Marshall, Denver, CO
Libby Martin, Chattanooga, TN
Sally M. Graham Martin, Nokesville, VA
Barb Mason, Paris, MO
Kelvin Meeks, Memphis, TN
Lori Meseke, CPA, Vandalia, IL
Sonia Miller, Garden Grove, CA
Heather Moraru, Suwanee, GA
Joanne Mullen, Pontiac, IL
Jennifer Mundy, O'Fallon, IL
Barb Nichols, Evansville, IN
Katherine Prange, Breese, IL
Eleanor Rankin, Rio Rico, AZ
Dr. Andrea B. Reiter, Dingman's Falls, PA
Nicole Reitz-Larson, Salt Lake City, UT
Dr. Harriet D. Rogers, Whitewater, WI
George Roth, Prairie du Sac, WI
Peggy J. Scott, Chesapeke, VA
Christopher G. Shaffer, Cincinnati, OH
Janet Shaw, Bailey, NC
Mary Ann Shea, Amherst, MA
Jenny V. Shippy, Naples, FL
Sherri Small, Las Vegas, NV
H. Leland Smith, Racine, WI
Tommie Stanaland, Perry, FL
Dottie Starkey, Milford, DE
Laurel Stein, Wall, NJ
Claire Thoke, Glendale, CA
Donnie Thompson, Pittsburgh, PA
John Tingley, Bradley, IL
Linda Underwood, Gilcrest, CO
Jennifer Wegner, Mishicot, WI
Linda White, Fayetteville, PA
Parnell Wiggins, Memphis, TN
Lonnie Wilson, Evansville, IN

CONTENTS

©GETTY IMAGES/PHOTODISC

PART 2
Accounting Adjustments and Valuation 140

PART 3
General Accounting Adjustments 196

©GETTY IMAGES/PHOTODISC

©GETTY IMAGES/PHOTODISC

1st Class

PART 6
Manufacturing Cost Accounting 556

©GETTY IMAGES/PHOTODISC

PART 7
Other Accounting Systems 618

©GETTY IMAGES/PHOTODISC

Additional Features in This Book

Chapter Review and Practice

Chapter Summary
25, 51, 77, 125, 160, 187, 214, 250, 280, 304, 333, 361, 393, 434, 463, 484, 518, 549, 573, 602, 636, 670, 702, 727

Application Problems
26, 27, 52, 78, 79, 126, 127, 128, 161, 162, 188, 189, 190, 215, 216, 251, 252, 253, 281, 282, 305, 334, 335, 362, 363, 394, 395, 435, 436, 464, 465, 466, 485, 486, 519, 520, 521, 550, 551, 574, 575, 603, 604, 637, 638, 671, 672, 703, 728

Mastery Problems
27, 53, 80, 128, 163, 190, 217, 254, 282, 306, 335, 363, 396, 437, 466, 486, 521, 552, 576, 604, 639, 672, 704, 729

Challenge Problems
28, 54, 81, 129, 163, 191, 218, 254, 283, 306, 336, 364, 397, 438, 467, 487, 522, 552, 577, 604, 640, 673, 705, 731

Applied Communication
29, 55, 82, 130, 165, 192, 219, 255, 284, 307, 337, 365, 398, 439, 468, 488, 524, 553, 578, 606, 642, 674, 706, 733

Cases for Critical Thinking
29, 55, 82, 130, 165, 192, 219, 255, 284, 307, 337, 365, 398, 439, 468, 488, 524, 553, 578, 606, 642, 674, 706, 733

SCANS Workplace Competency
29, 55, 82, 130, 165, 192, 219, 256, 284, 307, 337, 365, 398, 439, 468, 488, 524, 553, 578, 606, 642, 674, 706, 733

Graphing Workshop
56, 220, 285, 338, 399, 469, 525, 607, 675, 734

Auditing for Errors
30, 83, 131, 166, 193, 256, 308, 366, 439, 489, 554, 579, 643, 707

Analyzing Costco's Financial Statements
30, 56, 83, 131, 166, 193, 220, 256, 285, 308, 338, 366, 399, 439, 469, 489, 525, 554, 579, 607, 643, 675, 707, 734

Contents

Part 1 is a review of an accounting cycle for a merchandising business.

Chapter organization and content provide students with a review of what was learned in a first year of accounting study and expand their learning through applications relevant to a departmental accounting system.

- **Chapter 1** describes purchases and cash payments.
- **Chapter 2** describes sales and cash receipts.
- **Chapter 3** describes departmental payroll.
- **Chapter 4** describes financial reporting for a departmentalized business.

AUTOMATED ACCOUNTING

For those instructors who wish to fully integrate the accounting program, an Automated Accounting feature is provided at the end of each chapter.

SIMULATION

Chapters 1–4 review the entire accounting cycle for a corporation. It is important that the student see the entire accounting cycle as it applies to a particular form of business. It is also important that the student apply these concepts through the completion of the simulation, Sounds, Inc., and/or the reinforcement activity.

REINFORCEMENT ACTIVITY

Reinforcement Activity 1 may be completed after Chapter 4.

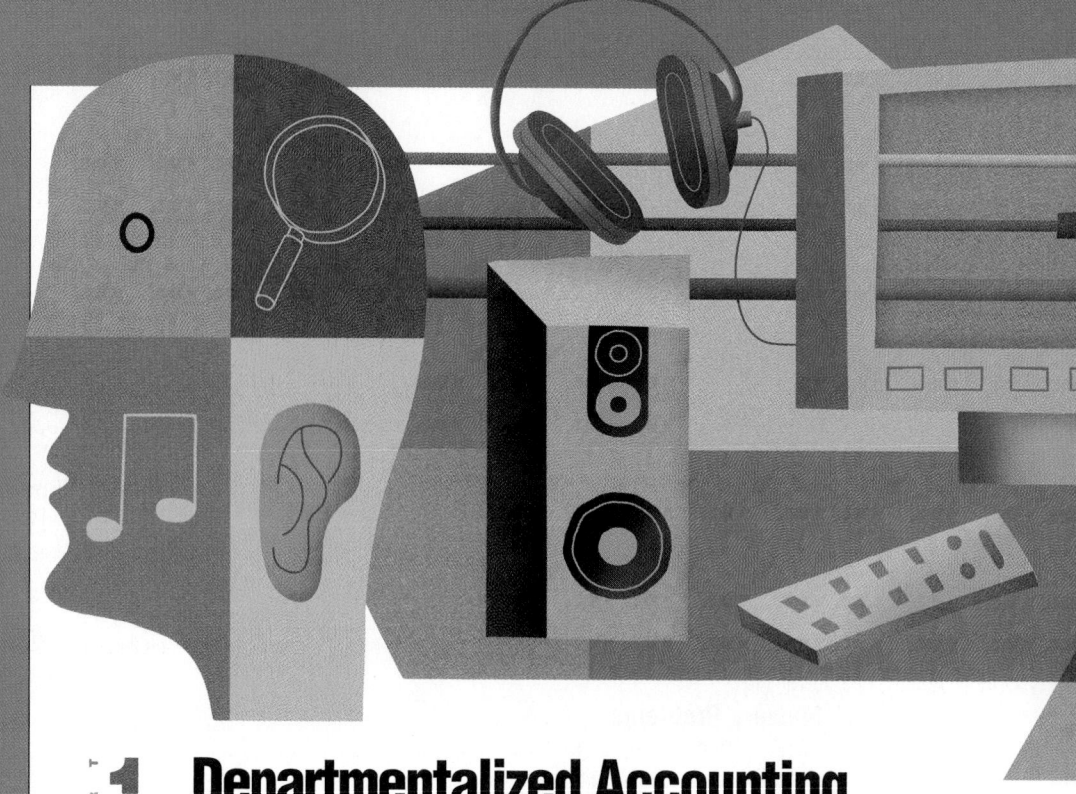

Departmentalized Accounting

PART 1

CHAPTER • CHAPTER • CHAPTER • CHAPTER

1   Recording Departmental Purchases and Cash Payments

2   Recording Departmental Sales and Cash Receipts

3   Calculating and Recording Departmental Payroll Data

4   Financial Reporting for a Departmentalized Business

THE BUSINESS • THE BUSINESS • THE BUSINESS

ZYTECH MEDIA CORPORATION

Zytech Media Corporation is the business that will be used in the chapters in Part 1 to illustrate the accounting concepts and procedures for a departmentalized merchandising business organized as a corporation. Zytech has two sales departments: Audio and Video.

2210 Employee Income Tax Payable—State
2215 Federal Income Tax Payable
2220 Social Security Tax Payable
2225 Medicare Tax Payable
2230 Sales Tax Payable
2235 Unemployment Tax Payable—Federal
2240 Unemployment Tax Payable—State
2245 Health Insurance Premiums Payable
2250 Life Insurance Premiums Payable
2305 Dividends Payable

(3000) STOCKHOLDERS' EQUITY
3105 Capital Stock
3110 Retained Earnings
3115 Dividends
3205 Income Summary—Audio
3210 Income Summary—Video
3215 Income Summary—General

Income Statement Accounts
(4000) OPERATING REVENUE
4105 Sales—Audio
4110 Sales Discount—Audio
4115 Sales Returns and Allowances—Audio
4205 Sales—Video
4210 Sales Discount—Video
4215 Sales Returns and Allowances—Video

(5000) COST OF MERCHANDISE
5105 Purchases—Audio
5110 Purchases Discount—Audio
5115 Purchases Returns and Allowances—Audio
5205 Purchases—Video
5210 Purchases Discount—Video
5215 Purchases Returns and Allowances—Video

(6000) DIRECT EXPENSES
6100 DIRECT EXPENSES—AUDIO
6105 Advertising Expense—Audio
6110 Depreciation Expense—Store Equipment, Audio
6115 Payroll Taxes Expense—Audio
6120 Salary Expense—Audio
6125 Supplies Expense—Audio

6200 DIRECT EXPENSES—VIDEO
6205 Advertising Expense—Video
6210 Depreciation Expense—Store Equipment, Video
6215 Payroll Taxes Expense—Video
6220 Salary Expense—Video
6225 Supplies Expense—Video

(7000) INDIRECT EXPENSES
7105 Broadband Expense
7110 Depreciation Expense—Office Equipment
7115 Insurance Expense
7120 Miscellaneous Expense
7125 Payroll Taxes Expense—Administrative
7130 Phone Expense
7135 Rent Expense
7140 Salary Expense—Administrative
7145 Supplies Expense—Administrative
7150 Uncollectible Accounts Expense
7155 Utilities Expense

(8000) INCOME TAX
8105 Federal Income Tax Expense

The chart of accounts for Zytech Media Corporation is illustrated above for ready reference as you study Part 1 of this textbook.

ZYTECH MEDIA CORPORATION
CHART OF ACCOUNTS

Balance Sheet Accounts
(1000) ASSETS
1100–1400 CURRENT ASSETS
1105 Cash
1110 Petty Cash
1205 Accounts Receivable
1210 Allowance for Uncollectible Accounts
1305 Merchandise Inventory—Audio
1310 Merchandise Inventory—Video
1315 Supplies—Administrative
1320 Supplies—Audio
1325 Supplies—Video
1400 Prepaid Insurance

1500–1600 PLANT ASSETS
1505 Office Equipment
1510 Accumulated Depreciation—Office Equipment
1605 Store Equipment—Audio
1610 Accumulated Depreciation—Store Equipment, Audio
1615 Store Equipment—Video
1620 Accumulated Depreciation—Store Equipment, Video

(2000) LIABILITIES
2105 Accounts Payable
2205 Employee Income Tax Payable—Federal

3

3

Recording Departmental Purchases

	SCOPE & SEQUENCE		ENHANCING	
	NEW	REVIEW/ EXTENSION	SPECIAL FEATURES	
Introduce the Chapter	✓		• Accounting in the Real World: New Balance	
Lesson 1-1 Using Accounting Principles and Records			• Making Ethical Decisions: Researching Codes of Conduct	
Accounting equation		✓		
General journal		✓	• Applied Communication	
Normal balances of accounts		✓		
Ledgers		✓		
Lesson 1-2 Journalizing and Posting Purchases and Purchases Returns				
Departmental accounting system	✓			
Journalizing purchases on account		✓		
Posting from a purchases journal		✓		
Posting the totals of a purchases journal		✓		
Journalizing purchases returns and allowances		✓		
Lesson 1-3 Journalizing and Posting Cash Payments			• Cultural Diversity: Professional Organizations	
Departmental cash payments		✓		
Journalizing a purchases discount		✓		
Taking a discount after a purchase return		✓		
Recording entries in a cash payments journal		✓		
Cash payment to replenish petty cash		✓		
Posting from a cash payments journal		✓		
Putting It All Together			• Explore Accounting	
			• Xtra! Web Site: Xtra! Enrichment	
			• Case for Critical Thinking	
			• SCANS Workplace Competency	
			• Auditing for Errors	
			• Analyzing Costco's Financial Statements	

and Cash Payments

INSTRUCTION		PRACTICE AND ASSESSMENT		
TECHNOLOGY AND MEDIA	**TEACHING STRATEGIES**	**GUIDED PRACTICE**	**INDEPENDENT PRACTICE**	**RETEACHING AND ENRICHMENT**
• Internet Research Activity • Accounting Xtra! Web Site	• Software Focus			
• Instructor's Resource CD: PowerPoint Slides • Xtra! Web Site: Xtra! Study Tools • Blackline Master: General Journal • Personal Trainer	• Print Learner • Specific Learning Disability (SLD) Students • Applied Skills: Communications	• Terms Review • Audit Your Understanding • Work Together 1-1	• On Your Own 1-1 • Application Problem 1-1 • Ongoing Assessment, p. 10 • Personal Trainer • Xtra! Web Site: Xtra! Study Tools	• Reteach, p. 10 • Enrich, p. 11
• Instructor's Resource CD: PowerPoint Slides • Xtra! Web Site: Xtra! Study Tools • Blackline Masters: Purchases Journal, Departmental Purchases Journal, General Journal, and Accounts Payable Subsidiary Ledger • Personal Trainer • Peachtree and QuickBooks	• Accounting Pedagogy • Cooperative Learning • Applied Skills: Writing Across the Curriculum	• Terms Review • Audit Your Understanding • Work Together 1-2	• On Your Own 1-2 • Application Problem 1-2 • Ongoing Assessment, p. 16 • Personal Trainer • Xtra! Web Site: Xtra! Study Tools	• Reteach, p. 16 • Enrich, p. 17 • Peachtree and QuickBooks
• Instructor's Resource CD: PowerPoint Slides • Xtra! Web Site: Xtra! Study Tools • Blackline Masters: Departmental Cash Payments Journal • Personal Trainer • Automated Accounting	• Applied Skills: Word Processing • Tactile Learner • Expanding Beyond the Classroom	• Terms Review • Audit Your Understanding • Work Together 1-3	• On Your Own 1-3 • Application Problem 1-3 • Ongoing Assessment, p. 23 • Personal Trainer • Xtra! Web Site: Xtra! Study Tools	• Reteach, p. 23 • Enrich, p. 24 • Automated Accounting
• Automated Accounting • Peachtree and QuickBooks • Personal Trainer • Xtra! Web Site: Xtra! Review, Quizzing, and Enrichment • Student Companion CD	• Visual Learner		• Mastery Problem 1-4 • Automated Accounting • Peachtree and QuickBooks • Personal Trainer • Xtra! Web Site: Xtra! Review and Quizzing • Study Guide 1 • Student Companion CD • Chapter 1 Test • ExamView Chapter 1 • Portfolio Assessment	• Challenge Problem 1-5 • Reteach, p. 25 • Enrich, p. 25 • Recycling Problem 1-1 • Automated Accounting • Xtra! Web Site: Xtra! Enrichment

CHAPTER 1

OBJECTIVES & TERMS

Recording Departmental Purchases and Cash Payments

After studying Chapter 1, you will be able to:

1. Define accounting terms related to departmental purchases and cash payments.

2. Identify accounting concepts and practices related to departmental purchases and cash payments.

3. Journalize and post departmental purchases and purchases returns.

4. Journalize and post departmental cash payments.

- asset
- liability
- equities
- owners' equity
- stockholders' equity
- accounting equation
- source documents
- double-entry accounting

- journal
- special journal
- account
- ledger
- general ledger
- subsidiary ledger
- controlling account
- file maintenance

- departmental accounting system
- merchandising business
- posting
- debit memorandum
- contra account
- cash discount
- purchases discount
- petty cash

Point Your Browser
accountingxtra.swlearning.com

• New Balance

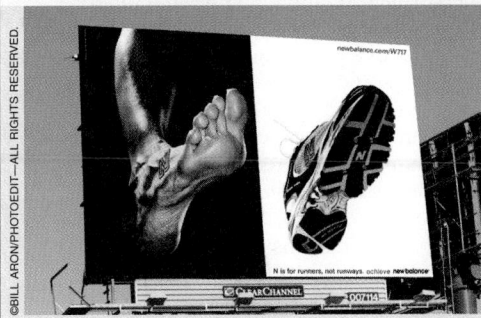

FUNCTION OVER FASHION

Since its inception in 1906, New Balance has focused on producing quality footwear to ensure proper fit and performance. The company believes that no two athletes are alike and that each foot is structurally unique. Consequently, New Balance manufactures a wide variety of running and sport shoes in assorted lengths, widths, and materials to meet individual requirements for shock absorption, arch, motion control, cushioning, and function. Throughout its existence, New Balance has always adhered to the philosophy "better fit and technology mean better performance."

In recent years, New Balance has expanded into athletic apparel using innovative fabrics and features. Each product is engineered for fit, durability, moisture management, and water resistance in order to ensure maximum performance and comfort.

Over the past decade, sales have increased substantially, from $221 million in 1992 to $1.1 billion in 2000. The company also refrains from paying famous athletes to endorse its products. New Balance strongly believes that product quality and performance speak for themselves. Rather than allocate large sums of money for endorsements, New Balance prefers to invest those same dollars in research, design, and manufacturing techniques.

Critical Thinking

1. What are some of the possible reasons for New Balance's success during the last decade?
2. Would you recommend that New Balance record apparel sales and expenses separately from shoe sales and expenses? Explain.

Source: www.newbalance.com

Xtra!
Today
accountingxtra.swlearning.com

vertical text: ACCOUNTING IN THE REAL WORLD • ACCOUNTING IN THE REAL WORLD • ACCOUNTING IN THE REAL WORLD

STUDENT CREDIT CARDS

Search the Internet for companies that offer a student credit card. Go to at least two different sites that offer such a card.

Instructions

1. Make a chart comparing the two companies' student credit cards, using the following criteria:
   a. Introductory interest rate (if any)
   b. Interest rate after the introductory period
   c. Annual fee
   d. Minimum finance charge (if any)
2. Comment on which card offers the better terms.

vertical text: internet activity

vertical text: INTERNET RESEARCH ACTIVITY • INTERNET RESEARCH ACTIVITY • INTERNET RESEARCH ACTIVITY •

5

INTERNET RESEARCH ACTIVITY

At the beginning of every chapter, students have an opportunity to search the Internet to answer questions related to the chapter content, giving them practice in developing technology and research skills.

Ask students if they have received a credit card application in the mail. Ask them if they own credit cards and, if so, what interest rates they are paying.

1. Student answers will vary.
2. Student answers will vary.

Each chapter introduction spotlights an actual business familiar to students. Intriguing questions demonstrate how the chapter's content applies to business today. Use this feature to demonstrate how the chapter's content applies to real businesses today.

Ask students to share any experiences they have had involving a New Balance product. Motivate students by asking them how they became familiar with New Balance (store fronts, news ads, television advertising, mail flyers, web sites, employment, etc.). Spark discussion by asking students if they agree with New Balance's policy of refraining from paying famous athletes to endorse its products.

Ask students to read the feature or have one or more students read the feature out loud. Remind them to pay close attention to details of the business as they read. Give students 5–10 minutes to jot down some ideas for answering the Critical Thinking questions; then discuss the answers in class.

As an alternative, you can organize students into groups of 3–4 individuals to generate possible solutions to the questions. With this approach you may also wish to record the suggestions and save them for additional discussion after the chapter is completed.

1. Student answers might include the following: a company dedication to quality and function resulting in satisfied, repeat customers; addition of apparel line; global sales; an investment in better manufacturing techniques, resulting in lower manufacturing costs; strict adherence to a non-endorsement policy; new and innovative products; wide variety of product sizes and fit.

2. New Balance should record all apparel sales and expenses separately in order to better evaluate the success of its new apparel line of products. Without separate information on apparel, New Balance will not be able to determine the profitability of its new line of products. Adequate information on apparel sales and expenses will help New Balance make better managerial decisions regarding apparel.

A link to the web site of this business can be accessed at the Accounting Xtra! Web Site.

1-1 Using Accounting Principles and Records

Financial information for a business can be recorded, summarized, and reported in a variety of ways. Accountants design accounting systems to meet the specific needs of the business. The way in which information is kept and reported in the accounting system is determined by the size, type, and complexity of the business. When designing financial records, the business should also consider the types of decisions that will be made, based on the financial statements.

If managers of individual departments want to use financial statements to assist in making decisions, information for each department must be recorded separately. The types of information

to be gathered by department include purchases, sales, and expenses. Payroll data may also be identified by department. Gathering information by department requires a somewhat different set of accounting procedures. Regardless of the accounting procedures used, the same accounting concepts and practices are followed.

If a business decides to record information by department, it must establish procedures to ensure that transactions are assigned to the correct department. Some businesses employ an accounting clerk for each department. The clerk's primary responsibility is to record day-to-day transactions for the department.

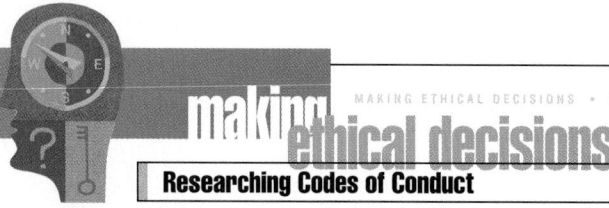

MAKING ETHICAL DECISIONS • MAKING ETHICAL DECISIONS • MAKING ETHICAL DECISIO

making ethical decisions

Researching Codes of Conduct

The Sarbanes-Oxley Act of 2002 requires publicly traded companies to have a code of conduct. Most companies make their codes available on the Internet. However, companies title and link their codes differently. Thus, accessing these codes on the Internet requires knowledge of common search terms and methods.

Begin your search by visually scanning the available links on the company's home page. "Code of Conduct," "Code of Ethics," and "Corporate Governance" are common links. A company whose web site is designed primarily to sell its product is unlikely to have an ethics-related link on its home page. In this case, look at the top or bottom of the web page and find a link such as "Investor Relations."

Most companies provide a search tool. Use the search tool to search for any of these terms: "ethics," "code of conduct," "code of ethics," and "corporate governance."

Instructions
Access the code of conduct for three publicly traded companies. Prepare a summary of the links and searches you used to access the code for each company.

MAKING ETHICAL DECISIONS
MAKING ETHICAL DECISIONS

This feature stimulates critical thinking and decision making. Situational ethical dilemmas assist students with decision making and critical thinking in light of current events, highlighting the ethical policies and business decisions of real companies. When these ethics cases are discussed in class, students can also gain a sense of individual diversity as they demonstrate individual opinions. A blackline master of the 3-Column Ethical Decision-Making Matrix is furnished in the Teacher's Resource Guide.

Throughout this textbook, the ethics features may require students to access the code of conduct of certain companies. This activity helps students access these codes regardless of the code title and how the code is linked on the company's web site. You may allow students to select their three companies or assign different companies to each student or group of students.

For the feature on this page, students' answers will vary.

Side column

INTRODUCTION

- Have the students read the text. Ask them why a large clothing store with separate men's, women's, and children's departments would be interested in knowing how well each department is doing.

- Ask students what types of information should be collected about each department. Write answers on the board or overhead.

- Emphasize that regardless of the accounting procedures used for a departmentalized business, the same accounting concepts and practices are followed.

OBJECTIVES

- Define accounting terms related to departmental purchases and cash payments.

- Identify accounting concepts and practices related to departmental purchases and cash payments.

MOTIVATE

- Discuss summer work experiences with students. Ask for examples of tasks that required a knowledge of accounting principles or concepts.

Preview

- Preview the accounting terms and definitions introduced in this lesson: asset, liability, equities, owners' equity, stockholders' equity, accounting equation, source documents, double-entry accounting, journal, special journal, account, ledger, general ledger, subsidiary ledger, controlling account, and file maintenance.

- Direct students to read the headings on each page in this lesson and to examine the illustrations given.

- Emphasize that in the first-year accounting course, the accounting concepts and practices related to recording, summarizing, and reporting the financial information for a merchandising business organized as a corporation were presented. Explain that this lesson will review the accounting equation, the use of special journals and the general journal, the use of general and subsidiary ledgers, and the chart of accounts numbering system and file maintenance.

ACCOUNTING EQUATION

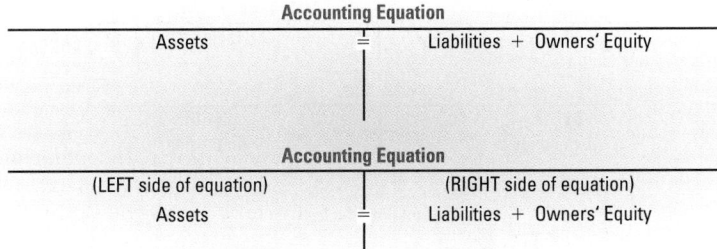

	Accounting Equation	
Assets	=	Liabilities + Owners' Equity

	Accounting Equation	
(LEFT side of equation)		(RIGHT side of equation)
Assets	=	Liabilities + Owners' Equity

Anything of value that is owned is called an **asset**. An amount owed by a business is called a **liability**. Financial rights to the assets of a business are called **equities**. The amount remaining after the value of all liabilities is subtracted from the value of all assets is called **owners' equity**. The owners' equity in a corporation is called **stockholders' equity**.

An equation showing the relationship among assets, liabilities, and owners' equity is called the **accounting equation**. The accounting equation may be stated as assets = equities. More commonly, the equation is stated as assets = liabilities + owners' equity.

The equation is often viewed as forming a "T." In the figure above, assets are listed on the left side of the T account and equities (liabilities and owners' equity) on the right side of the T account. Total assets must always equal total liabilities plus owners' equity.

Accounting Records

Accounting records show changes and the current account balance of each asset, liability, and owners' equity (or stockholders' equity) account. In the United States, the amounts are stated in dollars and cents. [*CONCEPT: Unit of Measurement*]

The unit of measurement concept states that business transactions are reported in numbers that have common values—that is, using a common unit of measurement. If part of the information in the accounting records is financial and part is nonfinancial, the financial statements will not be clear. For example, if Zytech Media Corporation states its sales in number of units sold (nonfinancial) and its expenses in dollars (financial), net profit cannot be calculated.

The preceding concept reference indicates the application of a specific accounting concept. For a complete statement and explanation of the concepts, refer to Appendix A in this text.

Information about business transactions is obtained from original business papers called **source documents**. Each journal entry must be supported by a source documents proving that a transaction occurred. [*CONCEPT: Objective Evidence*]

The source document is the original business paper indicating that the transaction did occur and that the amounts recorded in the accounting records are accurate and true. When accounting information reported on the financial statements needs to be verified, an accountant will first check the accounting record. If the details of an entry need further checking, an accountant will then check the source documents as objective evidence that the transaction did occur.

- Explain the accounting equation by discussing the relationship among assets, liabilities, and owners' equity, as shown in the illustration.
- Explain that source documents are used as the evidence that a business transaction occurred.
- Explain the Unit of Measurement concept.

DEMONSTRATE

Accounting equation

- Show the relationship among assets, liabilities, and owners' equity by writing the accounting equation on the board or overhead. Remind students that in a corporation the value of the owners' equity is referred to as stockholders' equity.
- Emphasize the relationship by asking the students to name an automobile. Write the approximate value of the auto under "assets" in the accounting equation. For example, $15,000. Ask the students if the owner put $5,000 down, where would the amount be recorded? Write $5,000 under "owners' equity." Ask the students to determine the amount owed, and write $10,000 under liabilities.
- Bring several source documents to class. Have students work in groups to create a T account analysis of the business transaction shown on the source document.

MATERIALS

- Instructor's Resource CD: PowerPoint Slides
- Xtra! Study Tools on the Xtra! Web Site
- Blackline Master: General Journal

- Working Papers: Teacher's Edition of the Working Papers for Lesson 1-1
- Software: Personal Trainer

7

- Review the accounting equation and explain how it is the basis for double-entry accounting.
- Review the use of a general journal and explain the relationship of the accounting equation to the amount columns in a general journal.
- Review the use of the four special journals.

DEMONSTRATE

Review the accounting equation

- Write the accounting equation. Remind students that any time there is a change in a company's assets, liabilities, or owners' equity, it is important to record that change. Point out that the accounting equation helps ensure the accuracy of recording changes, for at all times, Assets must equal Liabilities + Owners' Equity.

Review journals

- Show a general journal transparency. Discuss the use of the general journal as a form for recording transactions in chronological order. Remind students that with each transaction, at least two accounts change and that debits equal credits.

- Draw a *T* on the transparency over the debit and credit columns to emphasize that the left side of a T account represents the debit column of the general journal and that the right side of a T account represents the credit column. Point out to students that "debit" does not necessarily mean increase nor does "credit" necessarily mean decrease. Reinforce this concept by referring students to the illustration.

- Write the titles of the four special journals. Ask students the one kind of transaction recorded in each journal. Write correct responses next to the appropriate journal title.

GENERAL JOURNAL

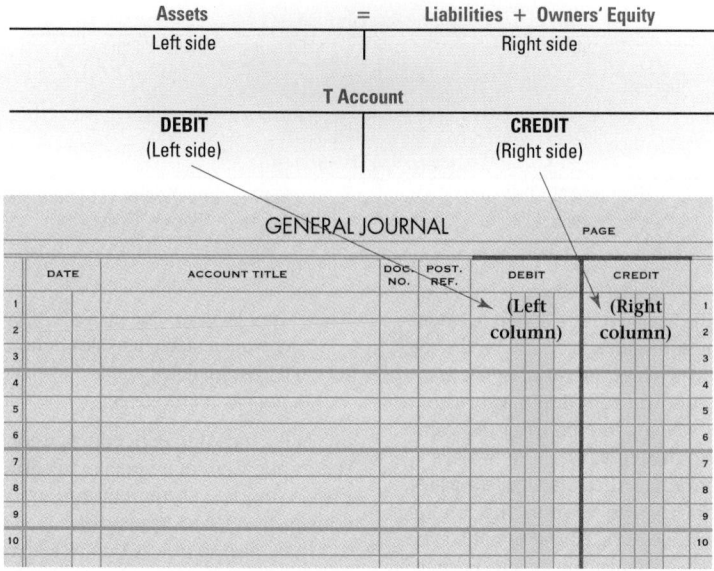

The recording of debit and credit parts of a transaction is called **double-entry accounting**. With every transaction, at least two accounts will change. Two accounting principles are common to double-entry accounting: (1) The total value of things owned by a business (assets) equals the total value of claims of outsiders (liabilities) and claims of owners (owners' equity). (2) Debits equal credits for each business transaction recorded.

A form for recording transactions in chronological order is called a **journal**. A general journal may be used to record all business transactions. A general journal includes amount columns for recording the dollars and cents of a transaction. [*CONCEPT: Unit of Measurement*] The general journal has two amount columns. The left amount column is labeled *Debit*. The right amount column is labeled *Credit*. An entry recorded in the debit column is known as a *debit*. Likewise, an entry recorded in the credit column is known as a *credit*.

The "T" previously described in the accounting equation is also present in a general journal's debit and credit amount columns.

A journal used to record only one kind of transaction is called a **special journal**. A business with many daily transactions may use special journals. Special journals include amount columns used to record debits or credits to specific accounts. For example, a cash payments journal includes a Cash Credit amount column. Zytech uses four special journals along with a general journal to record its transactions:

1. Purchases journal—for all purchases of merchandise on account
2. Cash payments journal—for all cash payments
3. Sales journal—for all sales of merchandise on account
4. Cash receipts journal—for all cash receipts

Zytech uses a general journal to record all other transactions.

> **REMEMBER** Total assets must always equal total liabilities plus total owners' equity.

TEACHING STRATEGIES   DIFFERENT LEARNING STYLES

Print Learner. The print learner prefers to see the data in print, preferably words. When being introduced to the T account, a print learner would prefer to study the illustration in the textbook that shows a T account, labeled with the words DEBIT and CREDIT.

TEACHING STRATEGIES   DIFFERENT LEARNING ABILITIES

Specific Learning Disability (SLD) Students. When you ask questions during class, ask SLD students questions that they can likely answer successfully. Save more difficult or unstructured questions for better students.

NORMAL BALANCES OF ACCOUNTS

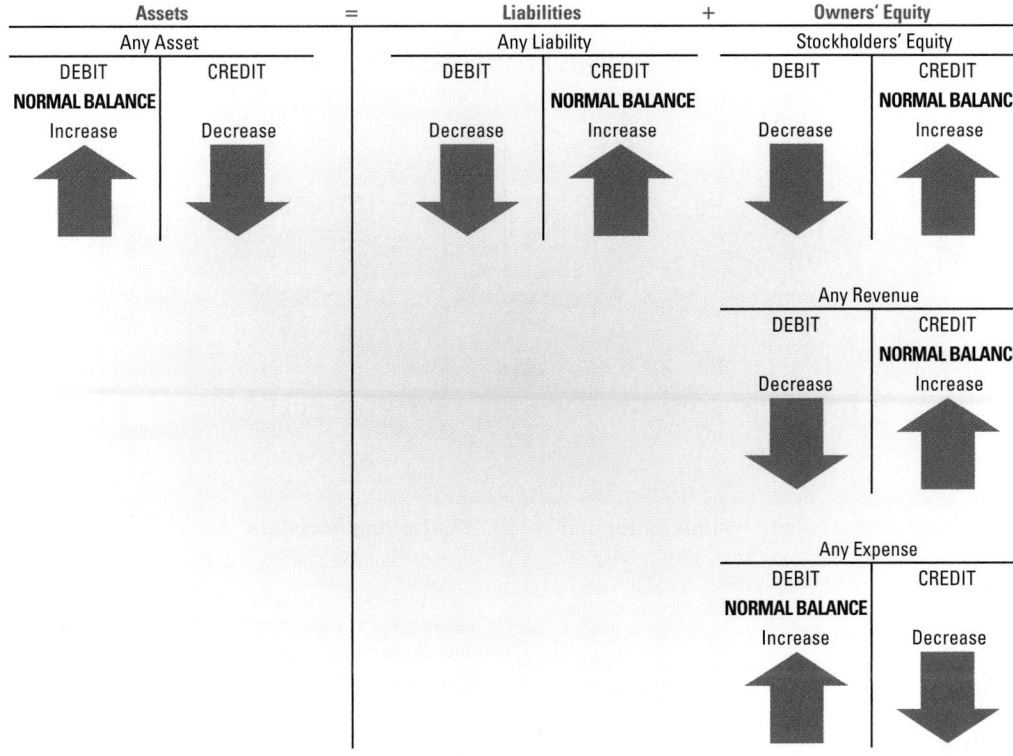

Transactions are journalized in chronological order. Periodically, information is sorted to summarize like kinds of information. A record summarizing all the information pertaining to a single item in the accounting equation is called an **account**.

The amount in an account is known as an *account balance.* Each business transaction causes a change in two or more account balances. Increases in an account balance are recorded in the same column as its normal balance. Decreases

in an account balance are recorded in the column opposite its normal balance. The normal balances of different classifications of accounts are shown in the figure above.

Asset account balances are increased by debits and decreased by credits. Liability and owners' equity account balances as well as revenue account balances are increased by credits and decreased by debits. Expense account balances are increased by debits and decreased by credits.

{ REMEMBER   Increases in revenue accounts increase owners' equity. Therefore, the normal credit balance of revenue accounts is the same as the normal balance of owners' equity. Increases in expense accounts decrease owners' equity. Therefore the normal debit balance of expense accounts is opposite the normal balance of owners' equity. }

- Review the definitions of ledger, general ledger, subsidiary ledger, and controlling accounts.
- Explain how the general ledger controlling account summarizes all accounts in a subsidiary ledger.
- Emphasize that the total of the subsidiary accounts must equal the balance in the appropriate controlling account.
- Explain the difference between accounts receivable and accounts payable.

DEMONSTRATE

Review subsidiary ledgers

- Use the illustration to show the relationship between accounts payable subsidiary accounts and the controlling account. Emphasize the individual account totals shown on the calculator tape equal the total in the controlling account.
- Ask students to prepare a similar example to show the relationship between accounts receivable subsidiary accounts and the controlling account. Ask a student to write her or his example on the board or overhead.
- Ask students to explain the difference between accounts payable and accounts receivable. Ask for examples.

EXPLAIN

- Review the definition of file maintenance.
- Review the chart of accounts numbering system.

DEMONSTRATE

File maintenance

- Direct student attention to the chart of accounts presented on page 3. Ask students to explain the purpose of each digit of the numbering system (first number indicates the division, second digit indicates the category, and third and fourth indicate position in category).

ONGOING ASSESSMENT

- Assessment is an ongoing process. Circulate through the classroom or lab, observing which students have problems with the assignments.
- Throughout the instructional process, ask individual students short questions to determine their knowledge of account classifications and basic accounting principles. Questions might include classifying different account titles as asset, liability, owners' equity, etc., or stating the

10

LEDGERS

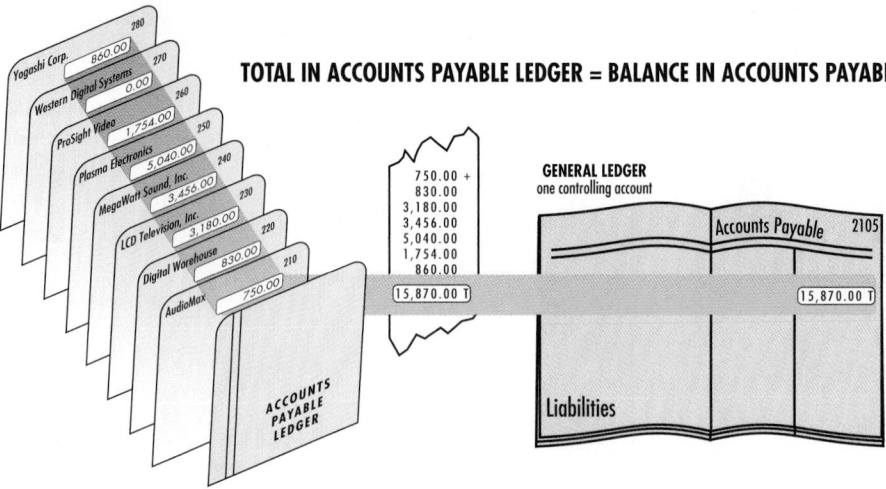

TOTAL IN ACCOUNTS PAYABLE LEDGER = BALANCE IN ACCOUNTS PAYABLE

A group of accounts is called a **ledger**. A ledger that contains all accounts needed to prepare financial statements is called a **general ledger**. A ledger that is summarized in a single general ledger account is called a **subsidiary ledger**. An account in a general ledger that summarizes all accounts in a subsidiary ledger is called a **controlling account**. Two subsidiary ledgers and two general ledger controlling accounts are commonly used:

Subsidiary Ledgers
Accounts Receivable Ledger
Accounts Payable Ledger

Controlling Accounts
Accounts Receivable
Accounts Payable

Accounts for customers who buy merchandise on account are kept in an accounts receivable ledger. The corresponding controlling account is Accounts Receivable. Separate accounts are kept in an accounts payable ledger for vendors to whom money is owed. The corresponding controlling account is Accounts Payable. The total of the subsidiary ledger account balances should equal the balance of the controlling account.

GENERAL AND SUBSIDIARY LEDGER FILE MAINTENANCE

Zytech uses a general ledger account numbering system that meets three needs: (1) A separate numeric listing is provided for each ledger division. (2) A predesigned arrangement of numbers is provided within each ledger division. (3) Account number digits are spaced to allow the addition of new accounts. The procedure for arranging accounts in a general ledger, assigning account numbers, and keeping records current is called **file maintenance**.

Zytech's general ledger chart of accounts has eight divisions. The first digit of each four-digit account number shows the general ledger division in which the account is located. The accounts in some divisions, such as Assets, are divided into categories. The second digit of the account number shows the category in which the account is located. The last two digits show the location of a specific account with respect to other accounts in that division and category.

rules for increasing and decreasing different accounts. These questions may also be completed as a written assessment.

- Troubleshooting: Students may have problems identifying account classifications and the rules for increasing and decreasing assets, liabilities, owners' equity, revenue, and expenses.
- Assess student understanding by checking solutions to Independent Practice assignments.

RETEACH

- Place the accounting equation and a list of accounts on the board. Select accounts from the chart of accounts on page 3. Ask students to classify each account and place it under the appropriate element of the equation. Using T accounts, ask students to indicate the increase and decrease sides of each account.

- Write a list of accounts. Ask students to arrange the accounts based on their classifications. Direct students to assign appropriate numbers.
- Ask a student to explain the relationship between a T account and the debit and credit columns of a general journal. Ask another student to illustrate the relationship using a transparency of the general journal.

terms review

asset
liability
equities
owners' equity
stockholders' equity
accounting equation
source documents
double-entry accounting
journal
special journal
account
ledger
general ledger
subsidiary ledger
controlling account
file maintenance

audit your understanding

1. How is the accounting equation most commonly stated?
2. What is the normal balance of an asset account? A revenue account?
3. What are the three needs met by Zytech's account numbering system?

work together 1-1

Determining the normal balance, increase, and decrease sides for accounts

Write the answers to the following problems in the *Working Papers*. Your instructor will guide you through the following examples.

Prepaid Insurance
Advertising Expense
Lee Enterprises (an account payable)
Capital Stock

Merchandise Inventory
Nguyen Entertainment (an account receivable)
Sales
Cash

For each of the accounts above, complete the following.
1. Prepare a T account for each account. Enter the title of the account.
2. In parentheses to the right of the account title, identify the account as asset, liability, owners' equity, revenue, or expense.
3. Label the *debit* and *credit* sides.
4. Label each side of the T account using the labels *Normal Balance, Increase Side,* or *Decrease Side.*

on your own 1-1

Determining the normal balance, increase, and decrease sides for accounts

Write the answers to the following problems in the *Working Papers*. Work this problem independently.

Rent Expense
Sales
Pacifico Studio (an account receivable)
Supplies

Gardena A/V Supply (an account payable)
Capital Stock
Petty Cash
Prepaid Insurance

For each of the accounts above, complete the following.
1. Prepare a T account for each account. Enter the title of the account.
2. In parentheses to the right of the account title, identify the account as asset, liability, owners' equity, revenue, or expense.
3. Label the *debit* and *credit* sides.
4. Label each side of the T account using the labels *Normal Balance, Increase Side,* or *Decrease Side.*

Using Accounting Principles and Records

GUIDED PRACTICE

Terms Review
Call on students to define each term in the Terms Review. After each definition, ask the class if the definition is correct and whether the complete definition has been given or if anything needs to be added. Suggested definitions are given in the Glossary.

Audit Your Understanding
Call on students to answer the Audit Your Understanding questions. Ask the class if the answer is correct and/or complete. Answers are given in Appendix E of the textbook.

Work Together
Have students write the solution to the Work Together problems as you guide the class through the examples.

- Direct students to record answers on the proper form as you elicit class participation in determining solution answers.
- Call on students for solutions.
- Ask a student to provide the rule for increasing and decreasing assets; another the rule for liabilities; and another for owner's equity.

INDEPENDENT PRACTICE

On Your Own
- Assign the On Your Own problems to be worked independently.
- Use the Ongoing Assessment techniques to diagnose student understanding.

Application Problem
- Assign Application Problem 1-1: Determining the normal balance, increase, and decrease sides for accounts.

Personal Trainer
- Students can access the Lesson 1-1 assessment material using this software.

Xtra! Web Site
- Students can access the Xtra! Study Tools for additional practice.

ENRICH

- Assign the Making Ethical Decisions feature on page 6.
- Assign the Applied Communication feature on page 29. This activity provides the opportunity to prepare a resume. Guide students through the steps of completing a resume.

CLOSE

- Ask students to name the classifications for accounts. As each classification is announced, ask students the rules for increasing and decreasing an account under that particular classification.
- Review the illustration on page 9 showing normal balances of accounts.
- Review the figure on page 10 showing ledgers to help students understand the relationship between subsidiary accounts and a controlling account.

1-2 Journalizing and Posting Purchases and Purchases Returns

DEPARTMENTAL ACCOUNTING SYSTEM

Management decisions depend on accounting information about each phase of a business. When a business has two or more departments, accounting information can help management decide whether a department's performance is acceptable or unacceptable. Accounting information can also determine the kinds of merchandise that produce the greatest or the least profit.

An accounting system showing accounting information for two or more departments is called a **departmental accounting system**. In a departmental accounting system, gross profit is calculated for each department. The general ledger, therefore, must include a number of separate departmental accounts. Shoe stores, furniture stores, computer stores, department stores, and sporting goods stores are examples of firms that commonly organize on a departmental basis.

A business that purchases and sells goods is called a **merchandising business**. Zytech Media Corporation sells audio equipment and video equipment. The business is a corporation organized on a departmental basis.

Merchandising businesses may have two types of equipment: (1) equipment purchased for sale to customers and (2) equipment used in the operation of the business. Zytech purchases and sells audio and video equipment. Zytech uses office equipment and store equipment to operate the business.

Zytech uses a departmental accounting system. Accounting information is recorded and reported for two departments: (1) Audio and (2) Video. The separate departmental accounts for Zytech are in the chart of accounts at the beginning of Part 1. All accounts for the audio department include "audio" in the account title. All accounts for the video department include "video" in the account title. For example, the audio department's inventory account is titled

Merchandise Inventory—Audio and is assigned number 1305. The first digit, *1*, indicates that the account is an asset. The second digit, *3*, shows the account is in the third category (inventory accounts) of the asset division. The last two digits, *05*, show the location of the account with respect to the other accounts in the inventory account category.

Purchase invoices are used as the source documents for all purchases on account. [*CONCEPT: Objective Evidence*]

All departmental purchases of merchandise on account are recorded in a purchases journal. A business with more than one department records a purchase on account in the same way as a business with a single department, except for two differences: (1) Each purchase invoice has a notation placed on it showing to which department the purchase applies. (2) Each department has a separate Purchases Debit column in the purchases journal. Zytech's purchases journal, shown on the next page, has special Purchases Debit columns for each department—Audio and Video.

Recording Departmental Purchases and Cash Payments

©GETTY IMAGES/PHOTODISC

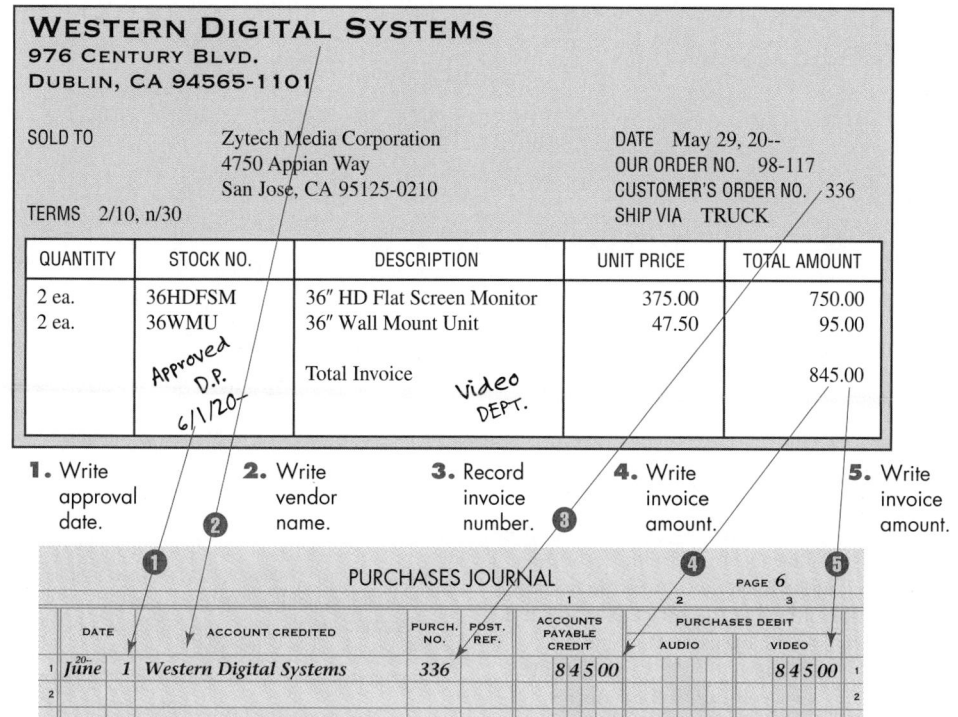

1. Write approval date. ❶

2. Write vendor name. ❷

3. Record invoice number. ❸

4. Write invoice amount. ❹

5. Write invoice amount. ❺

June 1. Purchased video equipment on account from Western Digital Systems, $845.00. Purchase Invoice No. 336.

In the general ledger, Purchases—Video increases by an $845.00 debit. Accounts Payable increases by an $845.00 credit. In the accounts payable ledger, Western Digital Systems increases by an $845.00 credit.

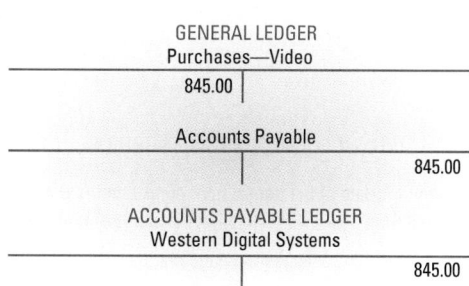

GENERAL LEDGER
Purchases—Video

845.00 |

Accounts Payable

| 845.00

ACCOUNTS PAYABLE LEDGER
Western Digital Systems

| 845.00

STEPS · STEPS · STEPS · STEPS · STEPS · STEPS · STEPS · STEPS · STEPS · STEPS · STEPS ·

JOURNALIZING A PURCHASE ON ACCOUNT

❶ Write the date the invoice was received and approved, *June 1,* in the Date column of the purchases journal. Since this is the first entry on page 6, include the current year, *20--.*

❷ Enter the vendor name, *Western Digital Systems,* in the Account Credited column.

❸ Record the invoice number, *336,* in the Purch. No. column. Since only purchase invoice numbers are recorded in the column, no identifying letter is necessary.

❹ Write the credit amount, *$845.00,* in the Accounts Payable Credit column. (Dollar signs are not written on ruled accounting forms.)

❺ Record the debit amount, *$845.00,* in the Purchases Debit Video column.

Journalizing and Posting Purchases and Purchases Returns

Lesson 1-2   **13**

- Ask students to explain the term *posting*. Write the definition.

- Direct students to the illustration. Review steps 1–5 for posting from a purchases journal to the accounts payable ledger.

- Ask students to read the Remember feature so they have a better understanding of what journal to use to record a charge purchase transaction.

Post the transaction

- Use transparencies of a departmental purchases journal and an accounts payable subsidiary ledger account to illustrate the five steps for posting from a purchases journal to the accounts payable ledger. Explain the abbreviation *P6* (Purchases Journal, page 6).

- Provide several numerical examples on the board to illustrate how a new balance in the accounts payable ledger is calculated.

POSTING FROM A PURCHASES JOURNAL

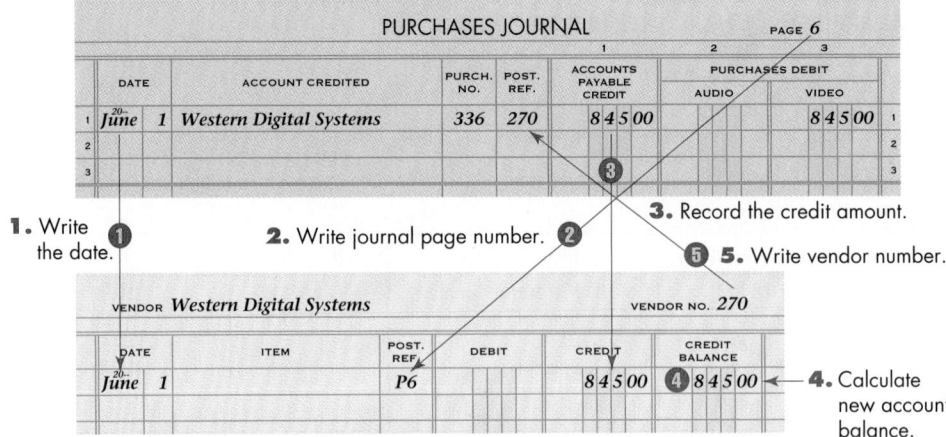

1. Write the date.
2. Write journal page number.
3. Record the credit amount.
5. Write vendor number.
4. Calculate new account balance.

Transferring transaction information from a journal entry to a ledger account is called **posting**. Zytech keeps vendor accounts in an accounts payable ledger. Individual amounts in the Accounts Payable Credit column of the purchases journal are posted often to the appropriate vendor accounts. The purchases journal is abbreviated as *P* in the Post. Ref. column of the ledger accounts. Posting from the Accounts Payable Credit column of the purchases journal to a ledger account is shown above.

FYI FOR YOUR INFORMATION

CPAs help small businesses avoid many of the pitfalls of doing business. Business owners rely on CPAs for advice in such areas as taxation, payroll requirements, banking policies, and business planning.

STEPS • STEPS • STEPS • STEPS • STEPS • STEPS • STEPS • STEPS • STEPS • STEPS

POSTING FROM THE PURCHASES JOURNAL TO THE ACCOUNTS PAYABLE LEDGER

1. Write the date of the transaction, *June 1,* in the Date column of the ledger account. Since this is the first ledger entry for Western Digital Systems, include the current year, *20--,* in the Date column.

2. Enter the purchases journal page number, *P6,* in the Post. Ref. column of the ledger account.

3. Record the credit amount, *$845.00,* in the Credit column of the account for Western Digital Systems. All postings from the purchases journal to the ledger accounts will be to the Credit amount column of the ledger.

4. Add the amount in the Credit amount column to the previous balance in the Credit Balance column. Write the new account balance in the Credit Balance column. Since Western Digital Systems has no balance, simply enter the amount, *$845.00,* in the Credit amount column in the Credit Balance column.

5. Record the vendor number in the Post. Ref. column of the journal. The vendor number shows that the posting for this entry is complete.

{ REMEMBER Only purchases of merchandise on account are recorded in the purchases journal. }

TEACHING STRATEGIES   COOPERATIVE LEARNING

Select a group of three students to prepare a bulletin board that includes the five steps for posting. Allow five days for this project. Appoint a spokesperson to make a presentation to the class of these five steps and how they are necessary in order to post correctly.

POSTING THE TOTALS OF A PURCHASES JOURNAL

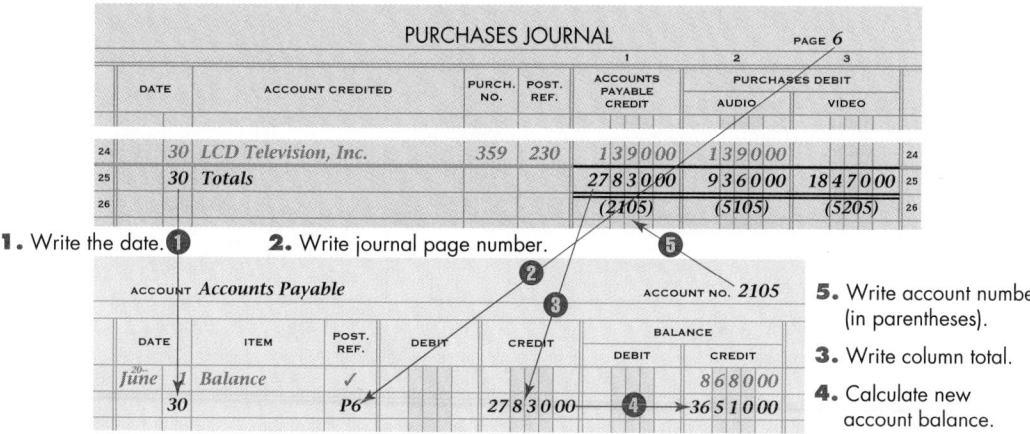

PURCHASES JOURNAL   PAGE *6*

	DATE	ACCOUNT CREDITED	PURCH. NO.	POST. REF.	ACCOUNTS PAYABLE CREDIT	PURCHASES DEBIT AUDIO	PURCHASES DEBIT VIDEO	
24	30	LCD Television, Inc.	359	230	1 3 9 0 00	1 3 9 0 00		24
25	30	Totals			27 8 3 0 00	9 3 6 0 00	18 4 7 0 00	25
26					(2105)	(5105)	(5205)	26

1. Write the date. ❶   **2.** Write journal page number.   ❺

ACCOUNT *Accounts Payable*   ACCOUNT NO. *2105*

DATE	ITEM	POST. REF.	DEBIT	CREDIT	BALANCE DEBIT	BALANCE CREDIT
June 1	Balance	✓				8 6 8 0 00
30		P6		27 8 3 0 00	❹ ➝ 36 5 1 0 00	

5. Write account number (in parentheses).

3. Write column total.

4. Calculate new account balance.

The purchases journal is proved and ruled at the end of each month. A purchases journal is proved by adding each column and then proving that the sum of the debit column totals equals the credit column total. Double lines are then ruled across the amount columns to show that the totals have been verified as correct. Each amount column total is posted to the general ledger account named in the column heading. The posting of the purchases journal's Accounts Payable Credit column total to the Accounts Payable account in the general ledger is shown above. The same procedure is used to post the totals of the Purchases Debit—Audio and the Purchases Debit—Video columns.

STEPS STEPS • STEPS • STEPS • STEPS
POSTING THE TOTAL OF THE ACCOUNTS PAYABLE COLUMN TO THE GENERAL LEDGER

❶ Write the date, *30,* in the Date column of the account.

❷ Write the purchases journal page number, *P6,* in the Post. Ref. column of the account.

❸ Write the Accounts Payable Credit column total, *$27,830.00,* in the Credit amount column of the *Accounts Payable* account.

❹ Calculate and record the new account balance, *$36,510.00,* in the Balance Credit column.

❺ Write the general ledger account number in parentheses, *(2105),* below the column total in the purchases journal.

©GETTY IMAGES/PHOTODISC

- Direct students to the illustration. Ask students to whom the merchandise was returned, what items were returned, what was the date of the return, and the total value of merchandise returned.

- Ask students what accounts would be used to indicate that (1) the amount of money owed to a company is less and (2) the amount of video purchases for the month should be reduced. Continue questioning until students answer Accounts Payable/Western Digital Systems and Purchases—Video. Introduce the contra cost account, Purchases Returns and Allowances—Video. Point out that the contra account allows businesses to see what proportion of the merchandise was returned to vendors.

- Draw the three T accounts (Purchases—Video, Accounts Payable, and Western Digital Systems), including the amounts shown on page 13, on the board or overhead. Ask students to describe the transaction (the purchase of video merchandise on account from Western Digital Systems, $845.00).

- Using only these three accounts, ask the students to record the entry for the purchases return. Without a return account, the credit amount would have to be placed under the Purchases—Video account. Discuss with students the disadvantages of doing so. Lead into a discussion of the importance of using a Purchases Returns—Video account so that businesses can determined what proportion of the merchandise was returned to vendors. A high percentage may indicate poor manufacturing, shoddy products, damage during shipping, etc.

Analyze the transaction

- Direct students to the illustration. Question students regarding quantity returned, model no., unit price, date, total amount, debit memo number, etc. Discuss the significance of using source documents in accounting.

- Use T accounts to explain the transaction presented.

- Use a transparency to illustrate the procedures for journalizing the return of merchandise in the general journal. Follows steps 1–7.

JOURNALIZING PURCHASES RETURNS AND ALLOWANCES

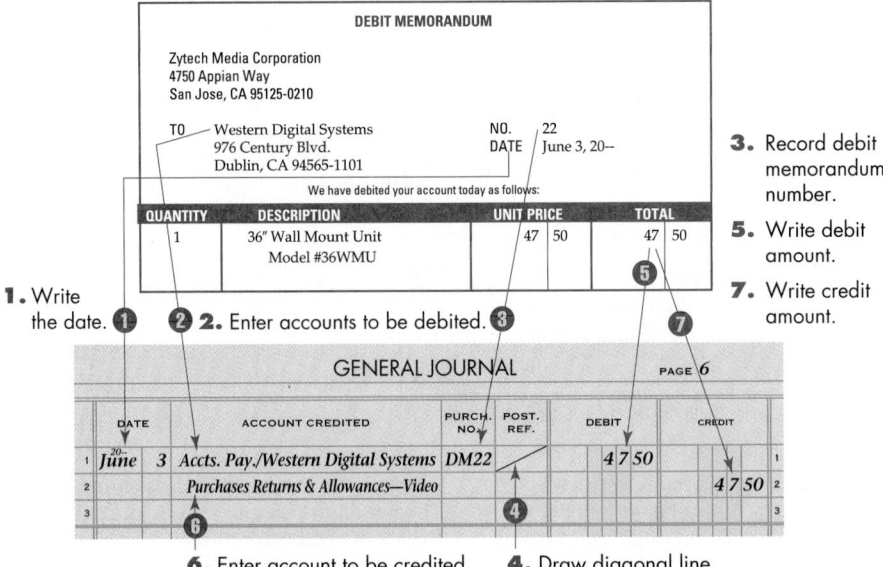

1. Write the date.
2. Enter accounts to be debited.
3. Record debit memorandum number.
4. Draw diagonal line.
5. Write debit amount.
6. Enter account to be credited.
7. Write credit amount.

When merchandise is returned to a vendor, the vendor's account and Accounts Payable are reduced by a debit. An allowance may also be given for merchandise that is not returned. A form prepared by the customer showing the price deduction for purchase returns and allowances is called a **debit memorandum**.

Zytech documents all purchases returns and allowances with a debit memorandum and records the transaction in a general journal. Zytech's general journal is shown above.

June 3. Returned video equipment (one damaged wall mount unit) to Western Digital Systems, $47.50, from Purchase Invoice No. 336. Debit Memorandum No. 22.

In the general ledger, Accounts Payable decreases by a $47.50 debit. An account that reduces a related account on a financial statement is known as a **contra account**. The purchases discount accounts are contra cost accounts. Purchases Returns and Allowances—Video increases by a $47.50 credit. In the accounts payable ledger, the vendor account, Western Digital Systems, decreases by a $47.50 debit.

GENERAL LEDGER
Accounts Payable

47.50	

Purchases Returns and Allowances—Video

	47.50

ACCOUNTS PAYABLE LEDGER
Western Digital Systems

47.50	

STEPS • STEPS • STEPS • STEPS • STEPS

JOURNALIZING A PURCHASES RETURN

1. Write the date, *June 3*, in the Date column of the general journal. Since this is the first entry on page 6 of the general journal, include the current year, *20--*.

2. Write the titles of the accounts to be debited, *Accts. Pay./Western Digital Systems*, in the Account Title column.

3. Record the debit memorandum number, *DM22*, in the Doc. No. column.

4. Draw a diagonal line in the Post. Ref. Column to indicate that the single debit amount is posted to two accounts.

5. Write the debit amount, *$47.50*, in the Debit column.

6. Indent and write the title of the account to be credited, *Purchases Returns and Allowances—Video*, in the Account Title column.

7. Record the credit amount, *$47.50*, in the Credit column.

16   Chapter 1

Recording Departmental Purchases and Cash Payments

- Troubleshooting: Diagnose what kinds of problems students have with this lesson. They sometimes become confused about when to post to the subsidiary ledger and when to post to the controlling account.

- Ask a student to explain the procedure for proving the accuracy of journal totals (the sum of debit column totals must equal the sum of credit column totals). Use the illustration on page 15. Write calculations on the board.

• terms review

TERMS REVIEW •

departmental accounting system
merchandising business
posting
debit memorandum
contra account

• audit your understanding

1. When Zytech's video department purchases merchandise on account, what general ledger accounts are affected, and how?

2. What general ledger accounts are affected, and how, by a purchases return of video equipment?

AUDIT YOUR

• work together 1-2

WORK TOGETHER • WORK TOGETHER • WORK TOGETHER • WORK TOGETHER

Journalizing and posting purchases on account and purchases returns and allowances

City Music has two departments: Discs and Tapes. A purchases journal, general journal, partial general ledger, and accounts payable ledger are provided in the *Working Papers*. The balances are recorded as of March 1 of the current year. Your instructor will guide you through the following examples.

Transactions:

Mar. 1. Purchased tapes on account from Raymond Wholesalers, $1,350.00. P283.
  2. Purchased discs on account from Artex Music, $965.00. P284.
  5. Returned discs to Dade, Inc., $165.00, from P280. DM36.
  6. Received an allowance on tapes from Raymond Wholesalers, $100.00, from P283. DM37.
  18. Purchased tapes on account from Quality Tapes, $268.00. P285.
  23. Purchased tapes on account from Castle Records and Tapes, $993.00. P286.

1. Journalize each transaction. Source documents are abbreviated as follows: debit memorandum, DM; purchase invoice, P.

2. Post the items that are to be posted individually from the purchases journal.

3. Post from the general journal.

4. Prove and rule the purchases journal. Post the totals.

The ledgers used in this problem are needed to complete On Your Own 1-2.

• on your own 1-2

ON YOUR OWN • ON YOUR OWN • ON YOUR OWN • ON YOUR OWN

Journalizing and posting purchases on account and purchases returns and allowances

Use the ledger accounts from Work Together 1-2 and the purchases journal in the *Working Papers*. Work this problem independently.

Transactions:

Apr. 4. Purchased tapes on account from Quality Tapes, $425.00. P287.
  12. Purchased tapes on account from Castle Records and Tapes, $2,100.00. P288.
  18. Purchased discs on account from Park Recording Company, $1,624.00. P289.
  20. Returned discs to Artex Music, $120.00, from P284. DM38.
  22. Purchased discs on account from Artex Music, $850.00. P290.
  30. Received an allowance on tapes from Castle Records and Tapes, $150.00, from P289. DM39.

1. Journalize each transaction.

2. Post the items that are to be posted individually from the purchases journal.

3. Post from the general journal.

4. Prove and rule the purchases journal. Post the totals.

GUIDED PRACTICE

Terms Review

Call on students to define each term in the Terms Review. After each definition, ask the class if the definition is correct and whether the complete definition has been given or if anything needs to be added. Suggested definitions are given in the Glossary.

Audit Your Understanding

Call on students to answer the Audit Your Understanding questions. Ask the class if the answer is correct and/or complete. Answers are given in Appendix E of the textbook.

Work Together

Have students write the solution to the Work Together problems as you guide the class through the examples.

- Direct students to record each transaction in the proper journal and ledger account as you elicit class participation in determining and calculating each amount.

- Ask students how to total and rule the purchases journal.

- Ask a student to describe the steps for posting journal totals.

INDEPENDENT PRACTICE

On Your Own

- Assign the On Your Own problems to be worked independently.

- Use the Ongoing Assessment techniques to diagnose student understanding.

Application Problem

- Assign Application Problem 1-2: Journalizing and posting departmental purchases on account and purchases returns and allowances.

Personal Trainer

- Students can access the Lesson 1-2 assessment using this software.

Xtra! Web Site

- Students can access the Xtra! Study Tools for additional practice.

ENRICH

- Students can use the Peachtree and QuickBooks data files to automate Application Problem 1-2.

CLOSE

- Use the illustrations on pages 13, 14, and 15 to briefly review the procedures for journalizing and posting transactions concerning the purchases of merchandise on account.

1-3 Journalizing and Posting Cash Payments

DEPARTMENTAL CASH PAYMENTS

Most of Zytech's cash payments are made by check. Therefore, checks are the source documents for most cash payments. [CONCEPT: Objective Evidence] All cash payments are recorded in the cash payments journal.

Cash Payment on Account

Purchases on account are expected to be paid within the stated credit period. A seller may encourage early payment by allowing a deduction from the invoice amount. A deduction that a vendor allows on the invoice amount to encourage prompt payment is called a **cash discount**. A cash discount on purchases taken by a customer is called a **purchases discount**.

A purchases discount is usually stated as a percentage. For example, the terms of an invoice may be written as *2/10, n/30*. The expression *2/10* means that 2% of the invoice amount may

be deducted from the amount due if payment is made within 10 days of the invoice date. The expression *n/30* means that payment of the total invoice amount must be made within 30 days of the invoice date. No discount can be deducted, however, if payment is made after 10 days from the invoice date. Zytech takes advantage of all discounts allowed by vendors.

A purchases discount reduces the net amount of cash paid for a purchase. The account Purchases Discount—Video is in the cost of merchandise division of Zytech's general ledger. Purchases discounts are kept in separate accounts and not deducted directly from the purchases accounts. This procedure helps the business see what proportion of purchases on account were allowed purchases discounts.

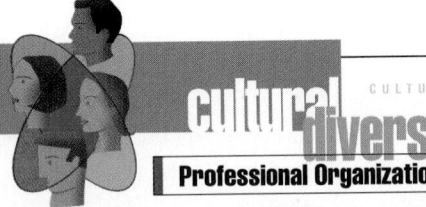

cultural diversity

Professional Organizations

How do you meet other people in your profession? Join a professional organization. Several professional accounting organizations exist to serve the needs of various ethnic groups. Among these organizations are The Association of Latino Professionals in Finance and Accounting (www.alpfa.org); The National Association of Black Accountants, Inc. (www.nabainc.org); and The Association of Asian American Attorneys and Certified Public Accountants.

These associations maintain an informal network among members. Such networks allow people in the profession to meet, to

use services of other association members, and to share ideas and career opportunities. They also promote career opportunities for their members, work to expand representation of their ethnic groups in the workforce, and offer various forms of continuing education.

In addition to their national organizations, each has various chapters around the country. All three offer student memberships to college students who are studying accounting.

JOURNALIZING A PURCHASES DISCOUNT

1. Write the date. 2. Enter vendor name. 3. Record the check number. 4. Write the debit amount. 5. Record the discount amount. 6. Enter the credit amount.

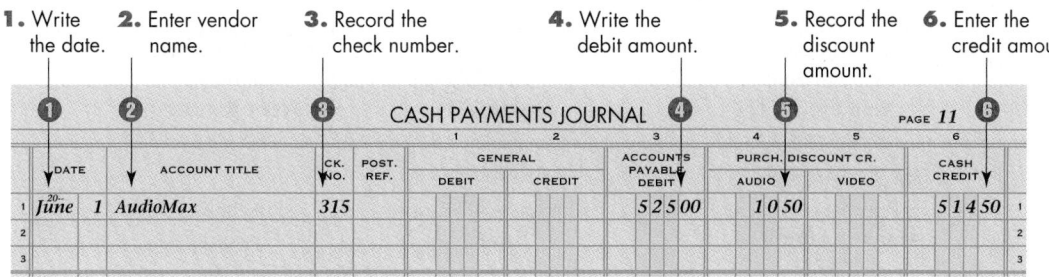

CASH PAYMENTS JOURNAL   PAGE 11

	DATE	ACCOUNT TITLE	CK. NO.	POST. REF.	GENERAL DEBIT	GENERAL CREDIT	ACCOUNTS PAYABLE DEBIT	PURCH. DISCOUNT CR. AUDIO	PURCH. DISCOUNT CR. VIDEO	CASH CREDIT	
1	June 1	AudioMax	315				525 00	10 50		514 50	1
2											2
3											3

Zytech's cash payments journal has two debit columns—General Debit and Accounts Payable Debit. The journal also has four credit columns—General Credit, a Purchases Discount Credit column for each of the two departments, and Cash Credit.

June 1. Paid cash on account to AudioMax, $514.50, covering Purchase Invoice No. 331 for surround sound audio equipment for $525.00, less 2% discount, $10.50. Check No. 315.

The source document for this transaction is a check. [CONCEPT: Objective Evidence]

In the general ledger, Accounts Payable decreases by a $525.00 debit. Cash decreases by a $514.50 credit. Purchases Discount—Audio increases by a $10.50 credit. In the accounts payable ledger, AudioMax decreases by a $525.00 debit.

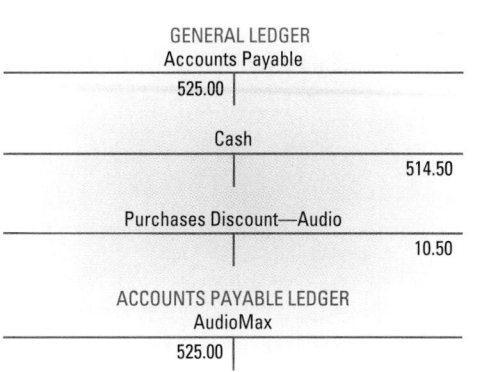

GENERAL LEDGER
Accounts Payable
525.00 |

Cash
| 514.50

Purchases Discount—Audio
| 10.50

ACCOUNTS PAYABLE LEDGER
AudioMax
525.00 |

STEPS

STEPS • STEPS • STEPS • STEPS • STEPS • STEPS • STEPS • STEPS • STEPS • STEPS •

JOURNALIZING A CASH PAYMENT THAT INCLUDES A PURCHASES DISCOUNT

1. Write the date, *June 1*, in the Date column of the cash payments journal. Since this is the first entry on page 11 of the cash payments journal, include the current year, *20--*.

2. Enter the vendor name, *AudioMax*, in the Account Title column.

3. Record the check number, *315*, in the Ck. No. column.

4. Write the debit amount, *$525.00*, in the Accounts Payable Debit column.

5. Record the discount credit amount, *$10.50*, in the Purchases Discount Credit Audio column.

6. Enter the cash credit amount, *$514.50*, in the Cash Credit column.

Journalizing and Posting Cash Payments   Lesson 1-3   **19**

EXPLAIN

- Show a transparency of a departmental cash payments journal. Ask students what is different from the cash payments journal previously used. Point out the Purchases Discount Credit columns for each department.

- Ask students the purpose of designing a journal that includes Purchases Discount Credit columns. *(It is easier to record numerous transactions of a like nature.)*

- Use the illustration to review the steps for journalizing a cash payment that includes a purchases discount.

DEMONSTRATE

Analyze the transaction

- Show the mathematical process for calculating the 2% discount described in the June 1 transaction. Create other discount problems and ask students to calculate discount amounts to assess comprehension levels.

- Draw a vertical stack of four T accounts and label them as shown on the page. Analyze the June 1 transaction into debit and credit parts. Emphasize that the discount amount, $10.50, is not recorded as a credit to Purchases—Audio to reduce the cost, but rather it is placed in a separate contra account, Purchases Discount—Audio.

Journalize the transaction

- Distribute copies of a blank cash payments journal. Use a transparency to explain the process for journalizing a cash payment that includes a purchases discount. Journalize the June 1 transaction using steps 1–6. Reinforce learning by creating other transactions for students to journalize. Ask students to save the cash payments journal for later use.

- Ask students to verify discount amounts through the use of a calculator.

APPLIED SKILLS   WORD PROCESSING

If you wish to integrate word processing in your accounting course, you may direct students to answer the end-of-chapter Explore Accounting, Applied Communication, and Cases for Critical Thinking features using their word processing software.

- Pose this problem to the students: A business purchases $100 of merchandise on account last week and returns $20 of the merchandise due to damage. If the company takes advantage of a 2% discount, how much is their payment? *($76)* Emphasize that the company owes $80 at the time the invoice is paid and therefore calculates the discount based on $80 and not $100. The amount of the return is deducted from the original purchase before the discount is calculated.

- Ask a student to read the June 2 transaction on this page. Use the math box to explain the procedures for calculating the proper amount of payment.

- Use the information shown on line 2 of the cash payments journal presented in the illustration to review steps 1–4.

DEMONSTRATE

Analyze the transaction

- Show the mathematical calculations for determining the 2% discount after a purchase return as described in the June 2 transaction.

- Show the remaining mathematical calculations for determining the total amount due. Create similar return and discount problems and ask students to solve them.

- Draw a vertical stack of four T accounts and label as shown on the page. Analyze the June 2 transaction into debit and credit parts.

Journalize the transaction

- Direct students to retrieve the previously distributed cash payments journal.

- Use a transparency of a cash payments journal to record the transaction.

- Have students calculate the amount due and record each item in the journal following the four steps shown.

- Reinforce learning by creating other transactions for students to journalize. Ask students to save the cash payments journal for later use.

- Ask students to verify all amounts with a calculator.

TAKING A DISCOUNT AFTER A PURCHASE RETURN

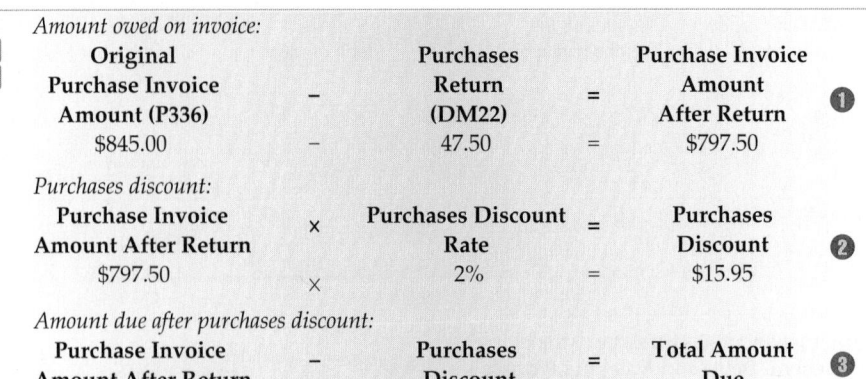

Amount owed on invoice:

Original Purchase Invoice Amount (P336)	−	Purchases Return (DM22)	=	Purchase Invoice Amount After Return	❶
$845.00	−	47.50	=	$797.50	

Purchases discount:

Purchase Invoice Amount After Return	×	Purchases Discount Rate	=	Purchases Discount	❷
$797.50	×	2%	=	$15.95	

Amount due after purchases discount:

Purchase Invoice Amount After Return	−	Purchases Discount	=	Total Amount Due	❸
$797.50	−	$15.95	=	$781.55	

CASH PAYMENTS JOURNAL — PAGE 11

	DATE		ACCOUNT TITLE	CK. NO.	POST. REF.	GENERAL DEBIT	GENERAL CREDIT	ACCOUNTS PAYABLE DEBIT	PURCH. DISCOUNT CR. AUDIO	PURCH. DISCOUNT CR. VIDEO	CASH CREDIT	
1	June	1	AudioMax	315				525 00	10 50		514 50	1
2		2	Western Digital Systems	316				797 50		15 95	781 55	2
3												3

❹

An additional calculation is necessary when a discount is taken after a purchase return or allowance has been granted. The discount is calculated on the amount owed at the time the invoice is paid. Therefore, the amount of the return or allowance must be deducted from the amount of the original purchase before the discount can be calculated.

> **June 2.** Paid cash on account to Western Digital Systems, $781.55, covering Purchase Invoice No. 336 for video equipment for $845.00, less Debit Memorandum No. 22 for $47.50, and less 2% discount, $15.95. Check No. 316.

The source document for this transaction is a check. [*CONCEPT: Objective Evidence*]

The total amount due for this purchase after the return and the discount is calculated as shown above.

This transaction is journalized in the same way as a payment of cash when there is no purchases return or allowance. The only difference is the way in which the amounts are calculated.

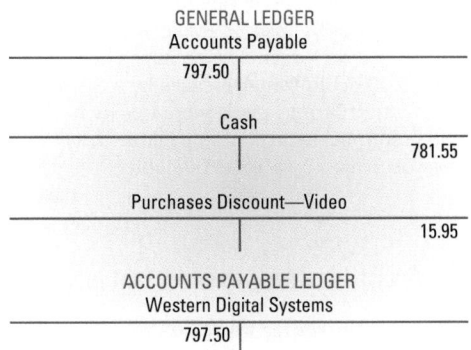

GENERAL LEDGER
Accounts Payable

797.50	

Cash

	781.55

Purchases Discount—Video

	15.95

ACCOUNTS PAYABLE LEDGER
Western Digital Systems

797.50	

STEPS • STEPS • STEPS • STEPS

CALCULATING A DISCOUNT AFTER A RETURN OR ALLOWANCE IS GRANTED AND JOURNALIZING THE CASH PAYMENT

❶ Calculate the amount owed on the invoice after the purchases return, $797.50.

❷ Calculate the purchases discount, $15.95.

❸ Find the amount due after the purchases return and the purchases discount, $781.55.

❹ Record the entry in the cash payments journal.

20 · Chapter 1

Recording Departmental Purchases and Cash Payments

RECORDING ENTRIES IN A CASH PAYMENTS JOURNAL

1. Write the date.　**2.** Enter the account title.　**3.** Record the check number.　**4.** Write the debit amount.　**5.** Enter the credit amount.

	DATE	ACCOUNT TITLE	CK. NO.	POST. REF.	GENERAL DEBIT	GENERAL CREDIT	ACCOUNTS PAYABLE DEBIT	PURCH. DISCOUNT CR. AUDIO	PURCH. DISCOUNT CR. VIDEO	CASH CREDIT	
					1	2	3	4	5	6	
3	2	Supplies—Admin.	317		1 3 6 00					1 3 6 00	3
4	2	Rent Expenses	318		1 5 0 0 00					1 5 0 0 00	4

CASH PAYMENTS JOURNAL　PAGE *11*

June 2. Paid cash for administrative supplies, $136.00. Check No. 317.

Supplies—Administrative increases by a $136.00 debit. Cash decreases by a $136.00 credit.

Supplies—Administrative
136.00 |

Cash
| 136.00

STEPS
JOURNALIZING BUYING OFFICE SUPPLIES FOR CASH

1. Write the date, *2,* in the Date column.

2. Enter the account title, *Supplies—Administrative,* in the Account Title column. It is acceptable to abbreviate account titles to fit the space in the journal.

3. Record the check number, *317,* in the Ck. No. column.

4. Write the debit amount, *$136.00,* in the General Debit column.

5. Record the credit amount, *$136.00,* in the Cash Credit column.

June 2. Paid cash for rent, $1,500.00. Check No. 318.

Rent Expense increases by a $1,500.00 debit. Cash decreases by a $1,500.00 credit.

Rent Expense
1,500.00 |

Cash
| 1,500.00

STEPS
JOURNALIZING THE CASH PAYMENT OF AN EXPENSE

1. Write the date, *2,* in the Date column.

2. Enter the account title, *Rent Expense,* in the Account Title column.

3. Record the check number, *318,* in the Ck. No. column.

4. Write the debit amount, *$1,500.00,* in the General Debit column.

5. Record the credit amount, *$1,500.00,* in the Cash Credit column.

Journalizing and Posting Cash Payments　　　　　　　　Lesson 1-3　　**21**

- Ask students the purpose of establishing a petty cash fund. Emphasize that a petty cash fund is used for making small payments for which writing a check is not time or cost effective.

- Ask students the process for replenishing petty cash. Remind them that a check is written for the amount spent from the fund, the check is then cashed, and the money is placed back into the fund.

DEMONSTRATE

Analyze the transaction

- Draw a stack of four blank T accounts on the board or overhead.

- Read the transaction statement regarding the replenishing of petty cash.

- Ask the students to analyze the transaction into debit and credit parts. Using the accounts and amounts shown in the illustration, complete the T accounts as the information is provided.

Journalize the transaction

- Use the transparency of a cash payments journal to illustrate recording the transaction to replenish petty cash.

- Students should copy the entry using the previously distributed cash payments journal.

CASH PAYMENT TO REPLENISH PETTY CASH

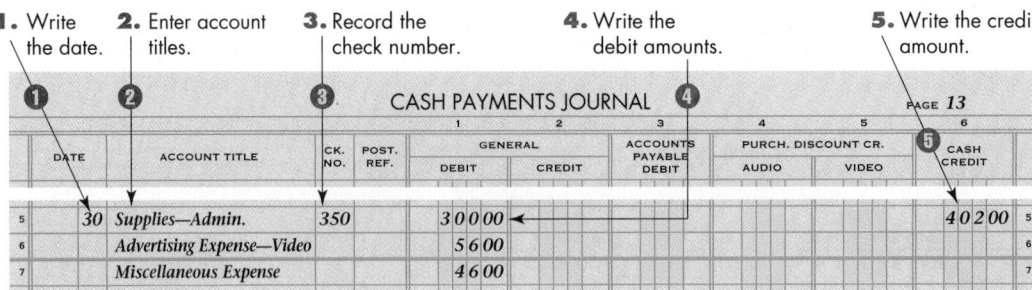

1. Write the date. **2.** Enter account titles. **3.** Record the check number. **4.** Write the debit amounts. **5.** Write the credit amount.

	DATE	ACCOUNT TITLE	CK. NO.	POST. REF.	GENERAL DEBIT	GENERAL CREDIT	ACCOUNTS PAYABLE DEBIT	PURCH. DISCOUNT CR. AUDIO	PURCH. DISCOUNT CR. VIDEO	CASH CREDIT	
5	30	Supplies—Admin.	350		3 0 0 00					4 0 2 00	5
6		Advertising Expense—Video			5 6 00						6
7		Miscellaneous Expense			4 6 00						7

An amount of cash kept on hand and used for making small payments is called **petty cash**. Zytech's petty cash fund is $500.00. It replenishes petty cash whenever the fund drops below $100.00. In addition, the petty cash fund is replenished on the last business day of each fiscal period, to assure that all expenses are recorded during the fiscal period in which they occurred. [CONCEPT: Matching Expenses with Revenue]

Business activities for an accounting period are summarized in financial statements. To adequately report how a business performed during an accounting period, all revenue earned as a result of business operations must be reported.

Likewise, all expenses incurred in producing the revenue during the same accounting period must be reported. Matching expenses with revenue gives a true picture of business operations for an accounting period.

To replenish petty cash, a check is written for the amount spent from the fund. The check is cashed and the money placed back in the fund.

June 30. Paid cash to replenish the petty cash fund, $402.00: administrative supplies, $300.00; advertising expense—video, $56.00; miscellaneous expense, $46.00. Check No. 350.

STEPS • STEPS • STEPS • STEPS • STEPS • STEPS • STEPS • STEPS • STEPS • STEPS • STEPS

JOURNALIZING THE CASH PAYMENT TO REPLENISH PETTY CASH

❶ Write the date, *30*, in the Date column.

❷ Enter the account titles, *Supplies—Administrative, Advertising Expense—Video,* and *Miscellaneous Expense,* in the Account Title column.

❸ Record the check number, *350*, in the Ck. No. column on the first line of the entry.

❹ Write the debit amounts for the appropriate accounts, *$300.00*, *$56.00,* and *$46.00*, in the General Debit column.

❺ Record the credit amount, *$402.00,* in the Cash Credit column on the first line of the entry.

©GETTY IMAGES/PHOTODISC

Recording Departmental Purchases and Cash Payments

POSTING FROM A CASH PAYMENTS JOURNAL

CASH PAYMENTS JOURNAL

PAGE 13

	DATE	ACCOUNT TITLE	CK. NO.	POST. REF.	GENERAL DEBIT	GENERAL CREDIT	ACCOUNTS PAYABLE DEBIT	PURCH. DISCOUNT CR. AUDIO	PURCH. DISCOUNT CR. VIDEO	CASH CREDIT	
12	30	Miscellaneous Expense	353	7120	4 1 80					4 1 80	12
13	30	Utilities Expense	354	7155	2 4 0 15					2 4 0 15	13
14	30	MegaWatt Sound, Inc.	355	240			4 3 0 00	8 60		4 2 1 40	14
15	30	Plasma Electronics	356	250			6 5 0 00		1 3 00	6 3 7 00	15
16	30	Totals			19 5 2 0 00	1 7 3 0 00	43 9 3 0 00	1 4 1 30	3 3 1 50	61 2 4 7 20	16
17					(√)	(√)	(2105)	(5110)	(5210)	(1105)	17
18											18

The accounting procedures for posting from a cash payments journal are the same as those followed for posting from the purchases journal. During the month, Zytech posts often from the General Debit and General Credit columns to the general ledger. Zytech also posts frequently from the Accounts Payable Debit column to the accounts payable ledger. Frequent posting permits Zytech to keep each vendor account balance in the accounts payable ledger up to date.

At the end of each month, the cash payments journal is proved and ruled. Totals of the special amount columns are posted to their respective accounts in the general ledger. The general ledger account number is written in parentheses immediately below the total. A check mark is recorded in parentheses below the totals of the General Debit and Credit columns to show that these totals are not posted. Zytech's departmental cash payments journal is shown after all posting has been completed.

STEPS

STEPS • STEPS • STEPS • STEPS • STEPS • STEPS • STEPS • STEPS • STEPS • STEPS •

POSTING FROM A CASH PAYMENTS JOURNAL

During the month:

1 Post individual amounts from the General Debit and General Credit columns to the appropriate accounts in the general ledger. Do this often during the month.

2 Post individual vendor amounts from the Accounts Payable Debit column to the appropriate accounts in the accounts payable ledger. Do this frequently during the month.

At the end of the month:

1 Post the total of each special amount column to the account named in the journal's column headings. Write the account number in parentheses under the totals as a posting reference.

2 Do *not* post the totals of the General Debit and Credit columns. (Place a check mark in parentheses under these columns to show that these totals are not posted.)

©GETTY IMAGES/PHOTODISC

Journalizing and Posting Cash Payments

Lesson 1-3 **23**

EXPLAIN

- Explain that amounts recorded in the General Debit and Credit columns are posted frequently to keep accounts in the general ledger up to date.

- Explain that amounts recorded in the Accounts Payable Debit column are posted frequently to the accounts payable ledger to keep vendor accounts up to date.

- Use the illustration to review the process for proving and ruling the cash payments journal. Explain the procedures for posting the totals of special columns.

ONGOING ASSESSMENT

- Assessment is an ongoing process. Circulate through the classroom, observing students having problems with handouts or assigned problems.

- Troubleshooting: Watch for students having difficulty calculating purchases discounts. Students may forget to deduct a return or allowance before determining the discount amount. Students may also have problems journalizing a cash payment that includes a discount after a return or allowance is granted. Students often debit accounts payable for the original amount of the invoice rather than the original amount less the return or allowance.

- Assess student understanding by checking solutions to Independent Practice assignments.

RETEACH

- Write several transactions on the board that include purchases discounts and purchases discounts after a return or allowance is granted. Arrange students into cooperative learning groups of 3–4 students. Ask the groups to analyze each transaction by answering: what accounts are affected, how each account is classified, whether they are increased or decreased, and whether they are debited or credited. Direct students to use T accounts for recording their responses.

- Distribute a blank cash payments journal and ask each cooperative learning group to journalize the transactions previously analyzed.

GUIDED PRACTICE

Terms Review

Call on students to define each term in the Terms Review. After each definition, ask the class if the definition is correct and whether the complete definition has been given or if anything needs to be added. Suggested definitions are given in the Glossary.

Audit Your Understanding

Call on students to answer the Audit Your Understanding questions. Ask the class if the answer is correct and/or complete. Answers are given in Appendix E of the textbook.

Work Together

Have students write the solution to the Work Together problems as you guide the class through the examples.

- Direct students to record each amount on the proper form as you elicit class participation in determining and calculating each amount.
- Call on students to describe the various steps used to complete each problem.

INDEPENDENT PRACTICE

On Your Own

- Assign the On Your Own problems to be worked independently.
- Use the Ongoing Assessment techniques to diagnose student understanding.

Application Problem

- Assign Application Problem 1-3: Journalizing and posting departmental cash payments.

Personal Trainer

- Students can access the Lesson 1-3 assessment material using this software.

Xtra! Web Site

- Students can access the Xtra! Study Tools for additional practice.

ENRICH

- Direct students to the Cultural Diversity feature on page 18. Perhaps invite a member from a local professional organization to discuss careers in accounting. Or, discuss the role of professional organizations in career networking. Emphasize that contacts throughout the industry can lead to new career opportunities.
- Assign the Automated Accounting feature on page 31 to automate Application Problem 1-3.

• terms review

cash discount
purchases discount
petty cash

• audit your understanding

1. What general ledger accounts are affected, and how, by a cash payment on account for video equipment that includes a purchases discount?

2. Where are cash payments affecting accounts that are not listed in the column headings recorded?

3. Why is a petty cash fund always replenished on the last day of a fiscal period?

• work together 1-3

Journalizing and posting departmental cash payments

Village Music Center has two departments: Guitars and Keyboards. Page 17 of a cash payments journal, a partial general ledger, and an accounts payable ledger are provided in the *Working Papers*. Source documents are abbreviated as follows: check, C; debit memorandum, DM; and purchase invoice, P. Your instructor will guide you through the following examples.

Transactions:

Sept. 5. Paid cash on account for guitars from Peninsula Guitar covering P358 for $1,150.00; no discount. C241.
      7. Paid cash for administrative supplies, $120.00. C242.
      9. Paid cash on account for keyboards from Magic Keyboards covering P360 for $2,210.00, less DM53 for $210.00, and less 2% discount. C243.
    16. Paid cash on account for keyboards from Magic Keyboard covering P361 for $1,800.00, less 2% discount. C244.
    19. Paid cash on account for guitars to Peninsula Guitar covering P359 for $1,680.00; no discount. C245.
    30. Paid cash to replenish the petty cash fund, $64.00: administrative supplies, $15.00; advertising expense, $22.00; miscellaneous expense, $27.00. C246.

1. Journalize the transactions.
2. Post items that are to be posted individually.
3. Prove and rule the cash payments journal. Post the totals.

• on your own 1-3

Journalizing and posting departmental cash payments

Design, Inc., has two departments: Carpet and Furniture. Use page 18 of a cash payments journal in the *Working Papers*. Work this problem independently.

Transactions:

Oct. 5. Paid cash on account for furniture from Sophos Furniture Co. covering P408 for $2,160.00. C218.
     7. Paid cash for carpet department supplies, $160.00. C219.
     8. Paid cash on account for furniture from Sophos Furniture Co. covering P412 for $3,210.00, less DM53 for $270.00, and less 2% discount. C220.
    12. Paid cash on account for carpet from Luxor Carpet, Inc. covering P413 for $1,200.00, less 2% discount. C221.
    17. Paid cash on account for carpet from Duro Weave, Inc. covering P414 for $2,600.00, less 2% discount. C222.
    19. Paid cash on account for carpet to Luxor Carpet, Inc. covering P411 for $1,775.00. C223.
    30. Paid cash to replenish the petty cash fund, $98.00: carpet department supplies, $52.00; advertising expense, $31.00; miscellaneous expense, $15.00. C224.

1. Journalize the transactions.
2. Post items that are to be posted individually.
3. Prove and rule the cash payments journal. Post the totals.

24   Chapter 1   Recording Departmental Purchases and Cash Payments

---

CLOSE

- Ask students to brainstorm and identify the most difficult concepts, transactions, or principles introduced in this lesson. Write student responses on the board or overhead.
- Ask students to vote on the top three areas of difficulty.
- Help students devise instructional lessons that will help explain and illustrate the problem areas identified.

After completing this chapter, you can

1. Define accounting terms related to departmental purchases and cash payments.

2. Identify accounting concepts and practices related to departmental purchases and cash payments.

3. Journalize and post departmental purchases and purchases returns.

4. Journalize and post departmental cash payments.

Explore Accounting

EXPLORE ACCOUNTING · EXPLORE ACCOUNTING · EXPLORE ACCOUN

Accounting Professionals

As a company grows, it can adopt two strategies to satisfy its need for accounting expertise. The company can add to its full-time accounting staff. As an alternative, the company could hire independent consultants. Regardless of which strategy is adopted, the search for accounting professionals should include examining their professional certification.

The *Certified Public Accountant (CPA)* is the most widely recognized certification. To become a CPA, an individual must pass a certifying examination and meet the educational and experience requirements of the board of accountancy in the individual's state. A CPA is qualified to perform a variety of accounting functions, including processing accounting information, auditing financial statements, preparing tax returns, and providing tax planning.

A partial list of additional certifications available in accounting and related areas follows:

Certified Management Accountant: Responsible for the accounting information system; assists managers in using accounting information in decision making; works to provide the company with adequate financial resources to conduct business.

Certified Internal Auditor: Audits the accounting information system and other operational reporting systems.

Certified Information Systems Analyst: Designs computer information systems that provide timely accounting information while assuring that the information is accessible only to authorized personnel.

Certified Fraud Examiner: Investigates alleged fraudulent activities by examining accounting records and interviewing personnel; prepares evidence for admission into court.

Certified Financial Planner: Manages the company's employee benefits and assists employees to develop investment strategies to meet future needs.

Certified Contingency Planner: Develops plans that enable the company and its accounting information system to continue operations in the event of a natural disaster.

Instructions: Identify an individual who has one of the certifications listed above. Ask the individual to describe how the certification has played a role in his or her professional career.

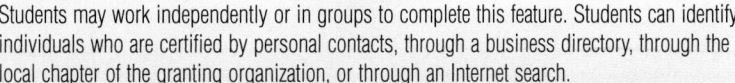

EXPLORE ACCOUNTING
EXPLORE ACCOUNTING

Students may work independently or in groups to complete this feature. Students can identify individuals who are certified by personal contacts, through a business directory, through the local chapter of the granting organization, or through an Internet search.

Students should be well-prepared for the interview before contacting the individual. Students should carefully record the responses to all questions. Direct students to prepare a brief written or oral report using the information from the interview.

1-1 APPLICATION PROBLEM

Determining the normal balance, increase, and decrease sides for accounts

Write the answers for the following problem in the *Working Papers*.

Sales—Video
Prepaid Insurance
Cash
Miscellaneous Expense

Supplies—Audio
Sanford Studios (an account receivable)
Capital Stock
TechCorp (an account payable)

1	2	3	4	5	6	7	8
Account Title	Account Classification	Account's Normal Balance		Increase Side		Decrease Side	
		Debit	Credit	Debit	Credit	Debit	Credit
Sales—Video	Revenue		✓		✓	✓	

Instructions:

Do the following for each account. The Sales—Video account is given above as an example.

1. Write the account title in Column 1.
2. Write the account classification in Column 2.
3. Place a check mark in either Column 3 or 4 to indicate the normal balance of the account.
4. Place a check mark in either Column 5 or 6 to indicate the increase side of the account.
5. Place a check mark in either Column 7 or 8 to indicate the decrease side of the account.

1-2 APPLICATION PROBLEM PEACHTREE QUICKBOOKS

Journalizing and posting departmental purchases on account and purchases returns and allowances

Zenix Communications has two departments: Cellular Phones and Pagers. A purchases journal, general journal, partial general ledger, and accounts payable ledger are provided in the *Working Papers*. The balances are recorded as of October 1 of the current year. Source documents are abbreviated as follows: debit memorandum, DM; purchase invoice, P.

Transactions:

Oct.
1. Purchased phones on account from CarPhone Wholesalers, $1,270.00. P183.
2. Purchased pagers on account from PageMax, Inc., $970.00. P184.
5. Purchased phones on account from ExecuPhone, $2,100.00. P185.
6. The order from Western Distributors contained 5 defective pagers. Returned pagers, $205.00, from P180. DM40.
9. Purchased pagers on account from Cell Advantage, Inc., $945.00. P186.
13. Purchased pagers on account from ComSystems, $2,240.00. P187.
17. Returned phones to CarPhone Wholesalers, $120.00, from P183. DM41.
    Posting. Post the items that are to be posted individually from the purchases journal. Post from the general journal. Post from the journals in this order: purchases journal and general journal.
19. Purchased phones on account from Telecom Corporation, $450.00. P188.
20. Returned pagers to PageMax, Inc., $90.00, from P184. DM42.
23. Issued P189 to purchase phones on account from ExecuPhone, $1,003.00.
30. Returned $75.00 of phones to Phone Solution, from P181. DM43.
    Posting. Post the items that are to be posted individually from the purchases journal. Post from the general journal.

Instructions:

1. Journalize the transactions completed during October of the current year. Use page 11 of a purchases journal and page 3 of a general journal.
2. Prove and rule the purchases journal. Post the totals.

1-3 APPLICATION PROBLEM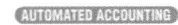

Journalizing and posting departmental cash payments

CraftMart has two departments: Crafts and Plants. A partial general ledger and accounts payable ledger are given in the *Working Papers*. The balances are recorded as of November 1 of the current year. Source documents are abbreviated as follows: check, C; memorandum, M.

Transactions:

Nov. 1. Paid cash for miscellaneous expense, $150.00. C303.
2. Paid cash for rent, $1,300.00. C304.
4. Paid cash on account to Wholesale Crafts, Inc. covering P287 for crafts for $885.00, less 2% discount. C305.
5. Paid cash for advertising, $83.50. C306.
8. Paid cash for administrative supplies, $95.50. C307.
10. Paid cash on account to Northtown Plants covering P288 for plants for $1,550.00, less DM107 for $300.00, less 2% discount. C308.
13. Paid cash on account to Century Crafts, Inc., covering P289 for crafts for $963.00, less 2% discount. C309.
15. Paid cash for miscellaneous, $33.50. C310.
   Posting. Post the items that are to be posted individually.
21. Paid cash for administrative supplies, $52.00. C311.
23. Paid cash on account to Evergreen Trees & Shrubs covering P290 for plants for $1,840.00, less 2% discount. C312.
27. Paid cash on account to Evergreen Trees & Shrubs covering P292 for plants for $1,460.00, less 2% discount. C313.
30. Paid cash to replenish the petty cash fund, $212.00: administrative supplies, $89.00; advertising, $83.40; miscellaneous, $39.60. C314.
   Posting. Post the items that are to be posted individually.

Instructions:

1. Journalize the transactions completed during November of the current year. Use page 21 of a cash payments journal. All of the vendors from which merchandise is purchased on account offer terms of 2/10, n/30.
2. Prove and rule the cash payments journal. Post the totals.

1-4 MASTERY PROBLEM AUTOMATED ACCOUNTING PEACHTREE QUICKBOOKS

Journalizing departmental purchases and cash payments

Outdoor Sport has two departments: Backpacks and Accessories. Source documents are abbreviated as follows: check, C; debit memorandum, DM; purchase invoice, P.

Transactions:

Apr. 1. Paid cash for advertising, $95.00. C273.
1. Paid cash for rent, $1,250.00. C274.
2. Purchased accessories on account from CampWorld Supplies, $800.00. P262.
3. Paid cash on account to PackGear covering P259 for backpacks for $500.00, less 2% discount. C275.
3. Purchased backpacks on account from SierraPack, $840.00. P263.
5. Paid cash on account to CampWorld Supplies covering P261 for accessories for $645.00, less 2% discount. C276.
7. Returned backpacks to SierraPack, $88.00, from P263. DM28.
10. Purchased backpacks on account from TahoeDesigns, $388.00. P264.
11. Paid cash for administrative supplies, $82.50. C277.
14. Paid cash on account to CampWorld Supplies covering P262 for accessories; no discount. C278.
   Posting. Post the individual items from the purchases journal, then the cash payments journal. Post from the general journal.

Application Problem 1-3
Cash Payments Journal totals: 1,926.50; 6,398.00; 36.96; 91.00; 8,196.54.

Mastery Problem 1-4
Purchases Journal totals: 4,660.40; 2,974.40; 1,686.00.

General Journal: Three entries dated April 7, 16, and 18.

Cash Payments Journal totals: 1,763.80; 4,680.00; 40.16; 22.40; 6,381.24.

Apr. 16. Returned accessories to Sequoia Sporting Goods, $132.50, from P260. DM29.

17. Purchased accessories on account from CampAll, Inc., $550.00. P265.

17. Paid cash on account to TahoeDesigns covering P264 for backpacks for $388.00, less 2% discount. C279.

18. Paid cash on account to SierraPack covering P263 for backpacks for $840.00, less DM28 for $88.00; no discount. C280.

18. Returned accessories to CampAll, Inc., $75.00, from P265. DM30.

19. Purchased backpacks on account from SierraPack, $1,120.00. P266.

21. Paid cash for administrative supplies, $62.30. C281.

23. Purchased accessories on account from Sequoia Sporting Goods, $336.00. P267.

24. Paid cash on account to CampAll, Inc. covering P265 for accessories for $550.00, less DM30 for $75.00, and less 2% discount. C282.

24. Purchased backpacks on account from PackGear, $626.40. P268.

26. Paid cash on account to SierraPack covering P266 for backpacks for $1,120.00, less 2% discount. C283.

28. Paid cash for administrative supplies, $53.00. C284

30. Paid cash to replenish the petty cash fund, $221.00: administrative supplies, $57.10; advertising, $62.50; miscellaneous, $101.40. C285.

Posting. Post the individual items from the purchases journal, then the cash payments journal. Post from the general journal.

Instructions:

1. Journalize the transactions completed during April of the current year. Use page 11 of a purchases journal, page 8 of a general journal, and page 21 of a cash payments journal. All of the vendors from which merchandise is purchased on account offer terms of 2/10, n/30.
2. Prove and rule the special journals.
3. Post the totals of the special journals.

1-5 CHALLENGE PROBLEM

Journalizing purchases at net amount and using the account Discounts Lost

Introductory remarks: Some businesses record purchases at the net amount to be paid when the cash discount is taken. For example, merchandise is purchased for $1,000.00 with a 2% discount allowed if the account is paid within 10 days. The discount will reduce the price from $1,000.00 to $980.00. To record this purchase on account transaction, Purchases is debited for $980.00 and Accounts Payable is credited for $980.00. When the account is paid, Accounts Payable is debited for $980.00 and Cash is credited for $980.00. Purchases returns and allowances are also recorded at the discounted amount. For example, a purchase return of $100.00 would be a debit to Accounts Payable of $98.00 and a credit to Purchases Returns and Allowances of $98.00.

If the discount period expires before payment is made, the entry in the cash payments journal for the example above would be as follows: debit Accounts Payable for $980.00, debit Discounts Lost for $20.00, and credit Cash for $1,000.00. Because most cash discounts are taken, there are few entries involving the discounts lost account. For this reason, no special amount column is provided for the account in the cash payments journal. Instead, the amounts debited to this account are recorded in the General Debit column.

Instructions:

1. Journalize the transactions for Mastery Problem 1-4 following the method described above. Use page 11 of a purchases journal, page 8 of a general journal, and page 21 of a cash payments journal. All of the vendors from which merchandise is purchased on account offer terms of 2/10, n/30.
2. Prove and rule the special journals.

Challenge Problem 1-5

Purchases Journal totals: 4,567.19; 2,914.91; 1,652.28.

General Journal: Three entries dated April 7, 16, and 18.

Cash Payments Journal totals: 1,794.84; 4,586.40; 6,381.24.

applied communication

The preparation of a *Career Portfolio* can be an extremely useful tool in helping you make the transition from school to work. The purpose of the portfolio is to assist you in collecting, organizing, and documenting data, information, work samples, achievements, and skills related to a specific career area. A *Career Portfolio* can be created very simply by purchasing a 1½- to 2-inch binder and inserting dividers.

One divider in your *Career Portfolio* should be labeled "Resume." A resume states your education, work experience, and qualifications. Your resume should be accurate, honest, and perfect in every respect. It is preferable to limit the resume to one typed page.

Instructions:

1. Research how to prepare an appropriate resume.
2. Prepare a personal resume that you could send to a prospective employer.
3. Keep several copies of your resume in your *Career Portfolio*.

case for critical thinking

Maria Hector manages a card and gift shop. The shop's general ledger includes a single sales account and a single purchases account. Periodically, Ms. Hector has an accountant review her accounting records and procedures. The accountant recommends that Ms. Hector change to a departmental accounting system. The accountant recommends that separate revenue and cost accounts be kept for the two types of merchandise sold—cards and gifts. Ms. Hector objects to the accountant's recommendation. She sees no advantage in complicating the accounting system by having separate departmental revenue and cost accounts. With whom do you agree? Why?

SCANS workplace competency

Interpersonal Competency: Participating as a Member of a Team

Concept: Effective employees work cooperatively with others and contribute to groups with ideas, suggestions, and effort. Good team members share tasks, encourage others, recognize individual strengths, resolve differences, and accept personal responsibility for accomplishing goals.

Application: Form a team of 3-4 students. Identify some departmentalized businesses in your community. List the name of each business, the merchandise sold, and possible departments within each company. Share your findings with the class.

APPLIED COMMUNICATION

CASE FOR CRITICAL

SCANS WORKPLACE

APPLIED COMMUNICATION

The resume should be keyed, one page in length, and in the most current style. Individual student resumes will vary; however, they should include the following elements: (1) name, address, and telephone number; (2) education, including grade average, courses, and any special skills; (3) work experience and any special training; (4) relevant school activities; and (5) honors or awards. The instructor should also consider writing style and mechanics (grammar, spelling, and punctuation) when evaluating this activity.

CASE FOR CRITICAL THINKING

Agree with the accountant. Department records would make it possible to determine gross profit for the two departments. This information would help make decisions about the efficiency of each phase of the business and would call attention to where changes might result in greater profits.

SCANS WORKPLACE COMPETENCY

Allow students 20–30 minutes to complete this activity. Circulate among class teams to ensure that groups stay on task. Ask each group for an example. Student answers will vary.

AUDITING FOR ERRORS

Account Title	Debit	Credit	Normal Balance
Cash	+	−	Dr.
Accts. Receivable	+	−	Dr.
All. for Uncoll. Accts.	−	+	Cr.
Mdse. Inventory	+	−	Dr.
Office Equipment	+	−	Dr.
Acc. Depr.—Off. Equip.	−	+	Cr.
Accounts Payable	−	+	Cr.
Dividends Payable	−	+	Cr.
Capital Stock	−	+	Cr.
Retained Earnings	−	+	Cr.
Dividends	+	−	Dr.
Income Summary	−	+	Cr.=Net Inc. Dr.=Net Loss
Sales	−	+	Cr.
Sales Ret. & Allow.	+	−	Dr.
Purchases	+	−	Dr.
Purchases Discount	−	+	Cr.
Advertising Expense	+	−	Dr.
Rent Expense	+	−	Dr.
Federal Inc. Tax Exp.	+	−	Dr.

ANALYZING COSTCO'S FINANCIAL STATEMENTS

1. Merchandise Costs = $37,235,000,000; Operating Income = $1,157,000,000

2. Gold Star members = 14,984,000

3. Net income per diluted share = $1.53

• auditing for errors

An office clerk at FastCom just prepared the chart below, which lists all the account titles from the firm's chart of accounts. For each account, a "+" or "−" was recorded in the appropriate debit and credit column to show the impact of a debit or credit to each account's balance. The last column indicates the normal balance for each account. The intent of creating the chart is to provide an easy reference tool to help new accounting clerks accurately record journal entries and calculate general ledger balances.

Review the office clerk's chart below. Make a new chart so that the reference tool is accurate.

Account Title	Debit	Credit	Normal Balance
Cash	+	−	Dr.
Accts. Receivable	−	+	Dr.
All. For Uncoll. Accts.	+	−	Dr.
Mdse. Inventory	+	−	Dr.
Office Equipment	+	−	Dr.
Acc. Depr.—Off. Equip.	−	+	Dr.
Accounts Payable	−	+	Cr.
Dividends Payable	−	+	Cr.
Capital Stock	−	+	Cr.
Retained Earnings	+	−	Cr.
Dividends	+	−	Cr.
Income Summary	−	+	Cr.=Net Inc. Dr.=Net Loss
Sales	−	+	Cr.
Sales Ret. & Allow.	−	+	Cr.
Purchases	+	−	Dr.
Purchases Discount	+	−	Dr.
Advertising Expense	+	−	Dr.
Rent Expense	+	−	Dr.
Federal Inc. Tax Exp.	+	−	Dr.

• analyzing Costco's financial statements

Selected published financial information for Costco Wholesale Corporation is reproduced in Appendix B of this textbook. Like many companies, Costco rounds off dollar amounts when reporting financial data on various financial statements. It is very important when reviewing data in Costco's annual report to determine if the amounts presented have been rounded off to the nearest million, nearest thousand, or not rounded at all. Look at page B-2 in Appendix B. Under the heading at the top of the page, notice the phrase "dollars in millions, except per share data." This means that all dollar amounts, except the dollar amounts reported under **Per Share Data-Diluted,** are rounded to the nearest million. For example, the reported 2003 Net Sales amount of $41,693 actually represents $41,693,000,000. Actual dollar amounts on this page are calculated by multiplying the amount reported by 1,000,000 ($41,693 × 1,000,000 = $41,693,000,000).

Instructions: Refer to the ten-year operating and financial highlights on page B-2.

1. List the actual dollar amount of Merchandise Costs and Operating Income for 2003.
2. List the number of Gold Star members at the end of 2003.
3. List Costco's net income per diluted share for 2003.

TEACHING STRATEGIES   PORTFOLIO ASSESSMENT

Analyzing transactions and journalizing and posting are the first steps in the accounting cycle and are critical to the accuracy of information in an accounting information system. Students should select an example of these activities that has been successfully completed to include in their portfolio. A copy of the Portfolio Assessment form (blackline master in the Teacher's Resource Guide; also on the Student Companion CD) should be completed by the student and the Description section should include any comments regarding how the student mastered these concepts and procedures. Alternatively, students might include in their portfolios a solution to the Automated Accounting feature that follows this chapter.

• Automated Accounting

Automated Entries for Purchases and Cash Payments

In the Automated Accounting software, transactions are recorded in journals similar to the purchases, general, and cash payments journals described in Chapter 1. The cash payments journal window is shown below. Journals are accessed by clicking the Journal Entries option from the Data menu or clicking the Journal toolbar button. Click the tab for the journal you wish to use.

The cash payments journal above shows three kinds of transactions: (1) two cash payments on account with purchase discounts; (2) cash payment for an asset (supplies); and (3) cash payment of an expense (Rent Expense).

Entries in the automated cash payments journal are similar to entries in a manual cash payments journal. The software automatically calculates the amount in the Cash Credit column; notice that these amounts are grey in the illustration. The Cash credit amount should be inspected and any errors corrected before an entry is posted. Entering an amount in the A.P. Debit column (Accounts Payable) automatically opens the Vendor column where an accounts payable ledger account must be selected.

The general ledger account number is entered in the Account No. column when amounts will be entered in the General Debit or General Credit column. No account number is entered for entries that are recorded entirely in special amount columns.

A journal entries report may be displayed or printed by clicking the Reports toolbar button, then clicking Journals and then the name of the journal.

AUTOMATING APPLICATION PROBLEM 1-3: Journalizing and posting departmental cash payments

AUTOMATING MASTERY PROBLEM 1-4: Journalizing departmental purchases and cash payments

Instructions:

1. Load the *Automated Accounting 8.0* or higher software.

2. Select data file A01-3 or A01-4 from the appropriate directory/folder ("A" indicates Advanced Course).

3. Select File from the menu bar and choose Save As. Key the path to the drive and directory that contains your data files. Save the data file with a filename of A01-3 or A01-4 XXX XXX (where the X's are your first and last name).

4. Access Problem Instructions through the Browser tool. Read the Problem Instruction screen.

5. Key the data listed in the problem on page 27.

6. Save your file and exit the Automated Accounting software.

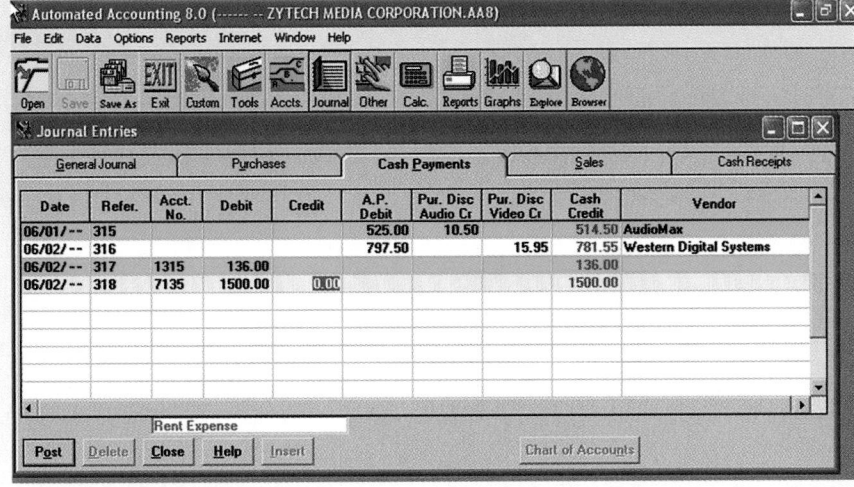

Recording Departmental Purchases and Cash Payments

Chapter 1   **31**

Recording Departmental Sales

	SCOPE & SEQUENCE		ENHANCING	
	NEW	REVIEW/ EXTENSION	SPECIAL FEATURES	
Introduce the Chapter	✓		• Accounting in the Real World: Blockbuster, Inc.	
Lesson 2-1 Departmental Sales on Account and Sales Returns and Allowances			• Making Ethical Decisions: At What Price Safety?	
Departmental sales on account	✓		• Small Business Spotlight	
Journalizing sales on account		✓	• Cases for Critical Thinking 1	
Posting from a sales journal to the accounts receivable ledger		✓		
Posting from a sales journal to a general ledger account		✓		
Journalizing sales returns and allowances		✓		
Posting from a general journal		✓		
Lesson 2-2 Journalizing and Posting Cash Receipts			• Global Perspective: International Terms of Sale	
Departmental cash receipts	✓		• Cases for Critical Thinking 2	
Cash receipts on account		✓		
Journalizing a cash receipt with a sales discount		✓		
Journalizing a cash receipt with a sales return and a sales discount		✓		
Journalizing cash and credit card sales		✓		
Posting from a cash receipts journal		✓		
Order of posting from journals		✓		
Putting It All Together			• Explore Accounting	
			• Xtra! Web Site: Xtra! Enrichment	
			• Applied Communication	
			• SCANS Workplace Competency	
			• Graphing Workshop	
			• Analyzing Costco's Financial Statements	

and Cash Receipts

INSTRUCTION		PRACTICE AND ASSESSMENT		
TECHNOLOGY AND MEDIA	**TEACHING STRATEGIES**	**GUIDED PRACTICE**	**INDEPENDENT PRACTICE**	**RETEACHING AND ENRICHMENT**
• Internet Research Activity • Accounting Xtra! Web Site	• Software Focus			
• Instructor's Resource CD: PowerPoint Slides • Xtra! Web Site: Xtra! Study Tools • Blackline Masters: Departmental Sales Journal and General Journal • Personal Trainer • Peachtree	• Cooperative Learning • Expanding Beyond the Classroom • Auditory Learner • Kinesthetic Learner • Limited English Proficiency (LEP) Students	• Term Review • Audit Your Understanding • Work Together 2-1	• On Your Own 2-1 • Application Problem 2-1 • Ongoing Assessment, p. 41 • Personal Trainer • Xtra! Web Site: Xtra! Study Tools	• Reteach, p. 42 • Enrich, p. 43 • Peachtree
• Instructor's Resource CD: PowerPoint Slides • Xtra! Web Site: Xtra! Study Tools • Blackline Masters: Departmental Cash Receipts Journal, General Ledger, and Accounts Receivable Ledger • Personal Trainer • Automated Accounting • Peachtree and QuickBooks	• Applied Skills: Building Study Skills • Visual Learner • Tactile Learner • Print Learner	• Terms Review • Audit Your Understanding • Work Together 2-2	• On Your Own 2-2 • Application Problem 2-2 • Ongoing Assessment, p. 49 • Personal Trainer • Xtra! Web Site: Xtra! Study Tools	• Reteach, p. 49 • Enrich, p. 50 • Automated Accounting • Peachtree and QuickBooks
• Automated Accounting • Peachtree and QuickBooks • Personal Trainer • Xtra! Web Site: Xtra! Review, Quizzing, and Enrichment • Student Companion CD	• Applied Skills: Language Arts • Applied Skills: Writing Across the Curriculum		• Mastery Problem 2-3 • Automated Accounting • Peachtree and QuickBooks • Personal Trainer • Xtra! Web Site: Xtra! Review and Quizzing • Study Guide 2 • Student Companion CD • Chapter 2 Test • ExamView Chapter 2 • Portfolio Assessment	• Challenge Problem 2-4 • Reteach, p. 51 • Enrich, p. 51 • Recycling Problem 2-1 • Automated Accounting • Xtra! Web Site: Xtra! Enrichment

CHAPTER 2

OBJECTIVES & TERMS

Recording Departmental Sales and Cash Receipts

After studying Chapter 2, you will be able to:

1. Define terms related to departmental sales and cash receipts.

2. Identify concepts and practices related to departmental sales and cash receipts.

3. Journalize and post departmental sales on account and sales returns and allowances.

4. Journalize and post departmental cash receipts.

- credit memorandum
- sales discount

- point-of-sale (POS) terminal
- terminal summary

Point Your Browser
accountingxtra.swlearning.com

Blockbuster, Inc.

©RICK MAIMAN/BLOOMBERG NEWS/LANDOV

BLOCKBUSTER ADAPTS TO CHANGES IN MEDIA FORMATS

Blockbuster opened its first video rental store in 1985 in Dallas, Texas. During the last two decades, the company has expanded from that single facility to approximately 8,900 company-owned and franchised stores throughout the world. Today, Blockbuster is recognized as one of the strongest entertainment brands in the world and is the leading renter of videos, DVDs, and video games. On an average day, over three million customers visit their neighborhood stores. In recent years, worldwide revenues have exceeded $5.9 billion.

Over the last 20 years, Blockbuster has wisely adapted its business model to keep pace with the changing formats in media reproduction. In 1985, movies were originally available only on videocassette tapes. Advancements in technology have prompted the company to now offer DVD and video game rentals. Other innovative management changes include opportunities for rental subscriptions, a store-within-a-store concept, movie and game trading, unlimited rentals without due dates, and the retail sale of movies and games.

In the upcoming years, Blockbuster will continue to be challenged by changing technologies and new competitors. As it has in the past, Blockbuster's managerial staff will have to remain diligent, adapt to the current business environment, and update its corporate strategies to remain competitive.

Critical Thinking

1. List several strategies that a company like Blockbuster might use to dramatically expand sales.
2. What types of challenges might Blockbuster face in the future?

Xtra!
Today
accountingxtra.swlearning.com

Source: www.blockbuster.com

ACCOUNTING IN THE REAL WORLD

internet activity

FEDERAL DEPOSIT INSURANCE CORPORATION (FDIC)

Go to the homepage for the Federal Deposit Insurance Corporation (FDIC) (www.fdic.gov). Search for information about the FDIC.

Instructions

1. Briefly describe the FDIC and its purpose.
2. Up to what amount are checking accounts, savings accounts, money market deposit accounts, and certificates of deposit insured by the FDIC?

ACCOUNTING IN THE REAL WORLD

Use this feature to demonstrate how the chapter's content applies to real businesses today. Motivate students by asking them how they became familiar with Blockbuster (store fronts, news ads, television advertising, mail flyers, web sites, employment, football sponsorship, etc.). Ask students to share any experiences they have had involving a Blockbuster store. Ask them why Blockbuster might be interested in tracking departmental sales and cash receipts. Write student answers on the board.

1. Student answers might include some of the following: open additional stores, buy other businesses, open global offices, sell franchises, offer new products and relevant services, incorporate technology, develop a web site, or add retail sales of movies and games in addition to rentals.

2. Besides other, smaller video rental businesses, challenges could come from extremely large retail corporations such as Wal-Mart, Target, and Best Buy that sell discounted DVDs and games. In addition, auction sites, such as Ebay, offer competing products for sale; NetFlix offers film rentals and subscriptions through the mail; Internet sites offer film rentals and subscriptions; DVD recorders are used to make inexpensive copies; satellite and cable TV companies offer pay-for-view movies; and TiVo trolls the airwaves for favorite TV shows and movies and records them for later viewing. Blockbuster will continue to face a variety of technological advancements in media recording, products, and transmission. More companies will offer digital downloads as broadband width and computer speeds increase. Several smaller video rental or media businesses may consolidate to create a larger, more competitive company. There will be increased global competition. High definition television could create issues. And, the ease and convenience of acquiring movies and games via the Internet may present a challenge.

INTERNET RESEARCH ACTIVITY

Ask students why a business would use a bank that provides FDIC insurance *(to protect its cash in checking and savings accounts).*

1. The FDIC is an independent agency of the United States government. The FDIC protects you against the loss of your deposits if an FDIC-insured bank or savings association fails. FDIC insurance is backed by the full faith and credit of the United States government.

2. Checking accounts, savings accounts, money market deposit accounts, and certificates of deposit (CDs) are insured up to $100,000 per depositor per insured bank.

2-1 Departmental Sales on Account and Sales Returns and Allowances

Managers use departmental data to make decisions relating to business operations. Companies such as Zytech Media Corporation are often organized into departments, based on the different types of products or services they sell. In order to maximize business operations, Zytech Media Corporation identified two departments based on the two categories of equipment it sells—audio and video. Zytech's management team uses departmental information to analyze the profitability of each department, set annual goals, evaluate managers, and determine company bonuses.

In order to have comprehensive departmental data, however, a business should record sales and cash receipts data separately for each department. For example, gross profit from operations for each department is one type of valuable information for management decision making. Departmental gross profit from operations helps business managers decide if each department is earning an appropriate profit. If not, departmental information can help managers determine which items are causing the problem. To determine departmental gross profit from operations, the business must keep records of sales and cost of merchandise sold by department.

©GETTY IMAGES/PHOTODISC

making ethical decisions

At What Price Safety?

Willcutt Industries assembles a safety system for passenger auto-mobiles. This system substantially reduces severe injuries to drivers involved in accidents. In an effort to increase profits, Willcutt recently took steps to cut costs and increase production. Willcutt began using some less expensive components, reducing the production costs by $50.00 per unit. The new components increase the system's estimated failure rate from 12 to 15 failures per 10,000 accidents. Despite this increased failure rate, the company continues to exceed the government's safety standard of 20 failures per 10,000 accidents. Willcutt has reduced the unit sales price by $40.00, which has substantially increased unit sales.

The ethical decision-making model has four steps:

1. Recognize you are facing an ethical dilemma.
2. Identify the action taken or the proposed action.
3. Analyze the action.
   a. Is the action illegal?
   b. Does the action violate company or professional standards?
   c. Who is affected, and how, by the action?
4. Determine if the action is ethical.

First analyze the first two steps. Then analyze the action. If the action is either illegal or violates company or professional standards, the action should not be taken. However, it is often necessary to analyze the action further to determine whether it is ethical by determining the parties that would be affected and whether they are affected in a negative or positive way. A sample solution follows.

Instructions

Access the *Ford Motor Company Standards of Corporate Conduct*. Using this code as a guide, use the ethical model to help determine whether the action by Willcutt Industries demonstrates ethical behavior.

Suggested Solution for Willcutt Industries' Ethical Dilemma:

1. *Recognize you are facing an ethical dilemma.* Willcutt Industries is intentionally increasing the failure rate of its safety system. Willcutt's managers should recognize that this decision requires ethical analysis.
2. *Identify the action taken or the proposed action.* Willcutt increased the failure rate of its safety system to reduce its production costs and increase profits.
3. *Analyze the action.*
   a. *Is the action illegal?* No. The new system still exceeds government quality standards.
   b. *Does the action violate company or professional standards?* Possibly. In the Product Safety and Quality section of the *Ford Motor Company Standards of Corporate Conduct,* the code states that "the issue of cost should not preclude consideration of possible alternatives, and priorities should be based on achieving the greatest anticipated practical safety benefit." The word "practical" implies that consumers may be willing or able to pay for only a certain level of safety. Further analysis using the ethics model is necessary.
   c. *Who is affected, and how, by the action?*
4. *Determine if the action is ethical.* Answers may vary.

Stakeholders	Negative	Positive
Willcutt Industries	Increases the risk of litigation.	Reduces production costs and increases profits by $10.00 per unit. Increases sales, further increasing profits.
Stockholders		Increases return on investment.
Car manufacturers		Lower costs promote higher car sales and profits.
Car owners who would have been willing to pay for a car with the original safety system.	Increases slightly the chance of incurring a serious injury if involved in an accident.	Reduces the cost of a car by $40.00.
Car owners who can now afford a car with a safety system (although a less reliable one).		Substantially reduces the chance of incurring a serious injury if involved in an accident.

Since personal ethics are unique, students' solutions will vary. Some students will view the increased failure rate as unethical under any circumstances and ignore the benefits received by other stakeholders. Other students may decide that the reduced price allows more drivers to have access to the safety system and, therefore, is ethical because it benefits the most people. Regardless of their conclusions, students may debate whether Willcutt Industries demonstrated ethical behavior by keeping $10.00 of the $50.00 cost savings.

Consider asking students to question whether their personal bias weighed in their decision. Students who drive cars with advanced safety features may focus more on the increased failure rate. Students driving cars lacking advanced safety features may focus more on the ability of more people to purchase a car having the safety system.

- Explain that Zytech is required to collect a sales tax of 8.25%.

- Explain that some of Zytech's customers are exempt from sales tax.

- Explain that sales on account are recorded separately for each of the two departments, Audio and Video.

- Explain the Realization of Revenue concept introduced in this lesson.

SMALL BUSINESS SPOTLIGHT

This feature describes the need for training in both large and small businesses. It emphasizes that the kinds of training needs may be the same, but the budget and staffing probably differ.

DEPARTMENTAL SALES ON ACCOUNT

In Chapter 1, you learned to record purchases transactions for a departmental merchandising business. To have complete departmental data, Zytech also records all sales transactions by department. Zytech makes sales on account to individuals, business firms, and schools. It sells merchandise in two departments. The audio department sells audio equipment such as surround sound systems, speakers for home theaters, 3-way tower speakers for small stadiums and large gymnasiums, and other sound-related equipment. The video department sells video equipment including high definition televisions, plasma monitors, flat screens, and jumbo video panels.

Zytech records all departmental sales on account in a sales journal. The sales journal has one debit column—Accounts Receivable Debit. The journal also has three credit columns—Sales Tax Payable Credit and special Sales Credit columns for Audio and Video.

The Sales Tax Payable Credit column is used to record all sales tax amounts that Zytech collects. Most states require vendors to collect sales tax from their customers. The city and state in which Zytech is located have a combined sales tax rate of 8.25%. In most states, some customers are not required to pay a sales tax. Many agencies supported by local and state government and nonprofit educational institutions are exempt from paying a sales tax. For example, the Wawona School District is a tax-exempt customer of Zytech.

Zytech prepares sales invoices in duplicate for each sale on account. [CONCEPT: Objective Evidence] Each sales invoice shows the amount of merchandise sold by department. The customer receives the original copy of the sales invoice. The duplicate copy is the source document for journalizing the transaction. Zytech records all departmental sales at the time of sale, regardless of when payment is made. [CONCEPT: Realization of Revenue]

The realization-of-revenue concept states that revenue is recorded at the time goods or services are sold. A business may sell either goods or services. Cash may be received at the time of sale, or an agreement may be made to receive payment at a later date. Regardless of when the business actually receives cash, the business records the sale amount in the accounting records at the time of sale. For example, a business sells office furniture for $2,000.00. The business agrees to an initial payment of $400.00 with the remaining balance to be divided in four monthly payments of $400.00 each. The business records the full $2,000.00 of revenue at the time of sale, even though $1,600.00 will be paid later.

©GETTY IMAGES/PHOTODISC

Most small businesses have the same kind of training needs as huge corporations. New employees, seasoned professionals, and executives all benefit from training throughout their careers. This includes everything from job-specific training to professional enrichment. While the needs may be the same, the budget and staffing might be quite different. Small businesses are finding solutions for their training needs within their own company and through outside sources. Small businesses frequently look to community colleges, trade groups, and professional associations for high-quality instruction. In many cases, small businesses are partnering with vendors for some of their training needs.

36   Chapter 2   Recording Departmental Sales and Cash Receipts

TEACHING STRATEGIES   COOPERATIVE LEARNING

Select a group of three students to create a bulletin board using source documents described in the first accounting cycle. Allow five days for completion of the activity. Appoint a spokesperson to report to the class as to where the documents came from, what each document represents, and how each document is used. These documents can be collected from local businesses, or documents from obsolete business simulations may be used. Documents such as receipts, checks, and cash register tapes can be collected through personal daily activities.

JOURNALIZING SALES ON ACCOUNT

1. Write the date.
2. Write the customer name.
3. Write the sales invoice number.

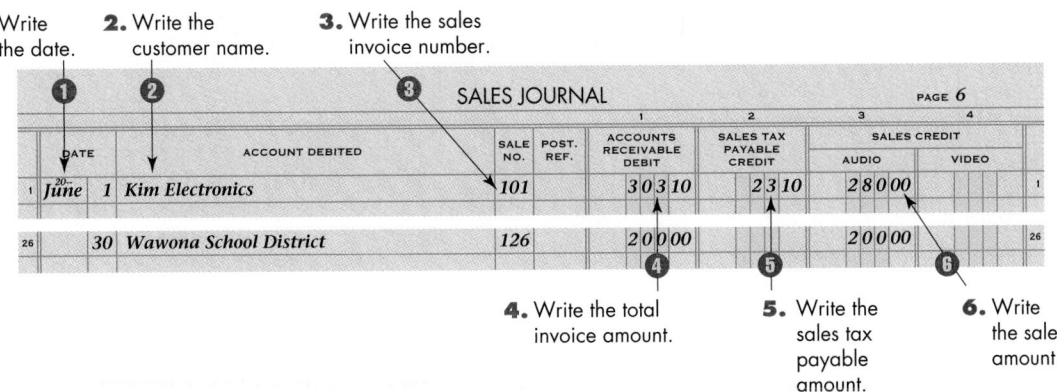

4. Write the total invoice amount.
5. Write the sales tax payable amount.
6. Write the sales amount.

June 1. Sold audio equipment on account to Kim Electronics, $280.00, plus sales tax, $23.10; total, $303.10. Sales Invoice No. 101.

This transaction is recorded in the departmental sales journal. The source document for this transaction is a sales invoice. [*CONCEPT: Objective Evidence*]

In the general ledger, Accounts Receivable is increased by a $303.10 debit. The amount that the customer owes represents the price of the merchandise plus the sales tax. All sales tax received is later remitted to the state in which Zytech is located. Therefore, the liability account Sales Tax Payable is increased by a $23.10 credit. Sales—Audio is increased by a $280.00 credit. In the accounts receivable ledger, Kim Electronics is increased by a $303.10 debit.

The transaction on line 26 of the sales journal shows a transaction for a tax-exempt customer.

Since the Wawona School District is an educational institution, it is not required by the state to pay sales tax.

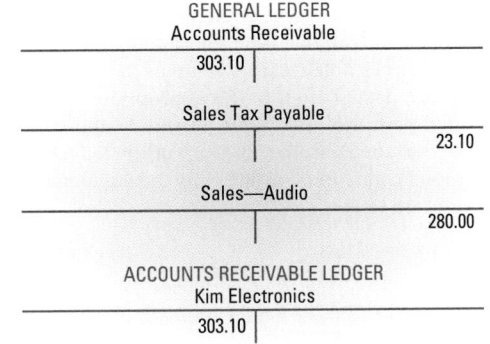

GENERAL LEDGER
Accounts Receivable
303.10 |

Sales Tax Payable
| 23.10

Sales—Audio
| 280.00

ACCOUNTS RECEIVABLE LEDGER
Kim Electronics
303.10 |

STEPS   STEPS • STEPS • STEPS • STEPS • STEPS
RECORDING THE SALE IN THE SALES JOURNAL

1 Write the date, *20--, June 1,* in the Date column.

2 Write the customer name, *Kim Electronics,* in the Account Debited column.

3 Write the sales invoice number, *101,* in the Sale No. column.

4 Write the total invoice amount, *$303.10,* in the Accounts Receivable Debit column.

5 Write the credit amount, *$23.10,* in the Sales Tax Payable Credit column.

6 Write the credit amount, *$280.00,* in the Sales Credit Audio column.

Departmental Sales on Account and Sales Returns and Allowances

Lesson 2-1   **37**

- Use a transparency from the blackline master of a departmental sales journal or direct students to the illustration to explain the columns used for a departmental sale on account. Point out that there is a separate Sales Credit column for each department.

- Remind students that a sales invoice is the source document for a sale on account.

- Remind students that a sale on account will always include an amount in the Accounts Receivable Debit column and that the name of the customer is written in the Account Debited column.

- Point out that the sales tax amount is recorded in the Sales Tax Payable Credit column. Remind students that a sale on account to a tax-exempt customer will not include a sales tax amount.

- Direct students to the F.Y.I. box for information about federal tax identification numbers.

DEMONSTRATE

Analyze the transaction

- Draw four blank T accounts on the board.

- Read the transaction statement.

- Ask students to analyze the transaction by answering: what accounts are affected, are they increased or decreased, and are they debited or credited. Complete the T accounts as the information is provided.

- Review the effect on the account for Kim Electronics in the accounts receivable ledger.

Record the transaction

- Use a transparency of the blackline master of a departmental sales journal to illustrate recording the transaction in the sales journal or direct students to the illustration.

- Record each item in the journal, following the six steps shown.

- Point out that no abbreviation for sales invoice is necessary in the Sales No. column. Sales invoices are the source document for all sales recorded on the sales journal.

TEACHING STRATEGIES   EXPANDING BEYOND THE CLASSROOM

Invite a representative of a business that is departmentalized to address the class. You might consider an accountant or information processing manager. The speaker should be encouraged to address how the business is departmentalized, what kind of account numbers are used for departments, and the advantages of a departmentalized business.

- Explain that individual amounts in the Accounts Receivable Debit column are posted from the sales journal to the accounts receivable ledger frequently so that customer accounts are up to date.

- Direct students to the F.Y.I. box for information about how businesses pay the liability for sales tax collected from customers to the appropriate government agency.

DEMONSTRATE

- Direct students to the illustration to explain the posting procedure from a sales journal to an accounts receivable ledger.

- As you read each step, ask students to point to the related arrows in the illustration.

- Remind students that the abbreviation for the sales journal, *S*, and the page number are recorded in the Post. Ref. column of every ledger account affected, in order to furnish an audit trail.

- Remind students that the accounts receivable account number is recorded in the sales journal's Post. Ref. column to show that posting has been completed and to furnish an audit trail.

POSTING FROM A SALES JOURNAL TO THE ACCOUNTS RECEIVABLE LEDGER

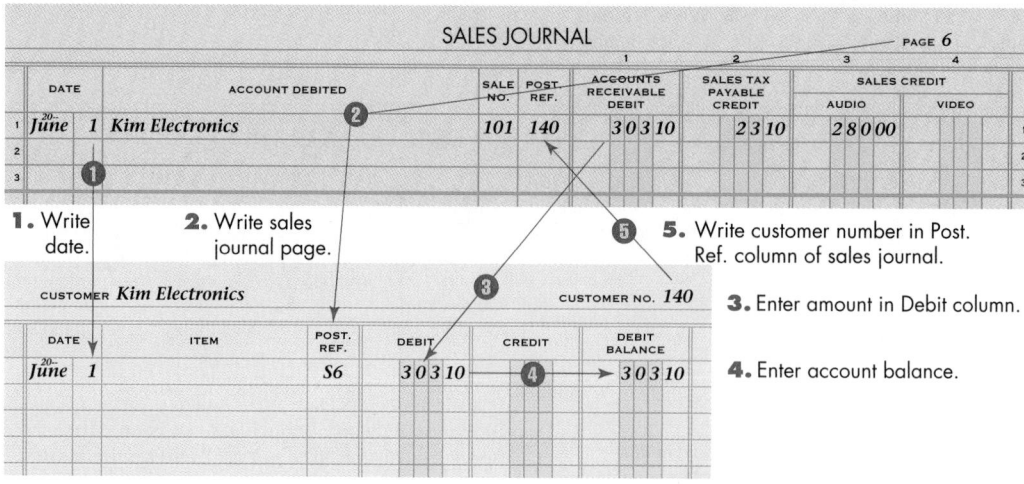

1. Write date.
2. Write sales journal page.
3. Enter amount in Debit column.
4. Enter account balance.
5. Write customer number in Post. Ref. column of sales journal.

Zytech keeps customer accounts in an accounts receivable ledger. Individual amounts in the Accounts Receivable Debit column of the sales journal are posted often to the appropriate customer accounts. The sales journal is abbreviated as *S* in the Post. Ref. column of the ledger accounts. Posting frequently keeps the customers' accounts up to date.

FYI
FOR YOUR INFORMATION

Sales taxes collected by businesses must be sent to the appropriate governmental agency. In many states, sales taxes are paid monthly. The payment is accompanied by a form that provides information such as total sales, sales tax collected, and sales exempt from sales tax.

STEPS • STEPS • STEPS • STEPS • STEPS • STEPS • STEPS • STEPS • STEPS • STEPS • STEPS

POSTING FROM THE SALES JOURNAL TO THE ACCOUNTS RECEIVABLE LEDGER

1. Write the date, *20--, June 1,* in the account's Date column.

2. Write *S6* in the Post. Ref. column of the subsidiary ledger account to indicate that the posting came from page 6 of the sales journal.

3. Write the debit amount, *$303.10,* in the account's Debit column. This is the total amount due from the customer. It includes the price of the audio equipment and the sales tax.

4. Write the new account balance in the Debit Balance column. When the customer has an existing balance, add the amount in the Debit column to the previous balance in the Debit Balance column. *Kim Electronics* had no account balance before this transaction.

5. Write the customer number, *140,* in the Post. Ref. column of the sales journal to show that posting is completed for this line.

Recording Departmental Sales and Cash Receipts

©GETTY IMAGES/PHOTODISC

TEACHING STRATEGIES DIFFERENT LEARNING STYLES

Auditory Learner. When learning how to post, the auditory learner would prefer to hear the steps involved in posting. This can be done via a live lecture or a taped tutorial. To reinforce learning, the student could recite the posting steps to another student or group of students.

POSTING FROM A SALES JOURNAL TO A GENERAL LEDGER ACCOUNT

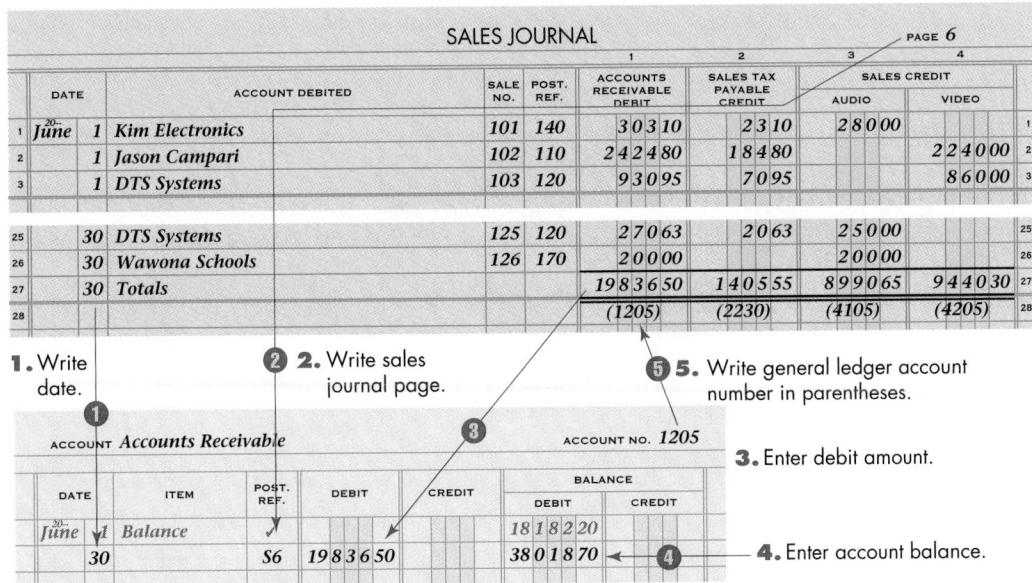

SALES JOURNAL   PAGE 6

	DATE	ACCOUNT DEBITED	SALE NO.	POST. REF.	ACCOUNTS RECEIVABLE DEBIT	SALES TAX PAYABLE CREDIT	SALES CREDIT AUDIO	SALES CREDIT VIDEO	
1	June 1	Kim Electronics	101	140	3 0 3 10	2 3 10	2 8 0 00		1
2	1	Jason Campari	102	110	2 4 2 80	1 8 4 80		2 2 4 0 00	2
3	1	DTS Systems	103	120	9 3 0 95	7 0 95		8 6 0 00	3
25	30	DTS Systems	125	120	2 7 0 63	2 0 63	2 5 0 00		25
26	30	Wawona Schools	126	170	2 0 0 00		2 0 0 00		26
27	30	Totals			19 8 3 6 50	1 4 0 5 55	8 9 9 0 65	9 4 4 0 30	27
28					(1205)	(2230)	(4105)	(4205)	28

1. Write date.

2. 2. Write sales journal page.

5. 5. Write general ledger account number in parentheses.

3. Enter debit amount.

ACCOUNT **Accounts Receivable**   ACCOUNT NO. **1205**

DATE	ITEM	POST. REF.	DEBIT	CREDIT	BALANCE DEBIT	BALANCE CREDIT
June 1	Balance	✓			18 1 8 2 20	
30		S6	19 8 3 6 50		38 0 1 8 70	

4. Enter account balance.

The sales journal is proved and ruled at the end of each month. Each amount column total is posted to the general ledger account named in the column heading.

STEPS · STEPS · STEPS · STEPS · STEPS · STEPS · STEPS · STEPS · STEPS · STEPS ·
POSTING A COLUMN TOTAL FROM THE SALES JOURNAL TO THE GENERAL LEDGER

1. Write the date, *30,* in the account's Date column.

2. Write *S6* in the Post. Ref. column of the ledger account to indicate that the posting came from page 6 of the sales journal.

3. Write the column total, *$19,836.50,* in the Debit column of the ledger account.

4. Add the amount in the Debit column, $19,836.50, to the previous balance of $18,182.20 to arrive at a new accounts receivable balance of *$38,018.70.*

5. Write the general ledger account number, *1205,* in parentheses immediately below the column total in the sales journal to show that the amount has been posted.

> REMEMBER   Proving a journal means verifying that the total debits equal the total credits. To prove a journal:
> 1. Add each amount column and write the total.
> 2. Add the column totals for all debit columns.
> 3. Add the column totals for all credit columns.
> 4. Verify that total debits and total credits are equal. Once a journal is proved, it should be ruled.

Departmental Sales on Account and Sales Returns and Allowances   Lesson 2-1   **39**

- Explain that a business may grant credit or give a cash refund for returned merchandise.

- Explain that a sales allowance does not involve the return of any merchandise.

- Explain that a vendor prepares a credit memorandum for a sales return or allowance because the return or allowance usually involves a credit to the customer's account receivable.

- Remind students that a credit memorandum is the source document for a sales returns and allowances transaction.

- Point out that sales returns and allowances on sales on account are recorded in the general journal. If a business accepted a return on a cash sale, cash would be paid to the customer and the transaction would be recorded in the cash payments journal.

- Remind students that a sales return or allowance for a sale on account will always include the name of the customer as written in the accounts receivable subsidiary ledger.

- Point out that the sales tax amount is calculated on the amount of the return.

- Direct students to the Remember note for an explanation of why Sales Returns and Allowances has a normal debit balance.

DEMONSTRATE

Analyze the transaction

- Draw a stack of four blank T accounts on the board.

- Read the transaction statement.

- Ask students to analyze the transaction by answering: what accounts are affected, are they increased or decreased, and are they debited or credited. Complete the T accounts as the information is provided.

- Review the effect on the account for Kim Electronics in the accounts receivable ledger.

Record the transaction

- Use a transparency of the blackline master of a general journal to illustrate recording the transaction in the general journal or direct students to the illustration.

- Record each item in the journal, following the seven steps shown.

- Point out that a credit memorandum is the source document for a return sale recorded in the general journal.

40

JOURNALIZING SALES RETURNS AND ALLOWANCES

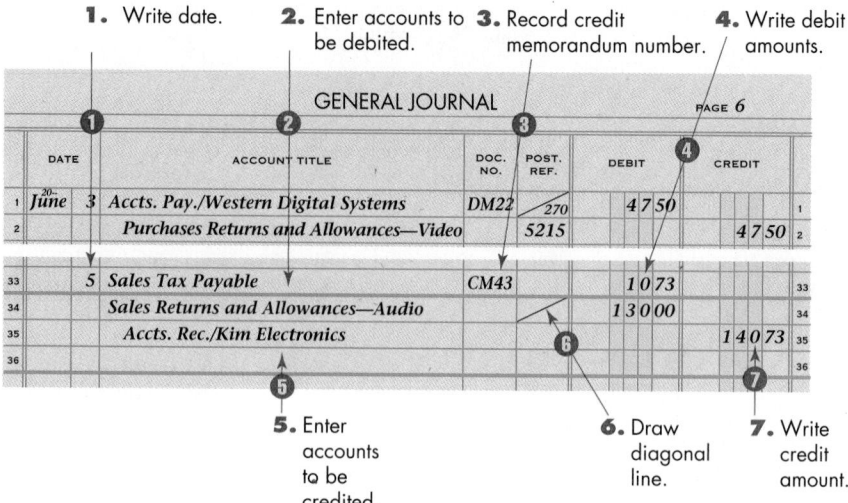

Zytech records all sales returns and allowances in a general journal. Zytech's general journal is shown above.

An account that reduces a related account on a financial statement is known as a *contra account*. An account showing deductions from a sales account is a contra revenue account. Sales Returns and Allowances—Audio is a contra revenue account. Sales returns and allowances are kept in a separate account and not deducted directly from the sales account. This procedure helps the business see what proportion of the merchandise sold was returned by customers. [CONCEPT: Adequate Disclosure]

June 5. Granted credit to Kim Electronics for audio equipment returned, $130.00, plus sales tax, $10.73, from Sales Invoice No. 101; total, $140.73. Credit Memorandum No. 43.

The source document prepared by the vendor showing the amount deducted for returns and allowances is called a **credit memorandum**. [CONCEPT: Objective Evidence]

When a sales return is accepted or an allowance is granted, the sales tax amount is no longer due. In the general ledger, Sales Tax Payable is decreased by a $10.73 debit. Sales Returns and Allowances—Audio is increased by a $130.00 debit. Accounts Receivable is decreased by a $140.73 credit. In the accounts receivable ledger, Kim Electronics is decreased by a $140.73 credit.

Details of the transaction involving Credit Memorandum No. 43 are recorded on lines 33, 34, and 35 of the general journal shown above.

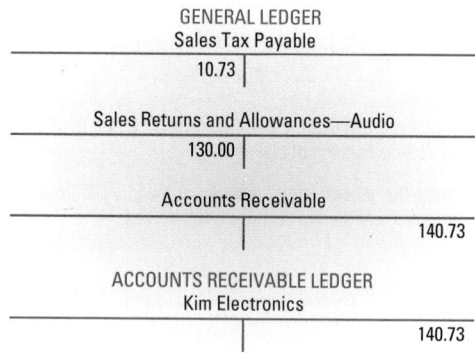

{ **REMEMBER** A contra account has a normal balance that is opposite its related account. For example, *Sales—Audio* has a normal credit balance. Therefore, *Sales Returns and Allowances—Audio* has a normal debit balance. }

Chapter 2

Recording Departmental Sales and Cash Receipts

TEACHING STRATEGIES DIFFERENT LEARNING ABILITIES

Limited English Proficiency (LEP) Students. Adjust the length of time allotted to complete assignments and tests. Remember that the primary objective is to assess knowledge of accounting rather than the ability to translate and comprehend the question or problem.

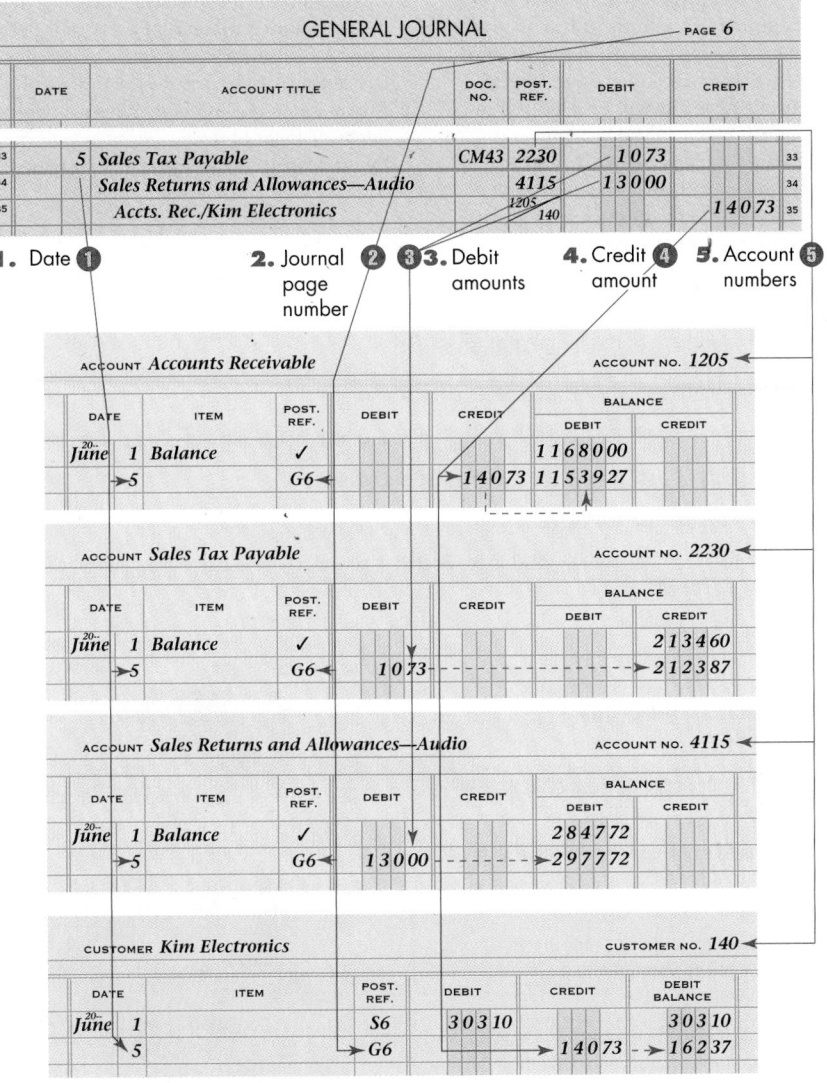

(Steps for posting from a general journal are shown on page 42.)

- Explain that sales returns and allowances are posted to the accounts receivable ledger frequently so that customer accounts are up-to-date.
- Note that the Sales Tax Payable amount is a debit.
- Point out that a sales return on a sale to an exempt organization will not include a debit to Sales Tax Payable.
- Mention that when a sales return or allowance is granted after the customer has paid for the purchase, the customer account after posting may have a credit balance instead of a normal debit balance. Use T accounts to demonstrate this dilemma.
- Remind students that the debit and credit columns of the general journal are never ruled and totaled.

DEMONSTRATE

Posting debit amounts from a general journal

- Direct students to the illustration to explain the posting procedure of debit amounts from a general journal to the general ledger.
- As you read each step, ask students to point to the related arrows in the illustration.
- Remind students that the journal page number and the ledger account number are recorded in the Post. Ref. column of the ledger and the journal in order to furnish an audit trail.

Posting a credit amount from a general journal

- Direct students to the illustration as you describe how to post a credit amount from the general journal to the general ledger and accounts receivable subsidiary ledger.
- As you read each step, ask students to point to the related arrows in the illustration.
- Remind students that the journal page number and the ledger account number are recorded in the Post. Ref. column of the ledger and the journal in order to furnish an audit trail.

- Assessment is an ongoing process. Circulate through the classroom or lab, observing which students have problems with the assignments.
- Troubleshooting: Diagnose what kinds of problems students have with this lesson. Students may have trouble recording transactions involving a tax-exempt organization or make careless mistakes recording amounts in the wrong departmental account.
- Assess student understanding by checking solutions to Independent Practice assignments.

- Ask a student to make up an original sale on account transaction statement that you write on the board. Ask another student to analyze the transaction using T accounts.

- Ask a student to name each column title in the sales journal and describe what is recorded in it, both in general and specifically for the transaction.

- Repeat for a sales returns and allowances transaction.

- Ask students to describe the effect of recording a sale or a return in the wrong departmental account.

STEPS FOR POSTING FROM A GENERAL JOURNAL

Sales returns and allowances are posted frequently to a customer's account in the accounts receivable ledger. This procedure keeps an individual customer's account up to date. Specifically, a customer's account will be credited to reduce the amount owed to the vendor. The posting of the June 5 sales return from Kim Electronics is shown on the previous page.

When a sales return or allowance is granted after the customer has paid for the purchase, the customer account after posting may have a credit balance instead of a normal debit balance. The credit balance, a contra balance, reduces the amount to be received from a customer for future sales on account. When a three-column account form is used, a contra balance is shown by enclosing the amount in parentheses.

STEPS • STEPS • STEPS • STEPS • STEPS • STEPS • STEPS • STEPS • STEPS • STEPS • STEPS

POSTING DEBIT AMOUNTS FROM A GENERAL JOURNAL

1. Write the date, *5*, in the Sales Tax Payable account's Date column.

2. Write *G* and the page number of the journal, *6*, in the Post. Ref. column of the *Sales Tax Payable* account.

3. Write the debit amount, *$10.73*, in the Sales Tax Payable Debit column.

4. Calculate and write the new balance, *$2,123.87*.

5. Record the appropriate account number, *2230*, in the Post. Ref. column of the journal. Follow the same steps for the debit entry on line 34.

STEPS • STEPS • STEPS • STEPS • STEPS

POSTING A CREDIT AMOUNT FROM A GENERAL JOURNAL

1. Write the date, *5*, in the Accounts Receivable and Kim Electronics accounts' Date columns.

2. Write *G* and the page number of the journal, *6*, in the Post. Ref. columns of the *Accounts Receivable* and *Kim Electronics* accounts.

3. Write the credit amount, *$140.73*, in the Credit columns of the *Accounts Receivable* and *Kim Electronics* accounts.

4. Calculate and write the new balances: *$11,539.27* in the *Accounts Receivable* account and *$162.37* in the *Kim Electronics* account.

5. Record the appropriate account numbers in the Post. Ref. column of the general journal. Write the account number for *Accounts Receivable*, *1205*, to the left of the diagonal line in the Post Ref. column of the general journal. Write the customer number for *Kim Electronics*, *140*, to the right of the diagonal line.

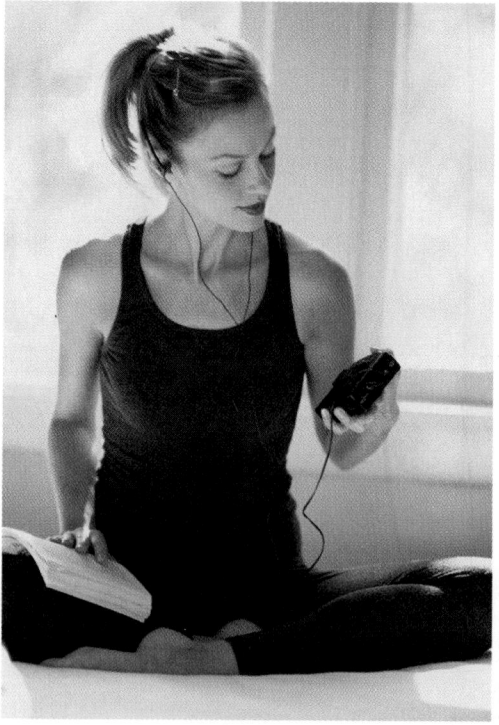

©GETTY IMAGES/PHOTODISC

Recording Departmental Sales and Cash Receipts

• term review

credit memorandum

• audit your understanding

1. What is a tax-exempt customer? Give an example.
2. For what purpose is a credit memorandum issued?

• work together 2-1

Journalizing and posting departmental sales on account and sales returns and allowances

The sales journal, general journal, and partial accounts receivable and general ledgers for Manhattan Beach Swimwear are provided in the *Working Papers*. Manhattan Beach has two departments: Swimwear and Accessories. Your instructor will guide you through the following examples.

1. Journalize each of the following sales on account and sales returns and allowances. The sales tax rate is 6%. Source documents are abbreviated as follows: sales invoice, S; credit memorandum, CM.

Transactions:

Sept. 1. Sold a bathing suit to Emily Branford for $40.00, plus sales tax. S12.
10. Sold three beach mats to Roger Minkow for $75.00, plus sales tax. S13.
14. Sold bathing suits to Oak Grove High School Swim Team for $310.00. No sales tax. S14.
15. Granted credit to Roger Minkow for one beach mat returned, $25.00, plus sales tax from sales invoice S13. Issued CM23.
Posting. Post the items that are to be posted individually from the sales journal and then from the general journal.
18. Sold beach towel to Sara Nunez for $15.00, plus sales tax. S15.
24. Sold a beach umbrella to Emily Branford for $70.00, plus sales tax. S16.
30. Granted credit to Sara Nunez as an allowance for a defective beach towel, $15.00, plus sales tax from sales invoice S15. Issued CM24.
Posting. Post the items that are to be posted individually from the sales journal and then from the general journal.

2. Prove and rule the sales journal. Post the totals to the general ledger.

• on your own 2-1

Journalizing and posting departmental sales on account and sales returns and allowances

The sales journal, general journal, and partial accounts receivable and partial general ledgers for Office Outfitters are provided in the *Working Papers*. Office Outfitters has two departments: Equipment and Supplies. Work this problem independently.

1. Journalize each of the following sales on account and sales returns. The sales tax rate is 6%. Source documents are abbreviated as follows: sales invoice, S; credit memorandum, CM.

Transactions:

Oct. 2. Sold a laser printer to Libby Products Co. for $515.00, plus sales tax. S410.
6. Sold office supplies to United Charities (tax exempt) for $410.00. S411.
10. Sold office copiers to Dunford, Inc., for $3,200.00, plus sales tax. S412.
13. Granted credit to Dunford, Inc., for one copier returned, $800.00, plus sales tax from sales invoice S412. Issued CM127.
Posting. Post the items that are to be posted individually from the sales journal and then from the general journal.
17. Sold office supplies to Professional Services Corporation for $602.00, plus sales tax. S413.
22. Sold laminating equipment to Libby Products Co. for $2,650.00, plus sales tax. S414.
28. Granted credit to Professional Services Corp. as an allowance for defective supplies, $55.00, plus sales tax from sales invoice S413. Issued CM128.
Posting. Post the items that are to be posted individually from the sales journal and then from the general journal.

2. Prove and rule the sales journal. Post the totals to the general ledger.

Departmental Sales on Account and Sales Returns and Allowances

Lesson 2-1 **43**

OBJECTIVES

- Define terms related to cash receipts.
- Identify concepts and practices related to cash receipts.
- Journalize and post departmental cash receipts.

MOTIVATE

This lesson involves cash receipts. Many businesses offer their customers discounts if their accounts are paid early. Ask students under what circumstances a business might not take advantage of a sales discount *(cash is not available to make the payment)*. Ask students to compare a 2% sales discount offered for payment within 10 days with interest offered on a savings account *(2% earned in 10 days is far superior to typical savings account interest rates earned in 365 days)*.

Preview

- Preview the accounting terms introduced in this lesson: sales discount, point-of-sale (POS) terminal, and terminal summary.
- Direct students to read the headings on each page in this lesson and to examine the illustrations given.
- Explain that this lesson introduces a departmentalized cash receipts journal and sales discounts.

EXPLAIN

- Explain that most cash receipts are from customers on account or for cash and credit card sales.
- Explain that to encourage early payment, a business may offer a deduction on the invoice amount called a *sales discount.*
- Emphasize that the discount amount is calculated on the total invoice amount, not just on the sales amount.
- Direct students to the F.Y.I. box for information on Internet sales tax.

DEMONSTRATE

Calculating sales discounts

- Direct students to the math box as you demonstrate how to calculate sales discounts.
- Demonstrate how to calculate the amount of discount on the total sales invoice amount.
- Demonstrate how to calculate the amount of cash received.
- Repeat the calculations using a variety of amounts and percentages.

44

2-2 Journalizing and Posting Cash Receipts

DEPARTMENTAL CASH RECEIPTS

Zytech keeps a record of all cash receipts. The sources of most cash receipts are (1) cash received from customer payments on account and (2) cash and credit card sales.

The amount of cash received when payment is made within a discount period is calculated as follows.

Sales Amount	+	8.25% Sales Tax	=	Total Invoice Amount
$1,700.00	+	$140.25	=	$1,840.25

Terms: 2/10, n/30
Invoice paid within 10 days:

Invoice Amount	×	Discount Rate	=	Sales Discount
$1,840.25	×	2%	=	$36.81

Total Invoice Amount	−	2% Sales Discount	=	Amount Due in 10 Days
$1,840.25	−	$36.81	=	$1,803.44

CASH RECEIPTS ON ACCOUNT

Each customer is expected to pay the amount due within the credit terms agreed upon. To encourage early payment, a business may grant a deduction on the invoice amount. A deduction that a vendor allows on the invoice amount to encourage prompt payment is known as a *cash discount.* A cash discount on sales is called a **sales discount.** Zytech sells on account using terms 2/10, n/30. These terms mean that a 2% sales discount may be deducted if sales on account are paid within 10 days of the invoice date (2/10). All sales on account must be paid within 30 days of the invoice date (n/30).

When a sale is made on account, the amount debited to Accounts Receivable reflects the total amount owed by the customer, including sales tax. Sales is credited only for the pre-tax selling price. An additional credit must be made to Sales

Tax Payable for the sales tax liability on the total sales invoice amount. Zytech prepares a receipt as the source document for cash received on account. [*CONCEPT: Objective Evidence*]

MATERIALS

- **Instructor's Resource CD:**
  PowerPoint Slides
- **Xtra! Study Tools on the Xtra! Web Site**
- **Blackline Masters:**
  Departmental Cash Receipts Journal
  General Ledger
  Accounts Receivable Ledger

- **Working Papers:**
  Teacher's Edition of the Working Papers for Lesson 2-2
- **Software:**
  Personal Trainer
  Student Companion CD
  Automated Accounting and Century 21 8E CD
  Peachtree and QuickBooks

JOURNALIZING A CASH RECEIPT WITH A SALES DISCOUNT

1. Write the date. **2.** Write the customer name. **3.** Record the receipt number. **4.** Write the accounts receivable credit amount. **5.** Write the sales discount debit amount.

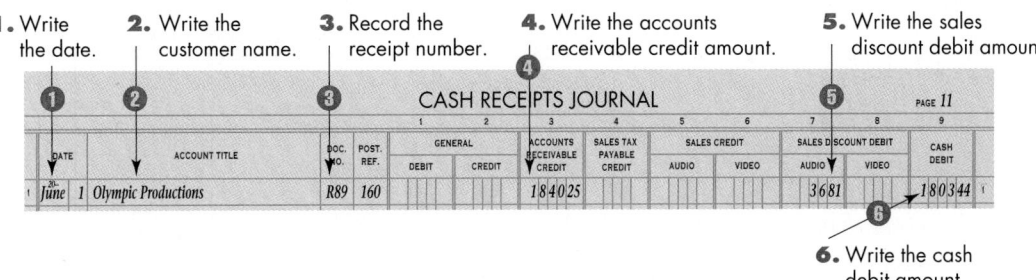

6. Write the cash debit amount.

Zytech records all cash receipts in a cash receipts journal. The journal has five credit columns—General Credit, Accounts Receivable Credit, Sales Tax Payable Credit, Sales Credit Audio, and Sales Credit Video. The journal also has four debit columns—General Debit, Sales Discount Debit—Audio, Sales Discount Debit—Video, and Cash Debit.

June 1. Received cash on account from Olympic Productions, $1,803.44, covering Sales Invoice No. 96 for audio equipment for $1,840.25 ($1,700.00 plus sales tax, $140.25), less 2% discount, $36.81. Receipt No. 89.

Cash is increased by a $1,803.44 debit. The contra revenue account, Sales Discount—Audio, is increased by a $36.81 debit. Using a separate account to record discounts allows the business to determine the proportion of available discounts that customers actually take. Accounts Receivable is

decreased by a $1,840.25 credit. In the accounts receivable ledger, Olympic Productions is decreased by a $1,840.25 credit.

The customer's payment on account is shown above. Use the following steps to make the journal entry.

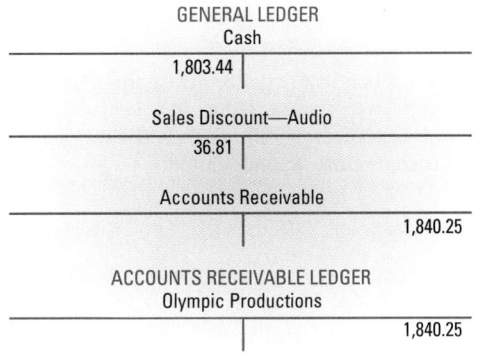

STEPS • STEPS • STEPS • STEPS • STEPS • STEPS • STEPS • STEPS • STEPS • STEPS • STEPS •

RECORDING THE RECEIPT OF CASH WHEN THE SALES DISCOUNT IS TAKEN

1 Write the date, *20--, June 1,* in the Date column.

2 Write the customer name, *Olympic Productions,* in the Account Title column.

3 Record the document number, *R89,* in the Doc. No. column.

4 Write the credit amount, *$1,840.25,* in the Accounts Receivable Credit column.

5 Write the debit amount, *$36.81,* in the Sales Discount Debit Audio column.

6 Write the debit amount, *$1,803.44,* in the Cash Debit column.

Journalizing and Posting Cash Receipts

Lesson 2-2   **45**

APPLIED SKILLS BUILDING STUDY SKILLS

A Quick Reference Guide (QRG) can be a useful study tool for several reasons. A QRG is simply a sheet of paper or notecard on which important information is written. When students create a QRG for an accounting topic, learning is reinforced because (1) the concept is reinforced through the act of writing it down; (2) students gain confidence in their knowledge of the subject; and (3) repeated use of a QRG reinforces the concept so students find that after a while they do not need to rely on the QRG. Creating a QRG also provides additional writing practice and often calls on students to order steps within a sequence. Direct students to prepare a QRG for the recommended order of posting. Students should use a QRG when they complete end-of-chapter problems, reinforcement activities, and simulations.

- Explain that cash received on account with a sales discount is recorded the same way whether there is a sales return or allowance or not. The only difference is the amounts used for the transaction.

- Explain that sales discounts are calculated on the amount owed at the time the invoice is paid. Therefore, a sales return or allowance reduces the amount owed.

DEMONSTRATE

Calculating sales discount

- Direct students to the math box as you demonstrate calculating a sales discount when there is a sales return.

- Demonstrate on the board the process for adjusting the original invoice amounts for the amount of the sales return.

- Demonstrate the steps for calculating sales discount and cash received based on the invoice amounts adjusted for a sales return.

Journalizing a cash receipt with a return and sales discount

- Use a transparency of a departmental cash receipts journal or direct students to the illustration to demonstrate journalizing a cash receipt on account with a sales return and a sales discount.

- Record each item in the cash receipts journal, following the six steps shown in the illustration. Point out that this is the same process for recording a cash receipt with a sales discount with no purchase return.

JOURNALIZING A CASH RECEIPT WITH A SALES RETURN AND A SALES DISCOUNT

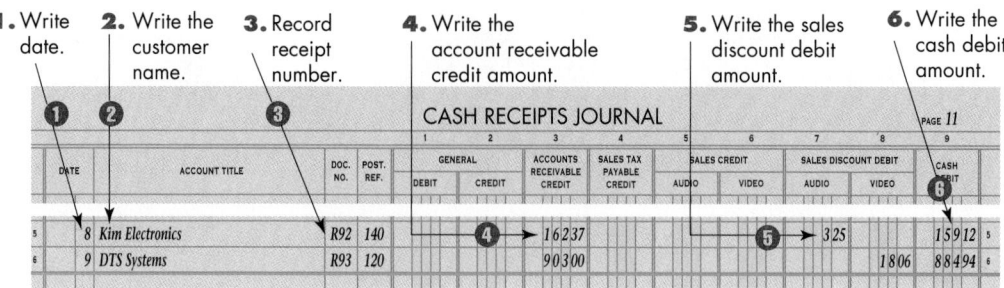

1. Write date.
2. Write the customer name.
3. Record receipt number.
4. Write the account receivable credit amount.
5. Write the sales discount debit amount.
6. Write the cash debit amount.

June 8. Received cash on account from Kim Electronics, $159.12, covering Sales Invoice No. 101 for $303.10 ($280.00 plus sales tax, $23.10), less Credit Memorandum No. 43 for $140.73 ($130.00 plus sales tax, $10.73), less 2% discount, $3.25. Receipt No. 92.

This transaction is journalized the same way as a receipt of cash when there is no sales return or allowance. The only difference is the way in which the amounts are calculated.

Sales discounts are calculated on the amount owed at the time the invoice is paid. When a customer takes a discount after being granted a return or an allowance, the amount of the return or allowance must be deducted from the amount of the original sale before the discount can be calculated. To calculate the amount of cash received, (1) find the sales discount amount and (2) determine the amount of cash to be received. The calculation for each of these items is shown below.

		Amount of Sale	+	Sales Tax	=	Total Receivable
	Original Sales Invoice Amount (S101)	$280.00	+	$23.10	=	$303.10
less	Sales Return (CM43)	130.00	+	10.73	=	140.73
equals	Sales Invoice Amount after Return	$150.00	+	$12.37	=	$162.37

Sales Invoice Amount after Return	×	Sales Discount Rate	=	Sales Discount
$162.37	×	2%	=	$3.25

Recording Departmental Sales and Cash Receipts

TEACHING STRATEGIES   DIFFERENT LEARNING STYLES

Visual Learner. When learning how to post, the visual learner would prefer to see how the posting process works. To encourage visual learners, therefore, the instructor could use a transparency to assist in the lecture. The transparency could be a blank transparency that the instructor completes.

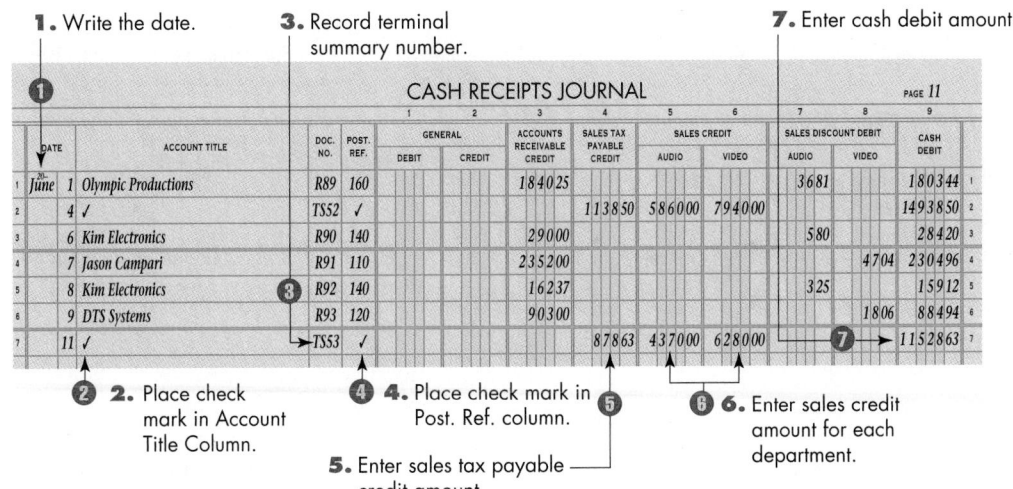

1. Write the date.

3. Record terminal summary number.

7. Enter cash debit amount.

CASH RECEIPTS JOURNAL — PAGE 11

	DATE	ACCOUNT TITLE	DOC. NO.	POST. REF.	GENERAL DEBIT	GENERAL CREDIT	ACCOUNTS RECEIVABLE CREDIT	SALES TAX PAYABLE CREDIT	SALES CREDIT AUDIO	SALES CREDIT VIDEO	SALES DISCOUNT DEBIT AUDIO	SALES DISCOUNT DEBIT VIDEO	CASH DEBIT	
1	June 1	Olympic Productions	R89	160			1 840 25				36 81		1 803 44	1
2	4	✓	TS52	✓				1 138 50	5 860 00	7 940 00			14 938 50	2
3	6	Kim Electronics	R90	140			290 00				5 80		284 20	3
4	7	Jason Campari	R91	110			2 352 00					47 04	2 304 96	4
5	8	Kim Electronics	R92	140			162 37				3 25		159 12	5
6	9	DTS Systems	R93	120			903 00					18 06	884 94	6
7	11	✓	TS53	✓				878 63	4 370 00	6 280 00			11 528 63	7

2. Place check mark in Account Title Column.

4. Place check mark in Post. Ref. column.

5. Enter sales tax payable credit amount.

6. Enter sales credit amount for each department.

Zytech accepts cash or credit cards from its customers. An independent company or bank hired by Zytech to process credit card sales automatically deposits the daily total of credit card sales to Zytech's bank account. Because credit card sales result in an immediate increase in the bank account balance, credit card sales and cash sales are recorded together in the cash receipts journal.

Both cash and credit card sales are entered into a modern version of a cash register. A computer used to collect, store, and report all the information of a sales transaction is called a **point-of-sale (POS) terminal**. The POS terminal prints a receipt for the customer and internally accumulates data about total sales. At the end of each week, Zytech instructs the POS terminal to print a report of all cash and credit card sales. The report that summarizes the cash and credit card sales of a point-of-sale terminal is called a **terminal summary**. The terminal summary is identified with a *TS* and a sequential number. Zytech uses the terminal summary as the source document for cash and credit card sales. [*CONCEPT: Objective Evidence*]

June 11. Recorded cash and credit card sales, audio equipment, $4,370.00; video equipment, $6,280.00; plus sales tax, $878.63; total, $11,528.63. Terminal Summary No. 53.

Cash increases by a $11,528.63 debit. Sales Tax Payable increases by a $878.63 credit. Sales—Audio is increased by a $4,370.00 credit, and Sales—Video increases by a $6,280.00 credit.

The details of Terminal Summary No. 53 are recorded on line 7 of the cash receipts journal. The steps needed to record this transaction are similar to those required to record other cash receipts transactions.

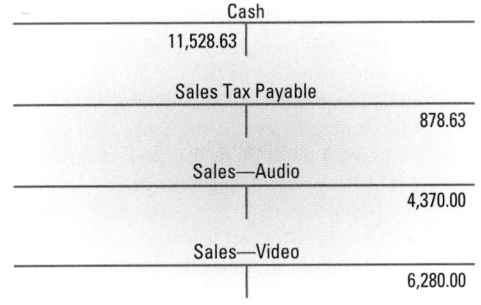

Cash	
11,528.63	

Sales Tax Payable	
	878.63

Sales—Audio	
	4,370.00

Sales—Video	
	6,280.00

FYI FOR YOUR INFORMATION

Even though a business may print a terminal summary and journalize cash and credit card sales weekly, it would normally deposit excess cash daily as a security measure.

Journalizing and Posting Cash Receipts

Lesson 2-2   47

EXPLAIN

- Explain that credit card sales are recorded together with cash sales because credit card sales are automatically deposited to the vendor's bank account.
- Explain that cash and credit card sales are entered into a point-of-sale (POS) terminal that prints a weekly summary, a *terminal summary*, of sales for the week that is used as the source document for cash and credit card sales transactions.

DEMONSTRATE

Analyze the transaction

- Draw four blank T accounts on the board.
- Read the transaction statement.
- Ask students to analyze the transaction by answering: what accounts are affected, are they increased or decreased, and are they debited or credited. Complete the T accounts as the information is provided.
- Point out the separate credits to the two departmental sales accounts.

Record the transaction

- Use a transparency of a departmental cash receipts journal to illustrate recording the transaction or direct students to the illustration.
- Record each item in the journal, following the seven steps shown.
- Point out that check marks are recorded in the Account Title column and the Post. Ref. column to indicate that no amounts on this line need to be posted individually.
- Point out that the abbreviation for terminal summary, *TS,* and the day of the month are recorded in the Doc. No. column.
- Point out that the sales tax amount is recorded in the Sales Tax Payable Credit column.

TEACHING STRATEGIES DIFFERENT LEARNING STYLES

Tactile Learner. The tactile learner can use a group of index cards to represent the general ledger. Each card should represent an account and should have three vertical lines to distinguish between the debit and credit columns and balance columns. Have the tactile learner post each example of a journal entry to the appropriate cards (accounts).

- Explain that individual amounts are posted often in order to keep customer accounts up to date.
- Explain that the departmental cash receipts journal is proved and ruled in a manner similar to that used with other journals at the end of each month.
- Explain that special amount columns are totaled and the totals are posted to the general ledger at the end of the month.
- Direct students to the F.Y.I. note for information about how merchants use computers to verify credit card transactions.

DEMONSTRATE

Proving and ruling the cash receipts journal

- Use a transparency of a departmental cash receipts journal or direct students to the illustration.
- Explain that all amount columns are totaled at the end of the month.
- Explain how the equality of debits and credits is proved for the cash receipts journal.
- Explain the ruling of the cash receipts journal.

Posting to the accounts receivable ledger

- Use a transparency of an account in the accounts receivable ledger to demonstrate posting the transaction on line 1 to the accounts receivable ledger.
- Emphasize recording the posting references in the ledger account and the cash receipts journal.

Posting to the general ledger

- Use a transparency of an account in the general ledger to demonstrate posting the total of the Sales Credit—Audio column total.
- Emphasize recording the posting references in the ledger account and the cash receipts journal.

POSTING FROM A CASH RECEIPTS JOURNAL

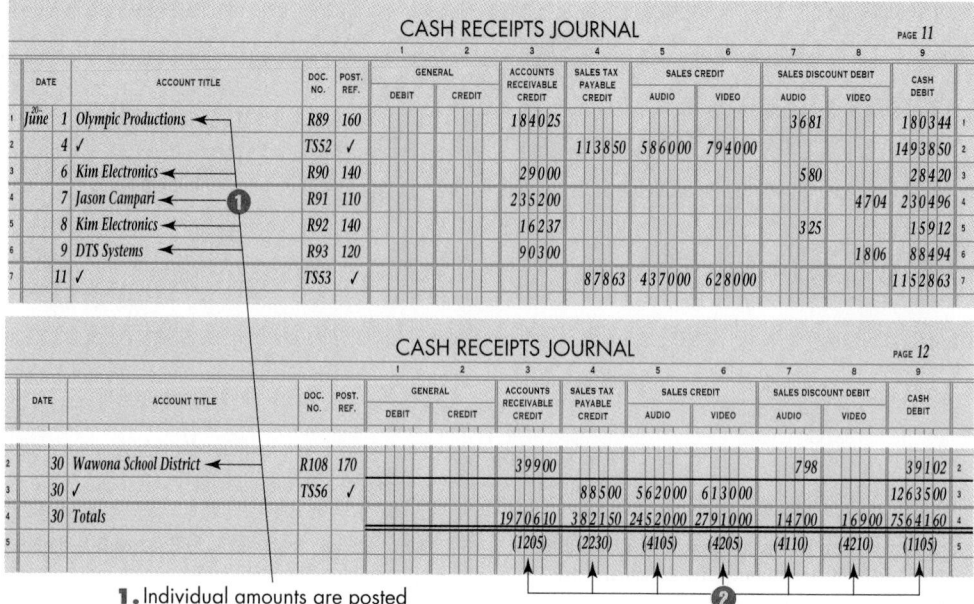

1. Individual amounts are posted to the accounts receivable ledger.

2. Column totals are posted to the account named in the column heading.

Individual amounts are posted often from the cash receipts journal. Frequent postings are required to keep the customers' accounts up to date. During the month, Zytech posts each amount written in the General Debit and Credit columns of the cash receipts journal to the general ledger. Each amount in the Accounts Receivable Credit column is also posted to the accounts receivable ledger. To indicate that the posting came from page 11 of the cash receipts journal, CR11 is recorded in the Post. Ref. column of the ledger account. The respective ledger account number is recorded in the Post. Ref. column of the journal to indicate completion of posting.

Transactions involving entries in the General Debit and Credit columns of a cash receipts journal are described in Chapter 10.

At the end of the month, the cash receipts journal is proved and ruled. Totals of the special amount columns are then posted to their respective accounts in the general ledger. The general ledger account number is written in parentheses immediately below the total. A check mark is placed in parentheses below the totals of the General Debit and Credit columns to show that the totals are not posted. Zytech's departmental cash receipts journal, page 12, after all posting has been completed, is shown above.

FYI FOR YOUR INFORMATION

Many businesses use automated equipment to verify credit card transactions. This verification process protects consumers and merchants and helps prevent fraud.

TEACHING STRATEGIES DIFFERENT LEARNING STYLES

Print Learner. When learning how to post, the print learner would prefer to see the process in print. This can be done by distributing a handout that explains the steps in the posting process. Allow the student to study the handout.

ORDER OF POSTING FROM JOURNALS

Businesses post transactions affecting vendor and customer accounts often during the month so that balances of subsidiary ledger accounts are kept up to date. General ledger account balances are needed only when financial statements are prepared. Therefore, posting to general ledger accounts may be done less frequently than posting to subsidiary ledgers. However, all transactions, including special amount column totals, must be posted at the end of a fiscal period. The recommended order in which to post journals is listed as follows.

1. Sales journal
2. Purchases journal
3. General journal
4. Cash receipts journal
5. Cash payments journal

This posting order generally places the debits and credits in the accounts in the order that the transactions occurred.

©GETTY IMAGES/PHOTODISC

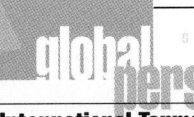

GLOBAL PERSPECTIVE • GLOBAL PERSPECTIVE • GLOBAL PERSPECTIV

International Terms of Sale

Terms of sale for international business are very similar to those used in the United States. However, it is important to make sure that all parties understand the terms before business is complete.

Selected international terms of sale are described below:

C.I.F. (Cost, Insurance, Freight) to the named port of import. Under this method, the seller quotes a price for the goods. The price includes insurance, all transportation, and all miscellaneous charges to the point of unloading the goods from the vessel.

F.A.S. (Free AlongSide a ship at the named U.S. port of export). Under this term, the seller quotes a price for goods that includes charges for delivery of the goods alongside a vessel at the port. The seller handles the cost of the unloading and wharf charges. All charges once goods are delivered to the vessel,

including loading, ocean transportation, and insurance, are the responsibility of the buyer.

F.O.B. VESSEL (named port of export). The seller quotes a price that includes all expenses up to, and including, delivery of goods upon an overseas vessel that is provided by or for the buyer. Once the goods are loaded "on board," all subsequent charges are the sole responsibility of the buyer.

EX ("EX" means "from" the named point of origin) such as EX FACTORY. Under this term, the price quoted applies only at the point of origin, and the seller agrees to place the goods at the disposal of the buyer at the specified place on the date or within the period fixed. All other charges are the responsibility of the buyer.

Journalizing and Posting Cash Receipts

GLOBAL PERSPECTIVE
GLOBAL PERSPECTIVE

The Global Perspective feature is intended to expose students to some of the ways in which accounting and business in general differ in other countries. This feature describes some terms of sale used in international sales:

1. *C. I. F. (Cost, Insurance, Freight) to the named port of import.* Under this method, the seller quotes a price for the goods that includes insurance, all transportation, and all miscellaneous charges to the

point of unloading the goods from the vessel.

2. *F.A.S. (Free AlongSide a ship at the named U.S. port of export).* The seller quotes a price for goods that includes charges for delivery of the goods alongside a vessel at the port. The seller handles the cost of the unloading and wharf charges. All charges once goods are delivered to the vessel are the responsibility of the buyer.

3. *F.O.B. VESSEL (named port of export).* The seller quotes a price that includes all expenses up to, and including, delivery of goods upon an overseas vessel that is provided by or for the buyer.

4. *EX ("from" the named point of origin).* The price quoted applies only at the point of origin, and the seller agrees to place the goods at the disposal of the buyer at the specified place on the date or within the period fixed.

GUIDED PRACTICE

Terms Review

Call on students to define the terms in the Terms Review. Ask the class if the definition is correct and whether the complete definition has been given or if anything needs to be added. The suggested definitions are given in the Glossary.

Audit Your Understanding

Call on students to answer the Audit Your Understanding questions. Ask the class if the answer is correct and/or complete. Answers are given in Appendix E of the textbook.

Work Together

Have students write the solution to the Work Together problems as you guide the class through the example.

- Direct students to record each transaction in the cash receipts journal as you elicit class participation in analyzing and recording each transaction.

- Call on students to describe each step in the process of posting separate amounts from the cash receipts journal to the accounts receivable journal.

- Call on students to describe each step in the process of proving and ruling a cash receipts journal.

- Call on students to describe each step in the process of posting the special column totals to the general ledger.

INDEPENDENT PRACTICE

On Your Own

- Assign the On Your Own problems to be worked independently.

- Use the Ongoing Assessment techniques to diagnose student understanding.

Application Problem

- Assign Application Problem 2-2: Journalizing and posting departmental cash receipts.

Personal Trainer

- Students can access the Lesson 2-2 assessment material using this software.

Xtra! Web Site

- Students can access the Xtra! Study Tools for additional practice.

50

• terms review

TERMS

sales discount
point-of-sale (POS) terminal
terminal summary

• audit your understanding

1. What does 2/10, n/30 mean?
2. Why are credit card sales and cash sales recorded together in the sales journal?

• work together 2-2

Journalizing and posting departmental cash receipts

The cash receipts journal, partial accounts receivable ledger, and partial general ledger for Norwalk Interiors are provided in the *Working Papers.* Norwalk Interiors has two departments, Furniture and Carpeting, and offers credit terms of 2/10, n/30.

1. Journalize each of the following cash receipts transactions. The sales tax rate is 6%; assume sales tax was paid on all cash and credit card sales. Source documents are abbreviated as follows: receipt, R; terminal summary, TS. Your instructor will guide you through the following examples.

Transactions:

Feb. 1. Received cash on account from Melinda Ashworth, $2,908.64 for five area carpets, purchased January 25 on S230 for $3,180.00, less CM29 ($200.00 plus sales tax), less discount. R343.
7. Recorded cash and credit card sales for the week: carpeting, $3,074.00; furniture, $3,286.00; plus sales tax. TS81.
12. Received a check from Filo Raines for furniture purchased February 3 on S231 for $1,272.00, less discount. R344.
14. Recorded cash and credit card sales for the week: carpeting, $2,112.00; furniture, $2,862.00; plus sales tax. TS82.
Posting. Post the items that are to be posted individually.
19. Received a check from Carlee Hanks for furniture purchased on February 12 on S232 for $848.00, less discount. R345.
21. Recorded cash and credit card sales for the week: carpeting, $2,851.00; furniture, $4,103.00; plus sales tax. TS83.
28. Recorded cash and credit card sales for the week: carpeting, $2,967.00; furniture, $2,803.00; plus sales tax. TS84.
Posting. Post the items that are to be posted individually.

2. Prove and rule the cash receipts journal. Post the totals to the general ledger.

• on your own 2-2

Journalizing and posting departmental cash receipts

The cash receipts journal, partial accounts receivable ledger, and partial general ledger for Electronic Warehouse, Inc., are provided in the *Working Papers.* Electronic Warehouse has two departments, Hardware and Software, and offers credit terms of 2/10, n/30.

1. Journalize each of the following cash receipts transactions. The sales tax rate is 7%; assume sales tax was paid on all cash and credit card sales. Source documents are abbreviated as follows: receipt, R; terminal summary, TS. Work this problem independently.

Transactions:

Feb. 1. Received cash on account from QuikPrint Co., for computers purchased on January 23 on S411 for $3,959.00, less CM29 ($300.00 plus sales tax), less discount. R343.
7. Recorded cash and credit card sales for the week: hardware, $3,264.00; software, $4,196.00; plus sales tax. TS81.
12. Received a check from Data Systems, Inc., for software purchased on February 3 on S413 for $1,230.50, less discount. R344.
14. Recorded cash and credit card sales for the week: hardware, $5,645.00; software, $2,098.00; plus sales tax. TS82.
Posting. Post the items that are to be posted individually.
19. Received a check from Gear Web Design Co. for scanners purchased on February 12 on S428 $1,203.75, less discount. R345.
21. Recorded cash and credit card sales for the week: hardware, $4,781.00; software, $2,876.00; plus sales tax. TS83.
28. Recorded cash and credit card sales for the week: hardware, $5,847.00; software, $1,955.00; plus sales tax. TS84.
Posting. Post the items that are to be posted individually.

2. Prove and rule the cash receipts journal. Post the totals to the general ledger.

ENRICH

- Assign the Global Perspective feature on page 49.

- Assign Cases for Critical Thinking 2.

- Assign the Automated Accounting feature on page 57 to automate Application Problem 2-2.

- Students can use the Peachtree and QuickBooks data files to automate Application Problem 2-2.

CLOSE

- Ask students to briefly summarize the procedure for journalizing and posting cash receipts from cash sales and sales on account with a sales discount.

SUMMARY

After completing this chapter, you can

1. Define terms related to departmental sales and cash receipts.
2. Identify concepts and practices related to departmental sales and cash receipts.
3. Journalize and post departmental sales on account and sales returns and allowances.
4. Journalize and post departmental cash receipts.

Explore Accounting

EXPLORE ACCOUNTING • EXPLORE ACCOUNTING • EXPLORE ACCOUN

Transfer Pricing

Departmental accounting allows managers to evaluate the performance of individual departments. Some companies use departmental income from operations as a basis for rewarding effective managers. A management incentive plan could base a manager's salary on the amount of departmental income from operations, the percentage of income to net sales, or some other measure of profitability.

This type of incentive program becomes difficult to administer when a manager is responsible for a department in which the product is transferred to another department. Consider the following example.

Cement Art has two departments: design and casting. The design department creates molds used by the casting department to make a variety of cement statues, bird baths, and planters. The casting department purchases its molds from the design department, pours cement in the molds, and sells the finished product to retail stores. The manager of each department receives a bonus equal to .05% of the department's profit on operations.

The incentive plan would seem to be a good idea. However, if the casting department is required to purchase molds from the design department at any price, the design department manager has no incentive to control production

costs. Thus, management must establish policies to determine the prices of molds transferred between the departments. Setting prices for the transfer of products between the departments is known as *transfer pricing*. Several transfer pricing methods are available:

1. Set the price consistent with the prices charged by other suppliers of the same or similar products.
2. Set the price based on the price that the product could be sold to other companies.
3. If the product is unique, use a percentage markup. This method must include a provision for containing increases in production costs.

Instructions: With another student, assume the roles of the design and casting department managers. Assume that the current cost of producing a mold is $20.00, and the mold is sold to the casting department for $25.00. The casting department adds $10.00 of other materials and labor to the product and sells the finished product to customers for $60.00. Negotiate a transfer pricing policy that provides an incentive salary for each manager. The policy should include a provision for the design manager to increase the price of a mold for an increase in production costs.

Recording Departmental Sales and Cash Receipts

Chapter 2   **51**

EXPLORE ACCOUNTING

Students will work in two-person groups for this activity. One student will be the design manager; the other will be the casting department manager. Specific answers will vary, but all should include one of the three pricing schemes described in the feature.

FORMAL EVALUATION

Chapter 2 Test
ExamView for Chapter 2
Assessment by Portfolio

- Review answers to all tests administered as a class activity. If time is limited, review only the items that were frequently incorrectly answered.

- Ask students if there are any questions about the chapter before proceeding to the next chapter.

CHECK FIGURES

Application Problem 2-1

Sales Journal totals: 1,631.15; 66.15; 1,070.00; 495.00.

General Journal: Four return entries dated April 5, 10, 15, and 24.

April 30 balance in Accounts Receivable: 2,822.65.

Application Problem 2-2

Cash Receipts Journal totals: 2,856.00; 2,534.50; 29,080.00; 21,610.00; 43.47; 9.45; 56,027.58.

See Teacher's Edition of the Working Papers for Chapter 2 for complete solutions.

2-1 APPLICATION PROBLEM (PEACHTREE)

Journalizing and posting departmental sales on account and sales returns and allowances

Sequoia Sport Apparel is a retail store with two departments: Clothing and Shoes. The general ledger and accounts receivable ledger are included in your *Working Papers.* The balances are recorded as of April 1 of the current year.

Instructions:

1. Journalize the transactions for April of the current year. Use page 4 of a sales journal and page 6 of a general journal. The sales tax rate is 5%. Source documents are abbreviated as follows: credit memorandum, CM; sales invoice, S.

Transactions:

April   1.   Sold shoes on account to Sridhar Duggirala, $85.00, plus sales tax. S63.
       2.   Sold clothing on account to Thuc Quan, $150.00, plus sales tax. S64.
       5.   Granted credit to Sridhar Duggirala for shoes returned, $85.00, plus sales tax from S63. CM12.
       5.   Sold shoes on account to Dean Fujiwara, $60.00, plus sales tax. S65.
       5.   Sold shoes on account to Gail Mahr, $180.00, plus sales tax. S66.
       7.   Sold clothing on account to Thuc Quan, $230.00, plus sales tax. S67.
     10.   Granted credit to Gail Mahr for shoes returned, $100.00, plus sales tax from S66. CM13.
     12.   Sold clothing on account to Jeffrey O'Connell, $350.00, plus sales tax. S68.
     15.   Granted credit to Thuc Quan for clothing returned, $140.00, plus sales tax from S67. CM14.

         Posting. Sequoia Sport Apparel posts items individually to the accounts receivable and general ledgers at mid-month and at the end of the month. Post the items accounted for through April 15. Post from the sales journal first and then from the general journal.

     17.   Sold shoes on account to Sridhar Duggirala, $46.00, plus sales tax. S69.
     19.   Sold clothing on account to the Andersen Vocational Center, $242.00. No sales tax. S70.
     24.   Granted credit to Jeffrey O'Connell for clothing returned, $120.00, plus sales tax from S68. CM15.
     27.   Sold clothing on account to Elias Carrasco, $98.00, plus sales tax. S71.
     30.   Sold shoes on account to Tianshu Jian, $124.00, plus sales tax. S72.

         Posting. Post the items individually to the accounts receivable and general ledgers.

2. Prove and rule the sales journal. Post the totals to the general ledger.

2-2 APPLICATION PROBLEM (AUTOMATED ACCOUNTING) (PEACHTREE) (QUICKBOOKS)

Journalizing and posting departmental cash receipts

Colonial Furnishings has two departments: Tables and Chairs. The general ledger and accounts receivable ledger are provided in the *Working Papers.* The balances are recorded as of June 1 of the current year.

Instructions:

1. Journalize the transactions for June of the current year. Use page 18 of a cash receipts journal. Colonial Furnishings offers credit terms of 2/10, n/30. The sales tax rate is 5%; assume sales tax was paid on all cash and credit card sales. Source documents are abbreviated as follows: receipt, R; terminal summary, TS.

Transactions:

June   1.   Received cash on account from Wayne Miller for chairs purchased May 25 on S147 for $157.50, less discount. R110.
      2.   Received cash on account from Amy Cannon for two tables purchased May 26 on S148 for $388.50, less discount. R111.

APPLIED SKILLS   LANGUAGE ARTS

Paraphrasing, Writing Complete Sentences, Identifying Singular and Plural Nouns. For additional practice in language arts skills, direct students to complete the Applied Communication activity. Students should use their own words and write complete sentences. To further practice language arts skills, ask students to underline the singular nouns and circle the plural nouns in their report.

6. Received cash on account from Bob Witt for chairs purchased on account for $210.00, no discount. R112.

6. Recorded cash and credit card sales for the week: tables, $6,240.00; chairs, $5,060.00; plus sales tax. TS66.

11. Received cash on account from Dawn Sanzone for a table purchased June 1 on S149 for $525.00, less discount. R113

13. Recorded cash and credit card sales for the week: tables, $5,640.00; chairs, $3,570.00; plus sales tax. TS67.
Posting. Post the items that are to be posted individually.

17. Received cash on account from Amy Cannon for a table purchased on June 9 on S150 for $336.00, less discount. R114.

18. Received cash on account from David Ring for a table purchased on June 9 on S151 for $451.50, less discount. R115.

20. Recorded cash and credit card sales for the week: tables, $7,110.00; chairs, $4,850.00; plus sales tax. TS68.

24. Received cash on account from Joe Ricardo for eight chairs and a table purchased June 15 on S152 for $892.50 ($420.00 for the chairs and $472.50 for the table), less CM42 for two chairs ($100.00 plus $5.00 sales tax), less discount. R116.

27. Recorded cash and credit card sales for the week: tables, $6,890.00; chairs, $5,150.00; plus sales tax. TS69.

30. Recorded cash and credit card sales for the period June 28–30: tables, $3,200.00; chairs, $2,980.00; plus sales tax. TS70.
Posting. Post the items individually to the accounts receivable ledger.

2. Prove and rule the cash receipts journal. Post the totals to the general ledger.

2-3 MASTERY PROBLEM (AUTOMATED ACCOUNTING) (PEACHTREE) (QUICKBOOKS)
Journalizing departmental sales, sales returns and allowances, and cash receipts

EuroFashions has two departments: Jewelry and Watches.

Instructions:

1. Journalize the transactions completed during April of the current year. Use page 9 of a sales journal and a general journal and page 12 of a cash receipts journal. EuroFashions offers its customers terms of 2/10, n/30. The sales tax rate is 5%; assume sales tax was paid on all cash and credit card sales. Source documents are abbreviated as follows: credit memorandum, CM; receipt, R; sales invoice, S; terminal summary, TS.

Transactions:

April 1. Sold jewelry on account to Ronn Hughes, $810.00, plus sales tax. S134.
3. Sold jewelry on account to Dara San, $520.00, plus sales tax. S135.
4. Received cash on account from Bill Melendez for watches purchased on March 27 covering S132 for $441.00, less discount. R83.
4. Recorded cash and credit card sales: jewelry, $2,560.00; watches, $2,130.00; plus sales tax. TS74.
6. Received cash on account from Katie Minko for jewelry purchased on March 29 on S131 for $640.50, less discount. R84.
8. Granted credit to Dara San for jewelry returned, $110.00, plus sales tax, from S135. CM28.
9. Received cash on account from Dara San for a watch purchased on April 1 for $302.40, less discount. R85.
11. Received cash on account from Ronn Hughes for jewelry purchased on April 4 on S134 for $850.50, less discount. R86.
11. Sold jewelry on account to Dan Tran, $780.00, plus sales tax. S136.

315 X .02

— X .02

Mastery Problem 2-3

Sales Journal totals: 3,747.00; 147.00; 2,430.00; 1,170.00.

General Journal: Two entries, both returns dated April 8 and 21.

Cash Receipts Journal totals: 3,483.90; 1,645.30; 17,960.00; 14,946.00; 54.81; 14.87; 37,965.52.

APPLIED SKILLS   WRITING ACROSS THE CURRICULUM

Writing Paragraphs and Short Essays. The Cases for Critical Thinking are short, practical applications of the accounting principles developed in the chapter. Some cases are planned to present problems related to the chapter but not specifically discussed and answered in the chapter. These cases present an opportunity for critical thinking and decision making. These cases also require more than a short objective-type response. Therefore, they provide ideal practice in writing paragraphs and short essays.

[handwritten notes in top margin:] 2% 5% AR 546 - 115.5 / ARX.02 - DIS

11. Recorded cash and credit card sales for the week: jewelry, $5,340.00; watches, $3,910.00; plus sales tax. TS75.

13. Received cash on account from Dara San, for jewelry purchased on S135 for $546.00, less CM28 ($110.00 plus sales tax), less discount. R87.

15. Sold two watches on account to Alana Austin, $510.00, plus sales tax. S137.

17. Sold jewelry on account to Katie Minko, $320.00, plus sales tax. S138.

18. Recorded cash and credit card sales: jewelry, $4,730.00; watches, $5,260.00; plus sales tax. TS76.

21. Received cash on account from Dan Tran, for jewelry purchased on S136 for $819.00, less discount. R88.

21. Granted credit to Alana Austin for returned watch, $150.00, plus sales tax, from S137. CM29.

25. Recorded cash and credit card sales for the week: jewelry, $3,470.00; watches, $2,681.00; plus sales tax. TS77.

28. Sold watches on account to The Hamilton Foundation, $660.00; no sales tax. S139.

30. Recorded cash and credit card sales: jewelry, $1,860.00; watches, $965.00; plus sales tax. TS78.

2. Prove and rule the sales journal.
3. Prove and rule the cash receipts journal.

2-4 CHALLENGE PROBLEM

Journalizing departmental sales, sales returns and allowances, and cash receipts

Assume that EuroFashions, the business described in Mastery Problem 2-3, is located in a state that does not charge a retail sales tax. Also assume that EuroFashions offers customers terms of 1/10, n/30. The journals with the proper headings are provided in the *Working Papers*.

Instructions:

1. Journalize the transactions given in Mastery Problem 2-3 without sales tax but with 1% sales discounts. Use page 9 of a sales journal, page 15 of a general journal, and page 12 of a cash receipts journal.

2. Prove and rule the special journals.

Challenge Problem 2-4

Sales Journal totals: 3,600.00; 2,430.00; 1,170.00.

General Journal: Two entries, both returns dated April 8 and 21.

Cash Receipts Journal totals: 3,318.00; 17,960.00; 14,946.00; 26.10; 7.08; 36,190.82.

©GETTY IMAGES/PHOTODISC

• applied communication

The preparation of a *Career Portfolio* was discussed in the Applied Communication activity in Chapter 1. In addition to labeling one divider "Resume," label another divider "Personal Letters." One type of personal letter is a cover letter. When sending your resume, a cover letter is your opportunity to introduce yourself to an employer and highlight your strongest qualifications.

The cover letter, or letter of application, consists of at least three paragraphs. In the first paragraph, introduce yourself, state the job for which you are applying, and express an interest in the job. The second paragraph should contain a description of your qualifications and related work experience. In the third paragraph, include an action statement—request an interview, ask for a phone call, indicate how you will follow-up, and—most importantly—thank the reader for her or his time and consideration.

Instructions:

1. Research how to write a strong cover letter.
2. In a newspaper or online, locate a job advertisement for a position for which you are qualified. Prepare a cover letter for the position you have selected.
3. Keep copies of all cover letters in the "Personal Letters" section of your *Career Portfolio*.

• cases for critical thinking

Case 1

Pacific Patio specializes in tables, umbrellas, and barbeques. All accounting records are kept on a departmental basis. When a customer returns merchandise or receives an allowance, a journal entry is made debiting the appropriate sales account and crediting Accounts Receivable and the customer account. Do you agree or disagree with this accounting procedure? Why?

Case 2

Ogden's, Inc., sells a complete line of hardware and lawn and garden products. To encourage early payment for sales on account, it offers a sales discount. The company has separate departmental accounts for purchases, sales, discounts, and returns and allowances. Thomas Gordon, who has been recording journal entries for sales and cash receipts, suggests that the Sales Tax Payable account also be split to have separate accounts for each of the two departments. The company's accountant disagrees with this suggestion. With whom do you agree? Why?

• SCANS workplace competency

Basic Skill: Speaking

Concept: Employers seek workers who possess the ability to organize their ideas and speak effectively. Employees spend much of their workday using oral communication skills to interact with other employees, managers, and customers.

Application: Prepare and give an oral report identifying the accounting and personal skills you possess that qualify you for entry-level employment.

APPLIED COMMUNICATION

Students' solutions will vary. The cover letter may be evaluated on both content and mechanics (format, grammar, and spelling).

CASES FOR CRITICAL THINKING

Case 1

Disagree. When the sales account is debited for a return or allowance, the balance of the sales account at the end of the fiscal period will represent net sales only. The income statement will not disclose the volume of sales returns and allowances. This omission would be considered a violation of the Adequate Disclosure accounting concept. Management should be informed of the volume of sales returns and allowances. A special account titled Sales Returns and Allowances should be established for each department. The balance of the account should be shown on the income statement as a reduction in sales for each respective department.

Case 2

Agree with the accountant. Sales tax is paid by the customer, collected by the business, and remitted to the appropriate governmental agency. Since the amount of sales tax payable generated in each department does not affect departmental operations or costs, there is no need to separate sales tax by departments.

SCANS WORKPLACE COMPETENCY

Use this end-of-the-chapter enrichment exercise to prepare your students with the SCANS skills necessary for a successful career. Emphasize to students that this specific oral report is excellent preparation for interviewing. Point out that during the interview process, students will likely be asked to review their skills and qualifications for employment.

Student dollar amounts for answers 2 and 3 may vary, due to determining exact amounts from graph.

1. Women's.

2. Palo Alto, with overall sales of approximately $265,000.

3. Atherton, due to overall sales of approximately $175,000.

ANALYZING COSTCO'S FINANCIAL STATEMENTS

1. Cash and Cash Equivalents for 2003 = $1,545,439,000.

2. "The company considers all highly liquid investments with a maturity of three months or less at the date of purchase and proceeds due from credit and debit card transactions with settlement terms of less than five days to be cash equivalents."

3. Credit and debit card receivables as of August 31, 2003 = $412,861,000. Cash remaining in checking, savings, and highly liquid investments = $1,132,578,000.

---

graphing workshop

Stanford Clothiers, an upscale department store, has locations in four different cities. Each quarter, the company charts departmental sales for each location. Use the information presented in the graph to estimate totals and answer the following questions.

Stanford Clothiers
4th Quarter Sales

1. Which department has the greatest sales at each location?

2. Which location appears to have the largest overall sales?

3. If you had to close a store based on total overall sales, which location would you select?

---

analyzing Costco's financial statements

Published financial statements include notes that provide a better understanding of some of the amounts, terms, and accounting policies used in preparing the financial statements. On a financial statement, the term "Cash and Cash Equivalents" includes more than just cash on hand. Checking accounts, savings accounts, highly liquid investments, and proceeds due from credit and debit card transactions are also included in this total.

Instructions:

1. Using the Consolidated Balance Sheets in Appendix B of this textbook, identify the actual amount of Costco's Cash and Cash Equivalents as of August 31, 2003.

2. Referring to the Notes to Consolidated Financial Statements in Appendix B, list the items Costco considers to be "cash equivalents."

3. Referring to the Notes to Consolidated Financial Statements in Appendix B, identify the amount of credit and debit card receivables with settlement terms of less than five days as of August 31, 2003. Calculate the amount of cash remaining in checking, savings, and highly liquid investments.

TEACHING STRATEGIES   PORTFOLIO ASSESSMENT

Analyzing transactions and journalizing and posting are the first steps in the accounting cycle and critical to the accuracy of information in an accounting information system. Students should select an example of these activities that has been successfully completed to include in their portfolio. A copy of the Portfolio Assessment form (blackline master in the Teacher's Resource Guide; also on the Student Companion CD) should be completed by the student and the Description section should include any comments regarding how the student mastered these concepts and procedures. Alternatively, students might include in their portfolios a solution to the Automated Accounting feature that follows this chapter.

· Automated Accounting

Recording Entries for Sales and Cash Receipts Using Special Journals

In the Automated Accounting software, transactions are recorded in journals similar to the sales, general, and cash receipts journals described in Chapter 2. The cash receipts journal window is shown below. Journals are accessed by clicking the Journal Entries option from the Data menu or clicking the Journal toolbar button. Click the tab for the journal you wish to use.

The cash receipts journal below shows two kinds of transactions: (1) three cash receipts on account with sales discounts; and (2) cash and credit card sales.

Entries in the automated cash receipts journal are similar to entries in a manual cash receipts journal. The software automatically calculates the amount in the Cash Debit column; notice that these amounts are grey in the illustration. Entering an amount in the A.R. Debit column (Accounts Receivable) automatically opens the Customer column where an accounts receivable ledger account must be selected.

The general ledger account number is entered in the Account No. column only when amounts will be entered in the general Debit or general Credit columns. Note that in the illustration, the Account No. and general Debit and Credit columns are not shown. The cash receipts journal window is too wide to display on most monitors. Therefore, the portions of the journal that are displayed change as you tab across the columns.

A journal entries report may be displayed or printed by clicking the Reports toolbar button, then clicking Journals and then the name of the journal.

AUTOMATING APPLICATION PROBLEM 2-2: Journalizing and posting departmental cash receipts

AUTOMATING MASTERY PROBLEM 2-3: Journalizing departmental sales, sales returns and allowances, and cash receipts

Instructions:

1. Load the *Automated Accounting 8.0* or higher software.
2. Select data file A02-2 or A02-3 from the appropriate directory/folder ("A" indicates Advanced Course).
3. Select File from the menu bar and choose Save As. Key the path to the drive and directory that contains your data files. Save the database with a filename of A02-2 or A02-3 XXX XXX (where the X's are your first and last name).
4. Access Problem Instructions through the Browser tool. Read the Problem Instruction screen.
5. Key the data listed in the problem on pages 52–54.
6. Save your file and exit the Automated Accounting software.

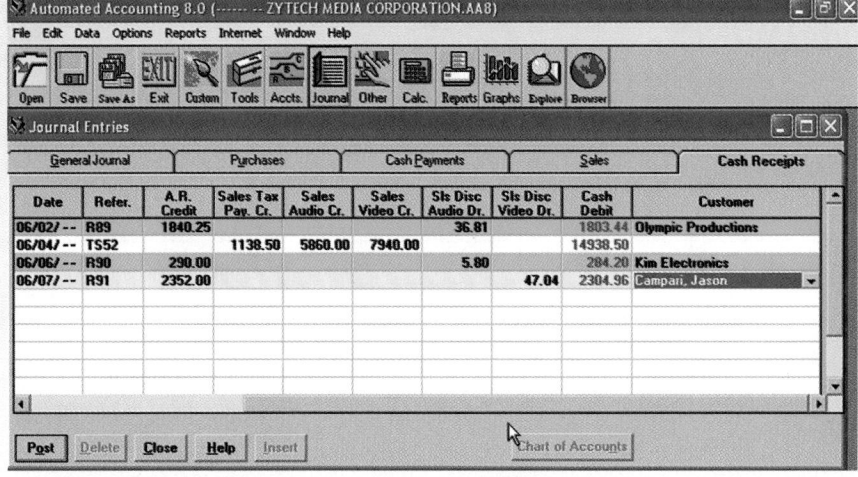

Recording Departmental Sales and Cash Receipts

AUTOMATED ACCOUNTING · AUTOMATED ACCOUNTING · AUTOMATED ACCOUNTING · AUTOMATED ACCOUNTING · AUTOMATED ACCOUNTING

Calculating and Recording

	SCOPE & SEQUENCE		ENHANCING	
	NEW	REVIEW/ EXTENSION	SPECIAL FEATURES	
Introduce the Chapter	✓		• Accounting in the Real World: Cisco Systems, Inc.	
Lesson 3-1 Completing Payroll Records for Employee Earnings and Deductions			• Making Ethical Decisions: Insider Trading	
Payroll deductions		✓		
Calculating employee earnings		✓		
Commissions record		✓		
Preparing a payroll register		✓		
Using the federal income tax withholding table		✓		
Preparing an employee earnings record		✓		
Lesson 3-2 Recording a Payroll and Payroll Taxes				
Payroll bank account, automatic check deposit, and employer payroll taxes		✓		
Journalizing payment of a payroll		✓		
Calculating employer payroll taxes		✓		
Journalizing employer payroll taxes		✓		
Journalizing payment of federal income tax, social security tax, and Medicare tax liability		✓		
Journalizing payment of federal unemployment tax liability		✓		
Putting It All Together			• Explore Accounting	
			• Xtra! Web Site: Xtra! Enrichment	
			• Applied Communication	
			• Case for Critical Thinking	
			• SCANS Workplace Competency	
			• Auditing for Errors	
			• Analyzing Costco's Financial Statements	

Departmental Payroll Data

INSTRUCTION		PRACTICE AND ASSESSMENT		
TECHNOLOGY AND MEDIA	TEACHING STRATEGIES	GUIDED PRACTICE	INDEPENDENT PRACTICE	RETEACHING AND ENRICHMENT
• Internet Research Activity • Accounting Xtra! Web Site	• Software Focus			
• Instructor's Resource CD: PowerPoint Slides • Xtra! Web Site: Xtra! Study Tools • Blackline Masters: Hours Worked Summary Sheet, Commissions Record, Payroll Register, Federal Income Tax Withholding Table, and Employee Earnings Record • Personal Trainer	• Expanding Beyond the Classroom • At-Risk Students • Print Learners • Limited English Proficiency (LEP) Students • Kinesthetic Learner	• Terms Review • Audit Your Understanding • Work Together 3-1	• On Your Own 3-1 • Application Problems 3-1, 3-2, and 3-3 • Ongoing Assessment, p. 67 • Personal Trainer • Xtra! Web Site: Xtra! Study Tools	• Reteach, p. 67 • Enrich, p. 69
• Instructor's Resource CD: PowerPoint Slides • Xtra! Web Site: Xtra! Study Tools • Blackline Masters: Payroll Register, Cash Payments Journal, and General Journal • Personal Trainer • Peachtree and QuickBooks	• Expanding Beyond the Classroom	• Terms Review • Audit Your Understanding • Work Together 3-2	• On Your Own 3-2 • Application Problems 3-4 and 3-5 • Ongoing Assessment, p. 75 • Personal Trainer • Xtra! Web Site: Xtra! Study Tools	• Reteach, p. 75 • Enrich, p. 76 • Peachtree and QuickBooks
• Automated Accounting • Personal Trainer • Xtra! Web Site: Xtra! Review, Quizzing, and Enrichment • Student Companion CD			• Mastery Problem 3-6 • Automated Accounting • Personal Trainer • Xtra! Web Site: Xtra! Review and Quizzing • Study Guide 3 • Student Companion CD • Chapter 3 Test • ExamView Chapter 3 • Portfolio Assessment	• Challenge Problem 3-7 • Reteach, p. 77 • Enrich, p. 77 • Recycling Problem 3-1 • Automated Accounting • Xtra! Web Site: Xtra! Enrichment

58

Calculating and Recording Departmental Payroll Data

INTRODUCE THE CHAPTER

Preview Chapter Objectives

- Introduce the topic of payroll by polling students as to how many have part-time jobs, how often they get paid, and whether their pay is by check or cash.

- Before introducing this chapter, ask students who have part-time jobs to bring in one of their pay check stubs.

- Have students review the different amounts recorded on their pay check stubs.

- Explain that in the first-year accounting course, the accounting concepts and practices related to a payroll system were presented.

- Explain that this chapter will review the basic payroll procedures and in addition will present the preparation of a payroll for a departmentalized business.

Preview Accounting Terms

- Read each term out loud to verify pronunciation for students.

- Point out terms or parts of terms that should already be familiar to most students such as salary, payroll, payroll taxes, and pay period.

INTERNET ACTIVITY

Point your browser to *accountingxtra. swlearning.com* to access the Accounting Xtra! Web Site.

SOFTWARE FOCUS

Software may be used for independent practice or enrichment as the instructor deems appropriate. For this chapter, the following software may be used: Automated Accounting and Century 21 8E CD with Mastery Problem 3-6; Peachtree and QuickBooks with Application Problem 3-5; the Student Companion CD; and Personal Trainer, Chapter 3.

Instructors may wish to cover the Automated Accounting feature on pages 84–85, even if the Automated Accounting software is not being used in the classroom, so students get a sense of how the chapter's accounting procedures would be implemented in an automated environment.

After studying Chapter 3, you will be able to:

1. Define accounting terms related to a departmental payroll system.

2. Identify accounting concepts and practices related to a departmental payroll system.

3. Prepare a commissions record and calculate commission on net sales.

4. Complete payroll records.

5. Journalize payroll transactions.

- salary
- pay period
- payroll
- payroll taxes

- withholding allowance
- tax base
- payroll register

- employee earnings record
- automatic check deposit
- electronic funds transfer (EFT)

Point Your Browser
accountingxtra.swlearning.com

Cisco Systems, Inc.

©NOAH BERGER/BLOOMBERG NEWS/LANDOV

CISCO SYSTEMS, INC. DELIVERS INFORMATION ACROSS THE INTERNET

Founded in 1984, Cisco Systems, Inc., has become the worldwide leader in networking for the Internet. Actually, the Internet would not be possible without an organized system that connects computer devices and databases around the world at corporations, universities, governmental agencies, and other institutions. Cisco's hardware, software, and routing technology allow bundles of information to be transferred across the Internet and delivered to the appropriate computer networks and devices.

Chapter 3 discusses payroll data. One payroll measure that Cisco uses to analyze the productivity of its employees is the dollar amount of sales generated per employee each year. For the year 2004, for example, Cisco's chairman reported productivity per employee of $690,000 revenue per employee, an increase of 23% over the previous year.

Critical Thinking

1. There are two ways businesses can improve their sales revenue per employee. What do you think they are?
2. Research two other companies and determine their sales revenues per employee for the past three years. What trends did you see for each company?

Xtra!
Today
accountingxtra.swlearning.com

Source: www.cisco.com

internet activity

PAYROLL TAX SUPPORT

Go to the homepage for the Internal Revenue Service (IRS) (www.irs.gov). Search the site for resources a small business owner can use to set up a system for deducting taxes and sending the taxes to the IRS.

Instructions

1. List at least three resources available to the small business owner related to payroll deductions.
2. Pick one of these resources and explain why you think it would be helpful to the small business owner.

Use this feature to demonstrate how the chapter's content applies to real businesses today. Motivate students by asking them if they are familiar with Cisco Systems or any of its products. Point out that if they have ever used the Internet, they have used Cisco technology. Ask students to read the feature or have one or more students read the feature out loud. Remind them to pay close attention to details of the business as they read. Give students 5–10 minutes to jot down some ideas for answering the Critical Thinking questions, then discuss the answers in class. As an alternative, you can organize students into groups of 3–4 individuals to generate possible solutions to the questions. With this approach you may also wish to record the suggestions and save them for additional discussion after the chapter is completed.

1. Companies can improve their sales revenue figure per employee by selling more merchandise or services or by using fewer employees. Sales might improve through the introduction of new products or the use of special promotions. Fewer employees might be needed with the introduction of new technologies or the reassignment of job tasks.
2. Student answers will vary. Students, however, should note any increases or decreases in sales and the number of employees.

INTERNET RESEARCH ACTIVITY

This activity provides students with an opportunity to search the Internet and answer questions related to the chapter content, giving them practice in developing technology and research skills. Point out that the correct site for the Internal Revenue Service is *www.irs.gov* and not *www.irs.com*.

Student answers to the questions will vary.

3-1 Completing Payroll Records for Employee Earnings and Deductions

INTRODUCTION

- Have students read the page. Having a student read this page out loud for the class can help develop the student's public speaking skills.

- This chapter stresses the importance of keeping accurate and complete payroll records.

- Ask students to identify the types of benefits they expect on their first full-time job.

OBJECTIVES

- Define accounting terms related to a departmental payroll system.

- Identify accounting concepts and practices related to a departmental payroll system.

- Prepare a commissions record and calculate commission on net sales.

- Complete payroll records.

MOTIVATE

- Get students involved in discussing some of the ways of setting wages earned *(hourly, monthly salary, commissions, etc.)*. As students respond, write the responses on the board or overhead.

- Discuss the importance of maintaining accurate payroll records. Ask the class who relies on all or part of the payroll information. Write the persons or organizations on the board as students respond.

Preview

- Preview the accounting terms and definitions introduced in this lesson: salary, pay period, payroll, payroll taxes, withholding allowance, tax base, payroll register, and employee earnings record.

- Direct students to read the headings on each page in this lesson and to examine the illustrations given.

MATERIALS

- Instructor's Resource CD: PowerPoint Slides

- Xtra! Study Tools on the Xtra! Web Site

- Blackline Masters:
  Hours Worked Summary Sheet
  Commissions Record
  Payroll Register
  Federal Income Tax Withholding Table
  Employee Earnings Record

Employees are an essential element of the business world. Businesses depend on competent employees in order to operate successfully. Employees provide services to a business in exchange for money. The money paid for employee services is called a **salary**. Federal, state, and local laws require employers to keep accurate records of the money paid to employees and of other payments related to employee services. Payroll records are maintained for the business and for each employee. The actual payroll system used differs among businesses. A business protects itself by keeping complete and accurate payroll records of all required information.

The period covered by a salary payment is called a **pay period**. The total amount earned by all employees for a pay period is called a **payroll**. In addition to salaries, a business must pay taxes based on the payroll. Taxes based on the

payroll of a business are called **payroll taxes**. Employers are also required by law to withhold certain payroll taxes from employee salaries each pay period.

Periodically, employers must pay government agencies all payroll taxes withheld from employee salaries as well as the employer payroll taxes. A business must also provide a yearly report to each employee showing the total salary earned and the total taxes withheld. The yearly report is provided to each employee on Form W-2. Businesses must distribute this form to their employees by January 31, reporting earnings and amounts withheld for the previous calendar year. Therefore, a business must keep records of each employee's earnings, amounts withheld, and net amount paid. Payroll records also must show the total amount of payroll taxes that a business must pay.

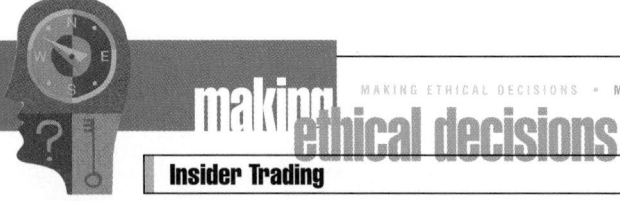

making ethical decisions

Insider Trading

Marcus Humphries, a loan officer for a regional bank, has just closed a loan agreement with Coastal Trucking Company. He was very impressed with the company's management and business plan. With the additional resources the loan will provide, Coastal Trucking Company should experience rapid growth during the next few years. The corporation's stock should also show a dramatic increase in market price.

Upon returning to the office, Marcus places an order to purchase 500 shares of the company's stock, currently trading

at $35.60 per share. This purchase is a substantial investment for Marcus.

Instructions

Access the *Code of Conduct* of Citigroup and insider trading information of the Securities and Exchange Commission (SEC). Using this information and the ethical decision-making model, determine whether Marcus's purchase of the stock of Coastal Trucking Company was ethical.

Calculating and Recording Departmental Payroll Data

- Working Papers:
  Teacher's Edition of the Working Papers for Lesson 3-1

- Software:
  Personal Trainer

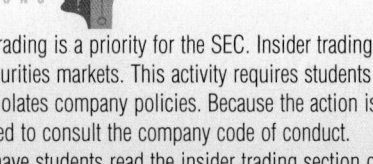

MAKING ETHICAL DECISIONS

Detecting and prosecuting illegal insider trading is a priority for the SEC. Insider trading undermines investor confidence in the securities markets. This activity requires students to analyze whether the action is illegal and violates company policies. Because the action is considered illegal, students are not required to consult the company code of conduct. However, as an extension of this activity, have students read the insider trading section of Citigroup's *Code of Conduct*. For suggested answers using the ethical decision-making model, see the front of this Wraparound Teacher's Edition.

PAYROLL DEDUCTIONS

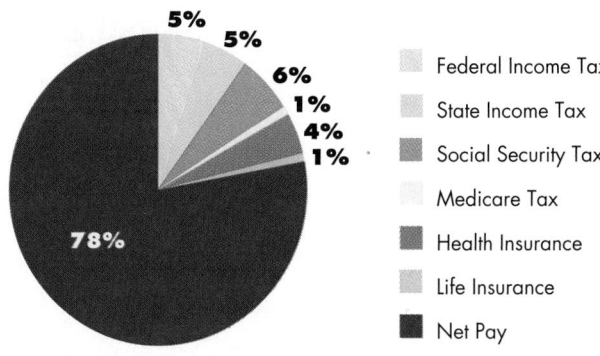

- 5% Federal Income Tax
- 5% State Income Tax
- 6% Social Security Tax
- 1% Medicare Tax
- 4% Health Insurance
- 1% Life Insurance
- 78% Net Pay

Zytech is required by law to withhold federal income tax and two FICA taxes (social security tax and Medicare tax) from each employee's pay. *FICA* is the abbreviation for the *Federal Insurance Contributions Act.*

The total earnings, marital status, and number of withholding allowances claimed by an employee determine the federal income tax amount to be withheld. For each person supported, including the employee, an employee is entitled to a reduction in the amount on which income tax is calculated. A deduction from total earnings for each person legally supported by a taxpayer is called a **withholding allowance**.

The Federal Insurance Contributions Act (FICA) provides for a federal system of old-age, survivors, disability, and hospital insurance. The old-age, survivors, and disability insurance portion is financed by the social security tax. The hospital insurance portion is financed by the Medicare tax. Each of these taxes is reported separately. Social security tax is calculated on employee earnings up to a maximum paid in a calendar year. The maximum amount of earnings on which a tax is calculated is called a **tax base**. Congress sets the tax base and the tax rates for social security tax. An act of Congress can change the tax base and tax rate at any time. The social security tax rate and base used in this textbook are 6.2% of earnings up to a maximum of $87,000.00 in each calendar year. Medicare does not have a tax base. Therefore, Medicare tax is calculated on total employee earnings. The Medicare tax rate used in this text is 1.45% of total employee earnings.

Some cities and states also require that employers deduct amounts for income and other taxes from employee earnings. Laws for handling state, city, and county taxes vary.

Some businesses also make deductions from employee earnings for health insurance, life insurance, pension plans, and savings deposits. Zytech makes deductions from its employee salaries for federal income tax, state income tax, social security tax, Medicare tax, health insurance, and life insurance. The payroll components for Mary Dennenberg are shown in the graph above.

©GETTY IMAGES/PHOTODISC

- Explain that Zytech has a biweekly pay period and that the employee hours worked report is designed for the two-week period. Other companies may have weekly, semimonthly, or monthly pay periods. These companies would have employee hours worked reports designed for their specific pay period.

- Point out that employees who are paid by the hour usually earn overtime pay after working 40 hours in a calendar week, regardless of the length of the pay period.

- Explain how regular hours worked are calculated.

- Explain how overtime hours worked are calculated.

- Explain how biweekly earnings are calculated.

DEMONSTRATE

- Prepare a transparency for an employee hours worked report. Use the transparency or the math box to illustrate how to calculate regular earnings, overtime earnings, and total earnings.

CALCULATING EMPLOYEE EARNINGS

| Hours Worked: ALL EMPLOYEES | | | | June 18–July 2, 20-- | |
Name	ID No.	Regular-1	Overtime-1	Regular-2	Overtime-2
Balero, Samantha R.	7	40	2	40	3
Dennenberg, Mary E.	10	-----		-----	
Dunnston, Shawn T.	16	40		40	2
Easthouse, Vern T.	9	40		40	
Fabio, Dante R.	15	-----		-----	
Famquez, Carlos M.	11	40	2	40	1
Yamaguchi, Sam F.	8	40		40	2

Zytech pays an hourly salary biweekly to sales-clerks and accounting department employees. Zytech's biweekly pay period is 80 hours, consisting of two regular 40-hour work weeks. The store is open six days a week. However, employees usually work only a five-day week of 40 hours. The pay rate for Zytech's salesclerks and accounting employees is stated as an hourly rate.

Zytech uses an employee identification card scanner to log employee hours. All employees have identification badges with a magnetic strip coded to include employee name and identification number. Employees slide the card through the card scanner when they begin and end each work period. At the end of a payroll period, a report listing employee hours worked is printed to provide the data for calculating employee earnings. The employee hours worked report for the biweekly period June 18 through July 2 is

shown above. The software that supports the card scanner can produce a variety of reports. For example, to monitor employee attendance, a report of the actual times an employee arrives and leaves work can also be generated.

All time worked in excess of 40 hours in any one week is considered overtime. Employees are paid $1\frac{1}{2}$ times the regular rate for overtime hours. However, managers are paid a base salary plus commissions, so their hours worked are indicated by dashes.

Employee regular earnings are calculated by multiplying the hourly rate by the number of regular hours. Employee overtime earnings are calculated by multiplying the regular rate by 1.5 and multiplying the result by the number of overtime hours. The calculations are shown below for Samantha R. Balero.

Regular Hours	×	Regular Rate	=	Regular Earnings		
80	×	$7.00 per hour	=	$560.00		
Overtime Hours	×	Regular Rate	×	1.5	=	Overtime Earnings
5	×	$7.00	×	1.5	=	$52.50
Regular Earnings	+	Overtime Earnings	=	Total Earnings		
$560.00	+	$52.50	=	$612.50		

TEACHING STRATEGIES DIFFERENT LEARNING ABILITIES

At-Risk Students. Together with the student, develop an individualized program that allows the student to attain both short-term and long-term goals. When identifying goals, consider the student's anticipated career goals.

COMMISSIONS RECORD

1 Record heading information.

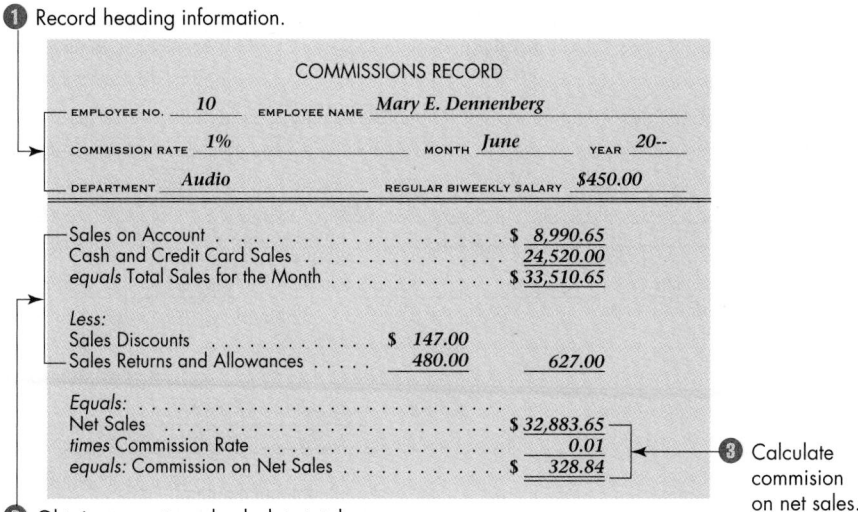

COMMISSIONS RECORD

EMPLOYEE NO. __10__ EMPLOYEE NAME __Mary E. Dennenberg__

COMMISSION RATE __1%__ MONTH __June__ YEAR __20--__

DEPARTMENT __Audio__ REGULAR BIWEEKLY SALARY __$450.00__

Sales on Account	. . . .	$ 8,990.65
Cash and Credit Card Sales	. . . .	24,520.00
equals Total Sales for the Month	. . . .	$ 33,510.65
Less:		
Sales Discounts	. . . . $ 147.00	
Sales Returns and Allowances	. . . . . 480.00	627.00
Equals:	. . . .	
Net Sales	. . . .	$ 32,883.65
times Commission Rate	. . . .	0.01
equals: Commission on Net Sales	. . . .	$ 328.84

3 Calculate commision on net sales.

2 Obtain amounts and calculate totals.

An employee's basic salary may be supplemented by other types of earnings. For example, an employee may receive commissions, cost-of-living adjustments, a share of profits, or a bonus.

At Zytech, department supervisors are paid a regular biweekly salary. They are not paid for overtime hours. However, to encourage increased sales, the supervisors are paid a 1% commission on the department's monthly net sales.

The store manager is also paid a regular biweekly salary and receives no salary for overtime hours. The store manager also earns an annual bonus based on the sales record for both departments.

Commissions for the previous month's net sales are included with the first biweekly pay period of a month. A commissions record is used to calculate each department supervisor's commission.

STEPS • STEPS • STEPS • STEPS • STEPS • STEPS • STEPS • STEPS • STEPS • STEPS •

STEPS PREPARING A COMMISSIONS RECORD

1 Record the employee number, employee name, commission rate, month, year, department, and regular biweekly salary at the top of the form.

2 Calculate department net sales for the month:
- Write the amount of sales on account for the department, *$8,990.65,* from the sales journal.
- Write the amount of cash and credit card sales for the month, *$24,520.00,* from the cash receipts journal.
- Add the two sales amounts and write the total sales for the month, *$33,510.65.*
- Write the amount of sales discounts, *$147.00,* from the cash receipts journal.
- Write the amount of sales returns and allowances, *$480.00.* This amount can be obtained from the general journal entries or the month's postings to the general ledger account.
- Write the total of sales discounts and sales returns and allowances, *$627.00.*

3 Calculate the commission on net sales for the month.
- Calculate the difference between total sales for the month, $33,510.65, less total sales discounts and returns and allowances, $627.00. Write the amount of net sales, *$32,883.65.*
- Write the commission rate of 1%, *0.01.*
- Multiply the commission rate times the net sales amount and write the commission on net sales, *$328.84.*

The June commission for Mary E. Dennenberg is calculated as shown in the illustration.

Completing Payroll Records for Employee Earnings and Deductions   Lesson 3-1   **63**

EXPLAIN

- Explain that to provide employees with an incentive to achieve higher levels of effectiveness, employers sometime pay employees a percentage of sales—a *commission.* Zytech pays departmental supervisors a 1% commission of the department's monthly net sales.
- Explain how to calculate commissions as a percent of net sales.

DEMONSTRATE

- Prepare a transparency for a commissions record. Use the transparency or the illustration to illustrate the preparation of a commission record.
- Demonstrate on the chalkboard, whiteboard, or overhead how to calculate commissions as a percentage of net sales using the process shown in the illustration.
- Record each item on the commissions record transparency, following the three steps shown.

TEACHING STRATEGIES DIFFERENT LEARNING STYLES

Print Learners. When learning how to prepare payroll records, the print learner would prefer to see the process in print. Prepare a series of handouts for benefits records, calculating employees' earnings, commissions records, etc. The handouts explain the various processes. Allow students to study the handouts.

- Explain that a payroll register is used to record all the essential payroll information for all employees for a specific payroll period.

- Explain that the amount of federal income tax withheld from an employee's gross pay is determined by the employee's marital status and number of dependents.

- Explain that total hours recorded in the payroll register are taken directly from the employee hours worked report.

- Point out that the store manager and the department supervisor are not paid on an hourly basis. Therefore, a dash is placed in the Total Hours column for these employees.

- Explain that each business is unique and may design a payroll register to accumulate information appropriate for the business as well as information required for federal and state reports.

- Explain that Zytech has three different types of earnings—regular, overtime, and commissions. To record each type, a separate column is provided in Zytech's payroll register for each type of earnings.

- Prepare a transparency of a payroll register. Use the transparency or the illustrations on this page and the next page to illustrate entries in the payroll register form.

- From data for a selected employee, record each item on the payroll register form, following the nine steps shown to prepare a payroll register.

- Emphasize the importance of accuracy.

PREPARING A PAYROLL REGISTER (LEFT PAGE)

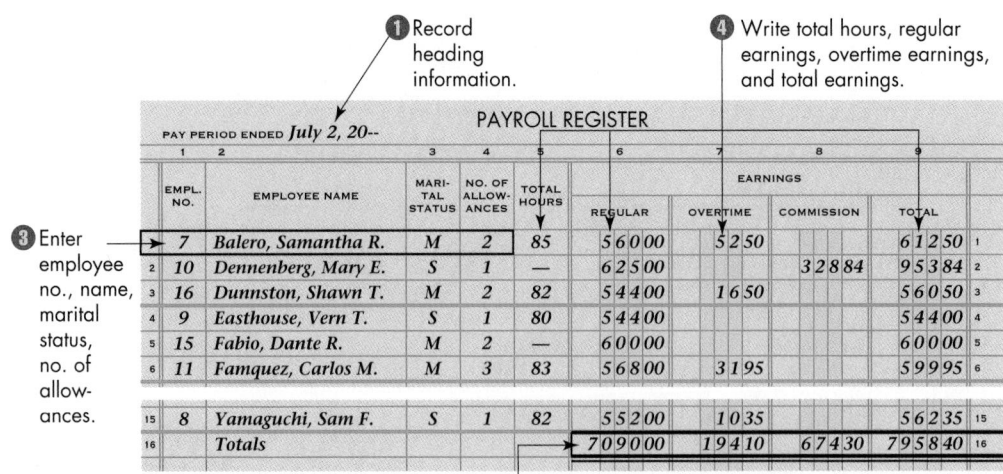

1 Record heading information.

4 Write total hours, regular earnings, overtime earnings, and total earnings.

3 Enter employee no., name, marital status, no. of allow-ances.

9 Total each amount column.

A business form used to record payroll information is called a **payroll register**. A payroll register summarizes the payroll for one pay period and shows total earnings, amounts withheld, and net pay for all employees. Zytech prepares a separate payroll register for each biweekly (every two weeks) payroll.

To provide better cost control, Zytech separates employee earnings into three classifications:

Audio Department, Video Department, and Administrative. The earnings of salesclerks and departmental managers are recorded in their respective departmental classification. The earnings of the store manager and accounting and office employees are recorded in the Administrative classification.

STEPS • STEPS • STEPS • STEPS • STEPS • STEPS • STEPS • STEPS • STEPS • STEPS

PREPARING A PAYROLL REGISTER

For each pay period:

1 Enter the last day of the biweekly payroll period, *July 2, 20--,* at the top of the payroll register.

2 Record the date of payment, *July 9, 20--,* also at the top of the payroll register. The time between the end of a pay period and the date of payment is needed in order to prepare the payroll records and payroll checks.

For each employee:

3 Enter employee number, *7;* name, *Balero, Samantha R.;* marital status, *M;* and number of allowances, *2,* in columns 1, 2, 3, and 4. This information is taken from personnel records kept for each employee.

4 Write total hours, *85;* regular earnings, *$560.00;* overtime earnings, *$52.50;* and total earnings, *$612.50,* in columns 5, 6, 7, and 9. The hours are from the employee hours worked report, and the earnings are calculated.

Department supervisors are not paid by the hour; therefore, a line is drawn through the Total Hours column, column 5, as shown on line 2 of the payroll register. The amount of a commission is entered in column 8. The salary amount is recorded in the Regular Earnings column, column 6. Regular earnings and commission earnings are added together to determine total earnings for the biweekly pay period.

The salaries of the store manager and non-sales employees, such as accounting department employees, are entered in the Admin. Salaries column, column 12 of the payroll register shown above.

5 Extend total earnings to the appropriate department column or Administrative Salaries.

TEACHING STRATEGIES DIFFERENT LEARNING ABILITIES

Limited English Proficiency (LEP) Students. Adjust the length of time allotted to complete assignments and tests. Remember that the primary objective is to assess knowledge of accounting rather than the ability to translate and comprehend the question or problem.

5 Record total earnings by department.

2 Record date of payment.

6 Enter payroll deductions.

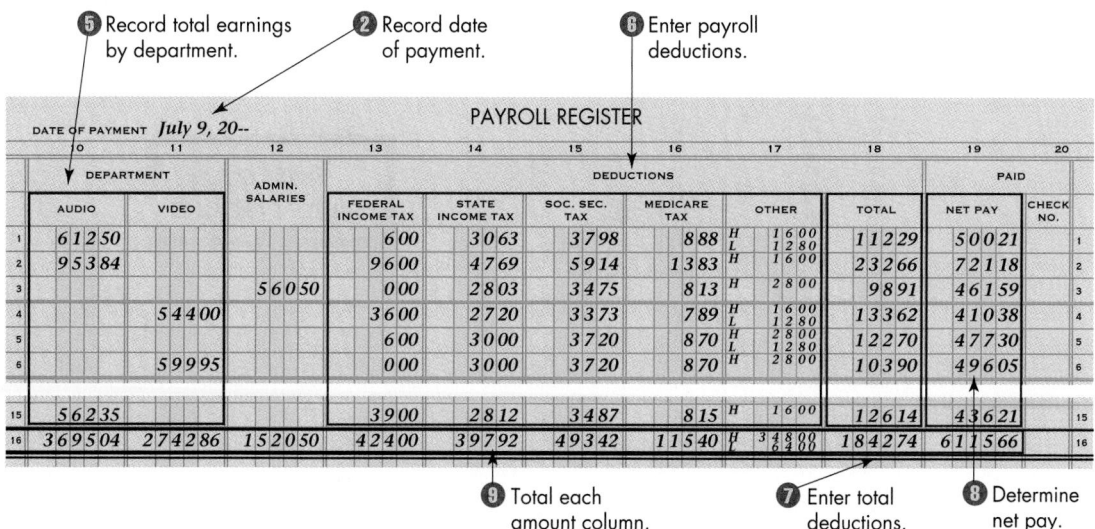

PAYROLL REGISTER

DATE OF PAYMENT *July 9, 20--*

	DEPARTMENT		ADMIN. SALARIES	DEDUCTIONS						PAID		
	AUDIO	VIDEO		FEDERAL INCOME TAX	STATE INCOME TAX	SOC. SEC. TAX	MEDICARE TAX	OTHER		TOTAL	NET PAY	CHECK NO.
1	6 12 50			6 00	30 63	37 98	8 88	H 16 00 / L 12 80		112 29	500 21	1
2	9 53 84			96 00	47 69	59 14	13 83	H 16 00		232 66	721 18	2
3			5 60 50	0 00	28 03	34 75	8 13	H 28 00		98 91	461 59	3
4		5 44 00		36 00	27 20	33 73	7 89	H 16 00 / L 12 80		133 62	410 38	4
5				6 00	30 00	37 20	8 70	H 28 00 / L 12 80		122 70	477 30	5
6		5 99 95		0 00	30 00	37 20	8 70	H 28 00		103 90	496 05	6
15	5 62 35			39 00	28 12	34 87	8 15	H 16 00		126 14	436 21	15
16	3 695 04	2 742 86	1 520 50	424 00	397 92	493 42	115 40	H 348 00 / L 64 00		1 842 74	6 115 66	16

9 Total each amount column.

7 Enter total deductions.

8 Determine net pay.

6 Enter the payroll deductions: federal income tax, *$6.00;* state income tax, *$30.63;* social security tax, *$37.98;* Medicare tax, *$8.88;* health insurance, *$16.00;* and life insurance, *$12.80.* Federal income tax withholding is calculated using withholding tables, such as the ones shown on page 66. The state in which Zytech operates calculates state income tax at 5% of total earnings. Samantha Balero's social security tax deduction for the biweekly pay period ended July 2 is calculated as shown here.

Total Earnings	×	Social Security Tax Rate	×	Social Security Tax Deduction
$612.50	×	6.2%	×	$37.98

Ms. Balero's Medicare tax deduction for the biweekly pay period ended July 2 is calculated as shown here.

Total Earnings	×	Medicare Tax Rate	=	Medicare Tax Deduction
$612.50	×	1.45%	=	$8.88

The health insurance deduction is $16.00 per biweekly pay period for each insured single employee claiming one allowance and each married employee who chooses single coverage. The deduction is $28.00 for all other married employees and single employees who claim more than one dependent. The health insurance deduction is identified by writing the letter *H* in front of the amount. The life insurance deduction is $12.80 per biweekly pay period for employees desiring life insurance. The deduction is identified by writing the letter *L* in front of the amount.

7 Add the amounts for deductions and enter the total, *$112.29,* in column 18.

8 Subtract the total deductions from total earnings to determine net pay, *$500.21.* The net pay for Samantha Balero is calculated as shown here.

Total Earnings (column 9)	−	Total Deductions (column 18)	=	Net Pay (column 19)
$612.50	−	$112.29	=	$500.21

At the end of the payroll period:

9 When the net pay has been entered for all employees, total each payroll register amount column. Subtract the Total Deductions column, $1,842.75, from the Total Earnings column. The result should equal the total of the Net Pay column. If the totals do not agree, find and correct the errors. Rule the payroll register.

65

EXPLAIN

- Explain that each employee is required to complete an Employee's Withholding Allowance Certificate, which provides the information needed by an employer to calculate the employee's income tax.

- Explain that to simplify the process for employers to calculate employees' income tax withholding, the federal government prepares a series of employee's income tax withholding tables.

- Explain that a table is made for single and married persons for the various payroll periods—weekly, biweekly, semimonthly, monthly, and daily or miscellaneous. Each table has columns for number of dependents and horizontal lines for the different wage brackets.

- Explain that employers determine each employee's federal income tax withholding for each pay period with these tables.

DEMONSTRATE

- Prepare a transparency of the tax withholding table for married persons or direct students to the illustration.

- Determine the amount of federal income tax withholding for Samantha Balero, following the three steps shown.

- Ask students to determine the amount of tax withholdings for two or three additional situations—given wages and number of dependents.

- Ask a student to provide his or her answer. Ask another student if the answer provided is correct.

BIWEEKLY SINGLE PERSONS

If the wages are—		And the number of withholding allowances claimed is—										
At least	But less than	0	1	2	3	4	5	6	7	8	9	10
		The amount of income tax to be withheld is—										
450	460	39	23	11	0	0	0	0	0	0	0	0
460	470	41	24	12	1	0	0	0	0	0	0	0
470	480	42	25	13	2	0	0	0	0	0	0	0
480	490	44	26	14	3	0	0	0	0	0	0	0
490	500	45	28	15	4	0	0	0	0	0	0	0
500	520	48	30	17	5	0	0	0	0	0	0	0
520	540	51	33	19	7	0	0	0	0	0	0	0
540	560	54	36	21	9	0	0	0	0	0	0	0
560	580	57	39	23	11	0	0	0	0	0	0	0
580	600	60	42	25	13	1	0	0	0	0	0	0
600	620	63	45	27	15	3	0	0	0	0	0	0
620	640	66	48	30	17	5	0	0	0	0	0	0
640	660	69	51	33	19	7	0	0	0	0	0	0
660	680	72	54	36	21	9	0	0	0	0	0	0
680	700	75	57	39	23	11	0	0	0	0	0	0
700	720	78	60	42	25	13	1	0	0	0	0	0
720	740	81	63	45	27	15	3	0	0	0	0	0
740	760	84	66	48	30	17	5	0	0	0	0	0
760	780	87	69	51	33	19	7	0	0	0	0	0
780	800	90	72	54	36	21	9	0	0	0	0	0
800	820	93	75	57	39	23	11	0	0	0	0	0
820	840	96	78	60	42	25	13	1	0	0	0	0
840	860	99	81	63	45	27	15	3	0	0	0	0
860	880	102	84	66	48	30	17	5	0	0	0	0
880	900	105	87	69	51	33	19	7	0	0	0	0
900	920	108	90	72	54	36	21	9	0	0	0	0
920	940	111	93	75	57	39	23	11	0	0	0	0
940	960	114	96	78	60	42	25	13	1	0	0	0
960	980	117	99	81	63	45	27	15	3	0	0	0
980	1,000	120	102	84	66	48	30	17	5	0	0	0

MARRIED Persons—BIWEEKLY Payroll Period

BIWEEKLY MARRIED PERSONS

If the wages are—		And the number of withholding allowances claimed is—										
At least	But less than	0	1	2	3	4	5	6	7	8	9	10
		The amount of income tax to be withheld is—										
440	450	14	2	0	0	0	0					0
450	460	15	3	0	0	0	0					0
460	470	16	4	0	0	0	0					0
470	480	17	5	0	0	0	0					0
480	490	18	6	0	0	0	0					0
490	500	19	7	0	0	0	0					0
500	520	20	8	0	0	0	0					0
520	540	22	10	0	0	0	0					0
540	560	24	12	0	0	0	0	0	0	0	0	0
560	580	26	14	2	0	0	0	0	0	0	0	0
580	600	28	16	4	0	0	0	0	0	0	0	0
600	620	30	18	6	0	0	0	0	0	0	0	0
620	640	32	20	8	0	0	0	0	0	0	0	0
640	660	34	22	10	0	0	0	0	0	0	0	0
660	680	36	24	12	0	0	0	0	0	0	0	0
680	700	38	26	14	2	0	0	0	0	0	0	0
700	720	40	28	16	4	0	0	0	0	0	0	0
720	740	42	30	18	6	0	0	0	0	0	0	0
740	760	44	32	20	8	0	0	0	0	0	0	0
760	780	46	34	22	10	0	0	0	0	0	0	0
1,380	1,400	135	117	99	81	63	49	37	25	13	1	0
1,400	1,420	138	120	102	84	66	51	39	27	15	3	0
1,420	1,440	141	123	105	87	69	53	41	29	17	5	0
1,440	1,460	144	126	108	90	72	55	43	31	19	7	0
1,460	1,480	147	129	111	93	75	57	45	33	21	9	0
1,480	1,500	150	132	114	96	78	60	47	35	23	11	0
1,500	1,520	153	135	117	99	81	63	49	37	25	13	1

1. Locate the range containing the total earnings.

2. Find the column with the correct number of withholding allowances.

3. Find the intersection of the row and column.

STEPS

STEPS • STEPS • STEPS • STEPS • STEPS • STEPS • STEPS • STEPS • STEPS • STEPS

EXAMPLE: SAMANTHA BALERO IS MARRIED AND CLAIMS 2 WITHHOLDING ALLOWANCES. HER TOTAL EARNINGS FOR THE PAY PERIOD ARE $612.50.

1. Use the left two columns of the Biweekly Married Persons tax table shown here to locate the range containing the total earnings—*At least 600 but less than 620.*

2. Find the column with the correct number of withholding allowances, *2.*

3. Find the intersection of the row and column. The amount of income tax to be withheld is *$6.00.*

PREPARING AN EMPLOYEE EARNINGS RECORD

2 Enter heading information.

1 Write last day of quarter.

3 Record beginning accumulated earnings.

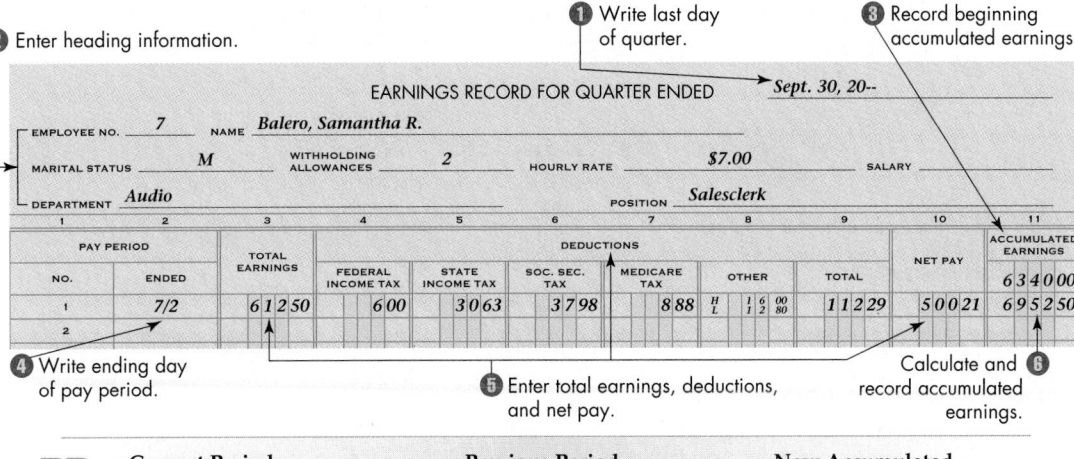

PAY PERIOD		TOTAL EARNINGS	DEDUCTIONS						NET PAY	ACCUMULATED EARNINGS
			FEDERAL INCOME TAX	STATE INCOME TAX	SOC. SEC. TAX	MEDICARE TAX	OTHER	TOTAL		
NO.	ENDED									6 3 4 0 00
1	7/2	6 1 2 50	6 00	3 0 63	3 7 98	8 88	H L 1 6 00 / 2 80	1 1 2 29	5 0 0 21	6 9 5 2 50
2										

EARNINGS RECORD FOR QUARTER ENDED   *Sept. 30, 20--*

EMPLOYEE NO. __7__   NAME *Balero, Samantha R.*

MARITAL STATUS *M*   WITHHOLDING ALLOWANCES *2*   HOURLY RATE *$7.00*   SALARY

DEPARTMENT *Audio*   POSITION *Salesclerk*

4 Write ending day of pay period.

5 Enter total earnings, deductions, and net pay.

6 Calculate and record accumulated earnings.

- Explain that a business must send a quarterly report to federal and state governments showing employee taxable earnings and taxes withheld from employee earnings. The employee earnings record is the form used to record the information needed for these reports.

- Emphasize that an earnings record is maintained for each employee.

- Explain that information for the earnings record is taken from the payroll register each pay period.

DEMONSTRATE

- Prepare a transparency of the employee earnings record. Use the transparency or the illustration to show entries in the earnings record.

- Record each item in the earnings record, following the six steps shown.

- Direct students to the math box to demonstrate the calculation of new accumulated earnings.

- Emphasize that accumulated earnings are the earnings the employee has earned for the year through the current pay period.

- Emphasize that total earnings, not the net pay, are added to the accumulated earnings.

ONGOING ASSESSMENT

- Assessment is an ongoing process. Circulate through the classroom or lab, observing which students have problems with the assignments.

- Troubleshooting: Diagnose what kinds of problems students have with this section. This section presents the procedures for preparing a commissions record, a payroll register, and an employee earnings record. Students may have trouble proving both the payroll register and employee earnings record. Students may need to be reminded that total earnings, not net pay, are added to the accumulated earnings.

- Assess student understanding by checking solutions to Independent Practice assignments.

	Current Period Total Earnings	+	Previous Period Accumulated Earnings	=	New Accumulated Earnings
	$612.50	+	$6,340.00	=	$6,952.50

A business must send a quarterly report to federal and state governments showing employee taxable earnings and taxes withheld from employee earnings. Detailed information about each employee's earnings is summarized in a single record for each employee. A business form used to record details affecting payments made to an employee is called an **employee earnings record**. An employee's total earnings and deductions for each pay period are summarized on one line of the employee earnings record.

Zytech prepares a new earnings record for each employee each quarter. Samantha Balero's earnings record for the third quarter is shown here.

Accumulated earnings are often referred to as *year-to-date earnings*. Accumulated earnings are needed for each employee because certain payroll taxes do not apply after an employee's earnings reach a certain tax base. For example, employers pay federal and state unemployment taxes only on the first $7,000.00 of each employee's earnings during a calendar year. Social security taxes also are paid only on a maximum amount determined by law. A tax base of $87,000.00 is used in this text. Medicare tax does not have a tax base. Therefore, Medicare tax is calculated on total employee earnings.

STEPS • STEPS • STEPS • STEPS • STEPS • STEPS • STEPS • STEPS • STEPS • STEPS •
PREPARING AN EMPLOYEE EARNINGS RECORD

1 Write the last day of the yearly quarter, *Sept. 30, 20--*, at the top of the earnings record.

2 Enter the employee's number, name, marital status, withholding allowances, hourly rate or salary, department, and position in the appropriate space. This information is taken from the employee's personnel records.

3 Record the fiscal year's accumulated earnings, *$6,340.00,* for the beginning of the current quarter. This information is taken from the ending accumulated earnings for the previous quarter. The Accumulated Earnings column of the employee earnings record shows the accumulated earnings since the beginning of the fiscal year.

4 Write the ending date of the current pay period, *7/2.*

5 Enter the total earnings, deductions, and net pay in the assigned columns of the earnings record. This information is taken from the current pay period's payroll register.

6 Calculate and record the new accumulated earnings, *$6,952.50,* on the same line as the other payroll information for the pay period ended July 2.

Completing Payroll Records for Employee Earnings and Deductions   Lesson 3-1   **67**

RETEACH

- Provide the payroll and withholdings information for several employees. Have students calculate the total deductions and net pay.

- Provide a partially completed employee's earnings record for each of the

employees in the point above. Have students calculate the accumulated earnings.

GUIDED PRACTICE

Terms Review

Call on students to define each term in the Terms Review. After each definition, ask the class if the definition is correct and whether the complete definition has been given or if anything needs to be added. Suggested definitions are given in the Glossary.

Audit Your Understanding

Call on students to answer the Audit Your Understanding questions. Ask the class if the answer is correct and/or complete. Answers are given in Appendix E of the textbook.

Work Together

Have students write the solution to the Work Together problems, as you guide the class through the examples.

- Direct students to record each entry in the commissions record, payroll register, and earnings record as you elicit class participation in calculating and recording each entry.

- Direct students to prepare the employee's earnings record as you elicit class participation in calculating accumulated earnings.

• terms review

salary
pay period
payroll
payroll taxes
withholding allowance
tax base
payroll register
employee earnings record

• audit your understanding

1. What three federal taxes are withheld from an employee's pay?
2. How is the amount of federal income tax withholding determined?
3. What is the formula for calculating net pay on the payroll register?
4. What amount is added to the accumulated earnings to get the new accumulated earnings to date?

• work together 3-1

Completing payroll records

Santa Clara Hardware's partial payroll register for the pay period ended July 3, 20-- and a blank earnings record form are provided in the *Working Papers*. Use the appropriate withholding tax tables shown in this lesson to determine the federal income tax. Deductions for all employees are 5% of total earnings for state income tax, 6.2% for social security tax, and 1.45% for Medicare tax. Use *H* to indicate health insurance and *L* to indicate life insurance. Your instructor will guide you through the following examples. Save your work to complete Work Together 3-2.

1. Prepare a commissions record for Allison Cavero, Supervisor of the Hardware Department, for June of the current year. Ms. Cavero, Employee No. 2, is paid a biweekly salary of $1,200.00 and receives a monthly commission of 1% of net sales. Commissions for the previous month are paid in the first pay period of the current month. Accounting records for the Hardware Department for the month ended June 30 of the current year are as follows: sales on account, $17,895.00; cash and credit card sales, $15,523.00; sales discount, $179.00; sales returns and allowances, $2,039.00.

2. Prepare the payroll register entries for the following two employees:
   a. On line 1: Allison Cavero, Employee No. 2, Hardware Department supervisor, married, two allowances, regular salary of $1,200.00 per pay period plus 1% of net sales. Use the commission calculated in instruction 1. Health insurance premium is $56.00, and life insurance premium is $25.60.
   b. On line 4: James Lee, Employee No. 4, Hardware Department salesclerk, single, one allowance, regular salary of $10.00 per hour with overtime paid at 1½ times the regular rate. He worked 80 hours regular time and 8 hours overtime. Health insurance premium is $28.00.

3. Prepare James Lee's earnings record for the first pay period of the quarter ended September 30, 20--. Accumulated earnings for the quarter ended June 30, 20-- are $11,900.00.

68

• on your own 3-1

Completing payroll records

Santa Clara Hardware's partial payroll register for the pay period ended October 2, 20-- and a blank earnings record form are provided in the *Working Papers.* Use the appropriate withholding tax tables to determine the federal income tax. Deductions for all employees are 5% of total earnings for state income tax, 6.2% for social security tax, and 1.45% for Medicare tax. Use *H* to indicate health insurance and *L* to indicate life insurance. Work this problem independently. Save your work to complete On Your Own 3-2.

1. Prepare a commissions record for Karla Ramirez, Supervisor of the Paint Department, for September of the current year. Ms. Ramirez, Employee No. 5, is paid a biweekly salary of $1,100.00 and receives a monthly commission of 1% of net sales. Commissions for the previous month are paid in the first pay period of the current month. Accounting records for the Paint Department for the month ended September 30 of the current year are as follows: sales on account, $18,561.20; cash and credit card sales, $13,970.80; sales discount, $196.90; sales returns and allowances, $1,835.10.

2. Prepare the payroll register entries for the following two employees:
   a. On line 11: Karla Ramirez, Employee No. 5, Paint Department supervisor, married, one allowance, regular salary of $1,100.00 per pay period plus 1% of net sales. Use the commission calculated in instruction 1. Health insurance premium is $28.00, and life insurance premium is $25.60.
   b. On line 12: Aaron Sutphin, Employee No. 12, Paint Department salesclerk, single, one allowance, regular salary of $9.50 per hour with overtime paid at 1½ times the regular rate. Sutphin worked 80 hours regular time and 10 hours overtime. Health insurance premium is $28.00.

3. Prepare Aaron Sutphin's earnings record for the first pay period of the quarter ended December 31, 20--. Accumulated earnings for the quarter ended September 30, 20-- are $19,000.00.

Completing Payroll Records for Employee Earnings and Deductions

Lesson 3-1   **69**

On Your Own

- Assign the On Your Own problems to be worked independently.
- Use the Ongoing Assessment techniques to diagnose student understanding.

Application Problems

- Assign Application Problem 3-1: Preparing departmental commissions records.
- Assign Application Problem 3-2: Completing a payroll register.
- Assign Application Problem 3-3: Completing an employee earnings record.

Personal Trainer

- Students can access the Lesson 3-1 assessment material using this software.

Xtra! Web Site

- Students can access the Xtra! Study Tools for additional practice.

ENRICH

- Assign students the Accounting in the Real World and Making Ethical Decisions features. Divide students into cooperative learning groups of 3–4 students. Have students work on their oral communication skills and SCANS competencies by asking a student from each group to present the group's answers.

CLOSE

- Ask students to briefly summarize the procedure for preparing a payroll register.
- Ask students to summarize the procedure for preparing an employee earnings record.

LESSON · LESSON · LESSON · LESSON · LESSON · LES

3-2 Recording a Payroll and Payroll Taxes

PAYROLL BANK ACCOUNT

Zytech pays its employees biweekly by check. A special payroll checking account and special payroll checks are used. After a biweekly payroll register has been completed, a check is written on Zytech's general checking account payable to Payroll for the total net pay. This check is deposited in a special payroll checking account against which payroll checks are written for each employee's net pay.

The amount of the biweekly deposit to the payroll account equals the sum of the biweekly salary payments. The special payroll account balance, therefore, is reduced to zero as soon as all employees have cashed their payroll checks. Because the special payroll bank account has a balance only until all payroll checks are cashed, no special account is needed in the general ledger.

AUTOMATIC CHECK DEPOSIT

Employees may authorize an employer to deposit payroll checks directly in their checking accounts at a specified bank. Depositing payroll checks directly to an employee's checking or savings account in a specific bank is called **automatic check deposit**. When automatic check deposit is used, the employer sends the check to the employee's bank for deposit.

Employers may also transfer payroll checks electronically from the employer's account directly to the employee's bank account. A computerized cash payments system that transfers funds without the use of checks, currency, or other paper documents is called **electronic funds transfer (EFT)**. Electronic funds transfer eliminates the need for preparing payroll checks. Under this system, each employee receives a statement of earnings and deductions similar to the detachable stub on a payroll check.

The use of automatic check deposit or electronic funds transfer for payroll does not change the accounting procedures for recording payroll. [CONCEPT: Consistent Reporting]

EMPLOYER PAYROLL TAXES

Most employers have four separate payroll taxes:

1. Employer social security tax
2. Medicare tax
3. Federal unemployment tax
4. State unemployment tax

Unemployment taxes are used to pay cash benefits to qualified workers for limited periods of unemployment.

FYI FOR YOUR INFORMATION

Federal income tax, social security tax, and Medicare tax withheld from employee earnings are taxes paid by the employee. The employer does not pay federal income tax on a payroll. However, an employer does pay the employer's share of social security and Medicare taxes.

JOURNALIZING PAYMENT OF A PAYROLL

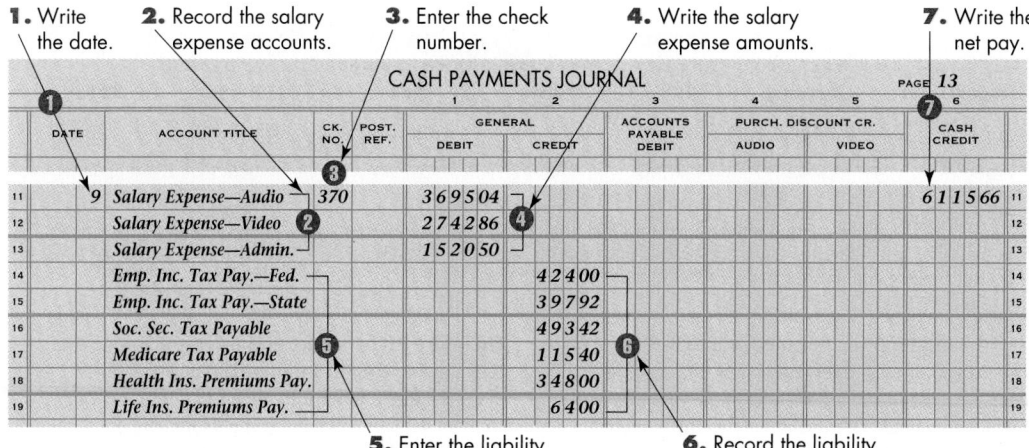

1. Write the date. **2.** Record the salary expense accounts. **3.** Enter the check number. **4.** Write the salary expense amounts. **7.** Write the net pay.

5. Enter the liability accounts. **6.** Record the liability amounts.

Zytech's payroll register contains the information needed to journalize a payroll as shown in the cash payments journal. The source document for journalizing a payroll payment is the check written for the net payroll amount. [*CONCEPT: Objective Evidence*]

July 9. Paid cash for biweekly payroll, $6,115.66 (total payroll: audio, $3,695.04; video, $2,742.86; administrative, $1,520.50; less deductions: employee income tax—federal, $424.00; employee income tax—state, $397.92; social security tax, $493.42; Medicare tax, $115.40; health insurance, $348.00; life insurance, $64.00). Check No. 370.

The T accounts show the debits and credits to all affected accounts.

Salary Expense—Audio		Social Security Tax Payable	
3,695.04			493.42

Salary Expense—Video		Medicare Tax Payable	
2,742.86			115.40

Salary—Expense Administrative		Health Insurance Premiums Payable	
1,520.50			348.00

Employee Income Tax Payable—Federal		Life Insurance Premiums Federal	
	424.00		64.00

Employee Income Tax Payable—State		Cash	
	397.92		6,115.66

STEPS • STEPS • STEPS • STEPS • STEPS • STEPS • STEPS • STEPS • STEPS • STEPS • STEPS •

JOURNALIZING PAYMENT OF A PAYROLL

1 Write the date, *9*, in the Date column of the cash payments journal.

2 Record the salary expense accounts, *Salary Expense—Audio*, *Salary Expense—Video*, *Salary Expense—Admin.*, in the Account Title column.

3 Enter the check number, *370*, in the Ck. No. column.

4 Write the salary expense amounts, *$3,695.04*, *$2,742.86*, and *$1,520.50*, in the General Debit column.

5 Enter the liability accounts, *Emp. Inc. Tax Pay.—Fed.*, *Emp. Inc. Tax Pay.—State*, *Soc. Sec. Tax Pay.*, *Medicare Tax Pay.*, *Health Ins. Premiums Pay.*, and *Life Ins. Premiums Pay.*, in the Account Title column.

6 Record the liability amounts, *$424.00*, *$397.92*, *$493.42*, *$115.40*, *$348.00*, and *$64.00*, in the General Credit column.

7 Write the net pay, *$6,115.66*, in the Cash Credit column.

EXPLAIN

- Explain that the payroll register column totals are the source of information needed to prepare a journal entry for the payroll.
- Explain that the departmental total earnings columns of the payroll register are the debit amounts for departmental salary expense.
- Explain that the net pay column is the credit amount for Cash.
- Explain that all other columns provide the credit parts of the entry. These credits become liabilities so if you add payable to the end of each column heading, you have the liability account.
- Explain that since cash is paid out (net pay to employees), the payroll transaction is recorded in a cash payments journal.
- Since this journal entry uses a multiple-line entry, it is important to reinforce the concept that debits must always equal credits.
- Read the transaction statement.

DEMONSTRATE

Analyze the transaction

- Use the transparency prepared for the previous lesson to review the information recorded in the various columns of a payroll register.
- Draw T accounts on the board.
- Read each column total from the payroll register.
- Ask students to analyze the treatment of each column total by determining: if the total is part of the payroll entry, what account the amount should be entered in, and whether it is a debit or credit entry. Complete the T accounts as the information is provided.
- Emphasize that only the column totals for departmental total earnings are journalized.

Record the transaction

- Prepare a transparency of a cash payments journal to illustrate journalizing the payroll transaction or direct students to the illustration.
- Record each item in the journal following the seven steps shown.
- Add the debit entries and add the credit entries to show that the total debit entries equal the total credit entries.

- Remind students that employers pay four separate payroll taxes: Two are the same amounts withheld from employees' pay—(1) social security tax and (2) Medicare tax. Two additional payroll taxes the employer must pay are (1) federal unemployment tax and (2) state unemployment tax.

- Explain that the total earnings subject to unemployment tax is referred to as *unemployment taxable earnings.*

- Explain that unemployment taxable earnings is calculated by subtracting accumulated earnings from $7,000.00, the unemployment tax base.

- Explain that information for calculating the unemployment taxable earnings is found on the employee's earnings record and the current payroll register.

- Explain that the effective tax rate in most states is 0.8% for federal unemployment tax and 5.4% for state unemployment tax. Both taxes are paid on the first $7,000.00 of each employee's earnings each year.

- Emphasize that payroll taxes are a direct result of the employees working in each department. For this reason, payroll taxes are reported by department.

- Emphasize that the total of all employer payroll taxes is an expense to the business.

Department	Taxable Earnings	Social Security 6.2%	Medicare 1.45%	Federal Unemployment 0.8%	State Unemployment 5.4%	Total
Audio	$3,695.04	$229.09	$ 53.58	$29.56	$199.53	$ 511.76
Video	2,742.86	170.06	39.77	21.94	148.11	379.88
Administrative	1,520.50	94.27	22.05	12.16	82.11	210.59
Total	$7,958.40	$493.42	$115.40	$63.66	$429.75	$1,102.23

Employer payroll taxes expense is based on a percentage of employee earnings. The employer social security tax (6.2%) and Medicare tax (1.45%) rates are the same as the rates used for employees. The federal unemployment tax is 6.2% of the first $7,000.00 earned by each employee. An employer generally can deduct the amounts paid to state unemployment funds from federal unemployment payments. This deduction cannot be more than 5.4% of taxable earnings. The effective federal unemployment tax rate in most states is, therefore, 0.8% on the first $7,000.00 earned by each employee. (Federal 6.2% − deductible for state 5.4% = 0.8%.) The employer pays all of the unemployment tax on the first $7,000.00 of salary.

Employees in a few states have deductions from their earnings for state unemployment tax. Employees do not pay federal unemployment tax.

None of Zytech's employees has earned $7,000.00 by the pay period ended July 2.

Therefore, Zytech's federal unemployment tax is 0.8% of $7,958.40 total earnings, or $63.67. Zytech's state unemployment tax is 5.4% of $7,958.40 total earnings, or $429.75.

Zytech reports employee earnings by department in order to be able to determine what expenses were incurred in earning a department's revenue. Likewise, some of Zytech's expenses are assigned to individual departments when they are directly related to the department. Payroll taxes are a direct result of the employees working in each department. Therefore, payroll taxes expenses are also reported by department.

The department salary column totals of the payroll register are used to calculate the employer's payroll taxes for each department. The calculations are summarized in the table at the top of the page. The calculations for the Audio Department are shown below as an example.

- Review the calculations shown in the illustration at the top of the page. Ask students to identify the page of the illustrations that show total taxable earnings (*page 64*), total social security tax (*page 65*), and total Medicare tax (*page 65*) for the pay period.

- Review the calculations shown in the illustration at the bottom of the page.

	Total Taxable Earnings		Tax Rate		Audio Department Tax
Social Security	$3,695.04	×	6.2%	=	$229.09
Medicare	$3,695.04	×	1.45%	=	53.58
Unemployment—Federal	$3,695.04	×	0.8%	=	29.56
Unemployment—State	$3,695.04	×	5.4%	=	199.53
Total Audio Department Payroll Taxes Expense					$511.76

Calculating and Recording Departmental Payroll Data

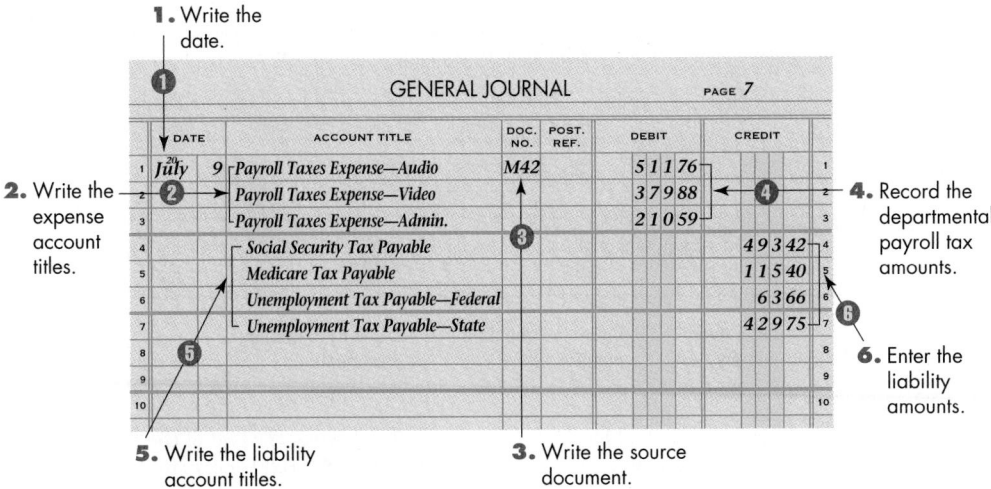

1. Write the date.

2. Write the expense account titles.

5. Write the liability account titles.

3. Write the source document.

4. Record the departmental payroll tax amounts.

6. Enter the liability amounts.

July 9. Recorded employer payroll taxes for the biweekly pay period ended July 2. Taxes owed are social security tax, $493.42; Medicare tax, $115.40; federal unemployment tax, $63.66; state unemployment tax, $429.75; total payroll taxes by department are Audio, $511.76; Video, $379.88; and Administrative, $210.59. Memorandum No. 42.

The journal entry to record the employer's payroll taxes is shown in the general journal above.

Payroll Taxes Expense—Audio		Medicare Tax Payable	
511.76			115.40

Payroll Taxes Expense—Video		Unemployment Tax Payable—Federal	
379.88			63.66

Payroll Taxes Expense—Administrative		Unemployment Tax Payable—State	
210.59			429.75

Social Security Tax Payable	
	493.42

STEPS • STEPS • STEPS • STEPS • STEPS • STEPS • STEPS • STEPS • STEPS •

STEPS JOURNALIZING EMPLOYER PAYROLL TAXES

1 Write the date, *July 9,* in the Date column of the general journal.

2 Write the expense account titles, *Payroll Taxes Expense—Audio, Payroll Taxes Expense—Video,* and *Payroll Taxes Expense—Admin.,* in the Account Title column.

3 Enter the source document, *M42,* in the Doc. No. column.

4 Record the amount of payroll taxes expense, *$511.76, $379.88,* and *$210.59,* in the debit column.

5 Enter the liability account titles, *Social Security Tax Payable, Medicare Tax Payable, Unemploy. Tax Payable—Fed.,* and *Unemploy. Tax Payable—State,* in the Account Title column.

6 Enter the liability amounts, *$493.42, $115.40, $63.66,* and *$429.75,* in the Credit column.

Recording a Payroll and Payroll Taxes

FYI FOR YOUR INFORMATION

Rounding differences can occur when percentage calculations are performed on parts of a total amount and then compared with the percentage of the total. For example, in the calculations on the previous page, federal unemployment tax calculations for the departments resulted in amounts of $29.56, $21.94, and $12.16, for a total of $63.66. However, if the federal unemployment tax rate of 0.8% is applied to the total payroll amount, $7,958.40, the result is $63.6672, which would be rounded to $63.67.

Lesson 3-2   **73**

EXPLAIN

- Explain that the frequency and method of payment of withheld employees' federal income tax, social security tax, and Medicare tax plus employer's social security tax and Medicare tax is determined by the total amount of tax paid each year.

- Explain that businesses with large amounts of payroll taxes must pay the amounts every few days. Businesses with lesser amounts pay once a month.

- Have students read the F.Y.I. Point out that submitting payments through the Electronic Federal Tax Payment System (EFTPS) is much more efficient for the federal government to process. Consequently, it is likely that all businesses will eventually have to submit their taxes through the EFTPS.

- Explain that employees' withheld income taxes, social security taxes, and Medicare taxes are paid in one payment.

- Explain that a deposit coupon, Form 8109, accompanies the payment.

- Explain that paying the liabilities for employee income tax, social security tax, and Medicare tax is a reduction in the liability accounts and a reduction in the cash account; thus, the liability accounts are debited and Cash is credited.

- Ask students if any part of this transaction can be entered in a special column of the cash payments journal.

- Explain that the only account titles entered in the Account Title column are for those entries in the General Debit or General Credit columns.

DEMONSTRATE

Analyze the transaction

- Draw a stack of four blank T accounts on the board.

- Read the transaction statement.

- Ask students to analyze the transaction into debit and credit parts. Complete the T accounts as the information is provided.

Record the transaction

- Use a cash payments journal transparency to illustrate recording the transaction or direct students to the illustration.

- Record each item in the journal, following the five steps shown in the illustration.

JOURNALIZING PAYMENT OF FEDERAL INCOME TAX, SOCIAL SECURITY TAX, AND MEDICARE TAX LIABILITY

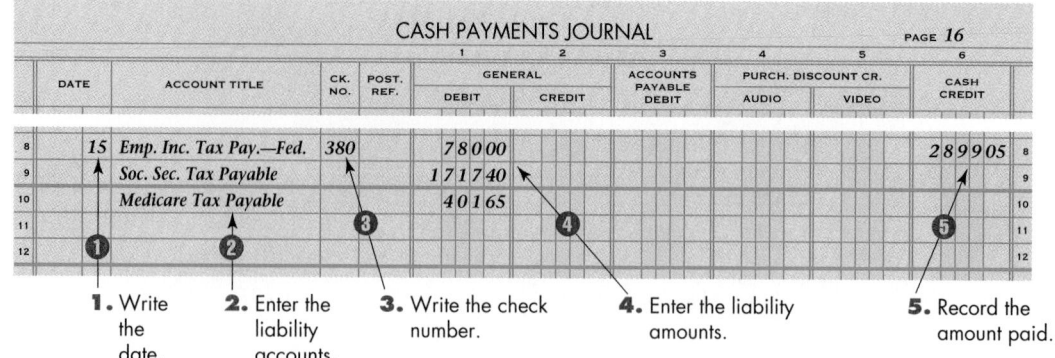

1. Write the date.
2. Enter the liability accounts.
3. Write the check number.
4. Enter the liability amounts.
5. Record the amount paid.

Employers must pay to federal, state, and local governments all payroll taxes withheld from employee earnings as well as the employer payroll taxes. The frequency of payments is determined by the amount owed.

Frequency and method of payment of withheld employees' federal income tax, social security tax, and Medicare tax plus employer's social security tax and Medicare tax are determined by the total amount of tax paid each year. If the total amount paid in the previous four quarters is $50,000 or less, a business is classified as a monthly schedule depositor. A monthly schedule depositor must pay the total amount due to an authorized financial institution by the 15th day of the following month accompanied by Form 8109, Federal Tax Deposit Coupon.

If the total amount paid in the previous four quarters is more than $50,000, a business is classified as a semiweekly schedule depositor. A semiweekly schedule depositor must deposit amounts accumulated on salary payments made on Saturday, Sunday, Monday, or Tuesday by the following Friday. For salary payments made on Wednesday, Thursday, or Friday, payment must be made by the following Wednesday. Companies depositing more than $200,000 in a calendar year must make payments directly to the Internal Revenue Service using the Electronic Federal Tax Payment System (EFTPS).

There are two exceptions to the standard tax payment schedules: (1) If less than $2,500 tax liability is accumulated during a three-month quarter, the deposit may be paid at the end of

the month following the end of the quarter. (2) If a tax liability of $100,000 or more is accumulated on any day, the amount must be deposited on the next banking day.

Zytech is classified as a monthly schedule depositor. The biweekly pay days are June 9 and 23. Therefore, the payroll taxes are deposited by August 15.

August 15. Paid cash for liability for employee federal income tax, $780.00, and for employees' and employer's social security tax, $1,717.40, and Medicare tax, $401.65; total, $2,899.05. Check No. 380.

Zytech's federal income tax, social security tax, and Medicare tax liabilities for the biweekly pay period ended July 2 and paid on July 9 are deposited on Friday, July 15 as shown here. Zytech's liability for state income tax withholding is paid at the end of each quarter.

FYI FOR YOUR INFORMATION

Methods of paying payroll taxes described on this page were in effect when this textbook was written. Businesses with payroll tax liabilities of more than $200,000.00 in 2003 must pay electronically using the EFTPS System. At some future date, all businesses probably will be required to pay payroll taxes electronically. The Treasury Department prefers receiving electronic payroll tax payments.

EXPLAIN (page 75)

- Explain that federal unemployment insurance is paid by the end of the month following each quarter if the liability amount is more than $100.00. Explain that the payment is paid to the federal government by sending the check to an authorized bank, accompanied by Form 8109.

- Explain that paying the liability for federal unemployment tax is a reduction in the liability account and a reduction in the cash account; thus, the liability account, Unemploy-

ment Tax Payable—Federal, is debited and Cash is credited.

- Ask students if any part of this transaction can be entered in a special column of the cash payments journal.

- Explain that the only account titles entered in the Account Title column are for those entries in the General Debit or General Credit column.

JOURNALIZING PAYMENT OF FEDERAL UNEMPLOYMENT TAX LIABILITY

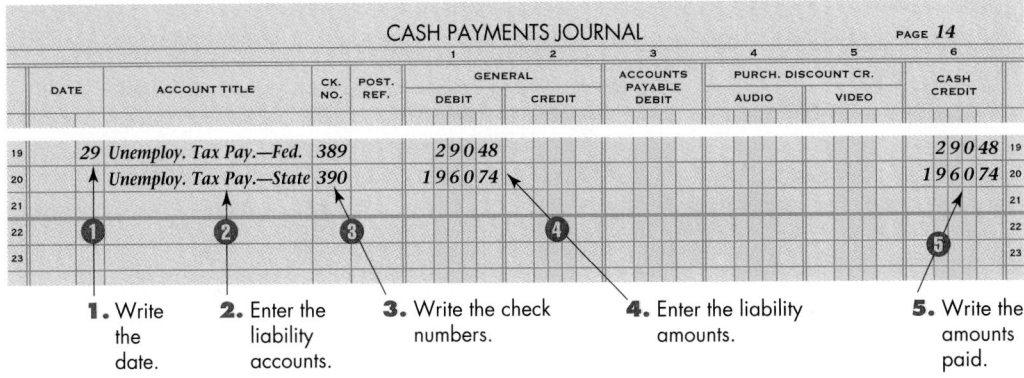

1. Write the date. **2.** Enter the liability accounts. **3.** Write the check numbers. **4.** Enter the liability amounts. **5.** Write the amounts paid.

If the annual federal unemployment tax for a business is $100.00 or less, it must pay the tax in one payment by January 31 of the following year. If its annual tax is more than $100.00, the business must make quarterly payments in the month following the end of the quarter.

Zytech's federal unemployment tax for the second quarter is $290.48. Therefore, it must make its payment during the first month of the following quarter, July.

July 29. Paid cash for federal unemployment tax liability for quarter ended June 30, $290.48. Check No. 389.

The T accounts show the debits and credits to all affected accounts.

Unemployment Tax Payable—Federal	
290.48	

Cash	
	290.48

JOURNALIZING PAYMENT OF STATE UNEMPLOYMENT TAX LIABILITY

Requirements for paying state unemployment taxes vary from state to state. Usually, employers are required to pay the state unemployment tax during the month following each calendar quarter.

Zytech's state unemployment tax for the second quarter is $1,960.74.

July 29. Paid cash for state unemployment tax liability for quarter ended June 30, $1,960.74. Check No. 390.

The T accounts show the debits and credits to all affected accounts.

Unemployment Tax Payable—State	
1,960.74	

Cash	
	1,960.74

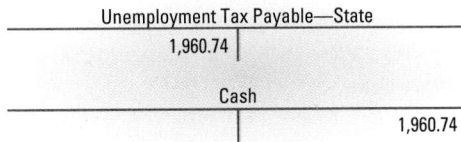

REMEMBER Employees do not pay federal unemployment tax.

Recording a Payroll and Payroll Taxes

Lesson 3-2 75

DEMONSTRATE

Analyze the transaction

- Draw two blank T accounts on the board.
- Read the transaction statement.
- Ask students to analyze the transaction into debit and credit parts. Complete the T accounts as the information is provided.

Record the transaction

- Use a cash payments journal transparency to illustrate recording the transaction in the cash payments journal or direct students to the illustration.
- Record each item in the journal, following the five steps shown.

EXPLAIN

- Explain that the transaction for payment of the liability for state unemployment tax is the same as for the liability for federal unemployment tax.

DEMONSTRATE

- Use the cash payments journal to illustrate recording the transaction in the cash payments journal or direct students to the illustration.
- Record each item in the journal, following the five steps shown in the illustration.

ONGOING ASSESSMENT

- Assessment is an ongoing process. Circulate through the classroom or lab, observing which students have problems with the assignments.
- Troubleshooting: Diagnose what kinds of problems students have with this lesson. Care must be taken to insure that all affected accounts are correctly entered in the journal since each account title except Cash must be entered in the Account Title column. Also, students must insure that total debits equal total credits for each transaction.
- Assess student understanding by checking solutions to Independent Practice assignments.

RETEACH

- Ask a student to make up an original payment of a payroll transaction statement. Write the statement on the board or an overhead transparency. Ask another student to tell how the transaction should be journalized, following the appropriate steps for journalizing payment of a payroll. Ask another student to make up an employer payroll taxes transaction using a company with two departments. Write the statement on the board. Ask another student to tell how the transaction should be journalized, following the appropriate steps.

GUIDED PRACTICE

Terms Review
Call on students to define each term in the Terms Review. After each definition, ask the class if the definition is correct and whether the complete definition has been given or if anything needs to be added. Suggested definitions are given in the Glossary.

Audit Your Understanding
Call on students to answer the Audit Your Understanding questions. Ask the class if the answer is correct and/or complete. Answers are given in Appendix E of the textbook.

Work Together
Have students write the solution to the Work Together problems as you guide the class through the examples.

- Direct students to record departmental payroll tax amounts as you elicit class participation in analyzing the transaction.
- Direct students to record each transaction in the cash payments or general journal as you elicit class participation in analyzing and recording the transaction.

INDEPENDENT PRACTICE

On Your Own
- Assign the On Your Own problems to be worked independently.
- Use the Ongoing Assessment techniques to diagnose student understanding.

Application Problems
- Assign Application Problem 3-4: Journalizing payment of a departmental payroll.
- Assign Application Problem 3-5: Calculating and journalizing payment of payroll tax liabilities.

Personal Trainer
- Students can access the Lesson 3-2 assessment material using this software.

Xtra! Web Site
- Students can access the Xtra! Study Tools for additional practice.

• terms review

automatic check deposit
electronic funds transfer (EFT)

• audit your understanding

1. When a payroll is journalized, which account is credited for the total net amount paid to all employees?
2. What four separate payroll taxes do most employers have to pay?

• work together 3-2

Journalizing and paying payroll and payroll taxes

Use the solution from Work Together 3-1. A cash payments journal, page 15, and general journal, page 7, are provided in the *Working Papers*. Your instructor will guide you through the following examples.

1. Use a grid similar to the one in this lesson to calculate departmental payroll taxes. You will need two taxable earnings columns, one for FICA Taxable Earnings and one for Unemployment Taxable Earnings, since the bases for these two classes of salaries are different for this period. Social security and Medicare taxes are due on total earnings for this period. Unemployment taxes are due on the following earnings for this period: Hardware, $2,132.00; Paint, $1,983.00; and Administrative, $985.00.
2. Journalize the following transactions for July of the current year.

Transactions:
July 10. Paid July 3 payroll. Check No. 260.
     10. Recorded employer's payroll taxes for the pay period ended July 3. Memo. No. 33.
     15. Paid employees' federal income tax withholding, social security tax, and Medicare tax liabilities for the pay period ended July 3. Check No. 265.
     29. Paid federal unemployment tax, $745.84, and state unemployment tax, $5,034.44, for the quarter ended June 30. Check No. 270.

• on your own 3-2

Journalizing and paying payroll and payroll taxes

Use the solution from On Your Own 3-1. A cash payments journal, page 18, and general journal, page 10, are provided in the *Working Papers*. Work independently to complete the following problem.

1. Use a grid similar to the one in this lesson to calculate departmental payroll taxes. You will need two taxable earnings columns, one for FICA Taxable Earnings and one for Unemployment Taxable Earnings, since the bases for these two classes of salaries are different for this period. Social security and Medicare taxes are due on total earnings for this period. Unemployment taxes are due on the following earnings for this period: Hardware, $2,050.00; Paint, $1,850.00; and Administrative, $1,010.00.
2. Journalize the following transactions for October of the current year.

Transactions:
Oct. 9. Paid October 2 payroll. Check No. 335.
    9. Recorded employer's payroll taxes for the pay period ended October 2. Memo. No. 48.
    14. Paid employees' federal income tax withholding, social security tax, and Medicare tax liabilities for the pay period ended October 2. Check No. 339.
    28. Paid federal unemployment tax, $91.65, and state unemployment tax, $618.64, for the quarter ended September 30. Check No. 344.

ENRICH

- Assign students to work in pairs to analyze transactions presented in the text. One student analyzes transactions by drawing T accounts. The other student journalizes the transaction. Then they switch activities. Allow 15–20 minutes for the exercise. Then ask students what they learned from the activity.
- Students can use Peachtree or QuickBooks data files to automate Application Problem 3-5.

CLOSE

- Ask students to briefly summarize the procedure for journalizing and paying payroll and payroll taxes.

Xtra!
Review
accountingxtra.swlearning.com

After completing this chapter, you can

1. Define accounting terms related to a departmental payroll system.

2. Identify accounting concepts and practices related to a departmental payroll system.

3. Prepare a commissions record and calculate commission on net sales.

4. Complete payroll records.

5. Journalize payroll transactions.

PUTTING IT ALL TOGETHER

- Review the Chapter Summary.

- Demonstrate at least one activity or transaction from each lesson. Ask if there are any specific activities or transactions anyone would like to review.

INDEPENDENT PRACTICE

- Assign Mastery Problem 3-6 to students who need the reinforcement of a problem that combines transactions from the chapter in one problem. This will be most students.

- Assign Challenge Problem 3-7 to accelerated students who do not require the reinforcement of the mastery problem.

- Assign Study Guide 3.

- Assign the Automated Accounting feature on pages 84–85 to automate Mastery Problem 3-6.

- Students can access Personal Trainer to work end-of-chapter problems on the computer.

- Students can access the Xtra! Web Site for the Xtra! Review and Quizzing.

- Students can access the Student Companion CD for additional review material.

Explore Accounting
EXPLORE ACCOUNTING • EXPLORE ACCOUNTING • EXPLORE ACCOUN

Pretax Benefits

Federal income tax is a major expense for most families. Current laws permit employers to set up retirement and cafeteria plans that allow employees to set aside a portion of their earnings on a pretax basis. Employees pay no taxes in that tax year on the amounts withheld.

Retirement Plans

For amounts placed in many qualified retirement accounts, income tax is "deferred" on earnings. Individuals will pay income taxes on the amounts withdrawn from their retirement accounts when they retire. Because of the income tax deferral, the amount available at retirement will be much larger.

The general requirements of most pretax retirement plans include the following:

1. The employer withholds the specified amount and deposits it in qualified investments, such as mutual funds.
2. The amount of earnings an employee can defer each year is limited.
3. Employees are assessed penalties if they withdraw amounts from their retirement account before the age of $59\frac{1}{2}$.

4. Withdrawals from retirement plan accounts must begin by the time the person reaches age $70\frac{1}{2}$.

Medical Savings Accounts and Cafeteria Plans

Medical savings accounts and cafeteria plans permit employees to have a portion of their pretax earnings deducted from their salaries. The amounts are used to reimburse out-of-pocket medical or childcare expenses. The advantage is that payment is made with pretax dollars. However, the amount of earnings withheld is available only for the purpose designated. For example, if an employee authorizes $50.00 a month to be withheld for medical costs but uses only $500.00 during the year, the remaining $100.00 that was withheld is not reimbursable to the employee.

Instructions: Answer the following questions.

1. Why would Congress allow employees to defer taxes?

2. Are there any disadvantages to participating in these tax deferral plans?

ONGOING ASSESSMENT

Review solutions to the assigned problems in class, diagnosing trouble spots.

RETEACH

- Call on students to describe how they avoid the trouble spots diagnosed.

- Use reteaching suggestions from section lesson plans as required.

- Assign Recycling Problem 3-1 if needed.

Calculating and Recording Departmental Payroll Data

Chapter 3   **77**

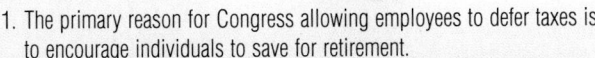

EXPLORE ACCOUNTING
EXPLORE ACCOUNTING

1. The primary reason for Congress allowing employees to defer taxes is to encourage individuals to save for retirement.

2. Some disadvantages: Money cannot be withdrawn from retirement plans until age $59\frac{1}{2}$ without penalties. Tax rates could be higher when individuals withdraw tax deferred funds, resulting in higher taxes paid. Amounts contributed to a cafeteria plan that are not spent cannot be reimbursed to the individual. Students may come up with additional disadvantages.

ENRICH

- Assign the Explore Accounting Feature. After students have had time to research the topic, discuss the topic in class.

- Students can access the Xtra! Web Site for the Xtra! Enrichment material.

- Assign the Applied Communication Activity.

- Assign the Case for Critical Thinking.

- Assign the SCANS Workplace Competency.

- Assign the Auditing for Errors activity.

- Assign the Analyzing Costco's Financial Statements activity.

- Assign the Automated Accounting feature on pages 84-85 to automate Mastery Problem 3-6.

3-1 APPLICATION PROBLEM
Preparing departmental commissions records

CarpetWorld employs a departmental supervisor for each of its two departments, Carpet and Drapery. Departmental supervisors receive a biweekly salary and monthly commissions of 1% of net sales. They receive their commissions for the previous month in the first pay period of the current month. The following data are from the accounting records for the month ended February 28 of the current year.

a. Carpet Department: sales on account, $8,623.40; cash and credit card sales, $12,936.20; sales discount, $148.90; sales returns and allowances, $1,699.30.

b. Drapery Department: sales on account, $7,223.89; cash and credit card sales, $13,987.11; sales discount, $337.17; sales returns and allowances, $654.33.

Instructions:

Prepare February's commissions record for each of the following departmental supervisors. Save your work to complete Application Problem 3-2.

a. **Carpet Department**
Employee name: Sarah Logan
Employee number: 9
Regular salary: $540.00

b. **Drapery Department**
Employee name: Ryan Paniaqua
Employee number: 14
Regular salary: $520.00

3-2 APPLICATION PROBLEM
Completing a payroll register

CarpetWorld has two departments, Carpet and Drapery. It uses a biweekly payroll system. It pays its salesclerks and employees in the accounting department on an hourly basis, and they receive 1½ times the regular hourly pay rate for all hours worked in excess of 40 hours in one week. The employee hours worked and pay rates for selected employees are shown below.

Name	Department	ID No.	Hours	Hourly Rate	Salary
Bodade, Nilesh	Carpet	7	83	$7.00	
Logan, Sarah	Carpet	10	—		$540.00
Paniaqua, Ryan	Drapery	16	—		$520.00
Quinn, Benjamin	Administrative	9	84	$6.50	
Ragasa, Corazan	Drapery	15	85	$8.00	

A partially completed payroll register for the biweekly pay period ended March 12 of the current year is provided in the *Working Papers*.

Use the commissions records from Application Problem 3-1 and the partially completed payroll register provided in the *Working Papers* to complete the payroll register. The following additional information is also needed:

a. A deduction for federal income tax is to be made from each employee's total earnings. Use the appropriate income tax withholding tables shown in Lesson 3-1.

b. A deduction of 2% for state income tax is to be made from each employee's total earnings.

c. A deduction of 6.2% for social security and 1.45% for Medicare tax is to be made from each employee's total earnings.

d. All employees have dental insurance, $9.40, and health insurance, $13.20, deducted from their pay each biweekly pay period. These deductions are to be recorded in the Other Deductions column of the payroll register. Use *D* to indicate the dental insurance deduction. Use *H* to indicate the health insurance deduction. Both of these deductions are written on one line of the payroll register for each employee.

Instructions:

Complete the payroll register for the pay period ended March 12 and paid on March 19 of the current year. Save your work to complete Application Problems 3-3 and 3-4.

3-3 APPLICATION PROBLEM

Completing an employee earnings record

Use the payroll register from Application Problem 3-2. A partially completed employee earnings record for each of CarpetWorld's employees appears in the *Working Papers*.

Instructions:

Complete the employee earnings record for each employee. This pay period is the sixth of the first quarter of the current year.

3-4 APPLICATION PROBLEM

Journalizing payment of a departmental payroll

Use the payroll register from Application Problem 3-2.

Instructions:

1. Record the March 19 payroll payment on page 6 of a cash payments journal. The source document is Check No. 463.
2. Use a grid similar to the one in Lesson 3-2 to calculate departmental payroll taxes. Because this payroll is early in the year, all employee earnings are subject to all payroll taxes.
3. Record the employer payroll taxes on page 6 of a general journal. Use March 19 of the current year as the date. The source document is Memorandum No. 41.

3-5 APPLICATION PROBLEM PEACHTREE QUICKBOOKS

Calculating and journalizing payment of payroll tax liabilities

Use the following payroll data for John's Automotive for the first quarter of the current year. Employer tax rates are social security, 6.2%; Medicare, 1.45%; federal unemployment, 0.8%; and state unemployment, 5.4%.

Period	Total Earnings	Social Security Tax Withheld	Medicare Tax Withheld	Federal Income Tax Withheld
Biweekly Period Ended March 28	$ 7,742.00	$480.00	$112.26	$911.00
First Quarter	46,452.00	—	—	

Instructions:

1. Calculate the liability for employee federal income tax, social security tax, and Medicare tax for the biweekly pay period ended March 28. Include both the employees' tax withheld and the employer liability for social security and Medicare taxes. Record the payment of federal income tax withholding, social security tax, and Medicare tax on page 7 of a cash payments journal. The payment is made on April 3 using Check No. 492 as the source document.
2. Calculate the federal unemployment tax liability for the first quarter. Record the payment on page 8 of a cash payments journal. The payment is made on April 30 using Check No. 515 as the source document.
3. Calculate the state unemployment tax liability for the first quarter. Record the payment on page 8 of a cash payments journal. The payment is made on April 30 using Check No. 516 as the source document.

Application Problem 3-3
Accumulated Earnings:
Bodade, 3,559.50
Logan, 3,887.11
Paniaqua, 4,072.20
Quinn, 3,315.00
Ragasa, 4,104.00

Application Problem 3-4
Total of payroll register: 1,102.23

Application Problem 3-5
Apr. 3 Cash Payments Journal Cash Credit: 2,095.54

Apr. 30 Unemploy. Tax Payable—Federal: 371.62

Apr. 30 Unemploy. Tax Payable—State: 2,508.41

Mastery Problem 3-6

Commissions:

Bullock, 132.14

Mondero, 130.95

Payroll Register:

Total Earnings: 3,893.04

Total Deductions: 687.61

Net Pay: 3,205.43

80

3-6 MASTERY PROBLEM (AUTOMATED ACCOUNTING)

Completing payroll records, journalizing payment of a payroll, and journalizing payroll taxes

ColdGuard has two departments, Windows and Doors. It uses a biweekly payroll system of 26 pay periods per year. ColdGuard pays salesclerks and employees in the accounting department on an hourly basis, and they receive 1½ times the regular hourly pay rate for all hours worked in excess of 40 hours in one week. The hours worked report shows the following information.

Name	ID No.	Dept.	Reg-1	OT-1	Reg-2	OT-2
Bullock, Andrea E.	2	Windows	—		—	
Demars, Scott R.	3	Doors	40	2	40	1
Kabic, Zora E.	1	Windows	40	1	40	2
Mondero, Teodora C.	4	Doors	—		—	
Purdy, Julie M.	5	Windows	40	2	40	1.5
Trang, Phuong M.	6	Admin.	40	4	40	3

Hourly rates and salaries are as follows:

Bullock, Andrea E.	$600.00
Demars, Scott R.	$7.50 per hour
Kabic, Zora E.	$7.40 per hour
Mondero, Teodora C.	$620.00
Purdy, Julie M.	$6.60 per hour
Trang, Phuong M.	$6.50 per hour

Department supervisors receive a biweekly salary and monthly commissions of 1% of net sales. Commissions for the previous month are paid in the first pay period of the next month.

ColdGuard's partially completed payroll records for selected employees for the pay period ended March 14 and paid on March 21 of the current year are provided in the *Working Papers*.

Instructions:

1. Complete the commissions record for each departmental supervisor. The following data are from the accounting records for the month of February of the current year:
   a. Windows Department: sales on account, $5,543.89; cash and credit card sales, $8,047.02; sales discount, $92.01; sales returns and allowances, $285.40.
   b. Doors Department: sales on account, $5,312.32; cash and credit card sales, $9,409.85; sales discount, $148.63; sales returns and allowances, $1,478.21.
2. Use the time records and completed commissions records to complete the payroll register for the pay period ended March 14 and paid March 21 of the current year. Use the following additional data to complete the payroll register:
   a. A deduction for federal income tax is to be made from each employee's total earnings. Use the appropriate income tax withholding tables shown in Lesson 3-1 in this chapter.
   b. A deduction of 3% for state income tax is to be made from each employee's total earnings.
   c. Deduction of 6.2% for social security tax and 1.45% for Medicare tax are to be made from each employee's total earnings.
   d. All employees have medical insurance, $14.80, and dental insurance, $8.20, deducted from their pay each biweekly pay period. Use *M* to indicate the medical insurance deduction. Use *D* to indicate the dental insurance deduction.
3. Complete the employee earnings record for each employee. This pay period is the fifth of the first quarter of the current year.
4. Journalize the March 21 payroll payment on page 5 of a cash payments journal. The source document is Check No. 211.
5. Use a grid similar to the one in this chapter to calculate departmental payroll taxes. You will need only one taxable earnings column, since no employee's accumulated earnings are greater than the base for unemployment tax. Employer tax rates are social security, 6.2%; Medicare, 1.45%; federal unemployment, 0.8%; and state unemployment, 5.4%.
6. Journalize the employer payroll taxes on page 7 of a general journal. Use March 21 of the current year as the date. The source document is Memorandum No. 33.

3-7 CHALLENGE PROBLEM

Completing a payroll register, journalizing payment of a payroll, and journalizing payroll taxes

Assume Congress recently past an Act raising all payroll taxes. The new rates are as follows:
- Social Security: 7.1% of earnings up to a maximum of $94,500 in each calendar year
- Medicare: 2.05% of all earnings in a calendar year
- Federal Unemployment: 6.8% of the first $10,000.00 earned by each employee during a calendar year. Employers are permitted to deduct up to a maximum of 5.9% paid to state unemployment funds. The effective unemployment rates for the state ColdGuard operates in are 0.9% for federal unemployment and 5.9% for state unemployment.

Instructions:
1. Use the earnings data from Mastery Problem 3-6. Complete a new payroll register for the pay period ended March 14. Use the new tax rates passed by Congress. Medical and dental insurance remains the same for each employee. (Compare the payroll registers completed in problems 3-6 and 3-7. Note the impact of higher taxes on each individual's net pay.)
2. Journalize the March 21 payroll payment on page 5 of a cash payments journal. The source document is Check No. 211.
3. Use a grid similar to the one in this chapter to calculate departmental payroll taxes.
4. Journalize the employer payroll taxes on page 7 of a general journal. Use March 21 of the current year as the date. The source document is Memorandum No. 33. (Compare the employer payroll taxes expense entries completed in problems 3-6 and 3-7. Note the impact of higher taxes on the employer.)

APPLIED COMMUNICATION

Students' responses will vary but should state clearly their request for information and the address to which the information should be sent. It may be wise to allow students to have the responses sent to your attention at the school's address.

CASE FOR CRITICAL THINKING

It should be explained to Ms. Dennenberg that her concern is appreciated and that it is a legitimate one. However, to prevent employees from unnecessarily overselling a customer, pressuring a customer, or selling a customer a product that isn't really needed, company policy is to deduct sales returns and sales discounts from sales before calculating commissions.

SCANS WORKPLACE COMPETENCY

Basic instruction or prior knowledge in the use of spreadsheet programs is necessary to complete this activity. Knowledgeable students may be paired with unskilled students.

• applied communication

Write a letter to two local payroll processing companies. Request information about their services. When you receive the information, compare and contrast the services offered by the two companies. Keep a copy of your letters in the "Personal Letters" section of your *Career Portfolio*.

• case for critical thinking

Zytech deducts department sales returns and allowances and sales discounts from sales before calculating manager discounts. Mary Dennenberg, manager of the Audio Department, does not think this policy is fair. "I work hard to train my salesclerks to close their sales, and I work hard on closing my own sales. Why should I be penalized if a customer returns the merchandise?" As the company president, how would you respond to Ms. Dennenberg?

• SCANS workplace competency

Information Competency: Using Computers to Process Information

Concept: Employers need individuals who can use computers to acquire, organize, analyze, and communicate information. Competent employees are familiar with word processing, spreadsheet, database, multimedia, and Internet software.

Application: Use a spreadsheet program to complete the payroll register in Application Problem 3-2. Use formulas to calculate totals, net pay, state income tax, social security and Medicare taxes, and column totals.

auditing for errors

Tony Parducci, a new payroll clerk for PowerGlide, prepared the commissions record shown here for Dianne Connelly. PowerGlide pays all salespersons a biweekly salary of $1,300.00 plus a monthly commission of 1.5% of department net sales. Commissions for the previous month are paid in the first pay period of the current month. Accounting records for Ms. Connelly's department for the month ended November 30 of the current year indicate: sales on account, $55,170.32; cash and credit card sales, $12,371.40; sales discount, $1,452.22; sales returns and allowances, $954.65.

Instructions: As the senior accounting clerk, you have responsibility for reviewing the work prepared by new hires. Examine the commissions record prepared by Mr. Parducci. Calculate the new commission on net sales if errors are found.

COMMISSIONS RECORD

EMPLOYEE NO. ___6___   EMPLOYEE NAME _Dianne Connelly_

COMMISSION RATE _1%_   MONTH _December_   YEAR _20--_

DEPARTMENT _Skates_   REGULAR BIWEEKLY SALARY _$1,300.00_

Sales on Account		$ 55,710.32
Cash and Credit Card Sales		12,371.40
equals Total Sales for the month		$ 68,081.72
Less:		
Sales Discounts	$ 145.22	
Sales Returns and Allowances	954.65	1,099.87
Equals:		
Net Sales		$ 66,981.85
times Commission Rate		0.01
equals: Commission on Net Sales		$ 6,698.19

analyzing Costco's financial statements

Expenses incurred in one fiscal period but not paid until a later date are called *accrued expenses*. During the last fiscal period of each year, Costco incurs salary and benefit expenses that are not paid until the following fiscal year. This occurs when a fiscal year ends in the middle of a payroll period. The accounting concept *Matching Revenue with Expenses* requires that financial statements must show all business expenses for a fiscal period. Consequently, Costco must report the unpaid salary and benefit amount even though it has not yet paid out cash. The unpaid amount owed for incurred employee salaries and benefits represents a liability. Use the material shown in Appendix B of this text to answer the questions below.

Instructions:

1. Referring to the consolidated balance sheets on page B-5, (a) list the title of the account that represents an amount owed for salaries and benefits and (b) list the amounts owed for this account on August 31, 2003, and September 1, 2002.

2. Referring to the ten-year operating and financial highlights on page B-2, identify one fact that would help explain the increase in this liability. List at least two other reasons that might explain the increase.

Calculating and Recording Departmental Payroll Data

Chapter 3   **83**

Errors are: incorrect commission rate, sales on account amount, total sales, sales discounts amount, total discounts and returns total, net sales, commission on net sales amount.

COMMISSIONS RECORD

EMPLOYEE NO. _6_

EMPLOYEE NAME _Dianne Connelly_

COMMISSION RATE _1.5%_

MONTH _December_   YEAR _20--_

DEPARTMENT _Skates_

REGULAR BIWEEKLY SALARY _$1,300.00_

Sales on Account		$ 55,170.32
Cash and Credit Card Sales		12,371.40
equals Total Sales for the Month		$ 67,541.72
Less:		
Sales Discounts	$ 1,452.22	
Sales Returns and Allowances	954.65	2,406.87
Equals:		
Net Sales		$ 65,134.85
times Commission Rate		1.5%
equals: Commission on Net Sales		$ 977.02

ANALYZING COSTCO'S FINANCIAL STATEMENTS

1. (a) Accrued Salaries and Benefits.
   (b) Accrued Salaries and Benefits for 2003, $734,261,000; for 2002, $589,927,000.

2. At the end of 2003, Costco was operating 23 more stores than during the previous year. Other reasons for the increase in Accrued Salaries and Benefits might include: more days in the accrued payroll period; an increase in salaries and wages; an increase in the cost of existing benefits (health care); the addition of new employee benefits; an increase in worker's compensation costs; changes in federal (Sarbanes-Oxley Act of 2002) or state regulations that might require the hiring of additional employees or the paying of overtime to comply with new requirements; or failures in technology or automation, requiring the rehire of employees.

TEACHING STRATEGIES   PORTFOLIO ASSESSMENT

An ideal specimen for inclusion in a portfolio to demonstrate mastery of the payroll procedures and concepts is the completion of the Mastery Problem. Students may wish to include both a manual version and an automated version for this problem.

83

AUTOMATED ACCOUNTING · AUTOMATED ACCOUNTING · AUTOMATED ACCOUNTING · AUTOMATED ACCOUNTING · AUTOMATED ACCOUNTING

EXPLAIN

- Point out that employee taxes may be entered or automatically calculated by the automated accounting program.

- Explain that the payroll register can be accessed on the Payroll tab in Other Activities.

- Explain that accuracy is very important when entering employee data, in order to eliminate under- or over-payments.

- Explain that employee transaction data is entered in the Payroll tab in the Other Activities window.

DEMONSTRATE

Entering payroll transactions

- Direct students to the illustrations as you demonstrate entering payroll transactions.

- Click on the Other button on the toolbar and then click the Payroll tab.

- Demonstrate entering the date of the check.

- Demonstrate selecting the employee from the Employee drop-down list.

- Demonstrate verifying the Check No. automatically generated or replacing it with a different number.

- Demonstrate striking the Tab key to advance to the Salary data field. Explain that a salary amount will appear if the employee is a salaried employee; otherwise regular and overtime hours will need to be entered in the appropriate fields.

- Click the Calculate Taxes button to calculate employee taxes.

- Enter the employee deductions.

- Click OK to generate the payroll check.

- Click the Close button to continue or click Print to print the check.

Automating Payroll Accounting Data—Payroll Procedures

Payroll Transactions

Every pay period, employee payroll information is entered into the payroll system. The information needed for each employee includes the date, pay information, and employee deductions. The employee taxes are entered or automatically calculated by the Automated Accounting program. Payroll transaction information is entered into the Payroll screen.

The payroll register can be accessed on the Payroll tab of the Other Activities window. The fields in the payroll register are shown in the two illustrations below. Use the horizontal scroll bar at the bottom of the work area to move to the right and left.

Entering Payroll Transactions

For each employee, the information shown on the payroll window is entered for each pay period:

hours worked, regular and overtime, tax deductions, and employee deductions. Accuracy is very important when entering this data in order to eliminate under- or overpayments.

Employee transaction data is entered in the Payroll tab in the Other Activities window. Click on the Payroll tab to display the payroll screen. Use the following steps to enter payroll transactions.

1. Enter the date of the check.

2. Select the employee from the Employee drop-down list or key the first letter of the last name until the correct name appears.

3. Verify that the check number displayed in the Check No. cell is correct. If it is not correct, enter the correct check number.

4. Use the Tab key to enter salary information. If the employee is salaried, the salary amount

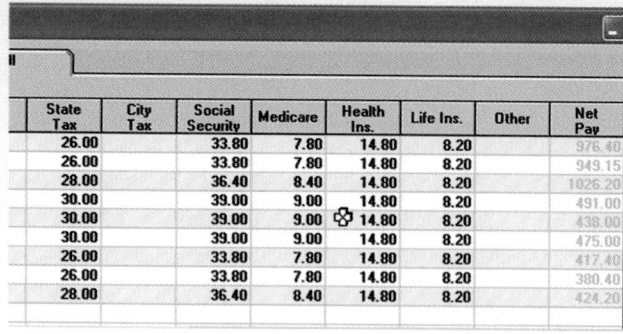

will be displayed. If it is necessary to key a different salary, the salary amount cell can be changed. Entering a new amount will override the salary amount in the cell.

5. If the employee is paid by the hour, enter the regular hours worked in the Reg. Hours cell.

6. If the employee is paid hourly and has worked overtime, enter the overtime hours worked in the O.T. Hours cell.

7. Click on the Calculate Taxes button to have the software automatically calculate the employee taxes. After the calculations are completed, the employee taxes are displayed in the various employee taxes cells. Visually check each cell to verify that an amount appears.

8. Enter all employee deductions.

9. Click OK. A display of the payroll check will be shown on the screen.

10. Click the Close button to continue or click Print to print the check.

Generating Payroll Journal Entries for the Period

The payroll journal entries can be generated automatically without any calculations by selecting the Current Payroll Journal Entry menu item from the Options menu. When the confirmation box appears, click Yes after checking the entry for accuracy. The general journal window automatically appears, displaying the payroll journal entries that were created. Click the Post button. Posting is done after verifying that the journal entry appears to be correct.

Generating the Journal Entry for Employer's Payroll Taxes

Generating the journal entry for the employer's payroll taxes can be done by using the menu item for employer's payroll taxes. Automated Accounting allows you to automatically generate the entry for the employer's portion of the payroll taxes. To automatically generate the journal entry, use the following steps.

1. Choose Employer's Payroll Taxes from the Options menu.

2. When the confirmation box appears, click Yes.

3. The entry is automatically generated. Click the Post button.

4. Click the Close button of the general journal.

AUTOMATING MASTERY PROBLEM 3-6: Completing payroll records, journalizing payment of a payroll, and journalizing payroll taxes

Instructions:

1. Load the *Automated Accounting 8.0* or higher software.

2. Select data file A03-6.

3. Select File from the menu bar and choose Save As. Key the path to the drive and directory that contains your data files. Save the database with a filename of A03-6 XXX XXX (where the X's are your first and last name).

4. Access Problem Instructions through the Browser tool. Read the Problem Instruction screen.

5. Key the data listed in the problem on page 80.

6. Save your file and exit the Automated Accounting software.

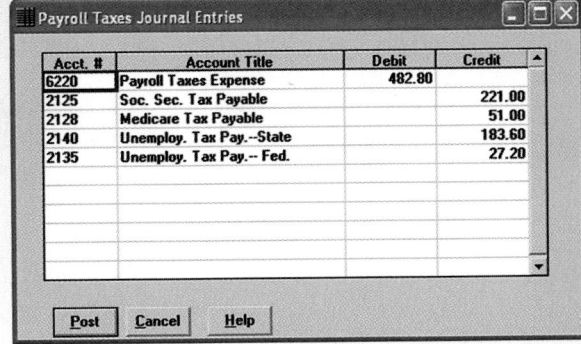

EXPLAIN

- Explain that payroll journal entries can be generated automatically without any calculations by selecting the Current Payroll Journal Entry menu item from the Options menu.

- Explain that posting is done after verifying that the journal entry appears to be correct.

- Explain that generating the journal entry for the employer's payroll taxes can be done by using the menu item for employer's payroll taxes. Automated Accounting allows you to automatically generate the entry for the employer's portion of the payroll taxes.

DEMONSTRATE

Generating payroll journal entries for the period

- Select the Current Payroll Journal Entry menu item from the Options menu.

- Demonstrate clicking Yes in the confirmation box after checking the entry for accuracy.

- Refer students to the illustration, which shows the payroll journal entry generated by the software. Explain that it should be verified and then the Post button should be clicked.

Generating the journal entry for employer's payroll taxes

- Demonstrate choosing the Employer's Payroll Taxes menu item from the Options menu.

- Demonstrate clicking Yes in the confirmation dialog box to display the journal entry.

- Demonstrate clicking the Post button to post the entry after it has been verified.

PRACTICE

- Assign Automating Mastery Problem 3-6: Completing payroll records, journalizing payment of a payroll, and journalizing payroll taxes.

ASSESSMENT

- Use the Electronic Auditor to assess student understanding. As an alternative, some instructors have found it effective to give students access to the Electronic Auditor to find their errors and correct their own work.

TEACHING STRATEGIES PORTFOLIO ASSESSMENT

Students should be encouraged to print at least one report from one of the Automated Accounting problems to include in their portfolio to demonstrate mastery of automated accounting systems. A copy of the Portfolio Assessment form (blackline master in the Teacher's Resource Guide; also on the Student Companion CD) should be completed by the student and the Description section should include any comments regarding how the student mastered these concepts and procedures.

Financial Reporting for

	SCOPE & SEQUENCE		ENHANCING	
	NEW	REVIEW/ EXTENSION	SPECIAL FEATURES	
Introduce the Chapter	✓		Accounting in the Real World: Trek Bicycles	
Lesson 4-1 Responsibility Accounting for a Merchandising Business			Making Ethical Decisions: Sharing Your Knowledge; Business Structures	
Features of a responsibility accounting system	✓			
Recording direct and indirect expenses	✓			
Lesson 4-2 Interim Departmental Statement of Gross Profit			Cases for Critical Thinking 1	
Interim financial statements		✓		
Estimating ending merchandise inventory		✓		
Interim departmental statement of gross profit	✓			
Cost of merchandise sold and gross profit percentages		✓		
Determining acceptable levels of performance		✓		
Lesson 4-3 Preparing a Work Sheet for a Departmentalized Business			Careers in Accounting; Cultural Diversity: African American Businesses; Cases for Critical Thinking 2	
Proving the accuracy of posting to subsidiary ledgers		✓		
Expanded work sheet		✓		
Adjustments		✓		
Departmental and company loss on a work sheet	✓			
Lesson 4-4 Responsibility Statements for a Merchandising Business			Cultural Diversity: Hispanic-Owned Firms Growing Rapidly	
Departmental margin statements	✓			
Income statement with departmental margin		✓		
Statement of stockholders' equity		✓		
Balance sheet		✓		
Lesson 4-5 End-of-Period Work for a Departmentalized Business				
Journalizing adjusting and closing entries		✓		
Post-closing trial balance		✓		
Summary of accounting cycle		✓		
Putting It All Together			Explore Accounting; Xtra! Web Site: Xtra! Enrichment; Applied Communication; SCANS Workplace Competency; Auditing for Errors; Analyzing Costco's Financial Statements	

a Departmentalized Business

INSTRUCTION			PRACTICE AND ASSESSMENT		
TECHNOLOGY AND MEDIA	**TEACHING STRATEGIES**		**GUIDED PRACTICE**	**INDEPENDENT PRACTICE**	**RETEACHING AND ENRICHMENT**
Internet Research Activity; Accounting Xtra! Web Site	Software Focus				
Instructor's Resource CD: PowerPoint Slides; Xtra! Web Site: Xtra! Study Tools; Blackline Masters; Personal Trainer			Terms Review; Audit Your Understanding; Work Together 4-1	On Your Own 4-1; Application Problem 4-1; Ongoing Assessment, p. 90; Personal Trainer; Xtra! Web Site: Xtra! Study Tools	Reteach, p. 90; Enrich, p. 92
Instructor's Resource CD: PowerPoint Slides; Xtra! Web Site: Xtra! Study Tools; Blackline Masters; Personal Trainer	Accounting Pedagogy; Cooperative Learning		Terms Review; Audit Your Understanding; Work Together 4-2	On Your Own 4-2; Application Problem 4-2; Ongoing Assessment, p. 96; Personal Trainer; Xtra! Web Site: Xtra! Study Tools	Reteach, p. 96; Enrich, p. 98
Instructor's Resource CD: PowerPoint Slides; Xtra! Web Site: Xtra! Study Tools; Blackline Masters; Personal Trainer; Automated Accounting; QuickBooks	Applied Skills: Building Study Skills; Limited English Proficiency (LEP) Students; Expanding Beyond the Classroom; Specific Learning Disability (SLD) Students; Print Learner; Kinesthetic Learner		Terms Review; Audit Your Understanding; Work Together 4-3	On Your Own 4-3; Application Problem 4-3; Ongoing Assessment, p. 109; Personal Trainer; Xtra! Web Site: Xtra! Study Tools	Reteach, p. 109; Enrich, p. 110; Automated Accounting; QuickBooks
Instructor's Resource CD: PowerPoint Slides; Xtra! Web Site: Xtra! Study Tools; Blackline Masters; Personal Trainer; Automated Accounting	Expanding Beyond the Classroom; Applied Skills: Writing Across the Curriculum		Terms Review; Audit Your Understanding; Work Together 4-4	On Your Own 4-4; Application Problem 4-4; Ongoing Assessment, p. 116; Personal Trainer; Xtra! Web Site: Xtra! Study Tools	Reteach, p. 116; Enrich, p. 117; Automated Accounting
Instructor's Resource CD: PowerPoint Slides; Xtra! Web Site: Xtra! Study Tools; Blackline Masters; Personal Trainer; Automated Accounting; Peachtree	Accounting Pedagogy; Visually-Impaired Students		Terms Review; Audit Your Understanding; Work Together 4-5	On Your Own 4-5; Application Problem 4-5; Ongoing Assessment, p. 123; Personal Trainer; Xtra! Web Site: Xtra! Study Tools	Reteach, p. 123; Enrich, p. 124; Automated Accounting; Peachtree; Sounds, Inc.: A Business Simulation
Automated Accounting; QuickBooks; Personal Trainer; Xtra! Web Site: Xtra! Review, Quizzing, and Enrichment; Student Companion CD				Mastery Problem 4-6; Automated Accounting; QuickBooks; Personal Trainer; Xtra! Web Site: Xtra! Review and Quizzing; Study Guide 4; Student Companion CD; Chapter 4 Test; ExamView Chapter 4; Portfolio Assessment	Challenge Problem 4-7; Reteach, p. 125; Enrich, p. 125; Recycling Problem 4-1; Automated Accounting; Xtra! Web Site: Xtra! Enrichment

CHAPTER 4

Financial Reporting for a Departmentalized Business

OBJECTIVES & TERMS

After studying Chapter 4, you will be able to:

1. Define accounting terms related to cost accounting and financial reporting for a departmentalized merchandising business.

2. Identify accounting concepts and practices related to cost accounting and financial reporting for a departmentalized merchandising business.

3. Distinguish between direct and indirect expenses.

4. Prepare an interim departmental statement of gross profit.

5. Prepare a work sheet for a departmentalized merchandising business.

6. Prepare financial statements for a departmentalized merchandising business.

7. Analyze financial statements using selected component percentages.

8. Complete end-of-period work for a departmentalized merchandising business.

- fiscal period
- responsibility accounting
- direct expense
- indirect expense
- departmental margin
- departmental margin statement
- gross profit
- departmental statement of gross profit
- periodic inventory
- perpetual inventory
- gross profit method of estimating an inventory
- component percentage
- schedule of accounts receivable
- schedule of accounts payable
- work sheet
- trial balance
- plant assets
- depreciation expense
- responsibility statements
- income statement
- statement of stockholders' equity
- capital stock
- retained earnings
- dividends
- balance sheet
- adjusting entries
- closing entries
- post-closing trial balance
- accounting cycle

Point Your Browser
accountingxtra.swlearning.com

86

Trek Bicycles

COURTESY OF TREK BICYCLE CORPORATION

TREK BICYCLES ADJUSTS PRODUCT LINE TO CONSUMER TRENDS AND TECHNOLOGICAL ADVANCEMENTS

Trek Bicycles started producing hand-built, steel bike frames in 1976 in an old barn located in Waterloo, Wisconsin. During the last 30 years, the company has grown into a global enterprise employing over 1,600 employees worldwide. Trek seized international recognition when Texan Lance Armstrong rode the first American bike frame to victory in the world's most prestigious bicycle race, the Tour de France.

Over the years, Trek has expanded its operation and now designs and produces a complete line of high-end bicycles, components, and accessories. The company manufacturers a variety of both road and mountain bicycles incorporating innovative designs and aerospace composites, as well as helmets, gloves, clothing, lights, tools, hydration packs, locks, pumps, and lubricants.

Initially, road bikes were 75% of Trek's business. Gradually, however, mountain bikes exceeded road bikes in popularity. By 1996, 80% of Trek's product offerings consisted of mountain bikes. Today, Trek continues to be a privately held corporation and has matured into the world's largest producer of bicycles sold through specialty retail stores.

Critical Thinking

1. Why is it important that Trek maintain separate sales records for road and mountain bikes?
2. Trek no longer manufactures bicycles solely using steel. What is the advantage of using technologically advanced materials in building bicycle frames, and how might that affect sales?

Xtra!
Today
accountingxtra.swlearning.com

Source: www.trekbikes.com

ACCOUNTING FIRMS

Go to the homepage for the following two international accounting firms:

PricewaterhouseCoopers: www.pwcglobal.com

Ernst & Young: www.ey.com/global/

Instructions

Create a table listing the following data for each company:

1. Number of global employees.
2. Amount of global revenue.
3. Number of countries in which it operates.

Use this feature to demonstrate how the chapter's content applies to real businesses today. Motivate students by asking them if they are familiar with Trek or any of its products. Ask students if any of them ride road or mountain bikes. Ask students why mountain bikes have become more popular than road bikes. Ask students to read the feature or have one or more students read the feature out loud. Remind them to pay close attention to details of the business as they read. Give students 5–10 minutes to jot down some ideas for answering the Critical Thinking questions; then discuss the answers in class. As an alternative, you can organize students into groups of 3–4 individuals to generate possible solutions to the questions. With this approach, you may also wish to record the suggestions and save them for additional discussion after the chapter is completed.

1. Separate sales records facilitate evaluating the success and profitability of the product lines, as well as their relevance to customer preferences. Often companies fail to keep pace with new customer trends, which can result in lost sales. Sales analysis will also help Trek better manage and allocate its manufacturing resources to meet the changing customer demand for its bicycles.

2. The use of technologically advanced materials often results in reduced material costs, more efficient production processes, and lighter bicycle frames that also increase rider efficiency. Generally, consumers perceive technologically advanced products more favorably, giving Trek a marketing advantage over other companies. The result has been an increase in sales.

INTERNET RESEARCH ACTIVITY

This activity provides students with an opportunity to search the Internet and answer questions related to the chapter content, giving them practice in developing technology and research skills. If possible, invite an employee from PWC or E & Y to speak to the class on accounting careers. Accountants from other firms in your community are acceptable as well.

At the time of this book's publication, the following figures were available:

	PricewaterhouseCoopers	Ernst & Young
Employees	120,000	103,000
Revenue	$14.5 billion	$13.1 billion
Countries	139 countries	140 countries

4-1 Responsibility Accounting for a Merchandising Business

OBJECTIVES

- Define accounting terms related to cost accounting for a departmentalized merchandising business.
- Identify accounting concepts and practices related to cost accounting for a departmentalized merchandising business.
- Distinguish between direct and indirect expenses.

MOTIVATE

Ask students to imagine a company with two sales departments and then to list the expenses of the company that do not directly involve either department. List these on the board and ask who is responsible for controlling each one of them.

Preview

- Preview the accounting terms and definitions introduced in this lesson: fiscal period, responsibility accounting, direct expense, indirect expense, departmental margin, and departmental margin statement.
- Direct students to read the headings on each page in this lesson and to examine the illustrations given.

EXPLAIN

- Have the students read the text on the page. Ask them why financial statements are prepared by a business. (*Financial statements report the progress of a business and help managers make sound business decisions.*)
- Ask students how often a business should prepare financial statements. Lead into a discussion of the fiscal period and the concept of accounting period cycle.
- Point out that for tax purposes, businesses must prepare financial statements at least once a year.

MATERIALS

- Instructor's Resource CD: PowerPoint Slides
- Xtra! Study Tools on the Xtra! Web Site
- Blackline Masters: 6-Column Cash Payments Journal
- Working Papers: Teacher's Edition of the Working Papers for Lesson 4-1
- Software: Personal Trainer

Financial statements summarize the financial information that a business records. These statements are then analyzed to evaluate the financial position and progress of the business. The managers of a business use the statements to make financial decisions for future operations. The financial statements are also used in preparing tax reports and other reports, such as those required by the SEC, which must be completed at least once a year. Therefore, financial statements are prepared at least once a year. The length of time for which a business summarizes and reports financial information is called a **fiscal period**. [*CONCEPT: Accounting Period Cycle*]

The accounting period cycle concept states that changes in financial information are reported for a specific period of time in the form of financial statements. The time period for which financial statements are prepared depends on the needs of the business. An accounting period may be one month, three months, six months, or one year. For tax purposes, every business prepares financial statements at the end of each year.

Successful businesses generally prepare financial statements monthly to analyze results and take corrective action when needed. A fiscal period may be any length of time, but it is generally considered to refer to a year. Each business determines the length of the fiscal period it uses. Zytech uses a calendar-year fiscal period.

©GETTY IMAGES/PHOTODISC

MAKING ETHICAL DECISIONS • MAKING ETHICAL DECISIONS • MAKING ETHICAL DECISIONS

making ethical decisions

Sharing Your Knowledge

John Oglesby is a certified public accountant who works as a computer consultant. He has just completed helping a local movie theater install a new ticketing system that tracks when and how often individuals come to the theater. The system will enable the theater to analyze its customers and select movies that target customers having specific movie preferences.

John has just received a phone call from another theater in the same city. The theater owner asks John to evaluate its existing computer systems and suggest any recommendations. After allowing the theater owner to present his request, John politely declines to accept the engagement.

Instructions

Use the AICPA *Code of Professional Conduct* to determine if John's actions violate the confidentiality rule. When researching the AICPA *Code of Professional Conduct*, begin by selecting the section title that most closely relates to the issue. Read the Rule and any related Interpretations. Then scan the titles of the Ethics Rulings for any case that may be similar to the issue.

Financial Reporting for a Departmentalized Business

MAKING ETHICAL DECISIONS

This activity was based on the following Ethics Ruling from Section 391. For a sample solution, see the front of this Wraparound Teacher's Edition.

.029 Question—A prospective client has asked a member's firm to study the desirability of his using a newly developed electronic ticketing system for his business. A recent study made for another client leads the member's firm to believe that the system would not be desirable for him. Must the firm state its reservations at the risk of disclosing information acquired while performing an assignment for a client competitor?

.030 Answer—Rule of conduct 301 [ET section 301.01] provides that a member shall not disclose any confidential information obtained in the course of a professional engagement except with the consent of the client. Knowledge and expertise that results in a special competence in a

(continued on p. 89)

1. Each manager is assigned responsibility for only those revenues, costs, and expenses for which the manager can make decisions and affect the outcome.
2. The revenues, costs, and expenses for which a manager is responsible must be readily identifiable with the manager's unit. For example, if a manager is responsible for advertising expense, that manager should make decisions about advertising. Also, a separate record should be kept for the manager's advertising expense. Thus, responsibility accounting traces revenues, costs, and expenses to the individual managers who are responsible for making decisions about those revenues, costs, and expenses.

Controlling costs is essential to a business's success. However, who should control a business's costs? Good management practices require that each manager be responsible for controlling all costs incurred by the manager's business unit. Assigning control of business revenues, costs, and expenses as a responsibility of a specific manager is called **responsibility accounting**. Merchandising businesses with effective cost controls generally use some kind of responsibility accounting. The two important features of a successful responsibility accounting system are described above.

A typical merchandising business income statement reports net income earned during a fiscal period. However, the statement usually does not report specific information that a department manager can use to control departmental costs. Therefore, merchandising businesses often prepare departmental statements to show each department's contribution to net income.

In responsibility accounting, operating expenses are classified as either direct or indirect expenses. An operating expense identifiable with and chargeable to the operation of a specific department is called a **direct expense**. The cost of supplies used by a specific department is an example of a direct expense. An operating expense chargeable to overall business operations and not identifiable with a specific department is called an **indirect expense**. Therefore, the cost of electricity used by a business's overall operation is an example of an indirect expense. A department manager has little or no control over the use of electricity in the department.

The revenue earned by a department less its cost of merchandise sold and less its direct expenses is called **departmental margin**. A statement that reports departmental margin for a specific department is called a **departmental margin statement**.

Zytech uses responsibility accounting to help control costs and expenses. Zytech has two merchandising departments: Audio and Video. Each department's revenue, cost of merchandise sold, and direct expenses are recorded in separate departmental general ledger accounts as shown in Zytech's chart of accounts.

Each business develops a chart of accounts to best meet its needs. Zytech groups its departmental accounts by type, such as operating revenue, cost of merchandise, direct expenses, and indirect expenses. For example, accounts under Direct Expenses—Audio are 6100 numbers. Accounts under Direct Expenses—Video are 6200 numbers.

©GETTY IMAGES/PHOTODISC

Responsibility Accounting for a Merchandising Business

MAKING ETHICAL DECISIONS

(continued from p. 88)

particular field can be provided to a client without violating the confidence of another client. Reservations that the firm may have concerning the electronic ticketing system should be communicated to the prospective client, provided the details of the other client's engagement are not disclosed. If, however, circumstances are such that the prospective client would clearly know the origin of the information on which the member's reservations are based, and such information is sensitive, the engagement should not be accepted without clearance with the first client.

Source: *www.aicpa.org/about/code/et_391.html#N15*

- Explain that responsibility accounting means assigning control of revenues, costs, and expenses only to the department that controls them.
- Direct students to the information at the top of the page to explain two principles of responsibility accounting.
- Explain the difference between direct and indirect expenses.

DEMONSTRATE

- Write the two department titles for Zytech, *Audio* and *Video*, on the board or overhead.
- Ask students for examples of direct expenses for each department. Write student answers under the appropriate department heading.
- Ask students for examples of indirect expenses Zytech might have. Write student answers under the heading *Indirect Expenses*.

- Point out that direct expenses are expenses that are under the control of and benefit a single department.

- Explain that the company has separate accounts in the general ledger for each department's direct expenses, such as advertising, salaries, payroll taxes, and supplies, as well as sales, merchandise inventory, and purchases.

- Emphasize that expenses that are not separated by department are indirect expenses.

- Emphasize that indirect expenses are not reported on departmental margin statements; however, they are reported on the income statement.

Recording a direct expense

- Use an instructor-made transparency of a 6-column cash payments journal or direct students to the illustration at the top of the page as you demonstrate journalizing a direct expense.

- Demonstrate that this transaction is recorded in the same way as any cash payment for an expense, with the difference that the department name is in the account title.

- Point out that this payment for advertising is debited to the departmental advertising expense account because the Audio Department manager made the decision to buy the advertising and it benefits the Audio Department directly.

Recording an indirect expense

- Use an instructor-made transparency of a 6-column cash payments journal or direct students to the illustration in the middle of the page as you demonstrate journalizing an indirect expense.

- Demonstrate that this transaction is recorded in the same way as any cash payment for an expense.

- Point out that this payment for rent is debited to the general Rent Expense account rather than a departmental account because neither department manager made the decision to rent the space and it benefits all departments.

ONGOING ASSESSMENT

- Assessment is an ongoing process. Circulate through the classroom or lab, observing which students have problems with the assignments.

RECORDING A DIRECT EXPENSE

	DATE	ACCOUNT TITLE	CK. NO.	POST. REF.	GENERAL DEBIT	GENERAL CREDIT	ACCOUNTS PAYABLE DEBIT	PURCH. DISCOUNT CR. AUDIO	PURCH. DISCOUNT CR. VIDEO	CASH CREDIT	
					1	2	3	4	5	6	
1	20-- Apr. 1	Advertising Exp.—Audio	610		4 0 0 00					4 0 0 00	1

CASH PAYMENTS JOURNAL — PAGE 16

Procedures for recording revenue, cost, and expense transactions are similar for most merchandising businesses. The journalizing procedures used by Zytech were discussed in Chapters 1 and 2. Zytech maintains separate accounts for each department's merchandise inventory, sales, purchases, and direct expenses. Departmental direct expenses include advertising, depreciation, payroll taxes, salaries, and supplies. Separate departmental accounts for sales, merchandise inventory, purchases, and direct expenses provide information needed to prepare departmental margin statements.

A journal entry prepared by Zytech to record a direct expense is shown above. Zytech's Audio Department manager decided to buy the advertising services. The advertising promotes the department's sale of audio equipment. Since the department manager controls the advertising expense and the department receives the benefits, the expense is classified as a direct expense. To ensure that such expenses are recorded as direct expenses, the account title also includes the department's name, Advertising Expense—Audio. Other direct expenses are shown in cash payments journal entries in Chapters 1 and 3. Debits to expense accounts that have a department name in the account title are entries for direct expenses.

RECORDING AN INDIRECT EXPENSE

CASH PAYMENTS JOURNAL — PAGE 16

	DATE	ACCOUNT TITLE	CK. NO.	POST. REF.	GENERAL DEBIT	GENERAL CREDIT	ACCOUNTS PAYABLE DEBIT	PURCH. DISCOUNT CR. AUDIO	PURCH. DISCOUNT CR. VIDEO	CASH CREDIT	
					1	2	3	4	5	6	
8	1	Rent Expense	611		1 5 0 0 00					1 5 0 0 00	8

A journal entry prepared by Zytech to record an indirect expense is shown above. The Audio Department uses a portion of the space rented by Zytech. However, the decision to rent the specific facility was made by the company president, not the Audio Department manager. In addition, rent expense is not separated by departments but is one payment for the entire facility used by all departments. Since this expense is not separated by departments, the expense is recorded as an indirect expense. Indirect expenses are reported in the company's income statement but not in departmental margin statements. Direct and indirect expenses are reported in the same way each fiscal period. [CONCEPT: Consistent Reporting]

Other journal entries for indirect expenses are shown in Chapter 1. The same accounting procedures must be followed in the same way in each accounting period. Business decisions are based on the financial information reported on financial statements. Some decisions require a comparison of current financial statements with previous financial statements. If accounting information is recorded and reported differently each accounting period, comparisons from one accounting period to another may not be possible.

- Troubleshooting: Diagnose what kinds of problems students have with this section. Students may have trouble understanding the concept of responsibility accounting or the procedures for recording direct and indirect expenses.

- Assess student understanding by checking solutions to Independent Practice assignments.

RETEACH

- Review the features of a responsibility accounting system.

- Review the illustrations on page 90, covering the recording of direct and indirect expenses.

• terms review

TERMS REVIEW • TERMS

fiscal period
responsibility accounting
direct expense
indirect expense
departmental margin
departmental margin statement

• audit your understanding

AUDIT YOUR UNDERSTANDING

1. What two features are required if responsibility accounting is to be successful?

2. For what type of accounts does Zytech have separate departmental accounts in the general ledger?

3. In order to ensure the features of a responsibility accounting system, what should be done if a direct expense used by departments is documented by a single invoice?

• work together 4-1

Identifying direct and indirect expenses

Mulberry, Inc., has two departments: Crafts and Fabrics. Mulberry completed the transactions below.

Use a form similar to the one below. For each transaction, indicate:

   a.   Whether the expense is a direct expense (identifiable with a specific department) or an indirect expense.

   b.   The title of the expense account.

The first transaction is completed as an example.

Trans. No.	Direct Expense or Indirect Expense	Expense Account Title
1	Indirect	Utilities Expense

1. Paid cash for utilities bill.

2. Paid cash for advertising in a craft fair program. The ad was prepared by the Craft Department and includes craft products only.

3. Paid cash for rush delivery (delivery expense) on a special order of fabric for a regular customer.

4. Paid cash for bimonthly payroll for all administrative, fabric, and crafts employees. Salesclerks are hired by specific department managers.

5. Paid cash for maintenance on the company's web site.

6. Paid a consultant to train all salesclerks in effective selling techniques.

7. Paid a retainer fee to an attorney for legal advice.

8. Paid cash for monthly payroll taxes (consider the taxes on the accounting employees only).

9. Paid cash for a promotional mailing to past customers to announce a new line of craft supplies.

10. Paid cash for food and beverages for the annual employee party.

WORK TOGETHER • WORK TOGETHER • WORK TOGETHER • WORK TOGETHER • WORK TOGETHER

GUIDED PRACTICE

Terms Review
Call on students to define the terms in the Terms Review. Ask the class if the definitions are correct and whether the complete definitions have been given or if anything needs to be added. Suggested definitions for all terms are given in the Glossary.

Audit Your Understanding
Call on students to answer the Audit Your Understanding questions. Ask the class if each answer is correct and/or complete. Answers are given in Appendix E of the textbook.

Work Together
Have students write the solution to the Work Together problems as you guide the class through the examples.

- Elicit student responses as you analyze each transaction.

Xtra!
Study Tools
accountingxtra.swlearning.com

INDEPENDENT PRACTICE

On Your Own

- Assign the On Your Own problems to be worked independently.
- Use the Ongoing Assessment techniques to diagnose student understanding.

Application Problem

- Assign Application Problem 4-1: Identifying direct and indirect expenses.

Personal Trainer

- Students can access the Lesson 4-1 assessment material using this software.

Xtra! Web Site

- Students can access the Xtra! Study Tools for additional practice.

ENRICH

- Assign the Business Structures feature on page 92.
- Assign the Internet Research Activity.

CLOSE

- Ask students to briefly state the distinction between direct and indirect expenses.

• on your own 4-1

Identifying direct and indirect expenses

Elegant Interiors, Inc., has two departments: Furniture and Accessories. Elegant Interiors completed the transactions below.

Use a form similar to the one used in Work Together 4-1 to summarize whether the following transactions are direct or indirect expenses.

1. Paid cash for rent of the company building.
2. Paid cash for newspaper advertising of a new furniture line.
3. Paid cash for overnight delivery of special accessories items.
4. Paid monthly bill for Internet service for all company computer stations.
5. Paid cash for refreshments for the opening of an art show in the Accessories Department.
6. Paid cash for company credit card fees charged on total monthly sales.
7. Reimbursed Furniture Department manager for travel costs to a seminar on furniture finishes.
8. Paid to have the carpeting in the store cleaned.
9. Paid cash for uniforms for the elementary school's girls' soccer team to promote the store.
10. Recorded the bank service charge on the store's checking account.

BUSINESS STRUCTURES • BUSINESS STRUCTURES • BUSINESS STRUCTUR

business structures

Differentiating Between Personal and Business Taxes

When running a business, owners must differentiate between the *personal taxes* collected from employees and customers and the *business taxes* incurred by a company as a consequence of daily operations. Each category is handled differently. For example, businesses similar to Zytech are required to withhold payroll taxes from their employees, such as federal income tax and Medicare tax, and forward the tax amounts to the appropriate government agency. Consequently, these personal payroll taxes represent a liability for Zytech until they are paid.

The sales tax collected on the sale of merchandise or services is also classified as a personal tax. Like personal payroll taxes, it is paid by individuals, collected by businesses, and later remitted to the required government agency. Until the sales tax is paid, it too represents a liability.

Like individuals, businesses also pay taxes. For example, successful businesses like Zytech must pay income tax on business profits. Zytech is also required by law to pay taxes on the earnings of its employees. Based on its payroll, Zytech must pay social security tax, Medicare tax, and unemployment taxes. Companies classify the taxes paid by a business as expenses, although they are temporarily recorded in liability accounts until they are paid.

Financial Reporting for a Departmentalized Business

BUSINESS STRUCTURES

- Direct students to this feature to help them understand the difference between the personal taxes paid by individuals and the business taxes paid by companies.
- Point out that some personal taxes, such as sales tax, are collected by businesses. Since businesses must turn these taxes in to the appropriate government agency, the amount is recorded on their financial statements as a liability until actually remitted.
- Write the headings *Personal Taxes* and *Business Taxes* on the board or overhead. Ask students for examples of both. Write answers in the appropriate column.

4-2 Interim Departmental Statement of Gross Profit

INTERIM FINANCIAL STATEMENTS

A departmentalized business prepares the same financial statements in the same form as a nondepartmentalized business. In addition, a departmentalized business usually prepares reports about the performance of each department. In the last lesson, you learned that companies interested in controlling costs often prepare a departmental margin statement. This statement shows the revenue earned by a department less its cost of merchandise sold and less its direct expenses. You will learn how to prepare a departmental margin statement in Lesson 4-4.

The amount of revenue from sales less the cost of goods sold is called **gross profit**. Gross profit, therefore, shows the direct relationship between sales and sales price and merchandise inventory and the cost of merchandise inventory. By analyzing a department's gross profit data, managers can determine the amount of revenue remaining after the cost of merchandise has been deducted from net sales. A statement showing gross profit for each department is called a **departmental statement of gross profit**. A review of gross profit information may show a need to do the following:

1. Change merchandise selling prices.
2. Change suppliers of merchandise.
3. Add, delete, or change products.
4. Discontinue a department.

Gross profit information reflects changes between costs and selling prices. Departmental gross profit data also provide information that can be used to quickly determine potential profits. Businesses prepare annual financial statements at the end of each fiscal year. However, a successful business does not wait a full year to analyze its gross profit and take action to reverse negative trends. Therefore, businesses often pre-

pare an interim departmental statement of gross profit at the end of a month or quarter. The word *interim* means *between terms* or *in the meantime*.

Determining Ending Merchandise Inventory

To prepare an interim departmental statement of gross profit, both beginning and ending inventory amounts are needed. The ending inventory for one month becomes the beginning inventory for the next month.

Two principal methods are used to determine actual amounts of merchandise on hand. A merchandise inventory determined by counting, weighing, or measuring items of merchandise on hand is called a **periodic inventory**. A periodic inventory is sometimes referred to as a *physical inventory*. A merchandise inventory determined by keeping a continuous record of increases, decreases, and balance on hand is called a **perpetual inventory**.

The cost of merchandise inventory is relatively easy to determine at any time when a perpetual inventory is kept. However, keeping a perpetual inventory for a merchandising business with many inventory items requires a good computer database system. The increased use of point-of-sale terminals or cash registers and barcodes on merchandise has made perpetual inventories increasingly common.

For a periodic inventory, the business takes a physical count of merchandise. However, a periodic inventory on a monthly basis may not be practical. When a perpetual inventory is not kept and a monthly periodic inventory is not practical, a business may estimate merchandise inventory. Estimating inventory by using the previous year's percentage of gross profit on operations is called the **gross profit method of estimating an inventory**.

MATERIALS

- **Instructor's Resource CD:**
  PowerPoint Slides
- **Xtra! Study Tools on the Xtra! Web Site**
- **Blackline Masters:**
  Estimated Merchandise Inventory Sheet, Gross Profit Method

Interim Departmental Statement of Gross Profit

- **Working Papers:**
  Teacher's Edition of the Working Papers for Lesson 4-2
- **Software:**
  Personal Trainer

- Refer students to the illustration at the top of the page as the steps for preparing an estimated merchandise inventory sheet are explained.

- Ask students to examine the math boxes so they understand the process for computing net purchases and net sales to date.

DEMONSTRATE

Prepare an estimated merchandise inventory sheet

- Guide the students through the preparation of an estimated merchandise inventory sheet for the Audio Department by using a transparency for an estimated merchandise inventory sheet, gross profit method.

- Read each step aloud or ask individual students to read the steps. Explain how each total for each step is calculated or determined.

- Show the students where each step's total appears on the estimated merchandise inventory sheet by completing the transparency on the overhead.

ESTIMATING ENDING MERCHANDISE INVENTORY

1. List beginning inventory.
2. Determine net purchases.
3. Calculate merchandise available for sale.
4. Determine net sales.
5. Calculate estimated gross profit.
6. Calculate the estimated cost of merchandise sold.
7. Calculate estimated ending inventory.

Zytech uses a periodic inventory system. It uses the gross profit method of estimating an inventory to determine monthly ending inventory. The Audio Department's estimated inventory sheet prepared on June 30 is shown above. Zytech used the following steps to prepare the estimated merchandise inventory sheet.

STEPS • STEPS • STEPS • STEPS • STEPS • STEPS • STEPS • STEPS • STEPS • STEPS

PREPARING AN ESTIMATED MERCHANDISE INVENTORY SHEET

1. Obtain the beginning inventory, January 1, from the general ledger. The balance of *Merchandise Inventory—Audio*, *$186,434.61*, is the actual merchandise inventory on hand at the beginning of the fiscal year. The amount is the result of the periodic inventory count from December 31 of the previous year.

2. Determine net purchases to date, *$56,550.10*, as follows:

	Purchases—Audio	$59,430.60
−	Purchases Discount—Audio	− 1,090.20
		$58,340.40
−	Purchases Returns and Allowances—Audio	− 1,790.30
=	Net Purchases to Date (January 1–June 30)	$56,550.10

3. Add lines 1 and 2 to determine the merchandise available for sale, *$242,984.71.*

4. Determine net sales to date, *$186,848.80*, as follows:

	Sales—Audio	$190,540.20
−	Sales Discount—Audio	− 680.60
		$189,859.60
−	Sales Returns and Allowances—Audio	− 3,010.80
=	Net Purchases to Date (January 1–June 30)	$186,848.80

5. Calculate the estimated gross profit, *$84,081.96*, by multiplying line 4 by 45.0%. The percentage used is a gross profit estimate based on records of previous years' operations.

6. Calculate the estimated cost of merchandise sold, *$102,766.84*, by subtracting line 5 from line 4.

7. Calculate the estimated ending inventory, *$140,217.87*, by subtracting line 6 from line 3. This estimate is used on the interim departmental statement of gross profit.

TEACHING STRATEGIES   ACCOUNTING PEDAGOGY

This textbook covers complete financial statement preparation including the statement of stockholders' equity. Students are given the opportunity to perform financial statement analysis, which will help improve their critical thinking skills.

Zytech Media Corporation
Interim Departmental Statement of Gross Profit
For Month Ended June 30, 20--

	Audio	*% of Net Sales	Video	% of Net Sales	Total	% of Net Sales
Operating Revenue:						
Net Sales	$32,883.65	100.0	$36,546.30	100.0	$69,429.95	100.0
Cost of Merchandise Sold:						
Est. Mdse. Inv., June 1.	$149,387.48		$145,799.62		$295,187.10	
Net Purchases	8,916.40		17,073.50		25,989.90	
Mdse. Available for Sale.	$158,303.88		$162,873.12		$321,177.00	
Less Est. End. Inv., June 30. .	140,217.87		138,772.66		278,990.53	
Cost of Merchandise Sold . . .		18,086.01	55.0	24,100.46	65.9	42,186.47	60.8
Gross Profit on Operations	$14,797.64	45.0	$12,445.84	34.1	$27,243.48	39.2

*Rounded to nearest 0.1%

Zytech's interim departmental statement of gross profit for the month ended June 30 is shown above. The data are organized into three sections:

1. Operating revenue.
2. Cost of merchandise sold.
3. Gross profit on operations.

The beginning inventory for each department is the estimated ending inventory from the interim departmental statement of gross profit for the month ended May 31 of the current year.

An interim departmental statement of gross profit can be prepared whether perpetual or periodic inventory methods are used. When a perpetual method is used, the up-to-date inventory amount for the end of a month is readily available. When a periodic inventory method is used, the inventory value at the end of the month is estimated using the gross profit method.

To help a manager analyze financial information, relationships between items in a financial statement are calculated. The percentage relationship between one financial statement item and the total that includes that item is called a **component percentage**. Component percentages may be shown in a separate column on a financial statement. Four basic components are included in every sales dollar:

1. Cost of merchandise sold.
2. Gross profit on operations.

3. Total operating expenses.
4. Net income before federal income tax.

Zytech analyzes its interim departmental statement of gross profit monthly by calculating a component percentage for cost of merchandise sold and gross profit on operations. The component percentages for operating expenses and net income are calculated and analyzed at the end of each fiscal period.

REMEMBER Gross profit is the difference between net sales and cost of merchandise sold. Direct and indirect expenses are not considered when calculating gross profit.

EXPLAIN

- Explain why the cost of merchandise sold figure is critical to a merchandising business *(to keep costs of merchandise as low as possible).*

- Emphasize that the gross profit on operations must be large enough to cover total operating expenses in order to produce a net income.

- Explain how the cost of merchandise sold percentage and the gross profit percentage are calculated.

DEMONSTRATE

Gross profit percentages

- Point out the cost of merchandise sold and the gross profit on operations amounts in the illustration.

- Use the board or overhead to demonstrate the procedure for calculating the percentages for cost of merchandise sold and gross profit.

- Ask students to verify the percentages through the use of a calculator.

EXPLAIN

- Point out that for component percentages to be useful, businesses must know acceptable levels of performance.

DEMONSTRATE

- Write Zytech's acceptable levels of performance for cost of merchandise sold *(60%)* and gross profit on operations *(40%)* on the board or overhead. Underneath these percentages, write the appropriate percentages from the illustration. Point out that both percentages indicate acceptable levels of performance.

ONGOING ASSESSMENT

- Assessment is an ongoing process. Circulate through the classroom or lab, observing which students have problems with assignments.

- Troubleshooting: Students may have problems with estimating ending inventory, calculating interim gross profit, and determining acceptable levels of performance.

- Assess student understanding by checking solutions to Independent Practice assignments.

COST OF MERCHANDISE SOLD AND GROSS PROFIT PERCENTAGES

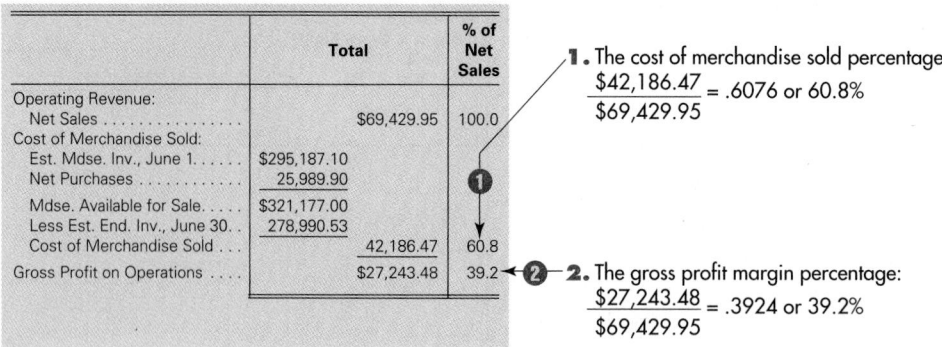

	Total	% of Net Sales
Operating Revenue:		
Net Sales	$69,429.95	100.0
Cost of Merchandise Sold:		
Est. Mdse. Inv., June 1.	$295,187.10	
Net Purchases	25,989.90	
Mdse. Available for Sale.	$321,177.00	
Less Est. End. Inv., June 30. .	278,990.53	
Cost of Merchandise Sold . . .		42,186.47	60.8
Gross Profit on Operations	$27,243.48	39.2

1. The cost of merchandise sold percentage:
$$\frac{\$42,186.47}{\$69,429.95} = .6076 \text{ or } 60.8\%$$

2. The gross profit margin percentage:
$$\frac{\$27,243.48}{\$69,429.95} = .3924 \text{ or } 39.2\%$$

The cost of merchandise sold is a significant cost for all merchandising businesses. Management attempts to keep this cost as low as possible. The calculation of Zytech's component percentage for total cost of merchandise sold is shown above. Both the cost of merchandise sold percentage and the gross profit percentage use net sales in the denominator of the equation. From these percentages, we learn that for every $100 in sales, Zytech spent $60.80 to obtain the

goods sold. The remainder, $39.20, represents the gross profit on operations. Gross profit on operations must be large enough to cover total operating expenses and produce a net income.

Since Zytech is a departmental business, similar calculations are made for each department. Zytech uses the departmental component percentages to analyze the results of each department.

DETERMINING ACCEPTABLE LEVELS OF PERFORMANCE

For component percentages to be useful, a business must know acceptable levels of performance. Two sources are frequently used to determine acceptable performance. A business's historical records provide percentages that can be compared across time. The business should investigate significant changes in component percentages over time.

Industry performance standards are another source that businesses use for comparison. Industry trade organizations survey businesses and publish significant data such as component percentages. While these percentages represent industry averages, they allow useful comparisons to be made.

Based on these sources, Zytech determines that the total cost of merchandise sold percentage should be 60.0% or less. As a result, total gross profit on operations should be 40.0% or more. Zytech further determines that these percentages are also good targets for each of the departments.

An analysis of the interim departmental statement of gross profit for the month ended June 30 indicates some unacceptable levels of performance. The component percentage for total cost of merchandise sold, 60.8%, is slightly more than 60.0%. The component percentage for total gross profit on operations, 39.2%, is less than 40.0%. Further review shows that the component percentages for the Audio Department are at acceptable levels but those of the Video Department are not. The company must find ways to improve gross profit on operations. Possible action could be to form strategies for increasing net sales or decreasing the cost of purchases. It is important to understand that if Zytech did not prepare monthly departmental statements of gross profit, the need for improvement in the Video Department might not have been discovered until the end of the year.

RETEACH

- Ask a student to explain the difference between periodic and perpetual inventory.

- Provide extensive practice in estimating merchandise inventory. Have students practice the procedures with a variety of net sales and net purchases amounts. Also, vary the estimated gross profit percentage to emphasize the significance of the percentage in arriving at an estimated ending inventory.

- Ask a student to explain and demonstrate on the board or overhead the procedure for computing the cost of merchandise sold percentage and gross profit percentage.

- Ask a student to explain the importance of determining acceptable levels of performance. Provide an example to the class of acceptable and unacceptable levels of performance.

terms review

TERMS REVIEW • TERMS

gross profit
departmental statement
  of gross profit
periodic inventory
perpetual inventory
gross profit method of estimating
  an inventory
component percentage

audit your understanding

AUDIT YOUR UNDERSTANDING

1. In addition to regular financial statements, what other reports does a departmentalized business prepare?

2. What are the two principal methods for determining amounts of merchandise on hand?

3. What are the three sections of a departmental statement of gross profit?

work together 4-2

WORK TOGETHER • WORK TOGETHER • WORK TOGETHER

Preparing an interim departmental statement of gross profit

The following data are obtained from the accounting records of Willow Glen Interior Design on May 31 of the current year. Estimated merchandise inventory forms and statement paper are provided in the *Working Papers.* Your instructor will guide you through the following examples.

	Kitchen	Bath
Beginning Inventory, January 1	$110,000.00	$84,000.00
Estimated Beginning Inventory, May 1	111,426.00	87,072.00
Net Purchases, January 1 to April 30	42,500.00	30,100.00
Net Sales, January 1 to April 30	78,600.00	52,300.00
Net Purchases for May	8,300.00	5,400.00
Net Sales for May	20,200.00	8,400.00
Estimated Gross Profit Percentage	48.0%	45.0%

1. Prepare an estimated merchandise inventory sheet for each department for the month ended May 31.

2. Prepare an interim departmental statement of gross profit for the month ended May 31. Calculate and record component percentages for cost of merchandise sold and gross profit on operations. Round percentage calculations to the nearest 0.1%.

Interim Departmental Statement of Gross Profit

Lesson 4-2   **97**

INDEPENDENT PRACTICE

On Your Own

- Assign the On Your Own problems to be worked independently.
- Use the Ongoing Assessment techniques to diagnose student understanding.

Application Problem

- Assign Application Problem 4-2: Preparing an interim departmental statement of gross profit; calculating component percentages.

Personal Trainer

- Students can access the Lesson 4-2 assessment material using this software.

Xtra! Web Site

- Students can access the Xtra! Study Tools for additional practice.

ENRICH

- Assign Case 1 of the Cases for Critical Thinking.

CLOSE

- Ask students to write a brief paragraph on the significance of preparing departmental records for a departmentalized merchandising business.

on your own 4-2

Preparing an interim departmental statement of gross profit

The following data are obtained from the accounting records of Lassen Heating and Air Conditioning, Inc., on April 30 of the current year. Estimated merchandise inventory forms and statement paper are provided in the *Working Papers*. Work this problem independently.

	Commercial	Residential
Beginning Inventory, January 1	$280,000.00	$108,000.00
Estimated Beginning Inventory, April 1	287,894.00	124,884.00
Net Purchases, January 1 to March 31	120,500.00	62,300.00
Net Sales, January 1 to March 31	196,600.00	88,400.00
Net Purchases for April	66,200.00	13,400.00
Net Sales for April	71,100.00	14,400.00
Estimated Gross Profit Percentage	42.0%	48.0%

1. Prepare an estimated merchandise inventory sheet for each department for the month ended April 30.

2. Prepare an interim departmental statement of gross profit for the month ended April 30. Calculate and record component percentages for cost of merchandise sold and gross profit on operations. Round percentage calculations to the nearest 0.1%.

©GETTY IMAGES/PHOTODISC

4-3 Preparing a Work Sheet for a Departmentalized Business

PROVING THE ACCURACY OF POSTING TO SUBSIDIARY LEDGERS

Zytech Media Corporation
Schedule of Accounts Receivable
December 31, 20--

Jason Campari	$ 950.60
DTS Systems	644.70
Kim Electronics	1,785.00
Links Golf Supply	1,592.50
Katie Matthews	245.70
Olympic Productions	1,391.25
Wawona School District	775.25
Bianca Velario	3,675.00
David Young	2,695.00
Total Accounts Receivable	$13,755.00

Zytech prepares a report showing the total of all accounts receivable ledger accounts. A list of customer accounts, account balances, and total amount due from all customers is called a **schedule of accounts receivable**. The total of a schedule of accounts receivable must equal the balance of the general ledger controlling account, Accounts Receivable. Zytech's schedule of accounts receivable is shown above.

Zytech also prepares a report showing the total of all accounts payable ledger accounts.

A list of vendor accounts, account balances, and total amount due all vendors is called a **schedule of accounts payable**. The total of a schedule of accounts payable must equal the balance of the controlling account, Accounts Payable. Zytech's schedule of accounts payable is shown below.

The balances of both controlling accounts, Accounts Receivable and Accounts Payable, agree with the totals shown on the two schedules. Therefore, posting to subsidiary ledgers is assumed to be correct.

Zytech Media Corporation
Schedule of Accounts Payable
December 31, 20--

AudioMax	$ 3,660.60
Digital Warehouse	9,420.00
LED Television, Inc.	1,590.00
MegaWatt Sound, Inc.	1,514.30
Plasma Electronics	10,840.00
Western Digital Systems	3,610.40
Yogashi Corporation	725.00
Total Accounts Payable	$31,360.30

Preparing a Work Sheet for a Departmentalized Business

- Explain that the rest of this lesson refers to procedures for completing an expanded work sheet, as shown on pages 102–103.

- Explain that information in the four additional Departmental Margin Statements columns is used to prepare departmental margin statements.

- Explain that there are three income summary accounts on the work sheet: Income Summary—Audio, Income Summary—Video, and Income Summary—General.

- Explain that the departmental income summary accounts are used for the adjustments for the departmental merchandise inventory accounts. In addition, the revenue, cost, and direct expense accounts of both departments are closed to these two income summary accounts.

- Explain that Income Summary—General is used for other closing entries.

- Remind students that adjusting entries are used to bring specific accounts up to date.

- Remind students that the information used to prepare the trial balance on the work sheet is taken from the general ledger accounts and that total debits must equal total credits.

- Point out that Federal Income Tax Expense is listed two lines below the last departmental margin amount.

EXPANDED WORK SHEET

Zytech completes the end-of-fiscal-period work as of December 31 each year. A columnar accounting form used to summarize the general ledger information needed to prepare financial statements is called a **work sheet**. Zytech uses an expanded work sheet to sort information needed for departmental margin statements. The 12-column work sheet prepared by Zytech on December 31 is shown on pages 102–103. Besides the standard eight amount columns that normally appear on a work sheet, Zytech uses four additional columns: Departmental Margin Statement—Audio Debit and Credit and Departmental Margin Statement—Video Debit and Credit. Information in these four additional columns is used to prepare departmental margin statements.

Trial Balance on a Departmental Work Sheet

If debits equal credits in journals and if posting is done correctly, debits will equal credits in a general ledger. A proof of the equality of debits and credits in a general ledger is called a **trial balance**. A trial balance can be prepared at any time to check the equality of debits and credits in the general ledger. A trial balance should always be prepared as part of the end-of-fiscal-period activities.

A trial balance is prepared in the Trial Balance columns of the work sheet. General ledger accounts are listed in the Account Title column in the same order in which they appear in the general ledger. All accounts are listed, regardless of whether there is a balance or not. Zytech's trial balance for the current year ended December 31 is shown on the work sheet. When Zytech prepares its departmental work sheet, notice that three income summary accounts are used. Two are used for adjusting inventory accounts related to separate departments, Income Summary—Audio and Income Summary—Video. They are also used to close the revenue, cost, and direct expense accounts of both departments. Income Summary—General is used for other closing entries.

Also notice that Zytech writes the account Federal Income Tax Expense on the work sheet two lines below Departmental Margin—Video. This location simplifies subtotaling the income statement columns and calculating additional income tax

expense. Procedures for calculating corporate income tax are described in Chapter 13.

After all general ledger accounts and balances have been entered, the Trial Balance columns are totaled, checked for equality, and ruled. The two column totals, $1,325,257.99, are the same.

Adjustments on a Work Sheet with Departmental Margins

Some of the general ledger accounts are not up to date. For example, uncollectible accounts expense has not been recorded. The entries needed to bring accounts up to date are planned in the Adjustments columns of the work sheet.

The information needed for adjusting Zytech's general ledger accounts for the year ended December 31 of the current year begins on the page following the work sheet illustration.

Zytech's adjustments are in the work sheet's Adjustments columns. The departmental merchandise inventory adjustments are recorded in each department's appropriate income summary account. Adjustments are made for uncollectible accounts expense, changes in departmental merchandise inventory, supplies used, insurance expired, depreciation, and estimated federal income tax expense.

Financial Reporting for a Departmentalized Business

APPLIED SKILLS BUILDING STUDY SKILLS

Direct students to create a Quick Reference Guide (QRG) on a small card or sheet of paper to use as an aid in analyzing adjustments. Students should write the four questions to analyze an adjustment on a card or sheet of paper to use as a QRG. Have them use this QRG whenever they analyze adjustments. The questions are: (1) What is the balance of the account? (2) What should the balance be for the account? (3) What must be done to correct the account balance? (4) What adjustment is made?

careers in accounting

Dianne Villanueva Conry, Part-Time Senior Accountant and Accounting Instructor

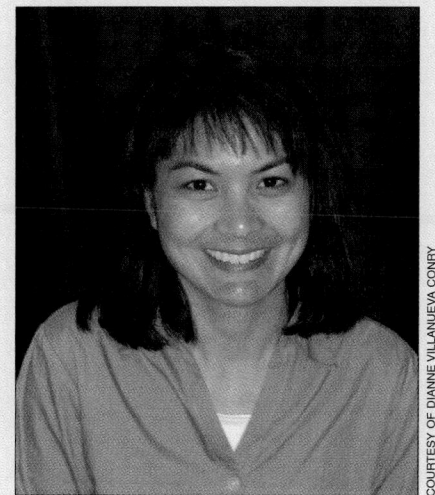

COURTESY OF DIANNE VILLANUEVA CONRY

Employment in the accounting profession is sometimes associated with working long, intense hours. In many instances, this association may be true but certainly not in all. For Dianne Villanueva Conry, a career in accounting has allowed her to keep her primary focus on her family. Presently, Dianne works as a part-time senior accountant at Clinimetrics Research Associates, Inc., and teaches an evening accounting class at the University of California Santa Cruz Extension Program in Cupertino, California.

To reach her current positions, Dianne earned a Bachelor of Science degree in Business Administration with the Accountancy Option from California State University, Fresno. Following graduation, she remained at CSUF for another year and earned a Master of Science degree in Financial Accounting. Because of her strong academic background and part-time work experience with a local CPA, she was hired by PricewaterhouseCoopers, one of the four largest accounting firms in the world. During her tenure at PWC, she acquired public accounting auditing experience and passed the certified public accountancy exam for the state of California. After three years of employment as a public accountant, she accepted a job offer from Sony Electronics. Dianne's new position helped satisfy her expanding interest in corporate accounting and allowed her to gain a more complete understanding of private industry practices.

After starting her family, Dianne had an opportunity to work part-time for Horn Murdock Cole. Working as the internal controller, start-up services instructor, and information technology troubleshooter, Dianne gained invaluable experience regarding all levels of consulting.

Presently, Dianne teaches an evening accounting class and works 24 to 28 hours per week at Clinimetrics Research Associates, Inc., a privately held firm that performs clinical research and drug trials related to the pharmaceutical, biotechnology, and medical device industries. At Clinimetrics, she has successfully combined her experience and knowledge in auditing, private industry, and consulting. Although Dianne has recurring accounting and payroll responsibilities, she finds special projects to be the most rewarding.

Salary Range: A senior accountant could expect to earn $70,000–$150,000, depending on the industry, company, part of the country, and level of experience.

Qualifications: To qualify for entry-level employment in the accounting industry, Dianne recommends that students develop the ability to multi-task, acquire strong written and oral communication skills, build a solid knowledge of accounting basics, and obtain proficient spreadsheet and word processing skills. Dianne also encourages students to view accounting as a flexible profession that offers individuals a variety of career options and alternatives that can assist them with the attainment of personal goals.

Occupational Outlook: For the future, Dianne envisions more analyses of variances and business activities. Accountants will be needed to assist managers in determining why revenues and expenses are fluctuating from original budget projections. This critical information will be used by managers to make sound financial decisions.

CAREERS IN ACCOUNTING

This feature presents interviews with individuals working in accounting and related fields. The various career paths selected by the interviewees are noted. Salary ranges, occupational outlooks, and educational requirements are highlighted.

Ask students to read the feature. Form the students into cooperative learning groups of 3–4 students. Ask groups to discuss the feature, noting the education and experience required for Dianne Villanueva Conry to reach her present position. Ask students why Dianne opted for part-time employment. Ask students to list some of the skills Dianne recommends for entry-level employment. Write student answers on the board or overhead. Ask students how many of these skills they honestly possess. Ask them what they can do to acquire such skills.

EXPLAIN

- Point out that the work sheet for a departmentalized business using responsibility accounting is shown on this page and on page 103.

- Explain that detailed instructions for completing this work sheet are explained on pages 104–108.

- Point out that the work sheet is the same as the 8-column work sheet studied previously, with the addition of four Departmental Margin Statements columns between the Adjustments columns and the Income Statement columns.

- Explain that under the heading Departmental Margin Statements, each department has a Debit and a Credit column. Explain that these columns are used for extending balances of departmentalized accounts.

- Explain to students that the completed work sheet is shown in order to give students a complete picture of the work sheet.

- Explain that this illustration should be used throughout this lesson for reference.

- Review the headings on the work sheet.

Zytech Media Corporation
Work Sheet
For Year Ended December 31, 20—

#	ACCOUNT TITLE	TRIAL BALANCE Debit	TRIAL BALANCE Credit	ADJUSTMENTS Debit	ADJUSTMENTS Credit	DMS AUDIO Debit	DMS AUDIO Credit	DMS VIDEO Debit	DMS VIDEO Credit	INCOME STATEMENT Debit	INCOME STATEMENT Credit	BALANCE SHEET Debit	BALANCE SHEET Credit
1	Cash	3891000										3891000	
2	Petty Cash	50000										50000	
3	Accounts Receivable	1375500										1375500	
4	Allow. for Uncoll. Accts.		24060		(a)210940								235000
5	Merchandise Inventory—Audio	18643461		(b)1842039								20485500	
6	Merchandise Inventory—Video	19984460			(c)936000							19048460	
7	Supplies—Administrative	697300			(d)292200							405100	
8	Supplies—Audio	1021500			(e)429400							592100	
9	Supplies—Video	984200			(f)775300							208900	
10	Prepaid Insurance	985000			(g)565000							420000	
11	Office Equipment	1690000										1690000	
12	Acc. Depr.—Office Equipment		596000		(h)149000								745000
13	Store Equipment—Audio	3890000										3890000	
14	Acc. Depr.—Store Equipment, Audio		1800000		(i)400000								2200000
15	Store Equipment—Video	2665200										2665200	
16	Acc. Depr.—Store Equipment, Video		1550000		(j)350000								1900000
17	Accounts Payable		3136030										3136030
18	Employee Income Tax Payable—Federal		268075										268075
19	Employee Income Tax Payable—State		111819										111819
20	Federal Income Tax Payable		85207		(k) 85207								85207
21	Social Security Tax Payable		273057										273057
22	Medicare Tax Payable		63013										63013
23	Sales Tax Payable		313964										313964
24	Unemployment Tax Payable—Federal		2360										2360
25	Unemployment Tax Payable—State		15930										15930
26	Health Insurance Premiums Payable		226116										226116
27	Life Insurance Premiums Payable		35019										35019
28	Dividends Payable		3000000										3000000
29	Capital Stock		34000000										34000000
30	Retained Earnings		5615550	(c)									5615550
31	Dividends	30000000										30000000	
32	Income Summary—Audio				(b)1842039		1842039						
33	Income Summary—Video			(c) 936000				936000					
34	Income Summary—General												
35	Sales—Audio		35103281				35103281						
36	Sales—Video		43834175						43834175				
37	Sales Discount—Audio	160585				160585							
38	Sales Returns and Allowances—Audio	495050				495050							
39	Sales Discount—Video	200525						200525					
40	Sales Returns and Allowances—Video	618180						618180					
41	Purchases—Audio	21574568				21574568							
42	Purchases—Video	23176662						23176662					
43	Purchases Discount—Audio		405895				405895						
44	Purch. Returns and Allowances—Audio		828248				828248						
45	Purchases Discount—Video		433455						433455				

TEACHING STRATEGIES   DIFFERENT LEARNING ABILITIES

Limited English Proficiency (LEP) Students. Rather than asking students whether they understand what you have said, ask them to restate what you have said in their own words.

Line	Account Title	Trial Balance Dr	Trial Balance Cr	Adjustments Cr	Dept. Margin—Audio Dr	Dept. Margin—Audio Cr	Dept. Margin—Video Dr	Dept. Margin—Video Cr	Income Statement Dr	Income Statement Cr	Balance Sheet Dr	Balance Sheet Cr
46	Purch. Returns and Allowances—Video		8897 52	(b) 8897 52				8897 52				
47	Advertising Expense—Audio	1650 00			1650 00							
48	Depr. Exp.—Store Equipment, Audio			(c) 4000 00	4000 00							
49	Payroll Taxes Expense—Audio	9401 80			9401 80							
50	Salary Expense—Audio	90924 19			90924 19							
51	Supplies Expense—Audio			(e) 4294 00	4294 00							
52	Advertising Expense—Video	2140 00					2140 00					
53	Depr. Exp.—Store Equipment, Video			(f) 3500 00			3500 00					
54	Payroll Taxes Expense—Video	7509 82					7509 82					
55	Salary Expense—Video	72627 02					72627 02					
56	Supplies Expense—Video			(j) 7753 00			7753 00					
57	Broadband Expense	1440 00							1440 00			
58	Depr. Exp.—Office Equipment			(h) 1490 00					1490 00			
59	Insurance Expense			(g) 5650 00					5650 00			
60	Miscellaneous Expense	5958 48							5958 48			
61	Payroll Taxes Expense—Administrative	4515 30							4515 30			
62	Phone Expense	2390 00							2390 00			
63	Rent Expense	18000 00							18000 00			
64	Salary Expense—Administrative	43667 19							43667 19			
65	Supplies Expense—Administrative			(d) 2922 00					2922 00			
66	Uncollectible Accounts Expense			(a) 2109 40					2109 40			
67	Utilities Expense	3202 28							3202 28			
68					332572 02	381794 63	342843 51	451573 82				
69	Department Margin—Audio				49222 61					49222 61		
70	Department Margin—Video						108730 31			108730 31		
71					381794 63	381794 63	451573 82	451573 82				
72	Federal Income Tax Expense	10800 00		(k) 852 07					11652 07			
73		1325257 99	1325257 99						102996 72	157952 92	577217 60	522261 40
74												54956 20
75	Net Income after Federal Income Tax	60350 86	60350 86						157952 92	157952 92	577217 60	577217 60

Preparing a Work Sheet for a Departmentalized Business

Lesson 4-3 **103**

EXPLAIN

- Point out the way in which the Departmental Margin Statements columns are totaled on lines 68–71 of the work sheet.
- Draw students' attention to the entries in the Account Title column for these columns.
- Point out that the amounts for the departmental margins are extended to the Income Statement Credit column.
- Point out that none of the departmental margin account balances are extended into the Income Statement or Balance Sheet columns.
- Point out that the Income Statement and Balance Sheet columns are totaled and ruled in the way previously learned for other work sheets.

TEACHING STRATEGIES EXPANDING BEYOND THE CLASSROOM

Invite an accountant from a merchandising business to the classroom to address the importance of responsibility accounting.

- Emphasize that not all accounts in the general ledger are up to date. Point out on the trial balance in the work sheet on pages 102–103 that no balance has been recorded for the Uncollectible Accounts Expense. Lead into a discussion of uncollectible accounts and the accounting concept of Matching Expenses with Revenue.

- Explain that Zytech considers Uncollectible Accounts Expense as an administrative expense and will list the amount in the indirect expense section of the income statement. Point out that other companies may divide this expense between departments.

DEMONSTRATE

Analyze the transaction

- Direct student attention to the math box in the middle of the page 104. Calculate the amount of uncollectible accounts expense manually by writing the appropriate amount and percentage on the board or overhead. Quickly review and illustrate the process of moving the decimal two places to the left when converting a percentage to a decimal amount.

- Use T accounts to show the adjustment for uncollectible accounts expense.

- Refer to the work sheet on pages 102–103 and ask students to locate the adjustment for uncollectible accounts expense. Emphasize that, as with all transactions, there must be at least one debit part and one credit part and that both parts must be equal.

ADJUSTMENT INFORMATION

Adjustment Information, December 31

Uncollectible accounts expense—estimated as 1.0% of total sales on account.

Total sales on account for year	$210,940.00
Merchandise Inventory—Audio	204,855.00
Merchandise Inventory—Video	190,484.60
Supplies Used—Administrative	2,922.00
Supplies Used—Audio	4,294.00
Supplies Used—Video	7,753.00
Value of Prepaid Insurance	4,200.00
Depreciation Expense—Office Equipment	1,490.00
Depreciation Expense—Store Equipment, Audio	4,000.00
Depreciation Expense—Store Equipment, Video	3,500.00
Federal Income Tax Expense for Year	11,652.07

ADJUSTMENTS SHOWN ON WORK SHEET

Uncollectible Accounts Expense Adjustment

Merchandise is sometimes sold on account to customers who later are unable to pay the amounts owed. Amounts that cannot be collected from customers are business expenses. All expenses must be recorded in the fiscal period in which the expenses contribute to earning revenue. [CONCEPT: Matching Expenses with Revenue]

Zytech has found from past experience that approximately 1% of the total sales on account will be uncollectible. Total sales on account for the current year are $210,940.00. Zytech's uncollectible accounts expense is calculated as follows:

	Total Sales on Account	×	Percentage	=	Estimated Uncollectible Accounts Expense
	$210,940.00	×	1%	=	$2,109.40

Zytech estimates that of the $210,940.00 sales on account during the year, $2,109.40 will eventually be uncollectible. Zytech considers the estimated uncollectible amount of $2,109.40 to be an administrative expense. Consequently, the amount is recorded in a separate account titled Allowance for Uncollectible Accounts and is listed in the indirect expense section of the income statement.

Uncollectible Accounts Expense increases by a $2,109.40 debit. Allowance for Uncollectible Accounts, a contra asset account, increases by a $2,109.40 credit. The Allowance for Uncollectible Accounts balance represents the total estimated amount that Zytech believes will not be collected from accounts receivable. This estimated amount is not deducted from the Accounts Receivable balance until Zytech knows for sure which customers will not pay.

Uncollectible Accounts Expense	
Adj. (a) 2,109.40	

Allowance for Uncollectible Accounts	
	Dec. 31 Bal. 240.60
	Adj. (a) 2,109.40
	(New Bal. 2,350.00)

The Uncollectible Accounts Expense adjustment is recorded on the work sheet, lines 4 and 66. The adjustment is labeled (a) because it is the first adjustment recorded. Entries related to uncollectible accounts expense are described in Chapter 7.

TEACHING STRATEGIES   DIFFERENT LEARNING ABILITIES

Specific Learning Disability (SLD) Students. Encourage students to maintain a daily log or journal that describes their academic progress. Students can share this log, if they desire, with the teacher when updating their individual program.

Merchandise Inventory Adjustments

The merchandise inventory account balances in the trial balance are the beginning inventory amounts for a fiscal period. The amount of the ending inventory is determined by taking a periodic inventory at the end of a fiscal period.

The beginning Audio merchandise inventory, $186,434.61, is shown on line 5 in the Trial Balance Debit column of the work sheet. The periodic inventory taken on December 31 shows that the cost of Audio merchandise inventory is $204,855.00. To bring the Audio merchandise inventory up to date, the balance of Merchandise Inventory—Audio needs to be increased by $18,420.39 ($204,855.00 ending inventory less $186,434.61 beginning inventory).

Merchandise Inventory—Audio	
Dec. 31 Bal.	186,434.61
Adj. *(b)*	18,420.39
(New Bal.	*204,855.00)*

Income Summary—Audio	
	Adj. *(b)* 18,420.39

The account Merchandise Inventory—Audio is debited for $18,420.39. Income Summary—Audio is credited for $18,420.39. The balance of Merchandise Inventory—Audio after this adjustment, $204,855.00, is equal to the actual ending inventory.

A similar adjustment is made for Merchandise Inventory—Video. The beginning Video merchandise inventory, $199,844.60, is shown on line 6 in the Trial Balance Debit column of the work sheet. The periodic inventory taken on December 31 shows that the cost of Video merchandise inventory is $190,484.60. Therefore, the balance of Merchandise Inventory—Video needs to be decreased by $9,360.00 ($199,844.60 beginning inventory less $190,484.60 ending inventory).

Income Summary—Video	
Adj. *(c)*	9,360.00

Merchandise Inventory—Video		
Dec. 31 Bal.	199,844.60	Adj. *(c)* 9,360.00
(New Bal.	*190,484.60)*	

Income Summary—Video is debited for $9,360.00. Merchandise Inventory—Video is credited for $9,360.00. The balance of Merchandise Inventory—Video after this adjustment, $190,484.60, is equal to the actual ending inventory.

The two inventory adjustments are entered on the work sheet. The Merchandise Inventory—Audio adjustment is labeled *(b)*. The Merchandise Inventory—Video adjustment is labeled *(c)*.

Supplies Adjustments

A supplies inventory account balance in a trial balance includes two items: (1) the account balance on January 1 and (2) the cost of supplies bought during the year. The account balance does not reflect the cost of any supplies used during the year, which is an operating expense. The amount of the ending inventory is determined by taking a periodic inventory at the end of a fiscal period.

©GETTY IMAGES/PHOTODISC

TEACHING STRATEGIES   DIFFERENT LEARNING STYLES

Print Learner. The print learner prefers to see the data in print, preferably printed in words. Direct students to the illustrations, particularly those that show the steps as callouts.

- Explain that the company keeps separate records for supplies used by each department, so there are separate Supplies Expense accounts and separate Supplies asset accounts for each department. Each of these accounts is affected by an adjustment.

- Review the adjustments for supplies. Emphasize that these adjustments are similar to the supplies adjustment made for a nondepartmentalized business.

DEMONSTRATE

Adjustments affecting one or more departments

- Draw three pairs of T accounts on the board and label them *Supplies Expense—Audio, Supplies—Audio, Supplies Expense—Video, Supplies—Video, Supplies Expense—Administrative*, and *Supplies—Administrative*. Record the beginning balance in each departmental Supplies asset account, as shown on the work sheet.

- Demonstrate that separate expense amounts are entered as debits in each department expense account and as a credit to the appropriate Supplies asset account.

- Direct students to point to each part of these adjustments in the Adjustments columns of the work sheet on pages 102–103.

- Ask students which letters are used for the adjustments to supplies.

EXPLAIN

- Review the adjustment for insurance. Point out that the account balance for prepaid insurance in the trial balance represents the balance on January 1 plus the amount of insurance premiums paid during the year.

- Refer students to the work sheet on pages 102–103. Ask them to state the amounts of the account balances for prepaid insurance and insurance expense.

- Review the concepts of plant assets and depreciation expense. Lead into a discussion of the accounting concept Matching Expenses with Revenue.

106

Zytech keeps a record of supplies used by each department so that supplies expense can be charged to the appropriate department. Zytech's records indicate that the following supplies amounts were used by each department: Audio, $4,294.00; Video, $7,753.00; and Administrative, $2,922.00.

Separate asset and expense accounts are maintained for each department and for administrative uses. The administrative account records the use of supplies by any person who does not work in one of the departments. For example, the use of supplies by the accounting staff would be recorded in the administrative account. The effect of the supplies adjustment for the year is shown in the T accounts.

Zytech's supplies account balances are shown on lines 7 to 9 in the Trial Balance Debit column of the work sheet. To bring Zytech's supplies inventories up to date, the balance of each supplies account needs to be decreased by the total amount used by each department and the administrative staff. Since supplies are an asset, the supplies accounts must be decreased with credits of $2,922.00, $4,294.00, and $7,753.00. The balances of the supplies accounts after these adjustments are equal to the actual ending inventories.

The supplies adjustments are entered on lines 7–9, 51, 56, and 65 on the work sheet and labeled *(d)*, *(e)*, and *(f)*.

Supplies Expense—Administrative	
Adj. *(d)* 2,922.00	

Supplies Expense—Audio	
Adj. *(e)* 4,294.00	

Supplies Expense—Video	
Adj. *(f)* 7,753.00	

Supplies—Administrative	
Dec. 31 Bal. 6,973.00	Adj. *(d)* 2,922.00
(New Bal. 4,051.00)	

Supplies—Audio	
Dec. 31 Bal. 10,215.00	Adj. *(e)* 4,294.00
(New Bal. 5,921.00)	

Supplies—Administrative	
Dec. 31 Bal. 9,842.00	Adj. *(f)* 7,753.00
(New Bal. 2,089.00)	

Prepaid Insurance Adjustment

The prepaid insurance account balance includes two items. (1) The account balance on January 1. (2) The amount of insurance premiums paid during the year. The account balance does not reflect the amount of any insurance used during the year, which is an operating expense. The amount of unexpired insurance is determined at the end of a fiscal period.

Zytech's prepaid insurance account balance, $9,850.00, is shown on line 10 in the Trial Balance Debit column of the work sheet. The actual unexpired prepaid insurance on December 31 is $4,200.00. To bring Zytech's prepaid insurance account up to date, the balance of Prepaid Insurance must be decreased by $5,650.00 (December 31 balance, $9,850.00, less unexpired insurance, $4,200.00).

Insurance Expense	
Adj. *(g)* 5,650.00	

Prepaid Insurance	
Dec. 31 Bal. 9,850.00	Adj. *(g)* 5,650.00
(New Bal. 4,200.00)	

Insurance Expense increases by a $5,650.00 debit. Prepaid Insurance is decreased by a $5,650.00 credit. The balance of Prepaid Insurance after this adjustment, $4,200.00, is equal to the actual unexpired prepaid insurance.

The prepaid insurance adjustment is entered on the work sheet. The adjustment is labeled *(g)*.

Depreciation Expense Adjustments

Assets that will be used for a number of years in the operation of a business are called **plant assets**. Plant assets are not bought for resale to customers in the normal course of business. Plant assets decrease in value because of use, the passage of time, and the availability of new models. The portion of a plant asset's cost that is transferred to an expense account in each fiscal period during a plant asset's useful life is called **depreciation expense**. The decrease in the value of equipment because of use and passage of time is an operating expense. [*CONCEPT: Matching Expenses with Revenue*]

DEMONSTRATE

Analyze the transaction

- Draw T accounts for insurance expense and prepaid insurance to illustrate the accounts used for the insurance adjustment. Ask students for the amount of prepaid insurance recorded on the trial balance. Write the amount in the prepaid insurance T account.

- Write the amount of unexpired insurance on the board or overhead. Referring to the ending insurance amount, point out that this is the amount that should be in the prepaid insurance account. Determine the difference between the current balance in the prepaid insurance account and the unexpired amount actually remaining. After illustrating to the students how the adjustment amount for the insurance account is calculated, record the adjustment amounts in the appropriate T accounts.

- Ask students to locate the insurance adjustment on the work sheet.

The amount of depreciation is an estimate. The actual decrease in equipment value is not known until equipment is disposed of or sold. For this reason, the estimated depreciation is recorded in a separate contra asset account for each type of equipment. Calculating the amount of depreciation is described more fully in Chapter 8.

Zytech estimates that the yearly depreciation on office equipment is $1,490.00. To adjust for the depreciation of office equipment, Depreciation Expense—Office Equipment increases by a $1,490.00 debit. The contra asset account, Accumulated Depreciation—Office Equipment, increases by a $1,490.00 credit. The depreciation expense adjustment is entered on the work sheet and labeled (h).

Depreciation Expense—Office Equipment	
Adj. (h) 1,490.00	

Accumulated Depreciation—Office Equipment	
	Dec. 31 Bal. 5,960.00
	Adj. (h) 1,490.00
	(New Bal. 7,450.00)

Similar adjustments are made for Depreciation Expense—Store Equipment, Audio and Depreciation Expense—Store Equipment, Video.

These two depreciation expense adjustments are entered on the work sheet. The Depreciation Expense—Store Equipment, Audio adjustment is labeled (i). The Depreciation Expense—Store Equipment, Video adjustment is labeled (j).

Federal Income Tax Expense Adjustment
Corporations anticipating federal income taxes of $500.00 or more are required to pay estimated taxes each quarter. The estimated tax is paid in quarterly installments in April, June, September, and December. Even though a corporation pays a quarterly estimated tax, the actual income tax must be calculated at the end of each fiscal year.

Zytech estimated $10,800.00 federal income tax for the current year. Each quarterly income tax payment is recorded in a cash payments journal as a debit to Federal Income Tax Expense and a credit to Cash. At the end of the fiscal year, Zytech determines that the federal income tax is $11,652.07. To bring its federal income tax expense account up to date, the balance of Federal Income Tax Expense must be increased by $852.07

(federal income tax amount, $11,652.07, less the December 31 balance in Federal Income Tax Expense, $10,800.00).

Federal Income Tax Expense increases by an $852.07 debit. Federal Income Tax Payable increases by an $852.07 credit. The balance of Federal Income Tax Expense after this adjustment, $11,652.07, is equal to the total federal income tax for the fiscal year.

The Federal Income Tax Expense adjustment, labeled (k), is entered on the work sheet.

Calculating the actual federal income tax is described in more detail in Chapter 13.

After all adjustments have been entered on a work sheet, the Adjustments columns are totaled and checked for equality. The two column totals, $60,350.86, are the same. The work sheet's Adjustments columns are ruled as shown on line 73 of the work sheet.

Federal Income Tax Expense	
Dec. 31 Bal. 10,800.00	
Adj. (k) 852.07	
(New Bal. 11,652.07)	

Federal Income Tax Payable	
	Adj. (k) 852.07

©GETTY IMAGES/PHOTODISC

<sup/>

- Draw T accounts for Depreciation Expense—Office Equipment and Accumulated Depreciation—Office Equipment; label the normal balance sides. Show the students how Zytech's estimate of $1,490 for yearly depreciation on office equipment is recorded. Emphasize that depreciation is an estimate. Stress that depreciation does not necessarily represent the actual decline in the value of an asset; instead it is a method of allocating the cost of an asset over the years it will be used to generate revenue. Thus, expenses are matched with revenue.

- Remind students that the adjustment for federal income tax is for corporations only.

- Ask students what it means to use quarterly installments to pay for estimated income tax. Point out that the amount of federal income tax in the trial balance column is the amount of tax that was paid in quarterly installments.

- Emphasize that at the end of the fiscal year, when net income is finally known, federal income tax for the year can be calculated. If the amount of federal income tax calculated for the year exceeds the quarterly installment total, an adjustment is required to show the amount of additional tax that must be paid.

DEMONSTRATE

- Continue to direct students to the illustrations on pages 102–103 as preparation of the work sheet is discussed.

- Draw T accounts for federal income tax expense and federal income tax payable to illustrate the accounts used for the federal tax adjustment. Ask students for the amount of federal tax expense recorded on the trial balance. Write the amount in the federal income tax expense T account.

- Write the amount of federal income tax, $11,652.07, as determined by Zytech at the end of the fiscal year. Demonstrate how to calculate the amount of federal income tax expense adjustment when the total amount of tax is known. Point out that the adjustment in this instance represents additional tax owed and is therefore credited to federal income tax payable.

- Ask the students to locate the federal income tax expense adjustment on the work sheet on pages 102–103. Also ask them to check the equality of the adjustments columns totals.

TEACHING STRATEGIES DIFFERENT LEARNING STYLES

Kinesthetic Learner. When learning how to plan adjustments, the kinesthetic learner would prefer to participate in the planning process. This can be done by using a transparency of the T accounts and having each student complete the analysis process for one adjustment at the overhead projector. Other students can be completing the adjustment planning process individually on printed T accounts.

EXPLAIN

- Remind students that the asset, liability, and stockholders' equity account balances appearing on the trial balance are extended to the balance sheet columns of the work sheet. For those accounts affected by adjustments, new balances are calculated and extended. Emphasize that the departmental merchandise inventory adjusted balances are also extended to the Balance Sheet columns.

- Explain how certain accounts are affected by adjustments by reviewing the extension for allowance for uncollectible accounts. Write the trial balance amount, $240.60, and add the adjustment, $2,109.40, to illustrate how a new balance, $2,350.00, is calculated and extended to the Credit column of the Balance Sheet.

- Explain that the up-to-date balances of the income summary, revenue, cost, and direct expense accounts are to be extended to the appropriate Departmental Margin Statement columns.

DEMONSTRATE

- Direct students to the work sheet on pages 102–103 as you demonstrate completing the work sheet.

- Demonstrate that balance sheet items are extended to the Balance Sheet columns in the same way as previously studied.

- Demonstrate that balances of all revenue, cost, and direct expense items for the audio department are extended to the Departmental Margin Statements—Audio columns. Direct students to point to each item and follow its extension.

- Repeat the demonstration of extending Video Department items.

- Demonstrate extending the indirect expense items to the Income Statement debit column.

- Demonstrate completing the Departmental Margin Statements columns and calculating the departmental margin for each department in the same way in which the Income Statement columns are normally completed.

- Demonstrate extending the departmental margin amounts to the Income Statement Credit column, as shown on lines 69–70. Emphasize writing the departmental margin titles in the Account Title column.

COMPLETING A WORK SHEET WITH DEPARTMENTAL MARGIN COLUMNS

Refer to the work sheet illustration to follow these steps:

1 Extend the asset, liability, and stockholders' equity account balances to the Balance Sheet Debit and Credit columns (Lines 1–31). When an account is not affected by an adjustment, the amount in the Trial Balance Debit or Credit column is extended to either the Balance Sheet Debit or Credit column. For those accounts affected by adjustments, new balances are calculated and extended. For example, *Allowance for Uncollectible Accounts*, line 4 of the work sheet, has a Trial Balance Credit balance of $240.60. The Adjustments Credit column amount of $2,109.40 makes the new account balance $2,350.00 ($240.60 plus $2,109.40). The new credit balance, $2,350.00, is extended to the Balance Sheet Credit column (Line 4).

2 Extend the up-to-date balances of the income summary, revenue, cost, and direct expense accounts for the Audio Department to the Departmental Margin—Audio Debit and Credit columns (Lines 32, 35–37, 41–43, and 47–51). When an account is affected by an adjustment, the new balance is calculated and extended. For example, the balance of *Supplies Expense—Audio* in the Trial Balance Debit column is zero. The zero balance is not up to date because this account is affected by an adjustment. The debit balance, $0.00, *plus* the debit adjustment, $4,294.00, *equals* the adjusted balance, $4,294.00. Extend the up-to-date adjusted debit balance, $4,294.00, to the Departmental Margin—Audio Debit column. Do not forget to extend the amount in the Adjustments columns for *Income Summary—Audio* to the Departmental Margin—Audio Debit or Credit columns (Line 32).

3 Extend the up-to-date balances of the income summary, revenue, cost, and direct expense accounts for the Video Department to the Departmental Margin Statements—Video Debit and Credit columns (Lines 33, 38–40, 44–46, and 52–56). The procedure for extending these income statement amounts is the same as that for the Audio Department amounts described in step 2.

4 Extend the indirect expense items to the Income Statement Debit column (Lines 57–67).

5 Calculate the departmental margin for each department (Lines 69 and 70).
   a. Rule a single line across the Departmental Margin Statements—Audio Debit and Credit columns on the line with the last expense account, line 67. Add each column and write the totals under the ruled line. Subtract the smaller total from the larger total ($381,794.63 − $332,572.02 = $49,222.61). Write the difference, *$49,222.61,* in the Departmental Margin Statements—Audio Debit column on the next line, line 69. Write the same amount in the Income Statement Credit column on the same line. Write the words *Departmental Margin—Audio* on the same line in the Account Title column. The amount written on this line, *$49,222.61,* is the departmental margin for the Audio Department for the year ended December 31 of the current year.
   b. The same procedure is followed to calculate departmental margin for the Video Department. The totals for the Video Debit and Credit columns are written on the same line as the totals of the Audio columns. This departmental margin is recorded in the work sheet's Departmental Margin Statements—Video Debit column and in the Income Statement Credit column. The amounts are written on the line below the departmental margin for the Audio Department, line 70.
   c. The Departmental Margin Statements columns for the two departments are totaled and ruled as shown on line 71.

6 Extend the adjusted balance of federal income tax expense amount ($10,800.00 + $852.07) and record it in the Income Statement Debit column (Line 72) on the work sheet. The procedure for calculating federal income tax expense is described in Chapter 13.

7 Total the Income Statement and Balance Sheet columns. Calculate and record net income after federal income tax. The difference between the two Income Statement column totals on the work sheet is the net income or net loss for a fiscal period. If the Credit column total is larger than the Debit column total as shown in the work sheet, the difference is the net income. The net income, *$54,956.20,* is written under the work sheet's Income Statement Debit column total to make the two Income Statement columns balance. The words *Net Income after Federal Income Tax* are written in the Account Title column.

8 The difference between the two Balance Sheet column totals on the work sheet also represents the net income or net loss for a fiscal period. A net income increases stockholders' equity. Since stockholders' equity is increased with a credit, Zytech's net income, *$54,956.20,* is written under the Balance Sheet Credit column total to make the two Balance Sheet columns balance.

9 After the net income amount is written in the two work sheet columns, the last four columns are totaled again. The totals for each pair of columns must be the same. The two Income Statement totals are the same, $157,952.92. The two Balance Sheet totals are the same, $577,217.60. If columns do not balance, errors must be found and corrected before final ruling is done.

10 Rule the work sheet as shown on lines 73–75.

- Demonstrate extending the adjusted federal income tax expense amount to the Income Statement debit column.

- Demonstrate completing the rest of the work sheet in the usual fashion.

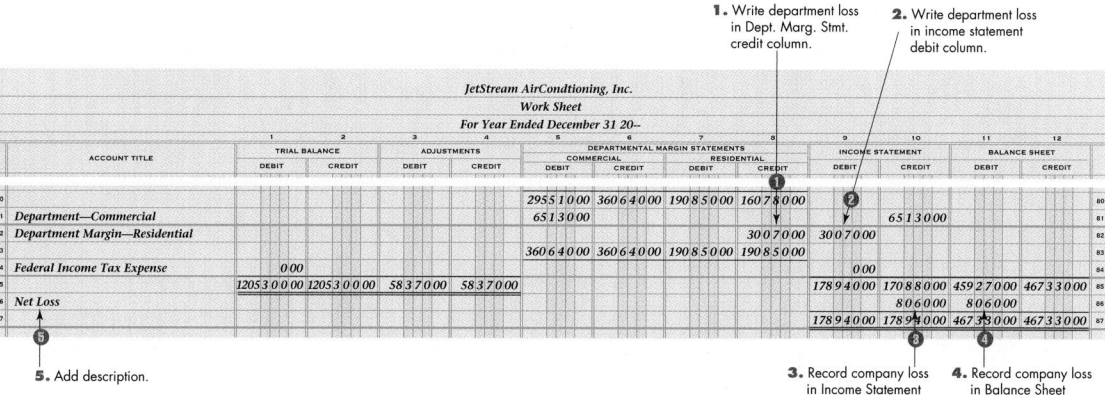

1. Write department loss in Dept. Marg. Stmt. credit column.

2. Write department loss in income statement debit column.

JetStream AirConditioning, Inc.
Work Sheet
For Year Ended December 31 20--

	TRIAL BALANCE		ADJUSTMENTS		DEPARTMENTAL MARGIN STATEMENTS				INCOME STATEMENT		BALANCE SHEET	
ACCOUNT TITLE					COMMERCIAL		RESIDENTIAL					
	DEBIT	CREDIT	DEBIT	CREDIT	DEBIT	CREDIT	DEBIT	CREDIT	DEBIT	CREDIT	DEBIT	CREDIT
Department—Commercial					2955100	3606400	1908500	1607800		6513000		
					651300							
Department Margin—Residential							300700		300700			
					3606400	3606400	1908500	1908500				
Federal Income Tax Expense	000								000			
	1205300000	1205300000	583700	583700					1789400	1708800	4592700	4673300
Net Loss										80600	80600	
									1789400	1789400	4673900	4673300

5. Add description.

3. Record company loss in Income Statement Credit Column.

4. Record company loss in Balance Sheet Debit column

If a department's Departmental Margin Statements Debit column total is larger than the Credit column total, as shown above for the Residential Department, the difference represents a departmental operating loss. A departmental operating loss occurs when the total of a department's cost of merchandise sold plus direct expenses exceeds its net sales. To record the departmental net loss on a work sheet, the net loss amount is written in the appropriate Departmental Margin Statements Credit column and the Income Statement Debit column.

If the Income Statement Debit column total is larger than the Credit column total, as also shown above, the difference represents a company net loss. When a company net loss occurs, the net loss amount is written on a work sheet in the Income Statement Credit and Balance Sheet Debit columns. The difference represents a decrease in stockholders' equity resulting from a net loss.

cultural diversity

CULTURAL DIVERSITY ◆ CULTURAL DIVERSITY ◆ CULTURAL DIVERSITY

African American Businesses

The Census Bureau's Survey of Minority-Owned Business Enterprises indicates that minority-owned enterprises are increasing in number and size. Firms owned by African Americans increased from 620,912 in 1992 to 823,000 in 1997. This represents a 32.5% increase. In 1997, these firms employed 718,300 people and generated $71.2 billion in revenue.

Six states—New York, California, Texas, Florida, Georgia, and Maryland—accounted for 47% of the nation's African American-owned businesses. The metropolitan areas of New York City, Washington, D.C., Los Angeles-Long Branch, Chicago, and Atlanta accounted for 28% of African American-owned firms.

Slightly more than half of businesses owned by African Americans operate in the service industries, such as health services, business services, and personal services. The retail trade accounted for the next largest concentration of African American-owned firms.

Black Enterprise magazine lists the nation's 100 largest black businesses in its "B.E. 100." The list is composed of industrial and service businesses that are at least 51% African American-owned. It maintains separate listings for the "Auto Dealer 100," which lists the largest auto dealerships that are at least 51% African American-owned. It also has lists for companies such as advertising agencies, banks, and insurance companies. From the 2004 "B.E. 100," World Wide Technology, Inc., of Maryland Heights, Missouri, was ranked in first place.

Source: U.S. Census and "Black Enterprise 100."

- Ask students how they can verify that a loss occurred by reviewing a work sheet. Point out that if the income statement debit column is greater than the credit column, the difference represents a net loss.

- Explain that a departmental operating loss occurs when the total of a department's cost of merchandise plus direct expenses exceeds its net sales.

- Point out that a departmental operating loss occurs if a department's Departmental Margin Statements Debit column total is larger than the Credit column total.

- Remind students that a net loss decreases stockholders' equity. Ask students how they would complete a work sheet if a net loss occurred.

DEMONSTRATE

Record a loss on a work sheet

- On the board or overhead, write the totals of the Departmental Margin Statements columns shown in the illustration. Point out that whenever the Debit column total is larger than the Credit column total, the difference is a departmental operating loss.

- Show students how to complete the Departmental Margin Statements columns using the figures on the board.

- Direct students' attention to the illustration. Review the remaining steps for completing a work sheet when there is a net loss.

- Write different pairs of amounts to represent totals of the income statement columns. Ask students if the totals in each pair represent a net income or net loss.

ONGOING ASSESSMENT

- Troubleshooting: Students may have difficulty with several of the adjusting entries, especially the uncollectible accounts expense, merchandise inventory, and federal income tax expense adjustments. Students might also have difficulty determining a net income or net loss, using the totals from a work sheet.

- Assess student understanding by checking solutions to Independent Practice assignments.

CULTURAL DIVERSITY

The Cultural Diversity feature shows the benefits of a culturally diverse society. Read the feature and discuss the specific information presented. Then clarify any terms or student questions.

RETEACH

- Analyze adjustments using four questions: (1) What is the balance of the account? (2) What should the balance be for the account? (3) What must be done to correct the account balance? (4) What adjustment is made?

- Call on students to describe the process of extending and completing the work sheet's Departmental Margin Statements columns.

- Distribute copies of several partial work sheets that show only the totals of the trial balance, adjustments, departmental margin statements, income statement, and balance sheet columns. Ask students to determine, label, and record the amount of net income or loss and to properly total and rule the work sheet.

- Review other procedures for completing a work sheet with Departmental Margin Statements.

GUIDED PRACTICE

Terms Review

Call on students to define the terms in the Terms Review. Ask the class if the definitions are correct and whether the complete definitions have been given or if anything needs to be added. Suggested definitions are given in the Glossary.

Audit Your Understanding

Call on students to answer the Audit Your Understanding questions. Ask the class if each answer is correct and/or complete. Answers are given in Appendix E of the textbook.

Work Together

Have students write the solution to the Work Together problems as you guide the class through the examples.

- Discuss each step before recording the answer in the *Working Papers*.
- Remind students to save their work to complete Work Together 4-4.

INDEPENDENT PRACTICE

On Your Own

- Assign the On Your Own problem to be worked independently.
- Use the Ongoing Assessment techniques to diagnose student understanding.

Application Problems

- Assign Application Problem 4-3: Preparing a work sheet with departmental margins.

Personal Trainer

- Students can access the Lesson 4-3 assessment material using this software.

Xtra! Web Site

- Students can access the Xtra! Study Tools for additional practice.

ENRICH

- Assign the Cultural Diversity feature on page 109.
- Assign Case 2 of the Cases for Critical Thinking.
- Assign the Automated Accounting feature on pages 132–133 to automate Application Problem 4-3.
- Students can use the QuickBooks data files to automate Application Problem 4-3.

110

• terms review

schedule of accounts receivable
schedule of accounts payable
work sheet
trial balance
plant assets
depreciation expense

• audit your understanding

1. What two reports are prepared to prove the accuracy of posting to subsidiary ledgers?

2. Why are adjustments made to certain accounts at the end of the fiscal period?

3. What account balances are extended to the Balance Sheet columns of a work sheet?

• work together 4-3

Preparing a work sheet with departmental margins

Callostay Co. has two departments: Books and Music. The trial balance and adjustment information for Callostay are provided in the *Working Papers*. Your instructor will guide you through the following examples. Save your work to complete Work Together 4-4.

1. Record the adjustments on the work sheet and total the adjustments columns.

2. Extend amounts to the proper debit and credit columns for the Departmental Margin Statements columns. Accounts on trial balance lines 56–65 are classified as indirect expenses. Total and rule the work sheet.

• on your own 4-3

Preparing a work sheet with departmental margins

Saratoga Spas has two departments: Accessories and Spas. The trial balance and adjustment information for Saratoga Spas are provided in the *Working Papers*. Work this problem independently. Save your work to complete On Your Own 4-4.

1. Record the adjustments on the work sheet and total the adjustments columns.

2. Extend amounts to the proper debit and credit columns for the Departmental Margin Statements columns. Accounts on trial balance lines 56–65 are classified as indirect expenses. Total and rule the work sheet.

CLOSE

- Ask students to briefly summarize the procedures for completing a work sheet with department margins.
- Use the work sheet on pages 102–103 to briefly review the procedures for planning adjustments, extending amounts, determining departmental margins, computing net income, and completing a work sheet.

4-4 Responsibility Statements for a Merchandising Business

DEPARTMENTAL MARGIN STATEMENT—AUDIO

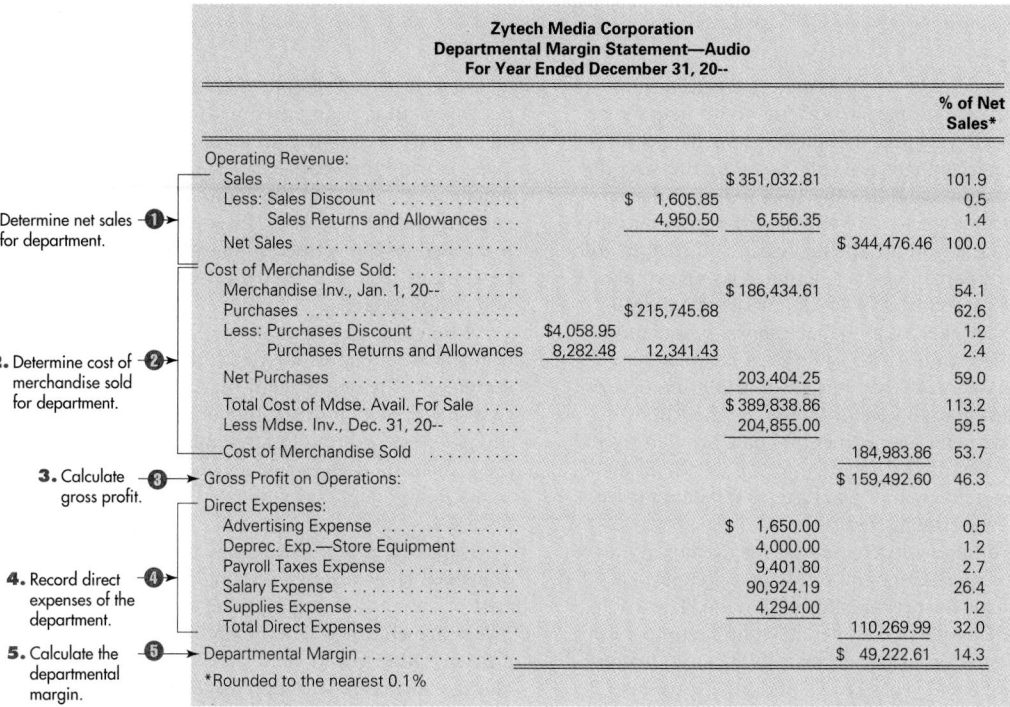

Zytech Media Corporation
Departmental Margin Statement—Audio
For Year Ended December 31, 20--

				% of Net Sales*
Operating Revenue:				
Sales			$ 351,032.81	101.9
Less: Sales Discount		$ 1,605.85		0.5
Sales Returns and Allowances		4,950.50	6,556.35	1.4
Net Sales			$ 344,476.46	100.0
Cost of Merchandise Sold:				
Merchandise Inv., Jan. 1, 20--			$ 186,434.61	54.1
Purchases		$ 215,745.68		62.6
Less: Purchases Discount	$4,058.95			1.2
Purchases Returns and Allowances	8,282.48	12,341.43		2.4
Net Purchases			203,404.25	59.0
Total Cost of Mdse. Avail. For Sale			$ 389,838.86	113.2
Less Mdse. Inv., Dec. 31, 20--			204,855.00	59.5
Cost of Merchandise Sold			184,983.86	53.7
Gross Profit on Operations:			$ 159,492.60	46.3
Direct Expenses:				
Advertising Expense			$ 1,650.00	0.5
Deprec. Exp.—Store Equipment			4,000.00	1.2
Payroll Taxes Expense			9,401.80	2.7
Salary Expense			90,924.19	26.4
Supplies Expense			4,294.00	1.2
Total Direct Expenses			110,269.99	32.0
Departmental Margin			$ 49,222.61	14.3

*Rounded to the nearest 0.1%

1. Determine net sales for department.
2. Determine cost of merchandise sold for department.
3. Calculate gross profit.
4. Record direct expenses of the department.
5. Calculate the departmental margin.

Financial statements reporting revenue, costs, and direct expenses under a specific department's control are called **responsibility statements**. Zytech prepares the usual end-of-fiscal-period financial statements: income statement, statement of stockholders' equity, and balance sheet. In addition, Zytech prepares two responsibility statements: (1) departmental margin statement—audio and (2) departmental margin statement—video. Since the departmental margin statements include information regarding each department's gross profit, Zytech does not prepare separate departmental statements of gross profit at the end of a fiscal period.

Zytech's departmental margin statement—audio for the year ended December 31 is shown above. Information for this statement is obtained from the Departmental Margin Statements—Audio columns of the work sheet, pages 102–103.

The departmental margin statement includes information about operating revenue, cost of merchandise sold, and the direct expenses that can be identified with Zytech's Audio Department. The format of the statement is similar to an income statement. However, only direct expenses for the Audio Department are included on the departmental margin statement.

The departmental margin statements help department managers determine how revenue, costs, and direct expenses affect department results. With this knowledge, managers can make informed decisions to improve department results.

Responsibility Statements for a Merchandising Business

Lesson 4-4   **111**

OBJECTIVES

- Define accounting terms related to cost accounting and financial reporting for a departmentalized merchandising business.
- Identify accounting concepts and practices related to cost accounting and financial reporting for a departmentalized merchandising business.
- Prepare financial statements for a departmentalized merchandising business.
- Analyze financial statements using selected component percentages.

MOTIVATE

Ask students to discuss what kinds of decisions might be made based on the results of departmental margin statements *(whether to discontinue a department, commit more resources to a department, add or change department personnel, etc.).*

Preview

- Preview the accounting terms and definitions introduced in this lesson: responsibility statements, income statement, statement of stockholders' equity, capital stock, retained earnings, dividends, and balance sheet.
- Direct students to read the headings at the top of each page in this lesson and to examine the illustrations given.

EXPLAIN

- Point out that information needed to prepare a departmental margin statement is taken from the work sheet.
- Explain that in the illustration, the name of the department is not included in the account titles since all the accounts are the departmental accounts for the Audio Department. This convention saves unnecessary repetition and makes the statement easier to read.

DEMONSTRATE

- Use an instructor-made transparency of a 4-column statement form with a % of Net Sales column or direct students to the illustration to demonstrate how to complete a departmental margin statement.
- Demonstrate the five steps shown in the illustration for completing the statement.

- Explain that component percentages on a departmental margin statement are calculated in the same way as for an income statement: the item is divided by net sales.

- Explain that a company may set departmental margin goals for each department in order to encourage acceptable performance or to evaluate acceptable performance.

- Explain that departmental goals are determined by reviewing previous performance and evaluating changes in selling prices and department costs.

- Explain that component percentages for the current period are also compared with the same percentages for previous periods in order to determine trends.

- Significant changes in a component percentage are evaluated in order to determine the reason for the change or to decide whether a policy resulting in a favorable change should be continued or one resulting in an unfavorable change should be discontinued.

DEMONSTRATE

Calculating component percentages

- Use the board or direct students to the math box to demonstrate calculating component percentages on a departmental margin statement.

- Demonstrate that the component percentage for departmental margin is calculated by dividing departmental margin by department net sales.

- Direct students to the math box to demonstrate the trend in the departmental margin component percentage over three months. Explain that the percentage is increasing each month—a positive trend for departmental margin.

- Emphasize that increasing component percentages for gross profit on operations and departmental margin is a favorable trend, while increasing component percentages for cost and expense items is an unfavorable trend.

COMPONENT PERCENTAGES ON DEPARTMENTAL MARGIN STATEMENTS

Departmental Margin	÷	Net Sales	=	Component Percentage for Departmental Margin
$49,222.61	÷	$344,476.46	=	14.3%

	Component Percentages		
	20X3	20X2	20X1
Departmental Margin	14.3%	13.4%	13.1%

Zytech calculates component percentages on departmental margin statements to help management interpret the information. The component percentages are calculated by dividing the amount on each line by the amount of departmental net sales. For the departmental margin statement—audio, the departmental margin component percentage is calculated as shown above.

A company may set departmental margin goals for each of its departments to encourage and determine acceptable performance by each department. Zytech has set a minimum departmental margin goal of 13.0% for the Audio Department. Departmental goals are determined by reviewing the department's previous achievements and evaluating changes in selling prices and department costs.

Component percentages for the current fiscal period also are compared to component percentages for previous fiscal periods. The audio department's departmental margin component percentages for the current (20X3) and two preceding fiscal years (20X2 and 20X1) are also shown above.

Since a department has control of and can affect its departmental margin by specific departmental action, this component percentage is an excellent measure of a department's performance. Zytech's Audio Department manager can determine whether the department is performing satisfactorily by making two comparisons: (1) current period's departmental margin component percentage compared with the company-assigned goal of at least 13.0% departmental margin and

(2) current period's departmental margin component percentage compared with previous periods' departmental margin component percentages. During the years 20X1 through 20X3, the department exceeded the company-assigned goal—a favorable result. The Audio Department increased its departmental margin component percentage from 13.1% to 14.3% in two years—a favorable trend.

When changes in component percentages occur for an item on the departmental margin statement, the department manager seeks the reasons for the changes. If changes are positive, the policies resulting in favorable changes are continued. If changes are negative, the manager seeks to change policies to prevent further declines.

Departmental revenue may increase because of special sales and advertising programs. The cost of merchandise may change because lower prices are obtained when merchandise is purchased. Other component percentages may change because of an increase or decrease in direct expenses. Without the information on the departmental margin statement, a department manager will not know which policies to continue and which to change.

Thus, departmental margin statements provide information to help managers identify unusual changes in revenue and cost amounts. The statements also provide information to assist company officers as well as department managers in evaluating departmental performance.

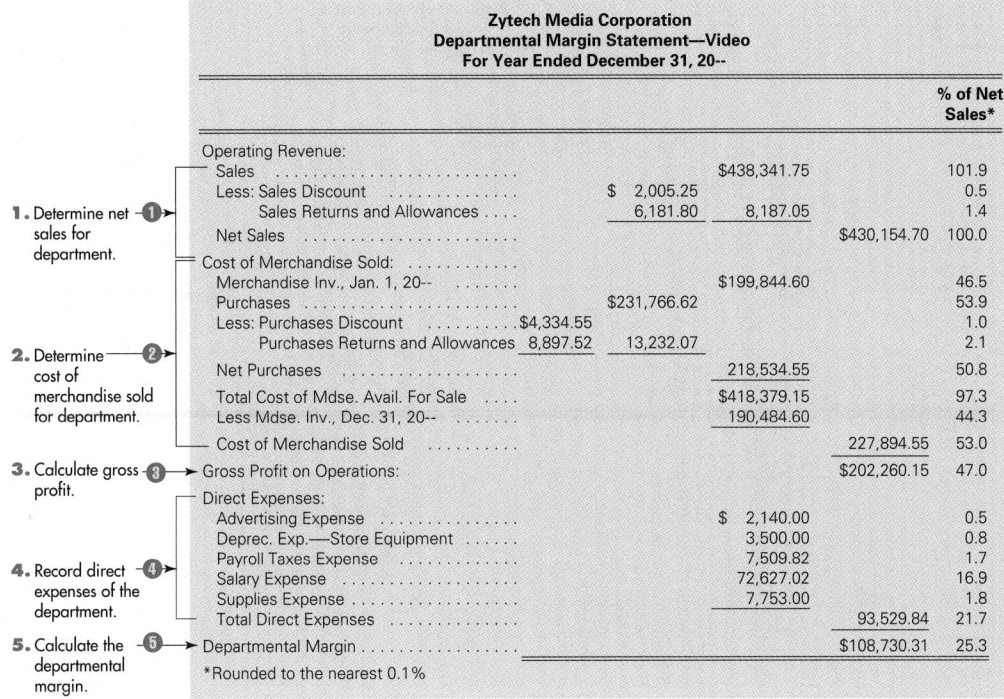

Zytech Media Corporation
Departmental Margin Statement—Video
For Year Ended December 31, 20--

			% of Net Sales*
Operating Revenue:			
Sales		$438,341.75	101.9
Less: Sales Discount	$ 2,005.25		0.5
Sales Returns and Allowances	6,181.80	8,187.05	1.4
Net Sales		$430,154.70	100.0
Cost of Merchandise Sold:			
Merchandise Inv., Jan. 1, 20--		$199,844.60	46.5
Purchases	$231,766.62		53.9
Less: Purchases Discount	$4,334.55		1.0
Purchases Returns and Allowances	8,897.52	13,232.07	2.1
Net Purchases		218,534.55	50.8
Total Cost of Mdse. Avail. For Sale		$418,379.15	97.3
Less Mdse. Inv., Dec. 31, 20--		190,484.60	44.3
Cost of Merchandise Sold		227,894.55	53.0
Gross Profit on Operations:		$202,260.15	47.0
Direct Expenses:			
Advertising Expense		$ 2,140.00	0.5
Deprec. Exp.—Store Equipment		3,500.00	0.8
Payroll Taxes Expense		7,509.82	1.7
Salary Expense		72,627.02	16.9
Supplies Expense		7,753.00	1.8
Total Direct Expenses		93,529.84	21.7
Departmental Margin		$108,730.31	25.3
*Rounded to the nearest 0.1%			

1. Determine net sales for department.
2. Determine cost of merchandise sold for department.
3. Calculate gross profit.
4. Record direct expenses of the department.
5. Calculate the departmental margin.

Zytech prepares a departmental margin statement for both the Video and Audio departments.

The departmental margin statement—video for the year ended December 31 is shown above.

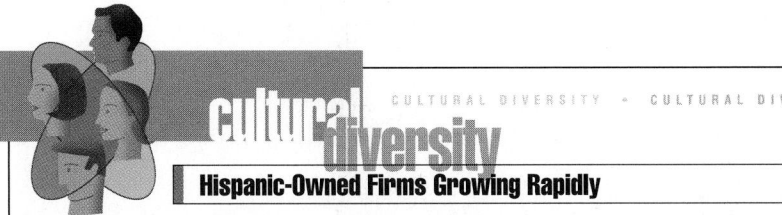

cultural diversity

Hispanic-Owned Firms Growing Rapidly

U.S. Census Bureau data indicates continuing growth in the Hispanic population in the United States. From 2000 to 2004, the number of Hispanics grew 13%, nearly half of the population growth in the country. With the growing population comes a Hispanic market that Hispanic-owned firms, among others, are racing to serve.

The U.S. Economic Census Survey of Minority-Owned Business Enterprises found a 76% increase from 1987 to 1992. Growth slowed to 30% from 1992 to 1997. However, the number of Hispanic-owned businesses was over 1,000,000. At the time of this text's publication, projections were that Hispanic-owned businesses would top 2 million in 2004, with revenues of $273.81 billion.

Source: www.hispanicbusiness.com and www.census.gov.

Responsibility Statements for a Merchandising Business

Lesson 4-4   **113**

- Ask students what type of information is presented on an income statement. Emphasize that the income statement shows revenue, gross profit, expenses, and net income or loss. Lead into a discussion as to why this information is important to managers, owners, stockholders, investors, lenders, and other individuals associated with or interested in the company.

- Explain that while the details of a departmental margin statement are not reported on the company's income statement, summary information *is* reported.

- Point out that the format used for the income statement shown uses the two columns to the left to report information about departmental margins for the two departments.

- Explain that the format uses the two columns to the right to report information for the company. Note that the departmental margin information is totaled to show departmental information combined in amounts for the whole company.

- Explain that component percentages are calculated for each item on the income statement. Point out that a company can show whichever component percentages it feels are relevant to understanding the income statement.

DEMONSTRATE

Preparing an income statement
Review preparation of an income statement.

- Show a transparency of a completed income statement. Use a marking pen and highlight the main sections of an income statement:
  - Total Revenue
  - Cost of Merchandise Sold
  - Gross Profit on Operations
  - Departmental Margin
  - Total Indirect Expenses
  - Net Income before Federal Inc. Tax
  - Net Income after Federal Inc. Tax

- Explain the origin of each number on the income statement or how it is calculated.

- Use an instructor-made transparency of a 4-column statement with a % of net sales column and headings for department and company results or direct students to the illustration as you demonstrate how to prepare an income statement with departmental margins.

- Demonstrate each of the nine steps described in the illustration.

INCOME STATEMENT WITH DEPARTMENTAL MARGIN

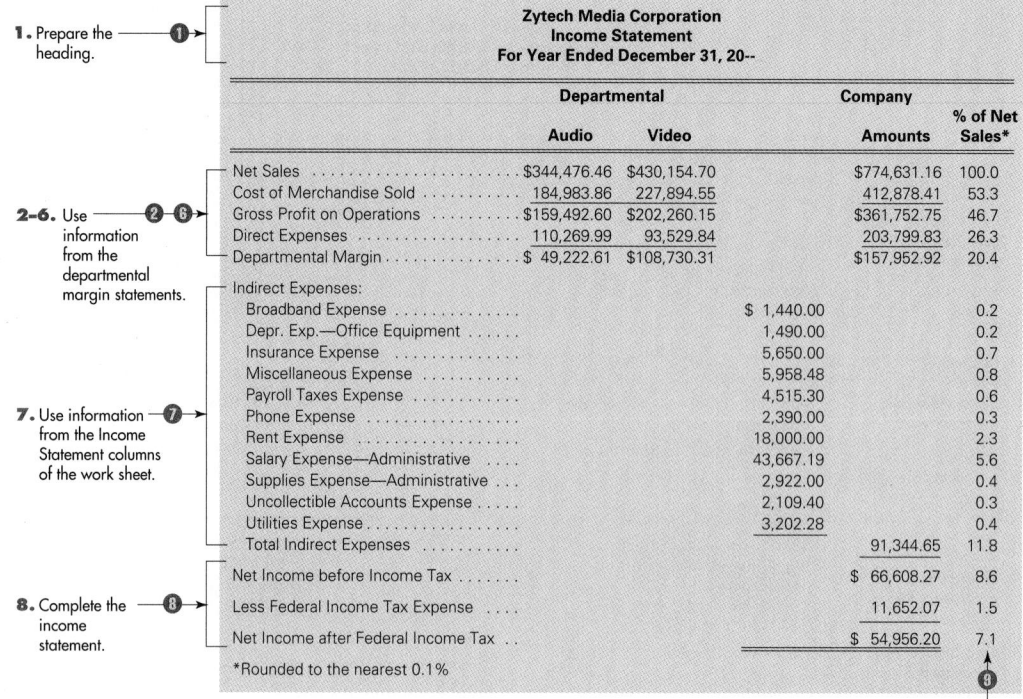

1. Prepare the heading.

2–6. Use information from the departmental margin statements.

7. Use information from the Income Statement columns of the work sheet.

8. Complete the income statement.

Zytech Media Corporation
Income Statement
For Year Ended December 31, 20--

| | Departmental | | Company | |
	Audio	Video	Amounts	% of Net Sales*
Net Sales	$344,476.46	$430,154.70	$774,631.16	100.0
Cost of Merchandise Sold	184,983.86	227,894.55	412,878.41	53.3
Gross Profit on Operations	$159,492.60	$202,260.15	$361,752.75	46.7
Direct Expenses	110,269.99	93,529.84	203,799.83	26.3
Departmental Margin	$ 49,222.61	$108,730.31	$157,952.92	20.4
Indirect Expenses:				
Broadband Expense			$ 1,440.00	0.2
Depr. Exp.—Office Equipment			1,490.00	0.2
Insurance Expense			5,650.00	0.7
Miscellaneous Expense			5,958.48	0.8
Payroll Taxes Expense			4,515.30	0.6
Phone Expense			2,390.00	0.3
Rent Expense			18,000.00	2.3
Salary Expense—Administrative			43,667.19	5.6
Supplies Expense—Administrative			2,922.00	0.4
Uncollectible Accounts Expense			2,109.40	0.3
Utilities Expense			3,202.28	0.4
Total Indirect Expenses			91,344.65	11.8
Net Income before Income Tax			$ 66,608.27	8.6
Less Federal Income Tax Expense			11,652.07	1.5
Net Income after Federal Income Tax			$ 54,956.20	7.1

*Rounded to the nearest 0.1%

9. Calculate component percentages.

A financial statement showing the revenue and expenses for a fiscal period is called an **income statement**. Zytech's income statement for the year ended December 31 is shown above. The income statement is prepared with five columns: two for departmental amounts and three for company amounts and component percentages.

STEPS • PREPARING AN INCOME STATEMENT

1 Write the heading. Center the name of the company, name of the report, and date of the report on three separate lines at the top of the statement.

2 Prepare the net sales section. Totals are obtained from the departmental margin statements.

3 Prepare the cost of merchandise sold section. Totals are obtained from the departmental margin statements.

4 Prepare the gross profit section. Totals are obtained from the departmental margin statements.

5 Prepare the direct expenses section. Totals are obtained from the departmental margin statements. Details about direct expenses are not listed. Managers can refer to departmental margin statements for the details.

6 Prepare the departmental margin section. Information is obtained from the departmental margin statements. Company amounts in steps 2–6 are totals of departmental amounts.

7 Prepare the indirect expenses section. Account titles and balances are obtained from the Income Statement columns of the work sheet.

8 Complete the income statement. Show the net income before and after Federal Income Tax.

9 Calculate the component percentages. The procedure is the same as calculating the percentages of net sales on departmental margin statements. However, the percentages are based on company net sales.

Financial Reporting for a Departmentalized Business

APPLIED SKILLS — WRITING ACROSS THE CURRICULUM

Writing Paragraphs and Short Essays. The Cases for Critical Thinking are short, practical applications of the accounting principles developed in the chapter. Some cases are planned to present problems related to the chapter but not specifically discussed and answered in the chapter. These cases present an opportunity for critical thinking and decision making. These cases also require more than a short, objective-type response. Therefore, they provide ideal practice in writing paragraphs and short essays.

STATEMENT OF STOCKHOLDERS' EQUITY

Zytech Media Corporation
Statement of Stockholders' Equity
For Year Ended December 31, 20--

Capital Stock:		
$170.00 Per Share		
January 1, 20--, 2,000 Shares Issued	$340,000.00	
Issued during Current Year, None	0.00	
Balance, December 31, 20--, 2,000 Shares Issued		$340,000.00
Retained Earnings:		
Balance, January 1, 20--	$ 56,155.50	
Net Income after Federal Income Tax for 20-- $54,956.20		
Less Dividends Declared during 20-- 30,000.00		
Net Increase during 20--	24,956.20	
Balance, December 31, 20--		81,111.70
Total Stockholders' Equity, December 31, 20--		$421,111.70

A financial statement that shows changes in a corporation's ownership for a fiscal period is called a **statement of stockholders' equity**. Zytech's statement of stockholders' equity for the fiscal year ended December 31 is shown above.

A statement of stockholders' equity contains two major sections:

1. *Capital stock.* Total shares of ownership in a corporation are called **capital stock**.
2. *Retained earnings.* An amount earned by a corporation and not yet distributed to stockholders is called **retained earnings**.

The first section shows that Zytech started the fiscal year with $340,000.00 in capital stock. This capital stock consisted of 2,000 shares of stock issued prior to January 1. During the year, Zytech did not issue any additional stock. Thus, at the end of the fiscal year, Zytech still had $340,000.00 in capital stock. This information is obtained from the previous year's statement of stockholders' equity and the capital stock account.

The second section of Zytech's statement of stockholders' equity shows that the business started the fiscal year with $56,155.50 in retained earnings. This amount represents previous years' earnings that have been kept in the business.

For the current fiscal year ended December 31, Zytech earned net income after federal income tax of $54,956.20. This amount is obtained from line 74 of the work sheet on page 103.

Net income increases the retained earnings of a corporation. Some income may be retained by a corporation for business expansion. Some income may be distributed to stockholders as a return on their investment. Earnings distributed to stockholders are called **dividends**.

Zytech's board of directors declared dividends of $30,000.00 during the year. The amount of dividends declared is obtained from line 31 of the Balance Sheet Debit column of the work sheet. The amount of dividends declared, $30,000.00, is subtracted from the amount of net income for the year, $54,956.20, to obtain the net increase in Retained Earnings for the year, $24,956.20. The net increase in Retained Earnings, $24,956.20, is added to the January 1 balance of Retained Earnings, $56,155.50, to obtain the December 31 balance, $81,111.70. Zytech's capital stock, $340,000.00, plus retained earnings, $81,111.70, equals total stockholders' equity on December 31, $421,111.70.

Declaration and payment of dividends are described in Chapter 11.

- Remind students that they have already prepared a number of 3-column balance sheets during their accounting instruction.

- Ask students what is reported on a balance sheet. Emphasize that a balance sheet is simply a snapshot of a business, showing what a business owns, owes, and is worth on a given day.

- Review the accounting concept that assets always must equal liabilities plus stockholders' equity. Point out that the balance sheet represents the accounting equation (A = L + OE) on paper.

- Discuss the difference between current assets and plant assets. Emphasize that these categories are based on the length of time the assets will be in use. For example, cash and other assets expected to be exchanged for cash or consumed within a year are known as *current assets*. Assets that will be used for a number of years in the operation of the business are known as *plant assets*.

- Remind students that the information for the preparation of the balance sheet is obtained from two sources—the balance sheet columns of the work sheet and the statement of stockholders' equity.

- Point out that a balance sheet is very similar for both a departmentalized and a nondepartmentalized corporation.

DEMONSTRATE

Study a balance sheet

- Ask students to provide examples of current assets and plant assets. Write their responses on the board under the headings *Current Assets* and *Plant Assets*.

- Use a transparency of a balance sheet similar to the one shown in the illustration. Circle the total assets amount and the total liabilities and stockholders' equity amount. Stress that assets always must equal liabilities and stockholders' equity.

- Point to different amounts on the balance sheet and ask students the origin of different amounts. Write *WS* next to amounts obtained from the work sheet and *SSE* next to amounts obtained from the statement of stockholders' equity.

- Use an instructor-made transparency of a 3-column statement or direct students to the illustration as you demonstrate how to prepare a balance sheet.

BALANCE SHEET

Zytech Media Corporation
Balance Sheet
December 31, 20--

ASSETS

Current Assets:			
Cash			$ 38,910.00
Petty Cash			500.00
Accounts Receivable		$13,755.00	
Less Allowance for Uncollectible Accounts		2,350.00	11,405.00
Merchandise Inventory—Audio			204,855.00
Merchandise Inventory—Video			190,484.60
Supplies—Administrative			4,051.00
Supplies—Audio			5,921.00
Supplies—Video			2,089.00
Prepaid Insurance			4,200.00
Total Current Assets			$462,415.60
Plant Assets:			
Office Equipment		$16,900.00	
Less Accumulated Depreciation–Office Equipment		7,450.00	$ 9,450.00
Store Equipment—Audio		38,900.00	
Less Accumulated Depreciation—Store Equipment, Audio		22,000.00	16,900.00
Store Equipment—Video		26,652.00	
Less Accumulated Depreciation—Store Equipment, Video		19,000.00	7,652.00
Total Plant Assets			34,002.00
Total Assets			$496,417.60

LIABILITIES

Current Liabilities:		
Accounts Payable		$ 31,360.30
Employee Income Tax Payable—Federal		2,680.75
Employee Income Tax Payable—State		1,118.19
Federal Income Tax Payable		852.07
Social Security Tax Payable		2,730.57
Medicare Tax Payable		630.13
Sales Tax Payable		3,139.64
Unemployment Tax Payable—Federal		23.60
Unemployment Tax Payable—State		159.30
Health Insurance Premiums Payable		2,261.16
Life Insurance Premiums Payable		350.19
Dividends Payable		30,000.00
Total Liabilities		$75,305.90

STOCKHOLDERS' EQUITY

Capital Stock		$340,000.00
Retained Earnings		81,111.70
Total Stockholders' Equity		421,111.70
Total Liabilities and Stockholders' Equity		$496,417.60

A financial statement that reports assets, liabilities, and owners' equity on a specific date is called a **balance sheet**. A balance sheet reports the financial condition of a business on a specific date. Zytech's balance sheet for December 31 is shown above. Data used in preparing a balance sheet come from two sources: Balance Sheet columns of the work sheet and Statement of Stockholders' Equity.

On a balance sheet, the total assets must equal the total liabilities plus stockholders' equity. Zytech's balance sheet shows total assets of $496,417.60 and total liabilities and stockholders' equity of the same amount. Therefore, Zytech's balance sheet is in balance and is assumed to be correct.

Financial analysis of balance sheet items is described in Chapter 17.

ONGOING ASSESSMENT

- Assessment is an ongoing process. Circulate through the classroom or lab, observing which students have problems with the assignments.

- Troubleshooting: Diagnose what kinds of problems students have with this lesson. Students should not have difficulty preparing financial statements because they are so similar to ones previously prepared. They may, however, have some difficulty with the format of the statements.

- Assess student understanding by checking solutions to Independent Practice assignments.

RETEACH

- Call on students to describe each step in preparing the various financial statements presented in this lesson.

Xtra!
Study Tools
accountingxtra.swlearning.com

• terms review

responsibility statements
income statement
statement of stockholders' equity
capital stock
retained earnings
dividends
balance sheet

• audit your understanding

1. Where does Zytech obtain the information to prepare the direct expenses section of the income statement?

2. How is the component percentage for departmental margin calculated?

3. What two comparisons can be made using the component percentage for departmental margin to determine if a department is performing satisfactorily?

4. Where does Zytech obtain the information to prepare the indirect expenses section of the income statement?

• work together 4-4

Preparing financial statements

Use the work sheet from Work Together 4-3. Statement paper is provided in the *Working Papers*. Your instructor will guide you through the following example.

1. Prepare departmental margin statements for the Books Department and the Music Department. Calculate and record the component percentages for each item on the statements. Round percentage calculations to the nearest 0.1%.

2. Prepare an income statement. Calculate and record the component percentages for each item on the statement. Round percentage calculations to the nearest 0.1%.

3. Prepare a statement of stockholders' equity. There are 2,000 shares of stock issued and none issued during the current year.

4. Prepare a balance sheet.

• on your own 4-4

Preparing financial statements

Use the work sheet from On Your Own 4-3. Statement paper is provided in the *Working Papers*. Work this problem independently.

1. Prepare departmental margin statements for the Spas Department and the Accessories Department. Calculate and record the component percentages for each item on the statement. Round percentage calculations to the nearest 0.1%.

2. Prepare an income statement. Calculate and record the component percentages for each item on the statement. Round percentage calculations to the nearest 0.1%.

3. Prepare a statement of stockholders' equity. There are 1,000 shares of stock issued and none issued during the current year.

4. Prepare a balance sheet.

GUIDED PRACTICE

Terms Review
Call on students to define the terms in the Terms Review. Ask the class if the definitions are correct and whether the complete definitions have been given or if anything needs to be added. Suggested definitions are given in the Glossary.

Audit Your Understanding
Call on students to answer the Audit Your Understanding questions. Ask the class if each answer is correct and/or complete. Answers are given in Appendix E of the textbook.

Work Together
Have students write the solution to the Work Together problems as you guide the class through the examples.

- Remind students to use their work completed in Work Together 4-3.

- Discuss each step of preparing the financial statements before recording the answer in the *Working Papers*.

INDEPENDENT PRACTICE

On Your Own
- Assign the On Your Own problem to be worked independently.

- Use the Ongoing Assessment techniques to diagnose student understanding.

Application Problem
- Assign Application Problem 4-4: Preparing financial statements.

Personal Trainer
- Students can access the Lesson 4-4 assessment material using this software.

Xtra! Web Site
- Students can access the Xtra! Study Tools for additional practice.

ENRICH

- Assign the Cultural Diversity feature on page 113.

- Assign the Automated Accounting feature on pages 132–133 to automate Application Problem 4-4.

CLOSE

- Use the illustrations on pages 111, 113, 114, 115, and 116 to briefly review the procedures for preparing financial statements.

4-5 End-of-Period Work for a Departmentalized Business

JOURNALIZING ADJUSTING ENTRIES FOR A DEPARTMENTALIZED BUSINESS

1. Write *Adjusting Entries* in Account Title column.

2. Enter the adjusting entries without additional explanation.

GENERAL JOURNAL — PAGE *13*

DATE		ACCOUNT TITLE	DOC. NO.	POST. REF.	DEBIT	CREDIT
		Adjusting Entries				
Dec 20--	31	Uncollectible Accounts Expense			2 1 0 9 40	
		Allowance for Uncoll. Accounts				2 1 0 9 40
	31	Merchandise Inventory—Audio			18 4 2 0 39	
		Income Summary—Audio				18 4 2 0 39
	31	Income Summary—Video			9 3 6 0 00	
		Merchandise Inventory—Video				9 3 6 0 00
	31	Supplies Expense—Administrative			2 9 2 2 00	
		Supplies—Administrative				2 9 2 2 00
	31	Supplies Expense—Audio			4 2 9 4 00	
		Supplies—Audio				4 2 9 4 00
	31	Supplies Expense—Video			7 7 5 3 00	
		Supplies—Video				7 7 5 3 00
	31	Insurance Expense			5 6 5 0 00	
		Prepaid Insurance				5 6 5 0 00
	31	Depreciation Exp.—Office Equip.			1 4 9 0 00	
		Accum. Depr.—Office Equip.				1 4 9 0 00
	31	Depreciation Exp.—Store Equip., Audio			4 0 0 0 00	
		Accum. Depr.—Store Equip., Audio				4 0 0 0 00
	31	Depreciation Exp.—Store Equip., Video			3 5 0 0 00	
		Accum. Depr.—Store Equip., Video				3 5 0 0 00
	31	Federal Income Tax Expense			8 5 2 07	
		Federal Income Tax Payable				8 5 2 07

Account balances are changed only by posting journal entries. Journal entries recorded to update general ledger accounts at the end of a fiscal period are called **adjusting entries**. At the end of a fiscal period, the temporary account balances are transferred to an income summary account. This procedure summarizes, in one account, the effect of operating the business.

Zytech's adjusting entries are shown above. After the adjusting entries are posted, general ledger accounts will be up-to-date as of December 31.

STEPS

JOURNALIZING ADJUSTING ENTRIES

1 Write the words *Adjusting Entries* in the Account Title column. This heading identifies the group of adjusting entries.

2 Enter each adjusting entry using information from the Adjustments column of the work sheet. The letters used to identify the adjustments provide the order for these entries. For example, adjustment *(a)* is the first adjusting entry to be recorded. No source document or explanation is written for each adjusting entry.

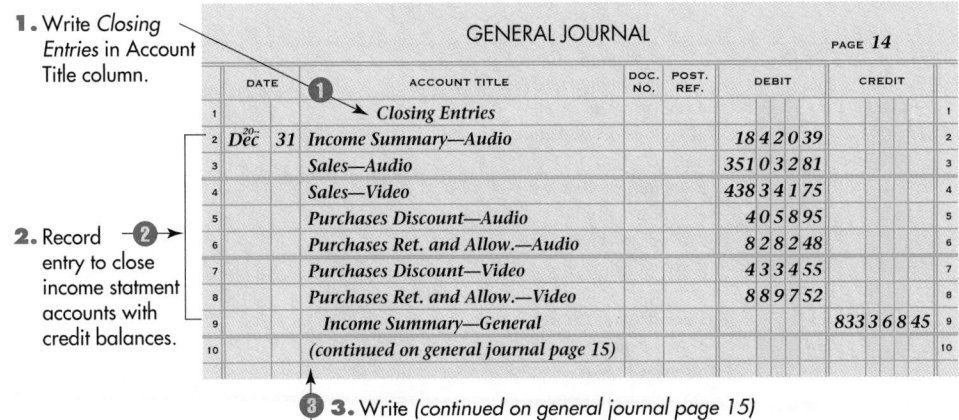

1. Write *Closing Entries* in Account Title column.

2. Record entry to close income statement accounts with credit balances.

3. Write *(continued on general journal page 15)* to show that the closing entries are continued.

Journal entries used to prepare temporary accounts for a new fiscal period are called **closing entries**. Zytech's closing entries made on December 31 are shown above and on the next page.

The information to journalize closing entries is obtained from the Departmental Margin Statements and the Income Statement columns of the work sheet.

EXPLANATION OF CLOSING ENTRIES

At the end of each fiscal period, Zytech records the following four closing entries:

1. Closing entry for income statement accounts with credit balances (revenue and contra cost accounts).
2. Closing entry for income statement accounts with debit balances (cost, contra revenue, and expense accounts).
3. Closing entry to record net income or net loss in the retained earnings account and to close the income summary account.
4. Closing entry for the dividends account.

Recording Closing Entries on Two General Journal Pages

Zytech's closing entries require 44 lines of the general journal to record. However, each page of the general journal is only 36 lines long. If all lines of the first page were filled and then the closing entries continued on the next page, the closing entry for income statement accounts would be split between two journal pages. It is not a good practice to split a journal entry between two pages because the debit and credit parts of the entry cannot be seen together. Therefore, Zytech uses the following procedure to be sure there is no misunderstanding when two general journal pages are used to record closing entries:

1. Record the first closing entry, using lines 1–9.
2. Write the note *(continued on general journal page 15)* on the line after the last line of the first closing entry.
3. Write the heading *Closing Entries (continued)* on the first line of the next page of the general journal.
4. Record the rest of the closing entries.

119

DEMONSTRATE

- Use the steps in the illustration to illustrate how Zytech's second, third, and fourth closing entries are journalized.
- Use several T account transactions to illustrate each closing entry. It is not necessary to write each expense for illustrative purposes.

4. Write *Closing Entries (continued)* in the Account Title Column.

5. Record entry to close income statement accounts with debit balances. **5**

6. Record entry to close Income Summary to Retained Earnings. **6**

7. Record entry for Dividends. **7**

GENERAL JOURNAL

PAGE 15

	DATE		ACCOUNT TITLE	DOC. NO.	POST. REF.	DEBIT	CREDIT	
1			*Closing Entries (continued)*					1
2	*Dec*	31	Income Summary—General			778 41 2 25		2
3			*Income Summary—Video*				9 3 6 0 00	3
4			*Sales Discount—Audio*				1 6 0 5 85	4
5			*Sales Returns and Allow.—Audio*				4 9 5 0 50	5
6			*Sales Discount—Video*				2 0 0 5 25	6
7			*Sales Returns and Allow.—Video*				6 1 8 1 80	7
8			*Purchases—Audio*				215 7 4 5 68	8
9			*Purchases—Video*				231 7 6 6 62	9
10			*Advertising Expense—Audio*				1 6 5 0 00	10
11			*Depr. Exp.—Store Equipment, Audio*				4 0 0 0 00	11
12			*Payroll Taxes Expense—Audio*				9 4 0 1 80	12
13			*Salary Expense—Audio*				90 9 2 4 19	13
14			*Supplies Expense—Audio*				4 2 9 4 00	14
15			*Advertising Expense—Video*				2 1 4 0 00	15
16			*Depr. Exp.—Store Equipment, Video*				3 5 0 0 00	16
17			*Payroll Taxes Expense—Video*				7 5 0 9 82	17
18			*Salary Expense—Video*				72 6 2 7 02	18
19			*Supplies Expense—Video*				7 7 5 3 00	19
20			*Broadband Expense*				1 4 4 0 00	20
21			*Depr. Exp.—Office Equipment*				1 4 9 0 00	21
22			*Insurance Expense*				5 6 5 0 00	22
23			*Miscellaneous Expense*				5 9 5 8 48	23
24			*Payroll Taxes Expense—Admin.*				4 5 1 5 30	24
25			*Phone Expense*				2 3 9 0 00	25
26			*Rent Expense*				18 0 0 0 00	26
27			*Salary Expense—Administrative*				43 6 6 7 19	27
28			*Supplies Expense—Administrative*				2 9 2 2 00	28
29			*Uncollectible Accounts Expense*				2 1 0 9 40	29
30			*Utilities Expense*				3 2 0 2 28	30
31			*Federal Income Tax Expense*				11 6 5 2 07	31
32		31	*Income Summary—General*			54 9 5 6 20		32
33			*Retained Earnings*				54 9 5 6 20	33
34		31	*Retained Earnings*			30 0 0 0 00		34
35			*Dividends*				30 0 0 0 00	35
36								36

Closing Entry for Income Statement Accounts with Credit Balances

The closing entry for Zytech's income statement debit balance accounts on December 31 is shown on lines 2–9 on page 14 of the general journal. Income statement credit balance accounts are the departmental income summary accounts with a credit balance (Income Summary—Audio), the revenue accounts (Sales—Audio and Sales—Video), and the contra cost accounts (Purchases Discount—Audio, Purchases Returns and Allowances—Audio, Purchases Discount—Video, and Purchases Returns and Allowances—Video).

Information needed for closing income statement credit balance accounts is obtained from the Departmental Margin Statements Credit columns of the work sheet.

Closing Entry for Income Statement Accounts with Debit Balances

The closing entry for Zytech's income statement debit balance accounts on December 31 is shown on lines 2–31 on page 15 of the general journal. Income statement debit balance accounts are the departmental income summary accounts with a debit balance (Income Summary—Video), the contra revenue accounts (Sales Discount—Audio, Sales Returns and Allowances—Audio, Sales Discount—Video, and Sales Returns and Allowances—Video), the cost accounts (Purchases—Audio and Purchases—Video), and the expense accounts.

Information needed for closing income statement debit balance accounts is obtained from the Departmental Margin Statements and Income Statement Debit columns of the work sheet.

©GETTY IMAGES/PHOTODISC

Closing Entry to Record Net Income or Net Loss in the Retained Earnings Account and to Close the Income Summary Account

The closing entry to record Zytech's net income in the retained earnings account and close the income summary account on December 31 is shown on lines 32–33 on page 15 of the general journal.

The balance of Income Summary—General is equal to the net income (or net loss) for the fiscal period. A corporation's net income is recorded in Retained Earnings. Information needed for this entry is obtained from line 74 of Zytech's work sheet.

After the entry to record net income is posted, Income Summary has a zero balance. The net income, $54,956.20, has been recorded as a credit to Retained Earnings.

Closing Entry for the Dividends Account

The closing entry for Zytech's dividends account on December 31 is shown on lines 34–35 on page 15 of the general journal. The debit balance of a dividends account is the total amount of dividends declared during a fiscal period. Since dividends decrease the earnings that a corporation retains, the dividends account is closed to Retained Earnings.

Information needed for closing Zytech's dividends account is obtained from line 31 of the Balance Sheet Debit column of the work sheet.

After the closing entry for the dividends account is posted, Dividends has a zero balance. The amount of the dividends, $30,000.00, has been recorded as a debit to Retained Earnings.

After closing entries are posted, all temporary accounts have zero balances and are prepared for a new fiscal period.

FYI FOR YOUR INFORMATION

In most commercial computerized accounting systems, year-end closing is performed by the computer. The accountant selects a menu item to close the accounting records for the year. The software automatically updates its database. In some systems, year-end closing cannot be undone.

POST-CLOSING TRIAL BALANCE FOR A DEPARTMENTALIZED BUSINESS

Zytech Media Corporation
Post-Closing Trial Balance
December 31, 20--

Account Title	Debit	Credit
Cash	$ 38,910.00	
Petty Cash	500.00	
Accounts Receivable	13,755.00	
Allowance for Uncollectible Accounts		$ 2,350.00
Merchandise Inventory—Audio	204,855.00	
Merchandise Inventory—Video	190,484.60	
Supplies—Administrative	4,051.00	
Supplies—Audio	5,921.00	
Supplies—Video	2,089.00	
Prepaid Insurance	4,200.00	
Office Equipment	16,900.00	
Acc. Depr.—Office Equipment		7,450.00
Store Equipment—Audio	38,900.00	
Acc. Depr.—Store Equipment, Audio		22,000.00
Store Equipment—Video	26,652.00	
Acc. Depr.—Store Equipment, Video		19,000.00
Accounts Payable		31,360.30
Employee Income Tax Payable—Federal		2,680.75
Employee Income Tax Payable—State		1,118.19
Federal Income Tax Payable		852.07
Social Security Tax Payable		2,730.57
Medicare Tax Payable		630.13
Sales Tax Payable		3,139.64
Unemployment Tax Payable—Federal		23.60
Unemployment Tax Payable—State		159.30
Health Insurance Premiums Payable		2,261.16
Life Insurance Premiums Payable		350.19
Dividends Payable		30,000.00
Capital Stock		340,000.00
Retained Earnings		81,111.70
Totals	$547,217.60	$547,217.60

Debits must always equal credits in general ledger accounts. The trial balance recorded on the work sheet proves that debits do equal credits before adjusting and closing entries are posted. After adjusting and closing entries are posted, equality of general ledger debits and credits is proved again. This procedure ensures that the equality of debits and credits has been maintained in preparation for a new fiscal period.

A trial balance prepared after the closing entries are posted is called a **post-closing trial balance**. Zytech's post-closing trial balance prepared on December 31 is shown above. The total of debit balances, $547,217.60, is the same as the total of credit balances. The equality of general ledger debits and credits is proved. Zytech's general ledger is ready for the next fiscal period. [CONCEPT: Accounting Period Cycle]

> REMEMBER Only temporary accounts are closed. Permanent account balances are needed to continue conducting business in the next accounting cycle.

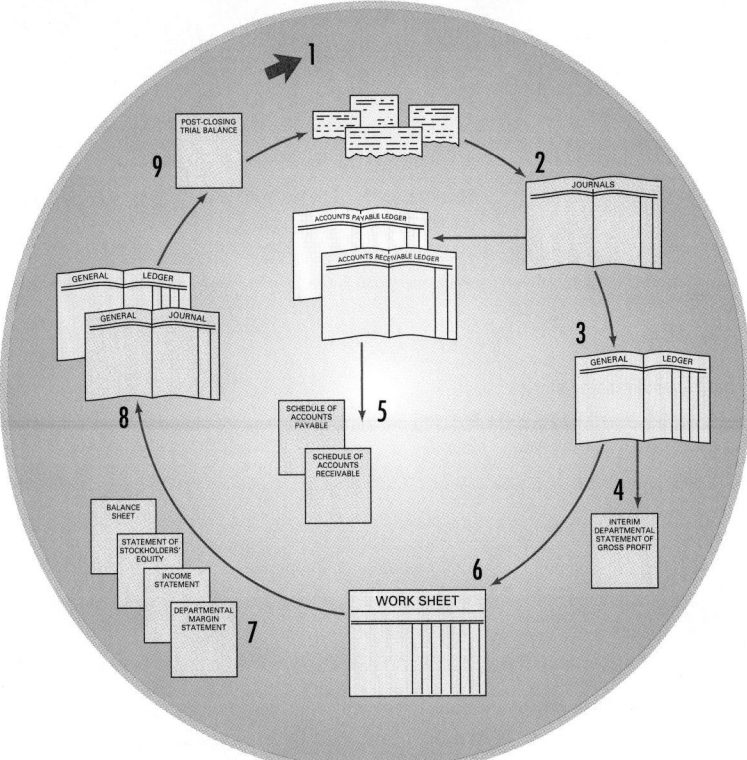

Accounting procedures used by Zytech, a departmentalized merchandising business, are described in Chapters 1 through 4. The same procedures are used from year to year. [CONCEPT: Consistent Reporting] The series of accounting activities included in recording financial information for a fiscal period is called an **accounting cycle**. Zytech's complete accounting cycle is shown above. Accounting cycle procedures provide information for preparing interim and end-of-fiscal-period financial statements. [CONCEPT: Accounting Period Cycle]

STEPS   STEPS • STEPS • STEPS • STEPS • STEPS • STEPS • STEPS • STEPS • STEPS • STEPS •

ACCOUNTING ACTIVITIES IN THE ACCOUNTING CYCLE FOR A DEPARTMENTALIZED BUSINESS

1. Verify source documents for accuracy. The source documents describe transactions and prove that the transactions did occur.
2. Record entries in journals using the information on the source documents.
3. Post journal entries to the ledgers.
4. Prepare an interim departmental statement of gross profit. Zytech prepares this statement monthly to assess the operating efficiency of each department.
5. Prepare schedules of accounts receivable and accounts payable from the subsidiary ledgers.
6. Prepare a trial balance on the work sheet. Complete the work sheet to summarize a business's financial condition.
7. Prepare financial statements using information on the work sheet and in the accounting records.
8. Journalize and post adjusting and closing entries using information from the work sheet.
9. Prepare a post-closing trial balance to check the equality of debits and credits in the general ledger. The accounting records for the fiscal period are complete and ready for the start of the next fiscal period.

GUIDED PRACTICE

Terms Review

Call on students to define each term in the Terms Review. After each definition, ask the class if the definition is correct and whether the complete definition has been given or if anything needs to be added. Suggested definitions are given in the Glossary.

Audit Your Understanding

Call on students to answer the Audit Your Understanding questions. Ask the class if the answer is correct and/or complete. Answers are given in Appendix E of the textbook.

Work Together

Have students write the solution to the Work Together problems as you guide the class through the examples.

- Direct students to record each amount on the proper form as you elicit class participation in determining and calculating each amount.

- Call on students to describe the source of information for preparing each closing entry.

- Ask students to recite each closing entry.

INDEPENDENT PRACTICE

On Your Own

- Assign the On Your Own problem to be worked independently.

- Use the Ongoing Assessment techniques to diagnose student understanding.

Application Problem

- Assign Application Problem 4-5: Journalizing adjusting and closing entries for a departmentalized business.

Personal Trainer

- Students can access the Lesson 4-5 assessment material using this software.

Xtra! Web Site

- Students can access the Xtra! Study Tools for additional practice

ENRICH

- Assign the Automated Accounting feature on pages 132–133 to automate Application Problem 4-5.

- Students can use the Peachtree data files to automate Application Problem 4-5.

- Assign Sounds, Inc.: A Business Simulation.

124

• terms review

adjusting entries
closing entries
post-closing trial balance
accounting cycle

• audit your understanding

1. What is the purpose of adjusting entries?
2. Which accounts are closed at the end of an accounting period?
3. What is the purpose of a post-closing trial balance?
4. Which accounting activities in the accounting cycle are performed at the end of a fiscal period?

• work together 4-5

Journalizing adjusting and closing entries

Use the work sheet from Work Together 4-3 and 4-4. Pages 13, 14, and 15 of a general journal are provided in the *Working Papers.* Your instructor will guide you through the following example.

1. Using the information presented in the Adjustments columns of Callostay's work sheet, journalize the adjusting entries on page 13 of a general journal.
2. Using Callostay's work sheet, journalize the closing entries on pages 14 and 15 of a general journal.

• on your own 4-5

Journalizing adjusting and closing entries

Use the work sheet from On Your Own 4-3 and 4-4. Pages 13, 14, and 15 of a general journal are provided in the *Working Papers.* Work this problem independently.

1. Using the information presented in the Adjustments columns of Saratoga Spa's work sheet, journalize the adjusting entries on page 13 of a general journal.
2. Using Saratoga Spa's work sheet, journalize the closing entries on pages 14 and 15 of a general journal.

CLOSE

- Review the illustration on page 123 showing the summary of the accounting cycle for a departmentalized business.

After completing this chapter, you can

1. Define accounting terms related to cost accounting and financial reporting for a departmentalized merchandising business.

2. Identify accounting concepts and practices related to cost accounting and financial reporting for a departmentalized merchandising business.

3. Distinguish between direct and indirect expenses.

4. Prepare an interim departmental statement of gross profit.

5. Prepare a work sheet for a departmentalized merchandising business.

6. Prepare financial statements for a departmentalized merchandising business.

7. Analyze financial statements using selected component percentages.

8. Complete end-of-period work for a departmentalized merchandising business.

Explore Accounting

EXPLORE ACCOUNTING · EXPLORE ACCOUNTING · EXPLORE ACCOUN

Exception Reports

The amount of financial information available to managers can become immense. Responsibility accounting is one way that managers focus accounting information on one aspect of the business. A departmental margin statement, for example, focuses on the revenue and expenses controlled by the manager of a single department. Even departmental margin statements can be overwhelming for a large company with hundreds of departments. How does an upper-level manager examine all of these statements to identify problems?

Rather than reviewing every line of every departmental statement, a manager can instruct the computer system to prepare a report of only those accounts for which the actual results differ significantly from expected results. These reports, often called *exception reports*, should identify both positive and negative situations. For example, an exception report could identify those accounts that differ by more than 10% from departmental budgets. This shorter report would allow the manager to quickly focus on areas that deserve attention.

Managers must gather information and be objective when investigating the reasons for excessive expenses. Does salary expense exceed-

ing budget by 20% indicate that workers lack discipline? Although this explanation is possible, other reasons could cause even the best employees to be unproductive. For example, note these factors:

1. Workers have not received adequate training.
2. Equipment is obsolete and often broken.
3. Parts are frequently out of stock.

It is natural for managers to focus on negative situations. The manager can work with the department manager to correct the problem. Too often, managers neglect to investigate the reasons for positive performances. If a department has generated sales 20% more than its budget, the manager should investigate what strategies and methods can account for the successful results. This information can then be shared with other departments to improve sales throughout the company.

Instructions: A manager of Summertime Furniture receives an exception report showing that lumber costs of its picnic table department are 32% above the budget. List possible explanations for the apparent problem in the purchase and use of lumber.

Financial Reporting for a Departmentalized Business

Chapter 4   **125**

EXPLORE ACCOUNTING
EXPLORE ACCOUNTING

Reasons for paying a higher-than-budgeted price for lumber might include:

1. Purchasing a higher quality of lumber than is required.
2. Failing to obtain competitive bids.
3. Having to buy lumber for immediate delivery and incurring higher-than-normal shipping costs.

Reasons that a higher-than-budgeted quantity of lumber might be used, resulting in a large amount of scrap, might include:

1. Purchasing lumber of inferior quality.
2. Failing to adequately train employees.
3. Using old or obsolete equipment.
4. Failing to control employee theft.

4-1 APPLICATION PROBLEM
Identifying direct and indirect expenses

Harbour House Interiors has two departments: Paint and Wallpaper. Harbor House completed the transactions below.

Instructions:

Use a form similar to the one below. For each transaction, indicate:

a. Whether the expense is a direct expense (identifiable with a specific department) or an indirect expense.

b. The title of the expense account.

The first transaction is completed as an example.

Trans. No.	Direct Expense or Indirect Expense	Expense Account Title
1	Indirect	Utilities Expense

1. Paid cash for utilities bill.
2. Paid cash for new accounting software for the company.
3. Paid cash for an instructor to conduct classes on wallpapering to encourage customers to enter the store.
4. Paid cash to a courier to deliver paint to a construction site.
5. Paid cash to rent a hall for the annual employee party.
6. Paid cash for bimonthly payroll for all administrative, paint, and wallpaper employees. Salesclerks are hired by specific department managers.
7. Donated paint and wallpaper to a group sponsoring a youth center.
8. Paid for advertising in the newspaper in a special home decorating supplement.
9. Paid monthly federal income tax expense.
10. Paid cash for monthly payroll taxes (consider the taxes on the Wallpaper Department employees only).

4-2 APPLICATION PROBLEM
Preparing an interim departmental statement of gross profit; calculating component percentages

LightSource has two departments, Office and Residential. The following data are obtained from the accounting records on March 31 of the current year:

	Office	Residential
Beginning Inventory, January 1	$124,640.00	$166,500.00
Estimated Beginning Inventory, March 1	101,344.00	135,660.00
Net Purchases, January 1 to February 28	23,360.00	24,840.00
Net Sales, January 1 to February 28	77,760.00	92,800.00
Net Purchases for March	13,497.00	9,978.00
Net Sales for March	29,200.00	33,600.00
Estimated Gross Profit Percentage	40.0%	50.0%

Instructions:

1. Prepare an estimated merchandise inventory sheet, similar to the one in this chapter, for each department for the month ended March 31 of the current year.

2. Prepare an interim departmental statement of gross profit. Calculate and record component percentages for departmental and total cost of merchandise sold and gross profit on operations. Round percentage calculations to the nearest 0.1%.

Preparing a work sheet with departmental margins

Application Problem 4-3
Net Income after Fed. Inc. Tax, 66,435.62.

AllSports Center is a merchandising business that sells sports clothing and equipment. AllSports Center's December 31 trial balance is recorded on a 12-column work sheet in the *Working Papers*. The following adjustment information is available:

Adjustment Information, December 31

Uncollectible accounts expense—equipment estimated as 1.0% of sales on account.

Sales on account for the year	$145,700.00
Merchandise Inventory—Clothing	88,950.00
Merchandise Inventory—Equipment	93,678.80
Supplies Used—Clothing	1,925.00
Supplies Used—Equipment	1,287.00
Supplies Used—Administrative	834.00
Insurance Expired	7,200.00
Depreciation Expense—Office Equipment	1,100.00
Depreciation Expense—Store Equipment, Clothing	3,720.00
Depreciation Expense—Store Equipment, Equipment	1,850.00
Federal Income Tax Expense for the Year	16,421.38

Instructions:

1. Complete the work sheet for the month ended June 30 of the current year. Record the adjustments on the work sheet using the adjustment information for December 31.
2. Extend amounts to the proper debit and credit columns for Departmental Margin Statement—Clothing, Departmental Margin Statement—Equipment, Income Statement, and Balance Sheet. Accounts on trial balance lines 51–65 are classified as indirect expenses. Save your work to complete Application Problems 4-4 and 4-5.

4-4 **APPLICATION PROBLEM** AUTOMATED ACCOUNTING

Preparing financial statements

Application Problem 4-4
Departmental Margin—Clothing, 96,255.00.
Departmental Margin—Equipment, 65,136.00.

Net Income after Fed. Inc. Tax, 66,435.62.

Total Stockholders' Equity, 322,807.62.

Total Assets, 270,522.30.

Instructions:

The work sheet from Application Problem 4-3 is needed to complete this problem.

1. Prepare departmental margin statements for AllSports Center's Clothing Department and Equipment Department. Calculate and record the component percentages for each item on the statements. Round percentage calculations to the nearest 0.1%. Save your work to complete Application Problem 4-5.
2. Prepare an income statement for AllSports Center. Calculate and record the component percentages for each item on the statements. Round the percentage calculations to the nearest 0.1%.
3. Prepare a statement of stockholders' equity. Use the following additional information:

January 1 balance of capital stock account	$100,000.00
(1,000 shares issued for $100.00 per share)	
No additional capital stock issued.	
January 1 balance of retained earnings account	68,372.00
Dividends declared during current quarter	5,000.00

4. Prepare a balance sheet.

Application Problem 4-5

Closing entry to close Income Summary to Retained Earnings: Debit Income Summary—General, 66,435.62; Credit Retained Earnings, 66,435.62.

Mastery Problem 4-6

Departmental Margin—Tennis, 58,259.00.
Departmental Margin—Golf, 139,280.30.
Net Income after Fed. Inc. Tax, 76,066.16.
Total Stockholders' Equity, 403,906.46.
Total Assets, 447,096.10.

Closing entry to close Income Summary to Retained Earnings: Debit Income Summary—General, 76,066.16; Credit Retained Earnings, 76,066.16.

4-5 APPLICATION PROBLEM 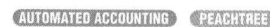 AUTOMATED ACCOUNTING PEACHTREE

Journalizing adjusting and closing entries for a departmentalized business

Instructions:

The work sheet from Application Problem 4-3 is needed to complete this problem.

1. Journalize the adjusting entries for AllSports Center. Use page 13 of a general journal.
2. Journalize the closing entries for AllSports Center. Use pages 14 and 15 of a general journal. Dividends declared during the current quarter were $12,000.00.

4-6 MASTERY PROBLEM AUTOMATED ACCOUNTING QUICKBOOKS

Completing end-of-fiscal-period work for a merchandising business using departmental margins

Klein Sporting Goods is a merchandising business that specializes in golf and tennis equipment. The company uses a yearly fiscal period. Klein's December 31 trial balance is recorded on a 12-column work sheet in the *Working Papers.* The adjustment information for December 31 follows.

Adjustment Information, December 31

Uncollectible accounts expense—estimated as 1.5% of sales on account.

Sales on account for year	$605,780.00
Merchandise Inventory—Golf	136,491.00
Merchandise Inventory—Tennis	154,040.00
Supplies Used—Administrative	2,013.00
Supplies Used—Golf	2,381.00
Supplies Used—Tennis	3,246.00
Insurance Expired	6,700.00
Depreciation Expense—Office Equipment	1,270.00
Depreciation Expense—Store Equipment, Golf	2,240.00
Depreciation Expense—Store Equipment, Tennis	1,850.00
Federal Income Tax Expense for the Year	21,173.44

Instructions:

1. Complete a work sheet for the year ended December 31 of the current year. Record the adjustments using the reported information for December 31.
2. Extend amounts to the proper debit and credit columns for Departmental Margin Statement—Golf, Departmental Margin Statement—Tennis, Income Statement, and Balance Sheet. Accounts on trial balance lines 57–65 are classified as indirect expenses.
3. Prepare departmental margin statements for each department. Calculate and record the percentages for each item on the statements. Round percentage calculations to the nearest 0.1%.
4. Prepare an income statement. Calculate and record the component percentages for each item on the statement. Round percentage calculations to the nearest 0.1%.
5. Prepare a statement of stockholders' equity. Use the following additional information:

January 1 balance of capital stock account (5,400 shares issued for $50.00 per share)	$270,000.00
No additional capital stock issued.	
January 1 balance of retained earnings account	67,840.30
Dividends declared during current year	10,000.00

6. Prepare a balance sheet.
7. Journalize the adjusting entries. Use page 13 of a general journal.
8. Journalize the closing entries. Use pages 14 and 15 of a general journal.

4-7 CHALLENGE PROBLEM

Analyzing a departmental margin statement

The departmental margin statement for the Personal Digital Assistant (PDA) department of Digital-Help, Inc., for the years 20X8 and 20X9 is provided in the *Working Papers*. The company has set a goal for the PDA Department to contribute a minimum of 25.0% departmental margin. For the years 20X3 through 20X8, the departmental margin for the PDA Department has varied from 25.5% to 29.0% of net sales.

Instructions:

1. Calculate and record the component percentages for each item on the 20X9 departmental margin statement. Round percentage calculations to the nearest 0.1%.
2. Calculate the changes in percentage of Net Sales from 20X8 to 20X9 for the following items: (a) cost of merchandise sold, (b) gross profit, (c) total direct departmental expenses, and (d) departmental margin.
3. From an analysis of the departmental margin statement and the amounts obtained from instructions 1 and 2, answer the following questions:
   a. Is the departmental margin for the PDA Department at a satisfactory percentage of sales? Explain why it is or is not satisfactory.
   b. Is the trend of the cost of merchandise sold percentage favorable or unfavorable? Explain why it is or is not favorable. Suggest some possible reasons for the change in cost of merchandise sold from 20X8 to 20X9.
   c. Is the trend of the total direct departmental expenses percentage favorable or unfavorable? Explain why the trend is or is not favorable.

Challenge Problem 4-7

1. Departmental Margin, 27.9%.
2. a. Cost of Merchandise Sold, 52.0%.
   b. Gross Profit, 48.0%.
   c. Total Direct Departmental Expenses, 20.1%.
   d. Departmental Margin, 27.9%.
3. a. Not satisfactory.
   b. Unfavorable.
   c. Unfavorable.

APPLIED COMMUNICATION

Students should connect qualities and activities they write about to specific employer needs. Personal characteristics and qualities should be documented with specific examples.

CASES FOR CRITICAL THINKING

Case 1

Nothing can be reported because the previous year's percentage of gross profit on operations is missing.

Case 2

Agree with the accountant. The major information needed by a manager to review how well each department is doing is the gross profit on operations. (Additional time would be required both for dividing the expenses and for preparing the statements.)

SCANS WORKPLACE COMPETENCY

Arrange students in cooperative learning groups consisting of 3–4 individuals. Allow 15 minutes for discussion. Allow another 15 minutes for groups to present their recommendations to the class.

• applied communication

One of the most frequently asked questions or requests during an interview is "Tell me about yourself." When responding to this inquiry, focus on how your education, skills, abilities, personal qualities, extracurricular activities, and work experience qualify you for the position. Emphasize information and accomplishments that are relevant to the job. Provide examples that document your traits and experience. And most important, be enthusiastic.

Instructions:

1. Write a paragraph about yourself. Emphasize those factors that would qualify you for employment. Don't forget to mention your accounting skills.

2. In your *Career Portfolio*, label a divider "Interviewing."

3. Keep a copy of your personal paragraph in the "Interviewing" section of your *Career Portfolio*. Be sure to review this paragraph before all interviews.

• cases for critical thinking

Case 1

The following data are obtained from financial information for InfoTech for the month ended August 31 of the current year:

Beginning Inventory, Jan. 1	$98,000.00
Net Purchases for the Period, Jan. 1 to Aug. 31	42,500.00
Net Sales for the Period, Jan. 1 to Aug. 31	66,800.00

You are asked to report the estimated ending inventory on August 31 using the gross profit method for estimating inventory. What will you report?

Case 2

Cyber Graphics is a departmentalized business. An interim statement of gross profit is prepared monthly. A departmental statement of gross profit is prepared at the end of each fiscal year. The manager suggests that the accountant extend the statements of gross profit by including a division of all expenses by department. The accountant indicates that the time required to divide the expenses by department would not add significantly to the information available for decision making. Do you agree or disagree with the accountant? Why?

• SCANS workplace competency

Resource Competency: Allocating Material and Facility Resources

Concept: Effective employees can acquire, store, and distribute supplies, parts, equipment, space, or final products in order to maximize their use.

Application: You are the manager of a small store consisting of three departments: Women's, Men's, and Children's. Presently, square footage is allocated as follows: Women's, 10,000 square feet; Men's, 5,000 square feet; Children's, 5,000 square feet. Gross profit on operations was $100,000 for the previous month. Each department contributed the following gross profit on operations amounts: Women's, $10,000 loss; Men's, $70,000 profit; Children's, $40,000 profit. Based on gross profit totals, how might you reallocate floor space for each department? Explain your answer. Is there a negative consequence to completely eliminating the Women's Department? Prepare an illustration indicating new department boundaries.

auditing for errors

A new accounting clerk for CalTech Corporation prepared the following trial balance using the general ledger account balances listed below.

1. Total the trial balance columns for the accounting clerk. If total debits do not equal credits, check your addition.

2. Review CalTech's trial balance for accuracy and make needed corrections. Re-total the trial balance columns. Continue checking until total debits = total credits.

3. Prepare a list identifying the general types of errors made.

Gen. Ledger	Account Title	Trial Balance	
42,370.00	Cash	4,237.00	
10,500.00	Accts. Receivable	10,500.00	
1,500.00	All. For Uncoll. Accts.	1,500.00	
30,510.00	Mdse. Inventory	30,510.00	
11,220.00	Office Equipment	11,220.00	
1,350.00	Acc. Depr.—Off. Equip.	1,350.00	
27,840.00	Accounts Payable		274,800.00
10,000.00	Dividends Payable		10,000.00
40,000.00	Capital Stock		40,000.00
2,150.00	Retained Earnings		2,150.00
10,000.00	Dividends		10,000.00
	Income Summary		
136,540.00	Sales		163,540.00
1,120.00	Sales Discount	1,120.00	
780.00	Sales Ret. & Allow.		780.00
48,230.00	Purchases	48,230.00	
1,850.00	Purchases Discount		1,850.00
20,000.00	Advertising Expense		
40,500.00	Rent Expense	40,500.00	
6,000.00	Federal Inc. Tax Exp.		6,000.00
	Totals		

analyzing Costco's Financial Statements

In this chapter, you have learned that the cost of merchandise is a significant cost for all merchandising businesses. In order to maximize profits, management attempts to keep this cost as low as possible. You also learned in Chapter 4 that there are four basic components included in every sales dollar. One of these components is the *cost of merchandise sold*. The component percentage for cost of merchandise sold is calculated by dividing merchandise costs by the amount of net sales.

Instructions:

1. Referring to the notes to consolidated financial statements on Appendix page B-12 in this textbook, describe what Costco considers to be the cost of merchandise sold beyond the purchase price of inventory sold.

2. Referring to the ten-year operating and financial highlights on Appendix pages B-2 and B-3:
   a. List the component percentages of net sales for merchandise costs for each year beginning with 1994 and ending with 2003.
   b. Looking at the component percentages for each year beginning with 1994, describe any trends regarding merchandise costs.
   c. Would you classify the trend identified in question 3 as "favorable" or "unfavorable" for Costco? Explain.
   d. For every $100 in net sales in 2003, how much did Costco spend to obtain merchandise? For every $100 in net sales in 1994, how much did Costco spend to obtain merchandise?

Financial Reporting for a Departmentalized Business

1. and 2.

Cash	42,370.00	
Accts. Receivable	10,500.00	
All. For Uncoll. Accts.		1,500.00
Mdse. Inventory	30,510.00	
Office Equipment	11,220.00	
Acc. Depr.—Off. Equip.		1,350.00
Accounts Payable		27,840.00
Dividends Payable		10,000.00
Capital Stock		40,000.00
Retained Earnings		2,150.00
Dividends	10,000.00	
Income Summary		
Sales		136,540.00
Sales Discount	1,120.00	
Sales Ret. & Allow.	780.00	
Purchases	48,230.00	
Purchases Discount		1,850.00
Advertising Expense	20,000.00	
Rent Expense	40,500.00	
Federal Inc. Tax Exp.	6,000.00	
	221,230.00	221,230.00

3. Errors include: transferring incorrect amounts, recording amounts in the incorrect debit or credit column, transposing numbers, leaving amounts off the trial balance, and possibly making addition errors.

ANALYZING COSTCO'S FINANCIAL STATEMENTS

1. "...inbound shipping charges and all costs related to our depot operations, including freight from depots to selling warehouses. Merchandise costs also include salaries, benefits, depreciation on production equipment, and other related expenses incurred in certain fresh foods and ancillary departments."

2a.
1994	90.7%	1999	89.6%
1995	90.6%	2000	89.6%
1996	90.3%	2001	89.6%
1997	89.9%	2002	89.4%
1998	89.7%	2003	89.3%

2b. The component percentage for merchandise costs has steadily declined since 1994.

2c. This decline is a favorable trend for Costco since less of every sales dollar is being spent on acquiring merchandise. This means more money is available to cover operating costs, which may lead to increased profits.

2d. For 2003, $89.30 ($100 × 89.3%). For 1994, $90.70 ($100 × 90.70%).

TEACHING STRATEGIES   PORTFOLIO ASSESSMENT

An ideal specimen for inclusion in a portfolio to demonstrate mastery of the procedures and concepts involved in the complete accounting cycle is an extended activity that simulates the accounting cycle. For this part, the accounting cycle for a departmentalized business, you may wish to have students complete and include in their portfolios either Reinforcement Activity 1 or Sounds, Inc.: A Business Simulation. You may also wish to include both a manual version and an automated version for either or both of these activities.

EXPLAIN

- Explain that the end-of-fiscal-period work described in this feature is similar to end-of-fiscal-period work in a manual accounting system.
- Explain that in an automated accounting system, adjusting entries are planned using a trial balance. A work sheet is not prepared.
- Explain that the Automated Accounting software can report an income statement either by fiscal period or by both month and year.
- Explain that closing entries are generated and posted by the software after financial statements are generated.
- Explain that there is no separate option for a post-closing trial balance, but that a trial balance prepared after closing entries have been recorded is a post-closing trial balance.

DEMONSTRATE

Processing a trial balance

- Direct students to the illustration as you demonstrate how to display and print a trial balance.
- Demonstrate clicking the Reports button.
- Demonstrate selecting Ledger Reports from the Report Selection dialog box.
- Demonstrate choosing Trial Balance from the Choose a Report to Display list.
- Demonstrate clicking the Print button to print a copy of the trial balance.

Recording adjusting entries

- Demonstrate clicking the General Journal tab within the Journal entries window.
- Demonstrate entering and posting adjusting entries in the General Journal screen.
- Explain that "Adj. Ent." is used as the reference for adjusting entries since there is no source document.

Processing financial statements

- Demonstrate that a financial statement is generated by clicking on the Reports button.
- Direct students to the illustration as you demonstrate selecting Financial Statements from the Select a Report Group options.
- Demonstrate choosing the gross profit statements from the Choose a Report to Display list and clicking OK.
- Demonstrate that other financial statements can be displayed by selecting other option buttons in the Choose a Report to Display list.
- Explain that displayed financial statements should be checked for accuracy before printing. Explain that if errors are

found on financial statements, corrections to journal entries should be made before financial statements are printed.

- Demonstrate clicking the Print button to print the statements.
- Repeat the demonstration for the income statement, balance sheet, and retained earnings statement.

Completing End-of-Fiscal-Period Work for a Departmental Business

During the fiscal period, many transactions are analyzed, journalized, and posted. When a transaction affects more than one accounting period, an adjusting entry may be needed to match revenues and expenses. To complete the accounting cycle, a trial balance is prepared. Adjusting entries are recorded, entered into the computer, and verified for accuracy. Financial statements are generated, and finally closing entries are generated and posted by the software. No work sheet is prepared in an automated accounting system.

Processing a Trial Balance

After all the usual transactions of the business are entered as journal entries, a preliminary trial balance is generated. A trial balance should be displayed and printed before adjusting entries are recorded. The trial balance indicates that debits equal credits. To display and print a trial balance:

1. Click the Reports button.
2. Select Ledger Reports from the Report Selection dialog box.
3. Choose Trial Balance from the Choose a Report to Display list.
4. Click the Print button to print a copy of the trial balance.

Adjusting Entries

This trial balance and period-end adjustment data are used as the basis for the adjusting entries. The General Journal tab within the Journal Entries window is used to enter and post the adjusting entries. All of the adjusting entries are dated the last day of the fiscal period and use *Adj. Ent.* as the reference.

Processing Financial Statements

The automated accounting system prepares financial statements from the information in the database. Financial statements can be displayed and printed at any time. They are always printed at the end of the fiscal period. These statements include:

- Departmental Gross Profit Statements
- Income statement
- Balance sheet
- Retained earnings statement

To display and print the statements:

1. Click the Reports button.
2. Select Financial Statements from the Report Selection dialog box.
3. Choose the statement you want to print from the Choose a Report to Display list.
4. Click the Print button to print a copy of the statement.

132   Chapter 4

Financial Reporting for a Departmentalized Business

TEACHING STRATEGIES   DIFFERENT LEARNING ABILITIES

Gifted Students. Students who are gifted often enjoy the challenge of working on the computer. Give gifted students an opportunity to automate other chapter problems after the assignment has been completed. It will challenge them to start a problem from scratch.

Closing Entries for a Departmentalized Business

In an automated accounting system, closing entries are generated and posted by the software. The software automatically closes net income to the retained earnings account after closing the revenue and expense accounts. The dividends account is closed as well.

1. Choose Generate Closing Journal Entries from the Options menu.
2. Click Yes to generate the closing entries.
3. The general journal will appear, containing the journal entries.
4. Click the Post button.
5. Display a post-closing trial balance report.
   a. Click on the Reports toolbar button, or choose the Reports Selection menu item from the Reports menu.
   b. Select the Ledger Reports option button from the Report Selection dialog box.
   c. Choose Trial Balance report.

AUTOMATING APPLICATION PROBLEMS 4-3, 4-4, and 4-5:
Preparing a work sheet with departmental margins
Preparing financial statements
Journalizing adjusting and closing entries for a departmentalized business

Instructions:

1. Load *Automated Accounting 8.0* or higher software.
2. Select data file A04-3 (Advanced Course Application Problem 4-3).

3. Select File from the menu bar and choose the Save As menu command. Key the path to the drive and directory that contains your data files. Save the database with a filename of A04-6 XXX XXX (where the Xs are your first and last names).
4. Access Problem Instructions through the Browser tool. Read the Problem Instruction screen.
5. Refer to pages 127 and 128 for data used in this problem.
6. Save your file and exit the Automated Accounting software.

AUTOMATING MASTERY PROBLEM 4-6:
Completing end-of-fiscal-period work for a merchandising business using departmental margins

Instructions:

1. Load *Automated Accounting 8.0* or higher software.
2. Select data file A04-6.
3. Select File from the menu bar and choose the Save As menu command. Key the path to the drive and directory that contains your data files. Save the database with a filename of A04-6 XXX XXX (where Xs are your first and last names).
4. Access Problem Instructions by clicking the Browser tool. Read the Problem Instruction screen.
5. Refer to page 128 for data used in this problem.
6. Save your file and exit the Automated Accounting software.

Generating closing entries and a post-closing trial balance

- Demonstrate choosing Generate Closing Journal Entries from the Options menu.
- Demonstrate choosing Yes to generate the closing entries.
- Demonstrate clicking the Post button after the general journal containing the closing entries is displayed and verified.
- Demonstrate clicking the Reports toolbar button or choosing the Report Selection menu item from the Reports menu.
- Demonstrate selecting the Ledger Reports option button from the Report Selection dialog box.
- Demonstrate choosing Trial Balance report to display the post-closing trial balance.

- Assign Automating Application Problem 4-3: Preparing a work sheet with departmental margins.
- Assign Automating Application Problem 4-4: Preparing financial statements.
- Assign Automating Application Problem 4-5: Journalizing adjusting and closing entries for a departmentalized business.
- Assign Automating Mastery Problem 4-6: Completing end-of-fiscal-period work for a merchandising business using departmental margins.

- Use the Electronic Auditor to assess student understanding. As an alternative, some instructors have found it effective to give students access to the Electronic Auditor to find their errors and correct their own work.

TEACHING STRATEGIES   PORTFOLIO ASSESSMENT

Students should be encouraged to print at least one report from one of the Automated Accounting problems to include in their portfolio to demonstrate mastery of automated accounting systems. A copy of the Portfolio Assessment form (blackline master in the Teacher's Resource Guide; also on the Student Companion CD) should be completed by the student and the Description section should include any comments regarding how the student mastered these concepts and procedures.

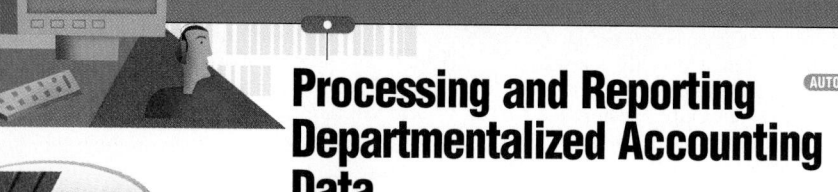

Processing and Reporting Departmentalized Accounting Data

AUTOMATED ACCOUNTING
PEACHTREE
QUICKBOOKS

This activity reinforces selected learning from Part 1, Chapters 1 through 4. The complete accounting cycle is for a departmentalized merchandising business organized as a corporation.

BOOKSPLUS, INC.

BooksPlus, Inc., has two departments: Books and Magazines. BooksPlus, Inc., is open for business Monday through Saturday. A monthly rent is paid on the building. The business owns the office and store equipment.

BooksPlus sells books and magazines to individuals and schools. Cash sales and sales on account are made. The business uses a national credit card service in addition to its own company credit card.

BooksPlus's fiscal year is January 1 through December 31. During the fiscal year, a monthly interim departmental statement of gross profit is prepared.

BooksPlus uses the chart of accounts shown on the following page. The journals and ledgers used by BooksPlus are similar to those illustrated in Part 1. The journal and ledger forms are provided in the *Working Papers.* Beginning balances have been recorded in the ledgers.

PREPARING AN INTERIM DEPARTMENTAL STATEMENT OF GROSS PROFIT

BooksPlus prepares an interim departmental statement of gross profit each month. The following data are obtained from the accounting records at the end of November of the current year.

	Books	Magazines
Beginning inventory, January 1	$164,164.20	$147,840.30
Estimated beginning inventory, November 1	180,205.05	157,195.78
Net purchases January 1 to October 31	133,839.60	130,449.20
Net sales, January 1 to October 31	214,179.55	220,170.40
Net purchases for November	13,007.20	14,162.58
Net sales for November	19,480.60	20,240.30
Gross profit on operation as a percent of sales	45.0%	55.0%

Instructions:

1. Use the gross profit method of estimating an inventory to prepare an estimated merchandise inventory sheet for each department for the month ended November of the current year.
2. Prepare an interim departmental statement of gross profit for the month ended November 30 of the current year. Calculate and record component percentages for departmental and total cost of merchandise sold and gross profit on operations. Round percentage calculations to the nearest 0.1%.

TEACHING STRATEGIES   PORTFOLIO ASSESSMENT

A reinforcement activity that covers the whole accounting cycle is an ideal exhibit to demonstrate mastery in a portfolio. A copy of the Portfolio Assessment form (blackline master in the Teacher's Resource Guide; also on the Student Companion CD) should be completed by the student, and the Description section should include any comments regarding how the student mastered these concepts and procedures.

GENERAL LEDGER CHART OF ACCOUNTS

Balance Sheet Accounts

(1000)	**ASSETS**
1100–1400	CURRENT ASSETS
1105	Cash
1110	Petty Cash
1205	Accounts Receivable
1210	Allowance for Uncollectible Accounts
1305	Merchandise Inventory—Books
1310	Merchandise Inventory—Magazines
1315	Supplies—Administrative
1320	Supplies—Books
1325	Supplies—Magazines
1405	Prepaid Insurance
1500–1600	PLANT ASSETS
1505	Display Equipment—Books
1510	Accumulated Depreciation—Display Equipment, Books
1515	Display Equipment—Magazines
1520	Accumulated Depreciation—Display Equipment, Magazines
1605	Office Equipment
1610	Accumulated Depreciation—Office Equipment
(2000)	**LIABILITIES**
2105	Accounts Payable
2205	Employee Income Tax Payable—Federal
2210	Employee Income Tax Payable—State
2215	Federal Income Tax Payable
2220	Social Security Tax Payable
2225	Medicare Tax Payable
2230	Sales Tax Payable
2235	Unemployment Tax Payable—Federal
2240	Unemployment Tax Payable—State
2245	Health Insurance Premiums Payable
2305	Dividends Payable
(3000)	**STOCKHOLDERS' EQUITY**
3105	Capital Stock
3110	Retained Earnings
3115	Dividends
3205	Income Summary—Books
3210	Income Summary—Magazines
3215	Income Summary—General

Income Statement Accounts

(4000)	**OPERATING REVENUE**
4105	Sales—Books
4110	Sales Discount—Books
4115	Sales Returns and Allowances—Books
4205	Sales—Magazines
4210	Sales Discount—Magazines
4215	Sales Returns and Allowances—Magazines
(5000)	**COST OF MERCHANDISE**
5105	Purchases—Books
5110	Purchases Discount—Books
5115	Purchases Returns and Allowances—Books
5205	Purchases—Magazines
5210	Purchases Discount—Magazines
5215	Purchases Returns and Allowances—Magazines
(6000)	**DIRECT EXPENSES**
6100	DIRECT EXPENSES—BOOKS
6105	Advertising Expense—Books
6110	Depreciation Expense—Display Equipment, Books
6115	Payroll Taxes Expense—Books
6120	Salary Expense—Books
6125	Supplies Expense—Books
(6200)	DIRECT EXPENSES—MAGAZINES
6205	Advertising Expense—Magazines
6210	Depreciation Expense—Display Equipment, Magazines
6215	Payroll Taxes Expense—Magazines
6220	Salary Expense—Magazines
6225	Supplies Expense—Magazines
(7000)	**INDIRECT EXPENSES**
7105	Credit Card Fee Expense
7110	Depreciation Expense—Office Equipment
7115	Insurance Expense
7120	Miscellaneous Expense
7125	Payroll Taxes Expense—Administrative
7130	Rent Expense
7135	Salary Expense—Administrative
7140	Supplies Expense—Administrative
7145	Uncollectible Accounts Expense
(8000)	**INCOME TAX**
8105	Federal Income Tax Expense

SUBSIDIARY LEDGERS CHARTS OF ACCOUNTS

Accounts Receivable Ledger

110	Marcella Amco
120	Matthew Barasso
130	Tanya Dockman
140	Brian Fadstad
150	Gilmore Public Schools
160	Belinda Judd
170	Janelle Kamschorr
180	Donald Lindgren
190	Renville Public Schools

Accounts Payable Ledger

210	A-1 Publishing
220	CBG Distributors
230	Grandway Products
240	H & B Books
250	Maryland Books & Magazines
260	Oliver Books, Inc.
270	Strup Publishers, Inc.

Instructions:

3. Use the appropriate journal to record the following transactions completed during December of the current year. Calculate and record sales tax on all sales and sales returns and allowances as described in Chapter 2. The sales tax rate is 5.0%. No sales tax is charged on sales to schools. BooksPlus offers its customers terms of 2/10, n/30. All of the vendors from which merchandise is purchased on account offer terms of 2/10, n/30. Source documents are abbreviated as follows: check, C; credit memorandum, CM; debit memorandum, DM; memorandum, M; purchase invoice, P; receipt, R; sales invoice, S; terminal summary, TS.

Dec. 1. Paid cash for monthly payroll, $7,899.83 (total payroll: books, $4,522.20; magazines, $4,310.40; administrative, $2,630.25, less deductions: employee income tax-federal, $1,204.00; employee income tax—state, $538.11; Social Security tax, $710.70; Medicare tax, $166.21; health insurance, $944.00). C340.

  1. Recorded employer payroll taxes, $924.26, for the monthly pay period ended November 30. Taxes owed are: Social Security tax, $710.70; Medicare tax, $166.21; federal unemployment tax, $6.11; state unemployment tax, $41.24. Payroll taxes are distributed among the departments as: books, $367.04; magazines, $356.00; and administrative, $201.22. M40.

  1. Paid cash for rent, $1,200.00. C341.

  2. Paid cash for supplies, $135.00. C342.

  2. Purchased books on account from Oliver Books, Inc., $1,933.00. P115.

  3. Recorded cash and credit card sales: books, $2,478.00; magazines, $2,588.50; plus sales tax. TS33.

     Posting. Post the items that are to be posted individually. Post from the journals in this order: sales journal, purchases journal, general journal, cash receipts journal, cash payments journal.

  5. Sold books on account to Matthew Barasso, $880.00, plus sales tax. S97.

  5. Received cash on account from Tanya Dockman, $493.92, covering S92 for magazines for $504.00 ($480.00 plus sales tax), less discount. R139.

  6. Paid cash on account to CBG Distributors, $2,185.50, covering P111 for books for $2,230.10, less discount. C343.

  7. Paid cash on account to H & B Books, $5,321.55, covering P112 for books for $5,430.15, less discount. C344.

  7. Returned books to Oliver Books, Inc., $300.00, from P115. DM59.

  8. Received cash on account from Gilmore Public Schools, $6115.40, covering S94 for magazines for $6,240.20, less discount. R140.

  8. Received cash on account from Belinda Judd, $257.25, covering S95 for books for $262.50 ($250.00 plus sales tax), less discount. R141.

  8. Received cash on account from Renville Public Schools, $9,389.87, covering S96 for books for $9,581.50, less discount. R142.

  8. Paid cash on account to Maryland Books & Magazines, $554.09, covering P113 for magazines for $565.40, less discount. C345.

  9. Paid cash on account to Oliver Books, Inc., $4,821.80, covering P114 for books for $4,920.20, less discount. C346.

  9. Granted credit to Matthew Barasso for books returned, $100.00, plus sales tax, from S97. CM33.

10. Recorded cash and credit card sales: books, $4,946.50; magazines, $3,650.00; plus sales tax. TS34.
    Posting. Post the items that are to be posted individually.
12. Paid cash on account to Oliver Books, Inc., $1,600.34, covering P115 for books for $1,933.00, less DM59, and less discount. C347.
13. Sold magazines on account to Marcella Amco, $450.00, plus sales tax. S98.
15. Paid cash for liability for federal employee income tax, $1,240.00; social security tax, $1,286.11; Medicare tax, $300.78; total, $2,826.89. C348.
15. Paid cash for quarterly federal income tax estimate, $1,200.00. C349. (Debit Federal Income Tax Expense; credit Cash.)
15. Received cash on account from Matthew Barasso, $802.62, covering S97 for books for $924.00 ($880.00 plus sales tax), less CM33, less discount. R143.
17. Recorded cash and credit card sales: books, $3,820.60; magazines, $3,240.50; plus sales tax. TS35.
    Posting. Post the items that are to be posted individually.
22. Sold magazines on account to Renville Public Schools, $4,750.00; no sales tax. S99.
22. Purchased magazines on account from Strup Publishers, Inc., $1,647.00. P116.
22. Purchased magazines on account from A-1 Publishing, $1,278.50. P117.
23. Sold books on account to Brian Fadstad, $1,720.00, plus sales tax, S100.
23. Sold magazines on account to Janelle Kamschorr, $920.00, plus sales tax. S101.
23. Received cash on account from Marcella Amco, $463.05, covering S98 for magazines for $472.50 ($450.00 plus sales tax), less discount. R144.
24. Purchased books on account from CBG Distributors, $1,500.00. P118.
24. Paid cash for advertising for the magazine department, $500. C351.
24. Recorded cash and credit card sales: books, $4,160.10; magazines, $3,420.50; plus sales tax. TS36.
    Posting. Post the items that are to be posted individually.
26. Sold magazines on account to Donald Lindgren, $540.00, plus sales tax. S102.
26. Returned magazines to A-1 Publishing, $265.00, from P117. DM60.
27. Purchased books on account from Maryland Books & Magazines, $2,440.50. P119.
27. Purchased magazines on account from Grandway Products, $3,157.99. P120.
28. Sold books on account to Donald Lindgren, $650.00, plus sales tax. S103.
30. Received bank statement showing December bank service charge, $11.40 (debit Miscellaneous Expense). M41.
30. Recorded credit card fee expense for December, $354.20. M42.
31. Granted credit to Renville Public Schools for magazines returned, $1,500.00, from S99. CM34.
31. Sold books on account to Gilmore Public Schools, $6,200.00; no sales tax. S104.
31. Paid cash to replenish petty cash fund, $415.00: supplies for the books department, $145.00; advertising—books, $160.00; miscellaneous, $110.00. C350.
31. Recorded cash and credit card sales: books, $3,580.40; magazines, $2,480.00; plus sales tax. TS37.
    Posting. Post the items that are to be posted individually.

COMPLETING JOURNALS

Instructions:

4. Prove and rule the sales journal. Post the totals of the special columns.
5. Prove and rule the purchases journal. Post the totals of the special columns.
6. Prove the cash receipts journal and the cash payments journal.
7. Prove cash. The balance on the next unused check stub is $59,773.67.
8. Rule the cash receipts journal. Post the totals of the special columns.
9. Rule the cash payments journal. Post the totals of the special columns.

END-OF-FISCAL-PERIOD WORK

Instructions:

10. Prepare a schedule of accounts receivable and a schedule of accounts payable. Compare each schedule total with the balance of the controlling account in the general ledger. The total and the balance should be the same.
11. Prepare a trial balance on a work sheet.
12. Complete the work sheet. Record the adjustments on the work sheet using the following information.

Adjustment Information, December 31

Uncollectible accounts expense estimated as 1.0% of sales on account.
Sales on account for year, $241,257.00.

Merchandise inventory—Books	$174,469.25
Merchandise inventory—Magazines	151,439.85
Supplies used—Books	940.00
Supplies used—Magazines	1,080.00
Supplies used—Administrative	706.00
Insurance Expired	880.00
Annual depreciation expense—Display Equipment, Books	870.00
Annual depreciation expense—Display Equipment, Magazines	940.00
Annual depreciation expense—Office Equipment	1,260.00
Federal income tax expense for the year	5,013.75

13. Prepare separate departmental margin statements for BooksPlus's Book Department and Magazine Department. Calculate and record component percentages for each item on the statements. Round percentage calculations to the nearest 0.1%.
14. Prepare an income statement. Calculate and record component percentages for each item on the statement. Round component percentage calculations to the nearest 0.1%.
15. Prepare a statement of stockholders' equity. Use the following additional information.

> January 1 balance of capital stock account $300,000.00
>   (3,000 shares issued for $100.00 per share)
> No additional capital stock issued.
> January 1 balance of retained earnings account 97,525.70

16. Prepare a balance sheet.
17. Use page 13 of a general journal. Journalize and post the adjusting entries.
18. Use pages 14 and 15 of a general journal. Journalize and post the closing entries.
19. Prepare a post-closing trial balance.

Activities in Sounds, Inc.:

1. Recording transactions in special journals and a general journal.

2. Calculating and recording departmental payroll data.

3. Posting items to be posted individually to a general ledger and subsidiary ledgers.

4. Proving and ruling journals.

5. Posting column totals to a general ledger.

6. Preparing schedules of accounts receivable and accounts payable.

7. Preparing a trial balance on a work sheet.

8. Planning adjustments and completing a work sheet.

9. Preparing financial statements.

10. Journalizing and posting adjusting entries.

11. Journalizing and posting closing entries.

12. Preparing a post-closing trial balance.

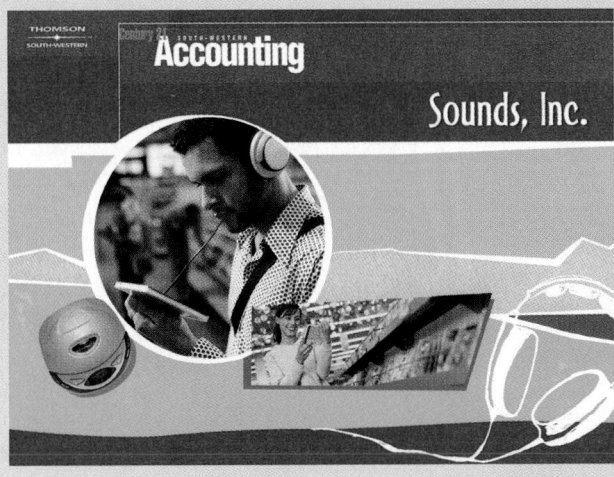

A Business Simulation
Sounds, Inc.

Sounds, Inc., is a departmentalized merchandising business organized as a corporation. This business simulation covers the realistic transactions completed by Sounds, Inc., which has two departments: Music and Accessories. The activities included in the accounting cycle for Sounds, Inc., are listed here.

This simulation is available from the publisher in either manual or automated versions.

INTRODUCE THE SIMULATION

- Sounds, Inc.: A Business Simulation is a self-contained simulation available in both manual and automated versions from the publisher.

- The simulation presents the complete accounting cycle for a departmentalized merchandising business organized as a corporation.

AUTOMATING THE SIMULATION

- Automated Accounting and Century 21 8E CD may be used to automate the Sounds, Inc., Business Simulation.

- Direct students to read the Problem Instructions screens for specific requirements for automating the simulation.

ASSESSMENT

- The Teacher's Key provides full solutions to the simulation.

- Blackline masters for audit tests for the simulation are included in the Teacher's Key.

- Use the Electronic Auditor to assess performance on the automated version of the simulation.

MATERIALS

- Manual Accounting:
  Sounds, Inc.: A Business Simulation
  Key for Sounds, Inc.: A Business Simulation
  Blackline Master of Audit Test

- Software:
  Sounds, Inc.: An Automated Business Simulation
  Key for Sounds, Inc.: An Automated Business Simulation
  Automated Accounting and Century 21 8E CD
  The Electronic Auditor

TEACHING STRATEGIES   PORTFOLIO ASSESSMENT

A simulation that covers the whole accounting cycle is an ideal exhibit to demonstrate mastery in a portfolio. A copy of the Portfolio Assessment form (blackline master in the Teacher's Resource Guide; also on the Student Companion CD) should be completed by the student, and the Description section should include any comments regarding how the student mastered these concepts and procedures.

Part 2 introduces accounting control systems and their importance to management. Of particular concern to management are procedures to control and protect assets. Many businesses, therefore, use two specific control systems to protect assets—vouchers and inventory planning and valuation.

Chapter 5 introduces vouchers as a system of controlling cash payments. Vouchers are described and the procedures for using a voucher system are thoroughly discussed.

Chapter 6 establishes the importance of managing inventory. Procedures for maintaining inventory must be established in order for a business to be successful. This chapter covers all the important elements of maintaining inventory.

AUTOMATED ACCOUNTING

For those teachers who wish to fully integrate the accounting program, an Automated Accounting feature is provided at the end of each chapter.

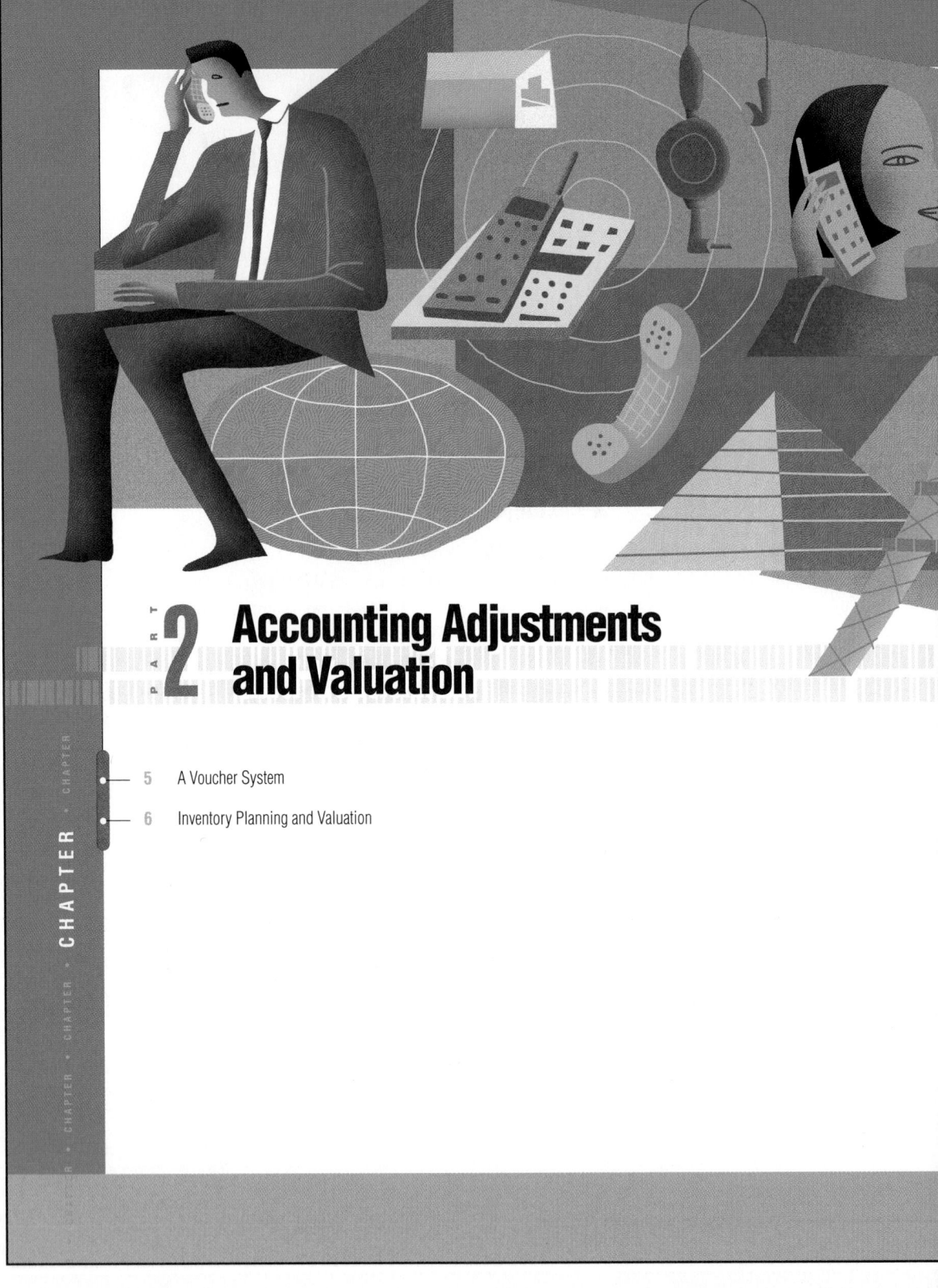

PART 2 Accounting Adjustments and Valuation

1200   Plant Assets
1205   Delivery Equipment
1210   Accumulated Depreciation—Delivery Equipment
1215   Office Equipment
1220   Accumulated Depreciation—Office Equipment
1225   Store Equipment
1230   Accumulated Depreciation—Store Equipment

(2000) LIABILITIES
2100   Current Liabilities
2105   Vouchers Payable
2110   Employee Income Tax Payable—Federal
2115   Employee Income Tax Payable—State
2120   Federal Income Tax Payable
2125   Social Security Tax Payable
2128   Medicare Tax Payable
2130   Sales Tax Payable
2135   Unemployment Tax Payable—Federal
2140   Unemployment Tax Payable—State
2145   Dividends Payable

(3000) STOCKHOLDERS' EQUITY
3105   Capital Stock
3110   Retained Earnings
3115   Dividends
3120   Income Summary

Income Statement Accounts

(4000) OPERATING REVENUE
4105   Sales
4110   Sales Discount
4115   Sales Returns and Allowances

(5000) COST OF MERCHANDISE
5105   Purchases
5110   Purchases Discount
5115   Purchases Returns and Allowances

(6000) OPERATING EXPENSES
6100   SELLING EXPENSES
6105   Advertising Expense
6110   Delivery Expense
6115   Depreciation Expense—Delivery Equipment
6120   Depreciation Expense—Store Equipment
6125   Miscellaneous Expense—Sales
6130   Salary Expense—Sales
6135   Supplies Expense—Sales
6200   ADMINISTRATIVE EXPENSES
6205   Depreciation Expense—Office Equipment
6210   Insurance Expense
6215   Miscellaneous Expense—Administrative
6220   Payroll Taxes Expense
6225   Rent Expense
6230   Salary Expense—Administrative
6235   Supplies Expense—Administrative
6240   Uncollectible Accounts Expense
6245   Utilities Expense

(7000) INCOME TAX EXPENSE
7105   Federal Income Tax Expense

The chart of accounts for OfficeMart, Inc. is illustrated above for ready reference as you study Part 2 of this textbook.

OFFICEMART, INC.
CHART OF ACCOUNTS

Balance Sheet Accounts

(1000) ASSETS
1100   CURRENT ASSETS
1105   Cash
1110   Petty Cash
1115   Accounts Receivable
1120   Allowance for Uncollectible Accounts
1125   Merchandise Inventory
1130   Supplies—Sales
1135   Supplies—Administrative
1140   Prepaid Insurance

CHART OF ACCOUNTS

- Emphasize that students should refer to this chart of accounts for both chapters in Part 2.
- Explain that this chart of accounts is used by a business that is a merchandising business organized as a corporation.
- Point out that charts of accounts are used for determining the classification of accounts and which accounts are temporary and permanent accounts.
- Stress that the chart of accounts is useful for completed automated accounting activities since account numbers are required for both data entry and file maintenance activities.

Point out the *similarities* between this chart of accounts and the one in Part 1.

- Typical divisions for a merchandising business:
  - Assets
  - Liabilities
  - Equity
  - Revenue
  - Cost of merchandise
  - Expenses
- Many familiar accounts within divisions.

Point out the *differences* between this chart of accounts and the one in Part 1:

- Because the business is not departmentalized, accounts are not divided into departments as they were for Zytech in Part 1.
- The liabilities section reflects the fact that OfficeMart uses a voucher system for controlling cash payments.
- In the stockholders' equity section, there is only one income summary account since the company is not departmentalized.
- The Operating Expenses section is divided into selling and administrative expenses. Administrative expenses are expenses of the business that do not clearly relate to the sales effort, such as salaries and supplies of the office staff.

A Voucher

	SCOPE & SEQUENCE		ENHANCING	
	NEW	REVIEW/ EXTENSION	SPECIAL FEATURES	
Introduce the Chapter	✓		• Accounting in the Real World: Procter & Gamble	
Lesson 5-1 Vouchers and Voucher Registers			• Making Ethical Decisions: Integrity in Management Accounting	
Using a voucher system	✓			
Preparing a voucher	✓		• Case for Critical Thinking 1	
Recording vouchers in voucher register		✓		
Lesson 5-2 Voucher Check and Check Registers			• Case for Critical Thinking 2	
Voucher checks		✓		
Recording cash payments in a check register		✓		
Proving, ruling, and posting a check register		✓		
Lesson 5-3 Selected Transactions in a Voucher System				
Journalizing a voucher for purchases returns and allowances on account		✓		
Journalizing a voucher for a payroll transaction		✓		
Putting It All Together			• Explore Accounting	
			• Xtra! Web Site: Xtra! Enrichment	
			• Applied Communication	
			• SCANS Workplace Competency	
			• Auditing for Errors	
			• Analyzing Costco's Financial Statements	

System

141B

INSTRUCTION		PRACTICE AND ASSESSMENT		
TECHNOLOGY AND MEDIA	**TEACHING STRATEGIES**	**GUIDED PRACTICE**	**INDEPENDENT PRACTICE**	**RETEACHING AND ENRICHMENT**
• Internet Research Activity • Accounting Xtra! Web Site	• Software Focus			
• Blackline Masters: Voucher Register • Instructor's Resource CD: PowerPoint Slides • Xtra! Web Site: Xtra! Study Tools • Personal Trainer	• Tactile Learner	• Terms Review • Audit Your Understanding • Work Together 5-1	• On Your Own 5-1 • Application Problem 5-1 • Ongoing Assessment, p. 148 • Personal Trainer • Xtra! Web Site: Xtra! Study Tools	• Reteach, p. 148 • Enrich, p. 149
• Blackline Masters: Check Register • Instructor's Resource CD: PowerPoint Slides • Xtra! Web Site: Xtra! Study Tools • Personal Trainer	• Applied Skills: Writing Across the Curriculum	• Terms Review • Audit Your Understanding • Work Together 5-2	• On Your Own 5-2 • Application Problem 5-2 • Ongoing Assessment, p. 152 • Personal Trainer • Xtra! Web Site: Xtra! Study Tools	• Reteach, p. 152 • Enrich, p. 154
• Blackline Masters: Voucher Register • Instructor's Resource CD: PowerPoint Slides • Xtra! Web Site: Xtra! Study Tools • Personal Trainer		• Audit Your Understanding • Work Together 5-3	• On Your Own 5-3 • Application Problem 5-3 • Application Problem 5-4 • Ongoing Assessment, p. 158 • Personal Trainer • Xtra! Web Site: Xtra! Study Tools	• Reteach, p. 158 • Enrich, p. 159
• Personal Trainer • Xtra! Web Site: Xtra! Review, Quizzing, and Enrichment • Student Companion CD			• Mastery Problem 5-5 • Personal Trainer • Xtra! Web Site: Xtra! Review and Quizzing • Study Guide 5 • Student Companion CD • Chapter 5 Test • ExamView Chapter 5 • Portfolio Assessment	• Challenge Problem 5-6 • Reteach, p. 160 • Enrich, p. 160 • Recycling Problem 5-1 • Automated Accounting • Xtra! Web Site: Xtra! Enrichment

INTRODUCE THE CHAPTER

Preview Chapter Objectives

- Point out that students have already learned how to record cash payments. This chapter will build on that knowledge.

- Note that using a voucher system to control cash payments will be introduced in this chapter.

Preview Accounting Terms

- Read each term out loud to verify pronunciation for students.

- Point out that the terms introduced this chapter are specific to a voucher system.

INTERNET ACTIVITY

Point your browser to *accountingxtra. swlearning.com* to access the Accounting Xtra! Web Site.

SOFTWARE FOCUS

Software may be used for independent practice or enrichment as the instructor deems appropriate. For this chapter, the following software may be used: the Student Companion CD and Personal Trainer, Chapter 5.

Instructors may wish to cover the Automated Accounting feature on page 167 even if the Automated Accounting software is not being used in the classroom so that students get a sense of how the chapter's accounting procedures would be implemented in an automated environment.

CHAPTER **5**

A Voucher System

OBJECTIVES & TERMS

After studying Chapter 5, you will be able to:

1. Define accounting terms related to a voucher system.

2. Identify accounting concepts and practices related to a voucher system.

3. Prepare a voucher.

4. Journalize data from vouchers in a voucher register.

5. Journalize voucher payment transactions in a check register.

6. Journalize purchases returns and allowances and payroll transactions in a voucher system.

- voucher
- voucher system
- voucher register
- voucher check
- check register

Point Your Browser
accountingxtra.swlearning.com

• Procter & Gamble

©DANIEL ACKER/BLOOMBERG NEWS/LANDOV

PURCHASING AT PROCTER & GAMBLE

Crest, Folgers, Pampers, Tide, Pringles, Charmin, Downey, and Clairol—these are just a few of the nearly 300 products marketed by the Procter & Gamble Company (P&G). Established in 1837 as a family-operated soap and candle company, P&G markets its products in over 160 countries.

With annual sales exceeding $40 billion, just imagine the amount of products and services P&G buys from other companies! P&G purchases buildings, equipment, raw materials, supplies, and packaging to produce its products. The company must install computer systems to fulfill its information needs. Administrative employees need office equipment and supplies. P&G's active research unit requires scientific supplies. The list can stagger the imagination.

To fulfill its mission to its stockholders, P&G must ensure that it receives the best value possible for every purchase. Before any payment for goods and services is completed, internal controls require that those individuals involved ensure that four objectives are met: (1) P&G buys only goods and services that it needs, (2) goods and services are ordered at the most favorable terms, (3) goods and services are received and meet quality standards, and (4) payment is made for the agreed-upon amount.

Critical Thinking

1. Two companies bid different amounts to supply P&G with a raw material. Why might P&G elect to purchase the materials from the company offering the higher price?
2. As a consumer, what do you do to ensure you receive the best price?

Source: www.pg.com/about_pg/sectionmain.jhtml, www.pg.com/annualreports/2002/pdf/pg_ar2002.pdf

Xtra!
Today
accountingxtra.swlearning.com

ACCOUNTING FIRMS (PART 2)

Go to the homepage for the following two international accounting firms:

Deloitte & Touche: http://deloitte.com

KPMG: http://kpmg.com

Instructions

Create a table listing the following items for each company:
1. Number of global employees
2. Amount of global revenue
3. Number of countries in which it operates

1. The company's product may be superior in quality. The company may also be able to deliver the material at a lower cost or with a shorter notice.
2. Consumers shop at different companies to search for the best price. For high-priced items, a consumer might bargain or ask the company to "give me your best deal."

INTERNET RESEARCH ACTIVITY

Answers at the time of the textbook's publication:

	Deloitte & Touche	KPMG
Employees	120,000	98,000
Revenue	$15.1 billion	$10.7 billion
Countries	144 countries	150 countries

143

5-1 Vouchers and Voucher Registers

An accounting system includes procedures for recording and reporting accurate and up-to-date financial information. An accounting system should also include procedures to assist management in controlling a company's daily operations. Management is particularly concerned with procedures and records to control and protect assets. One asset that should be controlled and protected is cash. Cash is the asset most likely to be misused because its ownership is easily transferred. Also, transactions generally affect the cash account more often than other general ledger accounts. Many businesses, therefore, use specific cash control procedures.

Among the procedures used to control cash are storing it in a safe place, making bank deposits regularly, and approving all cash payments. Cash payments should be approved before being paid to ensure that the goods or services were ordered, have been received, and the amounts due are correct. In small businesses, the owner or manager usually approves cash payments. In large businesses, several persons may have authority to approve cash payments. A business form used to show an authorized person's approval for a cash payment is called a **voucher**. A set of procedures for controlling cash payments by preparing and approving vouchers before payments are made is called a **voucher system**. In a voucher system, NO check can be issued without a properly authorized voucher.

MAKING ETHICAL DECISIONS • MAKING ETHICAL DECISIONS • MAKING ETHICAL DECISIO

making ethical decisions

Integrity in Management Accounting

The Institute of Management Accountants (IMA) is an organization dedicated to providing its members with professional development opportunities in management accounting, financial management, and information management. The Institute supports lifelong learning by its members through self-study courses, seminars, conferences, and webcasts. Members are encouraged to demonstrate their knowledge by becoming a Certified Management Accountant (CMA) or Certified in Financial Management (CFM).

An important element of the IMA's mission is to encourage its members and their organizations to adopt ethical business practices. One section of the IMA's *Standards of Ethical Conduct*

defines *integrity.* Individuals may attempt to influence management accountants to misrepresent facts to achieve short-term objectives that are contrary to the organization's long-term goals. Management accountants must be people of high integrity to resist these individuals and ensure that accounting information is accurate and reliable.

Instructions

Access the IMA's *Standards of Ethical Conduct.* How does the IMA define *integrity*?

144   Chapter 5

A Voucher System

VERIFYING AN INVOICE

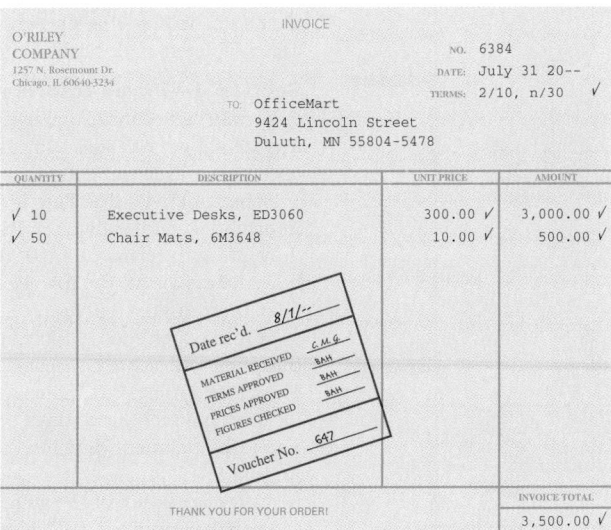

OfficeMart, a merchandising business, sells office furniture and supplies. When OfficeMart receives an invoice, a verification form is stamped on the invoice, as shown above.

OfficeMart's receiving clerk verifies that the items were received in the correct quantities. A clerk in OfficeMart's purchasing department verifies that the terms and prices are correct. The calculations on the invoice are also verified. Each person doing a part of the work places a check mark next to the items verified and initials the verification form to show responsibility for that part.

A VOUCHER

After an invoice is checked for accuracy, a voucher is prepared for each invoice received from a vendor.

August 1. Purchased merchandise on account from O'Riley Company, $3,500.00. Voucher No. 647.

When a voucher system is used, the source document for an approved cash payment is the voucher. The source document for this transaction is Voucher No. 647. [CONCEPT: Objective Evidence]

In a voucher system, the general ledger liability account, Vouchers Payable, is used instead of Accounts Payable. Accounts Payable has been used to record only amounts of items bought on account.

In a voucher system, Vouchers Payable is used to record *ALL* amounts to be paid by check. Since Vouchers Payable is a liability account, the normal balance is on the credit side of the account. With a voucher system, an accounts payable ledger is not kept. Instead, vouchers needing to be paid are kept in an unpaid vouchers file. The unpaid vouchers file shows all amounts owed and to whom they are owed.

Purchases	
3,500.00	

Vouchers Payable	
	3,500.00

EXPLAIN

- Discuss the verification form stamped on an invoice.
- Stress the purpose of a voucher system as a means of controlling cash payments.
- Introduce the vouchers payable account and compare it to the accounts payable account.

DEMONSTRATE

Analyze a T account

- Draw a T account on the board for Vouchers Payable and label the increase and decrease sides.
- Draw two sets of two T accounts side-by-side. Use the left set to record the transaction using Accounts Payable. Use the right set to record the transaction using Vouchers Payable. Compare the two entries.

- Explain how a voucher is prepared from an invoice.
- Emphasize the importance of each part of a voucher.
- Review terms of sale and calculating due dates.
- Emphasize that checks are written two days before they are due.
- Point out that a voucher can take many forms. Some vouchers are actually envelopes in which related documents may be placed.
- Stress that prenumbering voucher forms is another part of the control system.

DEMONSTRATE

Prepare a voucher

- Refer students to the illustration as preparation of a voucher is discussed.
- Have students point to each section of the voucher as you explain the information recorded in the section.

PREPARING A VOUCHER FROM AN INVOICE

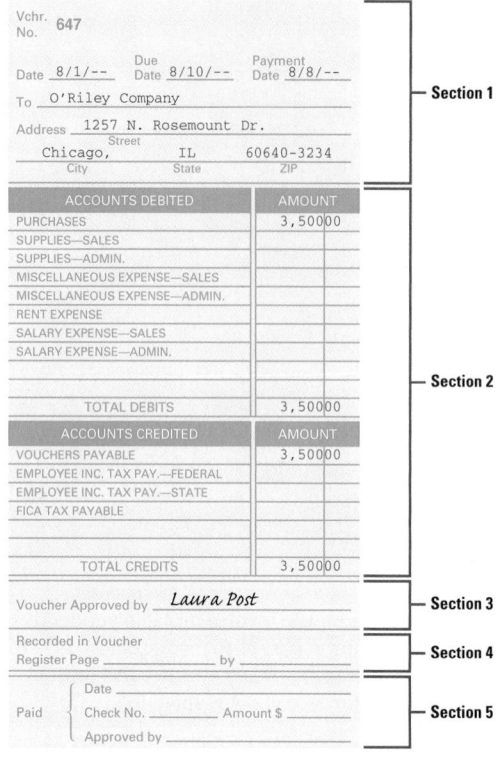

Sections 1, 2, and 3 of the voucher are completed at the time it is prepared. Sections 4 and 5 are completed as described later in this chapter.

Section 1—Payee Information

OfficeMart's accounting clerk uses the verified invoice shown on page 145 to enter information about the payee in Section 1 of the voucher.

The voucher's due date is calculated using information on the invoice. The invoice is dated July 31, with terms of 2/10, n/30. Therefore, to take the discount, the invoice must be paid no later than August 10.

From experience, OfficeMart has learned that most checks are received within two days. Therefore, OfficeMart writes and mails checks for cash payments two days before the due date. Thus, the payment date for Voucher No. 647 is August 8.

After Section 1 of the voucher is completed, the voucher number, 647, is recorded on the invoice's verification stamp, as shown on page 145.

Section 2—Accounts Affected

Two accounts are affected by this transaction: the cost account, Purchases, is debited, and the liability account, Vouchers Payable, is credited. Section 2 of the voucher lists preprinted account titles for accounts most often affected by cash payments. Purchases is preprinted under the heading Accounts Debited. Vouchers Payable is preprinted under the heading Accounts Credited. Therefore, only the amount of the invoice, $3,500.00, must be entered in Section 2. Total Debits and Total Credits are also calculated and entered. If additional account titles are needed, they are entered on the blank lines in Section 2.

Section 3—Voucher Approval

As a double check, many businesses authorize one person, sometimes more, to approve vouchers before they are journalized. Laura Post, accountant, is authorized to approve vouchers for OfficeMart. When Laura verifies that the voucher is correct, she approves it by signing her name in Section 3.

A form is printed on the outside of a voucher to summarize the contents and provide space for approving payments, as shown above. After the invoice is summarized on the voucher, the voucher is folded so that related documents can be placed inside. For this reason a voucher is sometimes known as a voucher jacket.

OfficeMart uses prenumbered voucher forms and must account for all voucher numbers. Therefore, the prenumbered vouchers serve as an additional control within OfficeMart's voucher system.

The outside of OfficeMart's voucher has five sections for recording information: (1) Information about the payee. (2) Information about the accounts affected. (3) Approval of the voucher. (4) Information about where the voucher is recorded. (5) Information about the payment of the voucher.

Tactile Learner. The tactile learner can use a folded piece of paper to represent the voucher. Have students divide the outside panel into five sections and label each section.

VOUCHER REGISTER (LEFT SIDE)

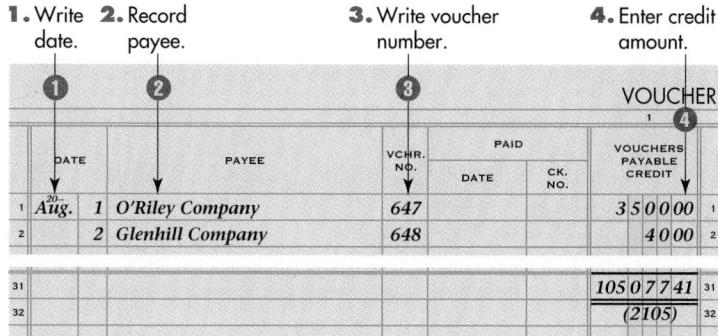

1. Write date. **2.** Record payee. **3.** Write voucher number. **4.** Enter credit amount.

	DATE	PAYEE	VCHR. NO.	PAID DATE	PAID CK. NO.	VOUCHERS PAYABLE CREDIT	
1	Aug. 1	O'Riley Company	647			3 5 0 0 00	1
2	2	Glenhill Company	648			4 0 00	2
31						105 0 7 7 41	31
32						(2105)	32

After it has been approved, a voucher is recorded, as shown above. A journal used to record vouchers is called a **voucher register**. A voucher register is similar to and replaces a purchases journal. Since OfficeMart's vouchers are prenumbered, all vouchers can be accounted for. A missing voucher number shows that a voucher has not been recorded.

Journalizing a Voucher in a Voucher Register's Special Columns

OfficeMart's voucher register has special columns for Vouchers Payable Credit, Purchases Debit, Supplies—Sales Debit, and Supplies—Administrative Debit. For accounts with no special amount columns, information is recorded in the General columns. Voucher 647 is recorded on line 1 of the voucher register.

Section 4 of a Voucher—Where the Voucher Is Recorded

The person who records the voucher in the voucher register also completes Section 4 of the voucher. The person makes a notation indicating the page on which the information is recorded in the voucher register. The person also initials the space provided on the voucher. Placing the voucher register page number on the voucher provides easy reference to the entry's location in the voucher register.

> Recorded in Voucher Register Page _____ 21 _____ by _____ G. R. S. _____

After Voucher No. 647 is journalized and the notation is made in Section 4, the voucher is filed in an unpaid vouchers file. The vouchers are placed in this file according to the payment date. Filing the vouchers by payment date makes it easier to determine which vouchers need to be paid each day. This method helps ensure payment of invoices within the discount period. Thus, Voucher No. 647 is filed under the date on which it is to be paid, August 8.

Payment of a voucher is described later in this chapter.

STEPS • STEPS • STEPS • STEPS • STEPS • STEPS • STEPS • STEPS • STEPS • STEPS • STEPS •

JOURNALIZING A VOUCHER IN THE SPECIAL COLUMNS OF A VOUCHER REGISTER

1 Write the date of the voucher, *Aug. 1, 20--,* in the Date column.

2 Record the name of the payee, *O'Riley Company,* in the Payee column.

3 Write the voucher number, *647,* in the Vchr. No. column.

4 Enter the credit amount, *3,500.00,* in the Vouchers Payable Credit column.

5 Record the debit amount, *3,500.00,* in the appropriate debit column. Since this is a purchase transaction, the debit is made to Purchases.

©GETTY IMAGES/PHOTODISC

Vouchers and Voucher Registers

- Emphasize that an account title is written in the account title column if there is not a special column in the voucher register.

- Remind students that once the entry is made in the voucher register, the voucher page number is recorded on the voucher along with the initials of the person making the entry. Point out that this is a good internal control process.

- Review the procedures for proving, ruling, and posting a voucher register.

DEMONSTRATE

Journalize a voucher

- Use a transparency of a voucher register or the illustration to show recording a voucher that includes an entry in the General columns.

- Record each item in the voucher register following the five steps shown.

- Continue using the transparency to illustrate proving, ruling, and posting from the register.

ONGOING ASSESSMENT

- Assessment is an ongoing process. Circulate through the classroom or lab observing which students have problems with the assignments.

- Troubleshooting: Diagnose what kinds of problems students have with this lesson. Students may have trouble remembering to record amounts owed in the Vouchers Payable account.

- Assess student understanding by checking solutions to Independent Practice assignments.

RETEACH

- Write a transaction involving vouchers on the board. Call on a student to state whether the entry would be recorded in the special columns or the General columns of the voucher register. Repeat this process several times. Students may refer to the illustrations on pages 147–148 for the headings of the special columns.

- Use a transparency of a blank voucher register. Ask students to record the transactions analyzed in the point above.

148

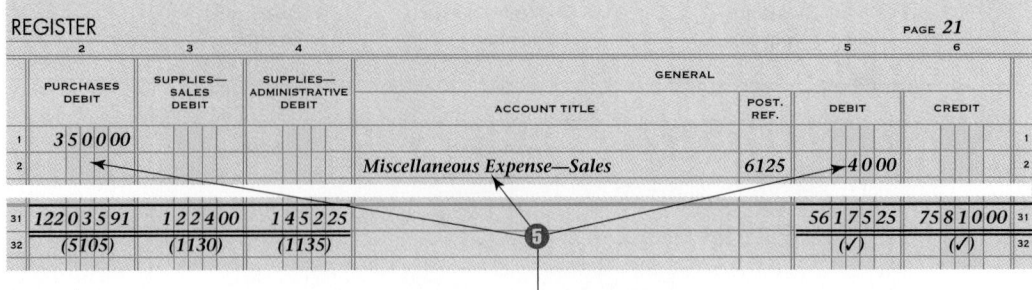

VOUCHER REGISTER (RIGHT SIDE)

5. Record debit amount.

Journalizing a Voucher in the General Columns of a Voucher Register

OfficeMart's voucher register has special debit amount columns for Purchases Debit, Supplies—Sales Debit, and Supplies—Administrative Debit. When an account other than these four is affected, the information is recorded in the General columns.

August 2. Received invoice for sales miscellaneous expense from Glenhill Company, $40.00. Voucher No. 648.

Voucher No. 648 is prepared in the same manner as Voucher No. 647. Voucher No. 648 is recorded on line 2 of the voucher register.

A notation is made on Voucher No. 648 in Section 4 to show where the voucher was recorded and by whom.

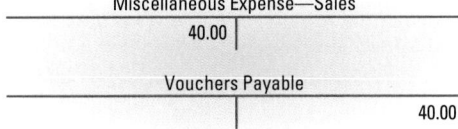

Proving, Ruling, and Posting a Voucher Register

Separate amounts recorded in the General Debit and General Credit columns of a voucher register are posted individually during the month. As each amount is posted, the account number is written in the Post. Ref. column of the voucher register.

At the end of each month, OfficeMart's voucher register is proved and ruled. The procedures for proving and ruling a voucher register are the same as those previously described for special journals.

As previously described for special journals, totals of special amount columns are posted to the general ledger accounts listed in the column headings. Totals of General Debit and General Credit amount columns are not posted.

STEPS • STEPS • STEPS • STEPS • STEPS

JOURNALIZING A VOUCHER IN THE GENERAL COLUMNS OF A VOUCHER REGISTER

1 Write the date of the voucher, *Aug. 2*, in the Date column.

2 Record the name of the payee, *Glenhill Company*, in the Payee column.

3 Enter the voucher number, *648*, in the Vchr. No. column.

4 Record the credit amount, *40.00*, in the Vouchers Payable Credit column.

5 Record the debit amount, *40.00*, in the General Debit column. Write the title of the account to be debited, *Miscellaneous Expense—Sales*, in the General Account Title column.

• terms review

voucher
voucher system
voucher register

• audit your understanding

1. In a voucher system, what general ledger account is used to record all amounts to be paid by check?
2. What is the purpose of using prenumbered voucher forms?
3. A voucher register is similar to and replaces what journal?

• work together 5-1

Preparing a voucher and journalizing vouchers in a voucher register

A voucher and page 10 of a voucher register for Cloverleaf Crafts is provided in the *Working Papers*. Your instructor will guide you through the following examples. The abbreviation for voucher is *V*.

Oct. 1. Purchased merchandise on account from Dickens Company, 11200 Irving Street, Minneapolis, MN 55411, terms 2/10, n/30, $600.00. V152.
  2. Received invoice for October rent from Land Development Co., $1,300.00. V153.
  4. Bought sales supplies on account from University Supplies, $350.00. V154.
  8. Received invoice for delivery service from City Delivery Co., $25.00. V155.

1. Prepare Voucher 152 for the October 1 transaction.
2. Journalize the transactions completed during October of the current year.
3. Prove and rule the voucher register. Save your work to complete Work Together 5-2.

• on your own 5-1

Preparing a voucher and journalizing vouchers in a voucher register

A voucher and page 8 of a voucher register for Trails End are provided in the *Working Papers*. Work independently to complete the following problem. The abbreviation for voucher is *V*.

Aug. 1. Purchased merchandise on account from Darst Corporation, 7020 Niles Lane, Centuria, WI 54824, terms 2/10, n/30, $300.00. V89.
  3. Received invoice for miscellaneous expense from G & G Company, $75.00. V90.
  5. Bought administrative supplies on account from Heartland Supplies, $200.00. V91.
  8. Received invoice for advertising from City News, $225.00. V92.

1. Prepare Voucher 89 for the August 1 transaction.
2. Journalize the transactions completed during August of the current year.
3. Prove and rule the voucher register. Save your work to complete On Your Own 5-2.

GUIDED PRACTICE

Terms Review
Call on students to define each term in the Terms Review. After each definition ask the class if the definition is correct and whether the complete definition has been given or if anything needs to be added. Suggested definitions are given in the Glossary.

Audit Your Understanding
Call on students to answer the Audit Your Understanding questions. Ask the class if the answer is correct and/or complete. Answers are given in Appendix E of the textbook.

Work Together
Have students write the solution to the Work Together problem as you guide the class through the examples.

- Call on students to analyze each transaction.
- Call on students to describe each step in the process for preparing the voucher.
- Direct students to record each transaction in the voucher register as you elicit class participation in recording each voucher.
- Ask a student to describe how to total and rule the voucher register.

INDEPENDENT PRACTICE

On Your Own
- Assign the On Your Own problem to be worked independently.
- Use the Ongoing Assessment techniques to diagnose student understanding.

Application Problem
- Assign Application Problem 5-1: Preparing a voucher and journalizing vouchers in a voucher register.

Personal Trainer
- Students can access the Lesson 5-1 assessment material using this software.

Xtra! Web Site
- Students can access the Xtra! Study Tools for additional practice.

CLOSE
- As a group, have students recall what they remember about a voucher and a voucher register. Ask a student to record the items on the board. Continue until all major concepts about a voucher and voucher register are listed.

ENRICH
- Assign Case 1 of Cases for Critical Thinking.
- Discuss how a company decides what special columns to use in a voucher register or any other special journal.

149

5-2 Voucher Check and Check Registers

PREPARING A VOUCHER CHECK

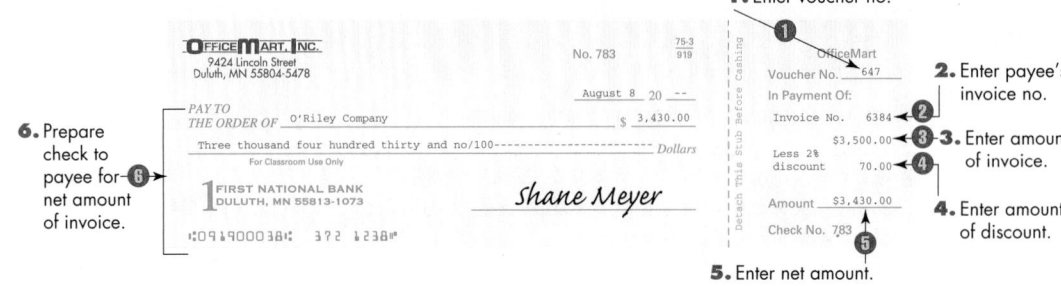

OfficeMart pays each voucher by check as shown above. It prepares a check for the amount of each voucher less any purchases discount. The check and voucher are presented to a person authorized to approve payment. A check with space for writing details about a cash payment is called a **voucher check**. OfficeMart prepares voucher checks in duplicate. The original is given to the payee and OfficeMart keeps the duplicate. The duplicate check is used as the source document for a cash payment transaction. [CONCEPT: Objective Evidence]

On August 8, vouchers to be paid on that day are removed from the unpaid vouchers file. Included in this group is Voucher No. 647. OfficeMart's cash payments clerk prepares the voucher checks.

OfficeMart uses the detachable section at the right of the voucher check to record details about the cash payment. On Check No. 783, the information includes the following items:

1. OfficeMart's voucher number, 647.
2. Payee's invoice number, 6384.
3. Amount of invoice, $3,500.00.
4. Amount of discount, $70.00.
5. Net amount for which check is written, $3,430.00.

Before a payee deposits or cashes a voucher check, the detachable section showing details

of the transaction is removed. It is kept by the payee as a record of the check.

Section 5 of a Voucher—Payment of a Voucher

The person who prepares the check also completes part of Section 5 of the voucher by noting the date paid, the check number, and the amount. The manager, Shane Meyer, verifies that the information on the check and on the voucher agrees and is accurate. After verification, he signs the check and initials Section 5 of the voucher.

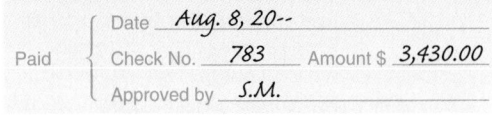

Information about this payment must also be recorded in the voucher register. The person who prepares the check usually makes this notation. The date on which this voucher is paid, Aug. 8, and the check number, 783, are written in the Paid columns of the voucher register. This information is written on the same line as the original entry for Voucher No. 647.

The check is given or sent to the payee, and the voucher is filed in the paid vouchers file according to the name of the vendor.

JOURNALIZING CASH PAYMENTS

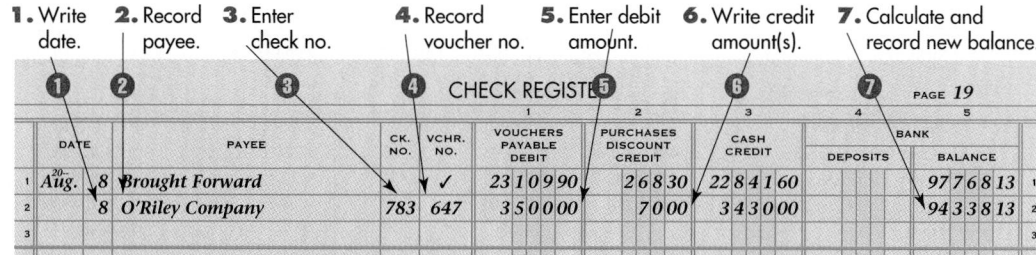

1. Write date.
2. Record payee.
3. Enter check no.
4. Record voucher no.
5. Enter debit amount.
6. Write credit amount(s).
7. Calculate and record new balance.

CHECK REGISTER   PAGE 19

	DATE	PAYEE	CK. NO.	VCHR. NO.	VOUCHERS PAYABLE DEBIT	PURCHASES DISCOUNT CREDIT	CASH CREDIT	BANK DEPOSITS	BANK BALANCE	
1	Aug. 8	Brought Forward		✓	23 1 0 9 90	2 6 8 30	22 8 4 1 60		97 7 6 8 13	1
2	8	O'Riley Company	783	647	3 5 0 0 00	7 0 00	3 4 3 0 00		94 3 3 8 13	2
3										3

A journal used in a voucher system to record cash payments is called a **check register**. The check register is similar to and replaces a cash payments journal.

Maintaining Bank Columns in a Check Register

OfficeMart uses a check register to maintain the checking account balance. OfficeMart's check register has two Bank columns, Deposits and Balance. Using these two Bank columns, Office-Mart keeps an up-to-date record of cash in the checking account. The Bank Deposits column is used to record the amounts deposited in the checking account. The Bank Balance column shows the checking account balance after each check and each deposit are recorded in the check register.

Journalizing Checks in a Check Register

OfficeMart prepares a voucher for each approved cash payment. Therefore, each check is issued in payment of a voucher. Checks are recorded in the check register in the order they are written.

In OfficeMart's voucher system, only three general ledger accounts are affected by a cash payment: Vouchers Payable, Purchases Discount, and Cash. Therefore, OfficeMart's check register has only three special amount columns: Vouchers Payable Debit, Purchases Discount Credit, and Cash Credit. Each check is recorded in a check register as a debit to the liability account, Vouchers Payable, and a credit to the asset account, Cash. If a discount is taken for prompt payment, the discount amount is recorded as a credit to the contra cost account, Purchases Discount.

August 8. Paid cash to O'Riley Company, $3,430.00, covering Voucher No. 647 for $3,500.00, less 2% discount, $70.00. Check No. 783.

The liability account, Vouchers Payable, is debited for $3,500.00. The contra cost account, Purchases Discount, is credited for $70.00. Cash is credited for the net amount paid, $3,430.00.

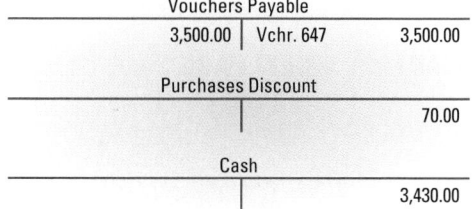

Vouchers Payable		
3,500.00	Vchr. 647	3,500.00

Purchases Discount	
	70.00

Cash	
	3,430.00

STEPS • STEPS • STEPS • STEPS • STEPS • STEPS • STEPS • STEPS • STEPS • STEPS •

JOURNALIZING CHECKS IN A CHECK REGISTER

1. Write the date of the payment, *8,* in the Date column.
2. Record the name of the payee, *O'Riley Company,* in the Payee column.
3. Enter the check number, *783,* in the Ck. No. column.
4. Record the number of the voucher being paid, *647,* in the Vchr. No. column.
5. Enter the debit amount, *3,500.00,* in the Vouchers Payable Debit column.
6. Write the credit amounts, *70.00* and *3,430.00,* in the Cash and the Purchases Discount Credit columns.
7. Calculate and record the new cash balance, *94,338.13,* in the Bank Balance column.

EXPLAIN

- Introduce the check register and explain the use of the bank columns.
- Emphasize that the register replaces the cash payments journal.
- Describe how checks are recorded in the check register and how the new bank balance is calculated.
- Point out that if a purchases discount is taken, the cash payment will be less than the amount of the voucher. Therefore, Purchases Discount and Cash will both be credited. Vouchers Payable will be debited for the total amount of the voucher.

DEMONSTRATE

Analyze the transaction

- Draw three blank T accounts on the board.
- Read the transaction statement.
- Ask students to analyze the transaction by answering: what accounts are affected, are they increased or decreased, and are they debited or credited. Complete the T accounts as the information is given.

Record the transaction

- Use a transparency of a check register or the illustration to show recording the transaction.
- Record each item in the register following the seven steps shown.
- Ask a student to verify that, for this transaction, debits equal credits.

APPLIED SKILLS   WRITING ACROSS THE CURRICULUM

Writing paragraphs and short essays. The Cases for Critical Thinking are short, practical applications of the accounting principles developed in the chapter. Some cases are planned to present problems related to the chapter but not specifically discussed and answered in the chapter. These cases present an opportunity for critical thinking and decision making. These cases also require more than a short objective-type response. Therefore they provide ideal practice in writing paragraphs and short essays.

- Review proving, ruling, and posting a check register. Point out that the special columns of the check register are posted in a similar manner as other special columns in special journals.

- Stress that the two Bank columns are neither ruled or posted.

DEMONSTRATE

Completing a check register
Use a transparency of a check register or the illustration to show how to prove, rule, and post a check register.

EXPLAIN

- Point out that a new page in the check register is prepared in a similar manner as a new page in other special journals.

ONGOING ASSESSMENT

- Assessment is an ongoing process. Circulate through the classroom or lab observing which students have problems with the assignments.

- Troubleshooting: Students may have trouble remembering to record the payment of vouchers in a check register.

- Assess student understanding by checking solutions to Independent Practice assignments.

RETEACH

- Provide several completed voucher checks to groups of three students (or list transactions on the board). Have each group analyze the transaction. Ask a representative of the group to record the transaction on a transparency of a check register while another member of the group describes the transaction.

- Ask the class if the transaction has been correctly analyzed and recorded.

- Give students groups of T accounts with transactions already recorded. For each set, ask students to determine the transaction by analyzing the way it was recorded in the T accounts.

PROVING, RULING, AND POSTING A CHECK REGISTER

	DATE		PAYEE	CK. NO.	VCHR. NO.	VOUCHERS PAYABLE DEBIT (1)	PURCHASES DISCOUNT CREDIT (2)	CASH CREDIT (3)	BANK DEPOSITS (4)	BANK BALANCE (5)	
1	Aug.	8	Brought Forward		✓	23 1 0 9 90	2 6 8 30	22 8 4 1 60		97 7 6 8 13	1
2		8	O'Riley Company	783	647	3 5 0 0 00	7 0 00	3 4 3 0 00		94 3 3 8 13	2
3		11	Jacobs Equipment	784	649	9 7 3 91	1 9 48	9 5 4 43		93 3 8 3 70	3
4		14	Petty Cash Cust., OfficeMart	785	656	2 1 2 50		2 1 2 50		93 1 7 1 20	4
5		14	Deposit		✓				18 7 6 7 15	111 9 3 8 35	5
22		31	Payroll	800	694	4 3 3 1 96		4 3 3 1 96		95 3 7 3 21	22
23		31	Deposit		✓				19 2 9 4 78	114 6 6 7 99	23
24		31	Totals			103 4 5 2 22	5 6 6 88	102 8 8 5 34			24
25						(2105)	(5110)	(1105)			25

At the end of each month, the special amount columns of the check register are proved, ruled, and posted.

OfficeMart's procedures for posting from its check register are the same as those previously described for special journals. However, no separate amounts are posted individually because the check register does not have a General Debit or General Credit column. The three special amount column totals are posted to the general ledger accounts listed in the column headings. After each total is posted, the account number is written in parentheses below the column total.

The two Bank columns are used to summarize the status of the checking account balance. These two columns are neither ruled nor posted.

A deposit in the checking account is shown on line 5 above. The Deposits column does not need to be totaled and posted because each cash receipt is recorded in the cash receipts journal and posted from that journal. At the end of each month, cash is proved by comparing the last amount in the Balance column of the check register with the balance in the general ledger cash account. Cash is proved if the two amounts are the same.

STARTING A NEW PAGE OF A CHECK REGISTER

	DATE		PAYEE	CK. NO.	VCHR. NO.	VOUCHERS PAYABLE DEBIT (1)	PURCHASES DISCOUNT CREDIT (2)	CASH CREDIT (3)	BANK DEPOSITS (4)	BANK BALANCE (5)	
1	Sept.	1	Brought Forward		✓					114 6 6 7 99	1
2											2

A new page of a check register may be needed either during a month or at the start of a new month. When a new page is started during a month, the totals of the Vouchers Payable Debit, Purchases Discount Credit, and Cash Credit columns are brought forward from the previous page. The balance of the Bank Balance column is also brought forward. No amount is brought forward for the Bank Deposits column.

OfficeMart begins a new page of the check register at the beginning of each month. Only the balance of the Bank Balance column is brought forward. The totals of the special amount columns are not brought forward because they were posted at the end of the previous month.

A Voucher System

• terms review

voucher check
check register

• audit your understanding

1. A check register is similar to and replaces what journal?

2. In what order are paid vouchers filed?

3. What account is debited for each check recorded in a check register?

• work together 5-2

Journalizing cash payments and deposits in a check register

Use the working papers from Work Together 5-1. Page 10 of a check register for Cloverleaf Crafts is provided in the *Working Papers*. Your instructor will guide you through the following examples. Source documents are abbreviated as follows: check, C; voucher, V.

Oct.   8.   Paid cash to Dickens Company, $588.00, covering V152 for $600.00, less 2% discount, $12.00. C309.
          9.   Paid cash to University Supplies, $350.00, covering V154. C310.
      11.   Paid cash to Land Development Co., $1,300.00, covering V153. C311.
      16.   Made a deposit in the checking account, $3,775.09.

1. Record the bank balance brought forward on October 1 of the current year, $18,765.55.

2. Journalize the transactions completed during October of the current year. As each cash payment is journalized, make the appropriate notation in the voucher register.

3. Prove and rule the check register.

Terms Review

Call on a student to define the terms in the Terms Review. Ask the class if the definitions are correct and whether the complete definitions have been given or if anything needs to be added. Suggested definitions are given in the Glossary.

Audit Your Understanding

Call on students to answer the Audit Your Understanding questions. Ask the class if the answer is correct and/or complete. Answers are given in Appendix E of the textbook.

Work Together

Have students write the solution to the Work Together problem as you guide the class through the examples.

• Call on students to analyze each transaction.

• Direct students to record each transaction in the check register as you elicit class participation in recording each entry.

• Ask a student to describe how to total and rule the check register.

INDEPENDENT PRACTICE

On Your Own

- Assign the On Your Own problem to be worked independently.
- Use the Ongoing Assessment techniques to diagnose student understanding.

Application Problem

- Assign Application Problem 5-2: Journalizing cash payments and deposits in a check register.

Personal Trainer

- Students can access the Lesson 5-2 assessment material using this software.

Xtra! Web Site

- Students can access the Xtra! Study Tools for additional practice.

ENRICH

- Assign Case 2 of Cases for Critical Thinking. Discuss the voucher system followed by Cayman Company.

CLOSE

- Gather examples of vouchers, voucher registers, and check registers from your school and/or local businesses. Create a bulletin board collage of these forms to illustrate that a voucher system is designed according to the needs of each business.

• on your own 5-2

Journalizing cash payments and deposits in a check register

Use the working papers from On Your Own 5-1. Page 8 of a check register for Trails End is provided in the *Working Papers*. Work this problem independently. Source documents are abbreviated as follows: check, C; voucher, V.

Aug. 8. Paid cash to Darst Corp., $294.00, covering V89 for $300.00, less 2% discount, $6.00. C222.
      9. Paid cash to Heartland Supplies, $200.00, covering V91. C223.
     11. Paid cash to C & G Company, $75.00, covering V90. C224.
     15. Made a deposit in the checking account, $1,388.12.

1. Record the bank balance brought forward on August 1 of the current year, $5,422.67.

2. Journalize the transactions completed during August of the current year. As each cash payment is journalized, make the appropriate notation in the voucher register.

3. Prove and rule the check register.

©GETTY IMAGES/PHOTODISC

5-3 Selected Transactions in a Voucher System

PURCHASES RETURNS AND ALLOWANCES

Vchr. No. 655

Date 8/12/--   Due Date 8/16/--   Payment Date 8/14/--

To Ramsey, Inc.

Address 1237 Cardinal Road
         Street
Springbrook,   WI   54824-3291
  City   State   ZIP

— Section 1

ACCOUNTS DEBITED	AMOUNT
PURCHASES	
SUPPLIES—SALES	
SUPPLIES—ADMIN.	
MISCELLANEOUS EXPENSE—SALES	
MISCELLANEOUS EXPENSE—ADMIN.	
RENT EXPENSE	
SALARY EXPENSE—SALES	
SALARY EXPENSE—ADMIN.	
Vouchers Payable	180 00
TOTAL DEBITS	180 00

ACCOUNTS CREDITED	AMOUNT
VOUCHERS PAYABLE	95 00
EMPLOYEE INC. TAX PAY.—FEDERAL	
EMPLOYEE INC. TAX PAY.—STATE	
FICA TAX PAYABLE	
Purchases Returns and Allowances	85 00
TOTAL CREDITS	180 00

— Section 2

Voucher Approved by *Laura Post*

— Section 3

Recorded in Voucher
Register Page _____ by _____

— Section 4

Paid { Date
Check No. _____ Amount $ _____
Approved by _____

— Section 5

STEPS • STEPS • STEPS • STEPS
CHANGING THE ORIGINAL AMOUNT OF A VOUCHER BECAUSE OF A PURCHASE RETURN

1 Remove the original voucher, No. 652, from the unpaid vouchers file. Write *Canceled* across Section 5.

2 Prepare a new voucher, No. 655. Place the canceled voucher and the debit memorandum inside.

3 In the voucher register, on the same line as the original voucher, write *See Vchr. 655* in the Paid columns. The number indicates the new voucher number.

4 Record the new voucher on the next available line of the voucher register. Enter the new credit amount, *95.00*, in the Vouchers Payable Credit column. Write the title of the account debited, *Vouchers Payable*, in the General Account Title column. Write the amount of the canceled voucher, *180.00*, in the General Debit column. On the next line of the register, write the other account title, *Purchases Returns and Allowances*, in the General Account Title column. Enter the amount of the return, *85.00*, in the General Credit column.

5 File the new voucher by its payment date in the unpaid vouchers file. The payment date is based on the terms of the original invoice. Therefore, the new voucher has the same payment date as the original voucher.

Selected Transactions in a Voucher System

Using a voucher system requires that some transactions follow different procedures. Two examples are purchases returns and allowances and payroll transactions.

A purchases returns and allowances transaction reduces the total amount owed for an invoice. Therefore, the voucher record for that invoice must be changed to show the reduction in the amount owed.

> **August 12. Issued Debit Memorandum No. 98 to Ramsey, Inc. for return of merchandise purchased, $85.00. Cancel Voucher No. 652. Voucher No. 655.**

Voucher No. 655 is prepared for this transaction and is the source document for the entry. [*CONCEPT: Objective Evidence*]

The liability account, Vouchers Payable, is debited for $180.00 to cancel Voucher No. 652. Vouchers Payable is credited for $95.00, the difference between Voucher No. 652 ($180.00) and Debit Memorandum No. 98 ($85.00). The contra cost account, Purchases Returns and Allowances, is credited for $85.00, the amount of merchandise returned.

OfficeMart follows five steps in changing the original amount owed for Voucher No. 652 because of the purchases return. The entry recording this voucher is on lines 6 and 9 of the voucher register on the next page.

Lesson 5-3   **155**

OBJECTIVES
- Identify accounting concepts and practices related to a voucher system.
- Journalize purchases returns and allowances and payroll transactions in a voucher system.

MOTIVATE
Ask students to recall how purchases returns and allowances were recorded by a business that does not use a voucher system. Have students try to determine how purchases returns and allowances will be recorded by a business that does use a voucher system.

Preview
- Direct students to read the headings at the top of each page in this lesson and to examine the illustrations given.
- The procedures for preparing, recording, and paying vouchers were presented earlier in this chapter. Explain that some transactions, such as purchases returns and allowances and payroll, require different procedures. In this lesson, the steps used to record these two transactions using a voucher system will be described.

EXPLAIN
- Review the purchases returns and allowances transaction.
- Use the illustration to explain how the purchases returns and allowances transaction appears on the voucher.
- Explain each step in canceling a voucher using the five steps listed.
- Point out that canceled vouchers are placed inside the new voucher.
- Describe recording the new voucher in a voucher register and canceling the original voucher for purchases returns and allowances transactions. Emphasize that the due date for canceled vouchers remains the same for the new voucher.
- Refer students to lines 6 and 9 of the illustration on page 156 as canceling and recording a new voucher for a purchases returns and allowances transaction are explained.

DEMONSTRATE

Analyze the transaction
- Draw two blank T accounts on the board.
- Read the transaction statement.
- Ask students to analyze the transaction by answering what accounts are affected, are they increased or decreased, and are they debited or credited. Complete the T accounts as the information is provided.

Record the transaction
- Use a transparency of the voucher register to illustrate recording the transaction.
- Ask a student to verify that, for this transaction, debits equal credits.

MATERIALS
- Instructor's Resource CD: PowerPoint Slides
- Xtra! Study Tools on the Xtra! Web Site
- Blackline Masters: Voucher Register
- Working Papers: Teacher's Edition of the Working Papers for Lesson 5-3
- Software: Personal Trainer Student Companion CD

- Explain how a voucher is prepared for a payroll transaction and journalized in a voucher register.
- Describe how payment of the payroll is journalized in the check register and a notation is made in the voucher register.
- Engage students in a conversation about the advantages of a voucher system.
- Refer students to the voucher at the bottom of this page and the voucher register at the top of the page as the payroll transaction is discussed.

Analyze the transaction
- Draw seven blank T accounts on the board.
- Read the transaction statement.
- Ask students to analyze the transaction by answering what accounts are affected, are they increased or decreased, and are they debited or credited. Complete the T accounts as the information is provided.

Record the transaction
- Use a transparency of the voucher register or the illustration at the top of the page to show recording the transaction.
- Ask a student to verify that, for this transaction, debits equal credits.

RECORDING PAYROLL IN A VOUCHER REGISTER (LEFT SIDE)

VOUCHER

	DATE		PAYEE	VCHR. NO.	PAID DATE	CK. NO.	VOUCHERS PAYABLE CREDIT	
1	Aug. 20--	1	O'Riley Company	647	Aug. 8	783	3 5 0 0 00	1
2		2	Glenhill Company	648			4 0 00	2
3		4	Jacobs Equipment	649	Aug. 11	784	9 7 3 91	3
4		5	Salem Wholesale Instruments	650			4 5 1 00	4
5		7	Bob's Delivery Service	651	Aug. 17	786	6 3 00	5
6		7	Ramsey, Inc.	652	See Vchr. 655		1 8 0 00	6
7		10	Superior Office Supplies	653			8 7 00	7
8		12	Kuker Company	654	Aug. 19	788	2 7 6 00	8
9		12	Ramsey, Inc.	655			9 5 00	9
10								10
11		14	Petty Cash Custodian, OfficeMart	656	Aug. 14	785	2 1 2 50	11
12								12
26		31	Payroll	694	Aug. 31	800	4 3 3 1 96	26

OfficeMart pays its employees semimonthly. A payroll register showing details for each payroll is prepared. The payroll register is prepared in a way similar to the description in Chapter 3. Information from a payroll register is used in preparing a voucher for payroll.

> *August 31. Recorded voucher for semimonthly payroll for period ended August 31, $4,331.96 (total payroll: sales, $3,000.00; administrative, $2,854.00; less deductions: employee income tax payable—federal, $878.10; employee income tax payable—state, $175.62; social security tax payable, $380.51; Medicare tax payable, $87.81). Voucher No. 694.*

A PAYROLL VOUCHER

VOUCHER

Vchr. No. **694**

Payment Date ___August 31___ 20 __--__

Date ___August 31___ 20 __--__ Terms _____ Due ___August 31___ 20 __--__

To ___Payroll___

Address _____

City _____ State _____ ZIP _____

For the following: Enclose all invoices or other papers.

DATE	VOUCHER DETAILS	AMOUNT
Aug. 31	Payroll for period ended 8/31/--	
	Salary Expense--Sales	$3,000.00
	Salary Expense--Administrative	2,854.00
	Deductions:	
	Employee Inc. Tax Pay.--Federal	$878.10
	Employee Inc. Tax Pay.--State	175.62
	Social Security Tax Payable	380.51
	Medicare Tax Payable	87.81
		1,522.04
	Net cash payment	$4,331.96

OFFICEMART, INC.

A payroll register is needed for several purposes, as described in Chapter 3. Therefore, the payroll register cannot be placed inside a voucher for payroll. For this reason, information from the payroll register is summarized on the inside of Voucher No. 694 as shown here.

The inside of the voucher allows additional space so that more detailed information about the transaction can be noted.

The outside of a payroll voucher is completed in a manner similar to the completion of other vouchers.

REGISTER

PAGE 21

	PURCHASES DEBIT	SUPPLIES— SALES DEBIT	SUPPLIES— ADMINISTRATIVE DEBIT	GENERAL				
	2	3	4	ACCOUNT TITLE	POST. REF.	DEBIT (5)	CREDIT (6)	
1	3 5 0 0 00							1
2				Miscellaneous Expense—Sales	6125	4 0 00		2
3	9 7 3 91							3
4	4 5 1 00							4
5		6 3 00						5
6	1 8 0 00							6
7			8 7 00					7
8	2 7 6 00							8
9				Vouchers Payable	2105	1 8 0 00		9
10				Purchases Returns and Allowances	5115		8 5 00	10
11		4 0 00	5 5 25	Advertising Expense	6105	4 7 00		11
12				Miscellaneous Expense—Administrative	6215	7 0 25		12
26				Salary Expense—Sales	6130	3 0 0 0 00		26
27				Salary Expense—Administrative	6230	2 8 5 4 00		27
28				Employee Income Tax Payable—Federal	2110		8 7 8 10	28
29				Employee Income Tax Payable—State	2115		1 7 5 62	29
30				Social Security Tax Payable	2125		3 8 0 51	30
31				Medicare Tax Payable	2128		8 7 81	31

The voucher register entry to record Voucher No. 694 is shown on lines 26 to 31. An entry is made in OfficeMart's general journal for the employer's payroll taxes. This entry is the same as the one described in Chapter 3. Later, when payroll taxes are due, vouchers are prepared, approved, and paid. One voucher is prepared for total payroll taxes owed to the federal government. Another voucher is prepared for total payroll taxes owed to the state government.

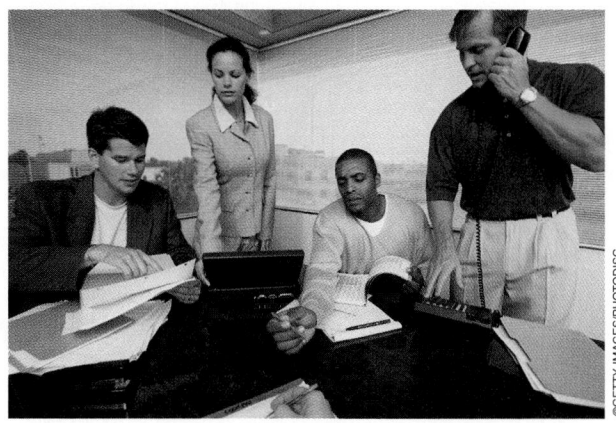

©GETTY IMAGES/PHOTODISC

- Discuss each advantage of the voucher system.
- Discuss how the voucher system helps a company with internal control of cash *(advantages 1 and 3).*

ONGOING ASSESSMENT

- Assessment is an ongoing process. Circulate through the classroom or lab observing which students have problems with the assignments.
- Troubleshooting: Students sometimes do not remember to cancel the original voucher when issuing a new voucher because of a purchase return.
- Assess student understanding by checking solutions to Independent Practice assignments.

RETEACH

- Prepare a voucher register transparency showing three purchases transactions.
- Ask a student to make up an original purchases returns and allowances transaction statement that you write on the board.
- Ask another student to analyze the transaction using T accounts.
- Ask a third student to record the cancellation of the old voucher and enter the transaction for the new voucher.

ADVANTAGES OF A VOUCHER SYSTEM

A voucher system has the following advantages for businesses that make many cash payments.

1. Only a few people can authorize and approve all cash payments. This procedure helps protect and control cash.
2. A voucher jacket provides a convenient way to file invoices and related business papers for future reference. This is especially true when invoices received from vendors are of different sizes.
3. Unpaid vouchers are filed by their payment dates to help ensure payment of invoices within the discount periods.
4. An unpaid vouchers file and a paid vouchers file eliminate posting to an accounts payable ledger.
5. A paid vouchers file provides three different and easy ways to find information about a paid voucher:
   a. *If only the voucher number is known,* look in the voucher register for that number and find the payee's name on the same line. The voucher will be in the paid vouchers file under the name of the payee.
   b. *If only the check number used to pay the voucher is known,* look in the check register for the check number. The payee's name is on the same line. The voucher will be in the paid vouchers file under the name of the payee.
   c. *If only the name of the payee is known,* look in the paid vouchers file where vouchers are filed under the name of the payee.

©GETTY IMAGES/PHOTODISC

A Voucher System

• audit your understanding

1. What accounts are affected, and how, when a debit memorandum is issued for the return of merchandise purchased and the original voucher is canceled?
2. What is the first step in canceling a voucher?
3. Where is the information obtained for preparing a voucher for payroll?

• work together 5-3

Journalizing purchases returns and allowances and payroll in a voucher register

A voucher register for Gille Company is provided in the *Working Papers*. Source documents are abbreviated as follows: debit memorandum, DM; voucher, V. Your instructor will guide you through the following examples.

May 1. Purchased merchandise on account from Casey Corporation, $1,500.00. V75.
4. Issued DM4 to Casey Corporation for return of merchandise purchased, $300.00. Cancel V75. V76.
15. Recorded voucher for semimonthly payroll for period ended May 15, $3,308.18 (total payroll: sales, $2,780.52; administrative, $1,690.00, less deductions: employee income tax payable—federal, $670.58; employee income tax payable—state, $134.12; social security tax payable, $290.58; Medicare tax payable, $67.06). V77.

1. Journalize the transactions completed during May of the current year. Use page 5 of a voucher register. When a voucher is canceled, make appropriate notations in the voucher register.

• on your own 5-3

Journalizing purchases returns and allowances and payroll in a voucher register

A voucher register for Geist Company is provided in the *Working Papers*. Source documents are abbreviated as follows: debit memorandum, DM; voucher, V. Work independently to complete the following problem.

June 1. Purchased merchandise on account from Prickett Corporation, $900.00. V110.
4. Issued DM56 to Prickett Corporation for return of merchandise purchased, $300.00. Cancel V110. V111.
15. Recorded voucher for semimonthly payroll for period ended June 15, $4,778.63 (total payroll: sales, $3,957.61; administrative, $2,500.00, less deductions: employee income tax payable—federal, $968.64; employee income tax payable—state, $193.73; social security tax payable, $419.75; Medicare tax payable, $96.86). V112.

1. Journalize the transactions completed during June of the current year. Use page 6 of a voucher register. When a voucher is canceled, make appropriate notations in the voucher register.

Selected Transactions in a Voucher System

Lesson 5-3 **159**

GUIDED PRACTICE

Audit Your Understanding
Call on students to answer the Audit Your Understanding questions. Ask the class if the answer is correct and/or complete. Answers are given in Appendix E of the textbook.

Work Together
Have students write the solution to the Work Together problem as you guide the class through the examples.
- Call on students to analyze each transaction.
- Direct students to record each transaction in the voucher register as you elicit class participation in recording each entry.

INDEPENDENT PRACTICE

On Your Own
- Assign the On Your Own problem to be worked independently.
- Use the Ongoing Assessment techniques to diagnose student understanding.

Application Problem
- Assign Application Problem 5-3: Journalizing purchases returns and allowances in a voucher register.
- Assign Application Problem 5-4: Preparing and journalizing a voucher for payroll.

Personal Trainer
- Students can access the Lesson 5-3 assessment material using this software.

Xtra! Web Site
- Students can access the Xtra! Study Tools for additional practice.

ENRICH

- Divide students into groups of three. Assign each group to contact two businesses in the community to inquire if the businesses use a voucher system. If possible, ask each business if they would supply a copy of a voucher and/or voucher register which they use. Have each group write a short report about their findings.

CLOSE

- Have each student write a summary of what they remember about preparing and recording: (1) a voucher to replace another when taking a purchases discount and (2) a payroll voucher.

159

PUTTING IT ALL TOGETHER

Use an overhead projector to display transparencies of a purchases journal and a cash payments journal. Record the following transactions in the journals: (a) purchase on account, (b) miscellaneous expense, (c) cash payment on account, (d) purchases returns and allowances, and (e) payroll. Show how these entries will be recorded in these journals. Then use transparencies for a voucher register and a check register. Demonstrate how the same transactions will be recorded in these registers. Help students recognize the similarities and differences between recording these transactions in previously studied journals and in the registers described in this chapter.

INDEPENDENT PRACTICE

- Assign Mastery Problem 5-5 to students who need the reinforcement of a problem that combines all activities from the chapter in one problem; this will be most students.
- Assign Challenge Problem 5-6 to accelerated students who do not require the reinforcement of the Mastery Problem.
- Assign Study Guide 5.
- Students can access Personal Trainer to work end-of-chapter problems on the computer.
- Students can access the Xtra! Web Site for the Xtra! Review and Quizzing.
- Students can access the Student Companion CD for additional review material.

ONGOING ASSESSMENT

Review solutions to the assigned problems in class, diagnosing trouble spots.

RETEACH

- Call on students to describe how they avoid the trouble spots diagnosed.
- Use reteaching suggestions from section lesson plans as required.
- Assign Recycling Problem 5-1 if needed.

ENRICH

- Assign the Explore Accounting feature. Write students' answers on the board or overhead.
- Students can access the Xtra! Web Site for the Xtra! Enrichment material.
- Assign the Applied Communication activity.

- Assign the SCANS Workplace Competency.
- Assign the Auditing for Errors activity.
- Assign the Analyzing Costco's Financial Statements activity.
- Assign the Automated Accounting feature on page 167.

160

After completing this chapter, you can

1. Define accounting terms related to a voucher system.
2. Identify accounting concepts and practices related to a voucher system.
3. Prepare a voucher.
4. Journalize data from vouchers in a voucher register.
5. Journalize voucher payment transactions in a check register.
6. Journalize purchases returns and allowances and payroll transactions in a voucher system.

Explore Accounting

EXPLORE ACCOUNTING · EXPLORE ACCOUNTING · EXPLORE AC

Internal Control Systems

A company should establish policies and procedures to protect the assets of the company and to insure the reliability of the company's accounting records. Such a set of policies and procedures is known as an internal control system. The American Institute of Certified Public Accountants defines an internal control structure as "the policies and procedures established to provide reasonable assurance that specific entity objectives will be achieved." A reliable internal control structure requires that *all* employees follow the policies and procedures established.

An accurate accounting system is an important part of a reliable internal control structure. Accounting controls must support internal controls. This chapter introduced one such accounting control, the voucher system.

A widely used internal control is "separation of duties." This means that no one employee is given authority to totally control an asset. For example, in this chapter's discussion, one employee prepared the voucher, another employee approved the voucher, and a third employee approved the check payment. Without this control mechanism, an employee has a better chance of stealing from the employer.

Required:

In-Class Assignment: In groups of 3 or 4, determine why internal controls are important. Who are they designed to protect?

Research Assignment: Contact at least one business in your community. Ask what internal controls have been established to protect the company's assets. Summarize and present your findings to your class.

EXPLORE ACCOUNTING
EXPLORE ACCOUNTING

Internal controls are important to ensure the accuracy of the accounting records and, therefore, the reliability of the financial statements. If the basic records of the company cannot be trusted, either because of intentional or unintentional errors, the financial statements are not reliable.

Internal controls are designed to protect the owners (stockholders) of the corporation. If assets are stolen, the owners are the ones to suffer the loss.

The auditor is concerned about the system of controls established by a company, because the auditor must be able to either check every transaction of the business (which is impossible) or rely to some degree on the accuracy of the records. A good internal control system ensures more accurate records.

5-1 APPLICATION PROBLEM

Quizzing
accountingxtra.swlearning.com

Preparing a voucher and journalizing vouchers in a voucher register

TeleTronics uses a voucher register similar to the one described in this chapter.

Transactions:

Sept. 1. Purchased merchandise on account from Eastern Company, 9424 Denison Pkwy., Corning, NY, 14830, terms: 2/10, n/30, $3,100.00. V87.
   2. Post Real Estate Developers sent an invoice for $1,150.00 for September's rent. V88.
   5. Bought sales supplies on account from Supra Supply Company, $258.00. V89.
   8. Received invoice for advertising from Newport News, $87.50. V90.
   11. Purchased merchandise on account from Hoyer Company, $3,347.75. V91.
   18. Received invoice for delivery service from Rapid Rabbit, $235.15. V92.
   19. Purchased $1,973.00 of merchandise on account from Beggen Company. V93.
   23. Bought office equipment on account from Syracuse Company, $1,315.00. V94.
   25. Received invoice for utilities from Northside Electric Cooperative, $185.00. V95.
   29. Bought administrative supplies on account from Northern Supply, $317.00. V96.
   30. Manley Maintenance Company sent an invoice for $25.00. The amount was for a miscellaneous sales expense. V97.

Instructions:

1. Prepare Voucher 87 for the September 1 transaction.
2. Journalize the transactions completed during September of the current year. Use page 9 of a voucher register. The abbreviation for voucher is V.
3. Prove and rule the voucher register.

The voucher register prepared in Problem 5.1 is needed to complete Problem 5.2.

5-2 APPLICATION PROBLEM

Journalizing cash payments and deposits in a check register

TeleTronics uses a check register similar to the one described in this chapter.

Transactions:

Sept. 2. Paid cash to Post Real Estate Developers, $1,150.00, covering V88. C83.
   8. Paid cash to Newport News, $87.50, covering V90. C84.
   9. Paid cash to Eastern Company, $3,038.00, covering V87 for $3,100.00, less 2% discount, $62.00. C85.
   13. Paid cash to Supra Supply Company, $258.00, covering V89. C86.
   18. Paid cash to Rapid Rabbit, $235.15, covering V92. C87.
   19. Paid cash to Hoyer Company, $3,280.79, covering V91 for $3,347.75, less 2% discount, $66.96. C88.
   24. Made a deposit in the checking account, $5,684.54.
   25. Paid cash to Northside Electric Cooperative, $185.00, covering V95. C89.
   30. Paid cash to Manley Maintenance Company, $25.00, covering V97. C90.

Instructions:

1. Use page 9 of a check register. Record the bank balance brought forward on September 1 of the current year, $19,443.13.
2. Continue using page 9 of the check register. Journalize the cash payments and deposits completed during September of the current year. As each cash payment is journalized, make the appropriate notation in the voucher register. Source documents are abbreviated as follows: check, C; voucher, V.
3. Prove and rule the check register.

FORMAL EVALUATION

Chapter 5 Test
Exam View for Chapter 5
Assessment by Portfolio

- Review answers to all tests administered as a class activity. If time is limited, review only the items that were frequently answered incorrectly.

- Ask students if there are any questions about the chapter before proceeding to the next chapter.

CHECK FIGURES

Application Problem 5-1
Total Vouchers Payable Credit column: 11,993.40

Application Problem 5-2
Check Register totals: Vouchers Payable Debit, 8,388.40
Purchases Discount Credit, 128.96
Cash Credit, 8,259.44
September 30 Bank Balance, 16,868.23

See Teacher's Edition of the Working Papers for Chapter 5 for complete solutions.

Application Problem 5-3
Amounts in Vouchers Payable Credit column: 2,700.00, 2,500.00, 1,778.00, 1,428.00

Application Problem 5-4
Accounts credited in the voucher:
Vouchers Payable, 3,120.97
Employee Inc. Tax Pay. Federal, 632.63
Employee Inc. Tax. Pay. State, 126.53
Social Security Tax Pay, 274.14
Medicare Tax Pay, 63.26

5-3 APPLICATION PROBLEM

Journalizing purchases returns and allowances in a voucher register

Nygren Supply Company uses a voucher register similar to the one described in this chapter.

Transactions:

Feb. 1. Purchased merchandise on account from Hamline Corporation, $2,700.00. V10.
      4. Issued DM2 to Hamline Corporation for return of merchandise purchased, $200.00. Cancel V10. V11.
     15. Purchased merchandise on account from Moorhead, Inc., $1,778.00. V12.
     17. Issued DM3 to Moorhead, Inc., for return of merchandise purchased, $350.00. Cancel V12. V13.

Instructions:

Journalize the transactions completed during February of the current year. Use page 2 of a voucher register. When a voucher is canceled, make appropriate notations in the voucher register. Source documents are abbreviated as follows: debit memorandum, DM; voucher, V.

5-4 APPLICATION PROBLEM

Preparing and journalizing a voucher for payroll

Bowman Service Center uses a voucher form and a voucher register similar to the ones described in this chapter. Bowman Service Center's payroll register for May 15 of the current year shows the following information. The abbreviation for voucher is V.

Transactions:

May 15. Recorded voucher for semimonthly payroll for period ended May 15, $3,120.97 (total payroll: sales, $2,530.53; administrative, $1,687.00, less deductions: employee income tax payable—federal, $632.63; employee income tax payable—state, $126.53; social security tax payable, $274.14; Medicare tax payable, $63.26). V51.

Instructions:

1. Prepare a voucher for the payroll on May 15 of the current year.
2. Use page 5 of a voucher register. Journalize the voucher for the payroll. Assume that the voucher has been approved. After the voucher is journalized, complete Section 4 of the voucher.

TEACHING STRATEGIES   COOPERATIVE LEARNING

Divide the class into groups of four or five students each. Using Cases for Critical Thinking, each group analyzes the cases and arrives at agreed-upon solutions. One member of each group is appointed the recorder and presents the group's analysis to the class. This cooperative learning activity should not take more than 20 to 25 minutes of class time.

5-5 MASTERY PROBLEM

Journalizing transactions in a voucher system

Mastery Problem 5-5
Voucher Register Vouchers Payable total,
12,447.34
Check Register Vouchers Payable total,
4,145.69
November 30 Bank Balance, 12,329.13

Jameson Company uses a voucher register and a check register similar to the ones described in this chapter.

Transactions:

Nov.
1. Purchased merchandise on account from Georgia Company, $975.00. V68.
2. Bought $216.80 of administrative supplies on account from Supply World. V69.
4. Bought store equipment on account from Equipment Plus, $1,998.00. V70.
8. Purchased merchandise on account from North Heights Corporation, $1,695.15. V71.
8. Paid $955.50 to Georgia Company covering V68 for $975.00, less 2% discount, $19.50. C57.
10. Made a deposit in the checking account, $3,579.00.
14. Received invoice for delivery service from Quick Delivery, $24.10. V72.
14. Paid cash to Quick Delivery, $24.10, covering V72. C58.
14. Issued DM10 to North Heights Corporation for return of merchandise purchased, $225.00. Cancel V71. V73.
15. Paid cash to North Heights Corporation, $1,440.75, covering V73 for $1,470.15, less 2% discount, $29.40. C59.
16. Recorded voucher for semimonthly payroll for period ended November 15, $1,459.64 (total payroll: sales, $1,183.50; administrative, $789.00; less deductions: employee income tax payable—federal, $295.88; employee income tax payable—state, $59.18; social security tax payable, $128.21; Medicare tax payable, $29.59). V74.
16. Paid cash for semimonthly payroll, $1,459.64, covering V74. C60.
22. Paid cash to Supply World, $216.80, covering V69. C61.
25. Issued Voucher No. 75 to buy office equipment on account from Fischer Equipment, $2,350.00.
29. Deposited $1,170.15 in the checking account.
30. Purchased merchandise on account from Georgia Company, $2,258.50. V76.

Instructions:

1. Use page 20 of a check register. Record the bank balance brought forward on November 1 of the current year, $11,676.77.
2. Journalize the transactions completed during November of the current year. Use page 22 of a voucher register and page 20 of a check register. When a voucher is paid or canceled, make appropriate notations in the voucher register. Source documents are abbreviated as follows: check, C; debit memorandum, DM; voucher, V.
3. Prove and rule both the voucher register and the check register.

5-6 CHALLENGE PROBLEM

Journalizing purchases invoices at the net amount in a voucher system

Challenge Problem 5-6
Voucher Register Vouchers Payable total,
5,011.00
Check Register Vouchers Payable total,
4,985.00
December 31 Bank Balance, 8,910.00

Cayman Company uses a voucher system. All of the vendors with whom Cayman Company does business offer terms of 2/10, n/30. Cayman has a policy of paying all invoices within the discount period. The business records invoice vouchers at the net amount (invoice total less a 2% discount). Thus, a $1,000.00 invoice, allowing a 2% discount of $20.00, is recorded at the net amount, $980.00. Purchases is debited and Vouchers Payable is credited for $980.00. A purchases discount account is not used.

If an invoice *is not* paid within the discount period, Cayman Company loses the discount. This loss is recorded in an account titled Discounts Lost. Thus, if the $1,000.00 invoice described above *is not* paid within the discount period, the business must pay the full $1,000.00. However, one of the controls in a voucher system is that no check can be written for more than the voucher amount. Therefore, for a check to be written for the full $1,000.00, the original voucher must be canceled. A new voucher for $1,000.00 must be prepared, approved, and recorded.

This new voucher would include a debit to Discounts Lost of $20.00, a debit to Vouchers Payable of $980.00 (the amount of the original voucher), and a credit to Vouchers Payable of $1,000.00. Once this voucher is approved, a check can be written for $1,000.00 to pay the full amount due.

If an invoice is recorded at its net amount, all purchases returns and allowances are recorded at net amounts. A $1,000.00 invoice recorded at net with a 2% discount has a $100.00 purchase return and allowance. Thus, the $100.00 return is discounted by 2% and recorded as $98.00. For the return, Vouchers Payable is debited $980.00 (the amount of original voucher), Purchases Returns and Allowances is credited for $98.00, and Vouchers Payable is credited for $882.00 (the amount of the new voucher).

Cayman's voucher register is similar to the one described for OfficeMart in this chapter. However, the third amount column is titled Discounts Lost. There is only one Supplies Debit column because there is only one supplies account. Cayman's check register has two special amount columns: Vouchers Payable Debit and Cash Credit.

Transactions:

Dec. 11. Purchased merchandise on account from Knotts Company, $2,000.00.
15. Made a deposit in the checking account, $1,000.00.
15. Bought supplies on account from Fairgate Supply Company, $200.00.
18. Bought store equipment on account from Hightop Company, $1,000.00.
18. Paid cash to Knotts Company covering V109. C80.
19. Purchased merchandise on account from Neal Company, $500.00.
22. Made a deposit in the checking account, $2,000.00.
25. Paid cash to Hightop Company covering V111. C81.
26. Paid cash to Fairgate Supply Company covering V110. C82.
28. Bought supplies on account from Peerless Supply Company, $300.00.
28. Issued DM30 to Neal Company for return of merchandise purchased, $50.00. Cancel V112.
29. Made a deposit in the checking account, $1,000.00.
31. Paid cash to Neal Company covering V115. C83.

Instructions:

1. Use page 20 of a check register. Record the amounts brought forward on December 11 of the current year.

Vouchers Payable Debit	$1,395.00
Cash Credit	1,395.00
Bank Balance	8,500.00

2. Journalize the transactions completed during December of the current year. Use page 25 of a voucher register. Assume that for all purchases of merchandise, equipment, or supplies, the invoice terms are 2/10, n/30. When a voucher is paid or canceled, make appropriate notations in the voucher register. Number vouchers consecutively starting with Voucher No. 109. Source documents are abbreviated as follows: check, C; debit memorandum, DM; voucher, V.

3. Prove and rule both the voucher register and the check register.

APPLIED SKILLS COMMUNICATIONS

Surveys of business managers show that communication skills are one of the most desired traits in new employees. The Applied Communication activity provides an opportunity for students to practice their communication and language arts skills on topics that directly relate to accounting. This activity requires students to prepare a report about computer viruses. In addition to learning about computer viruses, students learn how to do research in current periodicals. The instructor may need to assist students in the research process.

• applied communication

Information is the key to a successful business. The loss of information can inhibit the ability of accountants to prepare reports and managers to make business decisions. Computer viruses can cause the information in computer files to be destroyed and, therefore, are a serious problem for businesses of all sizes.

Required:

1. Go to the library and research computer viruses.

2. Write a short report about computer viruses. Include the following items:
   a. A description of one particular computer virus.
   b. The origin of the virus.
   c. Ways to prevent your computer from getting a virus.
   d. The action to take if you detect a virus.

• cases for critical thinking

Case 1

Kelly White, the bookkeeper for Greenfield, Inc., is setting up the company's voucher system. As she plans, she is trying to decide how many columns to use in the voucher register. She is also trying to decide what headings to use for the special columns in the voucher register. What should Ms. White consider in making her decision about these special columns?

Case 2

Review the entries you made for the Challenge Problem. Compare these entries with the entries for purchases on account made in the Mastery Problem. What is your opinion of recording purchases invoices at the net amount?

• SCANS workplace competency

Systems Competency: Understanding Systems

Concept: Competent employees know how social, organizational, and technological systems work and operate effectively within them. Capable individuals know which people to ask for information, how to respond to the demands of the organization, and how to function within a company's formal or informal codes.

Application: Design a flow chart, construct a bulletin board, or prepare a multimedia presentation that illustrates the complete accounting cycle for a departmental merchandising business. Include verifying source documents, journalizing, posting, preparing interim statements, preparing AR and AP schedules, completing a work sheet, preparing financial statements, journalizing and posting adjusting and closing entries, and preparing a post-closing trial balance.

APPLIED COMMUNICATION

Students' solutions will vary. In addition to the required information, the instructor should consider the following items when grading the activity: (1) understanding of computer viruses, (2) conciseness and completeness, (3) writing style, and (4) mechanics (grammar, spelling, punctuation).

CASES FOR CRITICAL THINKING

Case 1

Ms. White should consider what accounts are debited and how often each account is used. To do this, Ms. White could examine transactions from previous months. The accounts that are used most often are those that should be considered for special columns in the voucher register.

Case 2

One person, Mr. Bartell, is totally responsible for ALL aspects of the system. Because of this, it would be possible for Mr. Bartell to enter an unauthorized invoice into the system. He could then issue a check for this unauthorized invoice and cash the check himself. The invoice and voucher should be approved by persons who do not authorize, prepare, approve, or sign the checks. By dividing the responsibility, more employees are involved in each transaction. With more employees involved, illegal acts are more difficult to hide.

SCANS WORKPLACE COMPETENCY

Allow students to improve other SCANS skills by creating cooperative learning groups of 3–4 students to complete this assignment.

AUDITING FOR ERRORS

Proper control procedures are not being used in this voucher system. One person, Mr. Bartell, is totally responsible for *all* aspects of the system. Because of this, it would be possible for Mr. Bartell to enter an unauthorized invoice into the system. He could then issue a check for this unauthorized invoice and cash the check himself. The invoice and voucher should be approved by persons who do not authorize, prepare, approve, or sign the checks. By dividing the responsibility, more employees are involved in each transaction. With more employees involved, illegal acts are more difficult to hide.

ANALYZING COSTCO'S FINANCIAL STATEMENTS

The unit cost is $20.00 per unit [($1,200 + 100 + 400 + 300) / 100 = $20.00]. All costs of merchandise and shipping, plus depot costs, are included in the cost of the merchandise. Costs related to the warehouse employees are not a merchandise cost and would be included in selling, general, and administrative expenses.

• auditing for errors

Harper Company uses a voucher system for cash payments. Jonathan Bartell, the bookkeeper, receives and verifies the invoices. He then prepares the voucher and enters the voucher in the voucher register. When the voucher is due, Mr. Bartell prepares and signs the check and enters the payment in the check register.

Instructions:

Auditing involves more than checking the accuracy of amounts and calculations. It also includes checking processes to see whether proper procedures are being used. In this example, is Harper Company following proper procedures for its voucher system? Explain.

• analyzing Costco's financial statements

What Is Included in Merchandise Costs?

The cost of an asset should include all the costs necessary for making the asset available for its intended use. Costco considers merchandise inventory available for its intended use when the items are available for sale to a member.

Read the section "Merchandise Costs" in Note 1 (B-9–B-17) of Costco's financial statements in Appendix B of this textbook. Use the following information to determine the unit cost of inventory purchased on a purchase invoice:

100 units of BE-45 electronic can opener	$1,200
Shipping & handling	100
Wages and benefits of depot employees receiving items from vendor	400
Transportation costs from the depot to the warehouse	300
Wages and benefits of warehouse employees to stock the items on display shelves	100
Wages and benefits to warehouse employees to sell the items	200

TEACHING STRATEGIES　PORTFOLIO ASSESSMENT

Students should select an example of activities that have been successfully completed to include in their portfolio. A copy of the Portfolio Assessment form (blackline master in the Teacher's Resource Guide; also on the Student Companion CD) should be completed by the student and the Description section should include any comments regarding how the student mastered these concepts and procedures.

Automated Accounting

Safety Tips to Maintain Your Computer and Disks

Electrical Equipment

The following rules protect the operator of the equipment, other persons in the environment, and the equipment itself.

1. Do not unplug equipment by pulling on the electrical cord. Instead, grasp the plug at the outlet and remove it.
2. Do not stretch electrical cords across an aisle where someone might trip over them.
3. Avoid food and beverages near equipment where a spill might result in an electrical short.
4. Do not attempt to remove the cover of equipment for any reason while the power is turned on.
5. Do not attempt to repair equipment while it is plugged in. To avoid damage most repairs should be done by an authorized service technician.
6. Always turn the power off when finished using equipment.
7. Do not overload extension cords.
8. Follow manufacturer recommendations for safe use.
9. Replace frayed electrical cords immediately.

Computers

1. To avoid damage to the drives, do not insert pencils or other implements in floppy disk or CD-ROM drives.
2. To prevent overheating, avoid blocking air vents.
3. Position keyboards to prevent bumping or dropping them off the work surface.
4. Take care not to spill food or liquid on or in any computer component. If you do, turn off the computer immediately; unplug it; and notify your instructor before cleaning up the spill or turning on the equipment.

5. Avoid jolting or jostling your computer if it becomes necessary to move it.
6. Do NOT attempt to open or repair any part of the computer or monitor unless directed to do so by your instructor.

Monitors

1. Most manufacturers advise repair by authorized service technicians only.
2. Adjust brightness and focus for comfortable viewing.
3. Reposition computer or use glare visors to avoid glare on the monitor screen.
4. Do not leave fingerprints on the screen. Keep the screen clear of dust. Only use a soft cloth for cleaning the screen.

Printers

1. Do not let jewelry, ties, scarves, loose sleeves, or other clothing get caught in the machinery. This could result in damage to the machinery and could cause personal injury.
2. Exercise caution when using toxic chemicals such as toner in order to avoid spills.

Disks and Disk Drives

1. Do not bend disks.
2. Do not touch exposed surfaces of disks.
3. Be sure the disk drive is not running when you insert or remove a disk.
4. Keep disks away from extreme hot or cold temperatures. Do not leave disks in a car during very hot or cold weather.
5. Keep disks away from magnetic fields such as transformers and magnets.
6. Keep disks away from smoke, ashes, and dust, including chalk dust.
7. Be sure to make back-up copies.

EXPLAIN

- Review the safety tips and operation basics for electrical equipment.
- Review the safety tips and operation basics for computers.
- Review the safety tips and operation basics for monitors.
- Review the safety tips and operation basics for printers.
- Review the safety tips and operation basics for disks and disk drives.
- Explain policies and procedures related to the computers in your classroom or computer lab.
- Explain how to boot software in your classroom or computer lab. Explain specifically how to boot Automated Accounting.
- If you are using a network system, explain operating policies.
- Explain how students are to name their solution files. Note whether any students in the class have the same three initials so that these students can use alternate filenames. For *Automated Accounting 8.0*, direct students to use their full names when they save their files, such as "04-7 Firstname Lastname."
- Explain your policies on how Automated Accounting work is to be scheduled and completed.
- Explain how you will grade Automated Accounting problems and how Automated Accounting grades affect the course grade.

TEACHING STRATEGIES   DIFFERENT LEARNING ABILITIES

At-Risk Students. Instructors report that at-risk students are particularly successful when completing activities at the computer. Completing automated problems adds reality to the task at hand. Students can work at their own pace and experience immediate satisfaction. Encourage at-risk students to work at the computer as often as possible.

Inventory Planning

	SCOPE & SEQUENCE		ENHANCING	
	NEW	REVIEW/EXTENSION	SPECIAL FEATURES	
Introduce the Chapter	✓		• Accounting in the Real World: Toys "R" Us	
Lesson 6-1 The Nature of Merchandise Inventory			• Making Ethical Decisions: Is Someone Reading Your E-mail?	
Flow of inventory costs	✓			
Effects of errors in costing an inventory	✓			
Goods in transit	✓			
Goods on consignment	✓			
Inventory stock record		✓		
Periodic inventory		✓		
Lesson 6-2 Inventory Costing				
FIFO inventory costing method		✓		
LIFO inventory costing method		✓		
Weighted-average costing method		✓		
Lower of cost or market inventory costing method	✓			
Lesson 6-3 Estimating the Inventory			• Technology for Business: Spreadsheet Activity—Valuation of Inventory	
Gross profit method of estimating inventory		✓		
Retail method of estimating inventory	✓			
Calculating merchandise inventory turnover ratio	✓			
Calculating average number of days' sales in merchandise inventory	✓			
Putting It All Together			• Explore Accounting	
			• Xtra! Web Site: Xtra! Enrichment	
			• Applied Communication	
			• Cases for Critical Thinking	
			• SCANS Workplace Competency	
			• Auditing for Errors	
			• Analyzing Costco's Financial Statements	

and Valuation

INSTRUCTION		PRACTICE AND ASSESSMENT		
TECHNOLOGY AND MEDIA	**TEACHING STRATEGIES**	**GUIDED PRACTICE**	**INDEPENDENT PRACTICE**	**RETEACHING AND ENRICHMENT**
• Internet Research Activity • Accounting Xtra! Web Site	• Software Focus			
• Instructor's Resource CD: PowerPoint Slides • Xtra! Web Site: Xtra! Study Tools • Blackline Masters: Stock Record and Inventory Record • Personal Trainer • Automated Accounting • Peachtree and QuickBooks	• Applied Skills: Building Study Skills • Expanding Beyond the Classroom	• Terms Review • Audit Your Understanding • Work Together 6-1	• On Your Own 6-1 • Application Problem 6-1 • Ongoing Assessment, p. 174 • Personal Trainer • Xtra! Web Site: Xtra! Study Tools	• Reteach, p. 174 • Enrich, p. 175 • Automated Accounting • Peachtree and QuickBooks
• Instructor's Resource CD: PowerPoint Slides • Xtra! Web Site: Xtra! Study Tools • Personal Trainer • Automated Accounting • QuickBooks	• Cooperative Learning • Print Learner • Tactile Learner	• Terms Review • Audit Your Understanding • Work Together 6-2	• On Your Own 6-2 • Application Problem 6-2 • Ongoing Assessment, p. 180 • Personal Trainer • Xtra! Web Site: Xtra! Study Tools	• Reteach, p. 180 • Enrich, p. 181 • Automated Accounting • QuickBooks
• Instructor's Resource CD: PowerPoint Slides • Xtra! Web Site: Xtra! Study Tools • Personal Trainer	• Visual Learner • Kinesthetic Learner	• Terms Review • Audit Your Understanding • Work Together 6-3	• On Your Own 6-3 • Application Problem 6-3 • Application Problem 6-4 • Ongoing Assessment, p. 185 • Personal Trainer • Xtra! Web Site: Xtra! Study Tools	• Reteach, p. 185 • Enrich, p. 186
• Personal Trainer • Xtra! Web Site: Xtra! Review, Quizzing, and Enrichment • Student Companion CD	• Applied Mathematics • Specific Learning Disability (SLD) Students • Applied Skills: Writing Across the Curriculum • Applied Skills: Language Arts		• Mastery Problem 6-5 • Personal Trainer • Xtra! Web Site: Xtra! Review and Quizzing • Study Guide 6 • Student Companion CD • Chapter 6 Test • ExamView, Chapter 6 • Portfolio Assessment	• Challenge Problem 6-6 • Reteach, p. 187 • Enrich, p. 187 • Recycling Problem 6-1 • Automated Accounting • Xtra! Web Site: Xtra! Enrichment

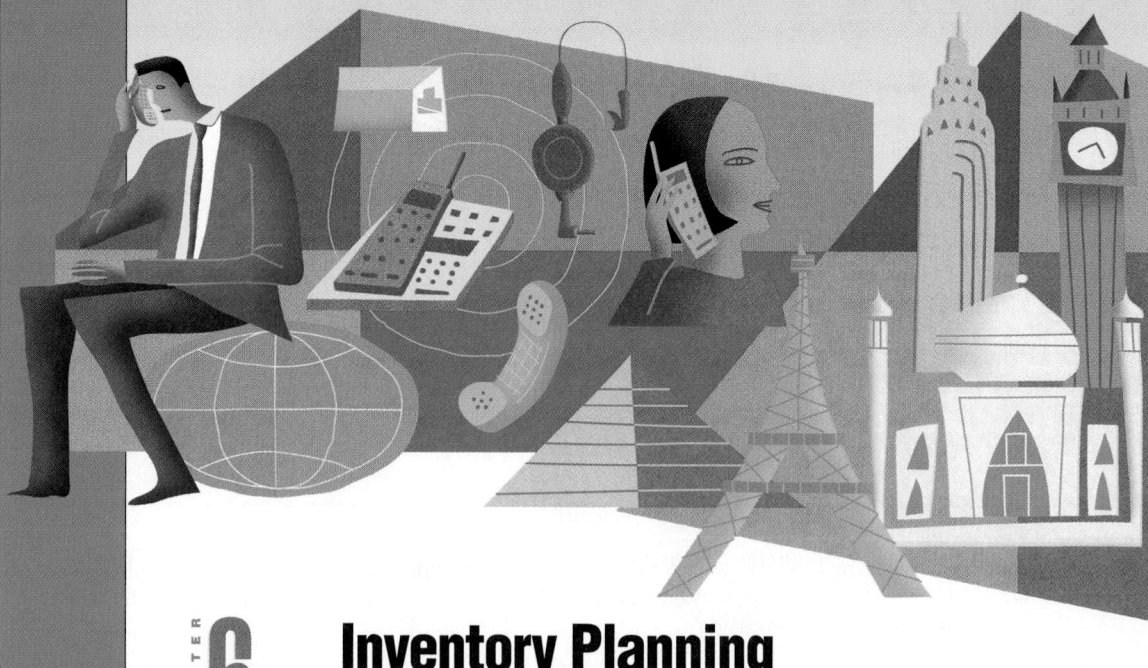

CHAPTER 6

OBJECTIVES & TERMS

Inventory Planning and Valuation

After studying Chapter 6, you will be able to:

1. Define accounting terms related to planning and costing inventory.

2. Identify accounting concepts and practices related to planning, counting, and costing inventory.

3. Describe the nature of merchandise inventory.

4. Determine the cost of merchandise inventory using selected costing methods.

5. Estimate the cost of merchandise inventory using selected estimating methods.

6. Calculate merchandise inventory turnover ratio and average number of days' sales in merchandise inventory.

- consignment
- consignee
- consignor
- stock record
- stock ledger
- purchase order
- inventory record
- first-in, first-out inventory costing method

- last-in, first-out inventory costing method
- weighted-average inventory costing method
- lower of cost or market inventory costing method

- retail method of estimating inventory
- merchandise inventory turnover ratio
- average number of days' sales in merchandise inventory

Point Your Browser
accountingxtra.swlearning.com

168

1. Without such a policy, an employee may by enticed to purchase inferior, unnecessary, or more expensive goods from a supplier because of the gifts the supplier gives to the employee.
2. Quantity discounts may be available when merchandise is purchased for all stores at the same time. It is also easier to control the actions of a few employees in one location rather than employees at each of the stores.

INTERNET RESEARCH ACTIVITY

1. The mission of the Financial Accounting Standards Board (FASB) is to establish and improve standards of financial accounting and reporting for the guidance and education of the public, including issuers, auditors and users of financial information.
2. To accomplish its mission, the FASB acts to:
   - Improve the usefulness of financial reporting by focusing on the primary characteristics of relevance and reliability and on the qualities of comparability and consistency.
   - Keep standards current to reflect changes in methods of doing business and changes in the economic environment.
   - Consider promptly any significant areas of deficiency in financial reporting that might be improved through the standard-setting process.
   - Promote the international convergence of accounting standards concurrent with improving the quality of financial reporting.
   - Improve the common understanding of the nature and purposes of information contained in financial reports.

• Toys"R"Us

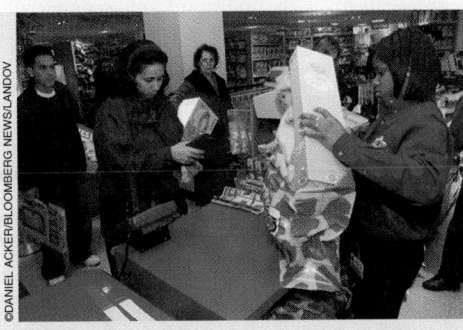

©DANIEL ACKER/BLOOMBERG NEWS/LANDOV

MANAGING INVENTORY AND EMPLOYEES AT TOYS"R"US

Say "Toys"R"Us" to most children, and their eyes light up with excitement. Their heads dance with a vision of rows of toys and games. With 1,600 stores worldwide and sales over $11 billion, Toys"R"Us buys and sells huge amounts of inventory each year.

Different stores within the Toys"R"Us family offer different merchandise. Toys"R"Us offers toys, children's apparel, and baby products. Kids"R"Us focuses on quality-name-brand children's wear at competitive prices. Babies"R"Us offers baby needs such as apparel, furniture, car seats, bedding, and strollers.

The Toys"R"Us employees who purchase this merchandise are expected to comply with a Professional Conduct code. Among other things, this code prohibits the employee from accepting gifts or gratuities from any supplier, prohibits the employee from buying merchandise from suppliers for personal use, and states that the selection of a supplier must be based on quality, need, performance, and cost and must promote the best interests of the company.

Exceptions to this policy have to be approved by someone in management—sometimes as high as the Chief Executive Officer of the company.

Critical Thinking

1. Why would a company like Toys"R"Us establish and enforce an employee policy controlling gifts from suppliers?
2. Why is it beneficial to a company to have a few employees buying merchandise for all stores rather than having each store purchase its own merchandise?

Source: www2.toysrus.com

Xtra!
Today
accountingxtra.swlearning.com

FASB MISSION STATEMENT

The Financial Accounting Standards Board (FASB) has the authority to make new accounting rules. FASB was given this authority by the Securities and Exchange Commission (SEC). Go to the homepage of the FASB (www.fasb.org). Click on "News Center" and then click on "Fact Sheet."

Instructions

1. List the one-paragraph mission of the FASB.
2. List at least two ways in which the FASB acts in order to accomplish its mission.

6-1 The Nature of Merchandise Inventory

For most merchandising businesses, merchandise inventory is the largest asset. Merchandising businesses implement good control measures in managing their inventory. A successful business must maintain an adequate amount of merchandise inventory that customers are willing to buy. A business may fail if it keeps too much or too little merchandise inventory on hand.

Business managers frequently analyze sales and inventory transactions to assist them in planning future inventory purchases. From this analysis, managers can determine the items of inventory that are selling well and the items that are not selling well. Managers also examine sales and inventory transactions to identify any seasonal trends in sales. This information allows managers to order the right kinds of merchandise at the right time.

Many businesses now maintain their inventory records on computer. Computerized inventory systems can keep more accurate records of the amount of inventory on hand than other systems can. Computerized systems also provide more frequent inventory information to managers. Managers use this information to make effective business decisions.

©GETTY IMAGES/PHOTODISC

making ethical decisions

MAKING ETHICAL DECISIONS • MAKING ETHICAL DECISIONS • MAKING ETHICAL DECISI

Is Someone Reading Your E-mail?

Janice Tillman had just been escorted from the plant by security guards. Twenty minutes earlier she lost her job for sending e-mail messages containing threatening statements directed toward Michael Ulman, her supervisor. When confronted with the messages, Janice tried to casually dismiss them as a joke. Then she accused Michael of invading her privacy, claiming that she selected the "private message" option when sending the e-mails to a friend.

The company's code of conduct states, "E-mail communication on the company computer systems is subject to electronic monitoring."

Instructions

Use the ethical model to evaluate Michael's decision to fire Janice.

FLOW OF INVENTORY COSTS

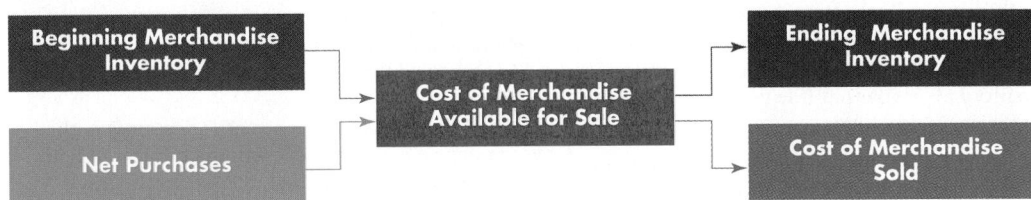

Merchandise is continually being purchased and sold. A business's actual merchandise inventory changes from day to day. The flow of inventory costs through the records of a business is shown above. The cost of the merchandise available for sale consists of:

1. The cost of the beginning merchandise inventory.
2. The cost of the net purchases added to the inventory during the fiscal period.

At the end of each fiscal period, the cost of the merchandise available for sale is divided into:

1. The cost of the ending merchandise inventory. The ending merchandise inventory represents a *current* asset that will be charged as costs in *future* fiscal periods.
2. The cost of the merchandise sold during the *current* fiscal period. This cost materially affects the amount of net income reported for the fiscal period. [*CONCEPT: Adequate Disclosure*]

EFFECTS OF ERRORS IN COSTING AN INVENTORY

Reports and Items Affected	If Ending Inventory Is	
	Understated	Overstated
Income Statement:		
Cost of Merchandise Sold	Overstated	Understated
Gross Profit	Understated	Overstated
Net Income	Understated	Overstated
Statement of Stockholders' Equity:		
Net Income	Understated	Overstated
Retained Earnings	Understated	Overstated
Stockholders' Equity	Understated	Overstated
Balance Sheet:		
Merchandise Inventory	Understated	Overstated
Total Assets.	Understated	Overstated
Stockholders' Equity	Understated	Overstated

The cost of both beginning and ending merchandise inventory affects items on an income statement, a statement of stockholders' equity, and a balance sheet. The effects are shown above.

An accurate merchandise inventory cost must be determined to adequately report the financial progress and condition of a merchandising business. [*CONCEPT: Adequate Disclosure*] If the ending inventory is understated, the cost of merchandise

sold will be overstated. Consequently, the net income will be understated. As a result, total assets and total stockholders' equity will be understated. If the ending inventory is overstated, the reverse will be true, and additional income tax must be paid on the overstated income. In neither situation will financial statements report accurate information. [*CONCEPT: Adequate Disclosure*]

- Explain that the cost of goods includes the price paid for them plus the cost involved in getting them delivered and ready for sale, including transportation charges paid by the buyer.

- Describe the two methods of determining the number of goods in inventory: taking a physical count and keeping a continuous record.

- Explain the importance of knowing who holds title to goods in determining whether the goods are counted in inventory.

- Explain the difference between FOB shipping point (goods in transit are part of the buyer's inventory) and FOB destination (goods in transit are not part of the buyer's inventory).

- Explain that the person or business that receives goods on consignment does not include those goods as part of inventory.

- Direct students to the F.Y.I. for a description of inventory management.

COSTING AND COUNTING THE INVENTORY

Items in the merchandise inventory of a merchandising business are frequently referred to as *goods*. Typically, a business counts as part of its inventory all goods that it legally owns. The cost of these goods includes:

1. The price paid to vendors for the merchandise. This price includes the purchase invoice amount less discounts, returns, and allowances granted by the vendors.
2. The cost involved in getting the goods to the place of business and ready for sale. This cost includes transportation charges paid by the buyer.

Merchandising businesses must know both the cost of the goods and the number of goods in inventory. Businesses use two methods to determine the number of goods in inventory:

1. Taking a physical count of the individual items in inventory. All goods in inventory as of a given date are included in a physical inventory count.
2. Keeping a continuous record for each merchandise item showing the number purchased and the number sold. Using this method, a business can determine the number of goods in inventory at any point in time.

Goods in Transit

Merchandising businesses purchase goods from suppliers. The suppliers ship the goods to the businesses. For goods in transit at the time of a physical count of inventory, the business must determine who holds title to the goods. When title to goods in transit passes from the supplier to the buyer, the goods become part of the buyer's inventory regardless of where they are physically located.

A vendor's terms of sale may include the provision *FOB shipping point*. FOB is an abbreviation for the phrase *Free On Board*. FOB shipping point means that the buyer pays the transportation charges. Under FOB shipping point terms, the title to the goods passes to the buyer as soon

as the vendor delivers the goods to a transportation business. These goods in transit, but not yet received by the buyer, are part of the *buyer's* inventory.

If the terms of sale are *FOB destination*, the vendor pays the transportation charges. Title to the goods passes to the buyer when the buyer receives the goods. These goods in transit, but not yet received by the buyer, are part of the *vendor's* inventory. The buyer does not include these goods in the cost of inventory.

Goods on Consignment

Goods that are given to a business to sell but for which title remains with the vendor, are called a **consignment**. The person or business that receives goods on consignment is called the **consignee**. The person or business that gives goods on consignment is called the **consignor**.

The consignee agrees to receive, care for, and attempt to sell the consigned goods. If the goods are sold, the consignee deducts a commission from the sale amount and sends the remainder to the consignor. In a consignment, title to the goods does not pass to the consignee. The goods on consignment are part of the consignor's inventory. The consignee does not include consigned goods in the cost of its inventory.

A consignee agrees to care for the goods on consignment and to make adequate attempts to sell them. Therefore, a consignee has implied liabilities if anything should happen to the goods before they are sold. A consignee often reports the cost of consigned goods as an attachment or footnote to its balance sheet.

FYI FOR YOUR INFORMATION

Inventory management consists of determining the quantity of goods on hand and developing procedures for ordering, receiving, and maintaining the inventory.

Inventory Planning and Valuation

APPLIED SKILLS BUILDING STUDY SKILLS

Direct students to prepare a Quick Reference Guide (QRG) by writing the formulas for calculating merchandise inventory turnover ratio and average number of days sales in merchandise inventory on an index card. Students should use this QRG as a reference.

STOCK RECORD FOR A PERPETUAL INVENTORY SYSTEM

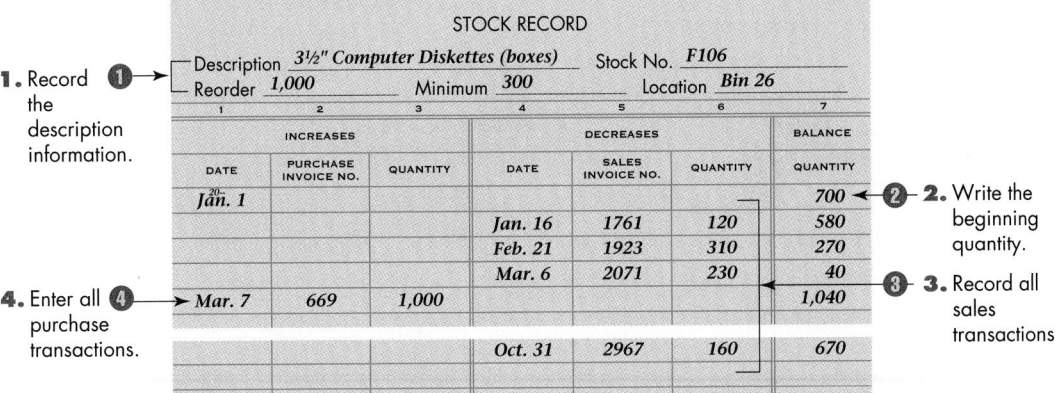

1. Record the description information.

2. Write the beginning quantity.

3. Record all sales transactions.

4. Enter all purchase transactions.

STOCK RECORD

Description: 3½" Computer Diskettes (boxes) Stock No. F106
Reorder: 1,000   Minimum: 300   Location: Bin 26

1	2	3	4	5	6	7
INCREASES			DECREASES			BALANCE
DATE	PURCHASE INVOICE NO.	QUANTITY	DATE	SALES INVOICE NO.	QUANTITY	QUANTITY
Jan. 1 20--						700
			Jan. 16	1761	120	580
			Feb. 21	1923	310	270
			Mar. 6	2071	230	40
Mar. 7	669	1,000				1,040
			Oct. 31	2967	160	670

EXPLAIN

- Emphasize that stock records are used to maintain the continuous count of a perpetual inventory.
- Explain that all stock records together comprise the stock ledger.
- Compare the stock record and stock ledger to accounts receivable accounts and an accounts receivable ledger.
- Ask students to identify information, other than the quantity on hand, that is recorded on a stock record.
- Explain how the Reorder and Minimum quantities are used in an inventory system.

DEMONSTRATE

- Use a stock record transparency or direct students to the illustration to demonstrate how to maintain a stock record.
- Explain the use of the information at the top of the stock record.
- Demonstrate how to do the calculation for the Balance Quantity column for an entry in the Increases columns.
- Demonstrate how to do the calculation for the Balance Quantity column for an entry in the Decreases columns.
- Ask students to determine on what date the diskettes should have been reordered. *(Feb. 21 when the balance quantity, 270, fell below the Minimum, 300.)*

A continuous record of merchandise inventory increases, decreases, and balance on hand is known as a perpetual inventory. OfficeMart, Inc., sells office furniture, equipment, and supplies. It maintains a perpetual inventory.

A perpetual inventory provides day-to-day records about the quantity of merchandise on hand. Based on the records, management knows when an item of inventory is low and needs to be reordered. For each inventory item, the record shows the number on hand, the number purchased, and the number sold. A form used to show the type of merchandise, quantity received, quantity sold, and balance on hand is called a **stock record**. A file of stock records for all merchandise on hand is called a **stock ledger**.

OfficeMart's stock record for the diskettes is shown above. It includes a notation of the minimum balance at which a reorder is to be placed. For example, OfficeMart determines that two

weeks are required to order and to receive a shipment of boxes of 3½" diskettes from a vendor. In a two-week period, OfficeMart will sell an average of 300 boxes of diskettes. Therefore, OfficeMart reorders diskettes when the inventory reaches 300 boxes, or units. Each reorder is for 1,000 units. On February 21, the inventory balance falls below the reorder point. An order is immediately placed for 1,000 boxes. The order is received on March 7.

A completed form authorizing a seller to deliver goods with payment to be made later is called a **purchase order**. OfficeMart prepares purchase orders for all purchases.

During the year, sales are recorded on the stock record when the sale is made. Purchases are recorded on the stock record when the goods are received. Unit prices are not recorded on the stock records. They are obtained from copies of the purchase invoices.

STEPS · STEPS · STEPS · STEPS · STEPS · STEPS · STEPS · STEPS · STEPS · STEPS · STEPS ·

MAINTAINING A STOCK RECORD

1. Record the description of the inventory item, *3½" Computer Diskettes (boxes)*, the stock number, *F106*, the reorder quantity, *1,000*, the minimum number, *300*, and the warehouse location, *Bin 26*.

2. Write the beginning quantity. On *Jan. 1, 20--*, the quantity on hand was *700*.

3. Record all sales transactions in the Decreases columns of the stock record. After each sale, enter the new quantity in column 7. For the sale on January 16, write *Jan. 16* in column 4, the sales invoice number, *1761*, in column 5, and the quantity sold, *120*, in column 6. In column 7, record the new balance of inventory, *580*.

4. Enter all purchase transactions in the Increases columns of the stock record when the goods are received. Enter the date, purchase invoice number, quantity, and balance.

The Nature of Merchandise Inventory

TEACHING STRATEGIES EXPANDING BEYOND THE CLASSROOM

Invite to class a local business person whose business maintains a perpetual inventory. Ask the speaker to explain how the perpetual inventory is used and to show students the inventory forms used. Have students compare and contrast the forms with those in the textbook to recognize similarities and differences.

EXPLAIN

- Explain what is involved in "taking an inventory."

- Emphasize that a business that uses a perpetual inventory will also conduct a physical inventory once a year, usually at year end.

- Explain that the inventory record is used in the process of taking a physical inventory to record the quantity of units on hand for each item. After the count is taken, the unit price is recorded and the total cost is calculated.

- Explain that any differences between the inventory record and the stock record are corrected on the stock record card.

- Mention that if large or frequent differences are found between stock records and inventory records, the inventory procedures need to be reviewed.

DEMONSTRATE

- Use an instructor-made transparency from the blackline master of an inventory record or direct students to the illustration to demonstrate how to complete an inventory record.

- As you read each of the six steps shown, direct students to point to the information on the inventory record.

ONGOING ASSESSMENT

- Assessment is an ongoing process. Circulate through the classroom or lab observing which students have problems with the assignments.

- Troubleshooting: Diagnose what kinds of problems students have with this lesson. Although the concepts presented in this lesson are relatively simple, students may have difficulty understanding the relationship of the inventory record, stock record, and stock ledger.

- Assess student understanding by checking solutions to Independent Practice assignments.

RETEACH

- Call on students to identify the two methods of determining the quantity of merchandise inventory.

- Call on students to explain the purpose of an inventory record.

- Call on students to identify the purpose of a stock record and its relationship to the stock ledger.

INVENTORY RECORD USED FOR THE PERIODIC INVENTORY

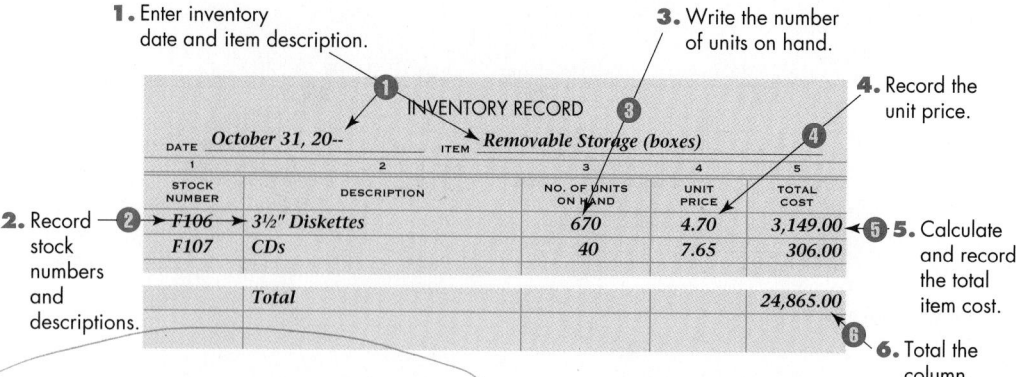

1. Enter inventory date and item description.

2. Record stock numbers and descriptions.

3. Write the number of units on hand.

4. Record the unit price.

5. Calculate and record the total item cost.

6. Total the column.

A merchandise inventory determined by counting, weighing, or measuring items of merchandise on hand is known as a periodic inventory. Counting, weighing, or measuring merchandise on hand for a periodic inventory is commonly referred to as "taking an inventory." For businesses with a large quantity of merchandise on hand, taking an inventory count is expensive. Therefore, businesses usually take a periodic inventory only once each fiscal period.

When only a periodic inventory is used, the low quantity of a merchandise item can be overlooked. When this happens, the business may not have the merchandise when customers want it. For this reason, OfficeMart uses the perpetual inventory method. Errors can occur, however, even when the perpetual inventory method is used. Therefore, OfficeMart takes a periodic inventory once each year to check the accuracy of the perpetual inventory.

A form used during a periodic inventory to record information about each item of merchandise on hand is called an **inventory record**. One inventory record is used for each item or category of items in inventory. When taking an inventory, OfficeMart uses an inventory record for categories of merchandise as shown above.

The periodic inventory count is compared to the perpetual inventory. Any differences are adjusted on the stock records. In the case of stock item F106, the physical count of boxes of the 3½" diskettes matched the quantity listed on the stock record. Therefore, no adjustment was needed. If large differences are found, the business should review its recording and control procedures to ensure that the inventory and the inventory records are being properly maintained.

STEPS • STEPS • STEPS • STEPS • STEPS • STEPS • STEPS • STEPS • STEPS • STEPS • STEPS

COMPLETE THE INVENTORY RECORD

1 Enter the date of the periodic inventory, *October 31, 20--,* and the item description, *Removable Computer Storage (boxes).*

2 Record the stock number, *F106,* and description, *3½" Diskettes.*

3 Write the actual number of units on hand, *670.*

4 Record the unit price, *4.70.* The unit price data are obtained from purchase invoices. In this case, all 3½" diskettes in inventory were purchased at the same price. Additional lines of the record are used to record units purchased at a different unit price.

5 Calculate and record the total cost, *3,149.00.* Total cost for each item is calculated by multiplying the unit price, column 4, by the number of items on hand, column 3.

6 Determine the total cost for these inventory items, *24,865.00.* The total of all inventory records is the total cost of the ending merchandise inventory.

• terms review

TERMS REVIEW • TERMS

consignment
consignee
consignor
stock record
stock ledger
purchase order
inventory record

• audit your understanding

AUDIT YOUR UNDERSTANDING

1. What two elements are included in the cost of merchandise available for sale?
2. If ending merchandise inventory is understated, will the net income be overstated or understated?
3. Name two ways to determine the number of inventory items on hand.

• work together 6-1

WORK TOGETHER • WORK TOGETHER • WORK TOGETHER • WORK

Completing a stock record for a perpetual inventory system

A stock record form and an inventory record form for Tower Television are provided in the *Working Papers*. Your instructor will guide you through the following examples.

1. Fill in the top portion of the stock record form with the following information: Description, 19″ color television set; Stock No., K087; Reorder, 80; Minimum, 20; and Location, Bin 12.

2. Record the following information. Save your work to complete On Your Own 6-1.

Date	Purchase Invoice No.	Sales Invoice No.	Quantity	Balance
Sept. 1				62
Sept. 12		475	40	
Sept. 16		508	8	
Sept. 17	183		80	
Sept. 20		653	15	

• on your own 6-1

ON YOUR OWN • ON YOUR OWN

Completing a stock record for a perpetual inventory system and comparing it to an inventory record

Use the working papers from the Work Together above. Work independently to complete the following problem.

1. Record the remaining information for product number K087 on the stock record.

Date	Purchase Invoice No.	Sales Invoice No.	Quantity	Balance
Sept. 23		714	40	
Sept. 25		761	22	
Sept. 26	255		80	
Sept. 30		850	12	

2. Compare the ending balance in units from the stock record with the number of units on hand for product K087 in the inventory record. Make sure they are equal.

The Nature of Merchandise Inventory

Lesson 6-1 **175**

6-2 Inventory Costing

FIRST-IN, FIRST-OUT INVENTORY COSTING METHOD

FIFO Inventory Costing Method

Purchase			Ending Inventory	
Date	Units	Unit Price	Units	Total Cost
January, beginning inventory....	500	$1.00	0	0.00
June	500	1.20	200	$240.00
November	500	1.25	500	625.00
Totals.....................			700	$865.00

3. Multiply ending inventory units by unit price.

1. Assign units from most recent purchase.

700 Units in ending inventory
− 500 From Nov. purchase
200 Units to be assigned
− 200 From June purchase
0 Units to be assigned

4. Total the ending inventory columns.

2. Assign units from the next most recent purchase.

Once OfficeMart takes a periodic inventory, it determines a dollar cost for each item. [CONCEPT: *Unit of Measurement*] The unit prices are obtained from purchase invoices. For example, as shown above, the 670 F106 boxes of diskettes have a unit price of $4.70 and a total cost of $3,149.00.

Various methods may be used to determine the cost of merchandise inventory. A business selects the method that best matches the revenue and costs for that business. [CONCEPT: *Matching Expenses with Revenue*]

Using the price of merchandise purchased first to calculate the cost of merchandise sold first is called the **first-in, first-out inventory costing method**. FIFO is an abbreviation for first in, first out. The FIFO method of determining the cost of

merchandise on hand assumes that the merchandise purchased first (first in) is the merchandise sold first (first out). Thus, the FIFO method uses the most recent purchase prices to determine the cost of merchandise inventory remaining. For example, OfficeMart has an inventory of 700 three-ring binders on November 30. If OfficeMart used the FIFO method, the binders would be costed as shown above.

Using the FIFO method, the remaining 300 units from the June purchase and the 500 units in beginning inventory are designated as the units that were sold. These binders are *first in*. Therefore, the business assumes that they are also the *first out*, or first sold.

CALCULATE INVENTORY COSTS USING THE FIFO METHOD

1 Assign ending inventory units from the most recent purchase. The number of units in ending inventory is 700. All *500* units from the November purchase are assigned to ending inventory.

2 If all units of ending inventory have not been assigned, assign units from the next most recent purchase. As shown above, 200 units have not been assigned. The next most recent purchase, June, includes 500 units. Therefore, all 200 units to be assigned will come from the June purchase. All 700 units in ending inventory have now been assigned.

3 Multiply the units in the Ending Inventory Units column by the unit prices. Enter the results, *$240.00* and *625.00*, in the Total Cost column.

4 Total the two Ending Inventory columns. The total number of units, *700*, is equal to the number of units on hand as determined by the periodic inventory. The total cost assigned to the ending inventory using the FIFO method is *$865.00*.

LAST-IN, FIRST-OUT INVENTORY COSTING METHOD

LIFO Inventory Costing Method

Date	Purchase		Ending Inventory	
	Units	Unit Price	Units	Total Cost
January, beginning inventory....	500	$1.00	500	$500.00
June	500	1.20	200	240.00
November	500	1.25	0	0.00
Totals.....................			700	$740.00

3. Multiply ending inventory units by unit price.

1. Assign units from earliest purchase.

700 Units in ending inventory
① – 500 From beginning inventory
200 Units to be assigned
② – 200 From June purchase
0 Units to be assigned

4. Total the ending inventory columns.

2. Assign units from next earliest purchase.

Using the price of merchandise purchased last to calculate the cost of merchandise sold first is called the **last-in, first-out inventory costing method.** LIFO is an abbreviation for last in, first out. The LIFO method assumes that the merchandise purchased last (last in) is the merchandise sold first (first out). Thus, the LIFO method uses the earliest purchase prices to determine the cost of merchandise inventory. If OfficeMart used the LIFO method, the 700 binders would be costed as shown above.

Of the 700 units on hand, 500 units are assumed to be the units in the beginning inventory at $1.00 per unit. The remaining 200 units are assumed to have been purchased on the next earliest date, June, at $1.20 each. None is considered to be part of the 500 units purchased on the most recent date, November. The total cost, using the LIFO method, is $740.00.

Using the LIFO method, the remaining 300 units from the June purchase and the 500 units from the November purchase are designated as the units that were sold. These binders are *last in.* Therefore, the business assumes that they are also the *first out,* or first sold.

WEIGHTED-AVERAGE INVENTORY COSTING METHOD

Weighted-Average Inventory Costing Method
Quantity on Hand, 700 units

Date	Purchase		Total Cost
	Units	Unit Price	
January, beginning inventory....	500	$1.00	$ 500.00
June	500	1.20	600.00
November	500	1.25	625.00
Totals.....................	1,500		$1,725.00

Total of Beginning Inventory and Purchases	÷	Total Units	=	Weighted-Average Price per Unit
$1,725.00	÷	1,500	=	$1.15

Units in Ending Inventory	×	Weighted-Average Price per Unit	=	Cost of Ending Inventory
700	×	$1.15	=	$805.00

{ **REMEMBER** FIFO uses the most recent purchase prices to determine the cost of merchandise inventory. }

- Explain that the weighted-average costing method is frequently used because it is the simplest to calculate.

- Explain that the same unit cost is used in the weighted-average method for all units in ending inventory.

- Explain that the three methods of costing ending inventory result in three different values.

- Remind students that the value assigned to the ending inventory affects items on the income statement, statement of stockholders' equity, and balance sheet.

- Explain that prices usually increase under normal economic conditions and that the costing method that uses the latest prices to value ending inventory will give the highest value, FIFO.

DEMONSTRATE

- Direct students to the illustration as you explain the effect of the three methods of costing ending inventory.

- Have students point to each item in the table as you explain the effects of the ending inventory cost.

- Demonstrate that the FIFO method gives the highest ending inventory, lowest cost of merchandise sold, and highest net income. Draw a skeleton income statement on the board and assign amounts to the items and calculate the net income to show that this holds true.

- Emphasize that the cost of goods available for sale (beginning inventory plus purchases) is the same for FIFO, LIFO, and weighted-average calculations.

- Summarize by pointing out that the FIFO method usually results in the highest net income, the LIFO method the lowest net income, and the weighted-average method somewhere in between the two, in a period of rising prices.

Using the average cost of beginning inventory plus merchandise purchased during a fiscal period to calculate the cost of merchandise sold is called the **weighted-average inventory costing method**. This method is based on the assumption that the cost is an average of the price paid for similar items purchased during the fiscal period. If OfficeMart used the weighted-average method, the 700 binders would be costed as shown at the bottom of page 177.

The total cost, $1,725.00, is divided by the total units purchased, 1,500, to calculate the weighted-average cost per unit, $1.15. The 700 units currently on hand are assumed to have been purchased at an average cost of $1.15 each. Therefore, the total cost of ending merchandise

inventory using the weighted-average method is $805.00. If OfficeMart used the weighted-average method, it would use the same weighted-average cost per unit, $1.15, to determine the cost of merchandise sold.

©GETTY IMAGES/PHOTODISC

COSTING INVENTORY DURING PERIODS OF INCREASING PRICES

Summary of Three Methods of Costing Inventory of 700 units of Ring Binders during a Period of Increasing Prices

Purchase		FIFO Method		LIFO Method		Weighted-Average Method
Date	Unit Price	Units	Cost	Units	Cost	
Jan., begin. inv.	$1.00	0	0.00	500	$500.00	Average Cost $1.15
June	1.20	200	$240.00	200	240.00	
Nov.	1.25	500	625.00	0	0.00	
Totals		700	$865.00	700	$740.00	$805.00

If prices are rising:

	FIFO	LIFO	Weighted-Average
Ending inventory valuation	Highest	Lowest	Always falls
Cost of merchandise sold	Lowest	Highest	between
Reported net income	Highest	Lowest	FIFO and LIFO

In the inventory costing situations described for the ring binders, prices increased from $1.00 to $1.25 per unit. Three ways of costing the inventory of 700 ring binders during a period of increasing prices are summarized above.

The cost of the ending inventory affects the cost of merchandise sold amount on the income statement. The higher the ending inventory, the lower the cost of merchandise sold amount, and vice versa. Therefore, during a period of *increasing prices*, the FIFO method usually results in the lowest cost of merchandise sold. The LIFO method usually results in the highest cost of merchandise sold.

The higher the cost of merchandise sold, the lower the net income reported on financial statements, and vice versa. Therefore, during a period of *increasing prices*, the FIFO method usually results in the highest reported net income. The LIFO method usually results in the lowest reported net income.

To reiterate: During a period of rising prices, the FIFO method shows a higher ending inventory than the other methods do. This results in a lower cost of merchandise sold, which in turn yields a higher reported net income. The opposite holds true for the LIFO method.

TEACHING STRATEGIES   DIFFERENT LEARNING STYLES

Print Learner. When learning formulas, the print learner would prefer to be able to study the formula as given in the textbook or as printed on a separate handout. The print material should show the formula as well as an example of performing the calculations.

COSTING INVENTORY DURING PERIODS OF DECREASING PRICES

**Summary of Three Methods of Costing Inventory of 700 units
of Ring Binders during a Period of Decreasing Prices**

Purchase		FIFO Method		LIFO Method		Weighted-Average Method
Date	Unit Price	Units	Cost	Units	Cost	
Jan., begin. inv.	$1.25	0	0.00	500	$625.00	Average Cost
June	1.20	200	$240.00	200	240.00	$1.15
Nov.	1.00	500	500.00	0	0.00	
Totals		700	$740.00	700	$865.00	$805.00

Prices for inventory items may also decrease. If OfficeMart determined the cost of inventory during a period of decreasing prices, the three inventory costing methods would be summarized as shown above.

During a period of *decreasing prices*, as shown in the figure above, the FIFO method usually results in the lowest merchandise inventory cost. This lower inventory cost results in a higher cost of merchandise sold and a lower net income. During a period of *decreasing prices*, the LIFO method usually results in the highest merchandise inventory cost. This higher inventory cost results in a lower cost of merchandise sold and a higher net income.

RESULTS OF THE THREE INVENTORY COSTING METHODS COMPARED

**Comparison of Three Methods of Costing
Inventory during Periods of Increasing
or Decreasing Prices**

Prices are	Total Inventory Cost Using		
	FIFO Method	LIFO Method	Weighted-Average Method
Increasing	$865.00	$740.00	$805.00
Decreasing	$740.00	$865.00	$805.00

A comparison of three methods of costing inventory during periods of increasing and decreasing prices is shown above.

The weighted-average method usually results in a total cost between the FIFO and LIFO total costs in both periods of increasing and decreasing prices. For businesses that purchase items with frequent fluctuations in price, the weighted-average method results in more consistent reporting of merchandise inventory costs.

Each business selects the method of costing merchandise inventory that best fits its policies and goals. A business selects one method of costing merchandise inventory and uses it for a number of years. In this way, the information on a series of financial statements can be compared easily. [CONCEPT: Consistent Reporting]

FYI FOR YOUR INFORMATION

The goal of the Japanese concept, the just-in-time (JIT) system, is to minimize inventory. Materials should be received only when they are needed for production; they should not be kept in inventory. The JIT system works well when vendors and buyers work together as a team to plan inventory levels.

179

- Point out that the lower of cost or market inventory costing method uses the current replacement cost for merchandise.

- Explain that the historical cost accounting cost refers to using actual amount paid rather than any preconceived idea of an item's value. In the example in the text, although the truck was valued at $20,000, OfficeMart paid $17,000. Therefore, the historical cost is $17,000, regardless of the estimated value. Often the historical cost is the cost that can be verified by a source document that states the amount paid.

- Explain that two values are needed to determine the lower of cost or market cost: The cost using FIFO, LIFO, or weighted-average and the current market price.

- Direct students to the F.Y.I. for an explanation of a practical application of the lower of cost or market costing method when the market value declines below the historical cost of an item.

- Direct students to the illustration to demonstrate how the lower of cost or market inventory costing method is applied.

- Point out that the amounts in the Cost column are the result of the inventory costing calculations shown on the preceding pages.

- Point out that the Market Price column is the result of multiplying the ending units times the last (market price) price paid for the item, $1.10.

- Show that the amount recorded in the Lower of Cost or Market column is whichever cost is lower when comparing the Cost amount and the Market Price amount.

- Assessment is an ongoing process. Circulate through the classroom or lab observing which students have problems with the assignments.

- Troubleshooting: Diagnose what kinds of problems students have with this lesson. Students may have difficulty (1) understanding which costs to use when calculating the cost of merchandise inventory using the FIFO and LIFO methods or (2) doing the calculations.

LOWER OF COST OR MARKET INVENTORY COSTING METHOD

Lower of Cost or Market Inventory Costing Method

Costing Method	Cost	Market Price (700 units × 1.10 current market price)	Lower of Cost or Market
Weighted Average	$805.00	$770.00	$770.00
FIFO	865.00	770.00	770.00
LIFO	740.00	770.00	740.00

1. Calculate the cost.

2. Calculate the market price.

3. Determine the smaller number to use as the lower of cost or market amount.

Using the lower of cost or market price to calculate the cost of ending merchandise inventory is called the **lower of cost or market inventory costing method**. In this context, *market* refers to the current replacement cost of the merchandise item. For example, OfficeMart may currently have to pay a vendor $1.10 to purchase a ring binder. The market price, therefore, is $1.10. When merchandise is purchased, the unit price is used to record inventory costs. [CONCEPT: Historical Cost]

The historical cost concept states that the actual amount paid for merchandise or other items bought is recorded. OfficeMart purchased a delivery truck valued at $20,000.00 and advertised at a sale price of $18,000.00. OfficeMart negotiated to purchase the delivery truck for $17,000.00. The amount recorded in accounting records for the delivery truck is the historical cost, $17,000.00—the actual amount paid.

Six months later, OfficeMart sells the delivery truck to Flowers by Giverney for $15,000.00. For Flowers by Giverney, the historical cost of the delivery truck is $15,000.00.

If the unit price is higher than the market price at the end of a fiscal period, the inventory cost is reduced to the current market price. However, if the unit price is lower than the market price, the inventory cost is maintained at the unit price.

Two amounts are needed to apply the lower of cost or market method:

1. The cost of the inventory using the FIFO, LIFO, or weighted-average method.
2. The current market price of the inventory.

These two amounts are then compared, and the lower of the two is used to cost the inventory. For example, OfficeMart uses the weighted-average method of costing inventory. The weighted-average cost and the current market price for 700 ring binders are shown above. The weighted-average cost is $805.00, and the current market price is $770.00. Using the lower of cost or market method, the market price of the binders is lower than the weighted-average cost. Therefore, the market value of $770.00 is used as the cost of the binders.

If OfficeMart used the FIFO method, the FIFO cost would be $865.00. The $770.00 market price is lower than the FIFO cost, so the market price would be used instead of the FIFO cost. If OfficeMart used the LIFO method, the LIFO cost would be $740.00. The LIFO cost is lower than the market price, so the LIFO cost would be used to cost the inventory.

FYI FOR YOUR INFORMATION

New models of computers tend to drive down the market prices of existing models. In this case, the market prices of the existing models may be less than the cost of the computers. Good inventory management attempts to minimize inventory for which the market price is lower than the cost.

- Put a set of inventory cost data on the board and direct students to walk through calculating the FIFO, LIFO, and weighted-average inventory costs.

- Ask students how to calculate the cost of merchandise sold.

- Ask students to describe the effect of rising prices on the cost of merchandise sold using the FIFO, LIFO, and weighted-average methods.

terms review

TERMS REVIEW • TERMS

first-in, first-out inventory costing method

last-in, first-out inventory costing method

weighted-average inventory costing method

lower of cost or market inventory costing method

audit your understanding

AUDIT YOUR UNDERSTANDING

1. What inventory costing method does a business usually use?
2. Which inventory costing method uses the earliest purchase prices to determine the cost of merchandise inventory?
3. During a period of increasing prices, what inventory costing method will result in the highest reported net income?
4. What two amounts are needed to apply the lower of cost or market inventory costing method?

work together 6-2

WORK TOGETHER • WORK TOGETHER

Costing ending inventory using FIFO, LIFO, and weighted average

Forms for calculating inventory costs for Cassie's Kitchen are provided in the *Working Papers*. Your instructor will guide you through the following examples.

1. Cassie's Kitchen had the following beginning inventory and purchases for a salad maker, stock number T1150. At the end of the year, 140 units remained in ending inventory. Determine the cost of the ending inventory using the FIFO, LIFO, and weighted-average inventory costing methods.

	Units	Unit Price
January, Beginning Inventory	120	$20.00
July, Purchase	100	$22.00
October, Purchase	100	$27.60

on your own 6-2

ON YOUR OWN • ON YOUR OWN

Costing ending inventory using FIFO, LIFO, and weighted average

Forms for calculating inventory costs for Cassie's Kitchen are provided in the *Working Papers*. Work independently to complete the following problem.

1. Cassie's Kitchen had the following beginning inventory and purchases for a frying pan, stock number M1030. At the end of the year, 75 units remained in ending inventory. Determine the cost of the ending inventory using the FIFO, LIFO, and weighted-average inventory costing methods.

	Units	Unit Price
January, Beginning Inventory	50	$4.20
March, Purchase	70	$4.50
November, Purchase	60	$5.05

Inventory Costing

GUIDED PRACTICE

Terms Review
Call on students to define the terms in the Terms Review. Ask the class if the definitions are correct and whether the complete definitions have been given or if anything needs to be added. Suggested definitions are given in the Glossary.

Audit Your Understanding
Call on students to answer the Audit Your Understanding questions. Ask the class if the answers are correct and/or complete. Answers are given in Appendix E of the textbook.

Work Together
Have students write the solution to the Work Together problems as you guide the class through the example. For the FIFO and LIFO methods,

- Call on a student to identify the first purchase to be used to cost the merchandise inventory.
- Call on another student to explain how to determine the number of units to be included from this purchase.
- Repeat this process until all the units have been identified.
- Ask a student to write the weighted-average method calculation on the board.

INDEPENDENT PRACTICE

On Your Own
- Assign the On Your Own problem to be worked independently.
- Use the Ongoing Assessment techniques to diagnose student understanding.

Application Problem
- Assign Application Problem 6-2: Determining inventory cost using FIFO, LIFO, weighted-average, and lower of cost or market.

Personal Trainer
- Students can access the Lesson 6-2 assessment material using this software.

Xtra! Web Site
- Students can access the Xtra! Study Tools for additional practice.

ENRICH

- Assign the Automated Accounting feature on pages 194–195 to automate Application Problem 6-2.
- Students can use the QuickBooks data files to automate Application Problem 6-2.
- Explain that many companies use LIFO because it results in a higher cost of merchandise sold during a period of rising prices and, therefore,

lower net income. Ask students why a business would want to report lower net income? *(First, the higher costs of merchandise sold better match the revenue earned during the fiscal period. Second, LIFO results in lower income taxes. To qualify to use the LIFO method for tax purposes, the IRS requires businesses to also use LIFO for financial reporting.)*

CLOSE

- Ask students to briefly summarize the procedures for calculating the cost of inventory using the FIFO, LIFO, and weighted-average inventory costing methods.

181

6-3 Estimating the Inventory

OBJECTIVES

- Define accounting terms related to planning and costing inventory.
- Identify accounting concepts and practices related to planning and costing inventory.
- Estimate the cost of merchandise inventory using selected estimating methods.
- Calculate merchandise inventory turnover ratio and average number of days' sales in merchandise inventory.

MOTIVATE

Taking a physical inventory is an expensive activity. Yet a company that does not keep a perpetual inventory needs to determine the cost of merchandise inventory in order to prepare monthly financial statements. Rather than incur the expense of a monthly physical inventory, a business can estimate its merchandise inventory.

Preview

- Preview the accounting terms and definitions introduced in this lesson: *retail method of estimating inventory, merchandise inventory turnover ratio,* and *average number of days' sales in merchandise inventory.*
- Direct students to read the headings at the top of each page in this lesson and to examine the illustrations given.

EXPLAIN

- Emphasize that the gross profit method yields an estimate of ending merchandise inventory.
- Emphasize that the gross profit percentage should be based on the prior periods' actual gross profit percentage.
- Remind students that they have already learned how to prepare an income statement with a cost of merchandise sold lesson.

DEMONSTRATE

- Direct students to the illustration as you demonstrate estimating ending inventory using the gross profit method.
- Have students point to each amount as you explain the seven steps for estimating ending inventory.

GROSS PROFIT METHOD OF ESTIMATING INVENTORY

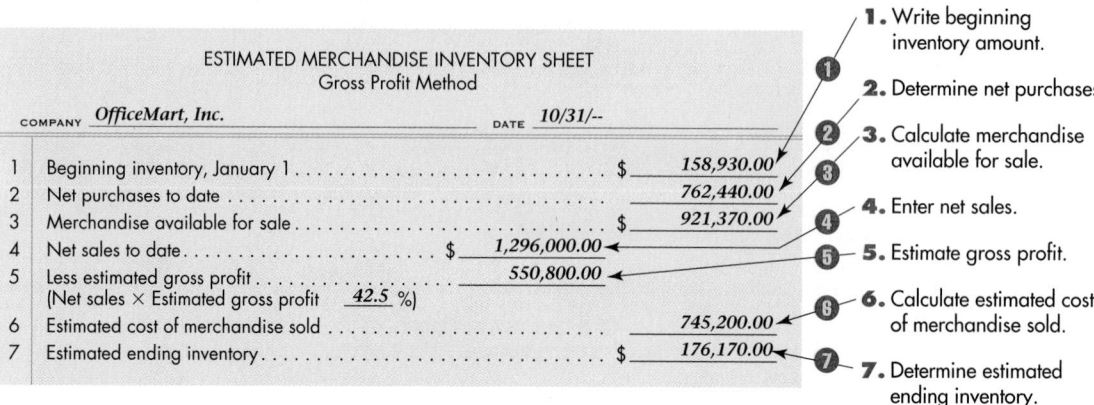

1. Write beginning inventory amount.
2. Determine net purchases.
3. Calculate merchandise available for sale.
4. Enter net sales.
5. Estimate gross profit.
6. Calculate estimated cost of merchandise sold.
7. Determine estimated ending inventory.

A business that keeps periodic inventory records and prepares monthly interim financial statements needs a cost to use for monthly ending merchandise inventory. Taking a monthly periodic inventory is usually too expensive. Therefore, monthly ending inventories may be estimated. Merchandisers who use perpetual inventory can take monthly ending inventory amounts from stock records (see the stock record on page 173), so they usually don't need to make estimates.

Estimating inventory by using the previous years' percentage of gross profit on operations is known as the gross profit method of estimating inventory. This method assumes that a continuing relationship exists between gross profit and net sales. Based on experience in previous fiscal periods, a gross profit to net sales percentage is calculated. On October 31, OfficeMart estimates its ending merchandise inventory using the gross profit method as shown above.

An ending merchandise inventory amount calculated using the gross profit method is an estimate and is not absolutely accurate. However, for monthly interim financial statements, the estimated amount is sufficiently accurate without taking a periodic inventory.

STEPS • STEPS • STEPS • STEPS • STEPS • STEPS • STEPS • STEPS • STEPS • STEPS • STEPS

ESTIMATE ENDING MERCHANDISE INVENTORY USING THE GROSS PROFIT METHOD

1. Write the January 1 beginning inventory, *158,930.00*, from the merchandise inventory account in the general ledger.
2. Determine net purchases to date, *762,440.00*. Using amounts from the general ledger, subtract purchases discounts and purchases returns and allowances from purchases.
3. Calculate merchandise available for sale, *921,370.00*, by adding lines 1 and 2.
4. Enter net sales to date, *1,296,000.00*. Using amounts from the general ledger, subtract sales discount and sales returns and allowances from sales.
5. Multiply the amount on line 4 by 42.5% to calculate estimated gross profit, *550,800.00*. The percentage, 42.5%, is an average of the gross profit percentages from OfficeMart's income statements for the past three years.
6. Calculate estimated cost of merchandise sold, *745,200.00*, by subtracting line 5 from line 4.
7. Determine estimated ending inventory, *176,170.00*, by subtracting line 6 from line 3.

MATERIALS

- Instructor's Resource CD: PowerPoint Slides
- Xtra! Study Tools on the Xtra! Web Site
- Working Papers: Teacher's Edition of the Working Papers for Lesson 6-3
- Software: Personal Trainer Student Companion CD

RETAIL METHOD OF ESTIMATING INVENTORY

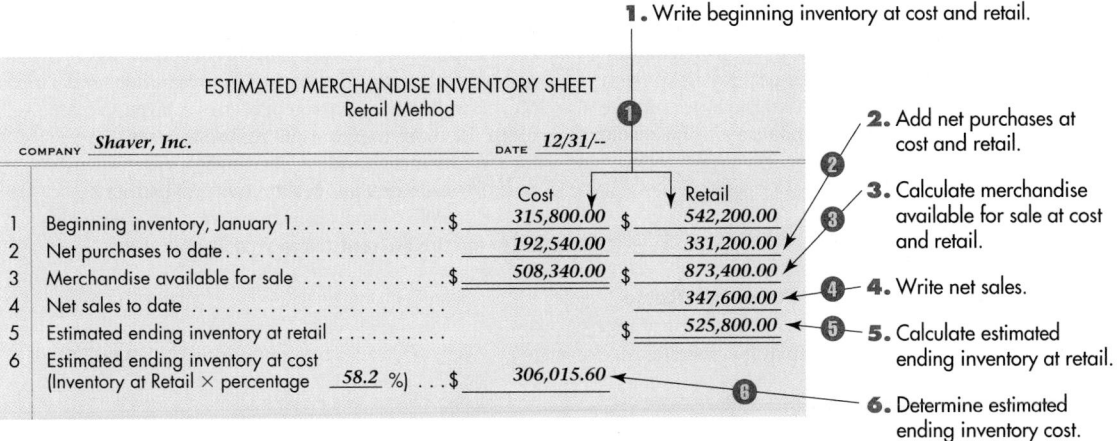

1. Write beginning inventory at cost and retail.

ESTIMATED MERCHANDISE INVENTORY SHEET
Retail Method

COMPANY *Shaver, Inc.*   DATE *12/31/--*

		Cost	Retail
1	Beginning inventory, January 1. . . . . $	315,800.00	$ 542,200.00
2	Net purchases to date.	192,540.00	331,200.00
3	Merchandise available for sale . . . . $	508,340.00	$ 873,400.00
4	Net sales to date		347,600.00
5	Estimated ending inventory at retail		$ 525,800.00
6	Estimated ending inventory at cost (Inventory at Retail × percentage *58.2* %) . . . $	306,015.60	

2. Add net purchases at cost and retail.

3. Calculate merchandise available for sale at cost and retail.

4. Write net sales.

5. Calculate estimated ending inventory at retail.

6. Determine estimated ending inventory cost.

Estimating inventory by using a percentage based on both cost and retail prices is called the **retail method of estimating inventory**. The retail method may be used instead of the gross profit method. To use the retail method, a business must keep separate records of both cost and retail prices for net purchases, net sales, and beginning merchandise inventory. An estimated ending merchandise inventory, using the retail method, for Shaver, Inc., is shown above.

STEPS   STEPS • STEPS • STEPS • STEPS • STEPS • STEPS • STEPS • STEPS • STEPS • STEPS •

ESTIMATE ENDING MERCHANDISE INVENTORY USING THE RETAIL METHOD

1 Write the January 1 beginning inventory at cost, *315,800.00*, from the merchandise inventory account in the general ledger. Write the beginning inventory at retail, *542,200.00*, which is obtained from the separate record of retail prices that must be maintained to use the retail method.

2 Add net purchases to date at cost, *192,540.00*. Using amounts from the general ledger, subtract purchases discounts and purchases returns and allowances from purchases to determine net purchases at cost. Add net purchases to date at retail, *331,200.00*, from the separate record of retail prices.

3 Calculate merchandise available for sale at cost, *508,340.00*, and at retail, *873,400.00*, by adding lines 1 and 2.

4 Write net sales to date at retail, *347,600.00*. Using amounts from the general ledger, subtract sales discount and sales returns and allowances from sales. Recall that a merchandising business always records sales at retail.

5 Calculate estimated ending inventory at retail, *525,800.00*, by subtracting line 4 from line 3.

6 Determine estimated ending inventory at cost, *306,015.60*, by multiplying line 5 by 58.2%. The percentage of merchandise available for sale at cost to merchandise available for sale at retail, 58.2%, is calculated from the amounts on line 3.

	Merchandise Available for Sale at Cost	÷	Merchandise Available for Sale at Retail	=	Percentage
+−÷×	$508,340.00	÷	$873,400.00	=	58.2%

Many businesses that need to estimate ending merchandise inventory use the gross profit method rather than the retail method. The gross profit method does not require separate records for cost and retail prices. Since OfficeMart uses a perpetual inventory, monthly ending inventories are available from the stock records without estimating or taking a monthly inventory.

Estimating the Inventory

Lesson 6-3   **183**

EXPLAIN

- Point out that ending inventory can also be estimated using the retail method.
- Explain that the retail method is based on the percentage ratio between the cost and retail prices of cost of merchandise available for sale.
- Point out that to use the retail method of estimating inventory a business must maintain separate records of both cost and retail prices for net purchases, net sales, and beginning merchandise inventory.
- Mention that many businesses that need to estimate inventory use the gross profit method because it does not require keeping separate cost and retail price records.
- State that a business that keeps a perpetual inventory or has a computerized inventory system may have the figures needed for the retail method readily available.

DEMONSTRATE

- Direct students to the illustration as you demonstrate the retail method of estimating inventory.
- Have students point to each item on the figure as you describe the six steps for estimating ending inventory.

- Explain that the more rapidly a business sells merchandise the more chance it has to make a satisfactory net income.
- Explain that there are two measures of the speed at which merchandise is sold: the merchandise inventory turnover ratio and the average number of days' sales in merchandise inventory.
- Explain that a merchandise inventory turnover ratio expresses a relationship between an average inventory and the cost of merchandise sold.
- Explain that a low merchandise inventory turnover ratio means inventory is not selling rapidly (turning over) and therefore return on investment is low.
- Explain that an inventory turnover ratio of 5.4 means that the average amount of merchandise inventory was sold 5.4 times during the fiscal period.
- Emphasize that inventory turnover ratios can be compared with those of similar businesses through national trade associations.
- Point out that if an inventory turnover ratio is too low, managers need to better control the quantity of merchandise inventory on hand.
- Explain that the inventory turnover ratio is used to calculate the average number of days' sales in merchandise inventory by dividing it into the number of days in a year.

MERCHANDISE INVENTORY TURNOVER

The more rapidly a business sells merchandise, the more chance it has to make a satisfactory net income. For example, more revenue results from selling 100 ring binders per day than from selling 60 binders per day. Two measures of the speed with which merchandise inventory is sold are:

1. Merchandise inventory turnover ratio.
2. Average number of days' sales in merchandise inventory.

Merchandise Inventory Turnover Ratio
The number of times the average amount of merchandise inventory is sold during a specific period of time is called the **merchandise inventory turnover ratio**. A merchandise inventory turnover ratio expresses a relationship between an average inventory and the cost of merchandise sold. Merchandise inventory represents a large investment for most merchandising businesses. Therefore, a low merchandise inventory turnover ratio usually indicates a low return on investment.

OfficeMart's merchandise inventory turnover ratio for the current fiscal year is calculated as follows.

	January 1 Merchandise Inventory	+	December 31 Merchandise Inventory	÷	2	=	Average Merchandise Inventory
	($168,365.00	+	$173,325.00)	÷	2	=	$170,845.00

Cost of Merchandise Sold	÷	Average Merchandise Inventory	=	Merchandise Inventory Turnover Ratio
$925,368.00	÷	$170,845.00	=	5.4 times

A 5.4 merchandise inventory turnover ratio means that the business sold the average merchandise inventory 5.4 times during the current year. National trade associations publish this ratio and others. OfficeMart can compare its ratio with the ratio for similar businesses which have an average merchandise inventory turnover ratio of 7.0 times. OfficeMart's turnover ratio of 5.4 is below the industry standard of 7.0. To correct this situation, OfficeMart's managers should consider taking action to better control the quantity of merchandise inventory on hand.

Average Number of Days' Sales in Merchandise Inventory
The period of time needed to sell an average amount of merchandise inventory is called the **average number of days' sales in merchandise inventory**. The average number of days' sales in merchandise inventory based on a 5.4 merchandise inventory turnover ratio is calculated as shown below.

Days in Year	÷	Merchandise Inventory Turnover Ratio	=	Average Number of Days' Sales in Merchandise Inventory
365	÷	5.4	=	68 days

The average number of days' sales in merchandise inventory is rounded to the nearest day. This level of accuracy provides managers with adequate information to make sound business decisions.

Inventory Planning and Valuation

TEACHING STRATEGIES   DIFFERENT LEARNING STYLES

Kinesthetic Learner. The kinesthetic learner should have the opportunity to perform the calculations to solve the formula. One way to accomplish this is to develop several examples using different amounts for beginning and ending inventory. The student should calculate the merchandise inventory turnover ratio for each example.

An average of 68 days means that, on average, each item in merchandise inventory is sold 68 days after it is purchased. Published averages from trade associations show that businesses similar to OfficeMart have an average number of days' sales in merchandise inventory of 53. OfficeMart's management should seek ways to increase its turnover of merchandise inventory.

The higher the number of days in merchandise inventory, the longer merchandise tends to remain unsold. A business can reduce the merchandise inventory turnover ratio and the number of days' sales in merchandise inventory by reducing the size of the inventory kept on hand. However, a lower inventory level may not allow a business to meet customers' demands. A business also can improve its turnover ratio and the number of days' sales in merchandise inventory by increasing the amount of merchandise sold during a month or a year.

©GETTY IMAGES/PHOTODISC

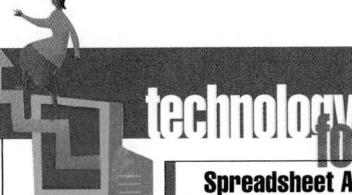

technology for business

TECHNOLOGY FOR BUSINESS • TECHNOLOGY FOR BUSINESS • TECHNOLOGY FOR BUSINE

Spreadsheet Activity—Valuation of Inventory

Front Porch, a small retail store, sells hand-crafted wooden porch furniture. Front Porch uses the weighted-average inventory costing method. Front Porch currently carries three items in its inventory: high-back chairs, rocking chairs, and porch swings.

The following inventory data are available for high-back chairs for the first six months of the year:

High-back Chairs

Purchases	Units	Unit Price
January, beginning inventory	18	$35.00
February	75	40.00
April	10	45.00
June	5	50.00
June 30, physical inventory	26	

Required

1. Create a spreadsheet to calculate the June 30 inventory for high-back chairs. Use the weighted-average inventory costing method, shown on page 177, as a model for creating the spreadsheet. Create formulas for the total cost of each purchase and for the column totals. Save the spreadsheet as

HIGHBACK. (Hint: The weighted-average cost of the ending inventory should be $1,042.41.)

2. Make copies of the spreadsheet you created in 1 to calculate the value of other inventory items for Front Porch. Use the information below.

Rocking Chairs

Purchases	Units	Unit Price
January, beginning inventory	2	$42.00
February	18	42.00
March	6	50.00
April	3	57.00
June 30, physical inventory	11	

Porch Swings

Purchases	Units	Unit Price
January, beginning inventory	1	$80.00
January	8	85.00
March	6	88.00
May	2	92.00
June 30, physical inventory	3	

Estimating the Inventory

TECHNOLOGY FOR BUSINESS

The Technology for Business feature is designed to show students common business applications of technology. Ask students if they can think of any other spreadsheet applications a small business that does not have an automated accounting system could use.

GUIDED PRACTICE

Terms Review

Call on students to define the terms in the Terms Review. Ask the class if the definitions are correct and whether the complete definitions have been given or if anything needs to be added. Suggested definitions for all terms are given in the Glossary.

Audit Your Understanding

Call on students to answer the Audit Your Understanding questions. Ask the class if each answer is correct and/or complete. Answers are given in Appendix E of the textbook.

Work Together

Have students write the solution to the Work Together problem as you guide the class through the examples.

- For each calculation, call on students to state the answer to a calculation.
- Call on another student to explain either how the amount was calculated or where the amount was obtained.

INDEPENDENT PRACTICE

On Your Own

- Assign the On Your Own problem to be worked independently.
- Use the Ongoing Assessment techniques to diagnose student understanding.

Application Problem

- Assign Application Problem 6-3: Estimating cost of merchandise inventory using estimating methods.
- Assign Application Problem 6-4: Calculating merchandise inventory turnover ratio and average number of days' sales in merchandise inventory.

Personal Trainer

- Students can access the Lesson 6-3 assessment material using this software.

Xtra! Web Site

- Students can access the Xtra! Study Tools for additional practice.

ENRICH

- Assign the Technology for Business feature. Students can practice writing formulas on paper rather than actually booting spreadsheet software if time is a factor.

CLOSE

- Ask students to summarize the purpose of estimating inventory.
- Ask students to explain the meaning of the merchandise inventory turnover ratio and the number of days' sales in merchandise inventory.

• terms review

TERMS REVIEW • TERMS

retail method of estimating inventory
merchandise inventory turnover ratio
average number of days' sales in merchandise inventory

• audit your understanding

AUDIT YOUR

1. On what assumptions is the gross profit method of estimating inventory based?
2. To use the retail method of estimating inventory, what records must be kept?
3. Explain a merchandise inventory turnover ratio of 5.0.
4. How is the average number of days' sales in merchandise inventory calculated?

• work together 6-3

WORK TOGETHER • WORK TOGETHER

Estimating inventory using the gross profit and retail methods

The following information is available for Handy Hardware for the month of April. Estimated merchandise inventory sheets are provided in the *Working Papers*. Your instructor will guide you through the following examples.

	Cost	Retail
Beginning Inventory, April 1	$124,850	$193,400
Net Purchases	73,230	110,340
Net Sales		138,500

Gross Profit Percentage: 37%
Percentage of merchandise available for sale at cost to merchandise available at retail: 65.2%

1. Estimate the ending inventory using the gross profit method.
2. Estimate the ending inventory using the retail method.

• on your own 6-3

ON YOUR OWN • ON YOUR OWN • ON YOUR OWN

Estimating inventory using the gross profit and retail methods

The following information is available for Handy Hardware for the month of October. Estimated merchandise inventory sheets are provided in the *Working Papers*. Work independently to complete the following problem.

	Cost	Retail
Beginning Inventory, October 1	$182,570	$276,380
Net Purchases	115,440	190,730
Net Sales		204,340

Gross Profit Percentage: 37%
Percentage of merchandise available for sale at cost to merchandise available at retail: 63.8%

1. Estimate the ending inventory using the gross profit method.
2. Estimate the ending inventory using the retail method.

After completing this chapter, you can

1. Define accounting terms related to planning and costing inventory.

2. Identify accounting concepts and practices related to planning, counting, and costing inventory.

3. Describe the nature of merchandise inventory.

4. Determine the cost of merchandise inventory using selected costing methods.

5. Estimate the cost of merchandise inventory using selected estimating methods.

6. Calculate merchandise inventory turnover ratio and average number of days' sales in merchandise inventory.

Explore Accounting
EXPLORE ACCOUNTING · EXPLORE ACCOUNTING · EXPLORE ACCOUN

Computerized Purchasing Systems

The traditional method for purchasing inventory requires many documents and manual steps to complete. The process involves many employees, requires several days to place an order, and is subject to many clerical errors.

A modern, computerized purchasing system might work as follows: The company's computer continually monitors stock levels against minimum quantities established by management. When the quantity of any inventory item falls below its reorder point, the computer automatically sends a message to a vendor's computer with the order information. (Management frequently enters into long-term contracts with selected vendors that govern prices and delivery schedules.) The vendor's computer immediately informs its warehouse to ship the items. When the items are received, the company's computer sends a message to its bank's computer instructing the bank to transfer funds to the vendor's account.

The direct transfer of information between computers of two or more companies is called electronic data interchange (EDI). EDI reduces the cost of placing an order by reducing paperwork and labor costs. The most important advantage, however, results from improved delivery times. The traditional manual ordering system required several days or weeks to process an order. An EDI system can have the order in transit on the same day the order is placed. Improved delivery time allows companies to reduce inventory levels, which results in substantial cost savings.

Required:
Contact your local bank and inquire if its computer system uses EDI to support its customers' purchasing systems.

Inventory Planning and Valuation

Chapter 6   **187**

EXPLORE ACCOUNTING
EXPLORE ACCOUNTING

This activity can be completed by groups of three or four students. Each group can be assigned a local bank, savings and loan, or credit union. Answers will vary depending on the willingness of the bank to supply the information. Since some groups may get a negative or limited response, evaluate the groups on their effort to obtain the information, rather than their actual findings. As an alternate approach, ask a local banker who is familiar with EDI to speak to the class.

PUTTING IT ALL TOGETHER

- Review the Chapter Summary.
- Ask students to prepare a list of the new concepts introduced in this chapter.
- Discuss that the methods presented in this chapter are used to determine the actual historical cost or an estimate of merchandise inventory.

INDEPENDENT PRACTICE

- Assign Mastery Problem 6-5 to students who need the reinforcement of a problem that combines all activities from the chapter in one problem; this will be most students.
- Assign Challenge Problem 6-6 to accelerated students who do not require the reinforcement of the Mastery Problem.
- Assign Study Guide 6.
- Students can access Personal Trainer to work end-of-chapter problems on the computer.
- Students can access the Xtra! Web Site for the Xtra! Review and Quizzing.
- Students can access the Student Companion CD for additional review material.

ONGOING ASSESSMENT

- Review solutions to the assigned problems in class, diagnosing trouble spots.

RETEACH

- Call on students to describe how they avoid the trouble spots diagnosed.
- Use reteaching suggestions from lesson plans as required.
- Assign Recycling Problem 6-1 if needed.

ENRICH

- Assign the Explore Accounting feature. Ask students to share the information they have gathered in a report to the class.
- Students can access the Xtra! Web Site for the Xtra! Enrichment material.
- Assign the Applied Communication activity.
- Assign the Cases for Critical Thinking.
- Assign the SCANS Workplace Competency.
- Assign the Auditing for Errors activity.
- Assign the Analyzing Costco's Financial Statements activity.
- Assign the Automated Accounting feature on pages 194–195.

6-1 **APPLICATION PROBLEM** (AUTOMATED ACCOUNTING) (PEACHTREE) (QUICKBOOKS)   accountingxtra.swlearning.com

Keeping perpetual inventory records

Bowman Lawn and Garden sells lawn and garden equipment to a variety of customers. For many years the business used a periodic inventory system. However, it switched to a perpetual merchandise inventory system two years ago. The perpetual system gives the company better control of its inventory.

Instructions:

1. Complete the heading of a stock record for each of the following two inventory items. Also record the balance on April 1 of the current year for each item.

   Lawn mower:
     Stock number R263
     Reorder, 60
     Minimum, 15
     Location, bin 41
     Number on hand April 1, 32
   Hedge trimmer:
     Stock number J184
     Reorder, 35
     Minimum, 8
     Location, bin 49
     Number on hand April 1, 17

2. Record on the stock records the merchandise items received and sold during April of the current year. Source documents are abbreviated as follows: sales invoice, S; purchase invoice, P.

Transactions:

April	2.	Sold 9 lawn mowers to Rogers Lawn and Garden, S211.
	3.	Sold 5 hedge trimmers to Besotral, Inc., S212.
	6.	Lawn Haven bought 6 lawn mowers and 6 hedge trimmers, S213.
	10.	Received 35 hedge trimmers from Hughes Manufacturing, P742.
	11.	Gilbert Co. bought 10 hedge trimmers, S214.
	15.	Five more lawn mowers were sold to Rogers Lawn and Garden, S215.
	16.	Lawn King Manufacturing shipped 60 lawn mowers, P743.
	19.	Sold 30 lawn mowers to Christie's Landscaping, S216.
	20.	Home Beautiful bought 20 lawn mowers and 15 hedge trimmers, S217.
	24.	Twelve more lawn mowers were sold to Lawn Haven, S218.
	25.	Received 60 lawn mowers from Lawn King Manufacturing, P744.
	28.	Sold 10 hedge trimmers to Greene, Inc., S219.
	29.	Hughes Manufacturing shipped 35 hedge trimmers, P745.
	30.	Sold 7 lawn mowers to Movin' Mowers, S220.

TEACHING STRATEGIES   APPLIED MATHEMATICS

End-of-chapter problems for Chapter 6 include a large amount of computational work. Students should be encouraged to use calculators to allow them to focus their attention on the procedures rather than on the arithmetic.

6-2 APPLICATION PROBLEM `AUTOMATED ACCOUNTING` `QUICKBOOKS`

Determining inventory cost using FIFO, LIFO, weighted average, and lower of cost or market

Accounting records at Wayne, Inc., show the following purchases, periodic inventory counts, and market prices.

Stock No.	January 1 Inventory		First Purchase		Second Purchase		Third Purchase		Fourth Purchase		December 31 Inventory	December 31 Market Price
	No.	Unit Price	No.	Unit Price	No.	Unit Price	No.	Unit Price	No.	Unit Price		
A30	15	$8.00	15	$10.00	15	$12.00	20	$14.00	20	$10.00	35	$12.00
B18	10	9.00	10	9.00	12	9.00	12	8.00	12	8.00	30	7.50
C45	22	5.00	30	6.00	30	6.00	30	7.00	30	8.00	64	8.00
D12	12	7.00	5	7.00	5	9.00	10	8.00	5	7.00	20	7.50

Instructions:

1. Calculate the inventory costs using the FIFO, LIFO, and weighted average inventory costing methods. Assume that the lower of cost or market method is applied to each inventory item separately. Use a form similar to the following. The inventory cost for Stock No. A30 is given as an example.

Stock No.	Dec. 31 Inventory	Market Price	Inventory Costing Method								
			FIFO			LIFO			Weighted Average		
			Unit Price	Total Cost	Lower of Cost or Market	Unit Price	Total Cost	Lower of Cost or Market	Unit Price	Total Cost	Lower of Cost or Market
A30	35	35 @ $12.00 = $420.00	20 @ $10.00 15 @ 14.00 }	$410.00	$410.00	15 @ $ 8.00 15 @ 10.00 5 @ 12.00 }	$330.00	$330.00	35 @ $10.94	$382.90	$382.90

2. Total the three Lower of Cost or Market columns.
3. Which of the three methods of costing inventory results in the highest inventory cost for Wayne, Inc.? Which results in the lowest inventory cost?

6-3 APPLICATION PROBLEM

Estimating cost of merchandise inventory using estimating methods

The records of Walker, Inc., show the following on December 31 of the current year.

Item	Cost	Retail
Beginning merchandise inventory...........	$ 42,400.00	$ 70,000.00
Net purchases to date....................	136,000.00	227,400.00
Net sales to date.......................	—	208,800.00
Gross profit percentage..................	40%	

Instructions:

1. Calculate the corporation's estimated ending inventory using the gross profit method of estimating inventory. Round the percentages to the nearest 0.1%.
2. Calculate the corporation's estimated ending inventory using the retail method of estimating inventory. Round the percentages to the nearest 0.1%.

Application Problem 6-2
Total cost of ending inventory: FIFO, 1,259.00; LIFO, 1,063.00; weighted-average, 1.172.59.

Application Problem 6-3
Estimated ending inventory, gross profit method: 53,120.00; Estimated ending inventory, retail method, 53,160.00.

6-4 APPLICATION PROBLEM

Calculating merchandise inventory turnover ratio and average number of days' sales in merchandise inventory

Selected information for three corporations follows.

	Corporation		
Item	A	B	C
Beginning Merchandise Inventory	$ 15,800.00	$ 80,500.00	$ 64,300.00
Ending Merchandise Inventory	21,200.00	78,900.00	54,600.00
Cost of Merchandise Sold	167,700.00	848,000.00	567,400.00

Instructions:

1. For each corporation, calculate the merchandise inventory turnover ratio. Round the ratio to the nearest 0.1%.
2. For each corporation, calculate the average number of days' sales in merchandise inventory. Round the amount to the nearest day.
3. Which corporation has the best merchandise inventory turnover ratio?

6-5 MASTERY PROBLEM

Determining cost of merchandise inventory; estimating cost of merchandise inventory using estimating methods; calculating merchandise inventory turnover ratio and average number of days' sales in merchandise inventory

On December 31 of the current year, Sowell, Inc., took a periodic inventory. The following information is obtained from Sowell's records.

Stock No.	January 1 Inventory		First Purchase		Second Purchase		December 31 Inventory	Market Price
	No.	Unit Price	No.	Unit Price	No.	Unit Price		
R46	14	$ 7.00	15	$ 8.00	15	$ 9.00	18	$ 9.50
S10	16	5.00	10	5.00	10	8.00	26	4.75
T76	8	12.00	15	11.00	15	11.00	25	10.00
U92	7	8.00	7	8.00	7	8.00	10	8.00
V17	5	4.00	10	6.00	10	7.00	5	6.00

Instructions:

1. Calculate the inventory costs using the FIFO, LIFO, and weighted-average inventory costing methods. Use the form in the *Working Papers*.
2. Total the three Total Cost columns.
3. Sowell uses the LIFO inventory costing method to determine the cost of inventory. Use the market price given in the form at the beginning of the problem to determine the cost of inventory using the lower of cost or market. Total the Lower of Cost or Market column. Use the form in the *Working Papers*.
4. Calculate the corporation's estimated ending inventory using the gross profit method of estimating inventory. The corporation's records show the following on December 31 of the current year.

Item	Cost	Retail
Beginning merchandise inventory.	$21,200.00	$ 35,000.00
Net purchases to date.	68,000.00	113,700.00
Net sales to date.	—	103,700.00
Gross profit percentage.	40%	

APPLIED SKILLS WRITING ACROSS THE CURRICULUM

Writing paragraphs and short essays. The Cases for Critical Thinking are short, practical applications of the accounting principles developed in the chapter. Some cases are planned to present problems related to the chapter but not specifically discussed and answered in the chapter. These cases present an opportunity for critical thinking and decision making. These cases also require more than a short objective-type response. Therefore they provide ideal practice in writing paragraphs and short essays.

5. Calculate the corporation's estimated ending inventory using the retail method of estimating inventory. Round the percentage to the nearest 0.1%.
6. Use the information and the estimated inventory calculated in Instruction 4. Calculate the corporation's merchandise inventory turnover ratio. Round the ratio to the nearest 0.1%.
7. Calculate the corporation's average number of days' sales in merchandise inventory. Round the amount to the nearest day.

6-6 CHALLENGE PROBLEM
Determining the unit price of merchandise inventory purchases

Minder, Inc., recently received a shipment of merchandise inventory. Minder maintains a perpetual inventory using unit prices including freight and cash discounts. The following information is from the purchase invoice for the shipment.

Stock No.	Quantity	Unit Price	Total Cost
A69	50	$2.00	$100.00
V56	15	6.00	90.00
X28	30	4.00	120.00
W12	20	3.00	60.00
S92	5	8.00	40.00
Subtotal			$410.00
Freight			20.50
Cash Discount			(8.20)
Total Cost			$422.30

Instructions:
1. Divide the total cost by the subtotal. Round the percentage to the nearest 0.1%.
2. Calculate the adjusted unit price of each item by multiplying the percentage calculated in Instruction 1 by the unit price of the item.
3. Calculate the adjusted total cost for each item by multiplying the quantity by the adjusted unit price.

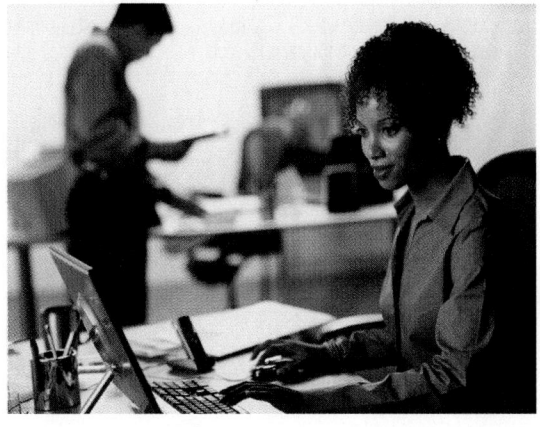

©GETTY IMAGES/PHOTODISC

Challenge Problem 6-6
Adjusted unit price percentage: 103.0%
Adjusted total costs: A69, 103.00; V56, 92.70; X28, 123.60; W12, 61.80; S92, 41.20.

APPLIED SKILLS LANGUAGE ARTS

Exploring spelling checker software. Students may wish to rely too heavily on the spelling checker feature of their word processing software. A word may be spelled correctly, but it may not be the word that should be used. Spend some time giving examples of incorrect words that the spelling checker cannot identify as misspelled. ("if" instead of "is"; "its" instead of "it's"; "the" instead of "them"; etc.) Ask students to supply other pairs of words.

APPLIED COMMUNICATION

Have students contact local retail businesses to determine the methods they use to control theft and fraud. Students may write a report or share their findings with the class, with one student making a list on the blackboard or an overhead transparency. Discuss how these methods may work and which ones should be most effective. Then discuss why theft and fraud results in higher consumer prices. (Theft and fraud adds to the business' costs without contributing to revenue, since no revenue is realized from any items lost or stolen.) When students discuss what actions they would take if a friend were shoplifting, they may be beginning to see the situation from the merchant's point of view.

CASES FOR CRITICAL THINKING

Case 1

This suggestion is not necessarily a good one. Benefits of keeping a perpetual inventory are: (a) The perpetual inventory method helps alert the business to the need to reorder individual items. (b) Actual inventory information is available for use on monthly interim financial statements without taking a periodic inventory or estimating ending inventories. If a business has relatively few different items of merchandise which can be counted easily and quickly, a perpetual inventory is not needed and a periodic inventory will be sufficient. However, most merchandising businesses carry many items and can benefit from a perpetual inventory.

Case 2

Hastings is probably taking a physical inventory too frequently. Since the company sells many different items, the cost of taking the quarterly inventory may not be worth the value received from it. However, the cost of maintaining a perpetual inventory system for a large variety of inventory may be just as costly unless a computerized inventory system with point-of-sale cash registers is used. If frequent inventory information is needed, the computerized system would be the recommendation. If such frequent information is not needed, recommend that physical inventory be taken once a year and estimated methods be used for quarterly statements.

• applied communication

Each year, retail businesses lose millions of dollars to theft and fraud. As consumers, we all pay for these illegal actions in the form of higher prices.

Required:

1. Research the actions that retail businesses take to control theft and fraud. Write a short report about your findings.
2. Explain why businesses must charge higher prices for their goods as a result of theft and fraud.
3. Discuss in class what actions you would take if you were with a friend who was shoplifting.

• cases for critical thinking

Case 1

Quitman, Inc., keeps a perpetual merchandise inventory. A new member of the board of directors notices that two employees work full time keeping the inventory records. The director suggests that the corporation stop using the perpetual inventory system and take a periodic inventory once a year when information is needed for financial statements. The director also suggests that the salaries saved by eliminating the positions of the two inventory employees will be more than the cost of an annual periodic inventory. What is your opinion of this suggestion? Explain your answer.

Case 2

Hastings, Inc., sells many different items of sports equipment. The corporation takes a periodic inventory once every three months for use in preparing quarterly financial statements. A newly employed accountant suggests that the corporation change over to a perpetual inventory. What would you recommend? Explain your recommendation.

• SCANS workplace competency

Resource Competency: Allocating Time

Concept: Employers need workers who can identify job tasks, rank tasks in order of importance, estimate time to accomplish tasks, develop a schedule for completing tasks, and adjust task schedules as needed. Wasted time costs employers money.

Application: Prepare a daily schedule for yourself for one week. List all activities that you need to complete daily, including classes, extracurricular activities, homework, employment hours, social events, meals, hygiene, etc. Allocate time slots during each day to complete each task. As you progress through the week, make changes to your schedule as needed.

Inventory Planning and Valuation

SCANS WORKPLACE COMPETENCY

Consider distributing copies of a daily calendar with hours broken down into 15-minute intervals or ask students to design a daily planner using a word processing or spreadsheet application.

auditing for errors

The following information was taken from the records of Centuria Music Store for the month of September.

	Cost	Retail
Beginning Inventory, September 1	$174,636	$279,418
Net Purchases	60,842	97,347
Net Sales		225,300

The bookkeeper prepared the following estimated merchandise inventory sheet. Verify the numbers on the report. List any errors and the correct amounts.

Estimated Merchandise Inventory Sheet
Retail Method

Company: Centuria Music Store   Date: September, 20--

	Cost	Retail
Beginning inventory, September 1	174,636	279,418
Net purchases to date	60,482	97,347
Merchandise available for sale	235,118	376,765
Net sales to date		225,300
Estimated ending inventory at retail		151,465
Estimated ending inventory at cost	94,514.16	
(Inventory at Retail × percentage 62.4%)		

analyzing Costco's financial statements

Most companies include information about inventory in the first note to the financial statement, "Summary of Significant Accounting Policies." This note usually tells the reader which method the company uses to value the cost of its ending inventory.

Instructions:

1. Using Note 1, beginning on page B-9 of Appendix B in this textbook, locate the paragraph titled "Merchandise Inventories." List the method Costco primarily uses to value the cost of its U.S. merchandise inventory and the method Costco primarily uses to value the cost of its foreign merchandise inventory.

2. Calculate Costco's merchandise inventory turnover ratio and average number of days' sales in merchandise inventory as of August 31, 2003. Use the information on the Ten Year Operating and Financial Highlights on pages B-2 and B-3 and the Consolidated Balance Sheets on page B-5.

3. Go to Costco's web site (www.costco.com) and locate the financial statements for the most current year available. (Look for "Investor Relations" or a similar link.) Calculate Costco's merchandise inventory turnover ratio and average number of days' sales in merchandise inventory for the current year.

4. Did these measures improve or worsen from 2003 to the current year?

Errors are as follows:

1. Net purchases to date at cost should be 60,842.

2. Merchandise available for sale at cost should be 235,478.

3. Percentage used to calculate estimated ending inventory at cost should be 62.5%. *(235,478/376,765 = .625)*

4. Estimated ending inventory at cost should be 94,665.63.

ANALYZING COSTCO'S FINANCIAL STATEMENTS

1. U. S. merchandise inventory is primarily valued using LIFO. Foreign merchandise inventory is primarily valued using FIFO.

2. Merchandise inventory turnover = 11.5 times

    a. (3,339,428,000 + 3,127,221,000) ÷ 2 = 3,233,324.50

    b. 37,235,000,000 ÷ 3,233,324.50 = 31.7 days

3. Answer depends on results found for the current year.

4. Answer depends on results found for the current year.

TEACHING STRATEGIES   PORTFOLIO ASSESSMENT

Proper and accurate accounting for merchandise inventory is critical to a business. Large businesses may have millions of dollars worth of merchandise inventory on hand and accurate records may make the difference in a business' success. Students should emphasize their learning of this topic by selecting an example of a comprehensive sample of their work in this chapter, either the mastery problem or a problem from a test to include in their portfolio. A copy of the Portfolio Assessment form (blackline master in the Teacher's Resource Guide; also on the Student Companion CD) should be completed by the student and the Description section should include any comments regarding how the student mastered these concepts and procedures. Alternatively, students might include in their portfolios printed reports from an Automated Accounting or Spreadsheet Accounting problem.

EXPLAIN

- Preview the terms used or introduced in this feature: inventory transaction report and inventory exceptions.

- Explain that a computerized inventory system allows businesses better access to accurate information about the inventory.

- Explain that inventory processing includes recording items sold, ordered, and received in the inventory records.

- Point out that inventory records are yet another database maintained by the Automated Accounting software.

- Explain that an inventory system must have a record for each item of merchandise in the inventory.

- Explain that inventory exceptions are those inventory items that require monitoring or action such as reordering.

- Explain that the inventory system can prepare a report of the value of ending inventory using either FIFO, LIFO, or average cost (weighted-average).

- Explain that the yearly sales report shows unit and dollar sales for each item in inventory on a year-to-date basis.

DEMONSTRATE

Inventory processing

- Demonstrate clicking the Other icon on the toolbar and then clicking the Inventory tab in the Other Activities screen.

- Demonstrate selecting the inventory item from the inventory drop-down list.

- Demonstrate entering transaction data in the appropriate fields.

- *Automated Accounting 8.0* integrates the inventory, purchases, and sales systems to keep a perpetual inventory. Demonstrate how purchase orders, purchase invoices, and sales invoices are entered in the Other Activities window to update inventory stock records.

- Demonstrate clicking OK to record the transaction.

Inventory Planning and Valuation

Inventory planning and valuation is necessary to accurately account for inventory and report asset values in financial statements. Merchandise inventory is usually the largest current asset of a merchandising business. Therefore, it is important to select an inventory system that provides the most accurate and up-to-date inventory valuations. Inventory planning and valuation may be accomplished by using either a manual or an automated inventory system. Today, most businesses use automated inventory systems.

Inventory Processing

Inventory processing includes recording items sold, ordered, and received in the inventory records. The inventory records are stored in a database that is separate from the general ledger database. To update the inventory records:

1. Click the Other Activities toolbar button.

2. Select the Inventory tab to display the data entry window.

3. Enter the data for items sold, ordered, and received.

4. Click OK.

Automated Accounting 8.0 has a more complete inventory system:

1. When inventory items are ordered, a purchase order is recorded in the Purch. Order tab of the Other Activities window.

2. When an order is received, a purchase invoice is issued and recorded in the Purch. Invoice tab of the Other Activities window.

3. When merchandise is sold, the sales invoice is entered in the Sales Invoice tab of the Other Activities window.

After all inventory processing data have been keyed, an Inventory Transaction report should be displayed, verified for accuracy, and printed. To print the Inventory Transaction report:

1. Click the Reports toolbar button.

2. Choose Inventory Reports from Select a Report Group.

3. Select Inventory Transactions from the Choose a Report to Display list.

4. Click OK.

5. Enter the Start and End date for the report.

6. Click OK.

The inventory transactions report is checked for accuracy by comparing the report totals with the totals on the inventory source documents or forms.

Inventory Exceptions

Inventory exceptions are those inventory items that require close monitoring. When inventory levels are low or there are no stock items, management will need to reorder or take action. The software provides an option for generating an exception report. This report lists items that are out of stock and items that are at or below the reorder point. To generate the report, select Inventory Exceptions from the list of inventory reports.

Inventory Valuation

Automated Accounting 8.0 or higher allows users to determine inventory costs using the average cost, LIFO, or FIFO costing methods. Reports can be generated to see the valuations using each of the inventory cost methods mentioned.

1. Click the Reports toolbar button.

2. Choose the Inventory Reports option button from the Select a Report Group list.

3. Select a valuation option from the Choose a Report to Display list.

Yearly Sales

The yearly sales report accumulates total sales throughout the year for each stock item. Therefore, a yearly sales report showing total sales for January, generated at month end, would include only sales for January. February's month-end report would show the accumulation of total sales for the months of January and February.

The yearly sales report provides management with unit and dollar sales for each inventory item.

1. Click the Reports toolbar button.

2. Select the Inventory Reports option from the Select a Report Group.

3. Choose the Yearly Sales option.

4. Click OK.

AUTOMATING ACCOUNTING PROBLEM 6-1

Instructions:

1. Load *Automated Accounting 8.0* or higher software.

2. Select database A06-1 (Advanced Course Application Problem 6-1) from the accounting template disk.

3. Select File from the menu bar and choose the Save As menu command. Key the path to the drive and directory that contains your data files. Save the database with a filename of XXX061 (where XXX are your initials).

4. Read the Problem Instruction screen by clicking the Browser toolbar button.

5. Refer to page 188 for data used in this problem.

6. Exit the Automated Accounting software.

AUTOMATING ACCOUNTING PROBLEM 6-2

Instructions:

1. Load *Automated Accounting 8.0* or higher software.

2. Select database A06-2 (Advanced Course Application Problem 6-2) from the accounting template disk.

3. Select File from the menu bar and choose the Save As menu command. Key the path to the drive and directory that contains your data files. Save the database with a filename of XXX062 (where XXX are your initials).

4. Read the Problem Instruction screen by clicking the Browser toolbar button.

5. Refer to page 189 for data used in this problem.

6. Exit the Automated Accounting software.

DEMONSTRATE

Generating inventory reports

- Demonstrate clicking the Reports toolbar button and choosing the Inventory Reports option button from the Select a Report Group list.

- Demonstrate choosing Inventory Transactions from the Choose a Report to Display list.

- Demonstrate clicking OK for the selection and entering the Start and End date for the report.

- Demonstrate clicking OK to display the report.

- Repeat the demonstration for each different inventory report.
  - Inventory Exceptions
  - Valuation (options include fifo, lifo, and average cost)
  - Yearly Sales

- Point out that each report should be checked for accuracy before printing the report.

PRACTICE

- Assign Automating Application Problem 6-1: Keeping perpetual inventory records.

- Assign Automating Application Problem 6-2: Determining inventory cost using fifo, lifo, weighted-average, and lower of cost or market.

ASSESSMENT

- Use the Electronic Auditor to assess student understanding.

Inventory Planning and Valuation

Chapter 6   **195**

TEACHING STRATEGIES   PORTFOLIO ASSESSMENT

Students should be encouraged to print at least one report from one of the Automated Accounting problems to include in their portfolio to demonstrate mastery of automated accounting systems. A copy of the Portfolio Assessment form (blackline master in the Teacher's Resource Guide; also on the Student Companion CD) should be completed by the student and the Description section should include any comments regarding how the student mastered these concepts and procedures.

Part 3 explores various general accounting adjustments. Adjustments sometimes involve more than just calculating amounts. Procedures for calculating some adjustments involve various aspects of accounting that must be explored before the actual adjustment figure is calculated.

Chapter 7 describes accounting for uncollectible accounts and the various methods of writing off accounts. These methods of writing off accounts lead directly to the adjusting entries for uncollectible accounts.

Chapter 8 explains plant assets and the methods for depreciating them. Depletion and property taxes are also covered in this chapter. A general description of the procedures for calculating depreciation using the MACRS method is also presented. Most businesses use one of the generally accepted accounting methods for recording depreciation. The MACRS method is generally used only for the preparation of federal income tax returns. Therefore, generally accepted accounting practices for the preparation of financial statements are emphasized in the text. More detailed information on MACRS can be obtained from the Internal Revenue Service.

Chapter 9 introduces accounting for notes payable, prepaid expenses, and accrued expenses. The procedures for calculating adjusting entries and recording reversing entries are covered for these topics. Chapter 10 then looks at the same aspects of notes receivable, unearned revenue, and accrued revenue.

AUTOMATED ACCOUNTING

For those teachers who wish to fully integrate the accounting program, an Automated Accounting feature is provided at the end of each chapter.

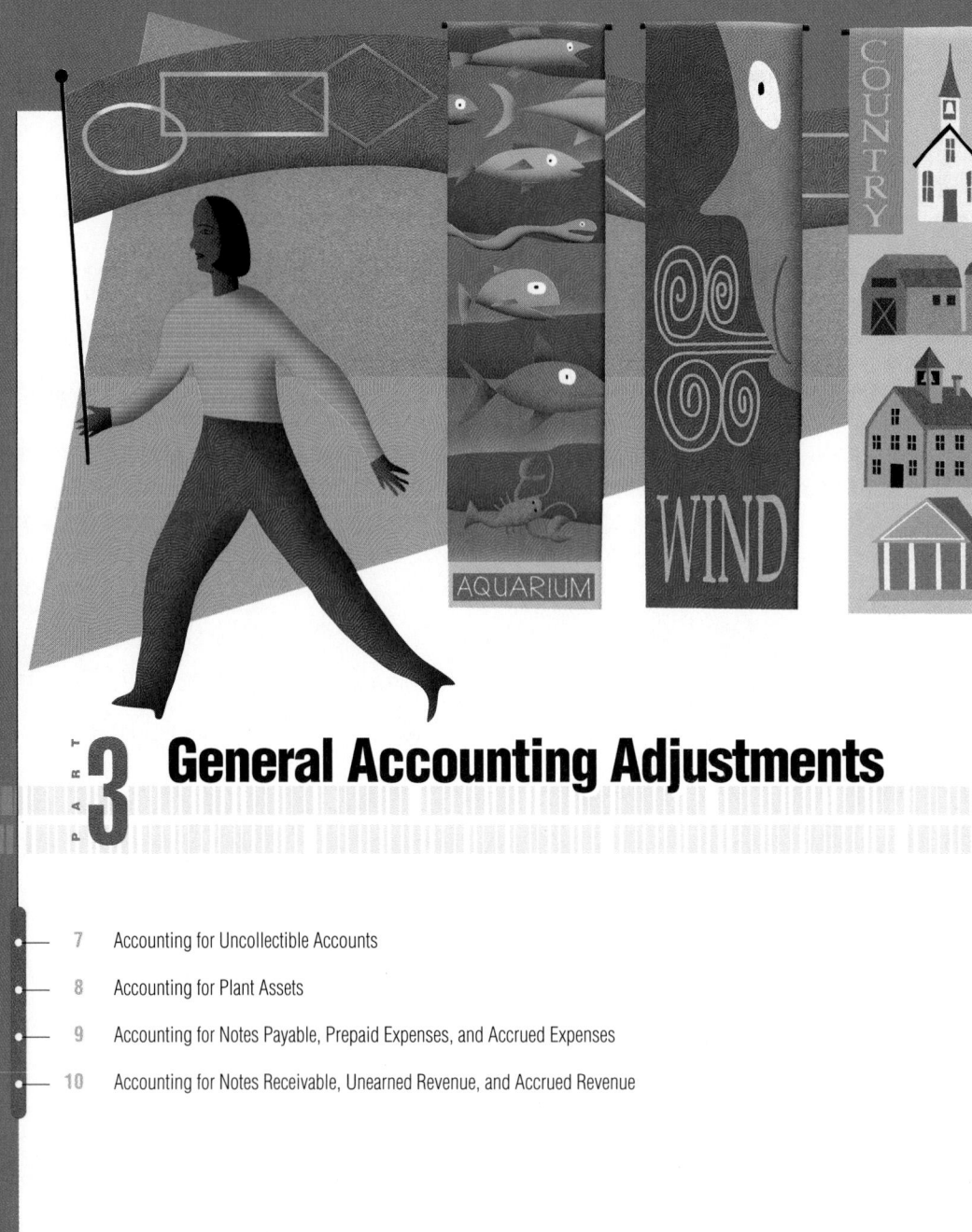

PART 3 **General Accounting Adjustments**

7   Accounting for Uncollectible Accounts

8   Accounting for Plant Assets

9   Accounting for Notes Payable, Prepaid Expenses, and Accrued Expenses

10   Accounting for Notes Receivable, Unearned Revenue, and Accrued Revenue

1250	Accumulated Depreciation—Warehouse Equipment
(2000)	**LIABILITIES**
2100	CURRENT LIABILITIES
2105	Notes Payable
2110	Interest Payable
2115	Accounts Payable
2120	Employee Income Tax Payable
2125	Federal Income Tax Payable
2130	Social Security Tax Payable
2133	Medicare Tax Payable
2135	Salaries Payable
2140	Sales Tax Payable
2145	Unearned Rent
2150	Unemployment Tax Payable—Federal
2155	Unemployment Tax Payable—State
2200	LONG-TERM LIABILITY
2205	Mortgage Payable
(3000)	**STOCKHOLDERS' EQUITY**
3105	Capital Stock
3110	Retained Earnings
3115	Income Summary

Income Statement Accounts

(4000)	**OPERATING REVENUE**
4105	Sales
4110	Sales Discount
4115	Sales Returns and Allowances
(5000)	**COST OF MERCHANDISE**
5105	Purchases
5110	Purchases Discount
5115	Purchases Returns and Allowances
(6000)	**OPERATING EXPENSE**
6100	ADMINISTRATIVE EXPENSES
6105	Depreciation Expense—Building
6110	Depreciation Expense—Office Equipment
6115	Insurance Expense
6120	Miscellaneous Expense—Administrative
6125	Payroll Taxes Expense
6130	Property Tax Expense
6135	Salary Expense—Administrative
6140	Supplies Expense—Administrative
6145	Uncollectible Accounts Expense
6200	SELLING EXPENSES
6205	Advertising Expense
6210	Credit Card Fee Expense
6215	Depreciation Expense—Store Equipment
6220	Miscellaneous Expense—Sales
6225	Salary Expense—Sales
6230	Supplies Expense—Sales
6300	WAREHOUSE EXPENSES
6305	Depreciation Expense—Warehouse Equipment
6310	Miscellaneous Expense—Warehouse
6315	Salary Expense—Warehouse
6320	Supplies Expense—Warehouse
(7000)	**OTHER REVENUE**
7105	Gain on Plant Assets
7110	Interest Income
7115	Rent Income
(8000)	**OTHER EXPENSES**
8105	Interest Expense
8110	Loss on Plant Assets
(9000)	**INCOME TAX**
9105	Federal Income Tax Expense

The chart of accounts for Appliance Center, Inc., is illustrated above for ready reference as you study Part 3 of this textbook.

CHART OF ACCOUNTS

Balance Sheet Accounts

(1000)	**ASSETS**
1100	CURRENT ASSETS
1105	Cash
1110	Petty Cash
1115	Notes Receivable
1120	Interest Receivable
1125	Accounts Receivable
1130	Allowance for Uncollectible Accounts
1135	Merchandise Inventory
1140	Supplies—Administrative
1145	Supplies—Sales
1150	Supplies—Warehouse
1155	Prepaid Insurance
1160	Prepaid Interest
1200	PLANT ASSETS
1205	Land
1215	Building
1220	Accumulated Depreciation—Building
1225	Office Equipment
1230	Accumulated Depreciation—Office Equipment
1235	Store Equipment
1240	Accumulated Depreciation—Store Equipment
1245	Warehouse Equipment

CHART OF ACCOUNTS

- Emphasize that students should refer to this chart of accounts throughout the chapters in Part 3.
- Explain that this chart of accounts is used by a merchandising business organized as a corporation.

Point out the *similarities* between this chart of accounts and the one in Parts 1 and 2.

- Typical divisions for a merchandising business:
  - Assets
  - Liabilities
  - Equity
  - Operating revenue
  - Cost of merchandise
  - Operating expenses
  - Other revenue
  - Other expenses
  - Income tax expense
- Many familiar accounts within divisions.

Point out the *differences* between this chart of accounts and the one in Parts 1 and 2:

- Only a single merchandise category is sold.
- Mortgage Payable, a long-term liability, is a new account.
- Only federal income taxes are withheld from employees' salaries.
- Operating expenses are categorized into administrative, selling, and warehouse expenses.
- Point out that Appliance Center, Inc., uses special journals and a general journal.

197

Gifted Students. This part presents a variety of accounting concepts, such as accounts receivable, plant assets, notes payable and receivable, prepaid and accrued expenses, and unearned and accrued revenue. Using gifted students as tutors for other students can be an effective way of teaching the topics students find most difficult. Allow the gifted students to complete one of these chapters while the class completes the first two chapters of the part. The gifted students can then assist you in presenting the concepts and procedures in their chapter to the class. Encourage the students to use visual aids and develop methods to assess student learning.

Accounting for

	SCOPE & SEQUENCE		ENHANCING	
	NEW	REVIEW/ EXTENSION	SPECIAL FEATURES	
Introduce the Chapter	✓		• Accounting in the Real World: J.C. Penney	
Lesson 7-1 Direct Write-Off Method of Recording Uncollectible Accounts			• Making Ethical Decisions: Sharing the News	
Uncollectible accounts		✓		
Direct write-off method	✓			
Lesson 7-2 Allowance Method of Recording Uncollectible Accounts Expense			• Explore Accounting	
Allowance method of recording uncollectible accounts expense		✓	• Global Perspective	
Estimating uncollectible accounts expense using a percentage of net sales		✓		
Estimating uncollectible accounts expense using a percentage of accounts receivable		✓		
Estimating the balance of uncollectible accounts by aging accounts receivable		✓		
Writing off an uncollectible account		✓		
Collecting a written-off account		✓		
Lesson 7-3 Accounts Receivable Turnover Ratio				
Accounts receivable turnover ratio	✓			
Average number of days for payment	✓			
Putting It All Together			• Explore Accounting	
			• Xtra! Web Site: Xtra! Enrichment	
			• Applied Communication	
			• Case for Critical Thinking	
			• SCANS Workplace Competency	
			• Graphing Workshop	
			• Analyzing Costco's Financial Statements	

Uncollectible Accounts

INSTRUCTION		PRACTICE AND ASSESSMENT		
TECHNOLOGY AND MEDIA	TEACHING STRATEGIES	GUIDED PRACTICE	INDEPENDENT PRACTICE	RETEACHING AND ENRICHMENT
• Internet Research Activity • Accounting Xtra! Web Site	• Software Focus			
• Instructor's Resource CD: PowerPoint Slides • Xtra! Web Site: Xtra! Study Tools • Blackline Masters: General Journal and Cash Receipts Journal • Personal Trainer • Automated Accounting		• Terms Review • Audit Your Understanding • Work Together 7-1	• On Your Own 7-1 • Application Problem 7-1 • Ongoing Assessment, p. 202 • Personal Trainer • Xtra! Web Site: Xtra! Study Tools	• Reteach, p. 202 • Enrich, p. 203 • Automated Accounting
• Instructor's Resource CD: PowerPoint Slides • Xtra! Web Site: Xtra! Study Tools • Blackline Masters: General Journal and Cash Receipts Journal • Personal Trainer • Automated Accounting • Peachtree	• Cooperative Learning • Applied Skills: Word Processing • Kinesthetic Learner	• Terms Review • Audit Your Understanding • Work Together 7-2	• On Your Own 7-2 • Application Problem 7-2 • Application Problem 7-3 • Application Problem 7-4 • Ongoing Assessment, p. 209 • Personal Trainer • Xtra! Web Site: Xtra! Study Tools	• Reteach, p. 209 • Enrich, p. 210 • Automated Accounting • Peachtree
• Instructor's Resource CD: PowerPoint Slides • Xtra! Study Tools • Blackline Masters: General Journal • Personal Trainer	• Auditory Learner	• Terms Review • Audit Your Understanding • Work Together 7-3	• On Your Own 7-3 • Application Problem 7-5 • Ongoing Assessment, p. 212 • Personal Trainer • Xtra! Web Site: Xtra! Study Tools	• Reteach, p. 212 • Enrich, p. 213
• Personal Trainer • Xtra! Web Site: Xtra! Review, Quizzing, and Enrichment • Student Companion CD • Automated Accounting	• Applied Skills: Writing Across the Curriculum • Applied Skills: Language Arts • Visual Learner • Print Learner		• Application Problem 7-6 • Mastery Problem 7-7 • Personal Trainer • Xtra! Web Site: Xtra! Review and Quizzing • Study Guide 7 • Student Companion CD • Chapter 7 Test • ExamView Chapter 7 • Portfolio Assessment	• Challenge Problem 7-8 • Reteach, p. 214 • Enrich, p. 214 • Recycling Problem 7-1 • Automated Accounting • Xtra! Web Site: Xtra! Enrichment

CHAPTER 7

Accounting for Uncollectible Accounts

After studying Chapter 7, you will be able to:

1. Define accounting terms related to uncollectible accounts.

2. Identify accounting concepts and practices related to uncollectible accounts.

3. Calculate and record estimated uncollectible accounts expense using the direct write-off method.

4. Calculate and record estimated uncollectible accounts expense using the allowance method.

5. Calculate and analyze accounts receivable turnover ratios.

- uncollectible accounts
- writing off an account
- direct write-off method of recording losses from uncollectible accounts

- allowance method of recording losses from uncollectible accounts
- aging accounts receivable

- accounts receivable turnover ratio
- book value of accounts receivable

OBJECTIVES & TERMS

Point Your Browser
accountingxtra.swlearning.com

ACCOUNTING IN THE REAL WORLD

• J.C. Penney

©NEAL HAMBERG/BLOOMBERG NEWS/LANDOV

J.C. PENNEY AND THE GOLDEN RULE

The J.C. Penney Company is one of the oldest department stores in the country. However, it has not always been known as the J.C. Penney Company. When James Cash Penney opened his first store in 1902 in Kemmerer, Wyoming, it was called the Golden Rule Store. It wasn't until 1913 that the chain incorporated as J.C. Penney Company, Inc.

It was not a coincidence that Mr. Penney chose this name for his store. "Do unto others as you would have others do unto you" became the cornerstone for setting his store apart from his competition. Mr. Penney stated, "In setting up a business under the name and meaning of the Golden Rule, I was publicly binding myself, in my business relations, to a principle which had been a real and intimate part of my family upbringing. To me the sign on the store was much more than a trade name. . . . We took our slogan 'Golden Rule Store' with strict literalness. Our idea was to make money and build business through serving the community with fair dealing and honest value."

Today, the J.C. Penney Company operates stores in all 50 states, Puerto Rico, and Mexico.

Critical Thinking

1. J.C. Penney Company allows customers to use bank credit cards (such as VISA) but also offers its own credit card. What is the cost to J.C. Penney Company of offering its own credit card? What are the benefits?
2. How could the Golden Rule philosophy apply to credit card customers?

Xtra!
Today
accountingxtra.swlearning.com

Source: www.jcpenney.com

RESUME WRITING

Go to the homepage for the American Institute of Certified Public Accountants (AICPA) (www.aicpa.org). Find the link for students. Search for information about how to prepare a resume and how to write appropriate letters.

Instructions

1. List the six items, in order, that this site recommends to include in a resume.
2. What two types of letters are recommended by this site?

ACCOUNTING IN THE REAL WORLD

1. Costs include the cost of the entire billing and collections department, including sending out bills, collecting and processing checks, and contacting customers who do not pay promptly. There is also the "opportunity" cost of loss of the use of the revenue until the money is collected. Finally, there is a cost associated with uncollectible accounts. Benefits include customer loyalty and the opportunity to offer special discounts to credit card holders, which encourage increased sales.
2. Applying the Golden Rule to credit card customers could include offering competitive interest rates and grace periods. It could also include such special offers as a frequent buyer program or special sales open to credit card holders.

INTERNET RESEARCH ACTIVITY

1. Heading, objective, education, work and experience, activities, and references.
2. This site recommends a cover letter and a follow-up letter.

OBJECTIVES

OBJECTIVES

- Define accounting terms related to uncollectible accounts receivable.
- Identify accounting concepts and practices related to uncollectible accounts receivable using the direct write-off method.
- Calculate and record estimated uncollectible accounts expense using the direct write-off method.

MOTIVATE

Ask students to identify businesses in their community that are likely to make sales on account. Point out that credit card sales are sales on account only if the credit card is issued and processed by the merchandise business.

Preview

- Preview the accounting terms and definitions introduced in this lesson: *uncollectible accounts, writing off accounts,* and *direct write-off method of recording losses from uncollectible accounts.*
- Direct students to read the headings at the top of each page in this lesson and to examine the illustrations given.
- This lesson presents an alternative method of accounting for uncollectible accounts. The direct write-off method is useful for small businesses that have few accounts receivable.

MATERIALS

- Instructor's Resource CD: PowerPoint Slides
- Xtra! Study Tools on the Xtra! Web Site
- Blackline Masters: General Journal Cash Receipts Journal
- Working Papers: Teacher's Edition of the Working Papers for Lesson 7-1
- Software: Personal Trainer Automated Accounting and Century 21 8E CD

7-1 Direct Write-Off Method of Recording Uncollectible Accounts

Many business transactions are completed on account rather than for cash. Businesses offer credit terms to attract new customers, increase sales to current customers, and encourage customer loyalty. Before a business sells merchandise on account, it should investigate the customer's credit rating to ensure that the customer will pay promptly.

Regardless of the care taken in granting credit, some customers will not pay when payment is due. Accounts receivable that cannot be collected are called **uncollectible accounts**. Uncollectible accounts are sometimes referred to as bad debts.

When a business makes a sale on account to a customer, it records the amount in a general ledger account titled Accounts Receivable. The amount remains recorded in this asset account until it is paid or until it is specifically known to be uncollectible.

When a customer account is believed to be uncollectible, the account is no longer an asset. An uncollectible account should be canceled and removed from the assets of the business. Canceling the balance of a customer account because the customer is not expected to pay is called **writing off an account**.

Occasionally an account that has been written off is collected. The account balance is restored and the receipt of cash is recorded. A complete history of the transactions for each customer is maintained.

©GETTY IMAGES/PHOTODISC

making ethical decisions

Sharing the News

Phillip Walters left the meeting and went straight to the phone to call his wife. "Corporate headquarters just informed us they plan to close the plant. They're going to announce the closing next Monday. I'll be able to keep my job if we're willing to move."

Instructions

Access the *Code of Business Conduct* of Dow. Using this information and the ethical model, determine whether Phillip acted ethically by informing his wife of the impending plant closing.

MAKING ETHICAL DECISIONS
MAKING ETHICAL DECISIONS

This activity deals with one of several confidentiality issues addressed in the *Safeguarding Important Information* section of the code. Students may contend that Phillip should be able to tell his wife of such a significant impending event in their lives. Other students may recognize that Phillip has now placed his wife in danger of committing insider trading if she shares the information with others. Phillip must either keep the information confidential until Monday's announcement or encourage the company to make the information public sooner to ensure that none of its employees mistakenly or intentionally reveals the information.
Source: *www.dow.com/about/aboutdow/code_conduct/ethics_conduct.htm*

RECORDING UNCOLLECTIBLE ACCOUNTS EXPENSE

GENERAL JOURNAL   PAGE 11

	DATE		ACCOUNT TITLE	DOC. NO.	POST. REF.	DEBIT	CREDIT	
1	Nov. 20--	15	Uncollectible Accounts Expense	M21		50 00		1
2			Accounts Rec./James Nordquist		/		50 00	2

An amount owed by a specific customer is part of the accounts receivable account balance until it is paid or is written off as uncollectible. An uncollectible account is closed by transferring the balance to a general ledger account titled Uncollectible Accounts Expense.

Northwest Cleaners dry cleans clothing for its customers. Most of the business's sales are made for cash or are paid with a credit card. The business does make a few sales on account. The business has a small number of accounts receivable and very few of these accounts become uncollectible. Therefore, Northwest Cleaners records uncollectible accounts expense only when a specific account is actually known to be uncollectible. Recording uncollectible accounts expense only when an amount is actually known to be uncollectible is called the **direct write-off method of recording losses from uncollectible accounts**.

On November 15, Northwest Cleaners learned that James Nordquist is unable to pay his account. Northwest Cleaners decides that James Nordquist's account is uncollectible. The entry to record the write-off is made in the general journal as shown above.

November 15. Wrote off James Nordquist's past due account as uncollectible, $50.00. Memorandum No. 21.

After this entry is journalized and posted, the balance of Accounts Receivable no longer includes the $50.00 as part of the business's assets. Also, James Nordquist's account has a zero balance and is written off.

GENERAL LEDGER
Uncollectible Accounts Expense

Write off	50.00	

Accounts Receivable

Bal.	54,789.05	Write off	50.00
(New Bal.	54,739.05)		

ACCOUNTS RECEIVABLE LEDGER
James Nordquist

Bal.	50.00	Write off	50.00
(New Bal. zero)			

REMEMBER Uncollectible accounts are also referred to as bad debts. Thus, the accounts used could be titled Bad Debt Expense and Collection of Bad Debts.

EXPLAIN

- Use a general journal transparency to illustrate the general journal or direct students to the illustration.
- Point out that the direct write-off method writes off an account only when the account is known to be uncollectible.
- Ask students to read the Remember feature to learn of alternative terms for uncollectible accounts.
- Ask students to read the F.Y.I. feature to learn one method that businesses can use to evaluate whether a business should sell to a customer on account.

DEMONSTRATE

Analyze the transaction

- Drawn three T accounts on the board.
- Read the transaction statement.
- Ask students to analyze the transaction by answering: what accounts are affected, are they increased or decreased, and are they debited or credited. Complete the T accounts as the information is provided.
- Review the effect on the account for James Nordquist in the accounts receivable ledger.

Record the transaction

- Use a general journal transparency to illustrate recording the transaction in the general journal or direct students to the illustration.

- Recording the collection of a written-off account requires two journal entries. One entry is documented by a memorandum. The second entry is documented by a receipt.

- Explain to students that the two entries enable the customer's accounts receivable account to fully reflect all of the account's activity. Managers use this information when making future credit decisions for the customer.

- Ask students to explain why the credit is recorded to Collection of Uncollectible Accounts rather than Uncollectible Accounts Expense. *(Keeping write-off and collection transactions separate provides more accounting information than netting the transactions in a single account.)*

DEMONSTRATE

Reopen the account

- Draw four T accounts on the board and enter the balance amounts.

- Read the transaction statement.

- Enter in the T accounts the transaction to reopen the customer's account. Ask students to analyze the transaction by answering: what accounts are affected, are they increased or decreased, and are they debited or credited.

- Use a general journal transparency to illustrate recording the transaction in the general journal or direct students to the illustration.

Record the cash received

- Read the transaction statement again.

- Enter in the T accounts the transaction to record the cash received. Ask students to analyze the transaction by answering: what accounts are affected, are they increased or decreased, and are they debited or credited.

- Use a cash receipts journal transparency to illustrate recording the transaction in the cash receipts journal or direct students to the illustration.

- Ask students to identify the current balance of James Nordquist's account.

COLLECTING A WRITTEN-OFF ACCOUNT—DIRECT METHOD

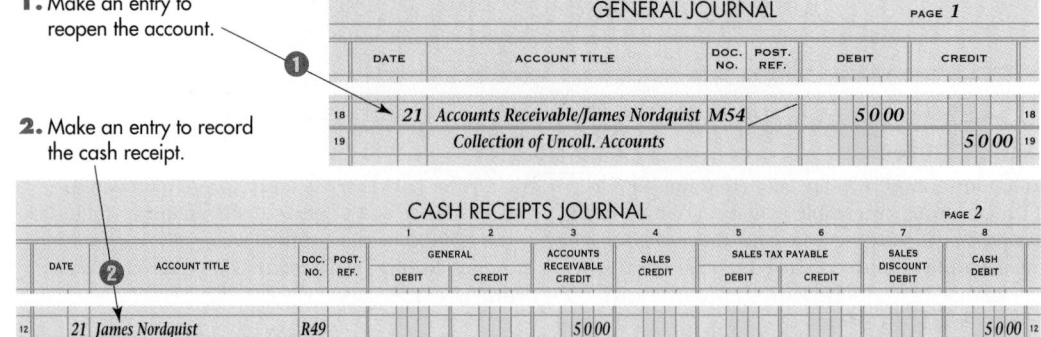

1. Make an entry to reopen the account.

2. Make an entry to record the cash receipt.

Sometimes a customer's written-off account is later collected. When the account is written off, the balance is recorded as an expense. When the account is later collected, the amount is recorded as other revenue.

January 21. Received cash in full payment of James Nordquist's account, previously written off as uncollectible, $50.00. Memorandum No. 54 and Receipt No. 49.

Northwest Cleaners needs a complete history of each customer's credit activities. Therefore, two journal entries are recorded for the collection of a written-off account receivable as shown above.

1. A general journal entry to reopen the customer account.
2. A cash receipts journal entry to record the cash received on account.

The account Collection of Uncollectible Accounts is used for recording collection of previously written-off accounts. The account is closed to Income Summary at the end of a fiscal period and is reported on an income statement as part of Other Revenue.

GENERAL LEDGER
Cash

Received	50.00		

Accounts Receivable

Bal.	54,789.05	Write off	50.00
Reopen	50.00	Received	50.00

Collection of Uncollectible Accounts

		Reopen	50.00

ACCOUNTS RECEIVABLE LEDGER
James Nordquist

Bal.	50.00	Write off	50.00
Reopen	50.00	Received	50.00
(New Bal. zero)			

STEPS • STEPS • STEPS • STEPS

COLLECTING A WRITTEN-OFF ACCOUNT USING THE DIRECT WRITE-OFF METHOD

1 Record an entry in the general journal to debit *Accounts Receivable/James Nordquist* and credit *Collection of Uncollectible Accounts* for the amount of the receipt, *50.00*.

2 Record an entry on the cash receipts journal to debit Cash and credit Accounts Receivable for the amount of the receipt, *50.00*.

FYI FOR YOUR INFORMATION

Uncollectible accounts are also referred to as bad debts. Thus, the accounts used could be titled Bad Debts Expense and Collection of Bad Debts.

ONGOING ASSESSMENT

- Circulate through the classroom or lab observing which students have problems with the assignments.

- Troubleshooting: Diagnose what kinds of problems students have with this section. Students may have trouble understanding why (1) the account is reopened when cash is received on a written-off account and (2) the receipt of cash results in a credit to Collection of Uncollectible Accounts.

- Assess student understanding by checking solutions to Independent Practice assignments.

RETEACH

- Call on students to list the transactions necessary to write off an uncollectible account and subsequently record the collection of the account.

- Write the five accounts affected by the transactions in this section. Ask a student to make up original transaction statements that you write on the board or an overhead transparency.

- Ask another student to analyze the transactions using T accounts.

202

GUIDED PRACTICE

• terms review

TERMS REVIEW

uncollectible accounts
writing off an account
direct write-off method of recording
losses from uncollectible
accounts

• audit your understanding

AUDIT YOUR

1. Why should the amount of an uncollectible account be removed from the assets of a business?

2. In the direct write-off method, how is an uncollectible account closed?

3. Why is the customer account reopened when cash is received for an account previously written off as uncollectible?

• work together 7-1

WORK TOGETHER • WORK TOGETHER

Journalizing entries to write off uncollectible accounts—direct write-off method

Cracker, Inc., uses the direct write-off method of recording uncollectible accounts expense. A general journal and a cash receipts journal are provided in the *Working Papers*. Source documents are abbreviated as follows: memorandum, M; receipt, R. Your instructor will guide you through the following examples.

1. Journalize the following transactions completed during the current year.

Jan. 10. Wrote off Melinda Sanford's past due account as uncollectible, $261.54. M13.
Mar. 12. Wrote off Mark Polk's past due account as uncollectible, $45.00. M24.
Apr. 13. Received cash in full payment of Andrew Leslie's account, previously written off as uncollectible, $67.42. M31 and R158.
Nov. 15. Received cash in full payment of Melinda Sanford's account, previously written off as uncollectible, $261.54. M84 and R313.

• on your own 7-1

ON YOUR OWN • ON YOUR OWN • ON YOUR

Journalizing entries to write off uncollectible accounts—direct write-off method

Kelley, Inc., uses the direct write-off method of recording uncollectible accounts expense. A general journal and a cash receipts journal are provided in the *Working Papers*. Source documents are abbreviated as follows: memorandum, M; receipt, R. Work this problem independently.

1. Journalize the following transactions completed during the current year.

Jan. 20. Wrote off Belinda Rafferty's past due account as uncollectible, $265.48. M15.
Feb. 15. Wrote off Ervin Bond's past due account as uncollectible, $52.00. M21.
Apr. 10. Received cash in full payment of Stephanie Byrd's account, previously written off as uncollectible, $178.43. M34 and R89.
Oct. 5. Received cash in full payment of Belinda Rafferty's account, previously written off as uncollectible, $265.48. M104 and R135.

Direct Write-Off Method of Recording Uncollectible Accounts

Lesson 7-1   **203**

GUIDED PRACTICE

Terms Review
Call on students to define the terms in the Terms Review. Ask the class if the definitions are correct and whether the complete definitions have been given or if anything needs to be added. Suggested definitions for all terms are given in the Glossary.

Audit Your Understanding
Call on students to answer the Audit Your Understanding questions. Ask the class if the answer is correct and/or complete. Answers are given in Appendix E of the textbook.

Work Together
Have students write the solution to the Work Together problem as you guide the class through the examples.

- Direct students to record each transaction in the journals as you elicit class participation in analyzing and recording each transaction.

- Call on students to describe how each transaction affects revenues and expenses.

INDEPENDENT PRACTICE

On Your Own
- Assign the On Your Own problem to be worked independently.
- Use the Ongoing Assessment techniques to diagnose student understanding.

Application Problem
- Assign Application Problem 7-1: Journalizing entries to write off uncollectible accounts—direct write-off method.

Personal Trainer
- Students can access the Lesson 7-1 assessment material using this software.

Xtra! Web Site
- Students can access the Xtra! Study Tools for additional practice.

ENRICH

- Assign the Automated Accounting feature on page 221 to automate Application Problem 7-1.

- Ask students to assume the role of a manager of Northwest Cleaners. They had written off James Nordquist's account but subsequently received payment. Under

what circumstances, if any, would they again sell to Mr. Nordquist on account? *(As with any sale on account, management must be reasonably assured of receiving payment. Students' responses should focus on this issue rather than dwelling too heavily on past events.)*

CLOSE

- Ask students to briefly summarize the procedures for journalizing transactions using the direct write-off method of accounting for uncollectible accounts.

7-2 Allowance Method of Recording Uncollectible Accounts Expense

ESTIMATING UNCOLLECTIBLE ACCOUNTS EXPENSE

Some businesses use the direct write-off method and record uncollectible accounts expense only when a specific customer account is determined to be uncollectible. However, when the direct write-off method is used, the expense may be recorded in a fiscal period different from the fiscal period of the sale. Uncollectible accounts expense should be recorded in the same fiscal period in which the sales revenue is received. [CONCEPT: Matching Expenses with Revenue]

At the time sales on account are made, a business has no way to know for sure which customer will not pay an amount due. Therefore, the business makes an estimate based on its past history of uncollectible accounts. Crediting the estimated value of uncollectible accounts to a contra account is called the **allowance method of recording losses from uncollectible accounts**. Two methods are commonly used to estimate uncollectible accounts expense:

1. Percentage of sales method.
2. Percentage of accounts receivable method.

The *percentage of sales method* assumes that a percentage of each sales dollar will become an uncollectible account. The *percentage of accounts receivable method* assumes that a percentage of accounts receivable at the fiscal year-end will become uncollectible. Regardless of the method used, the estimated amount is charged to Uncollectible Accounts Expense.

Explore Accounting

Representative Payees for Social Security Benefits

Retirees receive Social Security benefits. Supplemental Security Income (SSI) is received by disabled individuals and children of deceased workers. For those who need assistance managing their money, the Social Security Administration (SSA) allows a friend, relative, or other interested party to be appointed as a representative payee. The representative payee receives the Social Security or SSI payment on behalf of the beneficiary.

Before the SSA allows an individual to serve as a representative payee, it carefully investigates the individual's trustworthiness and ability to carefully manage the beneficiary's benefits. Among a representative payee's duties are:

- Regular contact with the beneficiary to determine how benefits can be used for his or her personal care or well-being.

- Good recordkeeping of how the funds were spent. Periodically, the SSA requires representative payees to complete a Representative Payee Report accounting for the funds received on behalf of the beneficiary.

All monies received from the SSA must be used for the personal care and well-being of the beneficiary. There is no specific list of approved expenditures; however, the SSA requires that the money first be used to ensure that the beneficiary's day-to-day needs for food and shelter are met.

Instructions
Go to the Web site of the Social Security Administration (www.ssa.gov) and report on an aspect of Social Security relevant to someone you know.

Accounting for Uncollectible Accounts

ADJUSTMENT USING THE PERCENTAGE OF SALES METHOD

	Net Sales	×	Percentage	=	Estimated Uncollectible Accounts Expense		**1.** Compute the estimated uncollectible accounts expense.
	$113,285.75	×	0.5%	=	$566.43		

Morgan, Inc.
Work Sheet
For Year Ended December 31, 20--

	ACCOUNT TITLE	TRIAL BALANCE		ADJUSTMENTS		INCOME STATEMENT		BALANCE SHEET		
		DEBIT	CREDIT	DEBIT	CREDIT	DEBIT	CREDIT	DEBIT	CREDIT	
4	Allowance for Uncoll. Accounts		25 87		(a) 566 43					4
49	Uncollectible Accounts Expense			(a) 566 43						49

2. Record an adjustment on a worksheet.

Past experience of Morgan, Inc., indicates that approximately 0.5% of its net sales will prove to be uncollectible. On December 31, Morgan estimated that 0.5% of its $113,285.75 net sales, $566.43, eventually will prove to be uncollectible. Morgan does not yet know which customer accounts in the accounts receivable ledger will become uncollectible. Therefore, the amount cannot be recorded directly in accounts receivable.

Before the adjustment is made, Morgan's general ledger shows Allowance for Uncollectible Accounts with a $25.87 credit balance. This balance is what remains of estimates made in previous fiscal periods but not yet specifically identified by customer. The new balance, $592.30, is an estimate of the accounts receivable that will become uncollectible.

At the end of a fiscal period, an adjustment for uncollectible accounts expense is planned on a work sheet as shown above.

The balance of Allowance for Uncollectible Accounts may increase from year to year. A large increase may indicate that an incorrect percentage is being used to calculate the uncollectible amount. When this occurs, a new percentage should be calculated based on actual experience for the past two or three years.

Uncollectible Accounts Expense

Adj.	566.43	

Allowance for Uncollectible Accounts

	Bal.	25.87
	Adj.	566.43
	(New Bal.	592.30)

STEPS · STEPS · STEPS · STEPS

ESTIMATING UNCOLLECTIBLE ACCOUNTS EXPENSE BY USING THE PERCENTAGE OF SALES METHOD

1. Compute the estimated uncollectible accounts expense by multiplying net sales, *113,285.75*, by the percentage estimate, 0.5%, which totals *566.43*.

2. Record an adjustment on the worksheet, recording a debit to Uncollectible Accounts Expense and a credit to Allowance for Uncollectible Accounts.

FYI FOR YOUR INFORMATION

A company can elect to base its estimate of uncollectible accounts expense on a percentage of total sales on account. The calculation of the allowance amount is the same as when total net sales is used.

- Explain that the percentage of accounts receivable is an alternative method to the percentage of sales method.
- Point out that although a business can use either method to estimate uncollectible accounts expense, the business should use the same method from year to year.
- Point out that the aging of accounts receivable in one month intervals is common practice but not a requirement of GAAP.

ADJUSTMENT USING AGING OF ACCOUNTS RECEIVABLE

Customer	Account Balance	Not Yet Due	Days Account Balance Past Due			
			1–30	31–60	61–90	Over 90
Louise Asmus	$ 735.51	$ 735.51				
Mark Darby	132.58		132.58			
⋮	⋮	⋮	⋮	⋮	⋮	⋮
Ann Gabriel	99.55					99.55
Kathy Quay	238.00	200.00	38.00			
Thomas Yost	133.67				133.67	
Totals	$12,891.97	$8,734.08	$2,952.90	$749.54	$238.45	$217.00
Percentages	—	0.1%	0.2%	0.4%	10.0%	80.0%

The *percentage of accounts receivable method* assumes that a percentage of the accounts receivable account balance is uncollectible. Therefore, emphasis is placed on estimating a percentage of accounts receivable that will not be collected. An amount that will bring the balance of Allowance for Uncollectible Accounts up to the estimated amount is recorded in that account.

Analyzing accounts receivable according to when they are due is called **aging accounts receivable**. Rosedale, Inc., ages accounts receivable at the end of each fiscal period, as shown above, to provide information for the uncollectible accounts expense adjustment. Rosedale sells on terms of 2/10, n/30. Rosedale expects customers to pay in full within 30 days. If Rosedale has not received cash within 30 days, it mails reminders to the customers. If it has not received cash after 60 days, the company makes special attempts to collect the amount due. If the business has not collected an amount from a customer after 90 days, it may stop selling on account to that customer until collection has been made.

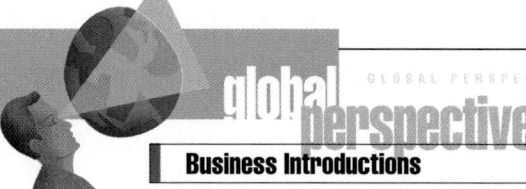

GLOBAL PERSPECTIVE • GLOBAL PERSPECTIVE • GLOBAL PERSPEC

Business Introductions

People from other countries may decide from your first meeting whether they want to do business with you. Therefore, it is very important that introductions be handled correctly.

Do not use first names with foreign business associates until invited to do so.

In Japan and India, address a person by adding Mr. or Mrs. to their last name. Use a title such as Dr. if appropriate. Address people from the Middle East as their name appears on their business card. Usually Mr. or Sheik will be used. If they are members of a royal family, use Your Excellency.

Chinese names appear in the reverse order of names in the United States. The family name or "last" name precedes the first name. For example, Mr. Wu Ho is called Mr. Wu because Ho is his given name.

In Latin America, address a person as Señor, Señora, or Señorita, followed by the last name. If they have a title such as doctor, be sure to use it.

Required

Research foreign business introductions. Find the appropriate introduction for meeting someone from Germany, South Africa, and England.

GLOBAL PERSPECTIVE
GLOBAL PERSPECTIVE

The Global Perspective feature is intended to expose students to some of the ways in which accounting and business in general differ in other countries. This Global Perspective feature allows students to explore international customs for handling introductions.

The activity requires students to research introductions and cultures for meeting foreign business people from a variety of countries. Student responses will vary depending on the countries that are chosen. Have students report their findings to the class.

ADJUSTMENT USING PERCENTAGE OF ACCOUNTS RECEIVABLE

Age Group	Amount	Percentage	Uncollectible	
Not Yet Due	$ 8,734.08	0.1%	$ 8.73	
1–30 Days	2,952.90	0.2%	5.91	
31–60 Days	749.54	0.4%	3.00	← ❶ — **1.** Compute an estimate for each age group.
61–90 Days	238.45	10.0%	23.85	
Over 90 Days	217.00	80.0%	173.60	
Totals	$12,891.97	—	$215.09	← ❷ — **2.** Compute the total estimate.

Current Balance of Allowance for Uncollectible Accounts	40.78
Estimated Addition to Allowance for Uncollectible Accounts	$174.31 ← ❸ — **3.** Compute the addition to the allowance account.

Based on past records, Rosedale determines that a percentage of each accounts receivable age group will become uncollectible in the future. For example, 0.4% of the accounts receivable overdue 31–60 days will probably become uncollectible. Also, 80.0% of the accounts overdue more than 90 days probably will become uncollectible.

Using these percentages, Rosedale calculates the total amount of estimated uncollectible accounts receivable, as shown above. Of the total accounts receivable on December 31, $12,891.97, the business estimates that $215.09 will prove to be uncollectible in the future.

Rosedale's general ledger shows that Allowance for Uncollectible Accounts has a $40.78 credit balance. This balance is what remains of estimates made in previous fiscal periods but not yet specifically identified by customer. The allowance account is increased by a $174.31 credit. The new balance of the allowance account, $215.09 (previous

balance, $40.78, *plus* adjustment, $174.31), equals the estimate of uncollectible accounts.

GENERAL LEDGER

Uncollectible Accounts Expense

Adj.	174.31	

Allowance for Uncollectible Accounts

	Bal.	40.78
	Adj.	174.31
	(New Bal.	*215.09)*

FYI FOR YOUR INFORMATION

An estimate of the amount of uncollectible accounts expense can also be computed by using a single percentage of the total accounts receivable account balance. Although this method is easier to compute, a method using age group information typically yields a better estimate of the expense.

STEPS • STEPS • STEPS • STEPS • STEPS • STEPS • STEPS • STEPS • STEPS • STEPS •

ESTIMATING THE BALANCE OF UNCOLLECTIBLE ACCOUNTS EXPENSE USING THE PERCENTAGE OF ACCOUNTS RECEIVABLE METHOD

❶ Compute the estimate for each age group. Multiply the amount of each age group by the percentage estimate.

❷ Compute the total, *$215.09*, of the uncollectible estimates.

❸ Subtract the current balance, *40.78*, from the total estimate to determine the addition to the allowance account, *$174.31*. (If the allowance account has a debit balance, add the current balance to the total estimate.)

Allowance Method of Recording Uncollectible Accounts Expense   Lesson 7-2   **207**

- Point out that both the direct and allowance methods write off an account when the account is known to be uncollectible.

- Ask students to compare how writing off an account affects Uncollectible Accounts Expense using the direct and allowance methods *(a direct method write off increases the expense, an allowance method write off has no affect on the expense).*

- Ask students to read the left F.Y.I. feature to learn the factors managers must consider when setting credit policies.

- Ask students to read the right F.Y.I. feature to learn more about internal controls.

DEMONSTRATE

Analyze the transaction

- Draw three T accounts on the board.

- Read the transaction statement.

- Ask students to analyze the transaction by answering: what accounts are affected, are they increased or decreased, and are they debited or credited. Complete the T accounts as the information is provided.

- Review the effect on the account for Candace Rhode in the accounts receivable ledger.

Record the transaction

- Use a general journal transparency to illustrate recording the transaction in the general journal or direct students to the illustration.

- Remind students that the abbreviation for the memorandum, M, and the memorandum number are recorded in the Doc. No. column.

	GENERAL JOURNAL				PAGE 1	
DATE	ACCOUNT TITLE	DOC. NO.	POST. REF.	DEBIT	CREDIT	
5	Allowance for Uncollectible Accts.	M71		42 80		4
	Accounts Rec./Candace Rhode				42 80	5
						6

The procedures for writing off an account are the same regardless of the allowance method used to calculate the estimated uncollectible accounts expense. When a specific customer account is thought to be uncollectible, the account balance is written off as shown above. Appliance Center determined that Candace Rhode will probably not pay the amount she owes, $42.80. The balance is no longer *estimated* to be uncollectible; it is *actually determined* to be uncollectible.

January 5. Wrote off Candace Rhode's past due account as uncollectible, $42.80. Memorandum No. 71.

After this entry is journalized and posted, Candace Rhode's account has a zero balance, and the account is written off.

Appliance Center did not notify Candace Rhode that it wrote off her account. Although Appliance Center believes the account is probably uncollectible, it may continue its attempts to collect the account. In some cases, customers do subsequently pay accounts that have been written off.

In a previous fiscal period, an adjusting entry was recorded for estimated uncollectible accounts expense resulting in an Allowance for Uncollectible Accounts balance of $1,363.88. This balance is the estimated amount of uncollectible accounts. The $42.80 debit entry in this account removes an amount that is no longer estimated but is actual.

Uncollectible Accounts Expense is not affected when a business writes off an account using the allowance method. The expense is recorded in an adjusting entry at the end of a previous fiscal period.

GENERAL LEDGER
Allowance for Uncollectible Accounts

Write off	42.80	Bal.	1,363.88

Accounts Receivable

Bal.	45,462.79	Write off	42.80

ACCOUNTS RECEIVABLE LEDGER
Candace Rhode

Bal.	42.80	Write off	42.80
(New Bal. zero)			

TEACHING STRATEGIES DIFFERENT LEARNING STYLES

Kinesthetic Learner. When covering journal entries with a kinesthetic learner, the instructor should give the student journal paper and have the student complete the entries as the instructor demonstrates on a cash receipts journal transparency or board.

COLLECTING A WRITTEN-OFF ACCOUNT—ALLOWANCE METHOD

1. Reopen the account.

2. Record the cash receipt.

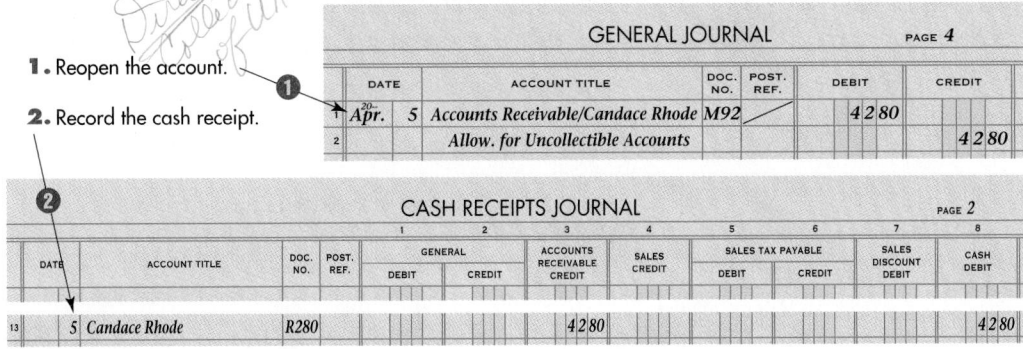

Later in the year, Appliance Center received a check in full payment of the amount owed by Candace Rhode.

April 5. Received cash in full payment of Candace Rhode's account, previously written off as uncollectible, $42.80. Memorandum No. 92 and Receipt No. 280.

Appliance Center's records must show a complete history of Ms. Rhode's credit dealings. The collection of a written-off account receivable involves two journal entries as shown above.

A general journal entry is recorded to reopen the customer account. The $42.80 debit increases Accounts Receivable and Candace Rhode's account in the accounts receivable ledger. The account balances now appear as they were before Ms. Rhode's account was written off as uncollectible.

The cash received from Ms. Rhode is then recorded in the cash receipts journal. The $42.80 credit decreases Accounts Receivable and Ms. Rhode's account in the accounts receivable ledger.

GENERAL LEDGER
Cash

Received	42.80		

Accounts Receivable

Bal.	45,462.79	Write off	42.80
Reopen	42.80	Recieved	42.80

Allowance for Uncollectible Accounts

Write off	42.80	Bal.	1,363.88
		Reopen	42.80

ACCOUNTS RECEIVABLE LEDGER
Candace Rhode

Bal.	42.80	Write off	42.80
Reopen	42.80	Received	42.80
(New Bal. zero)			

STEPS

STEPS • STEPS • STEPS • STEPS • STEPS • STEPS • STEPS • STEPS • STEPS • STEPS • STEPS •

JOURNALIZING THE COLLECTION OF A WRITTEN-OFF ACCOUNT—ALLOWANCE METHOD

1. Reopen the account by debiting Accounts Receivable and crediting Allowance for Doubtful Accounts for the amount of the receipt, *42.80*.

2. Record an entry in the cash receipts journal to debit Cash and credit Accounts Receivable for the amount of the receipt, *42.80*.

> **REMEMBER** Entries for the collection of a written-off account present evidence of the customer's credit history. Managers can use this information to make informed decisions about extending credit to the customer in the future.

Allowance Method of Recording Uncollectible Accounts Expense

Lesson 7-2   **209**

209

GUIDED PRACTICE

Terms Review

Call on students to define the terms in the Terms Review. Ask the class if the definitions are correct and whether the complete definitions have been given or if anything needs to be added. Suggested definitions are given in the Glossary.

Audit Your Understanding

Call on students to answer the Audit Your Understanding questions. Ask the class if the answer is correct and/or complete. Answers are given in Appendix E of the textbook.

Work Together

Have students write the solution to the Work Together problems as you guide the class through the example.

- Call on students to describe each step in calculating the allowance estimate.
- Ask students to describe how the current balance of the allowance account affects each allowance calculation method.
- Direct students to record each transaction in the journal as you elicit class participation in analyzing and recording each transaction.

INDEPENDENT PRACTICE

On Your Own

- Assign the On Your Own problem to be worked independently.
- Use the Ongoing Assessment techniques to diagnose student understanding.

Application Problem

- Assign Application Problem 7-2: Estimating amount of uncollectible accounts expense by using a percentage of net sales—allowance method; journalizing the adjusting entry.
- Assign Application Problem 7-3: Estimating the balance of Allowance for Uncollectible Accounts by aging accounts receivable—allowance method; journalizing the adjusting entry.
- Assign Application Problem 7-4: Journalizing entries to write off uncollectible accounts and collect written-off accounts—allowance method.

Personal Trainer

- Students can access the Lesson 7-2 assessment material using this software.

Xtra! Web Site

- Students can access the Xtra! Study Tools for additional practice.

210

terms review

allowance method of recording losses from uncollectible accounts
aging accounts receivable

audit your understanding

1. What are the two methods commonly used to estimate uncollectible accounts expense?
2. What is the formula for estimating uncollectible accounts expense based on net sales?
3. How is the addition to allowance for uncollectible accounts calculated using the percentage of accounts receivable method?

work together 7-2

Estimating amount of uncollectible accounts expense; journalizing the adjusting entry

General journal pages are provided in the *Working Papers*. Your instructor will guide you through the following independent examples.

1. Lynum, Inc., had net sales of $245,321.09 during the current year. It estimates that the amount of uncollectible accounts expense is equal to 0.5% of net sales. Journalize the adjusting entry for uncollectible accounts expense on December 31 of the current year.
2. The aging of accounts receivable for Kersten, Inc., as of December 31 of the current year and estimated percentages of uncollectible accounts by age group are presented in the Working Papers. Calculate the estimated balance of Allowance for Uncollectible Accounts. Then journalize the adjusting entry for uncollectible accounts expense. The balance of Allowance for Uncollectible Accounts on December 31 before adjusting entries are recorded is $63.24.

on your own 7-2

Estimating amount of uncollectible accounts expense; journalizing the adjusting entry

General journal pages are provided in the *Working Papers*. Work this problem independently.

1. Hillcrest, Inc., had net sales of $685,409.50 during the current year. It estimates that the amount of uncollectible accounts expense is equal to 0.8% of net sales. Journalize the adjusting entry for uncollectible accounts expense on December 31 of the current year.
2. The aging of accounts receivable for Malloy, Inc., as of December 31 of the current year and estimated percentages of uncollectible accounts by age group are presented in the *Working Papers*. Calculate the estimated balance of Allowance for Uncollectible Accounts. Then journalize the adjusting entry for uncollectible accounts expense. The balance of Allowance for Uncollectible Accounts on December 31 before adjusting entries are recorded is $391.75.

ENRICH

- Assign the Automated Accounting feature on page 221 to automate Application Problem 7-4.
- Students can use the Peachtree data files to automate Application Problem 7-4.
- Ask students to create a table that lists each method for computing uncollectible accounts expense using the allowance method. Instruct the students to identify the positive and negative features of each method. If they were managing a company, which method would they use?

CLOSE

- Ask students to briefly summarize the procedures for accounting for uncollectible accounts.

7-3 Accounts Receivable Turnover Ratio

CALCULATING THE ACCOUNTS RECEIVABLE TURNOVER RATIO

	Total Accounts Receivable	−	Allowance for Uncollectible Accounts	=	Book Value of Accounts Receivable	
Beginning	$50,329.14	−	$1,416.83	=	$48,912.31	
Ending	$45,462.79	−	$1,363.88	=	$44,098.91 ← ❶	**1.** Compute the beginning and ending book value.

(Beginning Book Value of Accounts Receivable	+	Ending Book Value of Accounts Receivable)	÷	2	=	Average Book Value of Accounts Receivable	
($48,912.31	+	$44,098.91)	÷	2	=	$46,505.61 ← ❷	**2.** Compute the average book value.

Net Sales on Account	÷	Average Book Value of Accounts Receivable	=	Accounts Receivable Turnover Ratio	
$330,312.85	÷	$46,505.61	=	7.1 times ← ❸	**3.** Compute the accounts receivable turnover.

Days in Year	÷	Accounts Receivable Turnover Ratio	=	Average Number of Days for Payment	
365	÷	7.1	=	51 ← ❹	**4.** Compute the average number of days for payment.

Appliance Center needs cash to purchase additional merchandise to sell to customers and to pay for operating expenses. If it does not collect amounts due from customers promptly, too large a share of the assets of the business will be in accounts receivable and not immediately usable. All businesses selling on account need prompt collection from credit customers.

Appliance Center analyzes how frequently customers make payments on account. If customers are not paying promptly, the business will adopt new procedures to speed collections. One way to analyze the collection efficiency of a business is to calculate the accounts receivable turnover ratio. The number of times the average amount of accounts receivable is collected during a specified period is called the **accounts receivable turnover ratio**. The accounts receivable turnover

ratio is calculated by dividing net sales on account by the average book value of accounts receivable. Businesses may calculate this ratio monthly, quarterly, or yearly.

The difference between the balance of Accounts Receivable and its contra account, Allowance for Uncollectible Accounts, is called the **book value of accounts receivable**.

An accounts receivable turnover ratio of 7.1 times means that Appliance Center turns over (or collects) its average accounts receivable about seven times a year. The number of days in a year, 365, divided by the accounts receivable turnover ratio, 7.1, yields the average number of days required to pay. Appliance Center's customers are taking an average of 51 days to pay their accounts in full.

Accounts Receivable Turnover Ratio

211

STEPS

STEPS • STEPS • STEPS • STEPS • STEPS • STEPS • STEPS • STEPS • STEPS • STEP

CALCULATING THE ACCOUNTS RECEIVABLE TURNOVER RATIO AND THE AVERAGE NUMBER OF DAYS FOR PAYMENT

1 Compute the beginning and ending book value of accounts receivable. The book values are computed by subtracting the allowance for doubtful accounts from the total accounts receivable.

2 Compute the average book value of accounts receivable, *$46,505.61*, by adding the beginning book value, *$48,912.31*, to the ending book value, *$44,098.91*, and dividing the total by 2.

3 Compute the accounts receivable turnover ratio by dividing net sales on account, *$330,312.85*, by the average book value of accounts receivable, *$46,505.61*.

4 Compute the average number of days for payment, *51*, by dividing *365* days by the accounts receivable turnover ratio, *7.1*.

ANALYZING ACCOUNTS RECEIVABLE TURNOVER RATIOS

Appliance Center, Inc.—Accounts Receivable Turnover Ratios

Year	20X1	20X2	20X3	20X4	20X5	20X6	20X7
Ratio	6.2	6.4	6.0	6.4	6.8	6.8	7.1
Days for Payment	59	57	61	57	54	54	51

Most of Appliance Center's customers do pay their accounts, but many customers take much longer than the expected 30 days.

From 20X1 through 20X7, the accounts receivable turnover ratio rose from 6.2 to 7.1 times as shown above. In 20X1, customers took an average of 59 days to pay their accounts in full. In 20X7, customers took an average of 51 days to pay their accounts in full, 8 fewer days than in 20X1.

With the exception of 20X3, the turnover ratio has been steadily increasing. On the average, customers have been paying their accounts in full in a fewer number of days each year. Appliance Center wants this favorable trend to continue.

Appliance Center needs to plan additional ways to encourage customers to pay their accounts in less time. With n/30 credit terms, the goal should be to have a turnover ratio of 12.0 times (365 days/12.0 accounts receivable turnover ratio = 30 average number of days for payment).

The business might take several steps to create a more favorable accounts receivable turnover ratio.

1. Send statements of account to customers more often, including a request for prompt payment.
2. Not sell on account to any customer who has an account for which payment is overdue more than 30 days.
3. Encourage more cash sales and fewer sales on account.
4. Conduct a more rigorous credit check on new customers before extending credit to them.

Sometimes the demand for quicker payment can result in a loss of business. Some customers might start buying from competitors. A business must weigh a change in credit policies against the effect the change will have on total sales.

FYI FOR YOUR INFORMATION

A business that does not record sales on account separately from cash sales uses total net sales to compute the accounts receivable turnover ratio.

TEACHING STRATEGIES DIFFERENT LEARNING STYLES

Auditory Learner. To reinforce the learning of journal entries, the auditory learner should verbally repeat the analysis of the transaction. The student should also verbally list the steps involved in making the entry.

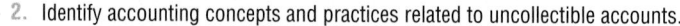

PUTTING IT ALL TOGETHER

- Ask students to prepare a list of the new concepts introduced in this chapter.
- Discuss that the journalizing and posting procedures learned in this chapter could also be used for any business that sells its product or service on account.

INDEPENDENT PRACTICE

- Assign Application Problem 7-6. This problem will emphasize transaction analysis skills because transactions are stated in a variety of different ways.
- Assign Mastery Problem 7-7 to students who need the reinforcement of a problem that combines all activities from the chapter in one problem; this will be most students.
- Assign Challenge Problem 7-8 to accelerated students who do not require the reinforcement of the Mastery Problem.
- Assign Study Guide 7.
- Students can use Automated Accounting 8.0 or higher to work Mastery Problem 7-7.
- Students can access Personal Trainer to work end-of-chapter problems on the computer.
- Students can access the Xtra! Web Site for the Xtra! Review and Quizzing.
- Students can access the Student Companion CD for additional review material.

ONGOING ASSESSMENT

Review solutions to the assigned problems in class, diagnosing trouble spots.

RETEACH

- Call on students to describe how they avoid the trouble spots diagnosed.
- Use reteaching suggestions from section lesson plans as required.
- Assign Recycling Problem 7-1 if needed.

ENRICH

- Assign the Explore Accounting feature. Ask students to share the information they have gathered in a report to the class.
- Students can access the Xtra! Web Site for the Xtra! Enrichment material.
- Assign the Applied Communication activity.

- Assign the Case for Critical Thinking.
- Assign the SCANS Workplace Competency.
- Assign the Graphing Workshop activity.
- Assign the Analyzing Costco's Financial Statements activity.
- Assign the Automated Accounting feature on page 221 to automate Mastery Problem 7-7.

214

SUMMARY

After completing this chapter, you can

1. Define accounting terms related to uncollectible accounts.
2. Identify accounting concepts and practices related to uncollectible accounts.
3. Calculate and record estimated uncollectible accounts expense using the direct write-off method.
4. Calculate and record estimated uncollectible accounts expense using the allowance method.
5. Calculate and analyze accounts receivable turnover ratios.

Explore Accounting

EXPLORE ACCOUNTING • EXPLORE ACCOUNTING • EXPLORE AC

Credit Scoring Systems

To help reduce the amount of uncollectible accounts, a business should evaluate the creditworthiness of potential customers before granting credit. The traditional credit evaluation involves a credit analyst manually evaluating financial information to determine if the customer has the financial resources to pay the account.

The benefit of reducing bad debt expenses should exceed the costs of performing credit evaluations. A business must consider the cost, in both time and money, involved in credit evaluations. A business should not, for example, spend $70,000 in salaries and other expenses to evaluate credit if the business can only reduce its annual bad debt expense by $50,000. In addition, customers may be unwilling to wait for a business to perform a traditional credit evaluation, favoring to purchase goods from another business.

A more cost-effective method for evaluating creditworthiness is available. A statistical method used to predict a customer's willingness to pay its account on a timely basis is called a credit scoring system. In addition to considering financial information, a credit scoring system considers other factors that have been shown to be

predictors of creditworthiness, such as: frequency of delinquent accounts, length of credit history, types of credit, available credit, frequency of credit applications, number of credit inquiries, industry comparative data, number of employees, management problems, and prior bankruptcies.

A score is assigned to each factor. The higher the score, the more creditworthy the customer. An effective credit scoring system will utilize information obtained from a credit application or available from public sources. A company can maintain its own system or use systems maintained by independent credit rating companies.

Credit scoring systems are optimally used for routine credit decisions that must be made quickly on relatively low-dollar sales on account. For sales on account that are relatively large, the credit decisions should involve the human decision of the traditional credit evaluation.

Regardless of how credit is evaluated, a company must assure that its decisions are consistent. Federal laws exist to assure that individuals and businesses have equal access to credit.

Required:
Research the Fair Credit Reporting Act. How does this act protect the rights of the consumer?

EXPLORE ACCOUNTING
EXPLORE ACCOUNTING

This activity presents an opportunity for students to research the Fair Credit Reporting Act. As consumers, students should be aware of their rights and responsibilities related to borrowing money and repaying the debt.

Evaluate student reports for content and for correct style, grammar, and punctuation.

7-1 APPLICATION PROBLEM (AUTOMATED ACCOUNTING)
Journalizing entries to write off uncollectible accounts—direct write-off method

Stallworth uses the direct write-off method of recording uncollectible accounts expense.

Instructions:
Journalize the following transactions completed during the current year. Use page 3 of a general journal and page 4 of a cash receipts journal. Source documents are abbreviated as follows: memorandum, M; receipt, R.

Transactions:
Feb.	16.	Wrote off William Rose's past due account as uncollectible, $215.64. M18.
Mar.	23.	Received cash in full payment of Emma Peden's account, previously written off as uncollectible, $175.00. M43 and R215.
May	7.	Wrote off Tom Ming's past due account as uncollectible, $187.32. M61.
Aug.	10.	Received cash in full payment of William Rose's account, previously written off as uncollectible, $215.64. M78 and R341.

7-2 APPLICATION PROBLEM
Estimating amount of uncollectible accounts expense by using a percentage of net sales—allowance method; journalizing the adjusting entry

Jacobs Market had net sales of $863,245.32 during the current year. The corporation estimates that the amount of uncollectible accounts expense is equal to 0.6% of net sales.

Instructions:
Journalize the adjusting entry for uncollectible accounts expense on December 31 of the current year. Use page 24 of a general journal.

7-3 APPLICATION PROBLEM
Estimating the balance of Allowance for Uncollectible Accounts by aging accounts receivable—allowance method; journalizing the adjusting entry

The following information has been taken from the records of Rosetta Company as of December 31 of the current year.

Customer	Account Balance	Not Yet Due	Days Account Balance Past Due			
			1–30	31–60	61–90	Over 90
Acorn & Karr	$623.74			$623.74		
Base Industries	723.22	$723.22				
.	.	.	.	.	.	.
.	.	.	.	.	.	.
Wright Stores	612.67					612.67
Yui Co.	1,723.33	1,048.99	$674.34			
Totals	$89,363.45	$44,434.51	$25,623.64	$10,535.20	$5,235.40	$3,534.70
Percentages	—	0.2%	0.5%	1.0%	5.0%	60.0%

Instructions:
1. Calculate the estimated balance of Allowance for Uncollectible Accounts.
2. Journalize the adjusting entry for uncollectible accounts expense on December 31 of the current year. Use page 12 of a general journal. The balance of Allowance for Uncollectible Accounts on December 31 before adjusting entries are recorded is $589.63.

Accounting for Uncollectible Accounts

Chapter 7   **215**

7-4 APPLICATION PROBLEM `AUTOMATED ACCOUNTING` `PEACHTREE`

Journalizing entries to write off uncollectible accounts and collect written-off accounts—allowance method

McCafferty, Inc., uses the allowance method of recording uncollectible accounts expense.

Instructions:

Journalize the following transactions completed during the current year. Use page 3 of a general journal and page 8 of a cash receipts journal. Source documents are abbreviated as follows: memorandum, M; receipt, R.

Transactions:

Feb.	14.	Wrote off Peggy King's past due account as uncollectible, $357.00. M16.
Apr.	25.	Wrote off Mel Kober's past due account as uncollectible, $84.98. M34.
May	12.	Received cash in full payment of Carolyn Kelly's account, previously written off as uncollectible, $74.00. M43 and R264.
Aug.	2.	Wrote off Lynn Hartman's past due account as uncollectible, $74.93. M71.
Oct.	6.	Received cash in full payment of Peggy King's account, previously written off as uncollectible, $357.00. M92 and R484.

7-5 APPLICATION PROBLEM

Calculating the accounts receivable turnover ratio

Fleming Company offers its customers n/30 credit terms. The turnover ratio for the prior year was 4.5. The following account balances were obtained from the records of Fleming Company for the current year:

Account	January 1	December 31
Accounts Receivable	$584,348.48	$604,285.25
Allowance for Doubtful Accounts	$20,153.35	$23,485.62
Net Sales		$3,848,348.27

Instructions:

1. Calculate the accounts receivable turnover ratio for the current year.
2. Calculate the average number of days for payment.
3. Is Fleming Company effective in collecting its accounts receivable?

7-6 APPLICATION PROBLEM

Accounts receivable transactions using the allowance method

Cofield Engineering uses the allowance method of recording uncollectible accounts expense.

Instructions:

Journalize the following transactions completed during the current year. Use page 4 of a general journal and page 10 of a cash receipts journal. Source documents are abbreviated as follows: memorandum, M; receipt, R.

Transactions:

Mar.	23.	A phone call to Larry Wade, president of Wade Supply, confirmed that the company is intending to file bankruptcy. Mr. Wade stated that no money would likely be available to pay its creditors. The Wade account of $4,000.00 is over 180 days past due. M32.

Accounting for Uncollectible Accounts

APPLIED SKILLS   LANGUAGE ARTS

Practicing punctuation skills. Special handouts for practicing punctuation skills can be created easily using word processing software. Key in some text, either something that you have written yourself or that has appeared in a newspaper or magazine. After checking to be sure you have keyed it correctly, use the change feature of the word processor to change all punctuation to an underline. This will create an answer space for students to supply the correct punctuation. Student solutions can then be compared with the original copy for correctness. For additional challenge, the answer blanks can be omitted.

Apr.	4.	Last year you wrote off the $3,200.00 balance of Creative Decor. The account was over 180 days past due and collection seemed doubtful. Today you received a $3,200.00 check from Creative Decor along with a letter stating that the company had just received a large contract and they wished to reestablish a credit account with your company. M45 and R156.
May	14.	Received a reply to a collection request letter sent to Raymond Fisher. Mr. Fisher refuses to pay the remaining $75.00 of his bill, stating that the original bill was larger than the agreed-upon price. Although your records clearly indicate the $75.00 was an appropriate charge, your manager believes that further efforts to collect this account are pointless. M54.
Oct.	10.	Today you received an $800.00 check from Wade Supply. In the enclosed letter, Mr. Wade stated that the bankruptcy court ordered the company to pay 20 cents for every dollar owed to its creditors. Thus, the $800.00 is the only amount that Wade Supply would ever be able to pay of its original account balance of $4,000.00. M72 and R348.
Nov.	21.	A letter sent to Mary Crawford was returned in the mail, with a U.S. Postal Service stamp stating that the party no longer lives at the address and has left no forwarding address. Ms. Crawford owed $600.00 from an invoice dated January 24. M89.

7-7 MASTERY PROBLEM `AUTOMATED ACCOUNTING`

Journalizing entries for uncollectible accounts—allowance method; calculating and journalizing the adjusting entry for uncollectible accounts expense

Northern, Inc., uses the allowance method of recording uncollectible accounts expense. The following information was obtained from Northern's records for the current year.

Account	January 1	December 31
Accounts Receivable	$49,576.17	$62,791.30
Allowance for Doubtful Accounts	$1,463.89	$3,813.98
Net Sales on Account		$349,562.10

Transactions:

Jan.	9.	Wrote off Jane Martinez's past due account as uncollectible, $634.65. M20.
Mar.	4.	Wrote off Jason Young's past due account as uncollectible, $782.50. M29.
Mar.	28.	Received cash in full payment of Jane Martinez's account, previously written off as uncollectible, $634.65. M40 and R24.
June	20.	Wrote off Allison Aanerud's past due account as uncollectible, $617.16. M58.
Oct.	7.	Wrote off Meredith Darst's past due account as uncollectible, $808.15. M74.
Dec.	11.	Received cash in full payment of Jason Young's account, previously written off as uncollectible, $782.50. M82 and R92.

Instructions:

1. Journalize the transactions above that were completed during the current year. Use page 1 of a general journal and page 1 of a cash receipts journal. Source documents are abbreviated as follows: memorandum, M; receipt, R.
2. Journalize the adjusting entry for uncollectible accounts expense on December 31 of the current year. Northern estimates that the amount of uncollectible accounts expense is equal to 1% of its net sales of $377,539.58.
3. Compute the accounts receivable turnover and average days for payment.

Mastery Problem 7-7
Uncollectible Accounts Expense, 3,775,40.
Accounts Receivable Turnover Ratio, 6.5;
Average Number of Days for Payment, 56.

TEACHING STRATEGIES   DIFFERENT LEARNING STYLES

Visual Learner. When covering journal entries with a visual learner, the instructor should discuss the entries, using a cash receipts journal transparency or the board to record the entry. In addition, the student should be asked to mentally picture each part of the entry before the instructor actually writes it on the cash receipts journal transparency or board.

7-8 CHALLENGE PROBLEM

Estimating and journalizing uncollectible accounts expense by aging accounts receivable—allowance method; calculating and journalizing the adjusting entry for uncollectible accounts expense

A complete list of the accounts receivable of Wind Refrigeration follows:

Account	Amount	Invoice Date
Atkins Co.	$2,523.64	May 16
Bankhead Supply	2,435.75	December 13
Coffman Distributing	943.74	November 30
Fleet Trucking	2,643.23	December 23
Griffin Industries	7,896.54	October 16
Miskelly & Sons	2,754.48	November 15
Oswalt, Inc.	8,723.54	December 4
Rice Shipping Co.	4,363.27	August 25
Smith Stores	1,324.76	September 20

Instructions:

1. Age the accounts receivable by determining the age group for each invoice and totaling the invoice amounts in each age group category.
2. Calculate the estimated balance of Allowance for Uncollectible Accounts using the following percentages: not yet due, 0.3%; 1–30 days past due, 1.0%; 31–60 days, 4.0%; 61–90 days, 20%; and over 90 days, 60%.
3. Journalize the adjusting entry for uncollectible accounts expense on December 31 of the current year. Use page 12 of a general journal. The Allowance for Uncollectible Accounts has a debit balance of $692.16 on December 31 of the current year before adjusting entries are recorded.

©GETTY IMAGES/PHOTODISC

Xtra!
Enrichment
accountingxtra.swlearning.com

• applied communication

Stegall Company had experienced no growth in sales or net income for several years. At your suggestion, the company changed its credit terms on January 1, 20X4, from n/60 to 2/10, n/30. In addition, the company loosened its requirements to extend credit to new customers. All sales are on account. Selected information, in thousands of dollars, taken from the December 31 financial statements for the past four years follows.

Item	20X1	20X2	20X3	20X4
Accts. Receivable	$496	$492	$514	$384
Allow. for Doubtful Accts.	17	17	18	42
Net Sales	2,653	2,676	2,689	2,945
Uncollectible Accts. Exp.	26	26	27	58
Net Income	253	259	262	284

Alice Shirley, a member of the board of directors, has suggested that the company return to its previous credit policies, citing the significant rise in the uncollectible accounts expense.

Required:

Write a memorandum to Alice supporting the new credit policy.

• case for critical thinking

Westermen, Inc., sells merchandise for cash and on account. The business uses the direct write-off method of recording uncollectible accounts expense. For the past two years, the amount of uncollectible accounts written off each year has been about 1.0% of the net sales. Net sales last year totaled $416,228.00. An accountant recommends that the business change to the allowance method of recording uncollectible accounts expense. However, management is reluctant to accept the recommendation because the business has used the direct write-off method for a long time and personnel fully understand it. What do you recommend and why?

• SCANS workplace competency

Systems Competency: Improving and Designing Systems

Concept: Employers value workers who make suggestions to modify existing systems to improve products or services, as well as develop new or alternative systems in order to enhance company performance.

Application: As the manager of accounts receivable, you have been directed to prepare a chapter for the new training manual. Your chapter must describe and illustrate the procedures for recording an uncollectible account using the allowance method, as well as collecting a past due account. In addition to your written explanation, design a flowchart that illustrates your system of handling uncollectibles.

APPLIED COMMUNICATION

Since beginning accounts receivable amounts are required to calculate these ratios, only three years of ratios can be calculated.

Although the company has experienced a dramatic increase in the amount of uncollectible accounts, the additional expense is more than offset by the additional income generated by loosening the company's credit policies. The company, therefore, should continue its new credit policies.

The memorandum should begin with a positive statement that, for example, thanks Ms. Shirley for her interest in the company's financial operations. The memo should then analyze the financial information and identify the student's solution. The memo could end by inviting Ms. Shirley to contact the student if she desires additional information.

CASE FOR CRITICAL THINKING

Generally accepted accounting practice is to record significant amounts of expenses in the same fiscal period as the revenue earned from paying the expenses. If it is determined the amount is sizable and significant, the business would be wise to consider changing to the allowance method.

SCANS WORKPLACE COMPETENCY

Assign half the class the same application task except using the direct write-off method. Allow students to improve other SCANS skills by creating cooperative learning groups of 3–4 students to complete this assignment.

1. As turnover increases, days for payment decreases.

2. Clifford Company's trend is good. Its turnover is increasing, which means it is taking fewer days to collect from its customers.

ANALYZING COSTCO'S FINANCIAL STATEMENTS

1. August 31, 2003 = 557,619,000 (556,090,000 + 1,529,000)
   September 1, 2002 = 477,085,000 (474,861,000 + 2,224,000)

2. Gross receivables has increased from 2002 to 2003, while the amount of the allowance for doubtful accounts has decreased. Costco is expecting to collect a higher percentage of its accounts receivable in 2003 than it did in 2002.

• graphing workshop

The Accounts Receivable Turnover and the Days for Payment for Clifford Company are given below in both table and graph formats.

Ratio	1	2	3	4	5	6	7
A/R Turnover	5.0	5.4	5.9	6.8	6.7	7.2	7.5
Days for payment	73.0	67.6	61.9	53.7	54.5	50.7	48.7

Instructions: Analyze the charts to answer the following questions.

1. What general statement can you make about the relationship between the Accounts Receivable Turnover and the Days for Payment?

2. Is the trend for Clifford Company a good or a bad trend?

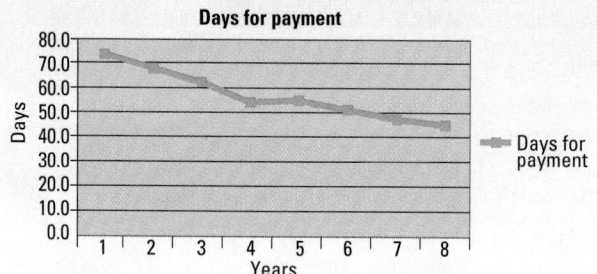

• analyzing Costco's financial statements

As shown in the financial statements in Appendix B of this textbook, Costco's balance sheet lists "Receivables, net" under the heading "Current Assets." This amount represents Costco's receivables after the allowance for doubtful accounts estimate has been deducted. Gross accounts receivable must be calculated. Additional information necessary for the calculation is usually included in Note No. 1, "Summary of Significant Accounting Policies."

Instructions:

1. Using Note 1, beginning on page Appendix B-9, locate the paragraph titled "Receivables, net." This paragraph lists the allowance for doubtful account balances for August 31, 2003, and September 1, 2002. Use this information and Costco's Balance Sheet to calculate the gross accounts receivable for August 31, 2003, and September 1, 2002.

2. How have the gross receivables and the allowance for doubtful accounts changed from 2002 to 2003? What does this say about Costco's expectations for collecting its receivables?

A clear understanding of uncollectible accounts is helpful for students who will work in accounts payable and credit departments. Students should emphasize their learning of this topic by selecting an example of a comprehensive sample of their work in this chapter, for example Mastery Problem 7-7, to include in their portfolio. A copy of the Portfolio Assessment form (blackline master in the Teacher's Resource Guide; also on the Student Companion CD) should be completed by the student and the Description section should include any comments regarding how the student mastered these concepts and procedures. Alternatively, students might include in their portfolios printed reports from an Automated Accounting or Spreadsheet Accounting problem.

Automated Accounting

Automated Entries for Uncollectible Accounts and Write-offs

Recording Uncollectible Accounts

Using the direct write-off method, Uncollectible Accounts Expense and Accounts Receivable are used to write off an uncollectible account.

Using the allowance method, an allowance for uncollectible accounts is maintained. Manual calculations are required to determine the amount of the allowance to be recorded as an adjusting entry at the end of the accounting period. The process is described in Chapter 7.

When an account is determined to be uncollectible, it is written off using the general ledger accounts: Allowance for Uncollectible Accounts and Accounts Receivable. In *Automated Accounting 8.0*, the journal entries should be entered after the amounts have been calculated.

Reinstating a Written-off Account

Occasionally a customer will make payment on an account that has been written off. When this occurs, the account receivable is reinstated and the payment is recorded as described in the chapter.

Other Computerized Accounting Systems

The automated accounting systems used in many businesses today will calculate the amounts that should be posted and will also do the posting based on how the system is set up to handle uncollectible accounts expenses and write-offs. In these cases, it is important to verify that the amounts posted to the accounts are accurate.

AUTOMATING APPLICATION PROBLEM 7-1

Instructions:

1. Load *Automated Accounting 8.0* or higher software.
2. Select database A07-1 (Advanced Course Application Problem 7-1) from the accounting template disk.
3. Select File from the menu bar and choose the Save As menu command. Key the path to the drive and directory that contain your data files. Save the database with a filename of XXX071 (where XXX are your initials).

4. Read the Problem Instruction screen by clicking the Browser toolbar button.
5. Key the data listed in the problem.
6. Exit the Automated Accounting software.

AUTOMATING APPLICATION PROBLEM 7-4

Instructions:

1. Load *Automated Accounting 8.0* or higher software.
2. Select database A07-4 (Advanced Course Application Problem 7-4) from the accounting template disk.
3. Select File from the menu bar and choose the Save As menu command. Key the path to the drive and directory that contain your data files. Save the database with a filename of XXX074 (where XXX are your initials).
4. Read the Problem Instruction screen by clicking the Browser toolbar button.
5. Key the data listed in the problem.
6. Exit the Automated Accounting software.

AUTOMATING MASTERY PROBLEM 7-7

Instructions:

1. Load *Automated Accounting 8.0* or higher software.
2. Select database A07-7 (Advanced Course Mastery Problem 7-7) from the accounting template disk.
3. Select File from the menu bar and choose the Save As menu command. Key the path to the drive and directory that contain your data files. Save the database with a filename of XXX077 (where XXX are your initials).
4. Read the Problem Instruction screen by clicking the Browser toolbar button.
5. Key the data listed in the problem.
6. Exit the Automated Accounting software

EXPLAIN

- Explain that the adjustment for uncollectible accounts expense is recorded in the general journal at the end of the fiscal period.
- Explain that uncollectible accounts receivable are written off when efforts to collect amounts due have been exhausted.
- Explain that the journal entry to write off an account receivable is recorded in the General Journal in the Journal Entries screen.
- Explain that when a previously written off account receivable is collected, two journal entries are needed: (1) An entry to reopen the account receivable, which is recorded in the General Journal in the Journal Entries screen and (2) an entry to record the cash received on account which is recorded in the Cash Receipts Journal in the Journal Entries Screen.
- Point out that after the Accounts Receivable account number is entered, the drop-down list of customers will be available for selecting the specific account receivable.

PRACTICE

- Assign Automating Application Problem 7-1: Journalizing entries to write off uncollectible accounts—direct write-off method.
- Assign Automating Application Problem 7-4: Journalizing entries to write off uncollectible accounts and collect written-off accounts—allowance method.
- Assign Automating Mastery Problem 7-7: Journalizing entries for uncollectible accounts—allowance method; calculating and journalizing the adjusting entry for uncollectible accounts expense.

ASSESSMENT

- Use the Electronic Auditor to assess student understanding.

Accounting for Uncollectible Accounts

Chapter 7 **221**

AUTOMATED ACCOUNTING • AUTOMATED ACCOUNTING • AUTOMATED ACCOUNTING • AUTOMATED ACCOUNTING • AUTOMATED ACCOUNTING

TEACHING STRATEGIES   PORTFOLIO ASSESSMENT

Students should be encouraged to print at least one report from one of the Automated Accounting problems to include in their portfolio to demonstrate mastery of automated accounting systems. A copy of the Portfolio Assessment form (blackline master in the Teacher's Resource Guide; also on the Student Companion CD) should be completed by the student and the Description section should include any comments regarding how the student mastered these concepts and procedures.

221

Accounting for

	SCOPE & SEQUENCE		ENHANCING	
	NEW	REVIEW/ EXTENSION	SPECIAL FEATURES	
Introduce the Chapter	✓		• Accounting in the Real World: Sysco	
Lesson 8-1 Buying Plant Assets			• Making Ethical Decisions: The Land of Opportunity?	
Completing a plant asset record	✓			
Buying a plant asset for cash or on account		✓		
Calculating and paying property tax		✓		
Lesson 8-2 Calculating and Journalizing Depreciation Expense			• Explore Accounting: Changes in Historic Cost	
Straight-line depreciation method		✓		
Adjusting entry for depreciation expense		✓		
Calculating partial year depreciation		✓		
Lesson 8-3 Disposing of Plant Assets			• Explore Accounting: Limitations of Historic Cost Concept	
Disposing of plant assets		✓		
Gain/loss on plant assets		✓		
Trading plant assets	✓			
Selling land and buildings		✓		
Lesson 8-4 Other Methods of Depreciation			• Technology for Business: Spreadsheet Activity— Depreciation Schedule	
Declining-balance depreciation method		✓		
Sum-of-the-years'-digits depreciation method		✓		
Production-unit depreciation method		✓		
Modified Accelerated Cost Recovery System	✓			
Depletion		✓		
Putting It All Together			• Explore Accounting • Xtra! Web Site: Xtra! Enrichment • Applied Communication • Cases for Critical Thinking • SCANS Workplace Competency • Auditing for Errors • Analyzing Costco's Financial Statements	

Plant Assets

INSTRUCTION		PRACTICE AND ASSESSMENT		
TECHNOLOGY AND MEDIA	**TEACHING STRATEGIES**	**GUIDED PRACTICE**	**INDEPENDENT PRACTICE**	**RETEACHING AND ENRICHMENT**
• Internet Research Activity • Accounting Xtra! Web Site	• Software Focus			
• Instructor's Resource CD: PowerPoint Slides • Xtra! Web Site: Xtra! Study Tools • Blackline Master: Cash Payments Journal • Personal Trainer	• Limited English Proficiency (LEP) Students	• Terms Review • Audit Your Understanding • Work Together 8-1	• On Your Own 8-1 • Application Problem 8-1 • Application Problem 8-2 • Ongoing Assessment, p. 227 • Personal Trainer • Xtra! Web Site: Xtra! Study Tools	• Reteach, p. 227 • Enrich, p. 228
• Instructor's Resource CD: PowerPoint Slides • Xtra! Web Site: Xtra! Study Tools • Blackline Master: General Journal • Personal Trainer	• Auditory Learner • Print Learner	• Terms Review • Audit Your Understanding • Work Together 8-2	• On Your Own 8-2 • Application Problem 8-3 • Application Problem 8-4 • Ongoing Assessment, p. 232 • Personal Trainer • Xtra! Web Site: Xtra! Study Tools	• Reteach, p. 232 • Enrich, p. 234
• Instructor's Resource CD: PowerPoint Slides • Xtra! Web Site: Xtra! Study Tools • Blackline Masters: General Journal Cash Receipts Journal Cash Payments Journal • Personal Trainer	• Visual Learner • Applied Skills: Language Arts	• Audit Your Understanding • Work Together 8-3	• On Your Own 8-3 • Application Problem 8-5 • Application Problem 8-6 • Ongoing Assessment, p. 240 • Personal Trainer • Xtra! Web Site: Xtra! Study Tools	• Reteach, p. 240 • Enrich, p. 241
• Instructor's Resource CD: PowerPoint Slides • Xtra! Web Site: Xtra! Study Tools • Blackline Master: General Journal • Personal Trainer • Automated Accounting	• Tactile Learner • Kinesthetic Learner • Applied Skills: Word Processing	• Terms Review • Audit Your Understanding • Work Together 8-4	• On Your Own 8-4 • Application Problem 8-7 • Application Problem 8-8 • Application Problem 8-9 • Application Problem 8-10 • Ongoing Assessment, p. 247 • Personal Trainer • Xtra! Web Site: Xtra! Study Tools	• Reteach, p. 247 • Enrich, p. 249 • Automated Accounting
• Personal Trainer • Xtra! Web Site: Xtra! Review, Quizzing, and Enrichment • Student Companion CD • Automated Accounting • Peachtree and QuickBooks	• Applied Skills: Writing Across the Curriculum • Cooperative Learning		• Mastery Problem 8-11 • Personal Trainer • Xtra! Web Site: Xtra! Review and Quizzing • Study Guide 8 • Student Companion CD • Chapter 8 Test • ExamView Chapter 8 • Portfolio Assessment	• Challenge Problem 8-12 • Reteach, p. 250 • Enrich, p.250 • Recycling Problems 8-1, 8-2, and 8-3 • Automated Accounting • Peachtree and QuickBooks • Xtra! Web Site: Xtra! Enrichment

TERMS • OBJECTIVES & TERMS • OBJECTIVES & TERMS

CHAPTER 8

Accounting for Plant Assets

After studying Chapter 8, you will be able to:

1. Define accounting terms related to plant assets and depreciation.
2. Identify accounting concepts and practices related to accounting for plant assets and depreciation.
3. Journalize entries for buying plant assets.
4. Calculate and record property tax expense.
5. Calculate and record depreciation expense for a plant asset using straight-line depreciation.
6. Journalize entries for disposing of plant assets.
7. Calculate depreciation expense using other methods.

- plant asset record
- real property
- personal property
- assessed value
- straight-line method of depreciation

- book value of a plant asset
- declining-balance method of depreciation
- sum-of-the-years' digits method of depreciation

- production-unit method of depreciation
- Modified Accelerated Cost Recovery System
- depletion

Point Your Browser
accountingxtra.swlearning.com

1. Increasing the useful life of an asset would decrease the amount of depreciation expense each year. Therefore, net income would increase.

2. Besides an estimate of how long the asset will be usable, helpful information would include how the asset will be used, if technology will make it beneficial to replace the asset before it actually wears out, and whether the asset is used in a process that is expected to remain unchanged.

INTERNET RESEARCH ACTIVITY

Answers will vary, depending on the occupation chosen.

• Sysco

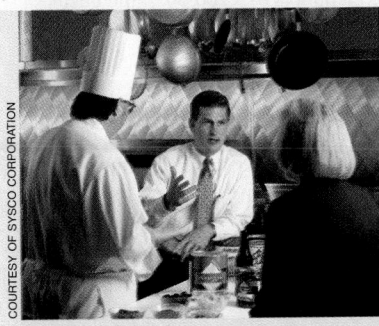

COURTESY OF SYSCO CORPORATION

SYSCO: TRANSPORTING GOODS ACROSS THE COUNTRY

Assume you just opened a restaurant. You have already purchased the equipment necessary to prepare meals and the dishes and silverware needed to serve meals and beverages. It's time to order supplies and food inventories. Where do you turn? Do you have to use a different supplier for each item you need? Isn't there a more efficient way?

Sysco Corporation strives to efficiently move food from "farm to fork." They do this by purchasing food and restaurant supplies from a variety of manufacturers and warehousing this inventory in over 145 locations across the country. They then distribute the food and supplies to restaurants, hospitals, schools, and other businesses involved in food service.

In order to accomplish this efficiently, Sysco has equipment to help move the inventory into and out of the warehouses. It also has trucks to deliver the goods to its customers. In a recent annual report, Sysco listed its cost of equipment at over $1.8 billion dollars and stated that the useful life of this equipment ranged from 3 to 20 years. This equipment is depreciated each year, which causes Depreciation Expense to lower net income on Sysco's income statement.

Critical Thinking

1. What effect would increasing the estimated useful life of an asset have on net income for a company like Sysco?
2. What information would you need to help identify the useful life of a piece of equipment?

Xtra!
Today
accountingxtra.swlearning.com

Source: www.sysco.com

OCCUPATIONAL OUTLOOK HANDBOOK

Go to the homepage of the U.S. Department of Labor's *Occupational Outlook Handbook* (www.stats.bls.gov/oco). Read the directions on how to search the *Handbook*. Pick an occupation connected to accounting or bookkeeping.

Instructions

Summarize the following information for the occupation chosen:
1. Working conditions
2. Minimum training required
3. Job outlook
4. Range of earnings
5. Related occupations

223

8-1 Buying Plant Assets

A business owns a variety of assets, all of which are used to help it earn a profit. Some assets such as cash, accounts receivable, and supplies are exchanged for cash or consumed within a year. Cash and other assets expected to be exchanged for cash or consumed within a year are known as current assets. Other assets, such as land, buildings, and equipment, are expected to help the business earn a profit for more than one year. Assets that will be used for a number of years in the operation of a business are known as plant assets. Plant assets are sometimes referred to as fixed assets or long-term assets.

Since businesses expect to remain in business indefinitely, the accounting records must be kept up-to-date as plant assets are bought and used. [CONCEPT: Going Concern]

The going concern concept states that financial statements are prepared with the expectation that a business will remain in operation indefinitely. A business bought store equipment for $30,000.00. The store equipment is expected to last 10 years. Yearly depreciation, therefore, is recorded and reported based on the expected life of the equipment. After six years of the expected 10-year life, the equipment's book value (cost less accumulated depreciation) is $13,200.00. If the business ended operations and the equipment had to be sold, the amount received may be less than the $13,200.00. However, accounting records are maintained with the expectation that the business will remain in operation indefinitely and that the cost will be allocated over the useful life of the equipment.

©GETTY IMAGES/PHOTODISC

MAKING ETHICAL DECISIONS • MAKING ETHICAL DECISIONS • MAKING ETHICAL DECIS

making ethical decisions

The Land of Opportunity?

As the director of corporate development, Kelly Maben is finishing the final touches on a proposal to locate a resort in Destin, Florida. Confident the proposal will be approved, Kelly is considering the purchase of a family-owned restaurant across the street from the proposed building site.

Instructions

Obtain the *Code of Business Conduct and Ethics* of Hilton Hotels Corporation. Using this information and the ethical model, provide Kelly with guidance on her proposed restaurant purchase. Is Kelly violating her company's code of conduct or simply seizing an opportunity?

1. Complete when asset is purchased. ①

2. Complete when asset is disposed of. ②

3. Complete each year to record annual depreciation expense. ③

PLANT ASSET RECORD, No. _72_   **General Ledger Account No.** _1225_

Description _Copying Machine_   **General Ledger Account** _Office Equipment_

Date Bought _January 2, 20--_   **Serial Number** _X3492D194_   **Original Cost** _$1,680.00_

Estimated Useful Life _5 years_   **Estimated Salvage Value** _$230.00_   **Depreciation Method** _Straight-Line_

Disposed of: **Discarded** _____   **Sold** _____   **Traded** _____

Date _____   **Disposal Amount** _____

YEAR	ANNUAL DEPRECIATION EXPENSE	ACCUMULATED DEPRECIATION	ENDING BOOK VALUE

- Ask students to provide a definition for plant asset.
- Point out a plant asset record contains information three distinct sections as shown in the illustration.
- Ask students to describe the purpose of the three sections of a plant asset record.
- Ask students to read the Remember feature to learn how individual prices are determined for land and a building purchased together.

DEMONSTRATE

- As you read each step, ask students to identify the information recorded in the plant asset record.
- Ask students to identify when information is recorded in each of the three sections of the plant asset record.

A business keeps a separate record of each plant asset it owns. An accounting form on which a business records information about each plant asset is called a **plant asset record**. Appliance Center uses a printed card as its plant asset record as shown above.

Appliance Center's plant asset record has three sections. Section 1 is prepared when the company buys a plant asset. Information in this section shows a description of the item,

the general ledger account title and number, date bought, serial number, and information needed to calculate annual depreciation expense for the plant asset. Section 2 provides space for recording the disposition of the plant asset. Section 3 provides space for recording annual depreciation expense.

Calculating depreciation and disposing of plant assets are described later in this chapter.

STEPS • STEPS • STEPS • STEPS • STEPS • STEPS • STEPS • STEPS • STEPS • STEPS •

PREPARE A PLANT ASSET RECORD

① When an asset is bought, enter the general information about the asset in the top section of the plant asset record.

② The center section will be completed when the asset is discarded, sold, or traded.

③ At the end of each year, record the annual depreciation expense, the accumulated depreciation, and the ending book value.

©GETTY IMAGES/PHOTODISC

{ **REMEMBER** A building and the land it is located on are typically purchased together for a single price. Separate values must be assigned to each asset. If a sales contract does not specify separate amounts for the land and building, a professional appraisal may be used to determine separate amounts. }

EXPLAIN

- Explain that students have learned to record the purchase of a plant asset in the first-year course.
- Explain that the asset category is recorded in the Account Title of the cash payments journal.

DEMONSTRATE

- Draw two T accounts on the board and enter the balance amounts.
- Read the transaction statement.
- Ask students to analyze the transaction by answering: what accounts are affected, are they increased or decreased, and are they debited or credited.
- Use a cash payments journal transparency to illustrate recording the transaction in the cash payments journal or direct students to the illustration at the top of the page.

EXPLAIN

- Ask students to identify why the purchase of this office equipment is recorded on a general journal rather than a cash payments journal (the asset is purchased on account and, therefore, no cash was paid).
- Ask students to read the F.Y.I. feature to learn more about distinguishing between merchandise inventory and plant assets.

DEMONSTRATE

- Draw three T accounts on the board and enter the balance amounts.
- Read the transaction statement.
- Ask students to analyze the transaction by answering: what accounts are affected, are they increased or decreased, and are they debited or credited.
- Use a cash payments journal transparency to illustrate recording the transaction in the general journal or direct students to the illustration in the middle of the page.

BUYING A PLANT ASSET FOR CASH

	DATE	ACCOUNT TITLE	CK. NO.	POST. REF.	GENERAL DEBIT	GENERAL CREDIT	ACCOUNTS PAYABLE DEBIT	PURCHASES DISCOUNT CREDIT	CASH CREDIT	
1	Jan. 2	Office Equipment	62		1 6 8 0 00				1 6 8 0 00	1

CASH PAYMENTS JOURNAL   PAGE 1

Appliance Center needs a new copying machine. Because this plant asset is to be used in the office, it is classified as office equipment.

January 2. Paid cash for new copying machine, $1,680.00. Check No. 62.

The entry is recorded in the cash payments journal as shown above. Appliance Center has three kinds of plant assets: office equipment, store equipment, and warehouse equipment. A separate general ledger account is used for each of these plant assets.

Office Equipment
1,680.00 |

Cash
| 1,680.00

BUYING A PLANT ASSET ON ACCOUNT

GENERAL JOURNAL   PAGE 1

	DATE	ACCOUNT TITLE	DOC. NO.	POST. REF.	DEBIT	CREDIT	
1	Jan. 2	Office Equipment	M70		3 3 0 0 00		1
2		Accts. Pay./Discount Computers		/		3 3 0 0 00	2

Not all plant assets are bought for cash. Appliance Center sometimes buys a plant asset on one date and pays for it on a later date.

January 2. Bought an office computer on account from Discount Computers, $3,300.00. Memorandum No. 70.

This transaction does not involve the purchase of merchandise. Therefore, the entry is not recorded in a purchases journal. It is recorded in the general journal as shown above. The entry is posted to both the general ledger and the accounts payable ledger.

GENERAL LEDGER
Office Equipment
3,300.00 |

Accounts Payable
| 3,300.00

ACCOUNTS PAYABLE LEDGER
Discount Computers
| 3,300.00

FYI FOR YOUR INFORMATION

An office equipment business may sell such things as desks, chairs, file cabinets, and typewriters. These items are for sale to customers and are not used in the operation of the office equipment business. Therefore, equipment purchased to sell to customers is classified as merchandise rather than as plant assets.

TEACHING STRATEGIES   DIFFERENT LEARNING ABILITIES

Limited English Proficiency (LEP) Students. Throughout the course, stress the accounting terms so that LEP students learn the language of accounting.

CALCULATING AND PAYING PROPERTY TAX

CASH PAYMENTS JOURNAL

PAGE **23**

	DATE	ACCOUNT TITLE	CK. NO.	POST. REF.	GENERAL DEBIT	GENERAL CREDIT	ACCOUNTS PAYABLE DEBIT	PURCHASES DISCOUNT CREDIT	CASH CREDIT	
					1	2	3	4	5	
1	Feb. 20-- 1	Property Tax Expense	122		3 2 5 0 00				3 2 5 0 00	1
2										2

In most states, businesses have to pay taxes on plant assets. For tax purposes, state and federal governments define two kinds of property: real and personal. Land and anything attached to it is called **real property**. Real property is sometimes referred to as real estate. All property not classified as real property is called **personal property**.

Assessed Value of Property

The value of an asset determined by tax authorities for the purpose of calculating taxes is called the **assessed value**. Assessed value is usually based on the judgment of persons referred to as assessors. Assessors are elected by citizens or are specially trained employees of a governmental unit.

An asset's assessed value may not be the same as the book value on the business's or individual's records. The assessed value is assigned to an asset for tax purposes only. Often the assessed value is only a part of the true value of the asset. However, many persons and businesses use the assessed value to estimate the market value of an asset.

Calculating Property Tax on Plant Assets

Most governmental units with taxing power have a tax based on the value of real property. The real property tax is used on buildings and land. Some governmental units also tax personal property such as cars, boats, trailers, and airplanes.

A governmental taxing unit determines a tax rate to use in calculating taxes. The tax rate is multiplied by an asset's *assessed* value, not the book value recorded on a business's records.

Appliance Center's buildings and land have been assessed for a total of $65,000.00. The city tax rate is 5%.

	Assessed Value	×	Tax Rate	=	Annual Property Tax
	$65,000.00	×	5%	=	$3,250.00

Paying Property Tax on Plant Assets

On February 1, Appliance Center paid its property tax as shown above.

> **Feb 1. Paid cash for property tax, $3,250.00. Check No. 122.**

Payment of property taxes is necessary if a firm is to continue in business. Therefore, Appliance Center classifies property tax as an operating expense.

Property Tax Expense	
3,250.00	

Cash	
	3,250.00

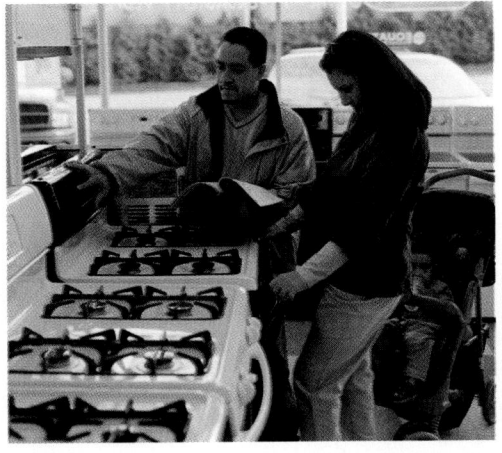

©GETTY IMAGES/PHOTODISC

Buying Plant Assets

Lesson 8-1   **227**

EXPLAIN

- Explain that property tax laws vary significantly from state to state. Local governments typically assess property taxes on real or personal property, or both.
- Ask students to identify the information needed to calculate property taxes.
- Point out that the assessed value is used for determining property taxes and may not be an appropriate value for making other business decisions.

DEMONSTRATE

Ask students to use a calculator to calculate the property tax as shown in the math box.

Analyze the transaction

- Draw two T accounts on the board and enter the balance amounts.
- Read the transaction statement.
- Ask students to analyze the transaction by answering: what accounts are affected, are they increased or decreased, and are they debited or credited.

Record the cash received

- Use a cash payments journal transparency to illustrate recording the transaction in the cash disbursements or direct students to the illustration.
- Remind students that the source document for this entry, a check, is recorded in the Ck No. column using the check number.

ONGOING ASSESSMENT

- Assessment is an ongoing process. Circulate through the classroom or lab observing which students have problems with the assignments.
- Troubleshooting: Diagnose what kinds of problems students have with this section. Students may have trouble understanding why the assessed value, rather than the cost of plant assets, is used to compute property taxes.
- Assess student understanding by checking solutions to Independent Practice assignments.

RETEACH

- Call on students to list the three sections of a plant asset record.
- Call on students to identify the transactions for purchasing plant assets for cash and on account.
- Ask students to describe how property taxes are calculated and journalized.

GUIDED PRACTICE

Terms Review

Call on students to define the terms in the Terms Review. Ask the class if the definitions are correct and whether the complete definitions have been given or if anything needs to be added. Suggested definitions for all terms are given in the Glossary.

Audit Your Understanding

Call on students to answer the Audit Your Understanding questions. Ask the class if the answer is correct and/or complete. Answers are given in Appendix E of the textbook.

Work Together

Have students write the solution to the Work Together problem as you guide the class through the examples.

- Direct students to record each transaction in the journals as you elicit class participation in analyzing and recording each transaction.

- Call on students to describe how to record the purchase of each plant asset on a plant asset record.

INDEPENDENT PRACTICE

On Your Own

- Assign the On Your Own problem to be worked independently.

- Use the Ongoing Assessment techniques to diagnose student understanding.

Application Problem

- Assign Application Problem 8-1: Journalizing entries to record buying plant assets.

- Assign Application Problem 8-2: Calculating and journalizing property tax.

Personal Trainer

- Students can access the Lesson 8-1 assessment material using this software.

Xtra! Web Site

- Students can access the Xtra! Study Tools for additional practice.

• terms review

plant asset record
real property
personal property
assessed value

• audit your understanding

1. What are the three sections of a plant asset record?
2. Why are asset purchases not recorded in a purchases journal?
3. What accounts are affected, and how, by an entry to pay property tax?

• work together 8-1

Journalizing asset purchase and property tax transactions

Depreciate all plant assets using the straight-line method. Plant asset records, a general journal, and a cash payments journal are provided in the *Working Papers*. Source documents are abbreviated as: check, C; memorandum, M. Your instructor will guide you through the following examples.

Jan. 3. Paid cash for scanner (plant asset no. 162), $600.00: no estimated salvage value; estimated useful life, three years; serial no. V2GR34. C310.

Jan. 5. Bought freight scale (plant asset no. 163) on account from Trent, Inc., $2,800.00: estimated salvage value, $400.00; estimated useful life, five years; serial no. GY52232B. M61.

Feb. 27. Paid property taxes on real property with an assessed value of $215,000.00. The tax rate in the city where the property is located is 3.5% of assessed value. C389.

1. Journalize the transactions completed during 20X1. General ledger accounts are: Office Equipment, 1225 and Warehouse Equipment, 1245.

2. Complete section 1 of a plant asset record for new asset purchases. Save your work to complete Work Together 8-2.

• on your own 8-1

Journalizing asset purchase and property tax transactions

Depreciate all plant assets using the straight-line method. Plant asset records, a general journal, and a cash payments journal are provided in the *Working Papers*. Source documents are abbreviated as: check, C; memorandum, M. Work independently to complete the following problem.

Jan. 2. Bought a cash register (plant asset no. 416) on account from JP Enterprises, $800.00: estimated salvage value, $200.00; estimated useful life, five years; serial no. G3HR644. M35.

Jan. 6. Paid cash for an office chair (plant asset no. 417), $500.00: estimated salvage value, $10.00; estimated useful life, seven years; serial no. FB1523. C415.

Feb. 26. Paid property taxes on real property with an assessed value of $280,000.00. The tax rate in the city where the property is located is 4.2% of assessed value. C489.

1. Journalize the transactions completed during 20X1. General ledger accounts are: Office Equipment, 1225 and Store Equipment, 1235.

2. Complete section 1 of a plant asset record for new asset purchases. Save your work to complete On Your Own 8-2.

Accounting for Plant Assets

ENRICH

- Ask students to research how property taxes are calculated in their community. Students should determine the meaning of the assessed value and how these amounts are determined. Students should also determine how the tax rates are set and how these rates may vary for different classes of property owners (for example, businesses, senior citizens, home owners).

- Assign Making Ethical Decisions on page 224.

CLOSE

- Ask students to briefly summarize the procedures for journalizing transactions to record the buying of plant assets.

8-2 Calculating and Journalizing Depreciation Expense

FACTORS USED TO CALCULATE DEPRECIATION

Plant assets may wear out, may no longer be needed in the operation of a business, or may become outdated by new models. To match revenue with the expenses incurred to earn it, the cost of a plant asset should be allocated to an expense account over the useful life of the plant asset. [CONCEPT: Matching Expenses with Revenue] The portion of a plant asset's cost that is transferred to an expense account in each fiscal period during a plant asset's useful life is known as depreciation expense.

Because of its permanent nature, land is not subject to depreciation. Increases or decreases in land value are usually recorded only when land is sold or otherwise disposed of.

Three factors are used to calculate a plant asset's annual depreciation expense:

1. Original cost.
2. Estimated salvage value.
3. Estimated useful life.

Original Cost
The original cost of a plant asset includes all costs paid to make the asset usable to a business. These costs include the purchase price, delivery costs, and any necessary installation costs. [CONCEPT: Historical Cost]

Estimated Salvage Value
When a plant asset is disposed of, some part of its original value may remain. When a plant asset is bought, its final value can only be estimated. The estimated salvage value is the amount an owner expects to receive when a plant asset is removed from use. Salvage value is also referred to as residual value, scrap value, or trade-in value.

Until a plant asset is disposed of, most businesses have difficulty determining its *exact* salvage value. Thus, until actually disposed of, a plant asset's salvage value can only be *estimated*. Because salvage value is used to calculate a plant asset's annual depreciation, the most accurate estimate possible is made when a plant asset is bought.

Estimated Useful Life
The estimated useful life of a plant asset is the number of years it is expected to be useful to a business. A plant asset's useful life differs from one situation to another. Most businesses use past experience as the basis for estimating a plant asset's useful life. If a calculator usually lasts five years for a specific business, then the business uses five years as the estimated useful life of a new calculator. Sometimes, however, a business has difficulty estimating a plant asset's useful life. In these cases, it may use the Internal Revenue Service's guidelines that give the estimated useful life for many plant assets.

Depreciation Methods
Various depreciation methods are illustrated in this chapter. A business should select the depreciation method that provides the best financial information. A business typically uses the same depreciation method for all assets within a plant asset category.

{ REMEMBER   Two of the three values used to compute depreciation are estimates. }

Calculating and Journalizing Depreciation Expense

- Define accounting terms related to plant assets and depreciation.
- Identify accounting concepts and practices related to accounting for plant assets and depreciation.
- Calculate and record depreciation expense for a plant asset using straight-line depreciation.

MOTIVATE

Plant assets represent a significant investment for most businesses. Therefore, the methods and estimates used to expense this investment over time has a significant impact on the financial statements.

Preview

- Preview the accounting terms and definitions introduced in this lesson: *straight-line method of depreciation* and *book value of a plant asset.*
- Direct students to read the headings at the top of each page in this lesson and to examine the illustrations given.
- Explain that this lesson is primarily a review of concepts and procedures presented in the first-year course.

EXPLAIN

- Remind students that depreciation is an estimate that attempts to match the cost of plant assets with the revenue earned using those plant assets.
- Ask students to identify the three factors used to calculate depreciation.
- Ask students to define each of the three factors.
- Ask students to identify the two depreciation methods that were presented in the first-year course *(straight-line* and *double declining-balance).*
- Ask students to read the Remember feature to reinforce that depreciation is an estimate.

MATERIALS

- Instructor's Resource CD:
  PowerPoint Slides
- Xtra! Study Tools on the Xtra! Web Site
- Blackline Masters:
  General Journal

- Working Papers:
  Teacher's Edition of the Working Papers for Lesson 8-2
- Software:
  Personal Trainer

- Ask students to identify how the estimated total depreciation expense is calculated.
- Point out that straight-line method esults in an equal amount of depreciation each year.
- Point out that the book value of a plant asset is the cost of the asset less accumulated depreciation. The term is more fully discussed on the following page.
- Ask students to read the F.Y.I. feature to learn an alternative way to calculate the annual depreciation expense.

DEMONSTRATE

Calculate annual depreciation

- Ask students to use a calculator to compute the annual depreciation expense calculated in the first math box.
- Ask students to prepare a new table assuming that the estimate salvage value is $300.00 and describe the impact of this change *(annual depreciation would decrease by $25.00)*.

Calculate the book value

- Ask students to use a calculator to compute the ending book value for any of the five years, as illustrated by the second math box.
- Ask students to identify the amounts that would appear on the balance sheet *(original cost, accumulated depreciation, and book value)*.

STRAIGHT-LINE DEPRECIATION

Plant asset: Computer		Original cost: $2,000.00	
Depreciation method: Straight-line		Estimated salvage value: $175.00	
		Estimated useful life: 5 years	

Year	Beginning Book Value	Annual Depreciation	Ending Book Value
1	$2,000.00	$ 365.00	$1,635.00
2	1,635.00	365.00	1,270.00
3	1,270.00	365.00	905.00
4	905.00	365.00	540.00
5	540.00	365.00	175.00
Total Depreciation	—	$1,825.00	—

Charging an equal amount of depreciation expense for a plant asset in each year of useful life is called the **straight-line method of depreciation**.

On January 2, 20X1, Appliance Center bought a computer for $2,000.00 with an estimated salvage value of $175.00 and an estimated useful life of five years. The details of the purchase and the depreciation amounts for each year of the asset's estimated useful life are shown above.

The estimated total depreciation expense is divided by the estimated useful life to compute the annual depreciation expense. The annual depreciation expense is the same for each year if the asset is used for the entire year.

	Original Cost	$ 2,000.00
−	Estimated Salvage Value	− 175.00
=	Estimated Total Depreciation Expense	$ 1,825.00
÷	Years of Estimated Useful Life	÷ 5
=	Annual Depreciation Expense	$ 365.00

The annual depreciation expense is subtracted from the beginning book value to compute the ending book value. The beginning book value for a year is the ending book value of the prior year.

	Beginning Book Value	−	Annual Depreciation	=	Ending Book Value
Year 3	$1,270.00	−	$365.00	=	$905.00

©GETTY IMAGES/PHOTODISC

TEACHING STRATEGIES   DIFFERENT LEARNING STYLES

Auditory Learner. The auditory learner can reinforce the learning of formulas by verbally explaining the formula and/or calculations to other students in a small group. In a group of three, for example, each student should get the opportunity to "teach" the formula to the other two students. Through this process, each student in the group will teach the formula once and learn the formula two times.

RECORDING DEPRECIATION ON PLANT ASSET RECORDS

PLANT ASSET RECORD, No. _86_	General Ledger Account No. _1225_
Description _Cabinet_	General Ledger Account _Office Equipment_

Date Bought _August 8, 20X1_	Serial Number _Z769D2_	Original Cost _$700.00_
Estimated Useful Life _5 years_	Estimated Salvage Value _$100.00_	Depreciation Method _Straight-Line_

Disposed of:	Discarded _____	Sold _____	Traded _____
Date _____		Disposal Amount _____	

YEAR	ANNUAL DEPRECIATION EXPENSE	ACCUMULATED DEPRECIATION	ENDING BOOK VALUE
20X1	50.00	50.00	650.00
20X2	120.00	170.00	530.00
20X3	→120.00	→290.00	410.00 ← ❸
20X4	120.00	410.00	290.00
20X5	❶ 120.00	❷ 530.00	170.00
20X6	70.00	600.00	100.00

3. Calculate ending book value.

1. Calculate annual depreciation expense.

2. Calculate accumulated depreciation.

	20X3 Depreciation Expense	+	20X2 Accumulated Depreciation	=	20X3 Accumulated Depreciation
20X3	$120.00	+	$170.00	=	$290.00

	Original Cost	−	Accumulated Depreciation	=	Ending Book Value
20X3	$700.00	−	$290.00	=	$410.00

Appliance Center records annual depreciation expense in two places for each plant asset:

1. On the plant asset record.
2. As part of the adjusting entries that are posted to general ledger accounts.

On December 31, Appliance Center recorded the annual depreciation expense on each plant asset record. The plant asset record for a cabinet used as office equipment is shown above.

In section 3 of the plant asset record, the year is recorded in the Year column. The depreciation expense for the plant asset is recorded in the Annual Depreciation Expense column. The amount recorded in the Annual Depreciation Expense column is $50.00, the depreciation expense for the months that the cabinet was used in 20X1. For a full year, the annual depreciation expense is $120.00. The amount of accumulated depreciation is recorded in the Accumulated

Depreciation column. The accumulated depreciation is the sum of the previous year's accumulated depreciation and the annual depreciation expense for the current year.

The original cost of a plant asset minus accumulated depreciation is called the **book value of a plant asset**. A new book value is calculated and recorded in the Ending Book Value column.

At the end of the estimated useful life, the cabinet should be depreciated down to its estimated salvage value. At the end of the sixth year, the ending book value is equal to the estimated salvage value, *$100.00*. The calculation for depreciation uses an *estimated* useful life. The cabinet's *actual* useful life may exceed the estimate made when the asset was put into use. If a plant asset is used longer than the estimated useful life, depreciation is *not* recorded once the book value equals the estimated salvage value.

JOURNALIZING ANNUAL DEPRECIATION EXPENSE

		GENERAL JOURNAL					PAGE 13
	DATE	ACCOUNT TITLE	DOC. NO.	POST. REF.	DEBIT	CREDIT	
1		*Adjusting Entries*					1
22	31	Depr. Exp.—Office Equipment			1 1 5 7 1 00		22
23		Accum. Depr.—Office Equipment				1 1 5 7 1 00	23
24							24

After depreciation expense is recorded on the plant asset records, depreciation amounts for the year are totaled.

An adjusting entry is made to record the total depreciation expense for the fiscal year for each category of plant assets. Appliance Center records separate adjusting entries for office equipment, store equipment, warehouse equipment, and building. The adjusting entry for office equipment is shown above.

Depreciation Expense—Office Equipment

| Dec. 31 Adj. | 11,571.00 | |

Accumulated Depreciation—Office Equipment

	Jan. 1 Bal.	37,434.00
	Dec. 31 Adj.	11,571.00
	Dec. 31 Bal.	*49,005.00*

CALCULATING DEPRECIATION EXPENSE FOR PART OF A YEAR

	Annual Depreciation Expense	$ 120.00
÷	Months in a Year	÷ 12
–	Monthly Depreciation Expense	$ 10.00
×	Number of Months Asset Is Used	× 5
–	Partial Year's Depreciation Expense	$ 50.00

A calendar month is the smallest unit of time used to calculate depreciation. A plant asset may be placed in service at a date other than the first day of a fiscal period. In such cases, depreciation expense is calculated to the nearest first of a month. To calculate depreciation expense for part of a year, the annual depreciation expense is divided by 12 to determine depreciation expense for a month. The monthly depreciation is then multiplied by the number of months the plant asset was used that year.

Appliance Center bought a cabinet on August 8, 20X1. The annual straight-line depreciation expense is $120.00. The depreciation expense for the part of the year that Appliance Center used the cabinet (August through December equals 5 months) is $50.00.

FYI FOR YOUR INFORMATION

Calculating depreciation expense for part of a year also is used when a plant asset is discarded or sold during a fiscal year. The partial year's depreciation expense is computed for the period from the start of the fiscal year to the date the asset is discarded or sold.

Accounting for Plant Assets

Explore Accounting

EXPLORE ACCOUNTING • EXPLORE ACCOUNTING • EXPLORE ACCOUNTING

Changes in Historic Cost

When a long-term asset is purchased, it is recorded at its *historic cost,* the actual amount paid for the asset. There are some circumstances when that historic cost could change over the life of the asset.

After an asset is put into service, money might have to be paid to maintain, repair, or replace a part of the asset. The accountant will have to decide if the payment qualifies as a repair or an improvement. The decision determines the accounts affected by the transaction.

If the expenditure merely maintains the asset in its normal operation, it should be treated as an expense in the period the payment is made. This category would include painting the inside or outside of a building, minor repairs on a delivery truck, regular maintenance on a piece of factory equipment, repairing gutters, and engine tune-ups. These costs typically bring the asset back to an original condition.

Therefore, the entry to record the payment of $500 for an engine tune-up would be as follows:

Repairs Expense	$500.00	
Cash		$500.00

If the expenditure adds to the value or extends the useful life of the asset, the cost must be added to the historic cost of the asset instead of treated as an immediate expense. This category would include adding a wing to a building, replacing the engine in a vehicle, and redoing the ventilation system of a building to include a state-of-the art air purification system.

The entry to record the payment of $10,000 to add an air purification system to a building would be:

Building	$10,000.00	
Cash		$10,000.00

By increasing the cost of the asset, the amount of depreciation to be recorded during the remaining useful life of the asset will also change.

Therefore, as odd as it may seem, the historic cost of an asset may not stay the same over the life of the asset.

Instructions

1. State whether each of the following expenditures would be treated as an expense or as an addition to the historic cost of the asset.
   a. Cost of plastering over a hole in a wall.
   b. Cost of replacing 20 shingles on the roof.
   c. Cost of lubricating a strapping machine.
   d. Cost of a major overhaul of the engine on the delivery truck, which will extend its useful life.
   e. Painting a machine to match other machines.

2. Suggest some other plant assets and the expenditures that might be made that would be considered as an addition to the historic cost of the asset.

EXPLORE ACCOUNTING
E X P L O R E   A C C O U N T I N G

1a. Expense
1b. Expense
1c. Expense
1d. Addition to the historic cost of the asset
1e. Expense
2. Answers will vary.

Calculating and Journalizing Depreciation Expense

234

GUIDED PRACTICE

Terms Review

Call on students to define the terms in the Terms Review. Ask the class if the definitions are correct and whether the complete definitions have been given or if anything needs to be added. Suggested definitions are given in the Glossary.

Audit Your Understanding

Call on students to answer the Audit Your Understanding questions. Ask the class if the answer is correct and/or complete. Answers are given in Appendix E of the textbook.

Work Together

Have students write the solution to the Work Together problems as you guide the class through the example.

- Call on a student to describe the calculation of the annual depreciation expense.
- Call on students to describe the calculation of the depreciation expense, accumulated depreciation, and book value for each year.
- Direct students to record each transaction in the general journal as you elicit class participation in analyzing and recording the transactions.

INDEPENDENT PRACTICE

On Your Own

- Assign the On Your Own problem to be worked independently.
- Use the Ongoing Assessment techniques to diagnose student understanding.

Application Problem

- Assign Application Problem 8-3: Calculating depreciation using the straight-line method.
- Assign Application Problem 8-4: Journalizing annual depreciation expense.

Personal Trainer

- Students can access the Lesson 8-2 assessment material using this software.

Xtra! Web Site

- Students can access the Xtra! Study Tools for additional practice.

• terms review

straight-line method of depreciation
book value of a plant asset

• audit your understanding

1. To match revenue with the expenses incurred to earn it, the cost of a plant asset should be allocated to an expense over what period of time?

2. Which accounting concept is being applied when depreciation expense is recorded for plant assets?

3. Why is annual depreciation for land not recorded?

4. What three factors are used to calculate a plant asset's annual depreciation expense?

5. What is the smallest unit of time used to calculate depreciation?

• work together 8-2

Calculating and journalizing depreciation

Use the plant asset records from Work Together 8-1. Depreciation tables and a general journal are provided in the *Working Papers*. Your instructor will guide you through the following examples.

1. Complete the depreciation table for each asset using the straight-line depreciation method. If the asset was not purchased at the beginning of 20X1, compute the depreciation expense for the part of 20X1 that the company owned the asset.

2. Complete each plant asset record for 20X1 through 20X4.

3. Journalize the adjusting entries to record depreciation expense for 20X1. Save your work to complete Work Together 8-3.

• on your own 8-2

Calculating and journalizing depreciation

Use the plant asset records from On Your Own 8-1. Depreciation tables and a general journal are provided in the *Working Papers*. Work this problem independently.

1. Complete the depreciation table for each asset using the straight-line depreciation method. If the asset was not purchased at the beginning of 20X1, compute the depreciation expense for the part of 20X1 that the company owned the asset.

2. Complete each plant asset record for 20X1 through 20X4.

3. Journalize the adjusting entries to record depreciation expense for 20X1. Save your work to complete On Your Own 8-3.

ENRICH

- Ask students to debate the following statement: "Some businesses use a half-year convention where a new plant asset is either depreciated an entire year or not at all in the first year." *(Any partial year method, applied consistently from year to year, will likely result in annual depreciation expense amounts that are materially the same.)*
- Assign Explore Accounting on page 233.

CLOSE

- Ask students to briefly summarize the procedures for calculating and recording depreciation expense using the straight-line method.

LESSON · LESSON · LESSON · LESSON · LESSON · LESSON

8-3 Disposing of Plant Assets

DISCARDING A PLANT ASSET WITH NO BOOK VALUE

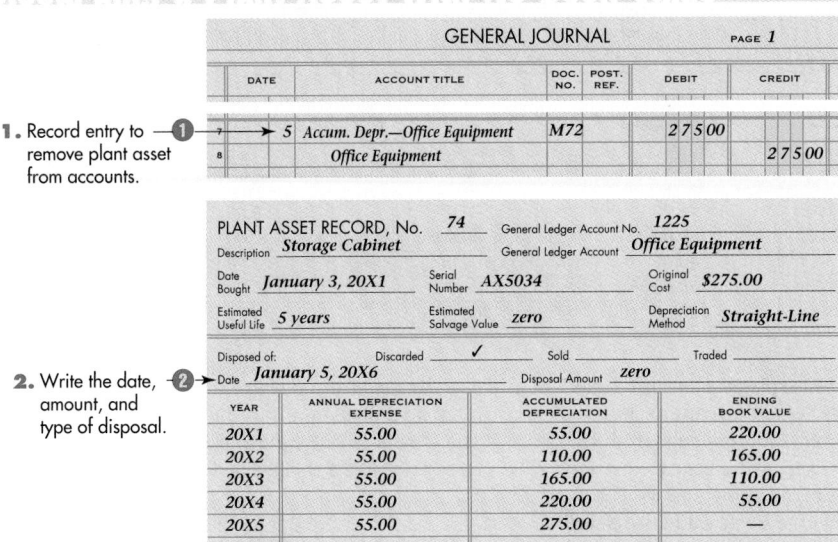

1. Record entry to remove plant asset from accounts.

GENERAL JOURNAL				PAGE 1	
DATE	ACCOUNT TITLE	DOC. NO.	POST. REF.	DEBIT	CREDIT
5	Accum. Depr.—Office Equipment	M72		275 00	
	Office Equipment				275 00

PLANT ASSET RECORD, No. _74_ **General Ledger Account No.** _1225_

Description _Storage Cabinet_ General Ledger Account _Office Equipment_

Date Bought _January 3, 20X1_ Serial Number _AX5034_ Original Cost _$275.00_

Estimated Useful Life _5 years_ Estimated Salvage Value _zero_ Depreciation Method _Straight-Line_

2. Write the date, amount, and type of disposal.

Disposed of: Discarded ✓ Sold _____ Traded _____

Date _January 5, 20X6_ Disposal Amount _zero_

YEAR	ANNUAL DEPRECIATION EXPENSE	ACCUMULATED DEPRECIATION	ENDING BOOK VALUE
20X1	55.00	55.00	220.00
20X2	55.00	110.00	165.00
20X3	55.00	165.00	110.00
20X4	55.00	220.00	55.00
20X5	55.00	275.00	—

Appliance Center usually disposes of plant assets in one of three ways:

1. The plant asset is discarded because no useful life remains.
2. The plant asset is sold because it is no longer needed even though it might still be usable.
3. The plant asset is traded for another plant asset of the same kind.

If a plant asset has a salvage value of zero and its total accumulated depreciation is equal to the original cost value, the plant asset has no book value. When a plant asset with no book value is discarded, a journal entry is recorded that removes the original cost of the plant asset and its related accumulated depreciation as shown above.

January 5, 20X6. Discarded storage cabinet: original cost, $275.00; total accumulated depreciation

through December 31, 20X5, $275.00. Memorandum No. 72.

Accumulated Depreciation—Office Equipment	
275.00	Bal. 275.00

Office Equipment	
Bal. 275.00	275.00

STEPS · STEPS · STEPS · STEPS · STEPS

DISCARDING A PLANT ASSET WITH NO BOOK VALUE

1 Record an entry on the general journal to remove the original cost, *275.00*, from Office Equipment and Accumulated Depreciation—Office Equipment. When this entry is posted, all amounts for the discarded cabinet are removed from the two accounts.

2 Check the type of disposal, *Discarded*, and write the date, *Jan. 5, 20X6*, and disposal amount, *zero*, on the plant asset record. These notations complete the history of the plant asset.

EXPLAIN

- Point out that most plant assets have a book value when discarded or sold.

- Ask students to describe the depreciation expense of a discarded plant asset. *(Calculate a partial year's depreciation for the period of time the plant asset was used.)*

- Ask students to explain why two journal entries are recorded to discard of a plant asset. *(One entry updates depreciation, the second entry records the disposition.)*

- Ask students to describe how to determine the loss on the disposal of a plant asset. *(Equals the book value after the depreciation entry.)*

- Ask students to explain why Loss on Plant Assets is not classified as an operating expense. *(The disposal of plant assets is not considered to be directly related to the production of revenue.)*

DEMONSTRATE

Update accumulated depreciation

- Draw four T accounts on the board.

- Read the transaction statement.

- Ask students to analyze the transaction. Complete the T accounts as the information is provided.

- As you read steps 1–3, have students record the journal entry and update the plant asset record.

Record the transaction

- Use a general journal transparency to illustrate recording the transaction in the general journal or direct students to the illustration.

- As you read step 4, ask students to analyze the adjustment by answering: what accounts are affected, are they increased or decreased, and are they debited or credited. Complete the T accounts as the information is provided.

DISCARDING A PLANT ASSET WITH A BOOK VALUE

GENERAL JOURNAL   PAGE 6

	DATE	ACCOUNT TITLE	DOC. NO.	POST. REF.	DEBIT	CREDIT	
4	30	Depr. Exp.—Office Equipment	M92		20 00		4
5		Accum. Depr.—Office Equipment				20 00	5
6	30	Accum. Depr.—Office Equipment	M92		160 00		6
7		Loss on Plant Assets			40 00		7
8		Office Equipment				200 00	8
9							9

1. Record a partial year's depreciation expense.

4. Record entry to remove plant asset from accounts.

3. Write the date, amount, and type of disposal.

Disposed of: Discarded ✓   Sold _____   Traded _____
Date **June 30, 20X6**   Disposal Amount *zero*

YEAR	ANNUAL DEPRECIATION EXPENSE	ACCUMULATED DEPRECIATION	ENDING BOOK VALUE
20X2	20.00	20.00	180.00
20X3	40.00	60.00	140.00
20X4	40.00	100.00	100.00
20X5	40.00	140.00	60.00
20X6	20.00	160.00	40.00

2. Record the partial year's depreciation.

A plant asset may be disposed of at any time during its useful life. When a plant asset is disposed of, its depreciation expense from the beginning of the current fiscal year to the date of disposal is recorded as shown above.

When an asset with a book value is discarded, a journal entry is recorded to: (1) Remove the original cost of the plant asset and its related accumulated depreciation. (2) Recognize the loss on disposal of the asset.

> *June 30, 20X6. Discarded office table: original cost, $200.00; total accumulated depreciation through December 31, 20X5, $140.00; additional depreciation to be recorded through June 30, 20X6, $20.00. Memorandum No. 92.*

The loss from discarding a plant asset with a book value is equal to the asset's book value. The loss is not an operating expense. Therefore, Loss on Plant Assets is classified as an Other Expense.

Depreciation Expense—Office Equipment

Add. Depr.	20.00

Accumulated Depreciation—Office Equipment

		Bal.	140.00
Disposal	160.00	Add. Depr.	20.00

Loss on Plant Assets

Disposal	40.00

Office Equipment

Bal.	200.00	Disposal	200.00

STEPS • STEPS • STEPS • STEPS • STEPS • STEPS • STEPS • STEPS • STEPS • STEPS • STEPS

DISCARDING AN ASSET WITH A BOOK VALUE

1 Record a partial year's depreciation expense, *20.00*, by debiting Depreciation Expense—Office Equipment and crediting Accumulated Depreciation—Office Equipment.

2 Record the depreciation in section 3 of the plant asset record.

3 Check the type of disposal, *Discarded*, and write the date, *June 30, 20X6*, and the disposal amount, *zero*, on the plant asset record. These notations complete the history of the plant asset.

4 Record an entry to remove the original cost, *200.00*, from Office Equipment and *160.00* from Accumulated Depreciation—Office Equipment. Record the loss on disposal, *40.00*, as a debit to Loss on Plant Assets.

SELLING A PLANT ASSET

Cash Received		$185.00
Book Value of Asset Sold:		
Cost	$600.00	
Accum. Depr.	400.00	200.00
Gain (Loss) on Sale of		
Plant Asset		$(15.00)

3. Record entry to remove plant asset from accounts.

1. Compute the gain or loss on the sale.

CASH RECEIPTS JOURNAL — PAGE 1

DATE	ACCOUNT TITLE	DOC. NO.	POST. REF.	GENERAL DEBIT	GENERAL CREDIT	ACCOUNTS RECEIVABLE CREDIT	SALES CREDIT	SALES TAX PAYABLE DEBIT	SALES TAX PAYABLE CREDIT	SALES DISCOUNT DEBIT	CASH DEBIT
20X6 Jan. 4	Accum. Depr.—Office Equip.	R60		400 00							185 00
	Loss on Plant Assets			15 00							
	Office Equipment				600 00						

Disposed of: Discarded _____ Sold ✓ Traded _____
Date **Jan. 4, 20X6** Disposal Amount **$185.00**

YEAR	ANNUAL DEPRECIATION EXPENSE	ACCUMULATED DEPRECIATION	ENDING BOOK VALUE

2. Write the date, amount, and type of disposal.

When a plant asset is sold, a journal entry is recorded to:

1. Remove the original cost of the plant asset and its related accumulated depreciation.
2. Recognize the cash received.
3. Recognize the gain or loss on disposal of the asset.

January 4, 20X6. Received cash from sale of fax machine, $185.00: original cost, $600.00; total accumulated depreciation through December 31, 20X5, $400.00. Receipt No. 60.

The amount of gain or loss is calculated by subtracting the book value from the cash received. The $15.00 loss on disposal is recorded as a debit to Loss on Plant Assets as shown above.

The sale of plant assets is not a normal operating activity of Appliance Center. A loss from the sale of plant assets is classified as Other Expense.

Cash	
185.00	

Accumulated Depreciation—Office Equipment	
400.00	Bal. 400.00

Loss on Plant Assets	
15.00	

Office Equipment	
Bal. 600.00	600.00

STEPS • SELLING A PLANT ASSET

1. Compute the gain or loss, *15.00 loss*, by subtracting the book value of the asset, *200.00*, from the cash received, *185.00*.
2. Check the type of disposal, *Sold*, and write the date, *January 4, 20X6*, and the disposal amount, *$185.00*, on the plant asset record. These notations complete the history of the plant asset.
3. Record an entry on the cash receipts journal to remove the original cost, *600.00*, from Office Equipment and *400.00* from Accumulated Depreciation—Office Equipment. Record the loss on **sale**, *15.00*, **as a debit to Loss on Plant Assets.**

Disposing of Plant Assets

Lesson 8-3   **237**

EXPLAIN

- Point out that plant assets can be sold as a productive asset or for scrap.
- Ask students to describe the calculation of the gain or loss on the sale of the plant asset.
- Ask students to explain why, unlike the entries on the previous two pages, this transaction is recorded on a cash receipts journal. *(Because the plant asset was sold for cash.)*
- Ask students to explain why a partial year's depreciation was not recorded. *(Because the plant asset was sold on Jan. 4, the plant asset was not considered to have been used during 20X6.)*

DEMONSTRATE

Analyze the transaction

- Read the transaction statement.
- As you read steps 1–2, have students compute the gain or loss and update the plant asset record.
- Draw four T accounts on the board.
- Ask students to analyze the transaction by answering: what accounts are affected, are they increased or decreased, and are they debited or credited. Complete the T accounts as the information is provided.

Record the transaction

- Use a general journal transparency to illustrate recording the transaction in the cash receipts journal or direct students to the illustration.
- As you read step 3, have students record the entry.
- Remind students that the abbreviation for the receipt, R, and the receipt number are recorded in the Doc. No. column.

TEACHING STRATEGIES   DIFFERENT LEARNING STYLES

Visual Learner. Formulas, such as those used to calculate depreciation expense, should be illustrated on the board or overhead to assist visual learners. The instructor should also complete the calculations for a few depreciable assets to show the process to visual learners.

237

- Point out that no gain or loss is recognized when a plant asset is traded for a similar plant asset.
- Ask students to describe the calculation of the cost of the new plant asset.
- Ask students to explain why the transaction is recorded on a payments journal. *(Because a portion of the purchase price was paid in cash.)*

DEMONSTRATE

Analyze the transaction
- Read the transaction statement.
- As you read steps 1–3, have students compute the gain or loss and update the plant asset record.
- Draw three T accounts on the board.
- Ask students to analyze the transaction by answering: what accounts are affected, are they increased or decreased, and are they debited or credited. Complete the T accounts as the information is provided.

Record the transaction
- Use a general journal transparency to illustrate recording the transaction in the cash payments journal or direct students to the illustration.
- As you read step 4, have students record the entry.
- Remind students that the source document is a check and the check number is recorded in the Ck. No. column.

TRADING A PLANT ASSET

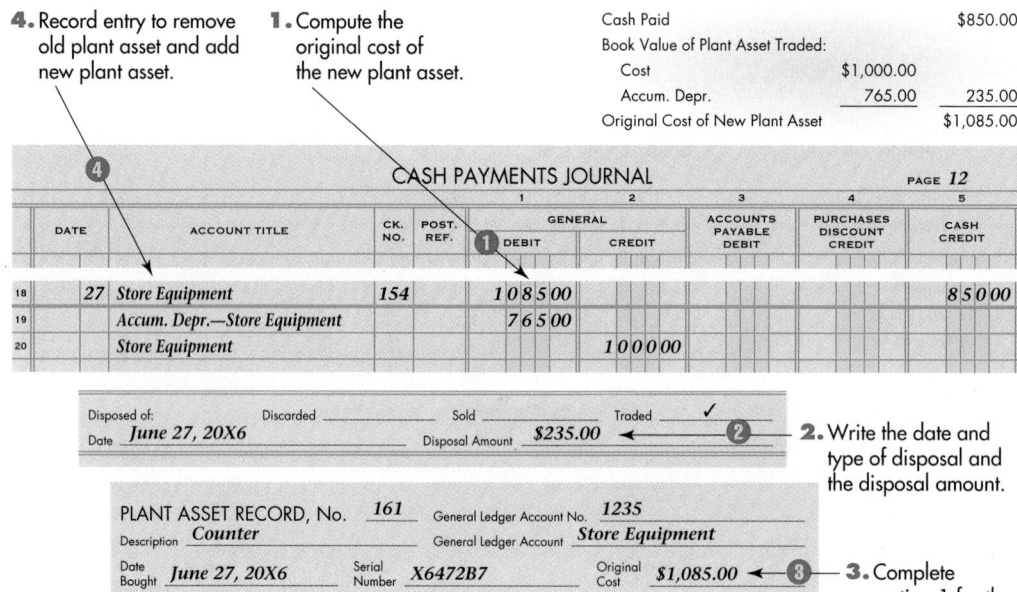

4. Record entry to remove old plant asset and add new plant asset.

1. Compute the original cost of the new plant asset.

Cash Paid			$850.00
Book Value of Plant Asset Traded:			
Cost		$1,000.00	
Accum. Depr.		765.00	235.00
Original Cost of New Plant Asset			$1,085.00

CASH PAYMENTS JOURNAL   PAGE *12*

	DATE	ACCOUNT TITLE	CK. NO.	POST. REF.	GENERAL DEBIT	GENERAL CREDIT	ACCOUNTS PAYABLE DEBIT	PURCHASES DISCOUNT CREDIT	CASH CREDIT	
18	27	*Store Equipment*	154		1085 00				850 00	18
19		*Accum. Depr.—Store Equipment*			765 00					19
20		*Store Equipment*				1000 00				20

Disposed of: Discarded _____   Sold _____   Traded ✓

Date *June 27, 20X6*   Disposal Amount *$235.00* ← ②

2. Write the date and type of disposal and the disposal amount.

PLANT ASSET RECORD, No. *161*   General Ledger Account No. *1235*

Description *Counter*   General Ledger Account *Store Equipment*

Date Bought *June 27, 20X6*   Serial Number *X6472B7*   Original Cost *$1,085.00* ← ③

3. Complete section 1 for the new plant asset.

Appliance Center needed a new store counter. The vendor agreed to take cash and an old store counter in trade. The new plant asset's original cost equals the cash *actually* paid plus the book value of the asset traded. [*CONCEPT: Historical Cost*]

When an old plant asset is traded for a new plant asset, the journal entry:

1. Removes the original cost of the old plant asset and its related accumulated depreciation.
2. Recognizes the cash paid.
3. Records the new plant asset at its original cost.

June 27, 20X6. Paid cash, $850.00, plus old counter for new store counter: original cost of old counter, $1,000.00; total accumulated depreciation through June 27, 20X6, $765.00. Memorandum No. 130 and Check No. 154.

Store Equipment

| Bal. | 1,000.00 | Trade-in | 1,000.00 |
| New Equip. | 1,085.00 | | |

Accumulated Depreciation—Store Equipment

| 765.00 | Bal. | 765.00 |

Cash

| | 850.00 |

STEPS   •   STEPS   •   STEPS   •   STEPS

TRADING A PLANT ASSET

① Compute the original cost of the new asset, *$1,085.00*, by adding the book value of the asset traded, *$235.00*, and the cash paid, *$850.00*.

② Check the type of disposal, *Traded*, and write the date, *June 27, 20X6*, and the disposal amount, *$235.00*, on the plant asset record of the traded asset.

③ Complete section 1 of the plant asset record for the new asset.

④ Record the journal entry to reflect the trade of plant assets.

APPLIED SKILLS   LANGUAGE ARTS

Paraphrasing, writing complete sentences, and identifying subjects. For additional practice in language arts skills, direct students to write the answers to the Audit Your Understanding questions in their own words and in complete sentences. To further practice language arts skills, ask students to underline the subject(s) in each sentence of their answers.

SELLING LAND AND BUILDINGS

2. Write the date, type, and amount of disposal.

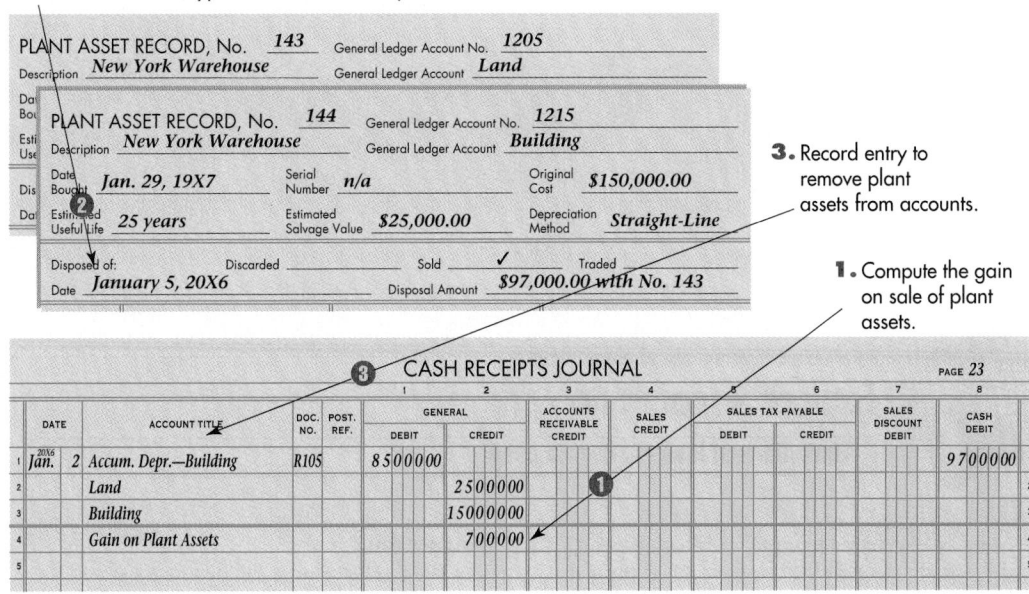

PLANT ASSET RECORD, No. **143**   General Ledger Account No. **1205**
Description **New York Warehouse**   General Ledger Account **Land**

PLANT ASSET RECORD, No. **144**   General Ledger Account No. **1215**
Description **New York Warehouse**   General Ledger Account **Building**

Date Bought **Jan. 29, 19X7**   Serial Number **n/a**   Original Cost **$150,000.00**

Estimated Useful Life **25 years**   Estimated Salvage Value **$25,000.00**   Depreciation Method **Straight-Line**

Disposed of: Discarded _____ Sold **✓** Traded _____
Date **January 5, 20X6**   Disposal Amount **$97,000.00 with No. 143**

3. Record entry to remove plant assets from accounts.

1. Compute the gain on sale of plant assets.

CASH RECEIPTS JOURNAL   PAGE 23

| | | | | | GENERAL | | ACCOUNTS RECEIVABLE CREDIT | SALES CREDIT | SALES TAX PAYABLE | | SALES DISCOUNT DEBIT | CASH DEBIT | |
DATE	ACCOUNT TITLE	DOC. NO.	POST. REF.	DEBIT	CREDIT				DEBIT	CREDIT			
20X6 Jan. 2	Accum. Depr.—Building	R105		85000 00								97000 00	1
	Land				25000 00								2
	Building				150000 00								3
	Gain on Plant Assets				7000 00								4
													5

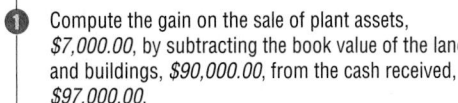

Land is considered to be a permanent plant asset. Therefore, its useful life is not estimated, and annual depreciation is not recorded for it. The book value of land is the original cost. [*CONCEPT: Historical Cost*]

Land is seldom discarded (abandoned). Usually land is sold at the same time that the buildings on it are sold. A separate plant record is maintained for the land and the building. Each record is updated when a sale is made.

> **January 2, 20X6. Fidelity Company sold land with a building for $97,000.00 cash; original cost of land, $25,000.00; original cost of building, $150,000.00; total accumulated depreciation on building through December 31, 20X5, $85,000.00. Receipt No. 105.**

The journal entry:

1. Removes the original cost of the land and building and the building's related accumulated depreciation.
2. Recognizes the cash received.
3. Recognizes the gain on disposal of the plant assets.

STEPS   STEPS • STEPS • STEPS • STEPS •
SELLING LAND AND BUILDINGS

1 Compute the gain on the sale of plant assets, *$7,000.00*, by subtracting the book value of the land and buildings, *$90,000.00*, from the cash received, *$97,000.00*.

2 Check the type of disposal, *Sold*, and write the date, *Jan. 2, 20X6*, and the disposal amount, *$97,000.00*, on each plant asset record. Include a reference to the other plant asset included in the sale.

3 Record an entry on the cash receipts journal to remove the original cost of land, *25,000.00*, and buildings, *150,000.00*, and to remove *85,000.00* from Accumulated Depreciation—Building. Record the gain on sale, *7,000.00*, as a credit to Gain on Plant Assets.

- Ask students to explain why land is not depreciated.
- Point out that buildings and land are typically sold for a single purchase price.
- Ask student to review the method to calculate the gain or loss on the sale of plant assets.

DEMONSTRATE

Analyze the transaction

- Draw five T accounts on the board.
- Read the transaction statement.
- Ask students to compute the gain or loss on the sale.
- Ask students to analyze the transaction by answering: what accounts are affected, are they increased or decreased, and are they debited or credited. Complete the T accounts as the information is provided.

Record the transaction

- Use a general journal transparency to illustrate recording the transaction in the cash receipts journal or direct students to the illustration.
- Record the entry in the journal and update the plant asset records using the three steps listed.

EXPLAIN

- Discuss how the gain or loss calculation method shown on the following page is the same as students have described, except that two plant assets are sold rather than one.

ONGOING ASSESSMENT

- Assessment is an ongoing process. Circulate through the classroom or lab observing which students have problems with the assignments.

- Troubleshooting: Diagnose what kinds of problems students have with this section. Students may have trouble understanding how to (1) calculate the gain or loss on the sale of a plant asset, (2) identify the accounts involved in a sale or disposition of a plant asset, or (3) identify the appropriate journal to use when recording a plant asset disposition.

- Assess student understanding by checking solutions to Independent Practice assignments.

RETEACH

- Ask students to prepare a list of all the transactions presented in this section.

- Remind students that a partial year's depreciation expense should be recorded before the gain or loss on any plant asset is calculated. Stated another way, students should make sure that the book value of the plant asset is up to date.

- Ask students to make up original entries that result in both gains and losses on the sales of plant assets.

- Direct the students to journalize the entries.

CALCULATING THE GAIN ON SALE OF LAND AND BUILDINGS

The amount of the gain is the cash received less the book value of the assets sold.

	Land	Building	Total
Cash Received			$97,000.00
Cost of Assets	$25,000.00	$150,000.00	
Accumulated Depreciation		85,000.00	
Book Values of Assets Sold	25,000.00	65,000.00	90,000.00
Gain on Sale of Plant Assets			$ 7,000.00

Explore Accounting

EXPLORE ACCOUNTING • EXPLORE ACCOUNTING • EXPLORE ACCOUNTING

Limitations of Historic Cost Concept

Most assets are recorded at their historic cost, the actual cost paid for the asset. Over time, this historic cost can be quite different than the fair market value of the asset, which is the amount for which the asset could be sold at any time.

The difference between the historic cost and the fair market value of an asset can make a difference when performing financial statement analysis during a period of changing prices. Any calculation that includes total assets will be affected by the required use of historic cost instead of fair market value for assets.

One example of the limitations of using historic cost is if two businesses own identical buildings. Company A bought the building 10 years ago and paid $50,000. Company B bought the building yesterday and paid $150,000. Company A can show an asset of only $50,000, while Company B will show an asset of $150,000 for the identical building. A potential investor could be led to believe that Company B has a more valuable building than Company A. A banker may be willing to give a bigger loan to Company B.

Regardless of which amount is more accurate, GAAP requires the use of historic cost for most assets.

Instructions

The table below shows the historic cost and the current market value for the assets owned by the Smith Company.

Account Title	Historic Cost	Market Value
Cash	$10,000	$10,000
Accounts Receivable	3,000	3,000
Equipment	15,000	10,000
Building	25,000	45,000
Land	20,000	75,000

1. Calculate the total assets using historic cost.

2. Calculate the market value of the assets owned by the Smith Company.

3. Which amount do you feel is more relevant to a bank loan officer in determining if Smith Company qualifies for a loan?

4. Why does GAAP require that most assets be listed at historic cost?

EXPLORE ACCOUNTING
EXPLORE ACCOUNTING

1. $73,000

2. $143,000

3. The current value of Smith Company's assets would probably be more relevant to the bank loan officer.

4. GAAP requires the use of historic cost because it is more reliable. It is felt that market value is too subjective.

• audit your understanding

1. What is recorded on a plant asset record for a plant asset that has been discarded?

2. When an asset is disposed of after the beginning of the fiscal year, what entry may need to be recorded before an entry is made for a discarded plant asset?

3. What is the formula to compute the gain or loss on the sale of a plant asset?

4. When cash is paid and old store equipment is traded for new store equipment, what is the formula for calculating the new equipment's original cost?

• work together 8-3

Recording the disposal of plant assets

Use the plant asset records from Work Together 8-2. The following transactions occurred in 20X5. A general journal, cash receipts journal, and plant asset records are provided in the *Working Papers*. Source documents are abbreviated as follows: check, C; memorandum, M; receipt, R. Your instructor will guide you through the following examples.

Jan.   3. Discarded scanner, no. 162. M65.
Mar. 30. Received cash for sale of freight scale, no.163, $600.00. M125 and R145.
June 26. Received cash for sale of a desk, no. 127, $500.00. M151 and R273.
Dec. 28. Paid cash, $30,000.00, plus old truck, no. 116, for new truck, no. 172. M222 and C671.
Dec. 30. Sold land, no. 105, and a building, no.106, for $110,000.00. M224 and R663.

1. Journalize additional depreciation, if needed. Journalize the disposal of each plant asset.

2. Make appropriate notations in the plant asset records.

• on your own 8-3

Recording the disposal of plant assets

Use the plant asset records from On Your Own 8-2. The following transactions occurred in 20X5. A general journal, cash receipts journal, and plant asset records are provided in the *Working Papers*. Source documents are abbreviated as follows: check, C; memorandum, M; receipt, R. Work this problem independently.

Jan.   4. Discarded office chair, no. 417. M5.
May   28. Received cash for sale of cash register, no. 416, $100.00. M52 and R243.
June 30. Sold land, no. 390, and a building, no. 391, for $106,000.00. M63 and R283.
Oct.   2. Discarded office file cabinet, no. 369. M121.
Dec. 29. Paid cash, $1,200.00, plus old computer, no. 428, for new computer, no. 439. M153 and C775.

1. Journalize additional depreciation, if needed. Journalize the disposal of each plant asset.

2. Make appropriate notations in the plant asset records.

Disposing of Plant Assets

Lesson 8-3   **241**

GUIDED PRACTICE

Audit Your Understanding

Call on students to answer the Audit Your Understanding questions. Ask the class if the answer is correct and/or complete. Answers are given in Appendix E of the textbook.

Work Together

Have students write the solution to the Work Together problem as you guide the class through the examples. For each transaction,

- Ask students to calculate the gain or loss, if any, on the disposition of the plant asset.

- Ask a student to identify the appropriate journal to record the entry.

- Direct students to record the transactions on the journal.

- Direct student to record the appropriate information on the plant asset record.

INDEPENDENT PRACTICE

On Your Own

- Assign the On Your Own problem to be worked independently.

- Use the Ongoing Assessment techniques to diagnose student understanding.

Application Problem

- Assign Application Problem 8-5: Recording disposal of plant assets.

- Assign Application Problem 8-6: Recording the sale of land and building.

Personal Trainer

- Students can access the Lesson 8-3 assessment material using this software.

Xtra! Web Site

- Students can access the Xtra! Study Tools for additional practice.

ENRICH

- Except for the gains and losses, financial statements do not report the amounts related to the disposition of plant assets. The Securities and Exchange Commission (SEC), however, requires publicly traded companies to report this information to the SEC in a separate report called the 10-K. These reports are not regularly distributed to stockholders but are available on-line or by request.

- Assign Explore Accounting on page 240.

CLOSE

- Ask students to list the information required to record the sale or disposition of a plant asset.

- Ask students to explain how to calculate the gain or loss on the sale or disposition of a plant asset.

8-4 Other Methods of Depreciation

DECLINING-BALANCE METHOD OF DEPRECIATION

Total Depreciation Expense		100%
÷	Estimated Useful Life	÷ 5 years
=	Straight-Line Rate	20%
×	Double the Rate	× 2
=	Declining-Balance Rate	40%

1. Calculate the declining-balance rate.

Plant asset: Computer
Depreciation method: Declining balance

Original cost: $2,000.00
Estimated salvage value: $175.00
Estimated useful life: 5 years

Year	Beginning Book Value	Declining-Balance Rate	Annual Depreciation	Ending Book Value
1	$2,000.00	40%	$ 800.00	$1,200.00
2	1,200.00	40%	480.00	720.00
3	720.00	40%	288.00	432.00
4	432.00	40%	172.80	259.20
5	259.20	40%	84.20	175.00
Total Depreciation	—		$1,825.00	—

	Beginning Book Value	×	Depreciation Rate	=	Annual Depreciation Expense
Year 3	$720.00	×	40%	=	$288.00

2. Calculate the annual depreciation.

Many plant assets depreciate more in the early years of useful life than in the later years. Charging more depreciation expense in the early years of a plant asset may be more accurate than charging the same amount each year.

Multiplying the book value at the end of each fiscal period by a constant depreciation rate is called the **declining-balance method of depreciation**. Although the depreciation rate is the same each year, the annual depreciation expense declines from year to year.

The declining-balance depreciation rate is based on the straight-line rate. A declining-balance rate that is twice the straight-line rate is commonly used. This method of depreciation is referred to as the double declining-balance method. For example, a plant asset with an

estimated useful life of five years would have a depreciation rate of 40%.

When the declining-balance method is used, the annual depreciation expense is calculated using the beginning book value for each year. The beginning book value is the same as the ending book value from the previous year. In the asset's first year of service, the beginning book value equals its original cost.

A plant asset is never depreciated below its estimated salvage value. Therefore, in the last year, only enough depreciation expense is recorded to reduce the book value of the plant asset to its salvage value. Thus, the depreciation expense in the fifth year is limited to $84.20 ($259.20 − $175.00).

> **REMEMBER** The declining-balance method does not use the estimated salvage value to compute annual depreciation. The estimated salvage value is used only to limit the last year's depreciation expense.

Accounting for Plant Assets

SUM-OF-THE-YEARS'-DIGITS METHOD OF DEPRECIATION

Years' Digits	Fraction
1	5/15
2	4/15
3	3/15
4	2/15
5	1/15
Total	15

1. Calculate the fraction.

Plant asset: Computer
Depreciation method: Sum-of-the-years'-digits

Original cost: $2,000.00
Estimated salvage value: $175.00
Estimated useful life: 5 years

Year	Beginning Book Value	Fraction	Total Depreciation	Annual Depreciation	Ending Book Value
1	$2,000.00	5/15	$1,825.00	$ 608.33	$1,391.67
2	1,391.67	4/15	$1,825.00	486.67	905.00
3	905.00	3/15	$1,825.00	365.00	540.00
4	540.00	2/15	$1,825.00	243.33	296.67
5	296.67	1/15	$1,825.00	121.67	175.00
Total Depreciation				$1,825.00	

Original Cost	$2,000.00
Estimated Salvage Value	−175.00
Estimated Total Depreciation Expense	$1,825.00
Year's Fraction	× 5/15
Annual Depreciation Expense	$608.33

2. Calculate the annual depreciation.

Another method of calculating depreciation is based on a fraction derived from the years' digits for the useful life of a plant asset. Using fractions based on the number of years of a plant asset's useful life is called the **sum-of-the-years'-digits method of depreciation**.

The fractions are determined as follows: The years' digits are added (1 + 2 + 3 + 4 + 5 = 15). Then, using the sum of the years' digits, a fraction is created for each year with the years' digits in reverse order. Year 1 has a fraction of 5/15. Year 5 has a fraction of 1/15.

The depreciation expense for each year is calculated by multiplying the total depreciation expense times the fraction for that year.

The sum-of-the-years'-digits method results in a last year ending book value equal to the plant asset's salvage value.

FYI
FOR YOUR INFORMATION

A company can select any generally accepted depreciation method. Once it has selected a method, however, the company cannot change the method unless it can show that the new method would better report the company's financial activities.

REMEMBER Like the straight-line method, the estimated salvage value is subtracted from the original cost to compute an estimated total depreciation expense. Thus, the estimated salvage value is used to compute each year's annual depreciation expense.

Other Methods of Depreciation

Lesson 8-4 **243**

- Point out that all three depreciation methods are generally accepted.

- Ask students to compare the annual depreciation for each year by referencing the illustration.

- Remind students that each depreciation method results in the same amount of depreciation over the useful life of the asset.

COMPARISON OF THREE METHODS OF DEPRECIATION

Plant asset: Computer
Depreciation method: Comparison

Original cost: $2,000.00
Estimated salvage value: $175.00
Estimated useful life: 5 years

Year	Straight-Line Method	Double Declining-Balance Method	Sum-of-the-Years'-Digits Method
1	$ 365.00	$800.00	$ 608.33
2	365.00	480.00	486.67
3	365.00	288.00	365.00
4	365.00	172.80	243.33
5	365.00	84.20	121.67
Total Depreciation	$1,825.00	$1,825.00	$1,825.00

Regardless of the depreciation method used, the total depreciation expense over the useful life of an asset is the same as that shown above.

Each of these depreciation methods conforms to generally accepted accounting principles. The straight-line method is easy to calculate. The same amount of depreciation expense is recorded for each of the five years of estimated life.

The double declining-balance method is relatively easy to calculate. This method records a larger depreciation expense in the early years than the straight-line method does.

The sum-of-the-years'-digits method is not as easy to use as the straight-line or declining-balance methods. This method also records a higher depreciation expense in the early years than the straight-line method does. Both the declining-balance method and the sum-of-the-years'-digits method are known as accelerated depreciation methods.

technology for business

TECHNOLOGY FOR BUSINESS • TECHNOLOGY FOR BUSINESS • TECHNOLOGY FOR BU

Spreadsheet Activity—Depreciation Schedule

Briarwood Center, an executive conference center, uses a spreadsheet to calculate depreciation. The following information is available for a high-volume photocopy machine:

Original cost	$22,700
Estimated salvage value	$4,500
Estimated useful life, in years	5

Required
1. Create a depreciation schedule spreadsheet. Use the schedule at the top of page 230 as a model. Write formulas to calculate annual depreciation, ending book value, and total depreciation.

2. Make copies of the spreadsheet you created in 1 to calculate the depreciation for the display equipment. Use the information below.

Original cost	$6,800
Estimated salvage value	$1,200
Estimated useful life, in years	3

Accounting for Plant Assets

The Technology for Business feature is designed to show students common business applications of technology. Ask students if they can think of any other spreadsheet applications a small business that does not have an automated accounting system could use.

If classroom computer time is limited, prepare a spreadsheet table showing row and column labels. Enter the basic data. Ask students to write the formulas to calculate annual depreciation, ending book value, and total depreciation. The formulas should use cell references.

PRODUCTION-UNIT METHOD OF DEPRECIATION

	Original cost	$ 18,200.00
−	Estimated Salvage Value	− 2,000.00
=	Estimated Total Depreciation Expense	$ 16,200.00
÷	Estimated Useful Life	÷ 90,000 miles
=	Depreciation Rate	$0.18/mile

Plant asset: Truck
Depreciation method: Production-unit
Original cost: $18,200.00
Estimated salvage value: $2,000.00

❶ 1. Calculate the depreciation rate.

Estimated total depreciation: $16,200.00
Estimated useful life: 90,000 miles
Depreciation rate: $0.18 per mile driven

Year	Beginning Book Value	Miles Driven	Annual Depreciation	Ending Book Value
1	$18,200.00	9,000	$ 1,620.00	$16,580.00
2	16,580.00	23,000	4,140.00	12,440.00
3	12,440.00	25,000	4,500.00	7,940.00
4	7,940.00	22,000	3,960.00	3,980.00
5	3,980.00	8,000	1,440.00	2,540.00
Totals		87,000	$15,660.00	

	Total Miles Driven	×	Depreciation Rate	=	Annual Depreciation Expense
Year 1	9,000	×	$0.18	=	$1,620.00

❷ 2. Calculate the annual depreciation.

Sometimes the useful life of a plant asset depends on how much the asset is used. For example, an automobile will wear out faster if it is driven 80,000 miles a year rather than 60,000 miles. Calculating estimated annual depreciation expense based on the amount of production expected from a plant asset is called the **production-unit method of depreciation**.

Mariah Delivery Service owns a small truck. The truck originally cost $18,200.00, and had an estimated salvage value of $2,000.00 and an estimated useful life of 90,000 miles. The depreciation rate for the truck is calculated by dividing the estimated total depreciation expense by the estimated useful life.

Depreciation expense for each year of the truck's estimated useful life is calculated at 18 cents per mile driven. The annual depreciation

expense for the truck is calculated by multiplying the total number of miles driven by the depreciation rate. After five years, $15,660.00 of depreciation has been expensed, as shown above. Additional depreciation expense will be recorded in future years as the truck approaches its 90,000 miles of useful life.

FYI FOR YOUR INFORMATION

Although relatively easy to compute, the production-units method of depreciation significantly increases the work required to compute depreciation. The company must collect the production units for each asset. For large companies with many locations, the collection of this information can be a difficult task.

{ **REMEMBER** The accounts used to record depreciation expense are the same regardless of the depreciation method used. }

Other Methods of Depreciation

- Point out that MACRS is not a generally accepted depreciation methods for financial reporting.
- Discuss that MACRS classifies all assets into property classes.
- Ask students to explain why the rates for 5-year property extend over 6 years. *(MACRS assumes all assets are placed into service during the middle of the year 1; thus, 5 years of depreciation ends in the middle of year 6.)*
- Ask students to read the F.Y.I. to understand how the MACRS system was created.

DEMONSTRATE

- Draw three columns on the board and label the columns as shown in the illustration.
- Ask a student to calculate and record the amounts for year 1.
- Ask students to take turns completing the table.
- Point out that MACRS totally depreciates the asset, leaving no salvage value.

CALCULATING DEPRECIATION EXPENSE FOR INCOME TAX PURPOSES

Plant asset: Printer		Original cost: $2,000.00
Depreciation method: MACRS		Property class: 5 year

Year	Depreciation Rate	Annual Depreciation
1	20.00%	$400.00
2	32.00%	640.00
3	19.20%	384.00
4	11.52%	230.40
5	11.52%	230.40
6	5.76%	115.20
Totals	100.00%	$2,000.00

Most businesses use one of the generally accepted accounting methods to calculate depreciation for financial reporting purposes. A depreciation method required by the Internal Revenue Service to be used for income tax calculation purposes for most plant assets placed in service after 1986 is called the **Modified Accelerated Cost Recovery System**. This depreciation system is generally referred to as MACRS, the initials of its full name.

MACRS is a depreciation method with prescribed periods for nine classes of useful life for plant assets. A property is assigned to a specified class based on its characteristics and general life expectancy. The two most common classes, other than real estate, are the five-year and the seven-year property classes. The five-year property class includes cars, general-purpose trucks, computers, manufacturing equipment, and office machinery.

The seven-year property class includes office furniture and fixtures. The depreciation for these two property classes approximates the use of the double declining-balance method.

To calculate depreciation using MACRS, the Internal Revenue Service has prescribed methods that use annual percentage rates to determine depreciation for each class of plant asset. These rates are applied to the total cost of the plant asset without considering a salvage value. All plant assets are assumed to be placed in service in the middle of the year and taken out of service in the middle of the year. For example, the five-year property class depreciation is spread over six years, as shown above.

Annual depreciation is calculated by multiplying the plant asset's original cost times the depreciation rate for its specific class. A printer is classified as five-year property.

	Original Cost	×	Depreciation Rate	=	Annual Depreciation Rate
Year 3	$2,000.00	×	19.20%	=	$384.00

FYI FOR YOUR INFORMATION

Congress writes the depreciation rules used in filing federal income taxes. The Internal Revenue Service is given the responsibility to enforce the tax laws.

APPLIED SKILLS   WORD PROCESSING

If you wish to integrate word processing into your accounting course, you may direct students to answer the various feature activities using their word processing software.

DEPLETION

	Original cost	$ 100,000.00
−	Estimated Salvage Value	−$12,250.00
=	Estimated Total Value of Coal	$ 87,750.00
÷	Estimated Tons of Recoverable Coal	÷ 50,000
=	Depletion Rate per Ton of Coal	$ 1.755

Plant asset: Coal mine
Depletion method: Production-unit
Original cost: $100,000.00
Estimated salvage value: $12,250.00

1. Calculate the depletion rate.

1 | Estimated total depletion: $87,750.00
Estimated tons of recoverable coal: 50,000 tons
Depletion rate: $1.755 per ton

Year	Beginning Book Value	Tons Recovered	Annual Depletion	Ending Book Value
1	$100,000.00	6,000	$10,530.00	$89,470.00
2	89,470.00	12,000	21,060.00	68,410.00
3	68,410.00	13,000	22,815.00	45,595.00
4	45,595.00	9,000	15,795.00	29,800.00
5	29,800.00	6,000	10,530.00	19,270.00
Totals		46,000	$80,730.00	

2 **2.** Calculate the annual depletion.

	Tons of Coal Removed	×	Depletion Rate	=	Annual Depletion Expense
Year 1	6,000	×	$1.755	=	$10,530.00

Some plant assets decrease in value because part of these plant assets is physically removed in the operation of a business. For example, a lumber business owns land on which many trees grow. The business removes the trees to use for lumber. The land with the trees still growing on it is more valuable than the land from which the trees have been removed. The decrease in the value of a plant asset because of the removal of a natural resource is called **depletion**.

McGladden Company owns land on which a coal mine is located. The land with the coal has an original cost of $100,000.00. The company's experts estimate that the land contains 50,000 tons of recoverable coal. The estimated value of the remaining land after the coal is removed is

$12,250.00. Therefore, each ton of coal taken from the land decreases the land's value by $1.755.

In the first year of operation, the business removed 6,000 tons of coal. The depletion expense for the first year is $10,530.00 as shown above. McGladden uses the general ledger accounts Mine, Accumulated Depletion—Mine, and Depletion Expense—Mine to record depletion.

FYI FOR YOUR INFORMATION

Depletion is used to charge the cost of a variety of natural resources, including oil, gas, coal, gravel, minerals, and timber.

REMEMBER The method used to compute depletion is the same as the production-unit method of depreciation. A rate per unit of production is multiplied by the amount of production to compute depletion.

- Explain that depletion is the depreciation of a natural resource.
- Discuss that the salvage value of the land is used to estimate the value of the resource being extracted.
- Ask students to explain how the depletion rate per unit is calculated.
- Ask students to read the F.Y.I. feature learn how depletion is used with other natural resources.
- Ask students to read the Remember feature to learn how the depletion and production-units methods are similar.

DEMONSTRATE

- Draw five columns on the board and label the columns as shown in the illustration.
- Ask a student to calculate the depletion rate.
- Ask a student to calculate and record the amounts for year 1.
- Ask students to take turns completing the table.

ONGOING ASSESSMENT

- Assessment is an ongoing process. Circulate through the classroom or lab observing which students have problems with the assignments.
- Troubleshooting: Diagnose what kinds of problems students have with this section. This section presents four depreciation methods that vary in their use of the book value, salvage value, useful life, and depreciation rate. Students may have trouble remembering how to apply each of the methods.
- Assess student understanding by checking solutions to Independent Practice assignments.

RETEACH

- List the information required to depreciate a plant asset using each of the depreciation methods.
- Ask students to explain each depreciation method.

GUIDED PRACTICE

Terms Review
Call on students to define each term in the Terms Review. After each definition ask the class if the definition is correct and whether the complete definition has been given or if anything needs to be added. Suggested definitions are given in the Glossary.

Audit Your Understanding
Call on students to answer the Audit Your Understanding questions. Ask the class if the answer is correct and/or complete. Answers are given in Appendix E of the textbook.

Work Together
Have students write the solution to the Work Together problem as you guide the class through the examples.

- Direct students to complete a depreciation table for one depreciation method as you elicit class participation in calculating each amount.

- Call on students to explain the calculations to assess their understanding before beginning the next depreciation table.

- Instruct students to complete the depletion table as you elicit class participation in calculating each amount.

• terms review

declining-balance method of depreciation

sum-of-the-years'-digits method of depreciation

production-unit method of depreciation

Modified Accelerated Cost Recovery System

depletion

• audit your understanding

1. Which depreciation method does not use the estimated salvage value to compute annual depreciation?

2. What is the basis for the production-unit method of calculating depreciation?

3. How does a mining company calculate the amount of depletion for a year?

• work together 8-4

Computing depreciation using various depreciation methods and calculating depletion

The following information relates to a delivery truck purchased on January 2, 20X1. Depreciation tables are provided in the *Working Papers*. Your instructor will guide you through the following examples.

		Miles Driven	
Original Cost	$90,000.00	20X1	34,600
Estimated Salvage Value	$6,000.00	20X2	47,300
Estimated Useful Life	3 years or 200,000 miles	20X3	52,800
MACRS Property Class	5-year	20X4	36,900

1. Complete depreciation tables showing depreciation expense calculated using the double declining-balance, sum-of-the-years'-digits, production-unit, and MACRS methods of depreciation.

The following data relate to a mineral mine owned by Kellogg, Inc. A depletion table is provided in the *Working Papers*.

		Tons Mined	
Original Cost	$260,000.00	20X1	3,500
Estimated Salvage Value	$60,000.00	20X2	12,500
Estimated Tons of Recoverable Minerals	60,000 tons	20X3	15,600

2. Complete a table showing depletion expense calculated using the production-unit method.

Accounting for Plant Assets

248

on your own 8-4

Computing depreciation using various depreciation methods and calculating depletion

The following information relates to a machine purchased on January 3, 20X1. Work independently to complete the following problem.

		Year	**Hours**
Original Cost	$13,500.00	20X1	600
Estimated Salvage Value	$1,500.00	20X2	1,200
Estimated Useful Life	5 years or 5,000 hours	20X3	900
MACRS Property Class	5 year	20X4	1,000
		20X5	800

1. Complete tables showing depreciation expense calculated using the double declining-balance, sum-of-the-years'-digits, production-unit, and MACRS methods of depreciation.

   The following data relate to a gas well owned by JH Enterprises.

		Year	**MCF Recovered**
Original Cost	$920,000.00	20X1	30,000
Estimated Salvage Value	$20,000.00	20X2	90,000
Estimated MCF of Recoverable Gas	600,000 MCF	20X3	100,000
		20X4	120,000

2. Complete a depletion table for this well; show depletion expense calculated using the production-unit method.

Other Methods of Depreciation

INDEPENDENT PRACTICE

On Your Own

- Assign the On Your Own problem to be worked independently.
- Use the Ongoing Assessment techniques to diagnose student understanding.

Application Problem

- Assign Application Problem 8-7: Calculating depreciation expense using the straight-line, declining-balance, and sum-of-the-years'-digits methods.
- Assign Application Problem 8-8: Calculating depreciation expense using the production-unit method.
- Assign Application Problem 8-9: Calculating depreciation expense using MACRS.
- Assign Application Problem 8-10: Calculating depletion expense.

Personal Trainer

- Students can access the Lesson 8-4 assessment material using this software.

Xtra! Web Site

- Students can access the Xtra! Study Tools for additional practice.

ENRICH

- Assign the Automated Accounting feature on page 257 to automate Application Problem 8-7.
- Ask students to obtain the financial statements of a publicly traded corporation. Instruct students to look in Note 1 of the Notes to the Financial Statements to identify the depreciation method(s) used. Survey the students to determine relative frequency of use for each method.
- Assign the Technology for Business feature on page 244.

CLOSE

- Ask students to briefly summarize the various depreciation and depletion methods.
- Ask students to compare the impact of the depreciation methods on the amount of depreciation expense recorded at the beginning and end of a plant asset's useful life.

PUTTING IT ALL TOGETHER

- Ask students to prepare a list of the new concepts introduced in this chapter.
- Discuss that the journalizing of depreciation expense and the gain or loss on the disposition of assets is the same regardless of the depreciation method used.

INDEPENDENT PRACTICE

- Assign Mastery Problem 8-11 to students who need the reinforcement of a problem that combines all activities from the chapter in one problem; this will be most students.
- Assign Challenge Problem 8-12 to accelerated students who do not require the reinforcement of the Mastery Problem.
- Assign Study Guide 8.
- Students can use *Automated Accounting 8.0* or higher to work Mastery Problem 8-11 and Challenge Problem 8-12.
- Students can use Peachtree or Quick-Books to automate Mastery Problem 8-11 and Challenge Problem 8-12.
- Students can access Personal Trainer to work end-of-chapter problems on the computer.
- Students can access the Xtra! Web Site for the Xtra! Review and Quizzing.
- Students can access the Student Companion CD for additional review material.

ONGOING ASSESSMENT

Review solutions to the assigned problems in class, diagnosing trouble spots.

RETEACH

- Call on students to describe how they avoid the trouble spots diagnosed.
- Use reteaching suggestions from section lesson plans as required.
- Assign Recycling Problem 8-1, 8-2, or 8-3 if needed.

ENRICH

- Assign the Explore Accounting feature. Ask students to share the information they have gathered in a report to the class.
- Students can access the Xtra! Web Site for the Xtra! Enrichment material.
- Assign Applied Communication.
- Assign the Cases for Critical Thinking.
- Assign the SCANS Workplace Competency.
- Assign Auditing for Errors.
- Assign Analyzing Costco's Financial Statements.
- Assign Automated Accounting on page 257.

250

SUMMARY

After completing this chapter, you can

1. Define accounting terms related to plant assets and depreciation.
2. Identify accounting concepts and practices related to accounting for plant assets and decpreciation.
3. Journalize entries for buying plant assets.
4. Calculate and record property tax expense.
5. Calculate and record depreciation expense for a plant asset using straight-line depreciation.
6. Journalize entries for disposing of plant assets.
7. Calculate depreciation expense using other methods.

Explore Accounting

EXPLORE ACCOUNTING • EXPLORE ACCOUNTING • EXPLORE A

Tax Laws Encourage Plant Assets Purchases

Tax law and generally accepted accounting principles (GAAP) often have conflicting objectives. Tax law is enacted to generate tax revenues. In contrast, GAAP are designed to report the results of operations.

The primary purpose of federal income tax laws is to guide the government's collection of tax revenue. However, Congress also uses income tax law to influence businesses. To promote economic development, Congress has periodically passed tax laws that provide businesses with financial incentives to purchase plant assets.

A business that purchases plant assets will likely hire more employees, purchase additional raw materials, and earn a higher net income—all resulting in increasing economic activity and income tax revenues. Congress has used the following three tax laws to enable businesses to recover a larger portion of their plant asset purchases in the first year than would be permitted by simply using straight-line depreciation.

Accelerated Depreciation: To spur the economy after World War II, Congress modified the tax laws in 1954 to permit the use of accelerated depreciation methods.

Investment Tax Credit: In 1962, President Kennedy proposed a tax credit for certain purchases of plant assets. Congress has periodically changed the percentage credits, purchase limitations, and qualifying assets. Unlike a tax deduction, a tax credit is a reduction in the tax paid. For example, a company purchasing an 8% qualifying asset for $50,000 could reduce its tax liability by $4,000.

Section 179 Property: In 1986, the rising federal debt motivated Congress to reduce the investment tax credit in favor of a tax law that enabled a business to expense up to $17,500 of plant asset purchases each year. For example, a company purchasing $50,000 of equipment could expense $17,500 of the equipment in the year of purchase and depreciate the remaining $32,500 using the current tax rates.

GAAP allow the use of accelerated depreciation methods. However, neither the investment tax credit nor Section 179 property rules can be used for financial reporting.

Required:
Obtain a copy of IRS Form 4562, Depreciation and Amortization. Identify the parts of the form used to report Section 179 property and MACRS depreciation. Prepare a list of amounts and other information that is required to prepare the form.

EXPLORE ACCOUNTING
EXPLORE ACCOUNTING

If needed, give students direction on resources for researching the requirements of this feature. You might suggest that the students begin their search in the Business Periodical Index or other periodical indexes or various other search engines on the Internet.

It is likely to be a wide distribution in the annual health care growth rates cited in various periodicals. Numerous organizations and government agencies attempt to estimate the annual growth rate in health care. The many assumptions regarding what activities constitute health care and the methods used to collect the data can have a significant impact on the resultant growth rate estimates. The variety of growth rates demonstrates the difficulty accountants face in their goal to calculate a reasonably accurate estimate of future health care costs.

8-1 APPLICATION PROBLEM

Journalizing entries to record buying plant assets

Mannings, Inc. uses three plant asset accounts: Office Equipment, Store Equipment, and Warehouse Equipment.

Transactions:

Jan. 2. Paid cash for office file cabinet (plant asset no. 1), $500.00: estimated salvage value, $50.00; estimated useful life, five years; serial no. FC2467. C130.

Jan. 3. Bought office word processor (plant asset no. 2) on account from Darst, Inc., $400.00: no estimated salvage value; estimated useful life, five years; serial no. X4672Y101. M11.

Apr. 4. Bought hand truck (plant asset no. 3) for warehouse on account from Boeser, Inc., $100.00: estimated salvage value, $25.00; estimated useful life, five years; serial no. 23D4689. M24.

May 1. Paid cash for used truck (plant asset no. 4) to be used between warehouses, $8,500.00: estimated salvage value, $1,000.00; estimated useful life, five years; serial no. 45J3257XF29. C210.

July 1. Paid cash for store shelving (plant asset no. 5), $500.00: estimated salvage value, $25.00; estimated useful life, 10 years; no serial no. C250.

Instructions:

1. Journalize the transactions completed during the current year. Use page 1 of a general journal and page 1 of a cash payments journal. General ledger accounts are: Office Equipment, 1225; Store Equipment, 1235; and Warehouse Equipment, 1245. Source documents are abbreviated as follows: check, C; memorandum, M.

2. Complete Section 1 of a plant asset record for each plant asset. Save the plant asset records from Application Problem 8-1 to complete Application Problems 8-3, 8-4, and 8-5.

8-2 APPLICATION PROBLEM

Calculating and journalizing property tax

Dependable Deliveries, Inc., has real property with an assessed value of $350,000.00. The annual tax rate in the city where the property is located is 4.5% of assessed value. Half of the annual tax is collected every six months.

Instructions:

1. Calculate Dependable Deliveries' total annual property tax.
2. Journalize the payment of the tax on February 26 with check No. 124. Use page 3 of a cash payments journal.

8-3 APPLICATION PROBLEM

Calculating depreciation using the straight-line method

Use the plant asset record from Application Problem 8-1. Complete a depreciation table for each of the plant assets bought by Mannings, Inc. Save the depreciation tables from Application Problem 8-3 to complete Application Problem 8-4.

8-4 APPLICATION PROBLEM

Journalizing annual depreciation expense

Use the plant asset records from Application Problem 8-1 and the depreciation tables from Application Problem 8-3.

Instructions:

1. Use the plant asset records prepared in Application Problem 8-1. For each plant asset, record depreciation for 20X1 in section 3 of the plant asset record.

Accounting for Plant Assets

Chapter 8   **251**

---

2. Use page 12 of a general journal and the depreciation tables prepared in Application Problem 8-3. Journalize the three adjusting entries for office, store, and warehouse depreciation expense on December 31, 20X1.

2. Use page 12 of a general journal and the depreciation tables prepared in Application Problem 8-3. Journalize the three adjusting entries for office, store, and warehouse depreciation expense on December 31, 20X1.
3. For each plant asset, record depreciation for 20X2, 20X3, and 20X4 in section 3 of the plant asset record.
4. Journalize the three adjusting entries for December 31, 20X2. Save the plant asset records from Application Problem 8-4 to complete Application Problem 8-5.

Application Problem 8-5

Gains and losses on disposal of plant assets: Jan. 21, 20X5, 73.33 loss; Jan. 28, 20X5, 132.50 loss; Mar. 29, 20X6, 15.00 loss, Dec. 31, 20X6, 11.25 gain.

8-5 APPLICATION PROBLEM
Recording disposal of plant assets

Use the plant asset records from Application Problem 8-4. Mannings, Inc., completed the following transactions. Use the appropriate plant asset records from Application Problem 8-4 for additional information needed. Use page 1 of a general journal, page 6 of a cash receipts journal, and page 12 of a cash payments journal. Source documents are abbreviated as follows: check, C; memorandum, M; receipt, R.

Transactions:

Jan. 21, 20X5. An office word processor, plant asset no. 2, was no longer being used. It was discarded. M522.
Jan. 28, 20X5. Discarded office file cabinet, plant asset no. 1. M523.
Mar. 29, 20X6. Received cash for sale of hand truck, $10.00, plant asset no. 3. M575 and R645.
Dec. 31, 20X6. Received cash for sale of store shelving, $250.00, plant asset no. 5. M631 and R733.
Dec. 31, 20X6. Paid $8,000.00 in cash plus old truck, plant asset no. 4, for new truck, plant asset no. 29. M632 and C815.

Instructions:

1. For each transaction in 20X5, do the following.
    a. Journalize an entry for additional depreciation if needed.
    b. Journalize the disposal of the plant asset.
    c. Make appropriate notations in the plant asset record.
2. Complete each plant asset record for the year.
3. Repeat instructions 1 and 2 for 20X6.

Application Problem 8-6

Journal entry for sale of land and buildings: Debit Cash, 73,000.00 and Accumulated Depreciation Building, 61,200.00; credit Land, 20,000.00, Building, 100,000.00, and Gain on Plant Assets, 14,200.00.

8-6 APPLICATION PROBLEM
Recording the sale of land and building

On January 2, 20X6, Jamestown, Inc., sold land and a company operations building it is no longer using. The following data relating to the land and building are obtained from the accounting records of Jamestown:

Cash Received	$73,000.00
Original Cost of Land	20,000.00
Original Cost of Building	100,000.00
Accumulated Depreciation on Building to 12/31/X5	61,200.00

Instructions:

1. Journalize the sale of the land and building. Use page 12 of a cash receipts journal. The source document is receipt no. 125.
2. Make appropriate notations in the plant asset records.

APPLIED SKILLS   WRITING ACROSS THE CURRICULUM

Writing paragraphs and short essays. The Cases for Critical Thinking are short, practical applications of the accounting principles developed in the chapter. Some cases are planned to present problems related to the chapter but not specifically discussed and answered in the chapter. These cases present an opportunity for critical thinking and decision making. These cases also require more than a short objective-type response. Therefore they provide ideal practice in writing paragraphs and short essays.

8-7 APPLICATION PROBLEM

Calculating depreciation expense using the straight-line, declining-balance, and sum-of-the-years'-digits methods

The following data relating to an office desk are obtained from the accounting records of Byrum, Inc.

Original Cost	$2,400.00
Estimated Salvage Value	200.00
Estimated Useful Life	4 years

Instructions:
Prepare a depreciation table showing depreciation expense calculated using the straight-line, declining-balance, and sum-of-the-years'-digits methods.

8-8 APPLICATION PROBLEM

Calculating depreciation expense using the production-unit method

The following data relating to a truck are obtained from the accounting records of Marcotte, Inc.:

Original Cost	$10,000.00
Estimated Salvage Value	1,000.00
Estimated Useful Life	120,000 miles

Instructions:
1. Calculate the depreciation rate.
2. Prepare a depreciation table for this truck showing depreciation expense calculated using the production-unit method.

8-9 APPLICATION PROBLEM

Calculating depreciation expense using MACRS

The following data relating to a computer are obtained from the accounting records of Caesar Company.

Original Cost	$3,300.00
Property Class	5-year property

Instructions:
Prepare a depreciation table showing depreciation expense calculated using MACRS.

8-10 APPLICATION PROBLEM

Calculating depletion expense using production-unit method

The following data relating to a coal mine are obtained from the accounting records of Geist, Inc.

Original Cost	$45,000.00
Estimated Salvage Value	1,000.00
Estimated Tons of Recoverable Coal	50,000 tons

Instructions:
Prepare a depletion table for this mine showing depletion expense calculated using the production-unit method.

Application Problem 8-7
First year depreciation: Straight-line method, 550.00; Declining-balance method, 1,200.00; Sum-of-the-years'-digits method, 880.00.

Application Problem 8-8
Annual depreciation: Year 1, 2,062.50; Year 2, 1,950.00; Year 3, 1,875.00; Year 4, 1,575.00; Year 5, 1,425.00.

Application Problem 8-9
Annual depreciation: Year 1, 660.00; Year 2, 1,056.00; Year 3, 633.60; Year 4, 379.50; Year 5, 379.50; Year 6, 191.40.

Application Problem 8-10
Book value end of Year 5, 4,432.00.

Mastery Problem 8-11

Gains and losses on disposal of plant assets: Jan. 2, 120.00 loss; Mar. 29, 25.00 loss; Mar. 30, 50.00 loss; June 29, 65.00 gain.

Challenge Problem 8-12

Amounts debited to Accumulated Depreciation accounts: General journal–July 1, 20X3, 46.00; Cash receipts journal–December 31, 20X3, 311.67; Cash payments journal–January 2, 20X3, 125.00 and September 1, 20X3, 3,900.00.

8-11 MASTERY PROBLEM   AUTOMATED ACCOUNTING   PEACHTREE   QUICKBOOKS

Recording entries for plant assets

Western, Inc., uses the straight-line method of calculating depreciation expense. Western uses one plant asset account, Office Equipment, account no. 1230. The plant asset records for Western are given in the *Working Papers*.

Transactions:

Jan. 2. Paid cash for new computer, plant asset no. 172, $1,900.00: estimated salvage value, $400.00; estimated useful life, five years; serial no. SD345J267. C122.

Jan. 2. Discarded desk, serial no. D3481, plant asset no. 167. M47.

Mar. 29. Discarded table, serial no. T3929, plant asset no. 168. M52.

Mar. 30. Received cash from sale of word processor, $100.00: serial no. TM48194H32, plant asset no. 170. M54 and R191.

June 29. Received cash from sale of filing cabinet, $150.00: serial no. FC125, plant asset no. 169. M62 and R224.

July 2. Paid cash, $500.00, plus old copying machine, serial no. C56M203, plant asset no. 171, for new copying machine: estimated salvage value of new machine, $100.00; estimated useful life of new machine, five years; serial no., C35194, plant asset no. 173. M70 and C239.

Instructions:

1. Journalize the transactions completed during 20X9. Journalize an entry for additional depreciation expense if needed. Use page 1 of a general journal, page 6 of a cash receipts journal, and page 8 of a cash payments journal. Source documents are abbreviated as follows: check, C; memorandum, M; receipt, R.

2. Make needed notations on plant asset records or prepare new records.

8-12 CHALLENGE PROBLEM   AUTOMATED ACCOUNTING   PEACHTREE   QUICKBOOKS

Recording entries for plant assets

McNeilley, Inc., uses the straight-line method to calculate depreciation expense. McNeilley uses two plant asset accounts, Office Equipment and Delivery Equipment.

Transactions:

Jan. 1, 20X1. Paid cash for new office word processor, plant asset no. 1, $600.00: estimated salvage value, $100.00; estimated useful life, eight years; serial no. T45M3409. C130.

Mar. 1, 20X1. Paid cash for office desk, plant asset no. 2, $700.00: estimated salvage value, $150.00; estimated useful life, five years; serial no. D345. C190.

June 30, 20X1. Paid cash for office chair, plant asset no. 3, $125.00: estimated salvage value, $10.00; estimated useful life, five years; no serial no. C200.

July 1, 20X1. Paid cash for delivery truck, plant asset no. 4, $10,000.00: estimated salvage value, $1,000.00; estimated useful life, five years; serial no. 345X32LD54. C220.

Jan. 2, 20X3. Paid cash, $400.00, plus old word processor, serial no. T45M3409, for new word processor: estimated salvage value of new word processor, $100.00; estimated useful life of new word processor, plant asset no. 5, five years; new word processor serial no. T64M4391. M50 and C300.

July 1, 20X3. Discarded office chair bought on June 30, 20X1. M66.

Sept. 1, 20X3. Paid cash, $5,500.00, plus old delivery truck, serial no. 345X32LD54, for new delivery truck: estimated salvage value of new truck, $2,000.00; estimated useful life of new truck, plant asset no. 6, five years; new truck serial no. 432XY30LE25. M70 and C310.

Instructions:

Journalize the transactions. Use page 7 of a general journal and page 12 of a cash payments journal. Source documents are abbreviated as follows: check, C; memorandum, M; receipt, R.

TEACHING STRATEGIES   COOPERATIVE LEARNING

Divide the class into groups of four or five students each. Using the Applied Communication activity, each group analyzes the case and arrives at an agreed-upon solution. One member of each group is appointed the recorder and presents the group's analysis to the class. This cooperative learning activity should not take more than 20 to 25 minutes of class time.

• applied communication

Examine the comparison of depreciation methods in the schedule at the top of page 244. Although the amount of depreciation recorded each year varies, the total depreciation over the asset's full life is the same.

Required:

Prepare a graph comparing the three depreciation methods. Make sure the graph is clearly labeled. The declining-balance method and the sum-of-the-years'-digits method are often referred to as accelerated depreciation methods. Use the graph to explain what is meant by accelerated depreciation.

• cases for critical thinking

Case 1

A corporation's plant assets include office equipment, a building, and the land on which the building is located. The corporation's general ledger includes a single account, Plant Assets, and a single account, Accumulated Depreciation—Plant Assets. The corporation's accountant suggests that the plant assets be divided into three accounts, Office Equipment, Building, and Land. The corporation's president does not think this is a good idea. With whom do you agree and why?

Case 2

A corporation owns land on which there are both an active coal mine and timber. The corporation also owns an office building and the land on which it is located. The corporation uses three plant asset accounts: (1) Land and Buildings (depreciation calculated using the straight-line method). (2) Timber (depreciation calculated using the declining-balance method). (3) Coal Mine (depreciation calculated using the declining-balance method). Do you agree with the accounting procedures being used? Explain your answers.

Case 3

A corporation currently uses straight-line depreciation for all plant assets. Its balance sheet reports accumulated depreciation and its income statement reports the depreciation expense for the current period. When the corporation's tax accountant prepares the corporate income tax return, all depreciation is reported using MACRS. Assume that all of the company's assets are one or two years old. Further assume that all the assets are in the 5-year property class. Will the net income reported on the tax return be greater than or less than the net income reported on the income statement? Explain your reasoning.

Case 4

The city in which a corporation is located has a business property tax. This tax is 1% of all business property over $50,000. The corporation is a small service business. Its assets that are subject to the tax are only $10,000. The law states that all businesses must file a return even if they owe no tax. The penalty for not filing is $100. The corporation's accountant has attempted to complete the tax return. However, some parts of the return are very technical. The accountant gets an estimate from a tax specialist to prepare the return. The estimate is $125 for the first year and $75 for the second and third years. What should the accountant do?

APPLIED COMMUNICATION

The graph will show straight-line depreciation as a straight line parallel to the X-axis. The declining-balance and sum-of-the-years'-digits lines will slope downward. The declining-balance line will have the steeper slope. Graphs should be properly labeled.

The graph can be used to explain that the declining-balance and sum-of-the-years'-digits methods record a greater amount of depreciation in the early years of the asset's life. Therefore, the depreciation is said to be accelerated.

CASES FOR CRITICAL THINKING

Case 1

Agree with the accountant. Annual depreciation expense should be recorded on the office equipment and the building but not on the land. When the amounts are recorded together, there is difficulty in keeping the information separate for financial statement reporting. (CONCEPT: Adequate Disclosure)

Case 2

Do not agree. Annual depreciation expense is calculated for buildings but not land. Therefore, the two kinds of plant assets should not be recorded in the same account. Timber and minerals are plant assets for which depletion expense rather than depreciation expense is recorded. Therefore, depletion expense should be calculated and recorded rather than using the declining-balance method of depreciation.

Case 3

The net income reported on the tax return will be less than the income reported on the income statement. Since the assets are all one or two years old, the accelerated rates for MACRS will result in a greater depreciation expense to be reported for income tax purposes.

Case 4

This is an ethical dilemma. The accountant should use the specialist to prepare the return for the current year, even though the cost will be greater than the penalty.

SCANS WORKPLACE COMPETENCY

Reinforce the concept of presenting information in a logical, organized, and visually pleasing format. Discuss with the students the importance of attending a college or university that is a good fit with their individual needs and abilities.

AUDITING FOR ERRORS

1. The error is in the depreciation expense for 20X3. It should be $6,000.00.

2. Answers will vary but should point out that the bookkeeper incorrectly used the salvage value in the calculation of the depreciation expense for 20X3. In the double-declining balance method of depreciation, the salvage value is not used in the yearly calculation of depreciation expense. The correct calculation should be: $15,000 \times .40 = $6,000.

ANALYZING COSTCO'S FINANCIAL STATEMENTS

1. Additions to property and equipment, 810,665,000.

2. Proceeds from the sale of property and equipment, 51,829,000.

3. 3,296,819,000 (810,665,000 + 1,038,605,000 + 1,447,549,000)

4. 194,680,000 (51,829,000 + 32,849,000 + 110,002,000)

• SCANS workplace competency (part I)

(The information collected and organized in this activity is used to complete the SCANS Workplace Competency in Chapter 9.)

Information Competency: Organizing and Maintaining Information

Concept: Competent employees possess the ability to organize, process, and maintain written or computerized records and other forms of information in a systematic fashion. The ability to sort, classify, and organize data from computerized databases, spreadsheets, videodisks, and paper files is critical.

Application: Visit the admissions pages of at least three college web sites. Select and organize information that compares a variety of admission data and requirements. Your comparison might include recommended high school subjects, cost of applying, required test scores, letters of recommendation, high school transcripts, entrance essays, deadlines, number of applicants, average GPAs and SAT scores of freshmen, ethnicity, average class size, and geographic origin of students. Save collected data for use in the next chapter's SCANS activity.

• auditing for errors

On June 5, 20X3, Fairborn, Inc., purchased a new cutting machine for use in its factory. The machine cost $15,000.00 and has an estimated salvage value of $1,000.00 and an estimated useful life of five years. Fairborn used the double-declining balance method of depreciation. The bookkeeper prepared the following plant asset record.

PLANT ASSET RECORD, No.	305	General Ledger Account No.	1150
Description *Cutting Machine*		General Ledger Account	*Factory Equipment*
Date Bought *June 5, 20X3*	Serial Number *G77U3JK298*	Original Cost	$15,000.00
Estimated Useful Life *5 years*	Estimated Salvage Value *$1,000.00*	Depreciation Method	*Double-declining Balance*

Disposed of:		Discarded ✓	Sold		Traded
Date *January 5, 20X6*			Disposal Amount *zero*		

YEAR	ANNUAL DEPRECIATION EXPENSE	ACCUMULATED DEPRECIATION	ENDING BOOK VALUE
20X3	5,600.00	5,600.00	9,400.00

Instructions:

1. Find the error in the plant asset record.
2. Write a written explanation of the error to the bookkeeper. In your explanation, give the correct calculation.

• analyzing Costco's financial statements

An income statement is a financial statement prepared on an accrual basis. A statement of cash flows is a financial statement prepared on a cash basis. It shows how and where the company received cash and spent cash. On a statement of cash flows, outflows of cash are usually shown in parenthesis. Inflows of cash are shown as positive amounts. These inflows and outflows of cash are organized into three categories—operating activities, investing activities, and financing activities. Buying and selling plant assets are classified as investing activities.

Instructions:

1. Go to the statement of cash flows for Costco on Appendix B page B-8. Find the heading "Cash flows from investing activities." Find the largest outflow of cash from investing activities for 2003. List the item and the amount of the outflow.
2. Find the largest inflow of cash from investing activities for 2003. List the item and the amount of the inflow.
3. How much cash has been used to purchase property and equipment over the last three years?
4. How much cash has been received from the sale of property and equipment over the last three years?

TEACHING STRATEGIES   PORTFOLIO ASSESSMENT

A clear understanding of plant assets and depreciation is useful for general accounting knowledge. In addition, familiarity with MACRS is helpful for students who plan to prepare tax returns. Students should emphasize their learning of this topic by selecting a comprehensive sample of their work in this chapter, for example the mastery or challenge problems to include in their portfolio. A copy of the Portfolio Assessment form (blackline master in the Teacher's Resource Guide; also on the Student Companion CD) should be completed by the student and the Description section should include any comments regarding how the student mastered these concepts and procedures. Alternatively, students might include in their portfolios printed reports from an Automated Accounting problem.

• Automated Accounting

Automated Depreciation and Creating Depreciation Schedules

In *Automated Accounting 8.0,* depreciation schedules can be maintained using the following methods: straight-line (SL), double-declining-balance (DDB), and sum-of-the-years'-digits (SYD).

Adding Plant Asset Data

Complete plant asset information is required for each plant asset. The information is entered in the Plant Assets tab of the Account Maintenance window. To add a new asset, enter all the requested information on a new line. Then click the Add Asset button.

Plant asset data can also be changed by clicking on the cell containing the data to be changed. The Add Asset button changes to the Change Asset button.

Displaying or Printing Plant Asset Reports

A plant asset list and depreciation schedules can be displayed and printed by selecting the appropriate report. When selecting the depreciation schedules report, select the asset or range of assets for the depreciation schedules you want to generate.

Generating Depreciation Adjusting Entries

Choose Depreciation Adjusting Entries from the Option menu. Click Yes to generate the depreciation adjusting entries. The software will analyze the plant asset records, calculate an amount based on the period, and generate the depreciation adjusting entries. The journal entries will display on the screen for your review and confirmation. Verify the accuracy of the entries, then click the Post button.

AUTOMATING APPLICATION PROBLEM 8-7

Instructions:

1. Load *Automated Accounting 8.0* or higher software.

2. Select database A08-07 (Advanced Course Application Problem 8-7) from the accounting template disk.

3. Select File from the menu bar and choose the Save As menu command. Key the path to the drive and directory that contain your data files. Save the database with a filename of XXX087 (where XXX are your initials).

4. Read the Problem Instruction screen by clicking the Browser toolbar button.

5. Refer to page 253 for data used in this problem.

6. Exit the Automated Accounting software.

AUTOMATING MASTERY PROBLEM 8-11

Instructions:

1. Load *Automated Accounting 8.0* or higher software.

2. Select database A08-11 (Advanced Course Mastery Problem 8-11) from the accounting template disk.

3. Select File from the menu bar and choose the Save As menu command. Key the path to the drive and directory that contain your data files. Save the database with a filename of XXX0811 (where XXX are your initials).

4. Read the Problem Instruction screen by clicking the Browser toolbar button.

5. Key the data listed in the problem.

6. Exit the Automated Accounting software.

AUTOMATING CHALLENGE PROBLEM 8-12

Instructions:

1. Load *Automated Accounting 8.0* or higher software.

2. Select database A08-12 (Advanced Course Challenge Problem 8-12) from the accounting template disk.

3. Select File from the menu bar and choose the Save As menu command. Key the path to the drive and directory that contain your data files. Save the database with a filename of XXX0812 (where XXX are your initials).

4. Read the Problem Instruction screen by clicking the Browser toolbar button.

5. Key the data listed in the problem.

6. Exit the Automated Accounting software.

EXPLAIN

- Explain that the software automatically calculates depreciation expense and can also automatically generate the adjusting entries for depreciation expense.

DEMONSTRATE

Maintaining plant asset records

- Demonstrate clicking the Accounts icon on the toolbar and clicking the Plant Assets tab.

- Enter each field of information about a new plant asset and click Add Asset to enter the information.

- Change or delete data by clicking the data field you wish to change, keying the new information, and clicking Change Asset to record the change or clicking the Delete button to remove the asset.

Generating plant asset reports

- Demonstrate clicking the Reports icon on the toolbar, selecting Plant Assets in Select a Report Group, and selecting Plant Assets List or Depreciation Schedules in Choose a Report to Display.

- Demonstrate clicking OK to set the asset range and clicking OK to display the depreciation schedules.

Generating adjusting entries

- Demonstrate clicking Depreciation Adjusting Entries from the Options menu.

- Demonstrate clicking Yes to generate the depreciation adjusting entries.

- Demonstrate clicking Post to post the adjusting entries after verification.

PRACTICE

- Assign Automating Application Problem 8-7: Calculating deprecation expense using the straight-line, declining balance, and sum-of-the-years'-digits methods.

- Assign Automating Mastery Problem 8-11: Recording entries for plant assets.

- Assign Automating Challenge Problem 8-12: Recording entries for plant assets.

ASSESSMENT

- Use the Electronic Auditor to assess student understanding.

TEACHING STRATEGIES   PORTFOLIO ASSESSMENT

Students should be encouraged to print at least one report from one of the Automated Accounting problems to include in their portfolio to demonstrate mastery of automated accounting systems. A copy of the Portfolio Assessment form (blackline master in the Teacher's Resource Guide; also on the Student Companion CD) should be completed by the student and the Description section should include any comments regarding how the student mastered these concepts and procedures.

CHAPTER 9

Accounting for Notes Payable,

	SCOPE & SEQUENCE		ENHANCING
	NEW	REVIEW/ EXTENSION	SPECIAL FEATURES
Introduce the Chapter	✓		• Accounting in the Real World: The Mall of America
Lesson 9-1 Notes Payable			• Making Ethical Decisions: Reporting Ethics Violations
Borrowing money with a note payable		✓	• Small Business Spotlight
Calculating maturity date and interest		✓	• Exploring Accounting: The Impact of Foreign Exchange Rates
Paying a note payable		✓	
Lesson 9-2 Prepaid Expenses			
Prepaid expenses		✓	
Supplies initially recorded as an asset		✓	
Supplies initially recorded as an expense		✓	
Prepaid insurance initially recorded as an expense		✓	
Adjusting, closing, and reversing entries for prepaid expenses		✓	
Lesson 9-3 Accrued Expenses			• Cultural Diversity: Hispanic American Businesses
Accrued interest expense		✓	• Exploring Accounting: Gains or Losses
Recording payment of note at maturity		✓	
Accrued salary expense		✓	
Accrued employer payroll taxes expense		✓	
Accrued federal income tax expense		✓	
Adjusting, closing, and reversing entries for accrued expenses		✓	
Putting It All Together			• Explore Accounting
			• Xtra! Web Site: Xtra! Enrichment
			• Applied Communication
			• Cases for Critical Thinking
			• SCANS Workplace Competency
			• Graphing Workshop
			• Analyzing Costco's Financial Statements

Prepaid Expenses, and Accrued Expenses

INSTRUCTION			PRACTICE AND ASSESSMENT		
TECHNOLOGY AND MEDIA	**TEACHING STRATEGIES**		**GUIDED PRACTICE**	**INDEPENDENT PRACTICE**	**RETEACHING AND ENRICHMENT**
• Internet Research Activity • Accounting Xtra! Web Site	• Software Focus				
• Instructor's Resource CD: PowerPoint Slides • Xtra! Web Site: Xtra! Study Tools • Blackline Masters: Cash Payments Journal, Cash Receipts Journal • Personal Trainer • Automated Accounting • Peachtree and QuickBooks			• Terms Review • Audit Your Understanding • Work Together 9-1	• On Your Own 9-1 • Application Problem 9-1 • Ongoing Assessment, p. 263 • Personal Trainer • Xtra! Web Site: Xtra! Study Tools	• Reteach, p. 263 • Enrich, p. 265 • Automated Accounting • Peachtree and QuickBooks
• Instructor's Resource CD: PowerPoint Slides • Xtra! Web Site: Xtra! Study Tools • Blackline Masters: General Journal • Personal Trainer	• Applied Skills: Building Study Skills • Cooperative Learning		• Term Review • Audit Your Understanding • Work Together 9-2	• On Your Own 9-2 • Application Problem 9-2 • Ongoing Assessment, p. 270 • Personal Trainer • Xtra! Web Site: Xtra! Study Tools	• Reteach, p. 270 • Enrich, p. 271
• Instructor's Resource CD: PowerPoint Slides • Xtra! Web Site: Xtra! Study Tools • Blackline Masters: General Journal • Personal Trainer	• Expanding Beyond the Classroom		• Term Review • Audit Your Understanding • Work Together 9-3	• On Your Own 9-3 • Application Problem 9-3 • Ongoing Assessment, p. 277 • Personal Trainer • Xtra! Web Site: Xtra! Study Tools	• Reteach, p. 277 • Enrich, p. 279
• Personal Trainer • Xtra! Web Site: Xtra! Review, Quizzing, and Enrichment • Student Companion CD • Automated Accounting • Peachtree and QuickBooks	• Cooperative Learning • Applied Skills: Language Arts • Applied Skills: Writing Across the Curriculum			• Mastery Problem 9-4 • Personal Trainer • Xtra! Web Site: Xtra! Review and Quizzing • Study Guide 9 • Student Companion CD • Automated Accounting • Peachtree and QuickBooks • Chapter 9 Test • ExamView Chapter 9	• Challenge Problem 9-5 • Reteach, p. 280 • Enrich, p. 280 • Recycling Problem 9-1 • Xtra! Web Site: Xtra! Enrichment

INTRODUCE THE CHAPTER

Preview Chapter Objectives

- Point out that students were introduced to notes, interest, prepaid expenses, and accrued expenses in the first-year course.

- Point out that this chapter will review the concepts presented in the first-year course and introduce many new concepts related to notes, prepaid expenses, and accrued expenses.

Preview Accounting Terms

- Read each term out loud to verify pronunciation for students.

- Point out terms or parts of terms that should already be familiar to most students, such as note, principal, interest, and prepaid expenses.

INTERNET ACTIVITY

Point your browser to *accountingxtra. swlearning.com* to access the Accounting Xtra! Web Site.

SOFTWARE FOCUS

Software may be used for independent practice or enrichment as the instructor deems appropriate. For this chapter, the following software may be used: Automated Accounting and Century 21 8E CD with Application Problem 9-1 and Mastery Problem 9-4; Peachtree and QuickBooks with Application Problem 9-1 and Mastery Problem 9-4; the Student Companion CD; and Personal Trainer, Chapter 9.

Instructors may wish to cover the Automated Accounting feature on pages 286–287 even if the Automated Accounting software is not being used in the classroom so that students get a sense of how the chapter's accounting procedures would be implemented in an automated environment.

CHAPTER 9

Accounting for Notes Payable, Prepaid Expenses, and Accrued Expenses

OBJECTIVES & TERMS

After studying Chapter 9, you will be able to:

1. Define accounting terms related to notes payable, prepaid expenses, and accrued expenses.

2. Identify accounting concepts and practices related to notes payable, prepaid expenses, and accrued expenses.

3. Journalize transactions for notes payable.

4. Journalize adjusting and reversing entries for prepaid expenses initially recorded as expenses.

5. Journalize adjusting and reversing entries for accrued expenses.

- promissory note
- notes payable
- date of a note
- principal of a note

- maturity date of a note
- interest
- interest rate of a note
- interest expense

- maturity value
- prepaid expenses
- reversing entry
- accrued expenses

Point Your Browser
accountingxtra.swlearning.com

• The Mall of America

©BILL ALKOFER/BLOOMBERG NEWS/LANDOV

AN ENTIRE CITY UNDER ONE ROOF— THE MALL OF AMERICA

Around the world, the Mall of America is considered the premier place to shop. However, the Mall of America (MOA) is not just a shopping mall. It is the largest retail and entertainment complex in the United States.

Many people are aware of some of the entertainment options available at the MOA, including Camp Snoopy (the nation's largest indoor theme park), Underwater Adventures (a $1.2 million walk-through aquarium), a 14-screen movie theater, and nearly 60 sit-down or fast food restaurants and nightclubs.

What really makes the MOA a city under one roof, however, is some of the other opportunities it offers. You can attend classes at the first-ever college campus in a mall. You can get health care at the Sage Clinic. You can complete all your banking needs, including foreign currency exchanges, at a bank in the mall. You can use the services of the post office—the only full-service post office located in a mall in the U.S. You can join the Walksport Mall Stars, a walking club with over 4,000 members who use the MOA as a place to exercise and socialize. You can even get married in the Chapel of Love Wedding Chapel!

The Mall of America certainly is an entire city under one roof.

Critical Thinking

1. Assume you are a tenant at the Mall of America and must pay your rent one year in advance. Besides Cash, what other account would you use to record this transaction?
2. The Mall of America calls itself a "retail and entertainment" complex. Why is the idea of combining retail stores and entertainment attractive to consumers?

Xtra!
Today
accountingxtra.swlearning.com

Source: www.mallofamerica.com

SERVICE CORPS OF RETIRED EXECUTIVES (SCORE)

Go to the homepage of the Service Corps of Retired Executives (SCORE) (www.score.org).

Instructions

1. Briefly describe SCORE.
2. Find the location of the SCORE chapter nearest you. List the address of this chapter.
3. Go to the web site for this SCORE chapter. List one requirement for becoming a SCORE consultant.

ACCOUNTING IN THE REAL WORLD

1. Prepaid Rent would be used to record the payment of rent in advance.
2. Answers will vary but could include the following:
   - It is possible for some members of a group to shop while others partake of the entertainment offerings.
   - The mall and parking facilities can be utilized outside normal retail shopping hours.
   - Once parked, a family can enjoy shopping, meals, and entertainment without having to drive from one location to another.

INTERNET RESEARCH ACTIVITY

1. SCORE is a nonprofit association dedicated to providing entrepreneurs with free, confidential face-to-face and e-mail business counseling.
2. Answers will vary.
3. Answers will vary, depending on the chapter selected.

259

9-1 Notes Payable

Business transactions occur throughout a fiscal period. Some transactions begin in one accounting period and are completed in a different accounting period. Accounting records for each period, however, must show all information needed to prepare the financial statements of a business. [CONCEPT: Adequate Disclosure] Therefore, some financial activities require the use of special accounting procedures.

Most expenses occur in the same period in which a cash payment is made for the expense. Some expenses, such as insurance and advertising, require cash payment before the benefit is received. Thus, a cash payment for these expenses may occur in the fiscal period before the related expense should be recognized. In addition, a business may borrow money in one period and repay it in another period. Interest owed in the current period must be included in the financial statements of the current period. [CONCEPT: Matching Expenses with Revenue]

©GETTY IMAGES/PHOTODISC

making ethical decisions

MAKING ETHICAL DECISIONS • MAKING ETHICAL DECISIONS • MAKING ETHICAL DECISIO

Reporting Ethics Violations

What should employees do when they witness another employee possibly violating a law or the company's code of conduct? Many companies instruct their employees to report the possible violation to an ethics officer or compliance department. A phone number that allows an individual to provide confidential information regarding possible ethics violations is often referred to as a *hotline.*

For a hotline to be effective, employees must have confidence that their information is being treated seriously. One way Hewlett-

Packard achieves this objective is to publish a report that describes the number and types of calls received by its Office of Business Practices.

Instructions

Access the global citizenship report of Hewlett-Packard. What are the five most common categories of issues reported to the Office of Business Practices? Identify the year of the report, total number of issues reported, and the percent of issues of the top five categories.

MAKING ETHICAL DECISIONS

Answers will vary, depending on the year of the report. The nature of the items reported is not the most important issue of this activity. Hewlett-Packard's reporting of these issues is evidence that the company takes business ethics seriously.

Suggested Solution: In 2002, Hewlett-Packard indicated 174 issues reported. The top five categories were:

Outside activities, employment	20%
Employee relations	16%
Discrimination, harassment	11%
Misuse of company resources	11%
Contract compliance	9%

Source: *www.hp.com*

				GENERAL		ACCOUNTS RECEIVABLE CREDIT	SALES CREDIT	SALES TAX PAYABLE		SALES DISCOUNT DEBIT	CASH DEBIT	
DATE	ACCOUNT TITLE	DOC. NO.	POST. REF.	DEBIT	CREDIT			DEBIT	CREDIT			
				1	2	3	4	5	6	7	8	
Mar. 2	Notes Payable	R143			1 5 0 0 00						1 5 0 0 00	1
												2
												3

CASH RECEIPTS JOURNAL PAGE 5

A written and signed promise to pay a sum of money at a specified time is called a **promissory note**. Promissory notes signed by a business and given to a creditor are called **notes payable**. The day a note is issued is called the **date of a note**. The original amount of a note is called the **principal of a note**. The date a note is due is called the **maturity date of a note**. An amount paid for the use of money for a period of time is called **interest**. The percentage of the principal that is paid for use of the money is called the **interest rate of a note**.

Appliance Center occasionally borrows money from a bank. It signs a note payable with the bank as evidence of the debt.

March 2. Signed a 180-day, 10% note, $1,500.00. R143.

Upon signing the note, Appliance Center receives the $1,500.00. It records the transaction in the cash receipts journal as shown above. Appliance Center issues a receipt that is used as the source document for the transaction. [*CONCEPT: Objective Evidence*]

Cash	
1,500.00	

Notes Payable	
	1,500.00

small business spotlight
SMALL BUSINESS SPOTLIGHT

Finding new markets is a key to growing any business. For many small businesses, those new markets span the globe. It is not unusual to find new markets as close to home as Canada and Mexico and as far away as Africa and the Pacific Rim. With the number of small businesses on the increase, the U.S. Commerce Department has developed and expanded programs aimed at helping small businesses export their products.

EXPLAIN

- Ask students to list and define each term.
- Point out that a note is a promise to pay between two individuals or businesses.
- Ask students to read the F.Y.I. feature to learn more about how notes payable are classified on the balance sheet.

DEMONSTRATE

- Draw two T accounts on the board.
- Read the transaction statement.
- Ask students to analyze the transaction. Enter in the transaction in the T accounts.
- Use a cash receipts journal transparency to illustrate recording the transaction in the cash receipts journal or direct students to the illustration.

SMALL BUSINESS SPOTLIGHT

This feature explores possible global markets for U.S. small businesses. The U.S. Department of Commerce helps small businesses with their exporting efforts.

- Explain that students have learned to calculate maturity dates in the first-year course.
- Remind students that the date of the note is not included as one of the days on which interest is incurred.
- Ask students to read the F.Y.I. feature to learn how to calculate the number of days for a note stated in months.

- Write the first month on the board and explain how to calculate the number of days.
- Write the next month on the board and ask students to calculate the total number of days.
- Continue the process of writing one month and updating the total number of days as shown in the illustration at the top of the page.
- Explain how to determine the maturity date.
- Ask students to make up original note principals, interest rates, and terms for several notes.
- Direct the students to calculate the maturity date for each note.

- Ask students to explain why time as a fraction of a year is included in the interest calculation.
- Multiply the principal by the interest rate and ask students to identify the meaning of the amount (the interest owed on $1,500.00 if borrowed for an entire year).
- Ask students to read the F.Y.I. feature to learn more about the number of days used in interest calculations.

- Ask students to use a calculator to calculate the interest as shown in the illustration at the bottom of the page.
- Ask students to make up original note principals, interest rates, and terms for several notes (or use the notes used in the previous demonstration).
- Direct the students to calculate the interest for each note.

CALCULATING THE MATURITY DATE

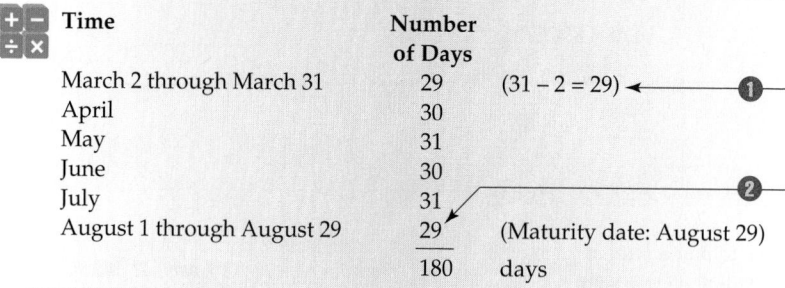

Time	Number of Days		
March 2 through March 31	29	(31 – 2 = 29)	1. Compute the number of days in the first month.
April	30		
May	31		
June	30		
July	31		2. Add the number of days in subsequent months until the total equals the number of days of the note.
August 1 through August 29	29	(Maturity date: August 29)	
	180	days	

The number of days in each month during the term of the note impacts the maturity date. The maturity date for Appliance Center's 180-day, March 2 note payable is August 29. The maturity date is determined as shown above.

STEPS · STEPS · STEPS · STEPS · STEPS
CALCULATING THE MATURITY DATE

1. Compute the number of days in the first month, *29*, by subtracting the date of the note, *2*, from the number of days in the month the note was signed, *31*.

2. Continue adding the number of days in each of the following months until the total equals the number of days of the note, *180*.

FYI FOR YOUR INFORMATION

The term of a note can be stated in months or years. Thus, a six-month note dated March 2 matures on September 2. The number of days between March 2 and September 2 must be determined to use in interest calculations.

CALCULATING INTEREST

Principal	×	Interest Rate	×	Time as Fraction of Year	=	Interest for Fraction of Year
$1,500.00	×	10%	×	$\frac{180}{360}$	=	$75.00

The interest rate of the note is stated as an annual rate. The interest paid on the note is calculated by applying the annual rate for the portion of the year that the note is outstanding as shown above. For ease of calculation, most banks use 360 rather than 365 as the number of days in a year.

FYI FOR YOUR INFORMATION

Agencies of the federal government generally use a 365-day year when calculating interest. Consumer interest also is generally calculated on a 365-day year. However, most banks use a 360-day year when calculating interest. Therefore, the interest calculations in this textbook use a 360-day year.

262   Chapter 9

Accounting for Notes Payable, Prepaid Expenses, and Accrued Expenses

PAYING A NOTE PAYABLE

1. Principal of note.

CASH PAYMENTS JOURNAL   PAGE 17

	DATE	ACCOUNT TITLE	CK. NO.	POST. REF.	GENERAL DEBIT	GENERAL CREDIT	ACCOUNTS PAYABLE DEBIT	PURCHASES DISCOUNT CREDIT	CASH CREDIT	
					1	2	3	4	5	
1	20-- Aug. 29	Notes Payable	359		1 500 00				1 575 00	1
2		Interest Expense			75 00					2

2. Interest on note.

3. Maturity value of note.

The interest accrued on money borrowed is called **interest expense**. On the maturity date, the borrower pays both the principal of the note payable and the interest expense. The payment of the note is recorded in the cash payments journal as shown above. The amount that is due on the maturity date of a note is called the **maturity value.** Appliance Center pays the maturity value of its note on the maturity date.

August 29. Paid cash for the maturity value of the Mar. 2 note: principal, $1,500.00, plus interest, $75.00; total, $1,575.00. Check No. 359.

Interest Expense is listed as an Other Expense on Appliance Center's chart of accounts. Expenses that are not a part of the normal operating expenses of a business are classified as other expenses.

Notes Payable	
1,500.00	Bal. 1,500.00

Interest Expense	
75.00	

Cash	
	1,575.00

©GETTY IMAGES/PHOTODISC

Notes Payable

Lesson 9-1   **263**

50,000 Canadian dollars
$$\times\ .87 = \$43{,}500$$
50,000 Canadian dollars
$$\times\ .82 = \underline{\$41{,}000}$$
Total loss $2,500
                  U.S. dollars

It will now cost Fashion Clothiers $43,500 American dollars to purchase 50,000 Canadian dollars. Fashion Clothiers will realize a loss of $2,500 U.S. dollars on the transaction.

Explore Accounting

The Impact of Changes in Foreign Exchange Rates on Accounts Payable and Notes Payable with Suppliers

Often U.S. companies purchase products from foreign suppliers. Even though a business purchases a foreign product in a foreign country using foreign currency, that transaction will ultimately have to be presented in dollars by the U.S. firm. [CONCEPT: Unit of Measurement] Consequently, any changes in foreign exchange rates can have an impact on a firm's accounts payable and notes payable.

Suppose an American firm, PhoneCom, purchases semiconductors on account from ChinaSemi, a Chinese corporation, priced at 800,000 yuan (a denomination of Chinese currency). The terms of the purchase are for the American company to pay 800,000 yuan in 60 days. If the rate for exchanging a yuan to the dollar rises or declines during the 60-day credit period, there will be an impact on the value of the final payment amount. Assume on the date of the purchase that the exchange rate is one yuan equals .10 dollars. In other words, one yuan costs 10 cents to buy. At this exchange rate, 800,000 yuan is equal to $80,000 ($800,000 × .10). Suppose, however, that during the 60-day credit period the exchange rate changes. If the new rate is one yuan equals .12 dollars (12 cents), PhoneCom will now have to pay more for each yuan. It will now cost PhoneCom $96,000 (800,000 × .12) to buy 800,000 yuan. The rise of 2 cents in the exchange rate for the yuan means the American company will have to pay $16,000 more to settle its purchase on account agreement.

It is also possible that the exchange rate for yuan to dollars may decline. Assume an American company, CalTech, purchases equipment for 2,000,000 yuan from a Chinese firm, XianCorp. The Chinese company accepts a 12-month, 5% note in lieu of cash at the time of sale. In 12 months, CalTech will pay 2,100,000 yuan (principal + 5% interest) in payment of the note. Assuming an exchange rate at the beginning and at the end of the note of one yuan equals .10 dollars, CalTech would need $210,000 (2,100,000 × .10) to pay its note. Suppose, however, that during the 12-month credit period the exchange rate declines. If the new rate is one yuan equals .09 dollars (9 cents), the American company will now pay less for each yuan. Due to the decline in the exchange rate, CalTech will need only $189,000 (2,100,000 × .09) to buy 2,100,000 yuan. The decline of one cent in the exchange rate for the yuan means that CalTech will pay $21,000 less to settle its purchase on account agreement.

Critical Thinking Activity

An American company, Fashion Clothiers, purchases men's clothing on account from a Canadian firm, Delmar, Inc., for 50,000 Canadian dollars. At the time of the sale, the exchange rate is one Canadian dollar equals .82 U.S. dollars. Thirty days later, when Fashion Clothiers pays the 50,000 Canadian dollars, the exchange rate has risen. One Canadian dollar can now be exchanged for .87 dollars. How much will it cost Fashion Clothiers to purchase Canadian dollars at the new rate? Will the American company realize a gain or a loss on the transaction? In your answer, state the amount of the gain or loss.

Optional Critical Thinking Activity

Use the Internet or newspaper to track the exchange rate between the Canadian dollar and U.S. dollar for one week. Did the rate for exchanging one Canadian dollar for one U.S. dollar increase or decrease? State the amount of change.

terms review

promissory note
notes payable
date of a note
principal of a note
maturity date of a note
interest
interest rate of a note
interest expense
maturity value

audit your understanding

1. What formula does Appliance Center use to calculate interest on notes?
2. How is the interest rate on a note stated?
3. The borrower pays what two amounts at the note's maturity?

work together 9-1

Journalizing notes payable transactions

A cash receipts journal and a cash payments journal are provided in the *Working Papers*. Source documents are abbreviated as: check, C; receipt, R. Your instructor will guide you through the following examples.

1. Using the current year, journalize the following transactions in the cash receipts journal.

   May 14. Signed a 90-day, 12% note with First National Bank, $5,000.00. R145.
   June 5. Signed a 180-day, 10% note with American Bank, $8,000.00. R213.

2. Calculate the maturity date of each note and the total amount of interest due at maturity for each note.

3. Journalize the following transactions in the cash payments journal. Use the maturity dates and interest amounts calculated in the previous steps.

   Paid cash for the maturity value of the $5,000.00 note. C345.
   Paid cash for the maturity value of the $8,000.00 note. C652.

on your own 9-1

Journalizing notes payable transactions

A cash receipts journal and a cash payments journal are provided in the *Working Papers*. Source documents are abbreviated as: check, C; receipt, R. Work this problem independently.

1. Using the current year, journalize the following transactions in the cash receipts journal.

   Mar. 23. Signed a 180-day, 10% note with Commerce Bank, $6,000.00. R84.
   July 12. Signed a 60-day, 12% note with Farmers National Bank, $12,000.00. R151.

2. Calculate the maturity date for each note and the total amount of interest due at maturity for each note.

3. Journalize the following transactions on page 14 of a cash payments journal. Use the maturity dates and interest amounts calculated in the previous steps.

   Paid cash for the maturity value of the $12,000.00 note. C455.
   Paid cash for the maturity value of the $6,000.00 note. C464.

Notes Payable

GUIDED PRACTICE

Terms Review

Call on students to define the terms in the Terms Review. Ask the class if the definitions are correct and whether the complete definitions have been given or if anything needs to be added. The suggested definitions are given in the Glossary.

Audit Your Understanding

Call on students to answer the Audit Your Understanding questions. Ask the class if the answer is correct and/or complete. Answers are given in Appendix E of the textbook.

Work Together

Have students write the solution to the Work Together problem as you guide the class through the examples.

- Direct students to record each transaction in the journals as you elicit class participation in analyzing and recording each transaction.
- Call on two students to describe how to calculate the maturity date for the notes.
- Call on another two students to write their interest calculations on the board.

INDEPENDENT PRACTICE

On Your Own

- Assign the On Your Own problem to be worked independently.
- Use the Ongoing Assessment techniques to diagnose student understanding.

Application Problem

Assign Application Problem 9-1: Journalizing notes payable transactions.

Personal Trainer

- Students can access the Lesson 9-1 assessment material using this software.

Xtra! Web Site

- Students can access the Xtra! Study Tools for additional practice.

ENRICH

- Assign Making Ethical Decisions on page 260.
- Assign Explore Accounting on page 264.
- Assign Automated Accounting on pages 286–287 to automate Application Problem 9-1.
- Students can use Peachtree and Quick-Books to automate Application Problem 9-1.

- Ask students to contact a local banker to learn how to apply for a $5,000.00 note to begin a small business. Have students list the information required on the loan application. What steps did the bank propose to assure that the students would be able to repay the note? *(Most banks would require other assets to be offered as collateral or a guarantee by another individual or business.)*

CLOSE

- Ask students to briefly summarize the procedures for journalizing transactions to record borrowing money with a note payable and later paying the maturity value of the note.

9-2 Prepaid Expenses

DESCRIPTION OF PREPAID EXPENSES

Expenses paid in one fiscal period but not reported as expenses until a later fiscal period are called **prepaid expenses**. Prepaid expenses include items such as supplies, insurance, advertising, and income taxes. Only that portion of cash payment for expenses that have been used in the current fiscal period should be reported as an expense in that fiscal period. [CONCEPT: Matching Expenses with Revenue]

Prepaid expenses may be recorded initially as assets or as expenses. Zytech, described in Part 1, initially records cash payments for supplies and insurance as assets. Appliance Center, in contrast, initially records these payments as expenses. Both methods are acceptable provided that the company consistently applies its chosen method from year to year.

Prepaid expenses are assets until they are actually used. For example, Appliance Center has a quantity of sales supplies on hand on any given day during the year. The company will use these sales supplies in the current and future fiscal periods. The amount recorded in the account Supplies Expense—Sales prior to the fiscal year-end adjustments represents a mixture of an expense (supplies already used) and an asset (supplies not yet used).

Appliance Center records an adjusting entry to recognize as an expense only those sales supplies used during the fiscal year. An adjusting entry could be made each day to recognize the sales supplies used that day. However, as a practical accounting procedure, this adjusting entry is made only when financial statements need to be prepared. [CONCEPT: Adequate Disclosure] Appliance Center records adjustments on December 31, the end of its fiscal year.

©GETTY IMAGES/PHOTODISC

SUPPLIES INITIALLY RECORDED AS AN ASSET

1. Debit the expense account.

		GENERAL JOURNAL				PAGE **13**	
	DATE	ACCOUNT TITLE	DOC. NO.	POST. REF.	DEBIT	CREDIT	
1		*Adjusting Entries*					1
2	Dec. 31	Supplies Expense—Office			9 9 5 0 00		2
3		Supplies—Office				9 9 5 0 00	3
4							4

2. Credit the asset account.

When Zytech, described in Part 1, buys office supplies, the asset Supplies—Office is debited and Cash is credited. Zytech recorded adjusting entries for supplies at the end of a fiscal period as shown above. Adjusting entries are recorded so that the supplies used during a fiscal period are reported as expenses and the supplies not used are reported as assets. [CONCEPT: *Matching Expenses with Revenue*]

Zytech initially recorded the prepaid supplies in the asset account Supplies—Office. The $12,700.00 debit balance represents the beginning inventory of supplies plus the total amount of all office supplies bought during the fiscal period. Nothing has been recorded in Zytech office supplies expense account during the fiscal period.

Zytech determined that the actual amount of office supplies inventory was $2,750.00. An adjusting entry of $9,950.00 ($12,700.00 – $2,750.00) is necessary.

After recording the adjustment, the new balance of Supplies—Office, *$2,750.00*, is the ending office supplies inventory on December 31. The new balance of Supplies Expense—Office, *$9,950.00*, represents supplies used during the current year.

Supplies—Office

12/31 Bal.	12,700.00	12/31 Adj.	9,950.00
(New Bal.	*2,750.00)*		

Supplies Expense—Office

12/31 Adj.	9,950.00

Closing Entries

To prepare a general ledger for the next fiscal period, closing entries are journalized and posted.

After its closing entries have been posted, Zytech's general ledger accounts are ready for the next fiscal period. On December 31, the amount of the office supplies inventory, *$2,750.00*, is recorded in the account in which it can be added to the amount of supplies that will be bought in the next fiscal period.

Income Summary

12/31 Clos.	9,950.00

Supplies Expense—Office

12/31 Adj.	9,950.00	12/31 Clos.	9,950.00
(New Bal. zero)			

EXPLAIN

- Point out that this method of recording prepaid expenses was used in both the first-year course and Part 1.
- Ask students to describe how the amount of an adjusting entry to Supplies—Office is determined.
- Ask students to explain why adjusting entries are recorded for prepaid expense accounts.
- Ask students to read the Remember feature to learn of other supply accounts.

DEMONSTRATE

Record the adjusting entry

- Draw three T accounts on the board.
- Describe the adjusting entry.
- Ask students to analyze the adjusting entry by answering: what accounts are affected, are they increased or decreased, and are they debited or credited. Enter the adjusting entry in the T accounts.
- Use a general journal transparency to illustrate recording the adjusting entry in the general journal or direct students to the illustration.

Record the closing entry

- Use the same three T accounts on the board.
- Describe the closing entry.
- Ask students to analyze the closing entry. Enter the closing entry in the T accounts and calculate new balances.
- Use a general journal transparency to illustrate recording the closing entry in the general journal.

{ **R E M E M B E R** Similar entries are made for each supply account, such as Supplies—Administrative and Supplies—Warehouse. }

APPLIED SKILLS BUILDING STUDY SKILLS

Direct students to create a Quick Reference Guide (QRG) for adjusting and reversing entries for prepaid and accrued expenses. (1) Label a QRG PREPAID EXPENSES. (2) List each prepaid expense situation out of the chapter narrative (for example, supplies initially recorded as an expense). (3) Indicate what accounts are debited and credited to record the adjusting and reversing entries for each situation. (4) Repeat the process for ACCRUED EXPENSES.

- Ask students to describe how the amount of the adjusting entry is determined.
- Point out that the procedure for recording a closing entry is the same regardless of the method used for initially recording supplies and other prepaid expenses.
- Ask students to read the Remember feature to reinforce that either method of accounting for prepaid expenses is acceptable.

DEMONSTRATE

Record the adjusting entry
- Draw three T accounts on the board.
- Describe the adjusting entry.
- Ask students to analyze the adjusting entry by answering: what accounts are affected, are they increased or decreased, and are they debited or credited. Enter the adjusting entry in the T accounts.
- Use a general journal transparency to illustrate recording the adjusting entry in the general journal or direct students to the illustration.

Record the closing entry
- Use the same three T accounts on the board.
- Describe the closing entry.
- Ask students to analyze the closing entry. Enter the closing entry in the T accounts and calculate new balances.
- Use a general journal transparency to illustrate recording the closing entry in the general journal.

SUPPLIES INITIALLY RECORDED AS AN EXPENSE

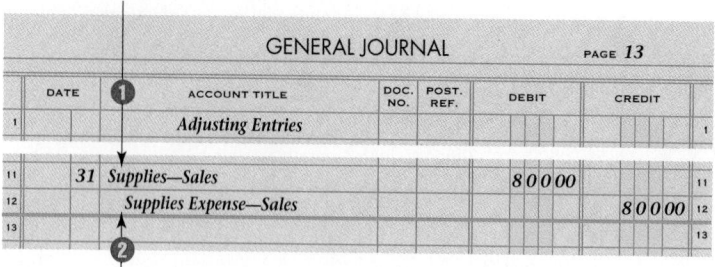

1. Debit the asset account.

2. Credit the expense account.

When Appliance Center buys sales supplies, Supplies Expense—Sales is debited and Cash is credited. The $2,000.00 debit balance of Supplies Expense—Sales represents the amount of the beginning sales supplies inventory plus the total amount of all sales supplies bought during the fiscal period. Nothing has been recorded in Appliance Center's sales supplies account during the fiscal period.

On December 31, Appliance Center takes a physical count of the sales supplies on hand. It determines that the sales supplies ending inventory is $800.00 and records the necessary adjusting entry as shown above.

The new balance of Supplies—Sales, *$800.00*, represents the ending sales supplies inventory on December 31. The new balance of Supplies Expense—Sales, *$1,200.00*, recognizes the amount of sales supplies used during the current year.

Supplies—Sales	
12/31 Adj. 800.00	

Supplies Expense—Sales	
12/31 Bal. 2,000.00	12/31 Adj. 800.00
(New Bal. 1,200.00)	

Closing Entry for Supplies Expense
To prepare a general ledger for the next fiscal period, closing entries are journalized and posted. After the closing entry is recorded, the Supplies Expense—Sales account balance is zero. The debit balance of $800.00 in Supplies—Sales represents the amount of sales supplies on hand on December 31.

Income Summary	
12/31 Clos. 1,200.00	

Supplies Expense—Sales	
12/31 Bal. 2,000.00	12/31 Adj. 800.00
(New Bal. zero)	12/31 Clos. 1,200.00

> **REMEMBER** Although Zytech and Appliance Center use different procedures, both correctly separate and record the asset and expense portions of the cost of supplies. Both procedures meet the requirements of the *Matching Expenses with Revenue* concept.

REVERSING ENTRY—SUPPLIES INITIALLY RECORDED AS AN EXPENSE

1. Debit the expense account.

	DATE	① ACCOUNT TITLE	DOC. NO.	POST. REF.	DEBIT	CREDIT	
		Reversing Entries					1
7	1	*Supplies Expense—Sales*			8 0 0 00		7
8		*Supplies—Sales*				8 0 0 00	8
9							9

GENERAL JOURNAL   PAGE *1*

2. Credit the asset account.

After the closing entries have been posted, Zytech's general ledger accounts are ready for the next fiscal period. However, Appliance Center's general ledger accounts are not ready for the next fiscal period.

Appliance Center initially records the amount of all supplies bought in an expense account. On December 31, the amount of Appliance Center's sales supplies inventory, *$800.00*, is the debit balance of Supplies—Sales. On January 1, the $800.00 should be returned as a debit in Supplies Expense—Sales. The $800.00 debit can then be added to the amount of sales supplies bought during the next year.

Some businesses that initially record prepaid items as expenses reverse the adjusting entries for prepaid expenses at the beginning of each fiscal period. An entry made at the beginning of one fiscal period to reverse an adjusting entry made in the previous fiscal period is called a **reversing entry**. Thus, a reversing entry is the exact opposite of the related adjusting entry.

Appliance Center initially records supplies as expenses and therefore needs to record reversing entries. Accountants use the following rule of thumb to determine whether a reversing entry is needed: If an adjusting entry *creates* a balance in an asset or a liability account, the adjusting entry is reversed.

Because Appliance Center's adjusting entry for sales supplies created a balance in Supplies—Sales, a reversing entry is needed. The reversing entry is shown above.

After the reversing entry is posted, the cost of the sales supplies inventory, *$800.00*, is recorded in the account where it can be added to the amount of supplies bought in the next fiscal period. The balance of Supplies—Sales is zero, as it was before the adjusting entry.

Supplies Expense—Sales			
12/31 Bal.	2,000.00	12/31 Adj.	800.00
1/1 Rev.	800.00	12/31 Clos.	1,200.00
(New Bal.	*800.00)*		

Supplies—Sales			
12/31 Adj.	800.00	1/1 Rev.	800.00
(New Bal. zero)			

> **REMEMBER** Zytech initially records supplies as assets but *does not* record reversing entries. On December 31, the amount of the office supplies inventory, $2,750.00, is recorded in the account where it can be added to the amount of supplies bought in the next fiscal period.

> **REMEMBER** Although Zytech and Appliance Center use different accounting procedures, both correctly separate and record the asset and expense portions of supply costs.

Prepaid Expenses

Lesson 9-2   **269**

EXPLAIN

- Point out that insurance premiums and supplies are both prepaid expenses.
- Ask students to describe how the amount of prepaid insurance at year-end would be determined.

DEMONSTRATE

- Draw two T accounts on the board and enter the pre-adjustment balances.
- Describe the adjusting entry.
- Ask students to analyze the adjusting entry. Complete the T accounts as the information is provided.
- Use a general journal transparency to illustrate recording the adjusting entry in the general journal or direct students to the illustration at the top of the page.

EXPLAIN

- Ask students to explain why prepaid insurance is reversed.
- Point out that the affect of the closing entry (not shown in the figure) is shown in the T accounts.
- Ask students to read the Remember feature to review why reversing entries are not recorded for prepaid expenses initially recorded as assets.

DEMONSTRATE

- Continue to use the T accounts from the prior demonstration.
- Describe the closing entry and record the entry in the T accounts.
- Describe the reversing entry.
- Ask students to analyze the adjusting entry. Complete the T accounts as the information is provided.
- Use a general journal transparency to illustrate recording the transaction in the general journal or direct students to the illustration in the middle of the page.

ONGOING ASSESSMENT

- Assessment is an ongoing process. Circulate through the classroom or lab observing which students have problems with the assignments.
- Troubleshooting: Diagnose what kinds of problems students have with this section. The concepts and procedures in this section are relatively simple and some concepts are a review of the first-year

PREPAID INSURANCE INITIALLY RECORDED AS AN EXPENSE

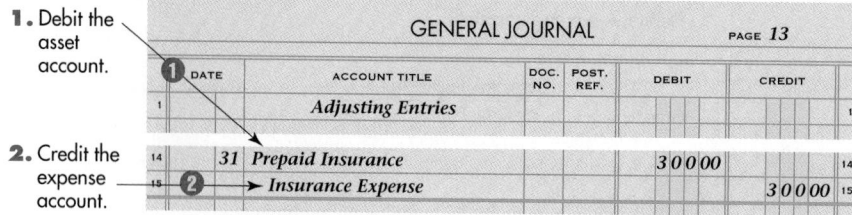

1. Debit the asset account.
2. Credit the expense account.

Appliance Center initially records insurance premiums as expenses. When Appliance Center pays insurance premiums, Insurance Expense is debited and Cash is credited.

On December 31, Appliance Center determines that the amount of the unexpired insurance premiums totals $300.00 and records the necessary adjusting entry as shown above.

The new balance of Prepaid Insurance, *$300.00*, represents the amount of unexpired insurance

premiums at the end of the fiscal period. The new balance of Insurance Expense *$600.00*, indicates the insurance expense for the fiscal period.

Prepaid Insurance		
12/31 Adj.	300.00	

Insurance Expense		
12/31 Adj.	900.00	12/31 Adj. 300.00
(New Bal.	*600.00)*	

REVERSING ENTRY FOR PREPAID INSURANCE

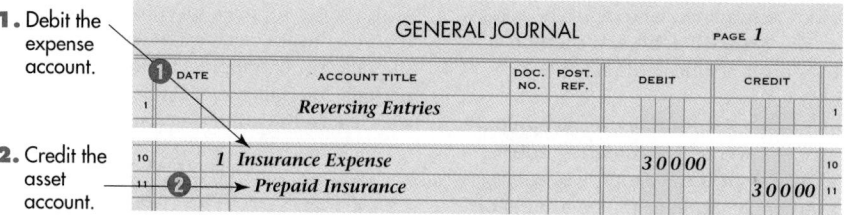

1. Debit the expense account.
2. Credit the asset account.

Insurance Expense is closed as part of Appliance Center's closing entries.

Appliance Center's adjusting entry for insurance expense created a balance in the asset account Prepaid Insurance. Therefore, on January 1, Appliance Center needs a reversing entry for insurance expense. The reversing entry is shown above.

The new balance of Insurance Expense, *$300.00*, can now be added to the amount of insurance premiums paid during the next fiscal period. The

new balance of Prepaid Insurance is zero, as it was before the adjusting entry.

Insurance Expense		
12/31 Bal.	900.00	12/31 Adj. 300.00
(New Bal. zero)		12/31 Clos. 600.00
1/1 Rev.	300.00	
(New Bal.	*300.00)*	

Prepaid Insurance		
12/31 Adj.	300.00	1/1 Rev. 300.00
(New Bal. zero)		

> **REMEMBER** No reversing entry is required when expenses are initially charged to a prepaid expense account.

course. Students may have difficulty understanding when to record a reversing entry.

- Assess student understanding by checking solutions to Independent Practice assignments.

RETEACH

- Ask students to describe the two methods for accounting for prepaid expenses.
- Ask students to explain how to determine the amount for the adjusting entry.
- Ask students to identify when a reversing entry should be recorded.

• terms review

prepaid expenses
reversing entry

• audit your understanding

1. Which accounting concept is being applied when an adjusting entry is recorded for prepaid expenses?

2. Why is an adjusting entry made for supplies at the end of a fiscal period?

3. What rule of thumb can accountants follow to determine whether a reversing entry is needed?

• work together 9-2

Journalizing adjusting and reversing entries for prepaid expenses initially recorded as expenses

Janson, Inc., has the following general ledger balances on December 31 of the current year before it records adjusting entries. A general journal is provided in the *Working Papers*. Your instructor will guide you through the following examples.

Supplies Expense—Administrative	$3,200.00	Insurance Expense	$2,000.00
Supplies Expense—Sales	1,500.00		

1. Using the following adjustment information, journalize the adjusting entries for supplies and insurance on December 31 of the current year.

Administrative Supplies Inventory	$500.00	Value of Prepaid Insurance	$600.00
Sales Supplies Inventory	400.00		

2. Journalize the reversing entries on January 1 of the next year.

• on your own 9-2

Journalizing adjusting and reversing entries for prepaid expenses initially recorded as expenses

Wren Industries has the following general ledger balances on December 31 of the current year before it records adjusting entries. A general journal is provided in the *Working Papers*. Work this problem independently.

Supplies Expense—Administrative	$4,600.00	Insurance Expense	$6,000.00
Supplies Expense—Sales	4,800.00		

1. Using the following adjustment information, journalize the adjusting entries for supplies and insurance on December 31 of the current year.

Administrative Supplies Inventory	$800.00	Value of Prepaid Insurance	$900.00
Sales Supplies Inventory	600.00		

2. Journalize the reversing entries on January 1 of the next year.

Prepaid Expenses

Lesson 9-2   **271**

GUIDED PRACTICE

Terms Review
Call on students to define the terms in the Terms Review. Ask the class if the definitions are correct and whether the complete definitions have been given or if anything needs to be added. The suggested definitions are given in the Glossary.

Audit Your Understanding
Call on students to answer the Audit Your Understanding questions. Ask the class if the answer is correct and/or complete. Answers are given in Appendix E of the textbook.

Work Together
Have students write the solution to the Work Together problems as you guide the class through the example.

- Direct students to record the three adjusting entries in the general journal as you elicit class participation in analyzing and recording the transactions.

- Ask students to explain why reversing entries should be recorded.

- Direct students to record the three reversing entries in the general journal as you elicit class participation in analyzing and recording the transactions.

INDEPENDENT PRACTICE

On Your Own
- Assign the On Your Own problem to be worked independently.
- Use the Ongoing Assessment techniques to diagnose student understanding.

Application Problem
- Assign Application Problem 9-2: Journalizing adjusting and reversing entries for prepaid expenses initially recorded as expenses.

Personal Trainer
- Students can access the Lesson 9-2 assessment material using this software.

Xtra! Web Site
- Students can access the Xtra! Study Tools for additional practice.

CLOSE
- Ask students to briefly summarize the recording of adjusting, closing, and reversing entries for prepaid expenses initially recorded as an expense.

ENRICH
- Ask students to debate which of the methods to account for prepaid expenses they prefer. Which method is easier to record? Easier to understand? Results in more accurate financial statements?

9-3 Accrued Expenses

JOURNALIZING ACCRUED INTEREST EXPENSE

Principal	×	Interest Rate	×	Time as Fraction of Year	=	Interest for 15 Days
$7,500.00	×	10%	×	$\frac{15}{360}$	=	$31.25

1. Determine the amount of accrued interest.

2. Debit the expense account.

3. Credit the liability account.

GENERAL JOURNAL   PAGE 1

	DATE	ACCOUNT TITLE	DOC. NO.	POST. REF.	DEBIT	CREDIT	
1		*Adjusting Entries*					1
25	Dec. 13	*Interest Payable*			3 1 25		25
26		*Interest Expense*				3 1 25	26
27							27

Expenses incurred in one fiscal period but not paid until a later fiscal period are called **accrued expenses**. In any fiscal period, Appliance Center may need to account for four types of accrued expenses.

1. Accrued interest expense.
2. Accrued salary expense.
3. Accrued employer payroll taxes expense.
4. Accrued federal income tax expense.

On December 31, Appliance Center has a 60-day, 10% note payable for $7,500.00, dated December 16, on which interest has accrued.

On December 31, Appliance Center owes 15 days worth of accrued interest on the note, $31.25. The accrued interest expense for this note should be reported in the current fiscal period. [CONCEPT: Matching Expenses with Revenue] The adjusting entry shown above records the accrued interest adjustment.

Interest Payable

12/31 Bal.	2,142.50
12/31 Adj.	31.25
(New Bal.	*2,173.75)*

Interest Expense

12/31 Adj.	31.25

STEPS • STEPS • STEPS • STEPS

RECORDING THE ADJUSTING ENTRY FOR ACCRUED INTEREST EXPENSE

1 Determine the interest expense for the current period, *$31.25*.

2 Record the debit to *Interest Expense, 31.25*. The debit increases the expense in the current period.

3 Record the credit to *Interest Payable, 31.25*. The credit increases the liability in the current period.

REMEMBER Any adjustment that creates an asset or liability should be reversed.

REVERSING ENTRY FOR ACCRUED INTEREST

1. Debit the liability account.

	DATE	①	ACCOUNT TITLE	DOC. NO.	POST. REF.	DEBIT	CREDIT	
1			*Reversing Entries*					1
14	Jan.	1	*Interest Payable*			3 1 25		14
15			*Interest Expense*				3 1 25	15
16		②						16
17								17
18								18

GENERAL JOURNAL   PAGE **1**

2. Credit the expense account.

Appliance Center's adjusting entry for accrued interest expense creates a balance in a liability account. After preparing its financial statements, Appliance Center journalizes and posts closing entries. To prepare the accounts for the next year, Appliance Center records a reversing entry for accrued interest expense, as shown above.

When Appliance Center pays the note on February 14 of the following year, the total interest expense payment is *$125.00*. The total interest expense should be divided between the two fiscal periods. Interest for the prior year, *$31.25*, is charged for the 15 days the note was outstanding

in that year. Interest for the current period, *$93.75*, relates to the 45 days from the start of the fiscal year to the maturity date.

Interest Payable

1/1 Rev.	31.25	12/31 Adj.	31.25
		(New Bal. zero)	

Interest Expense

12/31 Bal.	2,142.50	12/31 Clos.	2,173.75
12/31 Adj.	31.25		
(New Bal. zero)			
		1/1 Rev.	31.25

PAYMENT OF NOTE AT MATURITY

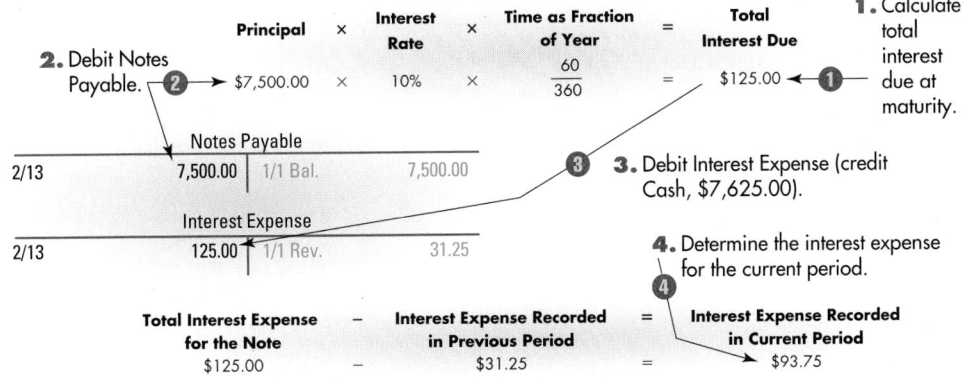

2. Debit Notes Payable.

Principal	×	Interest Rate	×	Time as Fraction of Year	=	Total Interest Due
$7,500.00	×	10%	×	$\frac{60}{360}$	=	$125.00

Notes Payable

2/13	7,500.00	1/1 Bal.	7,500.00

Interest Expense

2/13	125.00	1/1 Rev.	31.25

Total Interest Expense for the Note	−	Interest Expense Recorded in Previous Period	=	Interest Expense Recorded in Current Period
$125.00	−	$31.25	=	$93.75

1. Calculate total interest due at maturity.

3. Debit Interest Expense (credit Cash, $7,625.00).

4. Determine the interest expense for the current period.

On the maturity date, Appliance Center writes a check for the maturity value of $7,625.00. This decreases Notes Payable by a $7,500.00 debit. The $125.00 debit to Interest Expense, less the $31.25

credit balance created by the reversing entry, equals the $93.75 interest expense for the current period.

Accrued Expenses

Lesson 9-3   **273**

- Point out that the process for recording accrued salaries is the same as for accrued interest except that more accounts are involved.

- Ask students to compare the adjusting entry to the entry that will be recorded when the payroll is recorded at the end of the current payroll period *(the accounts are the same).*

- Ask students to read the Remember feature to review why salaries should be accrued.

DEMONSTRATE

Analyze the transaction

- Draw seven T accounts on the board.

- Describe the adjusting entry.

- Ask students to analyze the adjusting entry by answering: what accounts are affected, are they increased or decreased, and are they debited or credited. Complete the T accounts as the information is provided.

Record the transaction

- Use a general journal transparency to illustrate recording the adjusting entry in the general journal or direct students to the illustration.

		GENERAL JOURNAL					PAGE 13	
	DATE	ACCOUNT TITLE	DOC. NO.	POST. REF.	DEBIT		CREDIT	
1		*Adjusting Entries*						1
28	31	*Salary Expense—Administrative*			7 5 0 00			28
29		*Salary Expense—Sales*			8 5 0 00			29
30		*Salary Expense—Warehouse*			4 5 0 00			30
31		*Salaries Payable*					1 5 6 0 00	31
32		*Employee Income Tax Payable*					3 2 6 00	32
33		*Social Security Tax Payable*					1 3 3 25	33
34		*Medicare Tax Payable*					3 0 75	34
35								35

1. Debit the expense accounts.

2. Credit the liability accounts.

Appliance Center pays its employees each Friday for the time they worked during the previous week. On December 31, Appliance Center owes, but has not paid, the employees for Monday through Friday of the previous week. On Friday, January 5, the employees will receive a paycheck that includes five days' pay from the previous fiscal period.

On December 31, even though the employees have not been paid, salaries for five days are reported as an expense of the current fiscal period. [*CONCEPT: Matching Expenses with Revenue*] The financial statements must show all the business expenses for a fiscal period. [*CONCEPT: Adequate Disclosure*]

On December 31, Appliance Center owes $1,560.00 of salaries to employees who work in its three departments. To determine the adjusting entry, Appliance Center must prepare the payroll register. However, the checks are not prepared or distributed to employees until the normal payment date, January 5. The adjusting entry to record the accrued salary expense is shown above.

Salary Expense—Administrative

12/31 Bal.	37,062.50	
12/31 Adj.	750.00	
(New Bal.	*37,812.50)*	

Salary Expense—Sales

12/31 Bal.	45,075.00	
12/31 Adj.	850.00	
(New Bal.	*45,925.00)*	

Salary Expense—Warehouse

12/31 Bal.	22,037.50	
12/31 Adj.	450.00	
(New Bal.	*22,487.50)*	

Salaries Payable

| | | 12/31 Adj. | 1,560.00 |

Employee Income Tax Payable

| | | 12/31 Adj. | 326.00 |

Social Security Tax Payable

		12/31 Bal.	402.59
		12/31 Adj.	133.25
		(New Bal.	*535.84)*

Medicare Tax Payable

		12/31 Bal.	92.91
		12/31 Adj.	30.75
		(New Bal.	*123.66)*

REMEMBER   When a company incurs a salary expense, it must recognize this expense as a liability in the period in which employees provide their services to the company.

Accounting for Notes Payable, Prepaid Expenses, and Accrued Expenses

TEACHING STRATEGIES   EXPANDING BEYOND THE CLASSROOM

Assign students to contact various professional organizations to obtain information about the association. You may want to give the students some guidance as to what kind of information to request, such as purpose of the organization, membership enrollment, examples of activities, scholarship information, etc.

REVERSING ENTRY FOR ACCRUED SALARY

<table>
<tr><th colspan="7" align="center">GENERAL JOURNAL</th><th>PAGE 14</th></tr>
<tr><th></th><th>DATE</th><th>ACCOUNT TITLE</th><th>DOC.
NO.</th><th>POST.
REF.</th><th>DEBIT</th><th>CREDIT</th><th></th></tr>
<tr><td>1</td><td></td><td>*Reversing Entries*</td><td></td><td></td><td></td><td></td><td>1</td></tr>
<tr><td>15</td><td>1</td><td>Salaries Payable</td><td></td><td></td><td>1 5 6 0 00</td><td></td><td>15</td></tr>
<tr><td>16</td><td></td><td>Employee Income Tax Payable</td><td></td><td></td><td>3 2 6 00</td><td></td><td>16</td></tr>
<tr><td>17</td><td></td><td>Social Security Tax Payable</td><td></td><td></td><td>1 3 3 25</td><td></td><td>17</td></tr>
<tr><td>18</td><td></td><td>Medicare Tax Payable</td><td></td><td></td><td>3 0 75</td><td></td><td>18</td></tr>
<tr><td>19</td><td></td><td>Salary Expense—Administrative</td><td></td><td></td><td></td><td>7 5 0 00</td><td>19</td></tr>
<tr><td>20</td><td></td><td>Salary Expense—Sales</td><td></td><td></td><td></td><td>8 5 0 00</td><td>20</td></tr>
<tr><td>21</td><td></td><td>Salary Expense—Warehouse</td><td></td><td></td><td></td><td>4 5 0 00</td><td>21</td></tr>
<tr><td>22</td><td></td><td></td><td></td><td></td><td></td><td></td><td>22</td></tr>
<tr><td>23</td><td></td><td></td><td></td><td></td><td></td><td></td><td>23</td></tr>
</table>

1. Debit the liability accounts. ➊

2. Credit the expense accounts. ➋

After Appliance Center records closing entries for payroll, the three payroll expense accounts have zero balances. The salaries payable account reflects the $1,560.00 salaries to be paid on January 5.

The entry to reverse the payroll adjustment removes the adjusting entry amounts from the four payroll liability accounts, as shown above. The three salary expense accounts have contra (credit) balances after the reversing entry. When Appliance Center pays the payroll in January, the amount debited in each account is offset by the credit contra balance.

Fiscal years often end in the middle of payroll periods. Therefore, payroll expense must be accrued for the number of days of the payroll period in the current fiscal year. Estimates of the tax liabilities, based on previous payroll periods, are used to prepare the adjusting entry.

Salaries Payable

1/1 Rev.	1,560.00	12/31 Adj.	1,560.00
		(New Bal. zero)	

Employee Income Tax Payable

1/1 Rev.	326.00	12/31 Adj.	326.00
		(New Bal. zero)	

Social Security Tax Payable

1/1 Rev.	133.25	12/31 Bal.	535.84
		12/31 Adj.	133.25
		(New Bal.	*535.84)*

Medicare Tax Payable

1/1 Rev.	30.75	12/31 Bal.	123.66
		12/31 Adj.	30.75
		(New Bal.	*123.66)*

Salary Expense—Administrative

12/31 Bal.	37,062.50	12/31 Clos.	37,812.50
12/31 Adj.	750.00	1/1 Rev.	750.00
		(New Bal.	*750.00)*

Salary Expense—Sales

12/31 Bal.	45,075.00	12/31 Clos.	45,925.00
12/31 Adj.	850.00	1/1 Rev.	850.00
		(New Bal.	*850.00)*

Salary Expense—Warehouse

12/31 Bal.	22,037.50	12/31 Clos.	22,487.50
12/31 Adj.	450.00	1/1 Rev.	450.00
		(New Bal.	*450.00)*

FYI
FOR YOUR INFORMATION

Reversing entries eliminate the need to remember that the payroll liability accounts reflect an expense from the previous accounting period.

EXPLAIN

- Ask students to explain how to determine the amounts and accounts of a reversing entry *(debit the accounts credited by the adjusting entry for the same amount; credit the accounts debited by the adjusting entry by the same amounts).*
- Ask students to explain why the salary expense accounts have a credit balance after the adjusting entry is recorded.
- Ask students to read the F.Y.I. to learn another reason why reversing entries are recorded.

DEMONSTRATE

Analyze the transaction

- Draw seven T accounts on the board and record the balance before the adjusting entry.
- Review the adjusting and closing entries while recording these transactions in the T accounts.
- Describe the reversing entry.
- Ask students to analyze the reversing entry by answering: what accounts are affected, are they increased or decreased, and are they debited or credited. Complete the T accounts as the information is provided.

Record the transaction

- Use a general journal transparency to illustrate recording the reversing entry in the general journal or direct students to the illustration.

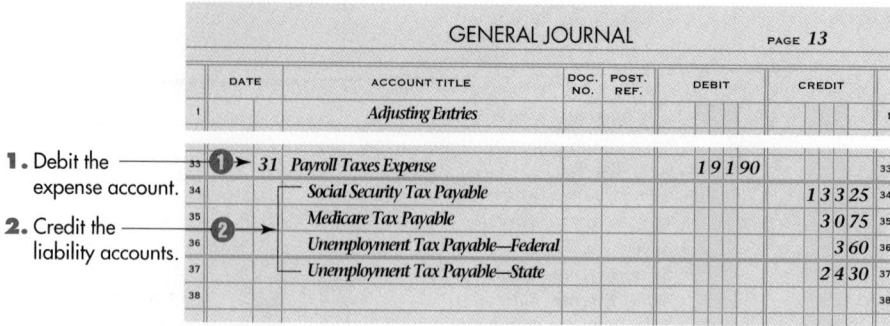

1. Debit the expense account.

2. Credit the liability accounts.

	DATE	ACCOUNT TITLE	DOC. NO.	POST. REF.	DEBIT	CREDIT	
1		*Adjusting Entries*					1
33	31	Payroll Taxes Expense			1 9 1 90		33
34		Social Security Tax Payable				1 3 3 25	34
35		Medicare Tax Payable				3 0 75	35
36		Unemployment Tax Payable—Federal				3 60	36
37		Unemployment Tax Payable—State				2 4 30	37
38							38

GENERAL JOURNAL — PAGE 13

Employer payroll taxes for accrued salaries must be recorded at the end of a fiscal period. Appliance Center has four employer payroll taxes:

1. Social security tax.
2. Medicare tax.
3. Federal unemployment tax
4. State unemployment tax.

The entry to record the accrued employer payroll taxes on December 31 of the current year is shown above.

REVERSING ENTRY FOR ACCRUED EMPLOYER PAYROLL TAXES

1. Debit the liability accounts.

2. Credit the expense account.

	DATE	ACCOUNT TITLE	DOC. NO.	POST. REF.	DEBIT	CREDIT	
1		*Reversing Entries*					1
18	1	Social Security Tax Payable			1 3 3 25		18
19		Medicare Tax Payable			3 0 75		19
20		Unemployment Tax Payable—Federal			3 60		20
21		Unemployment Tax Payable—State			2 4 30		21
22		Payroll Taxes Expense				1 9 1 90	22
23							23

GENERAL JOURNAL — PAGE 16

After Appliance Center records closing entries for payroll taxes, the payroll taxes expense account has a zero balance. The four payroll tax liability accounts reflect the tax payments to be made during the next fiscal year.

The entry to reverse the payroll taxes adjustment removes the adjusting entry amounts from the four payroll tax liability accounts, as shown above. The payroll tax expense account has a contra (credit) balance after the reversing entry. When the payroll taxes are paid, the amount debited to Payroll Taxes Expense will be offset by the credit contra balance. Thus, the transaction recorded is the same as other payroll tax payments during the fiscal year.

- Point out that the process for accruing payroll taxes expense is the same as for accrued salaries.
- Ask students to compare the adjusting entry to the entry that will be recorded when the payroll is recorded at the end of the current period *(the accounts are the same).*

DEMONSTRATE

Analyze the transaction

- Draw five T accounts on the board.
- Describe the adjusting entry.
- Ask students to analyze the adjusting entry. Complete the T accounts as the information is provided.

Record the transaction

- Use a general journal transparency to illustrate recording the adjusting entry in the general journal or direct students to the illustration at the top of the page.

EXPLAIN

- Ask students to explain why the salary expense accounts have a credit balance after the reversing entry is recorded.
- Review the benefit of using reversing entries *(eliminate the need to remember that the liability accounts reflect an expense from the previous accounting period).*

DEMONSTRATE

Analyze the transaction

- Use the five T accounts from the previous demonstration.
- Review the adjusting and closing entries.
- Describe the reversing entry.
- Ask students to analyze the reversing entry. Complete the T accounts as the information is provided.

Record the transaction

- Use a general journal transparency to illustrate recording the reversing entry in the general journal or direct students to the illustration in the middle of the page.

JOURNALIZING ACCRUED FEDERAL INCOME TAX EXPENSE

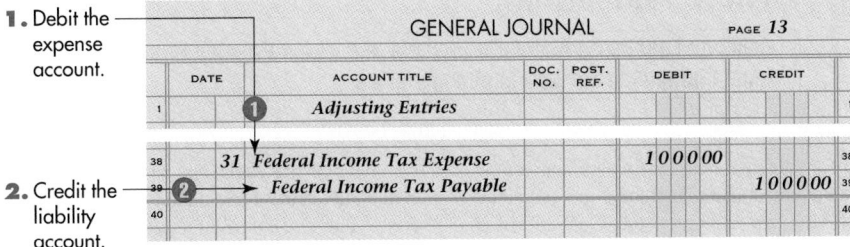

1. Debit the expense account.

2. Credit the liability account.

	DATE	ACCOUNT TITLE	DOC. NO.	POST. REF.	DEBIT	CREDIT	
1		*Adjusting Entries*					1
38	31	*Federal Income Tax Expense*			1 0 0 0 0 0		38
39		*Federal Income Tax Payable*				1 0 0 0 0 0	39
40							40

GENERAL JOURNAL   PAGE 13

Corporations must pay federal income tax on net income. At the beginning of each year, Appliance Center makes an estimate of its federal income tax obligation. It pays the estimated amount in four quarterly payments. At the end of a year, Appliance Center revises its income tax estimate for the year. Any unpaid federal income tax is an accrued expense for which an adjusting entry must be made.

On December 31, Appliance Center's records show that quarterly income tax payments have been made for a total of $9,000.00. On December 31, Appliance Center estimates that its income tax will be $10,000.00. Thus, the accrued federal income tax remaining to be paid is $1,000.00 (total tax, $10,000.00, *minus* amount paid, $9,000.00). The adjusting entry for the accrual is shown above.

Federal Income Tax Payable is a current liability account. Federal Income Tax Expense is an expense account located in the general ledger division titled *Income Tax*.

During the year, cash will be paid for accrued income tax expense for the previous year plus periodic payments for the current year's income tax expense. To avoid confusing the amount of tax expense recorded for each of these years and to provide year-to-date income tax expense information for each year, Appliance Center does not reverse this adjusting entry.

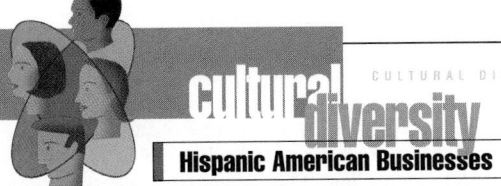

CULTURAL DIVERSITY • CULTURAL DIVERSITY • CULTURAL DIVERSITY

cultural diversity

Hispanic American Businesses

The Census Bureau's Survey of Minority-Owned Business Enterprises indicates that minority-owned enterprises are increasing in number and size. One of the fastest growing segments of U.S. business population during the period from 1987 to 1992 was businesses owned by Hispanic Americans. During this period, the number of Hispanic-owned businesses increased from 422,373 to 771,708. In addition, their total receipts more than tripled, from $24.7 billion to $72.8 billion.

With the impressive growth in Hispanic-owned businesses, *Hispanic Business* magazine has created lists of successful

Hispanic-owned businesses, including the Hispanic Business 500, the Hispanic Business High Tech 50, and the Fast-Growing 100. The 1997 Hispanic Business 500 gives the honor of largest Hispanic-owned corporation to Burt Automotive Network of Englewood, Colorado. Its chief executive office (CEO) is Lloyd G. Chavez. This automotive sales and service company was started in 1939, employs over 800, and had total revenue in 1996 of about $813 million.

Accrued Expenses

It will now cost the American company $43,500 American dollars to purchase 50,000 Canadian dollars. The American company will realize a loss of $2,500 U.S. dollars on the transaction.

50,000 Canadian dollars
$\times .87 = \$43,500$

50,000 Canadian dollars
$\times .82 = \underline{\$41,000}$

| Total loss | $ 2,500 |
| | U.S. dollars |

Accounts Payable/Delmar, Inc.	41,000	
Gain or Loss on Foreign		
Currency Exchange	2,500.00	
Cash		43,500.00

Explore Accounting

EXPLORE ACCOUNTING • EXPLORE ACCOUNTING • EXPLORE ACCOUNTING

Gains or Losses on Accounts Payable and Notes Payable Resulting from Changes in Foreign Exchange Rates

In the Explore Accounting feature in Lesson 9-1, PhoneCom purchases semiconductors priced at 800,000 yuan on account from ChinaSemi, a Chinese corporation. The terms of the purchase are for PhoneCom, an American company, to pay 800,000 yuan in 60 days. At the time of the purchase, the exchange rate between the yuan and the dollar is one yuan equals .10 dollars, meaning that one yuan costs 10 cents to buy. On the date of the purchase, 800,000 yuan equals $80,000 dollars (800,000 × .10). During the 60-day period credit period, however, the exchange rate for the yuan rises to .12 dollars. This higher exchange rate means that a single yuan now costs $.12 dollars (12 cents) to purchase. When PhoneCom makes a payment of 800,000 yuan in 60 days, the 800,000 yuan will cost $96,000.00 U.S. dollars (800,000 yuan × $.12). Due to the 2-cent increase in the exchange rate, PhoneCom will spend an extra $16,000 through the currency exchange process. PhoneCom accounts for the loss on accounts payable with the entry below. The account *Gain or Loss on Foreign Currency Exchange* is classified as an other revenue account.

Accounts Payable/ChinaSemi		
Corp.	80,000	
Gain or Loss on Foreign		
Currency Exchange	16,000	
Cash		96,000

In the previous Explore Accounting feature, another example was provided in which Cal-Tech, an American firm, gives XianCorp, a Chinese corporation, a 12-month, 5% note payable for 2,000,000 yuan. Including the interest of 100,000 yuan (2,000,000 yuan × .05), CalTech will pay XianCorp 2,100,000 yuan in

one year. If the exchange rate at the beginning and at the end of the note remains the same (one yuan = .10 dollar), 2,100,000 yuan will cost $210,000 dollars (2,100,000 yuan × $.10). Suppose, however, that during the 12-month period, the exchange rate between the yuan and the dollar declines from $.10 to $.09. Since a yuan costs less, CalTech can now purchase 2,100,000 yuan for $189,000 (2,100,000 yuan × $.09). Due to the one-cent decline in the exchange rate, CalTech realizes a gain of $21,000 ($210,000 − $189,000) through the currency exchange process. CalTech accounts for the gain on accounts payable using the entry below.

Accounts Payable/		
XianCorp	200,000	
Interest Expense	10,000	
Cash		189,000
Gain or Loss on Foreign		
Currency Exchange		21,000

Critical Thinking Activity
An American company, Fashion Clothiers, purchases men's clothing on account from a Canadian firm, Delmar, Inc., for 50,000 Canadian dollars. At the time of the sale, the exchange rate is one Canadian dollar equals .82 U.S. dollars. Thirty days later, when Fashion Clothiers pays the 50,000 Canadian dollars, the exchange rate has risen. One Canadian dollar can now be exchanged for .87 dollars. How much will it cost Fashion Clothiers to purchase Canadian dollars at the new rate? Will the American company realize a gain or a loss on the transaction? Use T accounts to show the impact of the gain or loss on accounts payable.

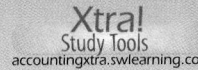
Xtra!
Study Tools
accountingxtra.swlearning.com

· term review

accrued expenses

· audit your understanding

1. What four kinds of accrued expenses might Appliance Center have at the end of a fiscal period?
2. What accounts are affected, and how, by an adjusting entry for accrued interest expense?
3. What accounts are affected, and how, by a reversing entry for accrued salary expense?

· work together 9-3

Journalizing adjusting and reversing entries for accrued expenses

Selected information relating to accruals for December 31 of the current year is given in the *Working Papers*. General journal pages are provided in the *Working Papers*. Your instructor will guide you through the following examples.

1. Journalize the adjusting entries for accrued interest, accrued payroll, accrued employer payroll taxes, and accrued federal income tax on December 31 of the current year.
2. Journalize the appropriate reversing entries on January 1 of the next year.

· on your own 9-3

Journalizing adjusting and reversing entries for accrued expenses

Selected information relating to accruals for December 31 of the current year is given in the *Working Papers*. General journal pages are provided in the *Working Papers*. Work independently to complete the following problem.

1. Journalize the adjusting entries for accrued interest, accrued payroll, accrued employer payroll taxes, and accrued federal income tax on December 31 of the current year.
2. Journalize the appropriate reversing entries on January 1 of the next year.

Accrued Expenses

Lesson 9-3   **279**

GUIDED PRACTICE

Term Review
Call on students to define the term in the Term Review. Ask the class if the definition is correct and whether the complete definition has been given or if anything needs to be added. The suggested definition is given in the Glossary.

Audit Your Understanding
Call on students to answer the Audit Your Understanding questions. Ask the class if the answer is correct and/or complete. Answers are given in Appendix E of the textbook.

Work Together
Have students write the solution to the Work Together problem as you guide the class through the examples. For each transaction,

- Ask students to write T accounts for each account affected by the adjusting entries.
- Direct students to record the adjusting entries to the general journal and T accounts.
- Ask students to record closing entries to the T accounts.
- Direct students to record the reversing entries to the general journal and T accounts.

INDEPENDENT PRACTICE

On Your Own
- Assign the On Your Own problems to be worked independently.
- Use the Ongoing Assessment techniques to diagnose student understanding.

Application Problem
- Assign Application Problem 9-3: Journalizing adjusting and reversing entries for accrued expenses.

Personal Trainer
- Students can access the Lesson 9-3 assessment material using this software.

Xtra! Web Site
- Students can access the Xtra! Study Tools for additional practice.

ENRICH

- Assign the Cultural Diversity feature on page 277.
- Assign Explore Accounting on page 278.
- Ask students to form into small groups and select a business with which they are familiar. Ask each group to prepare a list of expenses that could be prepaid or accrued. Is there any reason that an accrued expense might not be recorded? *(If an accrual amount is not material, recording an adjusting entry does not improve the accuracy of the financial statements.)*

CLOSE

- Ask students to list the accrued expenses adjusted and reversed in this section.
- Ask students to explain how to determine if an accrued expense should be reversed.

SUMMARY

After completing this chapter, you can

1. Define accounting terms related to notes payable, prepaid expenses, and accrued expenses.

2. Identify accounting concepts and practices related to notes payable, prepaid expenses, and accrued expenses.

3. Journalize transactions for notes payable.

4. Journalize adjusting and reversing entries for prepaid expenses initially recorded as expenses.

5. Journalize adjusting and reversing entries for accrued expenses.

Explore Accounting

EXPLORE ACCOUNTING • EXPLORE ACCOUNTING • EXPLORE ACC

Accounting for Warranty Expenses

Sunset Pools offers its customers a two-year warranty on its swimming pools. Sunset Pools makes all repairs resulting from defective parts free of charge to the customer.

When Sunset Pools sells a swimming pool, it does not know how much repair will be required during the warranty period. Some pools have no problems; other pools, called "lemons," require extensive repairs. Sunset Pools estimates that it spends an average of $150 on warranty repairs for each pool.

Applying the matching concept, expenses associated with earning revenue should be recorded in the same accounting period. Thus, the cost of repairing a pool during the warranty period should be recorded in the same period as the pool sale. For each pool sold, Sunset Pools records the following entry:

Warranty Exp. 150.00	
Accrued Warranty Exp.	150.00

When costs are incurred to repair a pool under warranty, Sunset Pools records the following entry:

Accrued Warranty Exp....... 45.00	
Cash	45.00

Accountants must periodically analyze the accrued warranty expense account. If the actual costs incurred are significantly more or less than the $150 per pool charge, a new warranty expense estimate is computed.

Warranty expenses demonstrate the impact of accounting estimates on financial statements. Companies must hire accountants with the proper training to ensure that these estimates are as accurate as possible.

Required:
Sunset Pools is starting to sell outdoor spas. It will maintain warranty expenses in a separate accrual account. Industry publications report that the average spa requires $50 of repairs during its one-year warranty period. After seven sales, Sunset Pools incurs a $500 repair. What is the balance in Accrued Spa Warranty Expense? Does the balance indicate that the $50 estimate is inaccurate? Explain.

280   Chapter 9   Accounting for Notes Payable, Prepaid Expenses, and Accrued Expenses

9-1 APPLICATION PROBLEM

Journalizing notes payable transactions

Raecker, Inc., completed the following transactions during the current year. Source documents are abbreviated as follows: check, C; receipt, R.

Transactions:

Aug.   1.   Signed a 90-day, 11% note with City National Bank for $1,100.00. R143.
Sept. 12. Signed a 60-day, 12% note with First American Bank for $1,200.00. R176.
Oct.   21. Signed a 60-day, 10% note with Commercial State Bank for $800.00. R203.

Instructions:

1. Journalize the transactions on page 15 of a cash receipts journal.
2. Calculate the maturity dates for each note.
3. Calculate the total amount of interest due at maturity for each note.
4. Journalize the following transactions on page 21 of a cash payments journal. Use the maturity dates and the interest amounts calculated in the preceding steps.

   Paid cash for the maturity value of the City National Bank note. C245.
   Paid cash for the maturity value of the First American Bank note. C352.
   Paid cash for the maturity value of Commercial State Bank note. C459.

9-2 APPLICATION PROBLEM

Journalizing adjusting and reversing entries for prepaid expenses initially recorded as expenses

Dupre, Inc., has the following general ledger balances on December 31 of the current year before adjusting entries are recorded.

Supplies Expense—Administrative	$1,500.00
Supplies Expense—Sales	2,500.00
Insurance Expense	3,000.00

Instructions:

1. Use the following adjustment information. Journalize the adjusting entries for supplies and insurance on December 31 of the current year. Use page 13 of a general journal.

Administrative Supplies Inventory	$450.00
Sales Supplies Inventory	800.00
Value of Prepaid Insurance	720.00

2. Journalize the reversing entries on January 1 of the next year. Use page 1 of a general journal.

FORMAL EVALUATION

Chapter 9 Test
ExamView for Chapter 9
Assessment by Portfolio

- Review answers to all tests administered as a class activity. If time is limited, review only the items that were frequently answered incorrectly.

- Ask students if there are any questions about the chapter before proceeding to the next chapter.

CHECK FIGURES

Application Problem 9-1

Maturity dates: October 30; November 11; and December 20. Interest at maturity: 30.25, 24.00, and 13.33.

Application Problem 9-2

Adjusting entries: debit Supplies—Administrative, 450.00; debit Supplies—Sales, 800.00; debit Prepaid Insurance, 720.00.

See Teacher's Edition of the Working Papers for Chapter 9 for complete solutions.

Accounting for Notes Payable, Prepaid Expenses, and Accrued Expenses

Chapter 9   **281**

TEACHING STRATEGIES   COOPERATIVE LEARNING

Complete the Applied Communication activity as a group project. Depending on how formal of a presentation is required, this project can require students an extended period of time to complete. The group should begin by identifying project tasks and delegating the primary responsibility for these tasks to group members. The group should establish a timetable for completing project phases, such as task delegation, task completion, review and revision, and presentation practice.

Application Problem 9-3
Adjusting entries: credit Interest Payable,
350.00; credit Salaries Payable, 772.00;
debit Payroll Taxes Expense, 156.20; debit
Federal Income Tax Expense, 1,300.00.

Mastery Problem 9-4
Maturity dates: August 30; November 24;
and January 30.

Adjusting entries: debit Supplies—
Administrative, 200.00; debit Supplies—
Sales, 300.00; debit Prepaid Insurance,
350.00; credit Interest Payable, 18.33;
credit Salaries Payable, 548.80; debit
Payroll Taxes Expense, 108.63; debit
Federal Income Tax Expense, 800.00.

9-3 APPLICATION PROBLEM

Journalizing adjusting and reversing entries for accrued expenses

Auxbury, Inc., has gathered the following information relating to accrued interest, accrued payroll, accrued employer payroll taxes, and accrued federal income tax on December 31 of the current year.

a. One note payable is outstanding on December 31: 180-day, 12% note with First National Bank, $15,000, dated October 22.

b. Payroll information from the December 31 payroll is as follows:

Payroll and Employee Payroll Taxes		Employer Payroll Taxes	
Salaries—Administrative	$600.00	Social Security Tax	$71.50
Salaries—Sales	500.00	Medicare Tax	16.50
Federal Income Tax Withheld	240.00	Federal Unemployment Tax	8.80
Social Security Tax Withheld	71.50	State Unemployment Tax	59.40
Medicare Tax Withheld	16.50		

c. Estimated federal income tax quarterly payment, $1,300.00.

Instructions:

1. Journalize the adjusting entries for accrued interest, accrued payroll, accrued employer payroll taxes, and accrued federal income tax on December 31 of the current year. Use page 13 of a general journal.

2. Journalize the appropriate reversing entries on January 1 of the next year. Use page 1 of a general journal.

9-4 MASTERY PROBLEM AUTOMATED ACCOUNTING PEACHTREE QUICKBOOKS

Journalizing adjusting and reversing entries for prepaid expenses initially recorded as expenses and for accrued expenses

Sass, Inc., completed the following transactions during the current year. Sass initially records prepaid expenses as expenses. Source documents are abbreviated as follows: check, C; receipt, R.

Transactions:

July   1.   Signed a 60-day, 12% note with Southern Bank for $700.00. R123.
Oct.   10.   Signed a 45-day, 10% note with American Bank for $1,500.00. R149.
Nov.   1.   Signed a 90-day, 11% note with Commercial Bank for $1,000.00. R152.

Instructions:

1. Journalize the transactions on page 15 of a cash receipts journal.
2. Calculate the maturity dates for each note.
3. Journalize the following transactions on page 21 of a cash payments journal. Use the maturity dates calculated in the prior step.

   Paid cash for the maturity value of the Southern Bank note. C105.
   Paid cash for the maturity value of the American Bank note. C195.

4. Sass, Inc., has the following general ledger balances on December 31 of the current year before adjusting entries are recorded.

Supplies Expense—Administrative	$400.00
Supplies Expense—Sales	600.00
Insurance Expense	900.00

Use the following information to journalize adjusting entries for prepaid expenses and accrued expenses on December 31 of the current year. The estimated federal income tax is $800.00. Use page 13 of a general journal.

Administrative Supplies Inventory	$200.00
Sales Supplies Inventory	300.00
Value of Prepaid Insurance	350.00

APPLIED SKILLS   LANGUAGE ARTS

Paraphrasing, writing complete sentences, and identifying direct objects. For additional practice in language arts skills, direct students to answer the Terms Review and Audit Your Understanding questions. Students should write the answers in their own words and in complete sentences. To further practice language arts skills, ask students to underline the direct object(s) in each sentence of their answers.

Payroll and Employee Payroll Taxes		Employer Payroll Taxes	
Salaries—Administrative	$350.00	Social Security Tax	$49.73
Salaries—Sales	415.00	Medicare Tax	11.47
Federal Income Tax Withheld	120.00	Federal Unemployment Tax	6.12
Social Security Tax Withheld	49.73	State Unemployment Tax	41.31
Medicare Tax Withheld	11.47		

5. Journalize the appropriate reversing entries on January 1 of the next year. Use page 1 of a general journal.

9-5 CHALLENGE PROBLEM

Journalizing entries for notes payable and prepaid insurance when no reversing entries are recorded

Reversing entries eliminate the balance of an asset or liability created by an adjusting entry. Unlike the Appliance Center's accounting procedures illustrated in this chapter, Baird Company has elected not to record reversing entries. Instead, Baird's accounting personnel must assign different accounts and amounts to subsequent transactions to correctly eliminate the asset or liability account balances.

The following transactions occurred related to a note payable.

Transactions:
Nov. 1, 20X1. Signed a 180-day, 12% note payable with First National Bank for $10,000.00. R142
Dec. 31, 20X1. Accrued interest expense.
Dec. 31, 20X1. Closed the interest expense account.
Apr. 30, 20X2. Paid the maturity value of the First National Bank note. C154

Instructions:
1. Journalize the transactions and record them in T accounts. Record the first three transactions correctly. Record the April 30 transaction, assuming that an accounting clerk fails to recognize that the transaction relates to a December 31 adjusting entry. Describe the error resulting from the accounting clerk's failure.
2. Create another set of T accounts and journalize the transactions again. Determine the correct accounts and amounts for the April 30 transaction to ensure that the final account balances are correct.

Challenge Problem 9-5
Adjusting entry, debit Interest Expense, 200.00; Maturity date, debit Interest Expense, 600.00, thus overstating 20X2 interest expense by 200.00.

APPLIED SKILLS   WRITING ACROSS THE CURRICULUM

Writing paragraphs and short essays. The Cases for Critical Thinking are short, practical applications of the accounting principles developed in the chapter. Some cases are planned to present problems related to the chapter but not specifically discussed and answered in the chapter. These cases present an opportunity for critical thinking and decision making. These cases also require more than a short objective-type response. Therefore they provide ideal practice in writing paragraphs and short essays.

APPLIED COMMUNICATION

This activity is an excellent opportunity for students to develop their leadership, communication, and presentation skills while reinforcing accounting concepts. Divide students into groups of four or five. Instruct the groups to develop a formal presentation that includes (1) an oral presentation, (2) visual aids, and (3) a written loan proposal. This activity could be assigned at the beginning of this chapter and the presentations after completing the chapter.

The experience gained from this activity can be enhanced by (1) having students make their presentation in business attire and (2) inviting a bank loan officer to attend the presentations and provide feedback.

CASES FOR CRITICAL THINKING

Case 1

No, Mrs. Wagner's reasoning is not sound. In most cases, vendors do not penalize customers if payment on account is received within 30 days. If Wagner Books is able to pay the notes in 15 days, it could do the same with the accounts payable. Fifteen days is well within the 30 days usually allowed. By paying the vendors directly, the business would save the interest on the monthly notes payable.

Case 2

Agree with the CPA. If adjusting entries are not made for accrued payroll in any specific fiscal period, then liabilities are understated on the balance sheet. Also, this means the net income or net loss for that period is not accurate. If adjusting entries are made for accrued payroll and accrued employer payroll taxes, then reversing entries should be made to facilitate recording the payroll entries in the next fiscal period.

SCANS WORKPLACE COMPETENCY

Encourage students to use multimedia software for their presentations. Prepare and distribute a grading rubric prior to presentations so that students will clearly understand which competencies must be demonstrated in order to earn a grade of A, B, C, D, or F.

284

• applied communication

As the financial vice president of Mason Co., you are responsible for ensuring that an adequate supply of cash exists to pay operating expenses. The marketing department has secured a huge order that will require funds for increased inventory and employee levels. A budget analysis reveals that a $100,000, 270-day note will be required to adequately fund the production of the order.

Over the past three years, Mason Co. has signed seven notes totaling $200,000 with First National Bank. Each note was for 90 days or less, was issued at prime plus 2-1/2, and was repaid on the due date.

Assume that the class is the bank loan committee of First National Bank. Make an oral presentation to persuade the loan committee to approve the $100,000, 270-day note at prime plus 2%. Recognize that the committee will be hesitant because of the amount of the note, the term of the note, and the lower interest rate. The following facts about Mason Co.'s five-year history may be used to support your request:

- 120% sales growth
- double number of items produced
- 20% annual increase in net income
- 100% increase in employment
- stable upper management

- 20% reduction in customer complaints
- increased market share from 25% to 33%
- 10% increase in dividends
- liabilities declined from 45% to 25% of assets

• cases for critical thinking

Case 1

Roberta Wagner owns Wagner Books. At the end of each month, Wagner Books borrows money from a bank and uses the proceeds to pay all of its outstanding accounts payable. The business signs a 15-day, 12.5% note payable for each loan. Each month to date, Wagner Books has been able to pay the notes payable when due. Mrs. Wagner uses this procedure to maintain good credit ratings with vendors. Is her reasoning sound? Explain your answer.

Case 2

Jennifer Pier, owner and manager of Pier, Inc., does not record adjusting or reversing entries for accrued payroll. Ms. Pier says that the matter is taken care of when the first payroll is recorded in the next month. The CPA who advises Ms. Pier suggests that the adjusting and reversing entries should be made. He states that omission of these entries affects the information reported on the business' financial statements. With whom do you agree? Explain your answer.

• SCANS workplace competency (part II)

(The data collected and organized in the SCANS Workplace Competency in Chapter 8 is needed to complete this activity.)

Information Competency: Interpreting and Communicating Information

Concept: Employers value employees who can select and analyze information and communicate the results to others, using oral, written, graphic, pictorial, or multimedia methods.

Application: Using the college admissions information you collected in the previous chapter's SCANS activity, prepare an oral report presenting your findings. A successful presentation will incorporate the use of handouts, charts, overhead transparencies, bar graphs, pie charts, line graphs, and other forms of organized visuals. Slideshow software may also make an effective presentation.

graphing workshop

Target Corporation lists the following current liabilities in its 2003 Annual Report. The data for January 31, 2004 are plotted in the pie chart below.

	January 31, 2004	February 1, 2003
Accounts Payable	5448	4684
Accrued Liabilities	1618	1545
Income Taxes Payable	382	319
Current Portion of Long Term Debt	866	975
Total Current Liabilities	8314	7523

Instructions: Create a pie chart using the data for February 1, 2003.

January 31, 2004

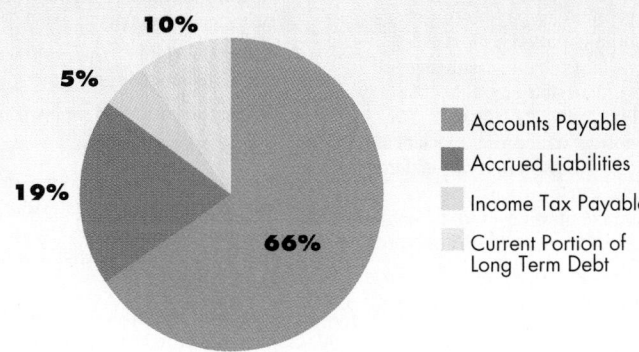

analyzing Costco's financial statements

Following the financial statements in an annual report is what is called the "Notes to Consolidated Financial Statements." These notes are an important part of the financial statements and can help clarify some of the amounts on the financial statements.

No. 1 is usually titled "Summary of Significant Accounting Policies."

Instructions:

1. In Appendix B of this textbook, read the last paragraph in Note No. 1, which is on page B-17. Summarize the note in one sentence.
2. Give at least one example of an estimate that is used in accounting.
3. Why is it necessary to use estimates in accounting?

Accounting for Notes Payable, Prepaid Expenses, and Accrued Expenses

Chapter 9   **285**

	February 1, 2003
Accounts Payable	4,684
Accrued Liabilities	1,545
Income Tax Payable	319
Current Portion of Long Term Debt	975
Total Current Liabilities	7,523

Source: Data taken from 2003 Annual Report of Target Corporation at *www.target.com*.

ANALYZING COSTCO'S FINANCIAL STATEMENTS

1. Answers will vary. One possible solution is: GAAP requires the use of estimates in the financial statements, which could result in inaccurate amounts.

2. Answers will vary, but could include the use of estimates for calculating depreciation (*estimated useful life, estimated salvage value*), estimates for calculating uncollectible accounts, estimates of expenses for the period, and estimates of unbilled but earned revenue.

3. Estimates are necessary because it is not possible to wait until the amounts are known. The estimates used in depreciation, for example, must be made in advance because when we purchase an asset, we do not know for certain how long it will be useful or how much it will be worth at the end of its useful life.

TEACHING STRATEGIES   PORTFOLIO ASSESSMENT

Students should emphasize their learning of this chapter's topic by selecting a comprehensive sample of their work, for example the Mastery or Challenge problems to include in their portfolio. A copy of the Portfolio Assessment form (blackline master in the Teacher's Resource Guide; also on the Student Companion CD) should be completed by the student and the Description section should include any comments regarding how the student mastered these concepts and procedures. Alternatively, students might include in their portfolios printed reports from an Automated Accounting problem.

- Explain that utilities such as the Notes and Interest Planner quickly perform calculations and display the results.
- Explain that results from utilities may also be printed.
- Explain that the Notes and Interest Planner will calculate the interest, maturity value, and maturity date for notes payable and receivable.
- Point out that the Notes and Interest Planner may also be used to determine the exact due date of a note when the term is stated as a number of days or months.
- Explain that once displayed, a report may be printed or copied to the clipboard for pasting into a spreadsheet or word processor.
- Explain that a report may also be printed out for use as a source document.

Notes and Interest Planner

- Direct students to the illustration on this page as you demonstrate how to use the Notes and Interest Planner.
- Demonstrate clicking the Tools icon on the toolbar and then clicking the Notes and Interest tab.
- Demonstrate selecting the appropriate time basis.
- Demonstrate entering the data for the note. Point out the calculated results at the bottom of the dialog box.

Generating a note analysis report

- Direct students to the illustration on page 287 as you demonstrate clicking the Report button to display a report of the calculations from the Notes & Interest Planner.
- Demonstrate clicking the Print button to print the report.

Calculating Notes and Interest Using Planning Tools

Planning Tools

Planning tools are easy-to-use applications for producing results for different types of financial investments. There are five different tabs included on the Planning Tools screen:

- College Planner
- Savings Planner
- Loan Planner
- Retirement Plan
- Notes and Interest

Notes and Interest

In this section, the Notes and Interest planning tool will be explored. As discussed in Chapter 9, a written and signed promise to pay a sum of money at a specified time is called a **promissory note**. Promissory notes signed by a business and given to a creditor are called **notes payable**. The day a note is issued is called the **date of the note**. The original amount of a note is called the **principal of a note**. The date a note is due is called the **maturity date of a note**.

The Notes and Interest planning tool is located on the Notes & Interest tab on the Planning Tools screen, as shown above. The tool is used to:

- Determine the maturity date of the note
- Calculate the amount of interest
- Calculate the maturity value of the note

Entering Note Data in the Notes and Interest Planning Tool

To use the tool, you must know the date of the note, the principal amount of the note, the interest rate, and the number of days (months) for which the note will be outstanding. The following steps are used for any note.

1. Click on the Tools toolbar button.
2. Select the Notes & Interest tab.
3. Select the time basis by clicking on the appropriate radio button. There are three time basis options: number of days (based on 360 days); number of days (based on 365 days); and number of months.
4. Enter the date of the note, which is the date the note was issued.
5. Enter the principal amount of the note.
6. Enter the interest rate.
7. Enter the number of days (time period for which the note is outstanding). If you select Number of Months as the time basis, you enter the number of months, rather than the number of days.

Once all the data are entered, the results are displayed at the bottom on the planner's screen.

Displaying or Printing the Note Analysis Report

A sample Notes Analysis report is shown on the next page. To display or print the report, use the following steps:

1. Click the Report button on the Notes & Interest screen.
2. Choose the Print button if you wish to print the report. (You may choose to view the report, instead of printing it.)
3. Click the Close button. You also have the option to copy the report to the clipboard so that you may include the note data in a separate document.

AUTOMATING APPLICATION PROBLEM 9-1

Instructions:

1. Load *Automated Accounting 8.0* or higher software.
2. Select database A09-1 (Advanced Course Application Problem 9-1) from the accounting template disk.
3. Select File from the menu bar and choose the Save As menu command. Key the path to the drive and directory that contains your data files. Save the database with a filename of XXX091 (where XXX are your initials).
4. Read the Problem Instruction screen by clicking the Browser toolbar button.
5. Key the data listed in the problem.
6. Exit the Automated Accounting software.

AUTOMATING MASTERY PROBLEM 9-4

Instructions:

1. Load *Automated Accounting 8.0* or higher software.
2. Select database A09-4 (Advanced Course Mastery Problem 9-4) from the accounting template disk.
3. Select File from the menu bar and choose the Save As menu command. Key the path to the drive and directory that contains your data files. Save the database with a filename of XXX094 (where XXX are your initials).
4. Read the Problem Instruction screen by clicking the Browser toolbar button.
5. Key the data listed in the problem.
6. Exit the Automated Accounting software.

Note Analysis

Note Analysis
05/22/

Date of the Note	05/22/ --
Time of the Note	90 Days
Principal of the Note	5000.00
Interest Rate of the Note	8.00
Amount of Interest	98.63
Maturity Date of the Note	8/20/ --
Maturity Value of the Note	5098.63

[**Print**] [**Help**] [**Close**] [**Copy**]

Copying reports to other documents

- Demonstrate clicking the Copy button to copy the results to the Clipboard. Explain that the next screen will require clicking either the spreadsheet or word processor option.
- Demonstrate clicking the Close button or pressing Esc to exit the Report and then repeating the action to exit the Notes and Interest Planner.

Using reports to prepare journal entries

- Display another report from the Notes & Interest Planner.
- Demonstrate opening the Cash Receipts Journal Entries Screen (click the Journal toolbar button and then click the Cash Receipts tab).
- Demonstrate recording the information in the appropriate fields. When the interest amount is needed, demonstrate pulling the Cash Receipts Journal Entries Screen down to reveal the interest calculations in the Notes & Interest Planner for keying the amount in the journal entry.

PRACTICE

- Assign Automating Application Problem 9-1: Journalizing notes payable transactions.
- Assign Automating Mastery Problem 9-4: Journalizing adjusting and reversing entries for prepaid expenses initially recorded as expenses and for accrued expenses.

ASSESSMENT

- Use the Electronic Auditor to assess student understanding.

TEACHING STRATEGIES PORTFOLIO ASSESSMENT

Students should be encouraged to print at least one report from one of the Automated Accounting problems to include in their portfolio to demonstrate mastery of automated accounting systems. A copy of the Portfolio Assessment form (blackline master in the Teacher's Resource Guide; also on the Student Companion CD) should be completed by the student and the Description section should include any comments regarding how the student mastered these concepts and procedures.

Accounting for Notes Receivable,

	SCOPE & SEQUENCE		ENHANCING	
	NEW	REVIEW/ EXTENSION	SPECIAL FEATURES	
Introduce the Chapter	✓		• Accounting in the Real World: Northwest Airlines	
Lesson 10-1 Notes Receivable			• Making Ethical Decisions: Conflicts of Interest	
Notes receivable		✓	• Exploring Accounting: The Impact of Changes in Foreign Exchange Rates	
Accepting a note receivable		✓		
Calculating interest		✓		
Receiving cash for a note receivable		✓		
Dishonored notes receivable		✓		
Lesson 10-2 Unearned and Accrued Revenue			• Technology in Business: The Federal Government Is Learning to Shop at Electronic Stores	
Unearned revenue initially recorded as revenue	✓		• Exploring Accounting: Gains or Losses	
Accrued interest income		✓		
Adjusting, closing, and reversing entries for unearned revenue		✓		
Adjusting, closing, and reversing entries for accrued revenue		✓		
Putting It All Together			• Explore Accounting	
			• Xtra! Web Site: Xtra! Enrichment	
			• Applied Communication	
			• Cases for Critical Thinking	
			• SCANS Workplace Competency	
			• Auditing for Errors	
			• Analyzing Costco's Financial Statements	

Unearned Revenue, and Accrued Revenue

INSTRUCTION		PRACTICE AND ASSESSMENT		
TECHNOLOGY AND MEDIA	**TEACHING STRATEGIES**	**GUIDED PRACTICE**	**INDEPENDENT PRACTICE**	**RETEACHING AND ENRICHMENT**
• Internet Research Activity • Accounting Xtra! Web Site	• Software Focus			
• Instructor's Resource CD: PowerPoint Slides • Xtra! Web Site: Xtra! Study Tools • Blackline Masters: General Journal Cash Receipts Journal • Personal Trainer • Automated Accounting • Peachtree and QuickBooks	• Visually-Impaired Students • Applied Skills: Word Processing	• Terms Review • Audit Your Understanding • Work Together 10-1	• On Your Own 10-1 • Application Problem 10-1 • Ongoing Assessment, p. 294 • Personal Trainer • Xtra! Web Site: Xtra! Study Tools	• Reteach, p. 294 • Enrich, p. 296 • Automated Accounting • Peachtree and QuickBooks
• Instructor's Resource CD: PowerPoint Slides • Xtra! Web Site: Xtra! Study Tools • Blackline Masters: General Journal • Personal Trainer	• Applied Skills: Building Study Skills	• Terms Review • Audit Your Understanding • Work Together 10-2	• On Your Own 10-2 • Application Problem 10-2 • Application Problem 10-3 • Ongoing Assessment, p. 300 • Personal Trainer • Xtra! Web Site: Xtra! Study Tools	• Reteach, p. 300 • Enrich, p. 303
• Personal Trainer • Xtra! Web Site: Xtra! Review, Quizzing, and Enrichment • Student Companion CD • Automated Accounting • Peachtree and QuickBooks	• Cooperative Learning • Applied Skills: Language Arts		• Mastery Problem 10-4 • Personal Trainer • Xtra! Web Site: Xtra! Review and Quizzing • Study Guide 10 • Student Companion CD • Automated Accounting • Peachtree and QuickBooks • Chapter 10 Test • ExamView Chapter 10	• Challenge Problem 10-5 • Reteach, p. 304 • Enrich, p. 304 • Recycling Problem 10-1 • Xtra! Web Site: Xtra! Enrichment

CHAPTER

OBJECTIVES & TERMS

10 Accounting for Notes Receivable, Unearned Revenue, and Accrued Revenue

After studying Chapter 10, you will be able to:

1. Define accounting terms related to notes receivable, unearned revenue, and accrued revenue.

2. Identify accounting concepts and practices related to notes receivable, unearned revenue, and accrued revenue.

3. Journalize transactions for notes receivable.

4. Journalize adjusting and reversing entries for unearned revenue initially recorded as revenue.

5. Journalize adjusting and reversing entries for accrued revenue.

- notes receivable
- dishonored note

- unearned revenue
- accrued revenue

Point Your Browser
accountingxtra.swlearning.com

Northwest Airlines

©REBECCA COOK/REUTERS/LANDOV

NORTHWEST AIRLINES GETS PAID IN ADVANCE

The "red tail" in the sky is famous worldwide as a trademark for Northwest Airlines. The first airplane tail was painted red in 1948. However, that wasn't the beginning of Northwest Airlines, Inc. The company began by flying mail between Minneapolis and Chicago in 1926. Passenger service started one year later. Today, Northwest and its global travel partners operate over 1,500 flights to more than 750 destinations in 120 countries on 6 continents, and have about 40,000 employees worldwide.

In many industries, the company provides the goods or services to a customer and either gets paid immediately or at a later date. However, the airline industry does not operate that way. In the airline industry, the company gets paid when the customer purchases a ticket, but it usually does not provide the service until sometime in the future. Another way in which the airline industry is unique is the frequent flyer program that many companies offer. This provides free transportation after the customer flies or accumulates a certain number of miles.

Both of these situations affect the financial statements of an airline company. Northwest Airlines records both of these events as a liability called "air traffic liability." This liability can make up a substantial portion of a company's current liabilities.

Critical Thinking:

1. Assume an airline company records a liability when a customer purchases a ticket for a future flight. When will the company decrease the liability?
2. When the company reduces the liability, what other account will be affected?

Source: www.nwa.com

Xtra!
Today
accountingxtra.swlearning.com

ACCOUNTING TERMS

Search the Internet for a site that lists the definition of accounting terms.

Instructions

1. List the definitions of the following words:
   a. unearned revenue (or unearned income)
   b. accrued revenue
   c. prepaid expense
2. Compare these definitions with those given in the textbook. How are they similar? How are they different?

1. The company will decrease the liability when the ticket is used for the flight for which it was purchased.
2. A revenue account will be increased when the liability is decreased because the airline will now have "earned" the revenue.

1. Answers will vary.
2. Textbook definitions:
   a. Unearned revenue: revenue received in one fiscal period but not earned until the next fiscal period.
   b. Accrued revenue: revenue earned in one fiscal period but not received until a later fiscal period.
   c. Prepaid expense: expenses paid in one fiscal period but not reported as expenses until a later fiscal period.

10-1 Notes Receivable

INTRODUCTION

- Have students read this page. Having a student read this page out loud for the class can help develop the student's public speaking skills.

- Ask students to identify transactions where the economic event *(a sale or expense)* occurs in one fiscal period and cash is exchanged in the later fiscal period *(sales on account and accrued expenses)*.

- Discuss that this chapter presents how to record transactions when cash is exchanged in one fiscal period but the economic event does not occur until a later fiscal period.

OBJECTIVES

- Define accounting terms related to notes receivable.

- Identify accounting concepts and practices related to notes receivable.

- Journalize transactions for notes receivable.

MOTIVATE

Banks help a community grow by providing individuals and businesses with loans. In the same way, a business can grow by providing its customers with loans to purchase its product, especially when the customer could not obtain the cash required with a bank loan.

Preview

- Preview accounting terms and definitions introduced in this lesson: *notes receivable* and *dishonored notes*.

- Direct students to read the headings at the top of each page in this lesson and to examine the figures given.

MATERIALS

- Instructor's Resource CD:
  PowerPoint Slides

- Xtra! Study Tools on the Xtra! Web Site

- Blackline Masters:
  General Journal
  Cash Receipts Journal

- Working Papers:
  Teacher's Edition of the Working Papers for Lesson 10-1

- Software:
  Personal Trainer
  Automated Accounting and Century 21 8E CD
  Peachtree and QuickBooks

A business entity must report accurate and up-to-date information about notes receivable and accrued revenue on its financial statements at the end of a fiscal period. [*CONCEPT: Adequate Disclosure*] Because of the nature of notes receivable and some types of revenue, special accounting procedures may be required at the end of a fiscal period. For example, a note receivable issued in one fiscal period with a maturity date in the following fiscal period requires special accounting procedures. Special accounting procedures also are required for two types of revenue:

1. Revenue received in one fiscal period but not earned until the next fiscal period.
2. Revenue earned in one fiscal period but not received until the next fiscal period.

The special accounting procedures are designed so that the correct amount of revenue earned in the fiscal period is recognized in the financial statements. [*CONCEPT: Matching Expenses with Revenue*]

©GETTY IMAGES/PHOTODISC

making ethical decisions

MAKING ETHICAL DECISIONS • MAKING ETHICAL DECISIONS • MAKING ETHICAL DECIS

Conflicts of Interest

Nicole Huckaby is a buyer for Extal Industries. An expert in raw metals, she is responsible for buying the company's copper requirements at the most favorable terms (price, delivery costs, metal purity, etc.). Nicole purchases from several suppliers to ensure a constant supply of copper at competitive prices.

Being an expert in metals, Nicole invests in the stock of metal companies. In fact, she just purchased 500 shares of Atlantic Metals, one of the companies that supplies Extal Industries with copper.

Instructions

Access the *Code of Ethics* of International Paper. Using this code as a guide, determine whether Nicole should own the stock of a vendor.

Accounting for Notes Receivable, Unearned Revenue, and Accrued Revenue

MAKING ETHICAL DECISIONS

Students may perceive it to be unfair that employees cannot invest in the companies of their choice. Students who express this opinion should be encouraged to identify the impact on the stakeholders. This process should enable them to understand why employees should not have an ownership interest in any company that does business with the employer.

In the section *Conflicts of Interest and Corporate Opportunities*, the company states that employees should not own a financial interest in a supplier. A financial interest does not include the ownership of the securities of a publicly traded company if the stock is less than the employee's salary and 5 percent of the employee's personal assets. Nicole's ownership of Atlantic Metals stock may violate the company's code of conduct. Nicole needs to assess her compliance with the code and, if necessary, seek the advice of the company's ethics officer.
Source: *www.internationalpaper.com*

ISSUING A NOTE RECEIVABLE FOR AN ACCOUNT RECEIVABLE

	DATE		ACCOUNT TITLE	DOC. NO.	POST. REF.	DEBIT	CREDIT	
	GENERAL JOURNAL						PAGE 4	
1	Apr. 20— 3		Notes Receivable	NR11		3 0 0 00		1
2			Accounts Rec./Duane Jansen				3 0 0 00	2

Promissory notes that a business accepts from customers are called **notes receivable**. Notes receivable are usually due within a year. Therefore, notes receivable are classified as current assets.

Notes receivable can be issued to customers who need an extension of time to pay on account.

April 3. Accepts a 30-day, 12% note from Duane Jansen for an extension of time on his account, $300.00. Note Receivable No. 11.

The amount to be received is changed from an account receivable to a note receivable, as shown above. In the accounts receivable ledger, the customer account, Duane Jansen, is decreased by a $300.00 credit. The balance of Mr. Jansen's accounts receivable account is zero.

GENERAL LEDGER
Notes Receivable

4/3	300.00	

Accounts Receivable

		4/3	300.00

ACCOUNTS RECEIVABLE LEDGER
Duane Jansen

Bal.	300.00	4/3	300.00
		(New Bal. zero)	

ISSUING A NOTE FOR A SALE

	DATE		ACCOUNT TITLE	DOC. NO.	POST. REF.	DEBIT	CREDIT	
	GENERAL JOURNAL						PAGE 4	
3		4	Notes Receivable	NR12		4 5 0 00		3
4			Sales				4 5 0 00	4

Most sales on account assume that the customer will pay within 30 days or less. To promote sales, a company may allow its customers to sign a note extending payment over a longer period of time. If no cash is received, the sale is recorded on a general journal, as shown above. If a cash down payment is received, the transaction could be recorded in a cash receipts journal.

April 4. Accepts a 90-day, 12% note from Mark Carver for the sale of an appliance, $450.00. Note Receivable No. 12.

Notes Receivable

4/4	450.00	

Sales

		4/4	450.00

EXPLAIN

- Explain that interest on a note receivable is calculated exactly the same as for a note payable.

- Remind students that the transaction to record the receipt of a note receivable is the same, regardless of why the note was initially issued.

- Ask students to explain why Interest Income is classified as an other revenue. *(The expense and revenue of notes do not directly impact how effectively a business buys and sells its product, as measured by the income from operations.)*

- Ask students to read the F.Y.I. feature to learn why a business might issue notes receivable to employees.

- Ask students to read the Remember feature to reinforce how annual interest rates are used in interest calculations.

DEMONSTRATE

Calculate interest income

- Ask students to use a calculator to calculate the interest using the formula in the illustration.

- Ask students to make up original note principals, interest rates, and terms for several notes.

- Direct the students to calculate the interest for each note.

Analyze the transaction

- Draw three T accounts on the board and enter the balance amounts.

- Read the transaction statement.

- Ask students to analyze the transaction.

Record the cash receipt

- Use a cash receipts journal transparency to illustrate recording the transaction in the cash receipts journal or direct students to the illustration.

- Remind students that the source document for this transaction is a receipt.

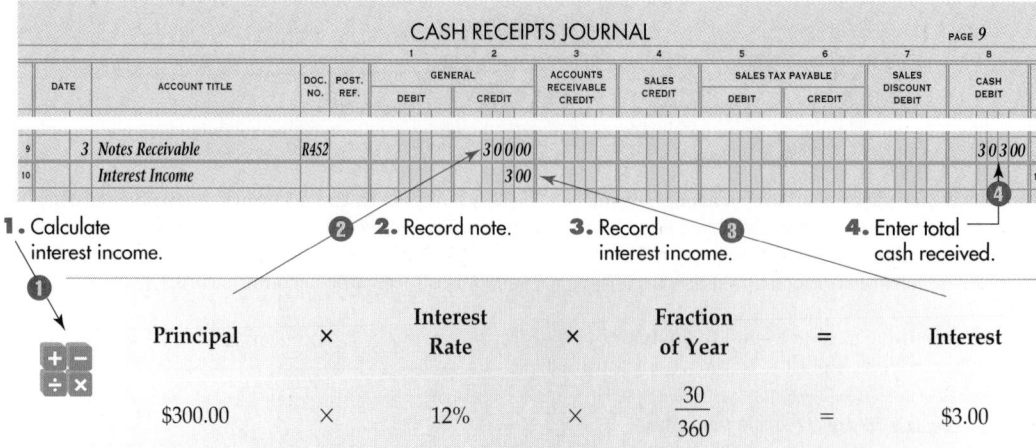

1. Calculate interest income.
2. Record note.
3. Record interest income.
4. Enter total cash received.

	Principal	×	Interest Rate	×	Fraction of Year	=	Interest
	$300.00	×	12%	×	$\frac{30}{360}$	=	$3.00

Interest is earned for the period of time a note is outstanding. Because the interest rate is stated as an annual rate, the actual interest earned must be computed as a fraction of a year. For ease of calculation, most companies use a 360-day year to calculate interest. The calculation of interest and the receipt of cash in payment of the note receivable are shown above.

Whether a note is accepted for the extension of time for an account receivable or for a sale, the transaction to record the receipt of cash on the maturity date is the same.

May 3. Received cash for the maturity value of Note Receivable No. 11: principal, $300.00, plus interest, $3.00; total, $303.00. Receipt No. 452.

Interest Income is classified as Other Revenue, as shown on Appliance Center's chart of accounts.

```
                  Cash
5/3      303.00 |

             Notes Receivable
Bal.     300.00 | 5/3      300.00
(New Bal. zero)

             Interest Income
                | 5/3        3.00
```

FYI FOR YOUR INFORMATION

A company may issue notes receivable to employees for a variety of reasons. To recruit a talented individual, a company may offer the individual a temporary loan to pay off education loans, pay moving costs, or fund a home down payment. A current employee may have a severe financial need caused by a personal tragedy, such as flood damage to a home or excessive uninsured medical bills. A loan to an employee is included in a group of transactions known as related-party transactions. Business owners should establish the policies used to determine the extent, if any, that managers may issue notes receivable to employees.

{ REMEMBER The interest rate on a note is stated as an annual rate. To compute the interest for a period of time, the interest rate must be multiplied by the fraction of a year that the note was outstanding. }

TEACHING STRATEGIES DIFFERENT LEARNING ABILITIES

Visually-Impaired Students. Many sources exist for providing alternative teaching materials. Most states have schools for the blind and rehabilitation service agencies that can enlarge the textbook and working papers. Consult these organizations to identify the latest technologies available for assisting the students.

RECORDING A DISHONORED NOTE RECEIVABLE

2. Record the debit for the total amount receivable.

3. Record a credit for the note principal.

1. Calculate interest income.

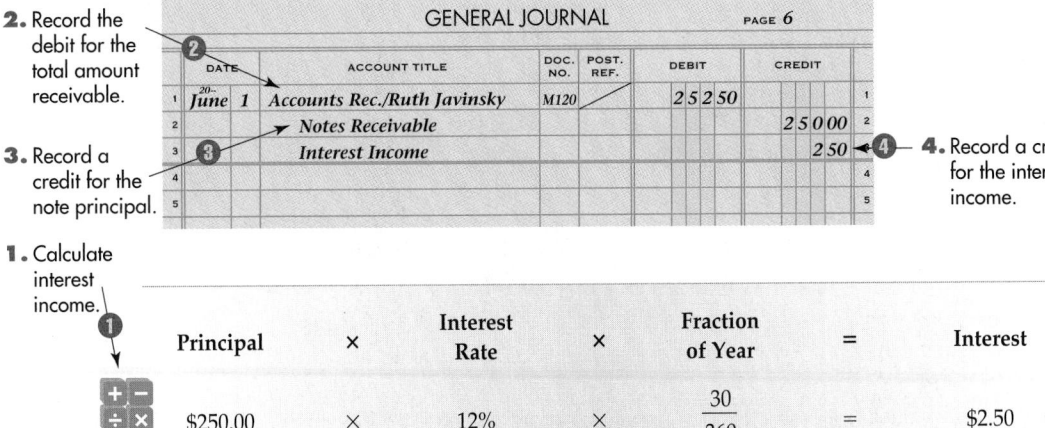

4. Record a credit for the interest income.

Principal	×	Interest Rate	×	Fraction of Year	=	Interest
$250.00	×	12%	×	$\frac{30}{360}$	=	$2.50

A note that is not paid when due is called a **dishonored note**. The notes receivable account balance should include only the amount of notes receivable that a business expects to collect. Otherwise, Notes Receivable will be reported incorrectly on a balance sheet. [CONCEPT: Adequate Disclosure]

On June 1, the maturity date of Note Receivable No. 8, Ruth Javinsky owes the principal, $250.00, plus accrued interest. Interest is accrued for the 30-day term of the note.

Although the note is dishonored, Ruth still owes the money to Appliance Center. A journal entry is recorded to transfer the maturity value of the note to accounts receivable, as shown above.

June 1. Ruth Javinsky dishonored Note Receivable No. 8, a 30-day, 12% note, maturity value due today: principal, $250.00; interest, $2.50; total, $252.50. Memorandum No. 120.

The journal entry for a dishonored note receivable does not cancel the debt. Appliance Center does not inform Ruth Javinsky that the note's maturity value was transferred to Accounts Receivable. Appliance Center continues to try to collect the account. However, the debt is transferred to Accounts Receivable and carried on the records until Ruth pays the amount or her account is declared uncollectible.

GENERAL LEDGER
Accounts Receivable

6/1	252.50	

Notes Receivable

5/1	250.00	6/1		250.00

Interest Income

		6/1	2.50

ACCOUNTS RECEIVABLE LEDGER
Ruth Javinsky

6/1	252.50	

> **REMEMBER** The accounting for uncollectible accounts was presented in Chapter 7. Dishonored notes receivable, when added to the balance of Accounts Receivable, are considered when computing adjustments to Allowance for Uncollectible Accounts. If the dishonored note, after being transferred to Accounts Receivable, is deemed uncollectible, the account is written off using the procedures discussed in Chapter 7.

Notes Receivable

EXPLAIN

- Explain that interest income is recorded for the term of the note, even though the note has been dishonored.
- Point out that a business should not inform the customer of transactions affecting their account and continue its attempt to collect the account.
- Ask students to read the Remember feature to reinforce procedures for accounting for uncollectible accounts.

DEMONSTRATE

Calculate interest income
- Ask students to use a calculator to calculate the interest using the formula shown in the illustration.

Analyze the transaction
- Draw four T accounts on the board and enter the balance amounts.
- Read the transaction statement.
- Ask students to analyze the transaction.

Record the transaction
- Use a general journal transparency to illustrate recording the transaction in the general journal or direct students to the illustration.
- Direct students to record the transactions following the four steps shown.
- Remind students that the source document for this transaction is a memorandum because no cash was exchanged.

APPLIED SKILLS   WORD PROCESSING

If you wish to integrate word processing into your accounting course, you may direct students to answer the various chapter features using their word processing software.

- Explain that a customer who pays the note would expect to pay interest from the date of the note through the payment date.

- Ask students to identify how much interest income has already been recorded. *(Interest has already been recorded during the term of the note.)*

- Explain that interest income must be recorded from the date the note was dishonored *(the maturity date)* through the payment date.

DEMONSTRATE

Calculate interest income

- Ask students to explain the number of days calculation as you write each month's days on the board.

- Ask students to use a calculator to calculate the interest using the formulas in the illustration.

Analyze the transaction

- Draw four T accounts on the board and enter the balance amounts.

- Read the transaction statement.

- Ask students to analyze the transaction.

Record the cash receipt

- Use a cash receipts journal transparency to illustrate recording the transaction in the cash receipts journal or direct students to the illustration.

ONGOING ASSESSMENT

- Assessment is an ongoing process. Circulate through the classroom or lab observing which students have problems with the assignments.

- Troubleshooting: Diagnose what kinds of problems students have with this section. Students may have trouble understanding (1) why interest income is recorded when a note is dishonored and (2) the number of days calculation for computing interest income when cash is received for a dishonored note.

- Assess student understanding by checking solutions to Independent Practice assignments.

RECEIVING CASH FOR A DISHONORED NOTE RECEIVABLE

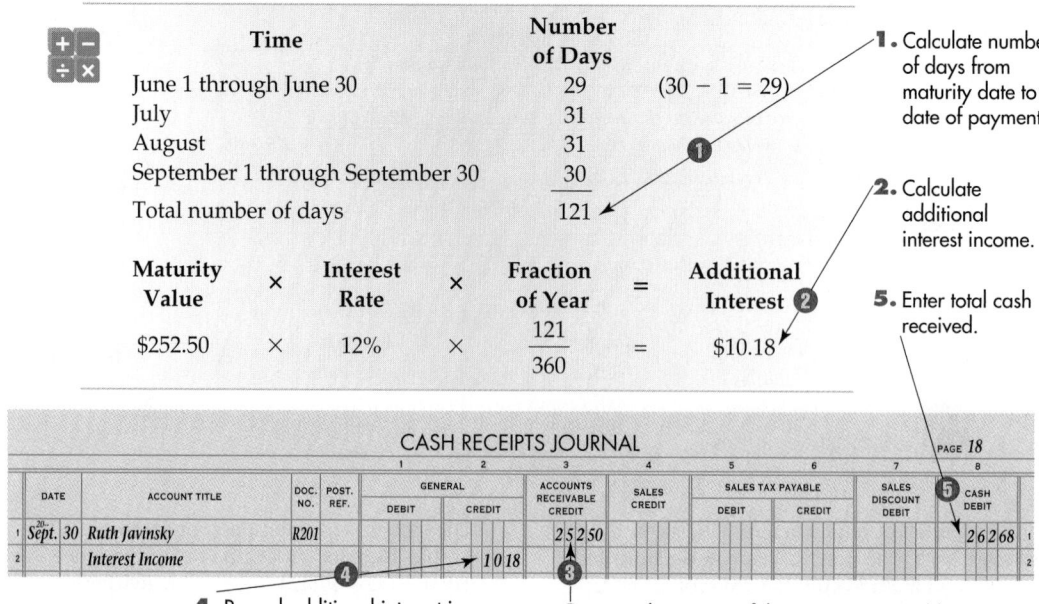

Time	Number of Days	
June 1 through June 30	29	(30 − 1 = 29)
July	31	
August	31	
September 1 through September 30	30	
Total number of days	121	

1. Calculate number of days from maturity date to date of payment.

Maturity Value	×	Interest Rate	×	Fraction of Year	=	Additional Interest
$252.50	×	12%	×	$\frac{121}{360}$	=	$10.18

2. Calculate additional interest income.

5. Enter total cash received.

CASH RECEIPTS JOURNAL   PAGE 18

				GENERAL		ACCOUNTS RECEIVABLE CREDIT	SALES CREDIT	SALES TAX PAYABLE		SALES DISCOUNT DEBIT	CASH DEBIT
DATE	ACCOUNT TITLE	DOC. NO.	POST. REF.	DEBIT	CREDIT			DEBIT	CREDIT		
Sept. 30	Ruth Javinsky	R201				252 50					262 68
	Interest Income				10 18						

4. Record additional interest income.

3. Record payment of the account receivable.

Sometimes payment may be received on a previously dishonored note. Additional interest is charged from maturity date to payment date.

On September 30, Ruth Javinsky paid Appliance Center the maturity value of her note plus interest. The time for computing additional interest begins when the note is dishonored and ends on the day cash is received. The number of days for which interest is owed is calculated using the same method as determining the due date of a note. Instead of adjusting the date of the last month to equal a predetermined number of days, the payment date is used to determine the number of days in the final month, as shown above.

The interest rate is adjusted for the fraction of the year from the date the note was dishonored to the payment date. The additional interest is based on the maturity value of the note on the date the note was dishonored, *$252.50*.

September 30. Received cash from Ruth Javinsky for dishonored Note Receivable No. 8: maturity value, $252.50, plus additional interest, $10.18; total, $262.68. Receipt No. 201.

Ruth Javinsky's account in the accounts receivable ledger provides a complete history of the transactions. Management should use this information when making any future decisions to extend credit to this customer.

GENERAL LEDGER
Cash

9/30	262.68		

Accounts Receivable

Bal.	252.50	9/30	252.50

Interest Income

		9/30	10.18

ACCOUNTS RECEIVABLE LEDGER
Ruth Javinsky

Bal.	252.50	9/30	252.50
(New Bal. zero)			

- Call on students to identify two transactions for recording a note receivable.

- Ask students to describe how to calculate interest income for a fraction of a year.

- Ask students what information is needed to journalize the dishonoring of a note receivable.

- Call on students to describe how to record the receipt of cash on a dishonored note.

Explore Accounting

EXPLORE ACCOUNTING • EXPLORE ACCOUNTING • EXPLORE ACCOUNTING

The Impact of Changes in Foreign Exchange Rates on Accounts Receivable and Notes Receivable

The American company will realize a gain of $2,000 on the transaction.

20,000 francs × .95 =	$19,000
20,000 francs × .85 =	$17,000
Total gain	$ 2,000

In Chapter 1 you learned that the unit of measurement concept states that business transactions are reported in numbers that use a common unit of measurement. In the United States, that common unit of measurement is the dollar. So what happens if a U.S. business completes a transaction in Italy? Should that transaction be measured in dollars or in euros, the currency of Italy? The unit of measurement accounting concept states that the transaction occurring in Italy will ultimately need to be presented in dollars for a U.S. company. Imagine how difficult it would be to analyze a company's income statement if some sales were presented in dollars and others in euros.

To understand the impact of changes in foreign currency exchange rates on a U.S. company's accounts receivable, let's analyze the following example. A U.S. company, CyclePart, sells road bike components to companies in both the United States and Italy. Recently, CyclePart sold on account a variety of American-made bicycle components priced at 10,000 euros to the Bicicletta Company in Italy. The terms of the sale on account are that Bicicletta will pay CyclePart 10,000 euros in 60 days. During the 60-day time period, the exchange rate between the euro and the dollar remains exactly even. An even exchange rate of 1 to 1 means that 1 euro can be exchanged for 1 dollar. Sixty days later, if the exchange rate is still even, CyclePart's 10,000 euros will be worth exactly $10,000. But what happens if during the 60-day credit period, the exchange rate for the euro rises to $1.20? This higher exchange rate means that a single euro can now be exchanged for more dollars ($1.20). When CyclePart receives payment of 10,000 euros in 60 days, the 10,000 euros can be exchanged for $12,000.00 U.S. dollars (10,000 euros × $1.20). The 20-cent

rise in the exchange rate means that CyclePart will gain an extra $2,000 through the exchange process.

It is also possible that the exchange rate for euros to dollars may decline. For example, assume the exchange rate for one euro declines from $1 to $.90. This means that if you exchange 10 euros for dollars, you will receive only $9.00 (10 euros × .90). A declining exchange rate for euros to dollars can have a significant impact on foreign transactions. Suppose on January 1 of the current year, Bicicletta gives CyclePart a 12-month, 6% note receivable for 100,000 euros. Including the interest of 6,000 euros (100,000 euros × .06), Bicicletta will pay CyclePart 106,000 euros in one year. If the exchange remains even (one euro = one dollar) during the entire 12 months, 106,000 euros will be worth $106,000. Suppose, however, that during the 12-month period, the exchange rate between the euro and the dollar declines from $1 to $.90. Since a euro now equals less than a dollar, CyclePart will exchange the 106,000 euros it receives on December 31 for only $95,400 (106,000 euros × .90).

Critical Thinking Activity

An American company sells watch parts on account to a Swiss firm, SwissTime, for 20,000 Swiss francs. At the time of the sale, the exchange rate for francs to dollars is one franc equals .85 dollars. Thirty days later, when the American company collects the 2,000 Swiss francs, the exchange rate has risen. One franc can now be exchanged for .95 dollars. If the American company exchanges the francs for dollars at the new rate, will the company realize a gain or a loss on the transaction? In your answer, identify the amount of the gain or loss.

GUIDED PRACTICE

Terms Review

Call on students to define the terms in the Terms Review. Ask the class if the definitions are correct and whether the complete definitions have been given or if anything needs to be added. The suggested definitions are given in the Glossary.

Audit Your Understanding

Call on students to answer the Audit Your Understanding questions. Ask the class if the answer is correct and/or complete. Answers are given in Appendix E of the textbook.

Work Together

Have students write the solution to the Work Together problem as you guide the class through the examples.

- If a transaction results in recording interest income, call on a student to describe how to calculate the amount.

- Direct students to record each transaction in the journals as you elicit class participation in analyzing and recording each transaction.

INDEPENDENT PRACTICE

On Your Own

- Assign the On Your Own problem to be worked independently.

- Use the Ongoing Assessment techniques to diagnose student understanding.

Application Problem

- Assign Application Problem 10-1: Journalizing transactions for notes receivable.

Personal Trainer

- Students can access the Lesson 10-1 assessment material using this software.

Xtra! Web Site

- Students can access the Xtra! Study Tools for additional practice.

ENRICH

- Assign Making Ethical Decisions on page 290.

- Assign Explore Accounting on page 295.

- Assign Automated Accounting on page 309 to automate Application Problem 10-1.

- Students can use Peachtree and Quick-Books to automate Application Problem 10-1.

296

• terms review

notes receivable
dishonored note

• audit your understanding

1. Why might a business accept a note receivable from a customer?

2. What happens to the maturity value of a note when a note receivable is dishonored?

3. What is the time for computing interest when payment is received on a dishonored note?

• work together 10-1

Journalizing notes receivable transactions

Page 5 of a general journal and page 8 of a cash receipts journal are provided in the *Working Papers*. Source documents are abbreviated as follows: memorandum, M; note receivable, NR; receipt, R. Your instructor will guide you through the following example.

1. Journalize the following transactions made during the current year.

May	1.	Accepted a 60-day, 15% note from Patrick Sampson for an extension of time on his account, $400.00. NR1.
June	1.	Accepted a 180-day, 18% note from Sandy Adams for the sale of equipment, $700.00. NR2.
June	30.	Patrick Sampson dishonored NR1; maturity value, $400.00 plus interest. M142.
Nov.	28.	Received cash for the maturity value of NR2: principal, $700.00 plus interest. R310.
Dec.	12.	Received cash from Patrick Sampson for dishonored NR1, $410.00 plus additional interest. R432.

• on your own 10-1

Journalizing notes receivable transactions

Page 6 of a general journal and page 9 of a cash receipts journal are provided in the *Working Papers*. Source documents are abbreviated as follows: memorandum, M; note receivable, NR; receipt, R. Work this problem independently.

1. Journalize the following transactions made during the current year.

May	14.	Accepted a 90-day, 18% note from Pamula Yates for an extension of time on her account, $320.00. NR19.
June	1.	Accepted a 120-day, 18% note from Walt Harrison for the sale of furniture, $1,500.00. NR20.
Aug.	12.	Pamula Yates dishonored NR19; maturity value, $320.00 plus interest. M82.
Oct.	26.	Received cash for the maturity value of NR20, $1,500.00 plus interest. R430.
Dec.	22.	Received cash on account from Pamula Yates for dishonored NR19, $334.40 plus additional interest. R753.

- Direct students to create and date a series of original note receivable transactions covering a six-month period. For example, a student could purchase goods on account, n/30, on Jan. 3, sign a 60-day, 15% note for an extension of time on Feb. 2, dishonor the note, and pay the note on June 4.

Assuming the role of the business, make a credit sale to five students. Using T accounts on the board, solicit class participation to record students' transactions in chronological order.

CLOSE

- Ask students to briefly summarize the procedures for journalizing transactions for notes receivable.

10-2 Unearned and Accrued Revenue

ADJUSTING ENTRY FOR UNEARNED REVENUE INITIALLY RECORDED AS A REVENUE

1. Debit the revenue account.

	DATE	❶ ACCOUNT TITLE	DOC. NO.	POST. REF.	DEBIT	CREDIT	
1		*Adjusting Entries*					1
36	31	Rent Income			4 0 0 0 00		36
37		Unearned Rent				4 0 0 0 00	37

GENERAL JOURNAL   PAGE *13*

2. Credit the liability account.

Some revenue is received during a fiscal period but is not actually earned until the next fiscal period. Revenue received in one fiscal period but not earned until the next fiscal period is called **unearned revenue**. Unearned revenue is also known as deferred revenue.

Unearned revenue may be recorded initially as a liability or as revenue. Appliance Center rents part of its building to Pace Delivery and initially records rent receipts as revenue.

On December 1, Appliance Center received $6,000.00 from Pace Delivery, $2,000.00 per month for December, January, and February rent. The receipt was recorded as rent income and is included in the $28,000.00 balance of Rent Income.

Only that part of rent actually earned should be recorded as revenue in a fiscal period. An adjusting entry is recorded to separate the earned and unearned portions of the rent recorded in Rent Income, as shown above. The January and February rent is unearned and should be reported in Unearned Rent.

The $4,000.00 balance of Unearned Rent, a liability account, represents the value of two months of rent owed to Pace Delivery. The new

balance of Rent Income, *$24,000.00*, correctly reflects 12 months of rent at $2,000.00 per month.

Unearned Rent is classified as a Current Liability and Rent Income is classified as Other Revenue, as shown on Appliance Center's chart of accounts.

Unearned Rent		
	Adj.	4,000.00

Rent Income			
Adj.	4,000.00	Dec. 31 Bal.	28,000.00
		(New Bal.	*24,000.00)*

FYI
FOR YOUR INFORMATION

A company can elect to record rent payments as Unearned Rent during the year. At December 31, it records an adjusting entry to recognize the revenue earned during the year. Initially recording unearned revenue either as a liability or as revenue is acceptable accounting practice. Appliance Center prefers recording unearned revenue as revenue because the unearned revenue eventually will become revenue as the building space is used.

297

EXPLAIN

- Point out that the rule for determining if an adjusting entry should be reversed applies to both revenue and expense adjusting entries.

- Ask students to describe each of the prior year's entries shown in the T accounts.

- Ask students to identify what the $4,000.00 credit balance in Rent Income represents.

DEMONSTRATE

- Draw two T accounts on the board and enter the pre-adjustment balances.

- Ask students to describe the adjusting and closing entries as these are recorded in the T accounts.

- Describe the reversing entry.

- Ask students to analyze the reversing entry by answering: what accounts are affected, are they increased or decreased, and are they debited or credited. Complete the T accounts as the information is provided.

- Use a general journal transparency to illustrate recording the transaction in the general journal or direct students to the illustration.

REVERSING ENTRY FOR UNEARNED REVENUE INITIALLY RECORDED AS A REVENUE

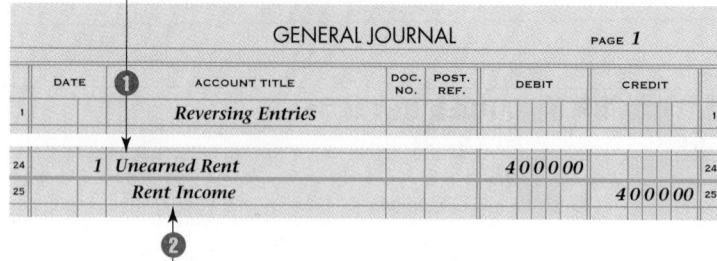

1. Debit the liability account.

2. Credit the revenue account.

On December 31, Rent Income is closed as part of Appliance Center's closing entries. After closing entries are posted, the balance in Rent Income is zero and ready to record transactions in the next fiscal period.

Reversing entries for prepaid and accrued expenses are described in Chapter 9. If an adjusting entry *creates* a balance in an asset or liability account, the adjusting entry is reversed. Reversing entries for unearned revenue are made for the same reason as for prepaid expenses. The amount of unearned revenue must be returned to the account in which it was initially recorded.

Appliance Center's adjusting entry created a balance in the liability account, Unearned Rent. Therefore, Appliance Center needs to make a

reversing entry for unearned rent on January 1, as shown above.

On January 1, after the reversing entry is posted, the new balance of Unearned Rent is zero as it was before the adjusting entry. Rent Income has a $4,000.00 credit balance. The rent received in advance for January and February, $4,000.00, is part of the rent revenue earned in the new fiscal period.

Unearned Rent			
Rev.	4,000.00	Adj.	4,000.00
		(New Bal. zero)	

Rent Income			
Adj.	4,000.00	Dec. 31 Bal.	28,000.00
Clos.	24,000.00	(New Bal. zero)	
		Rev.	4,000.00
		(New Bal.	4,000.00)

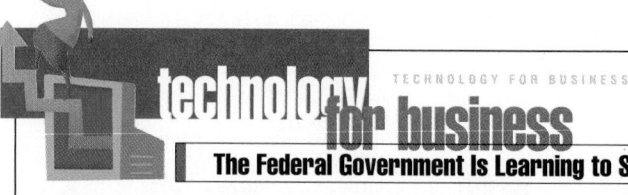

technology for business

TECHNOLOGY FOR BUSINESS • TECHNOLOGY FOR BUSINESS • TECHNOLOGY FOR BUS

The Federal Government Is Learning to Shop at Electronic Stores

The federal government purchases billions of dollars of goods and services every year. Various government agencies have developed Web-based electronic stores. The Government Services Administration (GSA) administers GSA Advantage, the largest of these electronic stores. GSA Advantage supplies more than 4 million items to other government agencies. Other departments and agencies, including NASA and the various branches of the Armed Services, operate smaller electronic stores.

Authorized federal employees can make purchases from these electronic stores. Currently, purchases are made by "credit cards" with various purchasing limits. Eventually, the credit cards will be replaced by smart cards.

The Web-based electronic stores reduce the purchasing cycle by more than 50 percent. Substantial cost savings result from lower inventory levels and reduced paperwork.

TECHNOLOGY FOR BUSINESS

The Technology for Business feature is designed to show students common business applications of technology. Ask students if they are familiar with the concept of electronic stores. As an optional activity, assign one or more groups of students to research electronic stores available to consumers.

ADJUSTING ENTRY FOR ACCRUED INTEREST INCOME

Note	Principal	×	Interest Rate	×	Fraction of Year	=	Accrued Interest Income
12	$500.00	×	10%	×	$\frac{30}{360}$	=	$4.17
13	$700.00	×	10%	×	$\frac{15}{360}$	=	2.92

Total accrued interest income, December 31.... $7.09 ◄─❶ **1.** Calculate interest earned on the notes.

2. Record entry to accrue interest income. ────────►

	GENERAL JOURNAL						PAGE 13	
❷ DATE	ACCOUNT TITLE	DOC. NO.	POST. REF.	DEBIT		CREDIT		
	Adjusting Entries							1
²⁰⁻ Dec. 31	*Interest Receivable*			7 09				2
	Interest Income					7 09		3

Revenue earned in one fiscal period but not received until a later fiscal period is called **accrued revenue**. For example, a business accepts a 30-day note on December 15. During December, the business earned interest for 16 days. However, the business will not receive any of the interest until the note's maturity in January. Interest for the first 16 days must be recorded in the current fiscal period. [*CONCEPT: Matching Expenses with Revenue*]

On December 31, Appliance Center has two notes receivable outstanding.

Note Receivable No. 12, a 60-day, 10% note dated December 1, $500.00.

Note Receivable No. 13, a 30-day, 10% note dated December 16, $700.00.

Accrued interest for each note is calculated from the date of the note through the end of the fiscal year, as shown above.

The accrued interest for all notes is totaled to compute the adjusting entry amount. The adjusting entry increases the balance of Interest Income to include interest that has been earned but not received in cash.

The amount of interest owed to the company is reported as Interest Receivable. Interest Receivable is classified as a Current Asset, as shown on Appliance Center's chart of accounts.

Interest Receivable	
Adj.	7.09

Interest Income	
Dec. 31 Bal.	65.70
Adj.	7.09
(New Bal.	72.79)

FYI FOR YOUR INFORMATION

A company that accepts a large number of notes might benefit from using a ledger system similar to an accounts receivable ledger. The ledger enables management to identify the total amount of notes outstanding with any single customer. Thus, management could make more informed decisions about extending additional credit to a particular customer.

REVERSING ENTRY FOR ACCRUED INTEREST INCOME

	DATE		ACCOUNT TITLE	DOC. NO.	POST. REF.	DEBIT	CREDIT	
1			*Reversing Entries*					1
2	20-- Jan.	1	Interest Income			7 09		2
3			Interest Receivable				7 09	3

GENERAL JOURNAL   PAGE 1

Interest Income is closed as part of Appliance Center's closing entries. After closing entries are posted, Interest Income has a zero balance. The $7.09 balance in Interest Receivable represents interest that Appliance Center has earned but has not yet received in cash.

The adjusting entry for accrued interest income created a balance in the asset account Interest Receivable. Therefore, on January 1, Appliance Center needs to reverse the adjusting entry that created the balance in Interest Receivable, as shown above.

The new balance of Interest Receivable is zero, as it was before the adjusting entry. The new

debit balance, $7.09, in Interest Income is a contra balance. When cash is received on the maturity date of each note, a credit to Interest Income will offset the debit balance.

Interest Income

Clos.	72.79	Dec. 31 Bal.	65.70
		Adj.	7.09
Rev.	7.09		
(New Bal.	*7.09)*		

Interest Receivable

Adj.	7.09	Rev.	7.09
(New Bal. zero)			

©GETTY IMAGES/PHOTODISC

REMEMBER Reversing entries eliminate the need for accounting personnel to remember to apply different account distributions to selected transactions. Without reversing entries, accounting personnel need to determine whether each interest payment was part of a prior year-end adjusting entry. If previously adjusted, the interest payment needs to be divided between Interest Receivable and Interest Income. With reversing entries, however, accounting personnel can simply record all interest payments to Interest Income.

Explore Accounting

Gains or Losses on Accounts Receivable and Notes Receivable Resulting from Changes in Foreign Exchange Rates

In the previous Explore Accounting feature, CyclePart sells on account a variety of American-made bicycle components priced at 10,000 euros to the Bicicletta Company in Italy. The transaction requires Bicicletta to pay CyclePart 10,000 euros in 60 days. At the time of the sale, the exchange rate between the euro and the dollar is exactly 1 to 1, meaning that 1 euro can be exchanged for 1 dollar. On the date of the sale, 10,000 euros equals $10,000 dollars. During the 60-day credit period, however, the exchange rate for the euro rises to $1.20. This higher exchange rate means that a single euro can now be exchanged for $1.20. When CyclePart receives payment of 10,000 euros in 60 days, the 10,000 euros are exchanged for $12,000.00 (10,000 euros × $1.20). Due to the 20-cent rise in the exchange rate, CyclePart gains an extra $2,000 through the currency exchange process. CyclePart accounts for the gain on accounts receivable with the entry below. The account Gain or Loss on Foreign Currency Exchange is classified as an other revenue account.

Cash 12,000
   Accounts Receivable/
     Bicicletta Company 10,000
   Gain or Loss on Foreign
     Currency Exchange 2,000

In the previous Explore Accounting feature, another example was provided in which Bicicletta gives CyclePart a 12-month, 6% note receivable for 100,000 euros. Including the interest of 6,000 euros (100,000 euros × .06), Bicicletta will pay CyclePart 106,000 euros in one year. If the exchange rate remains even (1 euro = 1 dollar) during the entire 12 months,

106,000 euros will be worth $106,000. Suppose, however, that during the 12-month period, the exchange rate between the euro and the dollar declines from $1 to $.90. Since a euro now equals less than $1, CyclePart will exchange the 106,000 euros it receives on December 31 for only $95,400 dollars (106,000 euros × .90). CyclePart accounts for the loss on notes receivable using the entry below. Due to the 10-cent decline in the exchange rate, CyclePart suffers a loss of $10,600 through the currency exchange process.

Cash 95,400
Gain or Loss on Foreign
     Currency Exchange 10,600
   Notes Receivable/
     Bicicletta Company 100,000
   Interest Income 6,000

Critical Thinking Activity

An American company sells watch parts on account to a Swiss firm, SwissTime, for 30,000 Swiss francs. At the time of the sale, the exchange rate for francs to dollars is 1 franc equals .9 dollars. The American company accepts a 6-month note from SwissTime at 8% interest. Six months later, when the American company collects the 30,000 Swiss francs for the note receivable plus the interest, the exchange rate has risen. One franc can now be exchanged for .95 dollars. If the American company exchanges the francs for dollars at the new rate, will the company realize a gain or a loss on the transaction? Show the impact of the gain or loss on accounts receivable as a journal entry similar to the example.

The American company will realize a gain of $1,560 on the transaction.

Interest:
   30,000 × 6/12 × .08 = 1,200 francs
Maturity value:
   30,000 + 1,200 = 31,200 francs

31,200 francs × .95 = $29,640
31,200 francs × .90 = $28,080
Total gain $ 1,560

Cash   32,760
   Notes Receivable/SwissTime   30,000
   Interest Income   1,200
   Gain or Loss on
     Foreign Currency Exchange   1,560

GUIDED PRACTICE

Terms Review

Call on students to define the terms in the Terms Review. Ask the class if the definitions are correct and whether the complete definitions have been given or if anything needs to be added. The suggested definitions are given in the Glossary.

Audit Your Understanding

Call on students to answer the Audit Your Understanding questions. Ask the class if the answer is correct and/or complete. Answers are given in Appendix E of the textbook.

Work Together

Have students write the solution to the Work Together problems as you guide the class through the example.

- Ask students to explain their calculation of total interest income.

- Direct students to record the adjusting entry in the general journal as you elicit class participation in analyzing and recording the transaction.

- Ask students to explain why a reversing entry should be recorded.

- Direct students to record the reversing entry in the general journal as you elicit class participation in analyzing and recording the transaction.

terms review

unearned revenue
accrued revenue

audit your understanding

1. What accounts are affected, and how, when rent received in advance is initially recorded as a revenue?

2. What is the rule for determining whether an adjusting entry should be reversed?

3. What accounts are affected, and how, by a reversing entry for rent revenue when rent receipts are initially recorded as a revenue?

4. What accounts are affected, and how, by an adjusting entry for accrued interest income?

5. What accounts are affected, and how, by a reversing entry for accrued interest income?

work together 10-2

Journalizing adjusting and reversing entries for unearned revenue initially recorded as revenue and for accrued revenue

Valentine, Inc., is preparing its December 31 financial statements for the current year. On December 1, the company received a $2,100.00 rent payment from Owens & Nolen, LLP. The payment is the $700.00 per month rent for December of the current year through February of the next year. Valentine initially records rent receipts as revenue. General journal pages are provided in the *Working Papers*. Your instructor will guide you through the following examples.

1. Journalize the adjusting entry for unearned rent. Use page 13 of a general journal.

2. Journalize the reversing entry for unearned rent. Use page 14 of a general journal.

Valentine, Inc., has two notes receivable outstanding on December 31 of the current year.

Note No.	Interest Rate	Term	Principal	Date
14	15%	60-days	$2,000.00	November 14
15	16%	60-days	$3,000.00	December 6

3. Journalize the adjusting entry for accrued interest income. Use page 13 of a general journal.

4. Journalize the reversing entry for accrued interest income. Use page 14 of a general journal.

on your own 10-2

Journalizing adjusting and reversing entries for unearned revenue initially recorded as revenue and for accrued revenue

Parker Discount Stores is preparing its December 31 financial statements for the current year. On October 30, the store paid $1,500.00 to K-98.1 Radio for advertising. The advertising contract requires K-98.1 to provide Parker with $500.00 of advertising time per month for November of the current year through January of the next year. K-98.1 initially records advertising receipts as revenue. General journal pages are provided in the *Working Papers*. Work this problem independently.

1. Journalize the adjusting entry for unearned advertising. Use page 19 of a general journal.
2. Journalize the reversing entry for unearned advertising. Use page 20 of a general journal.

Parker Discount Stores has two notes receivable outstanding on December 31 of the current year.

Note No.	Interest Rate	Term	Principal	Date
26	18%	90-days	$4,000.00	November 8
29	16%	60-days	$1,500.00	December 12

3. Journalize the adjusting entry for accrued interest income. Use page 19 of a general journal.
4. Journalize the reversing entry for accrued interest income. Use page 20 of a general journal.

303

After completing this chapter, you can

1. Define accounting terms related to notes receivable, unearned revenue, and accrued revenue.

2. Identify accounting concepts and practices related to notes receivable, unearned revenue, and accrued revenue.

3. Journalize transactions for notes receivable.

4. Journalize adjusting and reversing entries for unearned revenue initially recorded as revenue.

5. Journalize adjusting and reversing entries for accrued revenue.

Explore Accounting

EXPLORE ACCOUNTING • EXPLORE ACCOUNTING • EXPLORE AC

Factoring Accounts Receivable

New businesses must have an adequate amount of working capital to purchase inventory, rent or buy fixed assets, and pay employees during the planning, construction, and opening periods. Access to independent sources of working capital, such as bank loans, is often limited until a business proves it can maintain profitability.

Accounts receivable can become a significant drain on working capital. Inventory sold on account does not immediately provide cash to purchase new inventory. Customers unable to purchase out-of-stock items shop elsewhere. The more successful a business is at selling inventory on account, the greater its need for working capital.

A solution to this problem is that a business can sell its accounts receivable to another company for cash. Assigning the rights to accounts receivable to an independent company in exchange for cash is known as factoring. The factoring company pays 85% to 95% of the value of the accounts receivable sold. The factoring company assumes the responsibility and cost of collecting the accounts.

Factoring costs the business 5% to 15% of sales on account. However, the immediate cash received allows the business to continue operations. In addition, management can focus its attention on more important aspects of the business than on the collection of accounts receivable.

Required:

Accounting equations are provided in the *Working Papers.* Record transactions using the following assumptions for eight weeks, with and without factoring. Would you recommend that Chism Company factor accounts receivable at 90% of value?

1. All cash was used to purchase $10,000 of inventory.

2. Disregard other operating expenses.

3. With a complete inventory, sales are $2,000 per week ($1,000 cost). If the inventory levels drop below $10,000, however, sales for out-of-stock items are lost. Chism can still sell 20% of available inventory each week.

4. All sales are on account with n/30 terms. Cash collected is used to restock inventory up to $10,000.

5. Accounts receivable are factored at 90% of value.

- Ask students to prepare a list of the new concepts introduced in this chapter.

- Assign Mastery Problem 10-4 to students who need the reinforcement of a problem that combines all activities from the chapter in one problem; this will be most students.

- Assign Challenge Problem 10-5 to accelerated students who do not require the reinforcement of the Mastery Problem.

- Assign Study Guide 10.

- Students can use Automated Accounting 8.0 or higher to work Mastery Problem 10-4.

- Students can use Peachtree or Quick-Books to automate Mastery Problem 10-4.

- Students can access Personal Trainer to work end-of-chapter problems on the computer.

- Students can access the Xtra! Web Site for the Xtra! Review and Quizzing.

- Students can access the Student Companion CD for additional review material.

Review solutions to the assigned problems in class, diagnosing trouble spots.

- Call on students to describe how they avoid the trouble spots diagnosed.

- Use reteaching suggestions from section lesson plans as required.

- Assign Recycling Problem 10-1 if needed.

- Assign the Explore Accounting feature. Ask students to share the information they have gathered in a report to the class.

- Students can access the Xtra! Web Site for the Xtra! Enrichment material.

- Assign Applied Communication.

- Assign the Cases for Critical Thinking.

- Assign the SCANS Workplace Competency.

- Assign Auditing for Errors.

- Assign Analyzing Costco's Financial Statements.

- Assign Automated Accounting on page 309.

304

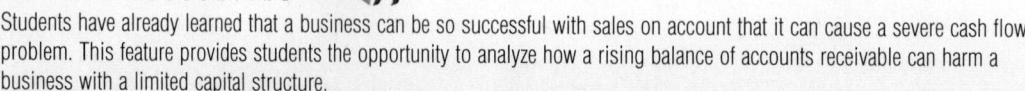

EXPLORE ACCOUNTING

EXPLORE ACCOUNTING

Students have already learned that a business can be so successful with sales on account that it can cause a severe cash flow problem. This feature provides students the opportunity to analyze how a rising balance of accounts receivable can harm a business with a limited capital structure.

This feature introduces the concept of factoring, the process of selling accounts receivable to another company.

Assist students in completing the first two weeks of the accounting equations.

After students complete the accounting equations with and without factoring, allow students to debate the advantages and disadvantages of factoring. Some students may express negative feelings about paying 10% to 15% of sales in factoring fees. Ask students if factoring is an appropriate strategy for all companies.

10-1 APPLICATION PROBLEM

Journalizing transactions for notes receivable

Bellingham, Inc., completed the following transactions during the current year.

Transactions:

Aug.	1.	Bellingham agreed to an extension of time on James Huber's account by accepting a 60-day, 10% note from him, $200.00. NR1.
Aug.	1.	Accepted a 60-day, 12% note from Frank Otto for a sale on account, $300.00. NR2.
Sept.	30.	The 60-day, 10% note from James Huber (NR1) was dishonored; $200.00 plus interest. M12.
Sept.	30.	Accepted a 60-day, 10% note from Melissa Carr for an extension of time on her account, $500.00. NR3.
Sept.	30.	Received cash for the maturity value of NR2, $300.00 plus interest. R10.
Nov.	30.	Principal, $500.00, plus interest was received for the maturity value of NR3. R32.
Dec.	1.	James Huber sent a check for dishonored NR1, $203.33 plus additional interest. R33.

Instructions:
Use page 8 of a general journal and page 15 of a cash receipts journal to journalize the transactions. Source documents are abbreviated as follows: memorandum, M; note receivable, NR; receipt, R.

10-2 APPLICATION PROBLEM

Journalizing adjusting and reversing entries for unearned revenue initially recorded as revenue

On November 1 of the current year, Billies, Inc., received a $2,700.00 rent payment from Simms & Ulman. The payment covers rent of office space for November through April, $450.00 per month. Billies initially records rent payments as revenue.

Instructions:
1. Journalize the adjusting entry for unearned rent on December 31 of the current year. Use page 13 of a general journal.
2. Journalize the reversing entry for unearned rent on January 1 of the next year. Use page 1 of a general journal.

10-3 APPLICATION PROBLEM

Journalizing adjusting and reversing entries for accrued revenue

On December 31 of the current year, McNeilson, Inc., has two notes receivable.

Note Receivable No. 1, a 90-day, 10% note dated November 1, $200.00.
Note Receivable No. 2, a 60-day, 10% note dated December 1, $300.00.

Instructions:
1. Calculate the accrued interest on the notes as of December 31.
2. Journalize the adjusting entry for accrued interest income on December 31 of the current year. Use page 13 of a general journal.
3. Journalize the reversing entry for accrued interest income on January 1 of the next year. Use page 1 of a general journal.

FORMAL EVALUATION

Chapter 10 Test
ExamView for Chapter 10
Assessment by Portfolio

- Review answers to all tests administered as a class activity. If time is limited, review only the items that were frequently answered incorrectly.

- Ask students if there are any questions about the chapter before proceeding to the next chapter.

CHECK FIGURES

Application Problem 10-1
August 1: debit Notes Receivable, credit Accounts Receivable/James Huber; August 1: debit Notes Receivable and credit Sales. September 30: debit Accounts Receivable/James Huber, credit Notes Receivable and Interest Income (3.33).

Application Problem 10-2
Adjusting entry: Debit Rent Income, 1,800.00; credit Unearned Rent, 1,800.00.

Application Problem 10-3
Accrued interest income: Note 1, $3.33; Note 2, 2.50. Adjusting entry: Debit Interest Receivable, 5.83; credit Interest Income, 5.83.

See Teacher's Edition of the Working Papers for Chapter 10 for complete solutions.

TEACHING STRATEGIES   COOPERATIVE LEARNING

Divide the class into groups. Each group stands and faces each other. The instructor chooses selected Accounting Terms from Chapters 7 through 10. When the instructor gives the term, the first student who raises his or her hand has the opportunity to give the correct definition. The group with the most correctly defined terms is declared the winner. This cooperative learning activity should not take more than 20 to 25 minutes of class time.

Mastery Problem 10-4

Adjusting entries: Debit Interest Receivable, 8.10; credit Interest Income, 8.10. Debit Rent Income, 500.00; credit Unearned Rent, 500.00.

Challenge Problem 10-5

July 31, debit Allowance for Uncollectible Accounts, 35.31, credit Accounts Receivable/Pierre Black, 27.81, and credit Accounts Receivable/John Hamilton, 7.50.

10-4 MASTERY PROBLEM 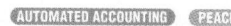 AUTOMATED ACCOUNTING PEACHTREE QUICKBOOKS

Journalizing notes receivable, unearned revenue, and accrued revenue initially recorded as revenue transactions

Marier, Inc., completed the following transactions during the current year. Marier initially records prepaid and unearned items as revenue.

Transactions:

July	1.	Accepted a 90-day, 10% note from Timothy Johnson for a sale on account, $500.00. NR12.
July	5.	Accepted a 90-day, 12% note from Gerald Kammer for an extension of time on his account, $600.00. NR13.
Sept.	29.	Timothy Johnson dishonored NR12, a 90-day, 10% note, $500.00 plus interest. M32.
Oct.	3.	Received cash for the maturity value of NR13, $600.00 plus interest. R65.
Nov.	1.	Received cash for November through January rent, $500.00 per month, in advance from Centuria, Inc., $1,500.00. R70.
Dec.	1.	Received cash from Timothy Johnson for dishonored NR12, $512.50 plus additional interest. R81.
Dec.	4.	Accepted a 90-day, 12% note from Jackie Webb for sale on account, $900.00. NR14.

Instructions:

1. Use page 7 of a general journal and page 19 of a cash receipts journal to journalize the transactions. Source documents are abbreviated as follows: memorandum, M; note receivable, NR; receipt, R.
2. Continue using page 7 of the general journal. Journalize the necessary adjusting entries.
3. Journalize the reversing entries on January 1 of the next year. Use page 1 of a general journal.

10-5 CHALLENGE PROBLEM

Journalizing accounts and notes receivable

Hillsdale, Inc., sells on account with n/30 terms. If the account is not paid within 30 days, Hillsdale begins charging customers 18% interest on their outstanding balance. At 120 days past due, Hillsdale asks customers to sign a 60-day, 18% note for the original amount of the sale plus 90 days of accrued interest. During the year, Hillsdale accrues interest income when notes are issued or payments on account are made.

Unfortunately, customers are not always willing to pay all or any of the interest charges. Because the amounts are often small, Hillsdale must consider the negative impact that attempting to collect these amounts may have on its image. Thus, it writes off many interest charges as uncollectible.

Transactions:

July	4.	Accepted a 60-day, 18% note from Steven Bozeman for an extension of time, $500.00 plus accrued interest. NR26.
July	12.	Received $618.00 cash from Pierre Black on payment of NR18, a $627.00 note ($600.00 plus $27.00 accrued interest) issued 60 days ago. Mr. Black included a letter stating that he would pay interest only on the note and only for the original sale amount. R70.
July	15.	Received $250.00 cash in payment of John Hamilton's account. The account balance resulted from a sale on account of $250.00 on May 16. R71.
July	31.	Hillsdale's credit manager decided not to attempt to collect the interest charges on the accounts of Pierre Black and John Hamilton. M46.

Instructions:

Journalize the transactions made during the current year. Calculate amounts as needed. Use page 7 of a general journal and page 7 of a cash receipts journal. Source documents are abbreviated as follows: memorandum, M; note receivable, NR; receipt, R.

Accounting for Notes Receivable, Unearned Revenue, and Accrued Revenue

APPLIED SKILLS LANGUAGE ARTS

Paraphrasing, writing complete sentences, and identifying verbs. For additional practice in language arts skills, direct students to answer the Terms Review and Audit Your Understanding questions. Students should write the answers in their own words and in complete sentences. To further practice language arts skills, ask students to underline the verbs in each sentence of their answers.

Xtra!
Enrichment
accountingxtra.swlearning.com

• applied communication

You have just been hired as the new credit manager for Harrell and Company, a chain of lumber stores. While evaluating the accounting system, you notice that many of the credit accounts are 120 to 180 days past due. Although these customers ultimately pay their accounts, they do not abide by the n/30 terms specified on the sales invoice.

At your suggestion, management has approved a plan to change the credit terms to 2/10, n/30, with 18% interest charged on overdue accounts. In addition, you will require a note receivable to be signed for accounts over 90 days past due as a condition for the customer to receive additional credit.

Required:

Prepare a letter to send to current credit customers informing them of the new credit terms.

• cases for critical thinking

Case 1

Farmland, Inc., issued a 60-day, 12%, $600.00 note receivable to a customer. The customer dishonored the note at maturity. The accounting clerk recorded the dishonored note receivable by debiting Accounts Receivable and crediting Notes Receivable for the maturity value, $612.00. Thirty days later, the customer paid $618.12 for the dishonored note. The accounting clerk recorded this amount by debiting Cash and crediting Notes Receivable. Farmland's bookkeeper checked the work and decided that the journal entries were both incorrect. Do you agree? Explain your answer.

Case 2

At the beginning of December, Maxim Floral, Inc., received three months' rent in advance. Maxim initially records rent payment as a revenue. On December 31, Maxim does not make an adjusting entry for unearned rent. What effect will this have on the firm's financial statements?

• SCANS workplace competency

Thinking Skills: Problem Solving

Concept: Business needs usually involve an underlying problem that must be first recognized and then solved. Solving a business problem involves devising a plan and then implementing the plan.

Application: Your construction company increasingly fails to win contracts for state and municipal construction jobs because of requirements for minority representation on your workforce. You know that many minority workers apply for jobs with your company but few are hired. Devise a plan for recruiting and hiring more minority workers for your company.

APPLIED COMMUNICATION

CASES FOR CRITICAL THINKING • CASES

SCANS WORKPLACE COMPETENCY

Accounting for Notes Receivable, Unearned Revenue and Accrued Revenue

Chapter 10   **307**

APPLIED COMMUNICATION

Students' answers to this activity will differ. Although the policy change has been made to benefit Harrell and Company, the letter should focus on benefits from the customer's point of view. Thus, the letter could announce a policy change that can save customers money by offering discounts for early payment. Should a customer need extra time to pay an account, the new plan provides for a fair interest rate and note policy. The letter should emphasize that the policy change will assist Harrell and Company to continue providing its customers with the highest quality products at the lowest possible prices.

CASES FOR CRITICAL THINKING

Case 1

Yes, the entries are incorrect. When dishonored, more than the note's value was transferred out of the notes receivable account. When cash was received, Accounts Receivable should have been credited instead of Notes Receivable. In both entries, interest should have been recorded in Interest Income. The correct entries are: (1) When dishonored, debit Accounts Receivable, $612.00; credit Notes Receivable, $600.00; credit Interest Income, $12.00. (2) When cash is received, debit Cash, $618.12; credit Accounts Receivable, $612.00; credit Interest Income, $6.12.

Case 2

On the income statement, rental income and net income will be overstated. *(Concept: Matching Expenses with Revenue)* On the balance sheet, owner's equity will be overstated and unearned rent, a current liability, will be understated.

SCANS WORKPLACE COMPETENCY

Students should recognize that there may not be just one problem or one solution. Are managers discriminating against minority job applicants? Or are qualified job applicants not applying for positions with the company? Solutions may require changes in the way applicants are reviewed and selected. Active recruiting plans may need to be implemented, such as participating in job fairs that attract minority workers. It may also be necessary to implement a training program so that the company can hire workers who may be less skilled but who can be trained to meet company labor standards.

307

AUDITING FOR ERRORS

Note 56 should be calculated using 110 days instead of 120 days.

Note 56:

110/360 × 10% × 1,600.00 = 48.89

Note 59 is rounded incorrectly.

Note 59:

89/360 × 10% × 1,600.00 = 22.25

Note 63 is correctly calculated.

ANALYZING COSTCO'S FINANCIAL STATEMENTS

ANALYZING COSTCO'S FINAN

1. Costco spreads the revenue out "over the one-year life of the membership."
2. Deferred membership income.
3. 401,357,000
4. 360,515,000

• auditing for errors

The Stephens Company has the following notes receivable outstanding on December 31.

No.	Date of Note	Term	Interest	Principal
56	September 12	120 days	10%	$1,600.00
59	October 3	90 days	10%	$900.00
63	November 30	60 days	9%	$2,000.00

In preparation for adjusting entries, the accounting clerk has calculated accrued interest as follows:

Note 56: 120/360 × 10% × 1,600.00 = 53.33

Note 59: 89/360 × 10% × 900.00 = 22.24

Note 63: 31/360 × 9% × 2,000.00 = 15.50

Instructions:

1. Verify the calculations.

2. If you find any errors, recalculate to find the correct amount of accrued interest.

• analyzing Costco's financial statements

Costco Wholesale Corporation is a membership company. Customers pay a yearly membership fee, which gives them the right to shop at Costco. When Costco receives the yearly fee from a customer, it cannot count all of it as revenue at that time. Revenue must be recognized as it is earned. Costco earns the revenue over the next year. Therefore, when Costco receives the cash for the fee, cash is debited, and a liability account is credited. This unearned revenue is a liability, because the company "owes" that customer the right of membership for the remainder of the membership period.

Instructions:

Using Appendix B in this textbook, find the paragraph in Note No. 1 titled "Revenue Recognition" on page B-12. Read the note related to membership fee revenue and answer the following questions.

1. When does Costco count the membership fee as revenue?

2. Look at Costco's balance sheet on page B5. What account title does Costco use for this liability account?

3. How much unearned revenue did Costco list as a liability for the fiscal period ending August 31, 2003?

4. How much unearned revenue did Costco list as a liability for the fiscal period ending September 1, 2002?

TEACHING STRATEGIES PORTFOLIO ASSESSMENT

A clear understanding of notes receivable, unearned revenue, and accrued revenue is helpful for students who will pursue accounting careers. Students should emphasize their learning of this topic by selecting an example of a comprehensive sample of their work in this chapter, for example the Mastery Problem to include in their portfolio. A copy of the Portfolio Assessment form (blackline master in the Teacher's Resource Guide; also on the Student Companion CD) should be completed by the student and the Description lesson should include any comments regarding how the student mastered these concepts and procedures. Alternatively, students might include in their portfolios printed reports from an Automated Accounting problem.

• Automated Accounting

Correction of Errors

When entering data into journals it is very easy to make errors unless you are careful. It is important to check your work as you enter transactions into the accounting system. People use different methods in order to lessen the likelihood of entering incorrect transactions and amounts, and entering transactions into the wrong journal.

Sometimes it may be necessary to locate and correct journal entries that have already been posted to the ledgers. The same procedure is used to locate and correct errors in all journals.

Finding a Journal Entry

Use the following steps to find a journal entry:

1. Click on the special journal tab to which the journal entry was made (General, Purchases, Cash Payments, Sales, Cash Receipts).

2. Choose the Find menu item from the Edit menu.

3. Enter the date, reference, vendor name, or amount of the transaction you want to find in the Find What text box. Then click OK.

4. If a matching transaction is found, it will be displayed onscreen so that it may be changed or deleted.

Changing Transactions

When changing or deleting journal transactions:

1. Click the journal tab in which you want to make a change.

2. Select the specific transaction that you wish to change.

3. Enter the correct journal entry and click the Post command button.

Accounting systems can be very efficient in processing data but it is the responsibility of the individual entering data to make accuracy a high priority. When producing a business's financial reports from an accounting system, if transactions were entered with errors, the reports will not represent the true financial position of the company.

An error can cause management to make business decisions based on inaccurate information, which could have serious consequences for a business.

AUTOMATING APPLICATION PROBLEM 10-1

Instructions:

1. Load *Automated Accounting 8.0* or higher software.

2. Select database A10-1 (Advanced Course Application Problem 10-1) from the accounting template disk.

3. Select File from the menu bar and choose the Save As menu command. Key the path to the drive and directory that contain your data files. Save the database with a filename of XXX101 (where XXX are your initials).

4. Read the Problem Instruction screen by clicking the Browser toolbar button.

5. Key the data listed in the problem.

6. Exit the Automated Accounting software.

AUTOMATING MASTERY PROBLEM 10-4

Instructions:

1. Load *Automated Accounting 8.0* or higher software.

2. Select database A10-4 (Advanced Course Mastery Problem 10-4) from the accounting template disk.

3. Select File from the menu bar and choose the Save As menu command. Key the path to the drive and directory that contain your data files. Save the database with a filename of XXX104 (where XXX are your initials).

4. Read the Problem Instruction screen by clicking the Browser toolbar button.

5. Key the data listed in the problem.

6. Exit the Automated Accounting software.

EXPLAIN

- Explain the importance of locating and correcting errors in journalizing and posting so that correct reports are available for decision making.

- Explain that transactions recorded in journals can be either changed or deleted depending on the nature of the correction needed.

- Point out that the Automated Accounting software will allow a search for journal entries on any data that appears in an entry, such as the date, reference, name, or amount.

- Explain that the Journal Entries screen must be open before the Edit Find option is active.

DEMONSTRATE

Finding a journal entry

- Open an existing Automated Accounting problem and save it under a new name.

- Open the Journal Entries screen. Click on the tab for the journal you wish to search.

- Choose the Find option from the Edit menu.

- Key data from a journal entry in the Find Journal entry dialog box and click OK. The journal entry containing the data is selected.

Changing or deleting a journal entry

- With an existing Automated Accounting problem still open under a different name, click one of the journal entry fields and key a change.

- Click the Post command button to post the changed transaction.

- Click another journal entry field and click the Delete command button to demonstrate how to delete a journal entry.

PRACTICE

- Assign Automating Application Problem 10-1: Journalizing transactions for notes receivable.

- Assign Automating Mastery Problem 10-4: Journalizing notes receivable, unearned revenue, and accrued revenue initially recorded as revenue transactions.

ASSESSMENT

- Use the Electronic Auditor to assess student understanding.

TEACHING STRATEGIES   PORTFOLIO ASSESSMENT

Students should be encouraged to print at least one report from one of the Automated Accounting problems to include in their portfolio to demonstrate mastery of automated accounting systems. A copy of the Portfolio Assessment form (blackline master in the Teacher's Resource Guide; also on the Student Companion CD) should be completed by the student and the Description section should include any comments regarding how the student mastered these concepts and procedures.

OVERVIEW

Part 4 gives an in-depth view of corporation accounting.

- **Chapter 11** begins with organizing a corporation and paying dividends. Transactions to get a corporation started are described and illustrated.

- **Chapter 12** moves on to cover the acquisition of additional capital for a corporation including a discussion of treasury stock and corporate bonds.

- **Chapter 13** wraps up the end-of-fiscal-period work for a corporation. The work sheet and financial statements, as well as calculating federal income tax, are given detailed coverage.

- **Chapters 11–13** cover the complete accounting cycle for a corporation. It is important that the student see the entire accounting cycle as it applies to a business organized as a corporation. It is equally important that the student begin to use the information generated during an accounting cycle to make good managerial decisions.

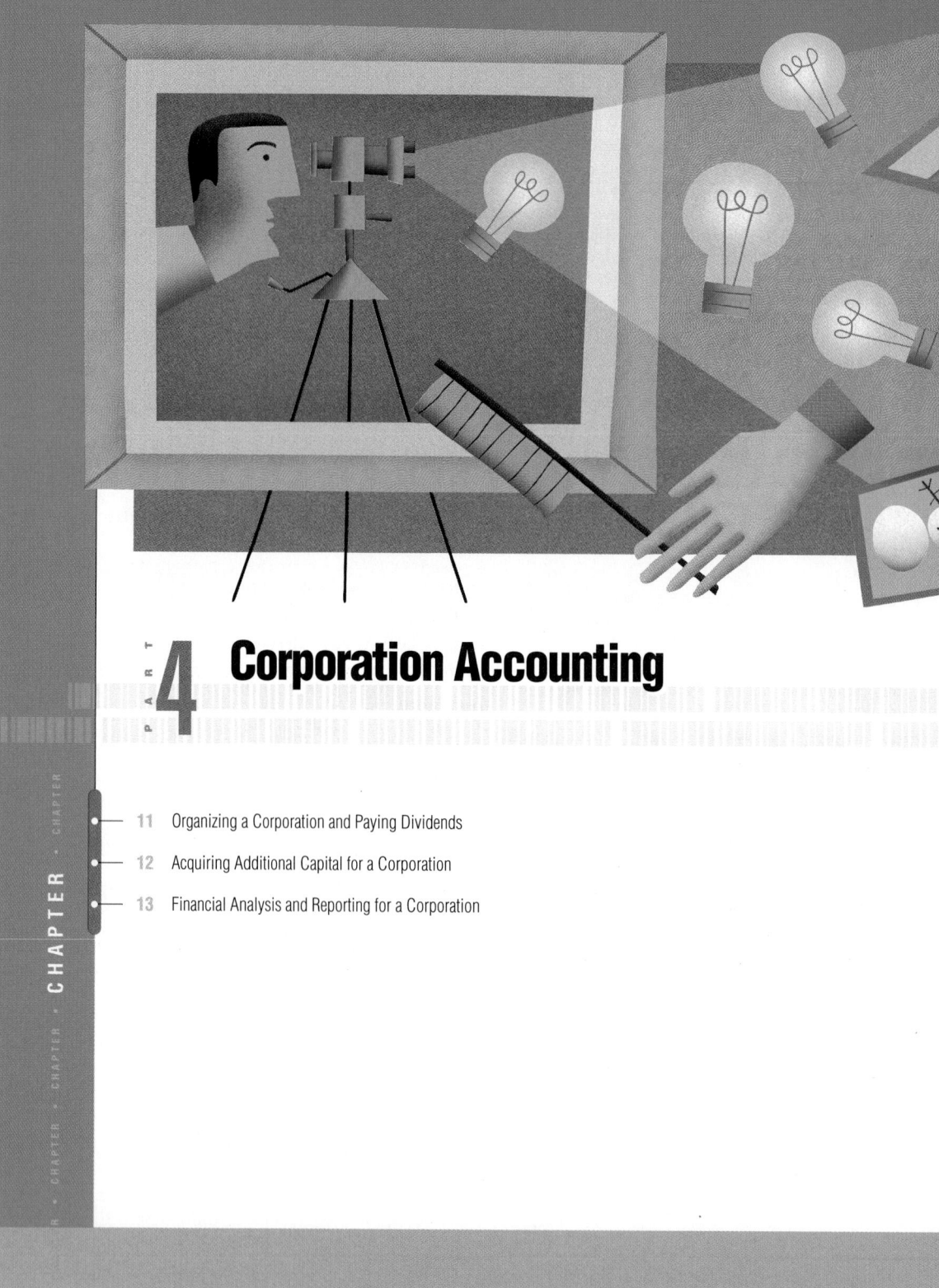

Corporation Accounting

PART 4

```
                          1400   INTANGIBLE ASSET
                          1405   Organization Costs
                          (2000) LIABILITIES
                          2100   CURRENT LIABILITIES
                          2105   Interest Payable
                          2110   Accounts Payable
                          2115   Employee Income Tax Payable
                          2120   Federal Income Tax Payable
                          2125   Social Security Tax Payable
                          2130   Medicare Tax Payable
                          2135   Salaries Payable
                          2140   Sales Tax Payable
                          2145   Unemployment Tax Payable—Federal
                          2150   Unemployment Tax Payable—State
                          2155   Health Insurance Premiums Payable
                          2160   Dividends Payable
                          2200   LONG-TERM LIABILITY
                          2205   Bonds Payable
                          (3000) STOCKHOLDERS' EQUITY
                          3105   Capital Stock—Common
                          3110   Stock Subscribed—Common
                          3115   Paid-in Capital in Excess of Stated Value—
                                 Common
                          3120   Capital Stock—Preferred
                          3125   Stock Subscribed—Preferred
                          3130   Paid-in Capital in Excess of Par Value—
                                 Preferred
                          3135   Discount on Sale of Preferred Stock
                          3140   Treasury Stock
                          3145   Paid-in Capital from Sale of Treasury Stock
                          3150   Retained Earnings
                          3155   Dividends—Common
                          3160   Dividends—Preferred
                          3165   Income Summary
```

Income Statement Accounts

```
(4000) OPERATING REVENUE
4105   Sales
4110   Sales Discount
4115   Sales Returns and Allowances
(5000) COST OF MERCHANDISE
5105   Purchases
5110   Purchases Discount
5115   Purchases Returns and Allowances
(6000) OPERATING EXPENSES
6100   SELLING EXPENSES
6105   Advertising Expense
6110   Credit Card Fee Expense
6115   Depreciation Expense—Store Equipment
6120   Miscellaneous Expense—Sales
6125   Salary Expense—Sales
6130   Supplies Expense—Sales
6200   ADMINISTRATIVE EXPENSES
6205   Depreciation Expense—Building
6210   Depreciation Expense—Office Equipment
6215   Insurance Expense
6220   Miscellaneous Expense—Administrative
6225   Payroll Taxes Expense
6230   Property Tax Expense
6235   Salary Expense—Administrative
6240   Supplies Expense—Administrative
6245   Uncollectible Accounts Expense
6250   Utilities Expense
(7000) OTHER REVENUE
7105   Gain on Plant Assets
7110   Interest Income
(8000) OTHER EXPENSES
8105   Interest Expense
8110   Loss on Plant Assets
8115   Organization Expense
(9000) INCOME TAX
9105   Federal Income Tax Expense
```

The chart of accounts for LampLight, Inc. is
illustrated above for ready reference as you study
Part 4 of this textbook.

311

LAMPLIGHT INC. CHART OF ACCOUNTS

Balance Sheet Accounts

```
(1000) ASSETS
1100   CURRENT ASSETS
1105   Cash
1110   Petty Cash
1115   Notes Receivable
1120   Interest Receivable
1125   Accounts Receivable
1130   Allowance for Uncollectible Accounts
1135   Subscriptions Receivable
1140   Merchandise Inventory
1145   Supplies—Store
1150   Supplies—Administrative
1155   Prepaid Insurance
1160   Prepaid Interest
1200   LONG-TERM INVESTMENT
1205   Bond Sinking Fund
1300   PLANT ASSETS
1305   Store Equipment
1310   Accumulated Depreciation—Store Equipment
1315   Building
1320   Accumulated Depreciation—Building
1325   Office Equipment
1330   Accumulated Depreciation—Office Equipment
1335   Land
```

- a
  beds
  syste
  receive
  without
  expense s.

- Emphasize t
  used for determi...
  of accounts and which...
  temporary and permanent a...

- Stress that the chart of accounts is
  for completed automated accounting
  activities since account numbers are
  required for both data entry and file
  maintenance activities.

Similarities
Point out the *similarities* between this chart
of accounts and the one used in Part 3:

- Typical divisions for a merchandising
  business:
  - Assets
  - Liabilities
  - Stockholders' Equity
  - Operating Revenue
  - Cost of Merchandise
  - Operating Expenses
  - Other Revenue
  - Other Expenses
  - Income Tax

- Many familiar accounts within divisions.

Differences
Point out the *differences* between this chart
of accounts and the one used in Part 3:

- Classifications within the assets and
  liabilities divisions.

- Large number of accounts now present
  under Stockholders' Equity division.

- New account, Organization Expense,
  added under the Other Expenses division.

Organizing a Corporation

	SCOPE & SEQUENCE		ENHANCING	
	NEW	REVIEW/ EXTENSION	SPECIAL FEATURES	
...ce the Chapter	✓		• Accounting in the Real World: General Mills	
...sson 11-1 Starting a Corporation			• Making Ethical Decisions: Just Following Orders	
...ature of a corporation		✓	• Global Perspective: International Packages and Customs Inspections	
Rights of stockholders	✓			
Common stock		✓	• Explore Accounting: Intangible Assets	
Preferred stock	✓		• Cultural Diversity: Businesses Owned by Asian Americans and Other Related Groups	
Capital accounts for a corporation		✓		
Transactions for forming a corporation	✓			
Lesson 11-2 Stock Subscriptions and the Balance Sheet			• Cases for Critical Thinking 1	
Subscription for capital stock	✓			
Organization costs of a corporation	✓			
Balance sheet of a newly formed corporation		✓		
Lesson 11-3 Calculating and Journalizing Dividends for a Corporation			• Business Structures: Advantages and Disadvantages of a Corporation	
Declaring and paying dividends		✓		
Calculating dividends for common and preferred stock	✓		• Careers in Accounting	
Putting It All Together			• Explore Accounting	
			• Xtra! Web Site: Xtra! Enrichment	
			• Applied Communication	
			• Cases for Critical Thinking 2	
			• SCANS Workplace Competency	
			• Graphing Workshop	
			• Analyzing Costco's Financial Statements	

and Paying Dividends

INSTRUCTION		PRACTICE AND ASSESSMENT		
TECHNOLOGY AND MEDIA	**TEACHING STRATEGIES**	**GUIDED PRACTICE**	**INDEPENDENT PRACTICE**	**RETEACHING AND ENRICHMENT**
• Internet Research Activity • Accounting Xtra! Web Site	• Software Focus			
• Instructor's Resource CD: PowerPoint Slides • Xtra! Web Site: Xtra! Study Tools • Blackline Masters: Cash Receipts Journal and Cash Payments Journal • Personal Trainer	• Accounting Pedagogy • Auditory Learner	• Terms Review • Audit Your Understanding • Work Together 11-1	• On Your Own 11-1 • Application Problem 11-1 • Ongoing Assessment, p. 320 • Personal Trainer • Xtra! Web Site: Xtra! Study Tools	• Reteach, p. 320 • Enrich, p. 323
• Instructor's Resource CD: PowerPoint Slides • Xtra! Web Site: Xtra! Study Tools • Blackline Masters: General Journal, Cash Receipts Journal, and 3-Column Financial Statement • Personal Trainer • QuickBooks		• Terms Review • Audit Your Understanding • Work Together 11-2	• On Your Own 11-2 • Application Problem 11-2 • Ongoing Assessment, p. 326 • Personal Trainer • Xtra! Web Site: Xtra! Study Tools	• Reteach, p. 326 • Enrich, p. 327 • QuickBooks
• Instructor's Resource CD: PowerPoint Slides • Xtra! Web Site: Xtra! Study Tools • Blackline Masters: General Journal, Cash Payments Journal • Personal Trainer • Peachtree and QuickBooks		• Terms Review • Audit Your Understanding • Work Together 11-3	• On Your Own 11-3 • Application Problems 11-3 and 11-4 • Ongoing Assessment, p. 330 • Personal Trainer • Xtra! Web Site: Xtra! Study Tools	• Reteach, p. 330 • Enrich, p. 332 • Peachtree and QuickBooks
• Automated Accounting • Peachtree • Personal Trainer • Xtra! Web Site: Xtra! Review, Quizzing, and Enrichment • Student Companion CD	• Visual Learner • Cooperative Learning • Kinesthetic Learner		• Mastery Problem 11-5 • Peachtree • Personal Trainer • Xtra! Web Site: Xtra! Review and Quizzing • Study Guide 11 • Student Companion CD • Chapter 11 Test • ExamView Chapter 11 • Portfolio Assessment	• Challenge Problem 11-6 • Reteach, p. 333 • Enrich, p. 333 • Recycling Problem 11-1 • Automated Accounting • Xtra! Web Site: Xtra! Enrichment

CHAPTER

11 Organizing a Corporation and Paying Dividends

OBJECTIVES & TERMS

After studying Chapter 11, you will be able to:

1. Define accounting terms related to corporate accounting.

2. Identify accounting concepts and practices related to corporate accounting.

3. Journalize transactions related to starting a corporation.

4. Journalize transactions related to stock subscriptions.

5. Prepare a balance sheet for a newly formed corporation.

6. Calculate dividends for a corporation.

7. Journalize transactions of a corporation related to declaring and paying dividends.

- corporation
- board of directors
- articles of incorporation
- charter
- common stock
- preferred stock

- stock certificate
- par value
- par-value stock
- no-par-value stock
- stated-value stock
- organization costs

- subscribing for capital stock
- intangible assets
- declaring a dividend
- date of declaration
- date of record
- date of payment

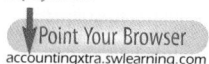
Point Your Browser
accountingxtra.swlearning.com

312

· General Mills

DANIEL ACKER/BLOOMBERG NEWS/LANDOV

THE "BIG G" COULD MEAN DIVIDENDS FOR AN INVESTOR IN GENERAL MILLS

Long before "Wheaties, the breakfast of champions," was available, General Mills was in existence. In fact, its history can be traced back more than 130 years.

What helps some companies, like General Mills, survive so long? It may be because General Mills has continually added products, either by internal development or by buying already-established product lines.

At General Mills, research and development is focused on new product development, product improvement, process design and improvement, packaging, and exploratory research in new business areas. In 2003, General Mills acquired Pillsbury. Overnight it doubled its revenues, workforce, and ownership of leading brands.

Regardless of how new products are brought into the General Mills family, they are all added with the hope that they will increase the bottom-line profit for the company. A steady stream of profit can mean a steady stream of dividends to stockholders.

General Mills has quite a record when it comes to paying dividends. It has "paid shareholder dividends, uninterrupted and without reduction, for 105 consecutive years." That's a long time.

Critical Thinking

1. Why would a company stress the fact that it has paid dividends for "105 consecutive years"?
2. Some companies have never paid a dividend and don't intend to pay a dividend in the near future. Why would an investor still be willing to invest in such a company?

Xtra!
Today
accountingxtra.swlearning.com

Source: www.generalmills.com

NEW YORK STOCK EXCHANGE (NYSE)

Go to the homepage for the New York Stock Exchange (NYSE) (www.nyse.com). Search the site for information about a "seat" on the exchange.

Instructions

1. Briefly summarize why a membership in the NYSE is called a "seat."
2. List how many seats are available on the NYSE.
3. What is the highest price ever paid for a seat on the NYSE?

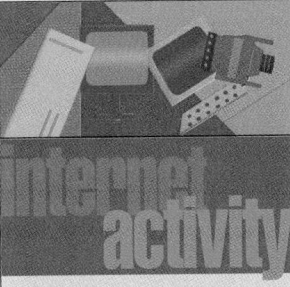

ACCOUNTING IN THE REAL WORLD

1. Some investors are very interested in dividends as a means of income. They look for stock that has a history of paying dividends in the hope that the company will continue this trend. A stock that pays regular dividends may also be more attractive to potential buyers.

2. The investor would buy stock hoping that the value of the stock would rise. The investor could then sell the stock for a profit.

INTERNET RESEARCH ACTIVITY

1. A membership on the NYSE is traditionally referred to as a "seat" because in the early years of its existence, members sat in assigned chairs during the roll call of stocks.

2. Currently, there are 1,366 seats on the NYSE.

3. The highest price ever paid for a seat on the NYSE was $2,650,000 on August 23, 1999.

313

11-1 Starting a Corporation

OBJECTIVES

- Define accounting terms related to corporate accounting.
- Identify accounting concepts and practices related to corporate accounting.
- Journalize transactions related to starting a corporation.

MOTIVATE

Ask students to review the financial or business section of the newspaper for announcements of new stock issues; they may bring copies to class. Discuss the number of shares offered, type of stock, price per share, and name of company offering stock issue. Review some of the vocabulary used in the announcements, such as "securities," "prospectus," or "solicitation."

Preview

- Preview the accounting terms and definitions introduced in this lesson: corporation, board of directors, articles of incorporation, charter, common stock, preferred stock, stock certificate, par value, par-value stock, no-par-value stock, stated-value stock, and organization costs.
- Direct students to read the headings at the top of each page in this lesson and to examine the illustrations given.
- Explain that students are already familiar with certain aspects of a corporation. In this lesson, they will receive additional information on organizing a corporation.

MATERIALS

- Instructor's Resource CD: PowerPoint Slides
- Xtra! Study Tools on the Xtra! Web Site
- Blackline Masters: Cash Receipts Journal Cash Payments Journal
- Working Papers: Teacher's Edition of the Working Papers for Lesson 11-1
- Software: Personal Trainer

Selecting the form of business ownership is an important decision of new business owners. An organization with the legal rights of a person and that may be owned by many persons is called a **corporation**. [CONCEPT: Business Entity] A corporation is organized by law to exist separately and apart from its owners. Corporations differ from other forms of businesses principally in the nature of ownership and management.

A corporation's ownership is divided into units. Each unit of ownership is known as a share of stock. Total shares of ownership in a corporation are known as capital stock. An owner of one or more shares of a corporation is known as a stockholder.

Stockholders share a corporation's earnings. Earnings distributed to stockholders are known as dividends. Corporations may retain some or all of their earnings to finance future business expansion and improvement. However, most corporations distribute a portion of their earnings to stockholders.

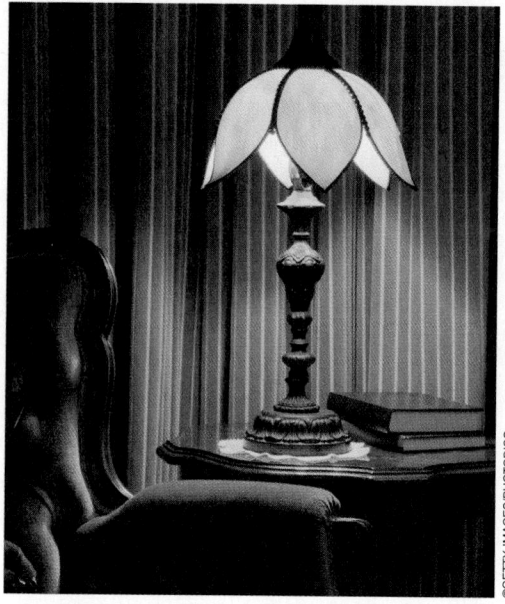

©GETTY IMAGES/PHOTODISC

making ethical decisions

MAKING ETHICAL DECISIONS • MAKING ETHICAL DECISIONS • MAKING ETHICAL DECISI

Just Following Orders

Step Productions is under contract with the federal government to produce training videos for the Environmental Protection Agency. The contract entitles Step Productions to charge its cost plus 15%. A government document outlines which expenditures qualify as "contract costs." The document specifically states that "expenses to entertain employees, suppliers, or other business partners do not qualify as contract costs."

After the annual company picnic, the company president told Jared Stern, who is a CPA, to record the picnic costs as a salary

expense. "This picnic will raise worker morale. The workers will be more productive—for every dollar we spend, we'll save two dollars on our payroll," stated the president, justifying his request.

Instructions

Use the ethical model to analyze whether the accountant's recording of the picnic costs as salary expense would demonstrate ethical behavior.

MAKING ETHICAL DECISIONS
MAKING ETHICAL DECISIONS

Some students may contend that the expense is justified because it will result in a net savings for the government. Without permission from the government, however, the company is violating the contract. The action could result in the company's disqualification for future contracts.

Although not required to analyze the action, the accountant would violate Rule 102 of the AICPA's Code of Professional Conduct (shall not knowingly misrepresent facts or subordinate his or her judgment to others).

A suggested solution is provided at the front of this Wraparound Teacher's Edition.

314

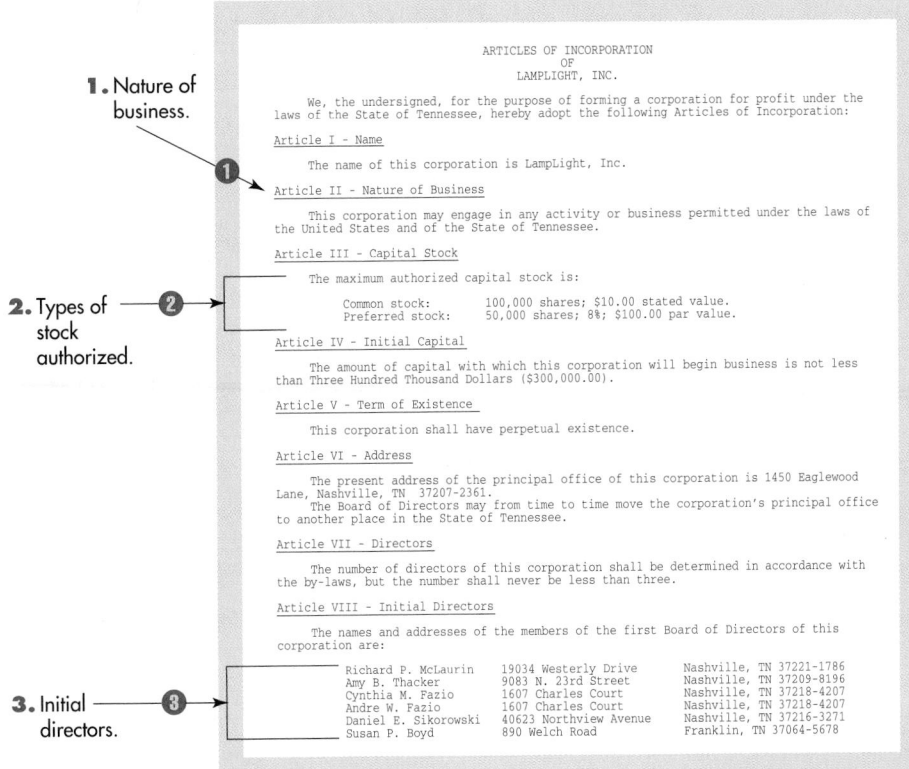

1. Nature of business.

2. Types of stock authorized.

3. Initial directors.

```
                        ARTICLES OF INCORPORATION
                                    OF
                             LAMPLIGHT, INC.

        We, the undersigned, for the purpose of forming a corporation for profit under the
   laws of the State of Tennessee, hereby adopt the following Articles of Incorporation:

   Article I - Name

        The name of this corporation is LampLight, Inc.

   Article II - Nature of Business

        This corporation may engage in any activity or business permitted under the laws of
   the United States and of the State of Tennessee.

   Article III - Capital Stock

        The maximum authorized capital stock is:

             Common stock:      100,000 shares; $10.00 stated value.
             Preferred stock:    50,000 shares; 8%; $100.00 par value.

   Article IV - Initial Capital

        The amount of capital with which this corporation will begin business is not less
   than Three Hundred Thousand Dollars ($300,000.00).

   Article V - Term of Existence

        This corporation shall have perpetual existence.

   Article VI - Address

        The present address of the principal office of this corporation is 1450 Eaglewood
   Lane, Nashville, TN  37207-2361.
        The Board of Directors may from time to time move the corporation's principal office
   to another place in the State of Tennessee.

   Article VII - Directors

        The number of directors of this corporation shall be determined in accordance with
   the by-laws, but the number shall never be less than three.

   Article VIII - Initial Directors

        The names and addresses of the members of the first Board of Directors of this
   corporation are:

        Richard P. McLaurin    19034 Westerly Drive      Nashville, TN 37221-1786
        Amy B. Thacker          9083 N. 23rd Street       Nashville, TN 37209-8196
        Cynthia M. Fazio        1607 Charles Court        Nashville, TN 37218-4207
        Andre W. Fazio          1607 Charles Court        Nashville, TN 37218-4207
        Daniel E. Sikorowski   40623 Northview Avenue     Nashville, TN 37216-3271
        Susan P. Boyd            890 Welch Road           Franklin, TN 37064-5678
```

- Explain the purpose of the board of directors is to represent the interests of owners not participating in the day-to-day management of the company.

- Explain that individuals seeking to form a corporation must submit an application to the state requesting permission to form a corporation. Point out that that even businesses organized as corporate not-for-profit entities must comply.

A corporation may have many owners. Most owners do not participate in the management of the business. Instead, they elect a small group to represent their combined interests and to be responsible for management of the corporation. A group of persons elected by the stockholders to manage a corporation is called a **board of directors**. A board of directors determines corporate policies and selects corporate officers to supervise the day-to-day management of the corporation.

Legal Requirements for Forming a Corporation

Persons seeking to form a corporation must submit an application to the state in which the company is to be incorporated. A written application requesting permission to form a corporation is called the **articles of incorporation**. Some articles of incorporation are submitted to the federal government, but most are submitted to a state government. When the articles of incorporation are approved, a corporation comes into existence. The approved articles of incorporation are called a **charter**. A charter is also referred to as a certificate of incorporation.

LampLight, Inc. is a corporation that sells lighting fixtures. The articles of incorporation submitted for LampLight, Inc. are shown above and on the next page.

- Direct students to read Article II of LampLight's articles of incorporation in the illustration. Ask them why this statement was written with such a broad purpose. Emphasize that companies often change as they evolve in an attempt to keep up with changing market demands. A narrow, specific statement would hinder a company's ability to expand into new business opportunities.

- Discuss the three basic rights of most stockholders.

- Point out that the type of stock, such as common or preferred, has an effect on certain stockholder rights. For example, preferred stock gives stockholders a preference in earnings.

- Direct students to the Remember feature to emphasize that although each company's articles of incorporation are unique, the articles address similar items.

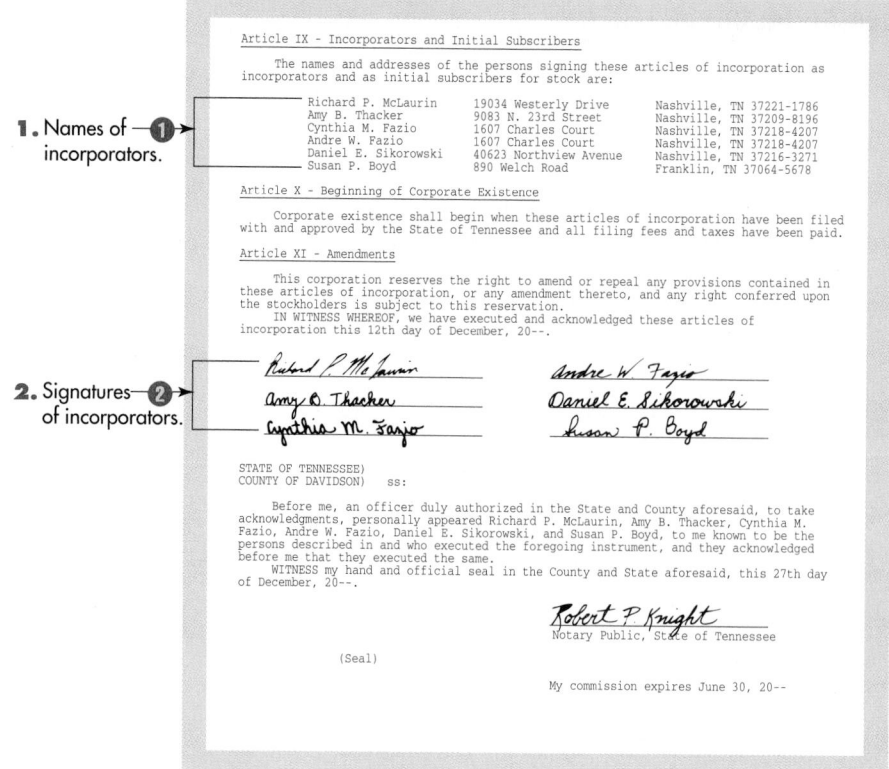

1. Names of incorporators.

2. Signatures of incorporators.

As stated, LampLight is organized as a corporation to sell lighting fixtures and accessories. However, Article II of its articles of incorporation describes the nature of the business in broad, general terms. This broad purpose enables LampLight to expand into other kinds of business activities, if it desires, without applying for a new charter.

Rights of Stockholders

Most stockholders have three basic rights.

1. To vote at stockholders' meetings unless an exception is made for holders of a particular kind of stock.

2. To share in a corporation's earnings.

3. To share in the distribution of the assets of the corporation if it ceases operations and sells all its assets.

Capital Stock of a Corporation

Corporations may issue two basic kinds of stock: common and preferred. Stock that does not give stockholders any special preferences is called **common stock**. Stock that gives stockholders preference in earnings and other rights is called **preferred stock**. LampLight is authorized to issue both common and preferred stock as described in Article III of the illustration on the previous page.

> **REMEMBER** Although the format of the articles of incorporation varies from one corporation to another, the articles usually address similar items.

TEACHING STRATEGIES   ACCOUNTING PEDAGOGY

This textbook acquaints students with procedures for organizing a corporation. It is important that students understand procedures for the start-up of all forms of business.

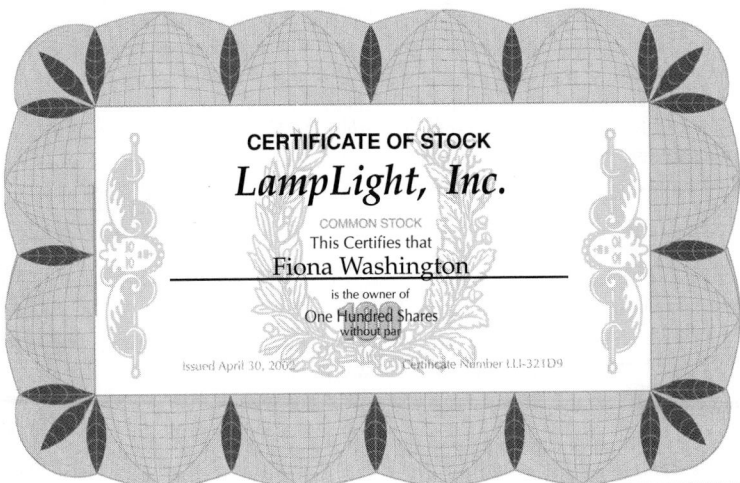

- Refer students to the illustration as stock certificates are discussed.
- Ask if any students or their parents have stock certificates. Ask what companies the stock certificates are for and the number of shares involved. Ask students the reasons for selecting those companies for investments.
- Ask students the distinction between par-value stock and stated-value stock. (*Par-value stock has an authorized value printed on the stock certificate; stated-value stock does not.*) Emphasize that from an accounting standpoint, par-value and stated-value stock are recorded in the same manner.
- Explain that if a company chooses to issue only one type of stock, that stock is common stock. Stress that each share of common stock gives the owner the right to share in earnings distributions, vote on matters brought before the stockholders, and share in the assets if the corporation liquidates.
- Direct students to the F.Y.I. to emphasize that most stock sold today is common stock.

Written evidence of the number of shares that each stockholder owns in a corporation is called a stock certificate. A corporation issues a stock certificate when it receives full payment for the stock. A **stock certificate**, such as the one shown above, usually states the issue date, certificate number, number of shares, and name of the stockholder.

A corporation keeps a record of stock issued to each stockholder. A stockholder may later decide to sell some or all shares of stock owned. Changing ownership of stock is referred to as a stock transfer. Some corporations handle the issuing and transferring of stock certificates as well as the record of stock ownership. Most corporations, however, engage a transfer agent, such as a bank, to issue certificates and keep stock ownership records.

Value of Stock

Shares of stock are frequently assigned a value. A value assigned to a share of stock and printed on the stock certificate is called **par value**. A share of stock that has an authorized value printed on the stock certificate is called **par-value stock**.

A share of stock that has no authorized value printed on the stock certificate is called **no-par-value stock**. Some states require that no-par-value stock be assigned a stated or specific value. No-par-value stock that is assigned a value by a corporation is called **stated-value stock**. Stated-value stock is similar to par-value stock except that the value is not printed on the stock certificates.

Common Stock

If a corporation issues only one type of stock, that stock is common stock. If a corporation issues only common stock, the common stockholders are entitled to all of the dividends. In most corporations, only owners of common stock have a right to vote on matters brought before the stockholders. LampLight is authorized to issue no-par-value common stock with a stated value of $10.00.

FYI FOR YOUR INFORMATION

Most stock sold today is common stock.

- Point out that some corporations issue two types of stock—common stock and preferred stock. Emphasize that preferred stock grants the holder certain preferences superior to those of common stock.

- Point out that one typical preference includes receiving dividends before common stockholders. Mention that sometimes unpaid dividends accumulate and that dividends above a stated percentage may be shared with common stockholders.

- Explain that preferred stockholders usually do not have voting rights and cannot influence the amount of dividend paid.

Preferred Stock

To attract more investors, a corporation may offer preferred stock with preferences as to some of the basic stockholders' rights. Preferred stockholders usually do not have voting rights and cannot influence when and how much is paid in dividends. Therefore, a typical preference given to preferred stockholders is to receive dividends before common stockholders. Other preferences granted preferred stockholders may include the following:

1. Unpaid dividends may accumulate from one year to another. In years that dividends are not paid, the preferred dividends accumulate and are paid in a later year. Accumulated preferred dividends must be paid before any common stock dividends are paid.
2. Dividends may be shared with common stockholders above a stated percentage or amount. Once the dividend to common stockholders equals the stated percentage of the preferred stock, additional dividends may be shared between preferred and common stockholders.

Every preference granted to preferred stockholders comes at the expense of common stockholders. For example, if preferred stockholders share in dividends above a stated percentage, common stockholders give up a right to some dividends. However, regardless of the type of stock issued, no stockholder is entitled to dividends until a corporation's board of directors votes to pay dividends.

Preferred stock dividends may be stated as a percentage of par value or as an amount per share. For example, LampLight has authorized the issuance of 8%, $100.00 par-value preferred stock.

©GETTY IMAGES/PHOTODISC

global perspective

GLOBAL PERSPECTIVE • GLOBAL PERSPECTIVE • GLOBAL PERSPECTIVE

International Packages and Customs Inspections

When sending a package overseas, appropriate documentation must accompany the package to verify its contents. Customs officials will read the documentation and may open the package to verify its contents.

All major trading nations use the Harmonized Commodity Description and Coding System (HS). HS establishes a single ten-digit code for each type of commodity. This code may be obtained from the Census Bureau's Foreign Trade Division.

Shipping restrictions apply to certain commodities. The Food and Drug Administration (FDA) regulates the import of items such as foods, pharmaceuticals, medical devices, and cosmetics. These restrictions protect American citizens from improperly tested items that could cause physical harm.

The U.S. Department of Agriculture (USDA) regulates the import of items such as meat and meat products, insects, plants,

fruits, and vegetables. Restrictions on shipments protect domestic horticulture from infection by disease or insects.

The Federal Communications Commission (FCC) regulates the import of such items as cordless telephones, video games, microwave ovens, and radio transmitters to protect the quality of consumer products.

Required

Obtain a guide from a carrier that provides the guidelines for sending a package internationally. Select a foreign country and assume that you are sending a package that contains a ten-page legal document. The package weighs less than two pounds.

1. Which forms must be completed to send the document?
2. How should you package the document?
3. How much will it cost?
4. When will it be delivered?

Organizing a Corporation and Paying Dividends

The Global Perspective feature is intended to expose students to some of the ways in which accounting and business in general differ in other countries. This feature allows students to explore international packages and customs inspections.

The Global Perspective activity requires students to research the forms and procedures required to send a small package to another country. Student responses will vary, depending on the countries that are chosen. Have students report their findings to the class.

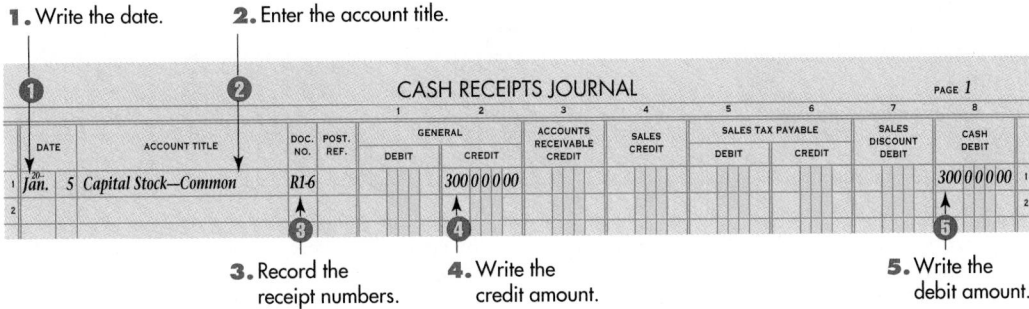

1. Write the date. **2.** Enter the account title.

3. Record the receipt numbers. **4.** Write the credit amount. **5.** Write the debit amount.

LampLight's charter is its legal authorization to begin business in the name of the corporation. The corporation needs assets to operate. It obtains its initial capital by selling stock to the incorporators.

Capital Accounts of a Corporation

Because of the number of owners, a corporation does not keep a separate capital account for each stockholder. Instead, it maintains a single summary general ledger capital account for each kind of stock issued. When a corporation issues only common stock, the value of all stock issued is recorded in a single capital stock account. When a corporation issues both common and preferred stock, separate capital stock accounts are used for common and preferred stock.

A corporation's net income is recorded in the capital account Retained Earnings. Using this account keeps the net income separate from the recorded values of issued capital stock. A net income is credited and a net loss is debited to Retained Earnings.

Issuing Capital Stock When Forming a Corporation

When the corporation is formed, each of Lamp-Light's six incorporators agrees to buy 5,000 shares of common stock at the stated value. Thus, a total of 30,000 shares of common stock, stated value $10.00, is issued for a total of $300,000.00.

> **January 5. Received cash from six incorporators for 30,000 shares of $10.00 stated-value common stock, $300,000.00. Receipt Nos. 1–6.**

Cash is debited for $300,000.00. Capital Stock—Common is credited for $300,000.00, the value of the issued common stock. The journal entry to record this transaction is shown above.

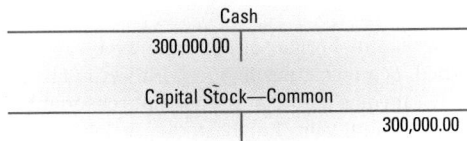

Cash	
300,000.00	

Capital Stock—Common	
	300,000.00

STEPS • STEPS • STEPS • STEPS • STEPS
JOURNALIZE THE ENTRY TO RECORD CASH RECEIVED FOR COMMON STOCK

1 Write the current year and the date in the Date column of the cash receipts journal.

2 Enter *Capital Stock—Common* in the Account Title column.

3 Record the receipt numbers, *R1–6*, in the Doc. No. column.

4 Write the credit amount, *300,000.00*, in the General Credit column.

5 Record the debit amount, *300,000.00*, in the Cash Debit column.

FYI FOR YOUR INFORMATION

A debit balance in Retained Earnings is often referred to as a deficit.

EXPLAIN

- Point out to students the difficulty of maintaining a separate general ledger capital account for each owner if there were 200,000 different stockholders. Emphasize that companies maintain a single summary account for each kind of stock issued such as Capital Stock—Common or Capital Stock—Preferred.

- Emphasize that the retained earnings account is used to record a corporation's earnings to keep income separate from issued stock.

DEMONSTRATE

Analyze the transaction

- Draw two blank T accounts on the board.
- Read the transaction statement.
- Ask students to analyze the transaction. Complete the T accounts as the information is provided.

Record the transaction

- Use the transparency of a cash receipts journal to illustrate the process for recording the entry in the journal or refer students to the illustration.

- Record each item in the journal following the five steps shown.

- Discuss the kinds of fees and expenses that may be included in organization costs, such as state incorporation fees, legal fees, and incidental expenses.

- Emphasize that these fees and expenses will benefit the corporation for many years to come. For this reason, these expenditures are recorded in an asset account, Organization Costs, until charged as an expense.

- Review the accounting concept of matching expenses with revenue.

- Direct students to the F.Y.I. to learn about stockholders right to purchase additional shares in proportion to the stockholder's present holding.

DEMONSTRATE

Analyze the transaction

- Draw two blank T accounts on the board.

- Read the transaction statement.

- Ask students to analyze the transaction. Complete the T accounts as the information is provided.

Record the transaction

- Use the cash payments transparency to illustrate the process for recording the entry in the journal or direct students to the illustration.

ONGOING ASSESSMENT

- Circulate through the classroom or lab, observing which students have problems with assignments.

- Troubleshooting: Students may have problems remembering the distinctions among the different classifications of stock.

- Assess student understanding by checking solutions to Independent Practice assignments.

RETEACH

- Divide the class into groups of six to eight students. Have each group plan the organization of a corporation. Each corporation is to be authorized 240,000 shares of $1.00 stated-value common stock and 50,000 shares of 10%, $100.00 par-value preferred stock. Have each group draft an articles of incorporation, following the illustrations on pages 315 and 316. Each group should decide on its own corporation name and address.

320

ORGANIZATION COSTS OF A CORPORATION

						GENERAL		ACCOUNTS PAYABLE DEBIT	PURCHASES DISCOUNT CREDIT	CASH CREDIT	
	DATE		ACCOUNT TITLE	CK. NO.	POST. REF.	DEBIT	CREDIT				
1	Jan.	5	Organization Costs	1		2 4 0 0 00				2 4 0 0 00	1
2											2
3											3

CASH PAYMENTS JOURNAL — PAGE 1

Fees and other expenses of organizing a corporation are called **organization costs**. Organization costs may include the following:

1. An incorporation fee paid to the state when the articles of incorporation are submitted.
2. Attorney fees for legal services during the process of incorporation.
3. Other incidental expenses incurred prior to receiving a charter.

A corporation cannot be formed without organization costs. Until it receives a charter, a corporation does not exist to pay the organization costs. The planning required to start a new corporation often takes months. Therefore, one of the incorporators usually agrees to pay these costs until the charter is granted. The incorporator or incorporators who agree to pay the organization cost should keep accurate and complete records of all amounts paid on behalf of the corporation. After it receives a charter, a corporation reimburses the incorporator for the organization costs.

If substantial organization costs were recorded as an expense in a corporation's first year, net income could be reduced unreasonably during that first year. Furthermore, benefits derived from these expenditures extend over

many years. Therefore, these costs are recorded in an asset account, Organization Costs, until charged as an expense. [*CONCEPT: Matching Expenses with Revenue*]

Adjusting entries to record portions of the organization costs as an expense each year are described in Chapter 13.

Amy Thacker agreed to pay the organization costs for LampLight until the company receives its charter. On January 5, Amy submitted a statement of organization costs, $2,400.00, that she had incurred prior to the receipt of the charter.

January 5. Paid cash to Amy Thacker as reimbursement for organization costs, $2,400.00. Check No. 1.

Organization Costs is debited for $2,400.00. Cash is credited for $2,400.00. The journal entry to record this transaction is shown above.

Organization Costs	
Jan. 5 2,400.00	

Cash	
	Jan. 5 2,400.00

©GETTY IMAGES/PHOTODISC

Explore Accounting

Intangible Assets

EXPLORE ACCOUNTING
EXPLORE ACCOUNTING

1. $50,000
2. $12,500
3. The company must write down the value of the patent to zero.

Assets of a nonphysical nature that have value for a business are known as *intangible assets*. Patents, trademarks, organization costs, brand names, copyrights, and goodwill (to be discussed in Chapter 21) are all examples of intangible assets.

When an intangible asset is acquired, it is recorded at its historic cost. On January 1, 20X1, Lyons Company purchased a patent from another company for $200,000. Lyons would make the following entry on the purchase date:

```
Patent............... $200,000
    Cash....................... $200,000
```

The portion of a plant asset's cost that is transferred to an expense account in each fiscal period during a plant asset's useful life is known as *depreciation expense*. The portion of an intangible asset's cost that is transferred to an expense account in each fiscal period during the life of the intangible asset is referred to as *amortization expense*.

The amount of yearly amortization expense should be based on the intangible asset's useful or legal life, whichever is less. When Lyons purchased the patent, it had a remaining legal life of five years. Lyons believed that the patent would be useful for at least five years. Therefore, the cost of the patent should be spread out over five years, the remaining useful life of the patent.

On December 31, 20X1, Lyons would make the following entry:

```
Amortization Expense .... $40,000
    Patent....................... $40,000
```

Under normal circumstances, Lyons would repeat this entry at the end of each of the next four years. At the end of the fifth year, when the patent expires, the balance of the Patent account would be zero. However, during 20X2 a competitor patents a device that makes Lyons's patent worthless. GAAP requires that a company must reevaluate the value of an intangible asset each year. If the asset value has been impaired, the asset must be written down immediately. Therefore, Lyons would make the following entry:

```
Amortization Expense ... $160,000
    Patent....................... $160,000
```

Instructions

On January 1, 20X1, Hayner Company purchased a copyright for $50,000. The copyright will expire on December 31, 20X4. Answer the following questions:

1. On January 1, 20X1, Hayner Company will debit Copyright for what amount?

2. On December 31, 20X1, Hayner Company will debit Amortization Expense for what amount?

3. On December 31, 20X2, Hayner Company determines that the copyright no longer has any value to the company. What must the company do?

GUIDED PRACTICE

Terms Review

- Ask students to write the definitions for each term presented in the Terms Review. Allow students to use their texts.

- Ask different students to read their definitions. After each definition is read, ask the class if the definition is correct and whether the complete definition has been given or if anything needs to be added. Suggested definitions are provided in the Glossary.

Audit Your Understanding

Call on students to answer the Audit Your Understanding questions. Ask the class if the answer is correct and/or complete. Answers are given in Appendix E of the textbook.

Work Together

- Have students write the solution to the Work Together problem as you guide the class through the examples.

• terms review

corporation
board of directors
articles of incorporation
charter
common stock
preferred stock
stock certificate
par value
par-value stock
no-par-value stock
stated-value stock
organization costs

• audit your understanding

1. What are the responsibilities of a corporation's board of directors?
2. What three basic rights do stockholders usually have?
3. What two basic kinds of stock may a corporation issue?
4. In place of a general ledger capital account for each owner, how does a corporation show stock ownership?
5. What accounts are affected, and how, when a corporation initially sells and issues common stock to incorporators?
6. What three items may be included in the organization costs of a corporation?

• work together 11-1

Journalizing transactions for starting a corporation

Presidential Limousine, Inc., received its corporate charter on April 2 of the current year. The corporation is authorized to issue 50,000 shares of $20.00 stated-value stock. A cash receipts journal and a cash payments journal are provided in the *Working Papers*. Source documents are abbreviated as follows: check, C; receipt, R. Your instructor will guide you through the following examples.

1.   Journalize the following transactions. Save your work to complete Work Together 11-2 on page 327.

Apr.   3.   Received cash from four incorporators for 30,000 shares of $20.00 stated-value common stock, $600,000.00. R1–4.
       4.   Paid cash to Julie Albrecht as reimbursement for organization costs, $10,000.00. C1.

---

on your own 11-1

Journalizing transactions for starting a corporation

Sierra Corporation received its corporate charter on June 3 of the current year. The corporation is authorized to issue 80,000 shares of $10.00 stated-value stock. A cash receipts journal and a cash payments journal are provided in the *Working Papers*. Source documents are abbreviated as follows: check, C; receipt, R. Work this problem independently.

1. Journalize the following transactions. Save your work to complete On Your Own 11-2 on page 327.

   June 3. Received cash from three incorporators for 40,000 shares of $10.00 stated-value common stock, $400,000.00. R1–3.
         5. Paid cash to Raul Mendoza as reimbursement for organization costs, $15,000.00. C1.

cultural diversity

CULTURAL DIVERSITY • CULTURAL DIVERSITY • CULTURAL DIVERSITY

Businesses Owned by Asian Americans and Other Related Groups

The Census Bureau's Survey of Minority-Owned Business Enterprises indicates that minority-owned enterprises are increasing in number and size. The Census Bureau groups together its statistics about businesses owned by Asian Americans, American Indians, Alaskan Natives, and Pacific Islanders. For this discussion, such businesses will be referred to as API/AIAN-owned businesses. Firms owned by this segment of the population increased from 376,711 in 1987 to 606,438 in 1992. This represents a 61 percent increase. During the same period, total receipts increased by 194 percent from $34 billion to $100 billion. These increases represent the fastest growing segment of the minority-enterprise business groups.

About 83 percent of API/AIAN-owned firms operated as proprietorships in 1992. These businesses accounted for 35.4 percent of the gross receipts of API/AIAN-owned businesses. During the period from 1987 to 1992, there was a large increase in both partnerships and Subchapter S corporations owned by Asian Americans, American Indians, Alaskan Natives, and Pacific Islanders.

Forty-five percent of API/AIAN-owned businesses operated in the service industries, primarily in business, personal, and health services. Another 22 percent of the API/AIAN-owned firms operated in the retail trades. Average receipts of API/AIAN-owned businesses were $165,000, compared with $193,000 for all U.S. firms. Average receipts of API/AIAN-owned companies exceeded those for all U.S. firms in the construction and service industries.

INDEPENDENT PRACTICE

On Your Own

- Assign the On Your Own problem to be worked independently.
- Use the Ongoing Assessment techniques to diagnose student understanding.

Application Problem

- Assign Application Problem 11-1: Journalizing transactions for starting a corporation.

Personal Trainer

- Students can access the Lesson 11-1 assessment material using this software.

Xtra! Web Site

- Students can access the Xtra! Study Tools for additional practice.

ENRICH

- Assign Making Ethical Decisions on page 314.
- Assign the Global Perspective feature on page 318.
- Assign Explore Accounting on page 321.
- Assign the Cultural Diversity feature on page 323.

CLOSE

- Ask students to write a brief paragraph on the significance of selecting the corporate form of business ownership. Students should define the term corporation and explain how corporations differ from other forms of businesses.

CULTURAL DIVERSITY

The Cultural Diversity feature is intended to expose students to the concept that our society is composed of people from many different cultural backgrounds. The features show the benefits of a culturally diverse society. (1) Read the feature. (2) Discuss the specific information in the feature. (3) Clarify any terms or questions.

11-2 Stock Subscriptions and the Balance Sheet

JOURNALIZING A STOCK SUBSCRIPTION

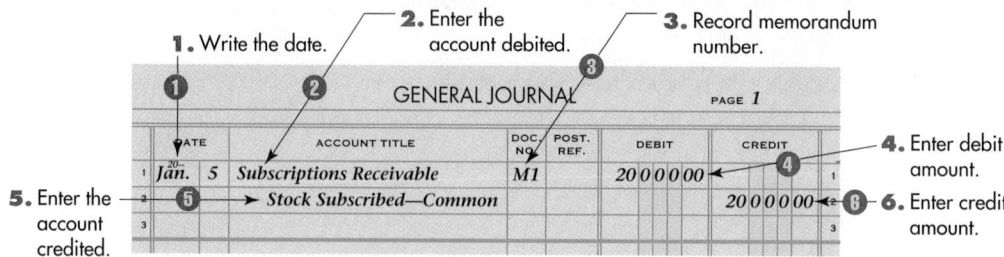

1. Write the date.
2. Enter the account debited.
3. Record memorandum number.
4. Enter debit amount.
5. Enter the account credited.
6. Enter credit amount.

	DATE		ACCOUNT TITLE	DOC. NO.	POST. REF.	DEBIT	CREDIT	
1	20-- Jan.	5	Subscriptions Receivable	M1		20 0 0 0 00		1
2			Stock Subscribed—Common				20 0 0 0 00	2
3								3

GENERAL JOURNAL — PAGE 1

Corporations frequently contract with investors to sell capital stock with payment to be received at a later date. Future payment for the stock may be made all at one time or on an installment plan. Entering into an agreement with a corporation to buy capital stock and pay at a later date is called **subscribing for capital stock**.

On January 5, Daniel Herring subscribed for 2,000 shares of LampLight's common stock at $10.00 a share. He agreed to pay $10,000.00 on March 1 and $10,000.00 not later than July 1.

January 5. Received a subscription from Daniel Herring for 2,000 shares of $10.00 stated-value common stock, $20,000.00. Memorandum No. 1.

The journal entry to record this transaction is shown above. Subscriptions Receivable is debited

for $20,000.00. The asset account Subscriptions Receivable shows the unpaid amount of all subscriptions. Stock Subscribed—Common is credited for $20,000.00. The capital account Stock Subscribed—Common shows the total amount of stock subscribed but not issued. This capital account is used because stock certificates are issued only when the stock is fully paid for. The amounts are recorded in Capital Stock—Common only when stock is fully paid for and stock certificates are issued.

Subscriptions Receivable	
20,000.00	

Stock Subscribed—Common	
	20,000.00

STEPS

JOURNALIZE THE ENTRY TO RECORD A STOCK SUBSCRIPTION

1. Write the current year and the date in the Date column of the general journal.
2. Enter the title of the account debited, *Subscriptions Receivable*, on line 1 in the Account Title column.
3. Record memorandum number, *M1*, in the Doc. No. column.
4. Write the debit amount, *20,000.00*, in the Debit column.
5. Enter the title of the account credited, *Stock Subscribed—Common,* in the Account Title column.
6. Write the credit amount, *20,000.00*, in the Credit column.

> **REMEMBER** Holders of subscribed stock have no voting rights.

JOURNALIZING CASH RECEIVED FOR A STOCK SUBSCRIPTION

CASH RECEIPTS JOURNAL   PAGE 3

					1 GENERAL DEBIT	2 GENERAL CREDIT	3 ACCOUNTS RECEIVABLE CREDIT	4 SALES CREDIT	5 SALES TAX PAYABLE DEBIT	6 SALES TAX PAYABLE CREDIT	7 SALES DISCOUNT DEBIT	8 CASH DEBIT
DATE	ACCOUNT TITLE	DOC. NO.	POST. REF.									
Mar. 1	Subscriptions Receivable	R45				10 000 00						10 000 00

On March 1, LampLight received cash from Daniel Herring in payment of half of his stock subscription. The journal entry to record this transaction is shown above.

March 1. Received cash from Daniel Herring in partial payment of stock subscription, $10,000.00. Receipt No. 45.

Cash is debited for $10,000.00. Subscriptions Receivable is credited for $10,000.00. The new balance of this account, $10,000.00, is the amount

that Daniel still owes for his stock subscription. A similar journal entry is made on July 1 when Daniel pays the second installment of the stock subscription.

Cash	
Mar. 1 10,000.00	

Subscriptions Receivable	
Jan. 5 20,000.00	Mar. 1 10,000.00
(New Bal. 10,000.00)	

JOURNALIZING ISSUANCE OF STOCK PREVIOUSLY SUBSCRIBED

GENERAL JOURNAL   PAGE 7

	DATE	ACCOUNT TITLE	DOC. NO.	POST. REF.	DEBIT	CREDIT	
1	July 1	Stock Subscribed—Common	M67		20 000 00		1
2		Capital Stock—Common				20 000 00	2

When a stock subscription is fully paid for, a stock certificate is issued to the stockholder. The journal entry to record the issuance of stock to Daniel is shown above.

July 1. Issued Stock Certificate No. 7 to Daniel Herring for 2,000 shares of $10.00 stated-value common stock. Memorandum No. 67.

Stock Subscribed—Common is debited for $20,000.00. Capital Stock—Common is credited for $20,000.00. The new balance of this account, $320,000.00, is the value of all common stock issued by LampLight.

LampLight records the issuance of stock only to the original stockholder. A stockholder may later

decide to sell shares of stock. LampLight does not journalize such stock transfers because these transactions do not generate additional capital for the corporation. However, the name of the new stockholder must be entered in LampLight's stock ownership records so that future dividend payments will be made to the correct person.

Stock Subscribed—Common	
July 1 20,000.00	Jan. 5 20,000.00
	(New Bal. zero)

Capital Stock—Common	
	Jan. 5 300,000.00
	July 1 20,000.00
	(New Bal. 320,000.00)

325

- Ask students to provide a list of assets. This list might include: cash, merchandise, office furniture, supplies, equipment, buildings, and land. Discuss the difference between regular assets and intangible assets. Emphasize that intangible assets are of a nonphysical nature; however, like regular assets they do have a value and provide future benefits.

- Review the concept of the balance sheet. Ask students what a balance sheet reports. Emphasize that the balance sheet shows what a company owns *(assets)*, owes *(liabilities)*, and is worth *(stockholders' equity)* on a specific date.

- Write the T accounts for the transactions discussed on pages 324 and 325. Using these six T accounts, ask the students what Lamplight currently owns, owes, and is worth.

- Ask students to prepare a list of assets, liabilities, and stockholders' equity accounts with up-to-date balances. Write this information on the board or overhead under the appropriate headings of assets, liabilities, and stockholders' equity.

- Use the information provided by the students and a blank transparency to prepare a balance sheet for LampLight as of January 5.

- Circulate through the classroom or lab, observing which students have problems with assignments.

- Troubleshooting: Students may have difficulty remembering which accounts to use when journalizing transactions involving stock subscriptions and issuing stock for paid-off subscriptions.

- Assess student understanding by checking solutions to Independent Practice assignments.

BALANCE SHEET OF A NEWLY FORMED CORPORATION

LampLight, Inc.
Balance Sheet
January 5, 20--

1. List intangible assets as the last category of assets. ➊

2. List sources of paid-in capital. ➋

ASSETS		
Current Assets:		
Cash	$297,600.00	
Subscriptions Receivable	20,000.00	
Total Current Assets		$317,600.00
Intangible Asset:		
Organization Costs		2,400.00
Total Assets		$320,000.00

STOCKHOLDERS' EQUITY		
Paid-in Capital:		
Capital Stock—Common (30,000 shares, $10.00 stated value)	$300,000.00	
Stock Subscribed— Common (2,000 shares)	20,000.00	
Total Paid-in Capital		320,000.00
Total Stockholders' Equity		$320,000.00

LampLight's balance sheet at the end of business on January 5 is shown above.

LampLight's cash on hand, January 5, is the original $300,000.00 paid by the incorporators *minus* the $2,400.00 paid for organization costs. The subscriptions receivable on January 5 is the amount due from Daniel Herring.

Assets of a nonphysical nature that have value for a business are called **intangible assets**. The heading, Intangible Asset, is listed on the balance sheet as the last subdivision in the Assets section. The asset account Organization Costs is presented in the intangible assets section. A corporation with long-term investments and plant assets shows them on a balance sheet before intangible assets.

Paid-in capital is a subdivision of the stockholders' equity section of a balance sheet. LampLight's paid-in capital on January 5 consists of $300,000.00 in issued common stock plus $20,000.00 in common stock subscribed. LampLight has not yet issued any preferred stock. Therefore, no amount for preferred stock is shown on the balance sheet.

FYI FOR YOUR INFORMATION

The Securities and Exchange Commission (SEC), established in 1934, helps regulate the offering, buying, and selling of securities, including capital stock.

REMEMBER To publicly sell large issues of stock, a corporation must have the approval of the Securities and Exchange Commission (SEC) to certify that information about the business is not being concealed.

Organizing a Corporation and Paying Dividends

- Draw four T accounts arranged in a vertical column on the board or overhead.

- Label the top account Cash, the second Subscriptions Receivable, the third Stock Subscribed—Common, and the bottom Capital Stock—Common.

- Start with a $10,000 stock subscription, show $10,000 received for the subscription, and finish with the issuance of stock.

- Emphasize that Cash and Capital Stock—Common now show balances of $10,000.00. The remaining accounts show zero balances.

terms review

subscribing for capital stock
intangible assets

audit your understanding

1. What accounts are affected, and how, when subscribed stock is issued?
2. How are assets of a nonphysical nature reported on the balance sheet?

work together 11-2

Journalizing transactions for stock subscriptions and preparing a balance sheet

Use the working papers from Work Together 11-1 on page 322. A general journal and statement paper are provided in the *Working Papers*. Source documents are abbreviated as follows: memorandum, M; receipt, R. Your instructor will guide you through the following examples.

1. Journalize the following transactions.

Apr. 7. Received a subscription from Robert Companari for 5,000 shares of $20.00 stated-value common stock, $100,000.00. M1.
24. Received cash from Robert Companari in payment of stock subscription, $100,000.00. R5.
25. Issued Stock Certificate No. 5 to Robert Companari for 5,000 shares of $20.00 stated-value common stock, $100,000.00. M2.

2. Prepare a balance sheet for Presidential Limousine as of April 30 of the current year.

on your own 11-2

Journalizing transactions for stock subscriptions and preparing a balance sheet

Use the working papers from On Your Own 11-1 on page 323. A general journal and statement paper are provided in the *Working Papers*. Source documents are abbreviated as follows: memorandum, M; receipt, R. Work this problem independently.

1. Journalize the following transactions.

June 11. Received a subscription from Jan Lee for 1,000 shares of $10.00 stated-value common stock, $10,000.00. M1.
19. Received a subscription from Bill Ackermann for 3,000 shares of $10.00 stated-value common stock, $30,000.00. M2.
24. Received cash from Jan Lee in payment of stock subscription, $10,000.00. R4.
25. Issued Stock Certificate No. 4 to Jan Lee for 1,000 shares of $10.00 stated-value common stock, $10,000.00. M3.

2. Prepare a balance sheet for Sierra Corporation as of June 30 of the current year.

Stock Subscriptions and the Balance Sheet
Lesson 11-2   **327**

327

11-3 Calculating and Journalizing Dividends for a Corporation

328

DIVIDENDS

Once operations begin, a new corporation usually retains a portion of net income to finance future business expansion and improvement. However, most corporations distribute a portion of the earnings to stockholders.

Corporate earnings distributed to stockholders are known as dividends. Action by a board of directors to distribute corporate earnings to stockholders is called **declaring a dividend**. The board determines when and what amount of the retained earnings will be distributed. A corporation has no obligation to distribute money to stockholders until the board of directors has declared a dividend.

Three important dates are involved in distributing a dividend:

1. Date of declaration. The date on which a board of directors votes to distribute a dividend is called the **date of declaration**.
2. Date of record. The date that determines which stockholders are to receive dividends is called the **date of record**. Stockholders may buy and sell stock at any time. However, only persons listed as stockholders on the date of record will receive dividends.
3. Date of payment. The date on which dividends are actually to be paid to stockholders is called the **date of payment**. Ordinarily, the date of payment occurs several weeks after the date of record. Thus, a corporation has time to determine who is entitled to receive dividends and to prepare dividend checks to mail on the date of payment.

Transactions are recorded in a corporation's accounts on two of the three dates: (1) date of declaration and (2) date of payment.

Calculating a Dividend

When a board of directors declares a dividend, the corporation is obligated to pay it. At the date of declaration, the corporation incurs a liability that must be recorded.

The board of directors of CompuForm, Inc. has decided to declare an annual dividend of $24,000.00. On the date of record, the corporation has issued 1,000 shares of 8%, $100.00 par-value preferred stock and 16,000 shares of $20.00 stated-value common stock. The value of the preferred and common stock is calculated as follows.

Number of Preferred Shares	×	Par Value	=	Value of Preferred Stock
1,000	×	$100.00	=	$100,000.00

Number of Common Shares	×	Stated Value	=	Value of Common Stock
16,000	×	$20.00	=	$320,000.00

REMEMBER No stockholder is guaranteed a dividend.

The value of preferred stock is used to calculate the dividend on preferred stock. The distribution of the $24,000.00 dividend between preferred and common stock is calculated as follows:

	Value of Preferred Stock	×	Preferred Dividend Rate	=	Preferred Dividend Amount
	$100,000.00	×	8%	=	$8,000.00

	Total Amount Available for Dividends	−	Preferred Dividend Amount	=	Amount Available for Common Dividends
	$24,000.00	−	$8,000.00	=	$16,000.00

The dividend rate for common stock is calculated as follows:

	Common Dividend Amount	÷	Value of Common Stock	=	Common Dividend Rate
	$16,000.00	÷	$320,000.00	=	5%

A summary of CompuForm's dividends follows.

	Amount	Rate
Preferred Stock Dividends	$ 8,000.00	8%
Common Stock Dividends	16,000.00	5%

In subsequent years, CompuForm may elect to increase its annual dividend. CompuForm's preferred stock dividend rate will never exceed 8%. Therefore, additional dividends will be distributed to common stock, increasing the common stock dividend rate. The common stock dividend rate may be less than, equal to, or more than the preferred stock dividend rate.

business structures

BUSINESS STRUCTURES • BUSINESS STRUCTURES • BUSINESS STRUCTURES

Advantages and Disadvantages of a Corporation

Organizing a corporation is as simple as filing an application with the appropriate state agency. The approved application establishes the corporation as a legal entity, giving the corporation many of the same legal rights and risks as individuals have, including owning assets, borrowing money, paying taxes, and being sued.

The corporate form of business organization has several advantages over a sole proprietorship:

• *Limited liability.* The liability of stockholders is limited to their investment in the corporation.
• *Supply of capital.* Individuals are more willing to invest in a corporation because their personal assets are protected by limited liability.

However, there are also some disadvantages to a corporation:

• *Shared decision making.* Significant business decisions must be approved by a vote of the stockholders.
• *Shared profits.* The earnings of the corporation are divided among the stockholders.
• *Taxation.* The earnings of a corporation may be subject to federal and state income taxes. When the earnings of the

corporation are distributed to the stockholders, individual stockholders may also have to pay income taxes on the dividends. Thus, the earnings of a corporation can be taxed twice, a concept known as *double taxation.*

Proper planning can offer stockholders the advantage of limited liability while avoiding the disadvantage of double taxation. Thus, although the application for incorporation can be prepared without the help of an attorney or accountant, consulting with these professionals is recommended.

Critical Thinking
1. Think of two businesses you might be interested in starting. Describe whether the proprietorship or corporation form of organization would be better suited for this business.
2. Often a person who has started a proprietorship and run it successfully for many years sells the business to a corporation. Why would a corporation be interested in buying such a business?

BUSINESS STRUCTURES
BUSINESS STRUCTURES

1. Students' solutions will vary. For the typical high school student starting a business, such as lawn maintenance, babysitting, etc., organizing the business as a sole proprietorship is easy and inexpensive. As the business grows, the student should consider spending the time and money required to organize the business as a corporation.

2. Most corporations are interested in increasing revenue. Purchasing an established business is the quickest method of increasing revenue.

- Remind students that once dividends are declared, they must be paid. Point out that since cash is not paid out the same day dividends are declared, the cash account cannot be credited.

- Emphasize that since cash is owed as a result of the declaration of dividends, Dividends Payable is credited.

- Ask students how they would classify Dividends—Common (contra capital).

DEMONSTRATE

Analyze the transaction

- Draw two blank T accounts on the board.
- Read the transaction statement.
- Ask students to analyze the transaction. Complete the T accounts as the information is provided.

Record the transaction

- Use the general journal transparency to illustrate the process for recording the entry or direct students to the illustration.

EXPLAIN

- Emphasize that when the dividends are paid Dividends Payable is debited to show the decrease in the amount owed.

- Ask students what journal should be used to record the cash payment of dividends.

DEMONSTRATE

Analyze the transaction

- Draw two blank T accounts on the board.
- Read the transaction statement.
- Ask students to analyze the transaction. Complete the T accounts as the information is provided.

Record the transaction

- Use the cash payments journal transparency to illustrate the process for recording the entry or direct students to the illustration.

JOURNALIZING DECLARATION OF DIVIDEND

	DATE		ACCOUNT TITLE	DOC. NO.	POST. REF.	DEBIT	CREDIT	
1	Dec.	15	Dividends—Common	M132		16 0 0 0 00		1
2			Dividends—Preferred			8 0 0 0 00		2
3			Dividends Payable				24 0 0 0 00	3

GENERAL JOURNAL   PAGE 12

The journal entry to record the transaction needed when the dividends are declared is shown above.

December 15. CompuForm's board of directors declared an annual dividend of $24,000.00. Preferred stock issued is $100,000.00 of 8%, $100.00 par-value preferred stock. Common stock issued is $320,000.00 of $20.00 stated-value common stock. Date of payment is January 15. Memorandum No. 132.

Dividends—Common is debited for $16,000.00. Dividends—Preferred is debited for $8,000.00. Dividends Payable is credited for $24,000.00.

JOURNALIZING PAYMENT OF A DIVIDEND

CASH PAYMENTS JOURNAL   PAGE 1

	DATE	ACCOUNT TITLE	CK. NO.	POST. REF.	GENERAL DEBIT	GENERAL CREDIT	ACCOUNTS PAYABLE DEBIT	PURCHASES DISCOUNT CREDIT	CASH CREDIT	
18	15	Dividends Payable	432		24 0 0 0 00				24 0 0 0 00	18

On January 15, CompuForm issued a single check for $24,000.00, the total amount of the dividends to be paid. The check is deposited in a special dividend checking account. A separate check to each eligible stockholder is written against the special checking account. This procedure avoids a large number of entries in CompuForm's cash payments journal. The special dividend checking account also reserves cash specifically for paying the dividends.

CompuForm's dividend check is given to an agent who handles the details of preparing and mailing stockholders' checks. CompuForm's agent is the bank with which the corporation has its checking account.

January 15. Paid cash for annual dividend declared December 15, $24,000.00. Check No. 432.

Dividends Payable is debited and Cash is credited for $24,000.00. The journal entry to record this transaction is shown above.

{ REMEMBER Dividends may be paid in additional capital stock, known as a stock dividend, instead of cash. Dividends Payable is debited and Capital Stock is credited when the stock is issued on the date of payment. }

ONGOING ASSESSMENT

- Circulate through the classroom or lab, observing which students have problems with assignments.

- Troubleshooting: Students may have difficulty remembering which accounts to use when journalizing transactions

involving the declaration and payment of dividends.

- Assess student understanding by checking solutions to Independent Practice assignments.

RETEACH

- Use three T accounts Dividends—Common, Dividends Payable, and Cash to demonstrate the declaration and payment of a $15,000 dividend.

careers in accounting

CAREERS IN ACCOUNTING • CAREERS IN ACCOUNTING • CAREERS IN ACCOUNTING

Steve Robertson, Diverse Accounting Background

CAREERS IN ACCOUNTING
CAREERS IN ACCOUNTING

The Careers in Accounting feature profiles people who are entrepreneurs, who are working in accounting-related fields, or who use accounting in their business lives.

Students can access the Careers section of the Xtra! Web Site for additional material about careers.

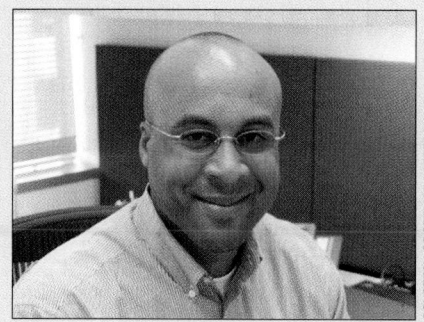

COURTESY OF STEVE ROBERTSON

Silicon Valley in California is recognized throughout the world for its innovation, development, and creative uses of technology. Many of the high-tech applications developed there have had an impact on movie making, the Internet, portable music players, computer games, semiconductors, computer security, wireless applications, cellular phones, personal digital assistants, telecommunications, and biotechnology. With such a diverse business environment in the San Francisco Bay area, a wide variety of career possibilities exists.

From the beginning of his professional life, Steve Robertson was determined to accumulate a variety of business experiences. Before changing employers during his career, however, Steve decided he would follow two important criteria: (1) each new job had to be more challenging and (2) each new job had to increase significantly in terms of responsibility and scope.

After graduating from Santa Clara University with a major in accounting, Steve accepted a position with Ernst & Young, LLP, where he audited a variety of companies and reviewed financial statements for accuracy. Shortly after becoming a certified public accountant (CPA), he moved into corporate finance at Silicon Graphics, Inc., where he gained valuable experience as a financial analyst.

Steve's next employment was as an assistant controller at HMT Technology Corporation. At HMT, he became very proficient at month-end closings, cost accounting, and creating financial reports for stockholders and other interested parties in the public domain. Steve's next position was controller at RockShox, Inc., where he was responsible for the entire accounting department, banking, insurance issues, and financial reporting as required by the Securities and Exchange Commission.

At this point in his career, Steve decided he needed to experience life at a startup company. He became controller at Counterpane Internet Security, Inc., where he handled not only the accounting duties but also human resources, contract administration, purchasing, and all corporate budgeting and forecasting.

Recently, Steve began working at Echelon Corporation. There, he is involved in all aspects of accounting and finance functions for the entire global organization, as well as treasury components, insurance, investor relations, and other regulatory issues.

Steve is not finished with his career yet. With his experience, he expects that eventually he will become a vice-president of finance, a corporate treasurer, a chief financial officer, or perhaps a financial consultant. Steve's diverse accounting and financial background makes it all very possible.

Salary Range: $135,000–$175,000 for accountants in upper-management positions.

Qualifications: Steve recommends earning a bachelor's degree in business and enrolling in a solid core of accounting classes. He feels that one of the most critical components for success in the accounting field is an individual's ability to identify the accounts being affected by an actual or hypothetical transaction and understanding the transaction's impact on a balance sheet and income statement. Steve also advocates that students participate in job shadowing experiences to acquaint themselves with the many career possibilities within accounting.

Occupational Outlook: During the next decade, Steve foresees a renewed interest in hiring experienced and competent certified public accountants. He believes that recent accounting scandals and the financial disasters occurring during the dot-com craze emphasize the need for sound accounting practices.

Calculating and Journalizing Dividends for a Corporation

GUIDED PRACTICE

Terms Review

Call on students to define each term in the Terms Review. After each definition ask the class if the definition is correct and whether the complete definition has been given or if anything else needs to be added. Suggested definitions are given in the Glossary.

Audit Your Understanding

Call on students to answer the Audit Your Understanding questions. Ask the class if the answer is correct and/or complete. Answers are given in Appendix E of the textbook.

Work Together

Have students write the solution to the Work Together problem as you guide the class through the examples.

- Call on students to assist in the calculation of stock values and dividend amounts.
- Ask students to verify calculations with a calculator.
- Call on students to read and analyze a transaction.
- Use T accounts to help student analysis and to record responses.
- Direct students to record each transaction in the appropriate journal as you guide the class through the examples.

INDEPENDENT PRACTICE

On Your Own

- Assign the On Your Own problem to be worked independently.
- Use the Ongoing Assessment techniques to diagnose student understanding.

Application Problems

- Assign Application Problem 11-3: Calculating dividends for a corporation.
- Assign Application Problem 11-4: Journalizing transactions for declaring and paying dividends.

Personal Trainer

- Students can access the Lesson 11-3 assessment material using this software.

Xtra! Web Site

- Students can access the Xtra! Study Tools for additional practice.

332

• terms review

declaring a dividend
date of declaration
date of record
date of payment

• audit your understanding

1. Who determines when and what amount of retained earnings that a corporation will distribute as dividends?
2. Why does a corporation record a liability when a dividend is declared?
3. What are two reasons for using a special dividend checking account?

• work together 11-3

Calculating and journalizing the dividends for a corporation

On January 10 of the current year, the board of directors of Eagle Express, Inc. declared an annual dividend of $60,000.00. On the date of record, the corporation had issued 2,000 shares of 6%, $100.00 par-value preferred stock and 30,000 shares of $22.00 stated-value common stock.

Page 4 of a general journal and page 11 of a cash payments journal are provided in the *Working Papers*. Source documents are abbreviated as follows: check, C; memorandum, M. Your instructor will guide you through the following examples.

1. Calculate the value of preferred stock.
2. Calculate the amount of dividends for the current year to be paid to preferred and common shareholders.
3. Journalize the entry to record the declaration of a dividend on January 10. M29.
4. Journalize the entry to record the payment of the dividend on January 30. C124.

• on your own 11-3

Calculating and journalizing the dividends for a corporation

On July 2 of the current year, the board of directors of StarVideo Corporation declared an annual dividend of $90,000.00. On the date of record, the corporation had issued 3,500 shares of 8%, $80.00 par-value preferred stock and 60,000 shares of $12.00 stated-value common stock.

Page 7 of a general journal and page 14 of a cash payments journal are provided in the *Working Papers*. Source documents are abbreviated as follows: check, C; memorandum, M. Work this problem independently.

1. Calculate the value of preferred stock.
2. Calculate the amount of dividends for the current year to be paid to preferred and common shareholders.
3. Journalize the entry to record the declaration of a dividend on July 2. M87.
4. Journalize the entry to record the payment of the dividend on August 2. C326.

ENRICH

- Assign the Business Structures feature on page 329.
- Assign the Careers in Accounting feature on page 331.
- Students can use the Peachtree or QuickBooks data files to automate Application Problem 11-4.

CLOSE

- Ask students to prepare a list of new accounts introduced in this lesson. These accounts include: Dividends—Common, Dividends—Preferred, and Dividends Payable.
- Ask students to draw T accounts for each under the appropriate headings Assets, Liabilities, and Stockholders' Equity.
- Ask students to place a "+" or "−" on the appropriate increase or decrease side on each account.

SUMMARY · SUMMARY

SUMMARY

After completing this chapter, you can

1. Define accounting terms related to corporate accounting.

2. Identify accounting concepts and practices related to corporate accounting.

3. Journalize transactions related to starting a corporation.

4. Journalize transactions related to stock subscriptions.

5. Prepare a balance sheet for a newly formed corporation.

6. Calculate dividends for a corporation.

7. Journalize transactions of a corporation related to declaring and paying dividends.

Explore Accounting

EXPLORE ACCOUNTING · EXPLORE ACCOUNTING · EXPLORE ACCOUN

Stock Splits

Most stock purchases are made in multiples of 100 shares. A stock trade of 100 shares is called a round lot. A stock trade in an amount other than a multiple of 100 shares is called an odd lot. Because brokerage firms typically charge additional fees for odd lot trades, investors have a financial incentive to trade stock only in round lots.

As the market price per share rises, the total cost of a round lot can exceed the financial resources of the average individual investor. For example, a round lot of a stock trading at $60 per share would cost $6,000 plus brokerage fees. The demand for the stock declines when individual investors become unable to purchase the stock. This decline in demand has a negative effect on the stock's market value.

One solution to this problem is to reduce the stock's market price to a reasonable amount. To reduce the market price, a corporation can increase the number of shares outstanding by dividing each outstanding share into two or more shares. Dividing a share of stock into a larger number of shares is called a stock split. In a 2-for-1 stock split, the company doubles the number of shares and reduces each share's par value by half. Thus, an investor holding 100 shares of $10 par value stock then owns 200 shares of $5 par value stock. More important, the market price of the stock, once at $60 per share, immediately drops to $30 per share.

Some investors mistakenly think that a stock split increases their ownership in the company and the value of their investment. Before the stock split, the investor owned 100 shares of $60 stock valued at $6,000. After the stock split, the investor owns 200 shares of $30 stock, also valued at $6,000. Because all stockholders now own twice the number of shares, each investor's percentage ownership in the corporation remains the same.

Required:
Explain the concept of stock splits using a pizza as a symbol for the total value of the corporation.

Organizing a Corporation and Paying Dividends

Chapter 11 **333**

EXPLORE ACCOUNTING
EXPLORE ACCOUNTING

The pizza represents the total of stockholders' equity in the corporation and each slice represents a share of stock. Suppose that four friends decide to share an 8-slice, $16.00 pizza. Each slice is worth $2.00 ($16.00 ÷ 8 pieces). Therefore, each person contributes $4.00 for two slices of pizza, and each person owns 2 of the 8 pieces, or 25%, of the pizza.

To make the pizza slices easier to eat, the friends instruct the server to cut each pizza slice in half. Thus, there are now 16 slices of pizza, each worth $1.00. Each person now has 4 of the 16 slices, or 25%, of the pizza, costing the same $4.00.

Cutting the pizza into 16 pieces from 8 pieces did not change the total size or total cost of the pizza. However, cutting the pizza did change the size and cost of each slice. Instead of having eight $2.00 slices of pizza, the friends now have sixteen $1.00 slices of pizza.

11-1 APPLICATION PROBLEM

Journalizing transactions for starting a corporation

Pacific Technologies Corporation received its charter on January 4 of the current year. The corporation is authorized to issue 200,000 shares of $10.00 stated-value common stock and 50,000 shares of 12%, $100.00 par-value preferred stock.

Transactions:

Jan. 4. Received cash from three incorporators for 48,000 shares of $10.00 stated-value common stock, $480,000.00. R1–3.

4. Paid cash to Joseph Garza as reimbursement for organization costs, $2,000.00. C1.

Instructions:

Journalize the transactions. Use page 1 of a cash receipts journal, a cash payments journal, and a general journal. Source documents are abbreviated as follows: check, C; receipt, R. Save your work to complete Application Problem 11-2.

11-2 APPLICATION PROBLEM   QUICKBOOKS

Journalizing transactions for stock subscriptions and preparing a balance sheet

Use the working papers for Application Problem 11-1.

Transactions:

Jan. 5. Received a subscription from Karen Yoshihara for 2,000 shares of $10.00 stated-value common stock, $20,000.00. M1.

16. Received a subscription from Tyronne Carter for 10,000 shares of $10.00 stated-value common stock, $100,000.00. M2.

Feb. 1. Received cash from Karen Yoshihara in payment of stock subscription, $20,000.00. R4.

1. Issued Stock Certificate No. 4 to Karen Yoshihara for 2,000 shares of $10.00 stated-value common stock, $20,000.00. M3.

8. Received cash from Tyronne Carter in partial payment of stock subscription, $50,000.00. R5.

15. Received a subscription from Cindy Coburn for 300 shares of $10.00 stated-value common stock, $3,000.00. M4.

Mar. 1. Received cash from Tyronne Carter in final payment of stock subscription, $50,000.00. R6.

1. Issued Stock Certificate No. 5 to Tyronne Carter for 10,000 shares of $10.00 stated-value common stock, $100,000. M5.

Instructions:

1. Journalize the transactions. Source documents are abbreviated as follows: memorandum, M; receipt, R.
2. Prepare a balance sheet for Pacific Technologies Corporation as of March 2 of the current year.

11-3 APPLICATION PROBLEM

Calculating dividends for a corporation

The information shown on page 335 is available from the accounting records of two different corporations.

Instructions:

1. Calculate the value of preferred stock.
2. Calculate the amount of dividends to be paid each year to preferred and common shareholders.

TEACHING STRATEGIES DIFFERENT LEARNING STYLES

Visual Learner. When covering journal entries with a visual learner, the instructor should discuss the entries, using a transparency or the board to record the entry. In addition, the student should be asked to mentally picture each part of the entry before the instructor actually writes it on the transparency or chalkboard.

	Corporations	
	Edison	**Carmac**
Preferred Stock:		
Description	$100.00 par-value	$50.00 par-value
Dividend Rate	10%	8%
Shares Issued	2,000	10,000
Common Stock:		
Description	$2.00 stated-value	$1.00 stated-value
Shares Issued	300,000	200,000
Annual Dividend:		
Year 1	$25,000.00	$50,000.00
Year 2	$30,000.00	$60,000.00
Year 3	$35,000.00	$75,000.00

11-4 APPLICATION PROBLEM PEACHTREE QUICKBOOKS

Journalizing transactions for declaring and paying dividends

PlasticTech, Inc. completed the following transactions during the current year.

Transactions:

Aug. 12. PlasticTech's board of directors declared an annual dividend of $180,000.00. Preferred stock issued is $500,000.00 of 10%, $100.00 par-value preferred stock. Common stock issued is $1,000,000.00 of $1,000.00 stated-value common stock. Date of payment is November 15. M65.

Nov. 15. Paid $180,000.00 cash for annual dividend declared August 12. C139.

Instructions:

Journalize the transactions. Use page 8 of a general journal and page 21 of a cash payments journal. Source documents are abbreviated as follows: check, C; memorandum, M.

11-5 MASTERY PROBLEM 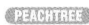 PEACHTREE

Journalizing transactions for starting a corporation, declaring and paying dividends, and preparing a balance sheet

SkyPark, Inc. received its charter on August 1 of the current year. The corporation is authorized to issue 150,000 shares of $5.00 stated-value common stock and 50,000 shares of 10%, $100.00 par-value preferred stock.

Transactions:

20X2

Aug. 4. Ten incorporators pay cash for 50,000 shares of $5.00 stated-value common stock, $250,000.00. R1–10.

4. Dan O'Brien was reimbursed for organization costs, $6,500.00. C1.

6. Diane Scalacci subscribed to purchase 500 shares of $5.00 stated-value common stock, $2,500.00. M1.

21. McCabe Daniels subscribed to purchase 3,000 shares of $5.00 stated-value common stock, $15,000.00. M2.

Sept. 16. Diane Scalacci made full payment on stock subscription, $2,500.00. R11.

16. Issued Stock Certificate No. 11 to Diane Scalacci for 500 shares. M3.

Oct. 1. McCabe Daniels made a partial payment on stock subscription, $7,500.00. R12.

15. Kay Mehta subscribed to purchase 6,000 shares of $5.00 stated-value common stock, $30,000.00. M4.

Nov. 1. McCabe Daniels made final payment on stock subscription, $7,500.00. R13.

1. Issued Stock Certificate No. 12 to McCabe Daniels for 3,000 shares. M5.

Application Problem 11-4
Pref. Dividend: 50,000
Com. Dividend: 130,000.

Mastery Problem 11-5
Pref. Dividend: 10,000
Com. Dividend: 30,000
Cap. Stk.: 267,500
Stk. Sub.: 30,000.

Instructions:

1. Journalize the transactions. Use page 1 of a cash receipts journal, a cash payments journal, and a general journal. Source documents are abbreviated as follows: check, C; memorandum, M; receipt, R.
2. Prepare a balance sheet for SkyPark, Inc. as of November 2 of the current year.
3. Journalize the following additional transactions completed during the following two years to record the declaration and payment of the dividends. Continue using page 1 of the general journal and the cash payments journal.

Additional Transactions:

20X3

Nov. 15. SkyPark's board of directors declared an annual dividend of $40,000.00. Preferred stock issued is $100,000.00 of 10%, $100.00 par-value preferred stock. Common stock issued is $400,000.00 of $5.00 stated-value common stock. Date of payment is January 15. M206.

20X4

Jan. 15. Paid cash for annual dividend declared November 15, $40,000.00. C339.

Challenge Problem 11-6

20X1 Pref.: 20,000 × 12% × 100 = 240,000; Com.: 400,000 − 240,000 = 160,000.

20X2 Com.: 450,000 − 240,000 = 210,000.

20X3 Pref.: 20,000 shares + 1,000 shares = 21,000; 21,000 × 12% × 100 = 252,000; Com.: 450,000 − 252,000 = 198,000.

11-6 CHALLENGE PROBLEM

Journalizing transactions for a corporation

On January 1, 20X1, Atlantic Semiconductor Corporation had issued the following stock:

250,000 shares of $10.00 stated-value common stock.
20,000 shares of 12%, $100.00 par-value preferred stock.

Transactions:

20X1

June 7. A subscription was received from Grace Young for 2,000 shares of $10.00 stated-value common stock, $20,000.00. M234.

Oct. 15. Grace Young paid cash in partial payment of stock subscription, $10,000.00. R245.

Nov. 1. Atlantic Semiconductor's board of directors declared an annual dividend of $400,000.00. Date of payment is January 15, 20X2. M245.

20X2

Jan. 15. The annual dividend declared November 1, $400,000.00, was paid. C1489.

Feb. 21. Grace Young paid cash in final payment of stock subscription, $10,000.00. R296.

21. Issued Stock Certificate No. 132 to Grace Young for 2,000 shares of $10.00 stated-value common stock, $20,000.00. M262.

Oct. 12. A subscription was received from James Richards for 1,000 shares of $100.00 par-value preferred stock, $100,000.00. M289.

Nov. 1. Atlantic Semiconductor's board of directors declared an annual dividend of $450,000.00. Date of payment is January 15, 20X3. M292.

20X3

Jan. 15. Paid annual dividend declared November 1, $450,000.00. C1654.

May 12. Cash was received from James Richards in full payment for 1,000 shares of $100.00 par-value preferred stock, $100,000.00. R312.

May 12. Stock Certificate No. 87 was issued to James Richards for 1,000 shares. M324.

Nov. 1. Atlantic Semiconductor's board of directors declared an annual dividend of $450,000.00. Date of payment is January 15, 20X4. M364.

Instructions:

Journalize the transactions. Use page 12 of a cash receipts journal, page 14 of a cash payments journal, and page 6 of a general journal. Source documents are abbreviated as follows: check, C; memorandum, M; receipt, R.

TEACHING STRATEGIES DIFFERENT LEARNING STYLES

Kinesthetic Learner. When covering journal entries with a kinesthetic learner, the instructor should give the student journal paper and have the student complete the entries as the instructor demonstrates on a board or transparency.

applied communication

Most accountants actively participate in professional organizations. The organizations have periodic dinner meetings at which guest speakers make presentations regarding current accounting topics. As a member of a professional organization, you may be asked to introduce a guest speaker.

Required:

Prepare an introduction for a business professional you know personally. Identify the individual's most significant professional qualifications that allow him or her to speak on the topic. Include information regarding the speaker's community service and personal information to highlight his or her personal qualities.

cases for critical thinking

Case 1

Jennifer Hester is considering whether she should buy stock as an investment. She asks you whether it would be better to buy common stock or preferred stock. How would you answer her? Explain your suggestions.

Case 2

Salvatoro, 22 years old, recently inherited $5,000.00. He has decided to invest the money in the stock market. He wants his investment to grow quickly. A friend recommended mutual funds as a good way to invest in the stock market. Salvatoro has asked you to research the types of mutual funds available and recommend how he should proceed.

SCANS workplace competency

Basic Skill: Writing

Concept: Employers seek workers who possess the ability to communicate thoughts, ideas, information, and messages in writing. During their workday, employees are often required to create documents such as letters, directions, manuals, reports, graphs, and flow charts.

Application: Prepare a memorandum to your staff announcing the addition of an accounts payable clerk position. Include a description of the job, skill and education requirements, desired personal traits, hours, salary, company benefits, and other relevant details.

APPLIED COMMUNICATION

Individual student outlines will vary; however, they should include the following elements: (1) Name. (2) Title. (3) Individual's most significant professional qualifications that establish the speaker's ability to speak on the topic. (4) Community service. (5) Personal information to highlight the personal qualities of the speaker. The instructor should also consider writing style and mechanics (grammar, spelling, punctuation, sentence structure) when grading this activity.

CASES FOR CRITICAL THINKING

Case 1

Each kind of stock has its advantages and disadvantages. If Jennifer Hester seeks a stock through which she will be able to participate in a corporation's stockholder meetings, she will buy common stock, which has voting rights. If Jennifer Hester desires only an income, she may want to buy preferred stock, which is assured of participating in dividends before common stock does. If Jennifer Hester is seeking a stock that will increase in value, she should check what has been happening to the value of various common and preferred stocks. Before deciding to invest in stock, Jennifer Hester would be wise to consult with a specialist in the stock market.

Case 2

Students will probably need to do some library or online research to answer this question. A mutual fund is a large, professionally managed group of investments. A mutual fund pools the money of many investors and buys a large selection of securities that meet the fund's investment goals. Since the fund invests in a wide variety of securities, it provides diversification that small investors could not otherwise achieve. General categories of mutual funds include growth funds, income funds, growth and income funds, and money market funds. Many funds require only a small minimum investment. Salvatoro would need to choose funds that match his investment goals and risk tolerance.

SCANS WORKPLACE COMPETENCY

Emphasize the importance of form, grammar, spelling, and significant details. Ask students to exchange memorandums for peer editing. Request that students prepare the final document using a word processing program.

337

Year	Dividend/Share
20X1	$3.00
20X2	$2.75
20X3	$2.35
20X4	$2.60

ANALYZING COSTCO'S
FINANCIAL STATEMENTS

1. 457,497,000 shares issued as of August 31, 2003.

2. .20 × 457,497,000 = 91,495,800.00.

3. .80 ÷ 37.43 = 2.1%.

graphing workshop

Northwest Floors, Inc., has paid dividends every year since it started business in 20X1.

The total dividend paid and the number of shares issued are given below for each year.

Year	Total Dividend	Number of Shares Issued
20X1	$45,000	$15,000
20X2	$55,000	$20,000
20X3	$51,700	$22,000
20X4	$65,000	$25,000

Instructions:

1. Calculate the dividend per share for each year.

2. Develop a bar chart of the dividend per share for all four years.

analyzing Costco's financial statements

As stated in this chapter, a corporation's board of directors decides the dividend policy for the corporation. As shown in Appendix B of this textbook, the 2003 Annual Report for Costco states, "Costco has never paid regular dividends and presently has no plans to declare a cash dividend." Changing tax laws have lowered the tax rate that a stockholder pays when receiving a dividend. This change has resulted in more companies paying dividends.

One ratio of interest to stockholders is the dividend yield. It is calculated as: dividend per share ÷ market price per share = dividend yield.

Instructions:

1. Look at Costco's Balance Sheet to determine the number of shares of common stock issued as of August 31, 2003.

2. Assume that Costco's board of directors declares a $.20 dividend per share. Calculate the total dividend Costco would pay.

3. The highest price for Costco's stock in 2003 was $37.43 per share. Calculate the dividend yield assuming Costco declared an $.80 dividend per share.

TEACHING STRATEGIES   PORTFOLIO ASSESSMENT

Payment of dividends is an important concept that students will likely encounter in their professional or personal lives. Students should select an example of the payment of dividends that has been successfully completed to include in their portfolio. A copy of the Portfolio Assessment form (blackline master in the Teacher's Resource Guide; also on the Student Companion CD) should be completed by the student and the Description section should include any comments regarding how the student mastered these concepts and procedures. Alternatively, students might include in their portfolios printed reports from an Automated Accounting problem.

• Automated Accounting

Using the Loan Planner

Planning Tools

Planning tools are easy-to-use applications within an accounting system that provide fast and easy ways of making calculations that are commonly needed for journal entries and reports. Five planning tools have been included in *Automated Accounting 8.0* and higher.

The Automated Accounting section in Chapter 9, pages 286 and 287, introduced the notes and interest planning tool. When a business uses notes receivable or notes payable to finance transactions, information about interest amounts, payment amounts, and due dates may be calculated using the appropriate planner. Planning tools are also efficient and easy-to-use tools to use for what-if scenarios.

Loan Planner

The Loan Planner is similar to the Notes and Interest tool. It is used to calculate the amount of a loan, the loan payment amount, and the number of payments. A common use of this tool is to compute the monthly payment when a loan is made using the stated interest rate. The loan planner may then be used to generate an amortization schedule that will show the amount of principal and interest associated with each payment. To use the Loan Planner:

1. Click on the *Tools* toolbar button or select Planning Tools from the Data menu.

2. Click the *Loan Planner* tab.

3. Select the Loan Amount, Loan Payment Amount, or the Number of Payments option button in the Calculate option group. The unknown amount to be calculated text box will be dimmed, based upon the option selected.

4. Enter the data in the text boxes and press the Tab key. The calculated results will appear at the bottom of the Planning dialog box.

5. Click on the *Report* command button to produce a Loan Amortization Schedule. Once displayed, the report may be printed or copied to the clipboard for entering into a spreadsheet or word processor.

6. Click on *Close* to exit the report and return to the planner. Steps 3–5 may then be repeated for different calculation options, or for different data sets.

7. Click on Close, or press ESC, to exit the planner.

Displaying or Printing the Loan Amortization Schedule

The Loan Amortization Schedule can be generated by following these steps:

1. Click on the Reports button on the Loan Planner screen after entering the data.

2. Choose the Print button if you wish to print the report or you may choose to view only.

3. Click the Close button. You also have the option to copy the report to the clipboard so that you may include the loan data on a separate document.

Using Special Tools: The Loan Planner

Instructions:

1. Load *Automated Accounting 8.0* or higher software.

2. Select New from the File menu. Enter your User name.

3. Click on the Tools toolbar button.

4. Click on the Loan Planner tab. Select Loan Payment Amount from the Calculate box. Enter a loan amount of $14,000.00, an interest rate of 8.00%, and 36 payments. The payment amount will be automatically calculated.

5. Click on the Report command button from within the Loan Planner tab. Print the report, or copy it to the clipboard for entering into a word processor or spreadsheet application.

6. Click Close to return to the planner. Steps 4 and 5 may then be repeated for different calculation options, or for different data sets.

7. Click Close to exit the planner. When you exit a planning tool, your data will not be saved. Be sure to print a report, or copy it to a word processor or spreadsheet and save it in that application.

8. Exit the Automated Accounting software.

Organizing a Corporation and Paying Dividends

Chapter 11 **339**

- Preview the terms used or introduced in this feature: Loan Planner and Amortization Schedule.

- Explain that the Loan Planner can be used to calculate the amount of a loan, the loan payment amount, and the number of payments.

Using the Loan Planner

- Click the Tools toolbar button and then click the Loan Planner tab.

- Click the Loan Payment Amount option button in the Calculate option group.

- Enter the loan amount, annual interest percentage rate, and number of payments desired.

- Repeat the demonstration for other options in the Calculate option group.

Displaying a report

- Click the Report button to display a report that shows the amortization table for the loan data entered.

Using reports in other documents

- Click the Copy button and select spreadsheet or word processor.

- Click OK. A dialog box indicating that the copy is complete appears if copy was done successfully. Click OK to exit the dialog box.

- Open word processing or spreadsheet software and demonstrate using the Edit Copy command to paste the report from the Clipboard to the document.

- Assign the Using Special Tools: The Loan Planner problem.

- Direct students to copy the results of the Loan Planner into either a word processing or spreadsheet file and print the results. If the word processor or spreadsheet software is not available, direct students to print the report from the Loan Planner.

TEACHING STRATEGIES PORTFOLIO ASSESSMENT

Students should be encouraged to print at least one report from the Automated Accounting problem to include in their portfolio to demonstrate mastery of using planning tools. Students might also copy an amortization table from the Loan Planner into a word processing document and compose additional copy to explain the results of the amortization table. A copy of the Portfolio Assessment form (blackline master in the Teacher's Resource Guide; also on the Student Companion CD) should be completed by the student and the Description section should include any comments regarding how the student mastered these concepts and procedures.

## CHAPTER 12

Acquiring Additional Capital

	SCOPE & SEQUENCE	
	NEW	REVIEW/ EXTENSION
Introduce the Chapter	✓	
Lesson 12-1 Capital Stock Transactions		
Issuing preferred stock at par value		✓
Issuing preferred stock for more or less than par value	✓	
Issuing preferred stock for assets other than cash	✓	
Issuing common stock with no par value	✓	
Issuing common stock with a stated value	✓	
Lesson 12-2 Treasury Stock Transactions		
Buying treasury stock	✓	
Selling treasury stock for original cost	✓	
Selling treasury stock for more or less than original cost	✓	
Lesson 12-3 Bonds Payable Transactions		
Issuing bonds	✓	
Paying interest on bonds	✓	
Recording deposit and interest earned on bond sinking fund	✓	
Retiring a bond issue	✓	
Putting It All Together		

ENHANCING

SPECIAL FEATURES

- Accounting in the Real World: Famous Dave's

- Making Ethical Decisions: Exercising Stock Options
- Explore Accounting: Stock Price Fluctuation in a Market Economy

- Small Business Spotlight

- Explore Accounting: Effective Interest Method

- Explore Accounting
- Xtra! Web Site: Xtra! Enrichment
- Applied Communication
- Case for Critical Thinking
- SCANS Workplace Competency
- Auditing for Errors
- Analyzing Costco's Financial Statements

for a Corporation

INSTRUCTION	
TECHNOLOGY AND MEDIA	**TEACHING STRATEGIES**
• Internet Research Activity • Accounting Xtra! Web Site	• Software Focus
• Instructor's Resource CD: PowerPoint Slides • Xtra! Web Site: Xtra! Study Tools • Blackline Masters: Cash Receipts Journal and General Journal • Personal Trainer • Peachtree and QuickBooks	• Applied Skills: Language Arts • Auditory Learner
• Instructor's Resource CD: PowerPoint Slides • Xtra! Web Site: Xtra! Study Tools • Blackline Masters: Cash Receipts Journal and Cash Payments Journal • Personal Trainer	
• Instructor's Resource CD: PowerPoint Slides • Xtra! Web Site: Xtra! Study Tools • Blackline Masters: General Journal, Cash Payments Journal, and Cash Receipts Journal • Personal Trainer	• Cooperative Learning • Visual Learner
• Automated Accounting • Peachtree and QuickBooks • Personal Trainer • Xtra! Web Site: Xtra! Review, Quizzing, and Enrichment • Student Companion CD	• Applied Skills: Writing Across the Curriculum • Kinesthetic Learner • Print Learner

PRACTICE AND ASSESSMENT		
GUIDED PRACTICE	**INDEPENDENT PRACTICE**	**RETEACHING AND ENRICHMENT**
• Term Review • Audit Your Understanding • Work Together 12-1	• On Your Own 12-1 • Application Problem 12-1 • Ongoing Assessment, p. 347 • Personal Trainer • Xtra! Web Site: Xtra! Study Tools	• Reteach, p. 347 • Enrich, p. 349 • Peachtree and QuickBooks
• Term Review • Audit Your Understanding • Work Together 12-2	• On Your Own 12-2 • Application Problem 12-2 • Ongoing Assessment, p. 353 • Personal Trainer • Xtra! Web Site: Xtra! Study Tools	• Reteach, p. 353 • Enrich, p. 354
• Term Review • Audit Your Understanding • Work Together 12-3	• On Your Own 12-3 • Application Problem 12-3 • Ongoing Assessment, p. 358 • Personal Trainer • Xtra! Web Site: Xtra! Study Tools	• Reteach, p. 358 • Enrich, p. 360
	• Mastery Problem 12-4 • Peachtree and QuickBooks • Personal Trainer • Xtra! Web Site: Xtra! Review and Quizzing • Study Guide 12 • Student Companion CD • Chapter 12 Test • ExamView Chapter 12 • Portfolio Assessment	• Challenge Problem 12-5 • Reteach, p. 361 • Enrich, p. 361 • Recycling Problem 12-1 • Automated Accounting • Xtra! Web Site: Xtra! Enrichment

CHAPTER

12 Acquiring Additional Capital for a Corporation

TERMS • OBJECTIVES & TERMS • OBJECTIVES & TERMS

After studying Chapter 12, you will be able to:

1. Define accounting terms related to acquiring capital for a corporation.

2. Identify accounting concepts and practices related to acquiring capital for a corporation.

3. Journalize entries for issuing additional capital stock.

4. Journalize entries for buying and selling treasury stock.

5. Journalize entries for bonds payable.

- discount on capital stock
- treasury stock
- bond

- bond issue
- trustee
- bond sinking fund

- retiring a bond issue
- term bonds
- serial bonds

Point Your Browser
accountingxtra.swlearning.com

1. Many factors determine the price of a share of stock, including economic conditions, company management, loyal customer base, competition, amount of research and development undertaken, and expected future earnings.

2. A company could borrow money by obtaining loans or by issuing bonds.

INTERNET RESEARCH ACTIVITY

1. Specific titles may vary somewhat but usually include: consolidated balance sheets and the related consolidated statements of income, stockholders' equity, and cash flow.

2. Consolidated financial statements are the responsibility of the company's management.

3. The auditor's responsibility is to express an opinion on the financial statements.

4. Answers will vary.

• Famous Dave's

©FAMOUS DAVE'S, INC.

MEETING THE CHALLENGES OF GROWTH AT FAMOUS DAVE'S

Are you hungry for some authentic hickory-smoked, flame-grilled barbecue ribs or chicken? Famous Dave's Barbecue offers these and many more choices, all served in a distinctive and comfortable environment. "Famous Dave" Anderson opened his first restaurant in 1995. Since then, his idea has expanded to 38 company-owned and 68 franchise-operated locations, with another 150 franchise restaurant commitments.

Famous Dave's features hickory-smoked St. Louis-style ribs, Texas beef brisket, and their award-winning Rich & Sassy® BBQ sauce. Additionally, the menu offers barbeque and country-roasted chicken, BBQ sandwiches, burgers, and salads.

While rapid growth is good, it also has its challenges. It takes a great deal of capital to expand a business, both in terms of opening new restaurants and in growing the administrative side of the business. More restaurants mean more employees to train. Information systems must grow with the company. More people are required to keep the company operating. All of this takes money.

Where can a company turn for this money? One option is to sell stock in the company. In 1996, Famous Dave's stock was first offered to the general public. This is called an "initial public offering," or IPO. Famous Dave's IPO of 2,645,000 shares of stock netted over $15 million dollars to help support the growth of the company.

Critical Thinking

1. What factors will help determine the price of a share of stock at the time of its IPO?
2. If a company needs more cash, but does not want to issue additional shares of stock, what else could it do to raise the capital?

Source: www.famousdaves.com

Xtra!
Today
accountingxtra.swlearning.com

AUDIT LETTER

Go to the homepage for two corporations of your choice. Search for the most recent annual report for each company. Within the annual report, find the "Report of the Independent Auditor." Answer the following questions about each corporation's report.

Instructions

1. Which financial statements did the auditors audit?
2. The consolidated financial statements are the responsibility of whom?
3. What is the auditor's responsibility related to the financial statements?
4. What company performed the audit?

341

12-1 Capital Stock Transactions

As a corporation grows, it may require additional capital to finance its expansion. The portion of a corporation's net income not paid to stockholders as dividends is a primary source of additional capital. Retained earnings may not, however, provide an adequate source of capital for a corporation. Both new and existing corporations may require a large increase in capital to finance rapid expansion. Thus, a corporation can acquire additional capital by selling stock to investors or borrowing money.

Articles of incorporation are usually written to permit a corporation to issue more shares of stock than it sold to initial investors. As the need arises for more capital, a corporation can issue some of the remaining authorized stock. LampLight, Inc. is authorized by its charter to issue a total of 100,000 shares of common stock

and 50,000 shares of preferred stock. [*CONCEPT: Business Entity*] However, LampLight initially issued only 32,000 shares of common stock during its first year as described in Chapter 11. Thus, LampLight may sell some of the remaining shares of common or some shares of preferred stock to raise additional capital.

Once capital stock has been issued it may be reacquired by the company. Special procedures are required to account for such shares.

©GETTY IMAGES/PHOTODISC

making ethical decisions

MAKING ETHICAL DECISIONS • MAKING ETHICAL DECISIONS • MAKING ETHICAL DECISIO

Exercising Stock Options

Corporations often compensate executives with more than a salary. The compensation package often includes the right to purchase company stock at a specified price (this right is called a *stock option*). The option price is typically set higher than the current market price. If the stock price increases above the option price, the option enables the individual to purchase the stock at less than the market price. If the stock's market price never exceeds the option price, the option is worthless.

Three years ago, the board of directors of Burnett Corp. offered its new chief executive officer, Brent McGowan, an annual salary of $500,000 plus 200,000 stock options at $30. The stock was selling for $18 at the time. Brent successfully improved the corporation's profitability. When the stock reached $40 per share,

Brent exercised the stock options and purchased 200,000 shares of stock from Burnett Corp. for $6 million. Over the next year, he sold the stock on the stock exchange for an average price of $42 per share and realized a profit of $2.4 million.

The company's code of conduct states that "employees should receive compensation consistent with their contributions toward the corporation's strategic objectives."

Instructions

Use the ethical model to analyze whether the corporation's use of stock options as executive compensation demonstrates ethical behavior.

MAKING ETHICAL DECISIONS

Most students will conclude that issuing stock options as part of the CEO's compensation package appears to be ethical. However, excessive management compensation continues to be a controversial issue. Although the management compensation packages of public corporations can seem excessive, the compensation is warranted if the executive can increase the profitability of the company and the wealth of its stockholders. In too many instances, however, executives have received excessive compensation even when their corporations were declining. For a sample solution, see the section at the front of this Wraparound Teacher's Edition.

As an extension of this activity, have students research current business magazines and newspapers for articles relating to excessive management compensation.

1. Calculate the amounts to be recorded.

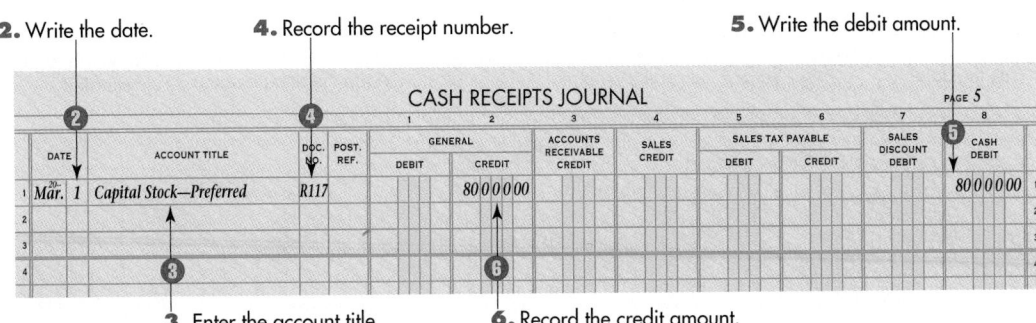

	No. of Shares	×	Par Value per Share	=	Total Par Value
	800	×	$100.00	=	$80,000.00

2. Write the date. **4.** Record the receipt number. **5.** Write the debit amount.

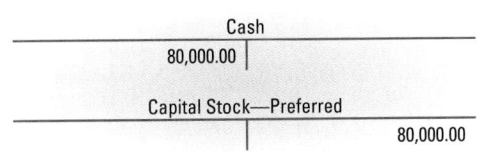

CASH RECEIPTS JOURNAL   PAGE 5

					GENERAL		ACCOUNTS RECEIVABLE CREDIT	SALES CREDIT	SALES TAX PAYABLE		SALES DISCOUNT DEBIT	CASH DEBIT	
	DATE	ACCOUNT TITLE	DOC. NO.	POST. REF.	DEBIT	CREDIT			DEBIT	CREDIT			
1	Mar. 1	Capital Stock—Preferred	R117			80 000 00						80 000 00	1
2													2
3													3
4													4

3. Enter the account title. **6.** Record the credit amount.

LampLight decided to issue preferred stock to raise additional capital. Brenda Henson paid par value, $100.00, for 800 shares of preferred stock, as shown above.

March 1. Received cash from Brenda Henson for 800 shares of $100.00 par value preferred stock at $100.00 per share, $80,000.00. Receipt No. 117.

Cash is debited for $80,000.00. Capital Stock—Preferred is credited for $80,000.00, the total par value of the issued preferred stock.

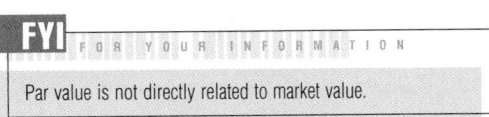

Cash	
80,000.00	

Capital Stock—Preferred	
	80,000.00

FYI   FOR YOUR INFORMATION

Par value is not directly related to market value.

STEPS • STEPS • STEPS • STEPS • STEPS • STEPS • STEPS • STEPS • STEPS • STEPS •

JOURNALIZE PREFERRED STOCK ISSUED AT PAR VALUE

1 Calculate the amounts to be recorded for the sale of 800 shares of preferred stock at par.

2 Write the date in the Date column of the cash receipts journal. Since this is the first entry on page 5 of the cash receipts journal, record the current year in the Date column.

3 Enter the account title, *Capital Stock—Preferred,* in the Account Title column.

4 Record the receipt number, *R117*, in the Doc. No. column.

5 Write the debit amount, *80,000.00*, in the Cash Debit column.

6 Record the credit amount, *80,000.00*, in the General Credit column.

- Explain that after a corporation is in operation, investors most often purchase stock from a shareholder that currently owns stock in the corporation. Remind students that the corporation receives no money from this stock transfer; therefore, no journal entry is recorded by the corporation. Explain that only when the corporation decides to issue additional stock, can an investor purchase stock from the corporation.

- Explain that a corporation may need to sell stock to raise additional capital for expansion. Emphasize that a corporation's articles of incorporation usually permit the corporation to issue more shares of stock than sold to initial investors.

- Point out that sometimes preferred stock is issued for more than its par value. In other words, the stock is sold for more than the authorized value printed on the stock certificate.

- Stress that regardless of the amount received, the credit to capital stock always equals the number of shares issued multiplied by the par value per share. Point out the use of two credit accounts in the illustration.

DEMONSTRATE

Analyze the transaction

- Draw three blank T accounts on the board.

- Ask a student to read the transaction statement.

- Review the math box provided so that students understand the mathematical procedure used for calculating the amount received in excess of par value. Repeat the math process on the board or overhead. Ask students to verify the amount using calculators.

- Ask students to analyze the transaction. Complete the T accounts as the information is provided.

Record the transaction

- Use the transparency of a cash receipts journal to illustrate the process for recording the entry in the journal.

- Record each item in the journal following the six steps shown.

ISSUING PREFERRED STOCK FOR MORE THAN PAR VALUE

	No. of Shares	×	Value per Share	=	Value
Total received	300	×	$120.00	=	$36,000.00
Par value	300	×	100.00	=	30,000.00
Amount received in excess of par value					$ 6,000.00

1. Calculate the amounts to be recorded.

2. Write the date.　　**4.** Record the receipt number.　　**5.** Write the debit amount.

3. Enter the account titles.

6. Enter the credit amounts.

Sometimes preferred stock is issued for more than its par value. LampLight sold 300 shares of preferred stock at $120.00 per share to Adam Kellogg, as shown above.

April 6. Received cash from Adam Kellogg for 300 shares of $100.00 par value preferred stock at $120.00 per share, $36,000.00. Receipt No. 127.

STEPS · STEPS · STEPS · STEPS

JOURNALIZE PREFERRED STOCK ISSUED FOR MORE THAN PAR VALUE

1 Calculate the amounts to be recorded for 300 shares of preferred stock sold at more than par value.

2 Write the date in the Date column of the cash receipts journal.

3 Enter the account titles, *Capital Stock—Preferred* and *Paid-in Capital in Excess of Par Value—Preferred*, on separate lines in the Account Title column.

4 Record the receipt number, *R127*, in the Doc. No. column.

5 Write the debit amount, *36,000.00*, in the Cash Debit column.

6 Enter the appropriate credit amounts, *30,000.00* and *6,000.00*, on separate lines in the General Credit column.

Cash is debited for $36,000.00, the total amount received. Capital Stock—Preferred is credited for $30,000.00, the total par value of the preferred stock issued. Paid-in Capital in Excess of Par Value—Preferred is credited for $6,000.00, the amount received in excess of the par value.

Regardless of the amount received, the credit to the capital stock account always equals the par or stated value of the stock issued.

Cash	
Apr. 6　36,000.00	

Capital Stock—Preferred	
	Balance　80,000.00
	Apr. 6　30,000.00
	(New Bal.　110,000.00)

Paid-in Capital in Excess of Par Value—Preferred	
	Apr. 6　6,000.00

FYI FOR YOUR INFORMATION

A limited liability company (LLC) and a limited liability partnership (LLP) provide the flexibility of a partnership by allowing earnings to flow through to its partners as personal income. This feature eliminates the double-taxation penalty of a corporation.

Acquiring Additional Capital for a Corporation

APPLIED SKILLS LANGUAGE ARTS

Practicing Capitalization Skills. Special handouts for practicing capitalization skills can be created easily using word processing software. Key in some text, either something that you have written yourself or that has appeared in a newspaper or magazine. After checking to be sure you have keyed it correctly, use the change case feature of your word processor to change all uppercase letters to lowercase letters. Students can be directed to underline or circle all letters that should be capitalized. Student solutions can then be compared with the original copy for correctness.

ISSUING PREFERRED STOCK FOR LESS THAN PAR VALUE

	No. of Shares	×	Value per Share	=	Value	
Par value	500	×	$100.00	=	$50,000.00	
Total received	500	×	90.00	=	45,000.00	**1.** Calculate the amounts to be recorded.
Total discount					$ 5,000.00	

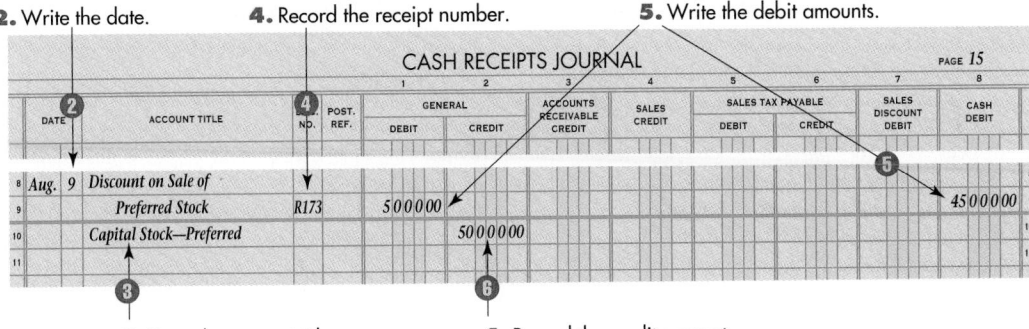

2. Write the date.   **4.** Record the receipt number.   **5.** Write the debit amounts.

3. Enter the account titles.   **6.** Record the credit amount.

An amount less than par or stated value at which capital stock is sold is called a **discount on capital stock**. The legal treatment of discounts on capital stock varies from state to state. In some states, a stockholder may be liable for the amount of discount on par value stock if a corporation is unable to pay creditors. In other states, a stockholder is not liable for the amount of the discount.

LampLight sold 500 shares of $100.00 par value preferred stock to Hazel Deloach at a price of $90.00 per share, as shown above.

August 9. Received cash from Hazel Deloach for 500 shares of $100.00 par value preferred stock at $90.00 per share, $45,000.00. Receipt No. 173.

Cash is debited for $45,000.00, the amount of cash received. Discount on Sale of Preferred Stock is debited for $5,000.00, the discount amount. Capital Stock—Preferred is credited for $50,000.00, the par value of the 500 shares of preferred stock.

```
                    Cash
        Aug. 9     45,000.00 |

        Discount on Sale of Preferred Stock
        Aug. 9      5,000.00 |

             Capital Stock—Preferred
                          | Balance    110,000.00
                          | Aug. 9      50,000.00
                          | (New Bal.  160,000.00)
```

FYI FOR YOUR INFORMATION

Discount on Sale of Preferred Stock is a contra stockholders' account; hence, it is increased with a debit.

FYI FOR YOUR INFORMATION

The credit to the capital stock account always equals the par or stated value of the stock issued regardless of the amount received.

- Point out that occasionally corporations issue stock in exchange for assets other than cash. Emphasize that the entry is similar to the entry for issuing stock for cash; only the asset account changes.
- Point out that Paid-in Capital in Excess of Par Value—Preferred is a stockholders' equity account, and therefore is increased with a credit.
- Direct students to the F.Y.I. feature to emphasize that companies often purchase other business with a payment of stock rather than cash.

DEMONSTRATE

Analyze the transaction

- Draw three blank T accounts on the board.
- Ask a student to read the transaction statement.
- Review the math illustration provided so that students understand the mathematical procedure used for calculating the amount received in excess of par value. Repeat the math process on the board or overhead. Ask students to verify the amount using calculators.
- Ask the students to analyze the transaction by answering: what accounts are affected, what is the classification of each account, are they increased or decreased, and are they debited or credited. Complete the T accounts as the information is provided.

Record the transaction

- Use the general journal transparency to illustrate the process for recording the entry in the journal.
- Record each item in the journal following the six steps shown in the illustration.

ISSUING PREFERRED STOCK FOR ASSETS OTHER THAN CASH

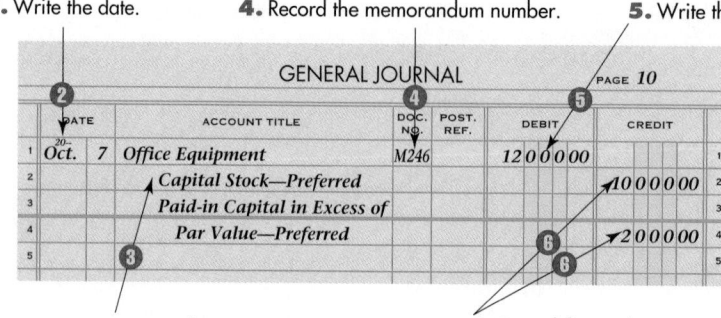

	No. of Shares	×	Value per Share	=	Value
Total received	100	×	$120.00	=	$12,000.00
Par value	100	×	100.00	=	10,000.00
Amount received in excess of par value					$ 2,000.00

1. Calculate the amounts to record.

2. Write the date. **4.** Record the memorandum number. **5.** Write the debit amount.

GENERAL JOURNAL
PAGE 10

DATE	ACCOUNT TITLE	DOC. NO.	POST. REF.	DEBIT	CREDIT
20—					
Oct. 7	Office Equipment	M246		12 0 0 0 00	
	Capital Stock—Preferred				10 0 0 0 00
	Paid-in Capital in Excess of				
	Par Value—Preferred				2 0 0 0 00

3. Enter the account titles.

6. Record the credit amount.

Occasionally, corporations issue capital stock in exchange for assets other than cash. When other assets are used to pay for capital stock, the investor and corporation must agree on the value of the assets and the capital stock.

LampLight issued 100 shares of preferred stock to Steven McBee in exchange for office equipment. The office equipment was accepted in full payment of the 100 shares of preferred stock. The agreed-upon total value of the equipment is $12,000.00. Therefore, the equipment fully pays for the 100 shares of preferred stock, as shown above.

October 7. Received office equipment from Steven McBee at an agreed value of $12,000.00 for 100 shares of $100.00 par value preferred stock. Memorandum No. 246.

Office Equipment is debited for $12,000.00. Capital Stock—Preferred is credited for $10,000.00, the total par value of the preferred stock issued.

Paid-in Capital in Excess of Par Value—Preferred is credited for $2,000.00, the amount received in excess of the par value.

Office Equipment	
Oct. 7 12,000.00	

Capital Stock—Preferred	
	Balance 160,000.00
	Oct. 7 10,000.00
	(New Bal. 170,000.00)

Paid-in Capital in Excess of Par Value—Preferred	
	Balance 6,000.00
	Oct. 7 2,000.00
	(New Bal. 8,000.00)

FYI FOR YOUR INFORMATION

Occasionally, a firm acquires a company by issuing stock in exchange for the company's assets.

TEACHING STRATEGIES   DIFFERENT LEARNING STYLES

Auditory Learner. To reinforce the learning of journal entries, the auditory learner should verbally repeat the analysis of the transaction. The student should also verbally list the steps involved in making the entry.

ISSUING COMMON STOCK WITH NO PAR VALUE

	DATE	ACCOUNT TITLE	DOC. NO.	POST. REF.	GENERAL DEBIT	GENERAL CREDIT	ACCOUNTS RECEIVABLE CREDIT	SALES CREDIT	SALES TAX PAYABLE DEBIT	SALES TAX PAYABLE CREDIT	SALES DISCOUNT DEBIT	CASH DEBIT	
12	July 8	Capital Stock—Common	R148			14000 00						14000 00	12

CASH RECEIPTS JOURNAL   PAGE *13*

Common stock often has no par value assigned to it or printed on the stock certificates. With no-par value stock, the entire amount paid by an investor is recorded in the capital stock account. Wheeler, Inc., sells no-par value common stock. The journal entry to record the transaction is shown above.

July 8. Received cash from Elizabeth Griffin for 1,000 shares of no-par value common stock at $14.00 per share, $14,000.00. Receipt No. 148.

Cash is debited for $14,000.00, the total amount received. Capital Stock—Common is credited for $14,000.00, the total amount received for the 1,000 shares of stock.

ISSUING COMMON STOCK WITH A STATED VALUE

CASH RECEIPTS JOURNAL   PAGE *19*

	DATE	ACCOUNT TITLE	DOC. NO.	POST. REF.	GENERAL DEBIT	GENERAL CREDIT	ACCOUNTS RECEIVABLE CREDIT	SALES CREDIT	SALES TAX PAYABLE DEBIT	SALES TAX PAYABLE CREDIT	SALES DISCOUNT DEBIT	CASH DEBIT	
1	Oct. 10	Capital Stock—Common	R181			1000 00						1200 00	1
2		Paid-in Capital in Excess of											2
3		Stated Value—Common				200 00							3
4													4

Corporations may assign a value to no-par value common stock. The value is known as the stated value. A stated value to no-par value shares serves the same function as par value. Therefore, no-par value common stock with a stated value is recorded using the same procedures as par value stock. An entry for issuing common stock at stated value is shown on page 319. An entry for issuing common stock at more than stated value is shown above.

LampLight's articles of incorporation, shown on pages 315 and 316, specify that the company's common stock has a stated value of $10.00. LampLight sold 100 shares of common stock to Alice Blake for $12.00 a share, as shown above.

October 10. Received cash from Alice Blake for 100 shares of $10.00 stated value common stock at $12.00 per share, $1,200.00. Receipt No. 181.

Cash is debited for $1,200.00, the total amount received. Capital Stock—Common is credited for $1,000.00, the total stated value of the 100 shares. Paid-in Capital in Excess of Stated Value—Common is credited for $200.00, the amount received in excess of the stated value.

GUIDED PRACTICE

Term Review

- Ask a student to define the term in the Term Review. Ask the class if the definition is correct and whether the complete definition has been given or if anything else needs to be added. The suggested definition is given in the Glossary.

- Ask a student to classify the account (contra stockholders' equity).

- Ask a student if the Discount on Capital Stock account is increased with a debit or credit (debit).

Audit Your Understanding

Call on students to answer the Audit Your Understanding questions. Ask the class if the answer is correct and/or complete. Answers are given in Appendix E of the textbook.

Work Together

Have students write the solution to the Work Together problem as you guide the class through the examples.

- Direct students to record each transaction in the appropriate journal as you guide the class through the examples.

- Call on students to read and analyze a transaction.

- Use T accounts and math illustrations to help student analysis.

---

term review

discount on capital stock

audit your understanding

1. To finance rapid expansion, how can a corporation acquire additional capital?

2. What accounts are affected, and how, when LampLight receives cash for preferred stock sold at par value?

3. What accounts are affected, and how, when LampLight receives cash for preferred stock sold for more than par value?

4. What accounts are affected, and how, when LampLight receives cash for preferred stock sold for less than par value?

5. What is the function of stated value?

work together 12-1

Journalizing capital stock transactions

Page 4 of a cash receipts journal and page 2 of a general journal are provided in the *Working Papers*. Your instructor will guide you through the following examples.

May 2. Received cash from Kari Kovaleski for 200 shares of $50.00 par value preferred stock at $60.00 per share, $12,000.00. Receipt No. 234.

3. Received cash from Phil Mullins for 100 shares of $50.00 par value preferred stock at $45.00 per share, $4,500.00. Receipt No. 235.

5. Received office equipment from Laura Nguyen at an agreed-upon value of $5,000.00 for 100 shares of $50.00 par value preferred stock. Memorandum No. 103.

5. Received cash from Arbus Kleinhoffer for 300 shares of $8.00 stated value common stock at $10.00 per share, $3,000.00. Receipt No. 236.

7. Received cash from Jenny Wasito for 100 shares of $8.00 stated value common stock at $8.00 per share, $800.00. Receipt No. 237.

1. Journalize each transaction completed during the current year.

• on your own 12-1

Journalizing capital stock transactions

Page 5 of a cash receipts journal and page 3 of a general journal are provided in the *Working Papers*. Work independently to complete the following problem.

June 3. Received cash from George Lyding for 200 shares of $80.00 par value preferred stock at $85.00 per share, $17,000.00. Receipt No. 174.

6. Received cash from Blanca Echauri for 200 shares of $80.00 par value preferred stock at $78.00 per share, $15,600.00. Receipt No. 175.

8. Received land from Asghar Ebadat at an agreed-upon value of $32,000.00 for 400 shares of $80.00 par value preferred stock. Memorandum No. 223.

9. Received cash from Barbara Parisot for 100 shares of $15.00 stated value common stock at $15.00 per share, $1,500.00. Receipt No. 176.

11. Received cash from Jin Myoung for 100 shares of $15.00 stated value common stock at $16.00 per share, $1,600.00. Receipt No. 177.

12. Received cash from Bernadine Barthel for 200 shares of $80.00 par value preferred stock at $80.00 per share, $16,000.00. Receipt No. 178.

14. Received office furniture from Rita Gomez at an agreed-upon value of $8,000.00 for 100 shares of $80.00 par value preferred stock. Memorandum No. 224.

1. Journalize each transaction completed during the current year.

Explore Accounting

EXPLORE ACCOUNTING • EXPLORE ACCOUNTING • EXPLORE ACCOUNTING

Stock Price Fluctuation in a Market Economy

The stocks of publicly traded corporations are traded freely on domestic and international stock exchanges. These companies also publish annual reports that usually show a 5-year history of the performance of their stock. In addition, historical information about the market price of stocks in public trading can be researched using the Internet.

Individuals buy and sell stocks as investments. Institutions such as retirement plans and philanthropic organizations may invest in stocks, too. Companies may also invest in stocks to earn a return on funds that are not immediately needed for the operations of the business.

In a market economy, stock prices fluctuate constantly, based on the interaction of supply and demand for a particular stock.

Instructions
Merito Retirement Systems wishes to invest $50,000. As comptroller, you have been asked to pick two stocks and research the performance of each stock over the past five years. Select two publicly traded stocks and research information about their selling prices during the past five years. Report the highest and lowest selling price of each stock during the past five years as well as any trends you may find in the market fluctuations.

Capital Stock Transactions

Lesson 12-1 **349**

EXPLORE ACCOUNTING
EXPLORE ACCOUNTING
Answers will vary, depending on the stocks selected. However, all answers should contain the highest and lowest price for each stock during the past five years as well as any trends that may be evident.

349

12-2 Treasury Stock Transactions

BUYING TREASURY STOCK

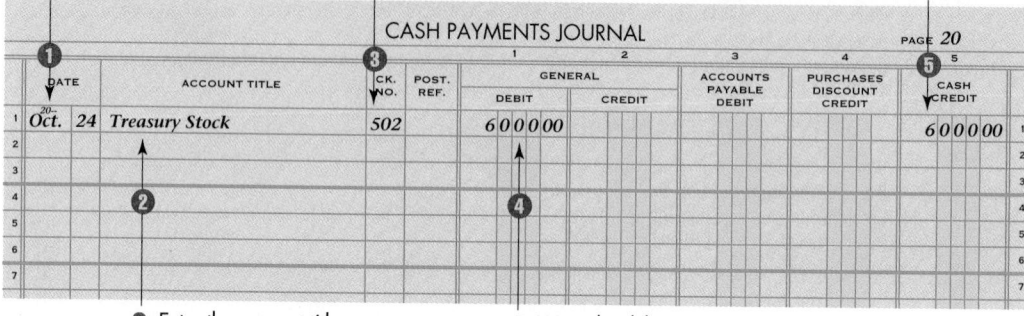

1. Write the date. **3.** Record the check number. **5.** Record the credit amount.

2. Enter the account title. **4.** Write the debit amount.

A corporation's own stock that has been issued and reacquired is called **treasury stock**. When a corporation buys treasury stock, it reduces the number of shares outstanding. However, treasury stock is still considered to be issued stock. A corporation usually intends to use the treasury stock for a specific purpose. For example, a corporation may acquire treasury stock to be given to employees as bonus payments.

Treasury stock is not an asset of a corporation. Since treasury stock is not owned by a stockholder, the stock does not involve voting rights. Dividends are not paid on treasury stock. Once treasury stock is given or sold to a stockholder, it ceases to be treasury stock and is again capital stock outstanding. A corporation records treasury stock at the price paid regardless of the stock's par or stated value. [CONCEPT: Historical Cost]

October 24. Paid cash to Francis Burns for 500 shares of $10.00 stated value common stock at $12.00 per share, $6,000.00. Check No. 502.

Treasury Stock is debited for $6,000.00, the amount paid for the 500 shares of treasury

stock. Cash is credited for $6,000.00. The journal entry to record this transaction is shown above.

Capital stock accounts have normal credit balances. Treasury Stock is a contra capital stock account and therefore has a normal debit balance.

Treasury Stock	
6,000.00	

Cash	
	6,000.00

STEPS • STEPS • STEPS • STEPS

STEPS — JOURNALIZE THE PURCHASE OF TREASURY STOCK

1 Write the date in the Date column of the cash payments journal.

2 Enter the account title, *Treasury Stock*, in the Account Title column.

3 Record the check number, *502*, in the Check Number column. Since only check numbers are recorded in the column, no identifying letter is necessary.

4 Write the debit amount, *6,000.00*, in the General Debit column.

5 Record the credit amount, *6,000.00*, in the Cash Credit column.

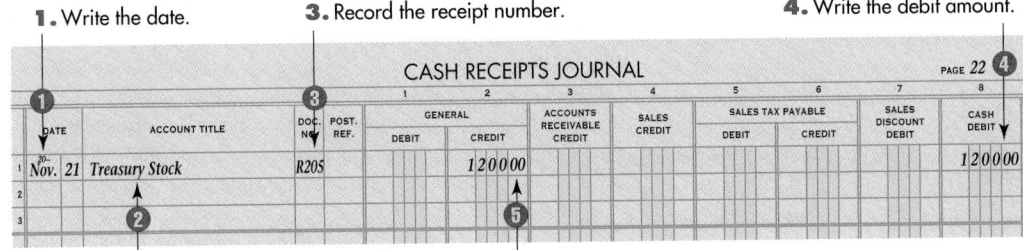

SELLING TREASURY STOCK FOR ORIGINAL COST

1. Write the date.
3. Record the receipt number.
4. Write the debit amount.

2. Enter the account title.
5. Record the credit amount.

CASH RECEIPTS JOURNAL — PAGE 22

	DATE	ACCOUNT TITLE	DOC. NO.	POST. REF.	GENERAL DEBIT	GENERAL CREDIT	ACCOUNTS RECEIVABLE CREDIT	SALES CREDIT	SALES TAX PAYABLE DEBIT	SALES TAX PAYABLE CREDIT	SALES DISCOUNT DEBIT	CASH DEBIT	
1	20-- Nov. 21	Treasury Stock	R205			1 2 0 0 00						1 2 0 0 00	1
2													2
3													3

Companies may sell treasury stock at any time. Treasury stock is generally reissued to investors who pay cash for the stock. Investors pay the current market price for the stock.

The market price of stock will be explained in Chapter 13.

The current value of stock in the marketplace may be the same as the original cost of the treasury stock. Assume LampLight sold some of its treasury stock at the $12.00 original cost, as shown above.

November 21. Received cash from Lisa Vance for 100 shares of treasury stock at $12.00 per share, $1,200.00. Treasury stock was originally bought by LampLight on October 24 at $12.00 per share. Receipt No. 205.

Cash is debited for $1,200.00. Treasury Stock is credited for $1,200.00.

Cash	
1,200.00	

Treasury Stock	
Balance 6,000.00	1,200.00
(New Bal. 4,800.00)	

STEPS

JOURNALIZE THE SALE OF TREASURY STOCK FOR ORIGINAL COST

1 Write the date in the Date column of the cash receipts journal.

2 Enter the account title, *Treasury Stock*, in the Account Title column.

3 Record the receipt number identified by the letter R, *R205*, in the Doc. No. column.

4 Write the debit amount, *1,200.00*, in the Cash Debit column.

5 Record the credit amount, *1,200.00*, in the General Credit column.

small business spotlight

SMALL BUSINESS SPOTLIGHT

There are many challenges associated with starting a new business or growing an existing one. Over 3.5 million small business owners and aspiring entrepreneurs have looked to SCORE to help them meet these challenges. SCORE (Service Corps of Retired Executives) includes over 12,000 trained volunteer business counselors dedicated to sharing real-world business experience with their clients. SCORE business counselors provide advice in areas such as writing a business plan, managing cash flow, assessing capital needs, starting or operating a business, and buying or selling a business. With almost 400 local chapters, SCORE provides face-to-face counseling along with low-cost workshops and seminars. Program topics are often tailored to meet the specific needs of a community.

EXPLAIN

- Point out that a corporation may acquire treasury stock to regain control of a corporation or to have additional stock to use for other purposes such as stock options, stock dividends, and stock bonuses.

- Explain that companies may sell treasury stock at any time.

- Emphasize that Treasury Stock is a contra stockholders' equity account and is therefore increased with a debit and decreased with a credit. Refer to illustration.

- Point out that when treasury stock is sold, it must be removed from the treasury stock account at the same value for which it was originally purchased. Once treasury stock is sold, it is again considered as outstanding stock for it is back in the hands of stockholders.

DEMONSTRATE

Analyze the transaction

- Draw two blank T accounts on the board.

- Ask a student to read the transaction statement.

- Ask students to analyze the transaction by answering: what accounts are affected, what is the classification of each account, are they increased or decreased, and are they debited or credited. Complete the T accounts as the information is provided.

Record the transaction

- Use the cash receipts journal transparency to illustrate the process for recording the entry in the journal.

- Record each item in the journal following the five steps shown.

SMALL BUSINESS SPOTLIGHT

SMALL BUSINESS SPOTLIGHT

The Small Business Spotlight feature describes how SCORE business counselors can help small business owners and aspiring entrepreneurs.

EXPLAIN

- Remind students that a corporation records treasury stock at the price paid regardless of the stock's par or stated value. It follows then that when treasury stock is sold, it is removed from the treasury stock account at the same value for which it was originally purchased.

- Point out that sometimes, however, treasury stock is sold for more than its original cost. In this instance, the amount received in excess of the treasury stock's original cost is credited to Paid-in Capital from Sale of Treasury Stock. Refer to the illustration.

- Emphasize that Paid-in Capital from Sale of Treasury Stock is a stockholders' equity account. It is increased with a credit and decreased with a debit.

DEMONSTRATE

Calculate excess amount

- Read the transaction statement.
- Use the math box on the page to explain the process for calculating the amount received in excess of original cost.
- Use the board or overhead to show how the excess amount is calculated manually.
- Ask students to verify amounts with a calculator.

Analyze the transaction

- Draw three blank T accounts on the board.
- Ask a student to read the transaction statement.
- Ask students to analyze the transaction by answering: what accounts are affected, what is the classification of each account, are they increased or decreased, and are they debited or credited. Complete the T accounts as the information is provided.

Record the transaction

- Use the cash receipts journal transparency to illustrate the process for recording the entry in the journal.
- Record each item in the journal following the six steps shown.

SELLING TREASURY STOCK FOR MORE THAN ORIGINAL COST

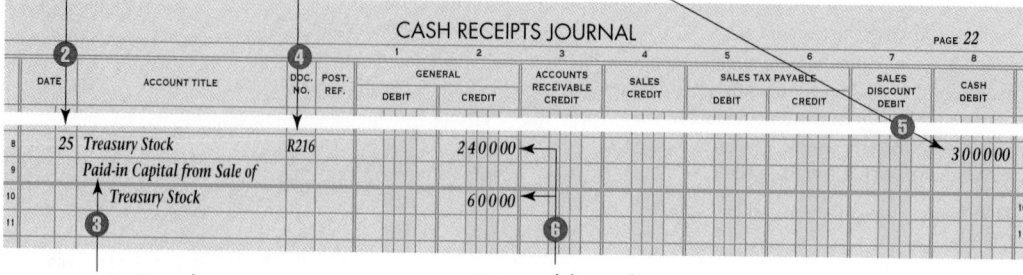

	No. of Shares	×	Value per Share	=	Value
Total received	200	×	$15.00	=	$3,000.00
Original cost	200	×	12.00	=	2,400.00
Amount received in excess of original cost					$ 600.00

1. Calculate the amounts to be recorded.

2. Write the date.   **4.** Record the receipt number.   **5.** Write the debit amount.

CASH RECEIPTS JOURNAL — PAGE 22

DATE	ACCOUNT TITLE	DOC. NO.	POST. REF.	GENERAL DEBIT	GENERAL CREDIT	ACCOUNTS RECEIVABLE CREDIT	SALES CREDIT	SALES TAX PAYABLE DEBIT	SALES TAX PAYABLE CREDIT	SALES DISCOUNT DEBIT	CASH DEBIT
25	Treasury Stock	R216			2 400 00						3 000 00
	Paid-in Capital from Sale of										
	Treasury Stock				6 0 0 00						

3. Enter the account titles.   **6.** Record the credit amounts.

LampLight sold 200 shares of treasury stock to Mary Long for $15.00 per share, as shown above.

November 25. Received cash from Mary Long for 200 shares of treasury stock at $15.00 per share, $3,000.00. Treasury stock was bought on October 24 at $12.00 per share. Receipt No. 216.

Cash is debited for $3,000.00, the total amount received from the sale of the treasury stock. Treasury Stock is credited for $2,400.00, the original cost of the 200 shares of treasury stock. Paid-in Capital from Sale of Treasury Stock is credited for $600.00, the amount received in excess of the treasury stock's original cost.

Cash	
3,000.00	

Treasury Stock	
Balance 4,800.00	2,400.00
(New Bal. 2,400.00)	

Paid-in Capital from Sale of Treasury Stock	
	600.00

 FYI FOR YOUR INFORMATION

A corporation may acquire treasury stock to regain control or to have additional stock to use for specific purposes such as stock dividends.

STEPS STEPS • STEPS • STEPS • STEPS • STEPS • STEPS • STEPS • STEPS • STEPS • STEPS • STEPS • STEP

JOURNALIZE THE SALE OF TREASURY STOCK FOR MORE THAN ORIGINAL COST

1 Calculate the amounts to be recorded for the sale of 200 shares of treasury stock at more than the original cost.

2 Write the date in the Date column of the cash receipts journal.

3 Enter the account titles in the Account Title column.

4 Record the receipt number, *R216*, in the Doc. No. column.

5 Write the debit amount in the Cash Debit column.

6 Record the credit amounts in the General Credit column.

Acquiring Additional Capital for a Corporation

SELLING TREASURY STOCK FOR LESS THAN ORIGINAL COST

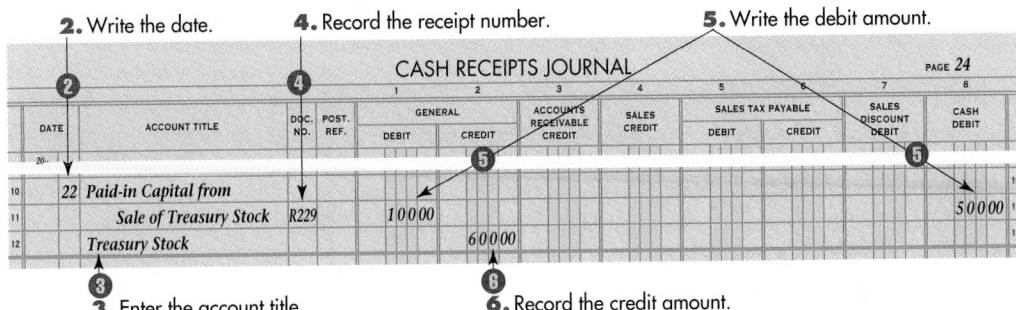

	No. of Shares	×	Value per Share	=	Value
Original cost	50	×	$12.00	=	$600.00
Total received	50	×	10.00	=	500.00
Amount received less than original cost					$100.00

1. Calculate the amounts to be recorded. ❶

2. Write the date. ❷ **4.** Record the receipt number. ❹ **5.** Write the debit amount. ❺

CASH RECEIPTS JOURNAL PAGE 24

					1	2	3	4	5	6	7	8	
	DATE	ACCOUNT TITLE	DOC. NO.	POST. REF.	GENERAL DEBIT	GENERAL CREDIT	ACCOUNTS RECEIVABLE CREDIT	SALES CREDIT	SALES TAX PAYABLE DEBIT	SALES TAX PAYABLE CREDIT	SALES DISCOUNT DEBIT	CASH DEBIT	
10	22	Paid-in Capital from											10
11		Sale of Treasury Stock	R229		1 0 0 00							5 0 0 00	11
12		Treasury Stock				6 0 0 00							12

3. Enter the account title. ❸ **6.** Record the credit amount. ❻

LampLight sold 50 shares of treasury stock to Frank Demetz for $10.00 per share, as shown above.

> **December 22. Received cash from Frank Demetz for 50 shares of treasury stock at $10.00 per share, $500.00. Treasury stock was originally bought October 24 at $12.00 per share. Receipt No. 229.**

Cash is debited for $500.00, the total amount of cash received. Paid-in Capital from Sale of Treasury Stock is debited for $100.00, the amount received that is less than the treasury stock's original cost. Treasury Stock is credited for $600.00, the original cost.

When treasury stock transactions occur, no entry is made in Capital Stock—Common or Capital Stock—Preferred. Treasury stock is considered to

Cash

| 500.00 | |

Paid-in Capital from Sale of Treasury Stock

| 100.00 | Balance | 600.00 |
| | (New Bal. | 500.00) |

Treasury Stock

| Balance | 2,400.00 | 600.00 |
| (New Bal. | 1,800.00) | |

be issued stock. The difference between the balances of the capital stock accounts and the treasury stock account is the value of outstanding stock. After the entry on December 22 for the sale of treasury stock, the number of LampLight's outstanding shares of capital stock is calculated as follows:

	No. of Shares Issued	−	No. of Shares of Treasury Stock	=	No. of Shares Outstanding
Preferred	1,700	−	0	=	1,700
Common	32,100	−	150	=	31,950

Treasury Stock Transactions

Lesson 12-2   **353**

EXPLAIN

- Point out that sometimes treasury stock is sold for less than its original purchase cost. In this instance, the amount received less than the treasury stock's original cost is debited to Paid-in Capital from Sale of Treasury Stock.
- Stress that the Capital Stock account is *not* affected when treasury stock is bought or sold.
- Point out that capital stock less treasury stock equals outstanding stock. Outstanding stock represents the value or the number of shares of stock in the hands of the stockholders.

DEMONSTRATE

Analyze the transaction

- Draw three blank T accounts on the board.
- Ask a student to read the transaction statement.
- Ask students to analyze the transaction. Use the math illustration to help students calculate the amount received less than original cost. Complete the T accounts as the information is provided.

Record the transaction

- Use the cash receipts journal transparency to illustrate the process for recording the entry in the journal.
- Record each item in the journal following the five steps shown in the illustration.

Compute shares outstanding

- Review the treasury stock transactions presented in this lesson. Point out that 500 shares of stock were originally purchased by the corporation and that 350 were then sold, leaving a balance of 150 shares.
- Use the math illustration and the board to show the process for calculating the number of shares outstanding.

ONGOING ASSESSMENT

- Circulate through the classroom or lab, observing which students have problems with assignments.
- Troubleshooting: Students may have difficulty remembering the rules for increasing and decreasing Treasury Stock and Paid-in Capital from Sale of Treasury Stock.
- Assess student understanding by checking solutions to the Independent Practice assignments.

RETEACH

- Draw three T accounts arranged in a vertical column on the board or overhead.
- Label the top account Cash, the middle Treasury Stock, and the bottom Paid-in Capital from Sale of Treasury Stock.
- Ask a student to record a corporation's $20,000 cash purchase of 1,000 shares of its own stock at $20 a share.
- Ask a student to record a transaction showing the sale of 200 shares of treasury stock at $23 a share.
- Ask a student to record a transaction showing the sale of 100 shares of treasury stock at $18 a share.

353

GUIDED PRACTICE

Term Review

Call on a student to define the term in the Term Review. After the definition ask the class if the definition is correct and whether the complete definition has been given or if anything else needs to be added. The suggested definition is given in the Glossary.

Audit Your Understanding

Call on students to answer the Audit Your Understanding questions. Ask the class if the answer is correct and/or complete. Answers are given in Appendix E of the textbook.

Work Together

Have students write the solution to the Work Together problem as you guide the class through the examples.

- Direct students to record each transaction in the appropriate journal as you guide the class through the examples.

- Call on students to read and analyze a transaction.

- Use T accounts to help student analysis and to record responses.

INDEPENDENT PRACTICE

On Your Own

- Assign the On Your Own problem to be worked independently.

- Use the Ongoing Assessment techniques to diagnose student understanding.

Application Problem

- Assign Application Problem 12-2: Journalizing treasury stock transactions.

Personal Trainer

- Students can access the Lesson 12-2 assessment material using this software.

Xtra! Web Site

- Students can access the Xtra! Study Tools for additional practice.

ENRICH

- Ask students to read the Small Business Spotlight feature on page 351. Ask students to discuss examples of retired executives helping small businesses.

354

---

term review

treasury stock

audit your understanding

1. What is treasury stock?

2. What accounts are affected, and how, when treasury stock is sold for more than its original cost?

3. What accounting concept is being applied when a corporation records the purchase of treasury stock at the price paid regardless of the stock's par or stated value?

work together 12-2

Journalizing treasury stock transactions

Page 11 of a cash receipts journal and page 8 of a cash payments journal are provided in the *Working Papers*. Your instructor will guide you through the following examples.

Mar. 9. Paid cash to Dana O'Brien for 300 shares of $20.00 stated value common stock at $22.00 per share, $6,600.00. Check No. 753.

12. Received cash from Doug Johnston for 100 shares of treasury stock at $24.00 per share, $2,400.00. Treasury stock was purchased on March 9 at $22.00 per share. Receipt No. 409.

13. Received cash from Ida Mann for 100 shares of treasury stock at $22.00 per share, $2,200.00. Treasury stock was purchased on March 9 at $22.00 per share. Receipt No. 410.

16. Received cash from Kathy Milhouse for 100 shares of treasury stock at $21.00 per share, $2,100.00. Treasury stock was purchased on March 9 at $22.00 per share. Receipt No. 411.

1. Journalize each transaction completed during the current year.

on your own 12-2

Journalizing treasury stock transactions

Page 7 of a cash receipts journal and page 6 of a cash payments journal are provided in the *Working Papers*. Work independently to complete the following problem.

Aug. 22. Paid cash to Tai Arriaga for 500 shares of $15.00 stated value common stock at $15.00 per share, $7,500.00. Check No. 172.

23. Received cash from Joyce Cariel for 250 shares of treasury stock at $14.00 per share, $3,500.00. Treasury stock was purchased on August 22 at $15.00 per share. Receipt No. 85.

25. Received cash from Stan Gavin for 250 shares of treasury stock at $15.00 per share, $3,750.00. Treasury stock was purchased on August 22 at $15.00 per share. Receipt No. 86.

26. Paid cash to Cindy Hopper for 750 shares of $15.00 stated value common stock at $16.00 per share, $12,000.00. Check No. 173.

27. Received cash from Tim Coburn for 100 shares of treasury stock at $17.00 per share, $1,700.00. Treasury stock was purchased on August 26 at $16.00 per share. Receipt No. 87.

1. Journalize each transaction completed during the current year.

CLOSE

- Ask students to prepare a list of all new accounts introduced in this lesson. These accounts include: Treasury Stock and Paid-in Capital from Sale of Treasury Stock.

- Ask students to draw T accounts for each under the appropriate headings Assets,

Liabilities, and Stockholders' Equity.

- Ask students to place a "+" or "−" on the appropriate increase or decrease side on each account.

- Ask students to write the definition or purpose of each account.

12-3 Bonds Payable Transactions

Read

CORPORATE BONDS PAYABLE

For a growing business, the capital needed to expand may come from three sources:

1. Using retained earnings.
2. Selling additional capital stock.
3. Borrowing the funds.

A business's management team may find that capital needed for expansion could be accumulated from retained net income during the next 5 to 10 years. However, the business may need the additional capital within the next year. A corporation's board of directors must decide whether to raise the needed capital by selling additional stock or borrowing the money.

An advantage of selling stock is that the additional capital becomes part of a corporation's permanent capital. Permanent capital does not have to be returned to stockholders as long as the business continues to operate. Another advantage is that dividends do not have to be paid to stockholders unless the earnings are sufficient to warrant such payments. A disadvantage of selling more stock to raise additional capital is that the ownership is spread over more shares and more owners.

An advantage of borrowing the additional capital is that stockholders' equity is not spread over additional shares of stock. A disadvantage

is that interest must be paid on the loan, which decreases the net income. This decrease in net income decreases the amount available for dividends. Another disadvantage of borrowing additional capital is that the amount borrowed must be repaid in the future.

Large loans are sometimes difficult to obtain for short periods. Corporations frequently borrow needed capital with the provision that the loan be repaid several years in the future. Therefore, the loan can be paid out of future earnings accumulated over several years.

Large loans may also be difficult to obtain from one bank or one individual. A printed, long-term promise to pay a specified amount on a specified date and to pay interest at stated intervals is called a **bond**. Bonds are similar to notes payable because both are written promises to pay. However, most notes payable are for one year or less, but bonds generally run for a long period of time, such as 5, 10, or 20 years. Also, bonds payable tend to be issued for larger amounts than notes payable.

All bonds representing the total amount of a loan are called a **bond issue**. A corporation usually sells an entire bond issue to a securities dealer who sells individual bonds to the public.

©GETTY IMAGES/PHOTODISC

DEMONSTRATE

Analyze the transaction

- Draw two blank T accounts on the board.
- Ask a student to read the July 1, 20X0, transaction statement.
- Ask students to analyze the transaction by answering: what accounts are affected, what is the classification of each account, are they increased or decreased, and are they debited or credited. Complete the T accounts as the information is provided.

Record the transaction

- Use the cash receipts journal transparency to illustrate the process for recording the entry in the journal.
- Repeat the same demonstration process for journalizing the payment of interest. Use the cash payments journal to record the entry. Refer to the math illustration so that students understand how to calculate the amount of annual interest to be paid on the bond issue.

ISSUING BONDS

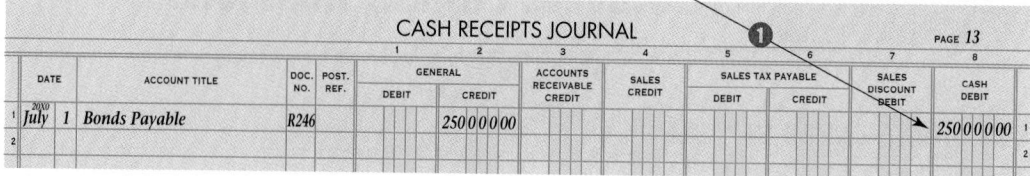

1. Record the issuance of the bonds.

	DATE	ACCOUNT TITLE	DOC. NO.	POST. REF.	GENERAL DEBIT	GENERAL CREDIT	ACCOUNTS RECEIVABLE CREDIT	SALES CREDIT	SALES TAX PAYABLE DEBIT	SALES TAX PAYABLE CREDIT	SALES DISCOUNT DEBIT	CASH DEBIT	
1	20X0 July 1	Bonds Payable	R246			250 000 00						250 000 00	1
2													2

CASH RECEIPTS JOURNAL — PAGE 13

On July 1, 20X0, LampLight borrowed $250,000.00 to expand its building. LampLight issued 250, 12%, $1,000.00 par value bonds. The bonds are scheduled to mature in five years. Annual interest on the bonds is to be paid on July 1 of each year. The bond issue was sold at par value to a securities dealer. The journal entry to record the sale of the bonds is shown above.

July 1, 20X0. Received cash for the face value of a five-year, 12%, $1,000.00 par value bond issue, $250,000.00. Receipt No. 246.

Cash is debited for $250,000.00. Bonds Payable is credited for $250,000.00.

Cash	
250,000.00	

Bonds Payable	
	250,000.00

PAYING INTEREST ON BONDS

Balance Owed on Bond Issue	×	Bond Interest Rate	=	Annual Interest
$250,000.00	×	12%	=	$30,000.00

1. Calculate the annual interest.

2. Record the payment of interest.

	DATE	ACCOUNT TITLE	CK. NO.	POST. REF.	GENERAL DEBIT	GENERAL CREDIT	ACCOUNTS PAYABLE DEBIT	PURCHASES DISCOUNT CREDIT	CASH CREDIT	
1	20X1 July 1	Interest Expense	562		30 000 00				30 000 00	1
2										2

CASH PAYMENTS JOURNAL — PAGE 13

A year's interest is paid to each bondholder on July 1 of each year until the bond's maturity date. A person or institution, usually a bank, given legal authorization to administer property for the benefit of property owners is called a **trustee**. LampLight pays the interest amount to a bond trustee who in turn handles the details of paying each individual bondholder.

July 1, 20X1. Paid cash to bond trustee for annual interest on bond issue, $30,000.00. Check No. 562.

Interest Expense is debited for $30,000.00. Cash is credited for $30,000.00. The journal entry to record this transaction is shown above.

Interest Expense	
30,000.00	

Cash	
	30,000.00

Acquiring Additional Capital for a Corporation

TEACHING STRATEGIES   COOPERATIVE LEARNING

Divide the class into groups of four or five students each. Using Cases for Critical Thinking, each group analyzes the cases and arrives at agreed-upon solutions. One member of each group is appointed the recorder and presents the groups analysis to the class. This cooperative learning activity should not take more than 20–25 minutes of class time.

DEPOSITING CASH IN A BOND SINKING FUND

1. Record the initial payment to the bond sinking fund.

					GENERAL		ACCOUNTS PAYABLE DEBIT	PURCHASES DISCOUNT CREDIT	CASH CREDIT	
	DATE	ACCOUNT TITLE	CK. NO.	POST. REF.	DEBIT	CREDIT				
	20X1									
2	1	Bond Sinking Fund	563		50 000 00				50 000 00	2
3										3

CASH PAYMENTS JOURNAL   PAGE 13

To assure bondholders that the bond issue will be paid at maturity, LampLight annually deposits a portion of the loan value with the bond trustee. An amount set aside to pay a bond issue when due is called a **bond sinking fund**. LampLight spreads the $250,000.00 amount over the five years that the bond issue is outstanding. The bond sinking fund is increased each year by $50,000.00, one-fifth of the total principal. On the bond issue's maturity date, a total of $250,000.00 will be available in the bond sinking fund to pay the bondholders.

July 1, 20X1. Paid cash to bond trustee for annual deposit to bond sinking fund, $50,000.00. Check No. 563.

Bond Sinking Fund is debited for $50,000.00. Cash is credited for $50,000.00. The entry to record the deposit for 20X1 is shown above.

DEPOSITING CASH TO SINKING FUND AND RECORDING INCOME EARNED

Amount of Increase in Sinking Fund	−	Interest Earned During Year	=	Amount to be Deposited
$50,000.00	−	$2,000.00	=	$48,000.00

1. Calculate the amount to be deposited in the fund.

2. Record the payment to the bond sinking fund.

CASH PAYMENTS JOURNAL   PAGE 13

					GENERAL		ACCOUNTS PAYABLE DEBIT	PURCHASES DISCOUNT CREDIT	CASH CREDIT	
	DATE	ACCOUNT TITLE	CK. NO.	POST. REF.	DEBIT	CREDIT				
1	20X2 July 1	Bond Sinking Fund	610		50 000 00				48 000 00	1
2		Interest Income				2 000 00				2

The bond trustee invests the sinking fund. The interest earned reduces the deposit that Lamp-Light must make. For example, the trustee reports to LampLight that the sinking fund investment earned $2,000.00. Thus, on July 1, 20X2, Lamp-Light pays only $48,000.00 to the trustee.

July 1, 20X2. Paid cash to bond trustee for annual deposit to bond sinking fund, $48,000.00, and recorded interest earned on bond sinking fund, $2,000.00. Check No. 610.

Bond Sinking Fund is debited for $50,000.00. Cash is credited for $48,000.00, the actual amount deposited. Interest Income is credited for $2,000.00, the amount of interest earned. The journal entry to record the deposit for 20X2 is shown above.

As the bond sinking fund balance increases, the amount of interest earned in a year usually increases. Thus, the amount LampLight must deposit each year decreases.

Bonds Payable Transactions

EXPLAIN

- Discuss the purpose of a bond sinking fund. Emphasize that bondholders are looking for security in their investments and like to feel confident that a bond issue will be paid at maturity. Annual deposits to a bond sinking fund provide assurance.

- Point out that Bond Sinking Fund is an asset account and therefore increased with a debit.

- Stress that the bond sinking fund earns interest, thereby reducing the amount of the annual deposit. Review the math illustration to emphasize this point.

DEMONSTRATE

Analyze the transaction

- Draw two blank T accounts on the board.

- Ask a student to read the July 1, 20X1, transaction statement.

- Ask students to analyze the transaction by answering: what accounts are affected, what is the classification of each account, are they increased or decreased, and are they debited or credited. Complete the T accounts as the information is provided.

Record the transaction

- Use the cash payments journal transparency to illustrate the process for recording the entry in the journal.

- Record each item in the journal as shown in the illustration.

- Repeat the same demonstration process for journalizing the July 1, 20X2, transaction. Three T accounts are needed to illustrate this transaction.

TEACHING STRATEGIES   DIFFERENT LEARNING STYLES

Visual Learner. When covering journal entries with a visual learner, the instructor should discuss the entries, using a transparency or the board to record the entry. In addition, the student should be asked to mentally picture each part of the entry before the instructor actually writes it on the transparency or board.

RETIRING A BOND ISSUE

	DATE		ACCOUNT TITLE	DOC. NO.	POST. REF.	DEBIT	CREDIT	
1	20X4 July	1	Bonds Payable	M600		250 0 0 0 00		1
2			Bond Sinking Fund				250 0 0 0 00	2
3								3

GENERAL JOURNAL   PAGE 6

A bond sinking fund is an asset to LampLight until the trustee makes payment to the bondholders. When LampLight's bonds are due, the bond trustee uses the bond sinking fund to pay the bondholders. Paying the amounts owed to bondholders for a bond issue is called **retiring a bond issue**. The journal entry to retire the bonds is shown above.

July 1, 20X4. Received notice from bond trustee that bond issue was retired using bond sinking fund, $250,000.00. Memorandum No. 600.

Bonds Payable is debited for $250,000.00, the total amount of the bond issue. Bond Sinking Fund is credited for $250,000.00, the amount in the fund used to retire the bond issue. After this entry is posted, both Bonds Payable and Bond Sinking Fund will have zero balances.

All of LampLight's bond issue matures on the same date. Bonds that all mature on the same date are called **term bonds**. Sometimes portions of a bond issue mature on different dates. Portions of a bond issue that mature on different dates are called **serial bonds**. For example, a 10-year bond issue with one-tenth of the bonds maturing every year is a serial bond issue. An advantage of serial bonds is that interest does not have to be paid on the total bond issue for the total 10 years.

Bonds Payable

Retired	250,000.00	Balance	250,000.00
		(New Bal. zero)	

Bonds Sinking Fund

Balance	250,000.00	Retired	250,000.00
(New Bal. zero)			

COMPARISON OF CAPITAL STOCK AND BONDS AS A SOURCE OF CORPORATE CAPITAL

Capital Stock

1. Stockholders are corporate owners.
2. Capital Stock is a stockholders' equity account.
3. Stockholders have a secondary claim against corporate assets.
4. Dividends are paid to stockholders out of corporate net income.
5. Dividends are not fixed costs and do not have to be paid if net income is insufficient.
6. Amount received from sale of stock is relatively permanent capital; amount invested by stockholders does not have to be returned to them in foreseeable future.

Bonds

1. Bondholders are corporate creditors.
2. Bonds Payable is a liability account.
3. Bondholders have a primary, or first, claim against corporate assets.
4. Interest paid to bondholders is a corporate expense.
5. Interest on bonds is a fixed expense; the expense must be paid when due; payment does not depend on amount of net income.
6. Amount received from sale of bonds is not permanent; amount invested by bondholders must be returned to them on bonds' maturity date.

358   Chapter 12   Acquiring Additional Capital for a Corporation

Explore Accounting

EXPLORE ACCOUNTING • EXPLORE ACCOUNTING • EXPLORE ACCOUNTING

Effective Interest Method

It can take a month or more for a company to issue bonds. The process begins when the company determines the number, par value, interest rate, and term of the bonds. The company must then arrange for a securities broker, known as an *underwriter*, obtain an audit, and receive the approval of the Securities and Exchange Commission. During this time, the market interest rate is almost certain to change from the interest rate of the bonds, known as the *stated interest rate*.

Investors will adjust the price they are willing to pay for the bond, based on the current market rate. If the market interest rate is above the stated interest rate, investors are not willing to pay full price for a bond that yields a below-market rate. Thus, the bond will be sold at a discount. However, if the market interest rate is below the stated interest rate, investors are willing to pay extra to earn an above-market rate. This bond will be sold at a premium.

Mentor Corporation is preparing to issue $2,000,000 in 7.5%, 10-year, $1,000.00 par value bonds. When the time finally arrives to issue the bonds, the market interest rate has risen to 8.0%. As a result, Mentor is able to sell the bonds for only $1,969,477.50, an amount that will enable investors to earn an 8.0% return on their investment. The interest rate earned by investors of bonds is referred to as the *effective interest rate*. Because the effective interest rate is greater than the stated interest rate, the bond is sold at a discount, as reflected in the journal entry to record the bonds.

Cash 1,969,477.50
Discount on Bonds
    Payable 30,522.50
    Bonds Payable 2,000,000.00

Discount on Bonds Payable is a contra liability account. At any time, the net balance of the Discount on Bonds Payable and Bonds Payable

accounts is the book value of the bonds payable. At the end of the bond term, Mentor must pay the investors $2,000,000.00 even though the bonds were sold for less than that amount. The $2,000,000.00 credit to Bonds Payable reflects this liability.

Mentor also owes the investors a semi-annual interest payment of 7.5% on the $2,000,000.00 face value of the bonds. The amount debited to Interest Expense is calculated using the book value of the bonds multiplied by the effective interest rate. The interest payment is calculated using the face value of the bonds multiplied by the stated interest rate.

Interest Expense 78,779.10
    ($1,969,477.50 × 8.0% × 6/12)
    Discount on Bonds Payable 3,779.10
    Cash 75,000.00
    ($2,000,000.00 × 7.5% × 6/12)

The difference between the two amounts, $3,779.10, is credited to Discount on Bonds Payable, reducing the balance of this account. At the final interest payment, the bonds' due date, the balance of Discount on Bonds Payable will be zero and the book value of the bonds will equal their face value.

Each year during the 5-year bond period, Mentor's interest expense will be 8.0% of the bonds' book value. Recording interest expense on bonds payable using the effective interest rate is referred to as the *effective interest rate method*.

Instructions

Equity Corporation is preparing to issue $3,000,000 in 8%, 10-year, $1,000.00 par value bonds. At the time of issue, the market interest rate has risen. What is the journal entry to record the bond issue if the bonds are sold for $2,843,213.00?

EXPLORE ACCOUNTING
EXPLORE ACCOUNTING

Cash 2,843,213.00
Discount on
    Bonds Payable 156,787.00
    Bonds Payable 3,000.00

The effective interest rate method can be difficult for students to understand. Ask students to explain why and how increases and decreases in market interest rates will change the price at which bonds can be sold. Write the illustrated transactions in T accounts and calculate the new balance of Discount on Bonds Payable. Explain that Mentor would have recorded a premium if the market interest rates had declined below 7.5%. However, the method used to calculate the interest payments is the same, except that the journal entry would contain a debit to Premium on Bonds Payable.

Challenge advanced students to prepare the journal entry for the second interest payment.

Interest Expense 78,930.26
    ($1,973,256.60 × 8.0% × 6/12)
    Discount on Bonds Payable . . 3,930.26
    Cash 75,000.00
    ($2,000,000.00 × 7.5% × 6/12)

Ask students to explain why the amount of interest expense increased from the first to the second interest payment *(the book value of the bonds increased with the credit to Discount on Bonds Payable).*

GUIDED PRACTICE

Terms Review

- Ask students to write the definition for each term in the Terms Review. Allow students to use their texts.

- Ask a student to read the definition for a selected term. Ask the class if the definition is correct and whether the complete definition has been given or if anything else needs to be added. The suggested definitions are given in the Glossary.

Audit Your Understanding

Call on students to answer the Audit Your Understanding questions. Ask the class if the answer is correct and/or complete. Answers are given in Appendix E of the textbook.

Work Together

Have students write the solution to the Work Together problem as you guide the class through the examples.

- Call on a student to read and analyze a transaction.

- Use T accounts to help student analysis and to record responses.

- Direct students to record each transaction in the appropriate journal as you guide the class through the examples.

INDEPENDENT PRACTICE

On Your Own

- Assign the On Your Own problem to be worked independently.

- Use the Ongoing Assessment techniques to diagnose student understanding.

Application Problem

- Assign Application Problem 12-3: Journalizing bonds payable transactions.

Personal Trainer

- Students can access the Lesson 12-3 assessment material using this software.

Xtra! Web Site

- Students can access the Xtra! Study Tools for additional practice.

ENRICH

- Assign Explore Accounting on page 359.

CLOSE

- Ask students to prepare a list of all accounts used in this lesson. These accounts include: Cash, Bonds Payable, Interest Expense, Bond Sinking Fund, and Interest Income.

360

- Ask students to draw T accounts for each under the appropriate headings Assets, Liabilities, Stockholders' Equity, Revenue, Cost, and Expense.

- Ask students to place a "+" or "−" on the appropriate increase or decrease side on each account.

- Ask students to write the definition or purpose of each account.

• terms review

bond
bond issue
trustee
bond sinking fund
retiring a bond issue
term bonds
serial bonds

• audit your understanding

1. What are two advantages of raising needed capital by selling stock?
2. What is an advantage of raising additional capital by borrowing?
3. What is a disadvantage of borrowing additional capital?
4. What accounts are affected, and how, when cash is deposited in a bond sinking fund in the second year of a bond issue?

• work together 12-3

Journalizing bonds payable transactions

On February 1, 20X1, Cyrotech, Inc., received $300,000.00 cash for a bond issue. The bond agreement provides that a bond sinking fund is to be increased annually by $37,500.00 for the next eight years. The bond trustee has guaranteed Cyrotech an interest rate of 4% on its sinking fund investment. A cash receipts journal, cash payments journal, and general journal are provided in the *Working Papers*. Your instructor will guide you through the following examples.

Feb. 1, 20X1. Received cash for face value of an 8-year, 10%, $500.00 par value bond issue, $300,000.00. Receipt No. 135.
1, 20X2. Paid cash to bond trustee for annual interest on bond issue, $30,000.00. Check No. 201.
1, 20X2. Paid cash to bond trustee for first annual deposit to bond sinking fund. Check No. 202.
1, 20X3. Paid cash to bond trustee for annual interest on bond issue, $30,000.00. Check No. 313.
1, 20X3. Paid cash to bond trustee for annual deposit to bond sinking fund and recorded interest earned on bond sinking fund. Check No. 314. (Interest earned equals 4% of the bond sinking fund deposit made on February 1, 20X2.)
3, 20X9. Received notice from bond trustee that bond issue was retired using bond sinking fund, $300,000.00. Memorandum 87.

1. Journalize the transactions.

• on your own 12-3

Journalizing bonds payable transactions

On May 1, 20X1, Biotech, Inc., received $500,000.00 cash for a bond issue. The bond agreement provides that a bond sinking fund is to be increased annually by $100,000.00 for the next five years. The bond trustee has guaranteed Biotech an interest rate of 5% on its sinking fund investment. A cash receipts journal, cash payments journal, and general journal are provided in the *Working Papers*. Work independently to complete the following problem.

May 1, 20X1. Received cash for face value of a 5-year, 8%, $1,000.00 par value bond issue, $500,000.00. Receipt No. 63.
1, 20X2. Paid cash to bond trustee for annual interest on bond issue, $40,000.00. Check No. 71.
1, 20X2. Paid cash to bond trustee for annual deposit to bond sinking fund. Check No. 72.
1, 20X3. Paid cash to bond trustee for annual interest on bond issue. Check No. 173.
1, 20X3. Paid cash to bond trustee for annual deposit to bond sinking fund and recorded interest earned on bond sinking fund. Check No. 174. (Interest earned equals 5% of the bond sinking fund deposit made on May 1, 20X2.)
2, 20X6. Received notice from bond trustee that bond issue was retired using bond sinking fund, $500,000.00. Memorandum 33.

1. Journalize the transactions.

360 Chapter 12   Acquiring Additional Capital for a Corporation

After completing this chapter, you can

1. Define accounting terms related to acquiring capital for a corporation.

2. Identify accounting concepts and practices related to acquiring capital for a corporation.

3. Journalize entries for issuing additional capital stock.

4. Journalize entries for buying and selling treasury stock.

5. Journalize entries for bonds payable.

Explore Accounting

EXPLORE ACCOUNTING • EXPLORE ACCOUNTING • EXPLORE ACCOUN

Convertible Bonds

Corporations often use long-term bonds to raise the investment capital required to expand operations. A bond is a contract between the corporation and the bondholder. The corporation promises to pay the bondholder interest during the life of the bond and the bond principle at the maturity date.

A corporation can add a variety of provisions to a bond contract. One such provision is referred to as a conversion option. A bond that can be exchanged for a specified number of capital stock is called a *convertible bond*. At the bondholder's request, the bond can be traded, or converted, for a specified number of shares of the corporation.

Assume that Chris Harrison purchased a 10%, 20-year, $1,000 convertible bond from Castle Corporation. The bond is convertible to 40 shares of Castle's capital stock. Castle's stock is traded at $12 per share on the bond issuance date. Chris can elect to convert the bond any time during the life of the bond.

Chris has no incentive to convert the bond to stock until the market value of the stock climbs above the $25 conversion price ($1,000 bond/ 40 shares = $25 per share). The market price of the stock in the future will determine whether Chris elects to convert his bond.

Suppose the market price climbs to $20 per share but is not expected to increase. Chris would

not convert his bond to stock, since the converted stock would only be worth $800 ($20 × 40 shares). Thus, Chris would hold the bond to maturity and receive the $1,000 maturity value.

If the market price climbs to $30 per share, Chris can convert his bond and receive 40 shares of stock. The stock is immediately worth $1,200 ($30 × 40 shares). Chris can sell his stock, earning an instant $200 gain. However, Chris can also hold the stock in hope that the stock price will continue to rise.

Why would a corporation issue convertible bonds? When purchasing the bond, Chris knew that there was the potential to earn money in addition to the interest income if the stock rose above $25. Thus, Chris accepted a 12% interest rate on the bond instead of the 13% market rate for bonds with no conversion feature. Thus, Castle Corporation's interest expense was reduced due to the conversion feature.

Required:
Assume Chris converted his stock and immediately sold the stock for a $200 gain. Research how this $200 gain should be recorded in the corporation's financial statements. Do you agree with the findings of your research?

Acquiring Additional Capital for a Corporation

EXPLORE ACCOUNTING
EXPLORE ACCOUNTING

When a corporation issues convertible bonds, it may choose to record the proceeds entirely as debt or as divided between a debt portion and an equity portion. In practice, most corporations record convertible bond proceeds entirely as debt. In this case, a corporation does not recognize any gain or loss when the bonds are converted. The carrying value of the bonds is simply transferred to the capital stock account. If the corporation separates debt and equity portions of the convertible bonds, then some recognition of the market value of the stock at the time of conversion is necessary. Student answers should reflect understanding of the differences between debt and equity in the issuing corporation's accounts.

- Ask students for examples of each summary item. List their responses on the board or overhead. Refer to illustrations in the text that match student responses.

INDEPENDENT PRACTICE

- Assign Mastery Problem 12-4 to students who need the reinforcement of a problem that combines all activities from the chapter in one problem; this will be most students.

- Assign Challenge Problem 12-5 to accelerated students who do not require the reinforcement of the Mastery Problem.

- Assign Study Guide 12.

- Students can use Peachtree or QuickBooks to automate Mastery Problem 12-4.

- Students can access Personal Trainer to work end-of-chapter problems on the computer.

- Students can access the Xtra! Web Site for the Xtra! Review and Quizzing.

- Students can access the Student Companion CD for additional review material.

ONGOING ASSESSMENT

Review solutions to the assigned problems in class, diagnosing trouble spots.

RETEACH

- Call on students to describe how they avoid the trouble spots diagnosed.

- Use reteaching suggestions from lesson plans as required.

- Assign Recycling Problem 12-1 if needed.

ENRICH

- Assign the Explore Accounting feature. Ask students to share the information they have gathered in a report to the class.

- Students can access the Xtra! Web Site for the Xtra! Enrichment material.

- Assign Applied Communication.

- Assign the Case for Critical Thinking.

- Assign the SCANS Workplace Competency.

- Assign Auditing for Errors.

- Assign Analyzing Costco's Financial Statements.

- Assign Automated Accounting on page 367.

12-1 APPLICATION PROBLEM   PEACHTREE   QUICKBOOKS
Journalizing capital stock transactions

PC Design, Inc., is authorized to issue 200,000 shares of $5.00 stated value common stock and 50,000 shares of 12%, $100.00 par value preferred stock. PC Design has 25,000 shares of common stock outstanding.

Transactions:

Feb. 8. Andre Cashman sent a check for 5,000 shares of $5.00 stated value common stock at $5.00 per share, $25,000.00. R398.

26. Jason Gutto exchanged a parcel of land at an agreed value of $30,000.00 for 300 shares of $100.00 par value preferred stock. M67.

Apr. 15. Jacquelyn Parker sent a $40,000.00 check for 400 shares of $100.00 par value preferred stock at $100.00 per share. R518.

Aug. 25. Received a $48,000.00 check from Lynn Kruschke for 500 shares of $100.00 par value preferred stock at $96.00 per share. R601.

Dec. 11. Received cash from Behrooz Behzadi for 200 shares of $100.00 par value preferred stock at $102.00 per share, $20,400.00. R698.

Instructions:

Journalize the transactions completed during the current year. Use page 2 of a cash receipts journal and a general journal. Source documents are abbreviated as follows: memorandum, M; receipt, R.

12-2 APPLICATION PROBLEM
Journalizing treasury stock transactions

Advanced Laser, Inc., is authorized to issue 150,000 shares of $10.00 stated value common stock. Advanced Laser has 50,000 shares of stock outstanding.

Transactions:

Feb. 21. Paid cash to Corey Fiske for 400 shares of $10.00 stated value common stock at $10.00 per share, $4,000.00. C87.

27. Received cash from Aurelia Gillien for 125 shares of treasury stock at $10.00 per share, $1,250.00. Treasury stock was bought on February 21 at $10.00 per share. R126.

Mar. 22. Paid cash to Leona Metzger for 750 shares of $10.00 stated value common stock at $11.00 per share, $8,250.00. C138.

Apr. 15. Received cash from Efren Merrill for 275 shares of treasury stock at $12.00 per share, $3,300.00. Treasury stock was bought on February 21 at $10.00 per share. R151.

July 30. Received cash from Susan Matsuda for 300 shares of treasury stock at $10.00 per share, $3,000.00. Treasury stock was bought on March 22 at $11.00 per share. R203.

Instructions:

Journalize the transactions completed during the current year. Use page 2 of a cash receipts journal and page 3 of a cash payments journal. Source documents are abbreviated as follows: check, C; receipt, R.

APPLIED SKILLS   WRITING ACROSS THE CURRICULUM

Writing Paragraphs and Short Essays. The Cases for Critical Thinking are short, practical applications of the accounting principles developed in the chapter. Some cases are planned to present problems related to the chapter but not specifically discussed and answered in the chapter. These cases present an opportunity for critical thinking and decision making. These cases also require more than a short objective-type response. Therefore, they provide ideal practice in writing paragraphs and short essays.

12-3 APPLICATION PROBLEM

Journalizing bonds payable transactions

On January 1, 20X1, Security Communications, Inc., received cash, $200,000.00, for a bond issue. The bond agreement provides that a bond sinking fund is to be increased by $20,000.00 every six months for the next five years.

Transactions:

Jan. 1, 20X1.   Received cash for the face value of a 5-year, 9%, $1,000.00 par value bond issue, $200,000.00. R104.

July 1, 20X1.   Paid cash to bond trustee for semiannual interest on bond issue, $9,000.00. C294.

July 1, 20X1.   Paid cash to bond trustee for semiannual deposit to bond sinking fund, $20,000.00. C295.

Jan. 1, 20X2.   Paid cash to bond trustee for semiannual interest on bond issue, $9,000.00. C504.

Jan. 1, 20X2.   Paid cash to bond trustee for semiannual deposit to bond sinking fund, $19,200.00, and recorded interest earned on bond sinking fund, $800.00. C505.

Jan. 4, 20X6.   Received notice from bond trustee that bond issue was retired using bond sinking fund, $200,000.00. M290.

Instructions:

Journalize the transactions. Use page 1 of a cash receipts journal, page 8 of a cash payments journal, and page 1 of a general journal. Source documents are abbreviated as follows: check, C; memorandum, M; receipt, R.

12-4 MASTERY PROBLEM   PEACHTREE   QUICKBOOKS

Journalizing stock and bond transactions

On January 1, 20X1, Sentry VideoLink, Inc., received cash, $50,000.00, for a bond issue. The bond agreement provides that Sentry VideoLink is to increase a bond sinking fund by $5,000.00 every six months for the next five years.

Transactions:

Jan. 1, 20X1.   Received cash for the face value of a 5-year, 12%, $1,000.00 par value bond issue, $50,000.00. R198.

Jan. 12, 20X1.   Received cash from Stuart Peterson for 1,000 shares of $10.00 stated value common stock at $10.00 per share. R210.

Feb. 21, 20X1.   Paid cash to Ruben Mendoza for 900 shares of $10.00 stated value common stock at $12.00 per share. C97.

Feb. 28, 20X1.   Received cash from Tai Banh for 500 shares of treasury stock at $12.00 per share. Treasury stock was bought on February 21 at $12.00 per share. R215.

Mar. 13, 20X1.   Received cash from Rebecca Munson for 200 shares of $10.00 stated value common stock at $15.00 per share. R220.

Mar. 22, 20X1.   Paid cash to Dermot Concannon for 2,000 shares of $10.00 stated value common stock at $16.00 per share. C138.

Apr. 8, 20X1.   Received cash from Rachel Kaplan for 100 shares of $100.00 par value preferred stock at $101.00 per share. R226.

Apr. 15, 20X1.   Received cash from Blake Kenefick for 300 shares of treasury stock at $18.00 per share. Treasury stock was bought on February 21 at $12.00 per share. R231.

May 15, 20X1.   Received cash from Paige Anderson for 800 shares of $100.00 par value preferred stock at $97.50 per share. R232.

July 1, 20X1.   Paid cash to bond trustee for semiannual interest on bond issue, $3,000.00. C200.

July 1, 20X1.   Paid cash to bond trustee for semiannual deposit to bond sinking fund, $5,000.00. C201.

July 14, 20X1.   Received delivery equipment from Travis Kimball at an agreed-on value of $20,000.00 for 200 shares of $100.00 par value preferred stock. M148.

Application Problem 12-3

Jan. 1, 20X1 entry: Cash is debited for 200,000.00.

July 1, 20X1 entry: debit Interest Expense, 9,000.00 and debit Bond Sinking Fund, 20,000.00.

Mastery Problem 12-4

April 15, 20X1 entry: Paid-in Capital from Sale of Treasury Stock is credited for 1,800.00.

Mar. 22, 20X2 entry: Cash is credited for 32,000.00.

TEACHING STRATEGIES   DIFFERENT LEARNING STYLES

Kinesthetic Learner. When covering journal entries with a kinesthetic learner, the instructor should give the student journal paper and have the student complete the entries as the instructor demonstrates on a transparency or board.

July 23, 20X1. Received cash from Brad Manning for 300 shares of treasury stock at $14.00 per share. Treasury stock consisted of 100 shares bought on February 21 at $12.00 per share and 200 shares bought on March 22 at $16.00 per share. R353.

Jan. 1, 20X2. Paid cash to bond trustee for semiannual interest on bond issue, $3,000.00. C504.

Jan. 1, 20X2. Paid cash to bond trustee for semiannual deposit to bond sinking fund, $4,600.00, and recorded interest earned on bond sinking fund, $400.00. C505.

Jan. 1, 20X6. Received notice from bond trustee that bond issue was retired using bond sinking fund, $50,000.00. M491.

Instructions:

Journalize the transactions. Use page 1 of a cash receipts journal, page 8 of a cash payments journal, and page 1 of a general journal. Source documents are abbreviated as follows: check, C; memorandum, M; receipt, R.

Challenge Problem 12-5
July 1 and Jan. 1 Interest Expense: 10,000.00.

12-5 CHALLENGE PROBLEM

Journalizing stock and bond transactions

Interspan Technologies, Inc., is authorized to issue 100,000 shares of $1.00 stated value common stock and 25,000 shares of 10%, $100.00 par value preferred stock. On January 1, 20X1, Interspan has the following outstanding stock: common stock, 40,000 shares; preferred stock, 10,000 shares. Provisions of a bond issue, January 1, 20X1, include (a) payment of interest on the bond issue on July 1 and January 1 of each year and (b) assurance by Interspan of an increase of $20,000.00 in a bond sinking fund on July 1 and January 1 of each year.

Transactions:

Jan. 1, 20X1. Cash was received for the face value of a 10-year, 10%, $1,000.00 par value bond issue, $200,000.00. R51.

Feb. 5, 20X1. Paid John Salas for 5,000 shares of $1.00 stated value common stock at $1.60 per share. C120.

Feb. 12, 20X1. Cash was received from Michael Donato for 15,000 shares of $1.00 stated value common stock at $1.20 per share. R64.

Feb. 20, 20X1. Carmen Romero paid cash for 500 shares of $100.00 par value preferred stock at $100.00 per share. R105.

Mar. 14, 20X1. Office equipment was received from Elaine Zaballos at an agreed-on value of $7,000.00 for 5,000 shares of $1.00 stated value common stock. M195.

Apr. 3, 20X1. Jennifer Chapman paid cash for 1,000 shares of treasury stock at $1.50 per share, $1,500.00. Treasury stock was bought on February 5 at $1.60 per share. R210.

May 10, 20X1. Deana Maxson paid cash for 300 shares of $100.00 par value preferred stock at $99.00 per share. R387.

July 1, 20X1. Paid semiannual interest to bond trustee on bonds payable. C389.

July 1, 20X1. Paid cash to bond trustee for semiannual deposit to bond sinking fund, $20,000.00. C390.

Sept.18, 20X1. Cash was received from Perry McCarthy for 2,500 shares of treasury stock at $2.00 per share. Treasury stock was bought on February 5 at $1.60 per share. R561.

Oct. 14, 20X1. Raj Vaudagna paid cash for 150 shares of $100.00 par value preferred stock at $103.00 per share. R600.

Jan. 1, 20X2. Paid cash to bond trustee for semiannual interest on bonds payable. C634.

Jan. 1, 20X2. Paid cash to bond trustee for semiannual deposit to bond sinking fund. Interest earned on money in sinking fund since last payment on July 1, $800.00. C635.

Jan. 2, 20X6. Received notice from bond trustee that bond issue was retired using bond sinking fund, $200,000.00. M428.

Instructions:

Journalize the transactions. Use page 1 of a cash receipts journal, page 2 of a cash payments journal, and page 1 of a general journal. Source documents are abbreviated as follows: check, C; memorandum, M; receipt, R.

TEACHING STRATEGIES   DIFFERENT LEARNING STYLES

Print Learner. When covering journal entries with a print learner, the instructor should discuss the entries, using the textbook examples and referring to the textbook. The print learner can later go back and study the entries.

• applied communication

The most important step in the employment process is the interview. During the interview, an employer will ask you a variety of questions about your abilities, qualifications, and attitudes. You must be thoroughly prepared to answer a prospective employer's questions. Two of the most frequently asked interview questions involve your qualifications for the job and your interest in working for the company.

Required:

1. Find a job advertisement in the newspaper or other source for a position for which you are qualified. Write several paragraphs discussing your qualifications for the job.

2. Research the company identified in the job advertisement. Write several paragraphs explaining your interest in working for the company, using specific facts about it.

• case for critical thinking

Cecil Thomas pays $12,000.00 for 2,000 shares of $5.00 stated value common stock of Datkins, Inc. A year later, Mr. Thomas sells the 2,000 shares of stock to Sally Gilliam for a total of $14,000.00. Ms. Gilliam sends a notice to Datkins so that ownership can be changed on the corporation's stock records. An accounting clerk at Datkins is not sure of the correct journal entry. What advice would you give the accounting clerk?

• SCANS workplace competency

Thinking Skills: Reasoning

Concept: Competent employees comprehend basic rules and principles and apply them in solving problems. Reasoning also includes the ability to prepare a series of conclusions, based on a set of given facts.

Application: You have learned a variety of accounting principles and concepts in Chapters 5-12. Using your reasoning ability, apply these new accounting principles and previously learned concepts by completing Reinforcement Activity 2, Part A.

APPLIED COMMUNICATION

CASE FOR

SCANS WORKPLACE COMPETENCY

APPLIED COMMUNICATION

1. Individual student answers will vary. However, when answering the question regarding qualifications, students should discuss those skills, attitudes, personal qualities, accomplishments, and classes related to the jobs for which they are applying. Answers should be brief and conclude with a strong statement emphasizing why the student should be hired.

2. When answering the question regarding interest in a company, students need to make a prospective employer feel as though the company was carefully selected. Topics might include management style, opportunities for advancement, product line, company size, community relations, geographic locations, continued education or training, research and development, or discussions with present employees. Students' answers should demonstrate to the employer that they have carefully researched the organization and that they are truly interested in working for the company.

CASE FOR CRITICAL THINKING

Change of stock ownership does not affect a corporation's general ledger accounts. Regardless of who owns the stock, the stock is still listed on the corporation's records as outstanding stock. No journal entry is made for stock transfer.

SCANS WORKPLACE COMPETENCY

Students may work independently or in small cooperative learning groups. If feasible, allow students to complete the project using Automated Accounting software. Other commercial accounting software may also be used.

ANALYZING COSTCO'S FINANCIAL STATEMENTS

1. Preferred stock and common stock

2. $.005 for each

3. Preferred, 100,000,000; Common, 900,000,000

4. Zero

5. 457,479,000

6. 457,479,000

7. Zero

AUDITING FOR ERRORS

(See the table at the bottom of this page.)

• auditing for errors

Gonzalez Corporation is authorized to issue 1,000,000 shares of $10.00 par value common stock and 100,000 shares of 10%, $100.00 par value preferred stock. The company has the following stock transactions:

June 1	Started the business by issuing 25,000 shares of common stock for $15 per share.
June 30	Issued 3,000 shares of preferred stock for $120 per share.
July 7	Bought 2,000 shares of common stock as treasury stock for $10 per share.
August 10	Sold 500 shares of treasury stock for $12 per share.
September 30	Issued 300 shares of preferred stock for $130 per share.

The bookkeeper has compiled the following data related to the preferred and common stock as of September 30.

Type of Stock	No. of Shares Issued	No. of Shares of Treasury Stock	No. of Shares Outstanding
Common	25,500	2,000	23,500
Preferred	3,000	0	3,300

Instructions:

On a separate piece of paper, redo the chart, making any necessary corrections.

• analyzing Costco's financial statements

Corporations can issue a variety of kinds or classes of stock. Most companies issue common stock. Some companies are also authorized to issue preferred stock. Information about the par value of each kind of stock and the number of shares authorized, issued, and outstanding can be found in the equity section of a corporation's balance sheet. The following definitions will help you with this activity.

If the number of shares issues and outstanding are equal, it means that company has no treasury stock.

Instructions:

1. Using Appendix B in this textbook, go to the balance sheet for Costco Corporation on page B-5. What kinds of stock is Costco authorized to issue?

2. What is the par value of each kind of stock?

3. How many shares of each kind of stock are authorized?

4. How many shares of preferred stock are issued as of 2003?

5. How many shares of common stock are issued as of 2003?

6. How many shares of common stock are outstanding as of 2003?

7. How many shares of treasury stock does Costco hold?

Auditing for Errors Table

Type of Stock	No. of Shares Issued	No. of Shares of Treasury Stock	No. of Shares Outstanding
Common	25,000	1,500	23,500
Preferred	3,300	0	3,300

TEACHING STRATEGIES   PORTFOLIO ASSESSMENT

Financing activities to raise additional capital can be critical to the success and growth of a corporation. Students should select an example of their successful completion of journal entries for acquiring additional capital to include in their portfolio. A copy of the Portfolio Assessment form (blackline master in the Teacher's Resource Guide; also on the Student Companion CD) should be completed by the student and the Description section should include any comments regarding how the student mastered these concepts and procedures.

• Automated Accounting

Understanding Graphs

Using Graphs and Charts

Graphs and charts are pictorial representations of data that may be used to effectively communicate summary information. Graphs and charts can be produced by the computer, displayed on the monitor, and printed to a printer. Graphs and charts are used to clarify the meanings of the words and numbers that appear in the financial statements. They are commonly used to enhance presentations, track sales, monitor expenses, identify trends, and make forecasts.

Graphs and charts can be used to enhance written or oral presentations. In reports, graphs and charts add a visual break for the reader. The reader will often review the graphs and charts to get a quick summary of written material or numerical data. Speakers may use electronic presentation software or overhead transparencies to illustrate important points. Graphs and charts are often an important part of these presentations.

Automated Accounting 8.0 and higher can generate the following types of graphs and charts:

- The Income Statement graph option will produce a bar graph of the major portions of an income statement: revenue, cost of goods sold, operating expenses, and net income.

- The Expense Distribution graph option will produce a pie chart of the expenses.

- The Top Customers option will produce a bar graph of the top five customers in the accounts receivable ledger. If there are no accounts receivable entries made in a sales journal, an "Insufficient data to graph" message will be displayed.

- The Balance Sheet graph option will produce a bar graph of assets, liabilities, and owners' equity.

- The Sales graph option will produce a line graph of the sales by day of the month. If sales have not been recorded in the sales journal data entry window, an "Insufficient data to graph" message will be displayed.

Creating a Graph

To prepare a graph based on financial data:

1. Choose the Graph Selection menu item from the Reports menu or click the Graphs toolbar button.

2. When the Graph Selection dialog box appears, as shown below, select an option.

3. A 3-D bar graph is shown below.

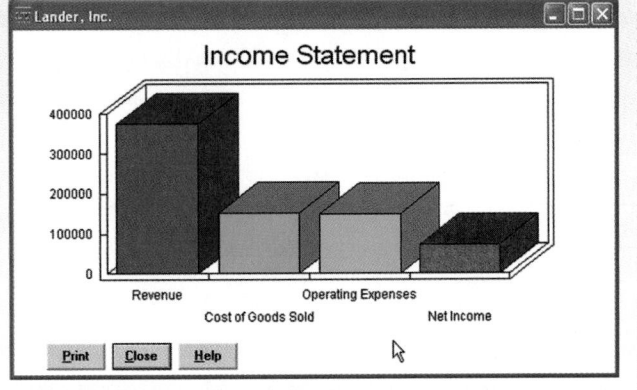

Acquiring Additional Capital for a Corporation

EXPLAIN

- Explain that computer presentations and printed reports frequently include charts and graphs.

- Explain that charts and graphs do not replace numeric data, but they help to effectively explain the data in a graphic way.

- Explain that different styles of graphs are used to display different types of financial information.

- Explain that a pie graph illustrates parts of a whole, such as component percentages.

- Explain that bar graphs show the relative size of related items, such as expenses.

- Explain that line graphs illustrate trends such as net income over a period of years.

- Explain that the Automated Accounting software can generate two and three-dimensional charts and graphs from data on the balance sheet and income statement, as well as additional reports.

DEMONSTRATE

Creating a graph

- Direct students to the illustration as you demonstrate choosing the Graph Selection menu item from the Reports menu or clicking the Graphs toolbar button.

- Demonstrate selecting an option from the Graph Selection dialog box.

- Repeat the demonstration for other types of reports and graphs.

PRACTICE

- Direct students to open an existing problem solution for a comprehensive problem, such as a Mastery Problem, and create a graph for the income statement or balance sheet.

ASSESSMENT

- Review student graphs to assess student understanding.

TEACHING STRATEGIES   PORTFOLIO ASSESSMENT

Students should be encouraged to print at least one graph from the Automated Accounting software to include in their portfolio to demonstrate mastery of automated accounting systems. A copy of the Portfolio Assessment form (blackline master in the Teacher's Resource Guide; also on the Student Companion CD) should be completed by the student and the Description section should include any comments regarding how the student mastered these concepts and procedures.

Financial Analysis and Reporting

	SCOPE & SEQUENCE		ENHANCING	
	NEW	REVIEW/ EXTENSION	SPECIAL FEATURES	
Introduce the Chapter	✓		• Accounting in the Real World: Medtronics	
Lesson 13-1 Work Sheet for a Corporation			• Making Ethical Decisions: Client Referrals	
Adjustment to amortize corporation organization costs	✓		• Explore Accounting: Contingent Liabilities	
Calculating federal income tax	✓			
Completing a work sheet for a corporation		✓		
Lesson 13-2 Financial Statements and Analysis			• Careers in Accounting	
Completing and analyzing financial statements		✓	• Cases for Critical Thinking 1 and 2	
Earnings per share		✓		
Equity per share	✓			
Price-earnings ratio	✓			
Accounts receivable turnover ratio		✓		
Rate earned on average stockholders' equity	✓			
Rate earned on average total assets	✓			
Lesson 13-3 Other End-of-Fiscal-Period Work			• Technology for Business: Electronic Backups	
Adjusting, closing, and reversing entries		✓	• Explore Accounting: Differences Between Generally Accepted Accounting Principles (GAAP) and Tax Law, and Net Income vs. Taxable Income	
Post-closing trial balance		✓		
Federal income tax return for a corporation	✓			
Dissolving a corporation		✓		
Putting It All Together			• Explore Accounting	
			• Xtra! Web Site: Xtra! Enrichment	
			• Applied Communication	
			• SCANS Workplace Competency	
			• Graphing Workshop	
			• Analyzing Costco's Financial Statements	

for a Corporation

INSTRUCTION		PRACTICE AND ASSESSMENT		
TECHNOLOGY AND MEDIA	**TEACHING STRATEGIES**	**GUIDED PRACTICE**	**INDEPENDENT PRACTICE**	**RETEACHING AND ENRICHMENT**
• Internet Research Activity • Accounting Xtra! Web Site	• Software Focus			
• Instructor's Resource CD: PowerPoint Slides • Xtra! Web Site: Xtra! Study Tools • Personal Trainer	• Expanding Beyond the Classroom • Tactile Learner	• Term Review • Audit Your Understanding • Work Together 13-1	• On Your Own 13-1 • Application Problems 13-1 and 13-2 • Ongoing Assessment, p. 375 • Personal Trainer • Xtra! Web Site: Xtra! Study Tools	• Reteach, p. 375 • Enrich, p. 376
• Instructor's Resource CD: PowerPoint Slides • Xtra! Web Site: Xtra! Study Tools • Personal Trainer	• Auditory Learner • Print Learner • Kinesthetic Learner • Visual Learner • Research Project	• Terms Review • Audit Your Understanding • Work Together 13-2	• On Your Own 13-2 • Application Problem 13-3 • Ongoing Assessment, p. 383 • Personal Trainer • Xtra! Web Site: Xtra! Study Tools	• Reteach, p. 383 • Enrich, p. 385
• Instructor's Resource CD: PowerPoint Slides • Xtra! Web Site: Xtra! Study Tools • Personal Trainer	• Expanding Beyond the Classroom • Applied Skills: Language Arts • Cooperative Learning	• Audit Your Understanding • Work Together 13-3	• On Your Own 13-3 • Application Problem 13-4 • Ongoing Assessment, p. 391 • Personal Trainer • Xtra! Web Site: Xtra! Study Tools	• Reteach, p. 391 • Enrich, p. 392
• Automated Accounting • Peachtree and QuickBooks • Personal Trainer • Xtra! Web Site: Xtra! Review, Quizzing, and Enrichment • Student Companion CD	• Applied Mathematics • Applied Skills: Writing Across the Curriculum • Applied Skills: Language Arts		• Mastery Problem 13-5 • Automated Accounting • Peachtree and QuickBooks • Personal Trainer • Xtra! Web Site: Xtra! Review and Quizzing • Study Guide 13 • Student Companion CD • Chapter 13 Test • ExamView Chapter 13 • Portfolio Assessment	• Challenge Problem 13-6 • Reteach, p. 393 • Enrich, p. 393 • Recycling Problem 13-1 • Automated Accounting • Xtra! Web Site: Xtra! Enrichment

INTRODUCE THE CHAPTER

Preview Chapter Objectives

- This chapter focuses on end-of-fiscal-period activities for a corporation, with an emphasis on financial analysis.

Preview Accounting Terms

- Read each term out loud to verify pronunciation for students.

- Point out terms or parts of terms that should already be familiar to most students, such as equity, market value, and average.

INTERNET ACTIVITY

Point your browser to *accountingxtra. swlearning.com* to access the Accounting Xtra! Web Site.

SOFTWARE FOCUS

Software may be used for independent practice or enrichment as the instructor deems appropriate. For this chapter, the following software may be used: Automated Accounting and Century 21 8E CD with Mastery Problem 13-5; Peachtree and QuickBooks with Mastery Problem 13-5; the Student Companion CD; and Personal Trainer, Chapter 13.

Instructors may wish to cover the Automated Accounting feature on pages 400–401 even if the Automated Accounting software is not being used in the classroom so that students get a sense of how the chapter's accounting procedures would be implemented in an automated environment.

CHAPTER

13 Financial Analysis and Reporting for a Corporation

OBJECTIVES & TERMS

After studying Chapter 13, you will be able to:

1. Define terms related to financial analysis and reporting for a corporation.

2. Identify concepts and practices related to financial analysis and reporting for a corporation.

3. Prepare a work sheet for a corporation.

4. Calculate federal income tax for a corporation.

5. Prepare and analyze financial statements for a corporation.

6. Prepare selected end-of-fiscal-period work for a corporation.

- amortization
- earnings per share
- equity per share
- market value

- price-earnings ratio
- rate earned on average stockholders' equity

- rate earned on average total assets

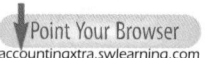
Point Your Browser
accountingxtra.swlearning.com

368

· Medtronics

accounting in the real world

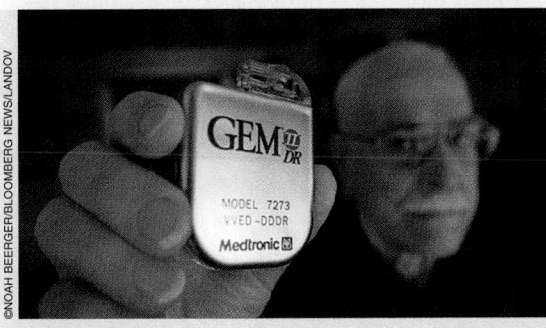

©NOAH BEERGER/BLOOMBERG NEWS/LANDOV

MEDTRONICS: IMPROVING A LIFE EVERY SEVEN SECONDS

An opening page of the Medtronics 2003 Annual Report states, "Every 7 seconds, we help improve another life." Medtronics is a leading manufacturer of medical devices such as pacemakers, heart pumps and valves, implantable brain stimulation systems, internal insulin pumps, thoracic and lumbar spine systems, and much more.

Medtronics' mission is "to contribute to human welfare by the application of biomedical engineering in the research, design, manufacture, and sale of products that alleviate pain, restore health, and extend life."

In order to accomplish this mission, Medtronics must constantly search for new medical devices, treatments, or processes. In a business, this is commonly referred to as "Research and Development," or "R & D." Medtronics has R & D facilities throughout the world. In addition, it sometimes purchases in-process R & D when it acquires another company. All of this R & D is designed to help Medtronics remain a leader in its field.

Critical Thinking

1. Medtronics spent $749.4 million on R & D in one year and $646.3 million the prior year. Calculate the percentage increase for R & D.
2. Pick a company outside the medical device industry. Identify the R & D in which this company would be involved.

Xtra!
Today
accountingxtra.swlearning.com

Source: www.medtronics.com

internet activity

COLLEGE ACCOUNTING PROGRAMS

Search the Internet for "public colleges accounting programs" in your state or a neighboring state. Search one such program and answer the following questions:

Instructions

1. What is the name of the college or university?
2. Does this college offer a bachelor's degree (4 years) or an associate's degree (2 years)?
3. How many semester hours are required for this degree?
4. List one class that is required for this degree.

369

13-1 Work Sheet for a Corporation

Corporations prepare three important financial statements at the end of each fiscal period to report their financial progress and condition. [*CONCEPT: Adequate Disclosure*]

1. Income statement.
2. Statement of stockholders' equity.
3. Balance sheet.

Corporations normally provide an analysis of the financial statements to help interested persons understand and use the information. Information on the income statement is used to analyze component percentages and earnings per share. Information on the statement of stockholders' equity is used to analyze equity per share and determine price-earnings ratio. Balance sheet information is used to determine accounts receivable turnover ratio, the rate earned on average stockholders' equity, and the rate earned on average total assets.

A corporation's board of directors uses the information on the financial statements for making management decisions. The board of directors also uses the information to determine whether to distribute earnings to stockholders. Stockholders and other investors use the information to determine whether to begin or continue investing in the corporation. Creditors use the information to determine whether the corporation will be able to meet its credit obligations.

©GETTY IMAGES/PHOTODISC

MAKING ETHICAL DECISIONS · MAKING ETHICAL DECISIONS · MAKING ETHICAL DECISI

making ethical decisions

Client Referrals

Mason Brick Company has asked its public accounting firm, Farris & Associates, to develop a comprehensive health and retirement program. Knowing that the firm lacks the expertise needed to perform these services, Sarah Farris, a CPA and the managing partner of Farris & Associates, refers Mason Brick Company to another CPA firm, Navarro & Simmons. In appreciation for the referral, Navarro & Simmons gives Sarah Farris an all-expense ski trip to Aspen. Neither accounting firm informs Mason Brick Company of the ski trip.

Instructions

Determine whether the referral was made in accordance with the AICPA *Code of Professional Conduct.*

Financial Analysis and Reporting for a Corporation

ORGANIZATION EXPENSE ADJUSTMENT

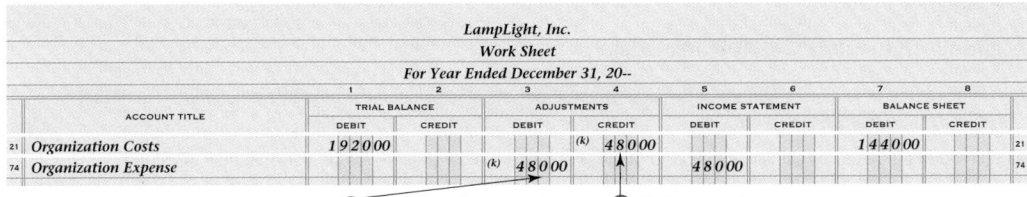

		TRIAL BALANCE		ADJUSTMENTS		INCOME STATEMENT		BALANCE SHEET		
	ACCOUNT TITLE	DEBIT	CREDIT	DEBIT	CREDIT	DEBIT	CREDIT	DEBIT	CREDIT	
21	Organization Costs	1920 00			(k) 480 00			1440 00		21
74	Organization Expense			(k) 480 00		480 00				74

LampLight, Inc.
Work Sheet
For Year Ended December 31, 20--

1. Increase the expense.   **2.** Decrease the asset.

LampLight prepares a work sheet at the end of the fiscal period. Most of its adjustments are similar to those described for Zytech in Part 1. LampLight also records adjustments for organization expense and federal income tax expense.

Corporate organization costs are intangible assets. A common accounting practice is to write off intangible assets over a period of years. Recognizing a portion of an expense in each of several years is called **amortization**.

LampLight incurred total organization costs of $2,400.00. LampLight spreads the $2,400.00 expense over five years. Thus, one-fifth of this amount, $480.00, is amortized in each of the first five years. In the first year, $480.00 was amortized as an expense. An adjustment is

planned on the work sheet for the second year's amortization, as shown above.

Organization Expense is debited for $480.00. Organization Costs is credited for $480.00. The new balance of Organization Costs, $1,440.00, is the amount to be amortized in the next three years.

FYI
FOR YOUR INFORMATION

A recent FASB rule change requires many companies to write off organization costs in the company's first fiscal year. This change will effectively eliminate the amortization of organization costs. However, amortization continues to apply to other intangible assets, such as patents and copyrights owned by a company.

FEDERAL INCOME TAX EXPENSE ADJUSTMENT

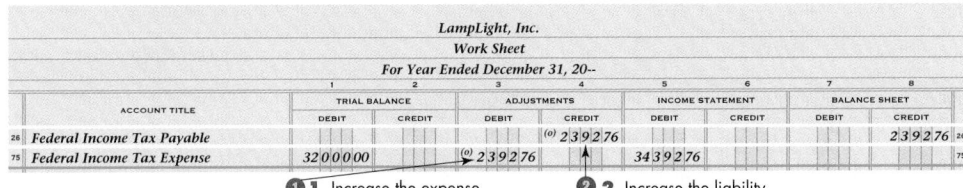

		TRIAL BALANCE		ADJUSTMENTS		INCOME STATEMENT		BALANCE SHEET		
	ACCOUNT TITLE	DEBIT	CREDIT	DEBIT	CREDIT	DEBIT	CREDIT	DEBIT	CREDIT	
26	Federal Income Tax Payable				(o) 2392 76				2392 76	26
75	Federal Income Tax Expense	32000 00		(o) 2392 76		34392 76				75

LampLight, Inc.
Work Sheet
For Year Ended December 31, 20--

1. Increase the expense.   **2.** Increase the liability.

At the beginning of the year, LampLight *esti-mated* its federal income tax for the year to be $32,000.00. LampLight paid the estimated tax to the federal government in four equal quarterly installments of $8,000.00 each. As of December

31, LampLight calculated its *actual* federal income tax to determine whether it owes additional income tax. An adjustment is planned on the work sheet for the additional amount owed, as shown above.

- Explain that organization costs are amortized over a period of years, similar to depreciation of a plant asset.
- Explain that corporations estimate their federal income tax at the beginning of the year and make quarterly estimated payments. At the end of the year the actual tax is calculated and any difference is paid.
- Direct students to the F.Y.I. box for additional information about amortization.

DEMONSTRATE

Organization Expense adjustment

- Direct students to the illustration at the top of the page to demonstrate planning the adjustment for organization costs on a work sheet. Point out that the asset account, Organization Costs, is credited and the expense account is debited.

Federal Income Tax Expense adjustment

- Direct students to the illustration at the bottom of the page as you demonstrate the adjustment planned on the work sheet for federal income tax. The adjustment records the amount of actual federal income tax that is greater or less than estimated payments.

Calculating net income before federal income tax

- Direct students to steps 1–3 and the first math box.

- Point out that all adjustments, except the one for federal income tax, must be completed and amounts extended to the Income Statement and Balance Sheet columns of the work sheet before net income before federal income tax can be calculated.

- Explain that the Income Statement Debit and Credit columns are totaled and the debit column is subtracted from the credit column total to obtain the net income before federal income tax.

Calculating federal income tax

- Demonstrate the calculation of federal income tax on the board or direct students to step 4 and the second math box.

- Point out that different tax rates apply for different net income brackets. Demonstrate the tax calculation for each bracket for the net income amount of $131,135.27.

- Repeat the demonstration with different amounts if needed.

Calculating accrued federal income tax expense

- Demonstrate the calculation of accrued federal income tax expense on the board or direct students to step 5 and the third math box.

- Direct students back to the illustration at the bottom of page 371 to review how to record the adjustment for accrued federal income tax expense on the work sheet.

CALCULATING FEDERAL INCOME TAX EXPENSE

STEPS · CALCULATING FEDERAL INCOME TAX EXPENSE

1 Complete the work sheet's Adjustments columns except for the federal income tax expense adjustment. Do not total the Adjustments columns at this time.

2 Extend all amounts, except Federal Income Tax Expense, to the work sheet's Income Statement columns.

3 Determine the work sheet's Income Statement column totals using a calculator. Do not record the column totals on the work sheet. Calculate the difference between the two totals. The difference is the net income before federal income tax. LampLight's net income before federal income tax is:

Income Statement Credit Column Total	−	Income Statement Debit Column Total before Federal Income Tax	=	Net Income before Federal Income Tax
$883,782.75	−	$752,647.48	=	$131,135.27

4 Calculate the amount of federal income tax using a tax rate table furnished by the Internal Revenue Service. The Internal Revenue Service distributes corporate tax rate tables each year. LampLight's actual federal income tax is calculated as shown using the following tax rate table:

15% of net income before taxes, zero to $50,000.00
Plus 25% of net income before taxes, $50,000.00 to $75,000.00
Plus 34% of net income before taxes, $75,000.00 to $100,000.00
Plus 39% of net income before taxes, $100,000.00 to $335,000.00
Plus 34% of net income before taxes over $335,000.00

Net Income before Taxes	×	Tax Rate	=	Federal Income Tax Amount
$50,000.00	×	15%	=	$ 7,500.00
Plus 25,000.00	×	25%	=	6,250.00
Plus 25,000.00	×	34%	=	8,500.00
Plus 31,135.27	×	39%	=	12,142.76
$131,135.27				$34,392.76

5 Calculate the amount of accrued federal income tax expense as follows:

Total Federal Income Tax Expense	−	Estimated Federal Income Tax Already Paid	=	Accrued Federal Income Tax Expense
$34,392.76	−	$32,000.00	=	$2,392.76

6 Record the federal income tax expense adjustment, as shown on page 371.

7 Extend the new balance of Federal Income Tax Payable, *2,392.76*, to the Balance Sheet Credit column.

8 Extend the new balance of Federal Income Tax Expense, *34,392.76*, to the Income Statement Debit column.

9 Total the work sheet's Adjustments, Income Statement, and Balance Sheet columns as shown on pages 374–375.

Federal Income Tax Expense is debited for $2,392.76. Federal Income Tax Payable is credited for $2,392.76. The new balance of Federal Income Tax Expense,

$34,392.76, is the total amount of federal income tax due based on the net income before federal income tax.

TEACHING STRATEGIES   EXPANDING BEYOND THE CLASSROOM

Invite an accountant from a merchandising business to the classroom to address the importance of the closing process, how long it takes, and what procedures are actually followed to close the books at the end of the period.

Explore Accounting

Contingent Liabilities

One of the duties of an accountant is to ensure that the financial statements of a company reflect a true picture of the financial position of that company. Business transactions affect the accounts of a business and are reflected in journal entries, which are posted to accounts. However, other items can affect the financial position of the company and these items are not automatically entered into the books of a business.

One such item is called a *contingent liability*. A contingent liability is a possible future obligation that arises from a current condition and is dependent upon a future event occurring. One example of a contingent liability is a pending lawsuit against a company. The possible future obligation is the chance that the company may lose the lawsuit and have to pay a penalty or fine. The current condition is the fact that the lawsuit has already been filed. The future event is the ruling of the court. Depending on the court ruling, the company may or may not have a financial obligation.

The accountant must analyze each contingent liability to determine if it must be included in the financial statements. The first step is to determine how likely it is that a loss will occur in the future. GAAP lists three possibilities: probable, possible, and remote. If it is probable that the loss will occur and if the loss can be reasonably estimated, the company must add a liability to the balance sheet in the amount of the probable loss. At the same time, a loss must be shown on the income statement.

If it is probable that the loss will occur but the loss cannot be reasonably estimated, the company does not have to add a liability to its balance sheet. However, the company must disclose the possible loss, which means that the company must tell about the lawsuit in the notes that accompany the financial statements. The same treatment is required if the chance of loss is possible.

If the chance of loss is remote, the company does not have to do anything.

Instructions

Listed below are activities that have already occurred for which the outcome is unknown at the end of the year. For each activity, state if a liability must be added to the balance sheet, if the company must disclose the activity in the notes, or if the company can do nothing.

1. The company is involved in a lawsuit. The legal team thinks it is probable that the company will lose the suit, but it has no idea of the amount of probable loss.

2. The company has published a $1-off coupon in the local paper. The company has estimated that 35% of the coupons will be redeemed.

3. The company is involved in a second lawsuit. The legal team feels that the chance of an unfavorable verdict is remote.

1. The loss is probable but cannot be estimated. Therefore, the company must disclose the lawsuit in the notes.

2. The chance of having to pay the coupon amount (for at least some of the coupons) is probable, and an estimate of the total cost can be made. The company must include a liability on the balance sheet for the estimate.

3. Because the chance of loss is remote, the company does not have to do anything related to this lawsuit.

EXPLAIN

- Explain that a corporation's work sheet is similar to that of any other form of business organization.
- Ask students to point out what accounts on this work sheet could also be found on the work sheet for a partnership or proprietorship.
- Ask students what accounts would appear only on a corporation's work sheet (accounts related to capital stock, organization costs, and federal income tax).

DEMONSTRATE

- Direct students to the illustration, which spreads over two textbook pages.
- Demonstrate preparing the trial balance on the work sheet and explain that amounts are obtained from the general ledger accounts.
- Demonstrate recording the adjustments on the work sheet except the adjustment for federal income tax. Remind students that the adjustment for organization costs was covered on page 371.
- Demonstrate extending adjusted balances to the Balance Sheet and Income Statement columns.
- Review the calculation of federal income tax covered on page 372 and the recording of the adjustment that was covered on page 371.

CORPORATE WORK SHEET (TOP HALF)

LampLight, Inc.
Work Sheet
For Year Ended December 31, 20—

	ACCOUNT TITLE	TRIAL BALANCE DEBIT	TRIAL BALANCE CREDIT	ADJUSTMENTS DEBIT	ADJUSTMENTS CREDIT	INCOME STATEMENT DEBIT	INCOME STATEMENT CREDIT	BALANCE SHEET DEBIT	BALANCE SHEET CREDIT
1	Cash	2543640						2543640	
2	Petty Cash	25000						25000	
3	Notes Receivable	1000000						1000000	
4	Interest Receivable			(a) 100000				100000	
5	Accounts Receivable	13523454						13523454	
6	Allow. for Uncoll. Accts.		42013		(b) 627750				669763
7	Subscriptions Receivable								
8	Merchandise Inventory	26745309			(c) 869790			25875519	
9	Supplies—Sales	1431567			(d) 586904			844663	
10	Supplies—Administrative	2261370			(e) 1445640			815730	
11	Prepaid Insurance	1690000			(f) 591131			1098869	
12	Prepaid Interest			(g) 1047				1047	
13	Bond Sinking Fund	5000000						5000000	
14	Store Equipment	14298334						14298334	
15	Accum. Depr.—Store Equip.		1512300		(h) 1675300				3187600
16	Building	16500000						16500000	
17	Accum. Depr.—Building		825000		(i) 825000				1650000
18	Office Equipment	7392823						7392823	
19	Accum. Depr.—Office Equip.		765200		(j) 973413				1738613
20	Land	13300000						13300000	
21	Organization Costs	192000			(k) 48000			144000	
22	Interest Payable				(l) 1500000				1500000
23	Accounts Payable		3058540						3058540
24	Employee Income Tax Pay.		1238890						1238890
25	Federal Income Tax Pay.				(o) 239276				239276
26	Social Security Tax Payable		62480		(m) 4119				66599
27	Medicare Tax Payable		14410		(m) 951				15361
28	Salaries Payable				(m) 63373				63373
29	Sales Tax Payable		215474						215474
30	Unemploy. Tax Pay.—Federal		8745		(m) 120				8865
31	Unemploy. Tax Pay.—State		59029		(m) 810				59839
32	Health Ins. Premiums Payable		42800						42800
33	Dividends Payable		2957500						2957500
34	Bonds Payable		25000000						25000000
35	Capital Stock—Common		321000000						321000000
36	Stock Subscribed—Common								

TEACHING STRATEGIES   DIFFERENT LEARNING STYLES

Tactile Learner. Suggest using a calculator with a printed tape to perform mathematical calculations. Better calculators also print the operational signs of calculations (+, −, etc.) for students to trace the steps in a calculation.

#	Account Title	Trial Balance Debit	Trial Balance Credit	Adjustments Debit	Adjustments Credit	Income Statement Debit	Income Statement Credit	Balance Sheet Debit	Balance Sheet Credit
37	Pd.-in Cap. in Exc. of St. Val.—Com.		200000						200000
38	Capital Stock—Preferred		17000000						17000000
39	Stock Subscribed—Preferred								
40	Pd.-in Cap. in Exc. of Par Val.—Pref.		800000						800000
41	Disc. on Sale of Preferred Stock	500000						500000	
42	Treasury Stock	180000						180000	
43	Pd.-in Cap. from Sale of Tr. Stock		50000						50000
44	Retained Earnings		5858835						5858835
45	Dividends—Common	1597500						1597500	
46	Dividends—Preferred	1360000						1360000	
47	Income Summary			(c) 869790		869790			
48	Sales		87295240				87295240		
49	Sales Discount	869512				869512			
50	Sales Ret. and Allow.	290056				290056			
51	Purchases	45539648				45539648			
52	Purchases Discount		671035				671035		
53	Purchases Ret. and Allow.		267000				267000		
54	Advertising Expense	1778200				1778200			
55	Credit Card Fee Expense	628500				628500			
56	Depr. Exp.—Store Equip.			(h) 1675300		1675300			
57	Miscellaneous Exp.—Sales	940612				940612			
58	Salary Expense—Sales	6322600		(m) 45789		6368389			
59	Supplies Expense—Sales			(d) 586904		586904			
60	Depr. Expense—Building			(i) 825000		825000			
61	Depr. Exp.—Office Equip.			(j) 973413		973413			
62	Insurance Expense			(l) 591131		591131			
63	Miscellaneous Exp.—Admin.	1257068				1257068			
64	Payroll Taxes Expense	990240		(m) 6000		996240			
65	Property Tax Expense	670000				670000			
66	Salary Expense—Admin.	2364333		(m) 17584		2381917			
67	Supplies Expense—Admin.			(e) 1445640		1445640			
68	Uncollectible Accounts Exp.			(b) 627750		627750			
69	Utilities Expense	2872725				2872725			
70	Gain on Plant Assets								
71	Interest Income		45000		(a) 100000		145000		
72	Interest Expense	1530000		(g) 1500000	(x) 1047	3028953			
73	Loss on Plant Assets								
74	Organization Expense			(k) 48000		48000			
75	Federal Inc. Tax Expense	3200000		(o) 239276		3439276			
76		178794491	178794491	9552624	9552624	78704024	88378275	106100579	96426328
77	Net Inc. after Fed. Inc. Tax					9674251			9674251
78						88378275	88378275	106100579	106100579

DEMONSTRATE

- Demonstrate totaling the Adjustments columns of the work sheet.
- Demonstrate totaling the Income Statement columns of the work sheet.
- Demonstrate calculating the net income after federal income tax by subtracting the Income Statement Debit total from the Income Statement Credit total.
- Demonstrate recording the words "Net Inc. after Fed. Inc. Tax" in the Account Title column and the amount of net income after federal income tax in the Income Statement Debit column.
- Demonstrate totaling the Income Statement columns again and checking for equality.
- Demonstrate totaling the Balance Sheet columns.
- Demonstrate recording the amount of net income after federal income tax in the Balance Sheet Credit column.
- Demonstrate totaling the Balance sheet columns again and checking for equality.

ONGOING ASSESSMENT

- Assessment is an ongoing process. Circulate through the classroom or lab, observing which students have problems with the assignments.
- Troubleshooting: Diagnose what kinds of problems students have with this lesson. Although the concepts presented in this lesson are relatively simple, students may have difficulty calculating the federal income tax.
- Assess student understanding by checking solutions to Independent Practice assignments.

RETEACH

- Call on students to describe the process of calculating the net income before federal income tax.
- Call on students to calculate the amount of federal income tax expense for a variety of net income amounts.

375

Xtra!

GUIDED PRACTICE

Term Review

Call on a student to define the term in the Term Review. Ask the class if the definition is correct and whether the complete definition has been given or if anything needs to be added. The suggested definition for the term is given in the Glossary.

Audit Your Understanding

Call on students to answer the Audit Your Understanding questions. Ask the class if each answer is correct and/or complete. Answers are given in Appendix E of the textbook.

Work Together

Have students write the solution to the Work Together problem as you guide the class through the examples.

- Discuss each step before recording the answer in the Working Papers.

- Remind students to save their work to complete Work Together 13-3.

INDEPENDENT PRACTICE

On Your Own

- Assign the On Your Own problem to be worked independently.

- Remind students to save their work to complete On Your Own 13-3.

- Use the Ongoing Assessment techniques to diagnose student understanding.

Application Problems

- Assign Application Problem 13-1: Preparing a work sheet for a corporation.

- Assign Application Problem 13-2: Calculating federal income taxes.

Personal Trainer

- Students can access the Lesson 13-1 assessment material using this software.

Xtra! Web Site

- Students can access the Xtra! Study Tools for additional practice.

ENRICH

- Assign Making Ethical Decisions on page 370.

- Assign Explore Accounting on page 373.

CLOSE

- Ask students to briefly summarize the procedures for completing a work sheet for a corporation.

376

• term review

amortization

• audit your understanding

1. What is amortization?
2. How often is estimated federal income tax paid?

• work together 13-1

Calculating federal income tax expense, recording the adjustment, and completing a work sheet

A work sheet for Provident Electronics, Inc., for the current year is provided in the *Working Papers*. Your instructor will guide you through the following examples.

1. Calculate net income before federal income tax.
2. Calculate the amount of federal income tax using the following rates:

    15% of net income before taxes, zero to $50,000.00
    Plus 25% of net income before taxes, $50,000.00 to $75,000.00
    Plus 34% of net income before taxes, $75,000.00 to $100,000.00
    Plus 39% of net income before taxes, $100,000.00 to $335,000.00
    Plus 34% of net income before taxes over $335,000.00

3. Calculate the accrued federal income tax expense.
4. Record the adjustment on the work sheet.
5. Complete the work sheet. Save your work to complete Work Together 13-3.

• on your own 13-1

Calculating federal income tax expense, recording the adjustment, and completing a work sheet

A work sheet for BRE Corporation for the current year is provided in the *Working Papers*. Work this problem independently.

1. Calculate net income before federal income tax.
2. Calculate the amount of federal income tax using the tax rates given in 4. above.
3. Calculate the accrued federal income tax expense.
4. Record the adjustment on the work sheet.
5. Complete the work sheet. Save your work to complete On Your Own 13-3.

13-2 Financial Statements and Analysis

INCOME STATEMENT FOR A CORPORATION

LampLight, Inc.
Income Statement
For Year Ended December 31, 20--

				Percentage of Net Sales*
Operating Revenue:				
Sales			$872,952.40	
Less: Sales Discount	$ 8,695.12			
Sales Returns and Allowances	2,900.56	11,595.68		
Net Sales			$861,356.72	100.0
Cost of Merchandise Sold:				
Merchandise Inventory, Jan. 1, 20--			$267,453.09	
Purchases		$455,396.48		
Less: Purchases Discount	$6,710.35			
Purchases Returns and Allowances	2,670.00	9,380.35		
Net Purchases			446,016.13	
Total Cost of Merchandise Available for Sale			$713,469.22	
Less Merchandise Inventory, Dec. 31, 20--			258,755.19	
Cost of Merchandise Sold			454,714.03	52.8
Gross Profit on Operations			$406,642.69	47.2
Operating Expenses:				
Selling Expenses:				
Advertising Expense	$ 17,782.00			
Credit Card Fee Expense	6,285.00			
Depreciation Expense—Store Equipment	16,753.00			
Miscellaneous Expense—Sales	9,406.12			
Salary Expense—Sales	63,683.89			
Supplies Expense—Sales	5,869.04			
Total Selling Expenses		$119,779.05		13.9
Administrative Expenses:				
Depreciation Expense—Building	$ 8,250.00			
Depreciation Expense—Office Equipment	9,734.13			
Insurance Expense	5,911.31			
Miscellaneous Expense—Administrative	12,570.68			
Payroll Taxes Expense	9,962.40			
Property Tax Expense	6,700.00			
Salary Expense—Administrative	23,819.17			
Supplies Expense—Administrative	14,456.40			
Uncollectible Accounts Expense	6,277.50			
Utilities Expense	28,727.25			
Total Administrative Expenses		126,408.84		14.7
Total Operating Expenses			246,187.89	28.6
Income from Operations			$160,454.80	18.6
Other Revenue:				
Interest Income		$ 1,450.00		
Other Expenses:				
Interest Expense	$ 30,289.53			
Organization Expense	480.00			
Total Other Expenses		$ 30,769.53		
Net Deduction			29,319.53	3.4
Net Income before Federal Income Tax			$131,135.27	15.2
Less Federal Income Tax Expense			34,392.76	4.0
Net Income after Federal Income Tax			$ 96,742.51	11.2

*Rounded to nearest 0.1%

LampLight uses net sales as the basis for calculating component percentages on its income statement as shown above.

Financial Statements and Analysis

- Explain that a company usually determines acceptable component percentages for each major cost, expense, and income item.
- Point out that acceptable component percentages for costs and expenses are usually stated as a maximum percentage or "Not more than" a certain percentage.
- Point out that acceptable component percentages for income are usually stated as a minimum percentage or "Not less than" a certain percentage.
- Explain that when a component percentage is not acceptable action must be taken to correct the situation.
- Explain that preferred stock's share of net income is based on the par value and dividend rate specified on the stock certificate.
- Explain that the share of net income assigned to common stock is the portion that is not assigned to preferred stock.

DEMONSTRATE

Analyzing component percentages
- Direct students to the illustration at the top of the page as you demonstrate analyzing component percentages.
- Analyze the component percentage for cost of merchandise sold, a cost item. Point out that 52.8% is "not more than 55.0%." In other words, the component percentage has not exceeded the maximum for this item.
- Analyze the component percentage for gross profit on operations, an income item. Point out that 47.2% is "Not less than 45.0%." In other words, the component percentage has not fallen below the acceptable minimum.
- Repeat the analysis for several other items. Ask students what kinds of actions could be taken to correct unacceptable percentages.
- Use the board or direct students to the illustration at the bottom of the page as you demonstrate the calculations for assigning shares of net income to the two classes of stock.

ACCEPTABLE AND ACTUAL COMPONENT PERCENTAGES

Income Statement Items	Acceptable Component Percentages	Actual Component Percentages
Cost of Merchandise Sold	Not more than 55.0%	52.8%
Gross Profit on Operations	Not less than 45.0%	47.2%
Total Selling Expenses	Not more than 12.0%	13.9%
Total Administrative Expenses	Not more than 18.0%	14.7%
Total Operating Expenses	Not more than 30.0%	28.6%
Income from Operations	Not less than 15.0%	18.6%
Net Deduction from Other Expenses	Not more than 4.0%	3.4%
Net Income before Federal Income Tax	Not less than 11.0%	15.2%

The percentage relationship between one financial statement item and the total that includes that item is known as a component percentage. LampLight determines acceptable component percentages for each major item of cost, expense, and income as shown above. Like Zytech in Chapter 4, LampLight does not analyze component percentages for federal income tax expense or net income after federal income tax.

For the current year, LampLight has achieved acceptable percentages for most items. However, the component percentage for total selling expenses, 13.9%, is higher than the maximum acceptable percentage, 12.0%, a negative result.

Thus, LampLight's managers further analyze the expense accounts that compose selling expenses. The managers' investigation reveals a sharp increase in the price of television advertising, one component of selling expenses. To correct this situation for the next fiscal period, LampLight's managers can do the following:

1. Reduce advertising costs and continue using 12.0% as the maximum acceptable component percentage.
2. Increase the maximum acceptable component percentage to recognize the increased advertising cost.

SHARE OF NET INCOME ASSIGNED TO PREFERRED AND COMMON STOCK

Total Par Value	×	Dividend Rate	=	Preferred Stock's Share of Net Income	
$170,000.00	×	8%	=	$13,600.00	◄— ❶ **1.** Calculate share of net income for preferred stock.

Total Net Income	−	Preferred Stock's Share of Net Income	=	Common Stock's Share of Net Income	
$96,742.51	−	$13,600.00	=	$83,142.51	◄— ❷ **2.** Calculate share of net income for common stock.

The total earnings for outstanding preferred stock equals the 8% dividend specified on the stock certificates. The total share of net income for common stock is the remainder of the net income after the preferred stock's share is deducted. These amounts are calculated as shown above.

Financial Analysis and Reporting for a Corporation

TEACHING STRATEGIES DIFFERENT LEARNING STYLES

Auditory Learner. The auditory learner can reinforce the learning of formulas by verbally explaining the formula and/or calculations to other students in a small group. In a group of three, for example, each student should get the opportunity to teach the formula to the other two students. Through this process, each student in the group will "teach" the formula once and "learn" the formula two times.

EARNINGS PER SHARE

	Share of Net Income	÷	Shares of Stock Outstanding	=	Earnings per Share
	$83,142.51	÷	31,950	=	$2.60

The amount of net income belonging to a single share of stock is called **earnings per share**. Earnings per share is typically calculated only on the number of common shares outstanding. For example, LampLight has 32,100 shares of common stock issued. However, 150 of these shares are treasury stock and, therefore, are not outstanding stock. LampLight has 31,950 shares of outstanding common stock (32,100 shares *less* 150 shares *equals* 31,950).

For the year ended December 31, LampLight's earnings per share on common stock is calculated as shown above.

STATEMENT OF STOCKHOLDERS' EQUITY FOR A CORPORATION

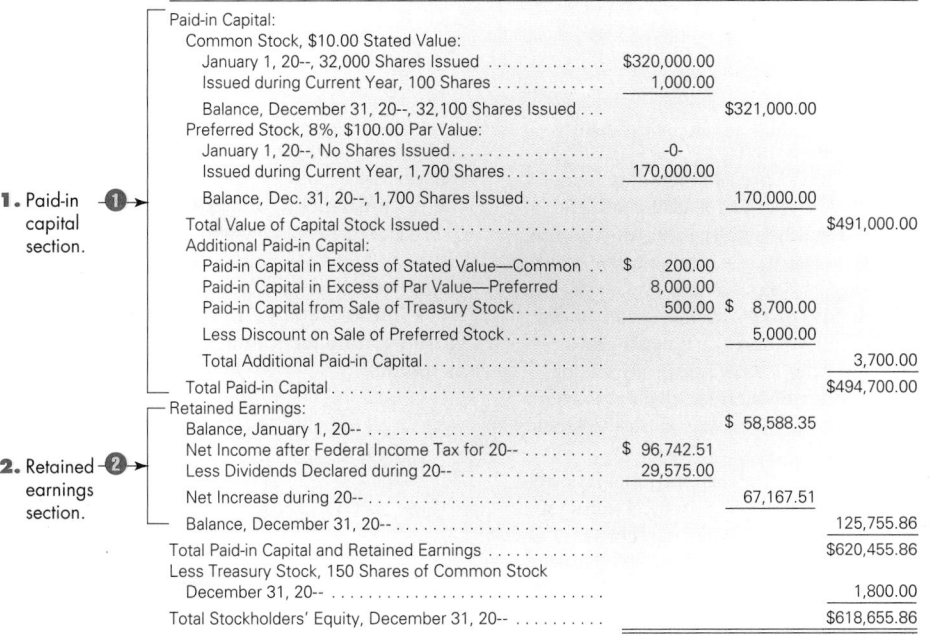

LampLight, Inc.
Statement of Stockholders' Equity
For Year Ended December 31, 20--

1. Paid-in capital section.

Paid-in Capital:
  Common Stock, $10.00 Stated Value:
    January 1, 20--, 32,000 Shares Issued $320,000.00
    Issued during Current Year, 100 Shares 1,000.00
    Balance, December 31, 20--, 32,100 Shares Issued ... $321,000.00
  Preferred Stock, 8%, $100.00 Par Value:
    January 1, 20--, No Shares Issued ....   -0-
    Issued during Current Year, 1,700 Shares 170,000.00
    Balance, Dec. 31, 20--, 1,700 Shares Issued 170,000.00
  Total Value of Capital Stock Issued $491,000.00
  Additional Paid-in Capital:
    Paid-in Capital in Excess of Stated Value—Common .. $ 200.00
    Paid-in Capital in Excess of Par Value—Preferred 8,000.00
    Paid-in Capital from Sale of Treasury Stock ....   500.00 $ 8,700.00
    Less Discount on Sale of Preferred Stock 5,000.00
    Total Additional Paid-in Capital 3,700.00
  Total Paid-in Capital $494,700.00

2. Retained earnings section.

Retained Earnings:
  Balance, January 1, 20-- .... $ 58,588.35
  Net Income after Federal Income Tax for 20-- .... $ 96,742.51
  Less Dividends Declared during 20-- 29,575.00
  Net Increase during 20-- 67,167.51
  Balance, December 31, 20-- 125,755.86
Total Paid-in Capital and Retained Earnings $620,455.86
Less Treasury Stock, 150 Shares of Common Stock
  December 31, 20-- 1,800.00
Total Stockholders' Equity, December 31, 20-- $618,655.86

A statement of stockholders' equity shows changes occurring in the stockholders' equity for a fiscal period. LampLight's statement of stockholders' equity has two major sections as shown above.

Some businesses prepare a statement of retained earnings instead of a statement of stockholders' equity. A statement of retained earnings includes information only about the changes in retained earnings during a fiscal period. The remainder of the information about changes in paid-in capital is placed on the corporation's balance sheet.

Financial Statements and Analysis

- Explain that the statement of stock-holders' equity is used to analyze equity per share, market value per share, and price-earnings ratio.

- Point out that the equity per share of preferred stock is equal to its par value. Explain that total equity of preferred stock is the par value times the number of shares outstanding.

- Explain that market value of a share of stock is the amount for which the stock can be sold on the stock market.

- Explain that the market value can vary from day to day but is never recorded in the company's ledgers. Instead, stock is recorded at par or stated value.

- Point out that higher price-earnings ratios are better than lower ones because investors are willing to pay more times what a share is earning to acquire the stock because it has some value other than just its earnings, such as growth potential.

DEMONSTRATE

Calculating equity per share

- Use the board or direct students to the first math box to demonstrate the calculation of equity per share for preferred and common stock.

- Explain that the total preferred stockholders' equity is calculated as number of shares times par value.

- Explain that common stockholders' equity is the total equity from the statement of stockholders' equity divided by the number of shares of common stock outstanding.

Calculating the price-earnings ratio

- Use the board or direct students to the second math box to demonstrate the calculation of the price-earnings ratio.

- Point out that the market price per share is obtained from the stock market. Explain that earnings per share is a calculated amount that was shown on page 379.

- Point out that a price-earnings ratio of 7.5 times means that investors are willing to pay 7.5 times the earnings of a share to acquire it.

ANALYZING A STATEMENT OF STOCKHOLDERS' EQUITY

As of December 31, LampLight has issued $321,000.00 in common stock and $170,000.00 in preferred stock. LampLight also has $1,800.00 in treasury stock. Therefore, the total stock outstanding is $489,200.00. The total stockholders' equity, *$618,655.86*, is shown on the last line of the statement of stockholders' equity. LampLight uses information on its statement of stockholders' equity to analyze (1) equity per share, (2) market value per share, and (3) price-earnings ratio.

Equity per Share
The amount of total stockholders' equity belonging to a single share of stock is called **equity per share**. The equity of preferred stock is equal to its total

par value, *$170,000.00*, or $100.00 per share. The remainder of the total stockholders' equity is the equity of the common stock, calculated as shown below. Common stock equity should at least equal its stated value to be acceptable. LampLight's common stock equity per share is higher than its stated value of $10.00 per share and therefore is acceptable.

©GETTY IMAGES/PHOTODISC

	Total Stockholders' Equity	÷	Shares of Capital Stock Outstanding	=	Equity per Share
Preferred	$170,000.00	÷	1,700	=	$100.00
Common	448,655.86	÷	31,950	=	14.04
Total	$618,655.86				

Market Value per Share
The price at which a share of stock may be sold on the stock market is called **market value**. The market value is established by investors' buying and selling the corporation's stock on the stock market. If a business is profitable and pays adequate dividends, investors often offer to pay a market price higher than the stock's par or stated value. If a business is not profitable or does not pay regular dividends, investors often offer to pay a market price lower than the stock's par or stated value.

Stock is recorded on a corporation's records at the par or stated value. The market value of stock is not recorded on corporate records.

Price-Earnings Ratio
The relationship between the market value per share and earnings per share of a stock is called the **price-earnings ratio**. Investors usually want to buy stock in companies that are earning a reasonable amount of net income. One way

to determine whether a company is earning a reasonable amount of net income is to calculate the price-earnings ratio. The ratio is then compared to standards for similar companies.

LampLight's earnings per share on common stock is $2.60 as previously described. Using stock market reports on December 31, the price-earnings ratio for common stock is calculated as follows:

Market Price per Share	÷	Earnings per Share	=	Price-Earnings Ratio
$19.50	÷	$2.60	=	7.5 times

The common stock price-earnings ratio, 7.5 times, means that the stock is selling for 7.5 times its share of the earnings. For businesses similar to LampLight, a common stock price-earnings ratio between 6.0 and 10.0 times is considered acceptable. LampLight's price-earnings ratio for common stock is acceptable.

Financial Analysis and Reporting for a Corporation

TEACHING STRATEGIES DIFFERENT LEARNING STYLES

Kinesthetic Learner. The kinesthetic learner should have the opportunity to perform the calculations to solve the formula. One way to accomplish this is to develop several situations using different data. The student should calculate the earnings per share for each situation.

LampLight, Inc.
Balance Sheet
December 31, 20--

ASSETS

Current Assets:

Cash		$ 25,436.40
Petty Cash		250.00
Notes Receivable		10,000.00
Interest Receivable		1,000.00
Accounts Receivable	$135,234.54	
Less Allowance for Uncollectible Accounts	6,697.63	128,536.91
Merchandise Inventory		258,755.19
Supplies—Sales		8,446.63
Supplies—Administrative		8,157.30
Prepaid Insurance		10,988.69
Prepaid Interest		10.47
Total Current Assets		$451,581.59

Long-Term Investment:

Bond Sinking Fund		50,000.00

Plant Assets:

Store Equipment	$142,983.34	
Less Accumulated Depreciation—Store Equipment	31,876.00	$111,107.34
Building	$165,000.00	
Less Accumulated Depreciation—Building	16,500.00	148,500.00
Office Equipment	$ 73,928.23	
Less Accumulated Depreciation—Office Equipment	17,386.13	56,542.10
Land		133,000.00
Total Plant Assets		449,149.44

Intangible Assets:

Organization Costs		1,440.00
Total Assets		$952,171.03

LIABILITIES

Current Liabilities:

Interest Payable		$ 15,000.00
Accounts Payable		30,585.40
Employee Income Tax Payable		1,238.90
Federal Income Tax Payable		2,392.76
Social Security Tax Payable		665.99
Medicare Tax Payable		153.61
Salaries Payable		633.73
Sales Tax Payable		2,154.74
Unemployment Tax Payable—Federal		88.65
Unemployment Tax Payable—State		598.39
Health Insurance Premiums Payable		428.00
Dividends Payable		29,575.00
Total Current Liabilities		$ 83,515.17

Long-Term Liability:

Bonds Payable		250,000.00
Total Liabilities		$333,515.17

STOCKHOLDERS' EQUITY

Total Stockholders' Equity		618,655.86
Total Liabilities and Stockholders' Equity		$952,171.03

A corporate balance sheet reports assets, liabilities, and stockholders' equity on a specific date. LampLight's December 31 balance sheet is shown above. LampLight calculates three ratios based on information from the balance sheet: (1) accounts receivable turnover ratio, (2) rate earned on stockholders' equity, and (3) rate earned on total assets.

- Explain that the accounts receivable turnover ratio is the number of times the average amount of accounts receivable is collected annually.

- Explain that the accounts receivable turnover ratio is a measure of a company's efficiency in collecting its accounts receivable.

- Point out that the expected accounts receivable turnover ratio is calculated by dividing the number of days in a year, 365, by the terms of sale.

- Point out that with 30-day terms of sale, the expected turnover ratio is 12.2 times *(365 days divided by 30 days)*. If a company's turnover ratio is lower than 12.2, then it needs to improve its collection procedures.

- Explain that beginning balances are obtained from the previous year's financial statements. The balance at the end of the previous year is the beginning balance of the next year.

- Use the board or direct students to the math boxes to demonstrate calculating the accounts receivable turnover ratio.

- Point out that the first step is to calculate the average book value of accounts receivable.

- Demonstrate calculating the beginning and ending book values of accounts receivable by subtracting the Allowance for Uncollectible Accounts balance from the Accounts Receivable balance.

- Demonstrate calculating the average book value of accounts receivable by adding the beginning and ending book values and dividing by 2.

- Demonstrate dividing the net sales on account from the income statement by the average book value of accounts receivable to get the accounts receivable turnover ratio.

- Demonstrate calculating the average number of days of payment (the number of days it takes customers to pay on account) by dividing days in a year, 365, by the accounts receivable turnover ratio.

ACCOUNTS RECEIVABLE TURNOVER RATIO

The number of times the average amount of accounts receivable is collected annually is known as the accounts receivable turnover ratio. LampLight calculates this ratio as described in the steps below.

LampLight's terms of sales are 2/10, n/30. Therefore, LampLight expects payment within 30 days. The expected accounts receivable turnover ratio is 12.2 times (365 days in a year ÷ 30 days). LampLight's average number of days for payment, 53, is higher than the expected level of 30 days. Therefore, LampLight's accounts receivable turnover ratio, 6.9 times, is unacceptable. LampLight needs to consider ways to encourage customers to pay their accounts within the credit period.

STEPS • CALCULATING ACCOUNTS RECEIVABLE TURNOVER RATIO

1 Calculate the average book value of accounts receivable. Beginning balances are obtained from the financial statements of the prior year. Ending balances are obtained from the work sheet for the current year.

Accounts Receivable Beginning Balance	−	Allowance for Uncollectible Accounts Beginning Balance	=	Beginning Book Value
$124,983.89	−	$4,362.18	=	$120,621.71

Accounts Receivable Ending Balance	−	Allowance for Uncollectible Accounts Ending Balance	=	Ending Book Value
$135,234.54	−	$6,697.63	=	$128,536.91

(Beginning Book Value of Accounts Receivable	+	Ending Book Value of Accounts Receivable)	÷	2	=	Average Book Value of Accounts Receivable
($120,621.71	+	$128,536.91)	÷	2	=	$124,579.31

2 Calculate the accounts receivable turnover ratio. Some businesses use separate accounts to record the amount of cash sales and net sales on account. Net sales as reported on the income statement should be used as net sales on account if the business does not record this information.

Net Sales on Account	÷	Average Book Value of Accounts Receivable	=	Accounts Receivable Turnover Ratio
$861,356.72	÷	$124,579.31	=	6.9 times

3 Calculate the average number of days for payment.

Days in Year	÷	Accounts Receivable Turnover Ratio	=	Average Number of Days for Payment
365	÷	6.9	=	53

TEACHING STRATEGIES — COOPERATIVE LEARNING

Research Project. Assign students to groups of two. Each group researches the financial statements (through the annual report) of a company in which they are interested, perhaps because they are familiar with the product. Students look for a list of specific items such as: the kinds of stock the corporation is authorized to issue, the categories of assets listed on the balance sheet, the total of current liabilities, the net increase/decrease in income from the previous period, etc. After the research is done, the group must plan and deliver a presentation of the data to the entire class. Time frame: Class time 25–45 minutes to plan presentation; additional time outside of class is needed to complete research and prepare presentation.

RATE EARNED ON AVERAGE STOCKHOLDERS' EQUITY

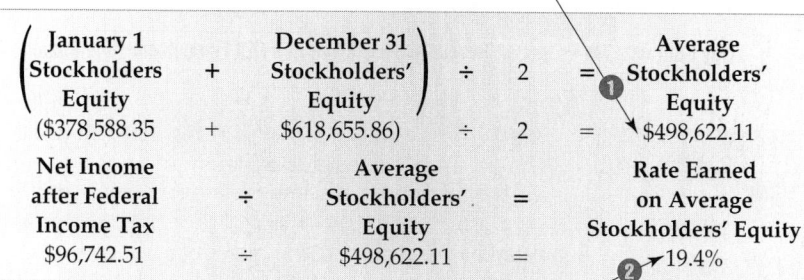

1. Calculate average stockholders' equity.

$$\left(\begin{array}{c}\text{January 1}\\\text{Stockholders}\\\text{Equity}\\(\$378{,}588.35)\end{array} + \begin{array}{c}\text{December 31}\\\text{Stockholders'}\\\text{Equity}\\\$618{,}655.86\end{array}\right) \div \begin{array}{c}2\\\\\\2\end{array} = \begin{array}{c}\text{Average}\\\text{Stockholders'}\\\text{Equity}\\\$498{,}622.11\end{array}$$

Net Income after Federal Income Tax	÷	Average Stockholders' Equity	=	Rate Earned on Average Stockholders' Equity
$96,742.51	÷	$498,622.11	=	19.4%

2. Calculate the rate earned.

The relationship between net income and average stockholders' equity is called the **rate earned on average stockholders' equity**. The rate earned on average stockholders' equity for LampLight is calculated as shown above.

For each dollar that stockholders have invested, LampLight is earning $0.194 in net income. The best investment is in a corporation with the highest rate earned on average stockholders' equity. For example, Midtown, Inc., has a rate earned on average stockholders' equity of 14.2% compared to LampLight's rate of 19.4%. Based on this one analysis, an investor would choose to invest in LampLight's stock rather than Midtown's.

RATE EARNED ON AVERAGE TOTAL ASSETS

1. Calculate average total assets.

$$\left(\begin{array}{c}\text{January 1}\\\text{Total Assets}\\(\$724{,}976.34)\end{array} + \begin{array}{c}\text{December 31}\\\text{Total Assets}\\\$952{,}171.03\end{array}\right) \div \begin{array}{c}2\\\\2\end{array} = \begin{array}{c}\text{Average}\\\text{Total Assets}\\\$838{,}573.69\end{array}$$

Net Income after Federal Income Tax	÷	Average Total Assets	=	Rate Earned on Average Total Assets
$96,742.51	÷	$838,573.69	=	11.5%

2. Calculate the rate earned.

The relationship between net income and average total assets is called **rate earned on average total assets**. This rate for LampLight is calculated as shown above.

For each dollar of assets that the corporation owns, the business has earnings of $0.115 after it pays federal income tax. Information published by trade organizations shows that businesses similar to LampLight tend to have a rate earned on average total assets between 10.0% and 14.0%. LampLight's rate, 11.5%, is acceptable.

Other methods to analyze corporate financial statement items are described in Chapter 17.

Financial Statements and Analysis

383

CAREERS IN ACCOUNTING

The Careers in Accounting feature profiles people who are entrepreneurs, who are working in accounting-related fields, or who use accounting in their business lives.

Students can access the Careers section of the Xtra! Web Site for additional material about careers.

careers in accounting

CAREERS IN ACCOUNTING • CAREERS IN ACCOUNTING • CAREERS IN ACCOU

Emily Gonzalez, Tax Preparer, Accounting Employee at a CPA Firm, Accounting Student, Future CPA

COURTESY OF EMILY GONZALEZ

Emily Gonzalez's story is that of hard work and continual self-improvement. She was in New York City and just out of high school, 18 years old, without enough money for four years of college. Emily had not taken any business classes in high school, so she turned to a technical school to jump-start a career in the banking industry. To help with expenses, she started a business preparing tax returns.

After completing her program, she obtained a job in the loan department of a savings and loan company. She spent the next nine years working in customer service at a lending company and in the accounting department of an insurance company. She also completed the requirements for her insurance license.

However, Emily realized that she was lacking computer skills, so she went back to a technical college at age 28 and enrolled in a computer technology program. Before she finished the program, the school hired her as assistant controller, where she could combine her accounting experience with her new technology skills.

Then Emily decided to move back to Puerto Rico to be near her family. For the next six years, she worked in a CPA (Certified Public Accountant) firm, but realized she could not advance further in the accounting field without a degree. She moved to Florida and began working for a CPA firm, specializing in accounting for condo associations, but she did not lose sight of her dream of getting a four-year degree.

Emily is still working full time with the CPA firm, and she still has her own business preparing tax returns. However, she is also finishing a bachelor's degree in accounting. She can do this because her college classes are all online. She can stay at home with her child and be enrolled in college classes at the same time. Once she completes her degree, Emily hopes to take the CPA exam.

She's not quite there yet, but since she has achieved every goal to this point, Emily is confident that she will be a CPA in the near future.

Salary Range: Salaries for CPAs vary greatly. Accountants and auditors with 1 to 3 years of experience earn between $34,000 and $49,500. Senior accountants and auditors earn between $41,000 and $61,500. The annual salary can be near $200,000 or more for partners in a CPA firm. The size and location of the firm account for the variation in salary.

Qualifications: CPAs must pass a four-part examination, and only about 25% of those who take the examination pass every part attempted. Most states require at least a bachelor's degree to sit for the exam. Many require more education. In addition, most states require some accounting experience. Accountants and auditors must be good at working with people, as well as with business systems and computers.

Occupational Outlook: The job market for CPAs is expected to grow, especially for those who are familiar with the laws that have been passed as a result of recent accounting scandals.

terms review

earnings per share

equity per share

market value

price-earnings ratio

rate earned on average
  stockholders' equity

rate earned on average total assets

audit your understanding

1. What does earnings per share represent?

2. What relationship is represented by the price-earnings ratio?

3. What amounts must be known to calculate the rate earned on average
    total assets?

work together 13-2

Analyzing Financial Statements

Financial statements for Provident Electronics, Inc., are given in the *Working Papers*. The *Working Papers* provide other selected information and forms needed to complete the problem. Your instructor will guide you through the following examples.

1. Calculate and record on the income statement the component percentages for the indicated items. Round the percentage calculations to the nearest 0.1%.

2. Calculate earnings per share. Round calculations to the nearest cent.

3. Use the statement of stockholders' equity and the additional information supplied to calculate: (a) equity per share of stock and (b) the price-earnings ratio.

4. Use the balance sheet and the additional information supplied to calculate the: (a) accounts receivable turnover ratio, (b) rate earned on average stockholders' equity, and (c) rate earned on average total assets.

on your own 13-2

Analyzing Financial Statements

Financial statements for BRE Corporation are given in the *Working Papers*. The *Working Papers* provide other selected information and forms needed to complete the problem. Work independently to complete the following problem.

1. Calculate and record on the income statement the component percentages for the indicated items. Round the percentage calculations to the nearest 0.1%.

2. Calculate earnings per share. Round calculations to the nearest cent.

3. Use the statement of stockholders' equity and the additional information supplied to calculate: (a) equity per share of stock and (b) the price-earnings ratio.

4. Use the balance sheet and the additional information supplied to calculate the: (a) accounts receivable turnover ratio, (b) rate earned on average stockholders' equity, and (c) rate earned on average total assets.

Financial Statements and Analysis

Lesson 13-2   **385**

GUIDED PRACTICE

Terms Review

Call on students to define the terms in the Terms Review. Ask the class if the definitions are correct and whether the complete definitions have been given or if anything needs to be added. The suggested definitions are given in the Glossary.

Audit Your Understanding

Call on students to answer the Audit Your Understanding questions. Ask the class if the answers are correct and/or complete. Answers are given in Appendix E of the textbook.

Work Together

Have students write the solution to the Work Together problems as you guide the class through the example.

- Discuss each calculation and, when the class has agreed on a calculation, direct students to enter the calculations and results in the Working Papers.

INDEPENDENT PRACTICE

On Your Own

- Assign the On Your Own problem to be worked independently.
- Use the Ongoing Assessment techniques to diagnose student understanding.

Application Problem

- Assign Application Problem 13-3: Preparing financial statements for a corporation.

Personal Trainer

- Students can access the Lesson 13-2 assessment material using this software.

Xtra! Web Site

- Students can access the Xtra! Study Tools for additional practice.

ENRICH

- Assign the Careers in Accounting feature on page 384.
- Assign Cases for Critical Thinking 1 and 2.

CLOSE

- Ask students to briefly summarize the analysis procedures described in this lesson.

13-3 Other End-of-Fiscal-Period Work

ADJUSTING ENTRIES

GENERAL JOURNAL — PAGE 13

	DATE		ACCOUNT TITLE	DOC. NO.	POST. REF.	DEBIT	CREDIT	
1			*Adjusting Entries*					1
2	Dec. 20--	31	*Interest Receivable*			1 0 0 0 0		2
3			*Interest Income*				1 0 0 0 0	3
4		31	*Uncollectible Accounts Expense*			6 2 7 7 50		4
5			*Allowance for Uncoll. Accts.*				6 2 7 7 50	5
6		31	*Income Summary*			8 6 9 7 90		6
7			*Merchandise Inventory*				8 6 9 7 90	7
8		31	*Supplies Expense—Sales*			5 8 6 9 04		8
9			*Supplies—Sales*				5 8 6 9 04	9
10		31	*Supplies Expense—Admin.*			14 4 5 6 40		10
11			*Supplies—Admin.*				14 4 5 6 40	11
12		31	*Insurance Expense*			5 9 1 1 31		12
13			*Prepaid Insurance*				5 9 1 1 31	13
14		31	*Prepaid Interest*			1 0 47		14
15			*Interest Expense*				1 0 47	15
16		31	*Depreciation Exp.—Store Equip.*			16 7 5 3 00		16
17			*Accum. Depr.—Store Equip.*				16 7 5 3 00	17
18		31	*Depreciation Exp.—Building*			8 2 5 0 00		18
19			*Accum. Depr.—Building*				8 2 5 0 00	19
20		31	*Depreciation Exp.—Office Equip.*			9 7 3 4 13		20
21			*Accum. Depr.—Office Equip.*				9 7 3 4 13	21
22		31	*Organization Expense*			4 8 0 00		22
23			*Organization Costs*				4 8 0 00	23
24		31	*Interest Expense*			15 0 0 0 00		24
25			*Interest Payable*				15 0 0 0 00	25
26		31	*Salary Expense—Sales*			4 5 7 89		26
27			*Salary Expense—Admin.*			1 7 5 84		27
28			*Salaries Payable*				6 3 3 73	28
29		31	*Payroll Taxes Expense*			6 0 00		29
30			*Social Security Tax Payable*				4 1 19	30
31			*Medicare Tax Payable*				9 51	31
32			*Unemploy. Tax Pay.—Federal*				1 20	32
33			*Unemploy. Tax Pay.—State*				8 10	33
34		31	*Federal Income Tax Expense*			2 3 9 2 76		34
35			*Federal Income Tax Payable*				2 3 9 2 76	35
36								36

In addition to a work sheet and financial statements, LampLight prepares adjusting entries, closing entries, a post-closing trial balance, and reversing entries. LampLight's December 31 adjusting entries are shown above.

GENERAL JOURNAL   PAGE 14

	DATE		ACCOUNT TITLE	DOC. NO.	POST. REF.	DEBIT	CREDIT	
1			*Closing Entries*					1
2	Dec. 20--	31	*Sales*			8 7 2 9 5 2 40		2
3			*Purchases Discount*			6 7 1 0 35		3
4			*Purchases Returns and Allowances*			2 6 7 0 00		4
5			*Interest Income*			1 4 5 0 00		5
6			*Income Summary*				8 8 3 7 8 2 75	6
7		31	*Income Summary*			7 7 8 3 4 2 34		7
8			*Sales Discount*				8 6 9 5 12	8
9			*Sales Returns and Allowances*				2 9 0 0 56	9
10			*Purchases*				4 5 5 3 9 6 48	10
11			*Advertising Expense*				1 7 7 8 2 00	11
12			*Credit Card Fee Expense*				6 2 8 5 00	12
13			*Depreciation Exp.—Store Equip.*				1 6 7 5 3 00	13
14			*Miscellaneous Exp.—Sales*				9 4 0 6 12	14
15			*Salary Expense—Sales*				6 3 6 8 3 89	15
16			*Supplies Expense—Sales*				5 8 6 9 04	16
17			*Depreciation Exp.—Building*				8 2 5 0 00	17
18			*Depreciation Exp.—Office Equip.*				9 7 3 4 13	18
19			*Insurance Expense*				5 9 1 1 31	19
20			*Miscellaneous Exp.—Admin.*				1 2 5 7 0 68	20
21			*Payroll Taxes Expense*				9 9 6 2 40	21
22			*Property Tax Expense*				6 7 0 0 00	22
23			*Salary Expense—Admin.*				2 3 8 1 9 17	23
24			*Supplies Expense—Admin.*				1 4 4 5 6 40	24
25			*Uncollectible Accounts Expense*				6 2 7 7 50	25
26			*Utilities Expense*				2 8 7 2 7 25	26
27			*Interest Expense*				3 0 2 8 9 53	27
28			*Organization Expense*				4 8 0 00	28
29			*Federal Income Tax Expense*				3 4 3 9 2 76	29
30		31	*Income Summary*			9 6 7 4 2 51		30
31			*Retained Earnings*				9 6 7 4 2 51	31
32		31	*Retained Earnings*			2 9 5 7 5 00		32
33			*Dividends—Common*				1 5 9 7 5 00	33
34			*Dividends—Preferred*				1 3 6 0 0 00	34
35								35

LampLight records four closing entries at the end of a fiscal period.

1. Closing entry for income statement accounts with credit balances (revenue and contra cost accounts).
2. Closing entry for income statement accounts with debit balances (cost, contra revenue, and expense accounts).

3. Closing entry to record net income or net loss in the retained earnings account and close the income summary account.
4. Closing entry for the dividends accounts.

LampLight's December 31 closing entries are shown above.

EXPLAIN

- Explain that a corporation prepares the same closing entries as any other kind of business organization.
- Emphasize that most of the closing entries can be recorded directly from the work sheet.
- Review the four closing entries: (1) an entry to close income statement accounts with credit balances; (2) an entry to close income statement accounts with debit balances; (3) an entry to record net income or net loss in the retained earnings account and close Income Summary; and (4) an entry to close the dividend accounts.
- Explain that when there are dividends accounts for both common and preferred stock, both accounts must be closed to Retained Earnings.

DEMONSTRATE

- Direct students to the illustration as you demonstrate the closing entries for a corporation.
- Refer students back to the work sheet on pages 374–375, as you demonstrate how all the Income Statement accounts with credit balances are debited in the first closing entry to close them. Demonstrate that the total of these accounts is credited to Income Summary.
- Refer students back to the work sheet on pages 374–375, as you demonstrate how all the Income Statement accounts with debit balances are credited in the second closing entry to close them. Demonstrate that the total of these accounts is debited to Income Summary.
- For the third closing entry, demonstrate how the debit to Income Summary is also the amount of net income on the work sheet. Explain that this debit will close Income Summary. Point out that the credit to Retained Earnings records the net income in the Retained Earnings account.
- Demonstrate how the fourth closing entry closes both of the dividends accounts to Retained Earnings.

TEACHING STRATEGIES   EXPANDING BEYOND THE CLASSROOM

Invite a stockbroker or investment counselor to the classroom to address how individual investors can use financial statement analysis in investment decisions. Brief the speaker in advance on which ratios the students have studied.

EXPLAIN

- Explain that a post-closing trial balance is prepared after closing entries are posted to check the accuracy of the general ledger.

- Point out that after closing entries are posted, the only accounts that should have balances are the asset, liability, and stockholders' equity accounts. All income statement accounts should have zero balances.

- Emphasize that when the post-closing trial balance totals are the same, the ledger is assumed to be correct.

- Explain that the word "post" means "after" and that the post-closing trial balance is therefore a trial balance prepared after closing entries are recorded.

DEMONSTRATE

- Direct students to the illustration as you demonstrate the preparation of a post-closing trial balance.

POST-CLOSING TRIAL BALANCE

LampLight, Inc.
Post-Closing Trial Balance
December 31, 20--

Account Title	Debit	Credit
Cash	$ 25,436.40	
Petty Cash	250.00	
Notes Receivable	10,000.00	
Interest Receivable	1,000.00	
Accounts Receivable	135,234.54	
Allowance for Uncollectible Accounts		$ 6,697.63
Subscriptions Receivable		
Merchandise Inventory	258,755.19	
Supplies—Sales	8,446.63	
Supplies—Administrative	8,157.30	
Prepaid Insurance	10,988.69	
Prepaid Interest	10.47	
Bond Sinking Fund	50,000.00	
Store Equipment	142,983.34	
Accumulated Depreciation—Store Equipment		31,876.00
Building	165,000.00	
Accumulated Depreciation—Building		16,500.00
Office Equipment	73,928.23	
Accumulated Depreciation—Office Equipment		17,386.13
Land	133,000.00	
Organization Costs	1,440.00	
Interest Payable		15,000.00
Accounts Payable		30,585.40
Employee Income Tax Payable		1,238.90
Federal Income Tax Payable		2,392.76
Social Security Tax Payable		665.99
Medicare Tax Payable		153.61
Salaries Payable		633.73
Sales Tax Payable		2,154.74
Unemployment Tax Payable—Federal		88.65
Unemployment Tax Payable—State		598.39
Health Insurance Premiums Payable		428.00
Dividends Payable		29,575.00
Bonds Payable		250,000.00
Capital Stock—Common		321,000.00
Stock Subscribed—Common		
Paid-in Capital in Excess of Stated Value—Common		200.00
Capital Stock—Preferred		170,000.00
Stock Subscribed—Preferred		
Paid-in Capital in Excess of Par Value—Preferred		8,000.00
Discount on Sale of Preferred Stock	5,000.00	
Treasury Stock	1,800.00	
Paid-in Capital from Sale of Treasury Stock		500.00
Retained Earnings		125,755.86
Totals	$1,031,430.79	$1,031,430.79

LampLight's December 31 post-closing trial balance is shown above.

REMEMBER If the totals on the post-closing trial balance are the same, the accounting records are ready for the next fiscal period.

Financial Analysis and Reporting for a Corporation

APPLIED SKILLS | LANGUAGE ARTS

Paraphrasing, Writing Complete Sentences, and Identifying Adjectives and the Words They Modify. For additional practice in language arts skills, direct students to answer the Cases for Critical Thinking in writing. Students should write in their own words and in complete sentences. To further practice language arts skills, ask students to underline the adjectives and circle the words they modify in their answers.

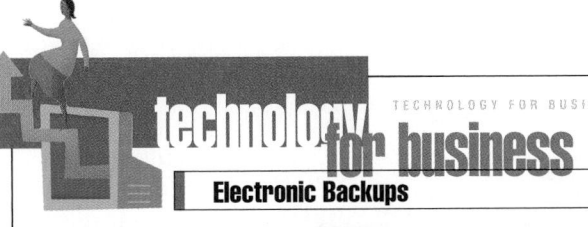

	DATE		ACCOUNT TITLE	DOC. NO.	POST. REF.	DEBIT	CREDIT	
1			*Reversing Entries*					1
2	20-- Jan.	1	Interest Income			1 0 0 0 0		2
3			Interest Receivable				1 0 0 0 0	3
4		1	Interest Expense			1 0 47		4
5			Prepaid Interest				1 0 47	5
6		1	Interest Payable			15 0 0 0 0		6
7			Interest Expense				15 0 0 0 0	7
8		1	Salaries Payable			6 3 3 73		8
9			Salary Expense—Sales				4 5 7 89	9
10			Salary Expense—Administrative				1 7 5 84	10
11		1	Social Security Tax Payable			4 1 19		11
12			Medicare Tax Payable			9 51		12
13			Unemploy. Tax Pay.—Federal			1 20		13
14			Unemploy. Tax Pay.—State			8 10		14
15			Payroll Taxes Expense				6 0 00	15
16								16

GENERAL JOURNAL — PAGE 15

If an adjusting entry creates a balance in an asset or liability account, LampLight reverses the adjusting entry. Like most corporations, however, LampLight does not reverse the adjust-ing entry that records federal income tax. Lamp-Light's reversing entries recorded on January 1 are shown above.

technology for business

TECHNOLOGY FOR BUSINESS • TECHNOLOGY FOR BUSINESS • TECHNOLOGY FOR BUSINE

Electronic Backups

Management information systems engineers design systems to back up and archive important electronic data. A backup creates a second set of all or part of the information stored on individual computers within a local area network.

Three techniques are commonly used. First is a complete backup. All the information on the system is backed up to a storage device such as a tape or an optical disk. Complete backup requires the most time to complete, but ensures that all information is stored in another location.

The second backup method is incremental backups. Using this method, only the files that have been changed or created since the last backup are saved to the storage device. The time to complete the backup is less than the time for a total backup. However, if a system failure occurs, restoring the files will take longer. The complete backup is restored first, then each incremental backup is restored.

The most complex method of backup is known as dynamic backup. Each time a file is saved, a backup is created. Thus, if a system failure occurs, virtually no data is lost. The technology for dynamic backups is more complex and more costly than the other two methods.

Whichever method is used, backing up files is an important part of any quality management information system.

Other End-of-Fiscal-Period Work

Lesson 13-3   **389**

TECHNOLOGY FOR BUSINESS

The Technology for Business feature is designed to show students common business applications of technology. Ask students if they are familiar with the concepts of electronic backups. Lead a class discussion on the advantages and disadvantages of the various backup methods.

TEACHING STRATEGIES   COOPERATIVE LEARNING

Using automated accounting software to complete accounting problems is an ideal cooperative learning experience. Students working in groups can collaborate on completing input forms and keying data.

- Explain that every corporation is required to complete a federal income tax return, Form 1120, and submit it and payment for outstanding federal income tax to the federal government.

- Point out that most of the information required for a Form 1120 is obtained from the work sheet or financial statements.

- Explain that some of the information required on the Form 1120 must be modified from what is reported on the work sheet. For example, the work sheet shows separate amounts for payroll tax expense and property tax expense, but the tax return requires all taxes to be combined in one amount.

- Explain that the government revises Form 1120 periodically as new tax laws are passed. Point out that some of the details of this form may therefore be different in future years.

DEMONSTRATE

- Direct students to the illustration as you demonstrate how to complete a Form 1120.

- Point out that on line 1, the amount of sales is Sales less Sales Discounts.

- Demonstrate that the amount of interest on line 5 is the interest income, not the income expense.

- Demonstrate how lines 12 and 13 report the total salary expense as two different kinds of compensation. Corporations need to account separately for the compensation paid to its officers.

- Demonstrate that the interest on line 18 is the interest expense, not the interest income.

- Demonstrate how the rest of the form is completed. Emphasize the importance of the signature at the bottom of the form.

FEDERAL INCOME TAX RETURN

Form 1120 — U.S. Corporation Income Tax Return
Department of the Treasury, Internal Revenue Service
OMB No. 1545-0123

For calendar year 20-- or tax year beginning ...., 20--, ending ...., 20 ...
▶ Instructions are separate. See page 1 for Paperwork Reduction Act Notice.
20--

A Check if a:
(1) Consolidated return (attach Form 851) ☐
(2) Personal holding co. (attach Sch. PH) ☐
(3) Personal service corp. (as defined in Temporary Regs. sec. 1.441-4T—see instructions) ☐

Name: LampLight, Inc.
Number, street, and room or suite no. (If a P.O. box, see page 6 of instructions.): 1450 Eaglewood Lane
City or town, state, and ZIP code: Nashville, TN 37207-2361

B Employer identification number: 74-1334457
C Date incorporated: 12/26/--
D Total assets (see Specific Instructions): $ 952,171.03

E Check applicable boxes: (1) ☐ Initial return (2) ☐ Final return (3) ☐ Change in address

Income			
1a	Gross receipts or sales	864,257.28	b Less returns and allowances 2,900.56	c Bal ▶ 1c	861,356.72
2	Cost of goods sold (Schedule A, line 8)	2	454,714.03
3	Gross profit. Subtract line 2 from line 1c	3	406,642.69
4	Dividends (Schedule C, line 19)	4	-0-
5	Interest	5	1,450.00
6	Gross rents	6	-0-
7	Gross royalties	7	-0-
8	Capital gain net income (attach Schedule D (Form 1120))	8	-0-
9	Net gain or (loss) from Form 4797, Part II, line 20 (attach Form 4797)	9	-0-
10	Other income (see instructions—attach schedule)	10	-0-
11	Total income. Add lines 3 through 10 ▶	11	408,092.69

Deductions (See instructions for limitations on deductions.)			
12	Compensation of officers (Schedule E, line 4)	12	28,432.50
13a	Salaries and wages 59,070.56 b Less jobs credit -0- c Balance ▶	13c	59,070.56
14	Repairs	14	-0-
15	Bad debts	15	6,277.50
16	Rents	16	-0-
17	Taxes	17	16,662.40
18	Interest	18	30,289.53
19	Charitable contributions (see instructions for 10% limitation)	19	-0-
20	Depreciation (attach Form 4562) 20 34,737.13		
21	Less depreciation claimed on Schedule A and elsewhere on return 21a -0-	21b	34,737.13
22	Depletion	22	-0-
23	Advertising	23	17,782.00
24	Pension, profit-sharing, etc., plans	24	-0-
25	Employee benefit programs	25	-0-
26	Other deductions (attach schedule)	26	83,705.80
27	Total deductions. Add lines 12 through 26 ▶	27	276,957.42
28	Taxable income before net operating loss deduction and special deductions. Subtract line 27 from line 11	28	131,135.27
29	Less: a Net operating loss deduction (see instructions) 29a -0-		
	b Special deductions (Schedule C, line 20) 29b -0-	29c	-0-

Tax and Payments			
30	Taxable income. Subtract line 29c from line 28	30	131,135.27
31	Total tax (Schedule J, line 10)	31	34,392.76
32	Payments: a 20-- overpayment credited to 20-- 32a -0-		
b	20-- estimated tax payments 32b 32,000.00		
c	Less 20-- refund applied for on Form 4466 32c (-0-) d Bal ▶ 32d 32,000.00		
e	Tax deposited with Form 7004 32e -0-		
f	Credit from regulated investment companies (attach Form 2439) 32f -0-		
g	Credit for Federal tax on fuels (attach Form 4136). See instructions 32g -0-	32h	32,000.00
33	Estimated tax penalty (see instructions). Check if Form 2220 is attached ▶ ☐	33	-0-
34	Tax due. If line 32h is smaller than the total of lines 31 and 33, enter amount owed	34	2,392.76
35	Overpayment. If line 32h is larger than the total of lines 31 and 33, enter amount overpaid	35	
36	Enter amount of line 35 you want: Credited to 19-- estimated tax ▶ Refunded ▶	36	

Under penalties of perjury, I declare that I have examined this return, including accompanying schedules and statements, and to the best of my knowledge and belief, it is true, correct, and complete. Declaration of preparer (other than taxpayer) is based on all information of which preparer has any knowledge.

Please Sign Here — Susan P. Boyd (Signature of officer) — 3/15/-- (Date) — Treasurer (Title)

Paid Preparer's Use Only — Preparer's signature / Date / Check if self-employed ☐ / Preparer's social security number — Firm's name (or yours if self-employed) and address / E.I. No. ▶ / ZIP code ▶

LampLight must file a federal income tax return and pay income taxes. Page 1 of LampLight's Form 1120, U.S. Corporation Income Tax Return, is shown above.

Some amounts reported on a corporation's income statement must be modified to complete the tax return. For example, LampLight presents both payroll tax expense and property tax expense on its income statement. LampLight's managers require this information to make sound business decisions. However, the tax form requires LampLight to report only the total of all taxes.

Financial Analysis and Reporting for a Corporation

DISSOLVING A CORPORATION

When a corporation is dissolved, it must meet legal requirements and follow correct accounting procedures. However, corporations are rarely dissolved. When an owner (stockholder) decides not to participate in the corporation, the stockholder merely sells all shares of stock owned. The corporation is not dissolved.

The dissolution of a corporation involves many legal procedures and documents. Documents that must be filed include a notice to the state in which the business was incorporated and a notice to all creditors of the corporation. Since the dissolution of a corporation is complex, the board of directors should seek legal advice.

Once a corporation is dissolved, the liquidation process can begin. The procedure for selling noncash assets is similar to that for proprietorships and partnerships. However, since a corporation is a taxable entity, the gains and losses on the sale of noncash assets are subject to taxation. Therefore, additional tax reports for the corporation must be filed. The accounting aspects of actually liquidating a corporation are extremely complex. Therefore, obtaining professional accounting services to assist in the liquidation of a corporation is recommended.

Explore Accounting

EXPLORE ACCOUNTING • EXPLORE ACCOUNTING • EXPLORE ACCOUNTING

Differences Between Generally Accepted Accounting Principals (GAAP) and Tax Law: Net Income vs. Taxable Income

The net income reported by a company on its income statement is usually not the same amount reported on the company's tax return as "taxable income." The difference between net income and taxable income is caused by the rules that must be followed to calculate each amount.

Net income is calculated following accounting rules, called *Generally Accepted Accounting Principles (GAAP)*. GAAP is developed by the Financial Accounting Standards Board and is designed to give investors and others information about the financial condition of a company.

Taxable income is calculated following U.S. tax laws. Tax laws are developed by Congress, enforced by the Internal Revenue Service, and designed to collect government revenue in an equitable manner.

Sometimes the difference is permanent. For example, interest on some investments is not

taxable. That means that the interest will be included in the company's net income on the income statement, but the company does not have to include the interest in taxable income for tax purposes.

Sometimes the difference is just a timing difference. For example, assume that in December 20X1, a company pays $1,000 for insurance for the next year. The company will not show the $1,000 as an income statement expense in 20X1, but it will show the expense on its 20X2 income statement. For tax purposes, the $1,000 will be a deduction against income in 20X1, not in 20X2.

Instructions
Use the Internet to research other differences between GAAP and tax laws. Report your findings to your class.

GUIDED PRACTICE

Audit Your Understanding
Call on students to answer the Audit Your Understanding questions. Ask the class if each answer is correct and/or complete. Answers are given in Appendix E of the textbook.

Work Together
Have students write the solution to the Work Together problem as you guide the class through the examples.

- Remind students that the problem started in Work Together 13-1 is needed to complete this problem.
- Discuss each entry and its source before having students complete the entries in their journals.

INDEPENDENT PRACTICE

On Your Own
- Assign the On Your Own problem to be worked independently.
- Remind students that the problem started in On Your Own 13-1 is needed to complete this problem.
- Use the Ongoing Assessment techniques to diagnose student understanding.

Application Problem
- Assign Application Problem 13-4: Completing other end-of-fiscal-period work.

Personal Trainer
- Students can access the Lesson 13-3 assessment material using this software.

Xtra! Web Site
- Students can access the Xtra! Study Tools for additional practice.

ENRICH

- Assign the Technology for Business feature on page 389.
- Assign Explore Accounting on page 391.

CLOSE

- Ask students to summarize the end-of-fiscal-period work described in Lesson 13-3.

392

• audit your understanding

1. What four closing entries are recorded at the end of the period?
2. What form is used to file the federal income tax return for a corporation?
3. How does the liquidation of a corporation differ from the liquidation of a proprietorship or partnership?

• work together 13-3

End-of-fiscal period work for a corporation

Use the work sheet for Provident Electronics, Inc. from Work Together 13-1. Statement paper and pages 14, 15, and 16 of a general journal are provided in the *Working Papers*. Your instructor will guide you through the following examples.

1. Journalize the adjusting entries on page 14 of the general journal.
2. Journalize the closing entries on page 15 of the general journal.
3. Prepare a post-closing trial balance as of December 31 of the current year.
4. Journalize the reversing entries on page 16 of the general journal.

• on your own 13-3

End-of-fiscal period work for a corporation

Use the work sheet for BRE Corporation from On Your Own 13-1. Statement paper and pages 8, 9, and 10 of a general journal are provided in the *Working Papers*. Your instructor will guide you through the following problem.

1. Journalize the adjusting entries on page 8 of the general journal.
2. Journalize the closing entries on page 9 of the general journal.
3. Prepare a post-closing trial balance as of December 31 of the current year.
4. Journalize the reversing entries on page 10 of the general journal.

accountingxtra.swlearning.com

After completing this chapter, you can

1. Define terms related to financial analysis and reporting for a corporation.

2. Identify concepts and practices related to financial analysis and reporting for a corporation.

3. Prepare a work sheet for a corporation.

4. Calculate federal income tax for a corporation.

5. Prepare and analyze financial statements for a corporation.

6. Prepare selected end-of-fiscal-period work for a corporation.

Explore Accounting

EXPLORE ACCOUNTING · EXPLORE ACCOUNTING · EXPLORE ACCOUN

Notes to Financial Statements

As today's business world becomes increasingly complex, investors' need for accounting information also continues to grow. Much of the information investors need goes beyond the general ledger account balances presented on financial statements. For example, the Financial Accounting Standards Board has determined that investors should have the scheduled payments on long-term debt for the next five years.

A complete set of financial statements includes four basic statements: income statement, balance sheet, statement of stockholders' equity, and statement of cash flows. The financial statements also include a variety of disclosures, called notes, that present additional information regarding amounts presented in the basic financial statements.

Each note begins with a heading that contains a number and title. The first note is typically a statement of significant account principles used to prepare the financial statements. This note would include the methods used to cost inventory, depre-

ciate assets, and other principles where management can select among acceptable alternatives.

Subsequent notes can cover a variety of topics, depending upon the individual characteristics of the company. For example, an oil company would explain how it values its crude oil reserves. Other notes might include information on inventory, fixed assets, income taxes, etc. Other significant events affecting the corporation, such as mergers, discontinued operations, and lawsuits, are also disclosed in the notes to financial statements.

Required:
Obtain the annual reports of three public corporations. What reference on each financial statement directs you to examine the notes to financial statements? Compare the titles of each note contained in each annual report. Which notes were presented in more than one annual report? Which notes were unique to one of the corporations?

Financial Analysis and Reporting for a Corporation

Chapter 13 **393**

PUTTING IT ALL TOGETHER

- Review the Chapter Summary.
- Ask students to prepare a list of the new concepts introduced in this chapter.
- Discuss ways the procedures described in this chapter are different from those of a partnership or proprietorship.

INDEPENDENT PRACTICE

- Assign Mastery Problem 13-5 to students who need the reinforcement of a problem that combines all activities from the chapter in one problem; this will be most students.
- Assign Challenge Problem 13-6 to accelerated students who do not require the reinforcement of the Mastery Problem.
- Assign Study Guide 13.
- Students can use Automated Accounting 8.0 or higher to work Mastery Problem 13-5.
- Students can use Peachtree or Quick-Books to automate Mastery Problem 13-5.
- Students can access Personal Trainer to work end-of-chapter problems on the computer.
- Students can access the Xtra! Web Site for the Xtra! Review and Quizzing.
- Students can access the Student Companion CD for additional review material.

ONGOING ASSESSMENT

Review solutions to the assigned problems in class, diagnosing trouble spots.

RETEACH

- Call on students to describe how they avoid the trouble spots diagnosed.
- Use reteaching suggestions from lesson plans as required.
- Assign Recycling Problem 13-1 if needed.

ENRICH

- Assign the Explore Accounting feature. Ask students to share the information they have gathered in a report to the class.
- Students can access the Xtra! Web Site for the Xtra! Enrichment material.
- Assign Applied Communication.
- Assign the SCANS Workplace Competency.
- Assign Graphing Workshop.
- Assign Analyzing Costco's Financial Statements.
- Assign Automated Accounting on pages 400–401.
- Assign First Class Image Wear, Inc.: A Business Simulation.

EXPLORE ACCOUNTING

Students' answers will vary. The reference to the notes to financial statements may vary from "The accompanying notes to financial statements are an integral part of these financial statements" to simply "See accompanying notes."

The first note describes the significant accounting principles used in the preparation of the financial statements and is typically titled "Summary of Significant Accounting

Policies." Notes commonly found in financial statements include "Inventory," "Property, Plant and Equipment," "Long-Term Commitments," "Income Taxes," "Leases," "Employee Benefit Plans," "Segment Information," and "Contingencies." Other notes might be related to the corporation's type of business; for example, an oil corporation might have a note titled "Oil Reserves."

13-1 APPLICATION PROBLEM

Preparing a work sheet for a corporation

General ledger account titles and balances for Trexler, Inc., are recorded on a work sheet in the *Working Papers* accompanying this textbook.

Instructions:

Complete the work sheet for the current year ended December 31. Record the adjustments on the work sheet using the following information. Save your work to complete Application Problems 13-3 and 13-4.

Adjustment Information, December 31

Accrued Interest Income	$ 160.17
Uncollectible Accounts Expense (estimated as 1.0% of sales on account)	
Sales on Account for Year	126,405.00
Merchandise Inventory	51,450.23
Sales Supplies Inventory	1,202.70
Administrative Supplies Inventory	959.85
Value of Prepaid Insurance	1,436.58
Prepaid Interest	1.85
Annual Depreciation Expense—Store Equipment	1,294.57
Annual Depreciation Expense—Building	2,900.00
Annual Depreciation Expense—Office Equipment	3,018.64
Organization Expense	50.00
Accrued Interest Expense	4,002.57
Accrued Salaries—Sales	153.97
Accrued Salaries—Administrative	593.49
Accrued Payroll Taxes—Social Security Tax	48.59
Accrued Payroll Taxes—Medicare	11.21
Accrued Payroll Taxes—Federal Unemployment Tax	1.72
Accrued Payroll Taxes—State Unemployment Tax	11.61

Federal income taxes are based on the tax rate table in this chapter.

13-2 APPLICATION PROBLEM

Calculating federal income taxes

During the past year, three corporations earned the following net income before federal income taxes:

Corporation A	$73,932.56
Corporation B	$467,032.45
Corporation C	$38,296.44

Instructions:

Calculate the amount of federal income tax expense for each of the three corporations. Use the tax rate table in this chapter.

TEACHING STRATEGIES   APPLIED MATHEMATICS

End-of-chapter problems for Chapter 13 include a large amount of computational work. Students should be encouraged to use calculators to allow them to focus their attention on the procedures rather than on the arithmetic.

13-3 APPLICATION PROBLEM

Preparing financial statements for a corporation

Use the work sheet prepared in Application Problem 13-1.

Instructions:

1. Prepare an income statement for the current year ended December 31.
2. Calculate and record the following component percentages: (a) cost of merchandise sold, (b) gross profit on operations, (c) total selling expenses, (d) total administrative expenses, (e) total operating expenses, (f) income from operations, (g) net addition or deduction resulting from other revenue and expenses, (h) net income before federal income tax, (i) federal income tax expense, and (j) net income after federal income tax. Round the percentage calculations to the nearest 0.1%.
3. Use the Income Statement Analysis table given in the *Working Papers.* Analyze Trexler's income statement by determining whether component percentages are within acceptable levels. If any component percentage is not within an acceptable level, suggest steps that the company should take.
4. Calculate earnings per share. Round the calculation to the nearest cent. Trexler has 10,900 shares of $10.00 stated-value common stock issued and 420 shares of $100.00 par-value preferred stock issued. Treasury stock consists of 70 shares of common stock. The dividend rate on preferred stock is 10%.
5. Prepare a statement of stockholders' equity for the current year ended December 31. Use the following additional information.

	January 1 Balance	Issued During the Year	December 31 Balance
Common Stock:			
No. of Shares	8,000	2,900	10,900
Amount	$80,000.00	$29,000.00	$109,000.00
Preferred Stock:			
No. of Shares	150	270	420
Amount	$15,000.00	$27,000.00	$ 42,000.00

Treasury stock consists of 70 shares of common stock.
The January 1 balance of Retained Earnings was $13,411.26.

6. Calculate the following items: (a) equity per share of stock and (b) price-earnings ratio. The market price of common stock on December 31 is $24.00.
7. Prepare a balance sheet for December 31 of the current year.
8. Calculate the following items:
   (a) Accounts receivable turnover ratio. Net sales on account are $126,405.00. Accounts receivable and allowance for uncollectible accounts on January 1 were $26,495.72 and $1,142.37, respectively.
   (b) Rate earned on average stockholders' equity. Total stockholders' equity on January 1 was $106,951.26.
   (c) Rate earned on average total assets. Total assets on January 1 were $233,699.75.

13-4 APPLICATION PROBLEM

Completing other end-of-fiscal-period work

Use the work sheet prepared in Application Problem 13-1.

Instructions:

1. Journalize the adjusting entries. Use page 13 of a general journal.
2. Journalize the closing entries. Use page 14 of a general journal.
3. Journalize the reversing entries. Use page 15 of a general journal. Use January 1 of the year following the current year as the date.

Application Problem 13-3
2. a. 46.7
   b. 53.3
   c. 12.0
   d. 17.3
   e. 29.3
   f. 24.0
   g. 3.3
   h. 20.7
   i. 3.1
   j. 17.6

Application Problem 13-4
Closing entry #3: Debit Income Summary, 34,008.51; credit Retained Earnings, 34,008.51.

Closing entry #4: Debit Retained Earnings, 9,073.50; credit Dividends Common, 4,873.50 and credit Dividends Preferred, 4,200.00.

Mastery Problem 13-5

1. Fed. Inc. Tax Exp., 20,126.97.

2. a. 40.6
   b. 59.4
   c. 17.8
   d. 13.6
   e. 31.5
   f. 27.9
   g. 2.9
   h. 25.0
   i. 5.4
   j. 19.6

4. Earnings per share: Pref., 10.00, Com., 3.63.

8. a. 50,528.60; 4.2
   b. 327,838.61; 22.5
   c. 432,311.07; 17.0

13-5 MASTERY PROBLEM   AUTOMATED ACCOUNTING   PEACHTREE   QUICKBOOKS

Completing end-of-fiscal-period work for a corporation

The general ledger account titles and balances for Lander, Inc., are recorded on a work sheet in the *Working Papers*.

Instructions:

1. Complete the work sheet for December 31 of the current year. Record the adjustments on the work sheet using the following information.

Adjustment Information, December 31

Accrued Interest Income	$ 277.18
Uncollectible Accounts Expense (estimated as 1.0% of sales on account)	
Sales on Account for Year	213,441.00
Merchandise Inventory	86,876.38
Sales Supplies Inventory	9,808.79
Administrative Supplies Inventory	3,620.75
Value of Prepaid Insurance	2,363.94
Prepaid Interest	3.12
Annual Depreciation Expense—Store Equipment	9,746.00
Annual Depreciation Expense—Building	2,400.00
Annual Depreciation Expense—Office Equipment	2,185.95
Organization Expense	75.00
Accrued Interest Expense	7,004.34
Accrued Salaries—Sales	375.65
Accrued Salaries—Administrative	1,002.13
Accrued Payroll Taxes—Social Security Tax	89.55
Accrued Payroll Taxes—Medicare	20.67
Accrued Payroll Taxes—Federal Unemployment Tax	1.27
Accrued Payroll Taxes—State Unemployment Tax	8.59

Federal income taxes are based on the tax rate table in this chapter.

2. Prepare an income statement. Calculate and record the following component percentages: (a) cost of merchandise sold, (b) gross profit on operations, (c) total selling expenses, (d) total administrative expenses, (e) total operating expenses, (f) income from operations, (g) net addition or deduction resulting from other revenue and expenses, (h) net income before federal income tax, (i) federal income tax expense, and (j) net income after federal income tax. Round percentage calculations to the nearest 0.1%.

3. Use the Income Statement Analysis table given in the *Working Papers*. Analyze Lander's income statement by determining whether component percentages are within acceptable levels. If any component percentage is not within an acceptable level, suggest steps that the company should take.

4. Calculate earnings per share. Round the calculation to the nearest cent. Lander has 18,400 shares of $10.00 stated-value common stock issued and 720 shares of $100.00 par-value preferred stock issued. Treasury stock consists of 90 shares of common stock. The dividend rate on preferred stock is 10%.

5. Prepare a statement of stockholders' equity for the current year ended December 31. Use the following additional information.

	January 1 Balance	Issued During the Year	December 31 Balance
Common Stock:			
No. of Shares	18,000	400	18,400
Amount	$180,000.00	$ 4,000.00	$184,000.00
Preferred Stock:			
No. of Shares	600	120	720
Amount	$ 60,000.00	$12,000.00	$ 72,000.00

The January 1 balance of Retained Earnings was $22,645.60.

APPLIED SKILLS   WRITING ACROSS THE CURRICULUM

Writing Paragraphs and Short Essays. The Cases for Critical Thinking are short, practical applications of the accounting principles developed in the chapter. Some cases are planned to present problems related to the chapter but not specifically discussed and answered in the chapter. These cases present an opportunity for critical thinking and decision making. These cases also require more than a short objective-type response. Therefore, they provide ideal practice in writing paragraphs and short essays.

6. Calculate the following items based on information on the statement of stockholders' equity: (a) equity per share of stock and (b) price-earnings ratio. The market price of common stock on December 31 is $30.00.
7. Prepare a balance sheet for December 31 of the current year.
8. Calculate the following items based on information from the balance sheet.
   (a) Accounts receivable turnover ratio. Net sales on account were $213,441.00. Accounts receivable and allowance for doubtful accounts on January 1 were $49,435.32 and $2,146.40, respectively.
   (b) Rate earned on average stockholders' equity. Total stockholders' equity on January 1 was $290,485.60.
   (c) Rate earned on average total assets. Total assets on January 1 were $392,691.70.
9. Journalize the adjusting entries. Use page 13 of a general journal.
10. Journalize the closing entries. Use page 14 of a general journal.
11. Journalize the reversing entries. Use page 1 of a general journal. Use January 1 of the year following the current year as the date.

13-6 CHALLENGE PROBLEM

Preparing a Form 1120, U.S. Corporation Income Tax Return

Goldstein, Inc., has completed its work sheet and financial statements for the fiscal year ending on December 31 of the current year. The income statement for Goldstein is in the *Working Papers*.

The following information required to prepare the tax return is obtained from company records.

Employer identification number: 65-074738
Date incorporated: January 5
Address: 7834 Industrial Road, Oxford, MS 38655-1500
Total assets: $786,986.50
Compensation of officers: $7,217.60
Estimated tax payments: $42,000.00

Instructions:
1. Complete the company name and address in the spaces provided on the tax form.
2. Use the information provided to complete lines D–F. Write the amount of compensation of officers on line 12. Write the estimated tax payments on line 32b.
3. Use the amounts on the income statement to complete the following lines of the tax form.

Tax Form

Line	Income Statement Account(s)
1a	Sales less Sales Discount
1b	Sales Returns and Allowances
2	Cost of Merchandise Sold
5	Interest Income
13a	Salary Expense—Sales plus Salary Expense—Administrative less Compensation of officers
15	Uncollectible Accounts Expense
17	Payroll Taxes Expense plus Property Taxes
18	Interest Expense
20	The sum of the three depreciation expense accounts
23	Advertising Expense
26	All other expenses not reported on other lines
31	Federal Income Tax Expense

4. Calculate the amounts on lines 1c, 3, 11, 13c, 21b, 27, 30, 32h, and 34 using the instructions provided on the tax form.
5. Check the accuracy of the completed tax form by comparing the amount on line 30 of the tax form to Net Income before Federal Income Tax on the income statement.
6. Write -0- on the remaining blank lines on the tax form.

Challenge Problem 13-6
Form 1120: Line 11: 443,611.80
Line 31: 45,977.13
Line 34: 3,977.13

APPLIED SKILLS LANGUAGE ARTS

Exploring Spelling Checker Software. Students may rely too heavily on the spelling checker feature of their word processing software. A word may be spelled correctly, but it may not be the word that should be used. Spend some time giving examples of incorrect words that the spelling checker cannot identify as misspelled ("if" instead of "is"; "its" instead of "it's"; "the" instead of "them"; etc.). Ask students to supply other pairs of words.

APPLIED COMMUNICATION

This activity may be evaluated on thoroughness of coverage, accuracy of research, and format of the report, as well as mechanics.

CASES FOR CRITICAL THINKING

Case 1

Recommend that the corporation prepare both a statement of stockholders' equity and a balance sheet. On the balance sheet show only summary information from the statement of stockholders' equity. This procedure will result in a shorter balance sheet, which will be easier to read.

Case 2

If Mr. Edwards is saving his money for sometime in the future, investing in the stock will likely be better. The higher rate of return from dividends over several years will offset the broker's commissions when stock is bought and sold. However, the full 6% interest on a savings account will be paid in each of the future years. A stockholder has no assurance that a corporation will pay dividends in future years.

SCANS WORKPLACE COMPETENCY

Allow students some freedom in organizing their budget format. Encourage the use of spreadsheet applications in the preparation of student budgets. At the end of the project, discuss with students their successes, as well as the different obstacles that arose.

398

• applied communication

The market price of a stock may change daily as its shares are traded on a stock exchange. Research and write a brief report about one of the stock exchanges. Describe such things as how a company is listed on the exchange, how shares are traded, and how an individual can find the current market price of a stock listed on the exchange.

• cases for critical thinking

Case 1

A corporation president suggests to the accounting department that the statement of stockholders' equity be dropped from the end-of-fiscal-period work. The president's reason is that the same information is reported on the corporation's balance sheet. The accounting department wants to continue using the statement. Which would you recommend? Why?

Case 2

Kevin Edwards has $20,000.00 in a savings account that is earning 6% interest. He is thinking of investing the money in stock that has a stated value and a current market price of $100.00 per share. For the past three years, the stock dividends have amounted to $9.00 per share per year. Mr. Edwards asks your advice. What would you recommend? Explain your answer.

• SCANS workplace competency

Resource Competency: Allocating Money

Concept: Employers need workers who can use or prepare budgets, including cost and revenue forecasts. Effective workers are able to maintain detailed records, track actual costs, calculate variances, measure budget performance, and make appropriate adjustments.

Application: Prepare a one-month budget projection for yourself. Identify all sources of income such as allowances, wages, monetary gifts, and other anticipated revenues. List all monthly expenses including meals, entertainment, gifts, car payments, insurance amounts, dues, savings, etc. As you track your revenues and expenses during the month, make necessary changes in order to meet your budgetary goals. At the end of the month, compare actual amounts with budgeted figures. Identify reasons for all variances.

graphing workshop

The corporate income tax for a year divided by the net income before taxes is the *effective tax rate.* Companies track their effective tax rate over the years to determine any trends that may be occurring.

Tax data for Superior Supply Corporation for the past five years is given below.

Year	Income Tax	Net Income before Tax
20X1	32,099.00	125,254
20X2	35,416.00	133,758
20X3	40,046.00	145,632
20X4	37,949.00	140,254
20X5	43,861.00	155,412

Instructions:

1. Calculate the effective tax rate for each year.

2. Create a line graph that will help Superior Supply Corporation determine any trends in its effective tax rate.

analyzing Costco's financial statements

The amount of net income belonging to a single share of stock is called *earnings per share (EPS).* EPS is shown on the income statement. In some cases, the company must calculate EPS two different ways. The formula for "basic" EPS is:

$$EPS = \text{Net Income/Number of Shares Outstanding}$$

The formula for "diluted" or "fully diluted" EPS is more complicated and can use different numbers for both the numerator and the denominator.

The formula for rate earned on average stockholders' equity is:

$$\text{Rate Earned on Average Stockholders' equity} = \text{Net Income/Average Stockholders' Equity}$$

Instructions:

1. Using Appendix B in this textbook, go to the income statement for Costco Corporation on page B-6. What is the basic EPS for the period ending August 2003?

2. Show the formula and amounts used to calculate the EPS for the period ending August 2003.

3. Compare the basic EPS for the three years shown on the income statement. What trend can you identify?

4. Calculate the rate earned on average stockholders' equity for the periods ending 2003 and 2002. Assume the beginning balance for the period ended 2002 was $4,882,940,000.

5. Compare the rate earned on average stockholders' equity for 2003 and 2002. What trend can you identify?

Financial Analysis and Reporting for a Corporation

1.

Year	Effective Tax Rate	Income Tax	Net Income Before Tax
20X1	25.63	32,099.00	125,254
20X2	26.48	35,416.00	133,758
20X3	27.50	40,046.00	145,632
20X4	27.06	37,949.00	140,254
20X5	28.22	43,861.00	155,412

As net income increases or decreases, the effective tax rate also increases or decreases. Since except for 20X4, the net income before tax has steadily increased, so the effective tax rate has increased.

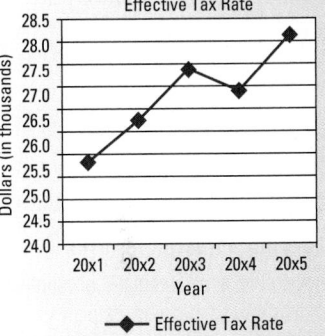

ANALYZING COSTCO'S FINANCIAL STATEMENTS
ANALYZING COSTCO'S FINAN

1. $1.58

2. 721,000,000/456,335,000 = 1.58

3. The basic EPS has improved each of the three years.

4. 2002: $699,983,000 ÷ ($4,882,940,000 + $5,694,237,000)/2 = 6.7%

   2003: &721,000,000 ÷ ($5,694,237,000 + $6,554,980,000)/2 = 5.9%

5. The rate earned on average stockholders' equity for 2002 was better than for 2003.

TEACHING STRATEGIES   PORTFOLIO ASSESSMENT

Proper and accurate end-of-fiscal-period work is critical to a business and to the internal and external users of the financial statements. Students should emphasize their learning of this topic by selecting an example of a comprehensive sample of their work in this chapter, either the mastery problem or a problem from a test to include in their portfolio. A copy of the Portfolio Assessment form (blackline master in the Teacher's Resource Guide; also on the Student Companion CD) should be completed by the student and the Description section should include any comments regarding how the student mastered these concepts and procedures. Alternatively, students might include in their portfolios printed reports from an Automated Accounting Problem or parts of Reinforcement Activity 2 or the simulation.

- Explain that the end-of-fiscal-period work described in this feature is a review of procedures studied in previous Automated Accounting features.

- Remind students that adjusting entries are analyzed from a trial balance in an automated accounting system. No work sheet is prepared.

DEMONSTRATE

Preparing a trial balance

- Demonstrate clicking the Reports toolbar button.

- Demonstrate choosing the Ledger Reports option button from the Select a Report Group list.

- Demonstrate selecting Trial Balance from the Choose a Report to Display list.

- Demonstrate clicking the OK button.

- Demonstrate clicking the Print button to print the trial balance.

Recording adjusting entries

- Explain that in an automated accounting system adjusting entries are planned using a trial balance. A work sheet is not prepared.

- Demonstrate clicking the Journal toolbar button and selecting the General Journal tab from the Journal Entries window.

- Demonstrate entering and posting the adjusting entries.

- Explain that "Adj. Ent." is used as the reference for adjusting entries since there is no source document.

Generating financial statements

- Demonstrate clicking the Reports toolbar button and selecting the Financial Statements option button from the Select a Report Group list.

- Demonstrate choosing the income statement from the Choose a Report to Display list and clicking OK.

- Demonstrate that other financial statements can be displayed by choosing other option buttons in the Choose a Report to Display list.

- Explain that displayed financial statements should be checked for accuracy before printing.

· Automated Accounting

End-of-Period Work for a Corporation

During the fiscal period, numerous transactions are analyzed, journalized, and posted. When a transaction affects more than one accounting period, an adjusting entry may be needed to match revenues and expenses with the appropriate accounting period. To complete the accounting cycle, adjusting entries are entered into the computer and verified for accuracy. The financial statements are generated, and then closing entries are generated and posted by the software.

Trial Balance

Before adjusting entries are recorded, a trial balance is displayed and printed. The trial balance proves the equality of debits and credits in the general ledger. To display the trial balance:

1. Click the Reports toolbar button, or choose the Report Selection menu item from the Reports menu.

2. When the Report Selection dialog appears, choose the Ledger Reports option button from the Select a Report Group list.

3. Select Trial Balance from the Choose a Report to Display list.

4. Click the OK button.

   From the Trial Balance display window, the report can be printed or copied to the Clipboard in spreadsheet or word processing format.

Adjusting Entries

The trial balance and period-end adjustment data are used as the basis for the adjusting entries. Adjusting entries are used to:

1. Transfer to expense the amount of assets consumed. For example, office supplies and prepaid insurance.

2. Update the merchandise inventory account.

3. Recognize accrued revenues and accrued expenses.

To record adjusting entries, use the following steps:

1. Click the Journal toolbar button, or choose the Journal Entries menu item from the Data menu.

2. Select the General Journal tab from the Journal Entries window, if necessary.

3. Key the adjusting entries. All adjusting entries are dated the last day of the fiscal period. *Adj. Ent.* is used as the reference for all adjusting entries.

4. Click the Post button.

Financial Statements

The reports that summarize information from the ledgers are known as financial statements. The most common financial statements for a business organized as a corporation are the balance sheet and the income statement. *Automated Accounting 8.0* or higher can also display a retained earnings statement.

After adjusting entries have been posted, financial statements are prepared. To display financial statements:

1. Click the Reports toolbar button, or choose the Report Selection menu item from the Reports menu. The Report Selection window displays.

2. Choose the Financial Statements option button from the Select a Report Group list.

3. Choose the financial statement report you would like to display from the Choose a Report to Display list.

4. Click the OK button.

   The up-to-date account balances stored by the software are used to calculate and display the current financial statements.

Closing Entries

In an automated accounting system, closing entries are generated and posted by the software. The software automatically closes net income to Retained Earnings after closing the revenue and expense accounts. The dividend account is closed as well. The steps required are as follows:

1. Choose Generate Closing Journal Entries from the Options menu.
2. Click Yes to generate the closing entries.
3. The general journal will appear, containing the journal entries. Verify the accuracy of the transactions.
4. Click the Post button.

AUTOMATING MASTERY PROBLEM 13-5

Instructions:

1. Load *Automated Accounting 8.0* or higher software.
2. Select database AA13-5 (Advanced Course Mastery Problem 13-5) from the accounting template disk.
3. Select File from the menu bar and choose the Save As menu command. Key the path to the drive and directory that contain your data files. Save the database with a filename of XXX135 (where XXX are your initials).
4. Read the Problem Instruction screen by clicking the Browser toolbar button.
5. Refer to page 396 for data used in this problem.
6. Exit the Automated Accounting software.

DEMONSTRATE

Generating closing entries and a post-closing trial balance

- Demonstrate choosing Generate Closing Journal Entries from the Options menu.
- Demonstrate clicking Yes to generate the closing entries.
- Demonstrate clicking the Post button after the general journal containing the closing entries is displayed and verified.
- Demonstrate clicking the Reports toolbar button.
- Demonstrate selecting the Ledger Reports option button from the Report Selection dialog box.
- Demonstrate choosing Trial Balance Report to display the post-closing trial balance.

PRACTICE

- Assign Automating Mastery Problem 13-5: Completing end-of-fiscal-period work for a corporation.

ASSESSMENT

- Use the Electronic Auditor to assess student understanding.

TEACHING STRATEGIES   PORTFOLIO ASSESSMENT

Students should be encouraged to print at least one report from one of the Automated Accounting problems to include in their portfolio to demonstrate mastery of automated accounting systems. A copy of the Portfolio Assessment form (blackline master in the Teacher's Resource Guide; also on the Student Companion CD) should be completed by the student and the Description section should include any comments regarding how the student mastered these concepts and procedures.

Processing and Reporting Accounting Data for a Corporation

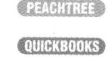

AUTOMATED ACCOUNTING

PEACHTREE

QUICKBOOKS

This activity reinforces learning from Parts 2 through 4, Chapters 5 through 13.

WHITEHURST, INC.

The accounting activities are for Whitehurst, Inc., a merchandising business organized as a corporation. Whitehurst sells plumbing and related products to building contractors, homeowners, and other consumers. Whitehurst's fiscal year is from January 1 through December 31.

PART A: JOURNALIZING TRANSACTIONS

In Part A of this reinforcement activity, selected transactions for Whitehurst, Inc., completed during December of the current year, are journalized.

Whitehurst uses the chart of accounts shown on page 403. The journals used by Whitehurst are similar to those illustrated in Parts 2 through 4.

RECORDING TRANSACTIONS

Instructions:

1. Journalize the following transactions completed during December of the current year. Use page 23 of a cash receipts journal, page 23 of a cash payments journal, and page 12 of a general journal. Whitehurst records prepaid interest expense initially as an expense and rent received in advance as revenue. Other prepaid and unearned items are recorded initially as assets and liabilities. Source documents are abbreviated as follows: check, C; memorandum, M; note payable, NP; note receivable, NR; receipt, R.

Dec. 1. Whitehurst's board of directors declared an annual dividend of $15,820.00. Preferred stock issued is $40,400.00 of 10%, $100.00 par-value preferred stock. Common stock issued is $11,780.00 of $10.00 stated-value common stock. Date of payment is December 30. M316.
1. Wrote off Susan Vine's past-due account as uncollectible, $427.50. M317.
1. Received cash for three months' rent in advance from Woodcrest, Inc., $2,400.00. R126.
1. Discarded a store fixture: original cost, $1,050.00; total accumulated depreciation through December 31 of last year, $840.00; additional depreciation to be recorded through December 1 of the current year, $210.00. M318.
1. Received a subscription from Delmar Adams for 30 shares of $100.00 par-value preferred stock, $3,000.00. M319.

TEACHING STRATEGIES   PORTFOLIO ASSESSMENT

A copy of the Portfolio Assessment form (blackline master in the Teacher's Resource Guide; also on the Student Companion CD) should be completed by the student, and the Description section should include any comments regarding how the student mastered these concepts and procedures.

Left sidebar

INTRODUCE THE ACTIVITY

- Reinforcement Activity 2 covers the complete accounting cycle for a merchandising business organized as a corporation. Students may begin this activity after they have completed their study of Chapter 13.

AUTOMATING THE ACTIVITY

- Automated Accounting 8.0 or higher may be used to automate Reinforcement Activity 2.
- Peachtree and QuickBooks may also be used to automate Reinforcement Activity 2.

ASSESSMENT

- Blackline masters for the audit test for Reinforcement Activity 2 are available in the Teacher's Resource Guide.
- Use the Electronic Auditor to assess performance on automating Reinforcement Activity 2 with Automated Accounting 8.0 or higher.

WINNING EDGE

Give students the *Winning Edge* by making competitive event prep part of their classroom materials throughout the year. Go to *http://winningedge.swlearning.com* for a list of materials that prepare students for specific competitive events.

MATERIALS

- Manual Accounting:
  Working Papers for Reinforcement Activity 2
  Teacher's Edition of the Working Papers for Reinforcement Activity 2
  Blackline Master of Audit Test
- Software:
  Automated Accounting and Century 21 8E CD
  The Electronic Auditor
  Peachtree and QuickBooks

GENERAL LEDGER CHART OF ACCOUNTS

Balance Sheet Accounts

(1000)	ASSETS
1100	CURRENT ASSETS
1105	Cash
1110	Petty Cash
1115	Notes Receivable
1120	Interest Receivable
1125	Accounts Receivable
1130	Allowance for Uncollectible Accounts
1135	Subscriptions Receivable
1140	Merchandise Inventory
1145	Supplies—Sales
1150	Supplies—Administrative
1155	Prepaid Insurance
1160	Prepaid Interest
1200	LONG-TERM INVESTMENT
1205	Bond Sinking Fund
1300	PLANT ASSETS
1305	Store Equipment
1310	Accumulated Depreciation—Store Equipment
1315	Building
1320	Accumulated Depreciation—Building
1325	Office Equipment
1330	Accumulated Depreciation—Office Equipment
1335	Land
1400	INTANGIBLE ASSET
1405	Organization Costs

(2000)	LIABILITIES
2100	CURRENT LIABILITIES
2105	Notes Payable
2110	Interest Payable
2115	Accounts Payable
2120	Employee Income Tax Payable
2125	Federal Income Tax Payable
2130	Social Security Tax Payable
2133	Medicare Tax Payable
2135	Salaries Payable
2140	Sales Tax Payable
2145	Unearned Rent
2150	Unemployment Tax Payable—Federal
2155	Unemployment Tax Payable—State
2160	Health Insurance Premiums Payable
2165	Dividends Payable
2200	LONG-TERM LIABILITY
2205	Bonds Payable

(3000)	STOCKHOLDERS' EQUITY
3105	Capital Stock—Common
3110	Stock Subscribed—Common
3115	Paid-in Capital in Excess of Stated Value—Common
3120	Capital Stock—Preferred
3125	Stock Subscribed—Preferred
3130	Paid-in Capital in Excess of Par Value—Preferred
3135	Treasury Stock
3140	Paid-in Capital from Sale of Treasury Stock
3145	Retained Earnings
3150	Dividends—Common
3155	Dividends—Preferred
3160	Income Summary

Income Statement Accounts

(4000)	OPERATING REVENUE
4105	Sales
4110	Sales Discount
4115	Sales Returns and Allowances
(5000)	COST OF MERCHANDISE
5105	Purchases
5110	Purchases Discount
5115	Purchases Returns and Allowances
(6000)	OPERATING EXPENSES
6100	Selling Expenses
6105	Advertising Expense
6110	Credit Card Fee Expense
6115	Depreciation Expense—Store Equipment
6120	Miscellaneous Expense—Sales
6125	Salary Expense—Sales
6130	Supplies Expense—Sales
6200	ADMINISTRATIVE EXPENSES
6205	Depreciation Expense—Building
6210	Depreciation Expense—Office Equipment
6215	Insurance Expense
6220	Miscellaneous Expense—Administrative
6225	Payroll Taxes Expense
6230	Property Tax Expense
6235	Salary Expense—Administrative
6240	Supplies Expense—Administrative
6245	Uncollectible Accounts Expense
6250	Utilities Expense
(7000)	OTHER REVENUE
7105	Gain on Plant Assets
7110	Interest Income
7115	Rent Income
(8000)	OTHER EXPENSES
8105	Interest Expense
8110	Loss on Plant Assets
8115	Organization Expense
(9000)	INCOME TAX
9105	Federal Income Tax Expense

Dec. 2. Paid cash for office equipment, $2,650.00. C476.
4. Patrick Carson dishonored NR4, a 30-day, 10% note, maturity value due today: principal, $150.00; interest, $1.25; total, $151.25. M320.
4. Discarded an office table: original cost, $250.00; total accumulated depreciation through December 31 of last year, $150.00; additional depreciation to be recorded through December 4 of the current year, $50.00. M321.
4. Received a 60-day, 10% note from Leigh Calhoun for an extension of time on her account, $500.00. NR5.
5. Issued a 6-month, 10% note, $10,000.00. NP6.
5. Paid cash to bond trustee for annual interest on bond issue, $24,000.00. C482.
5. Paid cash to bond trustee for annual deposit to bond sinking fund, $18,400.00, and recorded interest earned on bond sinking fund, $1,600.00. C487.
6. Received cash from Leslie Johns for 700 shares of $10.00 stated-value common stock at $11.00 per share, $7,700.00. R134.
7. Received cash for the maturity value of NR1, principal, $150.00, plus interest, $2.47; total, $152.47. R136.
11. Received cash from sale of office equipment, $70.00: original cost, $700.00; total accumulated depreciation through December 31 of last year, $500.00; additional depreciation to be recorded through December 11 of the current year, $100.00. M322 and R138.
11. Paid cash to Marlin Pratt for 60 shares of $10.00 stated-value common stock at $9.00 per share, $540.00. C502.
12. Paid cash for the maturity value of NP4: principal, $300.00, plus interest, $6.00; total, $306.00. C503.
13. Received cash from Robert Shull for 200 shares of $10.00 stated-value common stock at $10.00 per share, $2,000.00. R140.
14. Received cash for the maturity value of NR2: principal, $247.50, plus interest; $4.07; total $251.57. R141.
16. Paid cash for the maturity value of NP3: principal, $1,000.00, plus interest, $16.44; total, $1,016.44. C509.
19. Received office equipment from Valerie DeLong at an agreed value of $1,000.00 for 10 shares of $100.00 par-value preferred stock. M323.
20. Received cash in full payment of Susan Vine's account, previously written off as uncollectible, $427.50. M324 and R143.
21. Paid cash, $2,000.00, plus an office microcomputer, for a new microcomputer: original cost of old microcomputer, $3,500.00; total accumulated depreciation through December 31 of last year, $2,100.00; additional depreciation to be recorded through December 21 of the current year, $700.00. M325 and C515.
27. Discounted at 12% a 60-day non-interest-bearing note, $5,000.00; proceeds, $4,900.00; interest, $100.00. NP7.
28. Received cash from James Dier for 10 shares of treasury stock at $13.00 per share, $130.00. Treasury stock was bought on December 11 at $9.00 per share. R146.
29. Received cash from sale of an old cash register used in sales, $800.00: original cost, $1,600.00; total accumulated depreciation through December 31 of last year, $896.00; additional depreciation to be recorded through December 29 of the current year, $144.00. M326 and R147.
29. Received cash from Patrick Carson for dishonored NR4: principal, $151.25, plus additional interest, $1.05; total, $152.30. R148.
29. Received cash from Delmar Adams in payment of stock subscription, $3,000.00. R149.
29. Issued Stock Certificate No. 14 to Delmar Adams for 30 shares of $100.00 par-value preferred stock, $3,000.00. M327.
30. Paid cash for annual dividend declared December 1, $15,820.00. C519.

2. Prove and rule the cash receipts and cash payments journals.

In Part B, Whitehurst's end-of-fiscal-period work is completed. This work is similar to activities described in Chapter 14. The December 31 trial balance is recorded on a work sheet in the *Working Papers* accompanying this textbook.

Instructions:

3. Complete the work sheet for the year ended December 31 of the current year. Record the adjustments on the work sheet using the following additional information.

Adjustment Information, December 31

Accrued interest income	$ 95.70
Uncollectible accounts expense estimated as 0.1% of net sales on account.	
Net sales on account for year, $343,472.60.	
Merchandise inventory	206,618.63
Sales supplies inventory	1,456.06
Administrative supplies inventory	730.00
Value of prepaid insurance	970.00
Prepaid interest	93.33
Annual depreciation expense—store equipment	8,300.00
Annual depreciation expense—building	1,500.00
Annual depreciation expense—office equipment	1,150.00
Organization expense	300.00
Accrued interest expense	2,025.00
Accrued salaries—sales	3,232.04
Accrued salaries—administrative	716.50
Accrued payroll taxes—Social Security tax	256.65
Accrued payroll taxes—Medicare tax	59.23
Accrued payroll taxes—federal unemployment tax	15.79
Accrued payroll taxes—state unemployment tax	106.58
Rent received in advance and still unearned	1,200.00

Federal income tax expense for the year is calculated at the following rates:
  15% of net income before taxes, zero to $50,000.00.
  Plus 25% of net income before taxes, $50,000.00 to $75,000.00.
  Plus 34% of net income before taxes, $75,000.00 to $100,000.00.
  Plus 39% of net income before taxes, $100,000.00 to $335,000.00.
  Plus 34% of the net income before taxes over $335,000.00.

4. Prepare an income statement. Calculate and record the following component percentages. (a) Cost of merchandise sold. (b) Gross profit on operations. (c) Total selling expenses. (d) Total administrative expenses. (e) Total operating expenses. (f) Income from operations. (g) Net addition or deduction resulting from other revenue and expenses. (h) Net income before federal income tax. (i) Federal income tax expense. (j) Net income after federal income tax. Round percentage calculations to the nearest 0.1%.

5. Analyze Whitehurst's income statement by determining if component percentages are within acceptable levels. If any component percentage is not within an acceptable level, suggest steps that the company should take. Acceptable component percentages are given in the *Working Papers*.

6. Calculate earnings per share. Round the calculation to the nearest cent. Whitehurst has 12,680 shares of $10.00 stated-value common stock issued and 444 shares of 10%, $100.00 par-value preferred stock issued. Treasury stock consists of 50 shares of common stock.

7. Prepare a statement of stockholders' equity. Use the following additional information.

	January 1 Balance	Issued During the Year	December 31 Balance
Common stock:			
No. of shares	11,780	900	12,680
Amount	$117,800.00	$9,000.00	$126,800.00
Preferred stock:			
No. of shares	404	40	444
Amount	$ 40,400.00	$4,000.00	$ 44,400.00

The January 1 balance of Retained Earnings was $26,759.39.

8. Calculate the following items based on information on the statement of stockholders' equity. (a) Equity per share of stock. (b) Price-earnings ratio. The market price of common stock on December 31 is $13.50.

9. Prepare a balance sheet for December 31 of the current year.

10. Calculate the following items based on information from the balance sheet. (a) Accounts receivable turnover ratio. Accounts receivable and allowance for uncollectible accounts on January 1 were $36,785.45 and $698.35, respectively. (b) Rate earned on average stockholders' equity. Total stockholders' equity on January 1 was $186,459.39. (c) Rate earned on average total assets. Total assets on January 1 were $458,204.24.

11. Use pages 13 and 14 of a general journal. Journalize the adjusting entries.

12. Use pages 14 and 15 of a general journal. Do not skip a line. Journalize the closing entries.

13. Use page 1 of a general journal. Journalize the reversing entries. Use January 1 of the year following the current year as the date.

Activities in First Class Image Wear, Inc.:

1. Recording transactions in special journals and a general journal.

2. Posting items to be posted individually to a general ledger and subsidiary ledgers.

3. Proving and ruling journals.

4. Posting column totals to a general ledger.

5. Preparing schedules of accounts receivable and accounts payable.

6. Preparing a trial balance on a work sheet.

7. Planning adjustments and completing a work sheet.

8. Preparing financial statements.

9. Journalizing and posting adjusting entries.

10. Journalizing and posting closing entries.

11. Preparing a post-closing trial balance.

A Business Simulation
First Class Image Wear, Inc.

First Class Image Wear, Inc. is a merchandising business organized as a corporation. This business simulation covers the realistic transactions completed by First Class Image Wear, Inc., which sells a broad range of logo ware. The activities included in the accounting cycle for First Class Image Wear, Inc. are listed at left.

This simulation is available from the publisher in either manual or automated versions.

Part 5 takes a look at management accounting. One important aspect of management accounting, budgetary planning and control, is covered in **Chapter 14**. Topics such as budget functions, design procedures, and planning are discussed and illustrated.

- **Chapter 15** explores analyzing income statements so that managers can gain an understanding of the relationship among sales, costs, and expenses.

- **Chapter 16** describes how managers must consider the time value of money when comparing future profits to today's costs.

- **Chapter 17** progresses to financial statement analysis and how this information can be used to make wise management decisions.

- Part 5 concludes with **Chapter 18**, Statement of Cash Flows. This chapter describes and analyzes cash flows so that managers can determine if there will be enough cash to continue operating.

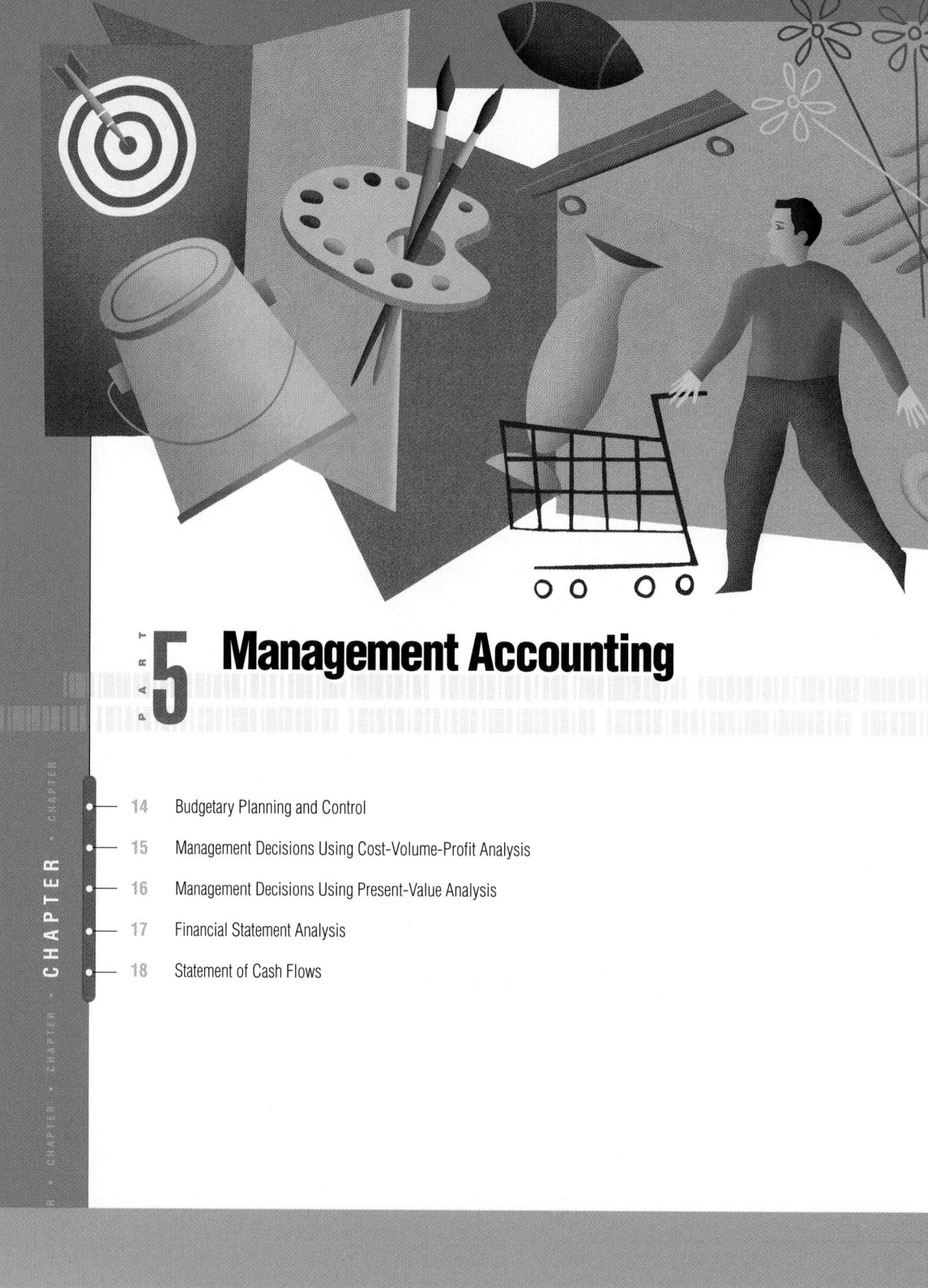

PART 5 Management Accounting

1235   Building
1240   Accumulated Depreciation—Building
1245   Land

(2000) LIABILITIES

2100   CURRENT LIABILITIES
2105   Notes Payable
2110   Interest Payable
2115   Accounts Payable
2120   Employee Income Tax Payable
2125   Federal Income Tax Payable
2128   Social Security Tax Payable
2130   Medicare Tax Payable
2135   Sales Tax Payable
2140   Unemployment Tax Payable—Federal
2145   Unemployment Tax Payable—State
2150   Dividends Payable

2200   LONG-TERM LIABILITY
2205   Mortgage Payable

(3000) CAPITAL
3105   Capital Stock
3110   Retained Earnings
3115   Dividends
3120   Income Summary

(4000) OPERATING REVENUE
4105   Sales
4110   Sales Discount
4115   Sales Returns and Allowances

(5000) COST OF MERCHANDISE
5105   Purchases
5110   Purchases Discount
5115   Purchases Returns and Allowances

(6000) OPERATING EXPENSES

6100   SELLING EXPENSES
6105   Advertising Expense
6110   Delivery Expense
6115   Depreciation Expense—Delivery Equipment
6120   Depreciation Expense—Warehouse Equipment
6125   Miscellaneous Expense—Sales
6130   Salary Expense—Commissions
6135   Salary Expense—Regular
6140   Supplies Expense—Sales

6200   ADMINISTRATIVE EXPENSES
6205   Depreciation Expense—Office Equipment
6210   Insurance Expense
6215   Miscellaneous Expense—Administrative
6220   Payroll Taxes Expense
6225   Rent Expense
6230   Salary Expense—Administrative
6235   Supplies Expense—Administrative
6240   Uncollectible Accounts Expense
6245   Utilities Expense

(7000) OTHER REVENUE
7105   Gain on Plant Assets
7110   Interest Income

(8000) OTHER EXPENSES
8105   Interest Expense
8110   Loss on Plant Assets

(9000) INCOME TAX
9105   Federal Income Tax Expense

The chart of accounts for Reflection, Inc. is illustrated above for ready reference as you study Part 5 of this textbook.

REFLECTION, INC.
CHART OF ACCOUNTS

Balance Sheet Accounts

(1000) ASSETS

1100   CURRENT ASSETS
1105   Cash
1110   Petty Cash
1115   Notes Receivable
1120   Interest Receivable
1125   Accounts Receivable
1130   Allowance for Uncollectible Accounts
1135   Merchandise Inventory
1140   Supplies—Sales
1145   Supplies—Administrative
1150   Prepaid Insurance

1200   PLANT ASSETS
1205   Equipment—Delivery
1210   Accumulated Depreciation—Delivery Equipment
1215   Equipment—Office
1220   Accumulated Depreciation—Office Equipment
1225   Equipment—Warehouse
1230   Accumulated Depreciation—Warehouse Equipment

409

CHART OF ACCOUNTS

- Emphasize that students should refer to this chart of accounts throughout the chapters in Part 5.

- Explain that this chart of accounts is used by a merchandising business organized as a corporation.

- Stress that charts of accounts are extremely important to companies because they drive the accounting system. Employees usually cannot even receive reimbursement for expenses without knowing which account the expense should be charged to.

- Emphasize that charts of accounts are used for determining the classification of accounts and determining which accounts are temporary and permanent accounts.

- Stress that the chart of accounts is useful for completing automated accounting activities since account numbers are required for both data entry and file maintenance activities.

Similarities

Point out the *similarities* between this chart of accounts and the ones used in Parts 3 and 4:

- Typical divisions for a merchandising business:
  - Assets
  - Liabilities
  - Stockholders' Equity
  - Operating Revenue
  - Cost of Merchandise
  - Operating Expenses
  - Other Revenue
  - Other Expenses
  - Income Tax
- Many familiar accounts within divisions.

Differences

Point out the *differences* between this chart of accounts and the ones used in Parts 3 and 4:

- Reflection, Inc., distinguishes between delivery equipment, office equipment, warehouse equipment, and building when accounting for plant assets and their related depreciation.

- Reflection, Inc., distinguishes between commissions, regular salaries, and salaries for administrative personnel when accounting for salary expenses.

	SCOPE & SEQUENCE		ENHANCING	
	NEW	REVIEW/ EXTENSION	SPECIAL FEATURES	
Introduce the Chapter	✓		• Accounting in the Real World: KPMG	
Lesson 14-1 Budget Planning			• Making Ethical Decisions: Confidentiality	
Budget function	✓			
Budget design	✓			
Lesson 14-2 Budgeted Income Statement			• Cultural Diversity: Who Owns This Small Business?	
Sales budget schedule	✓			
Purchases budget schedule	✓			
Selling expenses budget schedule	✓			
Administrative expense budget schedule	✓			
Other revenue and expenses budget schedule	✓			
Budgeted income statement		✓		
Lesson 14-3 Cash Budgets and Performance Reports			• Technology for Business: Numerical Format Options	
Cash receipts budget schedule	✓			
Cash payments budget schedule	✓			
Cash budget	✓			
Performance reports	✓			
Putting It All Together			• Explore Accounting	
			• Xtra! Web Site: Xtra! Enrichment	
			• Applied Communication	
			• Cases for Critical Thinking	
			• SCANS Workplace Competency	
			• Auditing for Errors	
			• Analyzing Costco's Financial Statements	

and Control

INSTRUCTION		PRACTICE AND ASSESSMENT		
TECHNOLOGY AND MEDIA	**TEACHING STRATEGIES**	**GUIDED PRACTICE**	**INDEPENDENT PRACTICE**	**RETEACHING AND ENRICHMENT**
• Internet Research Activity • Accounting Xtra! Web Site	• Software Focus			
• Instructor's Resource CD: PowerPoint Slides • Xtra! Web Site: Xtra! Study Tools • Personal Trainer	• Accounting Pedagogy	• Terms Review • Audit Your Understanding • Work Together 14-1	• On Your Own 14-1 • Ongoing Assessment, p. 416 • Personal Trainer • Xtra! Web Site: Xtra! Study Tools	• Reteach, p. 416 • Enrich, p. 417
• Instructor's Resource CD: PowerPoint Slides • Xtra! Web Site: Xtra! Study Tools • Blackline Masters: Budget Schedule • Personal Trainer	• Applied Skills: Communications	• Terms Review • Audit Your Understanding • Work Together 14-2	• On Your Own 14-2 • Application Problems 14-1 and 14-2 • Ongoing Assessment, p. 425 • Personal Trainer • Xtra! Web Site: Xtra! Study Tools	• Reteach, p. 425 • Enrich, p. 426
• Instructor's Resource CD: PowerPoint Slides • Xtra! Web Site: Xtra! Study Tools • Blackline Masters: Budget Schedule • Personal Trainer	• Cooperative Learning	• Terms Review • Audit Your Understanding • Work Together 14-3	• On Your Own 14-3 • Application Problem 14-3 • Ongoing Assessment, p. 432 • Personal Trainer • Xtra! Web Site: Xtra! Study Tools	• Reteach, p. 432 • Enrich, p. 433
• Automated Accounting • QuickBooks • Personal Trainer • Xtra! Web Site: Xtra! Review, Quizzing, and Enrichment • Student Companion CD	• Accounting Pedagogy • Teaching Tip • Specific Learning Disability (SLD) Students • Applied Skills: Writing Across the Curriculum		• Mastery Problem 14-4 • Personal Trainer • Xtra! Web Site: Xtra! Review and Quizzing • Study Guide 14 • Student Companion CD • Chapter 14 Test • ExamView Chapter 14 • Portfolio Assessment	• Challenge Problem 14-5 • Reteach, p. 434 • Enrich, p. 434 • Recycling Problem 14-1 • Automated Accounting • QuickBooks • Xtra! Web Site: Xtra! Enrichment

CHAPTER

14 Budgetary Planning and Control

OBJECTIVES & TERMS

After studying Chapter 14, you will be able to:

1. Define accounting terms related to budgetary planning and control.

2. Identify accounting concepts and practices related to preparing and analyzing budgeted income statements and cash budgets.

3. Gather information to prepare a budget.

4. Prepare a budgeted income statement.

5. Prepare a cash budget and performance report.

- budgeting
- budget
- budget period
- comparative income statement
- sales budget schedule
- purchases budget schedule
- selling expenses budget schedule
- administrative expenses budget schedule
- other revenue and expenses budget schedule
- budgeted income statement
- cash receipts budget schedule
- cash payments budget schedule
- cash budget
- performance report

Point Your Browser
accountingxtra.swlearning.com

410

• KPMG

©TONY WHITE//BLOOMBERG NEWS/LANDOV

FORENSIC ACCOUNTING AT KPMG

With nearly 100,000 employees and $11 billion in revenue, KPMG is one of the largest accounting firms in the world. In addition to providing traditional audit and tax services, KPMG has been a leader in the area of forensic accounting—the detection, prevention, and investigation of fraud.

KPMG published its first Fraud Survey in 1994. This renowned survey profiles the impact of fraud at hundreds of medium and large organizations. Its findings are clear—the instances of fraud are increasing.

What should an organization do if it suspects fraud has occurred? Most organizations elect to conduct an investigation. Unfortunately, most organizations do not have employees with the necessary knowledge or experience. KPMG, with its wealth of forensic accounting experience, is ideally suited to perform this investigation.

Organizations often require accounting firms to submit a bid or estimate of the professional fees that will be charged to complete the investigation. To calculate an estimate, KPMG must first determine the necessary experience level and expertise of the professional staff to be assigned to the client. The hourly billing rate of each professional staff member reflects that staff's experience and expertise.

Critical Thinking

1. What information would KPMG require in order to calculate an estimate of the professional fees to be charged for an advisory services project?
2. How does the level of experience and expertise affect the hourly billing rate of professional staff members?

Sources: www.us.kpmg.com/about/statistics2.asp; www.us.kpmg.com/
RutUS_prod/Documents/12/FINALFraudSur.pdf

Xtra!
Today
accountingxtra.swlearning.com

ORGANIZATIONAL CHARTS

Search the Internet for "organizational charts." Find the organizational charts for two organizations. Compare the charts by answering the following questions:

Instructions

1. What is the name of the organization?
2. What position(s) is at the top of the chart?
3. How many positions report directly to the top position? Name one such position.

The hourly billing rate and estimate of hours required by each professional staff member. Travel and other project-related expenses may also be included in the estimate.

The billing rate of a professional staff member increases as the level of experience increases. The more specialized the expertise, the higher the staff member's hourly billing rate.

INTERNET RESEARCH ACTIVITY

Answers will vary, depending on the charts selected.

411

14-1 Budget Planning

Business managers make a variety of business decisions each day. The quality of these decisions has a direct impact on the business's ability to improve profitability. Financial planning is one tool managers use to improve profitability. A business must earn a net income to continue in existence. [CONCEPT: Going Concern]

Planning the financial operations of a business is called **budgeting**. A written financial plan of a business for a specific period of time, expressed in dollars, is called a **budget**. [CONCEPT: Unit of Measurement] A business prepares a variety of budgets. Each budget provides managers with detailed information about a specific area of the business's operations.

A budget is a view into the future—a financial estimate of future business activities. Budget preparation begins with identifying company goals. Company goals might be to increase sales, reduce cost of merchandise sold, or increase net income. All of these goals affect budget preparation because the budget is a business's financial plan.

Two budgets commonly prepared in businesses are the budgeted income statement and the cash budget. The budgeted income statement is a projection of a business's sales, costs, expenses, and net income for a fiscal period. It is similar to a regular income statement and is sometimes known as an operating budget. The cash budget is a projection of a business's cash receipts and payments for a fiscal period. It is used to manage estimated cash shortages and overages.

©GETTY IMAGES/PHOTODISC

making ethical decisions

Confidentiality

Paxton Plastics manufactures molded plastic backyard play systems. Paxton is involved in several lawsuits as the result of children being injured while playing on Paxton's Slide by Slide, a double-wide sliding board. During a recent audit, Justin Portero, a CPA, learned that the company knew about structural problems with the sliding board and continued to manufacture and sell the products. Several company officers told Justin that they expect the company to lose the lawsuits but that the cost of these lawsuits

will be less than the cost of recalling and replacing the sliding boards. Later that week, Justin was visiting a friend who proudly displayed his son's new Paxton's Slide by Slide.

Instructions

Determine whether Justin, in accordance with the AICPA *Code of Professional Conduct*, can inform his friend of the problems with the play system. What recommendation would you give Justin?

BUDGET FUNCTIONS

Budgets are projections or estimates of what will happen in the future expressed in financial terms. A carefully prepared budget reflects the best projections possible by those persons who prepare it. A completed budget shows the projected course of action for a business. A budget serves three important business functions.

1. **Planning.** In preparing a budget, managers project what will happen in the future. This view of the future helps a manager plan actions that will meet desired goals. The budgeting process forces a manager to decide which actions should be emphasized to achieve the desired goals.
2. **Operational control.** A budget projects the accomplishments of a business. It specifies the type and the amount of projected activities. By comparing actual performance with projected performance, management can judge how well a business is achieving its goals. For example, managers compare actual expenses with budgeted expenses to identify differences. By identifying actual expense items that are higher than budgeted, a business can act to reduce these amounts.
3. **Department coordination.** Profitable business growth requires all managers to be aware of the company's plans. A budget reflects these plans. Each phase of a business operation must be coordinated with all related phases. For example, to achieve projected sales, the purchasing department must know when and how much merchandise to purchase. Therefore, all management personnel must help plan and use a budget as a guide to control and coordinate sales, costs, and expenses.

BUDGET PERIOD

The length of time covered by a budget is called the **budget period**. Usually this period is one year. Some companies also prepare a long-range budget of five years or more for special projects and plant and equipment purchases. However, the annual budget is the one used to compare current financial performance with budget plans.

An annual budget is normally prepared for a company's fiscal year. The annual budget is commonly divided into quarterly and monthly budgets. Such budget subdivisions provide frequent opportunities to evaluate how actual operations compare with budgeted operations.

A budget must be prepared in sufficient time to be communicated to the appropriate managers prior to the beginning of a budget period.

Large and complex companies start gathering budget information long before the beginning of a new budget year. Gathering information, performing analysis, making decisions, preparing the budget, and approving and communicating the budget take considerable time.

FYI FOR YOUR INFORMATION

Most budgets are based on forecasts of increases or decreases over previous years' performances. In zero-based budgeting, however, the data are prepared each year as though operations were being started for the first time.

EXPLAIN

- Point out to students that budgets are estimates of what will happen in the future.
- Emphasize the three functions of budgeting: planning, operational control, department coordination.
- Point out that planning helps managers create action plans to reach goals.
- Emphasize that operational control helps managers determine if their action plans were appropriate for reaching goals.
- Stress the importance of department coordination in reaching goals. All departments must contribute to the overall plan for it to be successful.
- Emphasize the effort necessary to prepare a budget. Budgets need to be prepared well in advance and require information gathering, analysis, estimating, and approval.

- Emphasize that although budgets rely on estimated figures, these projections need to be as accurate as possible. Stress that unless budgets are based on realistic assumptions, their value in operational control is lessened.

- Ask students where companies gather most of their information for the budget process. Stress that a company's own records and marketing research are extremely useful in projecting trends and identifying activities that will affect prices, promotional expenses, and other related items.

- Ask students what information or activities outside the company may affect a company's plans. Discuss economic factors, global competition, union contracts, new product development, technology, etc.

- Ask students which department or group of individuals within a corporation would be best suited to develop an estimate of projected sales for the upcoming year. Discuss the importance of involving sales personnel in this component of the budget process. Emphasize that sales personnel interact with customers on a daily basis and can often provide valuable input regarding projected sales for the next year.

SOURCES OF BUDGET INFORMATION

Budgets cannot be exact since they show only projected sales, costs, and expenses. However, a company should project future operations as accurately as possible. A company uses many information sources.

Company Records

The accounting and sales records of a business contain much of the information needed to prepare budgets. Accounting information about previous years' operations is used to determine trends in sales, purchases, and operating expenses. Expected price changes, sales promotion plans, and market research studies also are important in projecting activity for a budget period.

General Economic Information

A general slowdown or speedup in the national economy may affect budget decisions. Unusually high inflation rates affect budgeted amounts. A labor strike may affect some related industries and thus affect company operations. New product development, changes in consumer buying habits, availability of merchandise, international trade, and general business conditions all must be considered when preparing budgets.

Company Staff and Managers

Sales personnel estimate the amount of projected sales. Considering projected sales for the new budget period, other department managers project budget items for their areas of responsibility of the business.

Good Judgment

Good judgment by the individuals preparing the budgets is essential to realistic budgets. Even after evaluating all available information, answers to many budget questions are seldom obvious. Since some information will conflict with other information, final budget decisions are based on good judgment.

©GETTY IMAGES/PHOTODISC

{ **REMEMBER** National magazines and newspapers are a good source of information regarding general economic conditions. }

TEACHING STRATEGIES ACCOUNTING PEDAGOGY

This textbook presents budgetary planning and control as a tool to improve profitability. Internal control is continually emphasized as a key to success.

Reflection, Inc.
Comparative Income Statement
For Years Ended December 31, 20X1 and 20X2

	20X2	20X1	Increase (Decrease) Amount	Increase (Decrease) Percentage*
Operating Revenue:				
Net Sales	$1,880,000	$1,700,000	$180,000	10.6
Cost of Merchandise Sold	1,231,720	1,105,000	126,720	11.5
Gross Profit on Operations	$ 648,280	$ 595,000	$ 53,280	9.0
Operating Expenses:				
Selling Expenses:				
Advertising Expense	$ 45,120	$ 37,800	$ 7,320	19.4
Delivery Expense	150,410	140,640	9,770	6.9
Depr. Expense—Delivery Equipment	7,200	7,000	200	2.9
Depr. Expense—Warehouse Equipment	10,800	10,800	0	0.0
Miscellaneous Expense—Sales	11,490	11,960	(470)	(3.9)
Salary Expense—Commissions	75,200	68,000	7,200	10.6
Salary Expense—Regular	34,160	28,320	5,840	20.6
Supplies Expense—Sales	11,280	10,850	430	4.0
Total Selling Expenses	$ 345,660	$ 315,370	$ 30,290	9.6
Administrative Expenses:				
Depr. Expense—Office Equipment	$ 14,400	$ 12,000	$ 2,400	20.0
Insurance Expense	4,800	4,500	300	6.7
Miscellaneous Expense—Administrative	38,770	33,640	5,130	15.2
Depr. Expense—Warehouse Equipment	19,200	19,200	0	0.0
Payroll Taxes Expense	22,540	20,590	1,950	9.5
Rent Expense	30,000	30,000	0	0.0
Salary Expense—Administrative	77,830	75,240	2,590	3.4
Supplies Expense—Administrative	13,620	14,600	(980)	(6.7)
Uncollectible Accounts Expense	11,280	10,230	1,050	10.3
Utilities Expense	10,080	7,320	2,760	37.7
Total Administrative Expenses	$ 242,520	$ 227,320	$ 15,200	6.7
Total Operating Expenses	$ 588,180	$ 542,690	$ 45,490	8.4
Income from Operations	$ 60,100	$ 52,310	$ 7,790	14.9
Other Expenses:				
Interest Expense	$ 3,000	$ 6,500	($ 3,500)	(53.8)
Net Income before Federal Income Tax	$ 57,100	$ 45,810	$ 11,290	24.6
Federal Income Tax Expense	9,280	6,870	2,410	35.1
Net Income after Federal Income Tax	$ 47,820	$ 38,940	$ 8,880	22.8
Units (sq. ft.) of Mirror Sold	376,000	340,000	36,000	10.6

*Percentages rounded to the nearest 0.1%.

Preparation for planning a budget involves analyzing available financial information. An analysis of previous years' sales, cost, and expense amounts is an important part of budget preparation. An income statement containing sales, cost, and expense information for two or more years is called a **comparative income statement**.

Reflection, Inc., is a corporation that sells custom-cut mirrors. A comparative income statement provides the information for Reflection's analysis of previous years' sales, costs, and expenses. This statement shows trends that may be taking place in these items. The statement also highlights items that may be increasing or decreasing at a higher rate than other items on the statement. Reflection's comparative income statement is shown above.

- Ask students to state the percentage of increase or decrease for the cost of merchandise sold. Using the information presented in the illustration, ask students if the 11.5% change is favorable or unfavorable. Discuss with students that since the percent of increase (11.5) in the cost of merchandise sold exceeded the percent of increase (10.6) in net sales, this trend is unfavorable.

- Point out that unfavorable trends require additional investigation. In this instance, the percent of increase (11.5) for the cost of merchandise sold was greater than the percent of increase (10.6) in net sales due to a price increase in mirrors. The purchase price per square foot of mirrors increased during 20X2 from $3.25 per square foot to $3.30.

ONGOING ASSESSMENT

- Circulate through the classroom or lab, observing which students have problems with assignments.

- Troubleshooting: Students may have problems determining favorable and unfavorable trends when comparing the percentage change in expenses to the percentage change in sales.

- Assess student understanding by checking solutions to Independent Practice assignments.

RETEACH

- Arrange the class into cooperative learning groups of 3–4 individuals. Distribute copies of a blank 4-column financial statement form.

- Ask each group to create two simplified comparative income statements. The first comparative income statement is to show a percentage increase in sales; the second, a percentage decrease in sales.

- Direct students to use only five expense accounts and to ignore federal income tax.

- Ask students to indicate if the percent changes in expenses are favorable or unfavorable.

- Ask each group to write their examples on the board. Ask students in other groups if they spot any errors in calculations, percentage amounts, or trend analysis.

INTERPRETING THE COMPARATIVE INCOME STATEMENT

Compare the percentage change in expenses or costs to the percentage change in sales.

	Effect on net income
If the % increase ↑ in expenses or costs > the % increase ↑ in sales, net income ↓ decreases.	Unfavorable
If the % increase ↑ in expenses or costs < the % increase ↑ in sales, net income ↑ increases.	Favorable
If the % decrease ↓ in expenses or costs > the % decrease ↓ in sales, net income ↑ increases.	Favorable
If the % decrease ↓ in expenses or costs < the % decrease ↓ in sales, net income ↓ decreases.	Unfavorable

The first column of Reflection's comparative income statement shows actual sales, costs, and expenses for 20X2, the current year. The second column shows actual amounts for 20X1, the prior year. The third column shows the amount of increase or decrease from the prior year, 20X1, to the current year, 20X2. (For example, 20X2 cost of merchandise sold, $1,231,720, *less* 20X1 cost of merchandise sold, $1,105,000, *equals* the increase, $126,720.) The fourth column shows the percentage by which the current year amount increased or decreased from the prior year amount. (For example, the cost of merchandise sold increase, $126,720, *divided* by the 20X1 amount, $1,105,000, *equals* the percentage of increase, 11.5%.) Reflection rounds percentages to the nearest 0.1%.

Managers review each increase or decrease amount on the comparative income statement. The percentage of increase or decrease indicates whether the change is favorable, unfavorable, or normal compared with net sales. If a cost or expense item increase is a higher percentage than the net sales increase, net income is unfavorably affected. However, if the net sales increase is a higher percentage than cost and expense items, net income is favorably affected. Decreases have the opposite effect. If a cost or expense item decrease is a higher percentage than the net sales decrease, net income is favorably affected. If the net sales decrease is a higher percentage than cost and expense items, net income is unfavorably affected. A summary of the effect of changes in expenses or costs on net income is shown above.

Unfavorable results require further inquiry to determine the cause. Reflection's net sales increased 10.6% over 20X1. The goal for 20X2 was to increase sales volume by 10.0%. The actual 10.6% increase resulted from an increase in units sold from 340,000 to 376,000 square feet of mirrors. The unit sales price remained at $5.00. Management attributed the increase to two factors. (1) A more intensive advertising campaign increased market share from 42.0% to 45.0%. (2) Favorable economic conditions spurred new home building and created a greater demand for mirrors.

Reflection, Inc., analyzes each cost and expense amount and percentage. For example, the cost of merchandise sold increased 11.5% over 20X1. Most of the increase resulted from the 10.6% increase in the number of units sold. In addition, the purchase price per square foot of mirrors increased during 20X2 from $3.25 per square foot to $3.30. Advertising expense increased 19.4% over 20X1. The increase is consistent with the successful effort to expand market share. Management believes that more expensive television advertising resulted in a significant increase in third and fourth quarter unit sales.

During the annual budget process, Reflection also does the following:

1. Analyzes general and industry economic conditions to determine probable changes in sales volume for the coming year.
2. Sets company goals for costs and expenses as a percentage of sales.

> **REMEMBER** Comparative financial statements may be prepared for a fiscal year or a month.

· terms review

budgeting
budget
budget period
comparative income statement

· audit your understanding

1. How does the budgeting process help control expenses?
2. What is the length of time generally covered by a company's budget?
3. Will net income increase or decrease if the percentage change in expenses is less than the percentage change in net sales? Explain.

· work together 14-1

Analyzing a comparative income statement

The comparative income statement for San Francisco Sourdough Baking Company shows a percentage increase for net sales of 14.2%. A table is provided in the *Working Papers*. Your instructor will guide you through the following examples.

1. Indicate whether the following percentage change in cost and expense items is favorable or unfavorable:

Cost/Expense Item	Percentage of Increase (Decrease)
Cost of Merchandise Sold	11.0%
Advertising Expense	15.1%
Salary Expense	12.5%
Utilities Expense	(1.2%)

· on your own 14-1

Analyzing a comparative income statement

The comparative income statement for Precision Racing Components, Inc., indicates a percentage increase in net sales of 8.3%. A table is provided in the *Working Papers*. Work the following problem independently.

1. Indicate whether the following percentage change in cost and expense items is favorable or unfavorable:

Cost/Expense Item	Percentage of Increase (Decrease)
Cost of Merchandise Sold	11.0%
Advertising Expense	7.3%
Insurance Expense	(4.5%)
Rent Expense	2.0%

Budget Planning

Lesson 14-1   **417**

TERMS REVIEW · AUDIT YOUR · WORK TOGETHER · WORK TOGETHER · ON YOUR OWN · ON YOUR OWN

GUIDED PRACTICE

Terms Review
Call on students to define each term in the Terms Review. Ask the class if the definition is correct and whether the complete definition has been given or if anything else needs to be added. Suggested definitions are given in the Glossary.

Audit Your Understanding
Call on students to answer the Audit Your Understanding questions. Ask the class if the answer is correct and/or complete. Answers are given in Appendix E of the textbook.

Work Together
Have students write the solution to the Work Together problem as you guide the class through the examples.

- Direct students to record each answer as you guide the class through the examples.
- Call on students to explain why each percentage change is favorable or unfavorable.

INDEPENDENT PRACTICE

On Your Own
- Assign the On Your Own problem to be worked independently.
- Use the Ongoing Assessment techniques to diagnose student understanding.

Personal Trainer
- Students can access the Lesson 14-1 assessment material using this software.

Xtra! Web Site
- Students can access the Xtra! Study Tools for additional practice.

ENRICH

- Assign Making Ethical Decisions on page 412.
- Guide students through a comparison of the budget design procedures for a business with the budget design procedures for a family. Write on the board the headings *Business* and *Family*. As a group, discuss each design procedure given in the textbook and decide if a family would use the same or a different procedure. As a decision is reached, have a volunteer come to the board and write the procedure for a business and a family under the appropriate heading.

CLOSE

- Ask students to briefly summarize the three functions of a budget.

OBJECTIVES

- Define accounting terms related to budgetary planning and control.
- Identify accounting concepts and practices related to preparing and analyzing budgeted income statements and cash budgets.
- Prepare a budgeted income statement.

MOTIVATE

As an extra-credit assignment, ask students to prepare a budget for one week, estimating amounts of income from allowances, babysitting, or part-time employment. Students should also estimate the amount of their expenditures for the week for such categories as food, entertainment, clothing, savings, personal items, school-related purchases, and miscellaneous expenses. Inform students that they are to maintain a record of all actual expenditures and income earned. At the end of one week, ask students to compare estimated figures with actual amounts and write a paragraph about the results of their comparison.

Preview

- Preview the accounting terms and definitions introduced in this lesson: sales budget schedule, purchases budget schedule, selling expenses budget schedule, administrative expenses budget schedule, other revenue and expenses budget schedule, and budgeted income statement.
- Direct students to read the headings at the top of each page in this lesson and to examine the illustrations given.
- The importance and design of budgets were presented earlier in this chapter. In this lesson, the actual budgeting process begins by preparing a budgeted income statement. Explain that the budgeted income statement is actually a combination of several very specific budget schedules.

EXPLAIN

- Discuss how a business sets goals, develops operational plans, and projects sales, costs, and expenses. Point out that after a company's records for the preceding year(s) have been analyzed, goals and targets are set for the coming year. To help a company reach its targets, an operational plan is devised identifying estimated levels or dollar amounts to be obtained throughout the year. Refer to the list of goals at the top of the page.

418

14-2 Budgeted Income Statement

ANNUAL OPERATIONAL PLANS AND GOALS

Goals for 20X3:

1. The economy is projected to remain strong throughout 20X3. Therefore, the sales goal is to increase unit sales to 400,000 units, about a 6.4% increase. The unit sales price will be increased in the second quarter from $5.00 to $5.25 per square foot to recover merchandise cost increases in 20X2 and projected increases in the budget year.
2. Sales distribution by quarters is projected to be consistent with prior quarters.
3. The unit cost of merchandise is projected to rise from $3.30 to $3.40 in the first quarter, a 3.0% increase.
4. An automated cutting machine has been ordered. It will cost $20,000 and is projected to save approximately $10,000 per year in salary expense.
5. All employees on salary will receive a 5.0% increase in wage rate.
6. Rigid controls on all expenditures will be exercised.

After previous years' records have been analyzed, a business sets goals, develops operational plans, and prepares projection of sales, costs, and expenses for the coming year. Annual company goals establish targets that the company will work toward in the coming year. Goals help a company coordinate the efforts of all areas toward a common direction. An operational plan provides general guidelines for achieving the company's goals. Operational plans and goals generally are determined by a planning group consisting of the company's executive officers and department managers.

At Reflection, the planning group includes the president and all department managers. The planning group reviews the analysis of the previous years' comparative income statement and considers possible changes in economic conditions that may affect the company. From these discussions, the company's operational plan and goals for the coming year are determined. After reviewing company records and considering general economic conditions, Reflection's planning group develops the planning guidelines shown above.

The operational plan is converted into a more precise plan expressed in dollars by preparing a budgeted income statement. Reflection prepares separate schedules for the major parts of the bud-

geted income statement. Separate schedules are prepared for sales, purchases, selling expenses, administrative expenses, and other revenue and expenses. To permit more frequent comparisons with budgeted amounts, schedules for the budget are separated into quarterly projections.

At Reflection, the accounting department is responsible for coordinating budget preparation. The sales manager is responsible for preparing the sales, purchases, and selling expenses budget schedules. The administrative manager is responsible for preparing the administrative expenses budget and the other revenue and expenses budget schedules. The accounting department then prepares the budgeted income statement from these schedules. The completed budget, with attached schedules, is submitted to the budget committee for approval. The budget committee consists of the president and two members of Reflection's board of directors.

©GETTY IMAGES/PHOTODISC

Budgetary Planning and Control

MATERIALS

- **Instructor's Resource CD:** PowerPoint Slides
- **Xtra! Study Tools** on the Xtra! Web Site
- **Blackline Masters:** Budget Schedule

- **Working Papers:** Teacher's Edition of the Working Papers for Lesson 14-2
- **Software:** Personal Trainer

SALES BUDGET SCHEDULE

1. Enter actual and projected units.

2. Determine sales percentages:

20X2 Actual Unit Sales First Quarter	÷	20X2 Actual Unit Sales	=	20X2 Sales Percentage First Quarter
91,600	÷	376,000	=	24.4%

4. Enter unit sales prices.

6. Calculate total net sales.

$ 488,000
552,300
579,600
455,700
$ 2,075,600

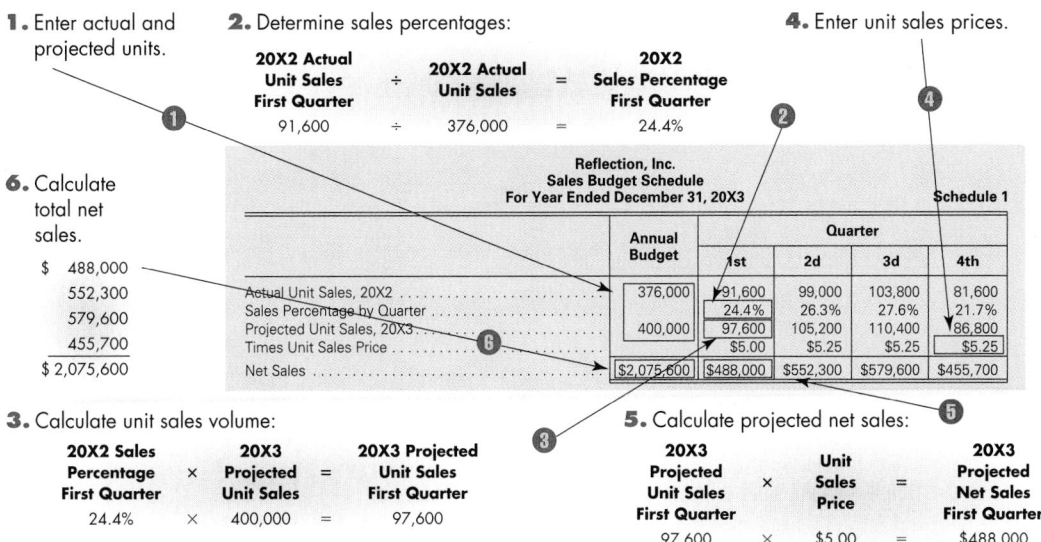

Reflection, Inc.
Sales Budget Schedule
For Year Ended December 31, 20X3
Schedule 1

	Annual Budget	Quarter			
		1st	2d	3d	4th
Actual Unit Sales, 20X2	376,000	91,600	99,000	103,800	81,600
Sales Percentage by Quarter		24.4%	26.3%	27.6%	21.7%
Projected Unit Sales, 20X3	400,000	97,600	105,200	110,400	86,800
Times Unit Sales Price		$5.00	$5.25	$5.25	$5.25
Net Sales	$2,075,600	$488,000	$552,300	$579,600	$455,700

3. Calculate unit sales volume:

20X2 Sales Percentage First Quarter	×	20X3 Projected Unit Sales	=	20X3 Projected Unit Sales First Quarter
24.4%	×	400,000	=	97,600

5. Calculate projected net sales:

20X3 Projected Unit Sales First Quarter	×	Unit Sales Price	=	20X3 Projected Net Sales First Quarter
97,600	×	$5.00	=	$488,000

A statement that shows the projected net sales for a budget period is called a **sales budget schedule**. The sales budget schedule is prepared first because the other schedules are affected by the projected net sales. Projected net sales are used to estimate the amount of merchandise to purchase and the amount that may be spent for salaries, advertising, and other selling and administrative expenses.

Reflection's sales manager, with knowledge of the budget guidelines and with the assistance of sales representatives, prepares the sales budget schedule shown above. Based on the planning group's goal of a 6.4% increase in unit

sales, the budget reflects an increase from 376,000 to 400,000 units. The sales manager plans to increase the unit sales price from $5.00 to $5.25 in the second quarter. The timing of the increase was planned after reviewing competitors' selling prices and analyzing projected costs of merchandise.

Accurate projections are important for effective budgeting. However, since budgets are based on estimates, most businesses round the projected amounts to simplify the budgeting process. Reflection Inc., rounds unit projections to the nearest hundred units and dollar projections to the nearest $10.

STEPS PREPARING A SALES BUDGET SCHEDULE

1 Enter the number of actual units, *376,000*, and projected units, *400,000*, in the Annual Budget column.

2 Determine the sales percentages by quarter. Dividing the annual budget into quarterly segments provides more frequent opportunities to compare actual with budgeted operations.

3 Calculate the unit sales volume for each quarter. Reflection's planning group believes that quarterly sales percentages will remain the same. Therefore, 24.4% of annual sales are expected to occur in the first quarter.

4 Enter the unit sales prices for each quarter.

5 Calculate projected net sales for each quarter.

6 Calculate total net sales for 20X3.

Budgeted Income Statement

Lesson 14-2   **419**

- Stress that the sales budget schedule is the basis for all other budget schedules. Refer back to the sales budget schedule as other budget schedules are introduced.

- Direct students to the illustration. Ask them to state the amount of projected sales for the coming year, 20X3. Ask students how 400,000 units were projected. Direct students to the list of goals on page 418 and review Reflection's first goal for 20X3.

- Discuss Reflection's policy for rounding off projected amounts. Point out that Reflection rounds unit projections to the nearest hundred units and dollar projects to the nearest $10. Emphasize that rounding off simplifies the budgeting process.

DEMONSTRATE

Prepare a sales budget schedule

- Distribute copies of a blank budget schedule. Guide students through the preparation of Reflection's sales budget schedule (in the illustration on this page), using the blackline master for a budget schedule.

- Read each step aloud or ask individual students to do so. Explain how each amount for each step is calculated or determined. Ask students to verify amounts with their calculators.

- Show the students where each step's amount appears on the sales budget schedule by completing the transparency on the overhead.

- Provide extensive practice in rounding off based on Reflection's policy. Have students practice rounding off with a variety of unit projections and dollar projections.

- Remind students that the sales budget is prepared first because the other schedules are affected by the projected net sales.

- Point out that projected sales determine the amount of purchases necessary during a particular budget period.

- Ask students what factors should be considered when determining the amount of purchases required for a budget period. Review the four factors presented in the text.

- Ask students what problems might be associated with owning an excessive inventory. Discuss the possibility of model changes, changes in consumer tastes, inability to recover cost if not sold, reduced prices due to technological advances, etc.

- Direct students to the list of goals on page 418. Review Goal #3.

DEMONSTRATE

Prepare a purchases budget schedule

- Distribute copies of a blank budget schedule. Guide students through the preparation of Reflection's purchases budget schedule (in the illustration on this page), using the blackline master for a budget schedule.

- Read each step aloud or ask individual students to do so. Explain or ask how each amount for each step is calculated or determined. Ask students to verify amounts with their calculators.

- Show the students where each step's amount appears on the purchases budget schedule by completing the transparency on the overhead.

PURCHASES BUDGET SCHEDULE

1. Calculate ending inventory for each quarter:

20X3 Unit Sales Second Quarter	×	Ending Inventory Unit Sales Percentage	=	20X3 Ending Inventory Second Quarter
105,200	×	40.0%	=	42,080 rounded to 42,100

5. Determine purchases.

139,700 units
− 39,200
100,500 units

4. Enter beginning inventory.

Reflection, Inc.
Purchases Budget Schedule
For Year Ended December 31, 20X3

Schedule 2

	1st	2d	3d	4th
Ending Inventory	42,100	44,200	34,700	40,000
Unit Sales for Quarter	97,600	105,200	110,400	86,800
Total Units Needed	139,700	149,400	145,100	126,800
Less Beginning Inventory	39,200	42,100	44,200	34,700
Purchases	100,500	107,300	100,900	92,100
Times Unit Cost	$3.40	$3.40	$3.40	$3.40
Cost of Purchases	$341,700	$364,820	$343,060	$313,140

6. Enter unit cost.

2. Enter projected unit sales.

3. Determine total units needed.

42,100 units
+ 97,600
139,700 units

7. Determine cost of purchases:

Purchases First Quarter	×	Unit Cost Percentage	=	Cost of Purchases First Quarter
100,500%	×	$3.40	=	$341,700

After the planning group approves the sales budget schedule, the remaining budget schedules are prepared. A statement prepared to show the projected amount of purchases that will be required during a budget period is called a **purchases budget schedule**. The following factors are considered when planning a purchases budget schedule:

1. Projected unit sales.
2. The quantity of merchandise on hand at the beginning of the budget period.

3. The quantity of merchandise needed to fill projected sales orders without having excessive inventory.
4. The price trends of merchandise to be purchased.

The sales manager prepares the purchases budget schedule shown above. The sales manager determines that the number of units in ending inventory should be about 40.0% of the number of units projected to be sold in the subsequent quarter.

STEPS • STEPS • STEPS • STEPS • STEPS • STEPS • STEPS • STEPS • STEPS • STEPS

PREPARING A PURCHASES BUDGET SCHEDULE

1 Calculate ending inventory for each quarter. Round estimates to the nearest hundred. Use *40,000* units for the fourth quarter's ending inventory (100,000 projected to be sold in the first quarter of 20X4 × 40%).

2 Enter projected unit sales for the quarter from the sales budget schedule.

3 Add ending inventory units and projected sales units to determine total units needed per quarter.

4 Enter beginning inventory, which is the same as ending inventory for the preceding quarter. Reflection's ending inventory of 39,200 units on December 31, 20X2, becomes its January 1 beginning inventory.

5 Subtract beginning inventory from total units needed to determine total unit purchases for the quarter.

6 Enter the unit cost for each quarter. Reflection's planning group has projected that material costs will rise from $3.30 to $3.40 per unit in the first quarter of 20X3.

7 Multiply the unit purchases each quarter by the unit cost to determine the cost of purchases.

Budgetary Planning and Control

APPLIED SKILLS   COMMUNICATIONS

Surveys of business managers show that communication skills are one of the most desired traits in new employees. The Applied Communication activity provides an opportunity for students to practice their communication and language arts skills on topics that directly relate to accounting. This activity requires students to create a skills list, write a short paper, and prepare teaching masters for a presentation that could be made to a high school counselor, student body, or incoming students to persuade the audience that everyone needs accounting.

SELLING EXPENSES BUDGET SCHEDULE

Reflection, Inc.
Selling Expenses Budget Schedule
For Year Ended December 31, 20X3   Schedule 3

	Annual Budget	Quarter			
		1st	2d	3d	4th
Advertising Expense	$ 49,820	$11,710	$13,260	$ 13,910	$10,940
Delivery Expense	160,000	39,040	42,080	44,160	34,720
Depr. Expense—Delivery Equipment	7,200	1,800	1,800	1,800	1,800
Depr. Expense—Warehouse Equipment	13,800	2,700	3,700	3,700	3,700
Miscellaneous Expense—Sales	10,380	2,440	2,760	2,900	2,280
Salary Expense—Commissions	83,020	19,520	22,090	23,180	18,230
Salary Expense—Regular	25,370	6,190	6,670	7,000	5,510
Supplies Expense—Sales	12,450	2,930	3,310	3,480	2,730
Total Selling Expenses	$362,040	$86,330	$95,670	$100,130	$79,910

A statement prepared to show projected expenditures related directly to the selling operations is called a **selling expenses budget schedule**. The sales manager projects the information for the selling expenses budget schedule. However, other sales personnel may provide specific information. For example, the advertising manager supplies much of the advertising expense information. After selling expenses information has been projected, a selling expenses budget schedule is prepared.

Some selling expense items are relatively stable and require little budget planning. For example, depreciation expenses for delivery and warehouse equipment are reasonably stable from year to year unless new equipment is bought. On the other hand, several selling expenses increase and decrease in relation to sales increases and decreases. Reflection has a seasonal business with higher sales during the second and third quarters. The company hires more personnel and spends more for advertising and sales supplies during the heavy sales season. All of these factors are considered when a selling expenses budget schedule is made. Reflection's selling expenses budget schedule is shown above.

Reflection's sales manager uses a number of approaches to project the various selling expenses. Most selling expenses are linked closely to the amount of quarterly net sales. Reflection's management uses the following

projection guides to prepare its selling expenses budget schedule.

1. **Advertising expense.** This expense is closely related to sales and sales promotions for the year. Advertising expense for 20X2 was 2.4% ($45,120 ÷ $1,880,000) of net sales. Sales promotion emphasis will be maintained at about the same level this year. Thus, 2.4% of each quarter's projected net sales will be allocated to advertising expense. First quarter projected advertising expense is $11,710 (2.4% × $488,000 = $11,712, rounded to $11,710).

2. **Delivery expense.** This expense is closely related to the number of units sold and delivered. The previous year's delivery expense increased significantly because an external freight company was used for increased deliveries until Reflection could acquire an additional truck. Rigid cost control measures will be applied to reduce future unit delivery expenses. Delivery expense is projected to be $0.40 per unit (sq. ft.) sold times each quarter's projected unit sales. First quarter projected delivery expense is $39,040 ($0.40 × 97,600 units).

3. **Depreciation expense—delivery equipment.** No new delivery equipment will be added. Thus, depreciation expense will remain the same as for the previous year ($1,800 per quarter).

- Ask students to state some of the factors a business must consider when projecting selling expenses for the coming year. Write student answers on the board or overhead and discuss. *(Answers might include: increases in sales goals, implementation of new advertising strategies, purchases of new vehicles for sales personnel, raises in salaries or commissions, purchases of cellular phones for sales force, etc.)*

- Point out that most of Reflection's selling expenses are closely related to the amount of quarterly net sales.

DEMONSTRATE

Use projection guides to determine expense amounts

- Distribute copies of a blank budget schedule. Guide students through the preparation of Reflection's selling expenses budget schedule (in the illustration on this page), using the blackline master for a budget schedule.

- Direct students to the illustration on page 415. Ask students to state the amounts of advertising expense and net sales for the year 20X2. Write these amounts on the board *($45,120, $1,880,000)*. Review with students the procedure for determining a component percentage of net sales *($45,120 ÷ $1,880,000 = 2.4%)*. Indicate to students that 2.4% of each quarter's projected net sales will be allocated to advertising expense.

- Direct students to the illustration on page 419. Ask students to state the amount of projected net sales for the first quarter *($488,000)*. Show students the mathematical process for calculating the advertising expense for the first quarter. Write the figures on the board or overhead *($488,000 × 2.4% = $11,712)*. Remind students that Reflection rounds dollar amounts to the nearest $10 amount *($11,710)*. Ask students to calculate the amount of advertising expense for the remaining quarters.

- Point out that Reflection's delivery expense is projected to be $.40 per unit. Direct students to the illustration on page 419. Ask students to state the amount of projected unit sales for the first quarter of 20X3 *(97,600 units)*. Show students the mathematical process for calculating the delivery expense for the first quarter. Write the figures on the board or overhead *(97,600 units × $.40 = 39,040)*.

421

Use projection guides to determine expense amounts

- Direct students to the illustration on page 415. Point out that the depreciation expense for delivery equipment was $7,200 for 20X2. Indicate that Reflection has determined this amount will remain the same for the year, or $1,800 per quarter *($7,200 ÷ 4).*

- Direct students to the list of goals on page 418. Ask a student to read Goal #4 for 20X3.

- Direct student attention to the illustration on page 415. Point out that the depreciation expense for warehouse equipment was $10,800 for 20X2. Explain to students that this amount equals $2,700 depreciation per quarter *($10,800 ÷ 4).* Point out that Reflection has determined that this amount will increase to $3,700 for the second, third, and fourth quarters, due to the purchase of the automated cutter.

- Use the illustration on page 415 to explain the .6% *($11,490 ÷ $1,880,000)* component percentage for miscellaneous expense for 20X2. Indicate that Reflection is determined to reduce miscellaneous expense to .5% of net sales for 20X3. Show students the calculation for first quarter miscellaneous expense, $2,440 *($488,000 × .5%).*

- Indicate that Reflection will continue to pay a 4% commission on net sales. Show students the calculation for first quarter salary expense—commissions amount, $19,520 *($488,000 × 4%).*

- Ask a student to read Goals # 4 & 5 in the list of goals on page 418. Use the math callout to explain the changes in salary expense—regular for 20X3. Point out that total salary expense—regular *($25,370)* is allocated among quarters using the same sales percentage rates shown in the illustration on page 419. Show the calculation for determining regular salaries for the first quarter, $6,190 *($25,370 × 24.4%).*

- Use the illustration on page 415 to explain the .6% *($11,280 ÷ $1,880,000)* component percentage for supplies expense—sales expense for 20X2. Indicate that Reflection will use the same rate for 20X3. Show students the calculation for first quarter supplies expense, $2,930 *($488,000 × .6% = $2,928, rounded to $2,930).*

4. **Depreciation expense—warehouse equipment.** A new automated cutter will be acquired at the beginning of the second quarter, increasing quarterly depreciation expense in the second, third, and fourth quarters from $2,700 to $3,700 per quarter.

5. **Miscellaneous expense—sales.** Miscellaneous expense was 0.6% ($11,490 ÷ $1,880,000) of net sales in 20X2. Management is committed to reducing miscellaneous expense to 0.5% of net sales in 20X3. First quarter miscellaneous expense is projected as $2,440 (0.5% × $488,000).

6. **Salary expense—commissions.** Salespersons will continue to earn a 4.0% commission on net sales. First quarter commissions are projected as $19,520 (4.0% × $488,000).

7. **Salary expense—regular.** Regular salary expense is determined by salary increases and changes in activity that affect the number of people employed. The new automated cutter will reduce regular salary expense by $10,000. A 5.0% raise will be added to remaining salaries. Thus, the projected annual amount is calculated as shown below.

Salary Expense: 20X2 Comparative Income Statement	$ 34,160
Less Reduction from Automated Cutter	– 10,000
Total	$ 24,160
Plus 5.0% Rate Increase	+ 1,210
Projected Salary Expense—Regular	$ 25,370

The projected amount is allocated among the four quarters in relation to the sales percentage from the sales budget schedule. First quarter regular salaries are projected as $6,190 (24.4% × $25,370).

8. **Supplies expense—sales.** Supplies expense was 0.6% ($11,280 ÷ $1,880,000) of net sales in 20X2. The same percentage relationship is expected in 20X3. First quarter supplies expense is projected as $2,930 (0.6% × $488,000 = $2,928, rounded to $2,930).

After the quarterly amounts have been calculated and entered, the annual budget amounts are determined by totaling the quarterly amounts.

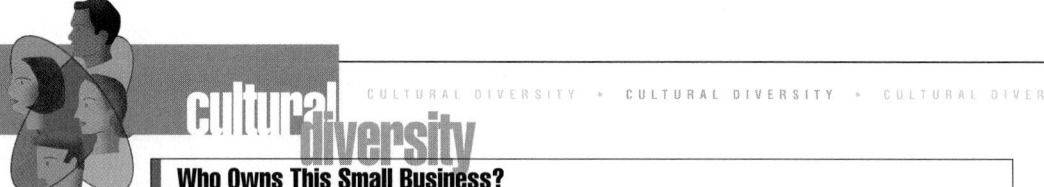

CULTURAL DIVERSITY • CULTURAL DIVERSITY • CULTURAL DIVERS

cultural diversity

Who Owns This Small Business?

In the 21st century, the answers to the question, "Who owns this small business?" is likely to be "A woman." In 1992, there were about 6 million women-owned firms. During the period of 1987 to 1992, the number of women-owned firms increased about 43 percent. The 1992 receipts of women-owned businesses were $1.574 trillion.

Women entrepreneurs start businesses at the rate of more than 4,000 per month. In 1996, women represented 36 percent of all small business owners. With the astonishing rate at which women are starting businesses, they will own a majority of all small businesses early in the 21st century.

Many of these "small businesses" employ over 100 people. Women-owned businesses are creating jobs at a faster rate than job growth in the overall economy. In fact, one out of four workers is employed in a woman-owned business.

Women-owned businesses are likely to be good community citizens. Many actively participate in their community, contribute to community projects, and provide a flexible work environment for their work force.

CULTURAL DIVERSITY
CULTURAL DIVERSIT

The Cultural Diversity feature is intended to expose students to the concept that our society is composed of people from many different cultural backgrounds. The features show the benefits of a culturally diverse society. (1) Read the feature. (2) Discuss the specific information in the feature. (3) Clarify any terms or questions.

Reflection, Inc.
Administrative Expenses Budget Schedule
For Year Ended December 31, 20X3

Schedule 4

	Annual Budget	Quarter			
		1st	2d	3d	4th
Depr. Expense—Office Equipment	$ 14,400	$ 3,600	$ 3,600	$ 3,600	$ 3,600
Insurance Expense	5,600	1,400	1,400	1,400	1,400
Miscellaneous Expense—Administrative	36,760	9,190	9,190	9,190	9,190
Payroll Taxes Expense	22,810	5,540	5,900	6,070	5,300
Rent Expense	30,000	7,500	7,500	7,500	7,500
Salary Expense—Administrative	81,720	20,430	20,430	20,430	20,430
Supplies Expense—Administrative........................	14,540	3,420	3,870	4,060	3,190
Uncollectible Accounts Expense	12,450	2,930	3,310	3,480	2,730
Utilities Expense	10,980	4,870	1,470	1,610	3,030
Total Administrative Expenses	$229,260	$58,880	$56,670	$57,340	$56,370

A statement that shows the projected expenses for all operating expenses not directly related to selling operations is called an **administrative expenses budget schedule**. The administrative manager prepares this budget schedule using information from these sources:

1. Past records.
2. Company plans.
3. Sales and selling expenses budget schedules.
4. Discussions with other managers.

After the administrative expenses have been projected, the administrative expenses budget schedule is prepared. Reflection's administrative expenses budget schedule is shown above.

Most administrative expenses are known and remain the same each period. Some administrative expenses need to be budgeted as a percentage of another amount from another budget. The following information was used to prepare the administrative expenses budget schedule.

1. **Depreciation expense—office equipment.** Recently purchased office equipment increased annual depreciation to $14,400. Annual depreciation is divided equally over the four quarters.
2. **Insurance expense.** Annual insurance is projected to increase to $5,600 primarily because of added coverage for the new automated cutting machine. An equal amount is paid each quarter.

3. **Miscellaneous expense—administrative.** Closely related to administrative salaries, miscellaneous expense was 49.8% ($38,770 ÷ $77,830) of administrative salaries in 20X2. Management is committed to reducing miscellaneous expense to 45.0% of projected administrative salaries in 20X3. First quarter miscellaneous expense is projected as $9,190 (45.0% × $20,430 = $9,194, rounded to $9,190).
4. **Payroll taxes expense.** Based on current payroll tax rates, payroll taxes expense is 12.0% of all salaries each quarter. First quarter salaries are projected as $46,140 ($19,520 + 6,190 + 20,430). Thus, payroll taxes expense is projected as $5,540 (12.0% × $46,140 = $5,537, rounded to $5,540).
5. **Rent expense.** Reflection leases the building for a known rental fee of $2,500 per month. Thus, rent expense can be projected accurately at $7,500 each quarter.
6. **Salary expense—administrative.** No new administrative personnel will be hired. Salary expense is projected as $81,720, equal to the 20X2 amount, $77,830, adjusted for a 5.0% salary rate increase. An equal amount is paid each quarter. Thus, each quarter's salary expense is projected as $20,430 ($81,720 ÷ 4).

- Direct students to the comparative income statement shown in the illustration on page 415. Ask students if Reflection earned any revenue or incurred any expenses outside the normal operations of the business during the year 20X2. Point out that the comparative income statement shows that Reflection earned no "other" revenue and incurred only one "other" expense, interest expense for $3,000.

- Emphasize that Reflection prepares an Other Revenue and Expenses Budget Schedule to account for revenue and expense amounts earned or incurred outside normal operations. These amounts might reflect interest income, interest expense, and gains or losses on the sale of plant assets.

DEMONSTRATE

Prepare another revenue and expense budget schedule

- Distribute copies of a blank budget schedule. Guide students through the preparation of Reflection's other revenue and expense budget schedule (in the illustration on this page), using the blackline master for a budget schedule.

- Show the students where each amount appears on the purchases budget schedule by completing the transparency on the overhead. Point out that Reflection intends to pay off a $20,000 loan at the start of the fourth quarter. Consequently, an interest expense of $750 is shown in each of the first three quarters and no interest expense for the fourth quarter.

7. **Supplies expense—administrative.** Supplies expense was 0.7% ($13,620 ÷ $1,880,000) of net sales for 20X2. The same percentage will be used in 20X3. First quarter supplies expense is projected as $3,420 (0.7% × $488,000 = $3,416, rounded to $3,420).

8. **Uncollectible accounts expense.** Closely related to net sales, uncollectible accounts expense was 0.6% ($11,280 ÷ $1,880,000) of net sales in 20X2. First quarter uncollectible accounts expense is projected as $2,930 (0.6% × $488,000 = $2,928, rounded to $2,930).

9. **Utilities expense.** Utilities expense is based on the amount of power, heat, telephone, and other utilities used in 20X2. Costs are projected to increase by 9.0%, consisting of a 5.0% projected increase in activity and a 4.0% increase in rates. Utilities expense by quarter in 20X2 is multiplied by 109% (100.0% + 9.0%) to calculate 20X3's projected utilities expense as follows:

20X2 Actual Utilities Expense	× 109% =	20X3 Projected Utilities Expense
1st Quarter $ 4,470	× 109% =	$ 4,870
2d Quarter 1,350	× 109% =	1,470
3d Quarter 1,480	× 109% =	1,610
4th Quarter 2,780	× 109% =	3,030
Total $10,080	× 109% =	$10,980

OTHER REVENUE AND EXPENSES BUDGET SCHEDULE

Reflection, Inc.
Other Revenue and Expenses Budget Schedule
For Year Ended December 31, 20X3

Schedule 5

	Annual Budget	Quarter			
		1st	2d	3d	4th
Other Expenses:					
Interest Expense	$2,250	$750	$750	$750	

Budgeted revenue and expenses from activities other than normal operations are shown in a statement called **other revenue and expenses budget schedule.** Typical items in this budget are interest income, interest expense, and gains or losses on the sale of plant assets. Reflection's other revenue and expenses budget schedule is shown above. Reflection has only one other expense item and no other revenue items.

Reflection's administrative manager is responsible for projecting the information in the other revenue and expenses budget schedule. Projected interest expense, the only item in the budget, is based on the interest due on a $20,000 loan used to acquire the automated cutter. Since Reflection plans to repay the $20,000 loan at the beginning of the fourth quarter, the budget schedule shows interest expense for only three quarters.

{ REMEMBER Even though budgets are based on estimates, much care is taken to ensure that the estimates are as accurate as possible. }

BUDGETED INCOME STATEMENT

Reflection, Inc.
Budgeted Income Statement
For Year Ended December 31, 20X3

	Annual Budget	Quarter			
		1st	2d	3d	4th
Operating Revenue:					
Net Sales (Schedule 1)	$2,075,600	$488,000	$552,300	$579,600	$455,700
Cost of Merchandise Sold:					
Beginning Inventory	$ 129,360	$129,360	$143,140	$150,280	$117,980
Purchases (Schedule 2)	1,362,720	341,700	364,820	343,060	313,140
Total Merchandise Available	$1,492,080	$471,060	$507,960	$493,340	$431,120
Less Ending Inventory	136,000	143,140	150,280	117,980	136,000
Cost of Merchandise Sold	$1,356,080	$327,920	$357,680	$375,360	$295,120
Gross Profit on Operations	$ 719,520	$160,080	$194,620	$204,240	$160,580
Operating Expenses:					
Selling Expenses (Schedule 3)	$ 362,040	$ 86,330	$ 95,670	$100,130	$ 79,910
Administrative Expenses (Schedule 4)	229,260	58,880	56,670	57,340	56,370
Total Operating Expenses	$ 591,300	$145,210	$152,340	$157,470	$136,280
Income from Operations	$ 128,220	$ 14,870	$ 42,280	$ 46,770	$ 24,300
Net Deduction (Schedule 5)	$ 2,250	$ 750	$ 750	$ 750	
Net Income before Federal Income Tax	$ 125,970	$ 14,120	$ 41,530	$ 46,020	$ 24,300
Federal Income Tax Expense	32,380	8,100	8,100	8,100	8,080
Net Income after Federal Income Tax	$ 93,590	$ 6,020	$ 33,430	$ 37,920	$ 16,220

1. Beginning inventory:
39,200 units × $3.30 = $129,360

2. Ending inventory:
42,100 units × $3.40 = $143,140

A statement that shows a company's projected sales, costs, expenses, and net income is called a **budgeted income statement**. Since the five budget schedules contain detailed items, Reflection prepares a shortened budgeted income statement and attaches the budget schedules. Reflection's budgeted income statement is shown above.

The first quarter beginning inventory is calculated using the 20X2 unit cost, $3.30. Other inventory amounts are calculated using the unit cost for 20X3, $3.40.

Amounts from the five budget schedules allow Reflection to project net income before federal income tax. Federal income taxes are estimated using a tax rate table furnished by the Internal Revenue Service. Reflection uses the tax rate table shown below. Using these rates, Reflection calculates its federal income tax.

Quarterly income tax payments are *$8,100* ($32,380 ÷ 4 = $8,095, rounded to $8,100). Thus, Reflection's payments equal $24,300 ($8,100 × 3 quarters) through the third quarter. The fourth quarter amount equals the unpaid amount of federal income taxes, *$8,080* ($32,380 – $24,300).

15% of net income before taxes, zero to $50,000.00.
25% of net income before taxes less $5,000.00, $50,001.00 to $75,000.00.
34% of net income before taxes less $11,750.00, $75,001.00 to $100,000.00.
39% of net income before taxes less $16,750.00, $100,001.00 to $335,000.00.

Net Income Before Federal Income Tax	×	Tax Rate	=	Federal Income Tax Expense
$125,970	×	39% less $16,750	=	$32,378.30 rounded to $32,380

GUIDED PRACTICE

Terms Review

Call on students to define the terms in the Terms Review. Ask the class if the definition is correct and whether the complete definition has been given or if anything else needs to be added. Suggested definitions are given in the Glossary.

Audit Your Understanding

Call on students to answer the Audit Your Understanding questions. Ask the class if the answer is correct and/or complete. Answers are given in Appendix E of the textbook.

Work Together

Have students write the solution to the Work Together problem as you guide the class through the examples.

- Direct students to record each answer and to show the appropriate work as you guide the class through the examples.
- Call on students to describe each step in the required computation.

INDEPENDENT PRACTICE

On Your Own

- Assign the On Your Own problem to be worked independently.
- Use the Ongoing Assessment techniques to diagnose student understanding.

Application Problems

- Assign Application Problem 14-1: Preparing a sales budget schedule and a budget schedule.
- Assign Application Problem 14-2: Preparing a budgeted income statement.

Personal Trainer

- Students can access the Lesson 14-2 assessment material using this software.

Xtra! Web Site

- Students can access the Xtra! Study Tools for additional practice.

ENRICH

- Assign the Cultural Diversity feature on page 422.
- Collect copies of budgets from organizations familiar to students, such as school clubs and local businesses, if available. Review the sales, cost, and expense items on the budget schedules. Emphasize the importance for each of these groups to accurately project sales and expenditures that can be made from the projected sales.

426

---

terms review

sales budget schedule
purchases budget schedule
selling expenses budget schedule
administrative expenses budget schedule
other revenue and expenses budget schedule
budgeted income statement

audit your understanding

1. How do annual goals help a company?
2. What factors are considered in preparing a sales budget schedule?

work together 14-2

Planning for a budgeted income statement

Actual unit sales for 20X1 were 230,000. Sterling Circuits, Inc., anticipates a 10.8% increase in unit sales for the upcoming year, 20X2. It projects that 18% of all yearly sales will occur during the first quarter. Sterling rounds unit projections to the nearest hundred units and dollar projections to the nearest $10. Your instructor will guide you through the following problem. Show your work.

1. How many units are projected to be sold during the first quarter of 20X2? If the unit sales price is $7.50, calculate the projected sales amount for the first quarter of 20X2.
2. If the desired ending inventory for the first quarter of 20X2 is 11,100 units, determine the number of units needed to meet the ending inventory and sales goals for the first quarter.
3. If the beginning inventory for the first quarter of 20X2 equals 9,400 units, how many units should be purchased to meet the inventory and sales goals for the first quarter?
4. Material costs per unit are projected to be $4.10. Compute the projected cost of purchases.

on your own 14-2

Planning for a budgeted income statement

Actual unit sales for 20X1 were 90,000. Graphite Co. forecasts a 6.1% increase in unit sales for the upcoming year, 20X2. It projects that 20% of all yearly sales will occur during the first quarter. Graphite rounds unit projections to the nearest hundred units and dollar projections to the nearest $10. Work independently to complete the following problem. Show your work.

1. How many units are projected to be sold during the first quarter of 20X2? If the unit sales price is $16.00, calculate the projected sales amount for the first quarter of 20X2.
2. If the desired ending inventory for the first quarter of 20X2 is 4,700 units, determine the number of units needed to meet the ending inventory and sales goals for the first quarter.
3. If the beginning inventory for the first quarter of 20X2 equals 3,400 units, how many units should be purchased to meet the inventory and sales goals for the first quarter?
4. Material costs per unit are expected to be $7.80. Compute the projected cost of purchases.

426   Chapter 14   Budgetary Planning and Control

CLOSE

- Ask students to name the five schedules and one statement they learned to prepare in Lesson 14-2. Write student responses on the board or overhead.
- Ask students to explain the basic content and purpose of each schedule or statement. Write responses under the appropriate heading.

14-3 Cash Budgets and Performance Reports

CASH RECEIPTS BUDGET SCHEDULE

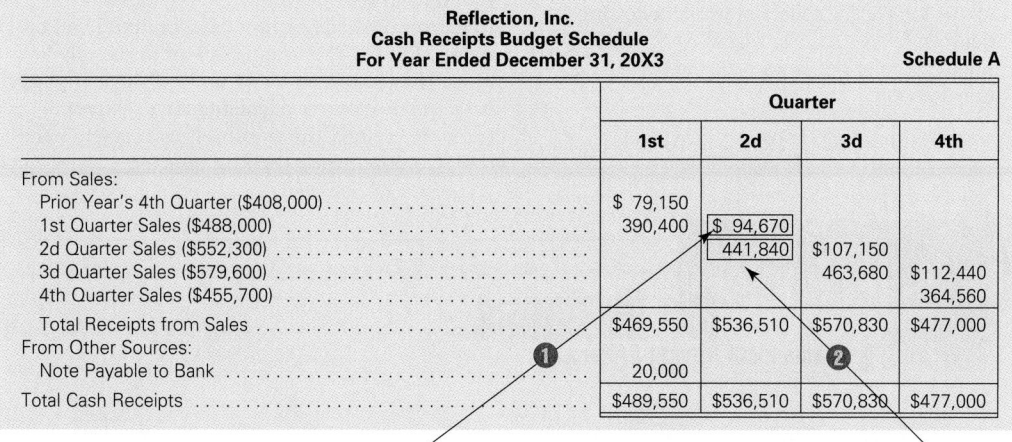

Reflection, Inc.
Cash Receipts Budget Schedule
For Year Ended December 31, 20X3   **Schedule A**

	Quarter			
	1st	**2d**	**3d**	**4th**
From Sales:				
Prior Year's 4th Quarter ($408,000)	$ 79,150			
1st Quarter Sales ($488,000)	390,400	$ 94,670		
2d Quarter Sales ($552,300)		441,840	$107,150	
3d Quarter Sales ($579,600)			463,680	$112,440
4th Quarter Sales ($455,700)				364,560
Total Receipts from Sales	$469,550	$536,510	$570,830	$477,000
From Other Sources:				
Note Payable to Bank	20,000			
Total Cash Receipts	$489,550	$536,510	$570,830	$477,000

Collection Percentage	×	First Quarter Net Sales	=	Second Quarter Cash Receipts
19.4%	×	$488,000	=	$94,672, rounded to $94,670

Collection Percentage	×	Second Quarter Sales	=	Second Quarter Cash Receipts
80.0%	×	$552,300	=	$441,840

Good cash management requires planning and controlling cash so that it will be available to meet obligations when they come due. Reflection prepares a cash budget to help analyze cash inflows and cash outflows. The treasurer prepares Reflection's cash budget in consultation with the budget committee. A corporation treasurer is an officer of the corporation who is usually responsible for planning the corporation's requirement for and use of cash. The treasurer analyzes

1. Projected receipts from cash sales, customers on account, and other sources.
2. Projected cash payments for ordinary expenses such as rent, payroll, and payments to vendors on account.
3. Other cash payments such as to buy plant assets or supplies.

Projected cash receipts for a budget period are reported on a statement called a **cash receipts budget schedule**. Reflection's cash receipts budget schedule is shown above. To prepare a cash receipts budget schedule, projections are composed of the following:

1. Quarterly cash sales.
2. Quarterly collections on account from customers. The amounts received from customers will not be the same as the amount of sales on account. Normally, cash is received for sales on account made during the previous one or two months. In addition, some sales returns and allowances and uncollectible accounts are likely.
3. Cash to be received quarterly from other sources.

REMEMBER   Many budget items are based on the budgeted estimate of sales. Therefore, the budget is only as accurate as the sales forecast.

Cash Budgets and Performance Reports   Lesson 14-3   **427**

- Discuss Reflection's pattern of net sales per quarter. Emphasize that approximately 80% of net sales are collected during the same quarter.

Prepare a cash receipts budget schedule

- Distribute copies of a blank budget schedule. Guide students through the preparation of Reflection's cash receipts budget schedule (in the illustration on page 427), using the blackline master of a budget schedule.

- Use the transparency to show students how each amount for the 1st quarter is calculated or determined.

- Direct students to the illustration on page 427. Ask students how the first figure in the first quarter column, $79,150, was calculated. Point out that 19.4% of prior quarter sales are collected the subsequent period ($408,000 × 19.4% = $79,152, rounded to $79,150).

- Ask students how the second figure, $390,400, in the 1st quarter column was calculated. Emphasize that 80% of all net sales are collected during the same period ($488,000 × 80% = $390,400).

- Ask students the origin of Reflection's first quarter net sales of $488,000. (See the illustration of the Sales Budget Schedule on page 419.)

- Show students that the total receipts from sales figure, $469,550, was simply calculated by adding $79,150 and $390,400.

- Point out to students that after cash receipts and cash payments were projected for the first quarter, Reflection's treasurer decided the company was very low on cash. To ensure there was adequate cash to pay company bills, the treasurer made arrangements to borrow $20,000 during the first quarter.

- Ask students to verify the amounts of Reflection's projected cash receipts for the 2nd, 3rd, and 4th quarters. Circulate through the classroom and assist students having difficulties.

ANALYSIS OF CASH RECEIPTS

An analysis of Reflection's sales for previous years shows the following pattern of net sales per quarter:

1. About 60.0% of all net sales are cash sales.
2. About 20.0% are sales on account collected in the same quarter. Thus, 80.0% of a quarter's net sales are collected during the same quarter.
3. About 19.4% are collected in the following quarter.
4. About 0.6% of net sales prove to be uncollectible.

Cash receipts in the first quarter include $79,150 from 20X2's fourth quarter sales on account (19.4% × $408,000 = $79,152, rounded to $79,150).

Cash sales and collections on account provide most of the cash receipts. If additional cash is needed, other sources of cash should be planned. After making a preliminary plan of projected cash receipts and cash payments, the treasurer determines that cash on hand will be reduced in the first quarter to an unusually low level. This condition could prevent the company from making timely payments for its expenditures. Therefore, the treasurer arranges to borrow $20,000 during the first quarter.

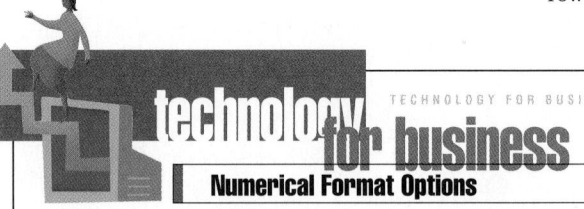

TECHNOLOGY FOR BUSINESS • TECHNOLOGY FOR BUSINESS • TECHNOLOGY FOR BU

technology for business

Numerical Format Options

Columns of data in a spreadsheet may include several different types of data. In columns E and F of the spreadsheet below, numbers are shown as currency amounts, percentage amounts, ratios, and general whole numbers.

Use of the numerical format options available on electronic spreadsheets makes the data easier to read and understand. For example, the rate earned on net sales in cells E7 and F7 are shown as percentages. In addition to numerous formatting options, the number of decimal places displayed may also be specified. Good spreadsheet design includes proper numerical formatting.

	A	B	C	D	E	F
1	Financial Statement Analysis					
2					Current	Prior
3					Year	Year
4	Rate Earned on Net Sales:					
5		Net Income after Federal Income Tax			$42,322	$38,976
6		Net Sales			514,560	465,430
7		Rate Earned on Net Sales			8.2%	8.4%
8	Earnings per Share:					
9		Net Income after Federal Income Tax			$42,322	$38,976
10		Shares of Stock Outstanding			10,000	10,000
11		Earnings per Share			$4.23	$3.90
12	Price-Earnings Ratio:					
13		Market Price per Share			$25.00	$22.00
14		Earnings per Share			$4.23	$3.90
15		Price-Earnings Ratio			5.9	5.6

TECHNOLOGY FOR BUSINESS

The Technology for Business feature is designed to show students common business applications of technology. Students should read user's manuals or online help screens to understand what numerical format options are available. Students should understand that different businesses may have different standards for numerical formats in spreadsheet files.

CASH PAYMENTS BUDGET SCHEDULE

Reflection, Inc.
Cash Payments Budget Schedule
For Year Ended December 31, 20X3   **Schedule B**

	Quarter			
	1st	2d	3d	4th
For Merchandise:				
Prior Year's 4th Quarter Purchases ($212,500)	$ 63,750			
1st Quarter Purchases ($341,700)	239,190	$102,510		
2d Quarter Purchases ($364,820)		255,370	$109,450	
3d Quarter Purchases ($343,060)			240,140	$102,920
4th Quarter Purchases ($313,140)				219,200
Total Cash Payments for Purchases	$302,940	$357,880	$349,590	$322,120
For Operating Expenses:				
Cash Selling Expenses	$ 81,830	$ 90,170	$ 94,630	$ 74,410
Cash Administrative Expenses	52,350	49,760	50,260	50,040
Total Cash Operating Expenses	$134,180	$139,930	$144,890	$124,450
For Other Cash Payments:				
Federal Income Tax Expense	$ 8,100	$ 8,100	$ 8,100	$ 8,080
Automated Cutting Machine	20,000			
Cash Dividend		50,000		50,000
Investment				25,000
Note Payable and Interest				22,250
Total Other Cash Payments	$ 28,100	$ 58,100	$ 8,100	$105,330
Total Cash Payments	$465,220	$555,910	$502,580	$551,900

Projected cash payments for a budget period are reported on a statement called a **cash payments budget schedule**. Reflection's cash payments budget schedule is shown above. To prepare the schedule, the accountant and treasurer make the following projections:

1. Quarterly cash payments for accounts payable or notes payable to vendors.
2. Quarterly cash payments for each expense item. This projection requires an analysis of the selling expenses, administrative expenses, and other revenue and expenses budget schedules.
3. Quarterly cash payments for buying equipment and other assets.
4. Quarterly cash payments for dividends.
5. Quarterly cash payments for investments.

Reflection's accountant and treasurer use the following projection guides to prepare the cash payments budget schedule.

1. **Cash payments for merchandise.** An analysis of past records for payments to vendors on account shows the following cash payment pattern:
   a. About 10.0% of all purchases are cash purchases.
   b. About 60.0% are purchases on account paid for in the quarter. Thus, 70.0% (10.0% + 60.0%) of a quarter's purchases are paid for during the same quarter.
   c. The remaining 30.0% are purchases on account paid for in the following quarter.

Cash payments are calculated using the same procedure used for cash receipts. Purchase amounts are from the purchases budget schedule. First quarter cash payments for first quarter purchases are $239,190 (70.0% × $341,700).

EXPLAIN

- Ask students to name the types of cash payments Reflection might make during a quarter. Lead into a discussion of cash payments for accounts or notes payable, various selling and administrative expenses, and purchasing equipment, dividends, and investments.
- Ask students the names of the budget schedules that provide information related to cash payments *(purchases, selling expenses, administrative expenses, and other revenue and expenses budget schedules).*
- Discuss the projection guides used by Reflection to determine cash payments for merchandise, operating expenses, and other cash payments.

DEMONSTRATE

Prepare a cash payments budget schedule

- Distribute copies of a blank budget schedule. Guide students through the preparation of Reflection's cash payments budget schedule (in the illustration on this page), using the blackline master of a budget schedule.
- Use the transparency to show students how each amount for the 1st quarter is calculated or determined.
- Direct students to the illustration on this page. Ask students how the first figure in the first quarter column, $63,750, was calculated. Point out that 30% of prior quarter purchases are paid for during the subsequent quarter *($212,500 × 30% = $63,750)*. Show all math calculations on the board or overhead.
- Ask students how the second figure, $239,190, in the 1st quarter column was calculated. Emphasize that 70% of all purchases are paid for during the quarter *($341,700 × 70% = $239,190)*.
- Ask students the origin of Reflection's first quarter purchases of $341,700. (See the illustration of the Purchases Budget Schedule on page 420.)

Prepare a cash payments budget schedule

- Use the math table in projection guide #2 to explain the process utilized to determine the cash payments for operating expenses. Ask students the origin of selling and administrative expenses. (See the illustration on page 421 and the illustration on page 423.) Emphasize that cash is not actually paid out for depreciation and uncollectible accounts expenses.

- Ask a student to read the projection guide for other cash payments. As the student reads, make notes on the board to identify other cash payments *(federal income tax, automated cutting machine, cash dividends, cash investment, repayment of promissory note).* After the student has finished reading the paragraph, ask the class to state the amount of cash payment for each category. Write appropriate student responses under each category.

- Identify the other cash payments related to the first quarter and enter amounts on the transparency. Calculate the totals for the first quarter.

- Ask students to verify the amounts of Reflection's projected cash payments for the 2nd, 3rd, and 4th quarters. Circulate through the classroom and assist students having difficulties.

- Explain that a cash budget summarizes cash receipts and cash payments and identifies the amount of cash available at the end of each quarter.

Prepare a cash budget

- Distribute copies of a blank budget schedule. Guide students through the preparation of Reflection's cash budget (in the illustration on this page), using the blackline master of a budget schedule.

- Use the transparency to show students how each amount for the 1st quarter is calculated or determined. Ask students the source of each amount.

- Ask students to verify the amounts of Reflection's cash budget figures for the 2nd, 3rd, and 4th quarters. Circulate through the classroom and assist students having difficulties.

430

2. **Cash payments for operating expenses.** Cash payments for most operating expenses are made in the quarter the expense is incurred. However, the selling expenses budget schedule, shown on page 421, and the administrative expenses budget schedule, page 423, include some projected items for which cash will not be paid. For example, cash is not paid for depreciation and uncollectible accounts expenses. Therefore, these amounts are not included in the cash payments budget schedule. The first quarter's cash payments for selling expenses and for administrative expenses are calculated as follows:

Selling Expenses		$86,330
Less: Depr. Exp.—Deliv. Equip.	$1,800	
Depr. Exp.—Ware. Equip.	2,700	4,500
Cash Payment for Selling Exp.		$81,830
Administrative Expenses		$58,880
Less: Depr. Exp.—Office Equip.	$3,600	
Uncollectible Accts. Exp.	2,930	6,530
Cash Payment for Admin. Exp.		$52,350

3. **Other cash payments.** Reflection also plans for cash payments other than for merchandise, selling expenses, and administrative expenses. Federal income tax payments equal the quarterly federal income tax expense amounts on the budgeted income statement. Reflection also plans to buy a new automated cutting machine for $20,000 at the end of the first quarter. The company expects to pay a $50,000 cash dividend to stockholders in the second and fourth quarters. Since a large cash balance is projected for the third quarter, Reflection plans a $25,000 interest-earning investment in the fourth quarter. Also, plans call for repaying the promissory note plus interest, *$22,250,* at the beginning of the fourth quarter.

The last line of the cash payments budget schedule shows the total cash payments projected each quarter. This total indicates the minimum amount of cash that must be available each quarter.

CASH BUDGET

Reflection, Inc.
Cash Budget
For Year Ended December 31, 20X3

	Quarter			
	1st	**2d**	**3d**	**4th**
Cash Balance—Beginning	$ 21,780	$ 46,110	$ 26,710	$ 94,960
Cash Receipts (Schedule A)	489,550	536,510	570,830	477,000
Cash Available	$511,330	$582,620	$597,540	$571,960
Less Cash Payments (Schedule B)	465,220	555,910	502,580	551,900
Cash Balance—Ending	$ 46,110	$ 26,710	$ 94,960	$ 20,060

A statement that shows for each month or quarter a projection of a company's beginning cash balance, cash receipts, cash payments, and ending cash balance is called a **cash budget**. Reflection's cash budget, shown above, is prepared from the information in the cash receipts budget schedule and the cash payments budget schedule. The first quarter beginning cash balance is taken from the balance sheet on December 31, 20X2.

At the end of each quarter of a budget period, Reflection compares the actual cash balance with the projected cash balance shown on the cash budget. If the actual cash balance is less than the projected balance, the reasons for the decrease are determined and action is taken to correct the problem. One reason may be that some customers are not paying their accounts when they should. Another may be that expenses are exceeding budget projections. If the decrease continues, the company could have a quarter in which there is not enough cash to make all the required cash payments. If this shortage does occur, the business will have to borrow money until receipts and payments are brought into balance.

PERFORMANCE REPORT

Reflection, Inc.
Performance Report
For Quarter Ended March 31, 20X3

	Budget	Actual	Increase (Decrease) Amount	Increase (Decrease) Percentage*
Unit Sales (sq. ft.)	97,600	98,500	900	0.9
Operating Revenue:				
Net Sales	$488,000	$492,500	$4,500	0.9
Cost of Merchandise Sold	327,920	330,680	2,760	0.8
Gross Profit on Operations	$160,080	$161,820	$1,740	1.1
Operating Expenses:				
Selling Expenses:				
Advertising Expense	$ 11,710	$ 12,050	$ 340	2.9
Delivery Expense	39,040	38,735	(305)	(0.8)
Depr. Expense—Delivery Equipment	1,800	1,800		
Depr. Expense—Warehouse Equipment	2,700	2,700		
Miscellaneous Expense—Sales	2,440	2,530	90	3.7
Salary Expense—Commissions	19,520	19,620	100	0.5
Salary Expense—Regular	6,190	6,190		
Supplies Expense—Sales	2,930	2,900	(30)	(1.0)
Total Selling Expenses	$ 86,330	$ 86,525	$ 195	0.2
Administrative Expenses:				
Depr. Expense—Office Equipment	$ 3,600	$ 3,600		
Insurance Expense	1,400	1,400		
Miscellaneous Expense—Administrative	9,190	9,350	$ 160	1.7
Payroll Taxes Expense	5,540	5,550	10	0.2
Rent Expense	7,500	7,500		
Salary Expense—Administrative	20,430	20,430		
Supplies Expense—Administrative	3,420	3,490	70	2.0
Uncollectible Accounts Expense	2,930	2,800	(130)	(4.4)
Utilities Expense	4,870	5,180	310	6.4
Total Administrative Expenses	$ 58,880	$ 59,300	$ 420	0.7
Total Operating Expenses	$145,210	$145,825	$ 615	0.4
Income from Operations	14,870	15,995	$1,125	7.6
Net Deduction	$ 750	$ 750	0	0.0
Net Income before Federal Income Tax	$ 14,120	$ 15,245	$1,125	8.0
Federal Income Tax Expense	8,100	8,100	0	0.0
Net Income after Federal Income Tax	$ 6,020	$ 7,145	$1,125	18.7

*Percentages rounded to the nearest 0.1%.

EXPLAIN

- Direct student attention to the illustration on page 430. Ask students to state the amount of the projected cash balance for the end of the first quarter *($46,110)*.

- Ask students where they would look to determine if Reflection met their cash goal for the end of the first quarter. *(Examine the March 31 balance of the cash account in the general ledger.)*

- Ask students why a business should be concerned if the actual cash balance is less than the projected balance in the cash budget. Lead into a discussion of how a cash shortage may prevent a company from paying its bills and other financial obligations on time. This could lead to a poor credit rating and make it difficult to borrow money in the future.

- Ask students why a company's actual cash balance might fall below the projected balance for cash. *(Answers may include: lower sales, sharp increase in sales returns, customers not making scheduled payments, increases in expenses, etc.)*

- Ask students what a company should do if it experiences a temporary cash shortage. Point out that the company must determine the cause(s) of the shortage and take corrective action, as well as consider borrowing money until cash receipts and payments are brought into balance.

TEACHING STRATEGIES   COOPERATIVE LEARNING

Divide the class into groups of three or four students each. Using the textbook as a guide, have each group compare the budget design procedures for a business with the budget design procedures for a family. Each group should appoint a leader who will present the list of similarities and differences to the class. This cooperative learning activity should not take more than 15–20 minutes of class time.

- Direct students to the illustration on page 431. Ask students what financial statement is very similar to a Performance Report (*Comparative Income Statement*).

- Direct students to the illustration on page 415. Ask students the difference between a comparative income statement and a performance report. Point out that the comparative income statement compares actual amounts of one fiscal period with the actual amounts of a prior fiscal period. A performance report compares actual amounts with projected amounts for the same fiscal period.

- Refer students to the illustration on page 431. Ask them to state the amount of increase or decrease for net sales (*$4,500 increase*). Quickly review with students how the amount was calculated (*$492,500 − $488,000 = $4,500*). Show and explain the calculations used to calculate the 0.9 percentage increase in net sales (*$4,500 ÷ $488,000 = .00922, rounded to .9%*).

- Select several other lines on the performance report and show the calculations required to compute amounts and percentages. Be sure to include a negative amount and percentage.

- Ask students to identify favorable and unfavorable percentage changes. Remind students that not all positive percentage changes are favorable. Point out that a percentage increase in an expense is unfavorable.

- Emphasize that unfavorable trends require additional investigation. Factors causing favorable trends should be encouraged.

- Point out that a performance report can be used to evaluate a company's budgeting process. Refer to Remember at the bottom of this page.

- Circulate through the classroom or lab, observing which students have problems with assignments.

- Troubleshooting: Students may have problems remembering or implementing projection guides when calculating various amounts.

- Assess student understanding by checking solutions to Independent Practice assignments.

At the end of each quarter, a business prepares an income statement that compares actual amounts with the budgeted income statement for the same period. This comparison shows variations between actual and projected items. A report showing a comparison of projected and actual amounts for a specific period of time is called a **performance report**.

Each quarter, Reflection prepares a quarterly performance report like the one shown on the previous page. This report is sent to the sales manager and the administrative manager. Knowing about significant differences between projected and actual income statement amounts helps the managers identify areas that need to be reviewed. By identifying large variations early, managers may be able to make changes that will correct negative effects on net income for the year. If conditions change significantly, the budget for the remainder of the year can be revised.

Preparation of a performance report is similar to preparation of a comparative income statement. However, a performance report compares actual amounts with projected amounts for the same fiscal period. A comparative income statement compares actual amounts of one fiscal period with actual amounts of a prior fiscal period.

The first amount column of the performance report shows the amounts projected for the first quarter. The second amount column shows the actual sales, costs, and expenses for the quarter. The third amount column shows how much the actual amount varies from the projected amount. For example, actual net sales, $492,500, *less* projected net sales, $488,000, *equals* the increase, $4,500. The fourth column shows the percentage, the actual amount increased or decreased from the projected amount. For example, the net sales increase, $4,500, *divided by* projected net sales, $488,000, *equals* the percentage of increase, 0.9%. Percentages are rounded to the nearest 0.1%.

An analysis is made of all significant differences to determine why the differences occurred. Normally, Reflection only considers changes of

5.0% or more to be significant. However, because the items influencing gross profit are large dollar amounts, small percentage changes affect net income significantly. Therefore, Reflection's sales manager reviews changes in net sales and cost of merchandise sold regardless of the amount of change.

Reflection's performance report indicates that three items should be reviewed:

1. Net sales.
2. Cost of merchandise sold.
3. Utilities expense.

Managers should determine what actions, if any, can correct the unfavorable situations such as the 6.4% increase in utilities expense. If the utility service cost has increased, the manager cannot change that. However, if power is being wasted, procedures may need to be changed to avoid the waste.

Managers should also determine what actions caused favorable results, such as the 0.9% increase in net sales, and encourage a continuation of those favorable actions.

©GETTY IMAGES/PHOTODISC

{ **REMEMBER** Actual performance must be compared with budgeted estimates in order for a business to evaluate its budgeting procedures. }

- Make transparencies of the budget schedule from the accounting forms masters provided in the Blackline Masters Section of the Teacher's Resource Guide. Using information from Recycling Problem 14-1 and the transparencies, demonstrate how the 1st

quarter amounts and percentages are calculated and recorded on Schedules A and B. Using these budget schedules, develop the 1st quarter of a cash budget. As each supporting schedule is used, display it on the overhead and circle the amounts used on the cash budget.

terms review

cash receipts budget schedule
cash payments budget schedule
cash budget
performance report

audit your understanding

1. Why is a cash budget important?
2. What information is reported in a cash budget?
3. How does a performance report differ from a comparative income statement?

work together 14-3

Planning for a cash budget

MicroVision's sales for previous years show that of total net sales, approximately 50% are cash sales, 30% are sales on account collected in the same quarter, 18% are sales on account collected in the next quarter, and 2% prove to be uncollectible. For the current year, net sales for the first quarter are $425,000.00 and for the second quarter, $360,500.00.

The cash payment budget schedule shows the following cash payments during the second quarter: total purchases, $289,000.00; total operating expenses, $97,840; federal income tax expense, $9,210.00; and notes payable and interest, $7,240.00. MicroVision rounds dollar projections to the nearest $10. Your instructor will guide you through the following examples.

1. Determine the total amount of cash received during the second quarter.
2. Calculate the total cash payments for the second quarter.
3. The beginning cash balance for the second quarter equals $61,560. Compute the ending cash balance for the second quarter.

on your own 14-3

Planning for a cash budget

MediaNet's sales for the previous years show that of total net sales, approximately 45% are cash sales, 40% are sales on account collected in the same quarter, 14% are sales on account collected in the next quarter, and 1% prove to be uncollectible. For the current year, net sales for the second quarter are $518,000.00 and for the third quarter, $670,250.00.

The cash payment budget schedule shows the following cash payments during the third quarter: total purchases, $410,000.00; total operating expenses, $101,630; federal income tax expense, $11,780.00; and cash dividend, $80,000.00. MediaNet rounds dollar projections to the nearest $10. Work the problem independently.

1. Determine the total amount of cash received during the third quarter.
2. Calculate the total cash payments for the third quarter.
3. The beginning cash balance for the third quarter equals $24,860.00. Compute the ending cash balance for the third quarter.

GUIDED PRACTICE

Terms Review

- Ask students to write the definition for each term in the Terms Review. Allow students to use their texts.
- Ask a student to read the definition for a selected term. Ask the class if the definition is correct and whether the complete definition has been given or if anything else needs to be added. Suggested definitions are given in the Glossary.

Audit Your Understanding

Call on students to answer the Audit Your Understanding questions. Ask the class if the answer is correct and/or complete. Answers are given in Appendix E of the textbook.

Work Together

Have students write the solutions to the Work Together problem as you guide the class through the examples.

- Call on a student to read and analyze a problem statement.
- Write required calculations on the board or overhead.

INDEPENDENT PRACTICE

On Your Own

- Assign the On Your Own problem to be worked independently.
- Use the Ongoing Assessment techniques to diagnose student understanding.

Application Problem

- Assign Application Problem 14-3: Preparing a cash budget with supporting schedules.

Personal Trainer

- Students can access the Lesson 14-3 assessment material using this software.

Xtra! Web Site

- Students can access the Xtra! Study Tools for additional practice.

ENRICH

- Assign the Technology for Business feature on page 428.

CLOSE

- Ask students to describe similarities and differences between preparing a budgeted income statement and a cash budget.

433

PUTTING IT ALL TOGETHER

- Review the Chapter Summary. Ask students for examples or figure numbers for each summary item. List student responses on the board or overhead.

INDEPENDENT PRACTICE

- Assign Mastery Problem 14-4 to students who need the reinforcement of a problem that combines all activities from the chapter in one problem; this will be most students.

- Assign Challenge Problem 14-5 to accelerated students who do not require the reinforcement of the mastery problem.

- Assign Study Guide 14.

- Students can use Automated Accounting 8.0 or higher to work Challenge Problem 14-5.

- Students can use QuickBooks to automate Challenge Problem 14-5.

- Students can access Personal Trainer to work end-of-chapter problems on the computer.

- Students can access the Xtra! Web Site for the Xtra! Review and Quizzing.

- Students can access the Student Companion CD for additional review material.

ONGOING ASSESSMENT

Review solutions to the assigned problems in class, diagnosing trouble spots.

RETEACH

- Call on students to describe how they avoid the trouble spots diagnosed.

- Use reteaching suggestions from section lesson plans as required.

- Assign Recycling Problem 14-1 if needed.

ENRICH

- Assign the Explore Accounting Feature. Ask students to share the information they have gathered in a report to the class.

- Students can access the Xtra! Web Site for the Xtra! Enrichment material.

- Assign Applied Communication.

- Assign the Cases for Critical Thinking.

- Assign the SCANS Workplace Competency.

434

After completing this chapter, you can

1. Define important accounting terms related to budgetary planning and control.

2. Identify accounting concepts and practices related to preparing and analyzing budgeted income statements and cash budgets.

3. Gather information to prepare a budget.

4. Prepare a budgeted income statement.

5. Prepare a cash budget and a performance report.

Explore Accounting

EXPLORE ACCOUNTING · EXPLORE ACCOUNTING · EXPLORE ACC

Spreadsheet Budgeting Tools

Budgeting has been a popular use for electronic spreadsheet programs since these software programs became readily available in the early 1980s. By entering labels for accounts and accounting periods in cells, the user can quickly tailor the structure of the budget to the nature of the business. Users create formulas to compute total revenues, expenses, and net income. Thus, with a knowledge of budgeting concepts, spreadsheet users can create a budget with a limited amount of effort.

Newer electronic spreadsheets have made budget creation even easier. These programs contain tools to assist the user in designing the budget and creating the formulas. The budget tools are especially useful for individuals with a limited knowledge of budgeting concepts. For most budgeting tools, the starting point is selecting the type and design of the budget.

Personal or Business
The budget tool suggests revenue and expense accounts commonly used in personal or business budgets. The user may add and delete accounts to customize the budget to the individual's needs.

Budget or Budget vs. Actual Analysis
The budget can be created to provide space for actual information to be entered at the end of each accounting period. The spreadsheet can be used to compute the amount or percentage difference between budget and actual amounts.

Number of Periods
The user identifies the starting period and the number of periods. A period can consist of a month, a quarter, or a year.

Quarterly and Yearly Totals
For a monthly budget, the budget tool can compute quarterly and yearly totals. With this information, the budget tool automatically creates the budget, including all labels and formulas. Format techniques, such as bolded text, numeric formats, and shaded cells, are applied to improve understanding.

Required
Use the budget tool of your electronic spreadsheet program to prepare a personal budget for your first year after high school.

434   Chapter 14

Budgetary Planning and Control

EXPLORE ACCOUNTING
EXPLORE ACCOUNTING

- Assign Auditing for Errors.
- Assign Analyzing Costco's Financial Statements.
- Assign the Automated Accounting feature on page 441 to automate Challenge Problem 14-5.

If spreadsheet programs are not available at the school site, students may share computer hardware and software applications available at home. Students might also check with family members, neighbors, and friends who have access to computers at work. Another possibility is the public library or organizations that rent computer time for general use.

Student answers will vary but should show sources of cash receipts and amounts of cash payments.

14-1 APPLICATION PROBLEM

Xtra!
Quizzing
accountingxtra.swlearning.com

Preparing a sales budget schedule and a purchases budget schedule

PhotoMax, Inc., plans to prepare a sales budget schedule and a purchases budget schedule for 20X3. Management has set a sales goal of 250,000 units. After reviewing price trends, the sales manager projects that PhotoMax will need to increase its unit sales price from $12.50 to $14.00 in the first quarter.

The sales manager, after checking with the company's merchandise suppliers, projects that the cost of merchandise will increase from $7.00 to $7.50 per unit in the first quarter of 20X3.

Quarterly unit sales for 20X2 are as follows:

| 1st quarter | 58,500 units | 3d quarter | 68,900 units |
| 2d quarter | 62,700 units | 4th quarter | 43,900 units |

After considering the time required to reorder merchandise, the sales manager requests that 30.0% of the next quarter's unit sales be available in the prior quarter's ending inventory. Ending inventory for 20X2 is 27,700 units. Management projects that 65,000 units will be sold in the first quarter of 20X4.

Instructions:
1. Prepare a sales budget schedule (Schedule 1) for the four quarters ended December 31, 20X3. PhotoMax rounds unit amounts to the nearest hundred units, dollar amounts to the nearest $10, and percentage amounts to the nearest 0.1%.
2. Prepare a purchases budget schedule (Schedule 2) for the four quarters ended December 31, 20X3.

14-2 APPLICATION PROBLEM

Preparing a budgeted income statement

The sales manager and administrative manager of Coffee Oasis have made the following projections to be used in preparing a budgeted income statement.
  a. Total net sales for 20X3 are projected to be $1,400,000. In each quarter the following percentages of total net sales were made:

| 1st quarter | 20.0% | 3d quarter | 25.0% |
| 2d quarter | 25.0% | 4th quarter | 30.0% |

  b. Purchases and merchandise ending inventories are projected as follows. Ending inventory for 20X2 was $88,250.

	Purchases	Ending Inventory
1st quarter	$201,000	$111,500
2d quarter	242,500	110,500
3d quarter	283,000	132,500
4th quarter	246,250	99,250

  c. Expenses for 20X3 are projected as follows. Except where noted, percentages are based on projected net sales. For these items, calculate each quarter's amount by multiplying the percentage times that quarter's net sales. Calculate the annual total by adding the four quarterly amounts. When a dollar amount is given, the total amount should be divided equally among the four quarters.

FORMAL EVALUATION

Chapter 14 Test
ExamView for Chapter 14
Assessment by Portfolio

- Review answers to all tests administered as a class activity. If time is limited, review only the items that were frequently answered incorrectly.

- Ask students if there are any questions about the chapter before proceeding to the next chapter.

CHECK FIGURES

Application Problem 14-1

1. Net Sales: 3,500,000; 875,000; 938,000; 1,029,000; 658,000.

2. Cost of Purchases: 411,750; 517,500; 491,250; 393,000.

Application Problem 14-2

1. Total Selling Expenses: 194,200; 40,010; 48,550; 48,550; 57,090.

2. Total Admin. Expenses: 126,200; 30,440; 31,550; 31,550; 32,660.

3. Net Inc. after Fed. Inc. Tax: 88,640; 24,500; 19,100; 1,600; 43,440.

See Teacher's Edition of the Working Papers for Chapter 14 for complete solutions.

TEACHING STRATEGIES ACCOUNTING PEDAGOGY

This textbook introduces the procedures for preparing a performance report before using the computer to prepare a performance report. It is important that students master accounting theory before using the computer to perform repetitive functions.

Selling Expenses		Administrative Expenses	
Advertising Expense	1.5%	Depreciation Expense—Office Equipment	$4,800
Delivery Expense	2.7%	Insurance Expense	$6,000
Depreciation Expense—		Miscellaneous Expense—	
Delivery Equipment	$3,400	Administrative	$5,600
Depreciation Expense—		Payroll Taxes Expense	13.2% of salaries
Store Equipment	$4,200	Rent Expense	$12,800
Miscellaneous Expense—Sales	$15,800	Salary Expense—Administrative	$46,000
Salary Expense—Sales	6.0%	Supplies Expense—Administrative	$4,240
Supplies Expense—Sales	2.0%	Uncollectible Accounts Expense	0.8%
		Utilities Expense	$18,400

Federal income taxes are calculated using the tax rate table shown in this chapter. Equal quarterly income tax payments are based on the projected annual federal income tax expense.

Instructions:
1. Prepare a selling expenses budget schedule (Schedule 3) for the four quarters ended December 31, 20X3. Coffee Oasis rounds all amounts to the nearest $10.
2. Prepare an administrative expenses budget schedule (Schedule 4) for the four quarters ended December 31, 20X3.
3. Prepare a budgeted income statement for the four quarters ended December 31, 20X3.

14-3 APPLICATION PROBLEM
Preparing a cash budget with supporting schedules

The following table shows SeaWest Fabrication's projected net sales, purchases, and cash payments for expenses for 20X3.

			Cash Payments for Expenses	
Quarter	Net Sales	Purchases	Selling	Administrative
1st	$646,300	$558,300	$32,100	$38,600
2d	674,900	571,600	36,200	38,900
3d	661,800	561,200	42,400	39,700
4th	681,600	582,300	36,800	39,800

Additional information is as follows:
a. Actual amounts for the fourth quarter of 20X2: sales, $639,200; purchases, $548,240.
b. The balance of cash on hand on January 1, 20X3, is $35,720.
c. In each quarter, cash sales are 10.0% and collections of accounts receivable are 50.0% of the projected net sales for the current quarter. Collections from the preceding quarter's net sales are 39.5% of that quarter. Uncollectible accounts expense is 0.5% of net sales.
d. In each quarter, cash payments for cash purchases are 10.0% and for accounts payable 30.0% of the purchases for the current quarter. Cash payments for purchases of the preceding quarter are 60.0% of that quarter.
e. Record only total projected cash payments for expenses as shown in the table above.
f. In the second quarter, SeaWest will borrow $35,000 on a promissory note and will purchase equipment costing $31,600 for cash. In the third quarter dividends of $30,000 will be paid in cash. In the fourth quarter, the promissory note plus interest will be paid in cash, $37,500.
g. Equal quarterly income tax payments are based on projected annual federal income tax expense of $7,720.

Instructions:
1. Prepare a cash receipts budget schedule (Schedule A) for the four quarters ended December 31, 20X3. Round all amounts to the nearest $10.
2. Prepare a cash payments budget schedule (Schedule B) for the four quarters ended December 31, 20X3.
3. Prepare a cash budget for the four quarters ended December 31, 20X3.

Application Problem 14-3

1. Total Cash Receipts: 640,260; 695,230; 663,670; 670,370.

2. Total Cash Payments: 624,890; 672,250; 681,470; 685,670.

3. Cash Balance-Ending: 51,090; 74,070; 56,270; 40,970.

TEACHING STRATEGIES TEACHING TIP

Demonstrate how the tax rate table is used to calculate projected federal income tax for a corporation. Change the amount of projected net income and work several different calculations. You may wish to have students calculate the tax at their desks as you demonstrate the procedure on the board or overhead projector.

14-4 MASTERY PROBLEM

Preparing a budgeted income statement and a cash budget with supporting budget schedules

On December 31, 20X2, the accounting records of Zylar, Inc., show the following unit sales for 20X2.

1st quarter	22,000 units	3d quarter	34,800 units
2d quarter	34,400 units	4th quarter	28,800 units

The following are additional actual amounts for the 4th quarter of 20X2.

Sales (28,800 units @ $5.60)	$161,280
Purchases (26,400 units @ $4.00)	105,600
Ending inventory	12,500 units

Management has established a unit sales goal of 130,000 units for 20X3 and 24,000 units for the first quarter of 20X4. The sales manager, after reviewing price trends and checking with the company's merchandise suppliers, projects that the unit cost of merchandise will increase from $4.00 to $4.25 in the first quarter of 20X3. Because of the increase in costs, the company will need to increase its unit sales price from $5.60 to $6.00 in the first quarter of 20X3.

After considering the time required to reorder merchandise, the sales manager requests that 40.0% of each quarter's unit sales be available in the prior quarter's ending inventory.

Expenses are projected as shown on the following page. Except where noted, percentages are based on quarterly projected net sales. For these items, calculate each quarter's amount by multiplying the percentage times that quarter's net sales. Calculate the annual total by adding the four quarterly amounts. When a dollar amount is given, the total amount should be divided equally among the four quarters.

Interest expense for each quarter is projected to be $1,250.

Federal income taxes are calculated using the tax rate table shown in this chapter. Equal quarterly income tax payments are based on the projected annual federal income tax expense.

Additional information is as follows:
  a. The balance of cash on hand on January 1, 20X3, is $41,600.
  b. In each quarter, cash sales are 10.0% and collections of accounts receivable are 40.0% of the projected net sales for the current quarter. Collections from the preceding quarter's net sales are 49.4% of that quarter. Uncollectible accounts expense is 0.6% of net sales.

Selling Expenses		Administrative Expenses	
Advertising Expense	1.2%	Depreciation Expense—Office Equipment	$3,600
Delivery Expense	0.6%	Insurance Expense	$4,200
Depreciation Expense—		Miscellaneous Expense—	
Delivery Equipment	$2,400	Administrative	$3,000
Depreciation Expense—		Payroll Taxes Expense	12.0% of salaries
Store Equipment	$6,680	Rent Expense	$9,600
Miscellaneous Expense—Sales	0.4%	Salary Expense—Administrative	$25,200
Salary Expense—Sales	5.0%	Supplies Expense—Administrative	$2,800
Supplies Expense—Sales	0.8%	Uncollectible Accounts Expense	0.6%
		Utilities Expense	1.8%

  c. In each quarter, cash payments for cash purchases are 10.0% and for accounts payable 55.0% of the purchases for the current quarter. Cash payments for purchases of the preceding quarter are 35.0% of that quarter.
  d. In the first quarter, $40,000 will be borrowed on a promissory note, and equipment costing $30,000 will be purchased for cash. In each quarter, dividends of $10,000 will be paid in cash. In the fourth quarter, the promissory note plus interest will be paid in cash, $45,000.

Mastery Problem 14-4

1. Net Sales: 780,000; 142,800; 223,800; 226,200; 187,200.

2. Cost of Purchases: 111,350; 159,380; 149,180; 120,280.

3. Total Selling Expenses: 71,480; 13,690; 20,180; 20,360; 17,250.

4. Total Admin. Expenses: 74,820; 17,140; 19,570; 19,640; 18,470.

5. Other Expenses: 5,000; 1,250; 1,250; 1,250; 1,250.

6. Net Inc. after Fed. Inc. Tax: 64,090; 8,890; 20,460; 20,910; 13,830.

7. Total Cash Receipts: 191,070; 182,440; 223,660; 205,340.

8. Total Cash Payments: 179,950; 191,620; 202,030; 220,610.

9. Cash Balance Ending: 52,720; 43,540; 65,170; 49,900.

TEACHING STRATEGIES   DIFFERENT LEARNING ABILITIES

Specific Learning Disability (SLD) Students. Exposing students to actual business situations can be an excellent motivational device. Arrange a field trip to a local business familiar to the students, such as a grocery store. Before the field trip, require the students to identify questions to ask the managers of the business. Allow students to ask these questions during the field trip. After the field trip, lead a class discussion that allows students the opportunity to share what they learned.

Instructions:

Prepare the following budget schedules for the year ended December 31, 20X3. Round percentage amounts to the nearest 0.1%, unit amounts to the nearest 100 units, and dollar amounts to the nearest $10.

    a. Prepare a sales budget schedule (Schedule 1).

    b. Prepare a purchases budget schedule (Schedule 2).

    c. Prepare a selling expenses budget schedule (Schedule 3).

    d. Prepare an administrative expenses budget schedule (Schedule 4).

    e. Prepare an other revenue and expenses budget schedule (Schedule 5).

    f. Prepare a budgeted income statement.

    g. Prepare a cash receipts budget schedule (Schedule A).

    h. Prepare a cash payments budget schedule (Schedule B).

    i. Prepare a cash budget.

14-5 CHALLENGE PROBLEM   AUTOMATED ACCOUNTING   QUICKBOOKS
Preparing a performance report

A partially completed performance report for Quasar Robotics, Inc., is in the *Working Papers*.

Quasar Robotics, Inc., has just completed its first quarter of the fiscal year ended December 31, 20X3. Management is interested in identifying significant favorable and unfavorable differences between projected and actual amounts. Quasar Robotics only considers changes of 5.0% or more to be significant. Management reviews changes in net sales and cost of merchandise regardless of the amount of change.

Instructions:

1. Complete the performance report by calculating the increase (decrease) from budget and percentage increase (decrease) from budget.

2. Place an asterisk (*) in the right margin by every item that is significant.

APPLIED SKILLS   WRITING ACROSS THE CURRICULUM

Writing Paragraphs and Short Essays. The Cases for Critical Thinking are short, practical applications of the accounting principles developed in the chapter. Some cases are planned to present problems related to the chapter but not specifically discussed and answered in the chapter. These cases present an opportunity for critical thinking and decision making. These cases also require more than a short objective-type response. Therefore, they provide ideal practice in writing paragraphs and short essays.

Xtra!
Enrichment
accountingxtra.swlearning.com

• applied communication

People often think that only accountants need to know accounting. Many students may not consider taking accounting because they have no interest in being an accountant. Whether students aspire to be doctors, teachers, lawyers, scientists, florists, or artists, they will need to use accounting to control the financial resources of their business or organization.

Required:

Create a presentation that could be made to your high school counselor, student body, or incoming students to persuade the audience that everyone needs accounting. Use the following guidelines.

1. Prepare a list of skills learned in accounting that can be used in everyday life.
2. Elaborate by writing a paragraph to discuss each skill and how advantageous it is for a person to gain the skill.
3. Prepare graphic aids such as transparency masters that could be used to present the material.

• cases for critical thinking

Case 1

Thomas Baker, president of Brundage Corporation, says he has observed that an increase in sales almost always results in an increase in net income. Therefore, he is considering recommending that the company set a sales goal increase of 15.0% for next year and "spare no expense" to achieve this goal. Thomas asks for your opinion regarding his recommendation. How would you respond?

Case 2

Camille Stibbe is general manager of Alden Corporation. She suggests that the budgeted income statement and the cash budget seem to show the same information. Therefore, she recommends that one of the statements be eliminated to reduce accounting costs. What response would you make to Camille?

• SCANS workplace competency

Interpersonal Competency: Teaching Others

Concept: Employers seek employees who are willing to help others learn. Effective employees recognize training needs, assess individual performance and provide constructive feedback, and help others apply concepts and theories through coaching, mentoring, or other means.

Application: Prior to the chapter test, pair up with another student who is having difficulty with the accounting concepts presented in this chapter. Identify weaknesses and thoroughly explain confusing material. Use visuals and rework related chapter problems. Be positive and encouraging during your study session. Conduct a complete chapter review for the upcoming test.

Budgetary Planning and Control

Chapter 14   **439**

APPLIED COMMUNICATION

This activity requires students to create a skills list, write a short paper, and prepare teaching masters. The instructor should consider the following items when grading the activity: (1) thorough list, (2) understandable explanation of each skill, (3) creativity, (4) writing style, and (5) mechanics (grammar, spelling, punctuation, and sentence structure).

CASES FOR CRITICAL THINKING

Case 1

If costs and expenses increase at a higher rate than sales, net income may actually decrease. Many factors should be considered when setting a sales budget schedule: projected economic conditions, projections of the sales personnel, an evaluation of previous years' sales, and the ability of the company to make and/or deliver the increased volume of sales. If the sales budget schedule is unrealistically high, the company may overspend in an effort to meet its sales goal, possibly resulting in lower net income. Recommend that Mr. Baker consider all the factors discussed above. Based on an evaluation of all these factors, set a realistic sales budget level.

Case 2

The statements are different, and each reports valuable information that should help managers run the company more efficiently and profitably. A budgeted income statement reports the projected net income and all the major items affecting net income of a company for a specified period. If the budgeted income statement has been carefully and accurately planned, it provides a reliable base for comparisons (monthly or quarterly) and provides managers with opportunities to identify and correct problems that are affecting net income. The principal purpose of this statement is to help managers manage efficiently so the company can maximize net income. The principal purpose of a cash budget is to plan for a company's cash needs so that adequate cash will be available to meet the company's obligations when due.

SCANS WORKPLACE COMPETENCY

It might be useful for the teacher to arrange pairings based on individual needs and strengths. Discuss with students the benefits of having a study buddy at the secondary and university level.

439

AUDITING FOR ERRORS

The following errors were noted:

1. The sales percentage by quarter for the 3d quarter should be 34.2%.

2. The label "Projected Dollar Sales, 20X3" should read "Projected Unit Sales, 20X3."

3. The unit prices should be formatted with dollar signs.

4. It is unlikely the 4th quarter unit sales price is $1.29. It is likely that the accounting clerk failed to enter a zero, intending to enter $12.90.

ANALYZING COSTCO'S FINANCIAL STATEMENTS

Students' operational goals based on these trends will differ. An example of a student's solutions follows:

1. Costco will open 36 stores in 2004, a 9% increase in the number of stores.

2. Costco will control expenses, reducing selling, general, and administrative expenses to 9.4% percent of net sales, reversing the increasing trend in these costs.

3. Costco will achieve a 5% percentage increase in comparable units, consistent with last year.

4. Costco will increase the number of business members by 4.5% and Gold Star members by 12.1%, the average growth of members over the past four years.

The schedule at the bottom of the page shows information related to the four items.

• auditing for errors

• auditing for errors

MPS Corporation manufactures and sells holiday towels. The number and unit price of the towels increase substantially during the third quarter. An accounting clerk has prepared the following sales budget for the next year. Determine if the budget has been prepared accurately.

MPS Corporation Sales Budget Schedule For Year Ended December 31, 20X3					
	Annual Budget	Quarter			
		1st	2d	3d	4th
Actual Unit Sales, 20X2	62,600	12,400	12,600	21,400	16,200
Sales Percentage by Quarter		19.8%	20.1%	32.4%	25.9%
Projected Dollar Sales, 20X3	72,000	14,256	14,472	23,328	18,648
Times Unit Sales Price		12.5	12.6	13.2	1.29
Net Sales	$692,533	$178,200	$182,347	$307,930	$24,056

analyzing Costco's financial statements

• analyzing Costco's financial statements

From net sales to the number of warehouses, the ten-year operating and financial highlights on pages B-2–B-3 of Appendix B in this textbook provide a historical perspective to Costco's growth. This summary reports trends that are an important input in the budgeting process.

The first step of the budget process is to establish operational goals.

Instructions: Use the information in this report to suggest operational goals for Costco in 2004. For each item, examine the trend from 2000 to 2003 and decide what operational goal you believe Costco should attempt to achieve in 2004. Be prepared to defend your goals in class.

1. Costco will open ___ stores in 2004. (*Hint:* Calculate the percent increase in the number of warehouses each year.)

2. Costco will control expenses, reducing selling, general, and administrative expenses to ___ percent of net sales.

3. Costco will achieve a ___ percentage increase in comparable units (same store sales).

4. Costco will increase the number of business members by ____ and Gold Star members by ___. (*Hint:* Calculate the percent increase in the number of members each year.)

Business Members:

End of year	4,636	4,476	4,358	4,170
Beginning of year	4,476	4,358	4,170	3,887
Increase in business members	160	118	188	283
Percentage increase in business members	3.6%	2.7%	4.5%	7.3%

Gold Star Members:

End of year	14,984	14,597	12,737	10,521
Beginning of year	14,597	12,737	10,521	9,555
Increase in Gold Star members	387	1,860	2,216	966
Percentage increase in Gold Star members	2.7%	14.6%	21.1%	10.1%

	2003	2002	2001	2000
Warehouses opened	29	35	39	25
Beginning warehouses	374	345	313	292
Percent increase in number of warehouses	7.8%	10.1%	12.5%	8.6%
SG&A expenses as percent of net sales (as reported in the highlights)	9.8%	9.4%	9.2%	8.7%
Sales—comparable units (as reported in the highlights)	5.0%	6.0%	4.0%	11.0%

TEACHING STRATEGIES   PORTFOLIO ASSESSMENT

Accounting knowledge can be used for more than recording actual transactions. Financial planning activities such as preparing budgets and performance reports are also very important. Students should select an example of these activities that have been successfully completed to include in their portfolio. A copy of the Portfolio Assessment form (blackline master in the Teacher's Resource Guide; also on the Student Companion CD) should be completed by the student and the Description section should include any comments regarding how the student mastered these concepts and procedures. Alternatively, students might include in their portfolios printed reports from an Automated Accounting problem.

Automated Accounting

Preparing a Performance Report

A budget is a financial plan for the future. It can be used to plan revenue and expenses. A performance report is a type of financial statement that compares budgeted and actual amounts. Once budgeted data have been entered into the accounting system, a performance report can be generated.

Entering and Changing Budget Amount Data

When the Other Activities menu item is chosen from the Data menu or the Other toolbar button is clicked, the Other Activities window containing the Budgets tab will appear. The Budgets tab allows you to enter the budgeted amounts for income statement accounts. To enter budget amounts:

1. Enter the budgeted amount for the first account (or highlight an amount you wish to change and enter a new amount).

2. Press the Tab key to move to the next account. The accounts are scrollable. When you have entered the amount for the last account visible, the accounts will scroll up so that you can enter the next budget amount.

3. When all budget amounts have been entered, click OK.

Preparing a Performance Report

Once the budgeted amounts have been entered, a performance report may be displayed or printed. Use the following steps to display the report:

1. Click the Reports toolbar button, or choose the Reports Selection menu item from the Reports menu.

2. When the Report Selection dialog appears, choose Financial Statements from the Select a Report Group list.

3. Choose Performance Report from the Choose a Report to Display list.

4. Click OK.

The report will be displayed in the scrollable Report Viewer Window. The report may be printed and/or copied for inclusion in another application, such as a spreadsheet or word processor.

AUTOMATING CHALLENGE PROBLEM 14-5

Instructions:

1. Load *Automated Accounting 8.0* or higher software.

2. Select database A14-5 (Advanced Course Challenge Problem 14-5) from the accounting template disk.

3. Select File from the menu bar and choose the Save As menu command. Key the path to the drive and directory that contain your data files. Save the database with a filename of XXX145 (where XXX are your initials).

4. Read the Problem Instruction screen by clicking the Browser tool button.

5. Refer to page 438 for data used in this problem.

6. Exit the Automated Accounting software.

TEACHING STRATEGIES   PORTFOLIO ASSESSMENT

Students should be encouraged to print at least one report from one of the Automated Accounting problems to include in their portfolio to demonstrate mastery of automated accounting systems. A copy of the Portfolio Assessment form (blackline master in the Teacher's Resource Guide; also on the Student Companion CD) should be completed by the student, and the Description section should include any comments regarding how the student mastered these concepts and procedures.

Management Decisions Using

	SCOPE & SEQUENCE	
	NEW	**REVIEW/ EXTENSION**
Introduce the Chapter	✓	
Lesson 15-1 Cost Characteristics That Influence Decisions		
Unit costs	✓	
Variable costs	✓	
Fixed costs	✓	
Calculating contribution margin	✓	
Lesson 15-2 Determining Breakeven		
Calculating breakeven point	✓	
Breakeven income statement	✓	
Lesson 15-3 Decisions That Affect Net Income		
Calculating sales to earn planned net income	✓	
Determining effects of changes on net income	✓	
Calculating sales mix	✓	
Putting It All Together		

ENHANCING	
SPECIAL FEATURES	
• Accounting in the Real World: RC Cola	
• Making Ethical Decisions: Due Care	
• Global Perspective: International Organizations	
• Explore Accounting: Differential Costs	
• Careers in Accounting	
• Technology for Business: Using a Spreadsheet to Perform Breakeven Analysis	
• Explore Accounting	
• Xtra! Web Site: Xtra! Enrichment	
• Applied Communication	
• Cases for Critical Thinking	
• SCANS Workplace Competency	
• Graphing Workshop	
• Analyzing Costco's Financial Statements	

Cost-Volume-Profit Analysis

INSTRUCTION		PRACTICE AND ASSESSMENT		
TECHNOLOGY AND MEDIA	**TEACHING STRATEGIES**	**GUIDED PRACTICE**	**INDEPENDENT PRACTICE**	**RETEACHING AND ENRICHMENT**
• Internet Research Activity • Accounting Xtra! Web Site	• Software Focus			
• Instructor's Resource CD: PowerPoint Slides • Xtra! Web Site: Xtra! Study Tools • Blackline Masters: 2-Column Statement Paper and 3-Column Statement Paper • Personal Trainer	• Auditory Learner • Print Learner	• Terms Review • Audit Your Understanding • Work Together 15-1	• On Your Own 15-1 • Application Problem 15-1 • Ongoing Assessment, p. 448 • Personal Trainer • Xtra! Web Site: Xtra! Study Tools	• Reteach, p. 448 • Enrich, p. 450
• Instructor's Resource CD: PowerPoint Slides • Xtra! Web Site: Xtra! Study Tools • Blackline Masters: 2-Column Statement Paper • Personal Trainer	• Applied Skills: Building Study Skills	• Term Review • Audit Your Understanding • Work Together 15-2	• On Your Own 15-2 • Application Problem 15-2 • Ongoing Assessment, p. 453 • Personal Trainer • Xtra! Web Site: Xtra! Study Tools	• Reteach, p. 453 • Enrich, p. 454
• Instructor's Resource CD: PowerPoint Slides • Xtra! Web Site: Xtra! Study Tools • Personal Trainer	• Tactile Learner • Kinesthetic Learner • Expanding Beyond the Classroom • Limited English Proficiency (LEP) Students • Visual Learner	• Term Review • Audit Your Understanding • Work Together 15-3	• On Your Own 15-3 • Application Problems 15-3, 15-4, and 15-5 • Ongoing Assessment, p. 462 • Personal Trainer • Xtra! Web Site: Xtra! Study Tools	• Reteach, p. 461 • Enrich, p. 462
• Automated Accounting • Personal Trainer • Xtra! Web Site: Xtra! Review, Quizzing, and Enrichment • Student Companion CD	• Applied Skills: Mathematics • Applied Skills: Language Arts • Applied Skills: Writing Across the Curriculum • Cooperative Learning		• Mastery Problem 15-6 • Personal Trainer • Xtra! Web Site: Xtra! Review and Quizzing • Study Guide 15 • Student Companion CD • Chapter 15 Test • ExamView Chapter 15 • Portfolio Assessment	• Challenge Problem 15-7 • Reteach, p. 463 • Enrich, p. 463 • Recycling Problem 15-1 • Automated Accounting • Xtra! Web Site: Xtra! Enrichment

CHAPTER

OBJECTIVES & TERMS

15 Management Decisions Using Cost-Volume-Profit Analysis

After studying Chapter 15, you will be able to:

1. Define terms related to accounting information for management decisions.

2. Identify accounting concepts and practices related to preparing accounting information for management decisions.

3. Prepare an income statement reporting contribution margin.

4. Calculate the contribution margin rate.

5. Calculate the breakeven point.

6. Calculate the sales dollars and sales units required to earn a planned amount of net income.

7. Determine the effect of changes in sales volume, unit costs, and unit sales prices on net income.

8. Calculate a sales mix.

- total costs
- unit cost
- variable costs

- fixed costs
- contribution margin

- breakeven point
- sales mix

Point Your Browser
accountingxtra.swlearning.com

442

ACCOUNTING IN THE REAL WORLD

1. Answers will vary; examples could be the Edsel or gravy in a tube.
2. By selling multiple beverage brands, the company can command more favorable shelf space with its retail store customers. The brands can also share the same distribution system and production facilities, thus reducing production costs.

INTERNET RESEARCH ACTIVITY

Answers will vary.

· RC Cola

©RC COLA IS A TRADEMARK OF DR PEPPER/ SEVEN UP, INC. © 2004 DR PEPPER/SEVEN UP, INC.

PRODUCT INNOVATION AT RC COLA

The forerunner of RC Cola was introduced in 1905, when a young pharmacist, Claud A. Hatcher, decided to supply the family grocery store with drinks. "Chero-Cola" was part of his "Royal Crown" line of beverages. In 1928, Hatcher renamed his company the Nehi Corporation, after his successful line of fruity beverages.

In the mid-1930s, the company introduced a reformulated version of Chero-Cola under the name "Royal Crown Cola." The new cola was such a success that the company was again renamed, this time to Royal Crown Cola Co. The company was recently acquired by Cadbury Schweppes, a London-based company that owns other beverage brands, including Dr. Pepper, 7UP, Canada Dry, Mott's, Snapple, and Hawaiian Punch. Throughout its history, the company has also been an innovator. First to introduce a low-calorie, caffeine-free diet cola, and diet cherry cola, the company also introduced the all-aluminum beverage can.

Before any company introduces a new product, its managers need to understand the relationship between the expected revenues and costs. How much of the new product must be sold to make the desired profit is an important question that must be answered before the new product is introduced.

Critical Thinking

1. Throughout its history, the Royal Crown Cola Co. was successful in introducing new products in the marketplace. Identify a company that was unsuccessful in introducing a new product.
2. Why would Cadbury Schweppes want to own so many well-known beverage brands?

Source: www.dpsu.com/rc.html; www.dpsu.com/dpsu_fact_sheets.html

Xtra!
Today
accountingxtra.swlearning.com

INSTITUTE OF MANAGEMENT ACCOUNTANTS

Go to the homepage for the Institute of Management Accountants (IMA) (www.imanet.org). Click on the Student link.

Instructions

1. List two resources provided for students.
2. Pick one of these two resources and examine it in more detail. List two interesting pieces of information you learned from this resource.

443

15-1 Cost Characteristics That Influence Decisions

Managers use financial statements to make good business decisions. An income statement is one source of information on which a manager can base decisions. An income statement includes information about operating revenue, cost of merchandise sold, gross profit on operations, operating expenses, and net income or net loss. By analyzing the income statement, managers can gain an understanding of the relationship among sales, costs, and expenses.

Managers can increase net income by increasing sales and/or decreasing costs and expenses. Managers, with the advice and assistance of accountants, analyze the relationships among sales, costs, and expenses to:

1. Determine the level of sales necessary to achieve planned net income.
2. Evaluate the impact of changes in sales volume, unit sales prices, and unit costs on net income.
3. Identify the strengths and weaknesses of a company.

©GETTY IMAGES/PHOTODISC

making ethical decisions

Due Care

Accountants will make mistakes—after all, they are human. Yet the codes of conduct for several accounting organizations require that their members exercise due care in the performance of professional services. The concept of *due care* requires accountants to strive for perfection and, as a result, earn the confidence of their clients and the financial community.

Instructions

Access the code of conduct for the American Institute of Certified Public Accountants and the Association of Certified Fraud Examiners. Identify adjectives the codes use to describe due care.

MAKING ETHICAL DECISIONS

Both codes provide more in-depth insight into the concept of due care. Without a knowledge of auditing, students may have difficulty understanding some of these concepts. However, they will be able to identify the key terms used. As an extension of this activity, lead a classroom discussion, asking students to define each of these terms in their own words.

Suggested Solution: Diligence, critical analysis, professional skepticism, and competence.

Sources: *www.aicpa.org/about/code/article5.htm* and *www.cfenet.com/about/ProfStandards.asp*

Reflection, Inc.
Income Statement
For Month Ended July 31, 20--

Operating Revenue:		
Net Sales		$180,000.00
Cost of Merchandise Sold		118,800.00
Gross Profit on Operations		$ 61,200.00
Operating Expenses:		
Selling Expenses	$31,930.00	
Administrative Expenses	20,820.00	
Total Operating Expenses		52,750.00
Income from Operations		$ 8,450.00
Other Expenses		2,450.00
Net Income		$ 6,000.00

Total Costs Versus Unit Cost

All costs for a specific period of time are called **total costs**. The abbreviated income statement above shows that the total cost of the merchandise sold by Reflection, Inc. during July was $118,800.00. Total selling expenses were $31,930.00. These totals show how much money was spent for these activities during a specific period of time. [CONCEPT: Accounting Period Cycle]

An amount spent for one unit of a specific product or service is called a **unit cost**. Reflection sold 36,000 square feet of mirrors during July at a total cost of $118,800.00. The unit cost of each square foot of mirrors is calculated as follows:

Cost of Merchandise Sold Total Cost	÷	Units Sold	=	Cost of Merchandise Sold Unit Cost
$118,800.00	÷	36,000	=	$3.30

Units may be expressed in many different terms. However, units should be expressed in terms that are meaningful to the people who are responsible for the costs. Some examples of other unit terms are gallons, liters, pounds, kilograms, inches, yards, meters, and hours. Knowing unit costs can be helpful to a manager in setting unit selling prices and in planning cost control.

FYI FOR YOUR INFORMATION

Spreadsheet software is often used to perform what-if analyses. Managers use what-if analyses to examine the financial results of various assumptions. For example, managers can project the net income for the next fiscal period if variable costs increase.

EXPLAIN

- Explain the difference between total costs and unit cost. The concept of unit cost is a key component of the analysis in this chapter.

- Explain that the abbreviated income statement in the illustration shows total costs for many items on the statement but does not furnish enough information to determine what it costs to manufacture or sell one unit of product.

- Explain that units may be expressed in many terms but should be expressed in terms that are meaningful to the people who are responsible for the costs.

- Direct students to the F.Y.I. for information about using spreadsheet software to perform what-if analysis.

DEMONSTRATE

- Use the board to demonstrate the calculation of unit cost as shown in the math box.

- Give a number of different amounts and direct students to calculate unit costs on their calculators at their desks.

- Explain that total variable costs change with the number of units while unit variable costs remain the same no matter how many units. For example, if the wood for a chair costs $10, then each chair will require $10 of wood. The total cost of wood will depend on how many chairs are produced.

- Explain that fixed costs remain the same no matter how many units. For example, the rent is the same each month no matter how many units are produced or sold.

DEMONSTRATE

Variable costs

- Direct students to the illustration at the top of the page as you demonstrate the nature of variable costs.

- Demonstrate how the amounts in the Total Cost column of the table on the left are calculated by multiplying the number of units (square feet) purchased by the unit cost per square foot.

- Draw on the board or a transparency a blank graph similar to the figure and ask students to suggest where the seven points should be placed for drawing the graph of unit costs.

- Point out that the total cost is different each month because the units purchased amount is different each month (variable cost).

Fixed costs

- Direct students to the illustration at the bottom of the page as you demonstrate the nature of fixed costs.

- Draw a blank graph similar to the figure on the board or a transparency and ask students to suggest where the seven points should be placed for drawing the graph of unit costs.

- Point out that the graph is a perfectly horizontal line because the rent is fixed at the same amount each month no matter how many units are purchased (fixed cost).

VARIABLE COST CHARACTERISTICS

Reflection, Inc. Mirror Purchases For Period January 1–July 31, 20--			
Month	Units Purchased	Unit Cost per sq. ft.	Total Cost
January	27,300	$3.30	$ 90,090.00
February	26,100	3.30	86,130.00
March	29,200	3.30	96,360.00
April	33,500	3.30	110,550.00
May	30,400	3.30	100,320.00
June	35,100	3.30	115,830.00
July	36,000	3.30	118,800.00

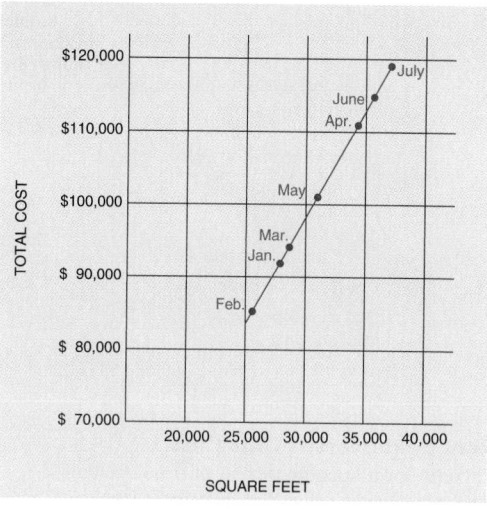

Costs may be separated into two parts: variable and fixed. Total costs that change in direct proportion to a change in the number of units are called **variable costs**. The *total* variable cost *varies* with a change in the number of units. Specifically, it increases. The *unit* variable cost *remains the same* regardless of the number of units.

For example, a business buys 1 hour of radio advertising for $150.00. Later the business buys 10 more hours of advertising for $1,500.00 (10 × $150.00 = $1,500.00). Regardless of the number of hours purchased, the unit cost of an hour of advertising is $150.00 per hour. Thus, radio advertising is a variable cost.

Reflection's mirror purchases for the months January through July are shown above. The volume of mirrors purchased ranges from a low

of 26,100 square feet in February to a high of 36,000 square feet in July. However, the price paid per square foot (unit cost) remained at $3.30 throughout the seven-month period. Therefore, these costs have the characteristics of variable costs.

Reflection's monthly costs for mirror purchases are plotted on the graph above. The line between the plotted points indicates the relationship between the number of square feet of mirrors purchased and the total cost of mirrors. The straight, upward sloped line shows that as the quantity of mirrors increases, the total cost also increases. The line is straight because Reflection's unit cost per square foot remained the same although the number of units purchased per month varied.

FIXED COSTS

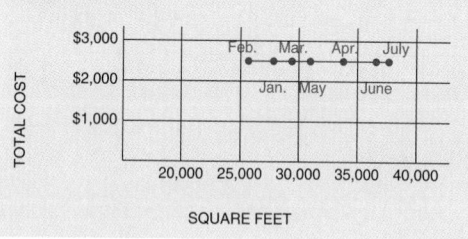

Total costs that remain constant regardless of change in business activity are called **fixed costs**. For example, Reflection's rent is $2,500.00 per month. Rent is *fixed* because the amount has been set at $2,500.00 per month regardless of how many square feet of mirrors are purchased. If each monthly rental cost is plotted on a graph and points are connected, the chart will appear as shown here. The fixed cost line is a straight line parallel to the base of the graph.

Management Decisions Using Cost-Volume-Profit Analysis

TEACHING STRATEGIES   DIFFERENT LEARNING STYLES

Auditory Learner. The auditory learner can reinforce the learning of formulas by verbally explaining the formula and/or calculations to other students in a small group. In a group of three, for example, each student should get the opportunity to teach the formula to the other two students. Through this process, each student in the group will "teach" the formula once and "learn" the formula two times.

GROSS PROFIT AND CONTRIBUTION MARGIN INCOME STATEMENTS

Reflection, Inc.
Income Statement
For Month Ended July 31, 20--

Operating Revenue:		
Net Sales (36,000 sq. ft. @ $5.00)		$180,000.00
Cost of Merchandise Sold (36,000 sq. ft. @ $3.30)		118,800.00
Gross Profit on Operations		$ 61,200.00
Operating Expenses:		
Selling Expenses:		
Sales Commission (36,000 sq. ft. @ $.20)	$ 7,200.00	
Delivery Costs (36,000 sq. ft. @ $.40)	14,400.00	
Other Variable Costs (36,000 sq. ft. @ $.15)	5,400.00	
Other Fixed Costs	4,930.00	$31,930.00
Administrative Expenses:		
Rent	$ 2,500.00	
Insurance	400.00	
Other Variable Costs (36,000 sq. ft. @ $.20)	7,200.00	
Other Fixed Costs	10,720.00	20,820.00
Total Operating Expenses		52,750.00
Income from Operations		$ 8,450.00
Other Expenses		2,450.00
Net Income		$ 6,000.00

Reflection, Inc.
Income Statement
For Month Ended July 31, 20--

Operating Revenue:		
Net Sales (36,000 sq. ft. @ $5.00)		$180,000.00
Variable Costs:		
Cost of Merchandise Sold (36,000 sq. ft. @ $3.30)	$118,800.00	
Sales Commission (36,000 sq. ft. @ $.20)	7,200.00	
Delivery Costs (36,000 sq. ft. @ $.40)	14,400.00	
Other Selling Costs (36,000 sq. ft. @ $.15)	5,400.00	
Other Administrative Costs (36,000 sq. ft. @ $.20)	7,200.00	
Total Variable Costs		153,000.00
Contribution Margin		$ 27,000.00
Fixed Costs:		
Rent	$ 2,500.00	
Insurance	400.00	
Other Selling Costs	4,930.00	
Other Administrative Costs	10,720.00	
Other Expenses	2,450.00	
Total Fixed Costs		21,000.00
Net Income		$ 6,000.00

An income statement reports operating revenue, cost of merchandise sold, gross profit on operations, operating expenses, and net income or net loss. Gross profit is determined by subtracting cost of merchandise sold from net sales. On a typical income statement, as shown in the top portion of the illustration above, costs are shown as cost of merchandise sold, selling expenses, and administrative expenses.

Income determined by subtracting all variable costs from net sales is called **contribution margin**. Reflection's income statement shown in the bottom portion of the illustration above reports contribution margin and net income by grouping costs into two categories: variable costs and fixed costs.

EXPLAIN

- Explain that the standard income statement reports gross profit on operations by subtracting cost of merchandise sold from net sales and then deducting expenses to arrive at net income. Variable and fixed costs are mixed together.

- Explain that contribution margin is the income left over after all variable costs are subtracted from net sales.

- Explain that an income statement reporting contribution margin separates fixed and variable costs and reports them in separate groups.

DEMONSTRATE

- Use an instructor-made transparency from the blackline master of 2-column statement paper.

- Direct students to the top income statement in the illustration. Explain each item on the statement and ask students to identify whether each selling and administrative expense is a fixed or a variable cost.

- Use the transparency to build the income statement reporting contribution margin by referring back to the gross profit income statement for each item.

- Point out that the variable costs all appear above the contribution margin and the fixed costs below it.

TEACHING STRATEGIES   DIFFERENT LEARNING STYLES

Print Learner. When learning formulas, the print learner would prefer to be able to study the formula as given in the textbook or as printed on a separate handout. The print material should show the formula as well as an example of performing the calculations.

447

CONTRIBUTION MARGIN PER UNIT

The concept of contribution margin is important to managers because it allows them to determine the income available to cover fixed costs and provide a profit. Reflection's managers can determine from this income statement that the total contribution margin in July was $27,000.00. The contribution margin per unit is calculated as follows.

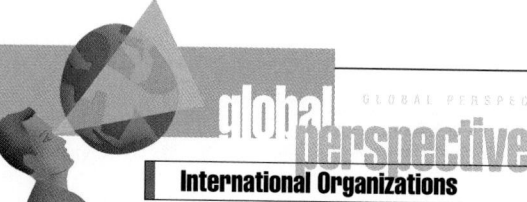

	Total Contribution Margin	÷	Units Sold	=	Contribution Margin per Unit
	$27,000.00	÷	36,000	=	$0.75

Thus, Reflection determined that it will earn a $0.75 contribution margin for each square foot of mirrors sold. The managers also know that the company will have $21,000.00 of fixed costs each month regardless of the number of square feet of mirrors sold. Therefore, in July Reflection earned net income of $6,000.00.

global perspective

GLOBAL PERSPECTIVE • GLOBAL PERSPECTIVE • GLOBAL PERSPECTIVE

International Organizations

There are many international organizations that establish trade regulations and standards to facilitate conducting business among the various countries in the world.

The United Nations plays an important role in foreign trade and has many organizations that make contributions. For example, The International Court of Justice (ICJ) decides disputes between nations, The International Monetary Fund (IMF) promotes international monetary cooperation and currency stabilization among member nations, The Universal Postal Union (UPU) promotes international cooperation in postal service, and the United Nations Children's Fund (UNICEF) provides aid to children and mothers in developing countries.

The International Chamber of Commerce (ICC) serves traders in over 100 countries. Its most important function is to issue rules on international trade practices. It is not a government agency and confines its activities to business issues rather than national policy issues.

The General Agreement on Tariffs and Trade (GATT) promotes economic growth by liberalizing world trade through requiring its member governments to reduce artificial trade restraints. There are 90 members of GATT, and the U.S. is a charter member.

The European Union (EU) is a group of 15 European democracies—Austria, Belgium, Denmark, Finland, France, Germany, Greece, the Republic of Ireland, Italy, Luxembourg, the Netherlands, Portugal, Spain, Sweden, and the United Kingdom. The EU has a short-term goal to integrate member nations' economies so members will act as a single nation for trade purposes. The EU's long-term goal is to unite member nations into a political union.

Required

Select one international trade organization and research the organization's creation, policies, and accomplishments.

Management Decisions Using Cost-Volume-Profit Analysis

Explore Accounting

Differential Costs

Some students will hesitate to discount the ticket, citing possible public relation problems with the other tourists who paid the full price. Note that this problem is a valid concern that managers must consider. Ask students to identify real companies that offer discounts on last-minute tickets (*airlines, cruise ships*).

Teton Tours is about to depart on a one-week bus tour with an empty seat. As the tourists are loading the bus, Sandy Tanaka offers to purchase the last ticket for $600.00—well below the regular $900.00 ticket price. Should Teton Tours depart with an empty seat or accept Sandy's offer?

Managers must understand the nature or characteristics of costs to make decisions that increase income. A cost that differs between alternative actions is referred to as a *differential cost*. Only differential costs are relevant to making a decision between alternatives.

Consider the costs of the tour for each of the alternatives.

Costs	43 Tourists (depart with an empty seat)	44 Tourists (accept Sandy's offer)
Food ($150.00 per person)	$ 6,450.00	$ 6,600.00
Hotel ($300.00 per person)	12,900.00	13,200.00
Admission Fees ($120.00 per person)	5,160.00	5,280.00
Bus Depreciation	1,000.00	$ 1,000.00
Bus Fuel	600.00	600.00
Bus Driver Wages	2,000.00	2,000.00
Total Costs	$28,110.00	$28,680.00
Cost per Tourist	$653.72	$651.82

A manager who compares the $600.00 ticket offer to the $651.82 cost per person and declines the offer is making the wrong decision. The three bus-related expenses do not change if an additional passenger joins the tour. Thus, these costs are not relevant to the decision.

The $600.00 offer should be compared only to differential costs. The food, hotel, and admission fees are $570.00 per person ($150.00 + $300.00 + $120.00 = $570.00). Thus, Teton Tours will earn an additional $30.00 ($600.00 − $570.00) by accepting Sandy's offer.

Certainly, Teton Tours cannot offer every passenger the $600.00 price and expect to earn any income. However, for this specific decision, Teton Tours earn more income by accepting a discounted ticket price than by leaving with an empty seat.

Critical Thinking: Recalculate the amounts shown in the table. Decide whether you agree with the decision to accept Sandy's offer.

Cost Characteristics That Influence Decisions

GUIDED PRACTICE

Terms Review

Call on students to define the terms in the Terms Review. Ask the class if the definitions are correct and whether the complete definitions have been given or if anything needs to be added. Suggested definitions for all terms are given in the Glossary.

Audit Your Understanding

Call on students to answer the Audit Your Understanding questions. Ask the class if each answer is correct and/or complete. Answers are given in Appendix E of the textbook.

Work Together

Have students write the solution to the Work Together problem as you guide the class through the examples.

- Discuss as a group what amounts are included in the Operating Revenue section. When all agree, direct students to complete that section in the working papers.

- Repeat for the Variable Costs section; then have students calculate the contribution margin.

- Repeat for the Fixed Costs section.

INDEPENDENT PRACTICE

On Your Own

- Assign the On Your Own problem to be worked independently.

- Use the Ongoing Assessment techniques to diagnose student understanding.

Application Problem

- Assign Application Problem 15-1: Preparing an income statement reporting contribution margin.

Personal Trainer

- Students can access the Lesson 15-1 assessment material using this software.

Xtra! Web Site

- Students can access the Xtra! Study Tools for additional practice.

ENRICH

- Assign Making Ethical Decisions on page 444.

- Assign the Global Perspective feature on page 448.

- Assign Explore Accounting on page 449.

CLOSE

- Ask students to describe the difference between fixed and variable costs and to explain why contribution margin is important.

450

• terms review

total costs
unit cost
variable costs
fixed costs
contribution margin

• audit your understanding

1. If total monthly fixed costs for a company were plotted on a graph for seven months, would the line drawn between the plotted points be parallel to the base or sloped? Explain why.

2. How does contribution margin differ from gross profit?

• work together 15-1

Preparing an income statement with contribution margin

An income statement for Wightman's Lumber is included in the *Working Papers.* Your instructor will guide you through the following examples.

1. Use the following information to prepare Wightman Lumber's January income statement reporting contribution margin. The February information will be used to complete the On Your Own below.

	January	February
Net Sales	52,000 square feet	47,000 square feet
Unit Sales Price	$7.50 per square foot	$7.50 per square foot
Cost of Merchandise Sold	$4.60 per square foot	$4.80 per square foot
Selling Expenses:		
Sales Commission	$.32 per square foot	$.32 per square foot
Delivery Cost	$.50 per square foot	$.55 per square foot
Other Variable Selling Expenses	$.35 per square foot	$.35 per square foot
Other Fixed Selling Expenses	$7,120.00	$7,120.00
Administrative Expenses:		
Rent	$3,800.00	$3,800.00
Insurance	$450.00	$450.00
Other Variable Administrative Expenses	$.30 per square foot	$.33 per square foot
Other Fixed Administrative Expenses	$12,540.00	$12,540.00

• on your own 15-1

Preparing an income statement with contribution margin

Use the February information from the Work Together above. An income statement for Wightman Lumber is included in the *Working Papers.* Work independently to complete this problem.

1. Prepare Wightman Lumber's February income statement reporting contribution margin.

15-2 Determining Breakeven

OBJECTIVES

- Define terms related to accounting information for management decisions.
- Identify accounting concepts and practices related to preparing accounting information for management decisions.
- Calculate the contribution margin rate.
- Calculate the breakeven point.

CALCULATING THE BREAKEVEN POINT

	Contribution Margin	÷	Net Sales	=	Contribution Margin Rate	❶
	$27,000.00	÷	$180,000.00	=	.15 or 15%	
	Total Fixed Costs Costs	÷	Contribution Margin Rate	=	Sales Dollar Breakeven Point	❷
	$21,000.00	÷	.15 or 15%	=	$140,000.00	
	Sales Dollar Breakeven Point	÷	Unit Sales Price	=	Unit Sales Breakeven Point	❸
	$140,000.00	÷	$5.00	=	28,000 units	

If a manager is to make decisions that yield a favorable net income for a company, the manager needs two important types of information. (1) The amount of merchandise or services the company must sell to earn a favorable net income. (2) The factors that contribute most to net income.

The amount of sales at which net sales is equal to total costs is called the **breakeven point**. At the breakeven point, neither a net income nor a net loss occurs. At sales levels above the breakeven point, net income occurs. Conversely, at sales levels below the breakeven point, net loss occurs. Knowing the breakeven point allows managers to determine the amount of sales needed to start earning a profit. The breakeven point can be stated in sales dollars or unit sales as shown above.

The amounts required to calculate a breakeven point are obtained from an income statement prepared to report contribution margin, such as the income statement on page 447.

MOTIVATE

Ask students what the word "breakeven" means to them. Ask students for examples from their personal lives when they "broke even." Point out that it is exactly the same in accounting.

Preview

- Preview the accounting term and definition introduced in this lesson: breakeven point.
- Direct students to read the headings at the top of each page in this lesson and to examine the illustrations given.

EXPLAIN

- Point out that to make decisions affecting net income, a manager needs to know the amount of sales necessary to earn a favorable net income and the factors that contribute most to net income.
- Point out that at the breakeven point, there is neither a net income nor a net loss, but that all costs are paid for by net sales.
- Point out that at sales levels above breakeven point, there is a net income. Conversely, at sales levels below breakeven point there is a net loss.
- Emphasize that the contribution margin rate must be calculated before breakeven sales can be calculated.
- Explain that the breakeven point can be calculated for either total sales dollars or total unit sales, but that the sales dollar breakeven point must be calculated first.

STEPS · STEPS · STEPS · STEPS · STEPS · STEPS · STEPS · STEPS · STEPS · STEPS ·

CALCULATING A BREAKEVEN POINT

❶ Calculate the contribution margin rate by dividing the total contribution margin by net sales. The amounts are taken from historical financial statements, which are often used to project future sales and costs. Reflection uses total amounts rounded to the nearest $10 in breakeven point calculations. This rate means that for every $1.00 of revenue, $0.15 is contribution margin. The contribution rate is available to pay for fixed costs and provide net income. Variable costs change in direct proportion to changes in sales activity. Therefore, for every $1.00 of revenue, $0.85 is required for variable costs.

❷ Calculate the sales dollar breakeven point by dividing total fixed costs by the contribution margin rate. The sales dollar breakeven point is the amount of sales at which the entire contribution margin is used to pay for fixed costs. Reflection must have total sales of $140,000.00 just to recover the fixed costs of doing business. More than $140,000.00 in sales must be made if the company is to earn a net income. At a sales level of exactly $140,000, total costs are $140,000 (fixed costs are $21,000 and variable costs are $119,000 [$140,000 × .85]), and Reflection achieves no net income. Any sales level less than $140,000 results in a net loss.

❸ Calculate the unit sales breakeven point by dividing the sales dollar breakeven point by the unit sales price. The unit sales breakeven point indicates the number of square feet of mirrors that Reflection must sell at $5.00 per square foot to achieve breakeven sales.

Determining Breakeven

MATERIALS

- Instructor's Resource CD:
  PowerPoint Slides
- Xtra! Study Tools on the Xtra! Web Site
- Blackline Masters:
  2-Column Statement Paper
- Working Papers:
  Teacher's Edition of the Working Papers for Lesson 15-2
- Software:
  Personal Trainer

DEMONSTRATE

- Demonstrate the calculation of the contribution margin rate on the board.
- Demonstrate the calculation of the sales dollar breakeven point on the board.
- Demonstrate the calculation of the unit sales breakeven point on the board.

CALCULATING BREAKEVEN POINT FOR NEW PRODUCTS

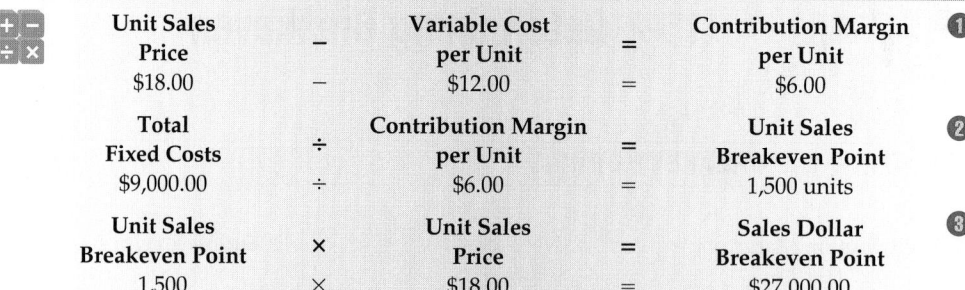

	Unit Sales Price	−	Variable Cost per Unit	=	Contribution Margin per Unit	①
	$18.00	−	$12.00	=	$6.00	
	Total Fixed Costs	÷	Contribution Margin per Unit	=	Unit Sales Breakeven Point	②
	$9,000.00	÷	$6.00	=	1,500 units	
	Unit Sales Breakeven Point	×	Unit Sales Price	=	Sales Dollar Breakeven Point	③
	1,500	×	$18.00	=	$27,000.00	

EXPLAIN

- Point out that when a business is going to introduce a new product, management wants to know how many units the company must sell to break even.

- Emphasize that for analyzing a new product introduction, there is obviously no historical income statement information available. Therefore, it is necessary to use the alternative contribution margin per unit rather than the historical contribution margin rate.

- Direct students to read the F.Y.I. for information about the magnitude of investment in fixed costs in some industries.

DEMONSTRATE

Demonstrate the three steps for calculating breakeven point based on contribution margin per unit on the board.

- Calculate contribution margin per unit by subtracting variable cost per unit from unit sales price. Point out that contribution margin per unit represents the amount per unit that is available to cover fixed costs and net income.

- Calculate unit sales breakeven point by dividing total fixed costs by contribution margin per unit. Explain that the unit sales breakeven point is the number of units that must be sold to cover all variable and fixed costs, before earning any net income.

- Calculate sales dollar breakeven point by multiplying unit sales breakeven point times unit sales price.

When a business plans to introduce a new product, management is interested in knowing how many units the company must sell to break even. Unfortunately, no financial statements exist from which sales and cost information can be obtained. Therefore, an alternative method to calculate the breakeven point using the *contribution margin per unit* rather than the *contribution margin rate* is necessary.

Reflection is considering selling desk lamps at $18.00 per unit. Management expects variable costs of $12.00 per unit with fixed costs of $9,000.00 per month. From the analysis, Reflection determines that it must sell more than 1,500 desk lamps per month before the company begins to make a net income. Thus,

management will begin selling desk lamps if it believes it can sell more than 1,500 per month.

This alternative method is also useful for calculating the breakeven point for existing products when complete financial statements are not available.

FYI FOR YOUR INFORMATION

The nature of some businesses requires a large investment in fixed costs. Businesses such as airlines, public utilities, and railroads have large fixed costs. These businesses may be considered riskier because much of their revenue is devoted to paying these fixed costs.

STEPS • STEPS • STEPS • STEPS • STEPS • STEPS • STEPS • STEPS • STEPS • STEPS

CALCULATING A BREAKEVEN POINT FOR A NEW PRODUCT

① Calculate the contribution margin per unit by subtracting the variable cost per unit from the unit sales price. The contribution margin per unit represents the amount available per unit to cover fixed costs and earn a profit.

② Calculate the unit sales breakeven point by dividing the total fixed costs by the contribution margin per unit. The unit sales breakeven point indicates the number of units that must be sold at the projected unit sales price to cover all variable and fixed costs. If Reflection sells exactly 1,500 units, it will earn no net income, nor will it incur a net loss.

③ Calculate the sales dollar breakeven point by multiplying the unit sales breakeven point by the unit sales price. This calculation gives the revenue earned by selling 1,500 units at the projected sales price, $18.00 per unit.

©GETTY IMAGES/PHOTODISC

Management Decisions Using Cost-Volume-Profit Analysis

Instruct students to prepare a Quick Reference Guide (QRG) for calculating breakeven point. (1) Label a QRG with the title CALCULATING BREAKEVEN POINT. (2) Copy the three steps and formulas out of the chapter narrative. This QRG can be used when students are completing end-of-chapter activities. Additional QRGs could be prepared for other calculations and formulas presented in the chapter.

BREAKEVEN INCOME STATEMENT

Reflection, Inc.
Breakeven Income Statement
For Month Ended July 31, 20--

Operating Revenue:		
Net Sales (28,000 sq. ft. @ $5.00)		$140,000.00
Variable Costs:		
Cost of Merchandise Sold (28,000 sq. ft. @ $3.30)	$92,400.00	
Sales Commission (28,000 sq. ft. @ $.20)	5,600.00	
Delivery Costs (28,000 sq. ft. @ $.40)	11,200.00	
Other Selling Costs (28,000 sq. ft. @ $.15)	4,200.00	
Other Administrative Costs (28,000 sq. ft. @ $.20)	5,600.00	
Total Variable Costs		119,000.00
Contribution Margin		$ 21,000.00
Fixed Costs:		
Rent	$ 2,500.00	
Insurance	400.00	
Other Selling Costs	4,930.00	
Other Administrative Costs	10,720.00	
Other Expenses	2,450.00	
Total Fixed Costs		21,000.00
Net Income		$ –0–

The breakeven income statement above shows the proof for Reflection's breakeven point for mirror sales. If the breakeven point is accurate, net income is zero.

The breakeven income statement is a projection of sales and costs under specific assumptions. Reflection reports projected amounts to the nearest $10. Total sales, *$140,000.00*, is equal to the sales dollar breakeven point. Each variable cost is calculated by multiplying the unit sales breakeven point, *28,000 units*, by the unit variable cost of each cost item. The amount of each fixed cost is taken from the July income statement. The contribution margin, *$21,000.00*, is 15% of net sales, *$140,000.00*. This verifies Reflection's contribution margin rate of 15%.

careers in accounting

CAREERS IN ACCOUNTING • CAREERS IN ACCOUNTING • CAREERS IN ACCOUNTIN

Licensure Requirements for Financial Careers

Do you want to be a nurse? A hairstylist? A teacher? An accountant? These and many other careers require you to have a license. The requirements for a license vary with the career and also vary across the country.

Within the accounting and financial career areas, there are many positions that require licensure. Generally, to get a license, a person must have the right combination of education and experience and also must pass a test. Within one licensure area, the amount of education and experience required can vary from state to state. For example, the Certified Public Accountant license is granted by a governing unit within each state. Therefore, the education and experience requirement in California may be very different from the education and experience requirements in Maine.

Someone hoping to obtain a license of any kind must be very careful to fulfill the requirements for the state in which he or she hopes to practice.

Instructions

Pick a career within the accounting or finance field. Research the requirements for licensure for your particular state. Share your findings with your class.

Determining Breakeven

CAREERS IN ACCOUNTING
CAREERS IN ACCOUNTI

Answers will vary, depending on the licensure chosen and the state. However, most licensures require some combination of work experience, education, and satisfactory completion of an examination.

GUIDED PRACTICE

Term Review

Call on students to define the term in the Term Review. Ask the class if the definition is correct and whether the complete definition has been given or if anything needs to be added. The suggested definition is given in the Glossary.

Audit Your Understanding

Call on students to answer the Audit Your Understanding questions. Ask the class if the answers are correct and/or complete. Answers are given in Appendix E of the textbook.

Work Together

Have students write the solution to the Work Together problems as you guide the class through the problem.

- Discuss each step of the calculation and when the class is in agreement on the method, direct students to write the solution in the Working Papers.

- Discuss each section of the breakeven income statement and when the class is in agreement on a section, direct students to write the solution in the working papers and then continue to the next section.

- Remind students to save their work to complete Work Together 15-3.

INDEPENDENT PRACTICE

On Your Own

- Assign the On Your Own problem to be worked independently.

- Use the Ongoing Assessment techniques to diagnose student understanding.

- Remind students to save their work to complete On Your Own 15-3.

Application Problem

- Assign Application Problem 15-2: Calculating contribution margin and breakeven point.

Personal Trainer

- Students can access the Lesson 15-2 assessment material using this software.

Xtra! Web Site

- Students can access the Xtra! Study Tools for additional practice.

ENRICH

- Assign the Careers in Accounting feature on page 453.

• term review

breakeven point

• audit your understanding

1. In what two ways can the breakeven point be stated?
2. How is the contribution margin per unit used?
3. What is the simplest way to verify the accuracy of a breakeven calculation?

• work together 15-2

Calculating breakeven in sales dollars and unit sales and preparing a breakeven income statement

An income statement for Cherie's Pizza is included in the *Working Papers*. Your instructor will guide you through the following examples.

1. Use the following information to calculate the breakeven point in sales dollars and unit sales for *July*. The August information will be used to complete the On Your Own below.

	July	August
Net Sales	$60,000.00	$80,000.00
Unit Sales Price	$8.00	$8.00
Contribution Margin	$12,000.00	$10,000.00
Total Fixed Costs	$8,000.00	$8,000.00
Unit Variable Cost	$6.40	$7.00

2. Prepare a breakeven income statement for July of the current year. Save your work to complete Work Together 15-3.

• on your own 15-2

Calculating breakeven in sales dollars and unit sales and preparing a breakeven income statement

Use the August information from the Work Together above. An income statement for Cherie's Pizza is included in the *Working Papers*. Work independently to complete this problem.

1. Calculate the breakeven point in sales dollars and unit sales for *August*.
2. Prepare a breakeven income statement for August of the current year. Save your work to complete On Your Own 15-3.

CLOSE

- Ask students to briefly summarize the procedures for calculating the breakeven point.

15-3 Decisions That Affect Net Income

CALCULATING SALES TO EARN PLANNED NET INCOME

Total Fixed Costs	+	Planned Net Income	=	Required Contribution Margin ❶
$21,000.00	+	$1,500.00	=	$22,500.00

Required Contribution Margin	÷	Contribution Margin Rate	=	Sales Dollars ❷
$22,500.00	÷	.15 or 15%	=	$150,000.00

Determining the breakeven point provides management with important information about the relationship of sales, variable costs, and fixed costs. Businesses do not, however, operate merely to break even. Managers need information that will assist them in achieving planned net income. The breakeven analysis can be used to calculate the dollar and unit sales needed to earn a specified amount of planned net income.

FYI
FOR YOUR INFORMATION

Fixed costs for your school might include the depreciation on the building and the principal's salary. These costs are the same no matter how many students are enrolled.

Variable costs for your school might include the cost of computers, cafeteria lunches, and textbooks. These costs will increase or decrease depending on the number of students enrolled.

Identify other costs involved with your school. Are they fixed or variable?

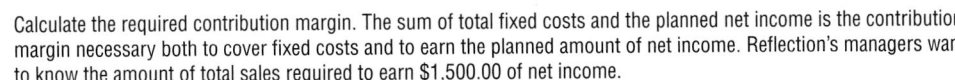

STEPS • STEPS • STEPS • STEPS • STEPS • STEPS • STEPS • STEPS • STEPS • STEPS •

CALCULATING SALES TO EARN PLANNED NET INCOME

❶ Calculate the required contribution margin. The sum of total fixed costs and the planned net income is the contribution margin necessary both to cover fixed costs and to earn the planned amount of net income. Reflection's managers want to know the amount of total sales required to earn $1,500.00 of net income.

❷ Calculate the amount of sales dollars by dividing the required contribution margin by the contribution margin rate. Thus, Reflection must sell 30,000 square feet of mirrors ($150,000.00 total sales *divided by* the unit sales price of $5.00) to earn $1,500.00 of net income.

The required contribution margin, $22,500.00, can be divided by the contribution margin per unit, $0.75, to calculate the number of units to be sold ($22,500.00/$0.75 = 30,000).

Decisions That Affect Net Income

Lesson 15-3   **455**

- Explain that now that students have an understanding of how sales, variable costs, and fixed costs affect contribution margin and net income, it is also desirable to be able to analyze how any change in one of these items would affect net income.

- Explain that some changes that can affect net income are: sales increases or decreases, changes in production methods, decreases in sales price, increases in sales volume, and so on.

- Explain that the relationship among sales, costs, and net income can be expressed as: net sales minus variable costs equals contribution margin; contribution margin minus fixed costs equals net income.

DEMONSTRATE

- Direct students to the illustration or demonstrate on the board how to analyze the effect of volume changes on net income.

- Draw five columns on the board and in the first column write an abbreviated income statement with contribution margin showing Net Sales, Variable Costs, Contribution Margin, Fixed Costs, and Net Income as shown in the table.

- In the second column, write the per unit costs shown in the table.

- Demonstrate calculating the items for each of the three levels of unit sales.

- Direct students to the graph in the illustration as you demonstrate where each level of sales appears on the graph.

- Point out that: when the Sales line is below the Total Costs line, there is a net loss; when the Sales line intersects with the Total Costs line, there is breakeven (no net income or loss); and when the Sales line is above the Total Costs line there is net income.

EFFECT OF VOLUME CHANGES ON NET INCOME

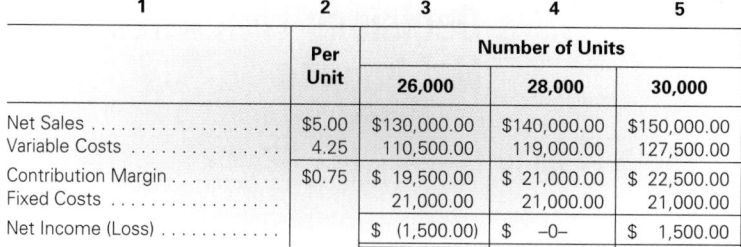

		1	2	3	4	5
			Per Unit	Number of Units		
				26,000	28,000	30,000
Net Sales			$5.00	$130,000.00	$140,000.00	$150,000.00
Variable Costs			4.25	110,500.00	119,000.00	127,500.00
Contribution Margin			$0.75	$ 19,500.00	$ 21,000.00	$ 22,500.00
Fixed Costs				21,000.00	21,000.00	21,000.00
Net Income (Loss)				$ (1,500.00)	$ –0–	$ 1,500.00

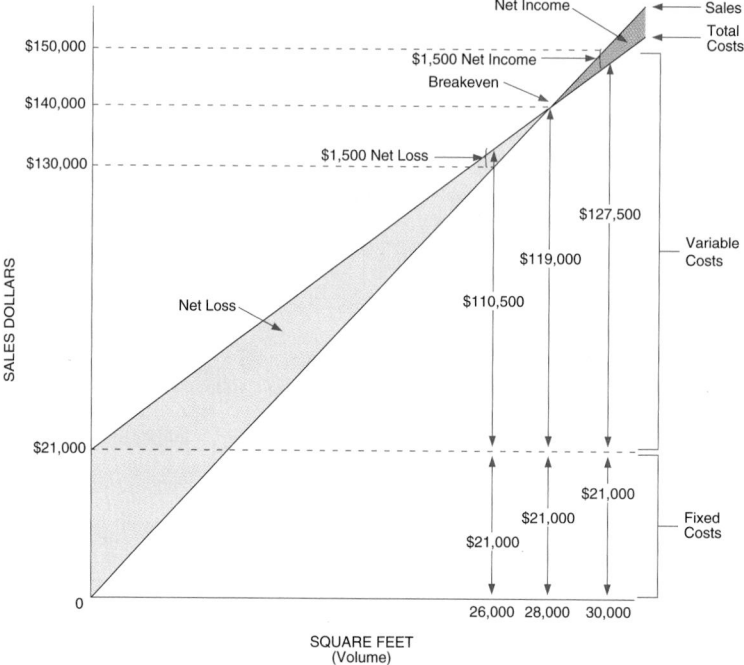

Businesses must be able to determine the change in net income that would result from changes in the relationship of sales, variable costs, and fixed costs. Reflection's managers desire answers to questions such as these: What would net income be if sales increase or decrease? Would it be profitable to change production methods? What would be the effect on net income of a decrease in unit sales price and an increase in sales volume?

Reflection has calculated its unit sales breakeven point to be 28,000 square feet. The table above shows how net income changes for a decrease or an increase of 2,000 units. For each square foot of mirrors Reflection sells, $0.75 of contribution margin is available for fixed costs and net income. At the 28,000 unit breakeven point, the $21,000.00 contribution margin pays for fixed costs, leaving no remaining amount for net income. For each square foot of mirrors above 28,000 units sold, the $0.75 per square foot contribution margin increases net income. Therefore, when 30,000 square feet of mirrors are sold, net income is expected to be $1,500.00 (2,000 square feet × $0.75 contribution margin per unit).

Management Decisions Using Cost-Volume-Profit Analysis

TEACHING STRATEGIES   DIFFERENT LEARNING STYLES

Tactile Learner. Suggest using a calculator with a printed tape to perform mathematical calculations. Better calculators also print the operational signs of calculations (+, −, etc.) for students to trace the steps in a calculation.

If only 26,000 square feet of mirrors are sold during the month, the contribution margin of $19,500.00 would not cover the fixed costs of $21,000.00. At this sales volume, a net loss of $1,500.00 would result.

The graph on the previous page shows the relationship of sales, costs, and net income as the volume changes. The sales line, beginning at zero, represents unit sales price times number of units sold. The total cost line starting at $21,000.00 (total fixed costs) represents the total fixed and variable costs for the number of units sold. No matter what the sales volume is, the fixed costs remain constant. The variable cost area represents 85% of sales regardless of volume.

At the breakeven point, the sales and total costs lines intersect, indicating that neither a net income nor a net loss will occur. If 30,000 square feet of mirrors are sold, the sales line is above the total cost line. At this sales volume, $150,000.00 of sales is higher than the sum of fixed costs ($21,000.00) and variable costs ($127,500.00), resulting in net income of $1,500.00. If sales volume is below 28,000 square feet, the total cost line is above the sales line indicating a net loss.

EFFECT OF COST CHANGES AT AVERAGE VOLUME

	Alternative 1 Manual Cutting			Alternative 2 Automated Cutting		
	Per Unit	Units Sold	Total	Per Unit	Units Sold	Total
Net Sales	$5.00	30,000	$150,000.00	$5.00	30,000	$150,000.00
Variable Costs	4.25	30,000	127,500.00	4.00	30,000	120,000.00
Contribution Margin	$0.75	30,000	$ 22,500.00	$1.00	30,000	$ 30,000.00
Fixed Costs			21,000.00			28,500.00
Net Income (Loss)			$ 1,500.00			$ 1,500.00

Two types of costs, variable and fixed, influence the decisions a company may make. Total variable costs increase or decrease as sales increase or decrease. Total fixed costs remain constant regardless of sales amount.

Reflection's management is concerned that the relatively low contribution margin rate makes increasing net income difficult for the company. Reflection is searching for ways to improve its percentage of net income per sales dollar. An alternate production method is being considered. The new method would automate the cutting of mirrors. A cost comparison of the two methods, Alternative 1 and Alternative 2, is shown above and is described below.

- *Alternative 1: Manual Cutting.* Variable costs per square foot of mirrors are $4.25. Reflection currently pays a crew to cut mirrors to dimensions ordered by its customers. Of the total variable costs, $0.25 per square foot represents the cost of this crew. Fixed costs are $21,000.00 per month.

- *Alternative 2: Automated Cutting.* The company buys an automated cutter and assigns the cutting crew to process orders of new product lines. The variable costs of the mirrors decrease by $0.25 per square foot to $4.00 per square foot. However, the new method requires buying the automated cutter and employing an experienced cutter at a fixed salary. Thus, fixed costs increase by $7,500.00 per month to $28,500.00.

Sales have been averaging about 30,000 square feet of mirrors per month. At a 30,000-unit sales level, net income is the same for both alternatives. With Alternative 2, the contribution margin is higher, but fixed costs also are higher. Thus, the higher fixed costs cancel the higher **contribution margin.**

- Point out that this demonstration is continued for a higher sales volume, 32,000 units instead of 30,000 units.

- Direct students to the illustration at the top of the page as you demonstrate the calculations for the two alternatives at the higher sales level.

- Point out that at this higher sales level, Alternative 2 results in larger contribution dollar amount and therefore greater net income than Alternative 1.

EXPLAIN

- Explain that when everything else is equal, the alternative with the highest contribution margin rate is the best alternative.

- Point out that everything else is rarely equal.

- Explain that the analysis just presented of the two alternatives favors Alternative 2 only at higher levels of sales. Point out that when sales fall below $30,000 Alternative 1 is preferable.

- Point out that higher contribution margin rates are usually desirable but that fixed costs must be in reasonable proportion to expected sales because the contribution margin must cover the fixed costs before there is any net income.

DEMONSTRATE

- Direct students to the illustration in the middle of the page to demonstrate the calculation of the contribution margin rates of the two alternatives.

EFFECT OF COST CHANGES AT ABOVE AVERAGE VOLUME

	Alternative 1 Manual Cutting			Alternative 2 Automated Cutting		
	Per Unit	Units Sold	Total	Per Unit	Units Sold	Total
Net Sales	$5.00	32,000	$160,000.00	$5.00	32,000	$160,000.00
Variable Costs	4.25	32,000	136,000.00	4.00	32,000	128,000.00
Contribution Margin	$0.75	32,000	$ 24,000.00	$1.00	32,000	$ 32,000.00
Fixed Costs			21,000.00			28,500.00
Net Income (Loss)			$ 3,000.00			$ 3,500.00

Reflection is planning to increase unit sales. A cost comparison with a sales volume of 32,000 units is shown above. With the increased sales volume, Alternative 2 earns a higher net income.

If Reflection expects a permanent sales increase, Alternative 2 would be more profitable than Alternative 1.

EFFECT OF CHANGES IN COSTS ON CONTRIBUTION MARGIN RATE

	Alternative 1 Manual Cutting		Alternative 2 Automated Cutting	
	Dollars	Percent	Dollars	Percent
Net Sales	$150,000.00	100%	$150,000.00	100%
Variable Costs	127,500.00	85%	120,000.00	80%
Contribution Margin	$ 22,500.00	15%	$ 30,000.00	20%

1. Contribution margin rate, Alternative 1.

2. Contribution margin rate, Alternative 2.

As long as sales increase as expected, Alternative 2 will be favored. However, if sales do not increase, the results will be much different. If the number of units actually sold falls below 30,000, the results will favor Alternative 1.

What is the reason for the change in favorable alternatives? The contribution margin rate favors Alternative 2. The illustration above shows that the contribution margin rate for Alternative 1 is 15% versus 20% for Alternative 2. This means that for every $1.00 of sales from Alternative 1, $0.15 is available for fixed costs and net income. But for every $1.00 of sales from Alternative 2, $0.20 is available for fixed costs and net income.

A higher contribution margin rate is usually desirable. However, fixed costs must also be reasonable since the contribution margin must

cover the fixed costs before any net income is earned. The contribution margin rate, *20%*, for the automated cutting method is more favorable. But fixed costs are $28,500.00—$7,500.00 more than fixed costs for the manual cutting method. If sales volume declines, the increased contribution margin is not enough to recover the increased fixed costs. Therefore a reduction in net income occurs.

A logical conclusion is "everything else being equal, the activity with the higher contribution margin rate is more profitable." If "everything else" is equal, selecting the more profitable choice is very simple. However, alternatives are seldom that simple because fixed costs probably differ for each alternative. Therefore, an effective business looks for the best combination of fixed and variable costs.

Management Decisions Using Cost-Volume-Profit Analysis

TEACHING STRATEGIES EXPANDING BEYOND THE CLASSROOM

Invite a manager from a local business to talk to the class about important cost considerations that influence a manager's business decisions. Advise the speaker in advance that students have been studying fixed and variable costs and breakeven analysis applied to business decisions so that the speaker is not blindsided on a topic he or she may not be prepared to discuss.

EFFECT OF CHANGE IN SALES PRICE

	Current Price			Price Reduction and Sales Volume Increase		
	Per Unit	Units Sold	Total	Per Unit	Units Sold	Total
Net Sales.................	$5.00	30,000	$150,000.00	$4.75	36,000	$171,000.00
Variable Costs..............	4.25	30,000	127,500.00	4.25	36,000	153,000.00
Contribution Margin...........	$0.75	30,000	$ 22,500.00	$0.50	36,000	$ 18,000.00
Fixed Costs.................			21,000.00			21,000.00
Net Income (Loss)...........			$ 1,500.00			$ (3,000.00)

Setting the sales price of a product is extremely important. If the price is set too high, potential customers will buy from another business. If the price is set too low, the company may not earn enough money to cover costs and may suffer a loss. The objective is to set sales prices that provide a reasonable amount of net income while keeping prices competitive.

Reflection earned record net income in July, selling 36,000 units. Unfortunately, Reflection's managers believe that a price reduction is necessary to sustain this sales volume. Management is considering a plan to reduce unit sales price by 5% (from $5.00 to $4.75). Management projects that the price decrease will result in a 20% increase in the average number of units sold

(from 30,000 to 36,000 units). Should Reflection implement this price reduction? The illustration above shows the effect of this price change on sales volume and net income.

Price cutting can be dangerous. In July, Reflection had a $0.75 contribution margin per square foot of mirrors sold. Average sales of 30,000 units resulted in $22,500.00 total contribution margin. A unit sales price reduction of 5% ($0.25 per unit) to $4.75 per unit reduces the contribution margin to $0.50, a 33⅓% reduction. The potential results of a price cut can be calculated. The unit sales required to maintain the net income using the new contribution margin is calculated as follows.

Contribution Margin	÷	New Contribution Margin per Unit	=	Unit Sales Required to Maintain Planned Net Income
$22,500.00	÷	$0.50	=	45,000 units

A decrease in unit sales price from $5.00 to $4.75 is projected to increase average sales from 30,000 to 36,000 units. However, at $4.75, the company would have to sell a total of 45,000 units to maintain the same net income as current sales at the $5.00 price. Reducing the unit sales price by $0.25 would not be a profitable decision if the company can sell only 36,000 units.

 FYI FOR YOUR INFORMATION

Spreadsheet software is an ideal tool to use for calculating breakeven and for analyzing the effect of price, cost, and sales mix changes. An effective spreadsheet identifies the variables used in an analysis, for example units sold, price per unit, variable costs, and fixed costs. The analysis is built by creating formulas that reference these variables. When the amounts of the variables are changed, the spreadsheet instantly recalculates the analysis and displays the results.

- Explain the importance of setting prices at levels that will not discourage customers but will earn enough to cover costs and net income.
- Point out that reducing prices also reduces contribution margin, so there must be an increase in sales volume to maintain the same net income.
- Explain that the abbreviated income statement format can be used to analyze the effect of a price cut.
- Direct students to the F.Y.I. for information about using spreadsheet software for breakeven analysis.

DEMONSTRATE

- Direct students to the illustration as you demonstrate the effects of a price cut and a sales volume increase.
- Explain that contribution margin dropped 33.3% *($0.25 decrease divided by $0.75)* while units sold increased only 20% *(6,000 increase divided by 30,000)*. Point out that even with the sales volume increase, a net loss resulted from the price decrease.
- Use the board to demonstrate the calculation for unit sales required to maintain net income with a price cut. Point out that in the example 45,000 units were required to maintain net income but sales were forecast to increase to only 36,000. Therefore, a price cut will not achieve the desired net income.

TEACHING STRATEGIES   DIFFERENT LEARNING ABILITIES

Limited English Proficiency (LEP) Students. LEP students, like visual learners, require a variety of visual clues to support the lesson and help them understand abstract ideas. Use transparencies, textbook illustrations, and software demonstrations to provide these clues.

- Explain that breakeven analysis can also be used for a sales mix (relative distribution of sales among various products).

- Point out that a sales mix must be calculated from information on the income statement before breakeven analysis can be calculated.

- Explain that after a sales mix percentage is calculated for each product, the usual breakeven analysis is calculated to determine the total sales dollars required for the desired net income. Then the sales mix percentages are applied to the total sales dollars to determine the quantity of sales for each product.

- Explain that in the example given, the goal is to increase monthly net income to $10,000 from the $6,000 shown on the income statement.

DEMONSTRATE

- Direct students to the income statement in the illustration as you demonstrate how the income statement shows information about net sales and variable costs for the two products, televisions and VCRs.

- Use the board to demonstrate the calculations for sales mix shown in the math box.

- Demonstrate the first step in the calculation: calculating the sales mix.

- Demonstrate dividing the total sales, $75,000, by the product sales for Televisions, $52,500. Explain that the percentage that results is the percentage of sales represented by televisions, 70%.

- Demonstrate dividing the total sales, $75,000, by the product sales for VCRs, $22,500. Explain that the percentage that results is the percentage of sales represented by VCRs, 30%.

USING BREAKEVEN TO PLAN SALES MIX

VideoPort, Inc.
Income Statement
For Month Ended November 30, 20--

Operating Revenue:		
Net Sales		
Televisions (150 units @ $350)	$52,500.00	
VCRs (90 units @ $250)	22,500.00	$75,000.00
Variable Costs:		
Televisions (150 units @ $210)	$31,500.00	
VCRs (90 units @ $150)	13,500.00	45,000.00
Contribution Margin		$30,000.00
Fixed Costs		24,000.00
Net Income		$ 6,000.00

	Product Sales	÷	Net Sales	=	Sales Mix	
Television	$52,500.00	÷	$75,000.00	=	70%	❶
VCR	$22,500.00	÷	$75,000.00	=	30%	

Contribution Margin	÷	Net Sales	=	Contribution Margin Rate	
$30,000.00	÷	$75,000.00	=	.40 or 40%	❷

Total Fixed Costs	+	Planned Net Income	=	Required Contribution Margin	
$24,000.00	+	$10,000.00	=	$34,000.00	❸

Required Contribution Margin	÷	Contribution Margin Rate	=	Total Sales Dollars	
$34,000.00	÷	.40 or 40%	=	$85,000.00	❹

	Sales Mix	×	Total Sales Dollars	=	Product Sales Dollars	
Television	70%	×	$85,000.00	=	$59,500.00	❺
VCR	30%	×	$85,000.00	=	$25,500.00	

	Product Sales Dollars	÷	Unit Sales Price	=	Product Unit Sales	
Television	$59,500.00	÷	$350.00	=	170 units	❻
VCR	$25,500.00	÷	$250.00	=	102 units	

Businesses that sell two or more products can also use breakeven point calculations to assist managers in planning. Relative distribution of sales among various products is called **sales mix**. The sales mix must be calculated to determine the breakeven point for a company that sells more than one product. VideoPort, Inc. sells televisions and videocassette recorders (VCRs). The income statement above reports VideoPort's sales and cost information for the month ended November 30.

VideoPort expects the relationship of television to VCR sales to remain relatively stable in future months. However, management has indicated its objective to improve monthly net income to $10,000.00. How many televisions and VCRs should VideoPort plan to purchase and sell?

The procedures used to calculate sales to earn a planned net income are similar to those previously described in this chapter. Six steps are used to calculate sales of more than one product to earn a planned net income.

Management Decisions Using Cost-Volume-Profit Analysis

TEACHING STRATEGIES   DIFFERENT LEARNING STYLES

Visual Learner. Formulas, such as those used to calculate contribution rate, should be illustrated on the chalkboard to assist visual learners. The instructor should also complete the calculations for several different situations to show the process to visual learners.

STEPS

SALES MIX NEEDED TO EARN PLANNED NET INCOME

1 Calculate the sales mix using information from the income statement. Net sales are divided by the sales amounts for each product. The total product mix must equal 100%.

2 Calculate the contribution margin rate by dividing the contribution margin shown on the income statement by net sales.

3 Add total fixed costs and the planned net income to determine the required contribution margin.

4 Divide the required contribution margin by the contribution margin rate to determine the total sales dollars.

5 Multiply the sales mix percentage by the total sales dollars to determine the sales dollars needed for each product.

6 Divide the product sales dollars by the unit sales price to determine product unit sales. The unit sales prices are found on the income statement. The product unit sales indicate the number of units of each product that must be sold to achieve the planned net income of $10,000.00.

Managers of the television and VCR departments can now plan to accomplish these sales objectives. For example, the television department manager knows that the department must sell 20 more televisions (170 − 150 = 20) each month. Thus, the manager can plan to increase purchases and devise new sales promotion and advertising campaigns to sell the increased number of televisions.

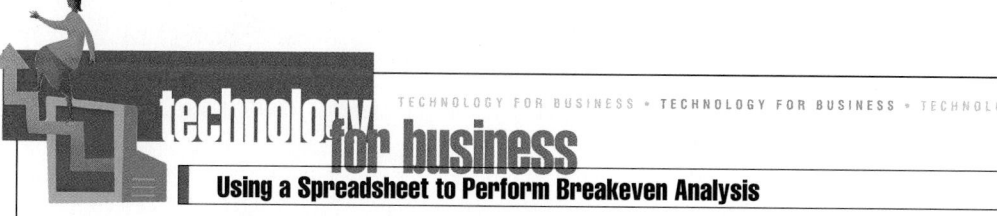

technology for business

TECHNOLOGY FOR BUSINESS · **TECHNOLOGY FOR BUSINESS** · TECHNOLOGY FOR BUSINE

Using a Spreadsheet to Perform Breakeven Analysis

Micron, Inc., a large wholesaler, plans to introduce a new product line next year. Three lines are being considered. Micron performs extensive market research on potential new product lines. The three lines being considered have tested well.

To make the final decision among the three product lines, management has decided that the line with the lowest breakeven point will be added. The following data are available for the three product lines:

Required

1. Create a spreadsheet that calculates the breakeven point for the three product lines. Use descriptive column headings and row titles. [Hint: Develop the breakeven formula for the Line A. Use the Copy command to copy the formula for Lines B and C.]

2. From your analysis, which line should Micron add next year?

	Line A	Line B	Line C
Sales price per unit	$42.00	$48.00	$46.00
Variable costs per unit	18.00	26.00	14.00
Fixed costs	$14,600.00	$11,800.00	$27,200.00

TECHNOLOGY FOR BUSINESS
TECHNOLOGY FOR BUSINESS

The Technology for Business feature is designed to show students common business applications of technology. This feature suggests the use of a spreadsheet for performing breakeven analysis.

GUIDED PRACTICE

Term Review

Call on students to define the term in the Term Review. Ask the class if the definition is correct and whether the complete definition has been given or if anything needs to be added. Suggested definitions for all terms are given in the Glossary.

Audit Your Understanding

Call on students to answer the Audit Your Understanding questions. Ask the class if each answer is correct and/or complete. Answers are given in Appendix E of the textbook.

Work Together

Have students write the solution to the Work Together problem as you guide the class through the examples. Remind students to use the problem started in Work Together 15-2.

- For each calculation, call on students to state the answer to a calculation.

- Call on another student to explain either how the amount was calculated or where the amount was obtained.

INDEPENDENT PRACTICE

On Your Own

- Assign the On Your Own problem to be worked independently. Remind students to use the problem started in On Your Own 15-2.

- Use the Ongoing Assessment techniques to diagnose student understanding.

Application Problems

- Assign Application Problem 15-3: Calculating plans for net income.

- Assign Application Problem 15-4: Calculating the effects on net income of changes in unit sales price, variable costs, fixed costs, and volume.

- Assign Application Problem 15-5: Calculating sales mix.

Personal Trainer

- Students can access the Lesson 15-3 assessment material using this software.

Xtra! Web Site

- Students can access the Xtra! Study Tools for additional practice.

• term review

sales mix

• audit your understanding

1. What two types of costs influence management's decisions?

2. To earn a planned net income, the required contribution margin must equal what two amounts?

• work together 15-3

Calculating sales to earn a planned net income, calculating the effect of volume changes on net income, and calculating the effect of changes in selling price

Use the working papers and data from Work Together 15-2. Forms for completing this Work Together are provided in the *Working Papers*. Your instructor will guide you through the following examples.

1. Assume that Cherie's Pizza wants a net income for July of $3,000. Calculate the amount of sales dollars needed to achieve this net income.

2. Determine the net income or loss if: (a) 4,000 units are sold; (b) 5,000 units are sold; (c) 6,000 units are sold.

3. Assume Cherie's Pizza normally sells 7,500 pizzas in July. If the selling price is reduced by $.50, Cherie's expects to sell 9,000 pizzas. Calculate the effect on net income of this change.

• on your own 15-3

Calculating sales to earn a planned net income, calculating the effect of volume changes on net income, and calculating the effect of changes in selling price

Use the working papers and data from On Your Own 15-2. Forms for completing this On Your Own are provided in the *Working Papers*. Work independently to complete this problem.

1. Assume Cherie's Pizza wants a net income for August of $3,000. Calculate the amount of sales dollars needed to achieve this net income.

2. Determine the net income or loss if: (a) 7,000 units are sold; (b) if 8,000 units are sold; (c) 9,000 units are sold.

3. Assume Cherie's Pizza normally sells 10,000 pizzas in August. If the selling price is increased by $.50, Cherie's expects to sell 9,500 pizzas. Calculate the effect on net income of this change.

---

462 Chapter 15 Management Decisions Using Cost-Volume-Profit Analysis

ENRICH

- Assign the Technology for Business feature on page 461. Students can practice writing formulas on paper rather than actually booting spreadsheet software if time is a factor.

CLOSE

- Ask students to summarize the purpose of breakeven analysis.

- Ask students to explain what the contribution margin must be large enough to cover.

SUMMARY · SUMMARY · SUMMARY

After completing this chapter, you can

1. Define terms related to accounting information for management decisions.

2. Identify accounting concepts and practices related to preparing accounting information for management decisions.

3. Prepare an income statement reporting contribution margin.

4. Calculate the contribution margin rate.

5. Calculate the breakeven point.

6. Calculate the sales dollars and sales units required to earn a planned amount of net income.

7. Determine the effect of changes in sales volume, unit costs, and unit sales prices on net income.

8. Calculate a sales mix.

Explore Accounting

EXPLORE ACCOUNTING · EXPLORE ACCOUNTING · EXPLORE ACCOUN

Mixed Costs

A cost having both fixed and variable characteristics is called a mixed cost. For example, Mason Castings uses natural gas to operate a casting furnace. Even if the company processes no castings, keeping the furnace heated incurs a cost—a fixed cost. The gas required to maintain a constant furnace temperature increases with the number of castings produced—a variable cost. Thus, natural gas expense is a mixed cost.

A statistical method used to determine the fixed and variable costs of a mixed cost is called regression analysis. Natural gas expense for the past six months can be used to estimate the fixed and variable costs.

Units	Temperature	Expense
4,653	28	$5,507
4,657	34	5,869
5,423	43	6,791
6,754	47	7,697
5,876	58	7,918
6,137	78	9,249

Using the number of units produced and the average outdoor temperature in the multiple regression equation allows management to estimate that the fixed cost is $1,500 and that variable costs are $60 for every degree of temperature and $.50 for every unit produced. With this information, management can accurately estimate future expenses.

Required:
Use the multiple regression tool of an electronic spreadsheet and the following six-month actual cost information to determine the fixed and variable amounts of labor costs. Assume that the number of units produced and the number of production days have an impact on labor costs. (Hint: Identify the cost as the dependent, y, variable and the units and days as independent, x, variables.)

Units	Days	Cost
675	15	$10,025
867	18	11,801
768	20	12,304
978	22	13,728
965	20	12,895
875	18	11,825

Management Decisions Using Cost-Volume-Profit Analysis

EXPLORE ACCOUNTING
EXPLORE ACCOUNTING

This Explore Accounting is intended for advanced or gifted students who have a good mathematics background. Although the computer will handle the complex array of calculations, the results may not be obvious. Students should look in the Help topics of the spreadsheet for information about multiple regression. In Excel, for example, the LINEST function is used to create the necessary array. The fixed and variable costs using the LINEST function are: $2,011.57 fixed + $3.00 per unit + $399.38 per day. The last two components are the variable components.

PUTTING IT ALL TOGETHER

- Review the Chapter Summary.
- Ask students to prepare a list of the new concepts introduced in this chapter.
- Discuss the methods presented in this chapter to make management decisions.

INDEPENDENT PRACTICE

- Assign Mastery Problem 15-6 to students who need the reinforcement of a problem that combines all concepts from the chapter in one problem; this will be most students.
- Assign Challenge Problem 15-7 to accelerated students who do not require the reinforcement of the Mastery Problem.
- Assign Study Guide Chapter 15.
- Students can access Personal Trainer to work end-of-chapter problems on the computer.
- Students can access the Xtra! Web Site for the Xtra! Review and Quizzing.
- Students can access the Student Companion CD for additional review material.

ONGOING ASSESSMENT

Review solutions to the assigned problems in class, diagnosing trouble spots.

RETEACH

- Call on students to describe how they avoid the trouble spots diagnosed.
- Use reteaching suggestions from lesson plans as required.
- Assign Recycling Problem 15-1 if needed.

ENRICH

- Assign the Explore Accounting Feature. Ask students to share the information they have gathered in a report to the class.
- Students can access the Xtra! Web Site for the Xtra! Enrichment material.
- Assign Applied Communication.
- Assign the Cases for Critical Thinking.
- Assign the SCANS Workplace Competency.
- Assign Graphing Workshop.
- Assign Analyzing Costco's Financial Statements.
- Assign the Automated Accounting feature on pages 470–471.

15-1 APPLICATION PROBLEM

Preparing an income statement reporting contribution margin

Milford Pump Company's income statement has been prepared for November of the current year.

Milford Pump Company Income Statement For Month Ended November 30, 20--		
Operating Revenue:		
Net Sales (8,700 units @ $210.00)		$1,827,000.00
Cost of Merchandise Sold (8,700 units @ $145.00)		1,261,500.00
Gross Profit on Operations		$ 565,500.00
Operating Expenses:		
Selling Expenses:		
Sales Commission (8,700 units @ $6.00)	$52,200.00	
Delivery Costs (8,700 units @ $4.80)	41,760.00	
Other Variable Costs (8,700 units @ $2.75)	23,925.00	
Other Fixed Costs	76,510.00	$194,395.00
Administrative Expenses:		
Rent	$15,000.00	
Insurance	9,750.00	
Other Variable Costs (8,700 units @ $5.50)	47,850.00	
Other Fixed Costs	45,290.00	117,890.00
Total Operating Expenses		312,285.00
Income from Operations		$ 253,215.00
Other Expenses		12,000.00
Net Income		$ 241,215.00

Instructions:
1. Prepare Milford Pump Company's November income statement reporting contribution margin.
2. Calculate the contribution margin per unit.
3. Calculate variable cost per unit. Plot variable costs and fixed costs on a graph.

15-2 APPLICATION PROBLEM

Calculating contribution margin and breakeven point

Farris Electronics is considering expanding its product line to include portable radios. Management projects that radios would sell for $60.00 each. Variable costs are projected to be $25.00 with total fixed costs of $42,000.00 per month.

Instructions:
1. Calculate the contribution margin per unit.
2. Calculate the unit sales breakeven point.
3. Calculate the sales dollar breakeven point.
4. Farris has projected that it could sell 1,000 units per month. Should the company expand its product line to sell the portable radios? Support your answer.

APPLIED SKILLS MATHEMATICS

This chapter introduces many different formulas and calculations that will be new to students. When necessary, create additional data for students to practice calculations they have problems with.

15-3 APPLICATION PROBLEM

Calculating plans for net income

Dennis Williams is projecting the coming year's net income potential for Williams Paint. The paint is sold for $15.00 a gallon. Variable costs per gallon are $10.00, and annual fixed costs are $135,000.00. Complete each of the following instructions independently of the others.

Instructions:
1. Calculate the (a) unit sales and (b) sales dollar breakeven points.
2. If a $50,000.00 annual net income is planned, calculate the required (a) number of gallons of paint to be sold and (b) sales dollars.
3. Dennis plans to purchase a new paint mixing machine that would reduce the cost of paint by $0.50 per gallon but increase annual fixed costs by $52,000.00. Calculate the (a) unit sales and (b) sales dollar breakeven points. Should Dennis purchase the mixing machine? Explain your answer.

15-4 APPLICATION PROBLEM

Calculating the effects on net income of changes in unit sales price, variable costs, fixed costs, and volume

The following information pertains to a product sold by Gomez Company:

Unit Sales Price	$12.00
Unit Variable Costs	$9.60
Unit Contribution Margin	$2.40
Fixed Costs	$48,000.00

Instructions:
1. Determine the net income or loss
   a. if 17,000 units are sold.
   b. if 20,000 units are sold.
   c. if 23,000 units are sold.
2. Gomez Company is considering purchasing equipment that would reduce the unit variable cost to $8.50. However, fixed costs would increase to $58,000.
   a. If 20,000 units were expected to be sold, would Gomez Company's net income increase if the new equipment were purchased and used?
   b. If only 17,000 units were expected to be sold, would Gomez Company's net income increase if the new equipment were purchased and used?
3. Gomez Company believes that a 10% reduction in the unit sales price would result in a 30% increase in the number of units sold. Assume that normal sales volume before any price reduction was 20,000 units. Assume also that the equipment described in instruction 2 was not purchased, so that the fixed costs and unit variable costs were $48,000.00 and $9.60, respectively. Would the reduction in sales price increase or decrease net income?

Application Problem 15-3

1. a. 27,000 units.
   b. 405,000.
2. a. 37,000 units.
   b. 555,000.
3. a. 34,000 units.
   b. 510,000.

Application Problem 15-4

1. a. 7,200 loss.
   b. 0.
   c. 7,200.
2. a. 0; 12,000.
   b. 7,200 loss; 1,500.
3. 0 at current price; 16,800 loss at price reduction.

APPLIED SKILLS LANGUAGE ARTS

Using Adjectives and Adverbs. When you assign one or more of the activities in this chapter that require a written response, direct students to underline the adjectives in their writing and circle the adverbs. Suggest that if their writing has very few adjectives and adverbs, using more of them could enhance their writing.

Application Problem 15-5

a. 40,000/100,000 = 40%;
   60,000/100,000 = 60%.

b. 40,000/100,000 = 40%.

c. 38,000 + 10,000 = 48,000;
   48,000/40% = 120,000.

d. 40% × 120,000 = 48,000;
   60% × 120,000 = 72,000.

e. 48,000/40 = 1,200 units;
   72,000/250 = 288 units.

Mastery Problem 15-6

1. Contribution Margin = 18,750.

2. 18,750/75,000 = 25%.

3. 11,600/25% = 46,400.

4. 46,400/25 = 1,856 units.

5. a. 26,000/25% = 106,400.

   b. 106,400/25 = 4,256 units.

6. Current machines, 7,150; Computer based machines, 9,750.

466

15-5 APPLICATION PROBLEM

Calculating sales mix

Schenk, Inc., sells desk lamps and desks. The following information is from the June income statement. Schenk's management is interested in knowing the number of lamps and desks it must sell to earn $10,000.00 of net income.

Schenk, Inc.
Income Statement
For Month Ended June 30, 20--

Net Sales:		
Lamps (1,000 @ $40.00)	$40,000.00	
Desks (240 @ $250.00)	60,000.00	
Total Net Sales		$100,000.00
Variable Costs:		
Lamps (1,000 @ $30.00)	$30,000.00	
Desks (240 @ $125.00)	30,000.00	
Total Variable Costs		60,000.00
Contribution Margin		$ 40,000.00
Fixed Costs		38,000.00
Net Income		$ 2,000.00

Instructions:

Schenk's managers need sales information assuming that the company earns $10,000.00 of monthly net income. Calculate the following amounts to achieve the $10,000.00 planned net income.

a. Sales mix.
b. Contribution margin rate.
c. Total sales dollars.

d. Product sales dollars.
e. Product unit sales.

15-6 MASTERY PROBLEM

Calculating contribution margin and breakeven point; calculating sales dollars and unit sales for planned net income

Ratliff Corporation produces lawn fertilizer spreaders. Ratliff's income statement shown on the next page has been prepared for August of the current year.

Instructions:

1. Prepare Ratliff's August income statement reporting contribution margin.
2. Calculate the contribution margin rate.
3. Calculate the sales dollar breakeven point.
4. Calculate the unit sales breakeven point.
5. If a $15,000.00 monthly net income is planned, calculate the required (a) sales dollars and (b) unit sales.
6. Ratliff is considering using computer-based machines to increase the productivity of the manufacturing process. The new machines would reduce variable costs by $4.20 per unit but increase monthly fixed costs by $10,000.00. Calculate the projected net income assuming that Ratliff sells 3,000 units. Should Ratliff purchase the machines? Explain your answer.

Management Decisions Using Cost-Volume-Profit Analysis

APPLIED SKILLS   WRITING ACROSS THE CURRICULUM

Writing Paragraphs and Short Essays. The Cases for Critical Thinking are short, practical applications of the accounting principles developed in the chapter. Some cases are planned to present problems related to the chapter but not specifically discussed and answered in the chapter. These cases present an opportunity for critical thinking and decision making. These cases also require more than a short objective-type response. Therefore they provide ideal practice in writing paragraphs and short essays.

Ratliff Corporation
Income Statement
For Month Ended August 31, 20--

Operating Revenue:		
Net Sales (3,000 units @ $25.00)		$75,000.00
Cost of Merchandise Sold (3,000 units @ $16.00)		48,000.00
Gross Profit on Operations		$27,000.00
Operating Expenses:		
Selling Expenses:		
Sales Commission (3,000 units @ $0.60)	$1,800.00	
Delivery Costs (3,000 units @ $0.75)	2,250.00	
Other Variable Costs (3,000 units @ $1.15)	3,450.00	
Other Fixed Costs	3,590.00	$11,090.00
Administrative Expenses:		
Rent	$1,000.00	
Insurance	600.00	
Other Variable Costs (3,000 units @ $0.25)	750.00	
Other Fixed Costs	5,610.00	7,960.00
Total Operating Expenses		19,050.00
Income from Operations		$ 7,950.00
Other Expenses		800.00
Net Income		$ 7,150.00

15-7 CHALLENGE PROBLEM

Calculating the effects on net income of changes in unit sales price, variable costs, and fixed costs

Millard, Inc., sold 68,000 computer printers last year with the following results.

Millard, Inc.
Income Statement
For Year Ended December 31, 20--

Net Sales (68,000 units @ $250.00)	$17,000,000.00
Less Variable Costs (68,000 units @ $200.00)	13,600,000.00
Contribution Margin	$ 3,400,000.00
Less Fixed Costs	2,980,000.00
Net Income	$ 420,000.00

Complete each of the following instructions independently of the others.

Instructions:

1. Millard projects that it can sell 75,000 printers next year at the current $250.00 unit sales price. However, management believes that it can increase net income by selling its printer below the unit sales price of its competitors. Millard's marketing department projects that it could sell 100,000 printers at a unit sales price of $230.00. Calculate the projected net income. Should Millard reduce the unit sales price to $230.00? Explain your answer.
2. Millard currently purchases the power cable from another manufacturer at a cost of $7.00 per unit. The company is considering producing the cable. Millard projects that it can produce the cable for $2.00 each plus annual fixed costs of $240,000.00. Calculate the projected net income assuming a sales volume of 75,000 printers. Should Millard produce the power cables? Explain your answer.

Challenge Problem 15-7

1. Current, 770,000; decreased, 20,000.
2. Purchase, 770,000; produce, 905,000.

• applied communication

APPLIED COMMUNICATION

Charts and graphs are often used to help people understand numbers. To be helpful, charts and graphs must be clearly labeled.

Required:

1. Use the data from Application Problem 15-4, Instruction 1, to prepare a graph similar to the one on page 456. Label the graph clearly.

2. Prepare a brief written explanation of the graph.

• cases for critical thinking

CASES FOR CRITICAL THINKING • CASES FOR CRITICAL THINKING

Case 1
George Edmonds, the new accountant for Zigler Company, has recommended the preparation of income statements reporting contribution margin rather than statements reporting gross profit. He states that the income statement with contribution margin provides better information. Kimberly Johnson, the manager, disagrees that one statement is better than the other. She says gross profit is the same as contribution margin, so it does not make any difference which statement is prepared. Which person is correct? Explain.

Case 2
Denise Young, an accountant for Chiles Corporation, has been asked to prepare an income statement that reports contribution margin. Miss Young has asked you to prepare an analysis of three months' costs. Provide Miss Young with an analysis of these data that include the unit cost of variable costs and monthly costs of fixed costs. Explain to Miss Young how you prepared your analysis.

	May	June	July
Unit Sales	400	500	600
Cost of Merchandise Sold	$8,000.00	$10,000.00	$12,000.00
Advertising Expense	2,300.00	2,300.00	2,300.00
Depreciation Expense	1,000.00	1,000.00	1,000.00
Payroll Taxes Expense	640.00	800.00	960.00
Rent Expense	2,000.00	2,000.00	2,000.00
Salary Expense	3,200.00	4,000.00	4,800.00
Supplies Expense	1,200.00	1,200.00	1,200.00
Utilities Expense	600.00	750.00	900.00

• SCANS workplace competency

SCANS WORKPLACE COMPETENCY

Interpersonal Competency: Serving Clients and Customers

Concept: Competent employees work and communicate with clients and customers to satisfy their expectations. They listen carefully to customer needs to avoid misunderstanding, remain positive when handling complaints, and are familiar with remedies to satisfy customer needs.

Application: Some companies promote the policy that "the customer is always right." Why do such businesses respect their clients or customers so highly? How important is good customer service? Form a task group of 3-4 students and brainstorm ideas. Discuss your group's suggestions with the class.

GRAPHING WORKSHOP

graphing workshop

Baumann Industries is considering purchasing NewMark Corporation. Baumann's board of directors has requested a breakeven analysis, based on cost data provided by NewMark's accounting department. Analyze the graph below by answering the following questions.

1. Identify each of the four lines (labeled A–D) in the graph.
2. Estimate the breakeven point in dollars and units.
3. Estimate NewMark's profit if the company can sell 9,000 units.

Breakeven Analysis for NewMark Corporation

analyzing Costco's financial statements

The average Costco warehouse in the United States generates an average of $112,000,000 of net sales, with 11 warehouses exceeding $200,000,000. When opening a new warehouse, Costco managers will measure the warehouse's success by how quickly its sales exceed the breakeven point.

Instructions:

Assume that Costco's selling, general, and administrative (SG&A) expenses are fixed costs and that merchandise costs are the only variable costs. Use this information for fiscal year 2003 to calculate a breakeven point per warehouse. Round dollar amounts to the nearest thousand dollars.

1. Calculate the average number of warehouses open during 2003 by adding the beginning- and end-of-year amounts and dividing by 2.
2. Calculate SG&A expenses per warehouse.
3. Calculate the contribution margin rate.
4. Use this information to calculate breakeven sales dollars for 2003.

Management Decisions Using Cost-Volume-Profit Analysis

Chapter 15 **469**

GRAPHING WORKSHOP

GRAPHING WORKSHOP

1. A - Sales
   B - Total Costs
   C - Variable Costs
   D - Fixed Costs
2. Sales of $150,000 and 6,000 units.
3. 30,000.

**ANALYZING COSTCO'S
FINANCIAL STATEMENTS**

ANALYZING COSTCO'S FINAN

1. (374 + 397)/2 = 385.5.
2. 4,097,000,000/385.5 = 10,628,000.
3. 100.0% − 89.3% = 10.7%.
4. 10,628,000/10.7% = 99,327,000.

TEACHING STRATEGIES PORTFOLIO ASSESSMENT

Proper and accurate accounting for fixed and variable costs is critical to a business because so many decisions are based on analyzing this information. If the information is incorrect, poor decisions may result and could cause a business to fail. Students should emphasize their learning of this topic by selecting an example of a comprehensive sample of their work in this chapter, either the mastery problem or a problem from a test to include in their portfolio. A copy of the Portfolio Assessment form (blackline master in the Teacher's Resource Guide; also on the Student Companion CD) should be completed by the student and the Description section should include any comments regarding how the student mastered these concepts and procedures. Alternatively, students might include in their portfolios printed reports from an Automated Accounting problem.

- Point out that the Automated Accounting software will generate financial statements with either horizontal trend analysis or vertical trend analysis.

- Describe horizontal trend analysis as analysis that compares the ending balance for the current period with the ending balance of the previous fiscal period and reports the difference and percentage change.

- Describe vertical trend analysis as analysis that shows the relationship of the component parts to the whole.

- Point out that income statement items are expressed as a percentage of total revenue.

- Point out that on the balance sheet, assets are expressed as a percentage of total assets while liabilities and stockholders' equity items are expressed as a percentage of total liabilities and stockholders' equity.

- Point out that in Automated Accounting 8.0, vertical analysis is included for both the current and previous fiscal periods for additional comparison.

Preparing a financial analysis report

- Click the Reports toolbar button.
- Click Financial Analysis from the Select a Report Group list.
- Choose one of the vertical or horizontal analysis reports from the Choose a Report to Display list.
- Click OK to display the report.
- Click the Print button to print the report or the Copy button to copy the report to another application.

Using Computerized Reports for Management Decisions

The accounting department of a business is responsible for generating financial reports. Managers use these reports to make informed business decisions. Individuals working as sales managers, production managers, purchasing managers, or in any other department of the business must be able to interpret accounting information to plan for and organize their business. Financial reports are also used for decision making by owners, investors, and lenders.

A computerized accounting system can provide a variety of timely reports to managers. These reports help managers compare and analyze the differences between the financial data for the current fiscal period and the previous fiscal period. Two types of financial analysis available are:

- Horizontal trend analysis
- Vertical trend analysis

Horizontal trend analysis compares the ending balance for the current fiscal period with the ending balance of the previous fiscal period for each item on the statement. The difference is reported as a percentage change. This type of analysis may be generated for both the balance sheet and the income statement.

Vertical trend analysis shows the relationship of the component parts to the total. On the income statement, total revenue (or sales) is expressed as 100%, and the other items are expressed as a percentage of total revenue. On the balance sheet, assets are expressed as a percentage of total assets, while liabilities and stockholders' equity items are expressed as a percentage of total liabilities and stockholders' equity. In *Automated Accounting 8.0* or higher, vertical analysis is included for both current and previous fiscal periods.

Preparing a Financial Analysis Report
Use the following steps to display the horizontal and vertical trend analysis reports:

1. Click the Reports toolbar button, or choose the Reports Selection menu item from the Reports menu.

2. When the Report Selection dialog appears, choose Financial Analysis from the Select a Report Group list.

3. Choose one of the vertical or horizontal analysis reports from the Choose a Report to Display list.

4. Click OK.

Management Decisions Using Cost-Volume-Profit Analysis

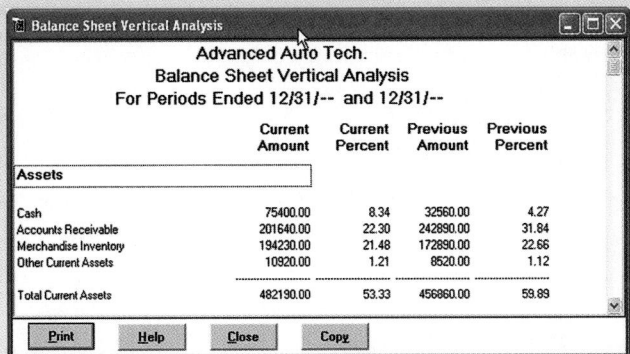

The report will be displayed in the scrollable Report Viewer Window. The report may be printed and/or copied for inclusion in another application, such as a spreadsheet or word processor.

1. To print the report, click the Print button.

2. To copy the report, click the Copy button and select the format for the report. The data are copied to the Clipboard in either the spreadsheet format or the word processing format.

PRACTICE

- Direct students to open an existing problem solution for a comprehensive problem, such as a Mastery Problem, and generate one or more of the financial analysis reports available.

ASSESSMENT

- Review student reports to assess understanding.

TEACHING STRATEGIES   PORTFOLIO ASSESSMENT

Students should be encouraged to print at least one report from one of the Automated Accounting problems to include in their portfolio to demonstrate mastery of automated accounting systems. A copy of the Portfolio Assessment form (blackline master in the Teacher's Resource Guide; also on the Student Companion CD) should be completed by the student, and the Description section should include any comments regarding how the student mastered these concepts and procedures.

Management Decisions Using

	SCOPE & SEQUENCE		ENHANCING	
	NEW	**REVIEW/ EXTENSION**	**SPECIAL FEATURES**	
Introduce the Chapter	✓		• Accounting in the Real World: Verizon	
Lesson 16-1 Business Decisions Using Present Values			• Making Ethical Decisions: Bribing Government Officials	
Future value of money	✓			
Present value of money	✓		• Cases for Critical Thinking 1	
Business decisions using present values	✓			
Lesson 16-2 Present Value and Annuities			• Technology for Business: Spreadsheet Functions for Present and Future Value Analysis	
Present value of an annuity	✓			
Financial planning and business decisions using present value of an annuity	✓		• Cases for Critical Thinking 2	
Putting It All Together			• Explore Accounting	
			• Xtra! Web Site: Xtra! Enrichment	
			• Applied Communication	
			• SCANS Workplace Competency	
			• Auditing for Errors	
			• Analyzing Costco's Financial Statements	

Present-Value Analysis

INSTRUCTION		PRACTICE AND ASSESSMENT		
TECHNOLOGY AND MEDIA	**TEACHING STRATEGIES**	**GUIDED PRACTICE**	**INDEPENDENT PRACTICE**	**RETEACHING AND ENRICHMENT**
• Internet Research Activity • Accounting Xtra! Web Site	• Software Focus			
• Instructor's Resource CD: PowerPoint Slides • Xtra! Web Site: Xtra! Study Tools • Personal Trainer		• Terms Review • Audit Your Understanding • Work Together 16-1	• On Your Own 16-1 • Application Problems 16-1, 16-2, and 16-3 • Ongoing Assessment, p. 477 • Personal Trainer • Xtra! Web Site: Xtra! Study Tools	• Reteach, p. 477 • Enrich, p. 478
• Instructor's Resource CD: PowerPoint Slides • Xtra! Web Site: Xtra! Study Tools • Personal Trainer		• Terms Review • Audit Your Understanding • Work Together 16-2	• On Your Own 16-2 • Application Problems 16-4, 16-5, and 16-6 • Ongoing Assessment, p. 482 • Personal Trainer • Xtra! Web Site: Xtra! Study Tools	• Reteach, p. 482 • Enrich, p. 483
• Automated Accounting • Personal Trainer • Xtra! Web Site: Xtra! Review, Quizzing, and Enrichment • Student Companion CD			• Mastery Problem 16-7 • Personal Trainer • Xtra! Web Site: Xtra! Review and Quizzing • Study Guide 16 • Student Companion CD • Chapter 16 Test • ExamView Chapter 16 • Portfolio Assessment	• Challenge Problem 16-8 • Reteach, p. 484 • Enrich, p. 484 • Recycling Problem 16-1 • Automated Accounting • Xtra! Web Site: Xtra! Enrichment

472

CHAPTER

OBJECTIVES & TERMS · TERMS · OBJECTIVES & TERMS

16 Management Decisions Using Present-Value Analysis

After studying Chapter 16, you will be able to:

1. Define accounting terms related to present values.

2. Identify accounting concepts and practices related to present values.

3. Calculate the future value of a single payment.

4. Calculate the present value of a future amount.

5. Make investment decisions using present values.

6. Make investment decisions using the present value of an annuity.

- time value of money
- future value
- compounding
- present value

- rate of return
- cash flows
- net cash flow
- net present value

- annuity
- present value of an annuity

Point Your Browser
accountingxtra.swlearning.com

ACCOUNTING IN THE REAL W

1. Communication network equipment is depreciated over its useful life. As a result, the cost of the communication system is matched against the revenue generated by the system.

2. Communication network equipment has a relatively short useful life. This equipment becomes technologically obsolete in a short time, forcing Verizon to constantly upgrade its equipment with the latest technologies.

INTERNET RESEARCH ACTIVITY

INTERNET RESEARCH ACTIVI

1. For an individual or business that is unable to pay its debts, a bankruptcy plan provides for the division of the available assets among the creditors.

2. Bankruptcy proceedings are supervised by and litigated in the United States Bankruptcy Courts, a part of the District Courts of the United States.

3. Liquidation is the most common type of bankruptcy. A court-appointed trustee collects the proceeds from the sale of available assets and distributes the proceeds to approved creditors.

---

accounting in the real world

• Verizon

©DANIEL ACKER/BLOOMBERG NEWS/LANDOV

VERIZON ASKS, "CAN YOU HEAR ME NOW?"

We've all seen it—a cellular phone user pacing about, asking, "Can you hear me now?" Verizon has cleverly branded this phrase to its cellular phone business. Verizon is the largest telecommunications company, with more than 200,000 employees and $165 billion of assets.

The Verizon name is derived from two words: *veritas,* the Latin word meaning certainty and reliability, and *horizon,* signifying forward-looking and visionary. To fulfill these objectives, Verizon must continually expand and upgrade its communication systems. At the beginning of the 21st century, Verizon invested approximately $10–$12 billion per year on its communication systems. Verizon made this enormous investment on the expectation that it will generate additional revenues for years to come.

Verizon operates in an industry in which depreciation is a significant component of its operating expenses. As a result, the cash generated from fees occurs after the year that cash is paid to purchase communication equipment. When evaluating additional investments, Verizon managers must consider the timing of the investment and the related revenues.

Critical Thinking

1. How are the costs of Verizon's communication equipment networks matched against the related revenues?
2. What does Verizon's continued investment in its communication networks indicate about today's communication technology?

Xtra!
Today
accountingxtra.swlearning.com

Source: www22.verizon.com/

internet activity

BANKRUPTCY

Go to the homepage of the Legal Information Institute of the Cornell Law School (www.law.cornell.edu). Search for "bankruptcy" and look for an overview about bankruptcy laws.

Instructions

Answer the following questions:
1. What kind of plan does bankruptcy law establish?
2. What agency supervises and litigates bankruptcy proceedings?
3. Which is the most common type of bankruptcy? What happens in this type of bankruptcy?

16-1 Business Decisions Using Present Values

Bank customers deposit their money in savings accounts and certificates of deposits to earn interest and increase their wealth. The expectation that invested money will increase over time is called the **time value of money**. Because of the time value of money, the promise of receiving $100.00 in three years is not worth $100.00 today. A bank customer would expect to deposit less than $100.00 today on the promise of receiving $100.00 in three years.

Like bank customers, managers must consider the time value of money when investing in plant assets. A business invests in plant assets, such as buildings, trucks, computers, and com-puter networks to expand its operations and increase profits. When deciding whether to purchase a plant asset, managers should compare the asset's cost to the additional profits that will be earned in the future. If future profits exceed the cost, then management should purchase the asset.

When those profits are earned is an important factor in that decision. The value of a dollar earned several years from now should not be compared directly to the cost of the asset today. Managers must consider the time value of money when comparing future profits to today's costs.

making ethical decisions

Bribing Government Officials

Companies that operate in countries throughout the world are exposed to different cultures, social norms, and acceptable business practices. In some countries, giving bribes to government officials to gain favorable business terms is both acceptable and expected. In contrast, giving a bribe to a government official in our society is both unethical and illegal. In 1977 Congress passed the Foreign Corrupt Practices Act, which made it illegal for U.S. companies to bribe foreign government officials.

Instructions

Access *Everyday Values*, the code of conduct for Harley-Davidson. (To find the code, go to *www.harley-davidson.com*. Click Company, and in Corporate Governance, click the English version under Code of Conduct. Note that Acrobat Reader is required to download and read this document.) What guidance does Harley-Davidson provide its employees in the following situations involving foreign government officials?

1. An employee, at the end of a business meeting with a government official, is considering paying for everyone's lunch.
2. To thank a mayor's staff for their help with a bike rally, an employee wants to give the mayor's staff Harley-Davidson hats or T-shirts.
3. An employee learns that a marketing company hired by Harley-Davidson has given a free motorcycle to a government official in thanks for closing a road to film a commercial.

FUTURE VALUE OF MONEY

Future Value of $1,000.00 at 10% Interest

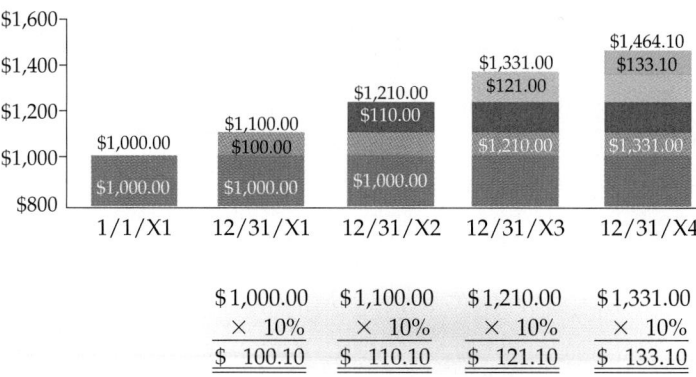

	$1,000.00	$1,100.00	$1,210.00	$1,331.00
	× 10%	× 10%	× 10%	× 10%
	$ 100.10	$ 110.10	$ 121.10	$ 133.10

Individuals and businesses expect invested money to grow over time. The value of money invested today at some point in the future is called a **future value**. The figure above shows how the value of a $1,000.00 investment on January 1, 20X1, at 10% annual interest will grow over time. The future value of $1,000.00 invested today at 10% interest is $1,464.10 in four years.

The interest earned each year is calculated by multiplying the current investment value by the interest rate. The calculation of interest earned in the third year is shown as follows.

Current Investment Value on 12/31/X2	×	Interest Rate	=	Interest Earned in 20X3
$1,210.00	×	10%	=	$121.00

Current Investment Value on 12/31/X2	+	Interest Earned in 20X3	=	Balance on 12/31/X3
$1,210.00	+	$121.00	=	$1,331.00

Each year, the interest earned increases the value of the investment. As the investment value increases, the amount of interest earned each year also increases. Interest earned in the fourth year, $133.10, is greater than the $121.00 interest earned in the third year. Earning interest on previously earned interest is called **compounding**. Compounding interest causes the annual interest earned to increase each year.

FYI FOR YOUR INFORMATION

A bank may advertise that its certificates of deposit earn "5% interest compounded annually." Each year the bank calculates interest earned of 5% on the outstanding account balance and adds this amount to the account. The more often (daily, monthly, or quarterly) interest is compounded, the more quickly the account balance will grow. For example, a $1,000.00 investment at 10% interest compounded semi-annually (twice each year) will grow to $1,628.90 in four years—$164.80 more than the $1,464.10 future value illustrated at the top of this page.

EXPLAIN

- Explain that present value is effectively the opposite of future value.
- Ask students to examine the figure as they say aloud "the present value of $1,464.10 at 10% interest for 4 years is $1,000.00."
- Use the math box to explain how each year's interest is calculated.
- Use the F.Y.I. to explain why the frequency that interest is compounded affects the amount of interest.

DEMONSTRATE

- On the chalkboard, create a table having four columns: Year, Investment on 1/1/--, Interest Earned, and Investment on 12/31/--.
- Ask a student to show how interest is calculated in year 1 for $3,000.00 invested at 8% interest.
- Ask individual students to complete the table for years 2–4 *(Interest earned: $259.20, $279.94, $302.33)*.
- Explain why interest earned increases each year *(interest is earned on larger amounts as interest accumulates)*.

- Explain that the present value table is used to calculate the present value for any amount. The number of periods and the periodic interest rate determine the present value factor.

- Discuss why the present value of $1,464.10 at 10% interest for 4 years is calculated to be $999.98 rather than $1,000.00. *(The decimal place accuracy of the present value table results in a two-cent rounding difference. A table with greater decimal place accuracy would yield exactly $1,000.00.)*

- Use the F.Y.I. to introduce students to a common statement used in business.

- On the board, work the calculation of the present value of $1,464.10.

- Ask students to use the present value table in the illustration to identify the factors for the following cases:

  12% for 5 periods *(0.567)*

  6% for 7 periods *(0.665)*

  8% for 6 periods *(0.630)*

- Assist students to calculate the future value of $2,000 at 8% annual interest for 3 years *($2,519.42)*. Then instruct students to use the present value table to calculate the present value of the future value. The present value, $2,000.42 *($2,519.42 × .794)* calculated using this present value table results in a $0.42 rounding difference.

PRESENT VALUE OF MONEY

Present Value of $1					
	Interest Rate				
Period	6%	8%	10%	12%	15%
1	0.943	0.926	0.909	0.893	0.870
2	0.890	0.857	0.826	0.797	0.756
3	0.840	0.794	0.751	0.712	0.658
4	0.792	0.735	0.683	0.636	0.572
5	0.747	0.681	0.621	0.567	0.497
6	0.705	0.630	0.564	0.507	0.432
7	0.665	0.583	0.513	0.452	0.376
8	0.627	0.540	0.467	0.404	0.327
9	0.592	0.500	0.424	0.361	0.284
10	0.558	0.463	0.386	0.322	0.247

The current value of a future cash payment or receipt is called a **present value**. At 10% interest, $1,000.00 invested today will be worth $1,464.10 in four years. Therefore, $1,000.00 is the present value of $1,464.10 in four years at 10% interest.

Present value tables enable managers to calculate the present value of any future amount. The amounts in the tables are known as *present value factors*. The present value factor is determined by finding the intersection of the interest rate in the columns and the number of years in the rows. The calculation of the present value of $1,464.10 is shown below.

The present value factors in the table are rounded to three digits. Some small rounding errors may occur. Calculating the present value of $1,464.10 using a rounded present value factor results in a $0.02 rounding error. Such minor rounding errors are acceptable when managers are using present values to make business decisions.

	Projected Net Cash Flows	$1,464.10
	times Present Value Factor	× 0.683
	Present Value	$ 999.98

FYI FOR YOUR INFORMATION

Managers may state that a future amount has been "discounted" to the present value.

©GETTY IMAGES/PHOTODISC

Management Decisions Using Present-Value Analysis

BUSINESS DECISIONS USING PRESENT VALUES

Year	Net Cash Flows		Present Value Factor		Present Value of Net Cash Flow
1	$ 500.00	x	0.926	=	$ 463.00
2	1,500.00	x	0.857	=	1,285.50
3	2,000.00	x	0.794	=	1,588.00
4	2,000.00	x	0.735	=	1,470.00
5	1,500.00	x	0.681	=	1,021.50
6	1,000.00	x	0.630	=	630.00
Present Value of Net Cash Flows					$6,458.00
Investment					6,000.00
Net Present Value					$ 458.00

Present Value of $1

Period	Interest Rate				
	6%	8%	10%	12%	15%
1	0.943	0.926	0.909	0.893	0.870
2	0.890	0.857	0.826	0.797	0.756
3	0.840	0.794	0.751	0.712	0.658
4	0.792	0.735	0.683	0.636	0.572
5	0.747	0.681	0.621	0.567	0.497
6	0.705	0.630	0.564	0.507	0.432
7	0.665	0.583	0.513	0.452	0.376
8	0.627	0.540	0.467	0.404	0.327
9	0.592	0.500	0.424	0.361	0.284
10	0.558	0.463	0.386	0.322	0.247

When individuals deposit money in a bank, they expect to earn interest. When businesses invest in plant assets, they expect to earn a specific amount of money beyond the cost of the asset. The relationship of money earned compared to the money invested is called the **rate of return**. Interest rates and the rate of return are stated as percentages.

As a measure of future profits, managers typically focus on the amount of cash received. The cash receipts and cash payments of a company are called **cash flows**. The difference between cash receipts and cash payments is called **net cash flow**. Managers discount future net cash flows using the desired rate of return.

Reflection, Inc. is considering purchasing a paint mixer for $6,000.00. The expected net cash flows during the mixer's six-year useful life are shown above. Management approves investments only if they earn an 8% rate of return.

Each year's cash flow is discounted using present values factors for 8%. For example, in Year 1, the first year the paint mixer is used, the net cash flow is

estimated to be $500.00. The present value factor for this year is one period at 8%—0.926. The next net cash flow will be for two periods. The sum of the present values for each year is the total present value of the investment. The difference between the discounted cash flows and the investment is called the **net present value**. The net present value is the amount the business is expected to earn above its desired rate of return.

The investment in the paint mixer is expected to earn a net present value of $458.00. Reflection, Inc. should invest in the mixer because the net present value is positive. The discounted cash flows exceed the desired 8% rate of return.

©GETTY IMAGES/PHOTODISC

GUIDED PRACTICE

Terms Review

- Ask students to write the definitions for each term presented in the Terms Review. Allow students to use their texts.

- Ask different students to read their definitions. After each definition is read, ask the class if the definition is correct and whether the complete definition has been given or whether anything needs to be added. Suggested definitions are provided in the Glossary.

Audit Your Understanding

Call on students to answer the Audit Your Understanding questions. Ask the class if the answer is correct and/or complete. Answers are given in Appendix E of the textbook.

Work Together

Have students write the solution to the Work Together problem as you guide the class through the examples.

- Direct students to record each amount on the proper form as you elicit class participation in determining and calculating each amount.

- Call on students to describe each step in the process for calculating the net present value.

INDEPENDENT PRACTICE

On Your Own

- Assign the On Your Own problem to be worked independently.

- Use the Ongoing Assessment techniques to diagnose student understanding.

Application Problems

- Assign Application Problem 16-1: Calculating future values.

- Assign Application Problem 16-2: Calculating present values.

- Assign Application Problem 16-3: Calculating net present value.

Personal Trainer

- Students can access the Lesson 16-1 assessment material using this software.

Xtra! Web Site

- Students can access the Xtra! Study Tools for additional practice.

478

---

terms review

time value of money
future value
compounding
present value
rate of return
cash flows
net cash flow
net present value

audit your understanding

1. Why does the amount of interest earned on an investment increase each year?

2. How is a present value factor determined?

3. How are interest rates and the rate of return stated?

work together 16-1

Calculating future and present values

Forms are provided in the *Working Papers*. Obtain the present value factors from the tables in the illustrations. Your instructor will guide you through the following examples.

1. Calculate the future value of a $2,000.00 investment in four years at 12% interest.

2. Calculate the present value of $25,000.00 received in four years at a 15% rate of return.

3. Lambert Company is considering the purchase of equipment costing $75,000.00 that will have a five-year useful life. Projected net cash flows from the investment are shown below. Determine the net present value of the investment, assuming a rate of return of 10%. Should the company purchase the equipment?

Year	Cash Flows
1	$ 8,000.00
2	25,000.00
3	36,000.00
4	22,000.00
5	15,000.00

on your own 16-1

Calculating future and present values

Forms are provided in the *Working Papers*. Obtain the present value factors from the tables in the illustrations. Work these problems independently.

1. Calculate the future value of a $25,000.00 investment in five years at 8% interest.

2. Calculate the present value of $48,000.00 received in five years at a 10% rate of return.

3. Daniel Supply Company is considering the purchase of equipment costing $150,000.00 that will have a seven-year useful life. Projected cash flows from the investment are shown below. Determine the net present value of the investment, assuming a rate of return of 8%. Should the company purchase the equipment?

Year	Cash Flows
1	$15,000.00
2	25,000.00
3	35,000.00
4	50,000.00
5	35,000.00
6	25,000.00
7	10,000.00

ENRICH

- Assign the Making Ethical Decisions feature on page 474.

- Assign Case 1 of the Cases for Critical Thinking.

CLOSE

- Ask students to identify any decision they have made that could have been evaluated using present value decision *(evaluating a cash back or low financing offer when buying a car).*

16-2 Present Value and Annuities

PRESENT VALUE OF AN ANNUITY

Year	Balance on January 1	+	10% Interest Earned	−	December 31 Payment	=	Balance on December 31
1	$3,170.00	+	$317.00	−	$1,000.00	=	$2,487.00
2	2,487.00	+	248.70	−	1,000.00	=	1,735.70
3	1,735.70	+	173.57	−	1,000.00	=	909.27
4	909.27	+	90.93	−	1,000.00	=	——*

* Inclues a $0.20 rounding error.

Some business transactions result in equal net cash flows each year. A series of equal cash flows is called an **annuity**. An amount invested at a given interest rate that supports the payments of an annuity is called the **present value of an annuity**.

The illustration above illustrates how an initial investment of $3,170.00 earns enough interest to make a payment of $1,000.00 at the end of each of the four years. The present value of the $1,000.00, four-year 10% annuity is $3,170.00.

Each year's interest is calculated on that year's investment balance. The annual payment is then deducted to calculate the next year's beginning balance. The calculation of the amounts for the first year is shown below.

Balance on January 1	×	Interest Rate	=	Interest Earned
$3,170.00	×	10%	=	$317.00

Balance on January 1	+	Interest Earned	=	Pre-Payment Balance
$3,170.00	+	$317.00	=	$3,487.00

Pre-Payment Balance	−	December 31 Payment	=	Pre-Payment Balance
$3,487.00	−	$1,000.00	=	$2,487.00

A present value of an annuity table contains the present value factors used to determine the net present value of an annuity. The factor is determined by the intersection of the interest rate and the number of years. The annual payment is multiplied by the present value factor to calculate the present value of the annuity.

MATERIALS

- Instructor's Resource CD: PowerPoint Slides
- Xtra! Study Tools on the Xtra! Web Site
- Working Papers: Teacher's Edition of the Working Papers for Lesson 16-2
- Software: Personal Trainer Student Companion CD

OBJECTIVES

- Define accounting terms related to present values.
- Identify accounting concepts and practices related to present values.
- Make investment decisions using the present value of an annuity.

MOTIVATE

Almost everyone has or will purchase an item, such as a car or house, and make equal monthly payments over the life of the loan. The value of the future payments can be determined using present values.

Preview

- Preview the accounting terms and definitions introduced in this lesson: annuity and present value of an annuity.
- Direct students to read the headings at the top of each page in this lesson and to examine the illustrations given.
- Explain that an annuity is simply a series of cash flows where each amount is the same. Thus, special present value factors are used to simplify the calculations.

EXPLAIN

- An annuity consists of a series of equal payments.
- A special table of factors is used to calculate the present value of an annuity.
- Explain that the term *annuity* also refers to a series of payments to investors. Many individuals purchase annuities to provide a steady income during retirement. Determining the present value of an annuity allows an individual to determine if enough money has been invested to ensure the desired periodic income.

DEMONSTRATE

- Ask students to describe or calculate each amount in the illustration. Write these amounts on the board. Refer students to the math box for help on certain calculations.
- Explain how to identify the present value factor for a 10% annuity for 3 years.
- To reinforce these concepts, assist students to calculate the present value of $3,000.00 annual payments for 10 years *($3,000.00 × 6.710 = $20,130.00)*. Ask students to explain the meaning of the $20,130.00 amount *(investing $20,130.00 at 10% interest will support $3,000.00 annual payments for 10 years)*.

This feature discusses the present value and future value functions available on electronic spreadsheets. Other commonly-used functions include =PV and =NPV. Students should be encouraged to experiment with these functions. More information about each function is available in Excel by clicking the Insert Function button on the Formula bar and selecting Financial in the category box. Excel provides a brief description of the function and assistance in entering the required amounts.

Present Value of an Annuity of $1					
	Interest Rate				
Period	6%	8%	10%	12%	15%
1	0.943	0.926	0.909	0.893	0.870
2	1.833	1.783	1.736	1.690	1.626
3	2.673	2.577	2.487	2.402	2.283
4	3.465	3.312	3.170	3.037	2.855
5	4.212	3.993	3.791	3.605	3.352
6	4.917	4.623	4.355	4.111	3.784
7	5.582	5.206	4.868	4.564	4.160
8	6.210	5.747	5.335	4.968	4.487
9	6.802	6.247	5.759	5.328	4.772
10	7.360	6.710	6.145	5.650	5.019

Annual Payment		$ 1,000.00
Present Value Factor	×	3.170
Present Value of an Annuity	=	$ 3,170.00

The calculation above shows the amount that would have to be invested today, $3,170.00 (present value of the annuity), earning 10% annual interest, with a withdrawal of $1,000.00 at the end of each year.

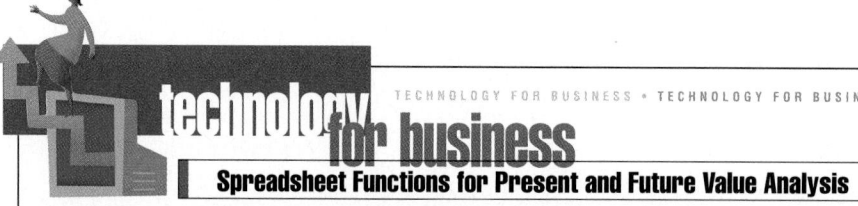

technology for business

TECHNOLOGY FOR BUSINESS • TECHNOLOGY FOR BUSINESS • TECHNOLOGY FOR BU

Spreadsheet Functions for Present and Future Value Analysis

A large company may have many investment decisions to make each day. There could be proposals for new equipment purchases; new factory, warehouse, or office buildings to buy, lease, or build; or new products to add. These decisions and many others can benefit from present and future value analysis. However, looking up factors on a table and performing the calculations on a calculator would not be efficient means of evaluating these business decisions.

Fortunately, modern spreadsheet software has present and future value functions. Using Excel as an example, the function for the future value of an annuity would be FV(rate, nper, pmt), where

rate is the interest rate, nper is the number of periods, and pmt is the amount of the regular payment. The present value function is similar.

In a large company, many different departments may compete for investment dollars to fund new product ideas. The accounting department may provide a spreadsheet for evaluating the different components of a proposal. Managers can use such a spreadsheet for evaluating and better defining their proposals before they are submitted to upper management, to increase the chances of approval.

			Interest Rate		
Period	6%	8%	10%	12%	15%
1	0.943	0.926	0.909	0.893	0.870
2	1.833	1.783	1.736	1.690	1.626
3	2.673	2.577	2.487	2.402	2.283
4	3.465	3.312	3.170	3.037	2.855
5	4.212	3.993	3.791	3.605	3.352
6	4.917	4.623	4.355	4.111	3.784
7	5.582	5.206	4.868	4.564	4.160
8	6.210	5.747	5.335	4.968	4.487
9	6.802	6.247	5.759	5.328	4.772
10	7.360	6.710	6.145	5.650	5.019
15	9.712	8.559	7.606	6.811	5.847
20	11.470	9.818	8.514	7.469	6.259
25	12.783	10.675	9.077	7.843	6.464
30	13.765	11.258	9.427	8.055	6.566

Present Value of an Annuity of $1

Annual Payment	$ 50,000.00
Present Value Factor	× 10.675
Present Value of an Annuity	= $ 533,750.00

Financial advisors use the present value of an annuity to assist their clients with financial planning decisions. A common decision is to determine the amount of money individuals need to have saved before their retirement.

John and Sally Neumann expect to retire at the age of 65 and hope to live until age 90, another 25 years. They project they need $50,000.00 per year to support themselves. Assuming they can invest their money to yield an 8% rate of return, what amount do the Neumanns need to save before they retire?

The present value for an 8%, $50,000.00, 25-year annuity is $533,750.00. The present value of an annuity is calculated by multiplying the present value factor, 10.675, by the annual payment, $50,000.00. The Neumanns need to have $533,750.00 saved for their retirement.

FYI FOR YOUR INFORMATION

The Neumanns risk running out of money if they live past 90 years of age. Insurance companies sell annuity policies to protect individuals against this risk. The annuity policy guarantees the insured will continue to receive an annual payment through lifetime. Insurance companies use the age and health of the insured to determine his or her life expectancy and, therefore, the expected life of the annuity. The present value of the annuity calculation is used to estimate the insurance company's cost of providing the annual payments.

EXPLAIN

- Explain how individuals planning for retirement manage their investments to ensure they can withdraw a constant level of cash each year during their retirement. This constant level of cash is an *annuity*.

- Explain that the present value of an annuity factors can be used to determine the amount of money a person must have invested to provide the desired annual cash payment.

DEMONSTRATE

- On the board, work the calculation of the present value of $533,750.00.

- Ask students to use the present value table in the illustration to identify the factors for the following cases:

  12% for 25 periods *(7.843)*

  6% for 30 periods *(13.765)*

  8% for 30 periods *(11.258)*

- Assist students to calculate the present value of a $40,000.00 annuity at 8% annual interest for 30 years *($40,000.00 × 11.258 = $450,320.00)*. Then instruct students to make the same calculation, assuming that the interest rate will be only 6% *($40,000.00 × 13.765 = $550,600.00)*. Discuss how the change in the interest rate had a significant impact on required investment, increasing the amount by $100,280.00 *($550,600.00 − $450,320.00 = $100,280.00)*.

BUSINESS DECISIONS USING THE PRESENT VALUE OF AN ANNUITY

Present Value of an Annuity of $1					
	Interest Rate				
Period	6%	8%	10%	12%	15%
1	0.943	0.926	0.909	0.893	0.870
2	1.833	1.783	1.736	1.690	1.626
3	2.673	2.577	2.487	2.402	2.283
4	3.465	3.312	3.170	3.037	2.855
5	4.212	3.993	3.791	3.605	3.352
6	4.917	4.623	4.355	4.111	3.784
7	5.582	5.206	4.868	4.564	4.160
8	6.210	5.747	5.335	4.968	4.487
9	6.802	6.247	5.759	5.328	4.772
10	7.360	6.710	6.145	5.650	5.019
15	9.712	8.559	7.606	6.811	5.847
20	11.470	9.818	8.514	7.469	6.259
25	12.783	10.675	9.077	7.843	6.464
30	13.765	11.258	9.427	8.055	6.566

Annual Net Cash Flows		$ 50,000.00
Present Value Factor	×	4.111
Present Value of an Annuity	=	$ 20,555.00
Investment	−	22,000.00
Net Present Value	=	$ (1,445.00)

The concept of the present value of an annuity is also useful in making decisions about investments in plant assets. Reflection, Inc. is considering purchasing equipment for $22,000.00. The equipment will enable the company to generate net cash flows of $5,000.00 annually over the equipment's six-year useful life. Management expects assets to yield a 12% rate of return.

At a 12% rate of return, the present value of an annuity of six $5,000.00 net cash flows is $20,555.00. The net present value is a negative $1,445.00 and, therefore, the investment fails to achieve the desired 12% rate of return.

Should management purchase the equipment? It may appear logical to purchase the equipment since the net cash flows of $30,000 ($5,000.00 per year multiplied by 6 years) are greater than the cost of the equipment. However, effective managers will not purchase equipment that does not yield a positive net present value. Rather, they will continue to search for alternative uses of the $22,000.00 investment that will achieve the desired rate of return.

• terms review

annuity
present value of an annuity

TERMS REVIEW

• audit your understanding

1. How is the present value of an annuity calculated?

2. How can individuals use the present value of an annuity to plan for retirement?

3. How does a company determine if it should invest in plant assets?

AUDIT YOUR

• work together 16-2

Calculating the present value of an annuity

Forms are provided in the *Working Papers*. Your instructor will guide you through the following examples.

1. Create a schedule that shows the payment of an annuity over a four-year period. The initial investment is $8,662.76, the annual payment is $2,500.00, and the interest rate is 6%.

2. Calculate the present value of an annuity of 10 payments of $10,000.00 at an interest rate of 8%.

3. Lambert Company is considering the purchase of equipment costing $75,000.00 having a five-year useful life. Projected net cash flows from the investment are $20,000.00 annually. Determine the net present value of the investment, assuming a rate of return of 10%. Should the company purchase the equipment?

WORK TOGETHER • WORK

• on your own 16-2

Calculating the present value of an annuity

Forms are provided in the *Working Papers*. Work this problem independently.

1. Create a schedule that shows the payment of an annuity over a five-year period. The initial investment is 25,000.00, the annual payment is $6,594.94, and the interest rate is 10%.

2. Calculate the present value of an annuity of 15 payments of $5,000.00 at an interest rate of 12%.

3. Daniel Supply Company is considering the purchase of equipment costing $35,000.00 having a seven-year useful life. Projected net cash flows from the investment are $8,000.00 annually. Determine the net present value of the investment, assuming a rate of return of 8%. Should the company purchase the equipment?

ON YOUR OWN • ON YOUR OWN

Present Value and Annuities

Lesson 16-2   **483**

GUIDED PRACTICE

Terms Review

- Ask students to write the definitions for each term presented in the Terms Review. Allow students to use their texts.

- Ask different students to read their definitions. After each definition is read, ask the class if the definition is correct and whether the complete definition has been given or whether anything needs to be added. Suggested definitions are also provided in the Glossary.

Audit Your Understanding

Call on students to answer the Audit Your Understanding questions. Ask the class if the answer is correct and/or complete. Answers are given in Appendix E of the textbook.

Work Together

Have students write the solution to the Work Together problem as you guide the class through the examples.

- Direct students to record each amount on the proper form as you elicit class participation in determining and calculating each amount.

- Call on students to describe each step in the process for calculating a present value of an annuity and net present value.

INDEPENDENT PRACTICE

On Your Own

- Assign the On Your Own problem to be worked independently.

- Use the Ongoing Assessment techniques to diagnose student understanding.

Application Problems

- Assign Application Problem 16-4: Preparing an annuity schedule.

- Assign Application Problem 16-5: Calculating the present value of an annuity.

- Assign Application Problem 16-6: Calculating the net present value using present value of an annuity.

Personal Trainer

- Students can access the Lesson 16-2 assessment material using this software.

Xtra! Web Site

- Students can access the Xtra! Study Tools for additional practice.

ENRICH

- Assign the Technology for Business feature on page 480.

- Assign Case 2 of the Cases for Critical Thinking.

CLOSE

- Ask students to develop a rule to decide which table to use for each business decision *(use the present value of an annuity table when there are equal periodic net cash flows; otherwise, use the present value table).*

- Ask students to summarize what they have learned in this lesson. How has learning about present values changed how they might plan for retirement?

PUTTING IT ALL TOGETHER

- Review the Chapter Summary. Ask students for examples of each summary item. List their responses on the board or overhead. Refer to illustrations in the text that match student responses.

INDEPENDENT PRACTICE

- Assign Mastery Problem 16-7 to students who need the reinforcement of a problem that combines many of the activities from the chapter in one problem; this will be most students.
- Assign Challenge Problem 16-8 to accelerated students who do not require the reinforcement of the Mastery Problem.
- Assign Study Guide Chapter 16.
- Students can access Personal Trainer to work end-of-chapter problems on the computer.
- Students can access the Xtra! Web Site for the Xtra! Review and Quizzing.
- Students can access the Student Companion CD for additional review material.

ONGOING ASSESSMENT

Review solutions to the assigned problems in class, diagnosing trouble spots.

RETEACH

- Call on students to describe how they avoid the trouble spots diagnosed.
- Use reteaching suggestions from section lesson plans as required.
- Assign Recycling Problem 16-1 if needed.

ENRICH

- Assign the Explore Accounting Feature. Ask students to share the information they have gathered in a report to the class.
- Students can access the Xtra! Web Site for the Xtra! Enrichment material.
- Assign Applied Communication.
- Assign the SCANS Workplace Competency.
- Assign Auditing for Errors.
- Assign Analyzing Costco's Financial Statements.
- Assign the Automated Accounting feature on pages 490–491.

484

SUMMARY

After completing this chapter, you can

1. Define accounting terms related to present values.
2. Identify accounting concepts and practices related to present values.
3. Calculate the future value of a single payment.
4. Calculate the present value of a future amount.
5. Make investment decisions using present values.
6. Make investment decisions using the present value of an annuity.

Explore Accounting

EXPLORE ACCOUNTING • EXPLORE ACCOUNTING • EXPLORE AC

The Power of Compounding

Investing early in your life enables the power of compounding interest to increase your investment portfolio. Consider the example of two individuals: Jim Early and Sally Late. Jim began saving early in his life, investing $1,000.00 every year beginning at age 18. For many years, this was a struggle for Jim as he paid for college, started his career, established a home, and raised his children. Sally began investing rather late in her life, electing to spend all of her money until after her children were out of college. But Sally believed she could catch up and began at age 48 to invest $4,000.00 annually.

By age 58, both Jim and Sally had invested $40,000 and were beginning to think about retirement. How well will their investments support their retirement? The graph compares how their investment portfolios grew over the 40 years.

At 8% interest, Jim's portfolio has grown to $279,781 whereas Sally's portfolio is only $71,909. Why is there such a significant difference? Because of the power of compounding, money earning 8% interest will double every 9 years. That means that Jim's first $1,000.00 investment at age 18 doubled to $2,000.00 by age 27, $4,000.00 by age 36, $8,000.00 by age 45, and $16,000.00 by age 54. The original $1,000.00 will reach $32,000.00 by age 63.

Instructions: Using an electronic spreadsheet, create a schedule to calculate the future value of annual investments. The headings and formulas for the first two years are shown below.

	A	B	C	D	E	F
1	Age	Investment	Balance on January 1	Interest Rate	Interest Earned	Balance on December 31
2	18	1000	=+B2	0.08	=+C2*D2	=+B2+E2
3	=+A2+1	=+B2	=+B3+F2	=+D2	=+C3*D3	=+C3+E3

Copy the year 2 formulas for the remaining years. Change the age in A2, annual investment in B2, and interest rate in D2 to develop a realistic plan that will guide you toward saving $1,000,000 for your retirement.

Management Decisions Using Present-Value Analysis

EXPLORE ACCOUNTING
EXPLORE ACCOUNTING

Following the instructions provided, students' solutions should be nearly identical. The level of assistance required will depend on students' existing knowledge of electronic spreadsheets. Instruct students to print a solution containing Jim Early's annual payment and interest rate assumptions to ensure their spreadsheet is accurate. Then instruct students to enter new assumptions for the annual payments and interest rate to develop their personal investment plan.

484

16-1 APPLICATION PROBLEM
Calculating future values

John Alexander is considering putting money into the following investments:
a. A $10,000.00, five-year certificate of deposit earning 4.5% interest compounded annually
b. A $2,500.00, seven-year certificate of deposit earning 5.0% interest compounded annually

Instructions:
1. Determine the future value of each certificate of deposit.

16-2 APPLICATION PROBLEM
Calculating present values

Logan Corporation loans money to start-up businesses that can't obtain traditional bank loans. The company loans the business money in exchange for a single future payment. Logan Company wants to make a 15% rate of return on each loan. The following future payments are expected.

Business	Payment	Number of Years to Payment
April Designs	$100,000.00	8
Putman Services	$250,000.00	10
Zigler Books	$300,000.00	6

Instructions:
1. Calculate the present value of each loan.

16-3 APPLICATION PROBLEM
Calculating net present value

MPS Industries is considering the purchase of equipment costing $100,000.00 having a seven-year useful life. Projected net cash flows from the investment are shown below. Determine the net present value of the investment, assuming a rate of return of 12%. Should the company purchase the equipment?

Year	Cash Flows
1	$ 2,000.00
2	10,000.00
3	26,000.00
4	32,000.00
5	44,000.00
6	35,000.00
7	30,000.00

Instructions:
1. Calculate the net present value of the investment.
2. Should MPS Industries purchase the equipment? Explain your answer.

16-4 APPLICATION PROBLEM
Preparing an annuity schedule

Barry Sudduth has deposited $28,367.61 in an account for his son's college education. The account yields a 5% interest rate. Barry's son is allowed to withdraw $8,000.00 at the end of each of the next four years.

Instructions:
1. Create a schedule that shows the payment of this annuity over a four-year period.

Management Decisions Using Present-Value Analysis

Chapter 16   **485**

16-5 APPLICATION PROBLEM

Calculating the present value of an annuity

Andrea Kent has won $600,000.00 in a state lottery. The state will pay her the prize in 30 annual payments of $20,000.00.

Instructions:

1. Assuming a 10% rate of return, calculate the present value of the prize.

16-6 APPLICATION PROBLEM

Calculating the net present value using present value of an annuity

Folk Landscaping is evaluating an offer to purchase Bruce Lawn Care, its main competitor, for $250,000.00. An accountant has projected that the purchase will increase Folk's annual net cash flow by $30,000.00. Folk wants its investment to earn a 15% rate of return.

Instructions:

1. Calculate the net present value of the purchase, assuming the $30,000.00 net cash flow will occur for 25 years.
2. Calculate the net present value of the purchase, assuming the $30,000.00 net cash flow will occur for 30 years.
3. Should Folk Landscaping purchase Bruce Lawn Care?
4. Management has asked you to evaluate the investment for 35 and 40 years. Do you believe these calculations will change the decision?

16-7 MASTERY PROBLEM

Calculating net present values

Forester Company is evaluating the purchase of equipment from two vendors. Differences in the technology and labor requirements to operate the equipment of each vendor affect the projected net cash flows. The equipment purchased from Neal Industries would cost $97,250.00 and is projected to generate total net cash flows of $168,000.00. The equipment from York Manufacturing would cost $135,200.00 and is projected to generate net cash flows totaling $235,000.00. The net cash flows for each year follow.

Year	Neal Industries	York Manufacturing
1	$30,000.00	$10,000.00
2	28,000.00	20,000.00
3	26,000.00	30,000.00
4	24,000.00	40,000.00
5	22,000.00	50,000.00
6	20,000.00	60,000.00
7	18,000.00	25,000.00

Instructions:

1. Assuming that Forester Company wants to earn a 12% rate of return, calculate the net present value of each equipment purchase.
2. Would you purchase the equipment and, if so, from which vendor?

Management Decisions Using Present-Value Analysis

16-8 CHALLENGE PROBLEM

Calculating the future value of an annuity

"How much do we need to invest each year to have $100,000.00 in a college fund when our child turns 18 years old?" New parents often seek similar advice from their financial advisors to establish college funds for their child. The future value of an amount invested each year at a given interest rate is known as the *future value of an annuity*. A table of future value factors is shown below.

	Future Value of an Annuity			
	Interest Rate			
Period	6%	8%	10%	12%
1	1.06	1.08	1.10	1.12
2	2.12	2.17	2.31	2.25
3	3.25	3.34	3.64	3.52
4	4.45	4.61	5.11	4.95
5	5.71	5.98	6.72	6.54
6	7.06	7.45	8.49	8.33
7	8.48	9.05	10.44	10.33
8	9.99	10.77	12.58	12.56
9	11.59	12.64	14.94	15.07
10	13.28	14.65	17.53	17.88
11	15.08	16.82	20.38	21.03
12	16.98	19.16	23.52	24.55
13	19.00	21.70	26.97	28.50
14	21.14	24.43	30.77	32.92
15	23.41	27.39	34.95	37.87
16	25.82	30.58	39.54	43.41
17	28.37	34.02	44.60	49.62
18	31.07	37.75	50.16	56.57
19	33.93	41.77	56.27	64.36
20	36.97	46.11	63.00	73.09

Instructions:

1. John and Kathy Finch want to know the expected amount of a college fund if they invest $2,500.00 each year for 18 years and earn 10% interest.
2. How will the future value of the college fund be affected if the Finches can only earn 8% interest?
3. How much will the Finches have to invest each year for 18 years (at 8% interest) if they want the fund to be $100,000.00 when their child enters college?

APPLIED COMMUNICATION

Students' articles will vary. The advertisement should be written to an audience who does not understand present value concepts. The tone of the advertisement should be encouraging but deliberate. Grade the advertisement for overall form, content, grammar, spelling, punctuation, and sentence structure.

Select the top two or three articles and submit them to a local financial planner for final editing. Then submit the articles to a student or local newspaper for publication.

CASES FOR CRITICAL THINKING

Case 1

No. Based on the time value of money, the future payment in current dollars is worth less than $40,000.00.

Case 2

Jeanne needs to consider her expected life expectancy and the interest rate she will be able to earn on the $80,000.00 payment. Examining the present value of an annuity table, any year/interest rate assumption having a present value factor less than 8 *($80,000.00/$10,000.00)* would favor Jeanne accepting the one-time payment.

SCANS WORKPLACE COMPETENCY

Students' solutions will vary. Before loaning a company $25 million, the bank should ensure that the company has the ability to repay the loan. Thus, the bank loan officer should evaluate projected financial statements of the company. Knowledge of present values will enable the bank loan officer to calculate a net present value to determine whether the company's investment will generate a rate of return adequate to repay the loan.

A bank loan officer can work with a company to pursue alternative sources of capital, such as issuing additional stock.

• applied communication

As a form of advertisement, financial advisors often publish in their local newspapers short articles about financial planning issues. The articles are meant to motivate readers to manage their money better and, as a result, to hire them as their financial advisor.

Instructions:

You have obtained a part-time job in the office of Dumetrius Dorsey, financial planner. Using your knowledge of future and present values, write a short newspaper article designed to motivate new high school graduates to begin investing early.

• cases for critical thinking

Case 1

John Pedrick has just completed a meeting with the credit manager of your company. Pedrick Company is 180 days late paying its $50,000.00 outstanding account receivable. The credit manager informs you that he has negotiated a settlement with John Pedrick that provides for Pedrick Company to pay only $40,000.00 to settle the account. The payment will be received in three years. "At least I got $40,000.00 on the account," states the credit manager. Do you agree with his statement?

Case 2

Jeanne Li was injured in a car accident caused by a negligent driver. A court settlement provides Jeanne with $10,000.00 annual payments for life to pay for her chronic medical expenses. An independent company has offered Jeanne a one-time payment of $80,000.00 in exchange for the annual payments. Jeanne has sought your advice on whether to accept this offer. What issues should Jeanne consider in making her decision?

• SCANS workplace competency

Thinking Skill: Decision Making

Concept: Effective employees specify goals, identify constraints, suggest alternatives, consider risks, and evaluate and select the best alternative. An effective decision maker is often the highest paid individual in a company.

Application: If you were a loan officer at a local bank or other financial institution, how might the financial analysis presented in this chapter affect your decision making regarding a $25 million loan to a company? If you did not feel comfortable lending the entire $25 million to a business, identify several alternatives for sharing the risk or raising needed funds. Share your ideas with your classmates.

· auditing for errors

LaBlanc, Inc., has the opportunity to purchase new equipment that will save the company $12,000.00 per year in manufacturing costs. The $62,000.00 of equipment is expected to be useful for 8 years, after which it could be sold for $2,500.00. Rosa Pedrillo, accountant, prepared the following analysis and concluded that the company should purchase the equipment.

	Cash Flows	Present Value Factors	Present Values
Annual savings	$12,000.00	5.747	$68,964.00
Salvage value	2,500.00	0.540	1,350.00
Total present value			$70,314.00
Investment			62,000.00
Net present value			$ 8,314.00

Evaluate Rosa's analysis to determine whether it is accurate. Did Rosa make the correct decision?

· analyzing Costco's financial statements

Numerous accounting principles require companies to discount future cash flows when estimating amounts that are reported on financial statements. For example, the present value of a $10,000 account receivable expected to be collected in two years should be reported on the balance sheet as $8,570, assuming an 8% discount rate.

Accounting principles require companies to write down the value of plant assets if the fair value of the assets is less than the recorded book value. When establishing these accounting principles, the Financial Accounting Standards Board (FASB) considered how present values should be applied to this situation. Costco presents its application of the FASB rules in the section "Impairment of Long-Lived Assets" of Note 1 on Appendix B pages B-9–B-17.

1.   Does the FASB require Costco to discount future cash flows related to asset impairments? Support your answer.

2.   What FASB statement provides Costco with the accounting principles required for accounting for asset impairments?

AUDITING FOR ERRORS
AUDITING FOR ERRORS

Rosa's analysis is correct. The company will earn a net present value of $8,314.00 and, therefore, should purchase the equipment.

This Auditing for Errors activity provides a unique challenge. Having learned to expect errors, students must be confident enough of their auditing skills to enable them to express a conclusion that is contrary to their expectations.

ANALYZING COSTCO'S FINANCIAL STATEMENTS
ANALYZING COSTCO'S FINAN

1. No. Costco's Note 1 states, "The Company evaluates the carrying value of the asset by comparing the estimated future undiscounted cash flows generated from the use of the asset and its eventual disposition with the asset's reported net book value."

2. SFAS No. 144.

Using the Retirement Planner

Planning Tools

The planning tools in *Automated Accounting* are easy-to-use applications for producing results for different types of financial investments. The calculations the software makes to produce the results are based on the present and future value concept—the time value of money.

Retirement Plan

The Retirement Plan feature is used to perform two different calculations: (1) the annual deposit needed to provide a specific retirement income and (2) the retirement income available after making specific annual investments.

The desired calculation is chosen from the Calculate box. The item to be calculated appears grayed (or dimmed). Enter the other items, and the planner will make the calculation. For example, Martin Kingsley wants to begin saving for retirement when he is 18 years old. He wants to retire at age 65 and estimates that he will need

an annual retirement income of $50,000 and assumes he will live to the age of 90. He uses an 8% annual interest rate on his investment.

When the information is entered in the appropriate fields in the Retirement Plan, the amount of the annual contribution is shown, $1,272.77. Martin Kingsley will need to make an annual investment of $1,272.77 each year from the ages of 18 to 65 in order to be able to withdraw $50,000 each year from age 65 to 90.

The Savings Planner Report

Click the Report button to display a report of the deposits and withdrawals. A report of the findings may be displayed or printed. Click the Print button from the Retirement Plan Report window to print a copy of the report. You may also click the Copy button to copy the report in a word processing or spreadsheet format to paste the report into a document or spreadsheet for further use.

Management Decisions Using Present-Value Analysis

Using the Planning Tools: The Retirement Plan

Instructions:

1. Load the *Automated Accounting 8.0* or higher software.

2. Select New from the File menu.

3. Enter your name in the User Name field. Your name will then appear when you print your report.

4. Click on the Retirement Plan tab. Select Annual Contribution from the Calculate box. Enter an Annual Yield of 8%. Enter the Current Age, 18, the Retirement Age, 65, and the Withdraw Until Age, 90. Enter the desired Annual Retirement Income, $50,000.00. The Annual Contribution amount, $1,272.77, will appear in the Annual Contribution field.

5. Click on the Report command button in the Retirement Plan tab. Print the report, or copy it to the clipboard for entering into a word processor or spreadsheet application.

6. Click Close to return to the Planning Tools. Steps 4 and 5 may then be repeated for different calculation options or different data sets. Experiment with different values. Enter an amount in the Beginning Retirement Savings field to see what effect this would have on the annual contribution requirement.

7. Click Close to exit the Planning Tools. Your data is not saved when you exit the Planning Tools. Therefore, be sure to print a report, or copy the report to a word processor or spreadsheet and save it in that application.

8. Exit the Automated Accounting software.

PRACTICE

- Ask students to decide on a personal retirement planning goal and enter realistic data. Then direct students to display the report, copy it to a word processing application, and write a report on their retirement plan.

ASSESSMENT

- Direct students to copy the results of the Retirement Planner into either a word processing or spreadsheet file and print the results. If the word processor or spreadsheet software is not available, direct students to print the report from the Retirement Planner.

TEACHING STRATEGIES   PORTFOLIO ASSESSMENT

Students should be encouraged to print at least one report from the Automated Accounting problem to include in their portfolio to demonstrate mastery of using Planning Tools. A copy of the Portfolio Assessment form (blackline master in the Teacher's Resource Guide; also on the Student Companion CD) should be completed by the student and the Description section should include any comments regarding how the student mastered these concepts and procedures.

Financial Statement

	SCOPE & SEQUENCE		ENHANCING	
	NEW	REVIEW/EXTENSION	SPECIAL FEATURES	
Introduce the Chapter	✓		• Accounting in the Real World: Yum! Brands, Inc.	
Lesson 17-1 Trend Analysis and Component Percentages			• Making Ethical Decisions: Could You Be a Whistle Blower?	
Trend analysis	✓			
Component percentage analysis		✓		
Lesson 17-2 Calculating Earnings Performance and Efficiency Analysis			• Global Perspective: International Mail	
Earnings performance analysis		✓		
Efficiency analysis		✓		
Lesson 17-3 Calculating Financial Strength Analysis			• Careers in Accounting	
Short-term analysis	✓			
Long-term analysis	✓			
Putting It All Together			• Explore Accounting	
			• Xtra! Web Site: Xtra! Enrichment	
			• Applied Communication	
			• Cases for Critical Thinking	
			• SCANS Workplace Competency	
			• Graphing Workshop	
			• Analyzing Costco's Financial Statements	

Analysis

INSTRUCTION		PRACTICE AND ASSESSMENT		
TECHNOLOGY AND MEDIA	**TEACHING STRATEGIES**	**GUIDED PRACTICE**	**INDEPENDENT PRACTICE**	**RETEACHING AND ENRICHMENT**
• Internet Research Activity • Accounting Xtra! Web Site	• Software Focus			
• Instructor's Resource CD: PowerPoint Slides • Xtra! Web Site: Xtra! Study Tools • Blackline Masters: Comparative Statement for Trend Analysis and Comparative Statement for Component Percentage Analysis • Personal Trainer • QuickBooks	• Cooperative Learning	• Terms Review • Audit Your Understanding • Work Together 17-1	• On Your Own 17-1 • Application Problems 17-1 and 17-2 • Ongoing Assessment, p. 501 • Personal Trainer • Xtra! Web Site: Xtra! Study Tools	• Reteach, p. 501 • Enrich, p. 502 • QuickBooks
• Instructor's Resource CD: PowerPoint Slides • Xtra! Web Site: Xtra! Study Tools • Personal Trainer		• Term Review • Audit Your Understanding • Work Together 17-2	• On Your Own 17-2 • Application Problems 17-3 and 17-4 • Ongoing Assessment, p. 510 • Personal Trainer • Xtra! Web Site: Xtra! Study Tools	• Reteach, p. 510 • Enrich, p. 511
• Instructor's Resource CD: PowerPoint Slides • Xtra! Web Site: Xtra! Study Tools • Personal Trainer	• Applied Skills: Writing Across the Curriculum	• Terms Review • Audit Your Understanding • Work Together 17-3	• On Your Own 17-3 • Application Problems 17-5 and 17-6 • Ongoing Assessment, p. 515 • Personal Trainer • Xtra! Web Site: Xtra! Study Tools	• Reteach, p. 515 • Enrich, p. 517
• Automated Accounting • Personal Trainer • Xtra! Web Site: Xtra! Review, Quizzing, and Enrichment • Student Companion CD	• At-Risk Students		• Mastery Problem 17-7 • Personal Trainer • Xtra! Web Site: Xtra! Review and Quizzing • Study Guide 17 • Student Companion CD • Chapter 17 Test • ExamView Chapter 17 • Portfolio Assessment	• Challenge Problem 17-8 • Reteach, p. 518 • Enrich, p. 518 • Recycling Problem 17-1 • Automated Accounting • Xtra! Web Site: Xtra! Enrichment

Preview Chapter Objectives

- Explain that this chapter brings together all of the tools of financial analysis presented in previous chapters and explains and demonstrates new measures such as trend analysis, debt and equity ratios, working capital, current ratio, and acid-test ratio.

- Mention that the chapter begins with a general description of financial analysis including objectives, information resources, analysis procedures, and acceptable levels of performance.

Preview Accounting Terms

- Read each term out loud to verify pronunciation for students.

- Point out that there are several different ratios presented in this chapter. Mention that each ratio has a different formula. Emphasize that knowledge of the correct formula will be critical.

INTERNET ACTIVITY

Point your browser to *accountingxtra. swlearning.com* to access the Accounting Xtra! Web Site.

SOFTWARE FOCUS

Software may be used for independent practice or enrichment as the instructor deems appropriate. For this chapter, the following software may be used: Automated Accounting and Century 21 8E CD with Mastery Problem 17-7; QuickBooks with Application Problem 17-1; the Student Companion CD; and Personal Trainer, Chapter 17.

Instructors may wish to cover the Automated Accounting feature on pages 526–527 even if the Automated Accounting software is not being used in the classroom so that students get a sense of how the chapter's accounting procedures would be implemented in an automated environment.

CHAPTER

17 Financial Statement Analysis

After studying Chapter 17, you will be able to:

1. Define accounting terms related to financial statement analysis.

2. Identify accounting concepts and practices related to financial statement analysis.

3. Analyze financial statements.

4. Calculate earnings performance.

5. Perform efficiency analysis.

6. Analyze the long-term financial strength of a business.

- ratio
- trend analysis
- rate earned on net sales

- working capital
- current ratio
- quick assets

- acid-test ratio
- debt ratio
- equity ratio

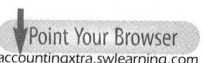
Point Your Browser
accountingxtra.swlearning.com

1. Changes in sales for a brand can result from a change in the number of stores as well as a change in same-store sales.

2. Answers may vary.

INTERNET RESEARCH ACTIVITY

Answers will vary.

Accounting in the real world

• Yum! Brands, Inc.

@BLOOMBERG NEWS/LANDOV

YUM! BRANDS FOCUSES ON SALES GROWTH

Yum! Brands, Inc., may be one of the most famous companies you've never heard of. The company owns some of the most respected quick-serve brands in the restaurant industry—Kentucky Fried Chicken, Pizza Hut, Taco Bell, Long John Silver's, and A&W.

Yum! managers use financial statement analysis to measure the performance of the company, each brand, and individual stores. Similar to managers of other retail businesses, Yum! managers use a measure known as *same-store sales* to evaluate sales trends at individual restaurant locations. The same-store sales measure is calculated by dividing the change in sales by the prior period's sales. Same-store sales can be calculated for a week, month, or year.

Restaurants strive to generate consistent increases in same-store sales. Popular methods of increasing sales include expanding menu options, offering value menus, providing late-night drive-up window service, and improving customer service.

To increase its same-store sales, Yum! Brands has been aggressive in opening multi-brand stores—buildings containing two brands, such as a Kentucky Fried Chicken and a Taco Bell. Families who may have difficulty agreeing where to eat enjoy the expanded menu options offered by a multi-brand store. Yum! has learned that multi-brand stores outperform single-brand stores by $300,000-$400,000 sales per year.

Critical Thinking

1. Why can calculating the change in total sales for Yum! be a misleading measure of how customers are reacting to changes designed to increase sales?
2. What two brands would you recommend that Yum! include in its multi-brand stores? Support your answer.

Source: www.yumbrands.com/investors/annualreport/03annualreport/

Xtra!
Today
accountingxtra.swlearning.com

NEW YORK STOCK EXCHANGE (NYSE)

Go to the homepage for the New York Stock Exchange (NYSE) (www.nyse.com). Click on "Symbol Lookup." Enter the name of a corporation to determine if its stock is traded on the NYSE and to find its trading symbol. Find the symbol for two different companies. Enter the symbol for each company into the "Quick Quote" box. Click on "Quick Quote."

Instructions

1. List the name and trading symbol for each company.
2. List the amount and time of the last stock trade for each company.
3. List the previous day's closing price for each company.

17-1 Trend Analysis and Component Percentages

Financial statements report the financial progress and condition of a business for a fiscal period. [CONCEPT: Adequate Disclosure]

The adequate disclosure concept states that financial statements contain the information necessary to understand a business's financial condition. Owners, managers, lenders, and investors rely on financial statements to make informed decisions. All relevant financial information must be adequately and completely disclosed on financial statements.

A business reports only the total liabilities of $200,000.00 on its balance sheet. However, the total liabilities include $75,000.00 in current liabilities and $125,000.00 in long-term liabilities. Therefore, the balance sheet does not adequately disclose the nature of the liabilities. The critical information not disclosed is that $75,000.00 is current and due within a few months.

Managers use financial information to identify areas for improving profitability. Banks and lending agencies use the information to decide whether to loan money to a business. Owners and potential owners use the information to decide whether to buy, sell, or keep their investment. Each group uses the financial information in a different way to assist with decision making.

Although financial statements provide useful information, they can be difficult to understand. For example, is a significant increase in the cost of merchandise sold an unfavorable trend? This question cannot be answered without considering information in other financial statement items, such as net sales. Financial statement analysis provides this information, since it calculates the relationships among financial statement items.

making ethical decisions

MAKING ETHICAL DECISIONS · MAKING ETHICAL DECISIONS · MAKING ETHICAL DECISIO

Could You Be a Whistle Blower?

You have just discovered that the management of your company is making improper accounting entries that substantially overstate its net income. You are concerned that if you disclose this information, the company's stock price will tumble, the company may be forced into bankruptcy, and your friends will lose their jobs. You will be branded a "whistle blower" and endure professional and personal hardships for your trouble.

The Association of Certified Fraud Examiners states that tips and complaints, rather than internal or external auditors, are the most common way that frauds are detected. Thus, it is important

that employees feel that they can communicate what they know without the fear of repercussions from their company. In an attempt to protect whistle blowers, Congress included a special whistle-blowing provision in the Sarbanes-Oxley Act of 2002 (Section 806).

Instructions

Write a summary of a news article that describes an individual who blew the whistle on unethical activities within a company. What sort of professional and personal hardships did he or she endure? What motivated that person to blow the whistle?

FINANCIAL ANALYSIS OBJECTIVES

Financial analysis objectives are determined by a business's characteristics and achievements that are important to the person making the analysis. Information is analyzed to obtain more knowledge about the business's strengths and weaknesses. Common objectives for analyzing financial information are to determine (1) profitability, (2) efficiency, (3) short-term financial strength, and (4) long-term financial strength.

Financial statements, with supporting schedules, are the primary information sources to be analyzed. A statement showing two or more years' information permits a reader to compare year-to-year differences. Financial statements providing information for each of two or more fiscal periods are known as comparative financial statements. Thus, consistent preparation and reporting of financial information are essential. [CONCEPT: Consistent Reporting]

The consistent reporting concept states that the same accounting procedures must be followed in the same way in each accounting period. Some business decisions require a comparison of current financial statements with previous financial statements. If accounting information is recorded and reported differently each accounting period, comparisons from one accounting period to another may not be possible. For example, in one period a business reports $170,000.00 for total operating expenses and in the next period it reports $120,000 as cost of merchandise sold and $50,000 as operating expenses. A user of this information cannot adequately compare the two accounting periods. Therefore, unless a change is necessary to make information more easily understood, accounting information is reported in a consistent way for each accounting period.

EXPLAIN

- Ask a student to read the accounting concept of Consistent Reporting. Discuss the example provided within the Consistent Reporting paragraph. Emphasize that it is difficult to compare oranges with apples. Although they are both fruits, they are two different kinds.

- Review the math box on this page. Point out that a ratio may be expressed as a stated ratio, percentage, or fraction and that all three methods provide the same information.

DEMONSTRATE

Calculate ratios

- Write the formulas on the board or overhead as they are presented. Review each formula and demonstrate how each is calculated. Have volunteers explain what each calculation measures and how it is used.

RATIO ANALYSIS

a.
Net Sales	÷	Net Income	=	Stated Ratio
$2,000,000.00	÷	$200,000.00	=	10 times (often stated as 10 to 1 or 10:1)

The stated ratio means net sales is 10 times net income. Another way of stating this ratio is 10:1, or for every $10.00 of net sales, the business earns $1.00 of net income.

b.
Net Income	÷	Net Sales	=	Percentage Ratio
$200,000.00	÷	$2,000,000.00	=	.10 or 10%

Net income is 10% of net sales.

c.
Net Income	÷	Net Sales	=	Fractional Ratio
$200,000.00	÷	$2,000,000.00	=	1/10

Net income is one-tenth of net sales.

A comparison between two numbers showing how many times one number exceeds the other is called a **ratio**. A ratio may be expressed as a stated ratio, percentage, or fraction. For a business with net sales of $2,000,000.00 and net income of $200,000.00, the relationship may be stated as any of the ratios calculated above. All three methods of calculating and expressing ratios are correct and essentially the same. The method selected is usually determined by the statement user's preference.

- Point out that the comparative income statement shown in the illustration is very similar to one studied in Chapter 14.

- Ask students to review the comparative income statement presented in the illustration on this page.

- Ask students what type of information is provided by the statement. Discuss net sales, cost of merchandise sold, gross profit on operations, expense amounts, and federal income. Point out that there are amounts for two years, as well as figures representing the dollar and percentage amounts of increase or decrease from the previous year.

- Review the math callout at the bottom of the illustration. Write the calculations on the board or overhead and explain each step. Ask for several student volunteers to come to the board and show the class how they would calculate the dollar and percentage amounts of increase or decrease for several other items shown on the comparative income statement.

- Ask students how Hamilton Corporation might use the information presented on the comparative income statement. Emphasize that one purpose for analyzing the comparative income statement is to identify trends in sales, costs, and expenses. Another is to develop reasonable expectations and amounts for the next fiscal period's sales, costs, and expenses.

- Point out that the comparative income statement is also helpful in identifying those items that are increasing or decreasing at a higher rate than normal.

- Emphasize that horizontal analysis is a comparison that presents the relationship among amounts from two or more years for a single item (for example, a comparison showing the percentage relationship of the net sales amount for the current year versus the net sales amount for the prior year).

TREND ANALYSIS ON THE INCOME STATEMENT

Hamilton Corporation
Comparative Income Statement
For Years Ended December 31, 20-- and 20--

	Current Year	Prior Year	Increase (Decrease)	
			Amount	Percentage*
Operating Revenue:				
Net Sales	$4,767,200	$3,633,000	$1,134,200	31.2
Cost of Merchandise Sold:				
Merchandise Inv., Jan. 1	$ 423,800	$ 232,300	$ 191,500	82.4
Net Purchases	2,726,900	2,226,900	500,000	22.5
Total Cost of Mdse. Avail. for Sale	$3,150,700	$2,459,200	$ 691,500	28.1
Less Mdse. Inventory, Dec. 31	547,900	423,800	124,100	29.3
Cost of Merchandise Sold	$2,602,800	$2,035,400	$ 567,400	27.9
Gross Profit on Operations	$2,164,400	$1,597,600	$ 566,800	35.5
Operating Expenses:				
Selling Expenses:				
Advertising Expense	$ 46,700	$ 30,100	$ 16,600	55.1
Delivery Expense	74,600	55,200	19,400	35.1
Salary Expense—Sales	912,400	696,800	215,600	30.9
Supplies Expense	81,600	63,800	17,800	27.9
Other Selling Expenses	102,900	78,700	24,200	30.7
Total Selling Expenses	$1,218,200	$ 924,600	$ 293,600	31.8
Administrative Expenses:				
Salary Expense—Administrative	$ 290,200	$ 229,600	$ 60,600	26.4
Uncollectible Accounts Expense	27,700	19,100	8,600	45.0
Other Administrative Expenses	229,500	189,200	40,300	21.3
Total Administrative Expenses	$ 547,400	$ 437,900	$ 109,500	25.0
Total Operating Expenses	$1,765,600	$1,362,500	$ 403,100	29.6
Income from Operations	$ 398,800	$ 235,100	$ 163,700	69.6
Other Expenses:				
Interest Expense	$ 62,000	$ 52,000	$ 10,000	19.2
Net Income before Fed. Inc. Tax	$ 336,800	$ 183,100	$ 153,700	83.9
Less Federal Income Tax Exp.	114,500	54,700	59,800	109.3
Net Income after Fed. Inc. Tax	$ 222,300	$ 128,400	$ 93,900	73.1

*Rounded to nearest 0.1%

①   Current Year Net Sales $4,767,200.00
   −   Prior Year Net Sales   3,633,000.00

②   =   Increase or Decrease in Net Sales $1,134,200.00
③   ÷   Prior Year Net Sales   3,633,000.00

④   =   % Increase or Decrease in Net Sales   31.2%

FYI   FOR YOUR INFORMATION

The prior year is always used as the base year to calculate the percentage increase or decrease.

Trends in a business's financial condition and operating results will not be apparent from a review of a single year's financial information. Comparison of information for two or more fiscal periods is needed to determine whether a business is making satisfactory progress. A comparison of the relationship between one item on a financial statement and the same item on a previous fiscal period's financial statement is called **trend analysis**. Trend analysis is sometimes referred to as horizontal analysis. A comparative income statement with trend analysis is shown above. The calculation of the favorable trend in net sales is included in the figure.

Financial Statement Analysis

TREND ANALYSIS ON THE STATEMENT OF STOCKHOLDERS' EQUITY

Hamilton Corporation
Comparative Statement of Stockholders' Equity
For Years Ended December 31, 20-- and 20--

	Current Year	Prior Year	Increase (Decrease) Amount	Percentage*
Capital Stock:				
$10.00 Per Share				
Balance, January 1	$ 500,000	$500,000	$ –0–	0.0
Additional Capital Stock Issued	100,000	–0–	100,000	—
Balance, December 31	$ 600,000	$500,000	$100,000	20.0
Retained Earnings:				
Balance, January 1	$ 349,300	$320,900	$ 28,400	8.9
Net Income after Federal Income Tax	222,300	128,400	93,900	73.1
Total	$ 571,600	$449,300	$122,300	27.2
Less Dividends Declared	120,000	100,000	20,000	20.0
Balance, December 31	$ 451,600	$349,300	$102,300	29.3
Total Stockholders' Equity, December 31	$1,051,600	$849,300	$202,300	23.8
Capital Stock Shares Outstanding	60,000	50,000	10,000	20.0

*Rounded to nearest 0.1%

The trend in stockholders' equity can be determined from information on Hamilton Company's comparative statement of stockholders' equity. Total stockholders' equity increased 23.8% from the prior year. Further review shows the increase in stockholders' equity was caused by an increase in both capital stock and net income. Management believes that the prior year's stockholders' equity was unsatisfactorily low; thus, the trend is favorable.

A percentage increase (decrease) cannot be calculated if the amount divided by is zero. Therefore, a dash (—) is recorded in the percentage column.

©GETTY IMAGES/PHOTODISC

- Ask students to review the comparative statement of stockholders' equity presented in the illustration.
- Ask students to state the January 1 balance of capital stock for the current year *($500,000)*. Ask them how many shares the beginning balance represents *($500,000 ÷ $10 share = 50,000 shares)*. Ask students the amount of additional capital stock that was sold during the current year *($100,000 or 10,000 shares)*.
- Ask students to state the amount of net income earned after federal income tax *($223,000)*. Ask students the origin of the net income figure *(Income statement on page 496)*. Ask students to state the percentage of increase in net income over the prior year *(73.1%)*.
- Ask students the amount of dividend for the current year *($120,000)*. Ask them if this represents a change in the amount of dividend declared per share. *(No, the amount of dividend per share, $.20, remained the same. There were 60,000 outstanding shares for the current year and 50,000 the prior year. Consequently, the dividend amount equals $120,000 for the current year and $100,000 for the prior year.)*
- Ask students to state the December 31 balance of stockholders' equity for the current year *($1,051,600)*. Ask students if this was an improvement over last year *(yes)*. Ask students to state the percentage of increase in stockholders' equity *(23.8%)*. Ask students to state the reasons for the increase *(additional capital stock sold, increase in net income)*.

- Remind students that a balance sheet shows what a company owns, owes, and is worth on a specific date. Emphasize that the balance sheet is a formal presentation of the accounting equation and that at all times assets must equal liabilities plus owner's equity.

- Ask students to look at the illustration and state the total amount of assets for the current and prior years. Ask students to state the amount and percentage of increase. Ask for a student volunteer to come to the board or overhead to explain and show the calculations required to calculate the amount and percentage of increase. Allow the student to use a calculator.

- Ask students for possible reasons to explain the decrease in the asset, accounts receivable *(fewer charge sales, greater cash sales, higher percentage of customers paying off accounts, selection of clients with lower credit risk).*

- Ask students to compare the percentages of increase for total assets and total liabilities. Ask students if this is a favorable or unfavorable trend and to explain their reasoning. *(Favorable trend. Assets increased at a greater rate than liabilities. This means Hamilton increased its assets without overborrowing.)*

- Emphasize that one purpose for analyzing the comparative balance sheet is to identify positive trends. Positive trends often indicate that the leadership team is properly managing the company. Another is to develop reasonable expectations for the long term. Potential lenders and investors are extremely interested in how well a company will perform in the future.

TREND ANALYSIS ON THE BALANCE SHEET

Hamilton Corporation
Comparative Balance Sheet
December 31, 20-- and 20--

	Current Year	Prior Year	Increase (Decrease) Amount	Increase (Decrease) Percentage*
ASSETS				
Current Assets:				
Cash	$ 206,100	$ 104,300	$101,800	97.6
Accounts Receivable (net)	474,000	569,200	(95,200)	(16.7)
Merchandise Inventory	547,900	423,800	124,100	29.3
Other Current Assets	26,100	21,300	4,800	22.5
Total Current Assets	$1,254,100	$1,118,600	$135,500	12.1
Total Plant Assets (net)	813,600	641,100	172,500	26.9
Total Assets	$2,067,700	$1,759,700	$308,000	17.5
LIABILITIES				
Current Liabilities:				
Notes Payable	$ 222,200	$ 241,600	$ (19,400)	(8.0)
Interest Payable	12,900	20,700	(7,800)	(37.7)
Accounts Payable	344,300	413,300	(69,000)	(16.7)
Federal Income Tax Payable	11,300	3,300	8,000	242.4
Other Current Liabilities	5,400	6,500	(1,100)	(16.9)
Total Current Liabilities	$ 596,100	$ 685,400	$ (89,300)	(13.0)
Long-Term Liability:				
Mortgage Payable	$ 420,000	$ 225,000	$195,000	86.7
Total Liabilities	$1,016,100	$ 910,400	$105,700	11.6
STOCKHOLDERS' EQUITY				
Capital Stock	$ 600,000	$ 500,000	$100,000	20.0
Retained Earnings	451,600	349,300	102,300	29.3
Total Stockholders' Equity	$1,051,600	$ 849,300	$202,300	23.8
Total Liabilities and Stockholders' Equity	$2,067,700	$1,759,700	$308,000	17.5

*Rounded to nearest 0.1%

Changes in Hamilton's balance sheet accounts are shown above. Accounts Receivable and Plant Assets are reported at book value. Information on this statement shows that total assets increased 17.5% during the current year. This increase was caused by an 11.6% increase in total liabilities and a 23.8% increase in total stockholders' equity. This trend is considered favorable because assets are increasing and the increase came more from the significant increase in stockholders' equity than the increase in liabilities.

Comparative financial statements report a business's current and past activity. However, most financial statement readers are also interested in how well a business will do in the future. Trend analysis is one method of financial analy-

sis used to help predict how well a business will perform in the future. [*CONCEPT: Adequate Disclosure*] Trend analysis is often performed using financial statements for a three-to-five-year period. Lenders and investors are very interested in how well a business will perform in the long term. Favorable trends over a period of several years often indicate that management is making good decisions.

FYI FOR YOUR INFORMATION

Financial statements are beneficial only to the extent that they are analyzed and used by the corporation to measure progress.

COMPONENT PERCENTAGES ON THE INCOME STATEMENT

Hamilton Corporation
Comparative Income Statement
For Years Ended December 31, 20-- and 20--

	Current Year		Prior Year	
	Amount	Percentage*	Amount	Percentage*
Operating Revenue:				
Net Sales	$4,767,200	100.0	$3,633,000	100.0
Cost of Merchandise Sold:				
Merchandise Inv., Jan. 1	$ 423,800	8.9	$ 232,300	6.4
Net Purchases	2,726,900	57.2	2,226,900	61.3
Total Cost of Mdse. Avail. for Sale........	$3,150,700	66.1	$2,459,200	67.7
Less Mdse. Inventory, Dec. 31	547,900	11.5	423,800	11.7
Cost of Merchandise Sold	$2,602,800	54.6	$2,035,400	56.0
Gross Profit on Operations	$2,164,400	45.4	$1,597,600	44.0
Operating Expenses:				
Selling Expenses:				
Advertising Expense.....................	$ 46,700	1.0	$ 30,100	0.8
Delivery Expense	74,600	1.6	55,200	1.5
Salary Expense—Sales..................	912,400	19.1	696,800	19.2
Supplies Expense	81,600	1.7	63,800	1.8
Other Selling Expenses	102,900	2.2	78,700	2.2
Total Selling Expenses	$1,218,200	25.6	$ 924,600	25.5
Administrative Expenses:				
Salary Expense—Administrative	$ 290,200	6.1	$ 229,600	6.3
Uncollectible Accounts Expense	27,700	0.6	19,100	0.5
Other Administrative Expenses	229,500	4.8	189,200	5.2
Total Administrative Expenses	$ 547,400	11.5	$ 437,900	12.1
Total Operating Expenses	$1,765,600	37.0	$1,362,500	37.5
Income from Operations	$ 398,800	8.4	$ 235,100	6.5
Other Expenses:				
Interest Expense	$ 62,000	1.3	$ 52,000	1.4
Net Income before Fed. Inc. Tax........	$ 336,800	7.1	$ 183,100	5.0
Less Federal Income Tax Exp...........	114,500	2.4	54,700	1.5
Net Income after Fed. Inc. Tax	$ 222,300	4.7	$ 128,400	3.5

*Rounded to nearest 0.1%.
Percentage totals may not equal sum of parts because of rounding.

The percentage relationship between one financial statement item and the total that includes that item is known as a component percentage. Component percentage analysis is also referred to as vertical analysis. Component percentages for items on an income statement are normally calculated as a percentage of net sales. The component percentage is shown in a separate percentage column. Hamilton's income statement with component percentages is shown above. This statement is similar to the one shown for Zytech in Chapter 4 and for LampLight in Chapter 13.

Component percentages on comparative statements show changes in a specific item from year to year. For example, Hamilton's cost of merchandise sold decreased from 56.0% to 54.6% of net sales. These percentages show a favorable trend since the cost of merchandise sold took a smaller part of each sales dollar in the current year. Similar comparisons can be made for each item on the comparative income statement. The cause of significant unfavorable changes should be investigated so that corrective action can be taken.

- Refer students to the illustration. Ask students to provide an example that demonstrates how a component percentage on a comparative statement of stockholders' equity is calculated. Ask a student to write an example on the board and to explain her/his calculations.

- Point out that component percentages on a comparative statement of stockholders' equity are usually calculated as a percentage of total stockholders' equity. Emphasize that this is the approach used by Hamilton Corporation. Stress that, in this instance, every amount appearing on Hamilton's comparative statement of stockholders' equity is divided by the total stockholders' equity figure.

- Ask students the difference in computing component percentages on a comparative income statement and computing component percentages on a comparative statement of stockholders' equity. *(On the income statement, the divisor is the net sales amount; on the statement of stockholders' equity, the divisor is the total stockholders' equity amount.)*

- Ask students to analyze the component percentages on Hamilton's comparative statement of stockholders' equity. Lead into a discussion of favorable and unfavorable trends.

- Emphasize that before any financial analysis can be productive, it is the company's responsibility to identify acceptable levels of performance. Point out that many firms determine acceptable standards of performance by reviewing prior company results, comparing results with published industry standards, and examining the rate of return for other types of investments.

Hamilton Corporation
Comparative Statement of Stockholders' Equity
For Years Ended December 31, 20-- and 20--

	Current Year		Prior Year	
	Amount	Percentage*	Amount	Percentage*
Capital Stock:				
$10.00 Per Share				
Balance, January 1	$ 500,000	47.5	$500,000	58.9
Additional Capital Stock Issued	100,000	9.5	0	0.0
Balance, December 31	$ 600,000	57.1	$500,000	58.9
Retained Earnings:				
Balance, January 1	$ 349,300	33.2	$320,900	37.8
Net Income after Federal Income Tax	222,300	21.1	128,400	15.1
Total	$ 571,600	54.4	$449,300	52.9
Less Dividends Declared	120,000	11.4	100,000	11.8
Balance, December 31	$ 451,600	42.9	$349,300	41.1
Total Stockholders' Equity, December 31	$1,051,600	100.0	$849,300	100.0
Capital Stock Shares Outstanding	60,000		50,000	

*Rounded to nearest 0.1%.
  Percentage totals may not equal sum of parts because of rounding.

Component percentages for items on a comparative statement of stockholders' equity are normally calculated as a percentage of total stockholders' equity. As shown above, capital stock represents 57.1% of Hamilton's stockholders' equity for the current year. The remaining 42.9% is retained earnings. Respective percentages for the prior year are 58.9% and 41.1%. Thus, little change has occurred in the component makeup of total equity. However, the percentage of dividends declared decreased slightly from 11.8% to 11.4%, an unfavorable trend for stockholders.

Acceptable Levels of Financial Performance

For financial analysis to be useful, a company must define acceptable levels of performance for each type of analysis. For example, Wiseman Grocery considers a component percentage of 3.0% for income from operations to be very good. However, Mitchell Manufacturing Co. considers a 12.0% component percentage for income from operations the minimum acceptable result. The difference is due to the different financial characteristics of the two businesses.

The grocery company has a low investment in plant assets and sells its inventory quickly. The manufacturing company has a high investment in plant assets and holds its inventory much longer. The manufacturing company's larger investment per sales dollar means that the company must earn a higher rate on sales. Each company's management team must determine the acceptable levels of performance for each financial analysis made.

Many businesses use two major guides to determine acceptable levels of performance: (1) prior company performance and (2) comparison with published trade performance standards.

Other sources of performance guides include (1) financial and credit-reporting companies such as Dun and Bradstreet, (2) the company's planned financial objectives (budget schedules), (3) current interest rates that could be earned by investing capital elsewhere, and (4) financial information available on the Internet.

Each company's management team should determine the acceptable performance level for each financial analysis made by the company.

COMPONENT PERCENTAGES ON THE BALANCE SHEET

Hamilton Corporation
Comparative Balance Sheet
December 31, 20-- and 20--

	Current Year		Prior Year	
	Amount	Percentage*	Amount	Percentage*
ASSETS				
Current Assets:				
Cash.................................	$ 206,100	10.0	$ 104,300	5.9
Accounts Receivable (book value)...............	474,000	22.9	569,200	32.3
Merchandise Inventory	547,900	26.5	423,800	24.1
Other Current Assets..........................	26,100	1.3	21,300	1.2
Total Current Assets	$1,254,100	60.7	$1,118,600	63.6
Total Plant Assets (book value)	813,600	39.3	641,100	36.4
Total Assets..................................	$2,067,700	100.0	$1,759,700	100.0
LIABILITIES				
Current Liabilities:				
Notes Payable	$ 222,200	10.7	$ 241,600	13.7
Interest Payable	12,900	0.6	20,700	1.2
Accounts Payable	344,300	16.7	413,300	23.5
Federal Income Tax Payable	11,300	0.5	3,300	0.2
Other Current Liabilities......................	5,400	0.3	6,500	0.4
Total Current Liabilities	$ 596,100	28.8	$ 685,400	38.9
Long-Term Liability:				
Mortgage Payable	$ 420,000	20.3	$ 225,000	12.8
Total Liabilities	$1,016,100	49.1	$ 910,400	51.7
STOCKHOLDERS' EQUITY				
Capital Stock	$ 600,000	29.0	$ 500,000	28.4
Retained Earnings	451,600	21.8	349,300	19.8
Total Stockholders' Equity......................	$1,051,600	50.9	$ 849,300	48.3
Total Liabilities and Stockholders' Equity	$2,067,700	100.0	$1,759,700	100.0

*Rounded to nearest 0.1%.
Percentage totals may not equal sum of parts because of rounding.

Component percentages for asset amounts on a comparative balance sheet are normally calculated as a percentage of total assets. Liabilities and stockholders' equity amounts are calculated as a percentage of total liabilities and stockholders' equity. Information on Hamilton's comparative balance sheet shows that current liabilities were 28.8% of total liabilities and stockholders' equity, down from 38.9% in the prior year.

Since current liabilities were at a high percentage in the prior year, Hamilton considers the reduction from 38.9% to 28.8% as a very favor-

able change. Hamilton's investors and lenders would also be pleased with this result. Similar comparisons can be made for each item on the comparative balance sheet.

EXPLAIN

- Refer students to the illustration. Ask them to prepare examples that demonstrate how the component percentages for asset, liability, and stockholders' equity items on a comparative balance sheet are calculated. Ask several students to write their examples on the board and to explain their calculations.

- Ask students if all the amounts on the comparative balance sheet are divided by the same figure, such as on the comparative income statement and comparative statement of stockholders' equity. Emphasize that each asset amount is divided by the total assets figure, $2,067,700, and that each liability and stockholders' equity item is divided by the total liabilities and stockholders' equity figure, $2,067,700.

- Ask students to analyze the component percentages on Hamilton's comparative balance sheet. Ask students to identify significant favorable and unfavorable trends of more than four percentage points *(cash, favorable; accounts receivable, favorable; accounts payable, favorable; total current liabilities, favorable; mortgage payable, unfavorable)*.

- Discuss with students possible reasons that might explain the favorable or unfavorable trends *(for example, cash increased due to the sale of additional stock, higher net income, and a large decrease in accounts receivable)*.

- Point out the F.Y.I. and the roles of judgment and experience in evaluating ratios.

ONGOING ASSESSMENT

- Circulate through the classroom or lab observing which students have problems with assignments.

- Troubleshooting: Students may become confused in selecting the proper divisor for calculating comparative and component percentages.

- Assess student understanding by checking solutions to Independent Practice assignments.

RETEACH

- Refer students to the illustration on page 496. Write *Comparative Income Statement—Horizontal Analysis* on the board. Using the amounts for advertising expense, show students how to calculate the amount and percentage of increase. Write all figures under the above heading. Emphasize that the divisor for

calculating the percentage of increase is the amount of advertising expense from the prior year. Highlight the divisor amount by circling it.

- Repeat the same process for the other comparative financial statements.

GUIDED PRACTICE

Terms Review

Call on students to define each term in the Terms Review. Ask the class if the definition is correct and whether the complete definition has been given or if anything else needs to be added. Suggested definitions are given in the Glossary.

Audit Your Understanding

Call on students to answer the Audit Your Understanding questions. Ask the class if the answer is correct and/or complete. Answers are given in Appendix E of the textbook.

Work Together

Have students write the solution to the Work Together problem as you guide the class through the examples.

- Direct students to record each answer on the appropriate income statement.
- Call on students to explain the process for calculating amounts and percentages.
- Ask a student to explain the difference between trend analysis and component percentage analysis.

INDEPENDENT PRACTICE

On Your Own

- Assign the On Your Own problem to be worked independently.
- Use the Ongoing Assessment techniques to diagnose student understanding.

Application Problems

- Assign Application Problem 17-1: Analyzing comparative financial statements using trend analysis.
- Assign Application Problem 17-2: Analyzing comparative financial statements using component percentage analysis.

Personal Trainer

- Students can access the Lesson 17-1 assessment material using this software.

Xtra! Web Site

- Students can access the Xtra! Study Tools for additional practice.

ENRICH

- Assign Making Ethical Decisions on page 494.
- Students can use QuickBooks data files to automate Application Problem 17-1.

• terms review

ratio
trend analysis

• audit your understanding

1. Why do managers, banks, lending agencies, owners, and potential owners need the financial information for a business?

2. What are four common objectives for analyzing a business's financial information?

3. Which accounting concept is being applied when comparative financial statements are prepared to provide useful information for statement users?

4. What two major guides do businesses use to determine acceptable levels of performance?

• work together 17-1

Analyzing comparative financial statements

Baycom Corporation's comparative income statement is provided in the *Working Papers*. Your instructor will guide you through the following examples.

1. Complete the partial income statement using trend analysis. Round percentage calculations to the nearest 0.1%.

2. Complete the income statement using component percentage analysis. Round percentage calculations to the nearest 0.1%.

• on your own 17-1

Analyzing comparative financial statements

Baycom Corporation's comparative balance sheet is provided in the *Working Papers*. Work independently to complete the following problem.

1. Complete the comparative balance sheet using trend analysis. Round percentage calculations to the nearest 0.1%.

2. Complete the balance sheet using component percentage analysis. Round percentage calculations to the nearest 0.1%.

Financial Statement Analysis

CLOSE

- Ask students why it is important that companies carefully analyze financial statements. Emphasize that one purpose for analyzing financial statements is to identify favorable and unfavorable trends. Identification of unfavorable trends may lead to corrective actions. Another purpose is to develop reasonable expectations for the next fiscal period.

- Ask students to briefly summarize the difference between trend analysis and component percentage analysis.

LESSON · LESSON · LESSON · LESSON · LESSON · LESSON

17-2 Calculating Earnings Performance and Efficiency Analysis

EARNINGS PERFORMANCE ANALYSIS

The amount and consistency of earnings are important measures of a business's success. The earnings of a business must be satisfactory to continue operations. [*CONCEPT: Going Concern*] Consequently, managers, owners, and creditors are interested in an analysis of earnings perfor-

mance. Hamilton calculates five earnings performance ratios for the two most recent years. (1) Rate earned on average total assets. (2) Rate earned on average stockholders equity. (3) Rate earned on net sales. (4) Earnings per share. (5) Price-earnings ratio.

RATE EARNED ON AVERAGE TOTAL ASSETS

Hamilton Corporation
Comparative Balance Sheet
December 31, 20-- and 20--

	Current Year		Prior Year	
	Amount	Percentage*	Amount	Percentage*
ASSETS				
Current Assets:				
Cash	$ 206,100	10.0	$ 104,300	5.9
Accounts Receivable (book value)	474,000	22.9	569,200	32.3
Merchandise Inventory	547,900	26.5	423,800	24.1
Other Current Assets	26,100	1.3	21,300	1.2
Total Current Assets	$1,254,100	60.7	$1,118,600	63.6
Total Plant Assets (book value)	813,600	39.3	641,100	36.4
Total Assets	$2,067,700	100.0	$1,759,700	100.0

*Rounded to nearest 0.1%.

① (January 1 Total Assets + December 31 Total Assets) ÷ 2 = Average Total Assets
(1,759,700.00 + $2,067,700.00) ÷ 2 = $1,913,700.00

② Net Income after Federal Income Tax ÷ Average Total Assets = Rate Earned on Average Total Assets
$222,300.00 ÷ $1,913,700.00 = 11.6%

Hamilton Corporation
Comparative Income Statement
For Years Ended December 31, 20-- and 20--

	Current Year		Prior Year	
	Amount	Percentage*	Amount	Percentage*
Other Expenses:				
Interest Expense	$ 62,000	1.3	$ 52,000	1.4
Net Income before Fed. Inc. Tax	$ 336,800	7.1	$ 183,100	5.0
Less Federal Income Tax Exp.	114,500	2.4	54,700	1.5
Net Income after Fed. Inc. Tax.	$ 222,300	4.7	$ 128,400	3.5

*Rounded to nearest 0.1%.

- Define accounting terms related to financial statement analysis.
- Identify accounting concepts and practices related to financial statement analysis.
- Calculate earnings performance.
- Perform efficiency analysis.

MOTIVATE

Obtain copies of annual reports from several major corporations as well as local corporations. Display these reports on the bulletin board. Discuss and highlight the way in which the corporations present their financial statements. Illustrate points in the written parts of the reports that show an analysis of items on the financial statements.

Preview

- Preview the accounting term and definition introduced in this lesson: rate earned on net sales.
- Direct students to read the headings at the top of each page in this lesson and to examine the illustrations given.
- Point out that general financial statement analysis was presented earlier in this chapter. In this lesson, analysis will focus on the amount and consistency of the earnings of a business and the measures available to determine how efficiently a business is using its assets.

EXPLAIN

- Review the accounting concept Going Concern. Emphasize that financial statements are prepared with the expectation that a business will remain in operation indefinitely. For example, if a company purchases a computer with an expected life of five years, yearly depreciation is calculated based on the computer's expected life. This is true even if the owner intends to sell the business in two years when she retires.
- Point out that for a company to continue operating, its earnings must maintain a satisfactory level. Emphasize that Hamilton Corporation measures company success by calculating the following five earnings performance ratios (write on board or overhead):
  1. rate earned on average total assets
  2. rate earned on average stockholders' equity
  3. rate earned on net sales
  4. earnings per share
  5. price-earnings ratio

MATERIALS

- Instructor's Resource CD:
  PowerPoint Slides
- Xtra! Study Tools on the Xtra! Web Site
- Working Papers:
  Teacher's Edition of the Working Papers for Lesson 17-2
- Software:
  Personal Trainer

- Ask students why companies invest large sums of money in assets. For example, why do companies purchase inventory, buy computers, or accumulate accounts receivable? Point out that companies need assets to help earn a net income.

- Stress that a company must use its assets effectively in order to earn income. One way companies measure this effectiveness is to determine the rate earned on average total assets.

- Emphasize that companies compare the rate earned on average total assets with the rates that can be earned on other investments. For example, if a company can earn more by placing extra cash in a special savings account, then perhaps the company needs to re-evaluate its earnings goals.

DEMONSTRATE

Calculate the rate of return on average total assets

- Direct students to the illustration on page 503.

- Review step 1 and demonstrate on the board how to calculate average total assets.

- Review step 2 and demonstrate on the board how to calculate the rate earned on average total assets. Ask students to state the source of the net income amount *(comparative income statement)*.

- Ask students to verify average total assets and the rate earned on average total assets with a calculator.

- Provide students with extra practice by writing additional January 1 and December 31 total asset amounts and the corresponding net income after federal income tax figures.

CALCULATING THE RATE EARNED ON AVERAGE TOTAL ASSETS

A business uses its assets to earn net income. If a business uses all assets as efficiently as possible, it should earn the best possible net income. The rate found by dividing net income after federal income tax by average total assets is known as the rate earned on average total assets. The rate earned on average total assets shows how well a business is using its assets to earn net income. Hamilton's rate of return on average total assets is calculated as shown on the previous page using income statement and balance sheet information.

STEPS · STEPS · STEPS · STEPS · STEPS · STEPS · STEPS · STEPS · STEPS · STEPS

CALCULATING THE RATE OF RETURN ON AVERAGE TOTAL ASSETS

1 Calculate average total assets. Average total assets is the average amount of assets held during a year.
   a. Add January 1 total assets and December 31 total assets. (Total assets for January 1 are the same as the total assets on the prior year's December 31 balance sheet.)
   b. Divide the total by 2.

2 Divide net income after federal income taxes by average total assets to determine the rate earned on average total assets.

An 11.6% rate earned on average total assets means that for each $1.00 of assets, the business earned 11.6 cents. A table comparing this result to the rate for the prior year is shown below. (Some information for the prior year is taken from financial statements that are not illustrated.)

	Current Year	Prior Year
Net Income after Federal Income Tax	$ 222,300.00	$ 128,400.00
January 1 Total Assets	1,759,700.00	1,437,600.00
December 31 Total Assets	2,067,700.00	1,759,700.00
Average Total Assets	1,913,700.00	1,598,650.00
Rate Earned on Average Total Assets	11.6%	8.0%

Hamilton compares this rate to rates of return on alternative investments. Hamilton's goal is to earn a rate of return that is at least as high as other types of investments. For example, if Hamilton can earn more by placing extra cash in government bonds, the company is not meeting its earnings goal.

Investment sources available to Hamilton are earning 10.0%. Although the prior year's investments fell below this goal, the trend in the rate earned improved significantly from 8.0% to 11.6%. Therefore, Hamilton believes that a rate earned on total assets of 11.6% is satisfactory.

FYI FOR YOUR INFORMATION

Publications such as *Dun and Bradstreet* list various ratios for a variety of businesses.

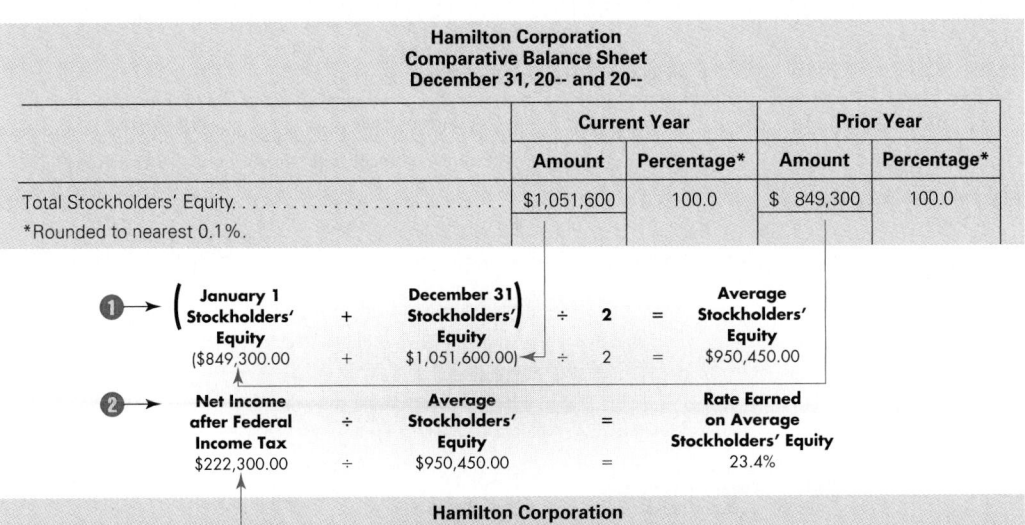

Hamilton Corporation
Comparative Balance Sheet
December 31, 20-- and 20--

	Current Year		Prior Year	
	Amount	Percentage*	Amount	Percentage*
Total Stockholders' Equity.........................	$1,051,600	100.0	$ 849,300	100.0

*Rounded to nearest 0.1%.

❶
$$\left(\begin{array}{c} \text{January 1} \\ \text{Stockholders'} \\ \text{Equity} \\ (\$849,300.00) \end{array} + \begin{array}{c} \text{December 31} \\ \text{Stockholders'} \\ \text{Equity} \\ \$1,051,600.00 \end{array} \right) \div 2 = \begin{array}{c} \text{Average} \\ \text{Stockholders'} \\ \text{Equity} \\ \$950,450.00 \end{array}$$

❷
$$\begin{array}{c} \text{Net Income} \\ \text{after Federal} \\ \text{Income Tax} \\ \$222,300.00 \end{array} \div \begin{array}{c} \text{Average} \\ \text{Stockholders'} \\ \text{Equity} \\ \$950,450.00 \end{array} = \begin{array}{c} \text{Rate Earned} \\ \text{on Average} \\ \text{Stockholders' Equity} \\ 23.4\% \end{array}$$

Hamilton Corporation
Comparative Income Statement
For Years Ended December 31, 20-- and 20--

	Current Year		Prior Year	
	Amount	Percentage*	Amount	Percentage*
Net Income before Fed. Inc. Tax......................	$ 336,800	7.1	$ 183,100	5.0
Less Federal Income Tax Exp......................	114,500	2.4	54,700	1.5
Net Income after Fed. Inc. Tax.......................	$ 222,300	4.7	$ 128,400	3.5

*Rounded to nearest 0.1%.

Investors compare the rate earned on stockholders' equity for several businesses to determine the best investment. Hamilton's rate earned on average stockholders' equity is calculated as shown above.

The following table compares the current year's rate to the rate for the prior year. (Some information for the prior year is taken from financial statements that are not illustrated.)

Hamilton's rate earned fell well below industry standards in the prior year. However, its rate of earnings has increased significantly from 15.4% to 23.4%. Based on the trend and a comparison with industry standards, Hamilton

achieved a satisfactory rate earned on average stockholders' equity.

STEPS · STEPS · STEPS · STEPS · STEPS · STEPS

CALCULATING THE RATE OF RETURN ON AVERAGE STOCKHOLDERS' EQUITY

❶ Calculate average stockholders' equity. (January 1 total stockholders' equity is the same as the total stockholders' equity on the prior year's December 31 balance sheet.)

❷ Divide net income after federal income taxes by average total stockholders' equity to determine the rate earned on average total assets.

	Current Year	Prior Year	Industry Standard (2 yrs.)
Net Income after Federal Income Tax	$ 222,300.00	$128,400.00	
January 1 Stockholders' Equity	849,300.00	820,900.00	
December 31 Stockholders' Equity	1,051,600.00	849,300.00	
Average Stockholders' Equity	950,450.00	835,100.00	
Rate Earned on Average Stockholders' Equity	23.4%	15.4%	20%

- Ask students the difference between total liabilities and total stockholders' equity. Remind students that liabilities represent funds invested by creditors and that stockholders' equity represents owners' worth or investment in a corporation. Stress that as investors, stockholders are very interested in knowing the amount of net income their investment is earning.

- Point out that another method of assessing a corporation's effectiveness in terms of earning capacity is to calculate the rate of return earned on average stockholders' equity.

- Emphasize that knowing this rate allows investors to compare the rates of several businesses in order to select the best investment.

DEMONSTRATE

Calculate the rate earned on average stockholders' equity

- Direct students to the illustration.

- Review step 1 and demonstrate on the board how to calculate average stockholders' equity.

- Review step 2 and demonstrate on the board how to calculate the rate earned on average stockholders' equity. Ask students to state the source of the net income amount (*comparative income statement*).

- Ask students to verify average stockholders' equity and the rate earned on average total assets with a calculator.

- Provide students with extra practice by writing additional January 1 and December 31 stockholders' equity amounts and the corresponding net income figures.

- Discuss with students that Hamilton's current year rate of 23.4% is a definite improvement over last year's rate of 15.4%, which was below the industry average of 20%.

- Point out that another indicator of a company's ability to earn income is the rate earned on net sales. This measure of profitability indicates if the company is properly managing the costs and expenses incurred to generate revenue.
- Stress that when this rate declines, it means the company is spending a greater portion of every sales dollar received on costs and expenses. If the rate earned on net sales increases, it indicates that the firm is carefully controlling costs and expenses by reducing the amount needed to generate each sales dollar.

DEMONSTRATE

Calculate the rate earned on net sales

- Direct students to the illustration.
- Review the single step on how to calculate the rate earned on net sales.
- Ask a student to write and explain the calculation on the board or overhead.
- Ask students to state the source of the net sales and net income after federal income tax amounts (comparative income statement).
- Ask students to verify the rate earned on net sales with a calculator.
- Provide students with extra practice by writing additional net sales and net income after federal income tax figures.
- Point out that Hamilton's current rate earned on net sales, 4.7%, exceeded last year's rate of 3.5%. Ask students if this rate increase is favorable or unfavorable and to state why. Lead into a discussion that the increase is a favorable trend and indicates that Hamilton Corporation did a better job of controlling costs and expenses this year than last year.

RATE EARNED ON NET SALES

Hamilton Corporation
Comparative Income Statement
For Years Ended December 31, 20-- and 20--

	Current Year		Prior Year	
	Amount	Percentage*	Amount	Percentage*
Operating Revenue: Net Sales	$4,767,200	100.0	$3,633,000	100.0
Other Expenses: Interest Expense	$ 62,000	1.3	$ 52,000	1.4
Net Income before Fed. Inc. Tax	$ 336,800	7.1	$ 183,100	5.0
Less Federal Income Tax Exp.	114,500	2.4	54,700	1.5
Net Income after Fed. Inc. Tax	$ 222,300	4.7	$ 128,400	3.5
*Rounded to nearest 0.1%.				

① Net Income after Federal Income Tax	÷	Net Sales	=	Rate Earned on Net Sales
$222,300.00	÷	$4,767,200.00	=	4.7%

A business that carefully controls costs should earn a consistent rate on net sales from year to year. The rate found by dividing net income after federal income tax by net sales is called the **rate earned on net sales**. However, if costs suddenly change, the rate earned on net sales also changes.

Hamilton's rate earned on net sales for the current year is calculated as shown above using information from the income statement.

The following table compares the current rate to the rate from the prior year.

	Current Year	Prior Year
Net Income after Federal Income Tax	$ 222,300.00	$ 128,400.00
Net Sales	4,767,200.00	3,633,000.00
Rate Earned on Net Sales	4.7%	3.5%

The component percentage for net income after federal income tax is the same percentage as the rate earned on net sales. In both calculations, net income is calculated as a percentage of net sales.

When determining an acceptable rate earned on net sales, Hamilton considers what is normal for similar businesses and the company's own past experience. Businesses similar to Hamilton have been earning about a 4.0% rate on net sales for the last two or three years. Based on a comparison of similar businesses, Hamilton's rate earned on net sales of 3.5% in the prior year was unsatisfactory. The trend in rate earned increased to 4.7% in the current year, a satisfactory rate. This trend should be watched closely for any future declines. When the rate earned on net sales declines, the company must increase sales or reduce costs to maintain an acceptable rate.

Hamilton Corporation
Comparative Income Statement
For Years Ended December 31, 20-- and 20--

	Current Year		Prior Year	
	Amount	Percentage*	Amount	Percentage*
Net Income before Fed. Inc. Tax.....................	$ 336,800	7.1	$ 183,100	5.0
Less Federal Income Tax Exp....................	114,500	2.4	54,700	1.5
Net Income after Fed. Inc. Tax......................	$ 222,300	4.7	$ 128,400	3.5

*Rounded to nearest 0.1%.

Hamilton Corporation
Comparative Balance Sheet
December 31, 20-- and 20--

	Current Year		Prior Year	
	Amount	Percentage*	Amount	Percentage*
Total Stockholders' Equity..........................	$1,051,600	100.0	$ 849,300	100.0
Capital Stock Shares Outstanding	60,000		50,000	

*Rounded to nearest 0.1%.

Net Income after Federal Income Tax	÷	**Shares of Capital Stock Outstanding**	=	**Earnings per Share**
①→ $222,300.00	÷	60,000	=	$3.71

The amount of net income earned on one share of common stock during a fiscal period is known as earnings per share. Stockholders and management frequently use earnings per share as a measure of success. As earnings per share increase, more people become interested in buying stock. This demand for stock causes stock prices to go up. The company then finds it easier to issue stock or borrow money.

Hamilton's earnings per share for the current year is calculated as shown above using information from the income statement and statement of stockholders' equity.

The earnings per share is calculated for the current and prior years as shown below.

	Current Year	Prior Year
Net Income after Federal Income Tax	$ 222,300.00	$128,400.00
Shares of Capital Stock Outstanding	60,000	50,000
Earnings Per Share	$3.71	$2.57

Increases in earnings per share signal stockholders that the company is continuing to increase the net income earned for each share. Hamilton knows that a positive trend is important to the company. Earnings per share increased significantly from $2.57 to $3.71, a very favorable trend.

FYI FOR YOUR INFORMATION

Earnings per share is one of the most widely recognized financial ratios.

507

- Remind students that the price-earnings ratio, or P/E ratio, was presented in Chapter 13.

- Ask students to define price-earnings ratio. Lead into a discussion that the P/E ratio shows the relationship between the market value per share and earnings per share of a stock. Point out the P/E ratio is based on a company's growth potential and future profitability. If investors think a company's future growth and earnings show excellent potential, they are usually willing to pay more for the stock.

- Stress that a high P/E ratio means that investors expect high growth and earnings in the future.

- Point out that the price-earnings ratio is often reported in the stock market section of the newspaper.

- Ask students what Hamilton's P/E ratio of 11.7 means. Explain to students in this instance that a single share of Hamilton's stock is selling for 11.7 times a single share's earnings.

DEMONSTRATE

Calculate price-earnings ratio

- Direct students to the math box.

- Review the information on how to calculate the earnings per share.

- Write and explain the calculation on the board or overhead.

- Ask students to verify the price earnings ratio with a calculator.

- Point out that Hamilton's current price-earnings ratio, 11.7, exceeded last year's price-earnings ratio of 9.5. Indicate that this is a favorable trend for Hamilton Corporation.

- Provide students with extra practice by writing additional amounts for market price per share and earnings per share.

PRICE-EARNINGS RATIO

	Market Price per share	÷	Earnings per Share	=	Price-Earnings Ratio
	$43.50	÷	$3.71	=	11.7 times

Investors want to buy stock in companies that will earn a reasonable return on their investment. The relationship between the market value per share of stock and the earnings per share is known as the price-earnings ratio. As described in Chapter 13, the price-earnings ratio of a company's stock relates profitability to the amount that the investors currently pay for the stock. The price-earnings ratio is usually expressed as a stated ratio.

Hamilton's capital stock sold for $43.50 per share on December 31 of the current year. Hamilton's price-earnings ratio for the current year is calculated as shown above.

The following price-earnings ratios are calculated for the current and prior years:

	Current Year	Prior Year
Market Price per Share	$43.50	$24.50
Earnings per Share	3.71	2.57
Price-Earnings Ratio	11.7 times	9.5 times

The market price of a share of stock is determined by the amount that investors are willing to pay for it. If investors think that a company's profitability is increasing, they are usually willing to pay more for the stock. Thus, the market price of a company's stock is influenced strongly by what potential investors think the company's earnings will be in the future. Hamilton's price-earnings ratio increased from 9.5 to 11.7. This change indicates that investors considered the stock more valuable and were willing to pay more for the stock per dollar earned by the corporation in the current year. This increased demand is a favorable trend for Hamilton.

GLOBAL PERSPECTIVE • GLOBAL PERSPECTIVE • GLOBAL PERSPEC

global perspective

International Mail

There are three categories of mail for sending documents internationally:

1. LC mail (initials for the French *lettres* and *cartes postale*—meaning "letters" and "postcards"). LC mail consists mainly of letters, letter packages, and postcards.

2. AO mail (initials for the French *Autres Objets*—meaning "other things"). AO mail usually consists of items considered printed materials, such as books, periodicals, and braille publications. This service is usually by ship and is slower than airmail.

3. CP mail (initials for the French par *Colis Postal*—meaning "by parcel post"). CP mail is the equivalent of American parcel post. CP mail resembles fourth class domestic mail. It is the only class of mail that can be insured. This service is also usually by ship.

Special services are also offered.

Required

Contact the local United States Postal Service or another mail service to obtain information about:

1. Express mail.
2. International Priority Airmail.
3. Registered mail.

Write a brief report about your findings.

Financial Statement Analysis

GLOBAL PERSPECTIVE
GLOBAL PERSPECTIVE

The Global Perspective feature is intended to expose students to some of the ways in which accounting and business in general differ in other countries. This particular feature allows students to explore international mail service and rates. The activity requires students to research the mailing options available and their costs.

Obtaining a schedule of costs and restrictions for international mail from the United States Postal Service or another mail service should be a relatively easy task. Student answers will vary, depending on the mail service and country that is chosen.

EFFICIENCY ANALYSIS

The profitability and continued growth of a business are influenced by how efficiently the business utilizes its assets. The operating cycle of a merchandising business consists of three phases. (1) Purchase merchandise. (2) Sell merchandise, frequently on account. (3) Collect the accounts receivable. Much of a business's assets are in accounts receivable and merchandise inventory. The faster a business can convert these assets to cash and begin another operating cycle, the more efficient and profitable the business will be.

ACCOUNTS RECEIVABLE TURNOVER RATIO

Hamilton Corporation
Comparative Balance Sheet
December 31, 20-- and 20--

	Current Year		Prior Year	
	Amount	Percentage*	Amount	Percentage*
ASSETS				
Current Assets:				
Cash.............................	$ 206,100	10.0	$ 104,300	5.9
Accounts Receivable (book value)...............	474,000	22.9	569,200	32.3
Merchandise Inventory......................	547,900	26.5	423,800	24.1
*Rounded to nearest 0.1%.				

Hamilton Corporation
Comparative Income Statement
For Years Ended December 31, 20-- and 20--

	Current Year		Prior Year	
	Amount	Percentage*	Amount	Percentage*
Operating Revenue:				
Net Sales..................................	$4,767,200	100.0	$3,633,000	100.0
*Rounded to nearest 0.1%.				

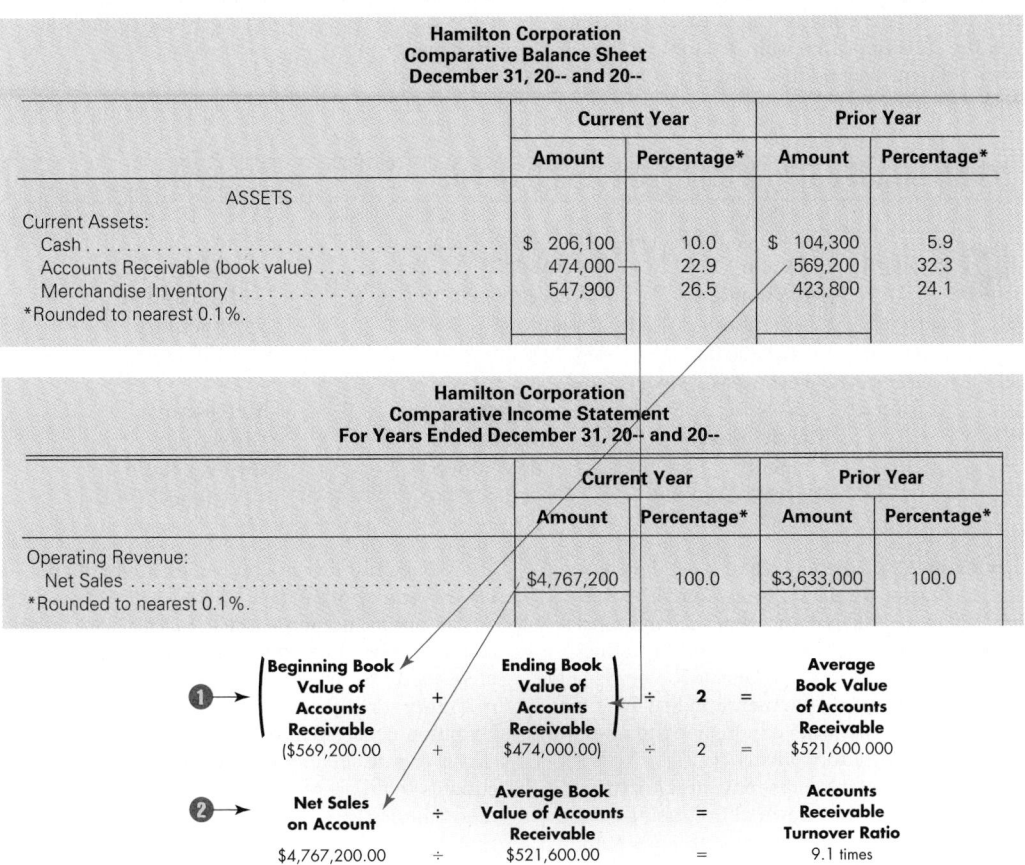

1
Beginning Book Value of Accounts Receivable	+	Ending Book Value of Accounts Receivable	÷	2	=	Average Book Value of Accounts Receivable
($569,200.00	+	$474,000.00)	÷	2	=	$521,600.000

2
Net Sales on Account	÷	Average Book Value of Accounts Receivable	=	Accounts Receivable Turnover Ratio
$4,767,200.00	÷	$521,600.00	=	9.1 times

A business accepts accounts receivable to encourage sales. However, the earnings process is not complete until the business receives cash for sales on account. Thus, an efficient company closely monitors the length of time required to collect its receivables. The number of times the average amount of accounts receivable is collected annually is known as the accounts receivable turnover ratio. This ratio monitors a business's accounts receivable collection efficiency.

Hamilton's accounts receivable turnover ratio for the current year is calculated as shown above, using the information from the balance sheet and income statement.

Calculating Earnings Performance and Efficiency Analysis

Lesson 17-2   **509**

AVERAGE NUMBER OF DAYS FOR PAYMENT

Hamilton's turnover ratio indicates that accounts are being collected 9.1 times a year. The average number of days for customers to pay their accounts is calculated:

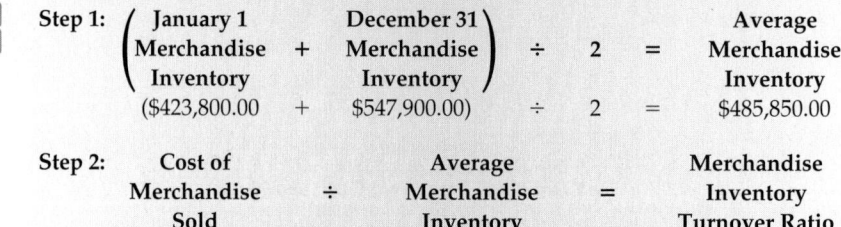

	Days in Year	÷	Accounts Receivable Turnover Ratio	=	Average Number of Days for Payment
	365	÷	9.1	=	40 days

is to collect accounts receivable in 30 days or less. Neither year's results meet that goal. However, the ratio improved from 7.0 to 9.1. This favorable trend means the company is becoming

The accounts receivable turnover ratio for the prior year was 7.0 times. The average number of days for payment was 52 days. Hamilton's credit terms are n/30. Thus, the company's goal

more efficient in its collection efforts by reducing collection of its accounts receivable from 52 to 40 days.

MERCHANDISE INVENTORY TURNOVER RATIO

		January 1 Merchandise Inventory		December 31 Merchandise Inventory	÷	2	=	Average Merchandise Inventory
Step 1:	(	($423,800.00	+	$547,900.00)	÷	2	=	$485,850.00

	Cost of Merchandise Sold	÷	Average Merchandise Inventory	=	Merchandise Inventory Turnover Ratio
Step 2:	$2,602,800.00	÷	$485,850.00	=	5.4 times

A company earns income when it sells merchandise. The faster it sells its merchandise inventory, the more efficient and generally more profitable the business. The number of times the average amount of merchandise inventory is sold annually is known as the merchandise inventory turnover ratio. This ratio can be used to monitor merchandise inventory efficiency.

Hamilton's merchandise inventory turnover ratio is calculated as shown above, using information from the income statement (page 499). The turnover ratio of 5.4 indicates that the inventory is being sold 5.4 times in a year. The average number of days' sales in merchandise inventory is 68 days (365 days ÷ 5.4 turnover ratio = 68 days). Last year, Hamilton had a merchandise turnover ratio of 6.2 times, resulting in

an average number of days' sales in merchandise inventory of 59 days.

An optimum merchandise inventory turnover ratio is determined by two factors. (1) Amount of sales. (2) Number of days needed to replenish inventory. Previous experience indicates that Hamilton needs to maintain an inventory turnover ratio of about 6.0. This 6.0 ratio equates to an average number of days' sales in merchandise inventory of 61 days. Last year, Hamilton's days' sales in inventory was 59 days. This lower-than-desired level of inventory resulted in lost sales because some items were out of stock before new inventory arrived. However, the current year inventory level, 68 days, is satisfactory.

• term review

rate earned on net sales

• audit your understanding

1. What does a rate earned on average total assets show?
2. What does a rate earned on average stockholders' equity show?
3. What does an accounts receivable turnover ratio of 9.1 indicate?

• work together 17-2

Calculating earnings performance and efficiency analysis ratios

Information from TeleNet Corporation's financial statements for the current year is provided in the *Working Papers*. Your instructor will guide you through the following examples.

1. Calculate the following earnings performance and efficiency ratios for the current year. Round percentage calculations to the nearest 0.1%, dollar amounts to the nearest $.01, and the price-earnings ratio to the nearest .1 (tenth).

   a. Rate earned on average total assets
   b. Rate earned on average stockholders' equity
   c. Rate earned on net sales
   d. Earnings per share
   e. Price-earnings ratio

   f. Accounts receivable turnover ratio
   g. Average number of days for accounts receivable payment
   h. Merchandise inventory turnover ratio
   i. Average number of days' sales in merchandise inventory

• on your own 17-2

Calculating earnings performance and efficiency analysis ratios

Information from Razure Adventures Company's financial statements for the current year are provided in the *Working Papers*. Work independently to complete the following problem.

1. Calculate the following earnings performance and efficiency ratios for the current year. Round percentage calculations to the nearest 0.1%, dollar amounts to the nearest $.01, and the price-earnings ratio to the nearest .1 (tenth).

   a. Rate earned on average total assets
   b. Rate earned on average stockholders' equity
   c. Rate earned on net sales
   d. Earnings per share
   e. Price-earnings ratio

   f. Accounts receivable turnover ratio
   g. Average number of days for accounts receivable payment
   h. Merchandise inventory turnover ratio
   i. Average number of days' sales in merchandise inventory

Calculating Earnings Performance and Efficiency Analysis

Lesson 17-2   **511**

GUIDED PRACTICE

Term Review
Call on a student to define the term in the Term Review. After the definition, ask the class if the definition is correct and whether the complete definition has been given or if anything else needs to be added. A suggested definition is given in the Glossary.

Audit Your Understanding
Call on students to answer the Audit Your Understanding questions. Ask the class if the answer is correct and/or complete. Answers are given in Appendix E of the textbook.

Work Together
Have students write the solution to the Work Together problem as you guide the class through the examples.

- Direct students to record each answer and to show the appropriate work as you guide the class through the examples.
- Call on students to describe each step in the required calculation.

INDEPENDENT PRACTICE

On Your Own
- Assign the On Your Own problem to be worked independently.
- Use the Ongoing Assessment techniques to diagnose student understanding.

Application Problems
- Assign Application Problem 17-3: Analyzing earnings performance from comparative financial statements.
- Assign Application Problem 17-4: Analyzing efficiency from comparative financial statements.

Personal Trainer
- Students can access the Lesson 17-2 assessment material using this software.

Xtra! Web Site
- Students can access the Xtra! Study Tools for additional practice.

CLOSE

- On the board, write the formulas used for earnings performance and efficiency analysis.
- Organize students into cooperative learning groups and have them prepare an example using each formula.

ENRICH

- Assign the Global Perspective feature on page 508.
- Invite an accountant or financial analyst into the classroom to discuss how she or he uses financial measures and ratios to analyze financial statements.

17-3 Calculating Financial Strength Analysis

SHORT-TERM FINANCIAL STRENGTH ANALYSIS

A successful business needs adequate capital. A business gets capital from two sources. (1) Owners' investments and retained earnings. (2) Loans. Some capital, either owned or borrowed, is to be used for long periods of time. Some capital is borrowed for short periods of time. A business can invest capital in assets (such as equipment and buildings) for long periods of time. A business also invests in assets (such as merchandise) that will be converted back to cash in a short period of time. Short-term assets are referred to as current assets because they are consumed in a business's daily activities or exchanged for cash. Long-term assets are referred to as plant assets and are used over a long period of time.

Hamilton uses three measures to analyze short-term financial strength. (1) Working capital. (2) Current ratio. (3) Acid-test ratio.

WORKING CAPITAL

	Total Current Assets	−	Total Current Liabilities	=	Working Capital
Current Year	$1,254,100.00	−	$596,100.00	=	$658,000.00
Prior Year	$1,118,600.00	−	$685,400.00	=	$433,200.00

The amount of total current assets less total current liabilities is called **working capital**. Working capital, stated in dollars, is the amount of current assets available to the business after current liabilities are paid. It is not the amount of cash available to the business. The amount of working capital can be compared from year to year to look for a trend. However, working capital cannot be used easily to compare Hamilton with other companies in the industry.

Hamilton's working capital for December 31 of the current year and December 31 of the prior year is calculated as shown above, using information from the balance sheet (page 501).

Hamilton's working capital increased from $433,200.00 to $658,000.00, a favorable trend. A review of other financial information suggests that part of the reason for the prior year's lower

working capital was the company's fast expansion. Frequently, when a business expands rapidly, it borrows money to buy more inventory and pay more employees. The rate of increased costs for merchandise and payroll may be initially greater than the rate of increase in sales and net income. In the current year, Hamilton lowered its current liabilities by issuing more capital stock and increasing long-term liabilities.

FYI
FOR YOUR INFORMATION

The *Wall Street Journal* and many local newspapers report price-earnings ratios in their stock quotations.

Financial Statement Analysis

CURRENT RATIO

	Total Current Assets	÷	Total Current Liabilities	=	Current Ratio
Current Year	$1,254,100.00	÷	$596,100.00	=	2.1 times
Prior Year	$1,118,600.00	÷	$685,400.00	=	1.6 times

A ratio that shows the numeric relationship of current assets to current liabilities is called the **current ratio**. Normally, current liabilities are expected to be paid from cash on hand plus cash soon to be received from other current assets.

The current ratio is calculated by dividing total current assets by total current liabilities. Hamilton's current ratio for the current year and the prior year are calculated as shown above, using information from the balance sheet.

The current ratio of 2.1 means that Hamilton owns $2.10 in current assets for each $1.00 needed to pay current liabilities.

Businesses similar to Hamilton try to maintain a current ratio of 2.0 times. Industry experience has shown that a business with a current

ratio of less than 2.0 times has difficulty raising ready cash to pay current liabilities on time. At the same time, industry experience shows that a current ratio can be too high. If the current ratio is 3.0 times or higher, the business has more capital invested in current assets than is needed to run the business.

In the prior year, Hamilton's current ratio, 1.6, was significantly below the desired ratio. However, the current year's ratio, 2.1, is at a satisfactory level. A review of financial information suggests that part of the reason for the prior year's lower current ratio was the company's fast expansion. In the current year, Hamilton lowered its current liabilities by issuing more capital stock and increasing long-term liabilities.

ACID-TEST RATIO

	Total Quick Assets (Cash + Accounts Receivable)	÷	Total Current Liabilities	=	Acid-Test Ratio
Current Year	($206,100.00 + $474,000.00)	÷	$596,100.00	=	1.1 times
Prior Year	($104,300.00 + $569,200.00)	÷	$685,400.00	=	1.0 times

Those current assets that are cash or that can be quickly turned into cash are called **quick assets**. Quick assets include cash, accounts receivable, and marketable securities, but not merchandise inventory or prepaid expenses. A ratio that shows the numeric relationship of quick assets to current liabilities is called the **acid-test ratio**. This ratio shows the ability of a business to pay all current liabilities almost immediately if necessary.

Hamilton's acid-test ratio for the current year and prior year is calculated as shown

above. The current year's ratio of 1.1 indicates that for each $1.00 needed to pay current liabilities, Hamilton has $1.10 available in quick assets. For companies similar to Hamilton, the desired industry standard for an acid-test ratio is between 0.9 and 1.3.

Hamilton's acid-test ratio has increased from 1.0 to 1.1, a favorable trend. Part of the cash received from the sale of capital stock and the increase in long-term liabilities was used to reduce the level of current liabilities and improve the acid-test ratio.

Calculating Financial Strength Analysis

Lesson 17-3   **513**

APPLIED SKILLS   WRITING ACROSS THE CURRICULUM

Writing Paragraphs and Short Essays. The Cases for Critical Thinking are short, practical applications of the accounting principles developed in the chapter. Some cases are planned to present problems related to the chapter but not specifically discussed and answered in the chapter. These cases present an opportunity for critical thinking and decision making. These cases also require more than a short objective-type response. Therefore, they provide ideal practice in writing paragraphs and short essays.

- Emphasize that long-term financial strength is demonstrated by companies that maintain the proper ratio between borrowed capital and owners' equity.

- Point out that companies with high percentages of borrowed capital sometimes find it difficult to make loan payments. Companies with high debt ratios do not have much of an operating cushion when earnings are low or there is a down cycle in the economy. During these declines, some businesses do not generate the cash flow needed to repay debts and consequently fail.

- Emphasize that the debt ratio shows the percentage of assets financed with borrowed capital that represent money owed or liabilities.

DEMONSTRATE

Calculate the debt ratio

- Direct students to the math box.

- Ask a student to review the amounts and demonstrate on the board how to calculate the debt ratio. Ask the student to state the source of total liabilities and total assets *(comparative balance sheet)*.

- Ask students to verify the debt ratio with a calculator.

- Ask a student to explain the meaning of Hamilton Corporation's debt ratio of 49.1%. Make sure the student emphasizes that for every $1.00 of assets owned by Hamilton, the company borrowed 49.1 cents.

- Note that Hamilton's debt ratio has improved considerably over last year's. Ask students how Hamilton could further improve its debt ratio. Point out that the funds secured through sale of additional capital stock could be used to reduce the total amount of liabilities.

LONG-TERM FINANCIAL STRENGTH ANALYSIS

Businesses that are successful and are able to continue operating through both strong and weak economic periods usually have long-term financial strength. Long-term financial strength requires a balance between stockholders' capital and borrowed capital. A profitable business can be even more profitable by using borrowed capital wisely. However, borrowed capital must be repaid with interest. Continuing operation of a business with a large percentage of borrowed capital may be jeopardized if net income declines and it cannot make loan payments. Also, creditors are reluctant to loan additional money to companies with a high level of liabilities. A well-managed company monitors its long-term financial strength to ensure that a reasonable balance between stockholders' capital and borrowed capital is maintained.

Hamilton uses three measures to analyze long-term financial strength: (1) debt ratio, (2) equity ratio, and (3) equity per share.

DEBT RATIO

	Total Liabilities	÷	Total Assets	=	Debt Ratio
Current Year	$1,016,100.00	÷	$2,067,700.00	=	49.1%
Prior Year	$ 910,400.00	÷	$1,759,700.00	=	51.7%

The ratio found by dividing total liabilities by total assets is called the **debt ratio**. This ratio shows the percentage of assets that are financed with borrowed capital (liabilities).

Hamilton's debt ratio for the current year and the prior year are calculated as shown above, using information from the balance sheet (page 501).

The current year ratio, 49.1%, indicates that for each $1.00 of assets owned by Hamilton, the company has borrowed 49.1 cents.

The average debt ratio for companies similar to Hamilton is 43.0%. Hamilton's ratios are above the industry average, an unfavorable condition. Rapid growth over the past two or three years, financed primarily through borrowed capital, has caused the unfavorable liabilities level. However, the additional capital stock that Hamilton issued this year helped lower the debt ratio from 51.7% to 49.1%. The company should consider issuing more capital stock to reduce the total liabilities to an industry average of 43.0%.

©GETTY IMAGES/PHOTODISC

EQUITY RATIO

	Total Stockholders' Equity	÷	Total Assets	=	Equity Ratio
Current Year	$1,051,600.00	÷	$60,000.00	=	50.9%
Prior Year	$ 849,300.00	÷	$50,000.00	=	48.3%

The ratio found by dividing stockholders' equity by total assets is called the **equity ratio**. This ratio shows the percentage of assets that are provided by stockholders' equity.

Hamilton's equity ratio for the current year and the prior year are calculated as shown above, using information from the statement of stockholders' equity (page 500) and the balance sheet (page 501).

Hamilton's ratio for the current year, 50.9%, indicates that for each $1.00 of assets owned by the company, 50.9 cents' worth was acquired with stockholders' capital. The average equity ratio for companies similar to Hamilton is 57.0%. Hamilton's ratios are below the industry average, an unfavorable condition.

The debt and equity ratios show the mix of capital provided by capital borrowed and capital provided by stockholders. The sum of the two ratios equals 100%, as shown here:

	Current Year	Prior Year
Debt Ratio	49.1%	51.7%
Equity Ratio	50.9%	48.3%
Totals	100.0%	100.0%

The totals always equal 100% because the total liabilities and stockholders' equity represent the source of all asset ownership. Due to rapid expansion, Hamilton's prior year's equity ratio declined to an unfavorable level. In the current year, Hamilton increased the percentage of ownership provided by stockholders' equity by issuing more capital stock. Hamilton plans to continue its efforts to increase the equity ratio by reducing its liabilities and issuing additional stock.

EQUITY PER SHARE

	Total Stockholders' Equity	÷	Shares of Capital Stock Outstanding	=	Equity per Share
Current Year	$1,051,600.00	÷	60,00.00	=	$17.53
Prior Year	$ 849,300.00	÷	50,00.00	=	$16.99

The amount of total stockholders' equity belonging to a single share of stock is known as equity per share. Hamilton's equity per share for the current year and the prior year are calculated as shown above, using information from the statement of stockholders' equity (page 500).

Hamilton's equity per share in the current year, $17.53, indicates that on December 31, each share of capital stock represents ownership in $17.53 of the assets.

Equity per share tells stockholders how much ownership of the company each share represents. For example, the stockholders of Hamilton know that each share represents $17.53 ownership of the total company assets. This ownership has increased from $16.99 per share in the prior year, a favorable trend.

- Point out that the debt ratio shows the percentage of assets financed with borrowed capital (liabilities), and the equity ratio shows the percentage of assets financed with owners' capital (stockholders' equity).

- Emphasize that the total of the debt ratio and the equity ratio must always equal 100%. In other words, all of Hamilton Corporation's assets were financed by either borrowed capital (liabilities) or stockholders' capital.

- Point out that the portion of stockholders' equity belonging to a single share of outstanding stock is called equity per share.

DEMONSTRATE

Calculate the debt ratio

- Direct students to the math box at the top of the page.

- Review the amounts and demonstrate on the board how to calculate the equity ratio. Ask a student to state the source of total stockholders' equity *(comparative statement of stockholders' equity)* and total assets *(comparative balance sheet)*.

- Ask a student to explain the meaning of Hamilton Corporation's equity ratio of 50.9%. Make sure the student emphasizes that for every $1.00 of assets owned by Hamilton, the stockholders provided 50.9 cents.

Calculate the equity per share

- Direct students to the math box in the middle of the page.

- Review the amounts and demonstrate on the board how to calculate the equity per share.

- Ask a student the meaning of Hamilton's equity per share of $17.53. Make sure the student emphasizes that each share of stock represents $17.53 ownership of the company's total assets.

ONGOING ASSESSMENT

- Circulate through the classroom or lab observing which students have problems with assignments.

- Troubleshooting: Students may have difficulty remembering the various formulas used for calculating financial strength.

- Assess student understanding by checking solutions to Independent Practice assignments.

RETEACH

- Have the students make a reference sheet listing the following formulas used for financial strength analysis:
  - working capital
  - current ratio
  - acid-test ratio
  - debt ratio
- equity ratio
- equity per share

- As an alternative assignment, assign a specific formula to a group and have them design a poster highlighting the formula. Posters may be placed throughout the classroom and used as a reference source.

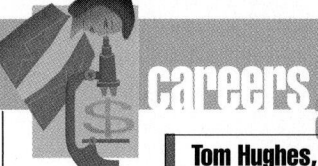

careers in accounting

CAREERS IN ACCOUNTING • CAREERS IN ACCOUNTING • CAREERS IN ACCOU

Tom Hughes, Forensic Accountant

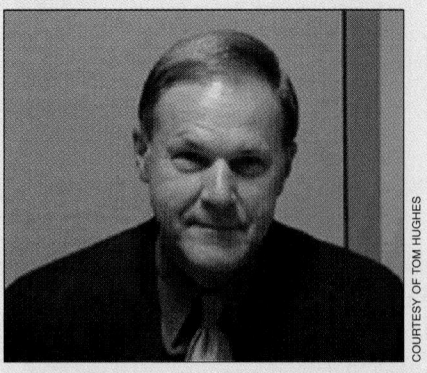

COURTESY OF TOM HUGHES

Forensic accounting has gained renewed attention due to recent accounting scandals, but it has always been a part of the profession. In fact, forensic accountants were credited with putting Al Capone in prison on tax-evasion charges.

Forensic accounting is a growth area of accounting today. Forensic accountants work in most major accounting firms and are needed for developing anti-fraud programs, conducting investigations, and supporting all kinds of civil litigation. Forensic accountants work throughout the business world, in public accounting, in corporations, and in all branches of government (from the FBI and SEC to the offices of the local authorities).

Tom Hughes is a Director in the Forensic & Dispute Services practice of Deloitte & Touche LLP. Based in the Los Angeles office, Tom conducts fraud and forensic investigative services on behalf of clients throughout the entire Pacific Southwest region, with a special focus on anti-fraud consulting and fraud investigations.

He is a certified fraud examiner with more than 30 years' experience in criminal and civil investigations, both domestic and international. His expertise in fraud investigations and security comes from 27 years with the Federal Bureau of Investigation, where he served as agent-in-charge of the San Diego and Boston offices. After the FBI, Tom joined a Fortune 100 company as the Director of Corporate Security, and in May 2001 joined the ranks of Deloitte & Touche LLP. He received his B.S. in Business Administration and Accounting from Quincy University and later earned his MBA at Bradley University in Illinois.

Tom has been involved in such cases as the following:

- The defrauding of a subsidiary bank in Moscow, Russia, by its senior management, leading to an out-of-court multi-million-dollar fidelity bond insurance settlement.
- Fraud in a county government by former county executives, consultants, and other vendors, leading to the filing of civil actions against a number of individuals and companies.
- Investigating purchasing activities at one of a hotel chain's properties in Rome, Italy, that identified fictitious vendors and fraudulent bids leading to changes in procurement policies and procedures.

Salary Range: $30,000–$110,000 and up. Can lead to high-level careers at law firms, corporations, and government agencies such as the FBI.

Qualifications: B.S. in accounting, and accounting/auditing experience. A Certified Public Accountant license is almost always required. Familiarity with legal concepts and procedures is important.

Occupational Outlook: Forensic accounting is one of eight "careers to count on." (*U.S. News and World Report,* February 18, 2002, pp. 46–48, 50)

• terms review

TERMS REVIEW • TERMS REVIEW

working capital
current ratio
quick assets
acid-test ratio
debt ratio
equity ratio

• audit your understanding

AUDIT YOUR UNDERSTANDING

1. What are two sources from which a business gets capital?
2. What three measures can be used to analyze short-term financial strength?
3. What is the major difference between current assets and quick assets?
4. What is the formula for the acid-test ratio?
5. Why does a well-managed company monitor its long-term financial strength?
6. What is the formula for calculating debt ratio?
7. What is the formula for calculating equity per share?

• work together 17-3

WORK TOGETHER • WORK TOGETHER

Analyzing short-term and long-term financial strength

Information taken from Applied Technology's comparative balance sheet is provided in the *Working Papers*. Your instructor will guide you through the following problem.

1. Calculate the following short-term financial strength analysis ratios for the current year and prior year. Round ratios to the nearest .1 (tenth). Your instructor will guide you through the examples.

   a. Working capital
   b. Current ratio
   c. Acid-test ratio
   d. Debt ratio
   e. Equity ratio
   f. Equity per share

• on your own 17-3

ON YOUR OWN • ON YOUR OWN

Analyzing short-term and long-term financial strength

Information taken from Online Office Supply's comparative balance sheet is provided in the *Working Papers*. Work independently to complete the following problem.

1. Calculate the following short-term financial strength analysis ratios for the current year and prior year. Round ratios to the nearest .1 (tenth). Work independently to complete the following problem.

   a. Working capital
   b. Current ratio
   c. Acid-test ratio
   d. Debt ratio
   e. Equity ratio
   f. Equity per share

Calculating Financial Strength Analysis
Lesson 17-3   **517**

GUIDED PRACTICE

Terms Review

- Ask students to write the definition for each term in the Terms Review. Allow students to use their texts.
- Ask a student to read the definition for a selected term. Ask the class if the definition is correct and whether the complete definition has been given or if anything else needs to be added. Suggested definitions are given in the Glossary.

Audit Your Understanding

Call on students to answer the Audit Your Understanding questions. Ask the class if the answer is correct and/or complete. Answers are given in Appendix E of the textbook.

Work Together

Have students write the solution to the Work Together problem as you guide the class through the examples.

- Direct students to record each answer and to show the appropriate work as you guide the class through the examples.
- Call on students to recite the formula and to describe each step in the required computation.

INDEPENDENT PRACTICE

On Your Own

- Assign the On Your Own problem to be worked independently.
- Use the Ongoing Assessment techniques to diagnose student understanding.

Application Problems

- Assign Application Problem 17-5: Analyzing short-term financial strength from a comparative balance sheet.
- Assign Application Problem 17-6: Analyzing long-term financial strength from a comparative balance sheet.

Personal Trainer

- Students can access the Lesson 17-3 assessment material using this software.

Xtra! Web Site

- Students can access the Xtra! Study Tools for additional practice.

ENRICH

- Ask students to read the Careers in Accounting feature on page 516.

CLOSE

- Write the formulas on the board used for financial strength analysis.
- Organize students into cooperative learning groups and have them prepare an example using each formula.

PUTTING IT ALL TOGETHER

- Review the Chapter Summary. Ask students for examples or figure numbers for each summary item. List student responses on the board or overhead.

INDEPENDENT PRACTICE

- Assign Mastery Problem 17-7 to students who need the reinforcement of a problem that combines all activities from the chapter in one problem; this will be most students.
- Assign Challenge Problem 17-8 to accelerated students who do not require the reinforcement of the mastery problem.
- Assign Study Guide Chapter 17.
- Students can use Automated Accounting to automate Mastery Problem 17-7.
- Students can access Personal Trainer to work end-of-chapter problems on the computer.
- Students can access the Xtra! Web Site for the Xtra! Review and Quizzing.
- Students can access the Student Companion CD for additional review material.

ONGOING ASSESSMENT

Review solutions to the assigned problems in class, diagnosing trouble spots.

RETEACH

- Call on students to describe how they avoid the trouble spots diagnosed.
- Use reteaching suggestions from section lesson plans as required.
- Assign Recycling Problem 17-1 if needed.

ENRICH

- Assign the Explore Accounting Feature. Ask students to share the information they have gathered in a report to the class.
- Students can access the Xtra! Web Site for the Xtra! Enrichment material.
- Assign Applied Communication.
- Assign the Cases for Critical Thinking.
- Assign the SCANS Workplace Competency.
- Assign Graphing Workshop.
- Assign Analyzing Costco's Financial Statements.
- Assign the Automated Accounting feature on pages 526–527 to automate Mastery Problem 17-7.

518

S U M M A R Y

After completing this chapter, you can

1. Define accounting terms related to financial statement analysis.

2. Identify accounting concepts and practices related to financial statement analysis.

3. Analyze financial statements.

4. Calculate earnings performance.

5. Perform efficiency analysis.

6. Analyze the long-term financial strength of businesses.

Explore Accounting

EXPLORE ACCOUNTING • EXPLORE ACCOUNTING • EXPLORE AC

Detailed Information on Financial Statements

Many of the financial statements used in this text report the balance of every account in the chart of accounts. These example companies have a relatively small number of accounts. Thus, every account balance can easily be reported on the financial statements. As companies grow, it becomes impractical for them to report every account. A company with hundreds of locations, for example, is likely to have a cash account for each location. Rather than reporting each cash account balance, the company combines all cash accounts and reports a single amount on the financial statements. The same method is used to report all accounts on the financial statements. For most users of the financial statements, a single cash amount provides adequate information. Most investors do not need to know the balance of each of the company's hundreds of cash accounts. Instead, the total cash amount is adequate for financial statement analysis. Detailed account information has rarely been available to individuals outside of the company. The cost of providing this information was not considered worth the benefit that a few individuals might

gain. However, computer technology has made the distribution of this detailed information significantly less expensive. Accountants are starting to recognize that the detailed information can be made available at a low cost using the Internet. The traditional financial statements are likely to remain as the primary method that companies use to report their financial information. The number of users accessing the detailed information is likely to increase, however, as users become more comfortable using the Internet and learn how to evaluate detailed information to improve business decisions.

Required:

Examine the annual report of a corporation and identify the balance in the inventory account. Why would you expect the amount to be the total of many inventory accounts? Suggest reasons that management might need many inventory accounts. Why might you, as a potential investor, want to know the inventory balance of a particular location?

Financial Statement Analysis

EXPLORE ACCOUNTING
EXPLORE ACCOUNTING

The inventory account balances of most commonly known corporations will likely surprise students. For example, Kmart Corporation's merchandise inventory exceeded $6 billion in 1998. This inventory balance is the total of many inventory accounts of individual stores and warehouses.

Effective managers need financial information regarding the assets for which they are responsible. An adequate level of detail enables managers to detect potential errors in accounting information. Detailed information could enable managers to identify several inventory problems, such as obsolete, overstocked, and understocked items.

Most investors do not need detailed information. However, an investor might be interested in the financial statements of a particular retail store in which he or she shops. For example, the investor might perceive the number of shoppers in the store to have increased. How has this increase impacted inventory and income? Armed with personal knowledge of a local store and its financial results, the investor has a unique insight that will be useful in making investment decisions about the larger corporation.

17-1 APPLICATION PROBLEM QUICKBOOKS

Xtra!
Quizzing
accountingxtra.swlearning.com

Analyzing comparative financial statements using trend analysis

The comparative financial statements for CyberOptic Corporation are in the *Working Papers*. The financial statements have been completed up to the trend analysis section. The following information is taken from the financial records of CyberOptic for two consecutive fiscal years ended December 31.

	Current Year	Prior Year
Accounts Receivable (book value), January 1	$ 76,820.00	$ 69,450.00
Total Assets, January 1	670,670.00	544,200.00
Market Price per Share of Stock, December 31	23.50	16.50

Instructions:

1. Complete the following comparative financial statements using trend analysis. Round percentage calculations to the nearest 0.1%.
   a. Comparative income statement
   b. Comparative stockholders' equity statement
   c. Comparative balance sheet
2. Use the financial statements' trend analysis to determine whether the trend from the prior to the current year for each of the following items appears to be favorable or unfavorable. Give reasons for these trends. Save your work to complete Application Problems 17-3, 17-4, 17-5, and 17-6.
   a. Net sales
   b. Net income
   c. Total stockholders' equity
   d. Total assets

17-2 APPLICATION PROBLEM

Analyzing comparative financial statements using component percentage analysis

The comparative financial statements for CyberOptic Corporation are in the *Working Papers*. The financial statements have been completed up to the comparative analysis section.

Instructions:

1. Complete the following comparative financial statements using component percentage analysis. Round percentage calculations to the nearest 0.1%.
   a. Comparative income statement
   b. Comparative stockholders' equity statement
   c. Comparative balance sheet
2. Use the financial statements' component percentage analysis to determine whether the current year's results for the following items, compared with those for the prior year, appear to be favorable or unfavorable. Give reasons for your responses.
   a. As a percentage of net sales:
      (1) Cost of merchandise sold
      (2) Gross profit on operations
      (3) Total operating expenses
      (4) Net income after federal income tax
   b. As a percentage of total stockholders' equity:
      (1) Retained earnings
      (2) Capital stock
   c. As a percentage of total assets or total liabilities and stockholders' equity:
      (1) Current assets
      (2) Current liabilities

Application Problem 17-3

1. a. 16.0%, 12.4% Fav.

   b. 29.1%, 22.6% Fav.

   c. 11.3%, 8.2% Fav.

   d. 2.35, 1.88 Fav.

   e. 10.0, 8.8 Fav.

Application Problem 17-4

1. a. 13.4, 12.5 Fav.

   b. 27, 29 Fav.

   c. 2.7, 4.0 Unfav.

   d. 135, 91 Unfav.

Application Problem 17-5

1. a. $284,380, $225,670 Fav.

   b. 2.1, 2.0 Fav.

   c. 0.8, 1.0 Unfav.

17-3 APPLICATION PROBLEM

Analyzing earnings performance from comparative financial statements

Use the comparative statements from Application Problem 17-1 to complete this problem.

Instructions:

1. Based on CyberOptic's comparative financial statements prepared in Application Problem 17-1 and the information given in the text for Application Problem 17-1, calculate the following for each year.
   a. Rate earned on average total assets
   b. Rate earned on average stockholders' equity
   c. Rate earned on net sales
   d. Earnings per share
   e. Price-earnings ratio
2. For each analysis, indicate whether a favorable or an unfavorable trend occurred from the prior to the current year. Give reasons for these trends.

17-4 APPLICATION PROBLEM

Analyzing efficiency from comparative financial statements

Use the comparative statements from Application Problem 17-1 to complete this problem.

Instructions:

1. Based on CyberOptic's comparative financial statements prepared in Application Problem 17-1 and the information given in the text for Application Problem 17-1, calculate the following for each year. All of CyberOptic's sales are on account.
   a. Accounts receivable turnover ratio
   b. Average number of days for payment
   c. Merchandise inventory turnover ratio
   d. Average number of days' sales in merchandise inventory
2. For each analysis, indicate whether a favorable or an unfavorable trend occurred from the prior to the current year. Give reasons for these trends.

17-5 APPLICATION PROBLEM

Analyzing short-term financial strength from a comparative balance sheet

Use the comparative balance sheet from Application Problem 17-1 to complete this problem.

Instructions:

1. Based on CyberOptic's comparative balance sheet prepared in Application Problem 17-1, calculate the following for each year.
   a. Working capital
   b. Current ratio
   c. Acid-test ratio
2. For each analysis, indicate whether a favorable or an unfavorable trend occurred from the prior to the current year. Give reasons for these trends.

TEACHING STRATEGIES DIFFERENT LEARNING ABILITIES

At-Risk Students. Assist students to understand how accounting is a useful skill in careers which interest them. This could be accomplished in many ways. For example, a student who shows interest in auto mechanics could be introduced to the owner of a local auto repair business. The student could then report his or her observations to the instructor in oral or written form. If no mentor is available, trade magazines often present articles to assist their readers in managing their businesses.

17-6 APPLICATION PROBLEM

Analyzing long-term financial strength from a comparative balance sheet

Use the comparative balance sheet from Application Problem 17-1 to complete this problem.

Instructions:

1. Based on CyberOptic's comparative balance sheet prepared in Application Problem 17-1, calculate the following for each year:
   a. Debt ratio
   b. Equity ratio
   c. Equity per share
2. For each analysis, indicate whether a favorable or an unfavorable trend occurred from the prior to the current year. Give reasons for these trends.

17-7 MASTERY PROBLEM `AUTOMATED ACCOUNTING`

Analyzing comparative financial statements

The comparative financial statements for Advanced Auto Technology, Inc., are in the Working Papers. The financial statements have been completed up to the financial analysis section. The following information is taken from the financial records of Advanced Auto Technology for two fiscal years ended December 31:

	Current Year	Prior Year
Accounts Receivable (book value), January 1	$242,890.00	$236,580.00
Merchandise Inventory, January 1	172,890.00	53,760.00
Total Assets, January 1	762,860.00	693,200.00
Stockholders' Equity, January 1	413,160.00	306,780.00
Shares of Capital Stock Outstanding	48,000	40,000
Market Price per Share of Stock, December 31	42.50	30.00

Instructions:

1. Complete the following comparative financial statements using trend analysis. Round percentage calculations to the nearest 0.1%.
   a. Comparative income statement
   b. Comparative stockholders' equity statement
   c. Comparative balance sheet
2. Use the financial statements' trend analysis to determine whether the trend from the prior to the current year for each of the following items appears to be favorable or unfavorable. Give reasons for these trends.
   a. Net sales
   b. Net income
   c. Total stockholders' equity
   d. Total assets
3. Complete the comparative income statement using component percentage analysis. Round percentage calculations to the nearest 0.1%.
4. Record from the statement prepared in Instruction 3 or calculate the component percentages for each of the following. Determine whether the current year's results, compared with those for the prior year, appear to be favorable or unfavorable. Give reasons for your responses.
   a. As a percentage of net sales:
      (1) Cost of merchandise sold
      (2) Gross profit on operations
      (3) Total operating expenses
      (4) Net income after federal income tax

Application Problem 17-6

1. a. 42.8%, 47.8% Fav.
   b. 57.2%, 52.2% Fav.
   c. $9.15, $8.75 Fav.

Mastery Problem 17-7

2. a. 32.0% Fav.
   b. 76.2% Fav.
   c. 44.2% Fav.
   d. 18.5% Fav.
4. a. (1) 59.8%, 63.3% Fav.; (2) 40.2%, 36.7% Fav.; (3) 25.4%, 25.8% Fav.; (4) 9.1%, 6.8% Fav.
   b. (1) 55.4%, 46.4% Fav.; (2) 44.6%, 53.6% Fav.
   c. (1) 53.3%, 59.9% Unfav.; (2) 21.1%, 32.7% Fav.
5. a. (1) 22.5%, 14.6% Fav.; (2) 41.1%, 31.3% Fav.; (3) 9.1%, 6.8% Fav.; (4) $3.90, $2.66 Fav.; (5) 10.9, 11.3 Unfav.
   b. (1) 9.3, 6.5 Fav.; (2) 6.7, 8.7 Unfav.
   c. (1) $291,060, $207,160 Fav.; (2) 2.5, 1.8 Fav.; (3) 1.4, 1.1 Fav.
   d. (1) 40.5%, 51.1% Fav.; (2) 59.5%, 48.9% Fav.; (3) $11.21, $9.33 Fav.

b. As a percentage of total stockholders' equity:
   (1) Retained earnings
   (2) Capital stock
c. As a percentage of total assets or total liabilities and stockholders' equity:
   (1) Current assets
   (2) Current liabilities

5. Based on Advanced Auto Technology's comparative financial statements, calculate the following ratios for each year.
   a. Profitability ratios:
      (1) Rate earned on average total assets
      (2) Rate earned on average stockholders' equity
      (3) Rate earned on net sales
      (4) Earnings per share
      (5) Price-earnings ratio
   b. Efficiency ratios:
      (1) Accounts receivable turnover ratio
      (2) Merchandise inventory turnover ratio
   c. Short-term financial strength ratios:
      (1) Working capital
      (2) Current ratio
      (3) Acid-test ratio
   d. Long-term financial strength ratios:
      (1) Debt ratio
      (2) Equity ratio
      (3) Equity per share

6. For each of the items in Instruction 5, indicate whether a favorable or an unfavorable trend occurred from the prior to the current year. Give reasons for these trends.

17-8 CHALLENGE PROBLEM

Analyzing comparative financial statements

The comparative financial statements for CompuCircuit Corporation are in the *Working Papers*. The financial statements have been completed up to the financial analysis section. The following information is taken from the financial records of CompuCircuit for two fiscal years ended December 31:

	Current Year	Prior Year
Accounts Receivable (book value), January 1	$105,500.00	$ 126,400.00
Total Assets, January 1	979,660.00	1,052,400.00
Market Price per Share of Stock, December 31	7.50	29.50

Instructions:

1. Prepare the following comparative financial statements using trend analysis. Round percentage calculations to the nearest 0.1%.
   a. Comparative income statement
   b. Comparative stockholders' equity statement
   c. Comparative balance sheet

2. Use the financial statements' trend analysis to determine whether the trend from the prior to the current year for each of the following items appears to be favorable or unfavorable. Give reasons for these trends.
   a. Net sales
   b. Net income
   c. Total stockholders' equity
   d. Total assets

3. Complete the comparative income statement using component percentage analysis. Round percentage calculations to the nearest 0.1%.

2. a. 16.0% Unfav.

   b. 61.4% Unfav.

   c. 4.6% Unfav.

   d. 6.5% Unfav.

4. a. (1) 70.9%, 66.5% Unfav.; (2) 29.1%, 33.5% Unfav.; (3) 24.1%, 25.7% Fav.; (4) 2.2%, 4.8% Unfav.

   b. (1) 10.2%, 14.4% Unfav.; (2) 89.8%, 85.6% Unfav.

   c. (1) 65.9%, 66.8% Unfav.; (2) 26.8%, 28.6% Fav.

5. a. (1) 3.0%, 7.3% Unfav.; (2) 6.2%, 16.2% Unfav.; (3) 2.2%, 4.8% Unfav.; (4) $1.42, $3.69 Unfav.; (5) 5.3, 8.0 Unfav.

   b. (1) 13.3, 13.2 Fav.; (2) 2.8, 3.3 Unfav.

   c. (1) $357,780, $373,360 Unfav.; (2) 2.5, 2.3 Fav.; (3) 0.5, 0.7 Unfav.

   d. (1) 51.4%, 52.3% Fav.; (2) 48.6%, 47.7% Fav.; (3) $22.27, 23.35 Unfav.

4. Record from the statement prepared in Instruction 3 or calculate the component percentages for each of the following. Determine whether the current year's results, compared with those for the prior year, appear to be favorable or unfavorable. Give reasons for your responses.
   a. As a percentage of net sales:
      (1) Cost of merchandise sold
      (2) Gross profit on operations
      (3) Total operating expenses
      (4) Net income after federal income tax
   b. As a percentage of total stockholders' equity:
      (1) Retained earnings
      (2) Capital stock
   c. As a percentage of total assets or total liabilities and stockholders' equity:
      (1) Current assets
      (2) Current liabilities
5. Based on CompuCircuit's comparative financial statements, calculate the following ratios for each year:
   a. Profitability ratios:
      (1) Rate earned on average total assets
      (2) Rate earned on average stockholders' equity
      (3) Rate earned on net sales
      (4) Earnings per share
      (5) Price-earnings ratio
   b. Efficiency ratios:
      (1) Accounts receivable turnover ratio
      (2) Merchandise inventory turnover ratio
   c. Short-term financial strength ratios:
      (1) Working capital
      (2) Current ratio
      (3) Acid-test ratio
   d. Long-term financial strength ratios:
      (1) Debt ratio
      (2) Equity ratio
      (3) Equity per share
6. For each of the items in Instruction 5, indicate whether a favorable or an unfavorable trend occurred from the prior to the current year. Give reasons for these trends.

APPLIED COMMUNICATION

This activity requires students to prepare a letter highlighting the positive or explaining the negative results of a corporation's fiscal year. Student solutions will vary.

CASES FOR CRITICAL THINKING

Case 1

Two trends are evident that can hurt the company's profits. First, cost of merchandise sold has been steadily rising. This means the cost of merchandise has been going up, but the company has not been increasing its selling prices to match the increased costs. Second, selling expenses have been steadily declining, which is desirable. The cost of merchandise has been increasing more rapidly than the total expenses have been decreasing. Recommend the company review its pricing policy as well as essential costs and expenses. If costs are reasonable, selling prices must be increased if the company is to continue making a profit.

Case 2

Ms. Perry's interpretation of the accounts receivable turnover ratio trend is incorrect. The trend is unfavorable, not favorable. The ratio indicates the number of times the average accounts receivable balance has been collected during the year. If the accounts receivable are collected 8.7 times per year, they are collected more often than if collected only 6.2 times in a year. The turnover ratio can be converted to number of days' sales in accounts receivable by dividing 365 (days in a year) by the accounts receivable turnover ratio.

	Current Year	Prior Year
Days in Year	365	365
Accounts Receivable Turnover Ratio	6.2 times	8.7 times
Number of Days for Payment	59 days	42 days

These results show that Ms. Perry's company had an average of 42 days from date of sale to date of collection for the average account receivable during the prior year. The amount increased to 59 days in the current year. Thus the trend is unfavorable.

applied communication

Corporate annual reports include a letter from the chief executive officer (CEO). The letter highlights achievements and positive results from the past year. If necessary, it delivers news of negative results with an explanation of the steps being taken to correct the problems.

Required:

Select one of the companies from the problems: CyberOptic Corporation, Advanced Auto Technology, Inc., or CompuCircuit Corporation. Assume that you are the CEO of the company. Using the information from your problem solutions, write a letter to stockholders that will appear in the company's annual report. You may add any details you would like, as long as the details are consistent with the financial analysis.

cases for critical thinking

Case 1

Alpha Network Solutions has had declining net income the past four years. The company president employs you as a consultant to review the company's operations in an effort to identify the reason for the decline. As part of your analysis, you make a component percentage analysis of the company's four most recent income statements. A part of that analysis is shown below. What are the implications from the information? What are the problems or potential problems evident from this analysis? What are your suggestions to the company?

	20X4	20X3	20X2	20X1
Cost of Merchandise Sold	62.1%	58.4%	55.2%	52.5%
Total Selling Expenses	12.1%	14.6%	15.7%	18.9%

Case 2

Minta Perry has received year-end information, including financial statements, from her accountant. Among the information is a report that the accounts receivable turnover ratio in the prior year was 8.7 and for the current year is 6.2. Ms. Perry is overjoyed at the trend of the accounts receivable turnover ratio. Do you agree with her reaction? Explain your answer.

SCANS workplace competency

Interpersonal Competency: Exercising Leadership

Concept: Competent leaders communicate thoughts, feelings, and ideas to justify a position. They encourage, persuade, convince, and motivate individuals or groups and responsibly challenge existing procedures, policies, or authority.

Application: Prepare a list of examples or cite situations in which you have displayed leadership. What do you think are the qualities of an effective leader?

SCANS WORKPLACE COMPETENCY

Solutions will vary. Students can obtain articles from national news or business magazines and newspapers. An Internet search can also identify articles on whistle blowing. The instructor could have students write their summary or present their summary in class.

graphing workshop

Tanisha Greggs, a stockholder in Mentar Corp., has just received a report of the company's ten-year financial performance that includes the following graph. In the report, management states that "the company has increased earnings per share for ten consecutive years." Tanisha is confused about the information presented in the graph. Help her understand the company's financial performance by answering the following questions.

Financial Performance Analysis for Mentar Corp.

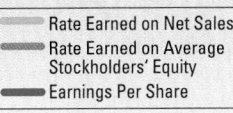

Instructions:

1. Has earnings per share increased each year?
2. Estimate the earnings per share for year 10.
3. Describe the trend in the rate earned on average stockholders' equity.
4. Describe the trend in the rate earned on net sales.

analyzing Costco's financial statements

The annual reports of publicly traded companies describe some of the financial ratios presented in this chapter. Other ratios must be calculated using the information provided in the financial statements.

Income statement amounts are the result of operations over an entire year or fiscal period. However, balance sheet amounts are the balance on a particular date. Therefore, when financial ratios use both an income statement amount and a balance sheet amount, the balance sheet amount is commonly expressed as an average of the amount at the beginning of the fiscal period and the amount at the end of the fiscal period. For example, average total assets would be the sum of total assets on January 1 plus total assets on December 31, divided by 2.

Because the balance sheet contains only two years of information, investors rely on information in multiple-year summaries to obtain the required information. Costco's ten-year operating and financial highlights (Appendix B pages B-2–B-3 in this textbook) enable readers to calculate financial ratios for several years.

Instructions:

Identify or calculate the following financial ratios from 2001 to 2003, using the financial statements and ten-year highlights, as appropriate.

1. Rate earned on average total assets
2. Rate earned on average stockholders' equity
3. Earnings per share
4. Price-earnings ratio (assume a market price of $46.25, $46.32, and $37.43 for 2001 to 2003, respectively)
5. Working capital
6. Current ratio
7. Debt ratio

Financial Statement Analysis

GRAPHING WORKSHOP

1. Yes, earnings per share has increased each year.
2. $1.79 per share.
3. The ratio has increased steadily from approximately 1.3% in year 1 to 1.9% in year 10. However, the rate of growth appears to have declined after year 5.
4. The rate began at approximately 2.2% in year 1 and declined for three years. In years 4 and 5, the rate increased slightly before continuing its decline to approximately 1.6% in year 10.

ANALYZING COSTCO'S FINANCIAL STATEMENTS

(See table at the bottom of the page)

TEACHING STRATEGIES   PORTFOLIO ASSESSMENT

Students should select an example of financial statement analysis that has been successfully completed to include in their portfolio. A copy of the Portfolio Assessment form (blackline master in the Teacher's Resource Guide; also on the Student Companion CD) should be completed by the student and the Description section should include any comments regarding how the student mastered these concepts and procedures. Alternatively, students might include in their portfolios printed reports from an Automated Accounting problem.

	2003	2002	2001
Rate earned on average total assets	5.8%	6.4%	6.4%
Rate earned on average stockholders' equity	11.8%	13.2%	13.2%
Earnings per share (reported in highlights)	$1.53	$1.48	$1.29
Price-earnings ratio	24.5	31.3	35.9
Working capital (reported in highlights)	$700	$181	$(230)
Current ratio	1.1	1.0	n/a
Debt ratio	50.3%	51.0%	n/a

(amounts in millions, except per share data)

n/a = Amounts not available on balance sheet or ten-year highlights.

EXPLAIN

- Explain that ratio analysis can be used to analyze a business and predict how well a business will do in the future.

- Explain that ratios may be compared to previous years' ratios, ratios of companies in similar industries, or to industry averages.

- Point out that ratios can be used to evaluate short-term and long-term financial strength, efficiency, and earnings performance.

- Point out that most of the data needed for the Automated Accounting software to calculate financial ratios is already available in the database, but that some information such as shares of stock outstanding and current market price per share may need to be entered to complete the analysis.

DEMONSTRATE

Performing ratio analysis

- Click the Reports toolbar button.

- Choose Financial Analysis from the Select a Report Group list.

- Choose Ratio Analysis from the Choose a Report to Display list and click OK.

- Enter the number of shares of stock outstanding and the current market price per share and click OK.

- Click the Print button to print the trial balance. Point out that the ratio analysis can also be copied into another application.

Analyzing Automated Financial Statements and Ratio Analysis

One method of evaluating relationships within the financial statements is the use of ratio analysis. Ratios obtained from numbers in the financial statements may be compared to the ratios of previous years, to those of companies in similar industries, or to industry averages computed by companies such as Dow Jones or Standard & Poor's. Ratio analysis is one of the tools managers, investors, and lenders use to predict how well a business will do in the future.

Ratios used by business are commonly grouped by their objectives:

- The evaluation of short-term financial strength
- The evaluation of long-term financial strength
- Efficiency
- Earnings performance

Most of the data needed to compute the common ratios are available within the database maintained by accounting software. Additional information that the accountant may need to input to complete the analysis include the number of shares of stock outstanding and the current market price per share.

Performing Ratio Analysis
Use the following steps to display the ratio analysis report:

1. Click the Reports toolbar button, or choose the Reports Selection menu item from the Reports menu.

2. When the Report Selection dialog appears, choose Financial Analysis from the Select a Report Group list.

3. Choose Ratio Analysis from the Choose a Report to Display list.

4. Click OK.

5. Enter the number of shares of stock outstanding and the market price per share.

6. Click OK.

The report will be displayed in the scrollable Report Viewer Window. The report may be printed and/or copied for inclusion in another application, such as a spreadsheet or word processor.

AUTOMATING MASTERY PROBLEM 17-7

Instructions:

1. Load *Automated Accounting 8.0* or higher software.

2. Select database AA17-7 (Advanced Course Mastery Problem 17-7) from the accounting template disk.

3. Select File from the menu bar and choose the Save As menu command. Key the path to the

drive and directory that contain your data files. Save the database with a filename of XXX177 (where XXX are your initials).

4. Read the Problem Instruction screen by clicking the Browser toolbar button.

5. Refer to page 521 for data used in this problem.

6. Exit the Automated Accounting software.

PRACTICE

- Assign Automating Mastery Problem 17-7: Analyzing comparative financial statements.

ASSESSMENT

- Use the Electronic Auditor to assess student understanding.

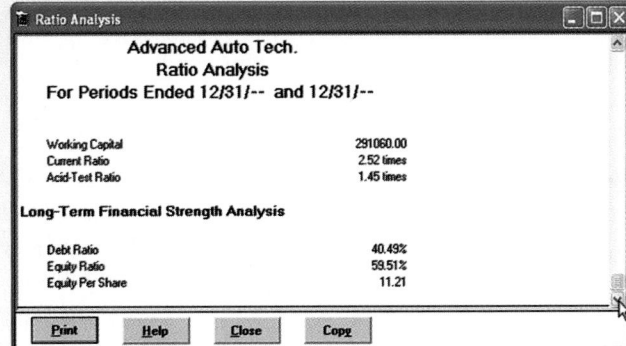

TEACHING STRATEGIES   PORTFOLIO ASSESSMENT

Students should be encouraged to print at least one report from one of the Automated Accounting problems to include in their portfolio to demonstrate mastery of automated accounting systems. A copy of the Portfolio Assessment form (blackline master in the Teacher's Resource Guide; also on the Student Companion CD) should be completed by the student, and the Description section should include any comments regarding how the student mastered these concepts and procedures.

CHAPTER 18

	SCOPE & SEQUENCE	
	NEW	**REVIEW/ EXTENSION**
Introduce the Chapter	✓	
Lesson 18-1 Understanding Cash Flow Analysis		
Cash flow analysis	✓	
Timing of revenue and expense recognition	✓	
Lesson 18-2 Preparing the Operating Activities Section of a Statement of Cash Flows		
Determining cash flows from operating activities	✓	
Reporting cash flows from operating activities	✓	
Lesson 18-3 Completing the Statement of Cash Flows		
Analyzing cash flows from investing activities	✓	
Analyzing cash flows from financing activities	✓	
Putting It All Together		

ENHANCING	
SPECIAL FEATURES	
• Accounting in the Real World: Hospitality Properties Trust	
• Making Ethical Decisions: Channel Stuffing • Small Business Spotlight • Technology for Business: Keeping Financial Transactions Safe	
• Careers in Accounting	
• Case for Critical Thinking	
• Explore Accounting • Xtra! Web Site: Xtra! Enrichment • Applied Communication • SCANS Workplace Competency • Auditing for Errors • Analyzing Costco's Financial Statements	

Cash Flows

INSTRUCTION			PRACTICE AND ASSESSMENT		
TECHNOLOGY AND MEDIA	**TEACHING STRATEGIES**		**GUIDED PRACTICE**	**INDEPENDENT PRACTICE**	**RETEACHING AND ENRICHMENT**
• Internet Research Activity • Accounting Xtra! Web Site	• Software Focus				
• Instructor's Resource CD: PowerPoint Slides • Xtra! Web Site: Xtra! Study Tools • Personal Trainer	• Auditory Learner		• Terms Review • Audit Your Understanding • Work Together 18-1	• On Your Own 18-1 • Application Problem 18-1 • Ongoing Assessment, p. 535 • Personal Trainer • Xtra! Web Site: Xtra! Study Tools	• Reteach, p. 535 • Enrich, p. 536
• Instructor's Resource CD: PowerPoint Slides • Xtra! Web Site: Xtra! Study Tools • Blackline Masters: 3-Column Financial Statement Form • Personal Trainer	• Cooperative Learning		• Audit Your Understanding • Work Together 18-2	• On Your Own 18-2 • Application Problem 18-2 • Ongoing Assessment, p. 541 • Personal Trainer • Xtra! Web Site: Xtra! Study Tools	• Reteach, p. 541 • Enrich, p. 542
• Instructor's Resource CD: PowerPoint Slides • Xtra! Web Site: Xtra! Study Tools • Blackline Masters: 3-Column Financial Statement Form • Personal Trainer • QuickBooks	• Limited English Proficiency (LEP) Students • Applied Skills: Language Arts		• Audit Your Understanding • Work Together 18-3	• On Your Own 18-3 • Application Problems 18-3 and 18-4 • Ongoing Assessment, p. 547 • Personal Trainer • Xtra! Web Site: Xtra! Study Tools	• Reteach, p. 547 • Enrich, p. 548 • QuickBooks
• Automated Accounting • QuickBooks • Personal Trainer • Xtra! Web Site: Xtra! Review, Quizzing, and Enrichment • Student Companion CD	• Applied Skills: Writing Across the Curriculum • Visual Learner			• Mastery Problem 18-5 • Personal Trainer • Xtra! Web Site: Xtra! Review and Quizzing • Study Guide 18 • Student Companion CD • Chapter 18 Test • ExamView Chapter 18 • Portfolio Assessment	• Challenge Problem 18-6 • Reteach, p. 549 • Enrich, p. 549 • Recycling Problem 18-1 • Automated Accounting • Xtra! Web Site: Xtra! Enrichment

CHAPTER

18 Statement of Cash Flows

OBJECTIVES & TERMS

After studying Chapter 18, you will be able to:

1. Define accounting terms related to cash flow analysis.

2. Identify accounting concepts and practices related to cash flow analysis.

3. Describe operating, investing, and financing activities and provide examples of each.

4. Prepare the operating activities section of a statement of cash flows.

5. Prepare the investing activities and financing activities sections of a statement of cash flows.

6. Prepare a statement of cash flows.

- accrual basis of accounting
- cash basis of accounting
- cash flows
- statement of cash flows
- operating activities
- investing activities
- financing activities

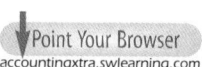
Point Your Browser
accountingxtra.swlearning.com

ACCOUNTING IN THE REAL WORLD

1. A REIT is required to distribute most of its income to stockholders and is not required to pay federal income tax on its income.

2. A large portion of a REIT's operating expense would be depreciation, a non-cash expense.

INTERNET RESEARCH ACTIVITY

Answers will vary.

Hospitality Properties Trust

©GETTY IMAGES/PHOTODISC

SPEND THE NIGHT WITH HOSPITALITY PROPERTIES TRUST

A common philosophy for business success is to delegate everything except your expertise. Hotel operators are experts at running the day-to-day operations of hotels and resorts. Building and owning hotel facilities, however, requires a different expertise. That's where Hospitality Properties Trust comes to the rescue.

Hospitality Properties Trust (HPT) leases its hotels to experienced hotel operators, including Prime Hotels and Resorts, AmeriSuites, Staybridge Suites, and several brands of Marriott. HPT owns 286 hotels with 38,577 rooms located in 38 states.

HPT is a real estate investment trust (REIT), a unique form of organization created under the tax laws of the United States. REIT tax laws require HPT to distribute most of its income to the stockholders. In exchange, the REIT is not required to pay federal income taxes.

For most corporations, earnings per share is the most recognized measure of financial performance. For a REIT, however, funds from operations (FFO) is the most important measure. HPT's board of directors uses its FFO to determine the amount of dividends to be paid. The quarterly dividend is important to HPT stockholders, who typically own the stock in order to earn HPT's regular quarterly dividend.

Critical Thinking

1. How does a REIT differ from a typical corporation?
2. Why would the FFO of a REIT be significantly different from its earnings per share?

Today
accountingxtra.swlearning.com

Source: www.hptreit.com

SOFTWARE FOR SPECIFIC INDUSTRIES

Search the Internet for "accounting software" for a specific industry, such as agriculture, physicians, construction, lawyers, etc.

Instructions

1. List the name of the company that sells the software.
2. List the name of the software program.

18-1 Understanding Cash Flow Analysis

The information presented on the income statement, balance sheet, and statement of stockholders' equity provides individuals insight into the financial condition of a business. Managers, investors, and other interested parties use this information to improve profitability, determine operating efficiency, and make informed managerial decisions. The accounting method that records revenues when they are earned and expenses when they are incurred is called the **accrual basis of accounting**. Generally accepted accounting principles (GAAP) require that most businesses use the accrual basis of accounting for their financial statements.

The accounting method that records revenues when they are received and expenses when they are paid is called the **cash basis of accounting**. Some small businesses use this method of accounting because it is easy to use and less expensive to maintain. However, cash-basis financial statements do not provide enough information about the financial condition of the business to satisfy most investors and creditors.

Accrual-based financial statements give a complete picture of the financial condition of a business. However, managers and investors may need additional information about the cash flows of a business. By analyzing cash flows, individuals can determine whether a company has enough cash to continue operating. Firms short on cash may experience problems paying expenses, purchasing new merchandise, replacing worn equipment, repaying debts, and providing owners with a return on their investment. It is critical that financial statement analysis include a study of a company's ability to produce and manage cash.

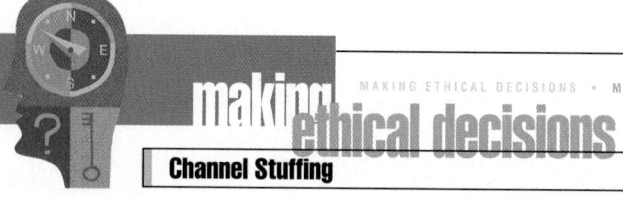

MAKING ETHICAL DECISIONS • MAKING ETHICAL DECISIONS • MAKING ETHICAL DECISION

making ethical decisions

Channel Stuffing

Rivera Manufacturing's president knows that the company's income is going to fall short of published estimates by stock analysts. The company's stock will surely drop on news of the income shortfall. Two weeks before the December 31 fiscal year end, Rivera's president instructs the sales department to offer substantial discounts to customers who will place their normal first-quarter orders in December. In addition, Rivera will hold the goods in its warehouse until delivery is requested by the customers.

Instructions

The practice described in this case is called *channel stuffing*. Define channel stuffing and determine whether the practice is legal.

Statement of Cash Flows

MAKING ETHICAL DECISIONS

A company can use channel stuffing to inflate its sales. Customers in the company's normal distribution channel are provided a financial incentive or simply pressured to order goods before they are needed. The goods are held by the company until delivery is requested by the customer. The problem with channel stuffing is that, in the subsequent fiscal period, customers either return unsold items or simply do not order additional goods. There is no business purpose for channel stuffing except to increase the company's stock price by inflating sales and income. Channel stuffing is illegal.

Internet sources are available that explain channel stuffing. The practice is a fraudulent method for inflating sales and income in the current fiscal period. Unless the practice is repeated in the subsequent year, sales and income will drop. Source: *www.theiia.org/itaudit/index.cfm?fuseaction= forum&fid=532* and *www.investopedia.com/terms/ c/channelstuffing.asp*

Case Study

Two years ago, in January, Gina and Kevin Harnley formed Snow Creek Corporation for the purpose of selling ski equipment, snowboards, and related accessories. During the first year, the company produced sales of over $300,000 and earned a net income of approximately $60,000. Last year was equally impressive. Assets increased, sales exceeded $500,000, and a net income of more than $100,000 was earned. Two months into the current year, however, Snow Creek Corporation lacked the amount of cash necessary to pay its current bills. If Snow Creek was growing and profits were rising, how does one explain the company's shortage of cash and inability to pay bills?

One of the main reasons for Snow Creek's financial problems was its generous credit policy, which created a large volume of accounts receivable. Snow Creek's credit policy of "no payments for six months" definitely attracted buyers. However, problems arose when a large number of Snow Creek's customers did not make their payments on time.

Another reason for Snow Creek's difficulties was a large increase in inventory. Snow Creek required a greater level of inventory to assure that it had an adequate selection of items for a growing number of customers. It paid for the merchandise within the 30-day credit terms, but it had not yet sold much of the inventory. The company ran out of money to pay its bills. Cash was going out to purchase inventory and not enough was coming in to pay expenses.

The Harnleys, who manage the company, failed to foresee their problems because they prepared their income statements using the accrual basis of accounting. Sale amounts were recognized when snow equipment and accessories left the store, not when cash was received. Consequently, Snow Creek Corporation showed strong sales and profits. However, an analysis of the company's cash receipts and cash payments shows a different picture.

Some investors and financial analysts rely heavily on an examination of income statements and balance sheets to judge a company's performance. However, impressive profits are not always a guarantee of success in the future. For example, despite reporting a substantial net income for the year, a business may experience a cash shortage and have difficulty paying its bills. Cash flow analysis helps owners, creditors, and other interested parties:

1. Determine a company's potential to produce cash in the future.
2. Judge a company's ability to pay bills and repay debts.
3. Explain changes in the cash account balance.
4. Evaluate a company's investment and equity transactions.

The U.S. Small Business Administration (SBA) is an independent agency of the federal government. Created by an act of Congress in 1953, the SBA is dedicated to helping Americans start and operate successful small enterprises. Today, the SBA is involved in financing, training, and advocacy for small firms.

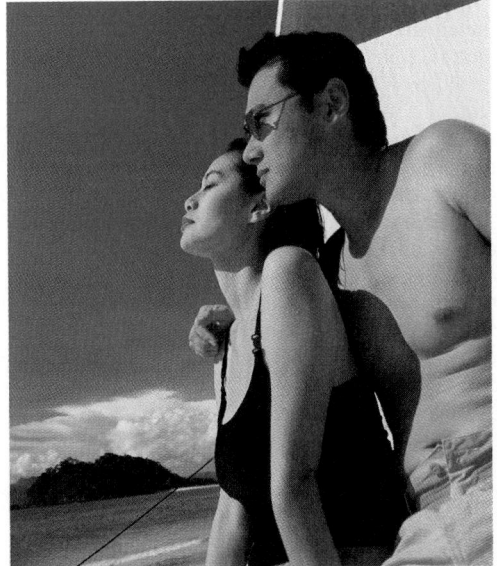

©GETTY IMAGES/PHOTODISC

Understanding Cash Flow Analysis

Lesson 18-1 **531**

SMALL BUSINESS SPOTLIGHT
The Small Business Spotlight feature explains the role of the Small Business Administration in helping businesspeople start and operate successful small enterprises.

- Emphasize that cash flows can be simply considered as money coming in (cash receipts) and money going out (cash payments).

- Point out that the statement of cash flows reports how money came in (sources of cash) and how money went out (uses of cash). By identifying the sources and uses of cash, the statement of cash flows explains the difference in the beginning and ending balances in the cash account.

- Ask students to identify the amount of net income presented in the statement of cash flows shown in the illustration. Emphasize strongly that net income does not usually match cash receipts. Explain that sales on account change the timing of cash received.

- Point out that the income statement does not address the issue of when cash is received from sales on account. Emphasize again that a net income of $100,000 reported on the income statement does not necessarily mean the company actually received $100,000 in cash during that same period. This discrepancy can mean a lack of cash to pay expenses.

- Point out that one reason for preparing the statement of cash flows is to determine if there will be enough cash on hand to pay bills.

- Ask students to identify the beginning and ending cash balances in the statement of cash flows shown in the illustration. Point out that cash decreased $4,135 during the fiscal year, meaning that Snow Creek used more cash than was received.

- Emphasize that the income statement and balance sheet are prepared using the accrual basis of accounting, whereas the statement of cash flows is prepared using the cash basis of accounting. Explain that the difference between the accrual and cash basis of accounting involves the timing as to when revenue and expenses are recognized, as explained on the next page.

Snow Creek Corporation
Statement of Cash Flows
For Year Ended December 31, 20X2

Cash Flows from Operating Activities:			
Net Income		$100,344.00	
Adjustments to Net Income:			
Depreciation Expense	$ 11,605.00		
Changes in current assets and liabilities:			
Increase in accounts receivable	(110,530.00)		
Decrease in supplies	399.00		
Increase in merchandise inventory	(116,640.00)		
Increase in notes payable	38,990.00		
Increase in accounts payable	54,924.00		
Total adjustments to net income		($121,252.00)	
Cash used for operating activities			($20,908.00)
Cash Flows from Investing Activities:			
Addition to equipment		($20,680.00)	
Proceeds from sale of property		30,000.00	
Cash provided by investing activities			$9,320.00
Cash Flows from Financing Activities:			
Repayment of mortgage		($547.00)	
Proceeds from issuance of common stock		40,000.00	
Dividend payment		(32,000.00)	
Cash provided by financing activities			$7,453.00
Net Decrease in Cash			($4,135.00)
Cash Balance, Beginning of Period			12,540.00
Cash Balance, End of Period			$8,405.00

The cash receipts and cash payments of a company are called **cash flows**. A statement that summarizes cash receipts and cash payments resulting from business activities during a fiscal period is called a **statement of cash flows**. The statement, as shown above, explains the change in Cash during a fiscal period by reporting the sources (inflows or receipts) and uses (outflows or payments) of a company's cash.

By studying a company's cash flows, a manager can analyze why there were profits and yet not enough cash to pay bills. No other financial statement provides this important information.

The Harnleys made business decisions based on information reported on the income state-ment and balance sheet. They failed to realize that the revenues reported on the income state-ment rarely match cash receipts. If a company reports sales on account of $100,000.00, it is unlikely that the company had $100,000.00 in actual cash receipts. Not all customers pay in a timely manner.

The income statement and balance sheet are prepared using an accrual basis of accounting. The statement of cash flows is prepared using the cash basis of accounting. The cash basis of accounting recognizes revenue when cash is received and expenses when cash is paid out.

REMEMBER   The cash inflows and outflows of a business are identified using the information presented on a company's financial statements.

TIMING OF REVENUE RECOGNITION

Accrual Basis		vs.	Cash Basis	
Revenue recognized at the time it is *earned*			Revenue recognized at the time cash is *received*	
Revenues	$25,000.00		Revenues	$ 0.00
Expenses	0.00		Expenses	0.00
Net Income	$25,000.00		Net Income	$ 0.00

Assume that Flomax Corporation has sales on account during the year and no expenses. Under the accrual basis for accounting, revenue is recognized at the time it is earned.

Accounts Receivable	
25,000.00	

Sales	
	25,000.00

Assume the account receivable remains outstanding at the end of the fiscal year. Using the accrual basis of accounting, Flomax reports revenues as shown above. However, the income calculation prepared under the cash basis shows no revenue for the period, hence, no net income. Under the cash basis of accounting, revenue is not recognized until cash is **received.**

TIMING OF EXPENSE RECOGNITION

Accrual Basis		vs.	Cash Basis	
Expense recognized at the time it is *incurred*			Expense recognized at the time cash is *paid*	
Revenues	$25,000.00		Revenues	$ 0.00
Expenses	3,000.00		Expenses	0.00
Net Income	$22,000.00		Net Income	$ 0.00

Similarly, the recognition of expenses does not always match the payments of cash. For example, Flomax Corporation recognizes one week of salaries earned by employees before the close of the current fiscal year. The salary expense will not be paid until the next fiscal period. Using

Salaries Expense	
3,000.00	

Salaries Payable	
	3,000.00

the accrual basis, Flomax recognizes the expense during the current fiscal year as shown in the T accounts.

Assume that this is Flomax Corporation's only expense of the year. Using the accrual basis of accounting, Flomax's net income is $22,000.00, as shown above. The accrual basis of accounting recognizes an expense at the time it is incurred. Using the cash basis of accounting, Flomax has no expenses to report in the current period. The cash basis recognizes an expense when cash is paid. Since no cash was received and no cash was paid, a net income of $0.00 is reported.

- Point out that the statement of cash flows summarizes cash receipts and cash payments for three separate categories: operating, investing, and financing activities.

- Point out that operating activities are the most important of the three business activities. Explain that operating activities are those cash receipts and cash payments connected to the production and delivery of goods and services to the customer, such as cash collections on sales or cash payments of expenses. Generally, operating activities are identified by determining the sources and uses of cash related to the calculation of net income and by noting the increases or decreases in current assets or current liabilities. Sources and uses of cash for operating activities will be further explained in Lesson 18-2.

- Point out that successful companies use the cash received from owners or the sale of stock to purchase assets that help produce revenue. For example, companies purchase office buildings and furniture so they may conduct business with customers at a central location. This strategy can help in generating sales and profits. Emphasize that cash receipts and cash payments related to the sale or purchase of assets used to earn revenue over time are called investing activities. Investing activities also include lending cash and collecting the loan principal. Generally, investing activities are identified by noting the increases or decreases in long-term assets. Sources and uses of cash for investing activities will be further explained in Lesson 18-3.

DEMONSTRATE

Prepare a list of common cash flows from operating activities

- Write the heading *Operating Activities* on the board or overhead.

- Ask students to provide examples of cash inflows and cash outflows resulting from operating activities. Write correct student responses on the board.

- After the list is completed, ask students to identify each example as a source of cash or use of cash. Record correct student responses.

534

CASH FLOWS FROM OPERATING ACTIVITIES

Operating Activities

Cash Inflows (sources of cash)
Cash sales of merchandise
Cash sales of services
Interest income
Dividends received from the ownership of stock in other companies
Cash received from charge customers

Cash Outflows (uses of cash)
Advertising
Credit card fees
Insurance expense
Interest payments
Payroll expenses
Property tax
Utility expenses
Income tax

The statement of cash flows is divided into three sections: cash flows from *operating activities*, cash flows from *investing activities*, and cash flows from *financing activities*. The cash flows for each of these sections are calculated by analyzing the information presented on the income statement, the balance sheet, and the statement of stockholders' equity.

The cash receipts and payments necessary to operate a business on a day-to-day basis are called **operating activities**. For example, a list of common cash inflows and cash outflows from operating activities is presented here. Snow Creek Corporation uses cash to add merchandise and to pay the daily expenses required to operate the business and earn a profit.

CASH FLOWS FROM INVESTING ACTIVITIES

Investing Activities

Cash Inflows (sources of cash)
Sale of property
Sale of equipment
Sale of building
Collections of long-term loans

Cash Outflows (uses of cash)
Purchase of land
Purchase of equipment
Purchase of building
Purchase of patents or special licenses
Loans to other companies
Purchase of stock in other companies
Purchase of bonds in other companies

Cash receipts and cash payments involving the sale or purchase of assets used to earn revenue over a period of time are called **investing activities**. A list of common cash inflows and cash outflows involving investing activities is shown here.

Creditors, owners, and potential investors examine the investing activities to assess the future financial strength and profitability of a business. Financial analysts know that investment activities are necessary if the business is to remain profitable. If a company sells buildings and equipment to raise cash for operations, there would soon be no buildings and equipment to produce or store the goods.

REMEMBER Sources of cash represent cash inflows and are added on the statement of cash flows. Uses of cash represent cash outflows and are subtracted on the statement of cash flows.

CASH FLOWS FROM FINANCING ACTIVITIES

Financing Activities

Cash Inflows (sources of cash)
Capital stock issue
Mortgage issue
Bond issue
Long-term loans

Cash Outflows (uses of cash)
Purchase of treasury stock
Payment of cash dividends
Repayment of loan/note principal
Retirement of bond principal

When Gina and Kevin Harnley decided to form Snow Creek Corporation, they had to obtain the necessary funding to carry out their plan. The Harnleys decided to sell common stock to acquire the financing they needed. Cash receipts and payments involving debt or equity transactions are called **financing activities**. These activities usually involve borrowing money from creditors and repaying the principal or acquiring capital from owners and providing a return on their investment.

Financing activities are often used to ensure that an adequate balance exists in the cash account. If a firm's business activities use more cash than it receives, it must obtain additional financing.

Some financing activities reduce the cash balance. This occurs when cash is used to pay dividends, repay the principal of a loan, or purchase treasury stock. These payments of cash decrease the amount available for operating and investing activities. A list of common cash inflows and cash outflows related to financing activities is shown above.

FYI
FOR YOUR INFORMATION

The Financial Accounting Standards Board (FASB), in *Statement No. 95*, classifies the interest paid on borrowed money as an operating activity. The reason for this classification is that the payment of interest expense on a loan is considered to have a direct impact on a firm's net income.

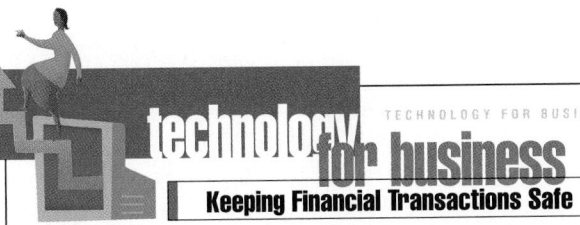

technology for business
TECHNOLOGY FOR BUSINESS • TECHNOLOGY FOR BUSINESS • TECHNOLOGY FOR BUSINE

Keeping Financial Transactions Safe

Each day, millions of financial transactions are electronically transmitted. Many of these transactions are made using the Internet. Several technologies exist to safeguard these transactions from electronic theft and fraud. Among the oldest of these technologies is encryption. Before data are transmitted, they are disguised through encryption. If the transmitted data are stolen, the thief cannot access the data. When the data reach the proper destination, the receiving party will decrypt the information. Two keys, or sets of codes, are needed. One is used to encrypt the information; the other is used to decrypt it.

A further safeguard for electronic data transmission is the use of digital certificates. These certificates are used to link the encryption key and the decryption key. Digital certificates are issued by third-party vendors. They link the encryption and decryption keys and prevent unauthorized parties from possessing the decryption key. Before digital certificates are issued, the identity of the business or individual is verified. This verification provides another level of security.

Understanding Cash Flow Analysis

Lesson 18-1   **535**

535

GUIDED PRACTICE

Terms Review

Call on students to define each term in the Terms Review. Ask the class if the definition is correct and whether the complete definition has been given or if anything else needs to be added. Suggested definitions are given in the Glossary.

Audit Your Understanding

Call on students to answer the Audit Your Understanding questions. Ask the class if the answer is correct and/or complete. Answers are given in Appendix E of the textbook.

Work Together

Have students write the solution to the Work Together problem as you guide the class through the examples.

- Direct students to record each answer on the appropriate form.
- Call on students to identify each transaction as a cash inflow or cash outflow.
- Call on other students to identify each transaction as an operating, investing, or financing activity.

INDEPENDENT PRACTICE

On Your Own

- Assign the On Your Own problem to be worked independently.
- Use the Ongoing Assessment techniques to diagnose student understanding.

Application Problem

- Assign Application Problem 18-1: Classifying cash flows.

Personal Trainer

- Students can access the Lesson 18-1 assessment material using this software.

Xtra! Web Site

- Students can access the Xtra! Study Tools for additional practice.

ENRICH

- Assign Making Ethical Decisions on page 530.
- Assign the Small Business Spotlight on page 531.
- Ask students to read the Technology for Business feature on page 535.

536

• terms review

accrual basis of accounting
cash basis of accounting
cash flows
statement of cash flows
operating activities
investing activities
financing activities

• audit your understanding

1. Using the accrual accounting basis, when are revenues and expenses recognized?

2. Using the cash accounting basis, when are revenues and expenses recognized?

3. Identify the three categories of business activities reported on the statement of cash flows.

• work together 18-1

Classifying cash flows

The following business transactions represent selected cash receipts (cash inflows) and cash payments (cash outflows) of Los Altos Cyclery. A blank form is provided in the *Working Papers*. Your instructor will guide you through the following problem.

1. Identify each transaction as (1) a cash inflow or cash outflow and (2) as an operating, investing, or financing activity.

   a. Receipts from the issue of capital stock.
   b. Cash purchase of office furniture.
   c. Dividend payment.
   d. Advertising expense.
   e. Receipts from the sale of merchandise.
   f. Cash received from the issue of a mortgage.
   g. Repayment of loan principal.
   h. Purchase of another company's stock.

• on your own 18-1

Classifying cash flows

The following business transactions represent selected cash receipts (cash inflows) and cash payments (cash outflows) of Burlingame Tuxedo. A blank form is provided in the *Working Papers*. Work independently to complete this problem.

1. Identify each transaction as (1) a cash inflow or cash outflow and (2) as an operating, investing, or financing activity.

   a. Receipts from the issue of bonds.
   b. Cash purchase of office furniture.
   c. Salary expense.
   d. Receipts from tuxedo rentals.
   e. Receipts from the issue of a mortgage.
   f. Cash receipt from sale of equipment.
   g. Cash purchase of treasury stock.
   h. Payment of property taxes.

CLOSE

- Emphasize that an analysis of cash flows helps individuals explain changes in the cash account balance and determine if a company may experience problems paying expenses, repaying loans, replacing worn equipment, purchasing new assets for expansion, or providing owners with a return on their investment.

18-2 Preparing the Operating Activities Section of a Statement of Cash Flows

DETERMINING CASH FLOWS FROM OPERATING ACTIVITIES

The operating activity section of the statement of cash flows reports the cash inflows and cash outflows resulting from the operation of a business. These cash flows can be indirectly determined by identifying the net income for the period and making several adjustments.

Net Income

Net income presented on an income statement summarizes revenues and expenses generated by the operating activities of a business during the fiscal period. For this reason, net income is a good starting point for calculating the cash

flows from operating activities. Since a net income eventually brings additional money into a firm, net income is viewed as a source of cash. A net loss reduces the amount of money available for expenditures and is considered to be a use of cash.

Since the income statement is prepared using the accrual basis of accounting and the statement of cash flows is prepared using the cash basis of accounting, the recognition of revenues and expenses occurs at different times. Adjustments are made to net income to recognize the timing differences.

ADJUSTING NET INCOME FOR DEPRECIATION

	Depreciation Expense	
Dec. 31	500.00	

	Accumulated Depreciation—Equipment	
		Dec. 31 500.00

← Effect on cash: None; add amount to net income

Depreciation expense is recognized on the income statement. However, it does not involve an outflow of cash. Since depreciation expense does not use cash, the amount is added back to the net income amount.

At the end of the fiscal year, Centaur Corporation expenses an appropriate amount of the original cost of equipment using the straight-line

method of depreciation. Depreciation for the year is recorded by debiting Depreciation Expense and crediting Accumulated Depreciation—Equipment as shown above.

Notice that the credit for this transaction is Accumulated Depreciation—Equipment, not Cash. Depreciation expense does not affect the balance in the cash account. However, depreciation expense is deducted from company revenues to determine net income. Since no cash is paid out, the amount of depreciation expense reported on the income statement must be added back to net income to determine the actual cash generated from operating activities. The amount of depreciation expense added back to net income is one of the adjustments to net income to determine the actual source of cash from operations.

Preparing the Operating Activities Section of a Statement of Cash Flows

Lesson 18-2   **537**

- Point out that the second adjustment to net income involves changes in current assets other than cash.

- Use the transactions provided to demonstrate to students that an increase in a noncash current asset represents a use of cash and that a decrease in a noncash current asset represents a source of cash. Write these two statements on the board.

Cash		
Dec. 15	80,000.00	

Sales		
	Nov. 15	100,000.00

Accounts Receivable		
Nov. 15	100,000.00	Dec. 15	80,000.00
Dec. 31 Bal.	20,000.00	

Increase in noncash current asset is a use of cash. ⟶

Analyze the increase in accounts receivable

- Draw three T accounts arranged vertically on the board or overhead. Label them *Accounts Receivable, Sales,* and *Cash.* Students can also refer to the illustration at the top of the page.

- Ask a student to read the Nov. 15 transaction. Ask the student what accounts are to be debited and credited. Record the correct student response in the T accounts. Be sure to emphasize that for illustration purposes this is the only sale on account for the entire year.

- Ask a student to read the Dec. 15 transaction. Ask the student what accounts are to be debited and credited. Record the correct student response in the T accounts.

- Ask students to review the T accounts. Ask them the amount of sales recorded for the year *($100,000).* Ask them how much of the $100,000 was actually collected in the form of cash *($80,000).*

- Emphasize that the $20,000 increase in accounts receivable, a current asset, represents a use of cash since this money is not available to the business for other purposes. Since $20,000 of the year's sales on account were not collected, this amount must be deducted from the net income figure so that the true cash flow from sales is accurately reported.

- Use the same approach described above for explaining that a decrease in a current asset represents a source of cash.

The second adjustment to net income involves changes in *noncash current assets* (current assets other than cash). Increases and decreases in noncash current assets impact cash flows and require an adjustment to net income. For example, an increase in the current asset Accounts Receivable indicates that not all of the sales on account reported for a fiscal period were collected. Consequently, an increase in accounts receivable means that cash received from sales is less than the sales amount reported on the income statement.

On November 1, Heritage Corporation began business. A T account analysis of the following transactions is shown above.

Nov. 15. Heritage Corporation makes its only sale on account, $100,000.00.

Dec. 15. Heritage receives $80,000.00 as a partial payment on the account. No other collections occur during the year.

The $20,000.00 increase in accounts receivable represents cash that has not yet been received and, therefore, must be deducted from net income to determine cash flow. This adjustment to net income informs analysts that the cash inflows from sales on account during the year were $80,000.00 ($100,000.00 – $20,000.00) and not the full $100,000.00 reported as sales on the income statement. An increase in a noncash current asset is considered to be a *use of cash.* This use of cash supports the company's daily operations by allowing the business to offer customers the option to buy now and pay later. A use of cash means a specified sum of money is no longer available for other business activities.

Noncash current assets may also decrease during a fiscal period. A decrease in a noncash current asset represents a *source of cash* and is added back to the net income amount. This concept is illustrated through the continued use of the previous example involving Heritage Corporation.

At the end of its second year in business, Heritage Corporation has a $10,000.00 balance in Accounts Receivable. From an analysis of the T account, we learn that:

1. The balance in *Accounts Receivable* at the beginning of the year was $20,000.00.
2. Sales on account of $130,000.00 were made during the year.
3. Payments on account of $140,000.00 were received.
4. The Accounts Receivable balance at the end of the year is $10,000.00.

How can a company collect $140,000.00 of receivables if sales on account for the year are only $130,000.00? In this instance, Heritage collected a portion of the $20,000.00 balance in accounts receivable due from the previous year. The balance in Accounts Receivable declined from $20,000.00 on January 1 to $10,000.00 on December 31. This decrease is added to net income to determine cash flow.

Each noncash current asset is analyzed in a similar manner to accounts receivable.

Accounts Receivable		
Jan. 1 Bal.	20,000.00	Cash received	140,000.00
Credit sales	130,000.00		
Dec. 31 Bal.	10,000.00		

Statement of Cash Flows

Select a group of three students to create a bulletin board matching various business transactions with the type of activity (operating, investing, or financing) and whether the transaction represents a cash inflow or cash outflow. Allow 3–4 days for completion of the activity.

ANALYZING CHANGES IN CURRENT LIABILITIES

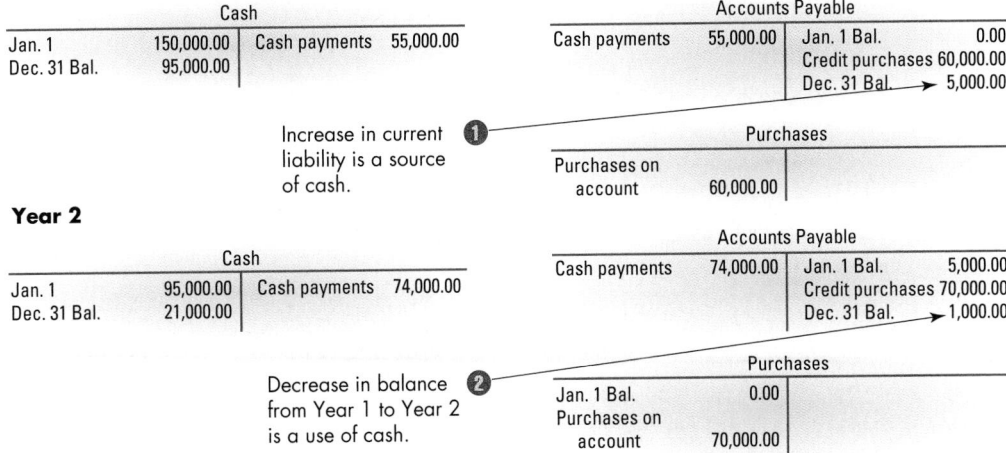

Year 1

Cash		
Jan. 1	150,000.00	Cash payments 55,000.00
Dec. 31 Bal.	95,000.00	

Accounts Payable		
Cash payments	55,000.00	Jan. 1 Bal. 0.00
		Credit purchases 60,000.00
		Dec. 31 Bal. → 5,000.00

① Increase in current liability is a source of cash.

Purchases	
Purchases on account	60,000.00

Year 2

Cash		
Jan. 1	95,000.00	Cash payments 74,000.00
Dec. 31 Bal.	21,000.00	

Accounts Payable		
Cash payments	74,000.00	Jan. 1 Bal. 5,000.00
		Credit purchases 70,000.00
		Dec. 31 Bal. → 1,000.00

② Decrease in balance from Year 1 to Year 2 is a use of cash.

Purchases	
Jan. 1 Bal.	0.00
Purchases on account	70,000.00

The third adjustment to net income involves changes in current liabilities. During the operating activities of a business, increases and decreases in current liabilities occur as debts are added and paid off in the process of generating revenues. For instance, an increase in accounts payable indicates that not all of the purchases on account made during a fiscal period were paid in full. An increase in current liabilities has a positive impact on cash flows as shown for the Fairtex Corporation above.

The $5,000.00 increase in accounts payable at the end of the first year means the actual cash outflow for purchases on account was $55,000.00 and not the full $60,000.00 reported as purchases on the income statement. For this reason, net income is adjusted by adding back

$5,000.00 for the increase in a current liability. Since the company has use of the $5,000.00, the increase in a current liability represents a *source of cash.*

During the second year of operation, Fairtex Corporation was extremely aggressive in paying off its debts. In fact, the company paid off $74,000.00 of accounts payable, $4,000.00 more than the total purchases on account of $70,000.00. Why would a company pay more than it owes? In this instance, Fairtex paid a portion of the $5,000.00 accounts payable balance owed for the previous year. A decrease in a current liability represents a *use of cash* and is subtracted from the net income figure.

Each current liability is analyzed in a similar manner to accounts payable.

SUMMARY

- Depreciation expense is *added* back to net income since it is a noncash expense
- Increases in noncash current assets (assets other than cash) and decreases in current liabilities represent *uses of cash* and are *deducted* from net income
- Decreases in noncash current assets and increases in current liabilities represent *sources of cash* and are *added* to net income

The operating activities section of the statement of cash flows shows the amount of cash actually received and paid as a result of operating a business. The adjustments to net income required to determine the cash flows from operating activities are reviewed here.

539

- Refer students to the illustration.

- Ask students to name the three financial statements presented in the illustration (*Income Statement, Statement of Cash Flows,* and *Balance Sheet*).

- Point out that the income statement is presented in abbreviated form for illustrative purposes.

- Ask students to state the amount of net income after federal income taxes for the current year *($100,344)*. Ask students if this is a source of cash or use of cash. Emphasize that net income eventually brings money into the firm and is therefore viewed as a source of cash.

- Ask students to state the amount of depreciation expense for equipment and building *($11,605)*. Ask students if this is a source of cash or use of cash *(source of cash)*. Emphasize that depreciation expense is recognized on the income statement but in actuality does not involve a cash payment during the identified fiscal period.

- Ask students to state the account titles of noncash current assets. Write the account titles on the board or overhead. Ask students to state the amount of increase or decrease from the prior year. Write the amounts beside the appropriate account titles. Ask students if the increase or decrease represents a source of cash or use of cash. Write the correct student responses *[Accts. Rec., $110,530, use of cash; Supplies, ($399), source of cash; Mdse. Inv., $116,640, use of cash]*.

- Ask students to state the account titles of current liabilities. Write the account titles on the board or overhead. Ask students to state the amount of increase or decrease from the prior year. Write the amounts beside the appropriate account titles. Ask students if the increase or decrease represents a source of cash or use of cash. Write the correct student responses *(Notes Pay., $38,990, source of cash; Accts. Pay., $54,924, source of cash)*.

- Emphasize that a source of cash is added to net income and that a use of cash is subtracted.

- Stress that an increase in an account does not necessarily mean that the amount is a use of cash. Point out that this is similar to the concept that not all accounts are increased with a debit.

REPORTING CASH FLOWS FROM OPERATING ACTIVITIES

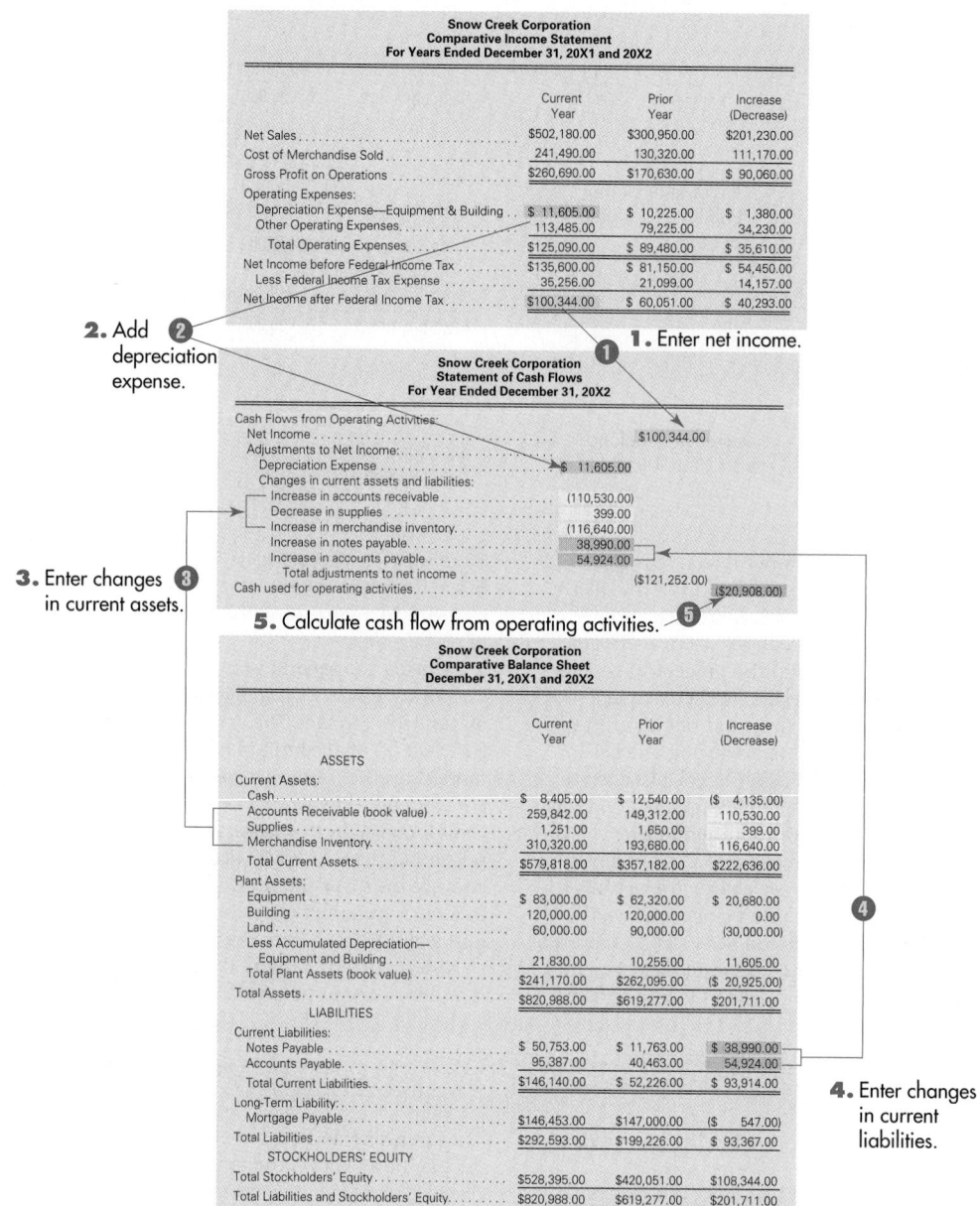

The first section of the statement of cash flows shows the cash flows from operating activities as shown above.

REPORTING CASH FLOWS FROM OPERATING ACTIVITIES

1 Enter net income, *$100,344.00* as shown on Snow Creek's comparative income statement.

2 Add the amount of depreciation expense, *$11,605.00*, to net income.

3 Enter the changes in current assets as indicated in the table below.

Change in Account	Current Year	Prior Year	Increase (Decrease)	Source or use of cash
Increase in Accts. Rec.	$259,842.00	$149,312.00	$110,530.00	use of cash
Decrease in Supplies	1,251.00	1,650.00	(399.00)	source of cash
Increase in Mdse. Inv.	310,320.00	193,680.00	116,640.00	use of cash

4 Enter the changes in current liabilities as indicated in the table below.

Change in Account	Current Year	Prior Year	Increase (Decrease)	Source or use of cash
Increase in Notes Payable	$50,753.00	$11,763.00	$38,990.00	source of cash
Increase in Accts. Payable	95,387.00	40,463.00	54,924.00	source of cash

5 Determine the cash provided by operating activities (if cash increases) or the cash used by operating activities (if cash decreases). After reporting the individual adjustments to net income, the statement of cash flows shows that the actual cash requirements for Snow Creek's operating activities exceeded net income by $20,908.00. This shortfall places Snow Creek in a very serious position regarding the company's ability to meet its short-term demands for cash.

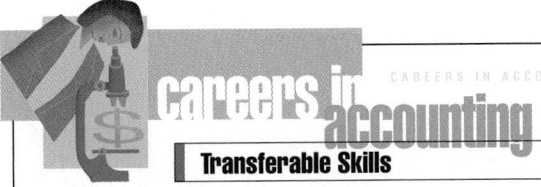

careers in accounting

CAREERS IN ACCOUNTING · CAREERS IN ACCOUNTING · CAREERS IN ACCOUNTING

Transferable Skills

In the process of developing specific accounting skills, you may also acquire a significant number of related skills. Many of these are listed below. These related skills are used in a variety of employment areas and are readily transferable to other occupations. Individuals who do not enter the accounting profession use many of the skills they acquired in accounting courses in whatever occupation they choose.

analyzing	explaining	prioritizing	speaking
attending to details	following directions	proofreading	spelling
calculating	interpreting	proving	summarizing
clarifying	listening	reading	thinking critically
communicating	managing time	reasoning mathematically	verifying
documenting	organizing	scheduling	writing
evaluating	planning	solving problems	

Instructions

Select one of the skills listed above and describe ways in which it would be useful in an accounting career.

Preparing the Operating Activities Section of a Statement of Cash Flows   Lesson 18-2   **541**

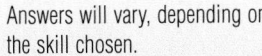

CAREERS IN ACCOUNTING

Answers will vary, depending on the skill chosen.

DEMONSTRATE

Prepare the operating activities section for the statement of cash flows

- Use a transparency of a three-column financial statement form to demonstrate the preparation of the operating activities section for the statement of cash flows.

- Review steps 1–5 for reporting cash flows from operating activities. Emphasize the origin of each amount by pointing out the financial statements used to determine amounts.

- Ask students to state the amount of cash flow from operating activities *(−$20,908)*. Ask students what a negative cash flow from operating activities means.

ONGOING ASSESSMENT

- Circulate through the classroom or lab, observing which students have problems with assignments.

- **Troubleshooting:** Students may get confused that an increase in a current asset presented on the balance sheet is subtracted as a decrease on the statement of cash flows while an increase in a current liability presented on the balance sheet is added as an increase on the statement of cash flows. Emphasize that it is easier to remember that a source of cash is added and a use of cash is subtracted.

- Assess student understanding by checking solutions to Independent Practice assignments.

RETEACH

- On the board or overhead, write the operating activities given below. Do not write the information shown in parentheses. Have the students identify the following increases and decreases as sources of cash or uses of cash:
  - net income (source of cash)
  - net loss (use of cash)
  - depreciation expense (source of cash)
  - increase in noncash current asset (use of cash)
  - decrease in noncash current asset (source of cash)
  - increase in current liability (source of cash)
  - decrease in current liability (use of cash)

GUIDED PRACTICE

Audit Your Understanding

Call on students to answer the Audit Your Understanding questions. Ask the class if the answer is correct and/or complete. As an alternative, arrange students into cooperative learning groups. Emphasize that each member in the group must be able to answer a question and explain the answer if called on. Answers are given in Appendix E of the textbook.

Work Together

Have students write the solution to the Work Together problem as you guide the class through the examples.

- Call on individual students to come to the overhead and to write the appropriate answers for each step. Ask students to explain their answers; supplement student explanations when necessary.

INDEPENDENT PRACTICE

On Your Own

- Assign the On Your Own problem to be worked independently.
- Use the Ongoing Assessment techniques to diagnose student understanding.

Application Problem

- Assign Application Problem 18-2: Calculating the cash flows from operating activities.

Personal Trainer

- Students can access the Lesson 18-2 assessment material using this software.

Xtra! Web Site

- Students can access the Xtra! Study Tools for additional practice.

ENRICH

- Assign the Careers in Accounting feature on page 541.
- Invite an accountant or financial analyst into the classroom to discuss how she or he uses the statement of cash flows to evaluate a company. Ask the speaker to provide examples of changes in current assets and liabilities and to explain why the change is viewed as a use of cash or source of cash.

• audit your understanding

1. Although depreciation expense is recognized on the income statement under the accrual basis of accounting, it does not involve an outflow of cash. Why?
2. What does an increase in the balance of accounts receivable indicate?
3. What does an increase in the balance of accounts payable indicate?
4. What is the starting point for calculating the cash flow from operating activities?

• work together 18-2

Preparing the operating activity section for a statement of cash flows

A comparative balance sheet for Zephyr Corporation is provided in the *Working Papers*. The income statement for the current year indicates that net income was $10,160.00 and the depreciation expense was $27,300.00. Statement paper and a form for analyzing changes in accounts are also provided in the *Working Papers*. Your instructor will guide you through the following examples.

1. For each item listed on the form, record the appropriate December 31 balances for the current and prior years.
2. For each item listed on the form, classify it as a current asset or current liability.
3. Compute the amount of increase or decrease from the prior year.
4. Indicate if the increase or decrease represents a source of cash or a use of cash.
5. Prepare the operating activity section of the statement of cash flows for the current year ended December 31. Save your work to complete Work Together 18-3.

• on your own 18-2

Preparing the operating activity section for a statement of cash flows

A comparative balance sheet for Cirrus Corporation is provided in the *Working Papers*. The income statement for the current year indicates that net income was $20,900.00 and the depreciation expense was $4,900.00. Statement paper and a form for analyzing changes in accounts are also provided in the *Working Papers*. Work independently to complete the following problem.

1. For each item listed on the form, record the appropriate December 31 balances for the current and prior years.
2. For each item listed on the form, classify it as a current asset or current liability.
3. Compute the amount of increase or decrease from the prior year.
4. Indicate if the increase or decrease represents a source of cash or a use of cash.
5. Prepare the operating activity section of the statement of cash flows for the current year ended December 31. Save your work to complete On Your Own 18-3.

CLOSE

- Label and write amounts on the board or overhead representing net income, net loss, depreciation expense, and changes in current assets and liabilities. Ask the students to state if the amounts represent sources of cash or uses of cash. Ask them to explain their answers.

18-3 Completing the Statement of Cash Flows

OBJECTIVES

- Identify accounting concepts and practices related to cash flow analysis.
- Prepare the investing activities and financing activities sections of a statement of cash flows.
- Prepare a statement of cash flows.

PREPARING THE INVESTING ACTIVITIES SECTION

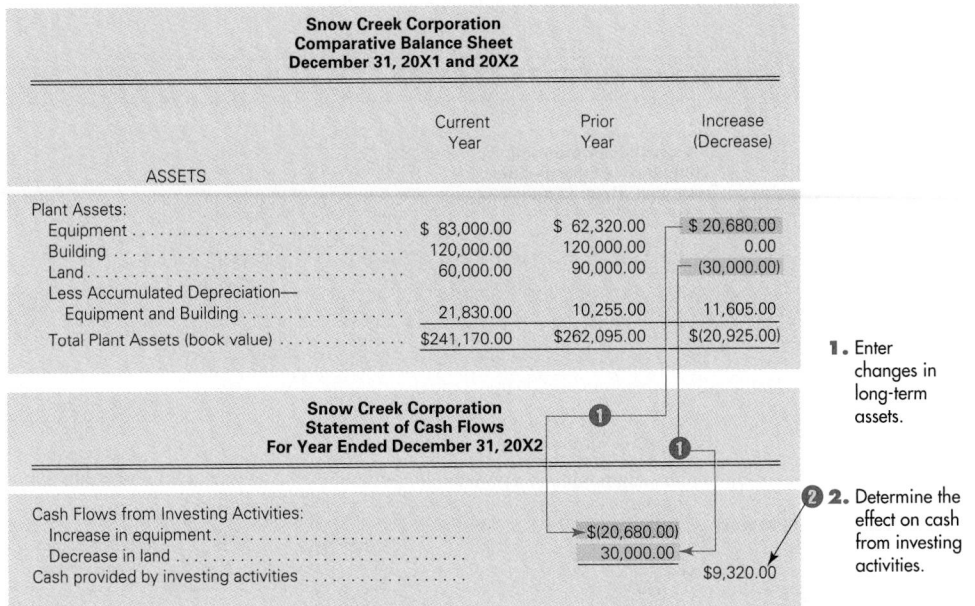

Snow Creek Corporation
Comparative Balance Sheet
December 31, 20X1 and 20X2

	Current Year	Prior Year	Increase (Decrease)
ASSETS			
Plant Assets:			
Equipment	$ 83,000.00	$ 62,320.00	$ 20,680.00
Building	120,000.00	120,000.00	0.00
Land	60,000.00	90,000.00	(30,000.00)
Less Accumulated Depreciation—			
Equipment and Building	21,830.00	10,255.00	11,605.00
Total Plant Assets (book value)	$241,170.00	$262,095.00	$(20,925.00)

1. Enter changes in long-term assets.

Snow Creek Corporation
Statement of Cash Flows
For Year Ended December 31, 20X2

2. Determine the effect on cash from investing activities.

Cash Flows from Investing Activities:	
Increase in equipment	$(20,680.00)
Decrease in land	30,000.00
Cash provided by investing activities	$9,320.00

Responsible investing activities are critical to the long-term success of a company. Cash flows resulting from a company's investing activities are identified by analyzing the changes in long-term assets (plant assets) presented on the comparative balance sheet. Snow Creek's investing activities section for the statement of cash flows is shown above.

STEPS • STEPS • STEPS • STEPS • STEPS • STEPS • STEPS • STEPS • STEPS • STEPS •

REPORTING CASH FLOWS FROM INVESTING ACTIVITIES

1 Analyze changes in long-term assets. The $20,680.00 increase in equipment represents a cash outflow. The increase in a long-term asset is a use of cash. During the year, Snow Creek Corporation sold a parcel of land for $30,000, the same amount paid for the land one year earlier. The $30,000.00 decrease in the long-term asset, Land, represents a cash inflow and is a source of cash. The following table summarizes the changes.

Change in Account	Current Year	Prior Year	Increase (Decrease)	Source or use of cash
Increase in Equipment	$83,000.00	$62,320.00	$20,680.00	use of cash
Decrease in Land	60,000.00	90,000.00	($30,000.00)	source of cash

2 Determine the cash provided by investing activities (if cash increases) or the cash used by investing activities (if cash decreases). Snow Creek's investing activities provided $9,320.00 in cash during the current year.

Completing the Statement of Cash Flows

Lesson 18-3 **543**

MOTIVATE

Obtain copies of printed annual reports from several major corporations as well as local corporations. Display statements of cash flows on the bulletin board. Discuss and highlight the way in which the corporations present their statement of cash flows. As an alternative, offer extra credit points to students who secure annual reports or go the public library and photocopy a company's statement of cash flows.

Preview

- Direct students to read the main headings presented throughout this lesson and to examine the illustrations provided.
- Point out that students are already familiar with investing and financing activities. In this lesson, students will learn the formal procedure for listing investing and financing activities on the statement of cash flows.

EXPLAIN

- Ask students why investing activities are critical to the long-term success of the firm. Point out that investing activities are primarily involved with the sale and purchase of long-term assets needed to operate a business. For example, investing activities include the purchases of land, buildings, furniture, equipment, machinery, and other items that will help the company earn revenue. Without such investments, it will be difficult for a business to earn revenue over the long run.
- Refer students to the illustration. Ask students to state the account titles of long-term assets *(plant assets)*. Write the account titles on the board or overhead. Ask students to state the amount of increase or decrease from the prior year. Write the amounts beside the appropriate account titles. Ask students if the increase or decrease represents a source of cash or use of cash. Write the correct student responses *[Equipment, $20,680, use of cash; Building, $0, no impact; Land, ($30,000), source of cash]*.
- Emphasize that a use of cash represents a negative cash flow and that a source of cash represents a positive cash flow.

MATERIALS

- Instructor's Resource CD: PowerPoint Slides
- Xtra! Study Tools on the Xtra! Web Site
- Blackline Masters: 3-Column Financial Statement Form
- Working Papers: Teacher's Edition of the Working Papers for Lesson 18-3
- Software: Personal Trainer Student Companion CD QuickBooks

- Refer students to the balance sheet shown in the illustration on page 543. Ask students why the increase of $11,605 in accumulated depreciation for equipment and building can be ignored. Ask them if they remember seeing $11,605 somewhere else *(depreciation expense under operating activities)*. Emphasize that the increase in accumulated depreciation equals the depreciation expense reported on the income statement and was already accounted for under operating activities.

- Review with students the two rules at the top of this page for cash flows regarding the increases and decreases in long-term assets.

DEMONSTRATE

Prepare the investing activities section for the statement of cash flows

- Continue to use the transparency started in Lesson 18-2 to demonstrate the preparation of the investing activities section for the statement of cash flows.

- Review steps 1 and 2 on the previous page for reporting cash flows from investing activities. Demonstrate how each step is recorded on the statement. Emphasize the origin of each amount by pointing out the financial statement used to determine amounts.

- Remind students that a use of cash is subtracted and that a source of cash is added.

- Ask students to verify the cash provided by the investing activities figure, $9,320, with a calculator.

ANALYZING CASH FLOWS FROM INVESTING ACTIVITIES

The increase in accumulated depreciation for equipment and building ($11,605.00) can be ignored. This increase matches the depreciation expense that was recorded on the income statement. The effect on cash flows was already accounted for under operating activities.

When calculating the cash flows from investing activities, it is useful to remember that:

- Increases in long-term assets generally result in cash outflows (*uses of cash*) that are subtracted on the statement of cash flows.

- Decreases in long-term assets generally result in cash inflows (*sources of cash*) that are added on the statement of cash flows.

PREPARING THE FINANCING ACTIVITY SECTION

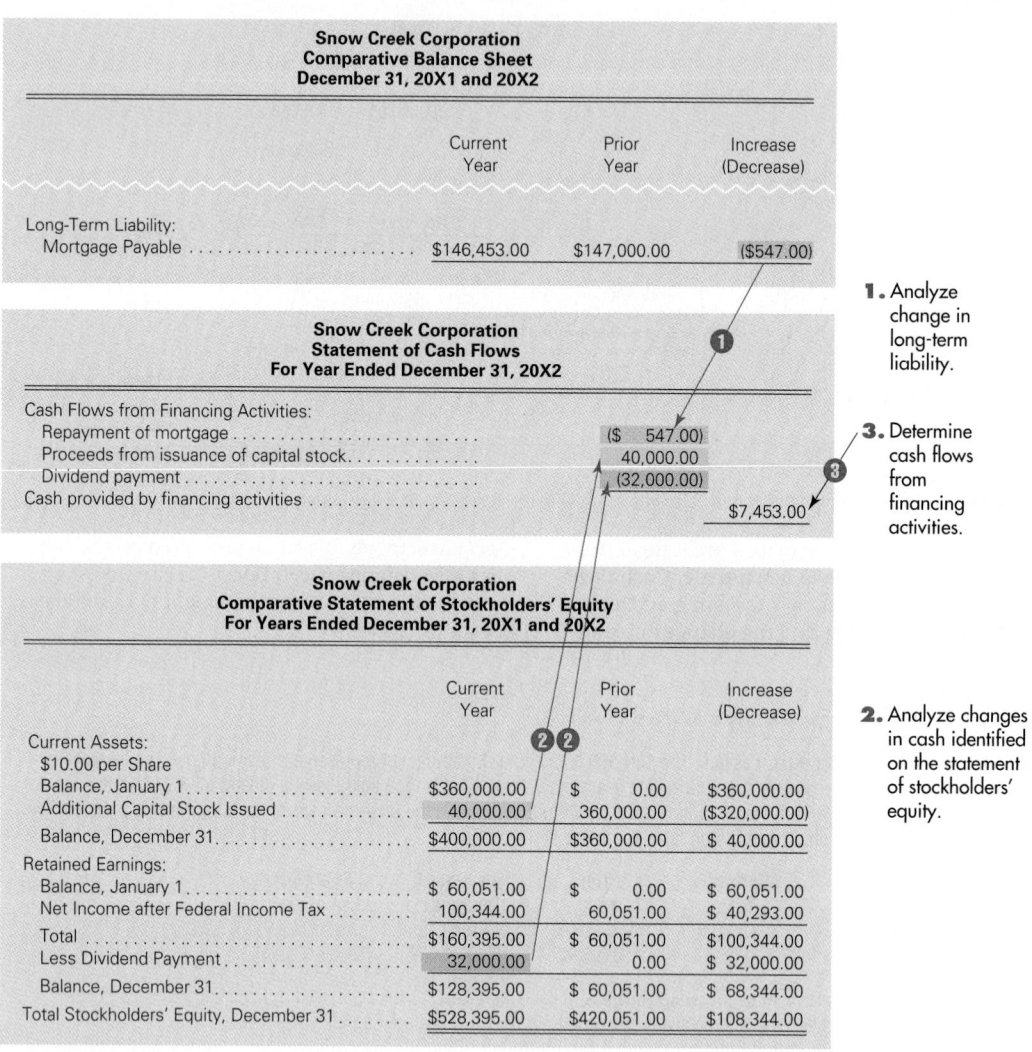

Snow Creek Corporation
Comparative Balance Sheet
December 31, 20X1 and 20X2

	Current Year	Prior Year	Increase (Decrease)
Long-Term Liability:			
Mortgage Payable	$146,453.00	$147,000.00	($547.00)

1. Analyze change in long-term liability.

Snow Creek Corporation
Statement of Cash Flows
For Year Ended December 31, 20X2

Cash Flows from Financing Activities:		
Repayment of mortgage	($ 547.00)	
Proceeds from issuance of capital stock	40,000.00	
Dividend payment	(32,000.00)	
Cash provided by financing activities		$7,453.00

3. Determine cash flows from financing activities.

Snow Creek Corporation
Comparative Statement of Stockholders' Equity
For Years Ended December 31, 20X1 and 20X2

	Current Year	Prior Year	Increase (Decrease)
Current Assets:			
$10.00 per Share			
Balance, January 1	$360,000.00	$ 0.00	$360,000.00
Additional Capital Stock Issued	40,000.00	360,000.00	($320,000.00)
Balance, December 31	$400,000.00	$360,000.00	$ 40,000.00
Retained Earnings:			
Balance, January 1	$ 60,051.00	$ 0.00	$ 60,051.00
Net Income after Federal Income Tax	100,344.00	60,051.00	$ 40,293.00
Total	$160,395.00	$ 60,051.00	$100,344.00
Less Dividend Payment	32,000.00	0.00	$ 32,000.00
Balance, December 31	$128,395.00	$ 60,051.00	$ 68,344.00
Total Stockholders' Equity, December 31	$528,395.00	$420,051.00	$108,344.00

2. Analyze changes in cash identified on the statement of stockholders' equity.

544 Chapter 18

Statement of Cash Flows

Limited English Proficiency (LEP) Students. Adjust the length of time allotted to complete assignments and tests. Remember that the primary objective is to assess knowledge of accounting rather than the ability to translate and comprehend the question or problem.

ANALYZING CASH FLOWS FROM FINANCING ACTIVITIES

Financing activities are often used to maintain an adequate balance in the cash account. These activities usually involve borrowing money from creditors and repaying the principal or acquiring capital from owners and providing a return on their investment. Cash flows originating from a company's financing activities are identified by examining the changes in long-term liabilities reported on the balance sheet and the changes in stockholders' equity reported on the statement of stockholders' equity. This analysis is shown on the previous page.

STEPS • STEPS • STEPS • STEPS • STEPS • STEPS • STEPS • STEPS • STEPS • STEPS •

REPORTING CASH FLOWS FROM FINANCING ACTIVITIES

1 Analyze changes in long-term liabilities. The $547.00 decrease in Mortgage Payable represents a cash outflow.

2 Analyze changes in cash identified on the statement of stockholders' equity. Snow Creek issued $40,000.00 of additional capital stock during the year. This activity resulted in a receipt of $40,000.00 from the issuance of 4,000 shares of capital stock at $10.00 per share. The sale of stock provides a source of cash. A cash dividend of $32,000.00 was paid during the year. The dividend payment represents a use of cash.

3 Determine the cash provided by financing activities (if cash increases) or the cash used by investing activities (if cash decreases). Snow Creek's financing activities provided $7,453.00 in cash during the current year.

The statement of stockholders' equity also shows a change in Retained Earnings due to the net income of the business. Net income was the starting point for the analysis of changes in the operating activities of the business. Net income results from the operating activities of the business. Net income does not affect the financing activities of the business.

When calculating the cash flows from financing activities, it is beneficial to remember that:

- Increases in long-term liabilities and the issuance of stock generally result in cash inflows (*sources of cash*) that are added on the statement of cash flows.
- Decreases in long-term liabilities and the payment of cash dividends generally result in cash outflows (*uses of cash*) that are subtracted on the statement of cash flows.

CALCULATE THE NET INCREASE OR DECREASE IN CASH

Cash used for operating activities (see page 540)	$(20,908.00)
Cash provided by investing activities (see page 543)	9,320.00
Cash provided by financing activities (see page 544)	7,453.00
Net change in cash	$ (4,135.00)

The illustration above shows the total change in cash resulting from operating, investing, and financing activities. During the current year, Cash decreased by $4,135.00.

> **REMEMBER** Financing activities involve debt or equity transactions.

Prepare the financing activities section for the statement of cash flows

- Continue to use the transparency originally started in Lesson 18-2 and used earlier in Lesson 18-3 to demonstrate the preparation of the financing activities section for the statement of cash flows.

- Review steps 1–3 on the previous page for reporting cash flows from financing activities. Demonstrate how each step is recorded on the statement. Emphasize the origin of each amount by pointing out the financial statements used to determine amounts. Refer students to the illustration on page 544 for a visual example.

- Remind students that a use of cash is subtracted and that a source of cash is added.

- Ask students to verify the cash provided by the financing activities figure, $7,453, with a calculator.

Complete the statement of cash flows

- Review steps 1–4 on the next page for completing the statement of cash flows. Demonstrate how each step is recorded on the statement. Emphasize the origin of each amount.

- Continue to use the transparency started earlier, which now shows completed operating, investing, and financing activities sections. Refer students to the illustration on this page for visual examples.

- Complete the transparency and emphasize that the statement of cash flows cannot be double ruled unless the Cash Balance, End of Period amount matches the current year cash account balance listed on the comparative balance sheet.

COMPLETING THE STATEMENT OF CASH FLOWS

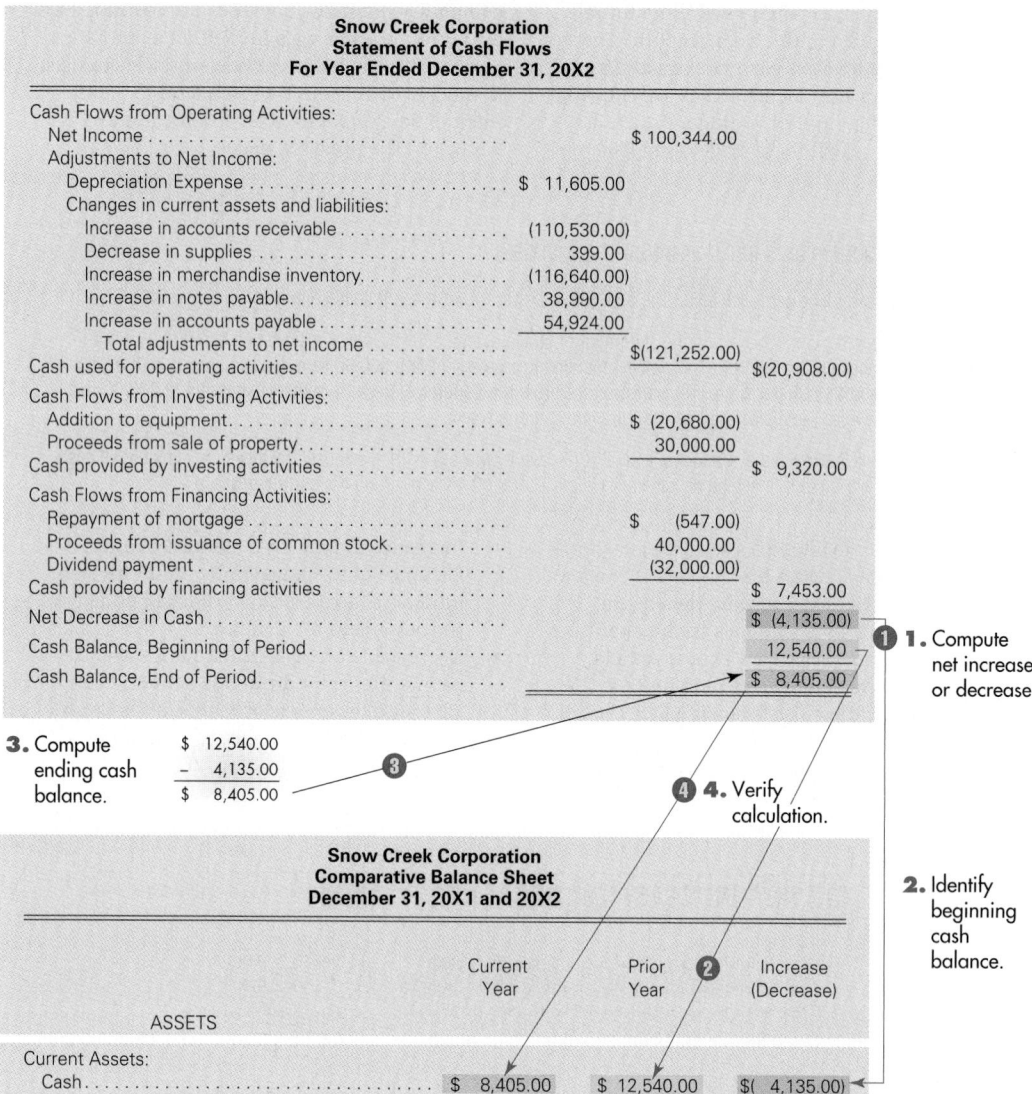

The completed statement of cash flows is shown above. The Cash balances at the beginning and end of the period shown on the statement of cash flows must match the amounts shown on the comparative balance sheet.

COMPLETING THE STATEMENT OF CASH FLOWS

1 Compute the net increase or decrease in Cash resulting from operating, investing, and financing activities.

2 Identify the beginning cash balance from the comparative balance sheet. The beginning cash balance for the current year is the ending cash balance from the prior year, $12,540.00.

3 Compute the ending cash balance, $8,405.00 ($12,540.00 – $4,135.00 decrease in cash).

4 Verify that the Cash Balance, End of Period matches the cash balance shown on the comparative balance sheet.

CASH FLOW ANALYSIS SUMMARY

The intent of the statement of cash flows is to report and explain the sources and uses of a company's cash and to clarify changes in other account balances. In the case of Snow Creek Corporation, the statement of cash flows helps explain the difference between solid profits and a decrease in the cash account. Among other things, the large increases in accounts receivable and merchandise inventory (uses of cash) hampered Snow Creek's ability to pay its bills. Studying cash flows along with analyzing the income statement, statement of stockholders' equity, and the balance sheet provides a more accurate overview of a company's present and future financial condition.

©GETTY IMAGES/PHOTODISC

GUIDED PRACTICE

Audit Your Understanding
Call on students to answer the Audit Your Understanding questions. Ask the class if the answer is correct and/or complete. Answers are given in Appendix E of the textbook.

Work Together
Have students write the solution to the Work Together problem as you guide the class through the examples.

- Call on individual students to come to the overhead and to write the appropriate answers for each step. Ask students to explain their answers; supplement student explanations when necessary.

INDEPENDENT PRACTICE

On Your Own
- Assign the On Your Own problem to be worked independently.
- Use the Ongoing Assessment techniques to diagnose student understanding.

Application Problems
- Assign Application Problem 18-3: Calculating the cash flows from investing activities.
- Assign Application Problem 18-4: Calculating the cash flows from financing activities and completing a statement of cash flows.

Personal Trainer
- Students can access the Lesson 18-3 assessment material using this software.

Xtra! Web Site
- Students can access the Xtra! Study Tools for additional practice.

ENRICH

- Assign the Case for Critical Thinking.
- Students can use QuickBooks data files to automate Application Problem 18-4.

CLOSE

- Direct students to the illustration on page 546.
- Ask students to state the origin of each amount shown. Answers should identify the financial statement used or indicate that the amount is the result of a calculation.

• audit your understanding

1. How are the cash flows resulting from a company's investing activities identified?
2. Why is an increase in accumulated depreciation on the balance sheet ignored when analyzing the cash flows from investing activities?
3. How are the cash flows originating from a company's financing activities identified?
4. How does an individual know if all cash transactions have been properly accounted for on the statement of cash flows?

• work together 18-3

Preparing the investing and financing activities sections for the statement of cash flows; completing the statement of cash flows

Use the working papers from Work Together 18-2. A comparative balance sheet and forms for analyzing changes in long-term assets, long-term liabilities, and stockholders' equity are provided in the *Working Papers*. Your instructor will guide you through the following examples.

1. Complete the changes in long-term assets and long-term liabilities form.
2. Prepare the investing activities section of the statement of cash flows.
3. Complete the changes in stockholders' equity form.
4. Prepare the financing activities section of the statement of cash flows.
5. Complete the statement of cash flows.

• on your own 18-3

Preparing the investing and financing activities sections for the statement of cash flows; completing the statement of cash flows

Use the working papers from On Your Own 18-2. A comparative balance sheet and forms for analyzing changes in long-term assets, long-term liabilities, and stockholders' equity are provided in the *Working Papers*. Work independently to complete the following problem.

1. Complete the changes in long-term assets and long-term liabilities form.
2. Prepare the investing activities section of the statement of cash flows.
3. Complete the changes in stockholders' equity form.
4. Prepare the financing activities section of the statement of cash flows.
5. Complete the statement of cash flows.

After completing this chapter, you can

1. Define accounting terms related to cash flow analysis.

2. Identify accounting concepts and practices related to cash flow analysis.

3. Describe operating, investing, and financing activities and provide examples of each.

4. Prepare the operating activities section of a statement of cash flows.

5. Prepare the investing activities and financing activities sections of a statement of cash flows.

6. Prepare a statement of cash flows.

Explore Accounting
EXPLORE ACCOUNTING · EXPLORE ACCOUNTING · EXPLORE ACCOUN

FASB Statement No. 95

The development of generally accepted accounting principles (GAAP) is a political process. After researching an accounting issue, the Financial Accounting Standards Board (FASB) issues a proposal for a new principle in a Discussion Memorandum (DM). Interested individuals and companies submit comments about the DM to the FASB. The FASB considers their comments in producing its final statement.

A good example of this political process is FASB Statement No. 95, Statement of Cash Flows. The statement allows companies to use two methods to report cash flows from operating activities. Although the FASB recommends the direct method, most companies use the alternative indirect method. The indirect method, as illustrated in this textbook, begins with net income and makes adjustments for changes in current assets and liabilities. In contrast, the direct method reports each major class of cash receipts and cash payments, as illustrated below.

If the FASB encourages the use of the direct method, why do most companies use the indirect method? First, the indirect method was used for many years for preparing a similar statement that was required prior to FASB No. 95. Second, the

direct method requires more effort to obtain the information. Most of the information for an indirect method statement can be obtained from other financial statements. The direct method requires the company to obtain more detailed information directly from the general ledger.

Required:
Obtain a copy of FASB No. 95. Read the portion of the statement (paragraph 106-121) that presents the FASB's reasons for allowing companies to use either the indirect or direct methods. Do you agree with the FASB's reasons? Identify other accounting principles where two or more methods are allowed. Should alternative methods be allowed to report the same accounting information?

Cash flows from operating activities:

Cash received from customers	$670,000.00
Cash paid to suppliers and employees	(540,000.00)
Interest paid	(34,000.00)
Income taxes paid	(29,000.00)
Net cash provided by operating activities	$ 67,000.00

Statement of Cash Flows

Chapter 18   **549**

EXPLORE ACCOUNTING
EXPLORE ACCOUNTING
Student answers will vary. Answers should demonstrate an understanding that there are advantages and disadvantages to different reporting methods.

18-1 APPLICATION PROBLEM

Classifying cash flows

The following business transactions represent selected cash receipts (cash inflows) and cash payments (cash outflows) of Ridge Development Corporation.

a. dividend payment

b. payment of insurance premium

c. receipts from the signing of a note payable

d. payment of payroll taxes

e. cash purchase of computer equipment

f. sale of treasury stock

g. receipts from consulting services

Instructions:

Use the form provided in the *Working Papers* to identify each transaction as (1) a cash inflow or cash outflow and (2) as an operating, investing, or financing activity.

18-2 APPLICATION PROBLEM

Calculating the cash flows from operating activities

The following information was taken from the financial statements of Flexcor Corporation on December 31 of the current year. The comparative income statement of Flexcor Corporation reveals the following net income and depreciation expense for the current year.

Net income	$91,460.00
Depreciation expense	12,500.00

The comparative balance sheet of Flexcor Corporation lists the following current assets and current liabilities and their ending balances for the current and prior years.

	Current Year	Prior Year
Accounts Receivable (book value)	$ 55,515.00	$ 48,000.00
Merchandise Inventory	118,316.00	121,000.00
Supplies	6,148.00	5,500.00
Accounts Payable	49,762.00	44,000.00

Instructions:

1. In the forms provided in the *Working Papers*, record the appropriate amount for net income. Indicate if this item represents a source of cash or use of cash.
2. Record the appropriate amount for depreciation expense. Indicate if this item represents a source of cash or use of cash.
3. For each current asset and current liability, write the balances for the current year and prior year. Classify each account as a current asset or current liability. Compute the amount of increase or decrease from the prior year. Indicate if the increase or decrease represents a source of cash or a use of cash.
4. Using the information collected, prepare the cash flows from operating activities section of the statement of cash flows for the current year ending December 31. Save your work to complete Application Problem 18-3.

Statement of Cash Flows

18-3 APPLICATION PROBLEM

Calculating the cash flows from investing activities

Use the statement of cash flows started in Application Problem 18-1. The comparative balance sheet of Flexcor Corporation lists the following long-term assets and their ending balances for the current and prior years.

	Current Year	Prior Year
Office equipment	$ 22,800.00	$ 12,500.00
Office furniture	12,210.00	9,000.00
Land (decrease due to sale)	100,000.00	140,000.00

Instructions:

1. For each account, write the balances for the current year and prior year. Compute the amount of increase or decrease from the prior year. Indicate if the increase or decrease represents a source of cash or a use of cash.
2. Using the statement of cash flows started in Application Problem 18-1, prepare the Cash Flows from Investing Activities section of the statement of cash flows. Save your work to complete Application Problem 18-4.

18-4 APPLICATION PROBLEM   QUICKBOOKS

Calculating the cash flows from financing activities and completing a statement of cash flows

Use the statement of cash flows started in Application Problem 18-1. The comparative balance sheet of Flexcor Corporation lists the following long-term liability and its ending balance for the current and prior years.

	Current Year	Prior Year
Mortgage payable	$80,100.00	$92,000.00

The comparative statement of stockholders' equity of Flexcor Corporation reveals the following stock and dividend information for the current year.

Sale of additional common stock	20,000.00
Payment of cash dividend	50,000.00

Instructions:

1. For the long-term liability, record the amount of increase or decrease from the prior year. Indicate if the increase or decrease represents a source of cash or a use of cash.
2. For each amount taken from the comparative statement of stockholders' equity, record the appropriate amount. Indicate if these activities represent a source of cash or use of cash.
3. Using the statement of cash flows started in Application Problem 18-1, prepare the cash flows from financing activities section of the statement of cash flows.
4. Compute the net increase or decrease resulting from operating, investing, and financing activities.
5. Record the cash balance for the beginning of the period in the form provided. Flexcor started the year with a beginning cash balance of $67,930.00.
6. Compute the cash balance for the end of the fiscal period by adding the amount of increase or decrease in cash and the beginning cash amount.
7. Complete the statement of cash flows for Flexcor Corporation by entering the net increase or decrease in cash, the beginning cash balance, and the ending cash balance.
8. Verify the accuracy of the statement of cash flows by comparing the statement's ending cash balance with the cash balance of $156,763.00 listed for the current year on Flexcor's comparative balance sheet.

Application Problem 18-3
Cash provided by investing activities, 26,490.00.

Application Problem 18-4
Cash used for financing activities, (41,900.00).
Net increase in cash, 88,833.00.
Cash balance, end of period, 156,763.00.

APPLIED SKILLS WRITING ACROSS THE CURRICULUM

Writing Paragraphs and Short Essays. The Cases for Critical Thinking are short, practical applications of the accounting principles developed in the chapter. Some cases are planned to present problems related to the chapter but not specifically discussed and answered in the chapter. These cases present an opportunity for critical thinking and decision making. These cases also require more than a short objective-type response. Therefore they provide ideal practice in writing paragraphs and short essays.

Mastery Problem 18-5

Total adjustments to net income, 30,086.00.
Cash provided by operating activities, 57,085.00.
Cash used for investing activities, (10,000.00).
Cash used for financing activities, (14,841.00).
Net increase in cash, 32,244.00.
Cash balance, end of period, 63,768.00.

Challenge Problem 18-6

Total adjustments to net income, (40,190.00).
Cash used for operating activities, (49,640.00).
Cash used for investing activities, (28,510.00).
Cash provided by financing activities, 84,090.00.
Net increase in cash, 5,940.00.
Cash balance, end of period, 46,710.00.

18-5 MASTERY PROBLEM   QUICKBOOKS
Preparing a statement of cash flows

Use the abbreviated comparative financial statements for West Coast Construction, Inc. in the *Working Papers*.

Instructions:
1. Review the comparative income statement and identify the amounts of net income (or net loss) and depreciation expense for the period. Indicate if each item represents a source of cash or use of cash.
2. Analyze the comparative balance sheet and complete the following steps:
   a. Prepare a list of current assets and current liabilities.
   b. Write the balances for the current year and prior year.
   c. Classify each account as a current asset or current liability.
   d. Compute the amount of increase or decrease from the prior year.
   e. Indicate if the increase or decrease represents a source of cash or a use of cash.
3. Analyze the comparative balance sheet and complete the following steps:
   a. Prepare a list of long-term assets.
   b. Write the balances for the current year and prior year.
   c. Compute the amount of increase or decrease from the prior year.
   d. Indicate if the increase or decrease represents a source of cash or a use of cash.
4. Reexamine the comparative balance sheet and complete the following steps:
   a. Prepare a list of long-term liabilities.
   b. Compute the amount of increase or decrease from the prior year.
   c. Indicate if the increase or decrease represents a source of cash or a use of cash.
5. Review the comparative statement of stockholders' equity and (1) identify the amounts of any additional stock issued or cash dividends paid and (2) indicate if each item represents a source of cash or use of cash.
6. Prepare the operating, investing, and financing activities sections of a statement of cash flows.
7. Enter the cash balance at the beginning of the year as shown on the comparative balance sheet.
8. Compute the cash balance for the end of the period to complete the statement of cash flows.
9. Verify the accuracy of the statement of cash flows by comparing the statement's ending cash balance with the cash balance listed for the current year on West Coast's comparative balance sheet

18-6 CHALLENGE PROBLEM
Preparing a statement of cash flows

Use the abbreviated comparative financial statements for Pacific Digital Corporation in the *Working Papers*. The comparative balance sheet for Pacific Digital Corporation lists an intangible asset, Patents. The patents were granted in the first year of the business's existence. Intangible assets like Patents are written off as an expense over a period of years. Although the expense is recognized on the income statement under the accrual basis of accounting, it does not involve an outflow of cash. The cash was actually spent in an earlier period. Since the amortized patent expense shown on Pacific Digital's comparative income statement does not use cash, it is handled the same way as depreciation expense. Both patents and depreciation expense are adjustments to net income (or net loss) and presented before changes in current assets and liabilities.

Instructions:
Prepare a statement of cash flows for the current year for Pacific Digital Corporation.

TEACHING STRATEGIES DIFFERENT LEARNING STYLES

Visual Learner. When learning how to prepare a statement of cash flows, the visual learner would prefer to see how the statement is prepared. To encourage visual learners, therefore, the instructor could use a transparency to assist in the lecture. The transparency could be a blank transparency that the instructor completes.

Xtra!
Enrichment
accountingxtra.swlearning.com

• applied communication

You are the President of a non-profit organization that has grown quickly over the last few years. For the first time, you have had an independent accountant audit your financial records. Upon the recommendation of the accountant, your staff has begun preparing a statement of cash flows.

The organization is overseen by a volunteer board of directors. They meet monthly to review the financial stability of the organization and to assist management in developing long-range plans. At each meeting, you present the financial statements from the previous month.

Required:

Since most of the members of your board are not familiar with the statement of cash flows, prepare a short explanation of the purpose and use of the statement.

• case for critical thinking

Techmart Corporation is a young start-up firm that produces components for high-resolution televisions. During the last two years, sales have grown dramatically. Currently, Techmart is experiencing a cash shortage and is having difficulty purchasing manufacturing supplies and meeting its weekly payroll. Lately, the company has not been very successful in collecting its accounts receivable. The company offers its clients 90 days to pay on all receivables and does not understand why there is a shortage of cash. What suggestions can you offer the president of Techmart regarding its collection policy? Explain your recommendations. What can Techmart do during the short run to overcome its shortage of cash?

• SCANS workplace competency

Resource Competency: Allocating Human Resources

Concept: Successful supervisors can assess an employee's job knowledge and skill base, distribute work accordingly, evaluate performance, and provide feedback.

Application: You are the manager of a small manufacturing firm. Employees must be at their stations before the production line can start each morning. One employee, Beth Stewart, is often 10–20 minutes late to work. Consequently, production is delayed. How might you counsel this employee to eliminate her tardiness? She is a good employee who has worked for the firm for 10 years. Write out your response.

APPLIED COMMUNICATION

Students' explanations will vary; however, statements should mention that the purpose of the statement of cash flows is to report and explain changes in the cash account by identifying the sources and uses of the organization's cash. Students should also emphasize that the statement of cash flows is used to determine if an organization has enough cash to operate, pay expenses, and repay debts.

CASE FOR CRITICAL THINKING

Techmart should re-examine its collection policy of 90 days. Perhaps credit terms of 2/10, n/30 might be more realistic. New terms and offering a cash discount might improve the accounts receivable turnover ratio and reduce the number of days for collections. Techmart should also analyze its policy for granting credit. If uncollectibles are increasing, Techmart needs to improve its credit checks. Techmart can also ease its credit crunch by seeking vendors who likewise offer extended terms of payment. During the interim, Techmart should consider a short-term loan or perhaps cutting those expenses that demand immediate payments of cash. Well-managed companies always try to reduce expenses to a minimum level that will accomplish the necessary activities. Another option for Techmart is to raise selling prices along with shortening credit terms. However, this practice may have a negative impact on overall revenues.

SCANS WORKPLACE COMPETENCY

Point out to students that firing trained employees may be costly and is not always the best solution. Allow students 10–15 minutes to complete the activity. Discuss with students the various strategies that might be used.

Statement of Cash Flows

Chapter 18   **553**

553

AUDITING FOR ERRORS

Errors include the following:

1. The statement should include "For Year Ended December 31, 20--."

2. Increases and decreases of current assets are reversed. An increase in a current asset is a use of cash; a decrease in a current asset is a source of cash.

3. The repayment of mortgage should be in the financing section. In addition, the amount is a use of cash.

4. The proceeds from issuance of common stock are a source of cash.

5. The dividend payment is a use of cash.

6. The end of period cash balance should be calculated by adding the beginning cash balance to the net increase in cash and the beginning cash balance.

The revised ending cash balance should be $213,400.00.

ANALYZING COSTCO'S FINANCIAL STATEMENTS

1. 2001: $1,447,549,000
   2002: $1,038,605,000
   2003: $810,665,000

2. Yes. Costco has spent over $3.2 billion to open 103 new warehouses (2001, 39; 2002, 35; 2003, 29). This represents a significant growth in the number of warehouses, from 313 at the start of 2001 to 397 at the end of 2003.

• auditing for errors

DuWayne Streitman, a newly hired accountant, has prepared the following statement of cash flows. DuWayne has asked you to examine his statement because the ending cash balance does not equal the balance of cash. Prepare a list of any errors you identify in the statement and calculate the correct ending cash balance.

Maher Products, Inc.
Statement of Cash Flows
December 31, 20--

Cash Flows from Operating Activities:			
Net Income		92,000.00	
Adjustments to Net Income:			
Depreciation Expense	124,000.00		
Changes in current assets and liabilities:			
Decrease in accounts receivable	(2,150.00)		
Increase in supplies	4,800.00		
Decrease in merchandise inventory	(21,500.00)		
Decrease in notes payable	(3,100.00)		
Increase in account payable	4,850.00		
Total adjustments to net income		106,900.00	
Cash provided by operating activities			198,900.00
Cash Flows from Investing Activities:			
Addition to equipment		(15,800.00)	
Repayment of mortgage		13,500.00	
Proceeds from sale of property		33,600.00	
Cash provided by investing activities			31,300.00
Cash Flows from Financing Activities:			
Proceeds from issuance of common stock		(10,000.00)	
Dividend payment		62,000.00	
Cash provided by financing activities			52,000.00
Net Increase in Cash			282,200.00
Cash Balance, Beginning of Period			24,500.00
Cash Balance, End of Period			257,700.00

• analyzing Costco's financial statements

Investors often evaluate the investing activities section of the statement of cash flows to measure the future growth of a company. A company that is investing in plant assets is more likely to generate sales growth and earn a higher level of net income.

Instructions:

1. Use the statement of cash flows on page B-8 of Appendix B in this textbook. Identify the cash expended on new property and equipment from 2001 to 2003.

2. Does Costco's statement of cash flows support the reported growth in the number of warehouses?

TEACHING STRATEGIES   PORTFOLIO ASSESSMENT

Successful businesses emphasize not only earning net income but also managing cash flow. A statement of cash flows provides information critical to cash flow analysis. Students should select an example of a statement of cash flows to include in their portfolio. A copy of the Portfolio Assessment form (blackline master in the Teacher's Resource Guide; also on the Student Companion CD) should be completed by the student and the Description section should include any comments regarding how the student mastered these concepts and procedures.

Automated Accounting

Using the Savings Planner

Planning Tools
Planning tools are easy-to-use applications for producing results for different types of financial investments. *Automated Accounting 8.0* and higher includes five such tools located on the different tabs included on the Planning Tools screen.

Savings Planner
The Savings Planner is similar to the loan planner introduced in the Automated Accounting section of Chapter 11. The Savings Planner is used to perform one of three calculations:

1. The monthly contribution required to meet a target ending savings balance
2. The ending savings balance of a series of contributions
3. The number of months required to meet a specified ending savings balance

One of the calculations is chosen from the Calculate box. The item to be calculated appears grayed (or dimmed). Enter the other items and the planner will make the calculation. For example, Andrew Ruiz is saving money to pay for his living expenses at college. He places $500.00 in a money market account. He plans to add $50.00 a month. Interest is earned on the account at the rate of 6.5%. How much will Andrew have at the end of three years (36 months)? Using the Savings Planner to make the calculation, Andrew will have $2,588.92 at the end of three years, as shown here.

The Savings Planner Report
A report of the findings may be displayed or printed. Click the Report button to display the report. Click the Print button from the Savings Plan report display to print it.

Using Special Tools: The Savings Planner

Instructions:

1. Load *Automated Accounting 8.0* or higher software.
2. Select New from the File menu.
3. Click on the Tools toolbar button.
4. Click on the Savings Planner tab. Select Number of Months from the Calculate box. Enter a beginning balance of $250.00. Enter an Annual Yield of 7%. Enter a Monthly Contribution of $100.00 and an Ending Savings Balance of $2,000.00. How many months are required for the savings balance to reach $2,000.00?
5. Click on the Report command button from within the Savings Planner tab. Print the report, or copy it to the clipboard for entering into a word processor or spreadsheet application.
6. Click Close or press ESC to return to the planner. Steps 4 and 5 may then be repeated for different calculation options, or for different data sets.
7. Click Close or press ESC to exit the planner. Upon exiting a planning tool, your data will not be saved. Be sure to print a report, or copy it to a word processor or spreadsheet and save it in that application.
8. Exit the Automated Accounting software.

EXPLAIN
- Explain that the Savings Planner can be used to calculate the monthly deposit required for a planned ending balance, the ending balance of a series of monthly deposits, or the number of months required to meet a planned ending balance.
- Point out that the Savings Planner is a Planning Tool that operates much the same as the Notes and Interest Planner and Loan Planner already studied.

DEMONSTRATE

Using the Savings Planner
- Click the Tools toolbar button and then click the Savings Planner tab.
- Click the Ending Savings Balance option button in the Calculate option group.
- Enter the Beginning Savings amount, Annual Yield (Percent), Number of Months, and Monthly Contribution. Point out that the Tab key is used to advance to the net field.
- Click the Report button to display a report that shows the amortization table for the savings data entered.
- Click the Print button to print the report or the Copy button to copy the report to the Clipboard for use in another application.
- Repeat the demonstration for other options in the Calculate option group.

PRACTICE
- Assign the Using Special Tools: The Savings Planner problem on this page.
- As an alternative, ask students to decide on a personal savings goal (for a car, college costs, etc.) and enter realistic data. Then direct students to display the report, copy it to a word processing application, and write a report on their savings plan.

ASSESSMENT
- Direct students to copy the results of the Loan Planner into either a word processing or spreadsheet file and print the results. If the word processor or spreadsheet software is not available, direct students to print the report from the Savings Planner.

TEACHING STRATEGIES   PORTFOLIO ASSESSMENT

Students should be encouraged to print at least one report from the Automated Accounting problem to include in their portfolio to demonstrate mastery of using planning tools. Students might also copy an amortization table from the Loan Planner into a word processing document and compose additional copy to explain the results of the amortization table. A copy of the Portfolio Assessment form (blackline master in the Teacher's Resource Guide; also on the Student Companion CD) should be completed by the student and the Description section should include any comments regarding how the student mastered these concepts and procedures.

Part 6 introduces cost accounting for manufacturing businesses.

- Chapter 19 shows how a manufacturing business buys materials and, by using labor and machines, changes the form of the materials into a finished product. The elements of manufacturing costs are covered, as well as the other important topics that relate to manufacturing and controlling inventory.

- Chapter 20 concludes Part 6 with the accounting transactions and financial reporting for a manufacturing business.

Part 6 wraps up with an opportunity for students to apply what they have learned about cost accounting for a manufacturing business through completion of the simulation Progressive Badge Company and/or Reinforcement Activity 3.

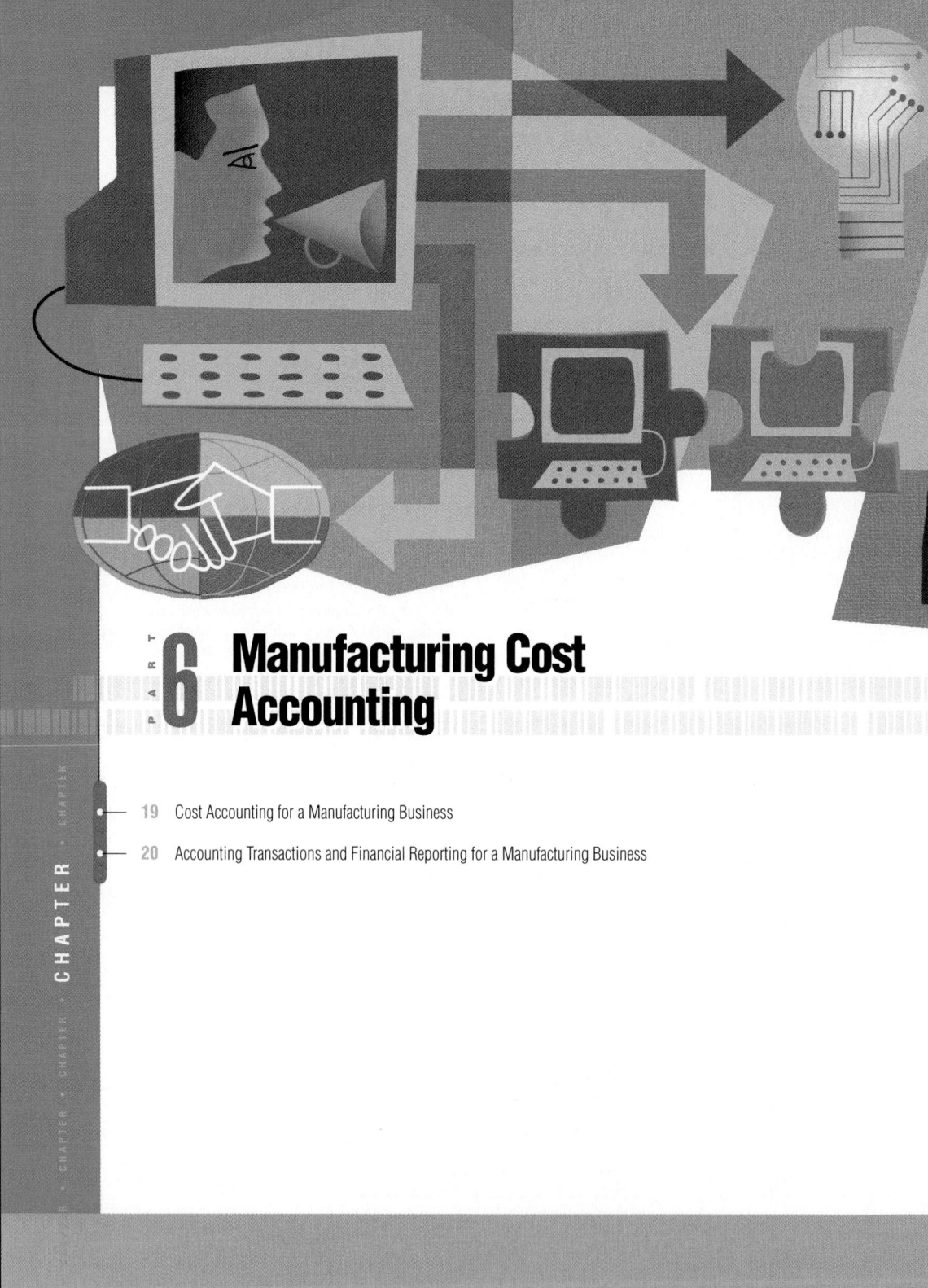

PART 6 Manufacturing Cost Accounting

19 Cost Accounting for a Manufacturing Business

20 Accounting Transactions and Financial Reporting for a Manufacturing Business

FAXAVISION, INC.
CHART OF ACCOUNTS

Balance Sheet Accounts

(1000) ASSETS
1100 CURRENT ASSETS
1105 Cash
1110 Petty Cash
1115 Accounts Receivable
1120 Allowance for Uncollectible Accounts
1125 Materials
1130 Work in Process
1135 Finished Goods
1140 Supplies—Factory
1145 Supplies—Sales
1150 Supplies—Administrative
1155 Prepaid Insurance
1200 PLANT ASSETS
1205 Factory Equipment
1210 Accumulated Depreciation—Factory Equipment
1215 Office Equipment
1220 Accumulated Depreciation—Office Equipment
1225 Store Equipment
1230 Accumulated Depreciation—Store Equipment
1235 Building
1240 Accumulated Depreciation—Building
1245 Land

(2000) LIABILITIES
2100 CURRENT LIABILITIES
2105 Accounts Payable
2110 Employee Income Tax Payable
2115 Federal Income Tax Payable
2120 Social Security Tax Payable
2123 Medicare Tax Payable
2125 Salaries Payable
2130 Unemployment Tax Payable—Federal
2135 Unemployment Tax Payable—State
2140 Dividends Payable
2200 LONG-TERM LIABILITY
2205 Mortgage Payable

(3000) STOCKHOLDERS' EQUITY
3105 Capital Stock
3110 Retained Earnings
3115 Dividends
3120 Income Summary

Income Statement Accounts

(4000) OPERATING REVENUE
4105 Sales

(5000) COST OF SALES
5105 Cost of Goods Sold

(5500) MANUFACTURING COSTS
5505 Factory Overhead
5510 Depreciation Expense—Factory Equipment
5515 Depreciation Expense—Building
5520 Heat, Light, and Power Expense
5525 Insurance Expense—Factory
5530 Miscellaneous Expense—Factory
5535 Payroll Taxes Expense—Factory
5540 Property Tax Expense—Factory
5545 Supplies Expense—Factory

(6000) OPERATING EXPENSES
6100 SELLING EXPENSES
6105 Advertising Expense
6110 Delivery Expense
6115 Depreciation Expense—Store Equipment
6120 Miscellaneous Expense—Sales
6125 Salary Expense—Sales
6130 Supplies Expense—Sales
6200 ADMINISTRATIVE EXPENSES
6205 Depreciation Expense—Office Equipment
6210 Insurance Expense—Administrative
6215 Miscellaneous Expense—Administrative
6220 Payroll Taxes Expense—Administrative
6225 Property Tax Expense—Administrative
6230 Salary Expense—Administrative
6235 Supplies Expense—Administrative
6240 Uncollectible Accounts Expense
6245 Utilities Expense—Administrative

(7000) OTHER REVENUE
7105 Gain on Plant Assets
7110 Miscellaneous Revenue

(8000) OTHER EXPENSES
8105 Interest Expense
8110 Loss on Plant Assets

(9000) INCOME TAX
9105 Federal Income Tax Expense

The chart of accounts for FaxaVision, Inc., is illustrated above for ready reference as you study Chapters 19 and 20 of this textbook.

EXPLAIN

- Emphasize that the chart of accounts shown on this page will be used throughout Chapters 19 and 20.

- Explain that this is a chart of accounts for a manufacturing business.

- Explain that because the business is not departmentalized, accounts are not divided into departments.

- Highlight that the major difference between a chart of accounts for a merchandising business and one for a manufacturing business can be found in the Cost sections. FaxaVision uses a Cost of Sales section and a Manufacturing Costs section to account for the costs associated with the three inventory accounts related to the products manufactured: (1) Materials, (2) Work in Process, and (3) Finished Goods.

- Explain that the three inventory accounts for products manufactured are in the Current Assets section.

- Point out that the Operating Expenses section is divided into selling and administrative expenses. Administrative expenses are expenses of the business that do not clearly relate to the sales effort, such as salaries and supplies of the office staff.

	SCOPE & SEQUENCE		ENHANCING	
	NEW	**REVIEW/ EXTENSION**	**SPECIAL FEATURES**	
Introduce the Chapter	✓		• Accounting in the Real World: Hershey	
Lesson 19-1 Elements of Manufacturing Cost			• Making Ethical Decisions: Occupational Fraud	
Cost accounting	✓		• Explore Accounting: Activity-Based Costing	
Direct materials	✓		• Cases for Critical Thinking 1	
Direct labor	✓			
Factory overhead	✓			
Manufacturing cost flows	✓			
Lesson 19-2 Maintaining Manufacturing Records			• Cases for Critical Thinking 2	
Recording direct materials on a cost sheet	✓			
Recording direct labor on a cost sheet	✓			
Calculating and recording factory overhead	✓			
Completing a finished goods ledger card	✓			
Putting It All Together			• Explore Accounting	
			• Xtra! Web Site: Xtra! Enrichment	
			• Applied Communication	
			• SCANS Workplace Competency	
			• Auditing for Errors	
			• Analyzing Costco's Financial Statements	

Manufacturing Business

INSTRUCTION		PRACTICE AND ASSESSMENT		
TECHNOLOGY AND MEDIA	TEACHING STRATEGIES	GUIDED PRACTICE	INDEPENDENT PRACTICE	RETEACHING AND ENRICHMENT
• Internet Research Activity • Accounting Xtra! Web Site	• Software Focus			
• Instructor's Resource CD: PowerPoint Slides • Xtra! Web Site: Xtra! Study Tools • Personal Trainer	• Expanding Beyond the Classroom • Visual Learners	• Terms Review • Audit Your Understanding • Work Together 19-1	• On Your Own 19-1 • Application Problem 19-1 • Ongoing Assessment, p. 563 • Personal Trainer • Xtra! Web Site: Xtra! Study Tools	• Reteach, p. 563 • Enrich, p. 564
• Instructor's Resource CD: PowerPoint Slides • Xtra! Web Site: Xtra! Study Tools • Blackline Masters: Materials Ledger Card, Cost Sheet, and Finished Goods Ledger Card • Personal Trainer • QuickBooks	• Visually-Impaired Students • Expanding Beyond the Classroom • Tactile Learners • Applied Skills: Building Study Skills • Kinesthetic Learners	• Term Review • Audit Your Understanding • Work Together 19-2	• On Your Own 19-2 • Application Problems 19-2, 19-3, 19-4, and 19-5 • Ongoing Assessment, p. 571 • Personal Trainer • Xtra! Web Site: Xtra! Study Tools	• Reteach, p. 571 • Enrich, p. 572 • QuickBooks
• Automated Accounting • Personal Trainer • Xtra! Web Site: Xtra! Review, Quizzing, and Enrichment • Student Companion CD	• Limited English Proficiency (LEP) Students • Cooperative Learning • Applied Skills: Writing Across the Curriculum • Applied Skills: Language Arts		• Mastery Problem 19-6 • Personal Trainer • Xtra! Web Site: Xtra! Review and Quizzing • Study Guide 19 • Student Companion CD • Chapter 19 Test • ExamView Chapter 19 • Portfolio Assessment	• Challenge Problem 19-7 • Reteach, p. 573 • Enrich, p. 573 • Recycling Problem 19-1 • Automated Accounting • Xtra! Web Site: Xtra! Enrichment

CHAPTER

19 Cost Accounting for a Manufacturing Business

OBJECTIVES & TERMS

After studying Chapter 19, you will be able to:

1. Define accounting terms related to cost accounting for a manufacturing business.

2. Identify accounting concepts and practices related to cost accounting for a manufacturing business.

3. Identify the elements of manufacturing costs: (1) direct materials, (2) direct labor, and (3) factory overhead.

4. Identify the flow of costs through the manufacturing process.

5. Prepare selected ledgers and cost sheets for a manufacturing business.

- direct materials
- direct labor
- factory overhead
- indirect materials
- indirect labor
- work in process
- finished goods
- materials ledger
- cost ledger
- finished goods ledger
- applied overhead

Point Your Browser
accountingxtra.swlearning.com

558

accounting in the real world

• Hershey

©TIM SHAFFER/REUTERS/LANDOV

THE WONDERFUL WORLD OF HERSHEY

Milton S. Hershey began his career as an apprentice to a candy maker in Lancaster, Pennsylvania. After a brief attempt to operate his own candy shop, he traveled to Denver, Colorado, where he learned the importance of fresh ingredients in the production of caramel. In 1886, he returned home to establish the Lancaster Caramel Company, the forerunner of today's Hershey Foods Corporation.

Mr. Hershey located his chocolate manufacturing operation in the heart of Pennsylvania's dairy country. A plentiful supply of fresh milk was a critical ingredient in the success of the company. Peanuts, cocoa, and milk are the primary raw materials in the production of Hershey products today. Equipment, labor, and packaging are just a few of the other items also included in the cost of the products.

Mr. Hershey believed that an individual is morally obligated to share the fruits of success with others. These beliefs led him to establish important components of the town that bears his name, including a bank, department store, park, churches, zoo, and a trolley system to transport workers from nearby communities. During the Great Depression, Mr. Hershey kept men at work constructing a hotel, community building, and sports arena. The Milton Hershey School continues to provide education for nearly 1,100 children whose lives have been disrupted.

Critical Thinking

1. What are the advantages of locating a manufacturing operation near a primary source of raw materials?
2. Do you believe Mr. Hershey's support of the community affected the success of his business?

Source: www.hersheys.com/about/milton.shtml

Xtra!
Today
accountingxtra.swlearning.com

internet activity

MANUFACTURING INVENTORY ACCOUNTS

Manufacturing companies use different inventory accounts than merchandising businesses do.

Instructions

Use the Internet to access the annual reports of two manufacturing companies. Using either the financial statements or the accompanying notes to the financial statements, answer the following questions for each company.

1. What three types of inventories are included in the heading "Inventories" on the balance sheet?
2. For each of the three types of inventories, calculate what percentage it is of the total inventories.

ACCOUNTING IN THE REAL WORLD

1. The raw material will be as fresh as possible, and transportation costs will be minimized. In addition, the company may have some control over the quantity and quality of the raw material production.
2. Mr. Hershey demonstrated a genuine concern and commitment to his employees, community, and people throughout the Pennsylvania dairy country. These people, touched by his generosity, would be more dedicated to help his company achieve its goals.

INTERNET RESEARCH ACTIVITY

1. Specific titles may vary somewhat but typically are: production materials, work in process, and finished goods.
2. Answers will vary.

559

19-1 Elements of Manufacturing Cost

The three general types of businesses are service, merchandising, and manufacturing. Service businesses provide a needed service for their customers. Examples of service business are accounting firms, law firms, and medical practices.

Merchandising businesses sell products to customers. A merchandising business purchases products and, without changing the products' forms, sells those products to customers. Department stores and grocery stores are examples of merchandising businesses.

A manufacturing business buys materials and uses labor and machinery to change the materials into a finished product. A manufacturing business generally sells the finished product to a merchandising business, which then sells the product to customers.

FaxaVision, Inc., a facsimile manufacturing business, buys modems, print motors, cutter assemblies, document sensors, and other materials. Using labor and machinery, FaxaVision combines the materials to make facsimile machines, commonly referred to as fax machines. Merchandising businesses buy the fax machines from FaxaVision for resale to customers.

A service business needs to know the cost of providing services to be able to calculate net income. A merchandising business needs to know the cost of merchandise sold to calculate net income. For the same reason, a manufacturing company needs to know the costs required to produce finished products that it sells. To know how much finished products cost, FaxaVision keeps records of all costs involved in making the products.

making ethical decisions

Occupational Fraud

Despite its best efforts, a company will have employees who will demonstrate unethical behavior. In fact, many employees will steal cash, inventory, and other items of value from their employers. The use of one's employment for personal gain through the deliberate misuse of company resources is called *occupational fraud*. The Association of Certified Fraud Examiners estimates that 6% of revenues are lost to occupational fraud. Fraud reduces the wages available to pay workers and limits stockholders' return on their investment.

Auditors and managers need an understanding of the most common forms of occupational fraud. Knowing how these frauds are committed enables auditors and managers to search for signs or "red flags" of fraud. Early detection of a fraud substantially reduces the loss incurred.

Instructions

Access the *Report to the Nation* of the Association of Certified Fraud Examiners. Identify and explain the five most common fraudulent disbursements.

The manufacturing cost of any finished product includes three cost elements: (1) direct materials, (2) direct labor, and (3) factory overhead.

Direct Materials

Materials that are of significant value in the cost of a finished product and that become an identifiable part of the product are called **direct materials**. Direct materials include all items used in the manufacturing process that have sufficient value to justify charging the cost directly to the product. [*CONCEPT: Materiality*] The materiality concept states that business activities creating dollar amounts large enough to affect business decisions should be recorded and reported as separate items in accounting records and financial statements. Dollar amounts that are small and not considered important in decision making may be combined with other amounts in the accounting records and financial statements. For example, modems and print motors used to manufacture fax machines are considered direct materials and accounted for separately. Connectors and gears used in the manufacture of fax machines are parts with a small enough dollar value that they are grouped together and only their total value is recorded in the accounting records.

Direct Labor

Salaries of factory workers who make a product are called **direct labor**. Direct labor includes salaries only of persons working directly on a product. Salaries of supervisors, maintenance workers, and others whose efforts do not apply directly to the manufacture of a product are not considered to be direct labor.

Factory Overhead

All expenses other than direct materials and direct labor that apply to making products are called **factory overhead**. Some materials used in manufacturing a product cost a very small amount for each unit produced. Materials used in the completion of a product that are of insignificant value to justify accounting for separately are called **indirect materials**. Indirect materials may include items such as glue, solder, bolts, and rivets. Materials and supplies used by the factory such as cleaning supplies and lubricants for the machinery are also classified as indirect materials.

Some factory workers devote their time to supervisory, clerical, and maintenance tasks necessary to operate the factory. Such workers include time clerks, supervisors, maintenance people, receiving clerks, and inspectors. Salaries paid to factory workers who are not actually making products are called **indirect labor**.

Other costs are also incurred in the manufacturing process. (1) Depreciation of factory buildings and equipment. (2) Repairs to factory buildings and equipment. (3) Insurance on building, equipment, and stock. (4) Taxes on property owned. (5) Heat, light, and power. All of these expenses, along with indirect materials and indirect labor, make up factory overhead.

INVENTORIES FOR A MANUFACTURING BUSINESS

A merchandising business normally has one general ledger account for merchandise inventory. However, a manufacturing business has three inventory accounts related to the products manufactured. (1) Materials. (2) Work in Process. (3) Finished Goods. These accounts are classified as current assets of FaxaVision, Inc.

A materials inventory account shows the costs of materials on hand that have not yet been used in making a product. Products that are being manufactured but are not yet complete are called **work in process**. A work in process inventory account, therefore, shows all costs that have been spent on products that are not yet complete. Manufactured products that are fully completed are called **finished goods**. A finished goods inventory account, therefore, shows the cost of completed products still on hand and unsold.

- List the three manufacturing cost elements: direct materials, direct labor, and factory overhead.
- Explain direct materials and ask for examples of direct materials used in manufacturing a local product.
- Explain direct labor. Discuss the kinds of labor that are not included in direct labor.
- Explain factory overhead. Discuss indirect materials and indirect labor. Discuss other elements of factory overhead.
- Explain the three kinds of inventory accounts for a manufacturing business. Discuss what is included in each.

TEACHING STRATEGIES   EXPANDING BEYOND THE CLASSROOM

Arrange a field trip to a manufacturing business. Inform the business contact that the major purpose of the trip is to learn what direct and indirect materials are used in production. After the trip, have students compile a list of the direct and indirect materials they identified.

- Explain three purposes for keeping manufacturing cost records.
- Explain that three subsidiary ledgers are maintained for the three manufacturing inventory accounts.
- Point out that a number of forms are used in a cost system for keeping detailed information.
- Explain that a materials ledger uses a materials ledger card for each kind of direct and indirect material.
- Explain that entries are recorded on a materials ledger card each time material is received and issued.
- Explain that a cost ledger uses a cost sheet for each manufacturing job.
- Point out that a materials requisition is completed for all direct materials issued for a particular job and the information is recorded on the cost sheet for that job.
- Point out that employees complete a job time record showing hours worked on each job and that those direct labor costs are recorded on the cost sheet for that job.
- Point out that when a job is completed, factory overhead is estimated and recorded on the cost sheet.
- Point out that a finished goods ledger card is kept for each type of product manufactured.
- Explain that entries are recorded on a finished goods ledger card each time a product is manufactured or received and each time a product is shipped or issued to a customer.
- Emphasize that the total of accounts in the subsidiary ledgers must equal the balance of the general ledger inventory account.
- The total of all materials ledger cards equals the balance of Materials in the general ledger.
- The total of all cost sheets for products in the process of being manufactured equals the balance of Work in Process in the general ledger.
- The total of all finished goods ledger cards equals the balance of Finished Goods in the general ledger.

COST RECORDS

Manufacturing businesses keep detailed cost records for three purposes. (1) To determine accurate costs for each product made. (2) To provide specific cost information to managers who must identify high cost areas so that corrective action can be taken. (3) To provide cost summary information for journal entries.

Subsidiary Cost Ledgers

Three subsidiary ledgers provide the detailed cost information for the three manufacturing inventory accounts.

1. **Materials Ledger.** FaxaVision uses a perpetual inventory system for direct and indirect materials. A perpetual inventory record provides detailed cost information about each type of material. A ledger containing all records of materials is called a **materials ledger**.

2. **Cost Ledger.** FaxaVision keeps a record of all charges for direct materials, direct labor, and factory overhead for each job. The record is known as a cost sheet. A cost sheet is maintained for each manufacturing job. A ledger containing all cost sheets for products in the process of being manufactured is called a **cost ledger**.

3. **Finished Goods Ledger.** The company keeps a record of each kind of finished good to provide a perpetual inventory of each product produced and its cost. A ledger containing records of all finished goods on hand is called a **finished goods ledger**. This ledger is similar to a materials ledger.

Journal entries for job costs are described in Chapter 20.

MANUFACTURING COST FLOWS

Manufacturing costs are recorded on cost forms as costs occur. The forms used and the sequence of steps followed for recording FaxaVision's manufacturing costs are shown above.

Visual Learners. The visual learner can benefit from illustrations such as the flowchart on this page and the other illustrations of cost accounting forms that show numbered steps of completion.

RECORDING MANUFACTURING COSTS

1 Record the number and cost of each kind of material purchased on materials ledger cards. This step is performed for both direct and indirect materials.

2 Prepare a materials requisition to use when direct materials are issued for use in the factory. The amount of direct materials issued is recorded as a reduction on the materials ledger card and an increase in the Direct Materials column of the cost sheet.

3 Prepare job-time records when direct labor is used. Time record amounts are recorded in the Direct Labor column of the cost sheet.

4 Estimate and record the amount of factory overhead when a product is completed. The amount of factory overhead is recorded in the Summary column of the cost sheet. Estimating factory overhead is described later in this chapter.

5 Total all costs on the cost sheet when a product is completed. Transfer the total to a finished goods ledger card.

Explore Accounting

EXPLORE ACCOUNTING · EXPLORE ACCOUNTING · EXPLORE ACCOUNTING

Activity-Based Costing

From the beginning of the Industrial Revolution in the mid-1800s, direct labor was a major component of manufacturing costs. Factory overhead costs, such as building depreciation, utilities, maintenance, and insurance, were costs incurred to provide workers with a safe and clean environment in which to work. As a result, it was natural for early accountants to allocate these factory overhead costs based on the direct labor (dollars or hours) incurred to manufacture a product.

Many of today's automated manufacturing processes involve little, if any, direct labor. Thus, accountants had to develop a new method for allocating factory overhead. One popular method requires accountants to identify significant activities in the manufacturing process. Allocating factory overhead based on the level of significant activities is referred to as *activity-based costing (ABC)*.

For example, the production of a pizza at a local pizza parlor involves two significant activities: assembling the ingredients and cooking the pizza. The first activity involves direct labor, but the second activity involves only cooking time in the oven. In contrast, the production of a sub sandwich involves three times as much direct labor as a pizza but no cooking in the oven. If factory overhead were applied based solely on

direct labor, the sub sandwich would improperly receive three times as much overhead cost as the pizza.

Using ABC, the accountant recognizes that a significant amount of overhead costs of the pizza parlor results from the ovens: the cost of the ovens, heating the ovens, and cooling the kitchen from the heat that escapes from the ovens. These overhead costs should be allocated to those products that require cooking. Thus, factory overhead costs related to the ovens would be applied to pizza production based on cooking time.

ABC is also used by service businesses to determine the cost of providing various services. ABC results in more accurate estimates on the cost of producing individual products and services. Managers can use this information to assist them in making better business decisions, such as the sales price of its products and the profitability of different product lines.

Critical Thinking: The challenge of implementing ABC is to match costs with related activities that are easy to measure. Identify the measurable activities in two different lawn maintenance services: mowing a lawn and cutting down a tree.

Elements of Manufacturing Cost

Lesson 19-1 **563**

EXPLORE ACCOUNTING
EXPLORE ACCOUNTING

Although both services require equipment, the cost of the equipment used to cut down trees is significantly more expensive. A company that cuts down trees will also incur more liability and medical insurance costs. ABC would allocate more costs to the tree cutting services, even if both required the same time to complete.

DEMONSTRATE

DEMONSTRATE

- Demonstrate the flow of costs from raw materials through work in process to finished goods, by sketching the flow on the chalkboard or overhead projector or direct students to the illustration on page 562.

- Demonstrate that the number and cost of each kind of direct and indirect material purchased is recorded on materials ledger cards (step 1).

- Demonstrate that a materials requisition is prepared for issuing direct materials to the factory (step 2a); the materials requisition is recorded on the materials ledger cards (step 2b); and the issued direct materials are recorded on the cost sheet (step 2b).

- Demonstrate that job time records are completed for direct labor and then recorded on the cost sheets (step 3).

- Demonstrate that factory overhead is estimated and recorded on the cost sheet when a job is completed (step 4).

- Demonstrate that the total cost of a completed job is transferred to the finished goods ledger cards (step 5).

ONGOING ASSESSMENT

- Assessment is an ongoing process. Circulate through the classroom or lab observing which students have problems with the assignments.

- Troubleshooting: Diagnose what kinds of problems students have with this lesson. Students may have difficulty (1) distinguishing between direct and indirect materials, (2) identifying the different kinds of manufacturing costs, or (3) understanding the flow of manufacturing costs through the manufacturing inventory accounts.

- Assess student understanding by checking solutions to Independent Practice assignments.

RETEACH

- Name a manufactured item, such as a desk, and ask students to describe the materials involved in its manufacture and describe the different kinds of workers in the company.

- Call on students to state whether each material item is a direct or indirect material.

- Call on students to state which employees contribute direct labor and which indirect labor.

- Call on students to sketch a chart of the components of the flow of manufacturing costs.

GUIDED PRACTICE

Terms Review
Call on students to define the terms in the Terms Review. Ask the class if the definitions are correct and whether the complete definitions have been given or if anything needs to be added. Suggested definitions for all terms are given in the Glossary.

Audit Your Understanding
Call on students to answer the Audit Your Understanding questions. Ask the class if each answer is correct and/or complete. Answers are given in Appendix E of the textbook.

Work Together
Have students write the solution to the Work Together problem as you guide the class through the examples.

- Discuss as a group the classification and ledger for each item.
- When agreement is reached, direct students to record the answer on the analysis sheet from the *Working Papers*.
- Remind students to save the work begun in this problem to complete On Your Own 19-1.

INDEPENDENT PRACTICE

On Your Own
- Remind students that the problem started in Work Together 19-1 is needed to complete this problem.
- Assign the On Your Own problem to be worked independently.
- Use the Ongoing Assessment techniques to diagnose student understanding.

Application Problem
- Assign Application Problem 19-1: Classifying manufacturing costs and determining which ledger to use for initial recording.

Personal Trainer
- Students can access the Lesson 19-1 assessment material using this software.

Xtra! Web Site
- Students can access the Xtra! Study Tools for additional practice.

ENRICH

- Assign Making Ethical Decisions on page 560.
- Assign Explore Accounting on page 563.
- Assign Cases for Critical Thinking 1.

564

• terms review

direct materials
direct labor
factory overhead
indirect materials
indirect labor
work in process
finished goods
materials ledger
cost ledger
finished goods ledger

• audit your understanding

1. What are the three manufacturing cost elements of a finished product?
2. What term is used to describe products that are being manufactured but are not yet complete?
3. What is the purpose of a cost sheet?

• work together 19-1

Classifying manufacturing costs; specifying the ledger used for initial recording

An analysis sheet for Gutman's Gutters, a firm that manufactures aluminum and steel gutters, is included in the *Working Papers*. Your instructor will guide you through the following examples.

1. For each of the following costs, determine whether the cost should be classified as direct materials, direct labor, or factory overhead.
2. Specify the subsidiary ledger (materials ledger, cost ledger, finished goods ledger) in which the cost is first recorded. Save your work to complete On Your Own 19-1 below.
   a. Wages earned by an employee working on the production of gutters.
   b. Aluminum used in the production of gutters.
   c. The rent expense of the factory in which the gutters are made.
   d. A cleaning solvent used to clean production machinery.
   e. Fringe benefits received by an employee working on the production of gutters.

• on your own 19-1

Classifying manufacturing costs; specifying the ledger used for initial recording

Use the working papers from Work Together 19-1 above. Work independently to complete the following problem.

1. For each of the following costs, determine whether the cost should be classified as direct materials, direct labor, or factory overhead.
2. Specify the subsidiary ledger (materials ledger, cost ledger, finished goods ledger) in which the cost is first recorded.
   a. Rivets used in the production of gutters.
   b. Wages earned by a maintenance employee.
   c. The property taxes of the factory.
   d. Fringe benefits of the factory supervisor.
   e. Wages earned by an employee who inspects finished gutters before they leave the factory.

CLOSE

- Ask students to describe the distinctions between the different kinds of manufacturing costs.

19-2 Maintaining Manufacturing Records

OBJECTIVES

- Define terms related to cost accounting for a manufacturing business.
- Identify accounting concepts and practices related to cost accounting for a manufacturing business.
- Prepare selected ledgers and cost sheets for a manufacturing business.

RECORDS FOR MATERIALS

1. Open a materials ledger card.

2. Record orders placed.

MATERIALS LEDGER CARD

Article _28S Print Motor_   Acct. No. _145_

Reorder _300_   Minimum _220_   Location _B-16_

ORDERED			RECEIVED					ISSUED					BALANCE			
DATE	PUR-CHASE ORDER NO.	QUAN-TITY	DATE	PUR-CHASE ORDER NO.	QUAN-TITY	UNIT PRICE	VALUE	DATE	REQUI-SITION NO.	QUAN-TITY	UNIT PRICE	VALUE	DATE	QUAN-TITY	UNIT PRICE	VALUE
													20-- Jan. 2	220	78.00	17,160.00
20-- Jan. 3	461	300						20-- Jan. 3	730	100	78.00	7,800.00	3	120	78.00	9,360.00
								10	752	100	78.00	7,800.00	10	20	78.00	1,560.00
			20-- Jan. 13	461	300	78.00	23,400.00						13	320	78.00	24,960.00

3. Record orders received.

4. Record the new balance.

A manufacturing business keeps a record of materials used in the manufacturing process. The business should have on hand sufficient materials so that the manufacturing process will not be interrupted. However, too large a stock of materials requires needless investment in inventory. To provide a perpetual inventory and detailed cost information about materials, Faxa-Vision keeps a materials ledger card for each type of material. A materials ledger card is shown above.

MOTIVATE

After quickly previewing the lesson, ask students to discuss whether they think all the records kept for manufacturing costs are worth the time and effort. Ask students to discuss both the advantages and disadvantages of the intensive recordkeeping. Ask if there is any technology available for streamlining the effort.

Preview

- Preview the accounting term and definition introduced in this lesson: applied overhead.
- Direct students to read the headings at the top of each page in this lesson and to examine the illustrations given.

EXPLAIN

- Explain that a manufacturing business keeps a perpetual inventory of the materials used in the manufacturing process.
- Emphasize that the total of the materials ledgers cards equals the balance of Materials in the general ledger.
- Point out that it is important to monitor the materials inventory and to reorder when quantities reach the minimum level because a shortage of one material might cause an expensive production process to be shut down.

STEPS • STEPS • STEPS • STEPS • STEPS • STEPS • STEPS • STEPS • STEPS • STEPS

OPENING A MATERIALS LEDGER CARD AND RECORDING MATERIALS ORDERED

1 Open a materials ledger card for each type of material kept in the storeroom.
 a. Enter the name and account number of the item.
 b. Determine and record the reorder quantity and minimum quantities to be kept in stock. When the number on hand equals the minimum, the materials clerk notifies the purchasing agent to place a new order.

2 Record the date of an order, _Jan. 3_, the purchase order number, _461_, and the quantity ordered, _300_, in the Ordered columns. The data are recorded from a purchase order. The purchase order authorizes a seller to deliver goods with payment to be made later. The order was placed because the quantity on hand, 220 units, equaled the minimum level at which a new order is placed. Note that the quantity ordered equals the reorder quantity shown at the top of the ledger card.

3 When the items ordered are received, record the date, _Jan. 13_, the purchase order number, _461_, the quantity, _300_, the unit price, _78.00_, and the total value of the order, _23,400.00_, in the Received columns of the materials ledger card. The total value is the quantity, 300, multiplied by the unit price, $78.00.

4 Add the quantity and value to the previous balances and extend the amounts to the Balance columns.

Notice that the materials ledger card also shows items that have been issued. The issuing of materials will be discussed later in the chapter. The total value for all the materials ledger cards equals the balance of the materials general ledger account.

The relationship of the general ledger accounts to the forms and ledgers described in this chapter is explained in Chapter 20.

DEMONSTRATE

Materials ledger card

- Use an instructor-made transparency of a materials ledger card or direct students to the illustration as you demonstrate maintaining a materials ledger card.
- Demonstrate how to open a materials ledger card by completing the top portion. Point out the Reorder quantity and the Minimum quantity.
- Demonstrate recording amounts ordered, received, and issued, as well as calculating the new balance after each entry. Point out that the unit price is also recorded.

Maintaining Manufacturing Records   Lesson 19-2   **565**

MATERIALS

- Instructor's Resource CD:
 PowerPoint Slides
- Xtra! Study Tools on the Xtra! Web Site
- Blackline Masters:
 Materials Ledger Card
 Cost Sheet
 Finished Goods Ledger Card

- Working Papers:
 Teacher's Edition of the Working Papers for Lesson 19-2
- Software:
 Personal Trainer
 Student Companion CD
 QuickBooks

- Explain that a new cost sheet is started each time a new job starts.
- Point out that materials cannot be transferred to the factory without a materials requisition.
- Explain that each materials requisition form is prepared in triplicate. One copy is kept in the factory where the materials will be used and the other two are sent to the materials storeroom. After the material is issued one of the two copies is forwarded to the cost accounting department for entry on the materials ledger card.
- Explain that a job is not started necessarily for sale to a customer; the products may just be needed to replenish stock for sale.

DEMONSTRATE

Opening a cost sheet (step 1)

- Direct students to the illustration to demonstrate how to open a cost sheet for a new job.
- Demonstrate recording the job number and item description in the top section of the cost sheet.
- Demonstrate recording the No. of items to be manufactured and the reason for the order, "Stock."
- Demonstrate recording the date the cost sheet was started and the date the job should be finished (Date wanted).
- Explain that the Date completed is left blank until the job is completed.
- Direct students to examine the remaining columns in anticipation of their use in step 4 on page 567.

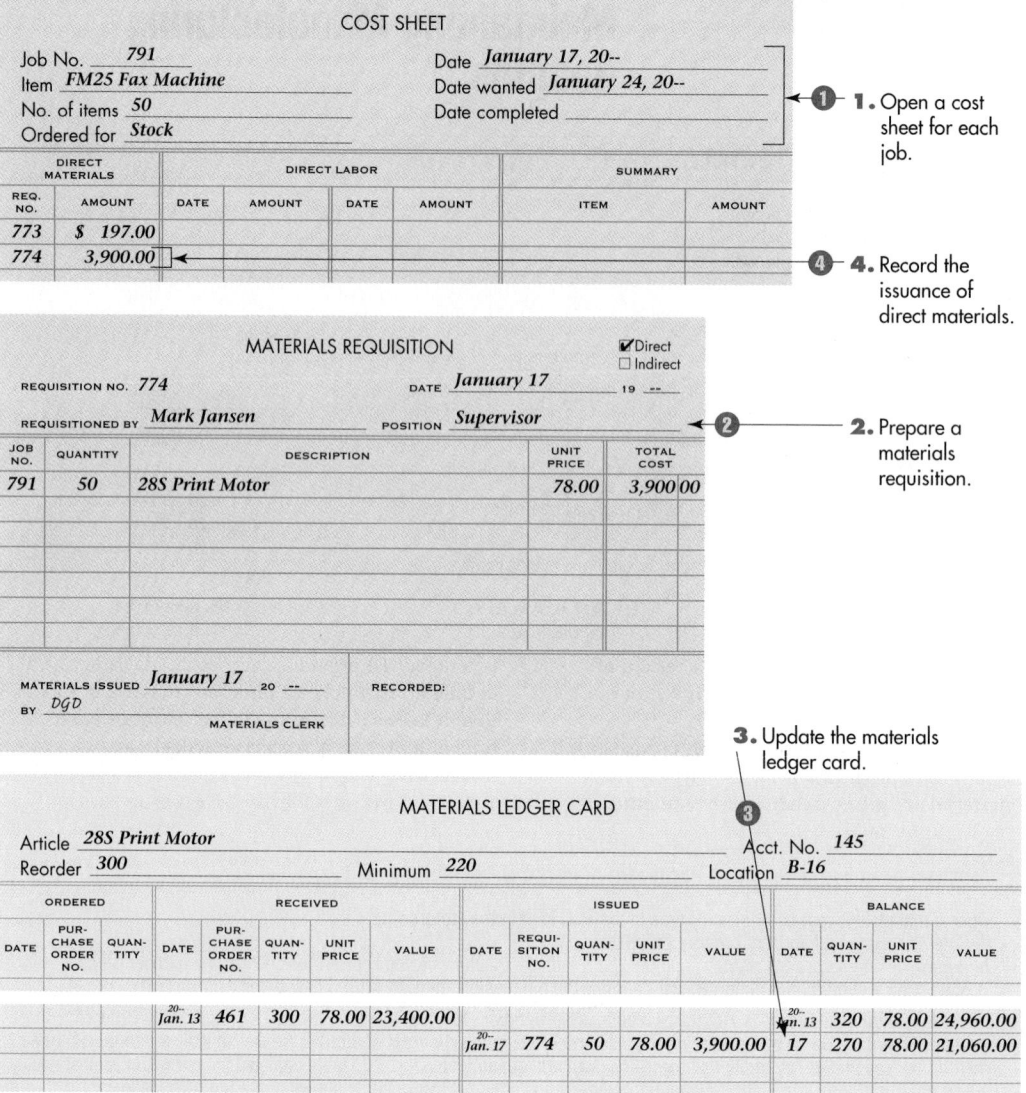

1. Open a cost sheet for each job.

4. Record the issuance of direct materials.

2. Prepare a materials requisition.

3. Update the materials ledger card.

During the manufacturing process, all costs of making a product must be recorded. All charges for direct materials, direct labor, and factory overhead for a particular job are recorded on a cost sheet, such as the one shown above.

When direct materials are needed for a job, they are requested from the storeroom using a materials requisition form. A materials requisition form is used to authorize transfer of items from the storeroom to the factory. When materials are issued to the factory from the storeroom, the materials ledger card is updated.

TEACHING STRATEGIES DIFFERENT LEARNING ABILITIES

Visually-Impaired Students. Many visually-impaired individuals are successful business professionals. It is important for visually-impaired students to have confidence in their ability to participate fully within the business world. Assign students to prepare an oral or written report which profiles a successful visually-impaired business professional.

RECORDING DIRECT MATERIALS ON A COST SHEET

1 Open a new cost sheet for each job started. When the cost accounting department receives a request from the factory department supervisor for a job number, it assigns the number and prepares a new job cost sheet. To open a new job cost sheet:

a. Enter the Job No., *791.*
b. Enter the stock number and the description of the product, *FM25 Fax Machine.*
c. Enter the number of items to be manufactured, *50.*
d. Enter the customer that ordered the item. In this case, the product will replenish FaxaVision's stock of the fax machine. Therefore, *Stock* is entered on the Ordered for line.
e. Enter the date the job number is assigned, *January 17, 20--.*
f. Enter the date the item is wanted, *January 24, 20--.*

2 Prepare a materials requisition in triplicate. One copy of a materials requisition is kept in the factory. Two copies are sent to the materials storeroom.

a. Enter the requisition number, *774.* Requisitions are numbered in order. The next available number is assigned.
b. Enter the name of the person who is making the requisition, *Mark Jansen.*
c. Check the appropriate box to indicate whether the requisition is for direct or indirect materials. In this case, a motor is a major part of the finished product. Therefore, the Direct box is checked.
d. Enter the date of the requisition, *January 17, 20--.*
e. Enter the position of the person making the requisition, *Supervisor.* Usually, a supervisor or a manager has the authority to make the requisition.
f. Enter the job number to which the materials are being issued, *791.*
g. Enter the quantity requisitioned, *50.*
h. Enter the stock number and description, *28S Print Motor.*
i. Enter the unit price of the materials, *78.00.*
j. Enter the total cost of the materials being issued to the factory, *3,900.00.* The total cost is determined by multiplying the quantity by the unit price (50 × $78.00 = $3,900.00).
k. Record the date on which the materials are issued to the factory, *January 17, 20--.*
l. The materials clerk initials the requisition to show that the materials have been issued. One copy of the completed materials requisition is kept in the storeroom. The original requisition is sent to the cost accounting department.

3 Update the materials ledger card. When the materials requisition is received by the cost accounting department, an entry is made in the materials ledger.

a. Enter the date the materials are issued to the factory, *January 17, 20--,* in the Date column of the Issued section of the materials ledger card.
b. Enter the requisition number, *774.*
c. Enter the quantity issued, *50.*
d. Enter the unit price, *78.00.*
e. Enter the total value of the materials issued, *3,900.00.*
f. Enter the date in the Balance Date column.
g. Enter the new quantity of the material, *270,* in the Balance Quantity column. Subtract the quantity issued from the current quantity in inventory (320 − 50 = 270) to determine the new quantity.
h. Enter the unit price, *78.00.*
i. Enter the total value of the material, *21,060.00* (270 units × $78.00 = $21,060.00).

4 Record the issuance of direct materials on the cost sheet. When the cost accounting department receives the materials requisition, an entry is made on the cost sheet.

a. Enter the requisition number, *774,* in the Req. No. column.
b. Enter the total value of the materials issued, *3,900.00,* in the Direct Materials Amount column.

Maintaining Manufacturing Records

Lesson 19-2   **567**

EXPANDING BEYOND THE CLASSROOM

Invite a manager from a cost accounting department of a manufacturing company to address the class on the methods his or her company uses for keeping cost account records. Prepare the speaker in advance with a description of the methods studied in this chapter. Do not be surprised if the speaker presents some alternative methods.

DEMONSTRATE

Preparing a materials requisition (step 2)

• Direct students to the materials requisition form in the middle of the illustration on page 566 as you demonstrate how to prepare a materials requisition.

• Demonstrate completing the top portion of the materials requisition. Point out that a company will either use pre-numbered forms or write a sequential requisition number on each form.

• Point out that the name and position of the person making the requisition and the date are also entered in the top portion.

• Emphasize the importance of checking whether the materials are direct or indirect. In this case a motor is a significant part of a finished fax machine so the Direct box is checked.

• Demonstrate completing the remainder of the requisition. Note that the job number is required for each material listed on the form. Point out that whoever actually issues the materials initials the bottom of the form.

Completing a materials ledger card (step 3)

• Use an instructor-made transparency of a materials ledger card or direct students to the bottom form in the illustration on page 566.

• Demonstrate entering the information from the materials requisition in the Issued columns of the materials ledger card.

• Demonstrate completing the line on the materials ledger card by recording the balance information.

Recording direct materials on a cost sheet (step 4)

• Continue with the instructor-made transparency of a cost sheet or direct students to the cost sheet in the illustration on page 566 as you demonstrate recording the direct materials on the cost sheet.

• Demonstrate recording the materials requisition number and the total cost of the issued materials on the cost sheet in the Direct Materials columns.

• Point out that the person making the entry would also sign the materials requisition in the Recorded box at the bottom.

- Explain that the time a factory employee works on a job is a direct labor cost to that job.

- Point out that factory employees may work on a number of different jobs in a single shift.

- Explain that factory employees must complete a job-time record for each job worked on during a shift.

- Emphasize that if employees did not complete a job-time record for each job worked on, there would be no way to accurately charge direct labor to specific jobs.

- Explain that the cost accounting department collects all job-time records, calculates the direct labor cost for a job by multiplying the employee hours times the employee rate of pay for each employee for each job, and records the total cost for each job on its cost sheet.

DEMONSTRATE

Completing a job-time record

- Direct students to the job-time record in the illustration as you demonstrate completing a job-time record.

- Point out that a job-time record is completed by each factory employee for each job worked on.

- Point out that the hours an employee works on a job are multiplied times the employee's hourly rate of pay to calculate the direct labor for that employee.

Recording direct labor

- Direct students to the illustration and continue using the instructor-made cost sheet transparency as you demonstrate recording direct labor costs on a cost sheet.

- Demonstrate that the direct labor costs of all employees for a particular job are added together and entered on the cost sheet in the Direct Labor column.

RECORDING DIRECT LABOR ON A COST SHEET

JOB – TIME RECORD

Employee Number __20__   Job Number __791__

Date ____1/17/--____

Time started ____1 p.m.____

Time finished ____5 p.m.____

Total time spent on job . . . . __4.0 hrs.__

1. Each employee prepares a job-time record for each job worked on.

COST SHEET

Job No. ____791____

Item __FM25 Fax Machine__

No. of items __50__

Ordered for __Stock__

Date __January 17, 20--__

Date wanted __January 24, 20--__

Date completed _____

REQ. NO.	AMOUNT	DATE	AMOUNT	DATE	AMOUNT	ITEM	AMOUNT
	DIRECT MATERIALS		DIRECT LABOR			SUMMARY	
773	$ 197.00	Jan. 17	$ 556.00				
774	3,900.00						

2. Record the total of all the job-time records for the job.

Factory employees may work on a number of different jobs each day. Therefore, a job-time record is kept to indicate the amount of time spent on each job. At the end of each day, all job-time records are summarized. The total direct labor cost for each job is recorded on each job's cost sheet.

A job-time record for one FaxaVision employee working 4 hours on Job No. 791 is shown above. All the direct labor costs for Job No. 791 are recorded in the Direct Labor columns of the cost sheet shown above.

STEPS • STEPS • STEPS • STEPS • STEPS • STEPS • STEPS
ASSIGNING DIRECT LABOR TO JOBS

Each factory employee:

1 Prepares a job-time record for each job worked on during the day. The record includes employee number, job number, date, time started, and time finished. The employee calculates and records the total time spent on the job.

Accounting department:

2 Totals the time on job-time records for each job and records the cost in the Direct Labor column of the cost sheet.

©GETTY IMAGES/PHOTODISC

Cost Accounting for a Manufacturing Business

TEACHING STRATEGIES   DIFFERENT LEARNING STYLES

Tactile Learners. The tactile learner learns best by touching or handling objects. Direct students to handle the cost accounting forms and to put their fingers on amounts that they are transferring to other forms in the system.

CALCULATING AND RECORDING FACTORY OVERHEAD

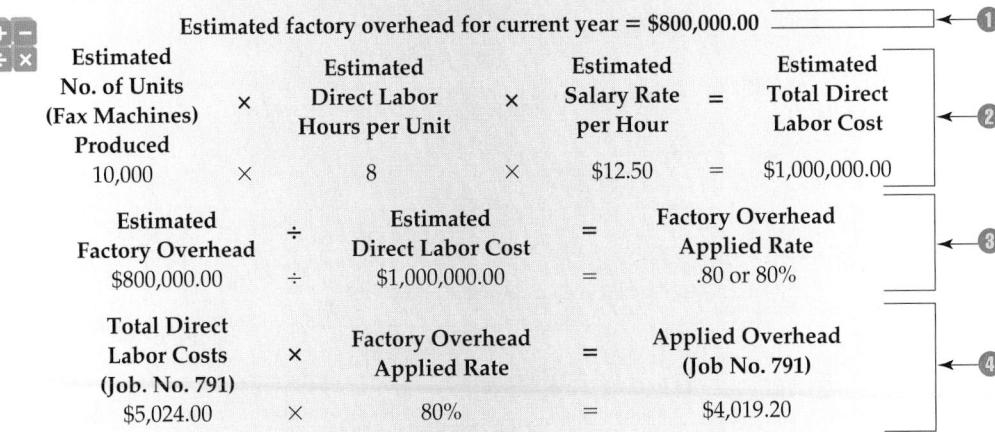

Some factory overhead expenses occur regularly throughout a fiscal period, and others occur irregularly. Many factory overhead expenses are not known until the end of a fiscal period. Therefore, factory overhead expenses normally are charged to jobs by using an application rate based on a known cost such as direct labor. This method applies factory overhead expenses to all jobs and permits a company to record overhead on a cost sheet when a job is completed. The estimated amount of factory overhead recorded on cost sheets is called **applied overhead**. The applied overhead is calculated for Job No. 791 as shown above.

Applied overhead is recorded on cost sheets during the fiscal period and before all factory overhead for the current period is known. [*CONCEPT: Matching Expenses with Revenue*] Therefore, the factory overhead applied rate is calculated before the fiscal periods begins.

STEPS · STEPS · STEPS · STEPS · STEPS · STEPS · STEPS · STEPS · STEPS · STEPS · STEPS ·
DETERMINING A FACTORY OVERHEAD APPLIED RATE

1 Estimate the amount of factory overhead costs for the next fiscal period. Generally, three factors are considered in estimating factory overhead. (a) Amount of factory overhead for the past several fiscal periods. (b) Number of products the factory expects to produce in the next fiscal period. (c) Expected change in unit costs of factory overhead items. FaxaVision expects to produce 10,000 fax machines during the coming year. Considering this volume, previous years' overhead, and anticipated cost increases, FaxaVision estimates factory overhead as $800,000.00.

2 Estimate the number of base units that will be used in the next fiscal period. Base units are usually cost items that can be identified easily. Direct labor cost, direct labor hours, and direct materials cost are common bases. A base unit should be selected that most closely relates to actual overhead costs. FaxaVision uses direct labor cost as a base unit because there is a close relationship between the amount of direct labor cost and factory overhead costs. FaxaVision estimates next year's direct labor cost as $1,000,000.00.

3 Calculate the factory overhead applied rate. Divide estimated factory overhead costs by the estimated base unit. FaxaVision's factory overhead applied rate is 80% of direct labor cost.

4 Calculate and record the amount of applied overhead, *4,019.20*, on the cost sheet for Job No. 791 (total direct labor for Job No. 791, $5,024.00, multiplied by the factory overhead rate, 80%).

- Explain that when a job is completed, the cost sheet columns are totaled and the totals are recorded in the Summary columns.
- Point out that the factory overhead is calculated using the applied rate and recorded in the Summary columns.
- Explain that the final step in completing a cost sheet is to calculate the cost per unit for the job.
- Explain that jobs that have not been completed at the end of a fiscal period need to be totaled to determine the ending inventory for Work in Process in the general ledger.

DEMONSTRATE

Completing a cost sheet

- Continue using the instructor-made transparency of a cost sheet or direct students to the illustration as you demonstrate how to complete a cost sheet.
- Demonstrate totaling the Direct Materials and Direct Labor columns.
- Demonstrate transferring the totals of the Direct Materials and Direct Labor columns to the Summary columns.
- Demonstrate calculating the applied factory overhead by multiplying the applied rate (80%) times the total Direct labor ($5,024). Point out that the method of calculation is also recorded.
- Demonstrate totaling the Summary column to obtain the total cost for the job.
- Demonstrate writing the number of units manufactured.
- Demonstrate calculating the cost per unit by dividing the total costs by the number of units, and recording the amount as the last item in the Summary Amount column.

COMPLETING A JOB COST SHEET

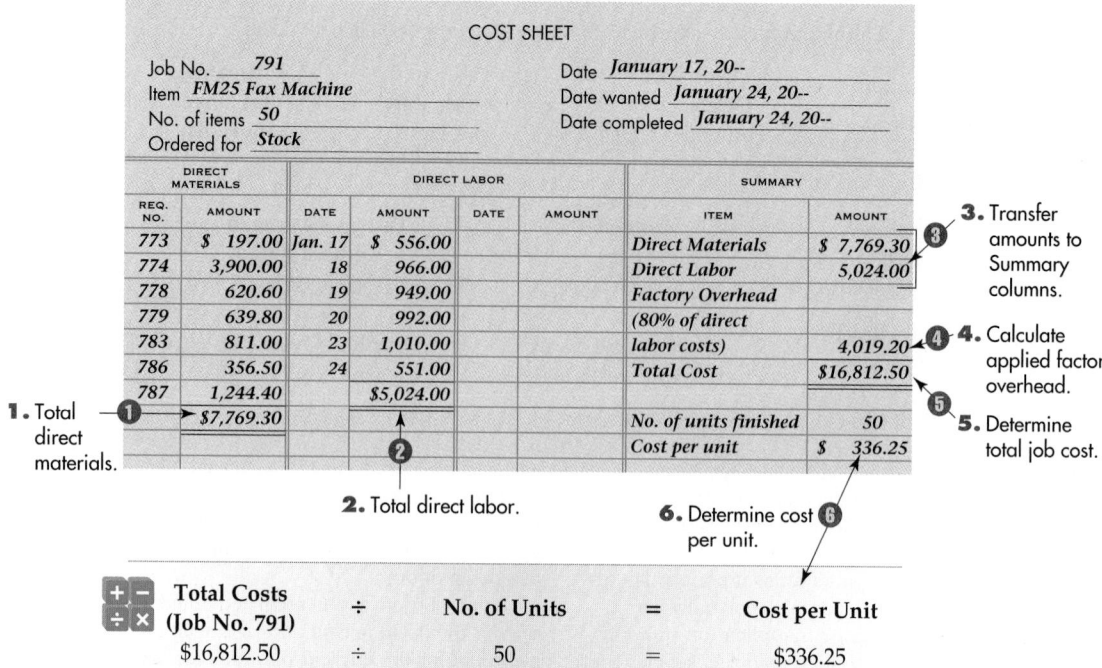

The completed cost sheet for Job No. 791 is shown above. When a job is completed, its total costs are calculated and recorded in the Summary columns of the cost sheet. Direct Materials and Direct Labor columns on the cost sheet are totaled and the totals are recorded in the Summary columns. Then factory overhead is applied to the job. A cost per unit is determined for each job.

Job No. 791 was completed on January 24. At the end of a fiscal period, cost sheets will also exist for jobs that have not been completed. The total value for all cost sheets for work still in process equals the balance of the work in process account in the general ledger. Thus, at the end of a fiscal period, cost sheets for work in process are totaled to determine ending inventory for the general ledger account Work in Process.

STEPS   STEPS • STEPS • STEPS • STEPS • STEPS • STEPS • STEPS • STEPS • STEPS • STEPS

COMPLETING A COST SHEET

1. Total the Direct Materials Amount column, *$7,769.30*.

2. Total the Direct Labor Amount column, *$5,024.00*.

3. Transfer the direct materials and direct labor amounts to the Summary columns.

4. Calculate and record the applied overhead, *$4,019.20*, in the Summary columns. Remember that factory overhead is applied at the rate of 80% of direct labor cost ($5,024.00 × 80% = $4,019.20).

5. Total the three cost elements in the cost sheet's Summary columns, *$16,812.50*. This is the total cost of the job.

6. Determine the cost per unit, *$336.25* ($16,812.50 total cost ÷ 50 units = $336.25).

TEACHING STRATEGIES   DIFFERENT LEARNING STYLES

Kinesthetic Learners. The kinesthetic learner learns best by taking an active part in instruction, usually involving motion. Students can role play different departments (materials, manufacturing, finished goods, and cost account) while the kinesthetic learner makes entries on forms in the working papers and physically delivers them to the appropriate departments.

FINISHED GOODS LEDGER CARD

1. Complete the Manufactured/Received columns.

2. Enter existing inventory balance.

FINISHED GOODS LEDGER CARD

Description **Fax Machine**
Minimum **75**

Stock No. **FM25**
Location **S-5**

	MANUFACTURED/RECEIVED				SHIPPED/ISSUED					BALANCE		
DATE	JOB NO.	QUANTITY	UNIT COST	TOTAL COST	DATE	SALES INVOICE NO.	QUANTITY	UNIT COST	TOTAL COST	DATE	QUANTITY	UNIT COST	TOTAL COST
										20-- Jan. 1	120	335.00	40,200.00
					17	528	20	335.00 ⎫					
							30	339.30 ⎭	16,879.00	17	110	339.30	37,323.00
24	791	50	336.25	16,812.50						24	110	339.30 ⎫	
											50	336.25 ⎭	54,135.50

3. Extend data for Job 791.

4. Calculate total cost.

	Quantity	×	Unit Cost	=	Total Cost
	110	×	$339.30	=	$37,323.00
	50	×	336.25	=	16,812.50
					$54,135.50

When a job is completed, the finished goods are placed in the finished goods stock area. At this time, summary information from the cost sheet is recorded on the completed product's finished goods ledger card. The entry for the completed Job No. 791 is recorded on the finished goods ledger card shown above.

The total value for all finished goods ledger cards equals the finished goods inventory account balance in the general ledger. After FaxaVision's Job No. 791 is completed and recorded, the company has 160 FM25 Fax Machines on hand at a total cost of $54,135.50. This amount will be added to the total costs of all other finished goods still on hand to determine the balance of finished goods inventory in the general ledger.

STEPS

STEPS • STEPS • STEPS • STEPS • STEPS • STEPS • STEPS • STEPS • STEPS • STEPS •

COMPLETING A FINISHED GOODS LEDGER CARD

1 Complete the Manufactured/Received columns of the finished goods ledger card.
a. Record the date the finished goods are transferred to the finished goods inventory, *24*.
b. Enter the Job No., *791*.
c. Enter the quantity, *50*.
d. Enter the unit cost, *336.25*.
e. Enter the total cost, *16,812.50*.

2 Enter the existing inventory in the Balance columns.
a. Enter the date, *24*.
b. Enter the previous quantity of fax machines in inventory, *110*, and the unit cost, *339.30*. Units costs for each job may differ since the amount of direct materials and direct labor used may vary. Therefore, the unit costs for each job are kept separate.

3 Extend the quantity, *50*, and the unit cost, *336.25*, for Job 791.

4 Calculate the total cost of all goods in inventory, *54,135.50*. Although unit costs are kept separate, the total cost balance is combined for all units in the finished goods inventory. FaxaVision uses the first-in, first-out inventory method. Thus, the cost recorded first is the cost removed from inventory first when units are sold.

Maintaining Manufacturing Records

Lesson 19-2   **571**

571

GUIDED PRACTICE

Term Review

Call on students to define the term in the Term Review. Ask the class if the definition is correct and whether the complete definition has been given or if anything needs to be added. The suggested definition is given in the Glossary.

Audit Your Understanding

Call on students to answer the Audit Your Understanding questions. Ask the class if the answers are correct and/or complete. Answers are given in Appendix E of the textbook.

Work Together

- Have students write the solution to the Work Together problems as you guide the class through the problem.
- Discuss each step and when the class is in agreement, direct students to write the solution in the *Working Papers*.

INDEPENDENT PRACTICE

On Your Own

- Assign the On Your Own problem to be worked independently.
- Use the Ongoing Assessment techniques to diagnose student understanding.

Application Problems

- Assign Application Problem 19-2: Classifying manufacturing costs and determining which ledger to use for initial recording.
- Assign Application Problem 19-3: Calculating factory overhead applied rate.
- Assign Application Problem 19-4: Preparing a cost sheet.
- Assign Application Problem 19-5: Recording entries in a finished goods ledger.

ENRICH

- Assign Cases for Critical Thinking 2.
- Students can use the QuickBooks data files to automate Application Problem 19-5.

CLOSE

- Ask students to briefly summarize the procedures for keeping cost records.

572

• term review

applied overhead

• audit your understanding

1. What are the four sets of columns on a materials ledger card?
2. What is the name of the form used to authorize a seller to deliver goods with payment to be made later?
3. What is the purpose of the materials requisition?
4. What is the formula for calculating the factory overhead applied rate?
5. Why are unit costs kept separate on the finished goods ledger card?

• work together 19-2

Determining total cost and unit cost for a job and determining total cost for a finished item

A cost sheet and partial finished goods ledger card for Leather Originals, a manufacturer of leather furniture, are provided in the *Working Papers*. Your instructor will guide you through the following examples.

1. Complete the cost sheet for Job No. 657 by filling in the Summary columns. Factory overhead is applied based on direct labor hours. Estimated factory overhead for the period was $3,000,000. The number of estimated direct labor hours was 200,000. A total of 530 direct labor hours was used on Job No. 657.
2. Calculate a new balance for item K-39 sofa on the partial finished goods ledger card.

• on your own 19-2

Determining total cost and unit cost for a job and determining total cost for a finished item

A cost sheet and partial finished goods ledger card for Leather Originals, a manufacturer of leather furniture, are provided in the *Working Papers*. Work independently to complete the following problem.

1. Complete the cost sheet for Job No. 711 by filling in the Summary columns. Factory overhead is applied based on direct labor hours. Estimated factory overhead for the period was $3,000,000. The number of estimated direct labor hours was 200,000. A total of 743 direct labor hours was used on Job No. 711.
2. Calculate a new balance for item S-68 chair on the partial finished goods ledger card.

SUMMARY

After completing this chapter, you can

1. Define accounting terms related to cost accounting for a manufacturing business.

2. Identify accounting concepts and practices related to cost accounting for a manufacturing business.

3. Identify the elements of manufacturing costs: (1) direct materials, (2) direct labor, and (3) factory overhead.

4. Identify the flow of costs through the manufacturing process.

5. Prepare selected ledgers and cost sheets for a manufacturing business.

Explore Accounting

EXPLORE ACCOUNTING • EXPLORE ACCOUNTING • EXPLORE ACCOUN

Equivalent Units of Production

Two general manufacturing costing methods exist: job order costing illustrated in this chapter and process costing.

Process costing is useful when a single production process uses a continuous flow of inputs to produce the same product. To illustrate process costing, assume that Hubble Inc. began the month with 200 televisions in production. Each unit is estimated to be 20% complete as to labor. During the month, Hubble began 1,000 units and completed 800 units. At the end of the month, the 400 units in production were 70% complete. Management budgeted $40.00 of direct labor per unit. During May, the company incurred $40,000 of direct labor. If the 800 completed units are used as a measure, it would appear that the laborers have not been efficient ($40,000 ÷ 800 = $50.00 per unit).

A better number would recognize the work performed on units incomplete at the end of the

month. An estimate of the number of units that could be started and completed during a period is known as the equivalent units of production (EUP). Hubble calculates EUP as shown below.

The workers were actually more efficient than projected in the budget ($40,000 ÷ 1,040 EUP = $38.46).

Required:

Determine the equivalent cost per unit of labor for the following problem. Nelson Company began the month with 600 units in production, each unit 60% complete as to labor. During the current month, these units were completed. During the month, Nelson also started 2,000 units and completed 1,800 units. At the end of the month, the 200 units in production were 10% complete. Labor costs, estimated to be $9.00 per unit, were actually $20,000.

Beginning Inventory	200 units	×	80%	=	160 EUP
Started and Completed	600 units	×	100%	=	600 EUP
Started and in Process	400 units	×	70%	=	280 EUP
Total EUP					1,1040 EUP

EXPLORE ACCOUNTING
EXPLORE ACCOUNTING

Students first determine equivalent units of production (EUP) and then divide the actual labor cost for the month by the EUP. EUP for the month were 2,060, determined as follows:

Beginning inventory	600 units	×	40%	=	240 EUP
Started and completed	1,800 units	×	100%	=	1,800 EUP
Started and in process	200 units	×	10%	=	20 EUP
Total EUP					2,060 EUP

Therefore, the equivalent cost per unit for the month is $9.71 *($20,000 ÷ 2,060 EUP)*. The workers were less efficient for the month than budgeted.

PUTTING IT ALL TOGETHER

• Review the Chapter Summary.

• Ask students to prepare a list of the new concepts introduced in this chapter.

• Discuss the methods presented in this chapter to keep records for manufacturing costs.

INDEPENDENT PRACTICE

• Assign Mastery Problem 19-6 to students who need the reinforcement of a problem that combines all concepts from the chapter in one problem; this will be most students.

• Assign Challenge Problem 19-7 to accelerated students who do not require the reinforcement of the mastery problem.

• Assign Study Guide Chapter 19.

• Students can access Personal Trainer to work end-of-chapter problems on the computer.

• Students can access the Xtra! Web Site for the Xtra! Review and Quizzing.

• Students can access the Student Companion CD for additional review material.

ONGOING ASSESSMENT

Review solutions to the assigned problems in class, diagnosing trouble spots.

RETEACH

• Call on students to describe how they avoid the trouble spots diagnosed.

• Use reteaching suggestions from lesson plans as required.

• Assign Recycling Problem 19-1 if needed.

ENRICH

• Assign the Explore Accounting Feature. Ask students to share the information they have gathered in a report to the class.

• Students can access the Xtra! Web Site for the Xtra! Enrichment material.

• Assign Applied Communication.

• Assign the SCANS Workplace Competency.

• Assign Auditing for Errors.

• Assign Analyzing Costco's Financial Statements.

• Assign the Automated Accounting feature on pages 580–581.

19-1 APPLICATION PROBLEM

Classifying manufacturing costs and determining which ledger to use for initial recording

Krasnoy Tire, a maker of tires for cars, trucks, and tractors, is trying to determine how to account for various factory costs. The costs include the following:
a. Wages earned by a factory supervisor.
b. Fringe benefits of the factory supervisor.
c. The rent expense of company headquarters, which is located 10 miles from the factory.
d. Rubber used in the production of tires.
e. The property taxes of the factory.
f. Wages earned by an employee working on the production of tires.
g. Inexpensive glue used sparingly in the production of tires.
h. A cleaning solvent used to clean production machinery.
i. Wages earned by an employee who inspects finished tires before they leave the factory.
j. Wages earned by a marketing manager at company headquarters.

Instructions:
1. For each of the costs above, determine whether the cost should be classified as direct materials, direct labor, factory overhead, or none. Hint: Only costs related to the factory or to production should be included as manufacturing costs.
2. Specify the subsidiary ledger (materials ledger, cost ledger, finished goods ledger) in which the cost is first recorded.

19-2 APPLICATION PROBLEM

Classifying manufacturing costs and determining which ledger to use for initial recording

Wilmington, Inc., manufactures heating systems. The company maintains a materials ledger for all direct materials.

Transactions:

Oct.		
	1.	Ordered 500 T-5 thermostats. Purchase Order No. 83.
	3.	Issued 110 T-5 thermostats. Materials Requisition No. 196.
	4.	Issued 45 T-5 thermostats. Materials Requisition No. 200.
	7.	Received 500 T-5 thermostats; unit price $39.50. Purchase Order No. 83.
	12.	Issued 220 T-5 thermostats. Materials Requisition No. 207.
	17.	Issued 85 T-5 thermostats. Materials Requisition No. 218.
	29.	Issued 55 T-5 thermostats. Materials Requisition No. 231.
	29.	Ordered 500 T-5 thermostats. Purchase Order No. 88.

Instructions:
1. Prepare a materials ledger card for T-5 thermostats. The thermostat is Account No. 76. Reorder quantity is set at 500 thermostats, minimum at 175 thermostats. Inventory location is Area A18.
2. Record the beginning balance on October 1 of the current year of 175 T-5 thermostats at a unit price of $39.50.
3. Record the transactions.

19-3 APPLICATION PROBLEM
Calculating factory overhead applied rate

Application Problem 19-3
Factory overhead applied rate, 80%.

AutoAnswer, Inc., a manufacturer of telephone answering machines, uses a factory overhead applied rate to charge overhead costs to its manufactured products.

The company manager estimates that AutoAnswer will manufacture 30,000 units next year. For this amount of production, the cost accountant estimates total factory overhead costs to be $336,000.00. Estimated direct labor cost for next year is $420,000.00.

Instructions:
Calculate AutoAnswer's factory overhead applied rate for next year as a percentage of direct labor cost.

19-4 APPLICATION PROBLEM
Preparing a cost sheet

Application Problem 19-4
Direct materials, 1,247.25; direct labor, 1,617.00; factory overhead, 1,212.75. Units finished, 45; 90.60 each.

On July 1, Esquire Tables, Inc., began work on Job No. 309. The order is for 45 No. ET42 game tables for stock; date wanted is July 10.

Transactions:

July	1.	Direct material, $641.25. Materials Requisition No. 432.
	1.	Direct labor, $465.00. Daily summary of job-time records.
	2.	Direct materials, $345.00. Materials Requisition No. 438.
	2.	Direct labor, $364.50. Daily summary of job-time records.
	3.	Direct labor, $301.50. Daily summary of job-time records.
	5.	Direct materials, $261.00. Materials Requisition No. 447.
	5.	Direct labor, $285.00. Daily summary of job-time records.
	8.	Direct labor, $201.00. Daily summary of job-time records.

Instructions:
1. Open a cost sheet and record the transactions.
2. Complete the cost sheet, recording factory overhead at the applied rate of 75% of direct labor costs.

19-5 APPLICATION PROBLEM
Recording entries in a finished goods ledger

Application Problem 19-5
April 30 balance: 90 units at 9.00 each; 100 units at 8.60 each; and 120 units at 8.85 each; finished goods final total, 2,732.00.

Decatur Industries, Inc., maintains a finished goods ledger for all of its manufactured products.

Transactions:

Apr.	2.	Received from production department 210 C45 bats at a unit cost of $8.80. Job No. 315.
	8.	Mike's Place, a store selling baseball equipment, cards, and memorabilia, ordered 90 C45 bats. Sales Invoice No. 511.
	9.	Production department completed 140 C45 bats and sent them to finished goods inventory. The unit cost for Job No. 334 was $9.00.
	14.	Sports Unlimited, a wholesale distributor of sports equipment, purchased 75 C45 bats. Sales Invoice No. 521.
	16.	Job No. 339 was completed, with 100 C45 bats sent to finished goods inventory. The unit cost was $8.60.
	23.	Mike's Place purchased 300 C45 bats. Sales Invoice No. 536.
	27.	Sold 75 bats to The Grand Old Game, a baseball retailer. Sales Invoice No. 543.
	28.	Received from production department 120 C45 bats at a unit cost of $8.85. Job No. 363.

TEACHING STRATEGIES COOPERATIVE LEARNING

Divide the class into groups of three or four students each. Have each group discuss and prepare a list of manufacturing businesses in the local community. Each group appoints a leader who will present the list and products being manufactured to the class. This cooperative learning activity should not take more than 15–20 minutes of class time.

Instructions:

1. Prepare a finished goods ledger card for stock no. C45 baseball bats. Minimum quantity is set at 250 units. Inventory location is Area R-12.
2. Record the beginning balance on April 1 of the current year for 280 C45 baseball bats at a unit cost of $8.70. Decatur Industries uses the first-in, first-out method to record inventory costs.
3. Record the transactions.

19-6 MASTERY PROBLEM

Preparing cost records

Gemini manufactures athletic shoes. The company records manufacturing costs by job number and uses a factory overhead applied rate to charge overhead costs to its products.

The company estimates Gemini will manufacture 50,000 shoes next year. For this amount of production, total factory overhead is estimated to be $398,800.00. Estimated direct labor costs for next year are $498,500.00.

Instructions:

1. Calculate Gemini's factory overhead applied rate for next year as a percentage of direct labor cost.

On May 3, Gemini began work on Job No. 283. The order is for 150 pairs of No. 52L athletic shoes for stock; date wanted May 13.

2. Open a cost sheet for Job No. 283 and record the following items.

May	3.	Direct materials, $862.50. Materials Requisition No. 392.
	3.	Direct labor, $129.00. Daily summary of job-time records.
	4.	Direct labor, $248.00. Daily summary of job-time records.
	5.	Direct materials, $472.50. Materials Requisition No. 399.
	5.	Direct labor, $175.00. Daily summary of job-time records.
	6.	Direct labor, $192.00. Daily summary of job-time records.
	7.	Direct labor, $295.00. Daily summary of job-time records.
	10.	Direct materials, $360.00. Materials Requisition No. 428.
	10.	Direct labor, $165.00. Daily summary of job-time records.
	11.	Direct labor, $152.00. Daily summary of job-time records.
	12.	Direct labor, $124.00. Daily summary of job-time records.

3. Complete the cost sheet, recording factory overhead at the rate calculated in Instruction 1.
4. Prepare a finished goods ledger card for Stock No. 52L athletic shoes. Minimum quantity is set at 100. Inventory location is Area C-50.
5. Record on the finished goods ledger card the beginning balance on May 1. The May 1 balance of 52L athletic shoes is 140 units at a unit cost of $30.45. Gemini uses the first-in, first-out method to record inventory costs.
6. Record the following transactions on the finished goods ledger card for 52L athletic shoes.

May	5.	Sold 60 pairs of 52L athletic shoes. Sales Invoice No. 633.
	12.	Received 150 pairs of 52L athletic shoes. Record cost from cost sheet for Job No. 283.
	18.	Sold 30 pairs of 52L athletic shoes. Sales Invoice No. 652.

Mastery Problem 19-6

1. Factory overhead applied rate, 80%.

3. Direct Materials, 1,695.00; direct labor, 1,480.00; factory overhead, 1,184.00. Units finished, 150; 29.06 each.

6. May 18 balance: 50 units at 30.45 each and 150 units at 29.06 each; finished goods final total, 5,881.50.

APPLIED SKILLS WRITING ACROSS THE CURRICULUM

Writing Paragraphs and Short Essays. The Cases for Critical Thinking are short, practical applications of the accounting principles developed in the chapter. Some cases are planned to present problems related to the chapter but not specifically discussed and answered in the chapter. These cases present an opportunity for critical thinking and decision making. These cases also require more than a short objective-type response. Therefore, they provide ideal practice in writing paragraphs and short essays.

19-7 CHALLENGE PROBLEM

Preparing cost records

Sea Explor manufactures deep-sea diving suits. The company records manufacturing costs by job number and uses a factory overhead applied rate to charge overhead costs to its products.

Sea Explor estimates they will manufacture 10,000 diving suits next year. For this amount of production, total factory overhead is estimated to be $600,000.00. Estimated direct materials costs for next year are $80.00 for each suit manufactured. Estimated direct labor for next year is 4 labor hours for each suit at $12.50 per hour.

Instructions:

1. Calculate Sea Explor's factory overhead applied rate for next year for each of the following three bases. (a) Direct materials cost. (b) Direct labor cost. (c) Direct labor hours.

On May 9, Sea Explor began work on Job No. 365. The order is for 55 SE80 diving suits for stock; date wanted May 19.

2. Open a cost sheet for Job No. 365 and record the following items.

May	9.	Direct materials, $1,160.50. Materials Requisition No. 421.
	9.	Direct labor, $274.75. Daily summary of job-time records.
	10.	Direct labor, $441.00. Daily summary of job-time records.
	11.	Direct materials, $2,321.00. Materials Requisition No. 430.
	11.	Direct labor, $392.00. Daily summary of job-time records.
	12.	Direct labor, $423.00. Daily summary of job-time records.
	13.	Direct labor, $440.00. Daily summary of job-time records.
	16.	Direct materials, $1,017.50. Materials Requisition No. 438.
	16.	Direct labor, $370.00. Daily summary of job-time records.
	17.	Direct labor, $352.00. Daily summary of job-time records.
	18.	Direct labor, $181.00. Daily summary of job-time records.

3. Complete the cost sheet, recording factory overhead at the direct materials cost rate calculated in Instruction 1.
4. Prepare a finished goods ledger card for Stock No. SE80 diving suit. Minimum quantity is set at 30. Inventory location is Area J16.
5. Record on the finished goods ledger card the beginning balance on May 1. The May 1 balance of SE80 diving suits is 40 units at a unit cost of $191.50. Sea Explor uses the last-in, first-out method to record inventory costs.
6. Record the following transactions on the finished goods ledger card for SE80 diving suits.

May	11.	Sold 10 SE80 diving suits. Sales Invoice No. 450.
	18.	Received 55 SE80 diving suits. Record cost from cost sheet for Job No. 365.
	23.	Sold 30 SE80 diving suits. Sales Invoice No. 494.
	25.	Sold 25 SE80 diving suits. Sales Invoice No. 523.

APPLIED SKILLS   LANGUAGE ARTS

Paraphrasing, Writing Complete Sentences, and Identifying Verbs. For additional practice in language arts skills, direct students to answer the Applied Communication activity in their own words and in complete sentences. To further practice language arts skills, ask students to underline all verbs in their answers.

APPLIED COMMUNICATION

Suggest that students use the library or the Internet to research bar code technology. They might also get useful information from local businesses. In addition to grading for clarity and mechanics, the report should also be evaluated on how well the student has supported the recommendation on bar codes for the situation described.

CASES FOR CRITICAL THINKING

Case 1

Several cost items are incorrectly classified. Correct classifications with reasons follow: (1) *Direct Materials*. The wood is a part of the finished product. (2) *Factory Overhead*. Insurance premiums are not part of the finished product. (3) *Direct Labor*. Time of the fan assembler is devoted to actual work on the finished product. (4) *Direct Materials*. The bolts are part of the finished product. However, because of their relatively small part of materials cost, they also may be classified as factory overhead. (5) *Factory Overhead*. The factory supervisor does not work directly on the finished product. (6) *Factory Overhead*. The brooms are not part of the finished product. (7) *Factory Overhead*. The packer does not work directly on the finished product. (8) *Direct Materials*. The paint and stain are part of the finished product. If the paint and stain are a relatively small part of the product's cost, they may be classified as factory overhead.

Case 2

Since Astro Company has found that total factory overhead is usually about 60% of total direct labor cost, applying factory overhead to each job at 60% of total direct labor cost on that job provides an easy and relatively accurate way of applying factory overhead. However, if the records are to be departmentalized, then a different method of applying factory overhead should be used since there are such wide variations in factory overhead expenses applicable to each department. Each factory overhead expense should be distributed to the three departments on an equitable basis, such as depreciation expense based on the value of the machinery in the department or rent expense based on the space occupied by the department.

• applied communication

You are appointed to participate on a time-efficiency team. The team includes factory workers, supervisors, and a representative from the accounting department. Currently the factory workers record their time on job–time sheets. They also calculate the total time worked on each job. A worker may work on three or four jobs each day. The accounting department receives about 200 job–time sheets each day. A clerk verifies the workers' calculations on the job–time records. Any changes to the total time must be initialed by a supervisor.

Required:

The company has appointed your team to explore ways to automate the time recording process. Your job on the team is to explore bar code technology. Write a report on bar code technology. Make a recommendation to the team indicating whether bar codes could be used to replace the job–time sheets.

• cases for critical thinking

Case 1

Century Fan Company manufactures ceiling fans. During the current year, payments were made for the following items. A new clerk classified the cost items. Are the cost items classified correctly? If not, give the correct classification and explain the reason for your corrected classification.

1. Wood to be used for fan blades. (Factory Overhead)
2. Insurance premium on the factory building. (Direct Materials)
3. Salary of factory workers assembling fans. (Factory Overhead)
4. Bolts used in assembling the fans. (Direct Materials)
5. Salary of factory supervisor. (Direct Labor)
6. Brooms used to sweep the factory floors. (Direct Materials)
7. Salary of packer who packs fan crates for shipping. (Direct Labor)
8. Paint and stain to be used on the fans. (Direct Materials)

Case 2

Astro Company has found that total factory overhead is usually about 60% of direct labor cost. The business manufactures one product that is processed in three different manufacturing departments: A, B, and C. In Department A, much expensive machinery is used. In Department B, some machinery is used. In Department C, virtually no machinery is used, all the work being manual work. There is a great difference in the amount of time required to process various jobs in the different departments. Under these circumstances do you believe that the company should charge factory overhead to each job at the rate of 60% of direct labor? If not, what would you recommend?

• SCANS workplace competency

Interpersonal Competency: Negotiating

Concept: Companies value employees who are skillful at working toward an agreement that involves exchanging specific resources or resolving divergent interests. Such individuals set attainable goals, research the history of the conflict, present arguments objectively, reflect on what has been stated, clarify problems, resolve conflicts, adjust quickly to new ideas, propose options, and make reasonable compromises.

Application: Prepare a new bell schedule or annual calendar for your school. Explain and justify your position. Discuss your views with the school's administration.

SCANS WORKPLACE COMPETENCY

Recent brain research supports late start times for teenagers. Some schools now start the school year earlier in order to conduct finals before Christmas vacation. Most bell schedules and school calendars are established based on the needs of adults rather than those of adolescents.

• auditing for errors

Advanced Systems is a new company that will produce a line of high-quality wood computer desks. The company's management is working on its accounting system and has prepared the following policy for classifying manufacturing costs. Determine whether any item in the policy violates generally accepted accounting principles.

Description	Direct Materials	Direct Labor	Overhead		
			Indirect Material	Indirect Labor	Other
Advertising and promotion					X
Delivery of finished goods to customer		X			
Depreciation of equipment					X
Heat, power, and light					X
Inspector wages		X			
Insurance on manufacturing building					X
Maintenance wages				X	
Packing materials			X		
Production wages		X			
Sandpaper	X				
Screws			X		
Supervisor salaries				X	
Varnish	X				
Wood	X				

• analyzing Costco's financial statements

Costco's selling, general, and administrative expenses (SG&A expenses) remained steady between 8.7% to 8.8% of net sales during fiscal years 1994 and 2000. For the past three years, however, these expenses have risen to between 9.2% and 9.8% of sales. Citing rising costs for healthcare, workers' compensation, and salaries, Costco's top officers state in their 2003 annual report, "These figures are unacceptable, and we are working hard to reverse this trend."

Trends in healthcare costs may prevent Costco from ever reducing SG&A expenses to 8.7% on net sales. Suppose Costco management sets a goal to reduce SG&A costs to 9.4% in 2004. Evaluate the impact this reduction would have had on the 2003 financial statements.

Instructions:
Calculate the following items, rounding amounts to the nearest million dollars:

1. Calculate how much SG&A expenses would have been in 2003 if Costco had been able to limit these expenses to 9.4% of net sales. Round your answer to the nearest million dollars.

2. Calculate the increase in 2003 income before federal income taxes that would result from lowering SG&A expenses to 9.4% of net sales.

3. Costco's effective tax rate was 37.75% in 2003, meaning that $37.75 of taxes were paid on every $100.00 of income before federal income taxes. Calculate the increase in net income of the reduction in SG&A expenses.

4. Calculate the increase in the earnings per share. Obtain the number of common shares in the Per Share Data-Diluted section of the ten-year operating and financial highlights on pages B-2–B-3 in Appendix B of this textbook.

5. Do you agree with the statement made by Costco's top officers? How do you believe their recognition of this problem will be perceived by current and potential investors? Support your answer.

AUDITING FOR ERRORS

1. Advertising and promotion is a selling expense.
2. Delivery of finished goods to customer is a selling expense.
3. Packing materials is a direct material.
4. Sandpaper is an indirect material.

ANALYZING COSTCO'S FINANCIAL STATEMENTS

1. $41,693,000,000 \times 9.4\% = \$3,919,000,000$.
2. $\$4,097,000,000 - \$3,919,000,000 = \$178,000,000$.
3. $\$178,000,000 \times (1 - 37.75\%) = \$111,000,000$.
4. $\$111,000,000/479,326,000 = \$0.23$.
5. Yes, earnings per share could be increased substantially if the company could return to having SGA expenses equal to 9.4% of net sales. Most investors will applaud the company for its willingness to admit there is a problem, thus providing more confidence that the company can lower these costs.

TEACHING STRATEGIES   PORTFOLIO ASSESSMENT

Proper and accurate accounting for manufacturing costs is critical to a business because so many decisions are based on this information. If the information is incorrect, poor decisions may result and could cause a business to fail. Students should emphasize their learning of this topic by selecting an example of a comprehensive sample of their work in this chapter, either the mastery problem or a problem from a test to include in their portfolio. A copy of the Portfolio Assessment form (blackline master in the Teacher's Resource Guide; also on the Student Companion CD) should be completed by the student and the Description section should include any comments regarding how the student mastered these concepts and procedures.

- Explain that the Automated Accounting software is not designed to provide every necessary form and report. Therefore, other forms may have to be prepared in spreadsheet software.
- Explain that electronic spreadsheets can be designed to replace most manually prepared documents, such as a cost sheet.
- Explain that formulas in the spreadsheet eliminate the need for calculations. Therefore, the spreadsheet can be more efficient to complete and may ensure a higher level of accuracy.
- Point out that the first step in creating a form on an electronic spreadsheet is to enter the labels contained on the document.
- Explain that it is important to check all formulas for accuracy before using the spreadsheet form.

DEMONSTRATE

The Auditing Toolbar

- Demonstrate that the Auditing Toolbar contains a series of tools that visually track the cells used by a formula. This feature is designed to detect errors.

Automated Accounting

Replacing Written Documents with Electronic Spreadsheets

The *Automated Accounting* software is not designed to provide every form and report a company may need. Reports generated in *Automated Accounting* may be copied and pasted into a spreadsheet for further use and analysis. Other forms may need to be prepared in spreadsheet software.

The electronic spreadsheet offers businesses the opportunity to increase the efficiency of employees who perform repetitive accounting tasks. Electronic spreadsheets can be designed to replace most manually prepared documents, such as a cost sheet. Formulas stored in the spreadsheet eliminate the need for the employee to make calculations and record the amount in the form. As a result, a spreadsheet form can be more efficient to complete and ensure a higher level of accuracy.

The first step in creating a form on an electronic spreadsheet is to enter the labels contained on the document. The columnar structure of the electronic spreadsheet may require the form to differ slightly from the original paper version. Making as few changes as possible in the style and layout will enable employees to quickly adapt to using a spreadsheet version of the form.

Before using the spreadsheet form, it is important to check all formulas for accuracy. Entering the data for a verified manual document should generate the same values. The spreadsheet form shown below results in the same cost per unit as the cost sheet on page 570.

The Auditing Toolbar

Microsoft Excel contains a feature especially designed to detect errors. The auditing toolbar (View>>Toolbars>>Formula Auditing) contains a series of tools that visually track the cells used by a formula. With the cell pointer on the total of direct material in H10, selecting Trace Precedents identifies the range of cells included in the cell's sum function. Notice that the blue outline surrounding cells B10:B16 only includes the seven direct material amounts for Job No. 791. Although this job's cost per unit calculated correctly, the cost per unit of any job having more than seven requisitions, entered in cells B17:B27, would be incorrectly excluded. The auditing feature alerts the spreadsheet designer of the error so that the function at H10 can be modified to include the entire range of cells B10:B27.

Protecting Formulas

Once the accuracy of the spreadsheet form has been verified, steps need to be taken to ensure that its accuracy is not compromised by an employee entering data where a formula is stored.

Any cell where the employee should enter data is known as an *input cell*. Changing the color of input cells (using the Font Color button on the Formatting toolbar) visually assists the employee in entering data in the correct cells. Entering a symbol, such as a question mark, in selected input cells also directs the employee's attention to these cells. In the spreadsheet below, input cells are shown in blue font with question marks.

Although the font color is helpful, cells containing formulas can be protected from being accidentally altered or erased. Protection of cells is a two-step process.

1. Change the properties of input cells to allow input (Format>>Cells>>Protection and remove the check from the Locked item). This command unlocks the input cells.

2. Turn on spreadsheet protection (Tools>> Protection>>Protect Sheet), protecting all the cells on the spreadsheet except the input cells unlocked in the previous step.

The spreadsheet form is now ready to be saved and used to create new documents. The extra time devoted to incorporating these modifications in spreadsheet forms helps ensure that accounting transactions and decisions are based on accurate data.

EXPLAIN

- Explain that once the accuracy of the spreadsheet form has been verified, it must not be compromised by entering data where a formula is stored.

- Explain that any cell where data should be entered is known as an *input cell*.

- Point out that changing the color of input cells visually assists an employee in entering data in the correct cells.

- Explain that cells containing formulas can be protected from being accidentally altered or erased.

DEMONSTRATE

Protecting formulas

- Demonstrate changing the properties of input cells to allow input, using the command that unlocks the input cells.

- Demonstrate turning on spreadsheet protection, protecting all the cells on the spreadsheet except the input cells unlocked in the previous step.

Accounting Transactions and Financial

	SCOPE & SEQUENCE	
	NEW	**REVIEW/ EXTENSION**
Introduce the Chapter	✓	
Lesson 20-1 Journalizing Manufacturing Accounting Transactions		
Journalizing manufacturing accounting transactions		✓
Recording materials transactions	✓	
Recording payroll transactions		✓
Recording factory overhead transactions	✓	
Overapplied and underapplied factory overhead	✓	
Recording finished goods transactions	✓	
Recording sales and cost of goods sold transactions		✓
Lesson 20-2 Preparing End-of-Fiscal-Period Statements		
Work sheet for a manufacturing business		✓
Statement of cost of goods manufactured	✓	
Income statement for a manufacturing business		✓
Balance sheet for a manufacturing business		✓
Putting It All Together		

ENHANCING
SPECIAL FEATURES

- Accounting in the Real World: Toyota

- Making Ethical Decisions: Fair Competition
- Global Perspective: International Banking
- Case for Critical Thinking
- Careers in Accounting

- Explore Accounting
- Xtra! Web Site: Xtra! Enrichment
- Applied Communication
- SCANS Workplace Competency
- Graphing Workshop
- Analyzing Costco's Financial Statements

Reporting for a Manufacturing Business

INSTRUCTION		PRACTICE AND ASSESSMENT		
TECHNOLOGY AND MEDIA	**TEACHING STRATEGIES**	**GUIDED PRACTICE**	**INDEPENDENT PRACTICE**	**RETEACHING AND ENRICHMENT**
• Internet Research Activity • Accounting Xtra! Web Site	• Software Focus			
• Instructor's Resource CD: PowerPoint Slides • Xtra! Web Site: Xtra! Study Tools • Blackline Masters: 5-Column Cash Payments Journal, Materials Purchases Journal, and General Journal • Personal Trainer • Peachtree and QuickBooks	• Auditory Learner • Kinesthetic Learner • Limited English Proficiency (LEP) Students • Print Learner • Tactile Learner • Expanding Beyond the Classroom	• Terms Review • Audit Your Understanding • Work Together 20-1	• On Your Own 20-1 • Application Problems 20-1 and 20-2 • Ongoing Assessment, p. 591 • Personal Trainer • Xtra! Web Site: Xtra! Study Tools	• Reteach, p. 591 • Enrich, p. 593 • Peachtree and QuickBooks
• Instructor's Resource CD: PowerPoint Slides • Xtra! Web Site: Xtra! Study Tools • Blackline Masters: 1-Column Statement Paper, 3-Column Income Statement with % of Net Sales Column, and 3-Column Statement Paper • Personal Trainer	• Limited English Proficiency (LEP) Students • Specific Learning Disability (SLD) Students • Visual Learner	• Term Review • Audit Your Understanding • Work Together 20-2	• On Your Own 20-2 • Application Problem 20-3 • Ongoing Assessment, p. 600 • Personal Trainer • Xtra! Web Site: Xtra! Study Tools	• Reteach, p. 600 • Enrich, p. 601
• Automated Accounting • Peachtree • Personal Trainer • Xtra! Web Site: Xtra! Review, Quizzing, and Enrichment • Student Companion CD	• Expanding Beyond the Classroom • Applied Skills: Language Arts • Applied Skills: Writing Across the Curriculum		• Mastery Problem 20-4 • Personal Trainer • Xtra! Web Site: Xtra! Review and Quizzing • Study Guide 20 • Student Companion CD • Chapter 20 Test • ExamView Chapter 20 • Portfolio Assessment	• Challenge Problem 20-5 • Reteach, p. 602 • Enrich, p. 602 • Recycling Problem 20-1 • Automated Accounting • Peachtree • Xtra! Web Site: Xtra! Enrichment

OBJECTIVES & TERMS

CHAPTER 20

Accounting Transactions and Financial Reporting for a Manufacturing Business

After studying Chapter 20, you will be able to:

1. Define accounting terms related to accounting transactions and financial reporting for a manufacturing business.

2. Identify accounting concepts and practices related to accounting transactions and financial reporting for a manufacturing business.

3. Journalize transactions for a manufacturing business.

4. Prepare selected financial statements for a manufacturing business.

- underapplied overhead
- overapplied overhead

- statement of cost of goods manufactured

Point Your Browser
accountingxtra.swlearning.com

582

accounting in the real world

• Toyota

©LUCAS SCHIFRES/LANDOV

GAAP AT TOYOTA

Toyota, the number-two automaker, is an international company with sales and production facilities in many countries. Yet a quick review of its financial statements indicates that this Japanese company has not strayed from its Japanese roots. Its latest financial statements indicate that the company had sales exceeding 17 trillion yen, or ¥17,000,000,000,000. That's roughly $150 billion U.S. dollars.

Toyota has historically prepared two sets of financial statements: one in accordance with generally accepted accounting principles (GAAP) in Japan, the other in accordance with generally accepted accounting principles in the United States (U.S. GAAP). Beginning with its 2004 report, Toyota prepared its financial statement only in accordance with U.S. GAAP. The company believed the change would make its financial statements easier to understand and would quicken the preparation process.

The new financial statements continue to be stated in yen. However, the accounting principles used to prepare the financial statements follow U.S. GAAP.

Critical Thinking

1. How should Toyota's financial statements, stated in yen, affect your ability to understand the reported financial information?
2. Where in the annual report do you think Toyota informs the reader of the financial statements that the statements are prepared in accordance with U.S. GAAP?

Today
accountingxtra.swlearning.com

Source: www.toyota.com/about/news/corporate/2004/05/11-1-finreport.html

internet activity

DIVIDENDS PAID BY CORPORATIONS

Go to the homepage for Kellogg's (www.kelloggs.com) and General Mills (www.generalmills.com). Search the site for information about dividends paid.

Instructions

1. List the date and the amount of the most recent dividend paid by Kellogg's.

2. List the date and the amount of the most recent dividend paid by General Mills.

ACCOUNTING IN THE REAL WORLD

1. Having the financial statements stated in yen should have little effect on the ability to understand the financial information. Using financial statement analysis and calculated financial ratios reveals a company's financial condition and results of operations, regardless of the currency used.

2. The notes to the financial statements would identify significant generally accepted accounting principles used in the preparation of financial statements.

INTERNET RESEARCH ACTIVITY

Answers will vary, depending on the year chosen.

583

583

20-1 Journalizing Manufacturing Accounting Transactions

Managing a manufacturing business requires more elaborate planning and control than managing a merchandising business. In addition to sales and administrative activities required of both types of businesses, a manufacturing business must provide the knowledge and resources needed to make the product.

Accounting for a manufacturing business is more complex than accounting for a merchandising business. To provide usable financial information for a manufacturing business, detailed cost records must be maintained throughout the manufacturing process. These detailed manufacturing cost records provide a business with information needed to price its product, analyze manufacturing costs, and make other important management decisions.

Procedures for maintaining detailed manufacturing cost records are described in Chapter 19.

In addition to detailed cost records, a manufacturing business also needs accurate financial statements. To provide financial statements, it must make journal entries to reflect cost transactions in general ledger accounts.

Manufacturing cost data are generally recorded daily to provide up-to-date cost information for managers. However, most manufacturing costs are recorded for financial reporting purposes only when up-to-date account balances are needed to prepare financial statements. These end-of-fiscal-period journal entries update the general ledger manufacturing accounts before financial statements are prepared.

MAKING ETHICAL DECISIONS • MAKING ETHICAL DECISIONS • MAKING ETHICAL DECISIO

making ethical decisions

Fair Competition

Grayson Corporation produces a line of personal care products. Last year the company invested a lot of money and effort to introduce a new shampoo. Unfortunately, the product's sales are significantly below expectations. Amy Stevens, the marketing manager, is under pressure to reverse the trend—and fast!

One of Amy's staff has suggested that they bundle the products to promote sales. In other words, the shampoo would be sold as part of a collection of products. Customers (retail stores) would have to buy the new shampoo in order to restock their shelves with the company's successful products.

Instructions

Access *Our Values and Policies,* the code of conduct for Procter & Gamble. What guidance does Procter & Gamble provide regarding a marketing plan such as the one described? Should Amy approve the plan? Assume that Grayson Corporation's policies are similar to Procter & Gamble's.

Source: www.pg.com/content/pdf/01_about_pg/01_about_pg_homepage/about_pg_toolbar/download_report/values_and_policies.pdf

FLOW OF MANUFACTURING COSTS

GENERAL LEDGER ACCOUNTS

All manufacturing costs flow through the manufacturing accounts. FaxaVision uses cost sheets to record direct materials, direct labor, and overhead costs of each job. This method permits the company to determine the unit costs of completed jobs. The unit costs are recorded in the company's perpetual inventory of finished goods.

Therefore, these costs are recorded through each phase of the manufacturing process. Summary journal entries update general ledger accounts for costs incurred in completing jobs, as shown above. Thus, end-of-fiscal-period inventory adjustments are not required.

Lesson 20-1   **585**

DEMONSTRATE

- Direct students to the illustration as you demonstrate the journal entries for cost accounts.
- Demonstrate recording materials purchased by debiting Materials and crediting Accounts Payable.
- Demonstrate recording direct materials by crediting Materials and debiting Work in Process and indirect materials by crediting Materials and debiting Factory overhead.
- Demonstrate recording payroll by debiting direct material to Work in Process and indirect material to Factory Overhead; and crediting payroll liability accounts and Cash.
- Demonstrate closing manufacturing expense accounts by debiting Factory Overhead and crediting the expense accounts.
- Demonstrate recording applied overhead by debiting Work in Process and crediting Factory Overhead.
- Demonstrate recording finished products by crediting Work in Process and debiting Finished Goods.
- Demonstrate recording products sold by crediting Finished Goods and debiting Cost of Goods Sold.

EXPLAIN

- Explain that a separate payroll register is prepared for factory employees.
- Point out that rather than debiting Salary Expense, the factory payroll costs are debited to Work in Process and Factory Overhead.

DEMONSTRATE

Analyzing factory cost accounts

- Draw T accounts on the board for Work in Process and Factory Overhead.
- Explain that Work in Process is an asset account and Factory Overhead is a cost account.
- Ask students to identify the increase, decrease, and normal balance sides of the accounts and label the accounts as the information is given.

Analyzing the factory payroll transaction

- Label six T accounts on the board with the account titles and balances shown.
- Explain that factory employee salaries are distributed as direct labor to Work in Process and indirect labor to Factory Overhead. Record the debit amounts in the T accounts.
- Record the employee withholding amounts as credits to the usual payroll tax liability accounts.
- Record the net salary as a credit to Cash.

Recording the transaction

- Use an instructor-made transparency of a cash payments journal or direct students to the illustration in the middle of this page as you demonstrate journalizing the transaction.
- Repeat the analysis and journalizing for the January 31 factory payroll.

STEPS • STEPS • STEPS • STEPS • STEPS • STEPS • STEPS • STEPS • STEPS • STEPS • STEPS

RECORDING JOURNAL ENTRIES FOR MANUFACTURING ACCOUNTS

1. Record materials purchased by debiting Materials and crediting Accounts Payable.

2. Record direct materials transferred to the factory by crediting Materials and debiting Work in Process. Record indirect materials transferred to the factory by crediting Materials and debiting Factory Overhead.

3. Record factory payroll by debiting direct labor to Work in Process, debiting indirect labor to Factory Overhead, crediting payroll liability accounts (e.g., Accounts Payable), and crediting Cash.

4. Close individual manufacturing expense accounts by debiting Factory Overhead and crediting each manufacturing expense account for its balance.

5. Record applied overhead by debiting Work in Process and crediting Factory Overhead for the total overhead amount applied during the fiscal period.

6. Record cost of products completed by crediting Work in Process and debiting Finished Goods.

7. Record cost of products sold by crediting Finished Goods and debiting Cost of Goods Sold.

JOURNAL ENTRIES TO RECORD FACTORY PAYROLL FOR A MONTH

3. Credit cash for the next payroll.

1. Debit the factory accounts.

2. Credit the three tax withholding accounts.

CASH PAYMENTS JOURNAL   PAGE 2

	DATE	ACCOUNT TITLE	CK. NO.	POST. REF.	GENERAL DEBIT	GENERAL CREDIT	ACCOUNTS PAYABLE DEBIT	PURCHASES DISCOUNT CREDIT	CASH CREDIT	
1	20-- Jan. 15	Work in Process	1194		39 24 5 00				41 32 5 38	1
2		Factory Overhead			11 77 4 00					2
3		Employee Income Tax Payable				5 61 2 10				3
4		Social Security Tax Payable				3 33 6 64				4
5		Medicare Tax Payable				7 44 88				5
21	31	Work in Process	1211		44 25 5 00				46 60 0 12	21
22		Factory Overhead			13 27 6 00					22
23		Employee Income Tax Payable				6 32 8 40				23
24		Social Security Tax Payable				3 76 2 53				24
25		Medicare Tax Payable				8 39 95				25

FaxaVision pays all factory employees twice each month. A separate payroll register is prepared for factory employees. A cash payments journal entry is prepared for each factory payroll. The journal entries for the January 15 and January 31 factory payroll for FaxaVision are shown above.

STEPS • STEPS • STEPS • STEPS

RECORDING FACTORY PAYROLL

1. Debit Work in Process for direct labor and Factory Overhead for indirect labor.

2. Credit Employee Income Tax Payable, Social Security Tax Payable, and Medicare Tax Payable for the amounts withheld from employees.

3. Credit Cash for the net pay.

Work in Process

Bal. 82,579.00	
1/15 39,245.00	
1/31 44,255.00	

Factory Overhead

1/15 11,774.00	
1/31 13,276.00	

Employee Income Tax Payable

	1/15 5,612.10
	1/31 6,328.40

Social Security Tax Payable

	1/15 3,336.64
	1/31 3,762.53

Medicare Tax Payable

	1/15 744.88
	1/31 839.95

Cash

	1/15 41,325.38
	1/31 46,600.12

586 Chapter 20   Accounting Transactions and Financial Reporting for a Manufacturing Business

---

TEACHING STRATEGIES   DIFFERENT LEARNING STYLES

Auditory Learner. To reinforce the learning of journal entries, the auditory learner should verbally repeat the analysis of the transaction. The student should also verbally list the steps involved in making the entry.

RECORDING MATERIALS PURCHASES

	DATE		ACCOUNT CREDITED	PURCH. NO.	POST. REF.	MATERIALS DR. ACCTS. PAY. CR.	
1	20-- Jan.	4	Oakley Electronics	621		7 0 9 7 80	1
24		31	Total			168 6 4 2 60	24

MATERIALS PURCHASES JOURNAL   PAGE 1

FaxaVision records the amount of direct and indirect materials purchased and issued in the general ledger account Materials. FaxaVision uses a perpetual inventory in the factory that permits the company to charge cost of materials to a job as materials are issued. [CONCEPT: Matching Expenses with Revenue]

FaxaVision uses a special materials purchases journal to record all materials purchases. Purchases are made on account; therefore, the journal has a single amount column. An entry in the materials purchases journal is shown above.

At the end of a month, the total of the materials purchases journal is posted to Materials and Accounts Payable in the general ledger.

In the materials account, the January 1 debit balance, $121,231.20, is the materials inventory at the beginning of the month. The January 31 debit, $168,642.60, is the total posted from the materials purchases journal. This represents the total cost of direct and indirect materials purchased during the month.

Materials	
Jan. 1 Bal. 121,231.20	
Jan. 31 168,642.60	

Accounts Payable	
	Jan. 31 168,642.60

RECORDING MATERIALS REQUISITIONS

	DATE		ACCOUNT TITLE	DOC. NO.	POST. REF.	DEBIT	CREDIT	
1	20-- Jan.	31	Work in Process	M240		156 4 7 7 00		1
2			Factory Overhead			11 4 4 7 50		2
3			Materials				167 9 2 4 50	3

GENERAL JOURNAL   PAGE 1

A materials requisition is prepared for direct materials issued for a specific job. After materials are issued, the requisition amount is recorded on a cost sheet and the requisition is filed. At the end of a month, the total value of all direct materials issued to specific jobs must be transferred from Materials to Work in Process.

A materials requisition is also prepared for indirect materials used in the factory. After the

indirect materials are issued to the factory, the requisition is filed. At the end of the month, the total value of all indirect materials issued is transferred from Materials to Factory Overhead.

FaxaVision prepares a memorandum with monthly summary information of the direct materials requisitions and the indirect materials totals. The general journal entry to transfer these amounts is shown above.

Journalizing Manufacturing Accounting Transactions

Lesson 20-1   **587**

Analyzing materials requisitions

- Draw three T accounts on the board for Work in Process, Factory Overhead, and Materials. Record the beginning Work in Process balance and the January 15 and 31 amounts for direct and indirect labor.

- Explain that direct materials are recorded in Work in Process and indirect materials in Factory Overhead, just like direct and indirect labor. Record the amounts in the T accounts.

- Record the credit entry for all materials requisitions, $167,924.50, in the Materials account.

Recording materials requisitions

- Use an instructor-made transparency of a general journal or direct students to the illustration at the bottom of page 587 as you demonstrate journalizing the transaction.

- Record the monthly entry for materials requisitions just analyzed in T accounts in the general journal.

- Explain that in addition to direct and indirect labor and materials, a factory has many other kinds of overhead costs, such as depreciation, utilities, insurance, and taxes.

- Remind students that some expense accounts are adjusted at the end of a fiscal period, such as depreciation expense.

- Explain that all adjusting entries are journalized and posted, and then the balances of the manufacturing expense accounts are transferred to Factory Overhead.

Recording actual factory overhead

- Draw a T account for Factory Overhead and record the entries for labor and materials already explained.

- Direct students to the illustration in the middle of this page as you demonstrate journalizing the transaction. Point out that all the expense accounts are credited and Factory Overhead is debited. Record the Factory Overhead amount in the T account. Emphasize that these are actual overhead amounts.

588

MATERIALS AND LABOR USED IN PRODUCTION

The balance in the Work in Process account, $82,579.00, is the beginning inventory of Work in Process. The other debits represent the total amounts of direct labor and direct materials used for all jobs during the month.

The debits to Factory Overhead represent the total amounts of indirect labor used and indirect materials issued during the month.

Work in Process

Bal.	82,579.00	
Jan. 15 Dir. Lab.	39,245.00	
Jan. 31 Dir. Lab.	44,255.00	
Jan. 31 Dir. Mat.	156,477.00	

Factory Overhead

Jan. 15 Ind. Lab.	11,774.00	
Jan. 31 Ind. Lab.	13,276.00	
Jan. 31 Ind. Mat.	11,447.50	

JOURNALIZING ACTUAL FACTORY OVERHEAD

GENERAL JOURNAL   PAGE **1**

DATE	ACCOUNT TITLE	DOC. NO.	POST. REF.	DEBIT	CREDIT	
31	Factory Overhead	M241		30 45 6 00		4
	Depr. Exp.—Factory Equip.				2 5 0 0 00	5
	Depr. Exp.—Building				1 3 0 0 00	6
	Heat, Light, and Power Exp.				6 1 5 8 50	7
	Insurance Exp.—Factory				6 2 0 00	8
	Miscellaneous Exp.—Factory				7 8 4 40	9
	Payroll Taxes Exp.—Factory				15 4 1 4 10	10
	Property Tax Exp.—Factory				1 4 6 3 60	11
	Supplies Exp.—Factory				2 2 1 5 40	12

Factory overhead includes various indirect factory expenses such as indirect labor, indirect materials, taxes, depreciation, and insurance. Actual factory overhead expenses are summarized in an account titled Factory Overhead.

Indirect labor and indirect materials are posted directly to the factory overhead account from the entries shown on pages 586 and 587. Other indirect expenses are recorded throughout the month in other manufacturing expense accounts. At the end of each month, these indirect expense account balances are transferred to the factory overhead account. The actual factory overhead can then be compared with the estimated amount of factory overhead recorded on the job cost sheets. Recall from Chapter 19 that factory overhead is estimated (applied) so that a company can record overhead on a cost sheet as soon as a job is completed.

Adjusting entries are made at the end of a fiscal period. These adjusting entries include debits to the depreciation expense, insurance expense, and supplies expense accounts. The closing entry to transfer actual overhead expenses to the factory overhead account is shown above.

After postings are completed, all actual factory overhead expense accounts are summarized in the factory overhead account.

Factory Overhead

Jan. 15 Ind. Lab.	11,774.00	
Jan. 31 Ind. Lab.	13,276.00	
Jan. 31 Ind. Mat.	11,447.50	
Jan. 31 Act. OH	30,456.00	
(New Bal.	*66,953.50)*	

TEACHING STRATEGIES   DIFFERENT LEARNING ABILITIES

Limited English Proficiency (LEP) Students. Rather than asking students whether they understand what you have said, ask them to restate what you have said in their own words.

RECORDING APPLIED OVERHEAD

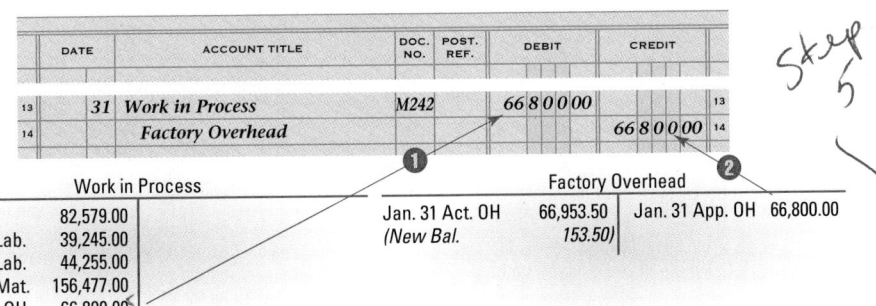

Step 5

	DATE	ACCOUNT TITLE	DOC. NO.	POST. REF.	DEBIT	CREDIT	
13	31	Work in Process	M242		66 80 00 00		13
14		Factory Overhead				66 80 00 00	14

① ②

Work in Process	
Bal.	82,579.00
Jan. 15 Dir. Lab.	39,245.00
Jan. 31 Dir. Lab.	44,255.00
Jan. 31 Dir. Mat.	156,477.00
Jan. 31 App. OH	66,800.00

Factory Overhead		
Jan. 31 Act. OH	66,953.50	Jan. 31 App. OH 66,800.00
(New Bal.	153.50)	

FaxaVision applies factory overhead to each job at the rate of 80% of direct labor charges. At the end of each month, FaxaVision totals the applied factory overhead recorded on all job cost sheets. Its applied factory overhead for January is $66,800.00. The journal entry to record applied factory overhead is shown above.

The factory overhead account debit, $66,953.50, is the actual factory overhead expense for the month. The credit, $66,800.00, is the applied factory overhead for the month. The account's $153.50 debit ending balance results from recording less applied factory overhead than the amount of actual factory overhead expenses.

DISPOSING OF OVERAPPLIED AND UNDERAPPLIED FACTORY OVERHEAD BALANCES

Under Step 5

	DATE	ACCOUNT TITLE	DOC. NO.	POST. REF.	DEBIT	CREDIT	
15	31	Income Summary	M243		1 5 3 50		15
16		Factory Overhead				1 5 3 50	16

The rate used to calculate applied factory overhead is only an estimate. Therefore, the factory overhead account may have an ending balance. The amount by which applied factory overhead is less than actual factory overhead is called **underapplied overhead**. The debit balance, $153.50, in FaxaVision's account indicates underapplied overhead for January. The journal entry to close the factory overhead account at the end of January is shown above.

A credit balance indicates that applied factory overhead is more than actual factory overhead. The amount by which applied factory overhead

is more than actual factory overhead is called **overapplied overhead**. If the factory overhead account has a credit balance, Factory Overhead is debited and Income Summary is credited for the overapplied overhead amount.

Overhead may be overapplied or underapplied for two reasons. (1) Actual expenses may be higher or lower than normal, an event that requires closer control over expenditures. (2) The factory overhead applied rate may be inaccurate. If the rate is found to be inaccurate, a revised rate is determined. The revised rate is used in the next fiscal period.

Debit more than Credit = Underapplied
Credit more than debit = Overapplied

TEACHING STRATEGIES DIFFERENT LEARNING STYLES

Print Learner. When covering journal entries with a print learner, the instructor should discuss the entries, using the textbook examples and referring to the textbook. The print learner can later go back and study the entries.

EXPLAIN

- Remind students that throughout the month as jobs are finished, an applied amount of factory overhead (an estimate) is recorded on each job cost sheet. At the end of the month, incomplete jobs also have an applied factory overhead amount recorded.

- Explain that this applied factory overhead amount must be journalized and posted.

DEMONSTRATE

Recording applied overhead

- Draw T accounts for Work in Process and Factory Overhead and record the balances shown or direct students to the illustration at the top of this page as you demonstrate recording applied overhead.

- Point out that the amount of applied overhead recorded on the job cost sheets is recorded as a debit to Work in Process and a credit to Factory Overhead, as shown in the general journal and the T accounts.

- Direct students to the Factory Overhead T account as you demonstrate that the Jan. 31 Act. OH amount, $66,953.50, is the amount of overhead transferred from the direct factory expense accounts, as shown on page 588. Point out that the journal entry on this page is for the applied (estimated) overhead recorded on the job cost sheets, $66,800.00.

Recording underapplied and overapplied factory overhead

- Direct students back to the T account for Factory Overhead shown at the top of the page. Point out that the actual overhead is greater than the applied overhead, so the overhead was underapplied and the debit balance must be closed.

- Explain that underapplied and overapplied overhead is closed by entries to Income Summary and Factory Overhead.

- Direct students to the illustration in the middle of the page as you demonstrate closing Factory Overhead when there is underapplied overhead (debit balance). Explain that if the estimated (applied) overhead had been greater than the actual overhead, Factory Overhead would have a credit balance and the closing entry would be just the opposite.

- Remind students that when jobs are finished the job cost sheets are completed. At the end of the month, the costs on these completed sheets are transferred to Finished Goods.

- Explain that the final two journal entries for the manufacturing accounts are to (1) transfer completed jobs out of Work in Process and into Finished Goods and (2) to transfer goods that have been sold out of Finished Goods and into Cost of Goods Sold.

- Students sometimes confuse the cost of products with the selling price of products. Point out that a company would have no net income if it sold products for the same price it cost to manufacture them.

- Explain that the cost of each unit sold is recorded on the company's copy of the sales invoice and these costs are totaled and recorded in Cost of Goods Sold at the end of the month. Explain that this is a feature of a perpetual inventory system.

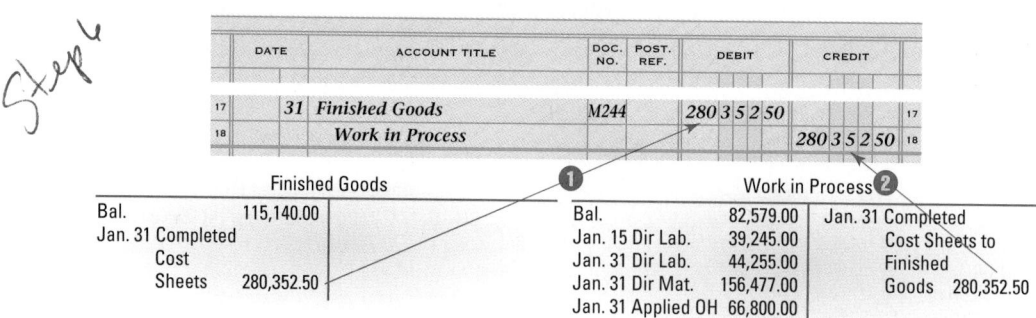

FaxaVision totals the cost sheets for all jobs completed during the month. Its January total, $280,352.50, is the cost of work finished during the month. This amount is transferred from Work in Process to Finished Goods. The journal entry to record this transaction is shown above.

The balance in the finished goods account, $115,140.00, represents beginning inventory.

The January 31 debit to Finished Goods and credit to Work in Process, $280,352.50, represents the cost of finished goods transferred from the factory to the stockroom. The work in process account balance, $109,003.50, is the total amount of direct materials, direct labor, and applied factory overhead charged to the jobs in the ending inventory of work in process.

DEMONSTRATE

Recording finished goods transactions

- Direct students to the illustration at the top of the page as you demonstrate the journal entry for transferring completed products from Work in Process to Finished Goods.

- Demonstrate that the total of the completed cost sheets, $280,352.50, is credited to Work in Process to remove those costs from that inventory account.

- Demonstrate that the total of the completed cost sheets is debited to Finished Goods to include those costs in that inventory account.

Recording sales and cost of goods sold

- Direct students to the illustration in the middle of the page as you demonstrate recording the cost of goods sold for products that have been sold during the month. Remind students that the amount is obtained by totaling the cost amounts recorded on each sales invoice during the month.

- Demonstrate that the costs are transferred out of Finished Goods with a credit, $264,020.00.

- Demonstrate that the costs are transferred into Cost of Goods sold with a debit for the same amount.

RECORDING SALES AND COST OF GOODS SOLD

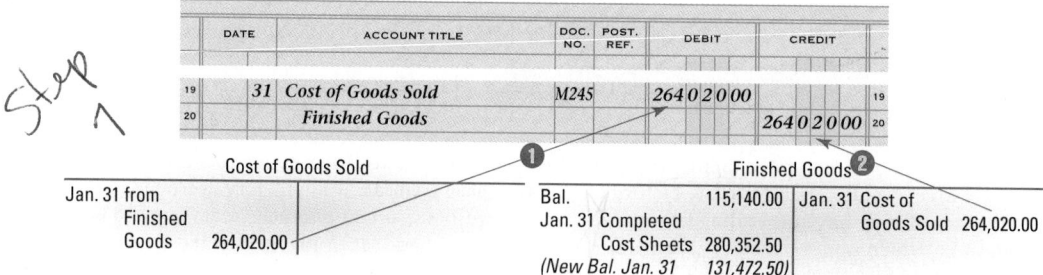

Since FaxaVision uses a perpetual inventory, a different procedure is used to determine and record cost of goods sold. For each sale, the number of products shipped, the unit cost, and the total amounts of products sold are recorded on the sales invoice.

At the end of the month, cost information on all sales invoices is totaled. The total costs recorded for FaxaVision's January sales, $264,020.00, is the cost of goods sold for the month. This number represents the total *cost* of products sold, not the revenue derived from

sales (which is determined by selling price). This total cost is transferred from the inventory account Finished Goods to the cost account Cost of Goods Sold, as shown above.

The debit to Cost of Goods Sold, $264,020.00, is the cost of goods sold during the month. The credit to Finished Goods, $264,020.00, is the cost of finished goods sold during the month and removed from inventory. The finished goods account balance, $131,472.50, is the ending inventory of finished goods.

590   Chapter 20   Accounting Transactions and Financial Reporting for a Manufacturing Business

---

TEACHING STRATEGIES   DIFFERENT LEARNING STYLES

Tactile Learner. Tactile learners should be given the opportunity to journalize transactions from at least one simulation that contains source documents which must be handled to analyze, journalize, and file.

MANUFACTURING ACCOUNTS IN THE GENERAL LEDGER

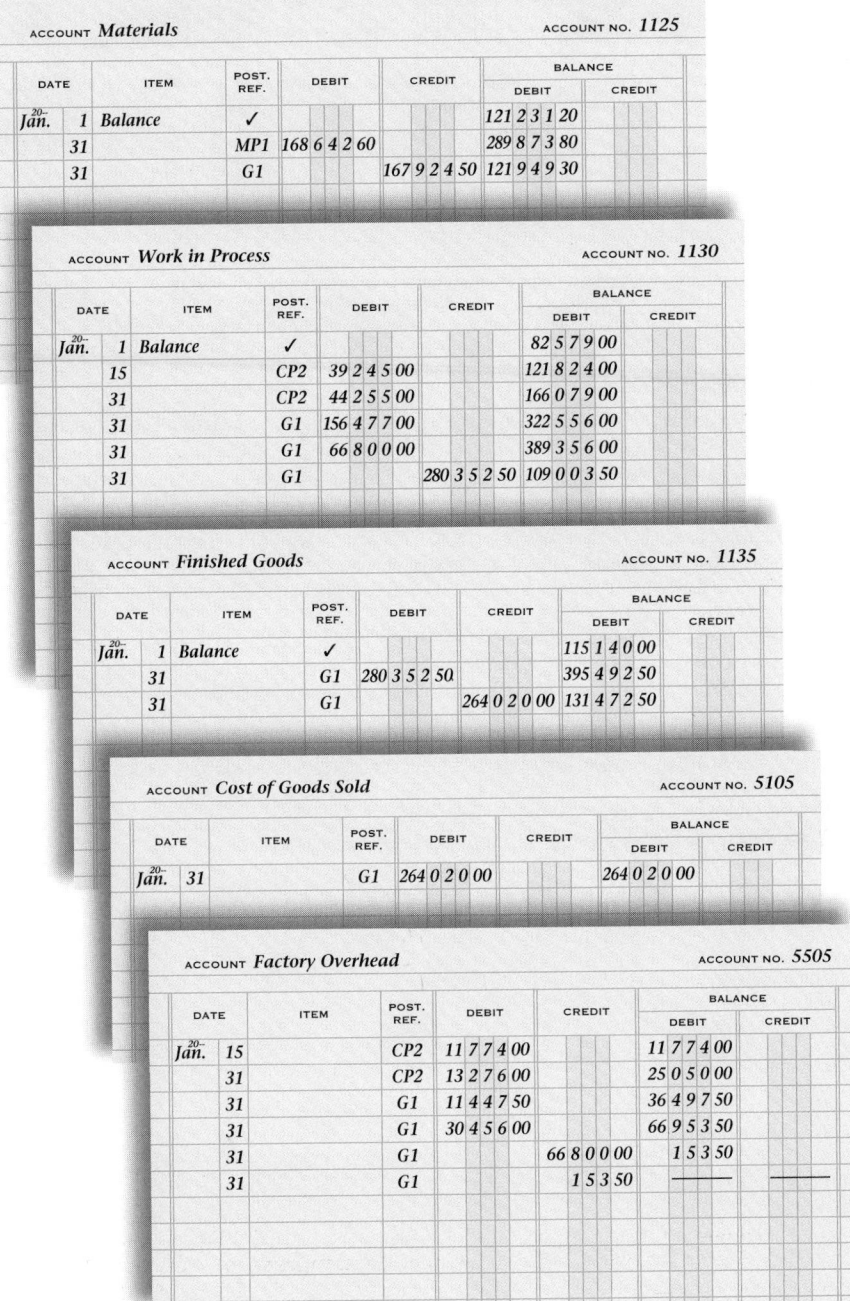

ACCOUNT **Materials** ACCOUNT NO. 1125

DATE		ITEM	POST. REF.	DEBIT	CREDIT	BALANCE DEBIT	BALANCE CREDIT
20-- Jan.	1	Balance	✓			121 2 3 1 20	
	31		MP1	168 6 4 2 60		289 8 7 3 80	
	31		G1		167 9 2 4 50	121 9 4 9 30	

ACCOUNT **Work in Process** ACCOUNT NO. 1130

DATE		ITEM	POST. REF.	DEBIT	CREDIT	BALANCE DEBIT	BALANCE CREDIT
20-- Jan.	1	Balance	✓			82 5 7 9 00	
	15		CP2	39 2 4 5 00		121 8 2 4 00	
	31		CP2	44 2 5 5 00		166 0 7 9 00	
	31		G1	156 4 7 7 00		322 5 5 6 00	
	31		G1	66 8 0 0 00		389 3 5 6 00	
	31		G1		280 3 5 2 50	109 0 0 3 50	

ACCOUNT **Finished Goods** ACCOUNT NO. 1135

DATE		ITEM	POST. REF.	DEBIT	CREDIT	BALANCE DEBIT	BALANCE CREDIT
20-- Jan.	1	Balance	✓			115 1 4 0 00	
	31		G1	280 3 5 2 50		395 4 9 2 50	
	31		G1		264 0 2 0 00	131 4 7 2 50	

ACCOUNT **Cost of Goods Sold** ACCOUNT NO. 5105

DATE		ITEM	POST. REF.	DEBIT	CREDIT	BALANCE DEBIT	BALANCE CREDIT
20-- Jan.	31		G1	264 0 2 0 00		264 0 2 0 00	

ACCOUNT **Factory Overhead** ACCOUNT NO. 5505

DATE		ITEM	POST. REF.	DEBIT	CREDIT	BALANCE DEBIT	BALANCE CREDIT
20-- Jan.	15		CP2	11 7 7 4 00		11 7 7 4 00	
	31		CP2	13 2 7 6 00		25 0 5 0 00	
	31		G1	11 4 4 7 50		36 4 9 7 50	
	31		G1	30 4 5 6 00		66 9 5 3 50	
	31		G1		66 8 0 0 00	1 5 3 50	
	31		G1	1 5 3 50		—	—

The effect of posting the entries described in this chapter is shown above.

Journalizing Manufacturing Accounting Transactions

Lesson 20-1 **591**

EXPLAIN

- Explain that the illustration shows the results of the manufacturing cost journal entries in the general ledger manufacturing inventory and cost accounts.

DEMONSTRATE

- Direct students to the illustration to demonstrate each of the journal entries for the manufacturing process.
- Demonstrate that the journal entry on page 586 that affects the cost accounts is on lines 2 and 3 of Work in Process (direct labor) and lines 1 and 2 of Factory Overhead (indirect labor).
- Demonstrate that the journal entry for purchases of materials on page 587 is on line 2 of Materials.
- Demonstrate that the journal entry on page 587 for materials requisitions is on line 3 of Materials, line 4 of Work in Process (direct materials), and line 3 of Factory Overhead (indirect materials).
- Demonstrate that the journal entry on page 588 for actual factory overhead is on line 4 of Factory Overhead.
- Demonstrate that the journal entry on page 589 for applied overhead is on line 5 of Work in Process and line 5 of Factory Overhead.
- Demonstrate that the journal entry on page 589 for disposing of underapplied overhead is on line 6 of Factory Overhead.
- Demonstrate that the journal entry on page 590 for transferring costs from Work in Process to Finished Goods is on line 2 of Finished Goods and line 6 of Work in Process.
- Demonstrate that the journal entry on page 590 for transferring costs from Finished Goods to Cost of Goods Sold for products that have been sold is on line 1 of Cost of Goods Sold and line 3 of Finished Goods.

ONGOING ASSESSMENT

- Assessment is an ongoing process. Circulate through the classroom or lab, observing which students have problems with the assignments.
- Troubleshooting: Diagnose what kinds of problems students have with this lesson. Students may have difficulty understanding the sequence, accounts, and amounts for the cost entries.
- Assess student understanding by checking solutions to Independent Practice assignments.

RETEACH

- Direct students to the illustration on page 585 and ask students to describe each step and list the journal used for each entry and the accounts debited and credited.
- Ask one student to describe an entry shown on pages 586–590 and call on students to name the journal in which the entry is recorded and where information for the entry is obtained.
- Direct students to the illustration on page 591 and call on students to describe what each amount in each account represents.

591

terms review

underapplied overhead
overapplied overhead

audit your understanding

1. Where are direct materials, direct labor, and overhead costs for each job initially recorded?

2. After factory overhead has been applied to work in process, what does a credit balance in Factory Overhead indicate?

3. Explain the difference between actual factory overhead and applied factory overhead.

work together 20-1

Preparing manufacturing journal entries

A materials purchases journal, a cash payments journal, and a general journal for Vanyo, Inc., a manufacturer of cardboard boxes, are provided in the *Working Papers*. Your instructor will guide you through the following examples.

1. Prepare journal entries for each of the following transactions or events.

May 3. Purchased $15,400.00 of materials on account from Bushnell Corrugated.

5. Requisitioned $2,650.00 of direct materials and $350.00 of indirect materials for the production department.

15. Paid employees their semimonthly pay. Gross (pretax) direct labor costs were $11,200. Gross indirect labor costs were $1,600.00. Employee income tax was $1,480.00. Social security tax was 6.2% and Medicare tax was 1.45% of gross wages.

21. Requisitioned $4,700.00 of direct materials and $2,100.00 of indirect materials for the production department.

31. Obtained factory costs for the month: depreciation on building, $750.00; depreciation on equipment, $1,200.00; insurance, $325.00; property taxes, $545.00; utilities, $1,880.00. Assume that these expenses have already been properly accounted for and now need to be closed.

31. Paid employees their semimonthly pay. Gross (pretax) direct labor costs were $10,150.00. Gross indirect labor costs were $1,370.00. Employee income tax was $1,220.00. Social security tax was 6.2% and Medicare tax was 1.45% of gross wages.

31. Applied overhead at the rate of 50% of direct labor costs.

31. Transferred cardboard boxes costing $29,920 to finished goods during the month.

31. Sold cardboard boxes costing $24,760 during the month.

• on your own 20-1

Preparing manufacturing journal entries

A materials purchases journal, a cash payments journal, and a general journal for Vanyo, Inc., a manufacturer of cardboard boxes, are provided in the *Working Papers*. Work independently to complete the following problem.

1.   Prepare journal entries for each of the following transactions or events.

June   4.   Purchased $8,100.00 of materials on account from Fresno, Inc.

7.   Requisitioned $3,770.00 of direct materials and $730.00 of indirect materials for the production department.

15.   Paid employees their semimonthly pay. Gross (pretax) direct labor costs were $12,590.00. Gross indirect labor costs were $1,940.00. Employee income tax was $1,780.00. Social security tax was 6.2% and Medicare tax was 1.45% of gross wages.

15.   Requisitioned $2,300.00 of direct materials and $1,530.00 of indirect materials for the production department.

30.   Obtained factory costs for the month: depreciation on building, $750.00; depreciation on equipment, $1,200.00; insurance, $325.00; property taxes, $570.00; utilities, $1,960.00. Assume that these expenses have already been properly accounted for and now need to be closed.

30.   Paid employees their semimonthly pay. Gross (pretax) direct labor costs were $10,860.00. Gross indirect labor costs were $1,785.00. Employee income tax was $1,615.00. Social security tax was 6.2% and Medicare tax was 1.45% of gross wages.

30.   Applied overhead at the rate of 50% of direct labor costs.

30.   Transferred cardboard boxes costing $35,500.00 to finished goods during the month.

30.   Sold cardboard boxes costing $32,160.00 during the month

ON YOUR OWN • ON YOUR OWN • ON YOUR OWN • ON YOUR OWN • ON YOUR OWN

global perspective

GLOBAL PERSPECTIVE • GLOBAL PERSPECTIVE • GLOBAL PERSPECTIV

International Banking

International business transactions usually require the use of international services from a commercial bank. More than 300 U.S. banks have international banking departments to assist customers with international business.

Some specific services that are offered by commercial banks are: exchange of currency; assistance in financing exports; and collection of invoices, drafts, letters of credit, and other foreign receivables.

Required

Contact a local bank that has an international department. Find out the following information.

1.   With what countries does the bank have specialized relationships?

2.   Does the bank handle letters of credit? If so, what is the procedure to negotiate a letter of credit?

3.   Is financial assistance available to exporters? If so, what are the guidelines?

Journalizing Manufacturing Accounting Transactions   Lesson 20-1   **593**

INDEPENDENT PRACTICE

On Your Own

• Assign the On Your Own problem to be worked independently.

• Use the Ongoing Assessment techniques to diagnose student understanding.

Application Problem

• Assign Application Problem 20-1: Journalizing cost accounting transactions for a manufacturing company.

• Assign Application Problem 20-2: Journalizing and posting entries that summarize cost records at the end of a fiscal period.

Personal Trainer

• Students can access the Lesson 20-1 assessment material using this software.

Xtra! Web Site

• Students can access the Xtra! Study Tools for additional practice.

ENRICH

• Assign Making Ethical Decisions on page 584.

• Assign the Global Perspective feature on page 593. You may also direct students to determine whether the bank researched will transfer money to other countries and whether it provides export counseling.

• Assign the Case for Critical Thinking.

• Assign Careers in Accounting on page 594.

• Students can use Peachtree or QuickBooks data files to automate Application Problem 20-1.

CLOSE

• Ask students to describe the journal entries for manufacturing costs.

GLOBAL PERSPECTIVE
GLOBAL PERSPECTIVE

The Global Perspective feature is intended to expose students to some of the ways in which accounting and business in general differ in other countries. Direct students to obtain answers to the questions given and then discuss the findings as a group.

CAREERS IN ACCOUNTING

The Careers in Accounting feature profiles people who are entrepreneurs, who are working in accounting-related fields, or who use accounting in their business lives.

Students can access the Careers section of the Xtra! Web Site for additional material about careers.

careers in accounting

CAREERS IN ACCOUNTING • CAREERS IN ACCOUNTING • CAREERS IN ACCOUN

Rochelle Klee, Director of Accounts Payable

COURTESY OF ROCHELLE KLEE

Accounts Payable (AP) has been viewed as the department whose employees are located in the basement paying the bills. They are neither qualified nor have the authority to challenge the spending preferences of middle and executive management.

Not so these days. AP leaders and their staff play a key role in helping to contain costs and maintain strict adherence to financial controls in an age of corporate scandals. Chief Financial Officers (CFOs) are looking to their AP leaders to implement processes and systems that create efficiencies in a paper-intensive environment. AP managers also implement financial controls and reports that give accounting managers and CFOs a true picture of the costs of the company. These costs make up a large portion of the general ledger assets, expenses, and risk. CFOs need to know that their AP operations are in capable hands and attention is being paid to those details that could result in major problems if not properly managed.

Rochelle Klee is the Director of Accounts Payable for a diversified *Fortune* 100 company. Accounting was the first high school class that interested her enough to motivate her to put effort into the homework assignments and achieve an *A*. After completing nearly two years of college with an emphasis in business, her focus was not on her studies, and she left college to take a job at a company as an accounting clerk reconciling bank statements.

A formal education is only one contributing factor to success. With a basic understanding of accounting, an ability to learn from others, a willingness to work hard, and the confidence to take on new roles and responsibilities, one can achieve many things in accounting. "There was a point in time where I stated to one of my co-workers, 'I will never work in AP.' It looked like a very dull and unrewarding job to me. Less than one year later I accepted a position as the supervisor of a small AP department." With little AP experience and no supervisory experience, this new position was a challenge. After many fulfilling years, Rochelle is currently the Director of AP and thoroughly enjoys the job.

A career in Accounts Payable provides an opportunity to work with many different individuals across a company but is not without challenges. There are pressures to do more with less and the challenge of working with internal and external AP customers. Rochelle says, "When an employee asks me how to handle a situation, I first ask them what they think. Most ideas and solutions are not made by referring to the idea and solution chart for the answer, but are made by using deductive reasoning and really thinking a situation through." As much as it would seem that AP is a very basic process with a very basic set of rules, the culture and the business needs of an organization dictate the solutions that are applied.

Salary Range: Salaries for accounts payable managers vary with the size of the company and the city, ranging from $55,000 to over $75,000. (Source: Bureau of Labor Statistics, U.S. Department of Labor, *Occupational Outlook Handbook, 2004–05 Edition,* Bookkeeping, Accounting, and on the Internet at http://www.bls.gov/oco/ocos144.htm [visited April 04, 2005].)

Qualifications: High school diploma for entry-level accounts payable clerks. Accounts payable experience usually required for supervisory positions in accounts payable.

Occupational Outlook: Slower than average growth is predicted in accounting clerk positions as technology improves employee efficiency. Clerks in specialized areas will be in less demand than those who have a broader range of knowledge and the ability to do a wider range of accounting activities.

20-2 Preparing End-of-Fiscal-Period Statements

OBJECTIVES

- Define accounting terms related to financial reporting for a manufacturing business.
- Identify accounting concepts and practices related to financial reporting for a manufacturing business.
- Prepare selected financial statements for a manufacturing business.

PREPARING THE WORK SHEET

The primary purpose of cost accounting information is to help managers make better decisions. However, some of this information is also used to prepare financial statements, which may be important not only to managers inside the firm but also to investors, creditors, and others outside the organization.

Several of the procedures used to prepare a manufacturing business's work sheet and financial statements are similar to the procedures used for a merchandising business.

A work sheet is used to plan a manufacturing business's financial information for fiscal period statements just as it is for merchandising businesses. However, a manufacturing business's work sheet includes three inventory accounts and a cost of goods sold account. FaxaVision's work sheet for January is shown on pages 596 and 597.

FaxaVision's work sheet, similar to the work sheets of other manufacturing businesses using the perpetual inventory method, has several unique characteristics:

1. The entries to record direct materials, work in process, and finished goods bring manufacturing inventory accounts up to date on January 31. Thus, the balances of Materials, Work in Process, and Finished Goods are brought up to date before a work sheet is prepared.

Adjustments for these inventory accounts do not need to be planned on a work sheet.

2. The factory keeps perpetual inventory subsidiary ledgers and detailed cost records. Based on these subsidiary records, summary journal entries are made to record the flow of costs through the manufacturing process to the cost of goods sold account. Since all manufacturing costs flow toward the account Cost of Goods Sold, no manufacturing cost accounts on the work sheet have balances. Amounts in these accounts have been transferred to either one of the inventory accounts or the cost of goods sold account. The cost of goods sold amount, $264,020.00, is extended to the Income Statement Debit column.

3. Income Summary has a debit balance of $153.50. This balance resulted from closing the underapplied overhead to Income Summary. The amount represents additional manufacturing costs that are not already in the inventory or cost of goods sold account. The amount is extended to the Income Statement Debit column.

Extending other accounts to the Income Statement and Balance Sheet columns and calculating net income are similar to the procedures described for corporations in Chapter 13.

MOTIVATE

Ask students to name the accounts that a manufacturing business has that a merchandising business does not. Ask students to predict which of these accounts will appear on the financial statements viewed by the general public and which will not. (*Balance sheet and income statement accounts that have balances will appear: three inventory accounts and Cost of Goods Sold.*)

Preview

- Preview the accounting term and definition introduced in this lesson: statement of cost of goods manufactured.
- Direct students to read the headings at the top of each page in this lesson and to examine the illustrations given.

EXPLAIN

- Explain that entries for Materials, Work in Process, and Finished Goods are made at the end of a fiscal period before the work sheet is prepared, so there are no adjusting entries for the inventory accounts on the work sheet.
- Explain that none of the manufacturing cost accounts on the work sheet have balances because these amounts have already been transferred to an inventory account or Cost of Goods Sold.
- Explain that the Income Summary account will have a balance representing the overapplied or underapplied overhead. A debit balance is underapplied overhead and a credit balance would be overapplied overhead. Remind students that this amount is the difference between the applied (estimated) overhead and the actual overhead.
- Direct students to the F.Y.I. for information on computer integrated manufacturing (CIM).

©GETTY IMAGES/PHOTODISC

FYI FOR YOUR INFORMATION

Robots and advanced electronic systems are used to manufacture products in many factories. The use of automated equipment to perform routine, repetitive manufacturing tasks is often referred to as "computer integrated manufacturing" (CIM).

MATERIALS

- **Instructor's Resource CD:**
  PowerPoint Slides
- **Xtra! Study Tools on the Xtra! Web Site**
- **Blackline Masters:**
  1-Column Statement Paper
  3-Column Income Statement with % of Net Sales Column
  3-Column Statement Paper

- **Working Papers:**
  Teacher's Edition of the Working Papers for Lesson 20-2
- **Software:**
  Personal Trainer
  Student Companion CD
  Peachtree

DEMONSTRATE

- Direct students to the illustration on pages 596–597, a work sheet for a manufacturing business, as you demonstrate completing a work sheet for a manufacturing business.

- Demonstrate that the three inventory accounts—Materials, Work in Process, and Finished Goods—do not have any work sheet adjustments because they were adjusted in the cost summary entries before the work sheet was begun.

- Demonstrate the usual adjustments for Allowance for Uncollectible Accounts, Prepaid Insurance, and Federal Income Tax Payable.

- Demonstrate the adjustments for Supplies—Sales and Supplies—Administrative. Point out that Supplies—Factory was already adjusted as part of the cost summary entries before the work sheet was begun.

- Demonstrate the adjustments for depreciation of office and store equipment. Point out that depreciation of factory equipment was already adjusted as part of the cost summary entries before the work sheet was begun.

FaxaVision, Inc.
Work Sheet
For Month Ended January 31, 20--

#	ACCOUNT TITLE	TRIAL BALANCE Debit	TRIAL BALANCE Credit	ADJUSTMENTS Debit	ADJUSTMENTS Credit	INCOME STATEMENT Debit	INCOME STATEMENT Credit	BALANCE SHEET Debit	BALANCE SHEET Credit
1	Cash	18263360						18263360	
2	Petty Cash	30000						30000	
3	Accounts Receivable	22420750						22420750	
4	Allow. for Uncoll. Accts.		454160		(a) 205660				659820
5	Materials	12194930						12194930	
6	Work in Process	10900350						10900350	
7	Finished Goods	13147250						13147250	
8	Supplies—Factory	725870						725870	
9	Supplies—Sales	953120			(b) 185020			768100	
10	Supplies—Administrative	2442580			(c) 46840			2395740	
11	Prepaid Insurance	419860			(d) 13060			406800	
12	Factory Equipment	18200000						18200000	
13	Accum. Depr.—Factory Equipment		5461000						5461000
14	Office Equipment	2526000						2526000	
15	Accum. Depr.—Office Equipment		620000		(e) 53000				673000
16	Store Equipment	2290000						2290000	
17	Accum. Depr.—Store Equipment		677000		(f) 49000				726000
18	Building	39700000						39700000	
19	Accum. Depr.—Building		5950000						5950000
20	Land	17700000						17700000	
21	Accounts Payable		18969850						18969850
22	Employee Income Tax Payable		1187140						1187140
23	Federal Income Tax Payable				(g) 2099500				2099500
24	Social Security Tax Payable		1397906						1397906
25	Medicare Tax Payable		322594						322594
26	Salaries Payable								
27	Unemploy. Tax Payable—Federal		126840						126840
28	Unemploy. Tax Payable—State		856170						856170
29	Dividends Payable								
30	Mortgage Payable		10000000						10000000
31	Capital Stock		60000000						60000000
32	Retained Earnings		46963880						46963880
33	Dividends								
34	Income Summary	15350				15350			

Accounting Transactions and Financial Reporting for a Manufacturing Business

TEACHING STRATEGIES — DIFFERENT LEARNING ABILITIES

Limited English Proficiency (LEP) Students. Create visual instructional methods, such as posters and bulletin boards, that reinforce accounting concepts in both English and the other dominant language(s).

#	Account Title	Trial Balance Debit	Trial Balance Credit	Adjustments Debit	Adjustments Credit	Income Statement Debit	Income Statement Credit	Balance Sheet Debit	Balance Sheet Credit
35	Sales		41148000				41148000		
36	Cost of Goods Sold	26402000				26402000			
37	Factory Overhead								
38	Depr. Expense—Factory Equipment								
39	Depr. Expense—Building								
40	Heat, Light, and Power Expense								
41	Insurance Expense—Factory								
42	Miscellaneous Exp.—Factory								
43	Payroll Taxes Exp.—Factory								
44	Property Tax Exp.—Factory								
45	Supplies Expense—Factory								
46	Advertising Expense	478440				478440			
47	Delivery Expense	1105860				1105860			
48	Depr. Expense—Store Equipment			(f) 49000		49000			
49	Miscellaneous Expenses—Sales	155450				155450			
50	Salary Expense—Sales	2807800				2807800			
51	Supplies Expense—Sales			(b) 185020		185020			
52	Depr. Expense—Office Equipment			(e) 53000		53000			
53	Insurance Expense—Admin.			(d) 13060		13060			
54	Miscellaneous Exp.—Admin.	218420				218420			
55	Payroll Taxes Exp.—Admin.	710000				710000			
56	Property Tax Exp.—Admin.	15980				15980			
57	Salary Expense—Admin.	2192200				2192200			
58	Supplies Expense—Admin.			(c) 46840		46840			
59	Uncollectible Accounts Expense			(a) 205660		205660			
60	Utilities Expense—Admin.	154380				154380			
61	Gain on Plant Assets								
62	Miscellaneous Revenue								
63	Interest Expense	150000				150000			
64	Loss on Plant Assets	14590				14590			
65	Federal Income Tax Expense			(g) 2099500		2099500			
66		194134540	194134540	2652080	2652080	37072550	41148000	159469150	155393700
67	Net Income after Fed. Inc. Tax					4075450			4075450
68						41148000	41148000	159469150	159469150

DEMONSTRATE

- Demonstrate that Income Summary has a debit balance in the Trial Balance columns. Explain that this is a result of the cost summary entries prepared before the work sheet was begun. Explain that it represents the amount of underapplied overhead. Point out that if overhead had been overapplied, this amount would be a credit balance for Income Summary.

- Demonstrate that the Income Summary account balance is extended to the Income Statement Debit column.

- Demonstrate that the Cost of Goods Sold account has a debit balance as a result of the cost summary entries prepared before the work sheet was begun. Point out that this account replaces the cost accounts of a merchandising business.

- Point out that Factory Overhead and the factory expense accounts do not have balances. Explain that adjustments for the factory cost accounts were recorded as part of the cost summary entries before the work sheet was begun. The cost accounts were adjusted and then their balances were recorded in Factory Overhead, which was then closed. Therefore, these amounts have already been absorbed into the inventory accounts and Cost of Goods Sold.

- Demonstrate that after all adjustments are recorded, the work sheet for a manufacturing business is completed the same way as one for a merchandising business.

- Demonstrate the extending of balance sheet account balances to the Balance Sheet columns.

- Demonstrate the extending of income statement account balances to the Income Statement columns. Emphasize that Income Summary is extended to the Income Statement columns.

- Demonstrate the totaling and ruling of the work sheet.

TEACHING STRATEGIES   DIFFERENT LEARNING ABILITIES

Specific Learning Disability (SLD) Students. When feasible, SLD students should become involved in work-study programs that are consistent with course content. When work-study opportunities are unavailable, simulations can be used to provide a simulated work environment. Field trips are an excellent method to expose students to the business world.

- Explain that a cost of goods manufactured statement is unique to a manufacturing business.

- Point out that a cost of goods manufactured statement is a supplement to the income statement because it shows the details of one of the items on the income statement—the cost of goods manufactured.

- Use an instructor-prepared transparency of a 1-column statement form or direct students to the illustration as you demonstrate how to prepare a cost of goods manufactured statement.

- Demonstrate calculating the total cost of work placed in process by adding: (a) direct materials from the total requisitions in the general journal entry on page 587; (b) direct labor from the cost sheets recorded in the cash payments journal entry on page 586; and (c) applied factory overhead from the job cost sheets in the general journal entry on page 589.

- Demonstrate adding the beginning balance of Work in Process from the general ledger to the total cost of work placed in process to get the total cost of Work in Process during the month.

- Demonstrate subtracting the ending balance of Work in Process to get the cost of goods manufactured.

STATEMENT OF COST OF GOODS MANUFACTURED

FaxaVision, Inc.
Statement of Cost of Goods Manufactured
For Month Ended January 31, 20--

Direct Materials	$156,477.00
Direct Labor	83,500.00
Factory Overhead Applied	66,800.00
Total Cost of Work Placed in Process	$306,777.00
Work in Process Inventory, Jan. 1, 20--	82,579.00
Total Cost of Work in Process During January	$389,356.00
Less Work in Process Inventory, Jan. 31, 20--	109,003.50
Cost of Goods Manufactured	$280,352.50

1. Enter direct materials, direct labor, and factory overhead applied.

2. Total the cost of work placed in process.

3. Add beginning work in process inventory.

4. Subtract ending work in process inventory.

A manufacturing business prepares an income statement, a statement of stockholders' equity, and a balance sheet. These statements are similar to those previously described for other kinds of businesses. A statement showing details about the cost of finished goods is called a **statement of cost of goods manufactured**. This statement shows the details of the cost elements—materials, direct labor, and factory overhead—spent on the goods completed in a fiscal period. A statement of cost of goods manufactured supplements the income statement. FaxaVision's statement of cost of goods manufactured is shown above.

STEPS • STEPS • STEPS • STEPS • STEPS • STEPS • STEPS • STEPS • STEPS • STEPS

PREPARING A STATEMENT OF COST OF GOODS MANUFACTURED

1 Enter direct materials, $156,477.00. This is the amount debited to Work in Process in the general journal, page 587. Enter direct labor, $83,500.00, from the cash payments journal, page 586. Enter factory overhead applied, $66,800.00. The amount of factory overhead is the total of the applied factory overhead recorded on cost sheets. The journal entry to record applied factory overhead was shown on page 589.

2 Total the cost of work placed in process by adding direct materials, direct labor, and factory overhead applied.

3 Add beginning work in process inventory, $82,579.00, to determine the total cost of work in process during the month.

4 Subtract ending work in process inventory, $109,003.50, to determine the cost of goods manufactured during the month.

SOURCES OF INCOME STATEMENT INFORMATION

FaxaVision's income statement for the month of January is shown on page 599. Information for FaxaVision's income statement comes from three sources:

1. Beginning and ending finished goods inventories, $115,140.00 and $131,472.50, come from the general ledger account, page 591.

2. Cost of goods manufactured, $280,352.50, comes from the statement of cost of goods manufactured shown above.

3. All other amounts come from the Income Statement columns of the work sheet, pages 596–597.

Accounting Transactions and Financial Reporting for a Manufacturing Business

TEACHING STRATEGIES DIFFERENT LEARNING STYLES

Visual Learner. When covering journal entries with a visual learner, the instructor should discuss the entries, using a transparency or the chalkboard to record the entry. In addition, the student should be asked to mentally picture each part of the entry before the instructor actually writes it on the transparency or chalkboard.

INCOME STATEMENT

FaxaVision, Inc.
Income Statement
For Month Ended January 31, 20--

			*% of Net Sales
Operating Revenue:			
Sales		$411,480.00	100.0
Cost of Goods Sold:			
Finished Goods Inventory, Jan. 1, 20--	$115,140.00		
Cost of Goods Manufactured	280,352.50		
Total Cost of Finished Goods Available for Sale	$395,492.50		
Less Finished Goods Inventory, Jan. 31, 20--	131,472.50		
Cost of Goods Sold	$264,020.00		
Underapplied Overhead ...Add...Over...Subtract	153.50		
Net Cost of Goods Sold		264,173.50	64.2
Gross Profit on Operations		$147,306.50	35.8
Operating Expenses:			
Selling Expenses:			
Advertising Expense	$ 4,784.40		
Delivery Expense	11,058.60		
Depreciation Expense—Store Equipment	490.00		
Miscellaneous Expense—Sales	1,554.50		
Salary Expense—Sales	28,078.00		
Supplies Expense—Sales	1,850.20		
Total Selling Expenses	$ 47,815.70		
Administrative Expenses:			
Depreciation Expense—Office Equipment	$ 530.00		
Insurance Expense—Administrative	130.60		
Miscellaneous Expense—Administrative	2,184.20		
Payroll Taxes Expense—Administrative	7,100.00		
Property Tax Expense—Administrative	159.80		
Salary Expense—Administrative	21,922.00		
Supplies Expense—Administrative	468.40		
Uncollectible Accounts Expense	2,056.60		
Utilities Expense—Administrative	1,543.80		
Total Administrative Expenses	$ 36,095.40		
Total Operating Expenses		83,911.10	20.4
Net Income from Operations		$ 63,395.40	15.4
Other Expenses:			
Interest Expense	$ 1,500.00		
Loss on Plant Assets	145.90		
Net Deduction		1,645.90	0.4
Net Income before Federal Income Tax		$ 61,749.50	15.0
Less Federal Income Tax Expense		20,995.00	5.1
Net Income after Federal Income Tax		$ 40,754.50	9.9

*Rounded to nearest 0.1%

This income statement differs in two ways from the income statements of merchandising businesses shown in previous chapters:

1. Cost of goods manufactured is used instead of purchases. Details of the cost of goods manufactured are given on the statement of cost of goods manufactured.
2. The amount of underapplied overhead, $153.50, is added to the cost of goods sold. The amount is added because applied overhead is less than the actual overhead. The

cost of goods manufactured, shown on page 598, includes the applied overhead amount rather than the actual amount. The income statement must be adjusted to reflect actual factory overhead costs. Theoretically, the underapplied or overapplied overhead should be apportioned among the work in process inventory, finished goods inventory, and cost of goods sold accounts. However, since the amount is small, it is charged entirely to cost of goods sold.

EXPLAIN

- Explain that information for preparing an income statement comes from three sources.
- Explain that the beginning and ending finished goods inventory amounts come from the general ledger account.
- Point out that the amount of cost of goods manufactured comes from the statement of cost of goods manufactured.
- Explain that all other income statement amounts come from the Income Statement columns of the work sheet.

DEMONSTRATE

- Use an instructor-prepared transparency of a 3-column statement form with a % of Net Sales column or direct students to the illustration as you demonstrate how to prepare an income statement for a manufacturing business.
- Demonstrate that the Cost of Goods Sold section is similar to the same section for a merchandising business. Demonstrate that the beginning inventory and the cost of goods manufactured are added to obtain the total cost of finished goods available for sale. Demonstrate that the ending finished goods inventory is then subtracted to obtain cost of goods sold.
- Demonstrate that the cost of goods sold needs to be adjusted by the amount of overapplied or underapplied overhead, which is obtained from the balance of Income Summary in the Income Statement columns of the work sheet. Demonstrate that underapplied overhead is added to cost of goods sold to obtain net cost of goods sold.
- Demonstrate the other portions of the income statement, which do not differ from the income statement of a merchandising business.

- Explain that there is little difference between the balance sheet of a merchandising and a manufacturing business.

- Point out that the primary difference in a balance sheet for a manufacturing business is that there are three manufacturing inventory accounts, Materials, Work in Process, and Finished Goods, rather than a single merchandise inventory account.

- Explain that although a statement of stockholders' equity is not illustrated, it would not differ from that for a merchandising business.

- Use an instructor-made transparency of a 3-column statement form or direct students to the illustration as you explain the preparation of a balance sheet.

- Demonstrate the preparation of the Assets section. Point out that the three inventory accounts are simply listed separately in the Current Assets section.

- Demonstrate the preparation of the Liabilities section.

- Demonstrate the preparation of the Stockholders' Equity section.

- Assessment is an ongoing process. Circulate through the classroom or lab, observing which students have problems with the assignments.

- Troubleshooting: Diagnose what kinds of problems students have with this lesson. Students should have little difficulty with the end-of-fiscal-period work in this lesson, but may have some difficulty with the format of the statement of cost of goods manufactured.

- Assess student understanding by checking solutions to Independent Practice assignments.

- Call on students to describe each line on the statement of cost of goods manufactured and how it is calculated.

- Review work sheet and financial statement preparation as needed.

BALANCE SHEET

Faxa Vision, Inc.
Balance Sheet
January 31, 20--

ASSETS

Current Assets:			
Cash		$182,633.60	
Petty Cash		300.00	
Accounts Receivable	$224,207.50		
Less Allowance for Uncollectible Accounts	6,598.20	217,609.30	
Materials		121,949.30	
Work in Process		109,003.50	
Finished Goods		131,472.50	
Supplies—Factory		7,258.70	
Supplies—Sales		7,681.00	
Supplies—Administrative		1,957.40	
Prepaid Insurance		4,068.00	
Total Current Assets			$ 783,933.30
Plant Assets:			
Factory Equipment	$182,000.00		
Less Accumulated Depreciation—Factory Equipment	54,610.00	$127,390.00	
Office Equipment	$ 25,260.00		
Less Accumulated Depreciation—Office Equipment	6,730.00	18,530.00	
Store Equipment	$ 22,900.00		
Less Accumulated Depreciation—Store Equipment	7,260.00	15,640.00	
Building	$397,000.00		
Less Accumulated Depreciation—Building	59,500.00	337,500.00	
Land		177,000.00	
Total Plant Assets			676,060.00
Total Assets			$1,459,993.30

LIABILITIES

Current Liabilities:		
Accounts Payable	$189,698.50	
Employee Income Tax Payable	11,871.40	
Federal Income Tax Payable	20,995.00	
Social Security Tax Payable	13,979.06	
Medicare Tax Payable	3,225.94	
Unemployment Tax Payable—Federal	1,268.40	
Unemployment Tax Payable—State	8,561.70	
Total Current Liabilities		$ 249,600.00
Long-Term Liability:		
Mortgage Payable		100,000.00
Total Liabilities		$ 349,600.00

STOCKHOLDERS' EQUITY

Capital Stock	$600,000.00	
Retained Earnings	510,393.30	
Total Stockholders' Equity		1,110,393.30
Total Liabilities and Stockholders' Equity		$1,459,993.30

The balance sheet prepared by FaxaVision on January 31, of the current year is shown above.

Except for the list of inventories, the balance sheet of a manufacturing business is similar to the balance sheet of a merchandising business. In a manufacturing business, the current assets section of the balance sheet lists three types of inventories: (1) materials, (2) work in process, and (3) finished goods.

A statement of stockholders' equity for a manufacturing business is similar to that of a merchandising business described in Chapter 13. The statement of stockholders' equity for FaxaVision is not illustrated.

• term review

statement of cost of goods manufactured

• audit your understanding

1. To which work sheet column is the debit balance of Cost of Goods Sold extended?

2. How is underapplied overhead accounted for on an income statement?

3. In which section of the balance sheet are the three inventory accounts of a manufacturing business listed?

• work together 20-2

Preparing statement of cost of goods manufactured, income statement, and balance sheet

Work sheets for Bedthings, Inc., a manufacturing firm, are included in the *Working Papers*. Additional information for Bedthings for the months of March and April follow. Your instructor will guide you through the following examples.

	March	April
Cost of Direct Materials Used to Produce Finished Goods	$110,950.00	$123,490.00
Cost of Direct Labor Used to Produce Finished Goods	82,165.00	88,205.00
Actual Factory Overhead	61,150.00	64,320.00
Applied Factory Overhead	62,310.00	63,730.00
Beginning Finished Goods Inventory	102,845.00	118,520.00
Beginning Work in Process Inventory	78,100.00	78,360.00

1. Prepare a statement of cost of goods manufactured for March of the current year.

2. Prepare an income statement for March of the current year.

3. Prepare a balance sheet as of March 31 of the current year.

• on your own 20-2

Preparing statement of cost of goods manufactured, income statement, and balance sheet

Work sheets for Bedthings, Inc., a manufacturing firm, are included in the *Working Papers*. Use the information for April from Work Together 20-2. Work independently to complete the following problems.

1. Prepare a statement of cost of goods manufactured for April of the current year.

2. Prepare an income statement for April of the current year.

3. Prepare a balance sheet as of April 30 of the current year.

GUIDED PRACTICE

Term Review
Call on students to define the term in the Term Review. Ask the class if the definition is correct and whether the complete definition has been given or if anything needs to be added. The suggested definition is given in the Glossary.

Audit Your Understanding
Call on students to answer the Audit Your Understanding questions. Ask the class if the answers are correct and/or complete. Answers are given in Appendix E of the textbook.

Work Together
Have students write the solution to the Work Together problems as you guide the class through the problem.

- Discuss each step and when the class is in agreement, direct students to write the solution in the *Working Papers*.

INDEPENDENT PRACTICE

On Your Own
- Assign the On Your Own problem to be worked independently.
- Use the Ongoing Assessment techniques to diagnose student understanding.

Application Problem
- Assign Application Problem 20-3: Preparing a statement of cost of goods manufactured.

Personal Trainer
- Students can access the Lesson 20-2 assessment material using this software.

Xtra! Web Site
- Students can access the Xtra! Study Tools for additional practice.

ENRICH

- Divide the class into two groups. Each group stands and faces each other. The instructor chooses selected terms from Terms Reviews in Chapters 19–20. The instructor gives the term. The first student who raises his or her hand has the opportunity to give the correct definition. The group with the most correctly defined terms is declared the winner.

CLOSE

- Ask students to briefly summarize the procedures for completing end-of-fiscal-period work for a manufacturing business.

PUTTING IT ALL TOGETHER

- Review the Chapter Summary.
- Ask students to prepare a list of the new concepts introduced in this chapter.
- Discuss the journal entries for summarizing costs at the end of a fiscal period.
- Discuss the differences between end-of-fiscal-period work for a manufacturing and a merchandising business.

INDEPENDENT PRACTICE

- Assign Mastery Problem 20-4 to students who need the reinforcement of a problem that combines all concepts from the chapter in one problem; this will be most students.
- Assign Challenge Problem 20-5 to accelerated students who do not require the reinforcement of the Mastery Problem.
- Students can use Peachtree data files to automate Challenge Problem 20-5.
- Assign Study Guide 20.
- Students can access Personal Trainer to work end-of-chapter problems on the computer.
- Students can access the Xtra! Web Site for the Xtra! Review and Quizzing.
- Students can access the Student Companion CD for additional review material.

ONGOING ASSESSMENT

- Review solutions to the assigned problems in class, diagnosing trouble spots.

RETEACH

- Call on students to describe how they avoid the trouble spots diagnosed.
- Use reteaching suggestions from lesson plans as required.
- Assign Recycling Problem 20-1 if needed.

ENRICH

- Assign the Explore Accounting Feature. Ask students to share the information they have gathered in a report to the class.
- Students can access the Xtra! Web Site for the Xtra! Enrichment material.
- Assign Applied Communication.
- Assign the SCANS Workplace Competency.
- Assign Graphing Workshop.
- Assign Analyzing Costco's Financial Statements.
- Assign the Automated Accounting feature on page 608.
- Assign Reinforcement Activity 3.
- Assign Progressive Badge Company: A Business Simulation.

602

SUMMARY

After completing this chapter, you can

1. Define accounting terms related to accounting transactions and financial reporting for a manufacturing business.

2. Identify accounting concepts and practices related to accounting transactions and financial reporting for a manufacturing business.

3. Journalize transactions for a manufacturing business.

4. Prepare selected financial statements for a manufacturing business.

Explore Accounting

ISO 9000 Certification

Downhill Cycle assembles mountain bikes from components manufactured by other companies. Rather than personally examining each supplier's manufacturing process, the managers of Downhill Cycle require its suppliers to be ISO 9000 certified. ISO 9000 certification assures customers that the company has an effective quality management system that continually evaluates and improves the production process.

The ISO certification program was developed by the International Organization of Standards (ISO), a worldwide federation of national standards organizations. ISO's role includes programs that certify the manufacturing process. To become ISO 9000 certified, a company must follow the ISO's standards for various phases of the production process, including design, development, production, inspection, and servicing. The company must maintain an information system to record its compliance with ISO standards. Finally, the company must hire an independent organization to audit its initial and continuing compliance with ISO standards. ISO 9000 certification does not assure or guarantee the production of quality products. However, ISO 9000 certification does make a positive statement about a company's commitment to quality.

Other than helping to control costs, how does ISO 9000 certification impact accounting? Accountants assist in designing and operating the information systems necessary to collect ISO 9000 compliance data. Accountants in public accounting firms are also involved in ISO 9000 certification. These firms can either assist a client to prepare for the ISO 9000 certification process or be the independent organization that audits the client and awards ISO 9000 certification.

Required:
Research answers to the following questions:

1. How is ISO 9000 certification similar to financial statement audits?

2. Several types of ISO certification are available. Explain the purpose of ISO 14000 standards.

3. An acronym for the International Organization of Standardization would logically be IOS. Explain why the ISO title is used for the organization and its certifications.

602   Chapter 20   Accounting Transactions and Financial Reporting for a Manufacturing Business

EXPLORE ACCOUNTING

1. An independent auditor tests documentation produced by the ISO information system to determine if the company is complying with the ISO standard. The auditor then issues a report that certifies the company is in conformance with the standard.

2. ISO 14000 standards deal with environmental management systems. The standards require a company to be in compliance with environmental laws and strive to improve the environmental impact of its manufacturing processes.

3. The word "ISO" means "equal." The word was chosen to identify standards that guide the manufacturing of products using the same or equal specifications.

20-1 APPLICATION PROBLEM PEACHTREE QUICKBOOKS

Journalizing cost accounting transactions for a manufacturing company

Perry, Inc., completed the following factory cost transactions during August of the current year:

Transactions:

Aug.   4.   Purchased $6,152.80 of materials from Sharon Company on account. P047.
      7.   Paid cash for machinery used for production, $3,458.00. C651.
    15.   Bought supplies for use in the factory by paying $583.83 cash. C658.
    21.   Had machinery repaired. Made cash payment of $1,123.00 to repairer. C667. (Miscellaneous Expense—Factory)
    24.   Purchased materials on account from Hubbard Company, $3,510.72. P048. Monthly factory payroll was paid in cash, $7,599.32 (direct labor, $7,200.00, and indirect labor, $1,920.00; less deductions: employee income tax, $823.00; Social security tax, $566.87; Medicare tax, $130.81). C679.

Instructions:

1. Journalize the following transactions. Use page 4 of a materials purchases journal and page 8 of a cash payments journal. Source documents are abbreviated as follows: check, C; purchase invoice, P.
2. Total and rule the materials purchases journal.
3. Prove and rule the cash payments journal.

20-2 APPLICATION PROBLEM

Journalizing and posting entries that summarize cost records at the end of a fiscal period

The following information is taken from the records of Cramer Corporation on March 31 of the current year. The accounts and balances needed to complete this problem are provided in the *Working Papers.*

a. The total factory payroll for the month from the payroll register is $122,530.00, distributed as follows:

Work in Process	$102,570.00	Employee Income Tax Payable	13,478.50
Factory Overhead	19,960.00	Social Security Tax Payable	7,964.45
Cash	99,249.10	Medicare Tax Payable	1,837.95

b. The total of all requisitions of direct materials issued during the month is $139,419.80. The total of all requisitions of indirect materials issued during the month is $4,505.00.
c. The factory overhead to be charged to Work in Process is 68% of the direct labor cost.
d. The total of all cost sheets completed during the month is $294,313.50.
e. The total of costs recorded on all sales invoices for March is $395,800.00.

Instructions:

1. Journalize the factory payroll entry on page 6 of a cash payments journal. C371. Post the general debit and general credit amounts.
2. Journalize the following entries on page 3 of a general journal. Post the entries.
   a. An entry to transfer the total of all direct materials requisitions to Work in Process and indirect materials to Factory Overhead. M34.
   b. An entry to close all individual manufacturing expense accounts to Factory Overhead. M35.
   c. An entry to record applied factory overhead to Work in Process. M36.
3. Continue using page 3 of the general journal. Journalize and post the entry to close the balance of the factory overhead account to Income Summary. M37.
4. Journalize and post the entry to transfer the total of all cost sheets completed from Work in Process to Finished Goods. M38.
5. Journalize and post the entry to transfer the cost of products sold from Finished Goods to Cost of Goods Sold. M39. Save your work to complete Application Problem 20-3.

FORMAL EVALUATION

Chapter 20 Test
ExamView for Chapter 20
Assessment by Portfolio

- Review answers to all tests administered as a class activity. If time is limited, review only the items that were frequently answered incorrectly.

- Ask students if there are any questions about the chapter before proceeding to the next chapter.

CHECK FIGURES

Application Problem 20-1

Materials Purchases Journal total, 9,663.52;
Cash Payments Journal totals, 14,284.83, 1,520.68, 12,764.15.

Application Problem 20-2

2. c. Applied factory overhead, 69,747.60.

3. Underapplied overhead, 767.80.

See Teacher's Edition of the Working Papers for Chapter 20 for complete solutions.

TEACHING STRATEGIES   EXPANDING BEYOND THE CLASSROOM

Invite an accountant from a manufacturing business to the classroom to address the importance of cost accounting to a manufacturing business.

20-3 APPLICATION PROBLEM

Preparing a statement of cost of goods manufactured

Use the working papers from Application Problem 20-2 to complete this problem.

Instructions:

Prepare a statement of cost of goods manufactured for Cramer Corporation. The statement is for the month ended March 31 of the current year.

20-4 MASTERY PROBLEM

Journalizing entries that summarize cost records at the end of a fiscal period

The following information is taken from the records of Simmons Corporation on May 31 of the current year. The accounts and balances needed to complete this problem are provided in the *Working Papers*.

a. The total factory payroll for the month according to the payroll register is $77,430.00, distributed as follows.

Work in Process	$58,160.00	Employee Income Tax Payable	8,627.50
Factory Overhead	19,270.00	Social Security Tax Payable	5,032.95
Cash	62,608.10	Medicare Tax Payable	1,161.45

b. The total of all requisitions of direct materials issued during the month is $64,344.00. The total of all requisitions of indirect materials issued during the month is $5,835.00.

c. The factory overhead to be charged to Work in Process is 80% of the direct labor cost.

d. The total of all cost sheets completed during the month is $166,425.00.

e. The total of costs recorded on all sales invoices for May is $258,705.00.

Instructions:

1. Journalize the factory payroll entry on page 10 of a cash payments journal. C711. Post the general debit and general credit amounts.

2. Journalize the following entries on page 5 of a general journal. Post the debit and credit amounts.

    a. An entry to transfer the total of all direct materials requisitions to Work in Process and indirect materials to Factory Overhead. M211.

    b. An entry to close all individual manufacturing expense accounts to Factory Overhead. M212.

    c. An entry to record applied factory overhead to Work in Process. M213.

3. Continue using page 5 of the general journal. Journalize and post the entry to close the balance of the factory overhead account to Income Summary. M214.

4. Journalize and post the entry to transfer the total of all cost sheets completed from Work in Process to Finished Goods. M215.

5. Journalize and post the entry to transfer the cost of products sold from Finished Goods to Cost of Goods Sold. M216.

6. Prepare a statement of cost of goods manufactured for the month ended May 31 of the current year.

20-5 CHALLENGE PROBLEM

Journalizing entries that summarize cost records at the end of a fiscal period; preparing financial statements

The following information is taken from the records of Cozart Company on July 31 of the current year. The accounts and balances needed to complete this problem are provided in the *Working Papers*.

APPLIED SKILLS   LANGUAGE ARTS

Paraphrasing, Writing Complete Sentences, and Identifying Subjects. For additional practice in language arts skills, direct students to answer the Applied Communication activity and Cases for Critical Thinking. Students should write the answers in their own words and in complete sentences. To further practice language arts skills, ask students to underline the subject(s) in each sentence of their answers.

a. The total factory payroll for the month from the payroll register is $63,000.00, distributed as follows.

Work in Process	$46,600.00	Employee Income Tax Payable	6,930.00
Factory Overhead	16,400.00	Social Security Tax Payable	4,095.00
Cash	51,030.00	Medicare Tax Payable	945.00

b. The total of all requisitions of direct materials issued during the month is $67,760.00. The total of all requisitions of indirect materials issued during the month is $6,990.00.
c. The factory overhead to be charged to Work in Process is 95% of the direct labor cost.
d. The total of all cost sheets completed during the month is $140,984.00.
e. The total of costs recorded on all sales invoices for July is $112,176.83.

Instructions:
1. Journalize the factory payroll entry on page 14 of a cash payments journal. C341. Post the general debit and general credit amounts.
2. Journalize the following entries on page 7 of a general journal. Post the entries.
   a. An entry to transfer the total of all direct materials requisitions to Work in Process and indirect materials to Factory Overhead. M698.
   b. An entry to close all individual manufacturing expense accounts to Factory Overhead. M699.
   c. An entry to record applied factory overhead to Work in Process. M700.
3. Continue using page 7 of the general journal. Journalize and post the entry to close the balance of the factory overhead account to Income Summary. M701.
4. Journalize and post the entry to transfer the total of all cost sheets completed from Work in Process to Finished Goods. M702.
5. Journalize and post the entry to transfer the cost of products sold from Finished Goods to Cost of Goods Sold. M703.
6. Prepare a statement of cost of goods manufactured for the month ended July 31 of the current year.

Cozart's general ledger accounts and their balances on July 31 of the current year are given on the work sheet in the *Working Papers*. (The Employee Income Tax Payable, Social Security Tax Payable, and Medicare Tax Payable balances differ from your ledger account balances due to additional postings completed for payroll taxes and sales and administrative salaries.)

7. Prepare an 8-column work sheet for the month ended July 31 of the current year. Record the adjustments on the work sheet using the following information.

Adjustment Information, July 31

Uncollectible Accounts Expense Estimated as 1.0% of Total Sales on Account.	
Sales on Account for Year	$76,275.00
Sales Supplies Inventory	1,762.50
Administrative Supplies Inventory	520.74
Value of Prepaid Administrative Insurance	1,383.30
Monthly Depreciation Expense—Office Equipment	68.51
Monthly Depreciation Expense—Store Equipment	61.88
Federal Income Tax Expense Estimated for the Month	7,807.00

8. Prepare an income statement for the month ended July 31 of the current year. Calculate and record the following component percentages: (a) net cost of goods sold, (b) gross profit on operations, (c) total operating expenses, (d) income from operations, (e) net addition or deduction resulting from other revenue and expenses, (f) net income before federal income tax, (g) federal income tax expense, and (h) net income after federal income tax. Round percentage calculations to the nearest 0.1%.
9. Prepare a balance sheet for July 31 of the current year. A statement of stockholders' equity is not prepared. Therefore, add the amount of net income after federal income tax to the beginning balance of Retained Earnings to obtain the ending balance.

APPLIED SKILLS WRITING ACROSS THE CURRICULUM

Writing Paragraphs and Short Essays. The Cases for Critical Thinking are short, practical applications of the accounting principles developed in the chapter. Some cases are planned to present problems related to the chapter but not specifically discussed and answered in the chapter. These cases present an opportunity for critical thinking and decision making. These cases also require more than a short objective-type response. Therefore, they provide ideal practice in writing paragraphs and short essays.

APPLIED COMMUNICATION

Student solutions can be compared to the illustration on page 585, but instructors should be aware that students may prepare other formats of charts that also present the cost flow appropriately. The written narrative of the report can also be graded for accuracy and mechanics.

CASE FOR CRITICAL THINKING

The accounting changes should not be made. The suggested procedure would require less time. However, without the information provided by the existing procedures, cost control would be more limited and management information less available.

Periodic inventory would not provide cost information for each job or unit manufactured. If an applied overhead rate is not used, overhead could not be charged to manufacturing costs until the end of the accounting period and then would be only a total amount. Overhead cost information would not be available for each job. If cost sheets were not used for each job, unit manufacturing costs could not be calculated. If all costs are closed into Income Summary, cost of goods sold could not be determined without separate computations.

SCANS WORKPLACE COMPETENCY

Schools might recognize various cultures through rallies featuring cultural dances, music, or martial arts. Other options include guest speakers, cultural fairs, food booths, or days set aside for cultural dress.

• applied communication

A new clerk has been hired at the company for which you work. You have been asked to explain the flow of materials from ordering through issuing to the factory.

Required:
Prepare a chart and a brief written explanation of the flow of materials.

• case for critical thinking

Kingston Corp., a manufacturing company, uses the perpetual inventory method for all inventory accounts. Direct materials, direct labor, and applied overhead are recorded on cost sheets similar to FaxaVision's. At the end of each month, general journal entries are made to update the general ledger manufacturing accounts. Overapplied or Underapplied Overhead is closed to Income Summary and reported on the income statement as an adjustment to the cost of goods sold.

A new accountant suggests that the company could save considerable time if a number of accounting changes are made: (1) use the periodic inventory method, (2) drop the use of applied overhead, and (3) close all manufacturing accounts to Income Summary similar to the procedure used by merchandising businesses. The accountant indicates that these new procedures would provide adequate information to prepare the income statement with a substantial time and cost saving.

Should the changes in accounting procedures be made? Will the changes provide adequate information? How will the changes affect the information now provided?

• SCANS workplace competency

Interpersonal Competency: Working with Cultural Diversity

Concept: Competent employees work well with both men and women and with people from a variety of ethnic, social, or educational backgrounds. These employees understand the cultures of others, respect the rights of others, make judgments and decisions on the basis of performance—not stereotypes—and understand the concerns of members of other ethnic and gender groups.

Application: Form a task group of 3-4 students, and brainstorm ideas on how your school can recognize and appreciate the diversity of cultures there. Discuss your views with the school's administration.

graphing workshop

John and Candy Moody operate Western Ski Centers, a small retail ski store in southwest Colorado. The couple is concerned that, despite increasing sales, they appear to be making less money each year. Using an option on their accounting software, you are able to prepare the following graph of income statement data.

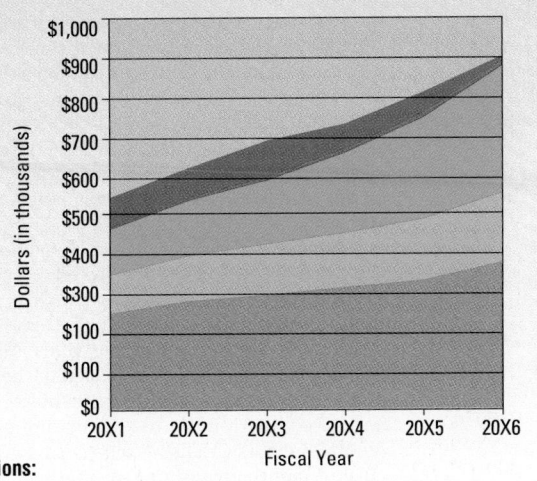

Analysis of Income Statement

Legend:
- Operating Income
- Other Expenses
- Administrative Expenses
- Selling Expenses
- Cost of Good Sold

Instructions:

1. What is represented by the top line of the graph?
2. Explain why the operating income of the business is declining.

analyzing Costco's financial statements

Like any retail company, Costco knows that some customers will return merchandise after the sale. When a June sale is returned in July, both the sale and the sales return are recorded in the same fiscal year. A problem occurs, however, when a sale in August (Costco's fiscal year end) is returned in September. The sale is recorded in one fiscal year while the sales return is recorded in the next fiscal year.

To solve this problem, Costco estimates the amount of its current-year sales it expects to be returned in the fiscal year. This procedure attempts to make sales and sales returns in the same fiscal year.

Instructions:

Read the first paragraph of the Revenue Recognition section of Note 1 in Costco's financial statements in Appendix B of this textbook.

1. How does Costco estimate sales returns?
2. Identify the amount of the reserve for sales returns reported on the 2003 financial statements. How is the amount reported on the financial statements?

---

1. Sales.
2. As sales increase, each of the sections of the graph should also increase. However, administrative expenses are increasing at a significantly higher rate than sales.

ANALYZING COSTCO'S FINANCIAL STATEMENTS

1. Costco "provides for estimated sales returns based on historical return levels."
2. $4,869,000.

TEACHING STRATEGIES   PORTFOLIO ASSESSMENT

Proper and accurate accounting and reporting of manufacturing costs is critical to a business because so many decisions are based on this information. If the information is incorrect, poor decisions may result and could cause a business to fail. Students should emphasize their learning of this topic by selecting an example of a comprehensive sample of their work in this chapter, either the Mastery Problem or a problem from a test to include in their portfolio. A copy of the Portfolio Assessment form (black-line master of the Teacher's Resource Guide; also on the Student Companion CD) should be completed by the student and the Description section should include any comments regarding how the student mastered these concepts and procedures. Alternatively, students might include in their portfolios all or part of Reinforcement Activity 3.

- Explain that the Automated Accounting software is not specifically designed to accommodate a cost accounting system; therefore, a company using software similar to this would need to use spreadsheet software for preparing some of its internal statements.

- Explain that a manufacturing company might wish to prepare a supplemental schedule of cost of goods manufactured. By doing so, statements can include detail from the ledger accounts while still maintaining the clarity of the individual statements they supplement.

- Explain that the statement of stockholders' equity is prepared the same for both a manufacturing and a merchandising business.

- Explain that a balance sheet of a manufacturing business differs from that of a merchandising business by showing the three types of inventory: Materials, Work in Process, and Finished Goods.

- Explain that the income statement of a manufacturing company may differ in several ways. A manufacturing business includes a cost of goods sold section but may also include supplemental schedules prepared with a spreadsheet program to present information about the cost of goods manufactured and the cost of goods sold.

- Explain that templates for spreadsheets should be created for frequently used schedules. A template is a skeleton design with a heading, titles, and formatting in place. Formulas are placed in the subtotal and total cells.

- Point out that each month a template can be opened and saved with a name to identify the report and month, such as COGS_March, and then the current data can be entered and verified before printing the report.

- Emphasize that when formulas are used in spreadsheets, the results calculated by the formulas should be checked for accuracy and corrected if need be before the spreadsheet can be used repeatedly with confidence.

Financial Statements for a Manufacturing Business

Manufacturing businesses, as well as merchandising businesses, prepare external financial statements reporting information for all the activities of the business taken as a whole. These statements include a balance sheet, an income statement, and a statement of stockholders' equity. The statement of stockholders' equity does not differ from that prepared for a corporation operating a merchandising business, but there are differences between the balance sheet and the income statement.

The asset section of the balance sheet for a manufacturing business will include the three types of inventory:

- Materials
- Work in process
- Finished goods

The partial balance sheet below shows the inventory accounts in the currents assets section.

The liabilities and stockholders' sections of the balance sheet do not differ from the financial statements of a merchandising business. The income statement of a manufacturing company may be presented in a number of ways. Like that of a merchandising company, the statement must include cost of goods sold information. Some companies include cost of goods sold as a section of the income statement. Many large corporations prefer to use supplemental schedules prepared with a spreadsheet program to present information about the cost of goods manufactured and the cost of goods sold. By preparing supplemental schedules before preparing the income statement, accounts can include detail from the ledger accounts while still maintaining the clarity of the individual statements.

Good spreadsheet design includes formulas and clear columns and row labels. Schedules prepared on a spreadsheet will resemble manual statements and schedules. Formulas will be used for all subtotals and totals. Formulas should be manually verified when the spreadsheet is created.

Many businesses create spreadsheet templates for frequently used schedules. The template is a skeleton design with a heading, titles, and formatting in place. Formulas are placed in the subtotal and total cells. Each month, the template is opened and saved with a name to identify the report and month, such as COGS_March. The data for the current month are entered and verified. Then the report is printed.

ABC Manufacturing
Partial Balance Sheet
Month Ended March 31, 20--

Assets

Current Assets	
Cash	$ 182,650
Accounts receivable, net	216,600
Materials	121,950
Work in process	108,400
Finished goods	131,475
Supplies	14,740
Total Current Assets	$ 775,815

Processing and Reporting Cost Accounting Data for a Manufacturing Business

This activity reinforces selected learning from Chapters 19 and 20. Job cost accounting processing and reporting is emphasized for a manufacturing company organized as a corporation.

FURNITURE DECOR, INC.

Furniture Decor, Inc., is a corporation that manufactures office furniture. Furniture Decor uses a job cost accounting system to record manufacturing costs. The fiscal year is from January 1 through December 31. Monthly financial statements are prepared.

PART A: RECORDING COST ACCOUNTING ACTIVITIES

In Part A of this reinforcement activity, Furniture Decor's daily cost accounting activities for one month will be recorded.

Furniture Decor uses the chart of accounts shown on the following page. The journals and ledgers used by Furniture Decor are similar to those illustrated in Chapters 19 and 20. The job cost sheets, selected general ledger accounts, and other accounting records or forms needed to do the cost accounting activities are provided in the *Working Papers*. Beginning balances have been recorded.

The January 31 general ledger balances are the result of posting completed during the month of January. Note that Accounts Payable has a debit balance for this reason. Also, the balances of the payroll liability accounts are the amounts posted for sales and administrative salaries for January.

CALCULATING FACTORY OVERHEAD APPLIED RATE

Instructions:
1. Calculate the factory overhead applied rate based on direct labor costs. Estimated annual factory overhead costs for the current year are $306,000.00. Estimated direct labor hours to be used during the current year are 17,000 hours at an estimated rate of $15.00 per hour. Retain the calculations for use later in this reinforcement activity.

- Reinforcement Activity 3 covers the complete accounting cycle for a manufacturing business organized as a corporation. Processing and reporting for job cost accounting is emphasized.

ASSESSMENT

- Blackline masters for the audit test for Reinforcement Activity 3 are available in the Teacher's Resource Guide.

WINNING EDGE

Give students the *Winning Edge* by making competitive event prep part of their classroom materials throughout the year. Go to *http://winningedge.swlearning.com* for a list of materials that prepare students for specific competitive events.

MATERIALS

Working Papers for Reinforcement Activity 3
Teacher's Edition of the Working Papers for Reinforcement Activity 3
Blackline Master of Audit Test

TEACHING STRATEGIES   PORTFOLIO ASSESSMENT

A copy of the Portfolio Assessment form (blackline master in the Teacher's Resource Guide; also on the Student Companion CD) should be completed by the student, and the Description section should include any comments regarding how the student mastered these concepts and procedures.

FURNITURE DECOR, INC. CHART OF ACCOUNTS

Balance Sheet Accounts

(1000)	ASSETS
1100	CURRENT ASSETS
1105	Cash
1110	Petty Cash
1115	Accounts Receivable
1120	Allowance for Uncollectible Accounts
1125	Materials
1130	Work in Process
1135	Finished Goods
1140	Supplies—Factory
1145	Supplies—Sales
1150	Supplies—Administrative
1155	Prepaid Insurance
1200	PLANT ASSETS
1205	Factory Equipment
1210	Accumulated Depreciation—Factory Equipment
1215	Office Equipment
1220	Accumulated Depreciation—Office Equipment
1225	Store Equipment
1230	Accumulated Depreciation—Store Equipment
1235	Building
1240	Accumulated Depreciation—Building
1245	Land
(2000)	LIABILITIES
2100	CURRENT LIABILITIES
2105	Accounts Payable
2110	Employee Income Tax Payable
2115	Federal Income Tax Payable
2120	Social Security Tax Payable
2123	Medicare Tax Payable
2125	Salaries Payable
2130	Unemployment Tax Payable—Federal
2135	Unemployment Tax Payable—State
2140	Dividends Payable
2200	LONG-TERM LIABILITY
2205	Mortgage Payable
(3000)	STOCKHOLDERS' EQUITY
3105	Capital Stock
3110	Retained Earnings
3115	Dividends
3120	Income Summary

Income Statement Accounts

(4000)	OPERATING REVENUE
4105	Sales
(5000)	COST OF SALES
5105	Cost of Goods Sold
(5500)	MANUFACTURING COSTS
5505	Factory Overhead
5510	Depreciation Expense—Factory Equipment
5515	Depreciation Expense—Building
5520	Heat, Light, and Power Expense
5525	Insurance Expense—Factory
5530	Miscellaneous Expense—Factory
5535	Payroll Taxes Expense—Factory
5540	Property Tax Expense—Factory
5545	Supplies Expense—Factory
(6000)	OPERATING EXPENSES
6100	SELLING EXPENSES
6105	Advertising Expense
6110	Delivery Expense
6115	Depreciation Expense—Store Equipment
6120	Miscellaneous Expense—Sales
6125	Salary Expense—Sales
6130	Supplies Expense—Sales
6200	ADMINISTRATIVE EXPENSES
6205	Depreciation Expense—Office Equipment
6210	Insurance Expense—Administrative
6215	Miscellaneous Expense—Administrative
6220	Payroll Taxes Expense—Administrative
6225	Property Tax Expense—Administrative
6230	Salary Expense—Administrative
6235	Supplies Expense—Administrative
6240	Uncollectible Accounts Expense
6245	Utilities Expense—Administrative
(7000)	OTHER REVENUE
7105	Gain on Plant Assets
7110	Miscellaneous Revenue
(8000)	OTHER EXPENSES
8105	Interest Expense
8110	Loss on Plant Assets
(9000)	INCOME TAX
9105	Federal Income Tax Expense

RECORDING TRANSACTIONS

Instructions:

2. Record the following transactions completed during January of the current year in the appropriate cost records and journals. Use page 1 of a materials purchases journal, general journal, and cash payments journal. Recording instructions are provided only for the first occurrence of each kind of transaction. Source documents are abbreviated as follows: check, C; memorandum, M; materials requisition, MR; purchase order, PO; sales invoice, S.

Jan. 3. Opened a cost sheet for Job No. 232, 250 C200 computer desks ordered for stock. Date wanted, January 12.

3. Issued direct materials to factory for Job No. 232, $5,100.00. MR750.

   Materials list: 6,000 square feet base wood @ $0.20 per square foot
                  6,000 square feet laminate @ $0.60 per square feet
                  187.5 pounds adhesive @ $1.60 per pound
   Record the direct materials in the materials ledger and the cost ledger.

5. Opened a cost sheet for Job No. 233, 200 P150 printer tables ordered for stock. Date wanted, January 17.

5. Issued direct materials to factory for Job No. 233, $3,400.00. MR751.

   Materials list: 4,000 square feet base wood @ $0.20 per square foot
                  4,000 square feet laminate @ $0.60 per square foot
                  125 pounds adhesive @ $1.60 per pound

5. Ordered 30,000 square feet base wood. P0520.

   Record the purchase order in the materials ledger.

5. Ordered 20,000 square feet laminate. P0521.

7. Ordered 1,600 casters. P0522.

7. Ordered direct materials to factory for Job No. 232, $1,250.00. MR752.

   Materials list: 1,000 casters @ $1.25 each

7. Ordered 1,000 sets hinges. P0523.

7. Recorded weekly summary of job-time records to cost ledger.

   Job No. 232 $3,300.00
   Job No. 233   1,125.00

7. Ordered 1,000 pounds adhesive. P0524.

10. Issued direct materials to factory for Job No. 233, $1,200.00. MR753.

    Materials list: 800 casters @ $1.25 each
                   200 sets metal glides @ $1.00 per set

10. Ordered 300 sets of metal glides. P0525.

10. Sold 100 C200 computer desks to Office Mart. S323.

    Record only the cost in the finished goods ledger. Furniture Decor uses the first-in, first-out inventory method. Thus, the cost recorded first is the cost removed from inventory first when units are sold.

Jan. 10. Ordered 1,000 fasteners. P0526.

10. Received at materials stockroom 20,000 square feet of laminate @ $0.60 per square foot. Materials were purchased on account from Plastics Unlimited, $12,000.00. P0521.

Record all receipts of materials in the materials ledger and purchases journal.

11. Completed Job No. 232. Apply factory overhead to job. Use the rate calculated in Instruction 1. Complete the cost sheet. Interim summary of job-time records for Job No. 232, $1,387.50.

When jobs are completed in the middle of a week, Furniture Decor makes a special interim summary of job-time records for these jobs. Therefore, direct labor costs will be complete. Record the finished goods in the finished goods ledger.

12. Opened a cost sheet for Job No. 234, 120 E400 entertainment centers ordered for stock. Date wanted, January 18.

12. Issued direct materials to factory for Job No. 234, $5,100.00. MR754.

Materials list: 6,000 square feet base wood @ $0.20 per square foot
6,000 square feet laminate @ $0.60 per square foot
187.5 pounds adhesive @ $1.60 per pound

12. Received at materials stockroom 30,000 square feet of base wood @ $0.20 per square foot. Materials were purchased on account from Wood Craft, Inc., $6,000.00. P0520.

12. Received at materials stockroom 1,600 casters @ $1.25 each. Materials were purchased on account from Wheels Galore, $2,000.00. P0522.

12. Received at materials stockroom 300 sets of metal glides @ $1.00 per set. Materials were purchased on account from Simpson Company, $300.00. P0525.

14. Opened a cost sheet for Job No. 235, 150 V110 video tape cabinets for stock. Date wanted, January 27.

14. Issued direct materials to factory for Job No. 235, $2,040.00. MR755.

Materials list: 2,400 square feet base wood @ $0.20 per square foot
2,400 square feet laminate @ $0.60 per square foot
75 pounds adhesive @ $1.60 per pound

14. Recorded weekly summary of job-time records to cost ledger.

Job No. 233 $1,875.00
Job No. 234   1,800.00
Job No. 235   225.00

14. Completed Job No. 233.

17. Paid cash for semimonthly factory payroll, $11,080.80 (direct labor, $9,712.50, and indirect labor, $3,967.50, less deductions: employee income tax, $1,504.80; Social security tax, $889.20; Medicare, $205.20). C782.

Record the payroll entry in the cash payments journal. Post the general debit and general credit amounts.

17. Recorded employer factory payroll taxes, $1,942.56, for the semimonthly pay period ended January 15. Taxes owed are Social security tax, $889.20; Medicare, $205.20; federal unemployment tax, $109.44; state unemployment tax, $738.72. M308.

Record the entry in the general journal. Post the amounts.

Jan. 17. Sold 150 P150 printer tables to CompuFurnishings. S324.
  18. Issued direct materials to factory for Job No. 234, $420.00. MR756.

  Materials list: 240 sets of hinges @ $1.00 per set
                  240 fasteners @ $0.75 each

  18. Opened a cost sheet for Job No. 236, 200 B160 bookcases ordered for stock. Date
      wanted, January 28.
  18. Issued direct materials to factory for Job No. 236, $6,800.00. MR757.

  Materials list: 8,000 square feet base wood @ $0.20 per square foot
                  8,000 square feet laminate @ $0.60 per square foot
                  250 pounds adhesive @ $1.60 per pound

  19. Completed Job No. 234. Interim summary of job-time record for Job No. 234, $1,800.00.
  20. Sold 60 T120 TV carts to Office Mart. S325.
  21. Issued direct materials to factory for Job No. 235, $825.00. MR758.

  Materials list: 300 sets metal glides @ $1.00 per set
                  300 sets hinges @ $1.00 per set
                  300 fasteners @ $0.75 each

  21. Received at materials stockroom 1,000 pounds adhesive @ $1.60 per pound. Materials
      were purchased on account from Cal Adhesives, $1,600.00. P0524.
  21. Received at materials stockroom 1,000 fasteners @ $0.75 each. Materials were pur-
      chased on account from Simpson Company, $750.00. P0526.
  21. Ordered 300 sets metal glides. P0527.
  21. Posted weekly summary of job-time records to cost ledger.

  Job No. 235 $1,125.00
  Job No. 236   2,250.00

  24. Ordered 20,000 square feet laminate. P0528.
  24. Received at materials stockroom 1,000 sets of hinges @ $1.00 per set. Materials were
      purchased on account from Simpson Company, $1,000.00. P0523.
  25. Issued direct materials to factory for Job No. 236, $700.00. MR759.

  Materials list: 400 sets of hinges @ $1.00 per set
                  400 fasteners @ $0.75 each

  25. Opened a cost sheet for Job No. 237, 160 T120 TV carts ordered for stock. Date wanted,
      January 31.
  25. Issued direct materials to factory for Job No. 237, $1,904.00. MR760.

  Materials list: 2,240 square feet base wood @ $0.20 per square foot
                  2,240 square feet laminate @ $0.60 per square foot
                  70 pounds adhesive @ $1.60 per pound

  26. Sold 90 E400 entertainment centers to BizFurn. S326.
  27. Completed Job No. 235. Interim summary of job-time records for Job No. 235, $900.00.
  27. Sold 200 V110 video tape cabinets to CompuFurnishings. S327.

Jan. 28. Issued direct materials to factory for Job No. 237, $800.00. MR761.

Materials list: 640 casters @ $1.25 each

28. Opened a cost sheet for Job No. 238, 200 C200 computer desks ordered for stock. Date wanted, February 8.

28. Issued direct materials to factory for Job No. 238, $4,080.00. MR762.

Materials list: 4,800 square feet base wood @ $0.20 per square foot
4,800 square feet laminate @ $0.60 per square foot
150 pounds adhesive @ $1.60 per pound

28. Posted weekly summary of job-time records to cost ledger.

Job No. 236 $2,250.00
Job No. 237   1,440.00
Job No. 238   630.00

28. Completed Job No. 236.

28. Sold 120 B160 bookcases to Office Mart. S328.

31. Received at materials stockroom 300 metal glides @ $1.00 per set. Materials were purchased on account from Simpson Company, $300.00. P0527.

31. Received at materials stockroom indirect materials (bolts, screws, and nails). Materials were purchased on account from Grant Hardware Supplies, $1,200.00. P0519.

Record indirect materials purchases only in the materials purchases journal.

31. Posted summary of job-time records for January 31 to cost ledger.

Job No. 237 $360.00
Job No. 238   630.00

31. Sold 200 C200 computer desks to Straight Arrow, Inc. S329.

31. Completed Job No. 237.

31. Paid cash for semimonthly factory payroll, $12,988.20 (direct labor, $11,385.00, and indirect labor, $4,650.00, less deductions: employee income tax, $1,764.00; Social Security tax, $1,042.28; Medicare tax, $240.52). C856.

31. Recorded employer factory payroll taxes, $2,276.97, for the semimonthly pay period ended January 31. Taxes owed are Social Security tax, $1,042.28; Medicare tax, $240.52; federal unemployment tax, $128.28; state unemployment tax, $865.89. M345.

Instructions:

3. Jobs not completed on January 31 are work in process. The factory overhead for the month of January on work in process must be recorded. Apply the factory overhead rate to the direct labor costs recorded on the cost sheet for work in process. Record this amount in the Summary column with the item description *Factory Overhead for January* and the explanation of how this was calculated.

4. Total and rule the materials purchases journal. Post the total. Do not post the individual amounts. The abbreviation for the materials purchases journal is MP.

5. Prove and rule the cash payments journal. Do not post the total of the Cash Cr. column.

6. Record the following entries. Continue using page 1 of the general journal. Use January 31 as the date. Post after journalizing each entry.

   a. An entry to transfer the total of all direct materials requisitions to Work in Process and indirect materials to Factory Overhead. The total of all requisitions of direct materials issued during January is $33,619.00. The total of all requisitions of indirect materials issued is $1,181.00. M346.

   b. An entry to close all individual manufacturing expense accounts to Factory Overhead. M347.

   c. An entry to record applied factory overhead to Work in Process. (Sum of factory overhead applied to cost sheets for the month.) M348.

7. Continue using page 1 of the general journal. Journalize and post the entry to close the balance of the factory overhead account to Income Summary. M349.

8. Journalize and post the entry to transfer the total of all cost sheets completed from Work in Process to Finished Goods. M350.

9. Journalize and post the entry to transfer the cost of products sold from Finished Goods to Cost of Goods Sold. The total cost recorded on all sales invoices for January is $61,137.50. M351.

10. Prove the subsidiary ledgers as follows.

    a. Add the ending balances in the materials ledger. The ending balance of the indirect materials is $1,369.00. The total of the materials ledger must equal the ending balance of Materials in the general ledger.

    b. Add the costs recorded on all cost sheets in the cost ledger that have not been completed. This total must equal the ending balance of Work in Process in the general ledger.

    c. Add the ending balances in the finished goods ledger. This total must equal the ending balance of Finished Goods in the general ledger.

11. Prepare a statement of cost of goods manufactured for Furniture Decor, Inc. for the month ended January 31 of the current year.

In Part B of this reinforcement activity, all accounting activities have been completed up to, but not including, a trial balance for the month of January.

The January 31 balances of the general ledger accounts not provided in Part A are recorded on an 8-column work sheet in the *Working Papers*.

Instructions:

12. Record the January 31 balances from the general ledger accounts used in Part A on the work sheet for Furniture Decor, Inc. Complete the Trial Balance columns of the work sheet.

13. Complete the work sheet for the month ended January 31 of the current year. Record the adjustments on the work sheet using the following information.

Adjustment Information, January 31

Uncollectible accounts expense estimated as 1.0% of sales on account.
   Sales on account for month, $27,000.00.

Sales supplies inventory	$1,111.35
Administrative supplies inventory	302.47
Value of prepaid administrative insurance	257.40
Monthly depreciation expense—office equipment	34.25
Monthly depreciation expense—store equipment	31.00
Federal income tax expense estimated for the month	3,682.38

14. Prepare an income statement for the month ended January 31 of the current year. Calculate and record the following component percentages. (a) Cost of goods sold. (b) Gross profit on operations. (c) Total operating expenses. (d) Income from operations. (e) Net addition or deduction resulting from other revenue and expenses. (f) Net income before federal income tax. (g) Federal income tax. (h) Net income after federal income tax. Round percentage calculations to the nearest 0.1%.

15. Prepare a balance sheet for January 31 of the current year. A statement of stockholders' equity is not prepared. Therefore, add the amount of net income after federal income taxes to the beginning balance of Retained Earnings to obtain the ending balance.

*Activities in Progressive Badge
Company:*

1. Recording transactions
   in special journals and a
   general journal.

2. Recording items in materials ledgers, cost sheets,
   and finished goods
   ledgers.

3. Posting items to be posted
   individually to a general
   ledger and subsidiary
   ledgers.

4. Proving and ruling
   journals.

5. Recording and posting
   general journal entries that
   summarize cost records.

6. Proving the subsidiary
   ledgers.

7. Preparing a trial balance
   on a work sheet.

8. Planning adjustments and
   completing a work sheet.

9. Preparing financial
   statements.

10. Journalizing and posting
    adjusting entries.

11. Journalizing and posting
    closing entries.

12. Preparing a post-closing
    trial balance.

THOMSON SOUTH-WESTERN

Century 21 SOUTH-WESTERN

Accounting

Progressive Badge Company

USA

A Business Simulation
Progressive Badge Company

Progressive Badge Company is a manufacturing business
organized as a corporation. This business simulation covers
the realistic transactions completed by Progressive Badge
Company, which manufactures badges for specialty retailing.
The activities included in the accounting cycle for Progressive Badge Company are listed at the left.

This simulation is available from the publisher in either
manual or automated versions.

INTRODUCE THE SIMULATION

- Progressive Badge Company: A Business
  Simulation is a self-contained simulation
  available from the publisher.

- The simulation presents the accounting
  cycle for a manufacturing business
  organized as a corporation.

ASSESSMENT

- The Teacher's Key provides full solutions
  to the simulation.

- Blackline masters for audit tests for
  the simulation are included in the
  Teacher's Key.

MATERIALS

- Progressive Badge Company: A Business
  Simulation

- Key for Progressive Badge Company:
  A Business Simulation

- Blackline Master of Audit Test

TEACHING STRATEGIES   PORTFOLIO ASSESSMENT

A simulation is an ideal exhibit to demonstrate mastery in a portfolio. A copy of the Portfolio Assessment form (blackline master
in the Teacher's Resource Guide; also on the Student Companion CD) should be completed by the student, and the Description
section should include any comments regarding how the student mastered these concepts and procedures.

Throughout Parts 1 through 6, the corporate form of business was used. Part 7 examines two other accounting systems: partnerships and not-for-profit organizations.

- Chapter 21 explores partnership formation and admitting partners to existing businesses.

- Chapter 22 addresses financial reporting for a partnership. The distribution of partnership equity using the common methods of distribution is illustrated.

- Chapter 23 defines not-for-profit organizations. Since income is not the objective of not-for-profits, other means of measuring activity are used. Budgeting and accounting for not-for-profit organizations are explored using a town government.

- Chapter 24 completes the discussion of not-for-profit organizations by illustrating the financial reports prepared by such entities.

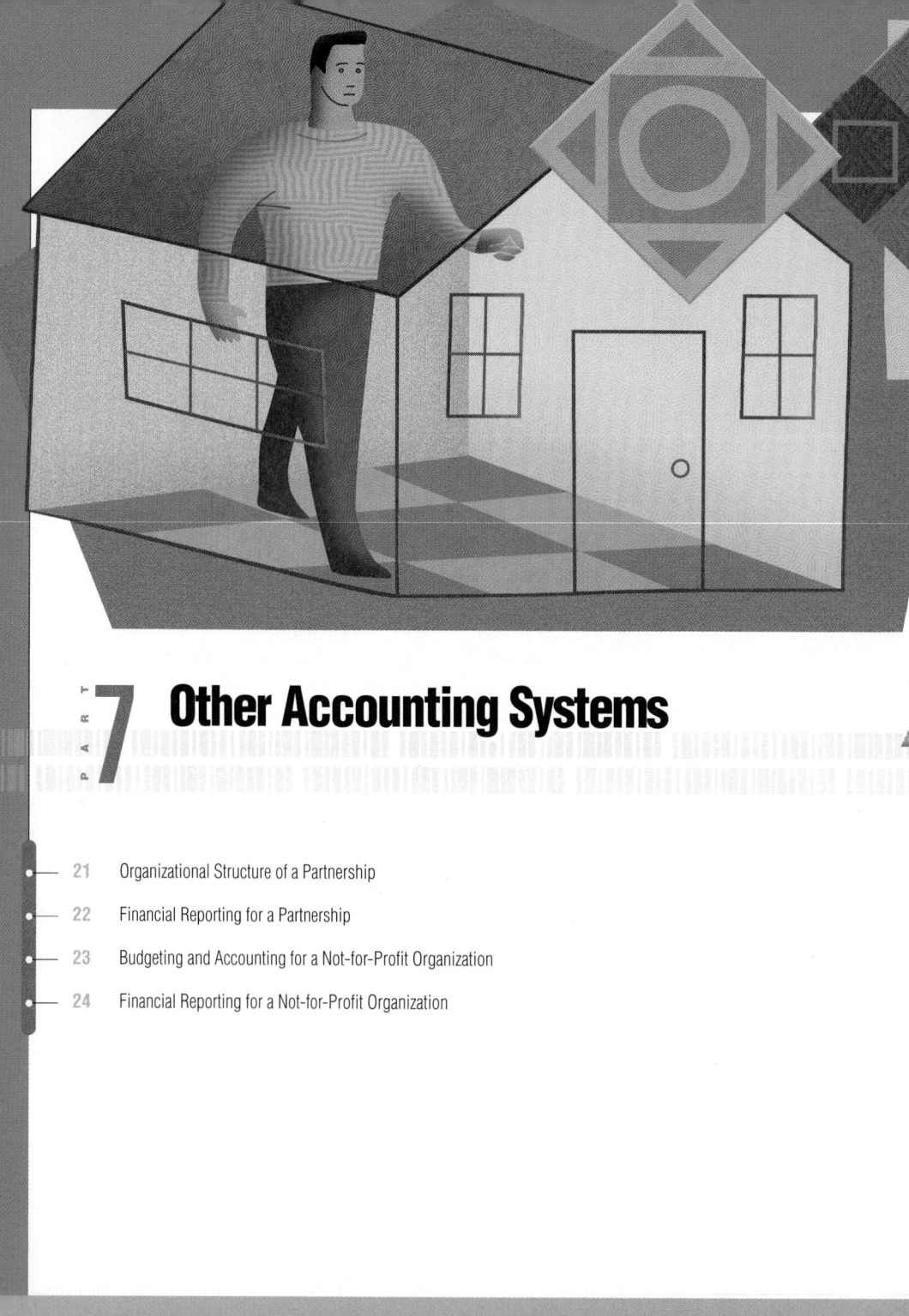

PART 7 Other Accounting Systems

MALIN CARPET DESIGN
CHART OF ACCOUNTS

Balance Sheet Accounts

(1000) ASSETS
1100   CURRENT ASSETS
1105   Cash
1110   Petty Cash
1115   Accounts Receivable
1120   Allowance for Uncollectible Accounts
1125   Supplies—Carpet
1130   Supplies—Office
1135   Prepaid Insurance
1200   Plant Assets
1205   Equipment
1210   Accumulated Depreciation—Equipment
1215   Truck
1220   Accumulated Depreciation—Truck

(2000) LIABILITIES
2100   CURRENT LIABILITIES
2105   Accounts Payable

(3000) OWNERS' EQUITY
3105   May Baker, Capital
3110   May Baker, Drawing
3115   Lindel Mattingly, Capital
3120   Lindel Mattingly, Drawing
3125   Income Summary

(4000) OPERATING REVENUE
4105   Sales

(5000) OPERATING EXPENSES
5105   Advertising Expense
5110   Depreciation Expense—Equipment
5115   Depreciation Expense—Truck
5120   Insurance Expense
5125   Miscellaneous Expense
5130   Rent Expense
5135   Supplies Expense—Carpet
5140   Supplies Expense—Office
5145   Truck Expense
5150   Uncollectible Accounts Expense
5155   Utilities Expense

The chart of accounts for MaLin Carpet Design is illustrated above for ready reference as you study Chapters 21 and 22 of this textbook.

CHART OF ACCOUNTS

- Emphasize that students should refer to this chart of accounts during the study of Chapters 21 and 22. (Note: The chart of accounts used for Chapters 23 and 24 is presented on page 685.)

- Explain that this chart of accounts is used by a business that is a service business organized as a partnership.

- Point out that charts of accounts are used for determining the classification of accounts and which accounts are temporary and permanent accounts.

- Stress that the chart of accounts is useful for completing automated accounting activities since account numbers are required for both data entry and file maintenance activities.

Organizational Structure

	SCOPE & SEQUENCE	
	NEW	**REVIEW/ EXTENSION**
Introduce the Chapter	✓	
Lesson 21-1 Forming a Partnership		
Characteristics of a partnership		✓
Formation of a partnership		✓
Partnership agreement		✓
Recording partners' initial investments		✓
Lesson 21-2 Admitting Partners to Existing Partnerships		
Admitting new partner with no change in total equity	✓	
Admitting new partner with equity equal to investment	✓	
Admitting new partner with equity greater than investment	✓	
Admitting new partner with goodwill	✓	
Putting It All Together		

ENHANCING

SPECIAL FEATURES

- Accounting in the Real World: Pricewaterhouse-Coopers, LLP

- Making Ethical Decisions: Accurate Accounting Records
- Cultural Diversity: Minority Recruiting

- Careers in Accounting

- Explore Accounting
- Xtra! Web Site: Xtra! Enrichment
- Applied Communication
- Cases for Critical Thinking
- SCANS Workplace Competency
- Auditing for Errors
- Analyzing Costco's Financial Statements

# of a Partnership

INSTRUCTION		PRACTICE AND ASSESSMENT		
TECHNOLOGY AND MEDIA	**TEACHING STRATEGIES**	**GUIDED PRACTICE**	**INDEPENDENT PRACTICE**	**RETEACHING AND ENRICHMENT**
• Internet Research Activity • Accounting Xtra! Web Site	• Software Focus			
• Instructor's Resource CD: PowerPoint Slides • Xtra! Web Site: Xtra! Study Tools • Blackline Masters: Cash Receipts Journal • Personal Trainer • Automated Accounting • Peachtree and QuickBooks	• Applied Skills: Communications	• Terms Review • Audit Your Understanding • Work Together 21-1	• On Your Own 21-1 • Application Problem 21-1 • Ongoing Assessment, p. 626 • Personal Trainer • Xtra! Web Site: Xtra! Study Tools	• Reteach, p. 626 • Enrich, p. 627 • Automated Accounting • Peachtree and QuickBooks
• Instructor's Resource CD: PowerPoint Slides • Xtra! Web Site: Xtra! Study Tools • Blackline Masters: Cash Receipts Journal and General Journal • Personal Trainer	• Applied Skills: Building Study Skills • Expanding Beyond the Classroom	• Term Review • Audit Your Understanding • Work Together 21-2	• On Your Own 21-2 • Application Problems 21-2, 21-3, 21-4, and 21-5 • Ongoing Assessment, p. 632 • Personal Trainer • Xtra! Web Site: Xtra! Study Tools	• Reteach, p. 632 • Enrich, p. 635
• Automated Accounting • Peachtree and QuickBooks • Personal Trainer • Xtra! Web Site: Xtra! Review, Quizzing, and Enrichment • Student Companion CD	• Gifted Students • Kinesthetic Learners		• Mastery Problem 21-6 • Personal Trainer • Xtra! Web Site: Xtra! Review and Quizzing • Study Guide 21 • Student Companion CD • Chapter 21 Test • ExamView Chapter 21 • Portfolio Assessment	• Challenge Problem 21-7 • Reteach, p. 636 • Enrich, p. 636 • Recycling Problem 21-1 • Automated Accounting • Peachtree and QuickBooks • Xtra! Web Site: Xtra! Enrichment

CHAPTER

OBJECTIVES & TERMS · TERMS · OBJECTIVES & TERMS · TERMS

21 Organizational Structure of a Partnership

After studying Chapter 21, you will be able to:

1. Define accounting terms related to forming and expanding a partnership.

2. Identify accounting concepts and practices related to forming and expanding a partnership.

3. Journalize transactions related to forming a partnership.

4. Journalize transactions related to expanding a partnership.

- partnership agreement
- mutual agency
- goodwill

Point Your Browser
accountingxtra.swlearning.com

PricewaterhouseCoopers, LLP

©GETTY IMAGES

PRICEWATERHOUSECOOPERS, LLP ASSURES CONFIDENCE IN FINANCIAL STATEMENTS

Suppose that you were shopping for a used automobile and you spotted your dream machine in the newspaper classified advertisements. The ad mentions that the vehicle is in excellent shape despite high mileage; however, the price seems a little high. Would you feel comfortable accepting the owner's word that the vehicle is in excellent condition or would you prefer an independent, third-party opinion? Most likely you would feel more confident and assured after a knowledgeable mechanic's thorough review and testing.

A major function of large accounting firms, such as PricewaterhouseCoopers, is providing assurance services. An example of assurance services is assessing the financial condition of a business and verifying the accuracy of its financial statements for clients or investors. Investors feel more confident about the financial reliability of a company after its records and operations have been reviewed by independent, knowledgeable experts.

PwC is one of the largest accounting firms in the world. It is a global enterprise employing over 122,000 individuals in offices located in 768 cities throughout 139 countries. The company is organized as a limited liability partnership with approximately 8,000 partners and generates annual revenues of over $15 billion. One of the more unusual responsibilities PwC has is its role as ballot counter for the annual Academy Awards presentation!

Critical Thinking

1. Why is it important that accounting firms such as PwC ensure that the financial statements of companies are indeed presented fairly?
2. Review the Explore Accounting feature at the end of this chapter. List two factors that make a limited liability partnership attractive.

Source: www.pwc.com

Xtra!
Today
accountingxtra.swlearning.com

FRANCHISES AVAILABLE

A franchise is a right purchased to operate a particular kind of business in a particular location. The value of a franchise is often the brand or company name that has been established. A franchise grants certain rights and also entails certain obligations to operate the business in a certain way to protect the reputation of the franchise brand.

Instructions

Search the Internet to find franchises that are available. Investigate two franchises.

1. List the name of each franchise investigated.
2. List the amount of initial investment required for each franchise.
3. List the services or goods that the franchisee will receive for the initial investment in each franchise.

621

621

21-1 Forming a Partnership

A corporation is one form of business that may be owned by many persons. Large corporations may have thousands of owners. These owners are known as shareholders because they own shares of stock.

Another form of business may also have more than one owner. A business in which two or more persons combine their assets and skills is known as a partnership. Each member of a partnership is known as a partner. Partnerships generally have only a few owners (partners). Partnerships do not issue shares of stock. Each partner has an equity account. Except for recording owners' equity and income taxes, accounting procedures for a partnership are similar to those for a corporation.

Unlike a corporation, however, a partnership does not have an unlimited life. Any change in the number of partners terminates an existing partnership. When a new partner is admitted, the partners sign a new partnership agreement. The old partnership's accounting records are often continued for the new partnership. As a result, initial investment journal entries for all partners are not always needed. Journal entries are needed, however, to show clearly how the partners' equity has changed. One or both of the following journal entries may be needed:

1. To show how much the new partner invests.
2. To show how the new partner's admission affects existing partners' capital accounts.

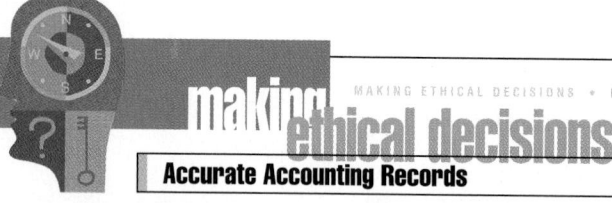

making ethical decisions

MAKING ETHICAL DECISIONS • MAKING ETHICAL DECISIONS • MAKING ETHICAL DECISION

Accurate Accounting Records

A company must keep an accurate and complete record of its accounting transactions. This seemingly obvious statement has, unfortunately, been forgotten at Marist Industries. Apparently the company's controller has been recording unsupported debits to Accounts Receivable and credits to Sales in order to inflate the company's sales and net income.

Nancy Nettleton, an accounting clerk, has just discovered the fraudulent accounting entries. Nancy is fearful of what might happen if she reports the transactions to the company's hotline.

Instead, she shares her discovery with friend and fellow employee Andrea Farris.

Instructions

Access *Setting the Standard*, the code of conduct of Lockheed Martin. What guidance does Lockheed Martin provide Nancy and Andrea? Should Andrea report the transactions even if Nancy asks her to remain silent?

Organizational Structure of a Partnership

MAKING ETHICAL DECISIONS
MAKING ETHICAL DECISIONS

Suggested Solution: Lockheed Martin's policy toward accounting records is very clear—it will not tolerate anyone who rationalizes or even considers misrepresenting accounting records and statements. In the section *Make Accurate Public Disclosures*, the company states that "any employee who is contacted by another employee expressing concerns about questionable accounting or auditing matters must immediately report those concerns to the Ethics Office." Thus, Nancy and Andrea must report the

discovery to the Ethics Office. Andrea must report the discovery even if Nancy asks her to remain silent.

Some students may argue that Andrea cannot violate the confidence of her friend, Nancy. However, the guidance in the code is quite emphatic—the employee must report the concerns. As an employee of the company, Nancy would be expected to know the code of conduct and realize that Andrea is obligated to report her concerns.

Source: *www.lockheedmartin.com/data/assets/540.pdf*

EXPLAIN

- Explain the purpose of a partnership agreement. Refer to the illustration.

- List and describe some of the stipulations that should be considered when preparing a partnership agreement.

PARTNERSHIP AGREEMENT

THIS CONTRACT is made and entered into this thirty-first day of December, 20--, by and between May Baker and Lindel Mattingly, of Petersburg, VA.

WITNESSETH: That the said parties have this date formed a partnership to engage in and conduct a business under the following stipulations which are a part of this contract. The partnership will begin operation January 1, 20--.

FIRST: The business shall be conducted under the name of MaLin Carpet Design, located initially at 1910 South Crater Road, Petersburg, VA 23801-2343.

SECOND: The investment of each partner is: May Baker: Equity in a business located at 1910 South Crater Road, Petersburg, VA 23801-2343, and as shown in a balance sheet to be provided by Ms. Baker on December 31, 20--. Total investment, $22,880.00. Lindel Mattingly: Cash equal to one-half of the initial investment of Ms. Baker. Total investment, $11,440.00.

THIRD: Both partners are to (a) participate in all general policy-making decisions, (b) devote full time and attention to the partnership business, and (c) engage in no other business enterprise without the written consent of the other partner. Ms. Baker is to be general manager of the business' operations.

FOURTH: Neither partner is to become a surety or bonding agent for anyone without the written consent of the other partner.

FIFTH: The partners' shares in earnings and losses of the partnership are: Ms. Baker: 5% interest on equity as of January 1 of each year; salary, $5,000.00 per year; remaining income or loss, 50%. Mr. Mattingly: 5% interest on equity as of January 1 of each year; salary, $3,000.00 per year; remaining income or loss, 50%.

SIXTH: No partner is to withdraw assets in excess of the agreed upon interest and salary without the other partner's written consent.

SEVENTH: All partnership transactions are to be recorded in accordance with standard and generally accepted accounting procedures and concepts. The partnership records are to be open at all times for inspection by either partner.

EIGHTH: In case of either partner's death or legal disability, the equity of the partners is to be determined as of the time of the death or disability of the one partner. The continuing partner is to have first option to buy the deceased/disabled partner's equity at recorded book value.

NINTH: This partnership agreement is to continue indefinitely unless (a) terminated by death of one partner, (b) terminated by either partner by giving the other partner written notice at least ninety (90) days prior to the termination date, or (c) terminated by written mutual agreement signed by both partners.

TENTH: At the termination of this partnership agreement, the partnership's assets, after all liabilities are paid, will be distributed according to the balance in partners' capital accounts.

IN WITNESS WHEREOF, the parties to this contract have set their hands and seals on the date and year written.

Signed _May Baker_____ (Seal) Date _December 31, 20--_____

Signed _Lindel Mattingly_____ (Seal) Date _December 31, 20--_____

A partnership is created when two or more persons agree orally or in writing to form a business using the partnership form of organization. As in other forms of business, a partnership's financial records are kept separate from those of the partners. [CONCEPT: Business Entity]

May Baker and Lindel Mattingly agree to form a partnership called MaLin Carpet Design. Prior to forming the partnership, May owned a similar business and Lindel was employed as a carpet installer.

Forming a Partnership

- Explain the meaning and importance of the term mutual agency. Emphasize the importance and impact this feature has to a partnership and its partners.
- Explain that the owners' equity division of a partnership's general ledger has two capital accounts for each partner.
- Explain that the two accounts are a capital account and a drawing account.
- Explain the purpose of each account.
- Explain how the accounts in the owners' equity section of a partnership differ from the accounts in the stockholders' equity section of a corporation.
- Explain that the initial investment to form a partnership may be cash or non-cash assets.
- Note that the MaLin partnership initial investment consists of the assets of May Baker's previous proprietorship business and Lindel Mattingly's cash investment.
- Call students' attention to the F.Y.I. There is no legal or accounting limit to the number of partners. Ask students what practical or organizational limits there may be to the number of partners.

MaLin Carpet Design provides carpet installation services to homeowners, housing developers, and businesses. The business does not sell merchandise. For this reason, it does not need general ledger accounts for merchandise inventory, purchases, purchases discount, and purchases returns and allowances. The partners, who provide all the services to customers, are not employees of the partnership. The Internal Revenue Service does not consider the money that partners receive from a partnership to be salaries. Therefore, the business does not need accounts for recording salaries and payroll taxes.

A written agreement setting forth the conditions under which a partnership is to operate is called a **partnership agreement**. A partnership's life is limited to the length of time agreed on by the partners. A partnership is terminated by the partners' mutual agreement, death of a partner, withdrawal of one partner, or admission of a new partner. In comparison, a corporation has unlimited life.

Each partner can bind a partnership to any contract. The right of all partners to contract for a partnership is called **mutual agency**. Each partner is an agent of the partnership unless restricted by agreement.

Legally, a partnership agreement may be either written or oral. However, to avoid misunderstandings, a partnership agreement should be in writing. Some but not all states require that a partnership agreement be in writing.

With an attorney's assistance, Ms. Baker and Mr. Mattingly prepare their partnership agreement, shown on the previous page. Both partners sign three copies of the partnership agreement. Each partner receives a copy for personal records, and the third copy becomes part of the partnership's records.

PARTNERSHIP CAPITAL ACCOUNTS

The owners' equity division of a partnership's general ledger has two capital accounts for each partner.

1. An account in which to record a partner's equity includes the word *capital* in the title. The two equity accounts in MaLin's general ledger are May Baker, Capital and Lindel Mattingly, Capital.
2. An account in which the earnings taken out of the partnership during the fiscal period are recorded includes the word *drawing* in the title. Assets taken out of a business for the owner's personal use are known as withdrawals. The two accounts in MaLin's general ledger used to record withdrawals are titled May Baker, Drawing and Lindel Mattingly, Drawing.

Partners' withdrawals can be a cause of misunderstandings. For this reason, most partnership agreements include a statement controlling withdrawals. MaLin's partnership agreement has a controlling statement in item 6 of the partnership agreement.

PARTNERS' INITIAL INVESTMENTS

Ms. Baker invests the assets of her existing business in the new partnership. According to item 2 of the partnership agreement, Ms. Baker will provide a December 31 balance sheet for her existing business.

The two partners agree on a value for all invested assets on the date the partnership begins, January 1. Ms. Baker's initial investment is $22,880.00, the agreed-upon value of her equity in her previous business. Mr. Mattingly's initial investment is cash of $11,440.00.

FYI FOR YOUR INFORMATION

A partnership can have an unlimited number of partners.

Organizational Structure of a Partnership

JOURNAL ENTRIES TO RECORD PARTNERS' INITIAL INVESTMENTS

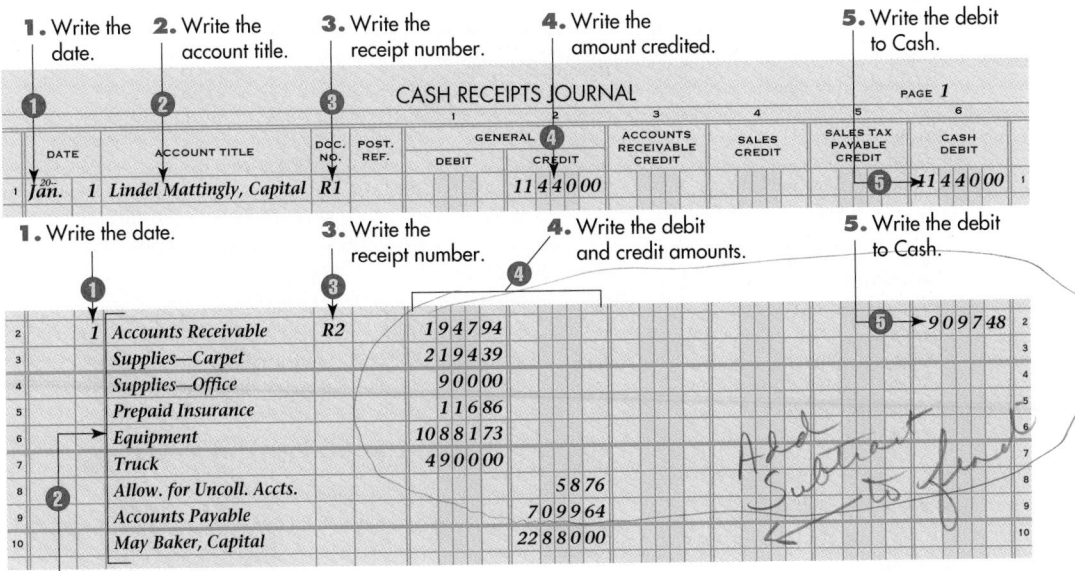

1. Write the date. 2. Write the account title. 3. Write the receipt number. 4. Write the amount credited. 5. Write the debit to Cash.

CASH RECEIPTS JOURNAL   PAGE 1

DATE	ACCOUNT TITLE	DOC. NO.	POST. REF.	GENERAL DEBIT	GENERAL CREDIT	ACCOUNTS RECEIVABLE CREDIT	SALES CREDIT	SALES TAX PAYABLE CREDIT	CASH DEBIT
Jan. 1	Lindel Mattingly, Capital	R1			11 4 4 0 00				11 4 4 0 00

1. Write the date. 3. Write the receipt number. 4. Write the debit and credit amounts. 5. Write the debit to Cash.

1	Accounts Receivable	R2		1 9 4 7 94					9 0 9 7 48
	Supplies—Carpet			2 1 9 4 39					
	Supplies—Office			9 0 0 00					
	Prepaid Insurance			1 1 6 86					
	Equipment			10 8 8 1 73					
	Truck			4 9 0 0 00					
	Allow. for Uncoll. Accts.				5 8 76				
	Accounts Payable				7 0 9 9 64				
	May Baker, Capital				22 8 8 0 00				

2. Write the account titles debited and credited.

A separate journal entry is made for each partner's initial investment as shown above.

January 1, 20--. Received cash from partner, Lindel Mattingly, as an initial investment, $11,440.00. Receipt No. 1.

    Cash is debited for $11,440.00. Lindel Mattingly, Capital is credited for $11,400.00.

January 1, 20--. Accepted assets and liabilities of May Baker's existing business as an initial investment, $28,880.00. Receipt No. 2.

    All asset amounts on the balance sheet are debited. Allowance for Uncollectible Accounts and Accounts Payable are credited.

STEPS · STEPS · STEPS · STEPS · STEPS · STEPS · STEPS · STEPS · STEPS · STEPS · STEPS ·

JOURNALIZING RECEIPT OF PARTNERS' INITIAL INVESTMENTS

1. Write the date, *20--, Jan 1*, in the Date column.

2. Write the account titles in the Account Title column. For Lindel Mattingly's investment, write the account to be credited, *Lindel Mattingly, Capital*. For May Baker's investment, write the accounts to be debited, *Accounts Receivable, Supplies—Carpet, Supplies—Office, Prepaid Insurance, Equipment*, and *Truck*. Also write the accounts to be credited, *Allowance for Uncollectible Accounts, Accounts Payable*, and *May Baker, Capital*.

3. Write the receipt numbers, *R1* and *R2*, in the Doc. No. column.

4. Write the amounts in the General Debit and Credit columns. The only credit amount for Lindel Mattingly is *11,440.00* for the cash investment. For May Baker's investment, debit the asset accounts, *1,947.94, 2,194.39, 900.00, 116.86, 10,881.73*, and *4,900.00*. Credit the contra asset, liability, and capital accounts, *58.76, 7,099.64*, and *22,880.00*.

5. Write the debits to Cash, *11,440.00* and *9,097.48*, in the Cash Debit column.

Forming a Partnership   Lesson 21-1   **625**

EXPLAIN

- Explain that a separate journal entry is made for each partner's initial investment.
- Explain that the value of non-cash assets invested in a partnership is recorded at a value agreed upon by the partners, not the book value of the assets recorded in the previous business.
- Explain that each partner's capital account is credited for the net amount of the partner's initial investment to the partnership.

DEMONSTRATE

- Draw T accounts on the overhead projector or board to analyze the transactions to record partners' initial investments.
- Use a transparency of a cash receipts journal to illustrate recording partners' initial investment in a partnership.
- Direct students to the illustration as you describe each of the five steps for recording partners' initial investment.

APPLIED SKILLS   COMMUNICATIONS

Surveys of business managers show that communication skills are one of the most desired traits in new employees. The Applied Communication activity provides an opportunity for students to practice their communication and language arts skills on topics that directly relate to accounting.

ONGOING ASSESSMENT

- Assessment is an ongoing process. Circulate through the classroom or lab observing which students have problems with the assignments.

- Troubleshooting: Diagnose what kinds of problems students have with this lesson. Since the initial investment is a receipt of cash and other assets, make sure students use a cash receipts journal to record the initial investments and make a separate journal entry for each partner's initial investment. If a partner should contribute all non-cash assets, then the entry would be recorded in a general journal.

- Assess student understanding by checking solutions to Independent Practice assignments.

RETEACH

- Write on the board initial investments to be made by two partners forming a new partnership, including one with non-cash assets.

- Draw some T accounts on the board. Ask a student to analyze the initial investment entry for one of the partners.

- Ask a student to describe the correct journal entry for recording each of the partner's initial investments as you write the entry in a transparency of a cash receipts journal.

BALANCE SHEET OF EXISTING BUSINESS

Baker's Carpet Design
Balance Sheet
December 31, 20--

ASSETS

Current Assets:		
Cash		$ 9,097.48
Accounts Receivable	$1,947.94	
Less Allowance for Uncollectible Accounts	58.76	1,889.18
Supplies—Carpet		2,194.39
Supplies—Office		900.00
Prepaid Insurance		116.86
Total Current Assets		$14,197.91
Plant Assets:		
Equipment	$10,881.73	
Truck	4,900.00	
Total Plant Assets		15,781.73
Total Assets		$29,979.64

LIABILITIES

Accounts Payable	$ 7,099.64

OWNER'S EQUITY

May Baker, Capital	22,880.00
Total Liabilities and Owner's Equity	$29,979.64

Ms. Baker's investment includes cash, other assets, and liabilities from her prior existing business. Both partners agree to any estimates shown on the balance sheet. For example, Allowance for Uncollectible Accounts is an estimate. After reviewing the accounts, Lindel and May agree that the $58.76 is a fair estimate of the amount that may become uncollectible.

A copy of the balance sheet from May Baker's previous business, shown above, is attached to a receipt to provide needed details for the journal entry. [CONCEPT: Objective Evidence]

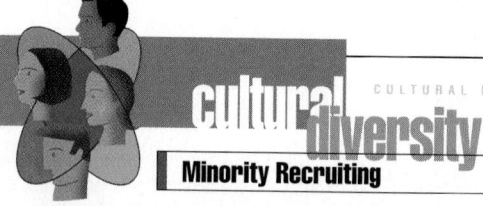

CULTURAL DIVERSITY • CULTURAL DIVERSITY • CULTURAL DIVERSI

cultural diversity

Minority Recruiting

Companies today are very interested in achieving a balance in their work force. They recognize that there are advantages in a work force that has the same ethnic and cultural composition as their customers. This attitude creates opportunity for minorities.

Many cities have annual "work force diversity" job fairs in which those looking for jobs meet employers looking for employees. At these minority job fairs, a wide range of jobs may be available. Companies are especially interested in minority hiring in sales, marketing, customer service, and technical and administrative positions.

Business interest in recruiting minorities grew in the 1990s and is expected to continue to grow in the 21st century.

Organizational Structure of a Partnership

CULTURAL DIVERSITY
CULTURAL DIVERSIT

The Cultural Diversity feature is intended to expose students to the concept that our society is composed of people from many different cultural backgrounds. The features show the benefits of a culturally diverse society. (1) Read the feature. (2) Discuss the specific information in the feature. (3) Clarify any terms or questions.

• terms review

partnership agreement
mutual agency

• audit your understanding

1. Why should a partnership agreement be in writing?
2. What happens to an existing partnership if a partner dies?
3. What does mutual agency mean?

• work together 21-1

Forming a partnership

A cash receipts journal is provided in the *Working Papers*. Your instructor will guide you through the following examples.

Betty Jensen and Glen Chau agree to form a partnership on April 1 of the current year. The partnership assumes the assets and liabilities of Ms. Jensen's existing business. Mr. Chau invests cash equal to Ms. Jensen's investment. Partners share equally in all changes in equity. The March 31 balance sheet for Ms. Jensen's existing business is shown in the *Working Papers*. Source documents are abbreviated as follows: memorandum, M; receipt, R.

Apr.   1.   Received cash from partner, Glen Chau, as an initial investment, $42,000.00. R1.
          1.   Accepted assets and liabilities of Betty Jensen's existing business as an initial investment, $42,000.00. R2.

1.   Journalize the transactions in a cash receipts journal on April 1 of the current year.

• on your own 21-1

Forming a partnership

A cash receipts journal is provided in the *Working Papers*. Work independently to complete the following problem.

David Rice and Tanya Taylor agree to form a partnership on July 1 of the current year. The partnership assumes the assets and liabilities of Mr. Rice's existing business. Ms. Taylor invests cash equal to Mr. Rice's investment. Partners share equally in all changes in equity. The June 30 balance sheet for Mr. Rice's existing business is shown in the *Working Papers*. Source documents are abbreviated as follows: receipt, R.

July   1.   Received cash from partner, Tanya Taylor, as an initial investment, $32,000.00. R1.
          1.   Accepted assets and liabilities of David Rice's existing business as an initial investment, $32,000.00. R2.

1.   Journalize the transactions in a cash receipts journal on July 1 of the current year.

Forming a Partnership

Lesson 21-1   **627**

Terms Review

Call on students to define each term in the Terms Review. Ask the class if the definition is correct and whether the complete definition has been given or if anything needs to be added. Suggested definitions are given in the Glossary.

Audit Your Understanding

Call on students to answer the Audit Your Understanding questions. Ask the class if the answer is correct and/or complete. Answers are given in Appendix E of the textbook.

Work Together

Have students write the solution to the Work Together problem as you guide the class through the examples.

- Direct students to record each initial investment in a cash receipts journal as you elicit class participation in recording each entry.

INDEPENDENT PRACTICE

On Your Own

- Assign the On Your Own problem to be worked independently.
- Use the Ongoing Assessment techniques to diagnose student understanding.

Application Problem

- Assign Application Problem 21-1: Forming a partnership.

Personal Trainer

- Students can access the Lesson 21-1 assessment material using this software.

Xtra! Web Site

- Students can access the Xtra! Study Tools for additional practice.

ENRICH

- Assign Making Ethical Decisions on page 622.
- Assign the Cultural Diversity feature on page 626.
- Assign the Automated Accounting feature on pages 644–645 to automate Application Problem 21-1.
- Students can use the Peachtree and QuickBooks data files to automate Application Problem 21-1.

CLOSE

- Ask students to briefly summarize the procedure for analyzing and journalizing partners' initial investments to form a partnership.

21-2 Admitting Partners to Existing Partnerships

OBJECTIVES

- Define the accounting term related to forming and expanding a partnership.
- Identify accounting concepts and practices related to forming and expanding a partnership.
- Journalize transactions related to expanding a partnership.

MOTIVATE

Forming a partnership and journalizing the partners' initial investments were presented in Lesson 21-1. Explain that a new partner may be admitted to an existing partnership. When this occurs, a new partnership agreement must be written. In this lesson, the journal entries used to record the admission of a new partner will be presented.

Preview

- Preview the accounting term and definition introduced in this lesson: goodwill.
- Direct students to read the headings at the top of each page in this lesson and to examine the illustrations given.

EXPLAIN

- Explain that partners might sell part of their equity to a new partner.
- Explain that the existing partners are selling part of their existing equity and the cash received is a personal transaction.
- The only entry in the journal is the transfer of capital from the existing partners to the new partner.

DEMONSTRATE

- Use a transparency of a general journal to illustrate recording the transfer of the existing partners' equity to the new partner.
- Direct students to the illustration as you describe the three steps for recording the transfer of partnership equity from the existing partners to the new partner.

ADMITTING A PARTNER WITH NO CHANGE IN TOTAL EQUITY

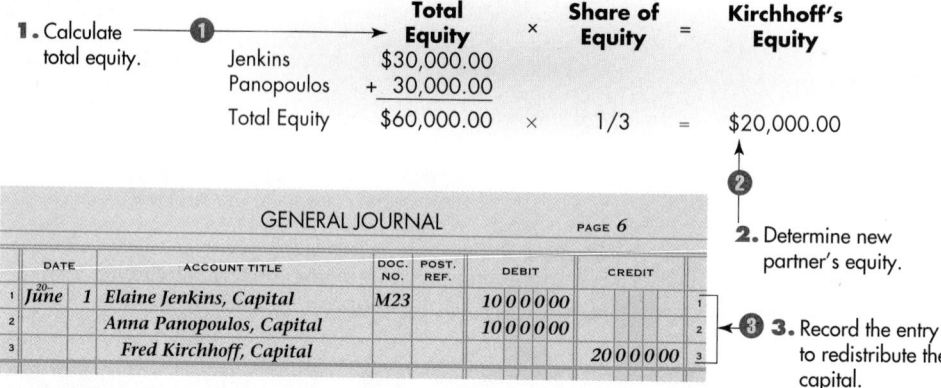

1. Calculate total equity.

	Total Equity	×	Share of Equity	=	Kirchhoff's Equity
Jenkins	$30,000.00				
Panopoulos	+ 30,000.00				
Total Equity	$60,000.00	×	1/3	=	$20,000.00

2. Determine new partner's equity.

GENERAL JOURNAL — PAGE 6

DATE	ACCOUNT TITLE	DOC. NO.	POST. REF.	DEBIT	CREDIT
June 1	Elaine Jenkins, Capital	M23		1000000	
	Anna Panopoulos, Capital			1000000	
	Fred Kirchhoff, Capital				2000000

3. Record the entry to redistribute the capital.

Elaine Jenkins and Anna Panopoulos are partners in an existing business. The partners agree to admit Fred Kirchhoff as a new partner. However, the business does not need additional capital at the present time. Therefore, Elaine and Anna agree to sell part of their existing equity to Fred.

The existing partners each have $30,000.00 equity in the existing partnership. The three partners agree that Fred is to pay $20,000.00 for a one-third equity in the new partnership. Elaine and Anna receive cash from Fred for equity in the partnership. The partnership does not receive the cash from the sale of equity.

The two existing partners are each entitled to one-half of the price Fred pays for one-third of the equity of the partnership. Therefore, Fred pays $10,000.00 to both Elaine and Anna. Also, $20,000.00 of the existing equity is transferred to Fred on the partnership's records, as shown above.

The receipt of cash, a personal transaction among Elaine, Anna, and Fred, is not recorded on the partnership's records. However, the redistribution of capital is a partnership entry and is journalized.

STEPS

ADMITTING A PARTNER WITH NO CHANGE IN TOTAL EQUITY

1 Calculate the total equity of the business, $60,000.00.

2 Determine the new partner's equity in the partnership, $20,000.00 ($60,000.00 × 1/3).

3 Record the entry in the general journal to transfer a portion of the existing equity to the new partner.

> **REMEMBER** If partners agree to sell part of their existing equity to a new partner, the receipt of cash is a personal transaction that is not recorded on the partnership's records.

MATERIALS

- Instructor's Resource CD:
  PowerPoint Slides
- Xtra! Study Tools on the Xtra! Web Site
- Blackline Masters:
  Cash Receipts Journal
  General Journal

- Working Papers:
  Teacher's Edition of the Working Papers for Lesson 21-2
- Software:
  Personal Trainer
  Student Companion CD
  Automated Accounting and Century 21 8E CD
  Peachtree and QuickBooks

	Total Equity	×	Share of Equity	=	Spears's Equity
Costello	$30,000.00				
Ramirez	30,000.00				
Spears	+ 20,000.00				
1. Calculate ① ➤ Total Equity	$80,000.00	×	1/4	=	$20,000.00

2. Determine new partner's equity.

1. Calculate total equity.

CASH RECEIPTS JOURNAL   PAGE *13*

	DATE	ACCOUNT TITLE	DOC. NO.	POST. REF.	GENERAL DEBIT	GENERAL CREDIT	ACCOUNTS RECEIVABLE CREDIT	SALES CREDIT	SALES TAX PAYABLE CREDIT	CASH DEBIT	
1	20-- Jan. 1	Alan Spears, Capital	R150			20 0 0 0 00				20 0 0 0 00	1

3. Record the entry to redistribute the capital.

Partnerships often seek to increase their total equity to allow the business to grow. Partnerships may seek to expand their current markets, move into new markets, or sell new types of merchandise. Additional capital gives partnerships added financial strength as the business grows.

John Costello and Juliet Ramirez are partners in an existing partnership. Each partner's equity is $30,000.00 for a total equity of $60,000.00. The existing partners agree to admit Alan Spears as a partner with a one-fourth interest for a $20,000.00 cash investment. Alan Spears's equity is calculated as shown above. Alan's investment does not change John or Juliet's equity.

July 1, 20--. Received cash from new partner, Alan Spears, for a one-fourth equity in the business, $20,000.00. Receipt No. 150.

STEPS   STEPS • STEPS • STEPS • STEPS

ADMITTING A PARTNER WITH EQUITY EQUAL TO NEW PARTNER'S INVESTMENT

① Calculate the total equity of the partnership including the new partner's equity.

② Determine the new partner's equity.

③ Record the entry to admit the new partner.

FYI   FOR YOUR INFORMATION

The use of several individuals' names in the name of a business is often an indication of a partnership.

REMEMBER The balance sheet for a partnership includes an equity account for each partner.

Admitting Partners to Existing Partnerships   Lesson 21-2   **629**

APPLIED SKILLS   BUILDING STUDY SKILLS

Direct students to prepare a Quick Reference Guide (QRG) for transactions to admit partners to existing partnerships. (1) Label the QRG ADMITTING PARTNERS. (2) Copy the transactions out of the chapter narrative. (3) Show the calculations to determine the new partner's equity. (4) Draw T accounts to analyze how the transactions affect capital accounts. This QRG can be used when students are completing end-of-chapter activities.

- Explain that in an effort to attract a new partner, existing partners may agree to admit the new partner with a larger share of equity than the amount of investment.

- Explain that two journal entries will be required to record this kind of transaction: (1) receipt of cash and (2) redistribution of existing equity.

- Point out the F.Y.I. The name of a business or the names of the partners can help in gaining public recognition.

DEMONSTRATE

- Illustrate on the board how the new partner's equity is calculated.

- Use transparencies of a cash receipts journal and a general journal to illustrate recording the new partner's investment and the redistribution of the existing partners' equity.

- Direct students to the illustration as you describe each of the four steps for admitting a new partner with equity greater than the new partner's investment.

ADMITTING A PARTNER WITH EQUITY GREATER THAN NEW PARTNER'S INVESTMENT

1. Calculate total equity.

	Total Equity	×	Share of Equity	=	Wood's Equity
Weisman	$33,000.00				
Redman	33,000.00				
Wood	+ 24,000.00				
Total Equity	$90,000.00	×	1/3	=	$30,000.00

2. Determine the new partner's equity.

3. Record the receipt of cash from the new partner.

CASH RECEIPTS JOURNAL — PAGE 17

	DATE	ACCOUNT TITLE	DOC. NO.	POST. REF.	GENERAL DEBIT	GENERAL CREDIT	ACCOUNTS RECEIVABLE CREDIT	SALES CREDIT	SALES TAX PAYABLE CREDIT	CASH DEBIT	
1	Sept. 1	Lois Wood, Capital	R125			24 0 0 0 00				24 0 0 0 00	1

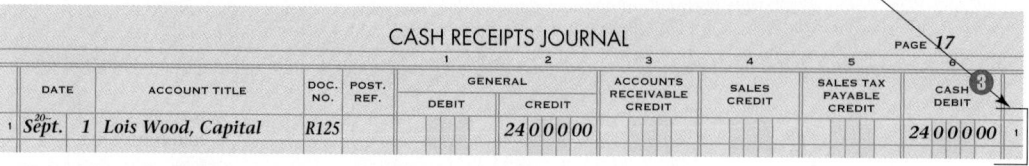

GENERAL JOURNAL — PAGE 9

	DATE	ACCOUNT TITLE	DOC. NO.	POST. REF.	DEBIT	CREDIT	
1	Sept. 1	James Weisman, Capital	M45		3 0 0 0 00		1
2		Lisa Redman, Capital			3 0 0 0 00		2
3		Lois Wood, Capital				6 0 0 0 00	3

4. Record the transfer of equity to the new partner.

James Weisman and Lisa Redman both have equity of $33,000.00 in an existing partnership. The existing partners agree to admit Lois Wood as a partner with a one-third interest for a $24,000.00 cash investment. Lois's equity is calculated as shown above.

September 1, 20--. Received cash from new partner, Lois Wood, for a one-third equity in the business, $24,000.00. Existing equity is redistributed as follows: from James Weisman, $3,000.00; from Lisa Redman, $3,000.00. Receipt No. 125 and Memorandum No. 45.

FYI
FOR YOUR INFORMATION

One reason for admitting a new partner with greater equity than investment is when a celebrity joins the partnership, bringing name recognition and increased sales.

Two journal entries are required to record this transaction. (1) Receipt of cash is recorded. (2) Redistribution of existing equity is recorded. These entries are shown above.

STEPS • STEPS • STEPS • STEPS • STEPS • STEPS • STEPS • STEPS • STEPS • STEPS • STEPS •

ADMITTING A PARTNER WITH EQUITY GREATER THAN NEW PARTNER'S INVESTMENT

1 Calculate the total equity, including the new partner's investment of cash.

2 Determine the new partner's equity. In this case, the cash investment by the new partner is less than the equity that will be assigned to her.

3 Record the receipt of cash from the new partner in the cash receipts journal.

4 Record the transfer of equity to Lois Wood from James Weisman and Lisa Redman. After the entry, each partner's capital account has a $30,000.00 balance.

ADMITTING A PARTNER WHEN GOODWILL IS RECOGNIZED

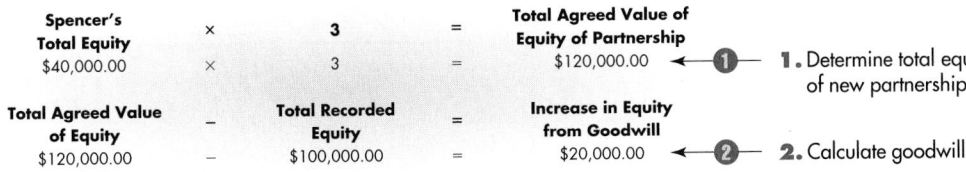

| Spencer's Total Equity | × | 3 | = | Total Agreed Value of Equity of Partnership | | **1.** Determine total equity of new partnership. |
| $40,000.00 | × | 3 | = | $120,000.00 | **①** | |

| Total Agreed Value of Equity | − | Total Recorded Equity | = | Increase in Equity from Goodwill | | **2.** Calculate goodwill. |
| $120,000.00 | − | $100,000.00 | = | $20,000.00 | **②** | |

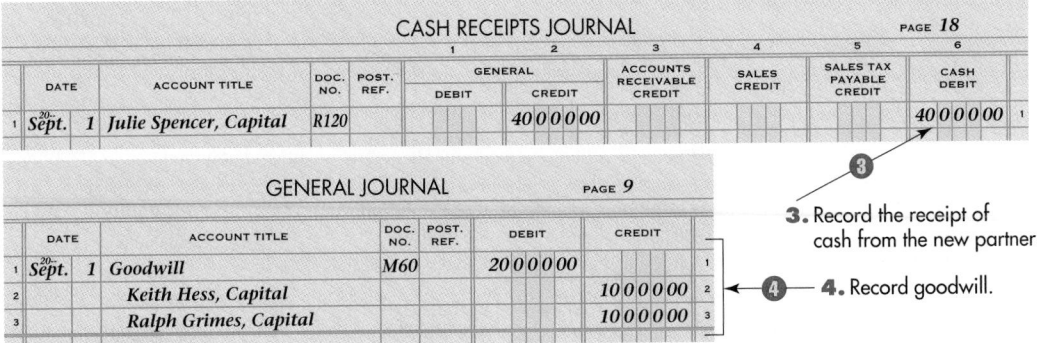

CASH RECEIPTS JOURNAL   PAGE 18

					1	2	3	4	5	6	
DATE	ACCOUNT TITLE	DOC. NO.	POST. REF.	GENERAL DEBIT	GENERAL CREDIT	ACCOUNTS RECEIVABLE CREDIT	SALES CREDIT	SALES TAX PAYABLE CREDIT	CASH DEBIT	
1	20-- Sept. 1	Julie Spencer, Capital	R120		40 0 00 00					40 0 00 00	1

3. Record the receipt of cash from the new partner. **③**

GENERAL JOURNAL   PAGE 9

	DATE	ACCOUNT TITLE	DOC. NO.	POST. REF.	DEBIT	CREDIT	
1	20-- Sept. 1	Goodwill	M60		20 0 00 00		1
2		Keith Hess, Capital				10 0 00 00	2
3		Ralph Grimes, Capital				10 0 00 00	3

④ **4.** Record goodwill.

Keith Hess and Ralph Grimes are partners in an existing business. Each partner's equity is $30,000.00, for a total equity of $60,000.00. The existing partners agree to admit Julie Spencer as a partner with a one-third interest for a $40,000.00 cash investment. Julie is willing to pay $40,000.00 for a one-third equity. She believes the total equity value is worth $120,000.00 after her investment.

The value of a business in excess of the total investment of owners is called **goodwill**. The partners agree that Julie's willingness to pay $40,000.00 for a one-third interest is evidence that goodwill exists. The value of goodwill is calculated as shown above.

September 1, 20--. Received cash from new partner, Julie Spencer, for a one-third equity in the business, $40,000.00. Goodwill, $20,000.00, is distributed as follows: Keith Hess, $10,000.00; Ralph Grimes, $10,000.00. Receipt No. 120 and Memorandum No. 60.

Two journal entries are required for this transaction. (1) Receipt of cash is recorded. (2) Distribution of goodwill is recorded. The $20,000.00 amount of equity in excess of the total recorded investment of the three partners is the value of goodwill.

STEPS • STEPS • STEPS • STEPS • STEPS • STEPS • STEPS • STEPS • STEPS • STEPS •

ADMITTING A PARTNER WHEN GOODWILL IS RECOGNIZED

① Determine the total equity of the new partnership by multiplying her investment, $40,000.00, by 3. The total, $120,000.00, will be the total agreed value of equity of the new partnership.

② Subtract the total recorded equity, $30,000.00 + $30,000.00 + $40,000.00 = $100,000.00 from the total agreed value of equity calculated in Step 1.

③ Record the cash investment by the new partner in a cash receipts journal.

④ Record the recognition of goodwill in the general journal.

Admitting Partners to Existing Partnerships   Lesson 21-2   **631**

- Explain that when goodwill is recognized, the account Goodwill is recorded as an intangible asset.

- Explain that goodwill may be recorded only at the time of a change in ownership of the business when some evidence of the value of goodwill is proven through the willingness of a new partner to invest a greater amount than the share of equity received.

ONGOING ASSESSMENT

- Assessment is an ongoing process. Circulate through the classroom or lab, observing which students have problems with the assignments.

- Troubleshooting: The most likely trouble spot is calculating the amount of owner's equity for the new partner. Students may also have trouble determining how to record a redistribution of existing partners' equity.

- Assess student understanding by checking solutions to Independent Practice assignments.

RETEACH

- Write on the board some situations for admitting a new partner.

- Ask students to individually calculate the amount of equity that each partner should have after the new partner is admitted.

EQUITY ACCOUNTS AFTER GOODWILL IS RECOGNIZED

Cash

Sept. 1	40,000.00

Goodwill

Sept. 1	20,000.00

Keith Hess, Capital

Bal.	30,000.00
Sept. 1	10,000.00
(New Bal.	*40,000.00)*

Ralph Grimes, Capital

Bal.	30,000.00
Sept. 1	10,000.00
(New Bal.	*40,000.00)*

Julie Spencer, Capital

Sept. 1	40,000.00

	Previous Equity	+	Share of Goodwill	=	New Equity
Hess	$ 30,000.00	+	$10,000.00	=	$ 40,000.00
Grimes	30,000.00	+	10,000.00	=	40,000.00
Spencer	+ 40,000.00	+	—	=	40,000.00
Total	$100,000.00	+	$20,000.00	=	$120,000.00

The analysis of the investment of cash by Julie Spencer and the distribution of goodwill is shown in the T accounts above. None of the goodwill is recorded in Julie Spencer's capital account. She invested $40,000.00 for a one-third share of the business. One-third of the total equity, *$120,000.00*, equals the current balance of Ms. Spencer's capital account, *$40,000.00*.

Goodwill may be recorded only at the time of a change in ownership of business. An ongoing business may be worth more than the equity value stated in the accounting records. However, goodwill may not be recorded without some evidence of its value. This evidence is provided by the willingness of an investor to pay a premium for an ownership interest in the business.

When used, the account Goodwill is located in a general ledger's Intangible Assets section. Intangible assets are nonphysical assets that have value to a business.

©GETTY IMAGES/PHOTODISC

Organizational Structure of a Partnership

Xtra!
Careers

accountingxtra.swlearning.com

careers in accounting

CAREERS IN ACCOUNTING • CAREERS IN ACCOUNTING • CAREERS IN ACCOUNTING

Jennifer Albrecht Young, Group Marketing Director—North America

COURTESY OF JENNIFER ALBRECHT YOUNG

As a student at Saint Mary's College in Moraga, California, Jennifer Albrecht Young participated in an internship program affiliated with Chancellor Broadcasting in San Francisco. At the time, Jennifer was working on a Bachelor of Arts in Communications with an emphasis in Marketing. The internship provided her with the opportunity to work at a local radio station and allowed her to explore the various careers available in broadcasting. Upon graduation from Saint Mary's, she was hired full-time.

Jennifer spent the next seven years in the broadcasting industry meeting country-western celebrities, attending concerts, working media events, researching listening preferences, coordinating advertising, and selling air time. Her goal was to gain experience in a variety of job categories within the broadcast industry in order to determine her primary area of interest. After evaluating her employment experiences, Jennifer realized she had a passion and talent for marketing. At this point in her career, she decided to seek out marketing opportunities with Fortune 500 companies. Her research lead her to Robert Half International (RHI), the world's leading firm in specialized staffing and the first to match professional workers with employers in the areas of accounting, finance, and information technology.

Currently, Jennifer holds the position of Group Marketing Director—North America. Her accounting skills play a significant role in the effective performance of her department. Each week, Jennifer reviews company revenue for both North America and global operations to ensure adherence to RHI's spending parameters for advertising. During the month, she reviews and approves departmental invoices, tracks budget expenditures as they accrue, and makes the necessary adjustments to remain within budget specifications. As the group marketing director for North America, Jennifer is responsible for the on-going management and development of an annual marketing budget in excess of $40 million dollars.

Salary Range: $84,000–$142,000

Qualifications: Jennifer is strongly convinced that the best way to enter the marketing profession is through an internship program. Marketing is a broad career area that includes consumer research, brand management, public relations, advertising, pricing, promotional campaigns, product distribution, product perception, and even product development. Most entry-level positions in this field require a 4-year college degree. Jennifer believes that success in the industry is directly related to one's ability to communicate, analyze, write, and think strategically.

Occupational Outlook: Jennifer foresees marketing-related jobs becoming increasingly important in today's environment of evolving technologies, industry consolidations, and rapid economic growth. As consumers are bombarded with more information than they can process, marketing personnel will remain to ensure that the right people get the right information.

CAREERS IN ACCOUNTING

The Careers in Accounting feature profiles people who are entrepreneurs, who are working in accounting-related fields, or who use accounting in their business lives.

Students can access the Careers section of the Xtra! Web Site for additional material about careers.

Admitting Partners to Existing Partnerships

Lesson 21-2   **633**

Term Review

Call on a student to define the term in the Term Review. Ask the class if the definition is correct and whether the complete definition has been given or if anything needs to be added. The suggested definition is given in the Glossary.

Audit Your Understanding

Call on students to answer the Audit Your Understanding questions. Ask the class if the answer is correct and/or complete. Answers are given in Appendix E of the textbook.

Work Together

Have students write the solution to the Work Together problem as you guide the class through the examples.

- Direct students to calculate and record each journal entry for admitting a partner to an existing partnership as you elicit class participation for each situation.

• term review

goodwill

• audit your understanding

1. What happens to an existing partnership when a new partner is admitted?
2. When admitting a new partner, how is the new partner's equity calculated?
3. What accounts are debited and credited to record the distribution of goodwill when a new partner is admitted?

• work together 21-2

Admitting partners to existing partnerships

Four independent situations are given below. Assume partners of the existing partnership are Maria Heath and Lisa Curtis. The new partner is Wade Torres. For each situation, prepare the appropriate journal entries to admit the new partner. Page 12 of a cash receipts journal and page 6 of a general journal are provided in the *Working Papers*. Source documents are abbreviated as follows: memorandum, M; receipt, R. Your instructor will guide you through the following examples.

1. Maria Heath and Lisa Curtis have equity of $24,000.00 each in an existing partnership. On April 1 of the current year, the two partners agree to admit Wade Torres as a third partner. Each partner agrees to sell Mr. Torres $8,000.00 of her equity and to give him a one-third share of ownership. Mr. Torres is to pay the money directly to the two original partners.

   Apr. 1. Journalized personal sale of equity to new partner, Wade Torres, $16,000.00, distributed as follows: from Maria Heath, $8,000.00; from Lisa Curtis, $8,000.00. M32.

2. Maria Heath and Lisa Curtis have equity of $80,000.00 each in the partnership. Partners share equally in all changes in equity. On April 1 of the current year, the two partners agree to admit Wade Torres as a partner with a one-third share of the total equity.

   Apr. 1. Received cash from new partner, Wade Torres, for a one-third equity in the business, $80,000.00. R101.

3. Maria Heath and Lisa Curtis have equity of $50,000.00 each in an existing partnership. The partners share equally in all changes in equity. On April 1 of the current year, the existing partners agree to admit Wade Torres with a one-third share of the total equity.

   Apr. 1. Received cash from new partner, Wade Torres, for a one-third equity in the business, $35,000. Existing equity is redistributed as follows: from Maria Heath, $5,000.00; from Lisa Curtis, $5,000.00. R125 and M31.

4. Maria Heath and Lisa Curtis have equity of $34,000.00 each in an existing business. The partners share equally in all changes in equity. On April 1 of the current year, Wade Torres is admitted as a new partner with a one-third share of the total equity.

   Apr. 1. Received cash from new partner, Wade Torres, for a one-third equity in the business, $40,000.00. Goodwill, $12,000.00, is distributed as follows: Maria Heath, $6,000.00; Lisa Curtis, $6,000.00. R89 and M22.

• on your own 21-2

Admitting partners to existing partnerships

Four independent situations are given below. Assume that partners of the existing partnership are Kyle Bowen and Susan Wong. The new partner is Angie Mills. For each situation, prepare the appropriate journal entries to admit the new partner. Page 18 of a cash receipts journal and page 9 of a general journal are provided in the *Working Papers*. Work independently to complete the following problem.

1. Kyle Bowen and Susan Wong have equity of $36,000.00 each in an existing partnership. On June 1 of the current year, the two partners agree to admit Angie Mills as a one-third partner. Each partner agrees to sell Ms. Mills $12,000.00 equity and to give her a one-third share of ownership. Ms. Mills is to pay the money directly to the two original partners.

   June 1. Journalized personal sale of equity to new partner, Angie Mills, $24,000.00, distributed as follows: from Kyle Bowen, $12,000.00; from Susan Wong, $12,000.00. M36.

2. Kyle Bowen and Susan Wong have equity of $75,000.00 each in the partnership. Partners share equally in all changes in equity. On June 1 of the current year, the two partners agree to admit Angie Mills as a partner with a one-third share of the total equity.

   June 1. Received cash from new partner, Angie Mills, for a one-third equity in the business, $75,000.00. R142.

3. Kyle Bowen and Susan Wong have equity of $36,000.00 each in an existing partnership. The partners share equally in all changes in equity. On June 1 of the current year, the existing partners agree to admit Angie Mills with a one-third share of the total equity.

   June 1. Received cash from new partner, Angie Mills, for a one-third equity in the business, $30,000.00. Existing equity is redistributed as follows: from Kyle Bowen, $2,000.00; from Susan Wong, $2,000.00. R130 and M40.

4. Kyle Bowen and Susan Wong each have $52,000.00 equity in an existing business. The partners share equally in all changes in equity. On June 1 of the current year, Angie Mills is admitted as a new partner with a one-third share of the total equity.

   June 1. Received cash from new partner, Angie Mills, for a one-third equity in the business, $60,000.00. Goodwill, $16,000.00, is distributed as follows: Kyle Bowen, $8,000.00; Susan Wong, $8,000.00. R160 and M46.

INDEPENDENT PRACTICE

On Your Own

- Assign the On Your Own problem to be worked independently.
- Use the Ongoing Assessment techniques to diagnose student understanding.

Application Problem

- Assign Application Problem 21-2: Admitting a partner with no change in total equity.
- Assign Application Problem 21-3: Admitting a partner with equity equal to new partner's investment.
- Assign Application Problem 21-4: Admitting a partner with equity greater than new partner's investment.
- Assign Application Problem 21-5: Admitting a partner when goodwill is recognized.

Personal Trainer

- Students can access the Lesson 21-2 assessment material using this software.

Xtra! Web Site

- Students can access the Xtra! Study Tools for additional practice.

ENRICH

- Assign the Careers in Accounting feature on page 633.
- Invite a lawyer, certified public accountant, or partner from a local partnership to speak to the class. Have the individual explain why the partnership form of organization is the best for that business.

CLOSE

- Ask students to briefly summarize the procedure for calculating and journalizing admitting new partners to existing partnerships.

PUTTING IT ALL TOGETHER

- Review the Chapter Summary.
- Demonstrate recording an initial investment in a partnership.
- Demonstrate one or two journal entries admitting a partner to an existing partnership.

INDEPENDENT PRACTICE

- Assign Mastery Problem 21-6 to students who need reinforcement.
- Assign Challenge Problem 21-7 to students who do not require reinforcement.
- Assign the Automated Accounting feature on pages 644–645 to automate Mastery Problem 21-6.
- Students can use Peachtree and QuickBooks data files to automate Mastery Problem 21-6.
- Assign Study Guide 21.
- Students can access Personal Trainer to work end-of-chapter problems on the computer.
- Students can access the Xtra! Web Site for the Xtra! Review and Quizzing.
- Students can access the Student Companion CD for additional review material.

ONGOING ASSESSMENT

- Review solutions to the assigned problems in class, diagnosing trouble spots.

RETEACH

- Use reteaching suggestions from section lesson plans as required.
- Assign Recycling Problem 21-1 if needed.

ENRICH

- Assign the Explore Accounting Feature. Ask students to share the information they have gathered in a report to the class.
- Students can access the Xtra! Web Site for the Xtra! Enrichment material.
- Assign Applied Communication.
- Assign the Cases for Critical Thinking.
- Assign the SCANS Workplace Competency.
- Assign Auditing for Errors.
- Assign Analyzing Costco's Financial Statements.

636

After completing this chapter, you can

1. Define accounting terms related to forming and expanding a partnership.
2. Identify accounting concepts and practices related to forming and expanding a partnership.
3. Journalize transactions related to forming a partnership.
4. Journalize transactions related to expanding a partnership.

Explore Accounting

EXPLORE ACCOUNTING · EXPLORE ACCOUNTING · EXPLORE ACC

Limited Liability Partnerships

The organizational structure of a corporation differs from a partnership in four ways.

1. Continuity of life. A partnership ends upon the death or withdrawal of an owner. Stockholders of a corporation buy and sell stock without affecting the life of the corporation.
2. Centralization of management. A partnership generally is managed by one or more of its partners. A corporation generally is managed by professional managers employed by the stockholders.
3. Limited liability. All partners are liable for contracts and liabilities incurred by the partnership. A corporation is treated as a separate legal entity. Thus the stockholders are not liable for the contracts or liabilities of the corporation.
4. Free transferability of interest. Generally, a partnership ends if a partner dies or withdraws. In addition, other partners must agree before a partner can sell his/her share to another person. Stockholders can buy and sell shares of a corporation without consulting other stockholders.

Because a corporation is a legal entity, a corporation must pay income taxes on its net income.

Most states allow a special kind of partnership, called a limited liability partnership and frequently referred to as an LLP. An LLP must file articles of organization with the state. The operating agreement is similar to a traditional partnership agreement. The LLP must be managed by the members or a group of managers who are elected by the members. To qualify to be taxed as a partnership, the partnership can have no more than two of the characteristics of a corporation. Most LLPs retain the two characteristics, centralization of management and limited liability.

The attractiveness of an LLP is twofold. (1) Partners can be taxed as a partnership (net income reported on individual partner's tax return). (2) Partners have limited liability for the actions of the partnership much like stockholders of a corporation. For these reasons, many partnerships have changed to an LLP.

Required

1. Make a list of the types of businesses that would be most appropriate organized as an LLP.
2. Through additional reading about LLPs or interviewing local partners of an LLP, determine other advantages and disadvantages of an LLP.

EXPLORE ACCOUNTING
EXPLORE ACCOUNTING

1. Businesses that would be most appropriate organized as an LLP include professional firms such as CPA or attorney firms and small family businesses.
2. Some advantages of an LLP:
   a. Can have an unlimited number of partners.
   b. Members can contribute property to an LLP without recognition of taxable gain.

   c. Fewer governmental reports, rules, and regulations than for a corporation.

   Some disadvantages of an LLP:

   a. Can have only two of the four characteristics of a corporation.
   b. Net income, which is distributed to the partners, is subject to self-employment taxes.

21-1 APPLICATION PROBLEM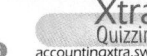
Forming a partnership

Xtra!
Quizzing
accountingxtra.swlearning.com

Carmen Estrada and Paula Jeter agree to form a partnership on June 1 of the current year. The partnership assumes the assets and liabilities of Carmen's existing business. Paula invests cash equal to Carmen's investment. Partners share equally in all changes in equity. The May 31 balance sheet for Carmen's existing business is as follows.

Carmen's Crafts		
Balance Sheet		
May 31, 20--		
ASSETS		
Current Assets:		
Cash		$14,532.00
Accounts Receivable	$3,746.47	
Less Allowance for Uncollectible Accounts	74.92	3,671.55
Merchandise Inventory		26,298.34
Supplies		670.59
Total Current Assets		$45,172.48
Plant Assets:		
Equipment		9,481.12
Total Assets		$54,653.60
LIABILITIES		
Accounts Payable		$ 8,653.60
OWNER'S EQUITY		
Carmen Estrada, Capital		46,000.00
Total Liabilities and Owner's Equity		$54,653.60

Transactions:

June   1.   Received cash from partner, Paula Jeter, as an initial investment, $46,000.00. R1.
       1.   Accepted assets and liabilities of Carmen Estrada's existing business as an initial investment, $46,000.00. R2.

Instructions:

Journalize the transactions using page 1 of a cash receipts journal. Source documents are abbreviated as follows: memorandum, M; receipt, R.

21-2 APPLICATION PROBLEM
Admitting a partner with no change in total equity

Steven Myer and William Riggs are partners in an existing business. Each partner has equity of $30,000.00. On October 1 of the current year, the two partners agree to admit Sandra DeVito as a third partner. Each of the partners agrees to personally sell Sandra $10,000.00 of his equity and to give her a one-third share of ownership. Sandra is to pay the money directly to the two original partners.

Transaction:

Oct.   1.   Journalized personal sale of equity to new partner, Sandra DeVito, $20,000.00, distributed as follows: from Steven Myer, $10,000.00; from William Riggs, $10,000.00. M24.

Instructions:

Journalize the transaction using page 12 of a general journal.

Application Problem 21-3

Debit Cash, credit new partner's capital, 60,000.00.

Application Problem 21-4

Debit Cash, credit new partner's capital account, 22,000.00.

Debit existing partners' capital, 6,000.00 each; credit new partner's capital 12,000.00.

Application Problem 21-5

Debit Cash, credit new partner's capital, 36,000.00.

Debit Goodwill 18,000.00; credit original partners' capital, 9,000.00 each.

21-3 APPLICATION PROBLEM

Admitting a partner with equity equal to new partner's investment

Susan Wang and Lelah Burch are partners in an existing business. Each partner has $60,000.00 equity in the partnership. Partners share equally in all changes in equity. On April 1 of the current year, the two partners agree to admit Daryl Wetzel as a partner with a one-third share of the total equity.

Transaction:

Apr. 1. Received cash from new partner, Daryl Wetzel, for a one-third equity in the business, $60,000.00. R95.

Instructions:

Journalize the transaction using page 13 of a cash receipts journal.

21-4 APPLICATION PROBLEM

Admitting a partner with equity greater than new partner's investment

Stanley Neal and Helen Jobe each have equity of $40,000.00 in an existing partnership. The partners share equally in all changes in equity. On August 1 of the current year, the existing partners agree to admit Greg Talbot with a one-third share of the total equity.

Transaction:

Aug. 1. Received cash from new partner, Greg Talbot, for a one-third equity in the business, $22,000.00. Existing equity is redistributed as follows: from Stanley Neal, $6,000.00; from Helen Jobe, $6,000.00. R116 and M25.

Instructions:

Journalize the transaction using page 14 of a cash receipts journal and page 7 of a general journal.

21-5 APPLICATION PROBLEM

Admitting a partner when goodwill is recognized

Arthur Jansky and Edward Thayer are partners, each with $27,000.00 equity in an existing business. The partners share equally in all changes in equity. On March 1 of the current year, Dean McGee is admitted as a new partner with a one-third share of the total equity.

Transaction:

Mar. 1. Received cash from new partner, Dean McGee, for a one-third equity in the business, $36,000.00. Goodwill, $18,000.00, is distributed as follows: Arthur Jansky, $9,000.00; Edward Thayer, $9,000.00. R67 and M10.

Instructions:

Journalize the transaction using page 5 of a cash receipts journal and page 3 of a general journal.

21-6 MASTERY PROBLEM   QUICKBOOKS

Forming and expanding a partnership

Mastery Problem 21-6
General journal transactions: Aug. 1, debit existing partners' capital, 4,000.00 each; credit new partner's capital, 8,000.00.
Oct. 20, debit original partners' capital, 200.00 each; credit new partner's capital, 800.00.
Dec. 5, debit Goodwill, 2,000.00, credit original partners' capital, 400.00 each.

On July 1 of the current year, Roy Hatfield and Michelle Allen form a partnership. The partners share equally in all changes in equity. The partnership assumes the assets and liabilities of Roy's existing business. Michelle invests cash equal to Roy's investment. The June 30 balance sheet for Roy's existing business is as follows.

Hatfield Financial Services
Balance Sheet
June 30, 20--

ASSETS

Current Assets:		
Cash		$4,291.23
Accounts Receivable	$3,303.60	
Less Allowance for Uncollectible Accounts	35.79	3,267.81
Supplies		290.19
Total Current Assets		$ 7,849.23
Plant Assets:		
Equipment		4,378.14
Total Assets		$12,227.37

LIABILITIES

Accounts Payable		$ 227.37

OWNER'S EQUITY

Roy Hatfield, Capital		12,000.00
Total Liabilities and Owner's Equity		$12,227.37

Transactions:

July 1. Received cash from partner, Michelle Allen, as an initial investment, $12,000.00. R1.

1. Accepted assets and liabilities of Roy Hatfield's existing business as an initial investment, $12,000.00. R2.

Aug. 1. Journalized personal sale of equity to new partner, Frank Boyd, $8,000.00, distributed as follows: from Michelle Allen, $4,000.00; from Roy Hatfield, $4,000.00. M8.

Oct. 1. Received cash from new partner, Danita McGrew, for a one-fourth equity in the business, $8,000.00. R80.

Oct. 20. Received cash from new partner, Donna Wells, for a one-fifth equity in the business, $7,000.00. Existing equity is redistributed as follows: from Michelle Allen, $200.00; from Roy Hatfield, $200.00; from Frank Boyd, $200.00; from Danita McGrew, $200.00. R92 and M18.

Dec. 5. Received cash from new partner, Pearl Morgan, for a one-sixth equity in the business, $8,200.00. Goodwill, $2,000.00, is distributed as follows: Roy Hatfield, $400.00; Michelle Allen, $400.00; Frank Boyd, $400.00; Danita McGrew, $400.00; Donna Wells, $400.00. R118 and M24.

Instructions:

Journalize the transactions using page 1 of a cash receipts journal and page 1 of a general journal.

TEACHING STRATEGIES　DIFFERENT LEARNING ABILITIES

Gifted Students. Partnerships are an effective form of business organization only when there is effective communication and cooperation among partners. Gifted students can best learn about the opportunities, problems, and challenges of a partnership by forming a real partnership. Encourage gifted students to form a partnership to sell a service or product of their selection. The students should prepare the partnership agreement, operate the business, and report the results of operations. Suggest that the students consult business persons, such as lawyers and accountants, for assistance.

Challenge Problem 21-7

General journal transactions: July 1, debit Merchandise Inventory and credit new partner's capital, 12,000.00.

July 20, debit new partner's capital, 2,250.00, credit existing partners' capital, 750.00 each.

Nov. 5, debit Goodwill, 1,000.00, credit existing partner's capital, 250.00 each.

21-7 CHALLENGE PROBLEM

Forming and expanding a partnership

On May 1 of the current year, Marsha Huerta and John Ward form a partnership. The partnership assumes the assets and liabilities of the two partners' existing businesses. Partners share equally in all changes in equity. The May 1 balance sheets for the existing businesses are as follows.

Marsha's Party Planner
Balance Sheet
May 1, 20--

ASSETS

Current Assets:		
Cash		$4,258.32
Accounts Receivable	$2,280.56	
Less Allowance for Uncollectible Accounts	35.43	2,245.13
Merchandise Inventory		6,237.29
Total Current Assets		$12,740.74
Plant Assets:		
Office Equipment		2,943.49
Total Assets		$15,684.23

LIABILITIES

Accounts Payable		$ 3,684.23

OWNER'S EQUITY

Marsha Huerta, Capital		12,000.00
Total Liabilities and Owner's Equity		$15,684.23

Ward's Wedding Chapel
Balance Sheet
May 1, 20--

ASSETS

Current Assets:		
Cash	$4,323.49	
Supplies	2,075.21	
Merchandise Inventory	6,342.04	
Total Current Assets		$12,740.74
Plant Assets:		
Office Equipment		2,959.88
Total Assets		$15,700.62

LIABILITIES

Accounts Payable		$ 3,700.62

OWNER'S EQUITY

John Ward, Capital		12,000.00
Total Liabilities and Owner's Equity		$15,700.62

Transactions:

May 1. Accepted assets and liabilities of Marsha Huerta's existing business as an initial investment. R1.

1. Accepted assets and liabilities of John Ward's existing business as an initial investment. R2.

July 1. Accepted assets of Dan Ogden's existing business as an investment of new partner for a one-third equity in the business. M80. Mr. Ogden's July 1 balance sheet is as follows.

Dan Ogden
Balance Sheet
July 1, 20--

ASSETS

Merchandise Inventory $12,000.00

OWNER'S EQUITY

Dan Ogden, Capital $12,000.00

July 20. Received cash from new partner, Pam Wise, for a one-fourth equity in the business, $15,000.00. R24 and M85.

Nov. 5. Accepted assets of Rodney Stein's existing business as an investment of new partner for a one-fifth equity in the business. Goodwill, $1,000.00, is distributed as follows: Marsha Huerta, $250.00; John Ward, $250.00; Dan Ogden, $250.00; Pam Wise, $250.00. R92 and M105. Mr. Stein's November 5 balance sheet is as follows.

Stein Supplies
Balance Sheet
November 5, 20--

ASSETS

Cash . . . . $ 5,000.00
Merchandise Inventory 8,000.00
Total Assets $13,000.00

OWNER'S EQUITY

Rodney Stein, Capital $13,000.00

Instructions:

Journalize the transactions using page 8 of a cash receipts journal and page 4 of a general journal.

APPLIED COMMUNICATION

Students' solutions will vary. Consider the following items when grading the activity: (1) identification of facts, (2) analysis of expenditure efficiency, (3) writing style, and (4) mechanics (grammar, spelling, punctuation, and sentence structure).

CASES FOR CRITICAL THINKING

Case 1

The vendor is correct. Each partner is an agent of the partnership and may bind the partnership to contracts with outside vendors.

Case 2

1. Can the business succeed as a two-owner partnership or are the skills and assets of the brother-in-law needed?

2. In a partnership, can Mrs. Cole and her son work together successfully as partners?

3. What will forming a corporation do to the income tax liabilities of the new business as compared to a partnership?

4. In a corporation, can the three persons work together successfully as stock-holders/officers?

SCANS WORKPLACE COMPETENCY

Inform students that most states have a society for CPAs. The American Institute of Certified Public Accountants (AICPA) is also a good source of information. Most ethics exams cover ethical theories, the professional code of ethics, rulings on ethics, identifying ethical dilemmas, tax ethics, rules and regulations, client confidentiality, conflicts of interest, and handling disagreements with one's supervisor.

• applied communication

Partnerships have operating expenses each month. Advertising, depreciation, and rent expense are examples of those operating expenses. Controlling these expenses affects the net income of the business.

Required:
Identify the operating expenses for MaLin Carpet Design in this chapter. Prepare a brief report, including a pie graph, that depicts the operating expenses for the year ended December 31. Do you think MaLin is controlling its operating expenses?

• cases for critical thinking

Case 1

Partner A contracted with a vendor to buy a computer for the partnership. Partner A did not discuss the transaction with Partner B or get Partner B's approval. Partner B refused to approve payment for the computer when it was delivered, claiming that the vendor cannot force payment because all partners did not agree to buy the computer. The vendor claims that the transaction is valid, and the partnership must pay for the computer. Is Partner B or the vendor correct? Explain.

Case 2

Helen Cole, her husband, and her son were partners in a business. Mrs. Cole's husband died, leaving his equity in the partnership to Mrs. Cole. Mrs. Cole and her son plan to form a new partnership and continue the business. Mrs. Cole's brother owns a similar business. The brother suggests that they combine the two businesses into a corporation. What questions do you suggest Mrs. Cole answer before she decides whether to form a partnership with her son or a corporation with her son and brother?

• SCANS workplace competency

Personal Qualities: Integrity/Honesty

Concept: Employers seek individuals who display integrity and choose ethical courses of action.

Application: In order to be licensed as a certified public accountant, candidates must past the uniform CPA exam and the American Institute of Certified Public Accountants Professional Ethics Exam. Some states also require the passing of a state ethics exam. Contact a local CPA or use the Internet to determine your state's requirements for an ethics exam. What is the exam's content? Why is it so critical that accountants demonstrate ethical behavior? Share your findings with the class.

auditing for errors

Amy Cardoza, Jeff Williams, and Claire Mangoni are partners in an existing music business. Each partner's equity is $32,000, for a total equity of $96,000. The partners agree to admit Russ Hodges as a partner with a one-fourth interest for a $24,000 cash investment. The firm's bookkeeper made the following entry in the partnership's general journal, based on information recorded on R213 and M89.

GENERAL JOURNAL   PAGE 12

	DATE		ACCOUNT TITLE	DOC. NO.	POST. REF.	DEBIT	CREDIT	
1	Oct.	1	Cash	R213		24 0 0 0 00		1
2			Goodwill			8 0 0 0 00		2
3			Russ Hodges, Capital				32 0 0 0 00	3
4								4

Instructions:

1. Do you agree with the bookkeeper's entry? Explain your answer.
2. If you disagree, what journal entries would you make?

analyzing Costco's financial statements

Financial statements are interrelated and connected to one another. A change on one financial statement will have an impact on other financial statements. For example, if a corporation neglected to record a $10,000 cash payment for July rent, the cash amount reported on the balance sheet would be overstated. On the income statement, the net income would also be overstated, due to the $10,000 missing in the rent expense account. Since net income increases the retained earnings, the amount of retained earnings listed on the statements of stockholders' equity would be incorrect. And finally, since the amount of net income and year-end cash balance are reported on the statement of cash flows, that financial statement would be incorrect as well.

Instructions:

Refer to Costco's financial statements shown on pages B-5–B-8 in Appendix B of this textbook to answer the following questions.

1. Determine the amount of the difference in retained earnings listed on the Consolidated Balance Sheets for August 31, 2003 and September 1, 2002. Remember, dollar amounts are reported in thousands.
2. Locate the dollar amount calculated in question 1 on Costco's Consolidated Statements of Income for the 52 Weeks Ended August 31, 2003. What is the title for the amount?
3. Locate the dollar amount calculated in question 1 on Costco's Consolidated Statements of Stockholders' Equity. What is the title for the amount?
4. Locate the dollar amount calculated in question 1 on Costco's Consolidated Statements of Cash Flows for the 52 Weeks Ended August 31, 2003. What is the title for the amount?
5. List the financial statements that would be affected by a failure to account for a $200,000 cash expenditure for advertising.

Organizational Structure of a Partnership

Chapter 21   **643**

AUDITING FOR ERRORS

1. The bookkeeper's entry is incorrect. Goodwill in this instance did not occur. Russ Hodges is purchasing a one-fourth capital share of the business ($30,000) for only $24,000 cash. The new value of the business is not in excess of the total investment of the owners.

2. *(See the journal at the bottom of the page.)*

ANALYZING COSTCO'S FINANCIAL STATEMENTS

1. $721,000,000 ($5,349,731,000 − $4,628,731,000).
2. Net income.
3. Net income or Total comprehensive income.
4. Net income.
5. Consolidated Balance Sheets, Consolidated Statements of Income, Consolidated Statements of Stockholders' Equity, and Consolidated Statements of Cash Flows.

TEACHING STRATEGIES   PORTFOLIO ASSESSMENT

The possibility exists that students will someday work for or provide accounting services to a partnership. Students should select examples of journalizing transactions to form and expand a partnership to include in their portfolios. A copy of the Portfolio Assessment form (blackline master in the Teacher's Resource Guide; also on the Student Companion CD) should be completed by the student and the Description section should include any comments regarding how the student mastered these concepts and procedures.

GENERAL JOURNAL   PAGE 12

	DATE		ACCOUNT TITLE	DOC. NO.	POST. REF.	DEBIT	CREDIT	
1	Oct.	1	Cash	R213		24 0 0 0 00		1
2			Russ Hodges, Capital				24 0 0 0 00	2
3		1	Amy Cardoza, Capital	M89		2 0 0 0 00		3
4			Jeff Williams, Capital			2 0 0 0 00		4
5			Claire Mangoni, Capital			2 0 0 0 00		5
6			Russ Hodges, Capital				6 0 0 0 00	6

643

- Explain that most accounting software packages can be tailored to the needs of a particular business.

- Explain that information about a company must be entered in the Customize Accounting System window before accounting data can be entered.

- Point out that different kinds of businesses have different kinds of reporting needs and these needs are specified in the Customize Accounting System window.

Setting up company info

- Demonstrate clicking the Custom toolbar button and choosing Company Info. Tab in the Customize Accounting System window.

- Demonstrate the different options that can be selected.

- Emphasize that the company name and problem name specified in this tab will be printed as part of the header for every report.

Setting up account classifications

- Demonstrate choosing the Classify Accts. tab in the Customize Accounting System window.

- Demonstrate changing a range of account numbers. Emphasize that the ranges for the classifications are used to generate financial statements.

Setting up required accounts

- Demonstrate choosing the Required Accts. tab in the Customize Accounting System window.

- Demonstrate specifying any unfound accounts by clicking the Chart of Accounts button, selecting the desired account, and clicking OK.

Setting Up Automated Accounting Systems for Partnerships

Accounting software packages can be tailored to the needs of various types of businesses. Before accounting data can be entered, information about the company must be entered. The Customize Accounting System window is used to enter company information.

Company Info Tab

General information about a new company is specified on this tab. The company name and problem number are printed as part of the header for every report. Other information required includes business organization, features, type of business, type of income statement, and which checks will be printed from the accounting system.

Classify Accounts Tab

For most businesses, the default account classifications will be used. However, the classification numbers can be edited if necessary.

Required Accts. Tab

To prepare reports and perform period-ending closing tasks, certain accounts are required. Based upon the information specified on the Company Information tab, the computer will automatically search the chart of accounts to determine and list the accounts it requires. Accounts that cannot automatically be determined must be keyed.

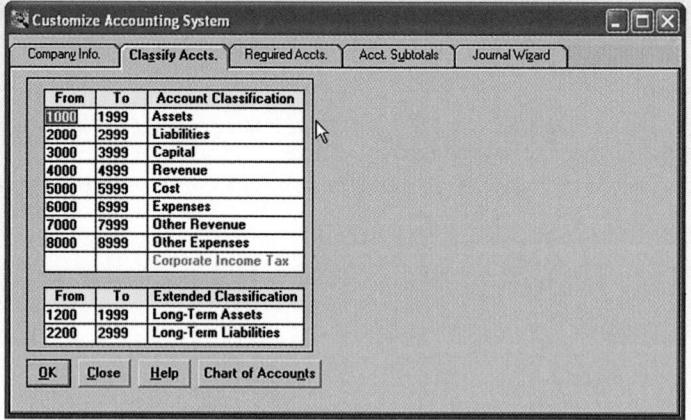

AUTOMATING APPLICATION PROBLEM 21-1

Instructions:

1. Load *Automated Accounting 8.0* or higher software.

2. Select database A21-1 (Advanced Course Application Problem 21-1) from the accounting template disk.

3. Select File from the menu bar and choose the Save As menu command. Key the path to the drive and directory that contains your data files. Save the database with a filename of XXX211 (where XXX are your initials).

4. Read the Problem Instruction screen by clicking the Browser toolbar button.

5. Key the data listed in the problem.

6. Exit the Automated Accounting software.

AUTOMATING MASTERY PROBLEM 21-6

Instructions:

1. Load *Automated Accounting 8.0* or higher software.

2. Select database A21-6 (Advanced Course Application Problem 21-6) from the accounting template disk.

3. Select File from the menu bar and choose the Save As menu command. Key the path to the drive and directory that contains your data files. Save the database with a filename of XXX216 (where XXX are your initials).

4. Read the Problem Instruction screen by clicking the Browser toolbar button.

5. Key the data listed in the problem.

6. Exit the Automated Accounting software.

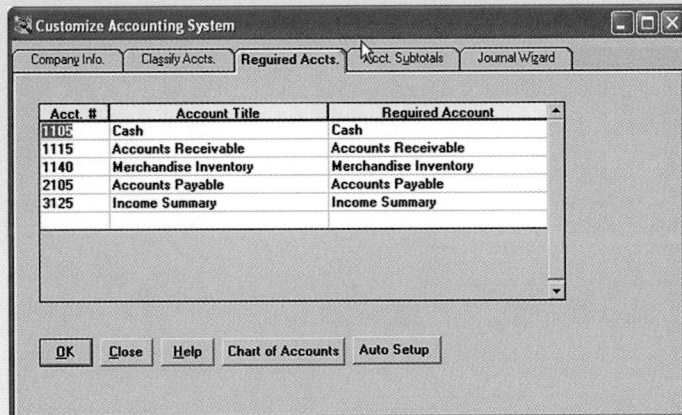

Organizational Structure of a Partnership

Chapter 21 **645**

TEACHING STRATEGIES   PORTFOLIO ASSESSMENT

Students should be encouraged to print at least one report from one of the Automated Accounting problems to include in their portfolio to demonstrate mastery of automated accounting systems. A copy of the Portfolio Assessment form (blackline master in the Teacher's Resource Guide; also on the Student Companion CD) should be completed by the student and the Description section should include any comments regarding how the student mastered these concepts and procedures.

Financial Reporting

	SCOPE & SEQUENCE	
	NEW	REVIEW/ EXTENSION
Introduce the Chapter	✓	
Lesson 22-1 Distribution and Withdrawal of Partnership Earnings		
Distributing partnership earnings using fixed percentages		✓
Distributing partnership earnings using percentage of total equity and using interest on equity	✓	
Distributing partnership earnings using salaries	✓	
Distributing partnership earnings using a combination of methods	✓	
Lesson 22-2 End-of-Fiscal-Period Work for a Partnership		
Work sheet for a partnership		✓
Distribution of net income statement	✓	
Financial statements for a partnership		✓
Adjusting and closing entries for a partnership		✓
Lesson 22-3 Liquidation of a Partnership		
Liquidation of a partnership		✓
Gains and losses on realization		✓
Putting It All Together		

ENHANCING

SPECIAL FEATURES

- Accounting in the Real World: Hewlett-Packard Company
- Making Ethical Decisions: Impending Merger Affects Student's Employment
- Explore Accounting: Accounting for Mortgage and Lease Payments
- Business Structures: The FTC Franchise Rule

- Technology for Business: Spreadsheet Activity— Distribution of Partnership Earnings

- Explore Accounting
- Xtra! Web Site: Xtra! Enrichment
- Applied Communication
- Cases for Critical Thinking
- SCANS Workplace Competency
- Graphing Workshop
- Analyzing Costco's Financial Statements

for a Partnership

INSTRUCTION		PRACTICE AND ASSESSMENT		
TECHNOLOGY AND MEDIA	**TEACHING STRATEGIES**	**GUIDED PRACTICE**	**INDEPENDENT PRACTICE**	**RETEACHING AND ENRICHMENT**
• Internet Research Activity • Accounting Xtra! Web Site	• Software Focus			
• Instructor's Resource CD: PowerPoint Slides • Xtra! Web Site: Xtra! Study Tools • Blackline Masters: Cash Payments Journal and General Journal • Personal Trainer		• Audit Your Understanding • Work Together 22-1	• On Your Own 22-1 • Application Problems 22-1 and 22-2 • Ongoing Assessment, p. 652 • Personal Trainer • Xtra! Web Site: Xtra! Study Tools	• Reteach, p. 652 • Enrich, p. 655
• Instructor's Resource CD: PowerPoint Slides • Xtra! Web Site: Xtra! Study Tools • Personal Trainer	• Print Learner	• Terms Review • Audit Your Understanding • Work Together 22-2	• On Your Own 22-2 • Application Problem 22-3 • Ongoing Assessment, p. 663 • Personal Trainer • Xtra! Web Site: Xtra! Study Tools	• Reteach, p. 663 • Enrich, p. 664
• Instructor's Resource CD: PowerPoint Slides • Xtra! Web Site: Xtra! Study Tools • Blackline Masters: Cash Receipts Journal and Cash Payments Journal • Personal Trainer	• Applied Skills: Writing Across the Curriculum	• Terms Review • Audit Your Understanding • Work Together 22-3	• On Your Own 22-3 • Application Problem 22-4 • Ongoing Assessment, p. 668 • Personal Trainer • Xtra! Web Site: Xtra! Study Tools	• Reteach, p. 668 • Enrich, p. 669
• Automated Accounting • Peachtree and QuickBooks • Personal Trainer • Xtra! Web Site: Xtra! Review, Quizzing, and Enrichment • Student Companion CD	• Applied Skills: Language Arts • Specific Learning Disability (SLD) Students		• Mastery Problem 22-5 • Personal Trainer • Xtra! Web Site: Xtra! Review and Quizzing • Study Guide 22 • Student Companion CD • Chapter 22 Test • ExamView Chapter 22 • Portfolio Assessment	• Challenge Problem 22-6 • Reteach, p. 670 • Enrich, p. 670 • Recycling Problem 22-1 • Automated Accounting • Peachtree and QuickBooks • Xtra! Web Site: Xtra! Enrichment

INTRODUCE THE CHAPTER

Preview Chapter Objectives

- Point out that students have already prepared an income statement and balance sheet for a merchandising business organized as a corporation.

- Emphasize that there are two major differences between end-of-fiscal-period work for a partnership and a corporation: (1) a corporation pays income tax on its net income; a partnership does not, and (2) a corporation maintains separate accounts for contributed and earned capital; partnerships maintain only one.

- Emphasize the importance of financial statements to all types of businesses.

Preview Accounting Terms

- Read each term out loud to verify pronunciation for students.

- Point out terms that should already be familiar to most students such as net income, owners' equity, and partnership.

INTERNET ACTIVITY

Point your browser to *accountingxtra. swlearning.com* to access the Accounting Xtra! Web Site.

SOFTWARE FOCUS

Software may be used for independent practice or enrichment as the instructor deems appropriate. For this chapter, the following software may be used: Automated Accounting and Century 21 8E CD with Mastery Problem 22-5 and Challenge Problem 22-6; Peachtree and QuickBooks with Mastery Problem 22-5 and Challenge Problem 22-6; the Student Companion CD; and Personal Trainer, Chapter 22.

Instructors may wish to cover the Automated Accounting feature on pages 676–677 even if the Automated Accounting software is not being used in the classroom so that students get a sense of how the chapter's accounting procedures would be implemented in an automated environment.

CHAPTER 22

Financial Reporting for a Partnership

After studying Chapter 22, you will be able to:

1. Define accounting terms related to distributing earnings and completing end-of-fiscal-period work for a partnership.

2. Identify accounting concepts and practices related to distributing earnings and completing end-of-fiscal-period work for a partnership.

3. Calculate the distribution of partnership earnings.

4. Journalize entries for withdrawal of partnership earnings.

5. Complete end-of-fiscal-period work for a partnership.

6. Prepare a distribution of net income statement for a partnership.

7. Journalize entries for liquidating a partnership.

- distribution of net income statement
- deficit
- owners' equity statement
- liquidation of a partnership
- realization

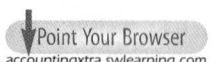
Point Your Browser
accountingxtra.swlearning.com

646

Hewlett-Packard Company

HEWLETT-PACKARD COMPANY: PARTNERING TO EXPAND GLOBAL IMPACT

In 1939, Bill Hewlett and Dave Packard formed a partnership that has evolved into one of the largest corporations in the world. The two partners began their business by developing a product known as an audio oscillator, an electronic device used by engineers to test sound equipment. In fact, one of the first companies to purchase Hewlett and Packard's audio oscillator was Walt Disney Studios, which used eight of the test instruments to create and develop a new sound system for its animated features. HP's revenues that first year totaled $5,369.

HP has grown considerably since 1939. The company recently launched 660 new products in a single year and closed that year with over 21,000 patents in force throughout the world. Today, with revenues of over $73 billion, HP is the leading consumer information technology company and sells its products in 110,000 retail outlets in more than 170 countries.

To remain competitive, the company continues to expand its operations and influence throughout the world. In 2003, HP merged with Compaq Computer Corporation. The merger allowed HP to improve cost efficiencies and offer a broad range of products and services to individual consumers, small businesses, and large corporations.

Critical Thinking

1. How would a merger between two technology companies help improve cost efficiencies?
2. How would a merger help expand sales?

Xtra!
Today
accountingxtra.swlearning.com

Source: www.hp.com

CPA DESIGNATION

Go to the homepage for the National Association of State Boards of Accountancy (NASBA) (www.nasba.org). This site has some information about each state's requirements for the Certified Public Accountant (CPA) designation and will link you to the State Board of Accountancy for your state.

Instructions

1. List the age, education, and work experience requirements to be licensed as a CPA in your state.
2. List the name, address, and phone number of the State Board of Accountancy for your state.

ACCOUNTING IN THE REAL WORLD

1. Student answers will vary but might include mention of improved cost efficiencies by eliminating duplicated costs related to R & D, engineering, support staff, manufacturing facilities, administration, marketing, product distribution, customer service, etc.
2. Student answers will vary, depending on the year revenues were reported. Students might suggest that mergers could improve sales figures by expanding product offerings and services, customer base, global presence, market share, consumer services, or corporate access.

INTERNET RESEARCH ACTIVITY

Answers will vary.

22-1 Distribution and Withdrawal of Partnership Earnings

Most end-of-fiscal-period work is similar for corporations, proprietorships, and partnerships. Two major procedures are different. (1) A corporation calculates and pays income tax on its net income, but partnerships and proprietorships do not. (2) A corporation maintains separate accounts for contributed capital (Capital Stock) and earned capital (Retained Earnings). Partnerships and proprietorships combine contributed and earned capital in one account for each owner.

A corporation may distribute some, but usually not all, of its earnings to stockholders as dividends. However, partnerships, like proprietorships, distribute all earnings of the business to the owners' capital accounts. The owners may then withdraw the earnings or leave them in the business.

©GETTY IMAGES/PHOTODISC

making ethical decisions

MAKING ETHICAL DECISIONS • MAKING ETHICAL DECISIONS • MAKING ETHICAL DECISION

Impending Merger Affects Student's Employment

Sallie Kaplan was a senior majoring in accounting at Southeastern State University when she accepted a position in the Columbus office of Jensen, Pearson & Marris, a public accounting firm. Sallie was not scheduled to begin working with the firm until after she completed her master's degree.

About the same time, John Jensen, the managing partner of the firm, agreed in principle to sell the firm to Patrel & Franklin, a large, international public accounting firm. The merger required extensive negotiations and planning. As a result, the merger was not announced to the public, existing clients, or employees (including Sallie) for over a year. Patrel & Franklin immediately announced that the Columbus office was going to be closed and its clients serviced from its New York office.

The day after the merger was announced, John offered Sallie a similar position in the New York office. For personal reasons, Sallie declined the offer. Thus, with only two months remaining before her graduation with a master's degree, Sallie again began searching for a new position in Columbus.

Instructions

Determine whether John Jensen's delay in telling Sallie Kaplan of the merger and office closing was ethical. Assume that the action is not illegal and does not violate any professional codes of conduct. Evaluate the impact of the decision on all the stakeholders.

MAKING ETHICAL DECISIONS

MAKING ETHICAL DECISIONS

Students' solutions will vary. Some students will conclude that Sallie should have been notified of the impending merger. Other students will recognize that John is in a very difficult position and cannot afford the possibility that Sallie might inform others of the merger.

For a sample solution, see the front section of this Wraparound Teacher's Edition.

DISTRIBUTION OF PARTNERSHIP EARNINGS

All earnings of a partnership are distributed to the partners. Five methods are commonly used for calculating the distribution of partnership earnings.

1. Fixed percentage.
2. Percentage of total equity.
3. Interest on equity.
4. Salaries.
5. Combination of methods

FIXED PERCENTAGE

	Total Net Income	×	Fixed Percentage	=	Share of Net Income
Costa	$20,000.00	×	60%	=	$12,000.00
McKee	$20,000.00	×	40%	=	8,000.00
Total					$20,000.00

The basis on which a partnership's earnings are distributed is usually stated in the partnership agreement. If a partnership agreement does not indicate how to divide the earnings, most state laws stipulate that partners share the earnings equally. For example, the earnings of two partners are shared on a fixed percentage of 50% and 50%. The law applies regardless of differences in the partners' investments, abilities, or time devoted to partnership business.

Scott Costa and Gary McKee are partners. On January 1, the partners' equities are Scott, $50,000.00 and Gary, $30,000.00. The net income for the year ended December 31 is

$20,000.00. The partnership agreement states that Scott is to receive 60% and Gary is to receive 40% of the net income or net loss. The distribution of net income is calculated as shown above.

FYI FOR YOUR INFORMATION

Limited partnerships include owners who have limited liability and limited operating responsibilities. Limited partnerships are sometimes formed for special projects such as Broadway plays.

©GETTY IMAGES/PHOTODISC

- Explain that the percentage of total equity is calculated in two steps: (1) calculate the percentage of equity each partner has of the total equity of the partnership and then (2) multiply the percentage of total equity each partner has times the total net income.

- Explain that partners often agree to use capital account balances on the first day of a fiscal year as the basis for calculating the equity percentage.

| DEMONSTRATE |

- Direct students to the math box at the top of the page. Illustrate on the board how to calculate partners' share of net income using the percentage of total equity.

| EXPLAIN |

- Explain that the interest on equity method is often used when partners invest different amounts in a partnership.

- Explain that partners often agree to use capital account balances on the first day of a fiscal year as the basis for this distribution. The partnership agreement should state the interest rate that is used.

- Direct students to the F.Y.I. box to learn that the interest rate specified in the partnership agreement is often related to the current bank prime lending rate.

- Explain that when this method is used, the remaining net income or net loss is distributed using another method.

| DEMONSTRATE |

- Direct students to the math box in the middle of the page. Illustrate on the board how to calculate partners' share of net income using the interest on equity method.

PERCENTAGE OF TOTAL EQUITY

	Partner's Equity	÷	Total Equity	=	Percentage of Total Equity
Costa	$50,000.00	÷	$80,000.00	=	62.5%
McKee	30,000.00	÷	$80,000.00	=	37.5%
Total	$80,000.00				

	Total Net Income	×	Percentage of Total Equity	=	Share of Net Income
Costa	$20,000.00	×	62.5%	=	$12,500.00
McKee	$20,000.00	×	37.5%	=	7,500.00
Total					$20,000.00

Partners often agree to use capital account balances on the first day of a fiscal year as the basis for calculating the distribution of partnership earnings. If Scott and Gary had agreed to use this method, referred to as the *percentage of total equity method*, the percentages would be calculated as shown above.

INTEREST ON EQUITY

	Partner's Equity	×	Interest Rate	=	Interest on Equity
Baker	$22,880.00	×	5%	=	$1,144.00
Mattingly	$11,440.00	×	5%	=	572.00

Interest on equity is often used as a method to distribute earnings when partners invest different amounts in a partnership. Partners often agree to use capital account balances on the first day of a fiscal year as the basis for this income distribution method. The partnership agreement states the interest rate.

MaLin Carpet Design's partnership agreement, Item Five, shown on page 623, stipulates that each partner is to receive 5% interest on equity. On January 1, May Baker's equity is $22,880.00 and Lindel Mattingly's equity is $11,440.00. The interest on equity is calculated as shown above.

When the interest on equity method is used, the remaining net income or net loss is distributed using another income distribution method as described later in this chapter.

FYI FOR YOUR INFORMATION

The rate of interest on equity is often related to the current bank prime lending rate.

SALARIES

Salaries are often used as a method to distribute earnings when partners contribute different amounts of personal service or bring different prior experience to a partnership. The amount of salary for each partner is stated in the partnership agreement.

MaLin's partnership agreement states that salaries are to be paid as follows: May Baker, $5,000.00; Lindel Mattingly, $3,000.00. When salaries are used, the remaining net income or net loss is distributed using a combination of methods described in the following paragraphs.

COMBINATION OF METHODS

	Interest on Equity	Salary	Distribution of Remaining Net Income or Net Loss
Baker	5%	$5,000.00	50%
Mattingly	5%	$3,000.00	50%

	Baker	Mattingly	Distribution
Total Net Income			$37,400.00
Interest on Equity	$ 1,144.00	$ 572.00	
Salary	5,000.00	3,000.00	
Total	$ 6,144.00	$ 3,572.00	9,716.00
Remaining Net Income			$27,684.00
Distribution of Remaining Net Income	13,842.00	13,842.00	
Total Distribution	$19,986.00	$17,414.00	$37,400.00

A combination of income distribution methods may be used for distributing partnership earnings. MaLin's partnership agreement states the earnings distribution as shown above. The distribution of MaLin's net income, *$37,400.00*, is calculated as shown above.

WITHDRAWAL OF PARTNERSHIP EARNINGS

A partner often needs a portion of the annual net income before the end of a fiscal year when the actual net income is known. Thus, during a fiscal year, partners take assets out of the partnership in anticipation of the net income for the year. Assets taken out of a business for the owner's personal use are known as withdrawals. Usually the partnership agreement indicates limits on the amount of assets that may be withdrawn.

> **REMEMBER** A partner may have a large capital balance yet be unable to withdraw any assets from the partnership. Cash or other assets must be available for a partner to make a withdrawal. A partner's salary is not an expense to the business.

- Explain that salaries are often allowed when partners contribute different amounts of time to the partnership or bring different prior experience to a partnership.

- Explain that the amount of net income distributed as a salary should be stated in the partnership agreement.

- Explain that when this method is used, the remaining net income or net loss is distributed using one or more additional methods.

- Explain that a combination of two or more of the previously described methods for distributing partnership net income may be used. When a combination of methods is used, generally the percentage of equity method is applied last to distribute any remaining net income or net loss remaining after the distributions have been made by the other methods.

DEMONSTRATE

- Illustrate on the board how to calculate partners' share of net income using a combination of methods or direct students to the math box to describe the calculation.

EXPLAIN

- Explain that partners may take assets out of the partnership during the year. Assets taken out of a business for the owner's personal use are known as withdrawals.

- Explain that usually the partnership agreement indicates limits on the amount of assets that may be withdrawn.

- Emphasize that a partner's salary is designated as a method of distribution or as a withdrawal from the partner's equity, not an expense to the business.

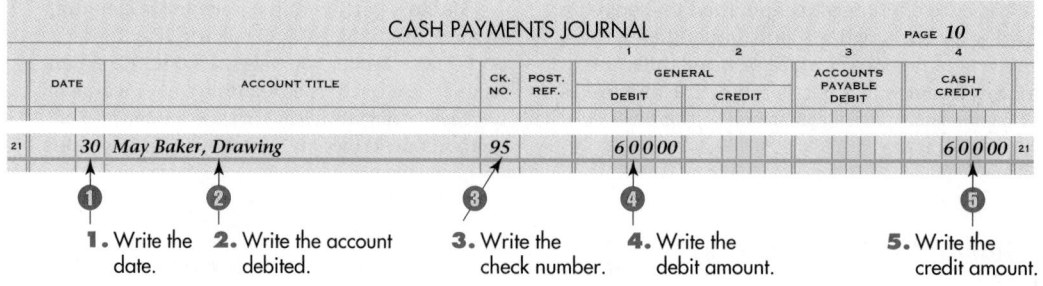

WITHDRAWAL OF CASH

	DATE		ACCOUNT TITLE	CK. NO.	POST. REF.	GENERAL DEBIT	GENERAL CREDIT	ACCOUNTS PAYABLE DEBIT	CASH CREDIT	
21	30	*May Baker, Drawing*		95		6 0 0 00			6 0 0 00	21

1. Write the date. **2.** Write the account debited. **3.** Write the check number. **4.** Write the debit amount. **5.** Write the credit amount.

May 30, 20--. May Baker, partner, withdrew cash for personal use, $600.00. Check No. 95.

May Baker, Drawing is debited for $600.00. Cash is credited for $600.00. The entry is made in the cash payments journal as shown above.

```
              May Baker, Drawing
           600.00  |

                  Cash
                      |  600.00
```

STEPS   STEPS • STEPS • STEPS • STEPS • STE

PARTNER'S WITHDRAWAL OF CASH

1. Write the date, *30*, in the Date column.

2. Write the title of the account debited, *May Baker, Drawing*, in the Account Title column.

3. Write the check number, *95*, in the Ck. No. column.

4. Write the debit amount, *600.00*, in the General Debit column.

5. Write the credit amount, *600.00*, in the Cash Credit column.

WITHDRAWAL OF ASSETS OTHER THAN CASH

1. Write the date. **2.** Write the account debited. **4.** Write the debit amount.

	DATE	ACCOUNT TITLE	DOC. NO.	POST. REF.	DEBIT	CREDIT	
1	July 20-- 10	*Lindel Mattingly, Drawing*	M14		5 0 00		1
2		*Supplies—Office*				5 0 00	2

5. Write the account credited. **3.** Write the memorandum number. **6.** Write the credit amount.

July 10, 20--. Lindel Mattingly, partner, withdrew office supplies for personal use, $50.00. Memorandum No. 14.

Office supplies withdrawn for personal use are not a business expense. This transaction reduces the partnership's office supplies inven-

tory and, therefore, Supplies—Office is credited. Lindel Mattingly, Drawing is debited for $50.00. Supplies—Office is credited for $50.00.

```
           Lindel Mattingly, Drawing
           50.00  |

                Supplies—Office
                      |  50.00
```

- Explain that a partner may withdraw cash or assets other than cash from the business. In either case, the withdrawal is recorded in the partner's drawing account.
- Explain that partner withdrawals of cash are recorded in a cash payments journal.

DEMONSTRATE

- Prepare a transparency of a cash payments journal to illustrate recording a partner's cash withdrawal.
- Direct students to the illustration at the top of the page as you describe each of the five steps for recording a partner's withdrawal of cash.

EXPLAIN

- Explain that a partner may withdraw assets other than cash from the business for personal use. Such a transaction is recorded in a general journal.
- Explain that the asset withdrawn should be decreased by a credit entry to the account of the asset withdrawn.

DEMONSTRATE

- Prepare a transparency of a general journal to illustrate recording a partner's withdrawal of an asset other than cash or direct students to the illustration at the bottom of the page.

ONGOING ASSESSMENT

- Assessment is an ongoing process. Circulate through the classroom or lab, observing which students have problems with the assignments.
- Troubleshooting: Diagnose what kinds of problems students have with this section. Students may have trouble in calculating correctly the complete distribution of partnership net income. Students may have trouble distributing net income when interest on equity or salaries method is used. Some students may have trouble determining what account to credit when assets other than cash are withdrawn by a partner.

RETEACH

- Write on the board a partnership's net income and distribution methods to be used.
- Ask the class to individually calculate the distribution of net income using the methods provided.
- Ask a student to give the answer and describe how the calculation was performed.
- Ask the class if the student description is correct.
- Repeat the process if some students need the review.

Explore Accounting

EXPLORE ACCOUNTING · EXPLORE ACCOUNTING · EXPLORE ACCOUNTING

Accounting for Mortgage and Lease Payments

Lexington Corporation has just signed a rental agreement with Metro Financing for the use of a delivery truck. Lexington must pay $600.00 each month for five years. A provision of the lease contract allows Lexington to purchase the truck from Metro Financing for $100.00 at the end of the lease term. Lexington's bookkeeper has recorded the first lease payment using the following entry:

Rent Expense 600.00
   Cash 600.00

Upon reviewing the monthly financial statements, Lexington's chief financial officer (CFO) recognizes that the transaction was not recorded properly. The CFO realizes that, although the form of the transaction is a lease, the substance of the transaction is a loan. GAAP provides accountants with four criteria to evaluate the substance versus the form of lease agreements. If any one of the criteria is met, the transaction is treated as a purchase. A lease with substantially the same provisions as a purchase is referred to as a *capital lease*.

The estimated cost of the asset is recorded as if the asset were purchased on account, with a bank loan or a mortgage. Lexington could have arranged a 10% bank loan to purchase the truck. Using this interest rate, the CFO estimates the value of the truck to be $28,239.22 and records the following entry:

Capitalize Lease
(truck) 28,239.22
   Lease Liability 28,239.22

The lease liability is recorded as a long-term liability. Similar to any loan or mortgage payment, each payment is divided between interest and loan repayment. After calculating the monthly interest expense, the remaining portion of the payment reduces the loan principal balance. In the first month of the lease, Lexington must pay 10% interest on the recorded value of the lease liability. Thus, the following entry would be recorded:

Interest Expense 235.33
   (28,239.22 × 10%/12)
Lease Liability 364.67
   (600.00 − 235.33)
   Cash 600.00

Since the truck is also recorded as an asset, a separate entry would be recorded to reflect depreciation expense. Thus, the accounting entries to record a capital lease are exactly the same as if Lexington had purchased the truck with a loan from Metro Financing.

Instructions: Determine the transaction for recording the second month's lease payment. Note that the principal for the interest calculation is reduced by the amount of reduction in the lease liability.

The concept of substance versus form is important in financial accounting and taxation. Stress that the rules for capitalizing leases ensure that financial statements reflect the economic reality of transactions. In this case, Lexington purchased the truck, regardless of the fact that the agreement is labeled as a lease.

Ask students to access the annual reports of several companies, such as retailers and airlines, which require substantial amounts of plant assets. Instruct students to identify if any capital (capitalized) leases are reported on the balance sheet or in the notes to the financial statements.

Interest Expense 232.29
(27,874.55 × 10%/12)
Lease Liability 367.71
(600.00 − 232.29)
   Cash 600.00

• audit your understanding

GUIDED PRACTICE

Audit Your Understanding

- Call on students to answer the Audit Your Understanding questions. Ask the class if the answer is correct and/or complete. Answers are given in Appendix E of the textbook.

Work Together

Have students write the solution to the Work Together problem as you guide the class through the examples.

- Direct students to calculate the distribution for each situation as you elicit class participation in calculating each situation.

- Direct students to record each transaction as you elicit class participation in recording each transaction.

• **audit your understanding**

1. Where should the method of distributing partnership earnings be stated?
2. What are five common methods for distributing partnership earnings?
3. What account is debited when a partner withdraws cash for personal use?
4. What account is debited when a partner withdraws supplies for personal use?

• **work together 22-1**

Calculating partnership earnings and journalizing partnership withdrawals

Scott Badger and Maxine Giesen are partners in a business. On December 31 of the current year, the partners' equities are Scott, $60,000.00 and Maxine, $90,000.00. The net income for the year is $60,000.00. A work sheet for calculating distribution of partners' earnings, a cash payments journal, and a general journal are provided in the *Working Papers*. Your instructor will guide you through the following examples.

1. For each of the following independent cases, calculate how the $60,000.00 net income will be distributed to the two partners.

   a. Each partner receives a fixed percentage of 50% of net income.

   b. Each partner receives a percentage of net income based on the percentage of total equity.

   c. Each partner receives 10% interest on equity. The partners share remaining net income equally.

   d. Scott receives 8% interest on equity and a salary of $18,000.00. Maxine receives 8% interest on equity and a salary of $22,500.00. The partners share remaining net income equally.

2. Record the following transactions in the appropriate journal.

   June 20, 20--. Scott Badger, partner, withdrew cash for personal use, $750.00. Check No. 133.
   July 1, 20--.   Maxine Giesen, partner, withdrew office supplies for personal use, $45.00. Memorandum No. 23.

TEACHING STRATEGIES   DIFFERENT LEARNING ABILITIES

Limited English Proficiency (LEP) Students. Rather than asking students whether they understand what you have said, ask them to restate what you have said in their own words.

654

on your own 22-1

Calculating partnership earnings and journalizing partnership withdrawals

Rose Nabors and Sam Ives are partners in a business. On December 31 of the current year, the partners' equities are Rose, $50,000 and Sam, $75,000.00. The net income for the year is $50,000.00. A work sheet for calculating distribution of partners' earnings, a cash payments journal, and a general journal are provided in the *Working Papers*. Work independently to complete the following problem.

1. For each of the following independent cases, calculate how the $50,000.00 net income will be distributed to the two partners.

   a. Each partner receives a fixed percentage of 50% of net income.

   b. Each partner receives a percentage of net income based on the percentage of total equity.

   c. Each partner receives 8% interest on equity. The partners share remaining net income equally.

   d. Rose receives 10% interest on equity and a salary of $16,000.00. Sam receives 10% interest on equity and a salary of $14,000.00. The partners share remaining net income equally.

2. Record the following transactions in the appropriate journal.
   Apr. 15, 20--. Rose Nabors, partner, withdrew cash for personal use, $800.00. Check No. 126.
   Oct. 3, 20--. Sam Ives, partner, withdrew store supplies for personal use, $120.00. Memorandum No. 18.

ON YOUR OWN • ON YOUR OWN • ON YOUR OWN

business structures

BUSINESS STRUCTURES • BUSINESS STRUCTURES • BUSINESS STRUCTURES

The FTC Franchise Rule

Successful business owners frequently seek ways to expand their businesses. One expansion technique is franchising. A franchise is a contractual arrangement in which the owner of a trademark, trade name, or copyright licenses others, under specified conditions or limitations, to use the trademark, trade name, or copyright to sell goods or services. The person or business entity granting the franchise is known as the franchisor. The person or business entity to whom the franchise is granted is known as the franchisee.

The Federal Trade Commission (FTC) Franchise Rule requires the franchisor to make a written disclosure of important information about the franchisor, the franchised business, and the franchise relationship. The disclosure should state information about the total cost, the amount of control the franchisor will have over the operations of the franchisee, the plan for termination of the franchise, and the conditions for renewal of the franchise. A franchisor must allow the potential franchisee at least 10 business days to review the disclosure document before asking the person to invest in the franchise.

Since the Franchise Rule is a trade regulation, it is enforced by the FTC. If the FTC finds that the rule has been violated, it may issue injunctions, freeze the assets of the franchisor, enact fines up to $10,000 per violation, and require that monetary compensation be given to those harmed by the actions of the franchisor.

Distribution and Withdrawal of Partnership Earnings

Lesson 22-1 **655**

22-2 End-of-Fiscal-Period Work for a Partnership

OBJECTIVES

- Define accounting terms related to end-of-fiscal-period work for a partnership.
- Identify accounting concepts and practices related to end-of-fiscal-period work for a partnership.
- Complete end-of-fiscal-period work for a partnership.
- Prepare a distribution of net income statement for a partnership.

MOTIVATE

Like a corporation, a partnership also prepares a work sheet, an income statement, and a balance sheet. Emphasize that in this section, the emphasis will be on preparing the two statements that are different from a corporation: a distribution of net income statement, and an owners' equity statement.

Preview

- Preview the accounting terms and definitions introduced in this lesson: distribution of net income statement, deficit, and owner's equity statement.
- Direct students to read the headings at the top of each page in this lesson and to examine the illustrations given.

EXPLAIN

- Explain that the adjustments for a partnership do not include an adjustment for federal income tax. A partnership net income is reported to the Internal Revenue Service on the partners' personal tax return.
- Explain that an income statement is used to report a partnership business's financial progress during a fiscal period.
- Explain that an income statement of a partnership service business has two main sections: (1) revenue section and (2) expenses section.

DEMONSTRATE

- Direct students to the income statement shown in the illustration.

ADJUSTMENTS ON A WORK SHEET

End-of-fiscal-period work for a partnership is similar to that for a corporation. In preparing partnership financial statements, accountants apply accounting principles in the same way during each fiscal period. [CONCEPT: Consistent Reporting]

All accounts in MaLin's general ledger are listed in a work sheet's Account Title column as shown on the next page. Adjustments are planned on a partnership work sheet in the same manner as on a corporate work sheet, with one exception. No adjustment for accrued federal income tax is *ever* planned on a partner-ship work sheet because partnerships do not pay federal income tax.

As described later in this chapter, partnership net income is reported to the Internal Revenue Service on the partners' personal tax returns.

Because MaLin Carpet Design does not sell merchandise, it does not need to make an adjustment for merchandise inventory. Adjustments for uncollectible accounts, supplies, insurance, and depreciation are planned on the work sheet.

INCOME STATEMENT

MaLin Carpet Design
Income Statement
For Year Ended December 31, 20--

			% of Sales*
Operating Revenue:			
Sales		$72,020.27	100.0
Operating Expenses:			
Advertising Expense	$ 985.00		
Depreciation Expense—Equipment	1,250.50		
Depreciation Expense—Truck	918.75		
Insurance Expense	503.20		
Miscellaneous Expense	2,869.21		
Rent Expense	8,400.00		
Supplies Expense—Carpet	7,676.50		
Supplies Expense—Office	1,420.00		
Truck Expense	8,477.56		
Uncollectible Accounts Expense	119.55		
Utilities Expense	2,000.00		
Total Operating Expenses		34,620.27	48.1
Net Income		$37,400.00	51.9

*Rounded to the nearest 0.1%.

MATERIALS

- Instructor's Resource CD: PowerPoint Slides
- Xtra! Study Tools on the Xtra! Web Site
- Working Papers: Teacher's Edition of the Working Papers for Lesson 22-2
- Software: Personal Trainer

MaLin Carpet Design
Work Sheet
For Year Ended December 31, 20--

	ACCOUNT TITLE	TRIAL BALANCE DEBIT	TRIAL BALANCE CREDIT	ADJUSTMENTS DEBIT	ADJUSTMENTS CREDIT	INCOME STATEMENT DEBIT	INCOME STATEMENT CREDIT	BALANCE SHEET DEBIT	BALANCE SHEET CREDIT	
1	Cash	4280247						4280247		1
2	Petty Cash	20000						20000		2
3	Accounts Receivable	1199251						1199251		3
4	Allow. for Uncollectible Accts.		1992		(a) 11955				13947	4
5	Supplies—Carpet	930500			(b) 767650			162850		5
6	Supplies—Office	184500			(c) 142000			42500		6
7	Prepaid Insurance	134970			(d) 50320			84650		7
8	Equipment	1250497						1250497		8
9	Accum. Depr.—Equipment				(e) 125050				125050	9
10	Truck	490000						490000		10
11	Accum. Depr.—Truck				(f) 91875				91875	11
12	Accounts Payable		852123						852123	12
13	May Baker, Capital		2288000						2288000	13
14	May Baker, Drawing	450000						450000		14
15	Lindel Mattingly, Capital		1144000						1144000	15
16	Lindel Mattingly, Drawing	275000						275000		16
17	Income Summary									17
18	Sales		7202027				7202027			18
19	Advertising Expense	98500				98500				19
20	Depr. Expense—Equipment			(e) 125050		125050				20
21	Depr. Expense—Truck			(f) 91875		91875				21
22	Insurance Expense			(d) 50320		50320				22
23	Miscellaneous Expense	286921				286921				23
24	Rent Expense	840000				840000				24
25	Supplies Expense—Carpet			(b) 767650		767650				25
26	Supplies Expense—Office			(c) 142000		142000				26
27	Truck Expense	847756				847756				27
28	Uncollectible Accounts Expense			(a) 11955		11955				28
29	Utilities Expense	200000				200000				29
30		11488142	11488142	1188850	1188850	3462027	7202027	8254995	4514995	30
31	Net Income					3740000			3740000	31
32						7202027	7202027	8254995	8254995	32

- Explain that the work sheet for a partnership is similar to the work sheet for a corporation.
- Point out that no federal income tax expense appears on the work sheet for a partnership.
- Since MaLin is a service business, there is no merchandise inventory account and no adjustment for merchandise inventory.

EXPLAIN

- Explain that MaLin Carpet Design calculates two component percentages on its income statement: (1) operating expenses and (2) net income.

DEMONSTRATE

- Calculate on the board component percentages for total operating expenses and net income.

EXPLAIN

- Explain that a financial statement unique to a partnership is a distribution of net income statement.

- Explain that this statement reports how the partnership net income is distributed to the partners.

DEMONSTRATE

- Prepare a transparency of the distribution of net income statement in the textbook or direct students to the illustration on this page.

- Describe each of the four steps, on page 659, for preparing a distribution of net income statement.

- Emphasize that the net income from the income statement is used to prepare the distribution of net income statement.

COMPONENT PERCENTAGES ON THE INCOME STATEMENT

A partnership income statement is similar to a corporation income statement with one exception. Federal income tax expense is *not* reported on a partnership income statement because a partnership does not pay federal income tax.

MaLin calculates two component percentages on its income statement as shown on page 656.

1. *Operating expenses component percentage.* MaLin expects a component percentage not more than 55.0%. Therefore, MaLin's operating expenses component percentage of 48.1% is acceptable. (Operating Expenses, $34,620.27 ÷ Sales, $72,020.27 = Operating Expense Component Percentage, 48.1%).
2. *Net income component percentage.* MaLin expects a component percentage not less than 45.0%. Therefore, MaLin's net income

component percentage of 51.9% is acceptable. (Net Income, $37,400.00; Sales, $72,020.27 = Net Income Component Percentage, 51.9%).

The net income component percentage is often high for partnerships that sell only services because they have no cost of merchandise sold. Also, the partners' salaries are not expenses of the partnership.

FYI FOR YOUR INFORMATION

Fields of accounting become extremely specialized as technical requirements increase. For example, some accountants specialize in accounting only for the gas and oil industry.

DISTRIBUTION OF NET INCOME STATEMENT SHOWING A NET INCOME

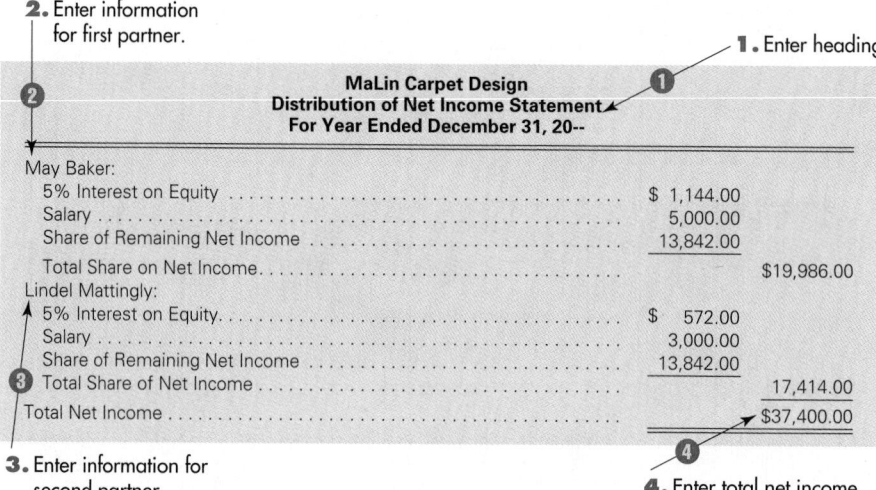

2. Enter information for first partner.

1. Enter heading.

MaLin Carpet Design
Distribution of Net Income Statement
For Year Ended December 31, 20--

May Baker:		
5% Interest on Equity	$ 1,144.00	
Salary	5,000.00	
Share of Remaining Net Income	13,842.00	
Total Share on Net Income		$19,986.00
Lindel Mattingly:		
5% Interest on Equity	$ 572.00	
Salary	3,000.00	
Share of Remaining Net Income	13,842.00	
Total Share of Net Income		17,414.00
Total Net Income		$37,400.00

3. Enter information for second partner.

4. Enter total net income.

A partnership financial statement showing distribution of net income or net loss to partners is called a **distribution of net income statement**.

MaLin's distribution of partnership earnings for the current year was calculated as shown on

page 651. The amounts calculated are reported on the Distribution of Net Income Statement shown above.

PREPARING A DISTRIBUTION OF NET INCOME STATEMENT

1 Enter the 3-line heading, *MaLin Carpet Design, Distribution of Net Income Statement, For Year Ended December 31, 20--.*

2 Enter the information for *May Baker*. List the distribution methods, *5% Interest on Equity, Salary,* and *Share of Remaining Net Income*. Enter the amounts of distribution for each method, *$1,144.00, $5,000.00,* and *$13,842.00,* respectively. Finally, enter the *Total Share of Net Income, $19,986.00.*

3 Enter the information for *Lindel Mattingly*. List the distribution methods, *5% Interest on Equity, Salary,* and *Share of Remaining Net Income.* Enter the distribution amounts for each method, *$572.00, $3,000.00,* and *$13,842.00,* respectively. Finally, enter the *Total Share of Net Income, $17,414.00.*

4 Enter *Total Net Income, $37,400.00.*

EXPLAIN

- Explain that partnership net income is divided in accordance with the partnership agreement.
- Explain that when salaries or interest on equity are stipulated, the amounts are allowed whether sufficient net income is available.
- Explain that if the net income is less than the total allowed, partners share in the resulting deficit according to the partnership agreement.

DEMONSTRATE

- Prepare a transparency of the distribution of net income statement showing a deficit or direct students to the illustration on this page.
- Describe each of the four steps, on page 660, for calculating and preparing a distribution of net income when there is a resulting deficit to distribute.

DISTRIBUTION OF NET INCOME STATEMENT SHOWING A DEFICIT

	Partner's Equity	×	Interest Rate	×	Time as Fraction of Year	=	Monthly Interest	
Ford	($60,000.00	×	10%)	×	1/12	=	$500.00	**1.** Calculate monthly interest.
Pope	($54,000.00	×	10%)	×	1/12	=	450.00	
Total							$950.00	

	Total Net Income	–	Total Allowance	=	Deficit		**2.** Determine the deficit.
	$750.00	–	$950.00	=	$200.00		

	Deficit	×	Fixed Percentage	=	Partner's Share of Deficit		**3.** Calculate each partner's share of the deficit.
Ford	$200.00	×	60%	=	$120.00		
Pope	$200.00	×	40%	=	80.00		
Total					$200.00		

Ford and Pope
Distribution of Net Income Statement
For Month Ended January 31, 20-- **4.** Prepare the statement.

Jason Ford:		
10% Interest on Equity	$500.00	
Less Share of Deficit	120.00	
Total Share of Net Income		$380.00
Celia Pope:		
10% Interest on Equity	$450.00	
Less Share of Deficit	80.00	
Total Share of Net Income		370.00
Total Net Income		$750.00

When salaries or interest on equity are stipulated, the amounts are allowed whether sufficient net income is available. The amount by which allowances to partners exceed net income is called a **deficit**. Partners share deficits according to the partnership agreement.

On January 1, the equity of two partners is as follows: Jason Ford, $60,000.00 and Celia

Pope, $54,000.00. Each partner receives a 10% annual interest on equity and shares any remaining income or deficit on a fixed percentage of 60% and 40%, respectively. For the month of January, the partnership earned a net income of $750.00. Their distribution of net income statement is shown above.

PREPARING A DISTRIBUTION OF NET INCOME STATEMENT SHOWING A DEFICIT

1 Calculate the monthly amounts due to each partner: *$500.00* for Ford and *$450.00* for Pope.

2 Determine the deficit amount, *$200.00* ($950.00 due to both partners − $750.00 net income).

3 Calculate each partner's share of the deficit, *120.00* for Ford and *80.00* for Pope.

4 Prepare the distribution of net income statement showing the deficit.

OWNERS' EQUITY STATEMENT

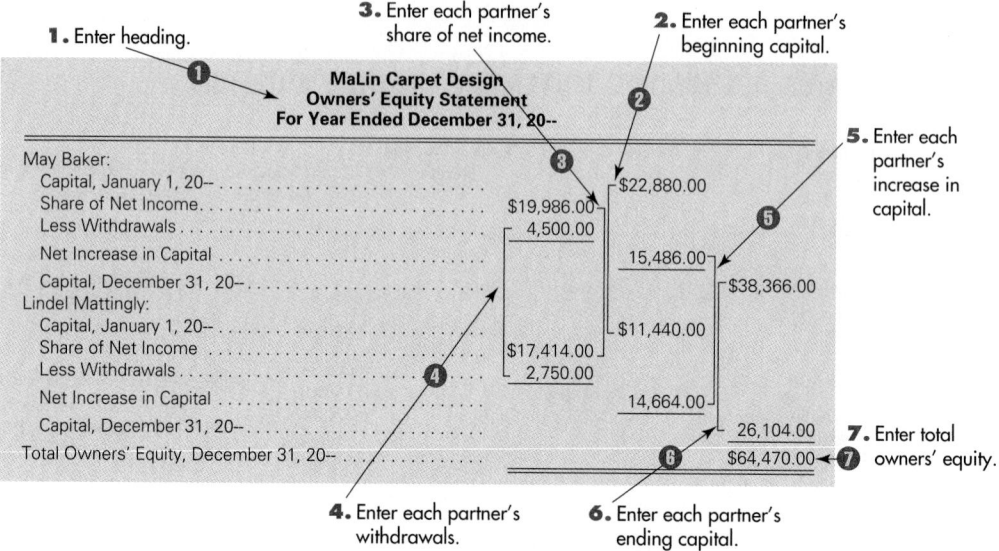

1. Enter heading.

3. Enter each partner's share of net income.

2. Enter each partner's beginning capital.

5. Enter each partner's increase in capital.

4. Enter each partner's withdrawals.

6. Enter each partner's ending capital.

7. Enter total owners' equity.

A corporation's equity is reported on a statement of stockholders' equity. A similar statement is prepared for a partnership. A financial statement that summarizes the changes in owners' equity during a fiscal period is called an **owners' equity statement**. The owners' equity statement shows the changes occurring in equity as shown above.

PREPARING AN OWNER'S EQUITY STATEMENT

1 Enter the 3-line heading, *MaLin Carpet Design, Owners' Equity Statement, For Year Ended December 31, 20--*.

2 Enter each partner's capital at the beginning of the fiscal period, *$22,880.00* and *$11,440.00*. This balance is found in each partner's capital account in the general ledger.

3 Enter each partner's total share of net income, *$19,986.00* and *$17,414.00*. These amounts are obtained from the distribution of net income statement.

4 Enter each partner's withdrawals during the fiscal period, *$4,500.00* and *$2,750.00*. These amounts are found on the work sheet.

5 Enter each partner's net increase in capital during the fiscal period, *$15,486.00* and *$14,664.00*.

6 Enter each partner's capital on the last day of the fiscal period, *$38,366.00* and *$26,104.00*.

7 Enter the partnership's total owners' equity on the last day of the fiscal period, *$64,470.00*.

Financial Reporting for a Partnership

- Explain that owner's equity represents the owner's share of the business.

- Explain that a successful business should continue to grow and owners' equity should also continue to grow.

- Explain that the owners' equity statement summarizes the changes in owners' equity during a fiscal period.

- Explain that there are three factors that can change owners' equity: (1) additional investments by the owners, (2) withdrawals by the owners, and (3) net income or net loss.

- Explain that information needed to prepare an owners' equity statement comes from the distribution of net income statement and the general ledger capital and drawing accounts.

- Explain that the general ledger capital and drawing accounts provide the following information used in preparing the owners' equity statement: (1) beginning capital amount, (2) any additional investments made during the fiscal period, and (3) each partner's withdrawal of assets during the fiscal period.

DEMONSTRATE

- Prepare a transparency of the owners' equity statement in the textbook or direct students to the illustration on this page.

- Describe each of the seven steps for preparing an owners' equity statement.

BALANCE SHEET

MaLin Carpet Design
Balance Sheet
December 31, 20--

ASSETS

Current Assets:		
Cash		$42,802.47
Petty Cash		200.00
Accounts Receivable	$11,992.51	
Less Allowance for Uncollectible Accounts	139.47	11,853.04
Supplies—Carpet		1,628.50
Supplies—Office		425.00
Prepaid Insurance		846.50
Total Current Assets		$57,755.51
Plant Assets:		
Equipment	$12,504.97	
Less Accumulated Depreciation—Equipment	1,250.50	$11,254.47
Truck	4,900.00	
Less Accumulated Depreciation—Truck	$ 918.75	3,981.25
Total Plant Assets		15,235.72
Total Assets		$72,991.23

LIABILITIES

Accounts Payable	$ 8,521.23

OWNERS' EQUITY

May Baker, Capital	$38,366.00	
Lindel Mattingly, Capital	26,104.00	
Total Owners' Equity		64,470.00
Total Liabilities and Owners' Equity		$72,991.23

On a partnership balance sheet, each partner's ending capital is reported under the heading *Owners' Equity* as shown above.

ADJUSTING ENTRIES

GENERAL JOURNAL   PAGE *12*

1. Adjusting entry for ❶ uncollectible accounts.

2. Adjusting entries ❷ for supplies.

3. Adjusting entry ❸ for insurance.

4. Adjusting entries ❹ for depreciation.

	DATE	ACCOUNT TITLE	DOC. NO.	POST. REF.	DEBIT	CREDIT
1		*Adjusting Entries*				
2	20-- Dec. 31	*Uncollectible Accounts Expense*			119 55	
3		*Allowance for Uncoll. Accts.*				119 55
4	31	*Supplies Expense—Carpet*			7676 50	
5		*Supplies—Carpet*				7676 50
6	31	*Supplies Expense—Office*			1420 00	
7		*Supplies—Office*				1420 00
8	31	*Insurance Expense*			503 20	
9		*Prepaid Insurance*				503 20
10	31	*Depreciation Expense—Equipment*			1250 50	
11		*Accum. Depreciation—Equipment*				1250 50
12	31	*Depreciation Expense—Truck*			918 75	
13		*Accum. Depreciation—Truck*				918 75

MaLin's adjusting entries, shown above, are made to record expenses in the fiscal period to which they apply. [*CONCEPT: Matching Expenses with Revenue*]

- Explain that closing entries for a partnership are similar to those of a corporation. The major difference is in recording distribution of earnings to the partners.

- Remind students that there are four kinds of closing entries: (1) to close income statement accounts with credit balances, (2) to close income statement accounts with debit balances, (3) to record net income or loss and close the income summary account, and (4) to close the partners' drawing accounts.

- Emphasize that the amounts needed for the closing entries are obtained from the Income Statement and Balance Sheet columns of the work sheet and from the distribution of net income statement.

DEMONSTRATE

- Prepare a transparency of the closing entries in the textbook or direct students to the illustration on this page.

- Describe each of the four steps for preparing closing entries for a partnership.

EXPLAIN

- Explain that the Internal Revenue Service classifies partners as self-employed persons whose salaries are not an expense of the partnership.

- Explain that although a partnership does not pay federal income tax on its net income, it does submit to the IRS a partnership tax return that reports the earnings distributed to each partner.

- Explain that partners include their share of the partnership net income or net loss on their personal income tax returns.

GENERAL JOURNAL — PAGE 12

	DATE	ACCOUNT TITLE	DOC. NO.	POST. REF.	DEBIT	CREDIT	
14		*Closing Entries*					14
15	31	Sales			72 020 27		15
16		Income Summary				72 020 27	16
17	31	Income Summary			34 620 27		17
18		Advertising Expense				9 85 00	18
19		Depreciation Exp.—Equipment				1 250 50	19
20		Depreciation Exp.—Truck				9 18 75	20
21		Insurance Expense				5 03 20	21
22		Miscellaneous Expense				2 869 21	22
23		Rent Expense				8 400 00	23
24		Supplies Expense—Carpet				7 676 50	24
25		Supplies Expense—Office				1 420 00	25
26		Truck Expense				8 477 56	26
27		Uncollectible Accts. Expense				1 19 55	27
28		Utilities Expense				2 000 00	28
29	31	Income Summary			37 400 00		29
30		May Baker, Capital				19 986 00	30
31		Lindel Mattingly, Capital				17 414 00	31
32	31	May Baker, Capital			4 500 00		32
33		May Baker, Drawing				4 500 00	33
34	31	Lindel Mattingly, Capital			2 750 00		34
35		Lindel Mattingly, Drawing				2 750 00	35

1. Close income statement accounts with credit balances.

2. Close income statement accounts with debit balances.

3. Close Income Summary.

4. Close partners' drawing accounts.

Closing entries for a partnership are similar to those of a corporation. The major difference is in recording distribution of earnings to the partners as shown above.

FEDERAL INCOME TAXES OF A PARTNERSHIP

MaLin's distribution of net income statement shows salaries for each of the partners. However, the Internal Revenue Service does not consider partners to be employees of the partnership they own. The IRS classifies the partners as self-employed persons whose salaries are not an expense of the partnership. Therefore, partners' salaries are considered to be withdrawals of partnership earnings, not expenses.

A partnership does not pay income tax on its earnings. However, a partnership does submit to the IRS a partnership tax return that reports the earnings distributed to each partner. This type of return is known as an information return. In addition, partners include their respective share of the partnership net income or net loss on their personal income tax returns.

As self-employed persons, partners are entitled to old-age, survivors, disability, and hospitalization insurance benefits known collectively as social security and Medicare. Each partner personally pays a self-employment tax to qualify for social security and Medicare coverage. Therefore, the self-employment tax rate is double that of an employed individual's social security and Medicare tax rates. Thus, the same total amount of social security and Medicare taxes are paid for both self-employed persons and employees. The self-employment taxes are personal expenses of the partners, not of the partnership. Therefore, partners' self-employment social security and Medicare taxes are not recorded on partnership records. [CONCEPT: Business Entity]

The business entity concept states that financial information is recorded and reported separately from the owner's personal financial information. A business's records must not be mixed with an owner's personal records and reports. For example, a business owner may buy insurance to protect the business and insurance to protect the owner's home. Only the insurance obtained for the business is recorded in the business's financial records. The insurance purchased for the owner's personal home is recorded in the owner's personal financial records. One bank account is used for the business and another for the owner. A business exists separately from its owners.

©GETTY IMAGES/PHOTODISC

POST-CLOSING TRIAL BALANCE

MaLin Carpet Design
Post-Closing Trial Balance
December 31, 20--

Account Title	Debit	Credit
Cash	$42,802.47	
Petty Cash	200.00	
Accounts Receivable	11,992.51	
Allowance for Uncollectible Accounts		$ 139.47
Supplies—Carpet	1,628.50	
Supplies—Office	425.00	
Prepaid Insurance	846.50	
Equipment	12,504.97	
Accumulated Depreciation—Equipment		1,250.50
Truck	4,900.00	
Accumulated Depreciation—Truck		918.75
Accounts Payable		8,521.23
May Baker, Capital		38,366.00
Lindel Mattingly, Capital		26,104.00
	$75,299.95	$75,299.95

After adjusting and closing entries have been posted, MaLin prepares a post-closing trial balance as shown above. MaLin's post-closing trial balance is similar to that of a corporation with the exception of the capital accounts.

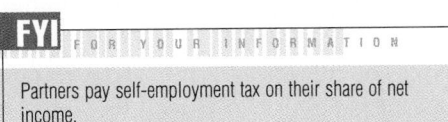
FYI FOR YOUR INFORMATION

Partners pay self-employment tax on their share of net income.

{ REMEMBER The post-closing trial balance indicates that the accounting records are ready for the next fiscal period. }

GUIDED PRACTICE

Terms Review

Call on students to define each term in the Terms Review. After each definition ask the class if the definition is correct and whether the complete definition has been given or if anything needs to be added. Suggested definitions are given in the Glossary.

Audit Your Understanding

Call on students to answer the Audit Your Understanding questions. Ask the class if the answer is correct and/or complete. Answers are given in Appendix E of the textbook.

Work Together

Have students write the solution to the Work Together problem as you guide the class through the examples.

- Direct students to prepare each financial statement as you elicit class participation.

- Direct students to prepare the closing entries as you elicit class participation.

INDEPENDENT PRACTICE

On Your Own

- Assign the On Your Own problem to be worked independently.

- Use the Ongoing Assessment techniques to diagnose student understanding.

Application Problem

- Assign Application Problem 22-3: Completing end-of-fiscal-period work for a partnership.

Personal Trainer

- Students can access the Lesson 22-2 assessment material using this software.

Xtra! Web Site

- Students can access the Xtra! Study Tools for additional practice.

ENRICH

- Accountants often write procedure manuals to provide accounting clerks with instructions for performing repetitive activities. Have students write instructions for preparing a distribution of net income statement. After students have prepared their written procedure, discuss the steps they have identified for their recommended procedure.

• terms review

distribution of net income statement
deficit
owners' equity statement

• audit your understanding

1. Why is an adjustment for accrued federal income tax never planned on a partnership work sheet?

2. When does a deficit occur?

3. What is the purpose of the owners' equity statement?

• work together 22-2

End-of-fiscal-period work for a partnership

Maria Delgado and Oren Kelso are partners in a business. Statement paper, page 15 of a general journal, and a portion of the partnership's completed work sheet for the year ended December 31 of the current year are provided in the *Working Papers*. Your instructor will guide you through the following examples.

1. Prepare an income statement. Calculate and record the component percentages for total operating expenses and net income. Round percentage calculations to the nearest 0.1%.

2. Prepare a distribution of net income statement. Each partner is to receive 8% interest on January 1 equity. Also, partners' salaries are Maria, $15,000.00 and Oren, $14,000.00. The remaining net income, net loss, or deficit is shared equally.

3. Prepare an owners' equity statement.

4. Journalize the closing entries.

• on your own 22-2

End-of-fiscal-period work for a partnership

Jeffrey Lowe and Mona Ray are partners in a business. Statement paper, page 12 of a general journal, and a portion of the partnership's completed work sheet for the year ended December 31 of the current year are provided in the *Working Papers*. Work independently to complete the following problem.

1. Prepare an income statement. Calculate and record the component percentages for total operating expenses and net income. Round percentage calculations to the nearest 0.1%.

2. Prepare a distribution of net income statement. Each partner is to receive 8% interest on January 1 equity. Also, partners' salaries are Jeffrey, $12,000.00 and Mona, $16,000.00. The remaining net income, net loss, or deficit is shared equally.

3. Prepare an owners' equity statement.

4. Journalize the closing entries.

CLOSE

- Ask students to briefly summarize the procedures for preparing a distribution of net income statement and an owners' equity statement.

22-3 Liquidation of a Partnership

ACCOUNT BALANCES BEFORE REALIZATION

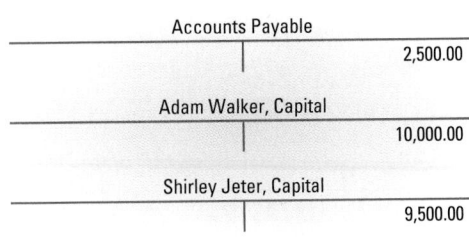

Cash	
11,000.00	

Supplies	
1,000.00	

Truck	
15,000.00	

Accumulated Depreciation—Truck	
	5,000.00

Accounts Payable	
	2,500.00

Adam Walker, Capital	
	10,000.00

Shirley Jeter, Capital	
	9,500.00

If a partnership goes out of business, its assets are distributed to the creditors and partners. The process of paying a partnership's liabilities and distributing remaining assets to the partners is called **liquidation of a partnership**.

Cash received from the sale of assets during liquidation of a partnership is called **realization**. Typically, when a partnership is liquidated, the noncash assets are sold, and the available cash is used to pay the creditors. Any remaining cash is distributed to the partners according to each partner's total equity.

On July 31, Adam Walker and Shirley Jeter liquidated their partnership. At that time, financial statements were prepared and adjusting and closing entries were journalized and posted. After the end-of-fiscal-period work was completed, the partnership had account balances as shown above.

GAIN ON REALIZATION

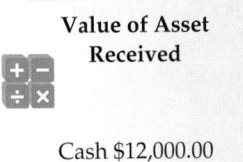

Value of Asset Received	−	Book Value of Asset Sold	=	Gain on Realization
		Cost $15,000.00		
		Accum. Depr. 5,000.00		
Cash $12,000.00	−	Book Value $10,000.00	=	$2,000.00

1. Calculate the gain. **①**

2. Record the entry. **②**

				CASH RECEIPTS JOURNAL					PAGE 15		
					1	2	3	4	5	6	
					GENERAL		ACCOUNTS RECEIVABLE CREDIT	SALES CREDIT	SALES TAX PAYABLE CREDIT	CASH DEBIT	
	DATE	ACCOUNT TITLE	DOC. NO.	POST. REF.	DEBIT	CREDIT					
1	20-- Aug. 1	Accum. Depr.—Truck	R316		5 0 0 0 00					12 0 0 0 00	1
2		Truck				15 0 0 0 00					2
3		Loss and Gain on Realization				2 0 0 0 00					3

EXPLAIN

EXPLAIN

- Explain that the first step in liquidating a partnership is to sell the noncash assets.

- Explain that the difference between the cash received for a noncash asset and the book value of that asset is the gain or loss on realization of that asset.

- Explain that after the gain or loss on realization has been calculated, a journal entry is recorded to recognize this realization and to recognize the disposal of the asset and any accumulated depreciation, if appropriate.

DEMONSTRATE

- Make a transparency of a cash receipts journal to illustrate recording a gain on realization.

- Direct students to the board as you describe how to calculate the gain on realization.

- Direct students to the transparency as you describe the cash receipts journal entry to record the gain on realization. Note that the gain on realization is a credit entry.

EXPLAIN

- Explain that sometimes during liquidation, the sale of an asset brings in less cash than the recorded book value.

DEMONSTRATE

- Use the cash receipts journal transparency to show recording a loss on realization or direct students to the illustration.

- Describe how to calculate the loss on realization, using the math box in the illustration.

- Direct students to the transparency as you describe the cash receipts journal entry to record the loss on realization or direct students to the illustration. Note that a loss on realization is a debit entry.

RECOGNIZING A GAIN ON REALIZATION

Noncash assets might be sold for more than the recorded book value. When this happens, the amount received in excess of the book value is recorded as a gain on realization. The gain is recorded as a credit in an account titled Loss and Gain on Realization.

August 1, 20--. Received cash from sale of truck, $12,000.00; original cost, $15,000.00; total accumulated depreciation recorded to date, $5,000.00. Receipt No. 316.

The partnership's gain on the sale of the truck is calculated as shown on the previous page.

STEPS • STEPS • STEPS • STEPS

RECOGNIZING A GAIN ON REALIZATION

1. Calculate the gain on the sale of the asset, *$2,000.00* ($12,000.00 cash received − $10,000.00 book value of asset).

2. Record the entry in the cash receipts journal.

LOSS ON REALIZATION

	Value of Asset Received	−	Book Value of Asset Sold	=	Loss on Realization
	Cash $800.00	−	Supplies $1,000.00	=	$(200.00)

1. Calculate the loss.

2. Record the entry.

CASH RECEIPTS JOURNAL — PAGE 15

	DATE	ACCOUNT TITLE	DOC. NO.	POST. REF.	GENERAL DEBIT	GENERAL CREDIT	ACCOUNTS RECEIVABLE CREDIT	SALES CREDIT	SALES TAX PAYABLE CREDIT	CASH DEBIT	
4	1	Loss and Gain on Realization	R317		2 0 0 00					8 0 0 00	4
5		Supplies				1 0 0 0 00					5

Sometimes during liquidation, the sale of an asset brings in less cash than the recorded book value.

August 1. Received cash from sale of supplies, $800.00; balance of supplies account, $1,000.00. Receipt No. 317.

The journal entry to record this transaction is shown above. After both liquidation entries have been journalized, the balance of Loss and Gain on Realization, *$1,800.00*, is the amount received in excess of the value of the truck and supplies combined.

STEPS • STEPS • STEPS • STEPS

RECOGNIZING A LOSS ON REALIZATION

1. Calculate the loss on the sale of the asset, *$200.00* ($800.00 cash received − $1,000.00 book value of supplies).

2. Record the entry in the cash receipts journal.

FYI FOR YOUR INFORMATION

A partnership usually tries to sell the business before it begins the process of liquidation.

LIQUIDATING LIABILITIES

						GENERAL		ACCOUNTS PAYABLE	CASH	
DATE		ACCOUNT TITLE	CK. NO.	POST. REF.	DEBIT	CREDIT		DEBIT	CREDIT	

CASH PAYMENTS JOURNAL   PAGE 15

						GENERAL		ACCOUNTS PAYABLE DEBIT	CASH CREDIT	
DATE		ACCOUNT TITLE	CK. NO.	POST. REF.	DEBIT	CREDIT				
Aug.²⁰⁻	4	*Accounts Payable*	422		2 50 0 00				2 50 0 00	1

The partnership's available cash is used to pay creditors. The entry is recorded in the cash payments journal as shown above.

> *August 4, 20--. Paid cash to all creditors for the amounts owed, $2,500.00. Check No. 422.*

ACCOUNT BALANCES AFTER LIQUIDATION OF NONCASH ASSETS AND PAYMENT OF LIABILITIES

Cash	
Bal. 21,300.00	

Shirley Jeter, Capital	
	Bal. 9,500.00

Adam Walker, Capital	
	Bal. 10,000.00

Loss and Gain on Realization	
	Bal. 1,800.00

When this transaction has been journalized and posted, the partnership has only four general ledger accounts with balances as shown above.

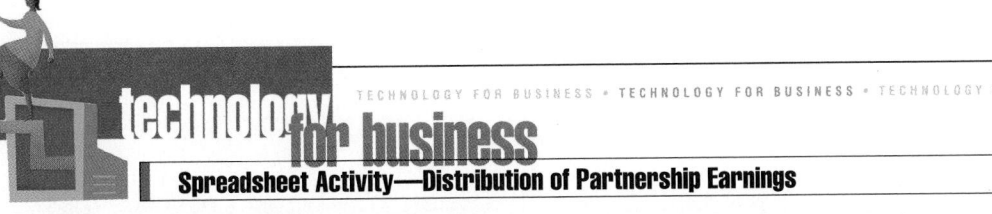

technology for business

TECHNOLOGY FOR BUSINESS • TECHNOLOGY FOR BUSINESS • TECHNOLOGY FOR BUSIN

Spreadsheet Activity—Distribution of Partnership Earnings

All Season Golf Center is an indoor golf facility with six computerized golf simulators. The partnership is owned by Arthur Wilson and Pamela Kim. According to the partnership agreement, Arthur receives 8% interest on equity and a salary of $22,000.00. Pamela receives 8% interest on equity and a salary of $18,000.00. The remainder of net income is divided equally. For the current year, net income for All Season Golf Center is $52,000.00.

Required

1. Create a distribution of partnership earnings spreadsheet. Use the calculation on page 651 as a model. Write formulas to calculate interest on equity, salary, division of remaining income, and the total distribution. Save the spreadsheet. Print a copy of the distribution of partnership earnings.

2. Use the spreadsheet to calculate the distribution of partnership earnings for the next year assuming net income is $66,000.00.

Lesson 22-3   **667**

APPLIED SKILLS   WRITING ACROSS THE CURRICULUM

Writing Paragraphs and Short Essays. The Cases for Critical Thinking are short, practical applications of the accounting principles developed in the chapter. Some cases are planned to present problems related to the chapter but not specifically discussed and answered in the chapter. These cases present an opportunity for critical thinking and decision making. These cases also require more than a short objective-type response. Therefore, they provide ideal practice in writing paragraphs and short essays.

- Explain that the balance in the account Loss and Gain on Realization is distributed to the partners' capital accounts in accordance with the partnership agreement.
- Explain that if gain is distributed, Loss and Gain on Realization is debited to close the account. If a loss is distributed, Loss and Gain on Realization is credited.

DEMONSTRATE

- Direct students to the board as you describe how to calculate each partner's share of gain or loss.
- Use a general journal transparency or the illustration at the top of the page as you describe the entry to record each partner's share of gain or loss in the capital accounts.

EXPLAIN

- Explain that the last step in liquidating the partnership is to distribute the remaining cash to the partners. At this point, the only accounts that have balances are the cash account and the partners' capital accounts.
- Explain that the cash is distributed according to each partner's capital account balance regardless of the method used to distribute net income or net loss.
- Explain that after this journal entry is journalized and posted, all of the accounts will have zero balances and the partnership is liquidated.

DEMONSTRATE

- Use the cash payments journal transparency or the illustration at the bottom of the page to show distributing the remaining cash to the partners.

ONGOING ASSESSMENT

- Assessment is an ongoing process. Circulate through the classroom or lab, observing which students have problems with the assignments.
- Troubleshooting: Diagnose what kinds of problems students have with this section. Students may have trouble calculating accurately the loss or gain on realization. Students may need to be reminded that the balance in the Loss or Gain on Real-

DISTRIBUTING LOSS OR GAIN ON REALIZATION TO PARTNERS

	Balance of Loss and Gain on Realization	×	Fixed Percentage	=	Share of the Balance of Loss and Gain on Realization	
Walker	$1,800.00	×	60%	=	$1,080.00	
Jeter	$1,800.00	×	40%	=	720.00	
Total					$1,800.00	

1. Calculate each partner's share of gain or loss.

2. Record entry to distribute gain or loss.

GENERAL JOURNAL   PAGE 8

	DATE		ACCOUNT TITLE	DOC. NO.	POST. REF.	DEBIT	CREDIT	
1	20-- Aug.	6	Loss and Gain on Realization	M412		1 80 0 00		1
2			Adam Walker, Capital				1 08 0 00	2
3			Shirley Jeter, Capital				72 0 00	3

When all creditors have been paid, the balance of Loss and Gain on Realization is distributed to the partners. A credit balance indicates a gain on realization. A debit balance indicates a loss. The distribution is based on the method of distributing net income or net loss as stated in the partnership agreement. The percentages for the Walker and Jeter partnership are Adam, 60%, and Shirley, 40%. The distribution of the balance of Loss and Gain on Realization is calculated as shown above.

August 6, 20--. Recorded distribution of gain on realization: to Adam Walker, $1,080.00; to Shirley Jeter, $720.00. Memorandum No. 412.

If a loss on realization is distributed to the partners, Loss and Gain on Realization is credited to close the account. Each partner's capital account is debited for the partner's share of the loss on realization.

DISTRIBUTING REMAINING CASH TO PARTNERS

CASH PAYMENTS JOURNAL   PAGE 15

		DATE	ACCOUNT TITLE	CK. NO.	POST. REF.	GENERAL DEBIT	GENERAL CREDIT	ACCOUNTS PAYABLE DEBIT	CASH CREDIT	
2		6	Adam Walker, Capital	423		11 08 0 00			21 30 0 00	2
3			Shirley Jeter, Capital	424		10 22 0 00				3

Any remaining cash is distributed to the partners. The cash is distributed according to each partner's capital account balance regardless of the method used to distribute net income or net loss.

August 6. Recorded final distribution of remaining cash to partners: to Adam Walker, $11,080.00; to Shirley Jeter, $10,220.00. Check Nos. 423 and 424.

After this journal entry is journalized, as shown above, and posted, all of the partnership's general ledger accounts will have zero balances. The partnership is liquidated.

Financial Reporting for a Partnership

---

ization account is distributed to the partners' capital accounts in accordance with the partnership agreement.

- Assess student understanding by checking solutions to Independent Practice assignments.

RETEACH

- Bring several inexpensive items to class to be the fixed assets of a hypothetical partnership. Prepare a balance sheet for the partnership, assigning values to each item, recording an accounts payable for the real cost of the items, and making the class equal partners. Auction the items to the students, recording the gain or loss on realization for each transaction. Liquidate the partnership by distributing the available cash. Record each transaction on the board using T accounts.

terms review

TERMS REVIEW

liquidation of a partnership
realization

audit your understanding

AUDIT YOUR

1. What is meant by the term "realization"?
2. What accounts are debited when distributing remaining cash to partners during liquidation?

work together 22-3

WORK TOGETHER • WORK TOGETHER

Liquidation of a partnership

Jason Edson and Peggy Karam agreed to liquidate their partnership on April 30 of the current year. On that date, after financial statements were prepared and closing entries were posted, the general ledger accounts had the balances shown in the *Working Papers.*

A cash receipts journal, page 6, a cash payments journal, page 8, and a general journal, page 4, are provided in the *Working Papers.* Your instructor will guide you through the following examples.

May 1. Received cash from sale of office equipment, $6,000.00. R86.
1. Received cash from sale of supplies, $950.00. R87.
3. Received cash from sale of truck, $7,500.00. R88.
5. Paid cash to all creditors for amounts owed. C116.
6. Distributed loss or gain to Jason Edson, 60%; to Peggy Karam, 40%. M21.
6. Distributed remaining cash to partners. C117 and C118.

1. Journalize the transactions.

on your own 22-3

ON YOUR OWN • ON YOUR OWN • ON YOUR OWN

Liquidation of a partnership

Denise Oxley and Charles Tatum agreed to liquidate their partnership on May 31 of the current year. On that date, after financial statements were prepared and closing entries were posted, the general ledger accounts had the balances shown in the *Working Papers.*

A cash receipts journal, page 8, a cash payments journal, page 10, and a general journal, page 5, are provided in the *Working Papers.* Work independently to complete the following problem.

June 1. Received cash from sale of office equipment, $6,200.00. R96.
1. Received cash from sale of supplies. $900.00. R97.
3. Received cash from sale of truck, $9,000.00. R98.
5. Paid cash to all creditors for amounts owed. C125.
6. Distributed loss or gain to Denise Oxley, 60%; to Charles Tatum, 40%. M29.
6. Distributed remaining cash to partners. C126 and C127.

1. Journalize the transactions.

Liquidation of a Partnership

Lesson 22-3 **669**

PUTTING IT ALL TOGETHER

- Review the Chapter Summary.
- Review each of the major chapter topics: (1) calculating the distribution of partnership earnings, (2) journalizing entries for withdrawal of partnership earnings, (3) completing end-of-fiscal-period work for a partnership, and (4) journalizing entries for liquidating a partnership.

INDEPENDENT PRACTICE

- Assign Mastery Problem 22-5 to students who need the reinforcement. This will be most students.
- Assign Challenge Problem 22-6 to students who do not require the reinforcement of the Mastery Problem.
- Assign the Automated Accounting feature on pages 676–677 to automate Master Problem 22-5 and Challenge Problem 22-6.
- Students can use Peachtree and QuickBooks data files to automate Mastery Problem 22-5 and Challenge Problem 22-6.
- Assign Study Guide 22.
- Students can access Personal Trainer to work end-of-chapter problems on the computer.
- Students can access the Xtra! Web Site for the Xtra! Review and Quizzing.
- Students can access the Student Companion CD for additional review material.

ONGOING ASSESSMENT

- Review solutions to the assigned problem in class, diagnosing trouble spots.

RETEACH

- Call on students to describe how they avoid the trouble spots diagnosed.
- Use reteaching suggestions from section lesson plans as required.
- Assign Recycling Problem 22-1 if needed.

ENRICH

- Assign the Explore Accounting Feature. Ask students to share the information they have gathered in a report to the class.

670

- Students can access the Xtra! Web Site for the Xtra! Enrichment material.
- Assign Applied Communication.
- Assign the Cases for Critical Thinking.
- Assign the SCANS Workplace Competency.
- Assign Graphing Workshop.
- Assign Analyzing Costco's Financial Statements.

SUMMARY

After completing this chapter, you can

1. Define accounting terms related to distributing earnings and completing end-of-fiscal-period work for a partnership.
2. Identify accounting concepts and practices related to distributing earnings and completing end-of-fiscal-period work for a partnership.
3. Calculate the distribution of partnership earnings.
4. Journalize entries for withdrawal of partnership earnings.
5. Complete end-of-fiscal-period work for a partnership.
6. Prepare a distribution of net income statement for a partnership.
7. Journalize entries for liquidating a partnership.

Explore Accounting

Determining Value of Partnership

When a partnership decides to add another partner or an existing partner wants to withdraw, the value of a partnership must be determined. The book value of a partnership is not necessarily an equitable value to the new or existing partners. Therefore, before admitting a new partner or retiring one, a current equitable value should be determined for the partnership. Three common methods used to value a partnership are (1) comparable sales, (2) appraisal, and (3) income capitalization.

Comparable sales method. This method attempts to compare other comparable businesses that have been sold recently with the partnership business being valued. Factors to be considered in selecting comparable businesses are type, size, and location of the business. If a comparable business recently sold for $500,000.00, this provides a sound basis for valuing the partnership at $500,000.00 regardless of the book value of the partnership.

Appraisal method. This method estimates the current fair market value of each of the assets and liabilities. A professional appraiser would be employed to determine the value of the assets and liabilities of the business.

Income capitalization method. This method places most emphasis on the expected future earnings capacity of the business. The buyer of a business or share of a partnership probably is making the investment for the anticipated future earnings of the business. This method places a value on the business based on those expected future earnings.

Required:

Assume that you are a doctor. You have been offered a one-quarter interest in a growing medical practice located in a fast-growth area. Which method of valuing the existing partnership would you prefer? Explain the reason for your choice.

EXPLORE ACCOUNTING

Student answers will vary, and there is no one correct answer. Student answers should include reasons for the choices made. Of the three methods, the appraisal method is the least likely to be useful, since the business is primarily a service business. The value of assets and liabilities may not give adequate value to the partnership. Students should be able to make a reasonable case for either of the other methods (comparable sales method and the income capitalization method).

22-1 APPLICATION PROBLEM
Calculating partnership earnings

Jill Fargo and Sheila Kain are partners in a business called Fargo and Kain. On December 31 of the current year, the partners' equities are Jill, $80,000.00 and Sheila, $120,000.00. The net income for the year is $80,000.00.

Instructions:

For each of the following independent cases, calculate how the $80,000.00 net income will be distributed to the two partners.
1. Each partner receives a fixed percentage of 50% of net income.
2. Each partner receives a percentage of net income based on the percentage of total equity.
3. Each partner receives 12% interest on equity. The partners share remaining net income, net loss, or deficit equally.
4. Jill receives a salary of $24,000.00; Sheila receives a salary of $30,000.00. The partners share remaining net income, net loss, or deficit on a fixed percentage of Jill, 40% and Sheila, 60%.
5. Jill is to receive 10% interest on equity and a salary of $24,000.00. Sheila is to receive 8% interest on equity and a salary of $30,000.00. The partners share remaining net income, net loss, or deficit equally.
6. Jill is to receive 15% interest on equity and a salary of $30,000.00. Sheila is to receive 15% interest on equity and a salary of $36,000.00. The partners share remaining net income, net loss, or deficit equally.

22-2 APPLICATION PROBLEM
Journalizing partners' withdrawals

Janet Agnew and Buford Franco are partners in a business. Each partner withdraws assets during May of the current year.

Transactions:

June   5.   Janet Agnew, partner, withdrew office supplies for personal use, $400.00. M46.
     26.   Buford Franco, partner, withdrew cash for personal use, $600.00. C284.

Instructions:

Journalize the transactions using page 12 of a cash payments journal and page 6 of a general journal.

22-3 APPLICATION PROBLEM
Completing end-of-fiscal-period work for a partnership

Susan Poole and Ann Dodd are partners in a business called Plantasia. The partnership's work sheet for the year ended December 31 of the current year is provided in the *Working Papers.*

Instructions:

1. Prepare an income statement. Calculate and record the component percentages for total operating expenses and net income. Round percentage calculations to the nearest 0.1%.
2. Prepare a distribution of net income statement. The partners share in net income, net loss, or deficit according to each partner's percentage of total equity. The January 1 equity is Susan, $23,400.00 and Ann, $12,600.00. Round percentage calculations to the nearest 0.1%.
3. Prepare an owners' equity statement.
4. Prepare a balance sheet.
5. Journalize the adjusting entries using page 12 of a general journal.
6. Journalize the closing entries on the same general journal page.

FORMAL EVALUATION

Chapter 22 Test
ExamView for Chapter 22
Assessment by Portfolio

- Review answers to all tests administered as a class activity. If time is limited, review only the items that were frequently answered incorrectly.
- Ask students if there are any questions about the chapter before proceeding to the next chapter.

CHECK FIGURES

Application Problem 22-1
40,000 each.
Fargo, 32,000; Kain, 48.000.
Fargo, 37,600; Kain, 42,400.
Fargo, 34,400; Kain, 45,600.
Fargo, 35,000; Kain, 45,000.
Fargo, 34,000; Kain, 46,000.

Application Problem 22-2
June 5, debit Janet Agnew, Drawing and credit Supplies—Office, 400.00.
June 26, debit Buford Franco, Drawing and credit Cash, 600.00.

Application Problem 22-3
Net Income, 24,600.00, 46.1%.
Poole, 15,900.00; Dodd, 8,610.00.
Poole, 34,990.00; Dodd 18,610.00.
Total Assets, 59,548.52; Total Owners' Equity, 53,600.00.

See Teacher's Edition of the Working Papers for Chapter 22 for complete solutions.

22-4 APPLICATION PROBLEM
Liquidating a partnership

Donald Winn and Judy Reed agreed to liquidate their partnership on June 30 of the current year. On that date, after financial statements were prepared and closing entries were posted, the general ledger accounts had the following balances.

Cash	$ 5,000.00
Supplies	500.00
Office Equipment	10,000.00
Accumulated Depreciation—Office Equipment	5,500.00
Truck	17,000.00
Accumulated Depreciation—Truck	12,200.00
Accounts Payable	500.00
Donald Winn, Capital	7,300.00
Judy Reed, Capital	7,000.00

The following transactions occurred during July of the current year.

Transactions:

July   1.   Received cash from sale of office equipment, $4,000.00. R114.

        1.   Received cash from sale of supplies, $200.00. R115.

        3.   Received cash from sale of truck, $5,000.00. R116.

        5.   Paid cash to all creditors for amounts owed. C156.

        6.   Distributed balance of Loss and Gain on Realization to Donald Winn, 65%; to Judy Reed, 35%. M34.

        6.   Distributed remaining cash to partners. C157 and C158.

Instructions:

Journalize the transactions. Use page 13 of a cash receipts journal, page 13 of a cash payments journal, and page 7 of a general journal.

22-5 MASTERY PROBLEM
Completing end-of-fiscal-period work for a partnership

Sarah Saxon and Jane Rolf are partners in a business called J & S Service. The partnership's work sheet for the year ended December 31 of the current year is provided in the *Working Papers*.

Instructions:

1. Prepare an income statement. Calculate and record the component percentage for total operating expenses and net income. Round percentage computations to the nearest 0.1%.
2. Prepare a distribution of net income statement. Each partner is to receive 10% interest on January 1 equity. The January 1 equity is Sarah, $15,000.00 and Jane, $12,000.00. Also, partners' salaries are Sarah, $10,000.00 and Jane, $15,000.00. The partners share remaining net income, net loss, or deficit equally.
3. Prepare an owners' equity statement.
4. Prepare a balance sheet.
5. Journalize the adjusting entries using page 12 of a general journal.
6. Journalize the closing entries on the same general journal page.

Completing end-of-fiscal-period work for a partnership

Theresa Doran and Roy Eden are partners in a business called D & E Sales. The partnership's work sheet for the year ended December 31 of the current year is provided in the *Working Papers*.

Instructions:

1. Prepare an income statement. Calculate and record the component percentages for cost of merchandise sold, gross profit on operations, total operating expenses, and net income or net loss. Round percentage calculations to the nearest 0.1%. If there is a net loss, use a minus sign with the component percentage.
2. Prepare a distribution of net income statement. Each partner is to receive 10% interest on January 1 equity. The January 1 equity is Theresa, $24,250.00 and Roy, $21,500.00. Also, partners' salaries are Theresa, $12,000.00 and Roy, $10,000.00. The remaining net income, net loss, or deficit is shared as follows: Theresa, 55%; Roy, 45%.
3. Prepare an owners' equity statement.
4. Prepare a balance sheet.

Challenge Problem 22-6
Net Loss, 4,600.00, 10.4%.
Doran, 2,721.25; Eden, 1,878.75.
Doran, 15,528.75; Eden, 14,621.25.
Total Assets, 34,989.02; Total Owners' Equity, 30,150.00.

TEACHING STRATEGIES   DIFFERENT LEARNING ABILITIES

Specific Learning Disability (SLD) Students. Exposing students to actual business situations can be an excellent motivational device. Arrange a field trip to a local business organized as a partnership. Before the field trip, require the students to identify questions to ask the partners. Allow students to ask these questions during the field trip. After the field trip, lead a class discussion which allows students the opportunity to share what they learned.

APPLIED COMMUNICATION

Students' reports will vary. Some of the advantages that may be included: (1) easy to form and (2) no federal income taxes paid by the partnership. Some disadvantages may include the following: (1) Unless restricted by agreement, any partner may bind the partnership to any contract; (2) the partnership ends any time a partner is added or deleted; and (3) it is more difficult to increase capital.

CASES FOR CRITICAL THINKING

Case 1

Use a combination of methods:
(a) *Interest on equity*. Mr. Santo should receive recognition for investing more equity. (b) *Salary*. Mr. Santo should receive recognition for working more hours, and Miss Stroud should receive recognition for her prior experience. (c) Divide remaining net income, net loss, or deficit according to a fixed percentage.

Case 2

The procedure is acceptable. However, the partnership's balance sheet is longer than it needs to be. The balance sheet is not as easy to read as it would be if some of the equity details were removed. Preparing the distribution of net income statement and the owners' equity statement reduces the size of the balance sheet. If interested persons still need the details, they can read the two statements in addition to the balance sheet.

SCANS WORKPLACE COMPETENCY

Students can gather information on accounting software by visiting electronics stores, talking with salespersons, using the Internet, reading packaging, or interviewing local business personnel.

• applied communication

Brian Hughes and Wendy Perez formed a partnership five years ago. The partnership has been very successful and is growing rapidly. The partners are evaluating future actions for the next five years. They are projecting continued growth of their business. Brian and Wendy are trying to decide whether they should incorporate their business.

Required:

Write a short report explaining the advantages and disadvantages of a partnership versus a corporation that Brian and Wendy can use in making their decision.

• cases for critical thinking

Case 1

Lola Stroud invests $30,000.00 in a partnership. Her partner, Juan Santo, invests $50,000.00. Miss Stroud has 10 years' experience in a similar business; Mr. Santo has no experience. Miss Stroud is to spend about 20 hours a week working for the partnership. Mr. Santo is to work full-time. Which method of distributing partnership earnings would you suggest for this partnership? Explain your answer.

Case 2

The P & A partnership does not prepare a distribution of net income statement or an owners' equity statement at the end of a fiscal period. Instead, the information is all reported in detail on the partnership's balance sheet. Is this an acceptable practice? Explain your answer.

• SCANS workplace competency

Technology Competency: Selecting Technology

Concept: Competent employees judge which set of procedures, tools, machines, computers, and software will produce the desired results. Capable employees evaluate a situation and select the appropriate technology.

Application: You are a partner in a small service business. Evaluate several accounting software programs and recommend one that best fits your company's needs in preparing financial statements similar to the ones presented in this chapter. Consider the type of computers your firm owns, memory capabilities, cost, ease of use, support services, and other potential uses. Justify your answer with an oral presentation that incorporates the use of technology.

Partner	Share
1. Katie Nguyen	50.0% ($30,000/$60,000)
Juan Mendoza	8.3% ($5,000/$60,000)
James Carlton	25.0% ($15,000/$60,000)
Carlee Anderson	16.7% ($15,000/$60,000)
2. Katie Nguyen	$20,000.00 ($40,000 × 50.0%)
Juan Mendoza	$3,320.00 ($40,000 × 8.3%)
James Carlton	$10,000.00 ($40,000 × 25.0%)
Carlee Anderson	$6,680.00 ($40,000 × 16.7%)
3. Katie Nguyen	$15,000.00 ($30,000 × 50.0%)
Juan Mendoza	$2,490.00 ($30,000 × 8.3%)
James Carlton	$7,500.00 ($30,000 × 25.0%)
Carlee Anderson	$5,010.00 ($30,000 × 16.7%)

• graphing workshop

The partnership of Nguyen, Mendoza, Carlton, and Anderson has agreed to use the capital account balances shown in the graph as the basis for calculating the distribution of partnership earnings.

Partner Capital Account Balances

Katie Nguyen — 30000
Juan Mendoza — 5000
James Carlton — 15000
Carlee Anderson — 10000
Total Equity — 60000

Instructions:

1. Using the *percentage of total equity method*, calculate the percentages for each partner that will be used to distribute partnership earnings. Round to the nearest tenth of a percent.

2. Determine each partner's share of $40,000 net income.

3. Determine each partner's share of a $30,000 net loss.

• analyzing Costco's financial statements

An American corporation must pay federal income tax based on the amount of its net income. The amount of income tax varies from year to year, based on earnings, corporate tax brackets, tax legislation, and changing tax regulations. For Costco, the amount of federal income tax paid during 2001 through 2003 represents a substantial expense. The effective tax rate for a corporation can be calculated by dividing the "provision for income taxes" amount by the "income before income taxes" amount. An awareness of the effective tax rate can help a corporation create a strategic plan for future earnings.

Instructions:

Refer to Costco's Consolidated Statements of Income on page B-6 of Appendix B in this textbook, and complete the following items.

1. List the "provision for income taxes" amounts for the 52 weeks ended August 31, 2003, September 1, 2002, and September 2, 2001.

2. Calculate the effective tax rates for the 52 weeks ended August 31, 2003, September 1, 2002, and September 2, 2001. Round calculations to the nearest .01%.

3. Determine how much Costco would have paid in federal income taxes in 2003 had the company used the 2001 effective tax rate. What was the amount of tax savings for 2003?

4. Determine the amount of federal income tax paid for every $100 of profit earned before taxes during the 52 weeks ended August 31, 2003.

ANALYZING COSTCO'S FINANCIAL STATEMENTS

1. 2003 = $437,233,000.
   2002 = $438,201,000.
   2001 = $401,392,000.

2. 2003 = 37.75% ($437,233,000/$1,158,233,000).
   2002 = 38.50% ($438,201,000/$1,138,184,000).
   2001 = 40.00% ($401,392,000/1,003,481).

3. $463,293,200 ($1,158,233,000 × 40%); savings, $26,060,200 ($437,233,000 − $463,293,200).

4. $37.75 ($100 × 37.75%).

TEACHING STRATEGIES   PORTFOLIO ASSESSMENT

Financial reporting for a partnership is similar to reporting for a corporation. Examples of financial statements for a partnership, in addition to those for a corporation, indicate a broad range of learning. Students should select an example of their work in this chapter to include in their portfolio. A copy of the Portfolio Assessment form (blackline master in the Teacher's Resource Guide; also on the Student Companion CD) should be completed by the student and the Description section should include any comments regarding how the student mastered these concepts and procedures. Alternatively, students might include in their portfolios printed reports from an Automated Accounting problem.

EXPLAIN

- Explain that partnership financial statements are similar to those of other forms of businesses, but the primary difference is the distribution of net income or loss to partners.

- Emphasize that if distribution is equal to all partners, the software will perform the closing entries needed; however, if distribution is unequal, the closing entries for net income and drawing need to be journalized.

- Point out that income statements can be generated for either year to date or month and year to date, as specified in the Customize Accounting System window.

DEMONSTRATE

Closing entries for unequal distribution

- Demonstrate clicking the Journal toolbar button and choosing the General Journal tab in the Journal Entries window.

- Demonstrate journalizing the closing entry to close Income Summary and distribute the net income or loss to the partners' capital accounts.

- Demonstrate journalizing the closing entry to close the balances of the partners' drawing accounts to the partners' capital accounts.

Setting up the income statement

- Demonstrate clicking the Custom toolbar button and choosing the Company Info. tab in the Customize Accounting System window.

- Demonstrate selecting the appropriate income statement format for either report by fiscal period or report by month and year.

Generating Financial Reports for a Partnership

Financial statements for partnerships are similar to the statements prepared for other types of business organizations. The primary difference is the distribution of net income or loss to the partners.

Partnership with Equal Distribution

When the Company Info. tab of the Customize Accounting System window specifies the business organization as Partnership Equal Distribution, *Automated Accounting 8.0* will perform all closing entries needed at the end of the fiscal period.

Partnership with Unequal Distribution

When the Company Info. tab specifies the business organization as Partnership Unequal Distribution, *Automated Accounting 8.0* will close revenue and expense accounts. However, journal entries must be entered to distribute the income or loss to the partners' accounts. The journal entries required to complete the closing process are:

1. Closing the amount in Income Summary to the partners' capital accounts.

2. Closing the partners' drawing accounts to their capital accounts.

Income Statement

The software will display net income or loss in two formats. The format is specified in the Company Info. tab of the Customize Accounting System window.

Report by Fiscal Period

This format shows the profitability of the business from the beginning of the fiscal year until the time when the income statement is displayed.

Report by Month and Year

This format shows profitability for the current month and for the year to date.

AUTOMATING MASTERY PROBLEM 22-5

Instructions:

1. Load *Automated Accounting 8.0* or higher software.

2. Select database A22-5 (Advanced Course Mastery Problem 22-5) from the accounting template disk.

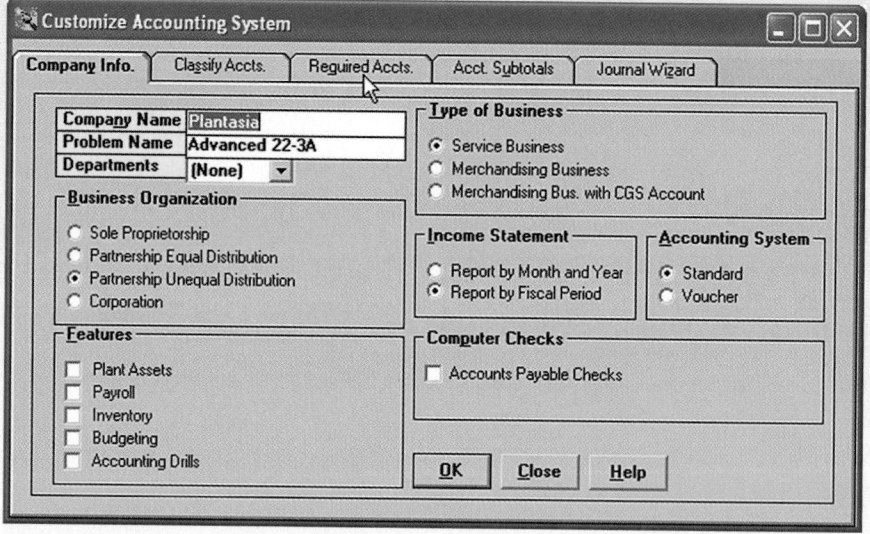

676

3. Select File from the menu bar and choose the Save As menu command. Key the path to the drive and directory that contains your data files. Save the database with a filename of XXX225 (where XXX are your initials).

4. Read the Problem Instruction screen by clicking the Browser toolbar button.

5. Refer to page 672 for data used in this problem.

6. Exit the Automated Accounting software.

AUTOMATING CHALLENGE PROBLEM 22-6

Instructions:

1. Load *Automated Accounting 8.0* or higher software.

2. Select database A22-6 (Advanced Course Mastery Problem 22-6) from the accounting template disk.

3. Select File from the menu bar and choose the Save As menu command. Key the path to the drive and directory that contains your data files. Save the database with a filename of XXX226 (where XXX are your initials).

4. Read the Problem Instruction screen by clicking the Browser toolbar button.

5. Refer to page 673 for data used in this problem.

6. Exit the Automated Accounting software.

- Assign Automating Mastery Problem 22-5: Completing end-of-fiscal-period work for a partnership.
- Assign Automating Challenge Problem 22-6: Completing end-of-fiscal-period work for a partnership.

ASSESSMENT

- Use the Electronic Auditor to assess student understanding.

TEACHING STRATEGIES   PORTFOLIO ASSESSMENT

Students should be encouraged to print at least one report from one of the Automated Accounting problems to include in their portfolio to demonstrate mastery of automated accounting systems. A copy of the Portfolio Assessment form (blackline master in the Teacher's Resource Guide; also on the Student Companion CD) should be completed by the student and the Description section should include any comments regarding how the student mastered these concepts and procedures.

Budgeting and Accounting for a

	SCOPE & SEQUENCE			ENHANCING	
	NEW	**REVIEW/ EXTENSION**		**SPECIAL FEATURES**	
Introduce the Chapter	✓			• Accounting in the Real World: The United States Postal Service	
Lesson 23-1 Not-for-Profit Organizations				• Making Ethical Decisions: Evaluating Auditor Independence	
Nature of not-for-profit organizations	✓			• Cases for Critical Thinking 1	
Characteristics of governmental accounting systems	✓				
Developing an operating budget	✓				
Journalizing an approved operating budget		✓			
Lesson 23-2 Journalizing Revenues				• Careers in Accounting	
Journalizing property tax revenues		✓			
Journalizing collection of current property taxes		✓			
Journalizing other revenue		✓			
Journalizing collection of delinquent property taxes		✓			
Lesson 23-3 Journalizing Expenditures, Encumbrances, and Other Transactions				• Global Perspective: International Travel	
Journalizing expenditures		✓		• Cases for Critical Thinking 2	
Journalizing encumbrances		✓			
Journalizing expenditures for amounts encumbered		✓			
Journalizing expenditures benefiting future periods		✓			
Journalizing issuance and payment of liabilities		✓			
Journalizing short-term investments		✓			
Putting It All Together				• Explore Accounting	
				• Xtra! Web Site: Xtra! Enrichment	
				• Applied Communication	
				• SCANS Workplace Competency	
				• Auditing for Errors	
				• Analyzing Costco's Financial Statements	

Not-for-Profit Organization

INSTRUCTION		PRACTICE AND ASSESSMENT		
TECHNOLOGY AND MEDIA	**TEACHING STRATEGIES**	**GUIDED PRACTICE**	**INDEPENDENT PRACTICE**	**RETEACHING AND ENRICHMENT**
• Internet Research Activity • Accounting Xtra! Web Site	• Software Focus			
• Instructor's Resource CD: PowerPoint Slides • Xtra! Web Site: Xtra! Study Tools • Blackline Masters: Multicolumn Journal • Personal Trainer	• Teaching Tips • Cooperative Learning	• Terms Review • Audit Your Understanding • Work Together 23-1	• On Your Own 23-1 • Application Problem 23-1 • Ongoing Assessment, p. 688 • Personal Trainer • Xtra! Web Site: Xtra! Study Tools	• Reteach, p. 688 • Enrich, p. 689
• Instructor's Resource CD: PowerPoint Slides • Xtra! Web Site: Xtra! Study Tools • Blackline Masters: Multicolumn Journal • Personal Trainer	• At-Risk Students	• Term Review • Audit Your Understanding • Work Together 23-2	• On Your Own 23-2 • Application Problem 23-2 • Ongoing Assessment, p. 692 • Personal Trainer • Xtra! Web Site: Xtra! Study Tools	• Reteach, p. 692 • Enrich, p. 694
• Instructor's Resource CD: PowerPoint Slides • Xtra! Web Site: Xtra! Study Tools • Blackline Masters: Multicolumn Journal • Personal Trainer	• Expanding Beyond the Classroom	• Terms Review • Audit Your Understanding • Work Together 23-3	• On Your Own 23-3 • Application Problem 23-3 • Ongoing Assessment, p. 700 • Personal Trainer • Xtra! Web Site: Xtra! Study Tools	• Reteach, p. 700 • Enrich, p. 701
• Automated Accounting • Peachtree and QuickBooks • Personal Trainer • Xtra! Web Site: Xtra! Review, Quizzing, and Enrichment • Student Companion CD			• Mastery Problem 23-4 • Peachtree and QuickBooks • Personal Trainer • Xtra! Web Site: Xtra! Review and Quizzing • Study Guide 23 • Student Companion CD • Chapter 23 Test • ExamView Chapter 23 • Portfolio Assessment	• Challenge Problem 23-5 • Reteach, p. 702 • Enrich, p. 702 • Recycling Problem 23-1 • Automated Accounting • Xtra! Web Site: Xtra! Enrichment

CHAPTER · OBJECTIVES & TERMS · TERMS · OBJECTIVES & TERMS

CHAPTER 23 Budgeting and Accounting for a Not-for-Profit Organization

After studying Chapter 23, you will be able to:

1. Define accounting terms related to budgeting and accounting for a not-for-profit governmental organization.

2. Identify accounting concepts and practices related to budgeting and accounting for a not-for-profit governmental organization.

3. Describe the process used to develop an operating budget.

4. Journalize budget transactions for a not-for-profit organization.

5. Journalize revenues for a not-for-profit organization.

6. Journalize expenditures, encumbrances, and other transactions for a not-for-profit organization.

- not-for-profit organization
- fund
- expenditure

- operating budget
- appropriations
- tax levy

- encumbrance
- general fixed assets
- certificate of deposit

Point Your Browser
accountingxtra.swlearning.com

678

• The United States Postal Service

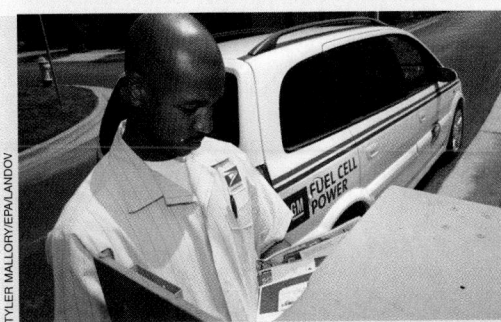

TYLER MALLORY/EPA/LANDOV

THE UNITED STATES POSTAL SERVICE ADAPTS TO A CHANGING BUSINESS ENVIRONMENT

The concept of a postal service for the United Colonies was initially approved by the members of the second Continental Congress at their July, 1775 assembly in Philadelphia. Do you know whom they appointed as the first Postmaster General? If you replied Benjamin Franklin, you are correct. Today, that agency has evolved into the United States Postal Service (USPS), whose mission is to provide every individual in America with convenient, affordable, efficient, and universal mail service regardless of geographic location.

Although the United States Postal Service is a non-profit governmental agency, it operates much like a profit-oriented corporation. For example, USPS has a board of governors that sets overall agency policy, employs a Postmaster General who functions as a CEO, publishes an annual report that lists financial information, and has even sponsored a professional bicycle racing team. Like other business entities, USPS is very concerned about its overall profitability. After reporting several losses for the years immediately after 2000, the agency responded by restructuring its operations and using technological advancements to improve postal efficiencies. Consequently, in 2003, USPS reported a net income of $3.9 billion.

Critical Thinking

1. In 2003, the postal system grew by 1.9 million delivery points. First-class mail volume, however, declined by over 3 billion pieces. What factors might contribute to the increasing number of delivery points and the decreasing amount of mail volume?
2. How might the mission of the USPS and its non-profit status affect profitability?

Xtra!
Today
accountingxtra.swlearning.com

Source: www.usps.com

internet activity

CMA DESIGNATION

Go to the homepage of the Institute of Management Accountants (IMA) (www.imanet.org). In order to have the Chartered Management Accountant (CMA) designation, a person must belong to the IMA. Search the site to find the following information.

Instructions

1. List the seven criteria necessary in order to become a CMA.
2. Find the IMA chapter nearest to you. List the city and state in which that chapter is located.

679

---

1. Student answers will vary. However, answers regarding the increase in mail delivery points might include mention of new business startups, business expansion to new locations, immigration, new housing developments, purchase of second homes or residences, separation of families, job relocation, and others. Students might attribute the reduction in mail volume to the increasing competition for mail services. Competition includes other mail and package carriers such as UPS or FedEx, free or inexpensive e-mail, creative e-greetings for all occasions, instant text messaging, increased cell phone usage, business use of pop-up advertising, and other technological advancements that provide faster and less expensive alternatives to standard mail service.

2. The USPS mission to provide affordable mail service regardless of geographic location prevents the USPS from charging more for hard-to-serve rural areas. USPS uses a fixed rate for delivery regardless of distance. Postal rates cannot be arbitrarily raised but must be approved by a special postal commission. The government mandate for convenience requires numerous locations and services that in many instances are extremely unprofitable.

INTERNET RESEARCH ACTIVITY

1. To become a CMA, a person must:
   a. Become a member of the IMA.
   b. Complete the certification information section on the IMA application and register for the CMA or CFM examination.
   c. Pass all four parts of the CMA or CFM examination.
   d. Fulfill or expect to fulfill the educational requirements.
   e. Be employed or expect to be employed in a position that meets the experience requirement.
   f. Be of good moral character.
   g. Comply with the *Standards of Ethical Conduct.*

2. Answers will vary.

23-1 Not-for-Profit Organizations

All businesses, whether organized as proprietorships, partnerships, or corporations, have a common objective—to earn a profit. Some organizations are formed for purposes other than earning a profit. An organization providing goods or services with neither a conscious motive nor expectation of earning a profit is called a **not-for-profit organization**. Not-for-profit organizations are also referred to as nonprofit organizations.

Both businesses and not-for-profit organizations provide goods and/or services. Business owners generally invest in a business for the purpose of earning a profit. Not-for-profit organizations, however, are formed to provide needed goods or services to a group of individuals without regard to earning a profit. The primary purpose of the organization is to make available the needed goods or services that may not be available otherwise.

FYI
FOR YOUR INFORMATION

GASB has proposed a new statement. If this new statement is adopted, governmental entities would be required to prepare financial statements from an entity-wide perspective and a fund perspective. Governmental entities would be required to place a value on all infrastructure assets, such as roads and curbs, and to set up depreciation schedules for these assets.

©GETTY IMAGES/PHOTODISC

making ethical decisions
MAKING ETHICAL DECISIONS • MAKING ETHICAL DECISIONS • MAKING ETHICAL DECISIO

Evaluating Auditor Independence

Martin Samuels has such a successful business that he is considering selling stock on one of the national stock exchanges. In order to sell the stock, the government requires that the business obtain an audit. Naturally, Martin turns to his brother Frank, a partner in an accounting firm, and asks that his firm perform the audit.

Instructions

Refer to the Code of Professional Conduct of the American Institute of Certified Public Accountants. Read Rule 101 related to independence. Can Frank's accounting firm perform the audit?

MAKING ETHICAL DECISIONS
MAKING ETHICAL DECISIONS

According to ET Section 101-1—Interpretation of Rule 101 of the AICPA's *Code of Professional Conduct,* a member cannot perform professional services for family members. The interpretation states that the accountant's independence is impaired if "a partner or professional employee of the firm, his or her immediate family, or any group of such persons acting together owned more than 5 percent of a client's outstanding equity securities or other ownership interests."

Because Frank's brother owns the business, Frank's accounting firm cannot perform the audit.

- Ask students to identify other not-for-profit organizations with which they may be familiar.

OBJECTIVES

- Define accounting terms related to budgeting and accounting for a not-for-profit organization.
- Identify accounting practices related to budgeting and accounting for a not-for-profit governmental organization.
- Describe the process used to develop an operating budget.
- Journalize budget transactions for a not-for-profit organization.

MOTIVATE

Explain that businesses are in business to make a profit. Not-for-profit organizations, on the other hand, are not interested in making a profit for owners. These organizations are concerned that control is exercised over expenditures and care is taken so that amounts over budget are not spent. In this lesson, the unique characteristics of not-for-profit accounting, the development of an annual budget, and the journal entry to record an approved operating budget will be presented.

Preview

- Preview the accounting terms and definitions introduced in this lesson: not-for-profit organization, fund, expenditure, operating budget, and appropriations.
- Direct students to read the headings on each page in this lesson and to examine the illustrations given.

MATERIALS

- Instructor's Resource CD: PowerPoint Slides
- Xtra! Study Tools on the Xtra! Web Site
- Blackline Masters: Multicolumn Journal
- Working Papers: Teacher's Edition of the Working Papers for Lesson 23-1
- Software: Personal Trainer

Types of Not-for-Profit Organizations

Not-for-profit organizations may differ as to the types of goods or services they provide, their sources of revenues, or the procedures they use to select their leaders or managers. Major types of not-for-profit organizations are as follows.

1. Governmental, such as federal, state, county, city, town, and village.
2. Educational, such as elementary, secondary, and post-secondary schools.
3. Health, such as hospitals and nursing homes.
4. Charitable, such as United Way, United Fund, and American Red Cross.
5. Foundational, including trusts and corporations organized for charitable and educational purposes, such as the Carnegie Foundation and the Ford Foundation.
6. Religious, such as churches and other religious organizations.

Since not-for-profit organizations have a common objective, they share many of the same needs for financial information. Thus, the accounting system and many of the financial reports are similar for all not-for-profit organizations. However, because of differences in goods or services provided, sources of revenues, or methods of leadership selection, their accounting procedures and reports are modified for the specific type of organization.

Purpose of Governmental Organizations

All individuals are affected by or are members of one or more governmental organizations. Also, more individuals are employed by governmental organizations than any other type of not-for-profit organization. Therefore, Chapters 23 and 24 emphasize accounting for local governmental organizations.

A governmental organization's purpose is normally to provide needed goods or services that would be impossible for individuals to provide for themselves. For example, the federal government provides national defense for all citizens of the nation. Individual states and cities would find it difficult and very inefficient to provide for their own defense from foreign pressures. Similarly, cities provide police and fire protection that would be very expensive and inefficient for individuals to provide for themselves.

©GETTY IMAGES/PHOTODISC

- Discuss the differences between a business corporation and a governmental organization (city or county).

- Have students develop a list of not-for-profit organizations.

CHARACTERISTICS OF GOVERNMENTAL ORGANIZATIONS

A governmental organization has four major characteristics that affect the accounting system.

1. *No profit motive exists.* A business's success can be measured by whether or not it earns a profit. A business that is inefficient, or not competitive, will not earn a profit. Without profits, a business will soon be unable to continue operations. However, since a governmental organization does not intend to earn a profit, success is much more difficult to measure. As long as money is available, a governmental organization can continue to operate regardless of its efficiency or inefficiency.

2. *Leadership is subject to frequent change.* Policy-making bodies of governmental organizations are generally elected by popular vote of the group's members. Thus, the leadership depends on the political process and may change frequently. Therefore, policies and long-range goals may change when the leadership changes. These frequent changes make effective long-range planning difficult.

3. *Users of services do not necessarily pay for the services.* Revenues for governmental organizations are provided primarily by taxation on property, retail sales, or income. Organization members who have the greatest amount of property or income provide the greatest amount of revenues. However, the goods or services are normally provided to all members of the organization based on need. The amount that individuals pay is not directly related to the benefits they receive. Therefore, individuals have decreased incentive for ensuring that services are administered efficiently.

4. *Conflicting pressures for differing objectives exist.* No direct relationship exists between who pays for and who receives the services provided by a governmental organization. Therefore, individuals generally support the organizational objective most advantageous

to themselves. For example, some citizens of a city may place the construction of a city library high on their list of priorities. Others, who seldom use a library, may place this project low on their list of priorities. Consequently, services provided by a governmental organization are usually determined through negotiation and compromise among the different interest groups. This procedure does not necessarily provide for the best services or the most efficiency.

The characteristics of governmental organizations have affected the development of governmental accounting systems. Therefore, numerous financial and legal regulations for determining the source and amount of revenues and for planning and executing expenditures of funds are required.

Characteristics of Governmental Accounting Systems

Six accounting practices are similar for business and governmental organizations.

1. The accounting equation (assets equal liabilities plus equities) is applied.
2. An appropriate chart of accounts is prepared.
3. Transactions are analyzed into debit and credit elements.
4. Transactions are journalized and posted to ledgers.
5. Financial statements are prepared for each fiscal period.
6. Most of the same accounting concepts are applied.

The characteristics of governmental organizations and the conditions in which they operate create information and control requirements that differ from those of businesses. Because of these differences, governmental accounting and financial reporting differ in several ways from business accounting and financial reporting.

TEACHING STRATEGIES   **TEACHING TIP**

The chart of accounts used in Chapters 23 and 24 is shown on page 685.

Eastfield General Fund	
ASSETS	
Cash...............	$350,000.00
Taxes Receivable..........	50,000.00
Total Assets.............	$400,000.00
LIABILITIES AND FUND EQUITY	
Liabilities:	
Accounts Payable........	$ 60,000.00
Fund Equity:	
Fund Balance	340,000.00
Total Liabilities and	
Fund Equity............	$400,000.00

Eastfield Library Fund	
ASSETS	
Cash.................	$70,000.00
LIABILITIES AND FUND EQUITY	
Liabilities:	
Accounts Payable........	$ 5,000.00
Fund Equity:	
Fund Balance	65,000.00
Total Liabilities and	
Fund Equity..........	$70,000.00

The accounting system for a business includes a single accounting entity. That is, all accounts used to record accounting transactions for the entire business are part of a single set of accounts. Within this set of accounts, assets must equal liabilities plus equities. A governmental accounting entity with a set of accounts in which assets always equal liabilities plus equities is called a **fund**. A governmental unit, such as a city, may have several different funds.

A fund accounting system emphasizes strong controls on the use of funds. The amount in a fund can be spent only for the specified purpose of the fund. Different funds may be created for different purposes. For example, the town of Eastfield has two funds: (1) a general fund and (2) a library fund. Balance sheets for the two funds are shown above.

The town of Eastfield has total assets of $470,000.00 (general fund, $400,00.00, *plus* library fund, $70,000.00). However, the assets are accounted for separately. Assets in the library fund may be used only for library purposes. General fund assets may be used for other authorized town expenditures. Each fund is kept as a separate set of accounts.

The fund equity, similar to owners' equity for a business, is the net amount of assets available for use. For example, Eastfield's library fund equity is $65,000.00 (assets, $70,000.00, *less* liabilities, $5,000.00). If $6,000.00 cash is spent for library salaries, total assets available for

spending would be reduced to $64,000.00 ($70,000.00 *less* $6,000.00). The fund equity account, Fund Balance, would be reduced to $59,000.00 (assets, $64,000.00, *less* liabilities, $5,000.00). After this transaction, the fund remains in balance. The governmental accounting equation, assets equal liabilities plus fund equity, is in balance.

Types of funds vary with the type of not-for-profit organization and the types of goods or services provided. A unique set of funds normally is used for each type of organization—federal government, state and local governments, hospitals, schools, etc.

Modified Accrual Accounting

Most businesses use accrual accounting so that revenue and expenses incurred during a fiscal period determine the resulting net income for the period. [CONCEPT: *Matching Expenses with Revenue*] In governmental accounting, modified accrual accounting is used. In modified accrual accounting, revenues are recorded in the accounting period in which they become measurable and available. For example, property taxes become measurable and available as soon as the amount is determined and tax statements are sent to property owners. However, sales taxes cannot be determined until sales are made. Thus, sales tax revenue is recognized when the taxes are received from merchants.

Not-for-Profit Organizations

EXPLAIN

- Review the differences and similarities between a corporation's and a governmental organization's financial statements.

DEMONSTRATE

- Illustrate the various financial statements for a business organization and a governmental organization.

DIFFERENCE BETWEEN EXPENSES AND EXPENDITURES

Cash disbursements and liabilities incurred for the cost of goods delivered or services rendered are called **expenditures**. In modified accrual accounting, expenditures are generally recognized when a liability is incurred. Therefore, governmental organizations record expenditures rather than expenses. An important distinction is made between expenditures and expenses. Businesses emphasize matching expenses with revenue in each fiscal period. However, governmental accounting emphasizes determining and controlling revenues and expenditures during a fiscal period. For example, if a business buys a

truck, Plant Asset or Truck is debited and Cash or Notes Payable is credited. No expense is incurred until the truck is used. If a governmental organization buys a truck, Expenditure is debited and Cash or Notes Payable is credited. The amount of money spent or liability incurred is recorded, not the expense. Thus, expenditures are decreases in net financial resources. Emphasis is placed on control of the net financial resources, not on matching expenses with revenue. Thus, modified accrual accounting is used for measuring financial position and operating results of governmental organizations.

FINANCIAL REPORTING EMPHASIS

Both business and governmental organizations prepare financial statements at the end of a fiscal period. [CONCEPT: Accounting Period Cycle] However, because the organizations have different objectives, their charts of accounts and statements differ. The chart of accounts for Sparta appears on the next page.

The two most common financial statements prepared by businesses are an income statement and a balance sheet. The two most common financial statements prepared by governmental organizations are a statement of revenues, expenditures, and changes in fund balance and a balance sheet (described in Chapter 24).

Businesses prepare income statements to report the amount of net income earned during

a fiscal period. Earning a net income is not an objective of governmental organizations. However, identifying and controlling the sources of revenues and the expenditure of funds are emphasized as part of the control process. Therefore, a statement of revenues, expenditures, and changes in fund balance is prepared.

A business' balance sheet reports the assets, liabilities, and owners' equity of the business at the end of a fiscal period. A governmental organization's balance sheet also reports the current assets and liabilities of the organization at the end of a fiscal period. However, no specific ownership of a governmental organization exists. Therefore, assets less liabilities is reported as fund equity.

BUDGETING

Both businesses and governmental organizations prepare budgets. The primary purpose of all budgets is planning and control. For businesses, planning is required to prepare the budget. During the fiscal period, budgeted amounts are compared with actual amounts to provide information to management about the

effectiveness of cost control. Planning is also required to prepare a budget for a governmental organization. However, an approved governmental budget becomes (1) a legal authorization to spend and (2) a legal limit on the amount that can be spent.

TOWN OF SPARTA GENERAL FUND CHART OF ACCOUNTS

Balance Sheet Accounts

(1000)	ASSETS
1010	Cash
1020	Taxes Receivable—Current
1030	Allowance for Uncollectible Taxes—Current
1040	Taxes Receivable—Delinquent
1050	Allowance for Uncollectible Taxes—Delinquent
1060	Interest Receivable
1070	Allowance for Uncollectible Interest
1080	Inventory of Supplies
1090	Investments—Short Term
(2000)	LIABILITIES
2010	Accounts Payable
2020	Notes Payable
(3000)	FUND EQUITY
3010	Unreserved Fund Balance
3020	Reserve for Encumbrances—Current Year
3030	Reserve for Encumbrances—Prior Year
3040	Reserve for Inventory of Supplies

Revenue and Expenditure Accounts

(4000)	REVENUES
4010	Property Tax Revenue
4020	Interest Revenue
4030	Other Revenue
(5000)	EXPENDITURES
5100	GENERAL GOVERNMENT
5110	Expenditure—Personnel, General Government
5120	Expenditure—Supplies, General Government
5130	Expenditure—Other Charges, General Government
5140	Expenditure—Capital Outlays, General Government
5200	PUBLIC SAFETY
5210	Expenditure—Personnel, Public Safety
5220	Expenditure—Supplies, Public Safety
5230	Expenditure—Other Charges, Public Safety
5240	Expenditure—Capital Outlays, Public Safety
5300	PUBLIC WORKS
5310	Expenditure—Personnel, Public Works

5320	Expenditure—Supplies, Public Works
5330	Expenditure—Other Charges, Public Works
5340	Expenditure—Capital Outlays, Public Works
5400	RECREATION
5410	Expenditure—Personnel, Recreation
5420	Expenditure—Supplies, Recreation
5430	Expenditure—Other Charges, Recreation
5440	Expenditure—Capital Outlays, Recreation

Budgetary Accounts

(6000)	BUDGETARY
6010	Estimated Revenues
6020	Appropriations
6030	Budgetary Fund Balance
6100	GENERAL GOVERNMENT
6110	Encumbrance—Personnel, General Government
6120	Encumbrance—Supplies, General Government
6130	Encumbrance—Other Charges, General Government
6140	Encumbrance—Capital Outlays, General Government
6200	PUBLIC SAFETY
6210	Encumbrance—Personnel, Public Safety
6220	Encumbrance—Supplies, Public Safety
6230	Encumbrance—Other Charges, Public Safety
6240	Encumbrance—Capital Outlays, Public Safety
6300	PUBLIC WORKS
6310	Encumbrance—Personnel, Public Works
6320	Encumbrance—Supplies, Public Works
6330	Encumbrance—Other Charges, Public Works
6340	Encumbrance—Capital Outlays, Public Works
6400	RECREATION
6410	Encumbrance—Personnel, Recreation
6420	Encumbrance—Supplies, Recreation
6430	Encumbrance—Other Charges, Recreation
6440	Encumbrance—Capital Outlays, Recreation

The chart of accounts for Sparta is illustrated above for ready reference as you study Chapters 23 and 24 of this textbook.

©GETTY IMAGES/PHOTODISC

> REMEMBER Governmental organizations record expenditures rather than expenses.

Not-for-Profit Organizations

- Emphasize that students should refer to this chart of accounts throughout Chapters 23 and 24.
- Explain that this chart of accounts is for a general fund of a not-for-profit organization.
- Explain that this chart of account reflects Sparta's use of a fund accounting system which emphasizes strong controls on the use of funds.
- Stress that because the differences between a business corporation and a governmental organization are significant, the differences in their respective charts of accounts will be significant.
- Explain that, unlike a business corporation, a not-for-profit organization uses modified accrual accounting. This fact is reflected in the Expenditures section of the chart of accounts.
- Point out that charts of accounts are used for determining the classification of accounts and which accounts are temporary and permanent accounts.
- Stress that the chart of accounts is useful for completed automated accounting activities since account numbers are required for both data entry and file maintenance activities.

Similarities
Point out the *similarities* between this chart of accounts and the one in Part 1:

- Typical divisions for a not-for-profit organization that are the same as a for-profit organization:
  - Assets
  - Liabilities
  - Revenue
- Many familiar accounts within divisions.

Differences
Point out the *differences* between this chart of accounts and the one in Part 1:

- Typical divisions for a not-for-profit organization that are different from a for-profit organization:
  - Fund Equity
  - Expenditure
  - Budgetary Accounts
- These sections will be explained as presented in the chapter. However, since the emphasis is on strong controls on the use of funds, encumbrance and expenditure accounts are used.

TEACHING STRATEGIES TEACHING TIP

Have students compare the differences between the chart of accounts for Chapters 23 and 24 and the corporation chart of accounts used in Part 5. As students identify those differences, list them on a chalkboard. Solicit responses until the major differences, such as the following, are identified: (a) Corporations use expense accounts. (b) Not-for-profit organizations use expenditure and encumbrance accounts. (c) Not-for-profit organizations do not have fund accounts for long-term assets or liabilities, nor do they have plant and equipment accounts.

DEVELOPING AN ANNUAL GOVERNMENTAL OPERATING BUDGET

Town of Sparta
Annual Operating Budget—General Fund
For Year Ended December 31, 20--

ESTIMATED REVENUES

Property Tax	$1,594,000.00	
Interest	10,000.00	
Other	2,500.00	
Total Estimated Revenues		$1,606,500.00

ESTIMATED EXPENDITURES AND BUDGETARY FUND BALANCE

General Government:		
Personnel	$ 263,280.00	
Supplies	12,150.00	
Other Charges	113,400.00	
Capital Outlays	16,220.00	
Total General Government		$ 405,050.00
Public Safety:		
Personnel	$ 589,200.00	
Supplies	20,000.00	
Other Charges	153,150.00	
Capital Outlays	90,300.00	
Total Public Safety		852,650.00
Public Works:		
Personnel	$ 113,400.00	
Supplies	5,600.00	
Other Charges	47,500.00	
Capital Outlays	51,500.00	
Total Public Works		218,000.00
Recreation:		
Personnel	$ 58,260.00	
Supplies	1,970.00	
Other Charges	25,250.00	
Capital Outlays	11,620.00	
Total Recreation		97,100.00
Total Estimated Expenditures		$1,572,800.00
Budgetary Fund Balance		33,700.00
Total Estimated Expenditures and Budgetary Fund Balance		$1,606,500.00

A plan of current expenditures and the proposed means of financing those expenditures is called an **operating budget**. A governmental fund's annual operating budget authorizes and provides the basis for control of financial operations during a fiscal year. Since each governmental fund is a separate accounting entity, an operating budget is normally prepared to show the estimated revenues, estimated expenditures, and budgetary fund balance for each fund. The operating budget shown above was prepared for the general fund of the town of Sparta.

Sparta organizes revenue accounts by source of revenue. Expenditure accounts are organized by department and type of expenditure. Some organizations maintain subsidiary accounts for each of the general ledger accounts to provide more detail about the sources of revenues and types of expenditures. Because of its small size, Sparta maintains only the general ledger accounts listed in its chart of accounts on the previous page.

Some basic procedures are followed to prepare an annual governmental operating budget.

1. Departments of the governmental organization submit budget requests to the chief executive of the organization. Requests are based on an analysis of expenditures for the previous year and expected changes in expenditures for the coming year.
2. The chief executive reviews budget requests with department heads. When budget requests are acceptable to the chief executive, departmental requests are consolidated into a single budget request for the organization. The chief executive then submits the operating budget to the legislative body. The legislative body is a group of persons normally elected by the citizens/members of the organization and granted authority to make laws for the organization.
3. The legislative body approves the operating budget. The approved operating budget becomes an authorization to spend the amounts listed in the budget. Before the operating budget can be approved, revenues plus the available amount of fund equity must be at least as great as the expenditures. If the expenditures are more than the total of expected revenues and available fund equity, the expected sources of revenue must be increased or expenditures decreased.

Sparta is a small town with a town manager and five town council members. The council members are elected to their positions. One member of the council serves as mayor. The council serves as the legislative body for Sparta. The council appoints the town manager who works full time as chief executive of the town. Sparta has three department heads: public safety director, public works director, and recreation director. Because Sparta is small and most of its revenues come from property taxes, the accounting system contains only one fund—a general fund.

At the request of the town manager, Sparta's three department heads analyze the current year's expenditures and expected changes, and then prepare budget requests for the next year. The town manager reviews the budget requests and prepares a single operating budget for Sparta's general fund for next year. The operating budget is submitted to the town council.

The town council represents the interests of all the town's citizens. Thus, the council should evaluate the operating budget from at least four perspectives. (1) Are adequate services being provided? (2) Are the services desired by a majority of citizens? (3) Are the amounts requested essential to provide the desired level of services? (4) Does the city have the financial capacity to support the budget?

The approved operating budget determines the amount of revenues needed for the year. The town's tax rate necessary to provide the needed funds for the approved operating budget is then determined.

After completing its review, the Sparta council formally approves next year's governmental operating budget. The approved governmental operating budget becomes authorization for the town manager and department heads to make expenditures as specified in the budget.

Approval of an annual governmental operating budget by the proper authorities provides legal authorization to make expenditures in accordance with the approved budget. Authorizations to make expenditures for specified purposes are called **appropriations**. Sparta's approved operating budget has appropriations that authorize expenditures up to the amounts stated in the budget. The tax rate is then set at a rate that will raise at least enough revenue to cover the appropriations.

> Many governmental organizations have restrictions as to the amount that taxes can be increased. Public hearings may be required before taxes can be increased. A formal vote in an election may also be required. If a proposed operating budget exceeds the amount of taxes and other estimated revenue, the budget may need to be reduced to the level of available revenues.

- Discuss the procedures followed to prepare the annual operating budget.

- Refer students to the illustration on page 686 and explain how an annual budget is prepared.

TEACHING STRATEGIES   TEACHING TIP

Explain that governmental organizations use a variety of journals, depending upon the size and complexity of the organization and the number of transactions. Medium and large cities generally use computers to record transactions. Small towns and villages may use a multicolumn journal, a general journal, or special journals adapted to the organizations' needs. Regardless of the method used, the accounting procedures for journalizing are similar. To keep the journalizing process as simple as possible for a small town, the chapter illustrations and end-of-chapter problems use a multicolumn journal.

DEMONSTRATE

Record the transaction

- Use a transparency to record the approved annual operating budget.

ONGOING ASSESSMENT

- Assessment is an ongoing process. Circulate through the classroom or lab, observing which students have problems with the assignments.
- Troubleshooting: Diagnose what kinds of problems students have with this lesson. Students may have trouble remembering the entry for journalizing an approved annual operating budget.
- Assess student understanding by checking solutions to Independent Practice assignments.

RETEACH

- Have students practice making the entry to journalize an approved annual operating budget. This could be done in groups of two students. One student develops a partial operating budget for a city. The partial operating budget should include the estimated revenue, appropriations, and budgetary fund balance. The other student must record the journal entry.

688

JOURNALIZING AN APPROVED ANNUAL OPERATING BUDGET

	DATE		ACCOUNT TITLE	DOC. NO.	POST. REF.	GENERAL DEBIT	GENERAL CREDIT	CASH DEBIT	CASH CREDIT	
1	Jan.	2	Estimated Revenues	M35		1606 50 0 00				1
2			Appropriations				1572 80 0 00			2
3			Budgetary Fund Balance				33 70 0 00			3

JOURNAL   PAGE 1

As an additional control measure, Sparta journalizes its approved operating budget as shown above. Budgetary accounts are for control purposes and are closed at the end of a fiscal period.

Governmental organizations, like businesses, record accounting transactions initially in a journal. Source documents are the basis for the journal entries. Governmental organizations may use a multi-column journal, a general journal, or special journals adapted to the organization's needs. Sparta uses a multi-column journal.

January 2. Recorded Sparta's approved operating budget: estimated revenues, $1,606,500.00; appropriations, $1,572,800.00; budgetary fund balance, $33,700.00. Memorandum No. 35.

Estimated Revenues is increased by a debit for the amount of budgeted revenues, $1,606,500.00. Estimated Revenues has a normal debit balance, opposite the normal credit balance of an actual revenue account. Appropriations is increased by a credit for the amount of Sparta's budgeted expenditures, $1,572,800.00. Appropriations has a normal credit balance, opposite the normal debit balance of the actual expenditure accounts. Budgetary Fund Balance is increased by a credit, $33,700.00 (estimated revenues, $1,606,500.00, less appropriations, $1,572,800.00).

A separate revenue account will be credited as revenues are earned. Balances of the two accounts, Estimated Revenues and Revenues, can be reviewed to compare the amount of actual revenues earned and the amount of revenues estimated to be earned. If actual revenues are not as great as expected, expenditures may need to be reduced to avoid exceeding available funds. Recording the estimated revenues in the budgetary account Estimated Revenues provides this planning and control information.

Estimated Revenues	
Jan. 2 1,606,500.00	

Appropriations	
	Jan. 2 1,572,800.00

Budgetary Fund Balance	
	Jan. 2 33,700.00

Separate expenditure accounts will be debited as actual expenditures are made. Ensuring that expenditures do not exceed the appropriations (budgeted expenditures) is essential for governmental organizations. Periodically, the appropriations account balance can be compared with the total of expenditure account balances to avoid overspending appropriations. Appropriations less total expenditures is the amount still available for spending. Recording appropriations in the budgetary account Appropriations provides this additional control information. Each department also keeps records of its appropriated and expended amounts to ensure that no department exceeds its appropriation amounts.

If appropriations exceed estimated revenues, Budgetary Fund Balance is debited to make the total debits equal the total credits. However, most governmental organizations normally set their revenue sources slightly above appropriations to avoid exceeding appropriations.

• terms review

not-for-profit organization
fund
expenditure
operating budget
appropriations

• audit your understanding

1. What four characteristics affect the accounting system for a governmental organization?

2. List the accounting practices that are similar for businesses and governmental organizations.

3. What is a fund?

4. What is the purpose of a governmental operating budget?

5. What accounts are debited and credited to journalize a governmental organization's approved operating budget?

Terms Review
Call on students to define each term in the Terms Review. Ask the class if the definition is correct and whether the complete definition has been given or if anything needs to be added. Suggested definitions are given in the Glossary.

Audit Your Understanding
Call on students to answer the Audit Your Understanding questions. Ask the class if the answer is correct and/or complete. Answers are given in Appendix E of the textbook.

• work together 23-1

Journalizing governmental operating budgets

The town of Powell approved its annual general fund operating budgets effective January 1 of the current year. Your instructor will guide you through the following example.

1. Journalize the entry to record the following operating budget for the town of Powell.

Estimated Revenues	Appropriations	Budgetary Fund Balance
$843,000.00	$836,800.00	$6,200.00

Work Together
Have students write the solution to the Work Together problem as you guide the class through the examples.

- Call on students to analyze the journal entry.
- Direct students to record each entry in a journal.

• on your own 23-1

Journalizing governmental operating budgets

The town of Worthington approved its annual general fund operating budgets effective January 1 of the current year. Work independently to complete the following problem.

1. Journalize the entry to record the following operating budget for the town of Worthington.

Estimated Revenues	Appropriations	Budgetary Fund Balance
$2,461,000.00	$2,423,000.00	$38,000.00

On Your Own
- Assign the On Your Own problem to be worked independently.
- Use the Ongoing Assessment techniques to diagnose student understanding.

Application Problem
- Assign Application Problem 23-1: Journalizing governmental operating budgets.

Personal Trainer
- Students can access the Lesson 23-1 assessment material using this software.

Xtra! Web Site
- Students can access the Xtra! Study Tools for additional practice.

- Assign Making Ethical Decisions on page 680.
- Assign Case 1 of the Cases for Critical Thinking. Discuss the necessity of using separate governmental funds in the town's accounting system.

- Have students write for five minutes on what they have learned about not-for-profit accounting. Ask for volunteers to read what they have written.

Sidebar text (vertical): TERMS REVIEW • TERMS REVIEW • TERMS REVIEW

AUDIT YOUR UNDERSTANDING

WORK TOGETHER • WORK

ON YOUR OWN • ON YOUR OWN

23-2 Journalizing Revenues

OBJECTIVES

- Define accounting terms related to budgeting and accounting for a not-for-profit governmental organization.
- Identify accounting concepts and practices related to budgeting and accounting for a not-for-profit governmental organization.
- Journalize revenues for a not-for-profit organization.

MOTIVATE

City governments may collect a variety of revenues from their citizens. Explain that this section will describe how to record the collection of such revenues.

Preview

- Preview the accounting term and definition introduced in this lesson: tax levy.
- Direct students to read the headings at the top of each page in this lesson and to examine the illustrations given.

EXPLAIN

- Direct students to the illustration. Discuss the necessity of having an allowance account for uncollectible taxes.
- Discuss journalizing property tax revenue before cash is received.

DEMONSTRATE

Analyze the transaction

- Draw three blank T accounts on the board.
- Read the transaction statement.
- Ask students to analyze the transaction by answering: what accounts are affected, are they increased or decreased, and are they debited or credited. Complete the T accounts as the information is provided.

Record the transaction

- Use a transparency to illustrate recording the transaction in a multicolumn journal.
- Record each item in the journal following the three steps shown.

JOURNALIZING CURRENT PROPERTY TAX REVENUES

1. Total taxes levied.

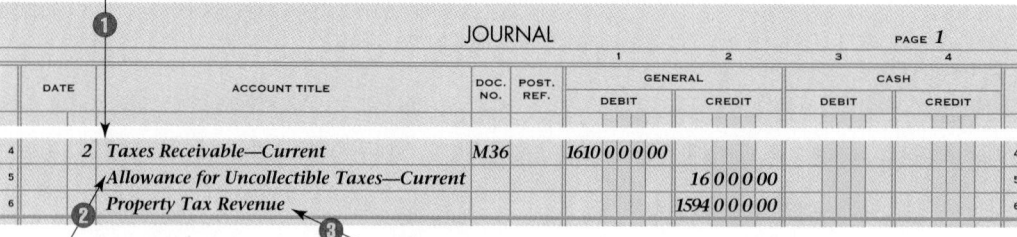

2. Estimated losses for taxes not collected.

3. Revenue recognized from tax levy.

Governmental fund revenues are recorded in the accounting period in which the revenues become measurable and available.

When property tax rates have been set and tax amounts calculated, taxes are levied on all taxable property. Authorized action taken by a governmental organization to collect taxes by legal authority is called a **tax levy**. Levied property taxes are considered measurable and available because they become a legal obligation of property owners. Therefore, when the levy is made, a journal entry is made to record property tax revenue as shown above. Although tax levies are legal obligations of property owners, some property owners do not pay their taxes. Legal action may eventually be taken against these property owners in an effort to collect the taxes. Even with these actions, a government generally does not collect all the taxes levied. On January 2, Sparta authorized its tax levy and sent out property tax statements to property owners. Sparta estimated that $16,000.00 of property taxes will not be collected.

January 2. Recorded property tax levy: taxes receivable—current, $1,610,000.00; allowance for uncollectible taxes—current, $16,000.00; property tax revenue, $1,594,000.00. Memorandum No. 36.

Taxes Receivable—Current	
Jan. 2 1,610,000.00	

Allowance for Uncollectible Taxes—Current	
	Jan. 2 16,000.00

Property Tax Revenue	
	Jan. 2 1,594,000.00

STEPS · STEPS · STEPS · STEPS
JOURNALIZING CURRENT PROPERTY TAX REVENUE

1 Debit *Taxes Receivable—Current* for the total amount of tax levied, *$1,610,000.00*. This amount is the total of the tax statements sent to taxpayers.

2 Credit the contra asset account, *Allowance for Uncollectible Taxes—Current*, for the amount of estimated loss, *$16,000.00*.

3 Credit the revenue account, *Property Tax Revenue*, for the amount of revenue recognized, *$1,594,000.00*. This amount is the total tax levy, $1,610,000.00, *less* the allowance for current uncollectible taxes, $16,000.00.

690   Chapter 23   Budgeting and Accounting for a Not-for-Profit Organization

---

MATERIALS

- Instructor's Resource CD:
  PowerPoint Slides
- Xtra! Study Tools on the Xtra! Web Site
- Blackline Masters:
  Multicolumn Journal

- Working Papers:
  Teacher's Edition of the Working Papers for Lesson 23-2
- Software:
  Personal Trainer

COLLECTION OF CURRENT PROPERTY TAXES

		JOURNAL								PAGE 3	
						1		2		3	4
						GENERAL			CASH		
DATE		ACCOUNT TITLE	DOC. NO.	POST. REF.		DEBIT	CREDIT		DEBIT	CREDIT	
12	10	Taxes Receivable—Current	R371				194 000 00	194 000 00			12

Cash received for property taxes reduces the taxes receivable account as shown above.

January 10. Received cash for current taxes receivable, $194,000.00. Receipt No. 371.

Cash is increased by a debit for the amount of cash received, *$194,000.00*. Taxes Receivable—

Current is decreased by a credit for the same amount, *$194,000.00*.

Cash	
Jan. 10 194,000.00	

Taxes Receivable—Current			
Bal. 1,610,000.00	Jan. 10	194,000.00

OTHER REVENUE

		JOURNAL								PAGE 3	
						1		2		3	4
						GENERAL			CASH		
DATE		ACCOUNT TITLE	DOC. NO.	POST. REF.		DEBIT	CREDIT		DEBIT	CREDIT	
17	15	Other Revenue	R386				8 5 00	8 5 00			17

1. Revenue that is not measurable until received.

Some revenues, such as fines, inspection charges, parking meter receipts, and penalties, are normally not known and, thus, are not measurable until cash is received. A journal entry to record such revenues, therefore, is generally made only when cash is received as shown above.

January 15. Received cash from traffic fines, $85.00. Receipt No. 386.

Cash is increased by a debit for the amount of cash received, *$85.00*. Other Revenue is increased by a credit for the same amount, *$85.00*.

Cash	
Jan. 15 85.00	

Other Revenue	
	Jan. 15 85.00

FYI FOR YOUR INFORMATION

In some states, the operating budget is not officially approved until it is reviewed by tax committees at the county and state level.

TEACHING STRATEGIES   DIFFERENT LEARNING ABILITIES

At-Risk Students. Many at-risk students can become motivated to begin self improvement only when they recognize that they have a need to improve. One method of promoting self evaluation is to have students identify the qualities they would require of another individual. Have students imagine that they are considering hiring employees for an office position. Require the student to prepare a job description that includes both skill and personal characteristics that applicants should possess. This activity should enable students to compare their qualifications with the job descriptions they have developed.

EXPLAIN

- Direct students to the illustration. Discuss the entry to record delinquent property taxes.

DEMONSTRATE

Analyze the transaction

- Draw four T accounts on the board.
- Read the transaction statement.
- Ask students to analyze the transaction by answering: what accounts are affected, are they increased or decreased, and are they debited or credited. Complete the T accounts as the information is given.

Record the transaction

- Use a transparency to illustrate recording the transaction in a multicolumn journal.
- Record the transaction as shown.

ONGOING ASSESSMENT

- Assessment is an ongoing process. Circulate through the classroom or lab, observing which students have problems with the assignments.
- Troubleshooting: Students may have trouble remembering how to record delinquent property taxes.
- Assess student understanding by checking solutions to Independent Practice assignments.

RETEACH

- Make a transparency of a multicolumn journal. Ask a student to come forward and record the first line of the transaction to record delinquent property taxes. Have a different student complete each line of the transparency.

1. Entry to record delinquent property taxes.

	DATE		ACCOUNT TITLE	DOC. NO.	POST. REF.	GENERAL		CASH		
						DEBIT	CREDIT	DEBIT	CREDIT	
1	Mar.	1	Taxes Receivable—Delinquent	M65		64 2 0 0 00				1
2			Allowance for Uncollectible Taxes—Current			16 0 0 0 00				2
3			Taxes Receivable—Current				64 2 0 0 00			3
4			Allowance for Uncollectible Taxes—Delinquent				16 0 0 0 00			4
20		20	Taxes Receivable—Delinquent	R420			12 0 0 0 00	12 0 0 0 00		20

JOURNAL   PAGE 21

2. Entry to record collection of delinquent property taxes.

Tax payments specify the date that property taxes are due and payable. Taxes not paid by the specified date are reclassified as delinquent. Sparta's property taxes are due on February 28. On March 1, taxes not paid are considered delinquent. On that date, a journal entry is made to transfer uncollected taxes from current to delinquent status as shown above.

Taxes that Sparta expects to collect are accounted for by using two accounts, Taxes Receivable—Current and Allowance for Uncollectible Taxes—Current. Delinquent taxes are accounted for using two accounts, Taxes Receivable—Delinquent and Allowance for Uncollectible Taxes—Delinquent. A journal entry transfers the balances of the two current accounts to the two delinquent accounts.

March 1. Recorded reclassification of current taxes receivable to delinquent status, $64,200.00, and the accompanying allowance for uncollectible accounts, $16,000.00. Memorandum No. 65.

Taxes Receivable—Delinquent
Mar. 1 64,200.00	

Allowance for Uncollectible Taxes—Current
Mar. 1 16,000.00	Bal. 16,000.00

Taxes Receivable—Current
Bal. 64,200.00	Mar. 1 64,200.00

Allowance for Uncollectible Taxes—Delinquent
	Mar. 1 16,000.00

STEPS · STEPS · STEPS · STEPS · STEPS · STEPS · STEPS · STEPS · STEPS · STEPS
JOURNALIZING ENTRY TO RECORD DELINQUENT PROPERTY TAXES

1 Debit *Taxes Receivable—Delinquent* for the amount of current taxes becoming delinquent, *$64,200.00*. Debit the contra asset account, *Allowance for Uncollectible Taxes—Current*, for the balance in that account, *$16,000.00*.

2 Credit *Taxes Receivable—Current* for the amount of current taxes becoming delinquent, *$64,200.00*. Credit *Allowance for Uncollectible Taxes—Delinquent* for the amount of allowance on the delinquent taxes, *$16,000.00*.

Collection of Delinquent Property Taxes

Although some taxes become delinquent, Sparta continues efforts to collect these taxes. Cash received for delinquent taxes reduces Taxes Receivable—Delinquent as shown above.

March 20. Received cash for delinquent taxes receivable, $12,000.00. Receipt No. 420.

Cash is increased by a debit for the amount received, *$12,000.00*. Taxes Receivable—Delinquent is decreased by a credit for the same amount, *$12,000.00*.

692   Chapter 23   Budgeting and Accounting for a Not-for-Profit Organization

Xtra!
Careers
accountingxtra.swlearning.com

careers in accounting

CAREERS IN ACCOUNTING • CAREERS IN ACCOUNTING • CAREERS IN ACCOUNTIN

Suresh Bhat, Financial Specialist

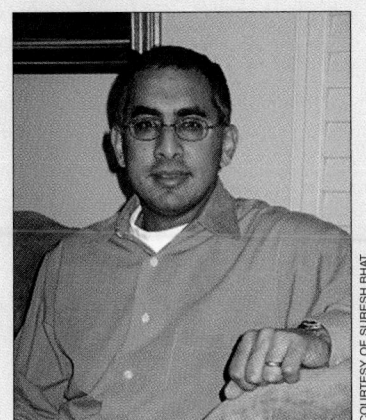

COURTESY OF SURESH BHAT

As a freshman at Oak Grove High School in San Jose, California, Suresh Bhat enrolled in classes that would ultimately prepare him for a career in medicine. His initial career plans were going well until he signed up for a business elective his junior year. That one class, accounting, changed everything. Suddenly, he was exposed to a curriculum that was both new and intellectually challenging. Throughout the year, he became aware of the many career opportunities within the field of business. His first year of accounting was such a success that he decided to enroll in advanced accounting for his senior year. After participating in two years of high school accounting, Suresh realized that his passion resided in the business arena and not in medicine.

Suresh pursued an undergraduate degree at the University of California, Berkeley. He graduated in 1990 with a Bachelor of Science in Business Administration. He obtained his certified public accountant (CPA) license in 1993 and later returned to UC Berkeley to acquire a Master's in Business Administration (MBA).

His first employment experience was with Deloitte & Touche, one of the world's largest and most prestigious accounting firms. Early in his accounting career, Suresh realized that the financial aspects of running a company appealed to him more than the accounting side of business. Finance personnel concentrate on money. Their responsibilities include finding funds to operate and expand a business and, in some instances, securing capital to acquire another company. They also manage cash resources on hand and help businesses plan for their financial futures.

After obtaining his CPA license, Suresh left Deloitte & Touche and accepted an employment offer from Bank of America. Here, he used his accounting background to evaluate the money requirements of businesses to fund growth, secure inventory, purchase new technologies, remodel facilities, and operate overseas.

Presently, Suresh is a vice-president of finance for Charles Schwab. This firm helps individuals and companies invest their money in stocks, bonds, and mutual funds. Suresh's duties at Charles Schwab include capital planning, budgeting, forecasting, strategic planning, risk analysis, and mergers and acquisitions. It is a demanding job but an exciting one that requires both accounting and finance skills.

Salary Range: $100,000–$200,000 + 20–40% bonus

Qualifications: To start your entry-level career in the financial services industry, Suresh recommends an undergraduate degree in business, strong people skills, and a talent for creative problem solving. Suresh believes that students seeking more information about careers in finance should secure an e-mail mentor.

Occupational Outlook: The future holds many possibilities for Suresh. Eventually, he sees himself as a managing partner at an accounting firm, a company treasurer, or perhaps a chief financial officer (CFO) for a major corporation. With his background in accounting and finance, all of these career options are available to Suresh.

CAREERS IN ACCOUNTING

The Careers in Accounting feature profiles people who are entrepreneurs, who are working in accounting-related fields, or who use accounting in their business lives.

Students can access the Careers section of the Xtra! Web Site for additional material about careers.

Journalizing Revenues

Lesson 23-2   **693**

693

• term review

tax levy

• audit your understanding

1. When is a journal entry made to record property tax revenue?

2. What accounts are affected, and how, when a taxpayer pays current property taxes?

3. What accounts are affected, and how, when a taxpayer pays property taxes two months after the due date?

• work together 23-2

Journalizing governmental revenue transactions

Groveport's town council recently approved the town's general fund operating budget for the current year. Use page 1 of the journal provided in the *Working Papers*. Your instructor will guide you through the following examples.

Jan. 1. Recorded property tax levy: taxes receivable—current, $2,400,000.00; allowance for uncollectible taxes—current, $24,000.00; property tax revenue, $2,376,000.00. M34.
14. Received cash from traffic fines, $1,354.00. R84. (Other Revenue)
Feb. 11. Received cash for current taxes receivable, $973,000.00. R113.
Mar. 1. Recorded reclassification of current taxes receivable to delinquent status, $96,200.00, and the accompanying allowance for uncollectible accounts, $24,000.00. M68.
12. Received cash for delinquent taxes receivable, $30,300.00. R157.

1. Journalize the selected transactions.

• on your own 23-2

Journalizing governmental revenue transactions

Centuria's town council recently approved the town's general fund operating budget for the current year. Use page 1 of the journal provided in the *Working Papers*. Work independently to complete the following problem.

Jan. 1. Recorded property tax levy: taxes receivable—current, $1,200,000.00; allowance for uncollectible taxes—current, $12,000.00; property tax revenue, $1,188,000.00. M163.
20. Received cash from parking meter receipts, $894.00. R541. (Other Revenue)
Feb. 11. Received cash for current taxes receivable, $485,200.00. R596.
Mar. 1. Recorded reclassification of current taxes receivable to delinquent status, $48,100.00, and the accompanying allowance for uncollectible accounts, $12,000.00. M225.
15. Received cash for delinquent taxes receivable, $15,150.00. R628.

1. Journalize the selected transactions.

23-3 Journalizing Expenditures, Encumbrances, and Other Transactions

JOURNALIZING EXPENDITURES

					GENERAL		CASH	
DATE	ACCOUNT TITLE	DOC. NO.	POST. REF.	DEBIT	CREDIT	DEBIT	CREDIT
Jan. 10	Expenditure—Other Charges, Public Safety	C355		2 9 0 00			2 9 0 00

JOURNAL — PAGE 3

A primary objective of governmental accounting is to control the financial resources. Governmental accounting focuses on measuring changes in financial resources rather than determining net income. Therefore, in governmental accounting, expenditures rather than expenses are recorded. The use of two special accounting procedures enhances the control of expenditures.

1. Expenditures are classified into categories to assign specific responsibility for the expenditure and to analyze the purpose of the expenditure. For example, Expenditure—Personnel, Public Safety is one of Sparta's expenditure accounts. Personnel indicates the type of expenditure (salaries for personnel). Public Safety indicates the department for which the personnel expenditures were made.

2. Budgetary accounts are used to record estimated amounts of expenditures to protect against overspending the budgeted amounts. To accomplish this control procedure, encumbrance accounts are used. A commitment to pay for goods or services that have been ordered but not yet provided is called an **encumbrance**. When an order that will require a future expenditure is placed, a budgetary encumbrance account is debited for the estimated amount. This entry reduces the fund balance and ensures that commitments and expenditures will not be greater than funds available.

Exact amounts of some expenditures are known as soon as the obligation is determined. For example, the amount and due date of payment for utility costs is known when the utility statement is received. The entry to record the expenditure is shown above.

January 10. Paid cash for electrical service in public safety department, $290.00. Check No. 355.

Expenditure—Other Charges, Public Safety is increased by a debit for the cost of the electrical service, *$290.00*. Cash is decreased by a credit for the same amount, *$290.00*.

Expenditure—Other Charges, Public Safety	
Jan. 10 290.00	

Cash	
	Jan. 10 290.00

The major control of expenditures is achieved by holding department heads accountable for expenditures in their department. Classification of expenditures is used to analyze major types of expenditures within each department. For Sparta, each department's expenditures are recorded in one of four classifications: personnel, supplies, other charges, or capital outlays. The other charges classification is used for all expenditures except salaries and related personnel expenditures, supplies expenditures, and capital outlays. Capital outlays is used for expenditures that will benefit future years.

- Remind students that an encumbrance ensures that funds are available to pay a bill when it arrives. Therefore, an encumbrance is recorded when an amount can be estimated for an expenditure.

- Explain that this encumbrance will be removed when the exact amount of the transaction is known.

- Explain that the appropriated amount for a category, less the encumbrances and expenditures, equals the amount that can still be spent in that category. Refer to the math box.

DEMONSTRATE

Analyze the transaction

- Draw two blank T accounts on the board.

- Read the transaction statement.

- Ask students to analyze the transaction by answering what accounts are affected, are they increased or decreased, and are they debited or credited. Complete the T accounts as the information is provided.

Record the transaction

- Use a transparency to illustrate recording the transaction in a multicolumn journal.

- Record each item in the journal.

- Ask a student to verify that, for this transaction, debits equal credits.

JOURNALIZING ENCUMBRANCES

	DATE	ACCOUNT TITLE	DOC. NO.	POST. REF.	GENERAL DEBIT	GENERAL CREDIT	CASH DEBIT	CASH CREDIT	
12	12	Encumbrance—Supplies, Public Works	M40		3 8 0 00				12
13		Reserve for Encumbrances—Current Year				3 8 0 00			13

JOURNAL   PAGE 3

To avoid spending more resources than are available, encumbrance accounts are used. When goods or services are ordered that will be provided at a later date, an obligation for a future expenditure is made. Resources have not yet been used, but there is a promise to give up those resources when ordered goods or services are delivered. Encumbering resources is a way of setting aside the amount estimated to be needed to pay for the ordered goods or services. When the goods or services are delivered, the estimated amount is removed from the encumbrance account and the exact amount of the expenditure is journalized in an expenditure account.

January 12. Encumbered estimated amount for supplies in public works department, $380.00. Memorandum No. 40.

The budgetary account Encumbrance—Supplies, Public Works is increased by a debit for the amount of the order, $380.00. The fund equity account Reserve for Encumbrances—Current Year is increased by

a credit for the amount of the supplies order, $380.00 as shown above. This account serves as an offsetting account for the encumbrance account and shows that this amount of the fund equity is reserved for an encumbrance.

Encumbrance—Supplies, Public Works	
Jan. 12 380.00	

Reserve for Encumbrance—Current Year	
	Jan. 12 380.00

Expenditures plus encumbrances for a specific account equal the total commitment that has been made against the appropriated amount for that account. The appropriated amount less the encumbrances and expenditures equals the amount that can still be spent. For example, Sparta appropriated $5,600.00 for supplies for the public works department. If expenditures are $900.00 and encumbrances are $380.00, then $4,320.00 is still available for public works supplies expenditures.

Appropriated for Supplies	−	Expenditures	−	Encumbrances	=	Amount Still Available
$5,600.00	−	$900.00	−	$380.00	=	$4,320.00

JOURNALIZING EXPENDITURES FOR AMOUNTS ENCUMBERED

1. Entry to cancel encumbrance.

	DATE	ACCOUNT TITLE	DOC. NO.	POST. REF.	GENERAL DEBIT	GENERAL CREDIT	CASH DEBIT	CASH CREDIT	
10	25	Reserve for Encumbrances—Current Year	M46		3 8 0 00				10
11		Encumbrance—Supplies, Public Works				3 8 0 00			11
12	25	Expenditure—Supplies, Public Works	C362		3 7 5 00			3 7 5 00	12

JOURNAL   PAGE 6

2. Entry to record expenditure.

When goods or services that have been encumbered are received, two entries must be made.

1. The encumbrance entry is reversed to remove the estimated amount from the encumbrance and reserve for encumbrance accounts.
2. The expenditure is recorded.

These entries are illustrated above.

January 25. Paid cash for public works department supplies, $375.00, encumbered January 12 per Memorandum No. 40. Memorandum No. 46 and Check No. 362.

Effect of first entry

Reserve for Encumbrances—Current Year

Jan. 25	380.00	Jan. 12	380.00
		(New Bal. zero)	

Encumbrance—Supplies, Public Works

Jan. 12	380.00	Jan. 25	380.00
(New Bal. zero)			

Effect of second entry

Expenditure—Supplies, Public Works

Jan. 25	375.00	

Cash

	Jan. 25	375.00

STEPS

STEPS • STEPS • STEPS • STEPS

JOURNALIZING EXPENDITURES FOR AMOUNT ENCUMBERED

1 Debit *Reserve for Encumbrances—Current Year* and credit *Encumbrance—Supplies, Public Works* for *380.00*. The entry cancels the encumbrance entry by removing the estimated amount from the encumbrance and reserve for encumbrance accounts. The encumbrance is no longer needed since it is no longer outstanding. The encumbrance was for an estimated amount, *$380.00*. When the supplies were delivered, the actual cost was $375.00. The actual amount of an expenditure sometimes differs from the amount estimated when an order is placed.

2 Debit *Expenditure—Supplies, Public Works* and credit *Cash* for the actual cost of supplies, *$375.00*.

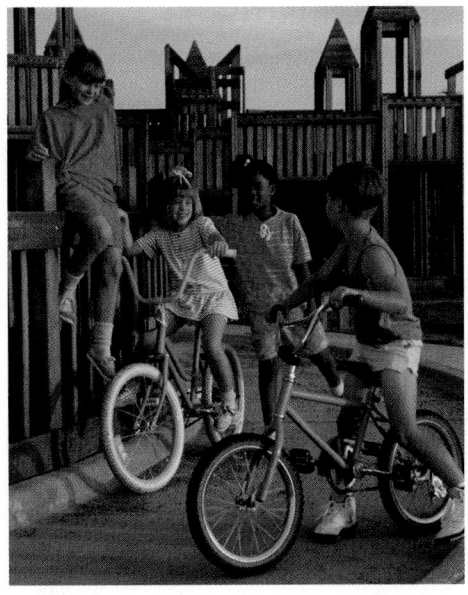

©GETTY IMAGES/PHOTODISC

- Remind students that once the goods or services encumbered are received, two entries must be made.
- The first entry reverses the encumbrance entry used to estimate the amount of the expenditure.
- The second entry records the actual expenditure.
- Refer to the illustration.

DEMONSTRATE

Analyze the transaction

- Draw four blank T accounts on the board.
- Read the transaction statement.
- Ask students to analyze the transaction by answering what accounts are affected, are they increased or decreased, and are they debited or credited. Complete the T accounts as the information is provided.

Record the transaction

- Use a transparency to illustrate recording the transaction in a multicolumn journal.
- Record each item in the journal, following the steps given.
- Ask a student to verify that, for this transaction, debits equal credits.

JOURNALIZING EXPENDITURES BENEFITING FUTURE PERIODS

JOURNAL   PAGE 21

	DATE	ACCOUNT TITLE	DOC. NO.	POST. REF.	GENERAL DEBIT	GENERAL CREDIT	CASH DEBIT	CASH CREDIT	
17	10	Expenditure—Capital Outlays, Gen. Gov't.	C400		9 0 0 00			9 0 0 00	17

Governmental organizations are formed to provide services that their members need, not to earn a profit. A business records the cost of property, such as a computer, as an asset. The business then depreciates the asset over its useful life. The depreciation expense is matched with revenue earned in each fiscal period. Since governmental organizations do not earn net income, they have no need for expense information. However, controlling the expenditure of funds is important. When money is spent for capital outlays, the amount is recorded as an expenditure in the period spent even though the item may benefit several accounting periods.

On March 10, Sparta's general government department bought a new computer.

March 10. Paid cash for a computer for general government department, $900.00. Check No. 400.

Expenditure—Capital Outlays, General Government is increased by a debit for the cost of the computer, $900.00. Cash is decreased by a credit for the same amount, $900.00. The journal entry is shown above.

Governmental properties that benefit future periods are called **general fixed assets**. Most governmental organizations keep a record of general fixed assets. This record helps to safeguard the government's ownership of the property. Sparta keeps a card file with information about each general fixed asset.

JOURNALIZING THE ISSUANCE OF LIABILITIES

JOURNAL   PAGE 1

	DATE	ACCOUNT TITLE	DOC. NO.	POST. REF.	GENERAL DEBIT	GENERAL CREDIT	CASH DEBIT	CASH CREDIT	
15	4	Notes Payable	NP26			100 0 0 00	100 0 0 00		15

Governmental organizations may need to borrow cash for short periods until tax money is received. At other times, these organizations have cash to invest for short periods until the cash is needed to pay expenditures. Sparta sends tax statements to property owners on January 1 each year. Taxes can be paid anytime from January 1 through February 28. Consequently, the town may need to borrow cash until taxes are received.

January 4. Issued a 1-month, 9% note, $100,000.00. Note Payable No. 26.

Cash is increased by a debit for the amount received, $100,000.00. Notes Payable is increased by a credit for the same amount, $100,000.00. The journal entry to record this transaction is shown above.

JOURNALIZING THE PAYMENT OF LIABILITIES

	DATE	ACCOUNT TITLE	DOC. NO.	POST. REF.	GENERAL DEBIT	GENERAL CREDIT	CASH DEBIT	CASH CREDIT	
					JOURNAL			PAGE 8	
					1	2	3	4	
22	4	Notes Payable	C370		100 000 00			100 750 00	22
23		Expenditure—Other Charges, Gen. Gov't.			7 50 00				23
24									24

When Sparta's note payable is due on February 4, the amount of the note plus interest expense is paid to the bank.

February 4. Paid cash for the maturity value of NP26: principal, $100,000.00, plus interest, $750.00; total, $100,750.00. Check No. 370.

Notes Payable is decreased by a debit, $100,000.00. Expenditure—Other Charges, General Government is increased by a debit for the amount of interest expense, $750.00. Cash is decreased by a credit for the total amount paid, $100,750.00. The journal entry is shown above.

INVESTING IN SHORT-TERM INVESTMENTS

	DATE	ACCOUNT TITLE	DOC. NO.	POST. REF.	GENERAL DEBIT	GENERAL CREDIT	CASH DEBIT	CASH CREDIT	
					JOURNAL			PAGE 21	
					1	2	3	4	
19	1	Investments—Short Term	C385		300 000 00			300 000 00	19
20									20

Most of Sparta's property taxes, the major portion of the town's revenue, are collected by March 1 each year. Cash that will not be needed for several months is placed in short-term investments. Interest on these investments provides additional revenue.

March 1. Paid cash for a 4-month, 8% certificate of deposit, $300,000.00. Check No. 385.

A document issued by a bank as evidence of money invested with the bank is called a **certificate of deposit**. The time and interest rate to be paid are included on the certificate.

Investments—Short Term is increased by a debit for the amount of the certificate, $300,000.00. Cash is decreased by a credit for the same amount, $300,000.00. The journal entry is shown above.

REMEMBER The interest rate of a certificate of deposit usually increases as the time period increases. Interest rates of certificates are frequently tied to the prime rate.

EXPLAIN

- Explain that the entry for receiving cash from short-term investments is the same for a governmental organization or a company.

DEMONSTRATE

Analyze the transaction

- Draw three blank T accounts on the board.
- Read the transaction statement.
- Ask students to analyze the transaction by answering what accounts are affected, are they increased or decreased, and are they debited or credited. Complete the T accounts as the information is provided.

Record the transaction

- Use a transparency to illustrate recording the transaction in a multicolumn journal.
- Record each item in the journal.
- Ask a student to verify that, for this transaction, debits equal credits.

ONGOING ASSESSMENT

- Assessment is an ongoing process. Circulate through the classroom or lab observing which students have problems with the assignments.
- Troubleshooting: Students sometimes do not remember to reverse the original encumbrance when recording the exact amount of the expenditure.
- Assess student understanding by checking solutions to Independent Practice assignments.

RETEACH

- Make a transparency of a multicolumn journal. Call on a student to come to the front of the room and record the first line of the entry to record the receipt of goods received that had been previously encumbered. Continue in this way until the entire entry is recorded on the transparency.

RECEIVING CASH FROM SHORT-TERM INVESTMENTS

	DATE	ACCOUNT TITLE	DOC. NO.	POST. REF.	GENERAL DEBIT	GENERAL CREDIT	CASH DEBIT	CASH CREDIT	
22	1	*Investments—Short Term*	R572			300 000 00	308 000 00		22
23		*Interest Revenue*				8 000 00			23

JOURNAL — PAGE 51

When the certificate of deposit is due on July 1, cash is received for the original cost of the investment plus interest revenue earned.

July 1. Received cash for the maturity value of certificate of deposit due today: principal, $300,000.00, plus interest, $8,000.00; total, $308,000.00. Receipt No. 572.

Cash is increased by a debit for the amount of cash received, $308,000.00. Investments—Short Term is decreased by a credit for the certificate of deposit's original cost, $300,000.00. Interest Revenue is increased by a credit for the amount of interest earned, $8,000.00. The journal entry is shown above.

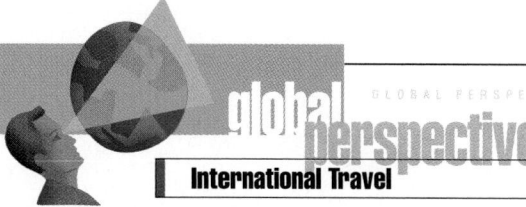

GLOBAL PERSPECTIVE • GLOBAL PERSPECTIVE • GLOBAL PERSPECTIVE

International Travel

International travel usually requires a passport. A passport is a formal document that allows exit from and reentry into a country. It proves citizenship and provides identity for the traveler.

First-time passport applicants must complete an application, which may be obtained from a United States Postal Service office. The application must be submitted with the following:

1. Proof of U.S. citizenship (usually a certified birth certificate).
2. Proof of identity (typically a document such as a driver's license).
3. Two identical 2" x 2" photographs (These photos must meet certain criteria. Many local photo studios advertise passport photo service.)
4. Fee. (The applicable fee when this textbook was written was $65.)

This information must be sent to a designated postal service office; a clerk of a federal or state court of records or a judge or clerk of a probate court who accepts applications; a U.S. consular official; or an agent at a passport agency in Boston, Chicago, Honolulu, Houston, Los Angeles, Miami, New Orleans, New York, Philadelphia, San Francisco, Seattle, Stamford, or Washington, D.C.

Required

Complete the following information that will be transferable to a passport application.

NAME: first, middle, and last name
ADDRESS: street, city, state, zip, country
PLACE OF BIRTH: city, state, country
DATE OF BIRTH: month, day, year
PERSONAL: Social Security number, height, color of hair, color of eyes
PHONE NUMBER: area code and home phone
FAMILY: father's name, birthplace, birth date, U.S. citizen (yes or no), mother's name, birthplace, birth date, U.S. citizen (yes or no)

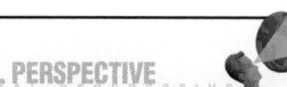

GLOBAL PERSPECTIVE

The Global Perspective feature is intended to expose students to some of the ways in which accounting and business in general differ in other countries. This particular feature allows students to explore international travel requirements. The activity requires students to provide the information that would be transferable to a passport application.

Students' solutions will vary. The instructor should consider the following items when grading the activity: (1) accuracy of information and (2) mechanics (grammar, spelling, punctuation).

terms review

encumbrance
general fixed assets
certificate of deposit

audit your understanding

1. What is an encumbrance?
2. What two entries are required when goods or services that have been encumbered are received?
3. Why does a governmental organization not record depreciation expense?
4. What is a certificate of deposit?

work together 23-3

Journalizing governmental encumbrances, expenditures, and other transactions

The town of River Falls uses a general fund for all financial transactions. Expenditures are recorded by type of expenditure and by department. The four categories of expenditures are personnel, supplies, other charges, and capital outlays. Departments are General Government, Public Safety, Public Works, and Recreation.

Page 1 of a journal is provided in the *Working Papers*. Source documents are abbreviated as follows: memorandum, M; check, C; notes payable, NP. Your instructor will guide you through the following examples.

Jan. 11. Paid cash for electrical service in public works department, $238.00. C482.
  16. Encumbered estimated amount for supplies in public safety department, $155.00. M111.
  19. Issued a one-month, 12% note, $200,000.00. NP15.
  27. Paid cash for public safety department supplies, $151.00, encumbered January 16 per M111. M125 and C497.
Feb. 6. Paid cash for printer for general government department, $395.00. C520. (Capital Outlays)
  19. Paid cash for the maturity value of NP15: principal, $200,00.00, plus interest, $2,000.00; total $202,000.00. C538.
Mar. 16. Paid cash for a 3-month, 10% certificate of deposit, $150,000.00. C567.
June 16. Received cash for the maturity value of certificate of deposit due today; principal, $150,000.00, plus interest, $3,750.00; total, $153,750.00. R312.

1. Journalize the transactions completed during the current year.

on your own 23-3

Journalizing governmental encumbrances, expenditures, and other transactions

The town of Annandale uses a general fund for all financial transactions. Expenditures are recorded by type of expenditure and by department. The four categories of expenditures are personnel, supplies, other charges, and capital outlays. Departments are General Government, Public Safety, Public Works, and Recreation.

Page 1 of a journal is provided in the *Working Papers*. Source documents are abbreviated as follows: memorandum, M; check, C; notes payable, NP. Work independently to complete the following problem.

Jan. 12. Paid cash for consultant's services in recreation department, $500.00. C267. (Personnel)
  17. Encumbered estimated amount for supplies in public works department, $215.00. M88.
  20. Issued a one-month, 10% note, $50,000.00. NP10.
  28. Paid cash for public works department supplies, $211.00, encumbered January 17 per M88. M95 and C282.
Feb. 7. Paid cash for desk for public safety department, $375.00. C294. (Capital Outlays)
  20. Paid cash for the maturity value of NP10: principal, $50,00.00, plus interest, $416.67; total $50,416.67. C322.
Mar. 17. Paid cash for a 3-month, 12% certificate of deposit, $75,000.00. C351.
June 17. Received cash for the maturity value of certificate of deposit due today; principal, $75,000.00, plus interest, $750.00; total, $75,750.00. R101.

1. Journalize the transactions completed during the current year.

Journalizing Expenditures, Encumbrances, and Other Transactions   Lesson 23-3   **701**

GUIDED PRACTICE

Terms Review
Call on students to define each term in the Terms Review. Ask the class if the definition is correct and whether the complete definition has been given or if anything needs to be added. Suggested definitions are given in the Glossary.

Audit Your Understanding
Call on students to answer the Audit Your Understanding questions. Ask the class if the answer is correct and/or complete. Answers are given in Appendix E of the textbook.

Work Together
Have students write the solution to the Work Together problem as you guide the class through the examples.

- Call on students to analyze each transaction.
- Direct students to record each transaction in the multicolumn journal as you elicit class participation in recording each entry.

INDEPENDENT PRACTICE

On Your Own
- Assign the On Your Own problem to be worked independently.
- Use the Ongoing Assessment techniques to diagnose student understanding.

Application Problem
- Assign Application Problem 23-3: Journalizing governmental encumbrances, expenditures, and other transactions.

Personal Trainer
- Students can access the Lesson 23-3 assessment material using this software.

Xtra! Web Site
- Students can access the Xtra! Study Tools for additional practice.

ENRICH
- Assign the Global Perspective feature on page 700.
- Assign Case 2 of Cases for Critical Thinking. Discuss the suggestion made by Edwin Mansky and the impact it could have on the controls which are the focus of governmental accounting.
- Students can use the Peachtree or QuickBooks data files to automate Application Problem 23-3.

CLOSE
- Have each student write a summary of what they remember about the entries used in governmental accounting to record transactions for encumbrances and expenditures.

PUTTING IT ALL TOGETHER

- Summarize the chapter by reviewing all the governmental transactions covered. Use an overhead projector to display a transparency of a multicolumn journal. Also review the purpose of governmental accounting—to control the expenditure of funds.

INDEPENDENT PRACTICE

- Assign Mastery Problem 23-4 to students who need the reinforcement of a problem that combines all transactions from the chapter in one problem; this will be most students.
- Assign Challenge Problem 23-5 to accelerated students who do not require the reinforcement of the Mastery Problem.
- Students can use Peachtree and QuickBooks data files to automate Mastery Problem 23-4.
- Assign Study Guide 23.
- Students can access Personal Trainer to work end-of-chapter problems on the computer.
- Students can access the Xtra! Web Site for the Xtra! Review and Quizzing.
- Students can access the Student Companion CD for additional review material.

ONGOING ASSESSMENT

- Review solutions to the assigned problems in class, diagnosing trouble spots.

RETEACH

- Call on students to describe how they avoid the trouble spots diagnosed.
- Use reteaching suggestions from section lesson plans as required.
- Assign Recycling Problem 23-1 if needed.

ENRICH

- Assign the Explore Accounting Feature. Ask students to share the information they have gathered in a report to the class.
- Students can access the Xtra! Web Site for the Xtra! Enrichment material.
- Assign Applied Communication.
- Assign the SCANS Workplace Competency.

- Assign Auditing for Errors.
- Assign Analyzing Costco's Financial Statements.
- Assign the Automated Accounting Activity on pages 708–709.

SUMMARY

After completing this chapter, you can

1. Define accounting terms related to budgeting and accounting for a not-for-profit governmental organization.
2. Identify accounting concepts and practices related to budgeting and accounting for a not-for-profit governmental organization.
3. Describe the process used to develop an operating budget.
4. Journalize budget transactions for a not-for-profit organization.
5. Journalize revenues for a not-for-profit organization.
6. Journalize expenditures, encumbrances, and other transactions for a not-for-profit organization.

Explore Accounting

EXPLORE ACCOUNTING • EXPLORE ACCOUNTING • EXPLORE ACC

Accounting in Not-for-Profit Organizations

When asked to think about accounting careers available in the not-for-profit sector, most people think about city, county, and state positions. Most often, these positions involve completing the accounting and reporting tasks required by these governmental agencies. However, there are other accounting-related careers in the not-for-profit sector that offer the opportunity for exciting and challenging positions. These opportunities include working for the Federal Bureau of Investigation (FBI), the Internal Revenue Service (IRS), and/or insurance companies in an area called "forensic accounting."

Forensic accounting is the investigation of accounting records and reports when fraud and/or embezzlement is suspected. Forensic accountants may help investigate crimes such as extortion, fraud, and embezzlement.

FBI agents may use interview and research techniques to investigate crimes. Requirements for employment as an FBI agent working in the accounting field include a four-year accounting degree from an accredited school and at least one year of experience in accounting or auditing. In addition, an agent must be a citizen of the U.S. between the ages of 23 and 35 and in good physical condition.

The IRS also employs accountants in various areas. Internal revenue agents are accountants who, by looking at the accounting records and tax returns of a business, determine if the business owes taxes and, if so, how much.

The IRS also employs internal auditors who examine the procedures and operations used with the IRS itself. A third position within the IRS is that of special agent. Special agents investigate tax fraud cases. Requirements for employment within the IRS vary, but most do include a four-year degree with some experience in the accounting field.

Insurance companies also hire accountants to assist in investigating cases involving suspected insurance fraud.

Required:
Contact the director of the FBI or a local IRS recruitment office to request more detailed information on job opportunities, requirements, and application procedures. Report your findings in written form.

Budgeting and Accounting for a Not-for-Profit Organization

EXPLORE ACCOUNTING
E X P L O R E   A C C O U N T I N G

Answers will vary according to the agency contacted by the student. As students write their reports, you may assign a group of students to create a bulletin board illustrating the job opportunities, requirements, and application procedures collected in the reports.

23-1 APPLICATION PROBLEM

Journalizing governmental operating budgets

Three towns, Appleton, Milltown, and Wilson, approved their annual general fund operating budgets effective January 1 of the current year. The available information about the budgets is as follows.

	Estimated Revenues	Budgetary Appropriations	Fund Balance
Appleton	$2,050,000.00	$2,009,000.00	$41,000.00
Milltown	794,500.00	789,200.00	5,300.00
Wilson	1,754,000.00	1,722,500.00	31,500.00

Instructions:

Journalize the entry to record the operating budgets for each of the three towns for the current year. Use page 1 of a journal.

23-2 APPLICATION PROBLEM

Journalizing governmental revenue transactions

Dalton's town council recently approved the town's general fund operating budget for the current year.

Transactions:

Jan.	1.	Recorded property tax levy: taxes receivable—current, $1,100,000.00; allowance for uncollectible taxes—current, $11,000.00; property tax revenue, $1,089,000.00. M88.
	8.	Received cash for current taxes receivable, $97,600.00. R134.
	14.	Received cash from traffic fines, $56.00. R147. (Other Revenue)
Feb.	11.	Received cash for current taxes receivable, $172,350.00. R194.
	16.	Received cash from parking meter receipts, $274.50. R212. (Other Revenue)
Mar.	1.	Recorded reclassification of current taxes receivable to delinquent status, $56,800.00, and the accompanying allowance for uncollectible accounts, $11,000.00. M107.
	12.	Received cash for delinquent taxes receivable, $10,700.00. R259.

Instructions:

Journalize the transactions for the current year. Use page 1 of a journal.

23-3 APPLICATION PROBLEM PEACHTREE QUICKBOOKS

Journalizing governmental encumbrances, expenditures, and other transactions

The town of Templeton uses a general fund for all financial transactions. Expenditures are recorded by type of expenditure and by department. The four categories of expenditures are personnel, supplies, other charges, and capital outlays. Departments are: General Government, Public Safety, Public Works, and Recreation.

Transactions:

Jan.	11.	Paid cash for supplies in public works department, $205.00. C244.
	15.	Encumbered estimated amount for supplies in public safety department, $235.00. M33.
Jan.	16.	Issued a one-month, 10% note, $150,000.00. NP6.
	28.	Paid cash for public safety department supplies, $232.00, encumbered January 15 per M33. M40 and C258.
Feb.	5.	Paid cash for calculator for general government department, $255.00. C267. (Capital Outlays)
	16.	Paid cash for the maturity value of NP6: principal, $150,000.00, plus interest, $1,250.00; total, $151,250.00. C279.
	28.	Encumbered estimated amount for supplies in public works department, $276.00. M49.

FORMAL EVALUATION

Chapter 23 Test
ExamView for Chapter 23
Assessment by Portfolio

- Review answers to all tests administered as a class activity. If time is limited, review only the items that were frequently answered incorrectly.

- Ask students if there are any questions about the chapter before proceeding to the next chapter.

CHECK FIGURES

Application Problem 23-1

Appleton: Debit Estimated Revenues, 2,050,000.00.
Milltown: Debit Estimated Revenues, 794,500.00.
Wilson: Debit Estimated Revenues, 1,754,000.00.

Application Problem 23-2

Cash Debit, 280,980.50.

Application Problem 23-3

Cash Credit, 352,580.00.

See Teacher's Edition of the Working Papers for Chapter 23 for complete solutions.

Mar. 15. Paid cash for a 3-month, 8% certificate of deposit, $200,000.00. C296.
18. Paid cash for public works department supplies, $278.00, encumbered February 28 per M49. M58 and C315.
21. Paid cash for consultant's services in recreation department, $360.00. C322. (Personnel)
June 15. Received cash for the maturity value of certificate of deposit due today: principal, $200,000.00, plus interest, $4,000.00; total, $204,000.00. R184.

Instructions:
Journalize the transactions for the current year. Use page 1 of a journal.

23-4 MASTERY PROBLEM PEACHTREE QUICKBOOKS
Journalizing governmental transactions

The town of Ingalls uses a general fund for all financial transactions. Expenditures are recorded by type of expenditure and by department. The four categories of expenditures are personnel, supplies, other charges, and capital outlays. Departments are: General Government, Public Safety, Public Works, and Recreation.

Transactions:
Jan. 2. Recorded current year's approved operating budget: estimated revenues, $1,270,000.00; appropriations, $1,224,000.00; budgetary fund balance, $46,000.00. M42.
2. Recorded current year's property tax levy: taxes receivable—current, $1,220,000.00; allowance for uncollectible taxes—current, $12,200.00; property tax revenue, $1,207,800.00. M43.
9. Received cash for current taxes receivable, $57,300.00. R105.
11. Paid cash for gas utility service in general government department, $234.00. C168.
12. Issued a 2-month, 9% note, $200,000.00. NP7.
16. Encumbered estimated amount for supplies in public works department, $165.00. M54.
20. Received cash from traffic fines, $225.00. R111. (Other Revenue)
30. Paid cash for lawn mower for public works department, $450.00. (Capital Outlays) C182.
Feb. 6. Paid cash for public works department supplies, $170.00, encumbered January 16 per M54. M58 and C190.
24. Encumbered estimated amount for supplies in recreation department, $133.00. M69.
Mar. 1. Recorded reclassification of current taxes receivable to delinquent status, $51,400.00, and the accompanying allowance for uncollectible accounts, $12,200.00. M76.
12. Paid cash for the maturity value of NP7: principal, $200,000.00, plus interest, $3,000.00; total, $203,000.00. C222.
20. Paid cash for a 3-month, 8% certificate of deposit, $400,000.00. C234.
22. Paid cash for recreation department supplies, $131.00, encumbered February 24 per M69. M88 and C241.
Apr. 10. Received cash for delinquent taxes receivable, $21,000.00. R355.
25. Paid cash for consultant's services in recreation department, $500.00. C266. (Personnel)
June 20. Received cash for the maturity value of certificate of deposit due today: principal, $400,000.00, plus interest, $8,000.00; total, $408,000.00. R497.

Instructions:
Journalize the transactions for the current year. Use page 1 of a journal.

Budgeting and Accounting for a Not-for-Profit Organization

23-5 CHALLENGE PROBLEM

Journalizing governmental transactions

Challenge Problem 23-5
Cash Debit, 778,358.00.

The town of Mabank uses a general fund for all financial transactions. Expenditures are recorded by type of expenditure and by department. The four categories of expenditures are personnel, supplies, other charges, and capital outlays. Departments are General Government, Public Safety, Public Works, and Recreation.

Transactions:

Jan. 2. Recorded current year's approved operating budget: estimated revenues, $1,528,000.00; appropriations, $1,542,100.00; budgetary fund balance, $14,100.00. M88.

(Note: Most towns prohibit deficit spending. In this case, a town would be prohibited from having a debit balance in the budgetary fund balance account. However, if sufficient fund equity is available at the beginning of a year, a town council may choose to appropriate more than the estimated revenues. The available fund equity would then be used for the amount that expenditures exceed revenues for the current period.)

2. Recorded current year's property tax levy: total amount of tax statements sent, $1,452,000.00; uncollectible taxes estimated at 1% of total tax levy. M89.

9. Received cash for current taxes receivable, $64,700.00. R111.

17. Paid cash for electric utility service in public works department, $286.00. C131.

20. Issued a 2-month, 12% note, $175,000.00. NP14.

25. Encumbered estimated amount for supplies in public safety department, $170.00. M102.

Feb. 3. Received cash from parking meter receipts, $1,158.00. R152.

10. Paid cash for public safety department supplies, $162.00, encumbered January 25 per M102. M130 and C188.

21. Paid cash for swing set for recreation department, $575.00. C199. (Capital Outlays)

Mar. 1. Recorded reclassification of current taxes receivable to delinquent status, $158,100.00, and the accompanying allowance for uncollectible accounts. M154.

Mar. 15. Paid cash for a 4-month, 9% certificate of deposit, $500,000.00. C220.

20. Paid cash for the maturity value of NP14: principal, $175,000.00, plus interest. C230.

21. Received cash for delinquent taxes receivable, $22,500.00. R206.

Apr. 4. Encumbered estimated amount for printer in general government department, $880.00. M178. (Capital Outlays)

16. Paid cash for general government department printer, $898.00, encumbered April 4 per M178. M190 and C267.

July 15. Received cash for the maturity value of certificate of deposit due today, $500,000.00, plus interest. R289.

Instructions:

Journalize the transactions for the current year. Use page 1 of a journal.

APPLIED COMMUNICATION

Student answers will vary. Answers should be grammatically correct and show an understanding of merge features in word processing programs.

CASES FOR CRITICAL THINKING

Case 1

Before any change in funds is considered, the original purpose for establishing the three funds should be determined. The funds may have been established by action of the town council. The funds may be required by county or state regulations. Normally, separate funds are created to place greater restrictions and control on the use of funds. Special taxing authority may have been approved by the town citizens to support specific services such as libraries or recreation. If a portion of the taxes is designated for the special purposes (libraries and recreation), then the separate funds should be retained. If there is no specific requirement or need for maintaining the special funds, such as town council authority or county or state regulations, then the three funds could be combined into a single general fund.

Case 2

When goods are ordered that will be delivered at some future date, a commitment is made to use resources when the goods arrive. However, to insure that commitments are not made for more than is authorized, entries for encumbrances are made. An encumbrance reserves the resources necessary to pay for the goods when they arrive. This process protects the organization from obligating itself for more than is authorized. Governmental organizations do not have a profit objective and thus cannot measure efficiency by the amount of profit earned. Consequently, greater control is placed on the use of financial resources by a governmental organization. An important part of the control is implemented through the development of budgets which, when approved, become authorizations to spend specific amounts for specific purposes.

SCANS WORKPLACE COMPETENCY

Remind students that technology education is critical for all students, regardless of where they are bound after high school. In today's global economy, a lack of technological skills results in lower-end employment opportunities.

706

• applied communication

When property taxes become delinquent, the city for which you work issues a Notice of Delinquency to the property owner. The notice is a form letter that includes:

- The address of the property
- The census tract number
- The name and address of the property owner
- The total tax due
- The amount of the tax that is delinquent

Required:

You have been asked to create a new form for the Notice of Delinquency. The form should be created to allow data to be merged into the form. Use the mail merge or similar feature of your word processor to create a suitable form letter.

• cases for critical thinking

Case 1

The town of Oneida has three funds in its accounting system: general, library, and recreation. Oneida's new town manager, Donna Ward, has questioned the necessity of having three separate governmental funds. Ms. Ward suggests combining all the funds into a single general fund. What do you recommend? Explain your answer.

Case 2

Edwin Mansky, a new accounting clerk with the town of Thornton, has been struggling with accounting entries involving encumbrances. He suggests that no entries be made until goods or services are received. When goods are received, an expenditure would be recorded. Encumbrances would not be necessary and the final results would be the same. What is your response to Mr. Mansky's suggestion? Explain your answer.

• SCANS workplace competency

Technology Competency: Applying Technology to Task

Concept: Technology-oriented employees use computers, software, and other related equipment to complete desired tasks.

Application: With your instructor's permission, contact a variety of local businesses, retailers, financial institutions, not-for-profit organizations, service providers, and educational institutions. Ask them to provide examples of how technology is used within their organizations to operate their businesses. Technology includes software, the Internet, e-mail, automated equipment, cellular phones, wireless systems, servers, data processing, networks, sensors, scanners, inventory tags, electronic registers, and fax machines. Present your findings to the class, using some form of technology.

• auditing for errors

An office clerk for the Town of Yorkville prepared the chart below, which lists all the account titles from the town's chart of accounts. For each account, a "+" (for an increase) or "−" (for a decrease) was recorded in the appropriate debit and credit column to show the impact of a debit or credit to each account's balance. The last column indicates the normal balance for each account. The intent of creating the chart is to provide an easy reference tool to help new accounting clerks accurately record journal entries and calculate general ledger balances.

Instructions:

Review the office clerk's chart below. Make a new chart so that the reference tool is accurate.

Account Title	Debit	Credit	Normal Balance
Cash	+	−	Dr.
Taxes Receivable—Current	−	+	Dr.
All. for Uncoll. Taxes—Current	+	−	Dr.
Taxes Receivable—Delinquent	−	+	Dr.
All. for Uncoll. Taxes—Delinquent	+	−	Dr.
Inventory of Supplies	−	+	Dr.
Accounts Payable	−	+	Cr.
Unreserved Fund Balance	−	+	Cr.
Reserve for Encumbrances—Current Year	+	−	Cr.
Reserve for Encumbrances—Prior Year	+	−	Cr.
Reserve for Inventory of Supplies	+	−	Dr.
Property Tax Revenue	−	+	Cr.
Other Revenue	−	+	Cr.
Expenditure—Personnel, General Government	+	−	Dr.
Expenditure—Supplies, General Government	+	−	Dr.
Expenditure—Other Charges, General Government	+	−	Dr.
Estimated Revenues	−	+	Cr.
Appropriations	−	+	Cr.
Budgetary Fund Balance	−	+	Cr.
Encumbrance—Personnel, General Government	+	−	Dr.
Encumbrance—Supplies, General Government	+	−	Cr.
Encumbrance—Other Charges, General Government	−	+	Cr.

• analyzing Costco's financial statements

Costco expects payment for merchandise at the time of sale. The company accepts cash, checks, debit cards, and credit cards. The company does not set up individual Costco accounts so that customers may buy now and pay Costco later. Therefore, the consolidated balance sheets do not show accounts receivable.

Instructions:

Using Appendix B in this textbook, refer to Costco's Notes to Consolidated Financial Statements to answer the following questions.

1. What is the content of net receivables?
2. What are the amounts for allowance for doubtful accounts on August 31, 2003 and September 1, 2002?
3. Do you think the allowance for doubtful accounts would increase or decrease if Costco granted credit to its customers?

Budgeting and Accounting for a Not-for-Profit Organization   Chapter 23   **707**

AUDITING FOR ERRORS

Account Title	Debit	Credit	Normal Balance
Cash	+	−	Dr.
Taxes Receivable—Current	+	−	Dr.
All. for Uncoll. Taxes—Current	−	+	Cr.
Taxes Receivable—Delinquent	+	−	Dr.
All. for Uncoll. Taxes—Delinquent	−	+	Cr.
Inventory of Supplies	+	−	Dr.
Accounts Payable	−	+	Cr.
Unreserved Fund Balance	−	+	Cr.
Reserve for Encumbrances—Current Year	−	+	Cr.
Reserve for Encumbrances—Prior Year	−	+	Cr.
Reserve for Inventory of Supplies	−	+	Cr.
Property Tax Revenue	−	+	Cr.
Other Revenue	−	+	Cr.
Expenditure—Personnel, General Government	+	−	Dr.
Expenditure—Supplies, General Government	+	−	Dr.
Expenditure—Other Charges, General Government	+	−	Dr.
Estimated Revenues	+	−	Dr.
Appropriations	−	+	Cr.
Budgetary Fund Balance	−	+	Cr.
Encumbrance—Personnel, General Government	+	−	Dr.
Encumbrance—Supplies, General Government	+	−	Dr.
Encumbrance—Other Charges, General Government	+	−	Dr.

ANALYZING COSTCO'S FINANCIAL STATEMENTS

1. "Receivables consist primarily of vendor rebates and promotional allowances, receivables from government tax authorities and other miscellaneous amounts due to the Company."

2. $1,529,000 for 2003; $2,224,000 for 2002.

3. Student answers will vary. Most likely the allowance for doubtful accounts would increase substantially. Presently, Costco essentially conducts cash transactions only. Granting customers credit would replace a portion of cash receipts with accounts receivable. It is doubtful that 100% of all accounts receivable would be collected.

TEACHING STRATEGIES   PORTFOLIO ASSESSMENT

It is possible that some students may work for governmental or other not-for-profit organizations. Students should select examples of journalizing not-for-profit transactions that have been successfully completed to include in their portfolio. A copy of the Portfolio Assessment form (blackline master in the Teacher's Resource Guide; also on the Student Companion CD) should be completed by the student and the Description section should include any comments regarding how the student mastered these concepts and procedures.

- Explain that Automated Accounting can be used to generate a performance report to compare budgeted and actual amounts for revenue and expense items.

- Emphasize that before a performance report can be prepared, budget amounts must be entered in the accounting database.

- Emphasize that to use budget information, the Budget option must be checked in the Company Info. Tab of the Customize Accounting System window.

Selecting the Budgeting feature

- Direct students to the top illustration on page 709 as you demonstrate clicking the Custom toolbar button and choosing the Company Info. tab in the Customize Accounting System window.

- Demonstrate clicking the checkbox for Budgeting under Features in the Company Info. tab.

Entering budget data

- Demonstrate clicking the Other toolbar button and choosing the Budgets tab of the Other Activities window.

- Direct students to the illustration on this page as you demonstrate entering the budget data for each revenue and expense account listed in the Account Title column.

- Explain that accounts may not be added from this screen.

- Explain that these budgeted amounts can be changed as often as necessary but that amounts are generally updated only once a year after the annual budget has been prepared and finalized.

Using Automated Reports for Analyzing Budget to Actual Business Activity

Businesses develop budgets as part of their planning processes. Budgets define in number terms the plans and expectations for the coming year. Budgets may be prepared by one or more managers or owners of the business. However, some businesses include all levels of management in their budgeting process. By including more people in the process, businesses expect greater success in meeting the goals established in the budgets.

The most common type of budget shows expected revenues and expenses for the coming year. Other types of budgets assist in planning for capital expenditures and cash management.

Entering Budget Data

Automated Accounting 8.0 and higher allows yearly budget amounts to be entered for all revenue and expense accounts. The data are entered using the Budgets tab of the Other Activities window. The complete list of revenue and expense accounts appears in the window as shown in the first illustration. Amounts are keyed for each account. The amounts should be the total planned revenue or expenditure for the year. (Note that accounts may not be added from this screen.)

Budgeted amounts can be changed as often as necessary. However, the amounts are generally updated only once a year. In many companies, budgets are prepared in November and December of the current year. The new budget amounts can then be entered into the software at the first of the year.

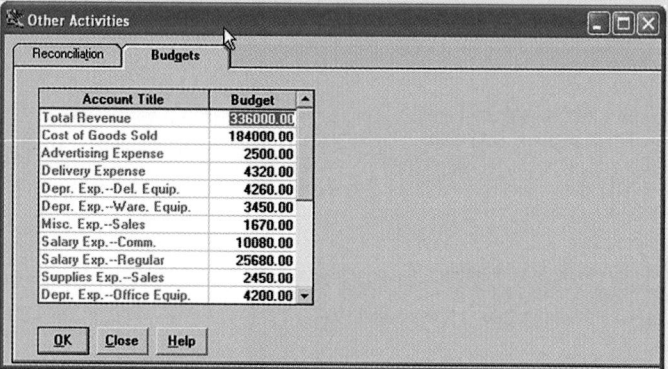

Using Budgets to Prepare Performance Reports

Before budgets can be used, two steps must be taken:

1. The Budgeting feature must be active. To activate this feature, click the check box beside Budgeting. This option is one of the features available in the Company Info. tab of the Customize Accounting System window as shown here.

2. Budget amounts must be entered for all revenue and expense accounts as described below.

When these steps have been taken, performance reports can be displayed as shown here. The performance report compares the budgeted amount to the actual amount for each revenue and expense. The report has four columns:

1. Budget. Shows the budgeted amount for the appropriate period.

2. Actual. Shows the amount reported for the revenue or expense on the income statement.

3. Diff. from Budget. Shows the difference between the budgeted amount and the actual amount

4. %. Displays the difference from budget expressed as a percentage.

The performance report is accessed through the Report Selection window. The report may be displayed or printed in the same manner as other financial reports.

Evaluating Performance Reports

Managers and business owners use performance reports to spot trends and to identify potential problem areas. If revenues are falling below budget, action can be taken to increase sales. If an expense category substantially exceeds budget, action may be needed to control the expenditure.

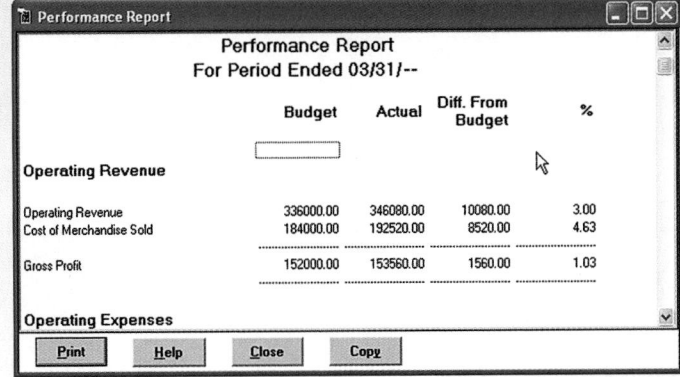

Budgeting and Accounting for a Not-for-Profit Organization

Chapter 23   **709**

EXPLAIN

- Remind students that the Budgeting feature must be turned on in the Company Info. Tab of the Customize Accounting System window.

- Explain that a performance report shows the budget and actual amounts for revenue and expense items as well as the difference between the actual and budgeted amounts and a percentage difference.

- Explain that budget amounts must be entered for all revenue and expense accounts before performance reports can be generated.

DEMONSTRATE

Generating a performance report

- Direct students to the illustration at the bottom of this page as you demonstrate how to generate a performance report.

- Demonstrate clicking the Reports toolbar button to open the Report Selection window.

- Demonstrate choosing Financial Statements from the Select a Report Group.

- Demonstrate choosing Performance Report from the Choose a Report to Display list.

- Demonstrate clicking the Print button to print the report of the Copy button to copy the report into another application.

PRACTICE

- Direct students to select a problem they have already completed, save it under a new name (such as XXXbudget), and experiment with the budgeting function. Direct students to print a performance report.

ASSESSMENT

- Review the performance report generated to assess student understanding.

TEACHING STRATEGIES   **PORTFOLIO ASSESSMENT**

Students should be encouraged to print at least one report from one of the Automated Accounting problems to include in their portfolio to demonstrate mastery of automated accounting systems. A copy of the Portfolio Assessment form (blackline master in the Teacher's Resource Guide; also on the Student Companion CD) should be completed by the student and the Description section should include any comments regarding how the student mastered these concepts and procedures.

Financial Reporting for a

	SCOPE & SEQUENCE	
	NEW	**REVIEW/ EXTENSION**
Introduce the Chapter	✓	
Lesson 24-1 Preparing a Work Sheet for a Governmental Organization		
Work sheet for a governmental organization		✓
Adjustments for a governmental organization		✓
Excess of revenues over expenditures		✓
Lesson 24-2 Preparing Financial Statements for a Governmental Organization		
Financial statements for a governmental organization		✓
Statement of revenues, expenditures, and changes in fund balance—budget and actual		✓
Balance sheet for a governmental organization		✓
Lesson 24-3 Recording Adjusting and Closing Entries for a Governmental Organization		
Adjusting and closing entries for a governmental organization		✓
Post-closing trial balance for a governmental organization		✓
Putting It All Together		

ENHANCING
SPECIAL FEATURES
• Accounting in the Real World: San Jose
• Making Ethical Decisions: Your Personal Code of Conduct
• Careers in Accounting • Cases for Critical Thinking 1
• Cases for Critical Thinking 2
• Explore Accounting • Xtra! Web Site: Xtra! Enrichment • Applied Communication • SCANS Workplace Competency • Graphing Workshop • Analyzing Costco's Financial Statements

Not-for-Profit Organization

INSTRUCTION		PRACTICE AND ASSESSMENT		
TECHNOLOGY AND MEDIA	**TEACHING STRATEGIES**	**GUIDED PRACTICE**	**INDEPENDENT PRACTICE**	**RETEACHING AND ENRICHMENT**
• Internet Research Activity • Accounting Xtra! Web Site	• Software Focus			
• Instructor's Resource CD: PowerPoint Slides • Xtra! Web Site: Xtra! Study Tools • Blackline Masters: Work Sheet • Personal Trainer	• Visually-Impaired Students	• Audit Your Understanding • Work Together 24-1	• On Your Own 24-1 • Application Problem 24-1 • Ongoing Assessment, p. 717 • Personal Trainer • Xtra! Web Site: Xtra! Study Tools	• Reteach, p. 717 • Enrich, p. 718
• Instructor's Resource CD: PowerPoint Slides • Xtra! Web Site: Xtra! Study Tools • Blackline Masters: Statement of Revenues, Expenditures, and Changes in Fund Balance • Personal Trainer	• Teaching Tip	• Audit Your Understanding • Work Together 24-2	• On Your Own 24-2 • Application Problem 24-2 • Ongoing Assessment, p. 722 • Personal Trainer • Xtra! Web Site: Xtra! Study Tools	• Reteach, p. 722 • Enrich, p. 723
• Instructor's Resource CD: PowerPoint Slides • Xtra! Web Site: Xtra! Study Tools • Blackline Masters: Multicolumn Journal and Post-Closing Trial Balance • Personal Trainer	• Applied Skills: Building Study Skills	• Audit Your Understanding • Work Together 24-3	• On Your Own 24-3 • Application Problem 24-3 • Ongoing Assessment, p. 725 • Personal Trainer • Xtra! Web Site: Xtra! Study Tools	• Reteach, p. 725 • Enrich, p. 726
• Automated Accounting • Peachtree and QuickBooks • Personal Trainer • Xtra! Web Site: Xtra! Review, Quizzing, and Enrichment • Student Companion CD			• Mastery Problem 24-4 • Peachtree and QuickBooks • Personal Trainer • Xtra! Web Site: Xtra! Review and Quizzing • Study Guide 24 • Student Companion CD • Chapter 24 Test • ExamView Chapter 24 • Portfolio Assessment	• Challenge Problem 24-5 • Reteach, p. 727 • Enrich, p. 727 • Recycling Problem 24-1 • Automated Accounting • QuickBooks • Xtra! Web Site: Xtra! Enrichment

CHAPTER

24 Financial Reporting for a Not-for-Profit Organization

OBJECTIVES & TERMS

After studying Chapter 24, you will be able to:

1. Identify accounting concepts and practices related to financial reporting for a not-for-profit governmental organization.

2. Prepare a worksheet for a governmental organization.

3. Prepare financial statements for a governmental organization.

4. Record adjusting and closing entries for a governmental organization.

Point Your Browser
accountingxtra.swlearning.com

710

ACCOUNTING IN THE REAL WORLD

1. Student answers will vary. However, students might recommend increasing city fees for building permits, inspections, and other city services, seeking new types of fees, selling surplus property or other assets, raising the city hotel tax for visitors, increasing the penalties for traffic violations, or possibly using past reserves.

2. Student answers will vary. Recommendations related to cost reductions might include eliminating employment positions within the city structure; reducing neighborhood services including library hours, recreation offerings, or street maintenance; closing city parks, police stations, and sport facilities; or postponing the construction of facilities that will increase staffing requirements.

INTERNET RESEARCH ACTIVITY

Answers will vary.

• San Jose

internet activity

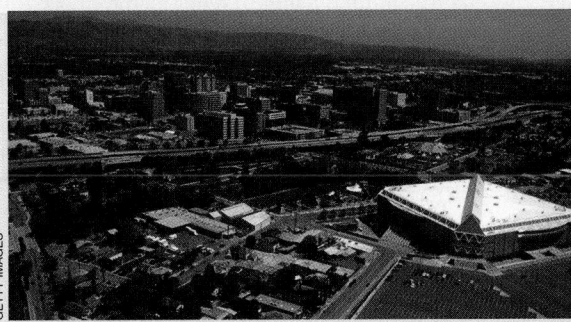

GETTY IMAGES

THE CITY OF SAN JOSE RESPONDS TO AN ECONOMIC DOWNTURN

San Jose was founded in 1777 and served as the first civilian settlement in California. Today, with a population of over 925,000, San Jose qualifies as the 11th largest city in the United States. It is recognized as the capital of Silicon Valley and is home for some of the most technologically oriented businesses in the world.

The city's total budget is normally in excess of $2 billion and is broken down into three main categories: general funds, special purpose funds, and capital funds. General funds are used to pay for expenses needed to operate the city. These might include maintaining police and fire services, libraries, public works, parks, recreation, cultural activities, and transportation. Special purpose funds are used for operations that receive special monies restricted for specific purposes, such as airports, water treatment, housing, waste management, storm sewers, or convention centers. Capital funds are used to improve the city's infrastructure, including road improvements, new police and fire stations, parks, community facilities, water pollution controls, library buildings, and additional street lights.

The economic downturn that began in 2001 had a significant impact on San Jose's operating budget. Sales tax receipts, the city's largest source of revenue for the general fund, declined considerably during the early 2000s. San Jose's proposed budget for the 2004–2005 operating year showed a $70 million funding gap for the general fund. Due to the shortage of revenues, the city was forced to make difficult decisions regarding its expenditures.

Critical Thinking

1. If you were a city manager or a city council member, what suggestions might you recommend to increase revenues in order to reduce the gap?
2. If you were a city manager or a city council member, what suggestions might you recommend to decrease expenditures in order to reduce the gap? Remember, if you are a city council member you need to keep in mind the best interests of your district's constituents. Election is just around the corner.

Source: www.sanjoseca.gov

Xtra!
Today
accountingxtra.swlearning.com

ONLINE COLLEGE ACCOUNTING CLASSES

Online learning can be very convenient for a person who cannot travel to a campus at set times to take a course or program of study. However, online learning still requires a commitment of time. An online course may take the same commitment of time as a conventional course, or even more.

Instructions

Search the Internet for "online accounting courses." Find two online accounting courses and answer the following questions about each course.

1. What are the names of the schools offering the online accounting courses?
2. How would you find out more information about the courses and the schools?

INTRODUCTION

24-1 Preparing a Work Sheet for a Governmental Organization

INTRODUCTION

- Have students read the paragraphs on this page. You may ask a student to read the paragraphs out loud for the class.

- Discuss the purposes of the financial statements for not-for-profit organizations.

- Have students try to visualize what differences they may expect to find in the financial statements for not-for-profit organizations.

OBJECTIVES

- Identify accounting concepts and practices related to financial reporting for a not-for-profit governmental organization.

- Prepare a worksheet for a governmental organization.

MOTIVATE

Remind students that a governmental organization does not have the goal of making a profit. Therefore, the financial statements of a governmental organization are different from those for a company. However, both organizations can use a work sheet to plan the adjustments and prepare financial statements.

Preview

- Direct students to read the headings on each page in this lesson and to examine the illustrations given.

MATERIALS

- **Instructor's Resource CD:** PowerPoint Slides

- **Xtra! Study Tools on the Xtra! Web Site**

- **Blackline Masters:** Work Sheet

- **Working Papers:** Teacher's Edition of the Working Papers for Lesson 24-1

- **Software:** Personal Trainer

Both businesses and not-for-profit organizations prepare financial statements periodically to report the results of financial activities. [CONCEPT: Accounting Period Cycle] However, financial information needed for not-for-profit organizations differs from that needed for businesses. A business measures performance primarily through determining the amount of net income. Thus, the accounting records are designed to emphasize the measurement of net income. In addition, the purpose of the income statement is to report the net income of the business. However, a not-for-profit organization's performance is measured primarily by the services provided and the efficiency with which resources are used. A not-for-profit organization does not prepare an income statement. Instead, it prepares a statement of revenues, expenditures, and changes in fund balance. A not-for-profit organization's financial statements are designed to provide information for the following purposes.

1. To make decisions about the use of resources.
2. To assess services provided and the ability to provide those services.
3. To assess management's financial accountability and performance.
4. To determine the assets, liabilities, and fund equity of the organization.

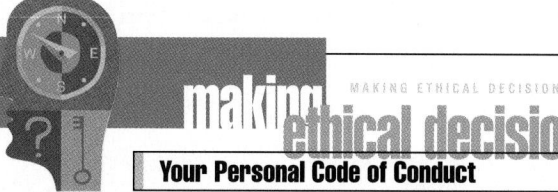

making ethical decisions

Your Personal Code of Conduct

Throughout this textbook you have evaluated a variety of ethical issues, researched the code of conduct of several professional organizations, and sought guidance in the code of conduct of real businesses. By completing these activities, you have learned one valuable lesson—ethical behavior is simply good business. Establishing and following a code of conduct provides direction for the business and its employees, ensuring that decisions are in the best long-term interest of the business and its stakeholders.

Do you have a code of conduct for your life? As an employee, colleague, business manager, or accountant, if you have a personal code of conduct you will be able to make both personal and business decisions that benefit your career and every stakeholder who is affected by your decisions in the long-term.

Instructions

Write a personal code of conduct. Begin by identifying six to ten major topics. Then write a single sentence that summarizes your beliefs for each major topic. Finish your code of conduct by adding additional information that will guide you in the future.

Financial Reporting for a Not-for-Profit Organization

MAKING ETHICAL DECISIONS
MAKING ETHICAL DECISIONS

This activity encourages students to establish a personal code of conduct. Encourage students to consult the codes of conduct for professional organizations and their favorite businesses for inspiration and ideas. Because students may be hesitant to share their answers, this activity should not be shared in class or submitted to the instructor.

RECORDING A TRIAL BALANCE ON A WORK SHEET

	ACCOUNT TITLE	TRIAL BALANCE DEBIT	TRIAL BALANCE CREDIT
	Town of Sparta General Fund		
	Work Sheet		
	For Year Ended December 31, 20--		
		1	2
1	Cash	78 3 6 0 00	
2	Taxes Receivable—Current		
3	Allow. for Uncoll. Taxes—Cur.		
4	Taxes Receivable—Delinquent	15 6 4 0 00	
5	Allow. for Uncoll. Taxes—Delin.		8 7 5 0 00
6	Interest Receivable		
7	Allow. for Uncoll. Interest		
8	Inventory of Supplies		
9	Investments—Short Term		
10	Accounts Payable		36 1 2 5 00
11	Notes Payable		
12	Unreserved Fund Balance		11 7 0 5 00
13	Res. for Encum.—Current Year		1 6 4 0 00
14	Res. for Encum.—Prior Year		
15	Reserve for Inv. of Supplies		
16	Property Tax Revenue		1594 0 0 0 00
17	Interest Revenue		8 7 8 5 00
18	Other Revenue		2 6 2 5 00
19	Expend.—Personnel, Gen. Gov't.	263 1 7 5 00	
20	Expend.—Supplies, Gen. Gov't.	11 9 4 0 00	
21	Expend.—Other Chgs., Gen. Gov't.	112 3 8 0 00	
22	Expend.—Cap. Outlays, Gen. Gov't.	16 0 0 0 00	
23	Expend.—Personnel, Public Safety	588 6 5 0 00	
24	Expend.—Supplies, Public Safety	19 7 9 0 00	
25	Expend.—Other Chgs., Pub. Safety	152 6 3 5 00	
26	Expend.—Cap. Outlays, Pub. Safety	89 3 5 0 00	
27	Expend.—Personnel, Public Works	113 3 0 0 00	
28	Expend.—Supplies, Public Works	5 5 4 0 00	
29	Expend.—Other Chgs., Pub. Works	47 3 4 0 00	
30	Expend.—Cap. Outlays, Pub. Works	51 1 7 5 00	
31	Expend.—Personnel, Recreation	58 1 1 0 00	
32	Expend.—Supplies, Recreation	1 9 6 0 00	
33	Expend.—Other Chgs., Recreation	25 1 0 5 00	
34	Expend.—Cap. Outlays, Recreation	11 5 4 0 00	
35	Estimated Revenues	1606 5 0 0 00	
36	Appropriations		1572 8 0 0 00
37	Budgetary Fund Balance		33 7 0 0 00
38	Encum.—Supplies, Public Safety	1 6 4 0 00	
39		3270 1 3 0 00	3270 1 3 0 00
40	Excess of Revenues Over Expend.		
41			

1. List all General Ledger accounts—except Encumbrances.

2. List encumbrance account with a balance.

3. Calculate totals.

The town of Sparta uses an eight-column work sheet similar to the one used by LampLight, Inc., in Part 4. However, the work sheets differ in one set of columns. Sparta's work sheet has Revenues/Expenditures Debit and Credit columns. LampLight's work sheet has Income Statement Debit and Credit columns.

A trial balance is entered in the Trial Balance columns as the first step in preparing a work sheet. All general ledger accounts except encumbrances are listed in the Account Title column in the same order as they appear in the general ledger, as shown here. Only encumbrance accounts with balances are listed. The Trial Balance columns are totaled to prove the equality of debits and credits.

STEPS   STEPS • STEPS • STEPS • STEPS • STEPS

RECORDING A TRIAL BALANCE ON A WORK SHEET

1 List all general ledger accounts except encumbrances in the Account Title column in the same order as they appear in the general ledger.

2 List only those encumbrance accounts with a balance in the Account Title column.

3 Total the trial balance columns. Compare totals to verify that the totals are equal.

FYI   FOR YOUR INFORMATION

Governments often issue bonds to pay for large projects, such as building schools and highways. Investors are not required to pay federal income tax on the interest income on these bonds.

EXPLAIN

- Review the definition of encumbrances: A commitment to pay for goods or services which have been ordered but not yet provided.
- Stress that the work sheet for a governmental organization begins with the trial balance columns—the same as a work sheet for a company.
- Emphasize that only encumbrances accounts with balances are listed in the Account Title column and included in the trial balance.

DEMONSTRATE

Record trial balance

- Use a transparency of a work sheet to demonstrate how to record the trial balance on the work sheet, following the three steps given.

- Point out that Sparta's work sheet uses the heading Revenues/Expenditures rather than Income Statement.

- Explain that the supplies remaining at the end of a period should be reported as an asset on the financial statements.

- Remind students that when an expenditure is made, it is reported during that fiscal period, regardless of the purpose of the payment. In addition, an amount equal to the inventory of supplies is recorded in a restricted fund equity account. This amount is not available for spending.

DEMONSTRATE

Record supplies adjustment

- Draw two blank T accounts on the board to analyze the adjustment for supplies.

- Direct students to the illustration as you show how to record the supplies adjustment on a work sheet.

- Use a transparency of a work sheet to demonstrate how to record the supplies adjustment on a work sheet.

ADJUSTMENT FOR INVENTORY OF SUPPLIES

Town of Sparta General Fund

Work Sheet

For Year Ended December 31, 20--

	ACCOUNT TITLE	TRIAL BALANCE		ADJUSTMENTS		REVENUES/EXPENDITURES		BALANCE SHEET		
		DEBIT	CREDIT	DEBIT	CREDIT	DEBIT	CREDIT	DEBIT	CREDIT	
6	Interest Receivable									6
7	Allow. for Uncoll. Interest									7
8	Inventory of Supplies			(a)2 8 2 0 00						8
9	Investments—Short Term									9
10	Accounts Payable		36 1 2 5 00							10
11	Notes Payable									11
12	Unreserved Fund Balance		11 7 0 5 00							12
13	Res. for Encum.—Current Year		1 6 4 0 00							13
14	Res. for Encum.—Prior Year									14
15	Reserve for Inv. of Supplies				(a)2 8 2 0 00					15
16	Property Tax Revenue		1594 0 0 0 00							16
17	Interest Revenue		8 7 8 5 00							17

Some general ledger accounts for governmental funds need to be brought up to date before financial statements are prepared. However, since governmental funds report expenditures and not expenses, no adjustments are needed for expense accounts. The actual amounts that have been spent and recorded as expenditures are the amounts reported.

Since governmental funds recognize revenues when the revenues become measurable and available, an adjustment may be needed to record some revenues.

Adjustments are planned on a work sheet. Sparta makes adjustments to three accounts: (1) Inventory of Supplies. (2) Interest Revenue. (3) Reserve for Encumbrances—Current Year.

Inventory of Supplies Adjustment

When supplies are bought, an expenditure account is debited. Some supplies may be unused at the end of a fiscal period. These unused supplies should be reported as an asset. [CONCEPT: Adequate Disclosure] Thus, an adjustment is made at the end of a fiscal period to record the remaining amount of supplies inventory as an asset, as shown above. Expenditure accounts debited when supplies were bought are

not adjusted. When an expenditure is made during a fiscal period, the expenditure is reported regardless of the purpose.

The total account balances of a governmental fund represent the equity of that fund. Thus, assets *less* liabilities *equals* total fund equity, which, unless reserved for a specified purpose, should represent resources that are available for appropriations and spending. The inventory of supplies, however, will be used by the organization. Therefore, this asset is not available for spending. To show that this asset, Inventory of Supplies, is not available for other uses, an equal amount of fund equity is reserved. Thus, the amount is credited to a restricted fund equity account titled Reserve for Inventory of Supplies.

Inventory of Supplies, an asset account, is increased by a debit for the amount of supplies on hand, *$2,820.00*. Reserve for Inventory of Supplies is increased by a credit for the same amount, *$2,820.00*.

Inventory of Supplies	
Adj. (a) 2,820.00	

Reserve for Inventory of Supplies	
	Adj. (a) 2,820.00

ADJUSTMENT FOR INTEREST REVENUE AND RESERVE FOR ENCUMBRANCES

		1	2	3	4	5	6	7	8	
		TRIAL BALANCE		ADJUSTMENTS		REVENUES/EXPENDITURES		BALANCE SHEET		
	ACCOUNT TITLE	DEBIT	CREDIT	DEBIT	CREDIT	DEBIT	CREDIT	DEBIT	CREDIT	
6	Interest Receivable			(b)2 5 6 5 00						6
7	Allow. for Uncoll. Interest				(b) 5 1 3 00					7
8	Inventory of Supplies			(a)2 8 2 0 00						8
9	Investments—Short Term									9
10	Accounts Payable		3 6 1 2 5 00							10
11	Notes Payable									11
12	Unreserved Fund Balance		1 1 7 0 5 00							12
13	Res. for Encum.—Current Year		1 6 4 0 00	(c)1 6 4 0 00						13
14	Res. for Encum.—Prior Year				(c) 1 6 4 0 00					14
15	Reserve for Inv. of Supplies				(a)2 8 2 0 00					15
16	Property Tax Revenue		1 5 9 4 0 0 0 00							16
17	Interest Revenue		8 7 8 5 00		(b)2 0 5 2 00					17
38	Encum.—Supplies, Public Safety	1 6 4 0 00								38
39		3 2 7 0 1 3 0 00	3 2 7 0 1 3 0 00	7 0 2 5 00	7 0 2 5 00					39

Town of Sparta General Fund
Work Sheet
For Year Ended December 31, 20--

Interest is assessed on all delinquent taxes. Interest on delinquent taxes becomes measurable and available when it is assessed. Thus, to bring the accounts up to date and record revenue earned but not collected at the end of the year, an adjustment is made, as shown above.

Sparta's interest due but not yet collected on December 31 is $2,565.00. Experience has shown that approximately 20% of this amount, $513.00 ($2,565.00 × 20%), will not be collected. Thus, the amount expected to be collected, $2,052.00 ($2,565.00 − $513.00), is recorded as revenue.

Interest Receivable	
Adj. (b) 2,565.00	

Allowance for Uncollectible Interest	
	Adj. (b) 513.00

Interest Revenue	
	Adj. (b) 2,052.00

At the end of a fiscal year, a governmental organization may have outstanding encumbrances—orders that have not yet been delivered. When goods are delivered that were encumbered against the preceding year's appropriations, the amount should not be recorded as an expenditure of the current period. Therefore, at the end of a fiscal period, the balance of Reserve for Encumbrances—Current Year, the amount of encumbrances outstanding, should be reclassified to prior year status. Then, when the prior year's orders arrive, they can be debited to Reserve for Encumbrances—Prior Year, rather than current year's expenditures. This procedure prevents charging expenditures of one year to another year's appropriations.

Reserve for Encumbrances—Current Year	
Adj. (c) 1,640.00	Bal. 1,640.00
	(New Bal. zero)

Reserve for Encumbrances—Prior Year	
	Adj. (c) 1,640.00

- Explain that an adjustment must be made to bring the accounts related to delinquent taxes up to date. These include interest receivable, interest revenue, and allowance for uncollectible interest.
- Explain that outstanding encumbrances (orders that have not yet been delivered) should not be recorded as an expenditure in the period received. Therefore, an adjustment must be made to reclassify these encumbrances to the prior year.

DEMONSTRATE

Record interest adjustment

- Draw three blank T accounts on the board to analyze the adjustment for interest on delinquent taxes.
- Direct students to the illustration as you show how to record the interest adjustment on a work sheet.
- Use a transparency of a work sheet to demonstrate how to record the interest adjustment on a work sheet.

Record encumbrance adjustment

- Draw two blank T accounts on the board to analyze the adjustment for reserve for encumbrances—prior year.
- Direct students to the illustration as you show how to record the adjustment on a work sheet.
- Use a transparency of a work sheet to demonstrate how to record the adjustment on a work sheet.

- Explain that all asset, liability, and fund equity account balances, except Reserve for Encumbrances—Prior Year, are extended to the Balance Sheet column.

DEMONSTRATE

Extend balance sheet accounts

- Direct students to the illustration as you show how to extend balance sheet accounts on a work sheet.

EXTENDING AMOUNTS TO REVENUES/EXPENDITURES AND BALANCE SHEET COLUMNS

Town of Sparta General Fund

Work Sheet

For Year Ended December 31, 20--

	ACCOUNT TITLE	TRIAL BALANCE DEBIT	TRIAL BALANCE CREDIT	ADJUSTMENTS DEBIT	ADJUSTMENTS CREDIT	REVENUES/EXPENDITURES DEBIT	REVENUES/EXPENDITURES CREDIT	BALANCE SHEET DEBIT	BALANCE SHEET CREDIT	
1	Cash	78360 00						78360 00		1
2	Taxes Receivable—Current									2
3	Allow. for Uncoll. Taxes—Cur.									3
4	Taxes Receivable—Delinquent	15640 00						15640 00		4
5	Allow. for Uncoll. Taxes—Delin.		8750 00						8750 00	5
6	Interest Receivable			(b)2565 00				2565 00		6
7	Allow. for Uncoll. Interest				(b) 513 00				513 00	7
8	Inventory of Supplies			(a)2820 00				2820 00		8
9	Investments—Short Term									9
10	Accounts Payable		36125 00						36125 00	10
11	Notes Payable									11
12	Unreserved Fund Balance		11705 00						11705 00	12
13	Res. for Encum.—Current Year		1640 00	(c)1640 00						13
14	Res. for Encum.—Prior Year				(c)1640 00		1640 00			14
15	Reserve for Inv. of Supplies				(a)2820 00				2820 00	15
16	Property Tax Revenue		159400 00				159400 00			16
17	Interest Revenue		8785 00		(b)2052 00		10837 00			17
18	Other Revenue		2625 00				2625 00			18
19	Expend.—Personnel, Gen. Gov't.	26317 50 00				26317 50 00				19
20	Expend.—Supplies, Gen. Gov't.	1194 0 00				1194 0 00				20
21	Expend.—Other Chgs., Gen. Gov't.	11238 0 00				11238 0 00				21
22	Expend.—Cap. Outlays, Gen. Gov't.	1600 0 00				1600 0 00				22
23	Expend.—Personnel, Public Safety	58865 0 00				40349 5 00 / 58865 0 00				23
24	Expend.—Supplies, Public Safety	1979 0 00				1979 0 00				24
25	Expend.—Other Chgs., Pub. Safety	15263 5 00				15263 5 00				25
26	Expend.—Cap. Outlays, Pub. Safety	8935 0 00				8935 0 00				26
27	Expend.—Personnel, Public Works	11330 0 00				85042 5 00 / 11330 0 00				27
28	Expend.—Supplies, Public Works	554 0 00				554 0 00				28
29	Expend.—Other Chgs., Pub. Works	4734 0 00				4734 0 00				29
30	Expend.—Cap. Outlays, Pub. Works	5117 5 00				5117 5 00				30
31	Expend.—Personnel, Recreation	5811 0 00				21735 5 00 / 5811 0 00				31
32	Expend.—Supplies, Recreation	196 0 00				196 0 00				32
33	Expend.—Other Chgs., Recreation	2510 5 00				2510 5 00				33
34	Expend.—Cap. Outlays, Recreation	1154 0 00				1154 0 00				34
35	Estimated Revenues	160650 0 00				9671 5 00 / 160650 0 00				35
36	Appropriations		157280 0 00				157280 0 00			36
37	Budgetary Fund Balance		3370 0 00				3370 0 00			37
38	Encum.—Supplies, Public Safety	1640 0 00				1640 0 00				38
39		327013 0 00	327013 0 00	7025 00	7025 00	317613 0 00	321560 2 00	99385 00	59913 00	39
40	Excess of Revenues Over Expend.					3947 2 00			3947 2 00	40
41						321560 2 00	321560 2 00	99385 00	99385 00	41

All asset, liability and fund equity account balances except Reserve for Encumbrances—Prior Year are extended to the Balance Sheet columns on the work sheet.

Financial Reporting for a Not-for-Profit Organization

TEACHING STRATEGIES   DIFFERENT LEARNING STYLES

Visually-Impaired Students. New technologies are continually being developed that assist visually-impaired students to participate fully in both school and business. Students must be aware of these technologies and know how to continually learn of new technologies. Using government agencies as a resource, assist the students in preparing a report concerning anticipated technologies.

The reserve for encumbrances accounts are listed as balance sheet accounts in the chart of accounts. During a fiscal period, the current year reserve for encumbrances account is used as a balancing account for the encumbrance accounts. Fund equity is not actually reduced when encumbrances are recorded. Therefore, the current year's reserve for encumbrances account is considered to be a budgetary account until accounts are closed at the end of a fiscal period. Therefore, the balance of Reserve for Encumbrances—Prior Year is extended to the Revenues/Expenditures columns of the work sheet, as shown on the previous page.

The balances of all temporary accounts are also extended to the work sheet's Revenues/Expenditures columns. Temporary accounts are closed at the end of each fiscal period. Temporary accounts include all revenue, expenditure, and budgetary accounts.

CALCULATING THE EXCESS OF REVENUES OVER EXPENDITURES

	Revenues/Expenditures Credit column total (line 39)	$ 3,215,602.00
Less	Revenues/Expenditures Debit column total (line 39)	3,176,130.00
Equals	Excess of revenues over expenditures	$ 39,472.00

The Revenues/Expenditures and Balance Sheet columns are totaled. Totals are written as shown on line 39 of the work sheet shown on the previous page. The difference between the Revenues/Expenditures Credit column total and the Debit column total is the excess of revenues over expenditures. If the Debit column total is larger, the difference is the excess of expenditures over revenues. Sparta's excess of revenues over expenditures is calculated as shown above.

COMPLETING THE WORK SHEET

The excess of revenues over expenditures, *$39,472.00*, is written under the work sheet's Revenues/Expenditures Debit column total on line 40 to make the two Revenues/Expenditures columns balance. The words *Excess of Revenues Over Expend.* are written in the Account Title column on the same line.

Sparta's excess of revenues over expenditures, *$39,472.00*, is also written under the Balance Sheet Credit column total on line 40 to make the two Balance Sheet columns balance.

When there is an excess of expenditures over revenues, the excess amount is written on a work sheet in the Revenues/Expenditures Credit and Balance Sheet Debit columns.

After the excess of revenues over expenditures is recorded on the work sheet, the last four columns are totaled again and ruled. Both pairs of Sparta's totals are the same. When the totals of each pair of columns are the same, the work sheet is assumed to be correct.

After the work sheet is completed, expenditures in the Revenues/Expenditures Debit column are totaled for each department. These totals are used in the preparation of financial statements. Departmental totals are written in small numbers below the amount of the last listed expenditure for the department. For General Government, lines 19 through 22, the total, *$403,495.00*, is written below line 22. For Public Safety, lines 23 through 26, the total, *$850,425.00*, is written below line 26. For Public Works, lines 27 through 30, the total, *$217,355.00*, is written below line 30. For Recreation, lines 31 through 34, the total, *$96,715.00*, is written below line 34.

GUIDED PRACTICE

Audit Your Understanding

Call on students to answer the Audit Your Understanding questions. Ask the class if the answer is correct and/or complete. Answers are given in Appendix E of the textbook.

Work Together

Have students write the solution to the Work Together problem as you guide the class through the examples.

- Call on students to analyze each adjusting entry.
- Direct students to record each adjusting entry on a work sheet.
- Direct students to complete the work sheet.

INDEPENDENT PRACTICE

On Your Own

- Assign the On Your Own problem to be worked independently.
- Use the Ongoing Assessment techniques to diagnose student understanding.

Application Problem

- Assign Application Problem 24-1: Preparing a work sheet for a governmental organization.

Personal Trainer

- Students can access the Lesson 24-1 assessment material using this software.

Xtra! Web Site

- Students can access the Xtra! Study Tools for additional practice.

ENRICH

- Assign Making Ethical Decisions on page 712.
- With your permission, have students contact a not-for-profit organization and interview someone in the accounting area. Develop a list of questions the student should ask regarding the training and education required to work in that person's position. Each student should prepare a written report of his/her findings.

• audit your understanding

1. What columns on a governmental organization's work sheet replace the Income Statement columns on a business's work sheet?
2. What accounts are affected, and how, when an interest revenue adjustment is recorded for a governmental organization?
3. To which column of a work sheet is the balance of Reserve for Encumbrances—Prior Year extended?
4. How is the excess of revenues over expenditures calculated on the work sheet?

• work together 24-1

Preparing a work sheet for a governmental organization

The town of Anoka uses a general fund. The trial balance for December 31 of the current year is recorded on a work sheet in the *Working Papers*. Your instructor will guide you through the following examples.

1. Analyze the following adjustment information and record the adjustments on the work sheet.

Supplies Inventory	$2,925.00
Interest Revenue Due but not Collected	2,490.00

An estimated 20% of the interest revenue due will not be collected.
The reserve for encumbrances for the current year is reclassified to prior year status.

2. Complete the work sheet. Save your work to complete Work Together 24-2 and 24-3.

• on your own 24-1

Preparing a work sheet for a governmental organization

The town of Annandale uses a general fund. The trial balance for December 31 of the current year is recorded on a work sheet in the *Working Papers*. Work independently to complete the following problem.

1. Analyze the following adjustment information and record the adjustments on the work sheet.

Supplies Inventory	$1,870.00
Interest Revenue Due but not Collected	2,180.00

An estimated 20% of the interest revenue due will not be collected.
The reserve for encumbrances for the current year is reclassified to prior year status.

2. Complete the work sheet. Save your work to complete On Your Own 24-2 and 24-3.

CLOSE

- As a group, have students recall the procedures for preparing a work sheet for a governmental organization. Ask one student to begin by stating the first step. Call on another student to state the next step. Continue until all steps are discussed.

LESSON • LESSON • LESSON • LESSON • LESSON • LESSON •

24-2 Preparing Financial Statements for a Governmental Organization

STATEMENT OF REVENUES, EXPENDITURES, AND CHANGES IN FUND BALANCE—BUDGET AND ACTUAL

2. List expenditures.   **1.** List revenues.

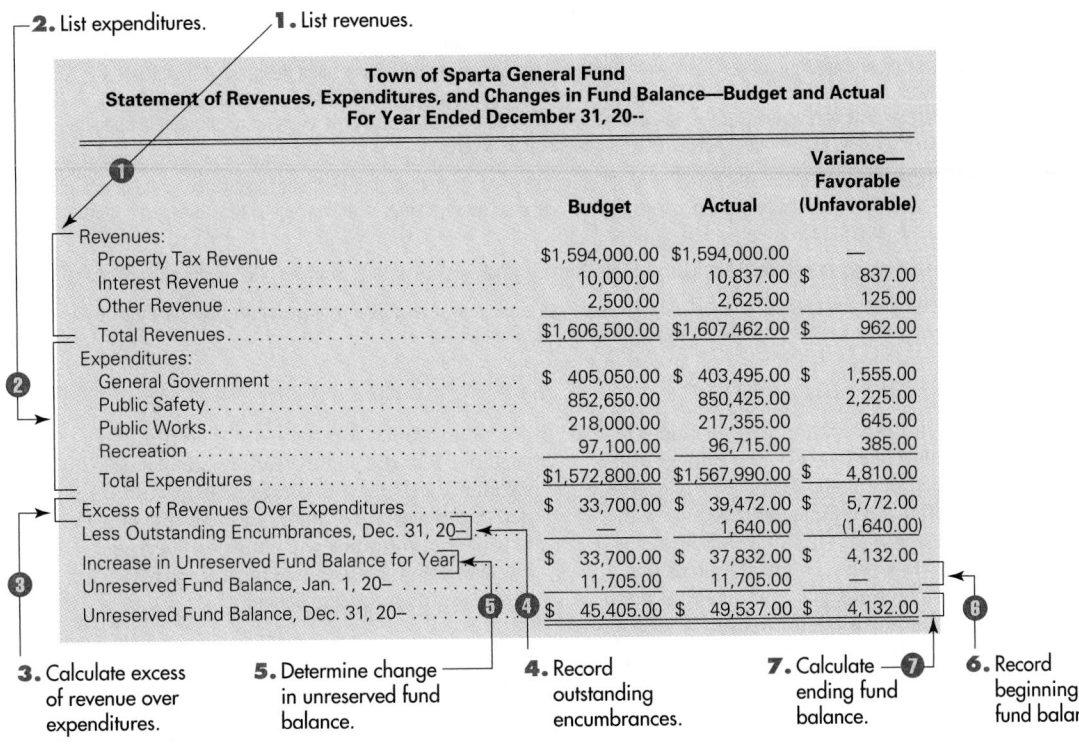

Town of Sparta General Fund
Statement of Revenues, Expenditures, and Changes in Fund Balance—Budget and Actual
For Year Ended December 31, 20--

	Budget	Actual	Variance— Favorable (Unfavorable)
Revenues:			
Property Tax Revenue	$1,594,000.00	$1,594,000.00	—
Interest Revenue	10,000.00	10,837.00	$ 837.00
Other Revenue	2,500.00	2,625.00	125.00
Total Revenues	$1,606,500.00	$1,607,462.00	$ 962.00
Expenditures:			
General Government	$ 405,050.00	$ 403,495.00	$ 1,555.00
Public Safety	852,650.00	850,425.00	2,225.00
Public Works	218,000.00	217,355.00	645.00
Recreation	97,100.00	96,715.00	385.00
Total Expenditures	$1,572,800.00	$1,567,990.00	$ 4,810.00
Excess of Revenues Over Expenditures	$ 33,700.00	$ 39,472.00	$ 5,772.00
Less Outstanding Encumbrances, Dec. 31, 20–	—	1,640.00	(1,640.00)
Increase in Unreserved Fund Balance for Year	$ 33,700.00	$ 37,832.00	$ 4,132.00
Unreserved Fund Balance, Jan. 1, 20–	11,705.00	11,705.00	—
Unreserved Fund Balance, Dec. 31, 20–	$ 45,405.00	$ 49,537.00	$ 4,132.00

3. Calculate excess of revenue over expenditures.

5. Determine change in unreserved fund balance.

4. Record outstanding encumbrances.

7. Calculate ending fund balance.

6. Record beginning fund balance.

Financial statements are prepared for each governmental fund. [*CONCEPT: Adequate Disclosure*] Sparta prepares two financial statements for its general fund. (1) Statement of revenues, expenditures, and changes in fund balance—budget and actual. (2) Balance sheet.

A statement of revenues, expenditures, and changes in fund balance—budget and actual reports the amount of revenues earned and expenditures made for a fiscal period. The changes in the unreserved fund balance from the beginning to the end of the fiscal period are also reported. In addition, actual revenues, expenditures, and unreserved fund balance are

compared with budgeted amounts for a fiscal period. [*CONCEPT: Accounting Period Cycle*]

Sparta's general fund statement of revenues, expenditures, and changes in fund balance—budget and actual for the fiscal year ended December 31 is shown above.

Information used to prepare the Budget column is obtained from the annual operating budget shown in Chapter 23, page 686. Information needed to prepare the Actual column is obtained from the work sheet's Revenues/Expenditures columns. The beginning fund balance that is used in both the Budget and Actual columns is obtained from the prior year's balance sheet.

Preparing Financial Statements for a Governmental Organization

Lesson 24-2 **719**

- Review the steps to complete the statement of revenues, expenditures, and changes in fund balance—budget and actual.

- Discuss how variances are calculated and which are favorable and unfavorable.

DEMONSTRATE

Complete the statement

- Use a blank transparency of the statement of revenues, expenditures, and changes in fund balance—budget and actual to illustrate how to complete the statement. Follow the steps given.

- Direct students to the illustration on page 719 as you use the steps given to complete the statement.

STEPS   STEPS • STEPS • STEPS • STEPS • STEPS • STEPS • STEPS • STEPS • STEPS • STEPS

PREPARING THE STATEMENT OF REVENUES, EXPENDITURES, AND CHANGES IN FUND BALANCE—BUDGET AND ACTUAL

1. List revenues by source. Sparta has three sources of revenues: property taxes, interest, and other. The total of all three sources of revenues is also shown.

2. List expenditures as totals for each department. Departments are responsible for controlling expenditures through budgeting and appropriations of specific amounts for each department. Thus, to aid the control process, amounts actually spent are reported for each responsible department. The total expenditures for the whole fund are also shown on the statement.

3. Calculate the excess of revenues over expenditures. If expenditures exceed revenues, the difference is labeled "excess of expenditures over revenues."

4. Record any outstanding encumbrances for the current year. Outstanding encumbrances are not deducted in figuring excess of revenues over expenditures. However, funds will be required in the future when the goods for which the encumbrances were made are delivered. Therefore, current year's encumbrances should be reported as a reduction in the current year's excess of revenues rather than in the next year when goods are paid for. Because no amount is budgeted for the encumbrances, the amount shown in the budget column is zero.

5. Deduct outstanding encumbrances from excess of revenues over expenditures to determine the change in the unreserved fund balance for the year. The remaining excess of revenues over expenditures is an increase in the unreserved fund balance for the current year.

6. Record the beginning unreserved fund balance. This January 1 balance is obtained from the prior year's balance sheet.

7. Calculate the ending unreserved fund balance. The increase in the unreserved fund balance for the year plus the beginning unreserved fund balance equals the ending unreserved fund balance.

Each amount recorded in the Variance column is the difference between the budget and actual amounts for the item. For example, the variance for other revenue is $125.00 (actual, $2,625.00, *less* budget, $2,500.00). Variances are considered favorable if actual results are better than the amount budgeted for that item. When actual revenues are more than budgeted revenues, variances are favorable. When actual revenues are less than budgeted revenues, variances are unfavorable. When actual expenditures are less than budgeted expenditures, variances are favorable. When actual expenditures are more than budgeted expenditures, variances are unfavorable. A reserve for encumbrances variance has the same effect as an expenditure variance. Because encumbrances are not budgeted, any variance will be unfavorable since an actual encumbrance will cause an increase. Unfavorable variances are indicated by placing the amounts in parentheses.

FYI   FOR YOUR INFORMATION

Governmental financial statements are often published in local newspapers.

REMEMBER   Parentheses are placed around unfavorable variances to show negative results.

Financial Reporting for a Not-for-Profit Organization

TEACHING STRATEGIES   TEACHING TIP

Instruct students to compare the differences and similarities between the statement of revenues, expenditures, and changes in fund balance—budget and actual in this chapter, and the income statement for a corporation in Chapter 14. List the differences and similarities on the chalkboard as students identify them.

CAREERS IN ACCOUNTING • CAREERS IN ACCOUNTING • CAREERS IN ACCOUNTIN

careers in accounting

Jerry Bienias, Vice President of Finance and Technical Operations

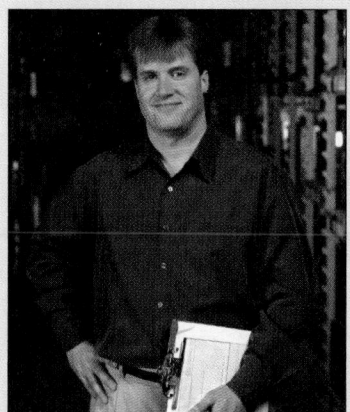

COURTESY OF JERRY BIENIAS

Do you have to be an expert in plastics in order to be successful as the Vice President of Finance and Technical Operations at a plastic molding company? Not according to Jerry Bienias, the person in that position. With over 20 years of experience, Jerry feels that "business is business, no matter what industry you are in."

Jerry's education includes a B.S. degree in Finance. He is also a Certified Management Accountant (CMA). He began his career holding numerous accounting positions at one company, including inventory accountant, cost accountant, cost analyst, and cost accounting supervisor. These positions gave him a great opportunity to not only expand his managerial and cost accounting skills but also offered the opportunity to develop his business skills. By working on many project teams looking at expanding into new markets, implementing new business systems, and analyzing business processes to reduce costs and remain competitive, he learned important lessons about business in general.

Jerry summarizes the importance of a broad background when he says, "In all cases, a strong grasp of how to identify and understand the costs in a business and then use that information to make informed business decisions is critical to success."

They are continually facing challenges at Donnelly Custom Manufacturing in Alexandria, Minnesota. Jerry says,"We are now faced with trying to reconfigure our businesses to compete in a world market where some companies pay employees 25 cents per hour—with no health benefits." These challenges may seem insurmountable, but Jerry believes that "a strong understanding of managerial and cost accounting principles and a willingness to expand beyond just accounting into the overall discipline of business can present a person with a challenging and rewarding career that can last a lifetime."

Salary Range: Salaries for financial managers vary with the size of the company and the industry, ranging from $75,000 to over $200,000.

Qualifications: Minimum educational level is a bachelor's degree in finance, accounting, economics, or business administration. A professional certification is also helpful. Interpersonal skills, especially working as part of a team, are important. Broad business knowledge, clear communications, creative thinking, and problem solving are also required skills.

Occupational Outlook: This occupational area moves with the economy. When the economy expands, newly created companies as well as established companies that are expanding will be looking for financial managers. Economic downturns will decrease the need for financial managers.

CAREERS IN ACCOUNTING

The Careers in Accounting feature profiles people who are entrepreneurs, who are working in accounting-related fields, or who use accounting in their business lives.

Students can access the Careers section of the Xtra! Web Site for additional material about careers.

- Present the governmental fund balance sheet and discuss how it is different from the balance sheet of a corporation.

- Stress that since a governmental fund does not have specific owners, the balance sheet has no owners' equity section.

- The difference between assets and liabilities is reported as fund equity.

- Emphasize that total assets must equal total liabilities and fund equity.

DEMONSTRATE

Complete the balance sheet

- Refer students to the illustration as the balance sheet for a governmental organization is explained.

ONGOING ASSESSMENT

- Assessment is an ongoing process. Circulate through the classroom or lab observing which students have problems with the assignments.

- Troubleshooting: Students may have trouble preparing the statement of revenues, expenditures, and changes in fund balance—budget and actual.

- Assess student understanding by checking solutions to Independent Practice assignments.

RETEACH

- Working in groups, have students make a list of the similarities and differences between the statement of revenues, expenditures, and changes in fund balance—budget and actual prepared for a governmental fund and the income statement prepared for a company.

- Call on an individual from one group to list one similarity. Call on an individual from another group to list another similarity. Continue in this way until all similarities and differences have been discussed.

BALANCE SHEET

Town of Sparta General Fund
Balance Sheet
December 31, 20--

ASSETS

Cash		$78,360.00
Taxes Receivable—Delinquent	$15,640.00	
Less Allowance for Uncollectible Taxes—Delinquent	8,750.00	6,890.00
Interest Receivable	$ 2,565.00	
Less Allowance for Uncollectible Interest	513.00	2,052.00
Inventory of Supplies		2,820.00
Total Assets		$90,122.00

LIABILITIES AND FUND EQUITY

Liabilities:		
Accounts Payable		$36,125.00
Fund Equity:		
Unreserved Fund Balance	$49,537.00	
Reserve for Encumbrances—Prior Year	1,640.00	
Reserve for Inventory of Supplies	2,820.00	
Total Fund Equity		53,997.00
Total Liabilities and Fund Equity		$90,122.00

A governmental fund balance sheet reports information about assets, liabilities, and fund equity for a specific date, usually the last day of a fiscal period. [CONCEPT: Adequate Disclosure] Assets and liabilities on a governmental fund balance sheet have characteristics similar to those on a corporation's balance sheet. However, a governmental fund does not have specific owners. Therefore, a governmental fund has no owners' equity section. Instead, the difference between assets and liabilities is reported as fund equity. Thus, unless restricted, fund equity represents the amount that is available for expenditures or encumbrances.

On December 31, Sparta's fund equity, consisting of three fund equity account balances, is $53,997.00. The Unreserved Fund Balance, *$49,537.00*, represents equity in the fund that has no restrictions (Total fund equity, $53,997.00, less Reserve for Encumbrances—Prior Year, $1,640.00, and less Reserve for Inventory of Supplies, $2,820.00). With proper authorization, Sparta may appropriate this amount for expenditures.

The other two fund equity account balances are reserved for specific purposes. The Reserve for Encumbrances—Prior Year, *$1,640.00*, is an amount of equity set aside for an encumbrance outstanding on December 31 of the prior year. When the goods arrive and are paid for in the current year for an order that was encumbered in a prior year, Reserve for Encumbrances—Prior Year is debited rather than Expenditures. Payment of the prior year's order closes the reserve for encumbrances account. The entry also avoids recording an expenditure in the current year for goods ordered in a prior year.

The Reserve for Inventory of Supplies, *$2,820.00*, represents the equity in inventory of supplies. Although supplies are assets, they are available for use, not spending. Therefore, part of the fund equity is reserved for the amount of supplies on hand. This reserve avoids appropriating the amount of equity that is represented by the asset supplies.

On a governmental fund balance sheet, total assets must equal total liabilities and fund equity. Sparta's balance sheet has total assets of $90,122.00. The total liabilities and fund equity is the same amount. The balance sheet is in balance and assumed to be correct.

Financial Reporting for a Not-for-Profit Organization

audit your understanding

1. What are the three columns found on a statement of revenues, expenditures, and changes in fund balance—budget and actual?

2. Where is the information obtained to prepare the Actual column of the statement of revenues, expenditures, and changes in fund balance—budget and actual?

3. When actual expenditures are less than budgeted expenditures, is the variance favorable or unfavorable?

4. What must total assets equal on a governmental fund balance sheet?

work together 24-2

Preparing financial statements for a governmental organization

Use the working papers from Work Together 24-2. The town of Anoka's general fund operating budget for the current year is given in the *Working Papers*. Your instructor will guide you through the following examples.

1. Prepare a statement of revenues, expenditures, and changes in fund balance—budget and actual for the year ended December 31 of the current year.

2. Prepare a balance sheet for December 31 of the current year.

on your own 24-2

Preparing financial statements for a governmental organization

Use the working papers from On Your Own 24-1. The town of Annandale's general fund operating budget for the current year is given in the *Working Papers*. Work independently to complete the following problem.

1. Prepare a statement of revenues, expenditures, and changes in fund balance—budget and actual for the year ended December 31 of the current year.

2. Prepare a balance sheet for December 31 of the current year.

Preparing Financial Statements for a Governmental Organization   Lesson 24-2   **723**

GUIDED PRACTICE

Audit Your Understanding
Call on students to answer the Audit Your Understanding questions. Ask the class if the answer is correct and/or complete. Answers are given in Appendix E of the textbook.

Work Together
Have students write the solution to the Work Together problem as you guide the class through the examples.

- Guide students through the preparation of the Revenues section of the statement of revenues, expenditures, and changes in fund balance—budget and actual.

- Working as a group, determine the budget and actual amounts to be recorded for Property Tax Revenue. When all students agree on the amounts, direct them to record the amounts on the form provided in the working papers.

- Continue to work as a group to determine the variance. When all students agree, direct them to record the amount on the form in the working papers. Repeat the process until the entire statement has been completed.

- Use the same process to complete the balance sheet.

INDEPENDENT PRACTICE

On Your Own
- Assign the On Your Own problem to be worked independently.
- Use the Ongoing Assessment techniques to diagnose student understanding.

Application Problem
- Assign Application Problem 24-2: Preparing financial statements for a governmental organization.

Personal Trainer
- Students can access the Lesson 24-2 assessment material using this software.

Xtra! Web Site
- Students can access the Xtra! Study Tools for additional practice.

CLOSE

- Have students outline the steps to prepare the financial statements for a governmental organization. Discuss the outlines prepared by the students, allowing students to edit their outlines as necessary.

ENRICH

- Assign the Careers in Accounting feature on page 721.
- Assign Case 1 of Cases for Critical Thinking. Discuss the revision of the financial statement suggested in the case.

24-3 Recording Adjusting and Closing Entries for a Governmental Organization

ADJUSTING AND CLOSING ENTRIES

JOURNAL PAGE 48

	DATE	ACCOUNT TITLE	DOC. NO.	POST. REF.	GENERAL DEBIT	GENERAL CREDIT	CASH DEBIT	CASH CREDIT	
1		*Adjusting Entries*							1
2	Dec. 31	Inventory of Supplies			2 8 2 0 00				2
3		Reserve for Inventory of Supplies				2 8 2 0 00			3
4	31	Interest Receivable			2 5 6 5 00				4
5		Allowance for Uncollectible Interest				5 1 3 00			5
6		Interest Revenue				2 0 5 2 00			6
7	31	Reserve for Encumbrances—Current Year			1 6 4 0 00				7
8		Reserve for Encumbrances—Prior Year				1 6 4 0 00			8
9		*Closing Entries*							9
10	31	Property Tax Revenue			1594 0 0 0 00				10
11		Interest Revenue			10 8 3 7 00				11
12		Other Revenue			2 6 2 5 00				12
13		Unreserved Fund Balance				1607 4 6 2 00			13
14	31	Unreserved Fund Balance			1567 9 9 0 00				14
15		Expenditure—Personnel, General Government				263 1 7 5 00			15
16		Expenditure—Supplies, General Government				11 9 4 0 00			16
17		Expenditure—Other Charges, General Government				112 3 8 0 00			17
18		Expenditure—Capital Outlays, General Government				16 0 0 0 00			18
19		Expenditure—Personnel, Public Safety				588 6 5 0 00			19
20		Expenditure—Supplies, Public Safety				19 7 9 0 00			20
21		Expenditure—Other Charges, Public Safety				152 6 3 5 00			21
22		Expenditure—Capital Outlays, Public Safety				89 3 5 0 00			22
23		Expenditure—Personnel, Public Works				113 3 0 0 00			23
24		Expenditure—Supplies, Public Works				5 5 4 0 00			24
25		Expenditure—Other Charges, Public Works				47 3 4 0 00			25
26		Expenditure—Capital Outlays, Public Works				51 1 7 5 00			26
27		Expenditure—Personnel, Recreation				58 1 1 0 00			27
28		Expenditure—Supplies, Recreation				1 9 6 0 00			28
29		Expenditure—Other Charges, Recreation				25 1 0 5 00			29
30		Expenditure—Capital Outlays, Recreation				11 5 4 0 00			30
31		Appropriations			1572 8 0 0 00				31
32	31	Budgetary Fund Balance			33 7 0 0 00				32
33		Estimated Revenues				1606 5 0 0 00			33
34		Unreserved Fund Balance			1 6 4 0 00				34
35	31	Encumbrance—Supplies, Public Safety				1 6 4 0 00			35

Sparta's adjusting entries are recorded on December 31, as shown above. Information needed for Sparta's adjusting entries is obtained from the work sheet's Adjustment columns.

> **REMEMBER** Governmental budgetary accounts are temporary accounts that are extended to the work sheet Revenue/Expenditures columns and closed at the end of the fiscal year.

CLOSING ENTRIES

Sparta's closing entries are also recorded on December 31, as shown on the previous page. Information needed for the closing entries is obtained from the work sheet's Revenues/Expenditures columns. The following four entries are made:

1. Close all revenue accounts to the unreserved fund balance account.
2. Close all expenditure accounts to the unreserved fund balance account.
3. Close the budgetary accounts. At the beginning of the fiscal year, estimated revenues and appropriations were recorded based on the approved operating budget. At the end of the fiscal year, these budgetary accounts are closed. This entry is the opposite of the original entry to record the operating budget.
4. Close the outstanding encumbrance accounts to the unreserved fund balance account. This entry reduces the unreserved fund balance account by the amount of the outstanding encumbrance for supplies, public safety, *$1,640.00.*

The balance of Reserve for Encumbrances—Prior Year, *$1,640.00*, has been a budgetary account balance. Thus, the account balance is listed in the work sheet's Revenues/Expenditures Credit column. However, after the outstanding encumbrance account is closed to Unreserved Fund Balance, Reserve for Encumbrances—Prior Year is considered a fund equity account. The account, therefore, is not closed. This account balance now is the amount of total fund equity that is reserved for outstanding encumbrances.

After posting the closing entries, all temporary accounts have zero balances and are prepared for a new fiscal period. The difference between revenues and expenditures has been transferred to the unreserved fund balance account. Fund equity amounts that are not available for appropriations are recorded in reserve accounts.

PREPARING A POST-CLOSING TRIAL BALANCE FOR A GOVERNMENTAL ORGANIZATION

Town of Sparta General Fund
Post-Closing Trial Balance
December 31, 20--

Cash	$78,360.00	
Taxes Receivable—Delinquent	15,640.00	
Allowance for Uncollectible Taxes—Delinquent		$ 8,750.00
Interest Receivable	2,565.00	
Allowance for Uncollectible Interest		513.00
Inventory of Supplies	2,820.00	
Accounts Payable		36,125.00
Reserve for Encumbrances—Prior Year		1,640.00
Reserve for Inventory of Supplies		2,820.00
Unreserved Fund Balance		49,537.00
Totals	$99,385.00	$99,385.00

After all end-of-fiscal-period activities are complete, a post-closing trial balance is prepared to prove the equality of debits and credits in the account balances, as shown above. Because the debit and credit balance totals equal, the general ledger accounts are ready for the new fiscal period. [*CONCEPT: Accounting Period Cycle*]

GUIDED PRACTICE

Audit Your Understanding

Call on students to answer the Audit Your Understanding questions. Ask the class if the answer is correct and/or complete. Answers are given in Appendix E of the textbook.

Work Together

Have students write the solution to the Work Together problem as you guide the class through the examples.

- Call on students to analyze each transaction.
- Direct students to record each transaction in the multi-column journal as you elicit class participation in recording each entry.

INDEPENDENT PRACTICE

On Your Own

- Assign the On Your Own problem to be worked independently.
- Use the Ongoing Assessment techniques to diagnose student understanding.

Application Problem

- Assign Application Problem 24-3: Journalizing adjusting and closing entries for a governmental organization.

Personal Trainer

- Students can access the Lesson 24-3 assessment material using this software.

Xtra! Web Site

- Students can access the Xtra! Study Tools for additional practice.

ENRICH

- Assign Case 2 of Cases for Critical Thinking. Discuss the suggestion made by Miss Bonilla and the impact it could have on the controls which are the focus of governmental accounting.
- Students can use the Peachtree data files to automate Application Problem 24-3.

CLOSE

- As a group, develop a summary of adjusting and closing entries for a governmental organization. Have a student write the summary on the board as it is being developed by the other students.

• audit your understanding

1. What are the sources of information for a governmental organization's adjusting entries?

2. Into what account are revenue and expenditure accounts closed?

3. What accounts are debited and credited to close the budgetary accounts?

4. Which of the following accounts will appear on a post-closing trial balance?

    Appropriations
    Reserve for Encumbrances—Prior Year
    Property Tax Revenue
    Taxes Receivable—Delinquent
    Budgetary Fund Balance
    Unreserved Fund Balance

• work together 24-3

Journalizing adjusting and closing entries for a governmental organization

Use the working papers from Work Together 24-1. Page 40 of a journal form is provided in the *Working Papers*. Your instructor will guide you through the following examples.

1. Journalize the adjusting entries.

2. Journalize the closing entries.

• on your own 24-3

Journalizing adjusting and closing entries for a governmental organization

Use the working papers from On Your Own 24-1. Page 52 of a journal form is provided in the *Working Papers*. Work independently to complete the following problem.

1. Journalize the adjusting entries.

2. Journalize the closing entries.

After completing this chapter, you can

1. Identify accounting concepts and practices related to financial reporting for a not-for-profit governmental organization.

2. Prepare a worksheet for a governmental organization.

3. Prepare financial statements for a governmental organization.

4. Record adjusting and closing entries for a governmental organization.

Xtra!
Review
accountingxtra.swlearning.com

Explore Accounting

EXPLORE ACCOUNTING · EXPLORE ACCOUNTING · EXPLORE ACCOUN

Governmental Accounting Standards Board

Governmental accounting is governed by the Governmental Accounting Standards Board (GASB). GASB was organized in 1984 to establish standards of financial accounting and reporting for governmental entities. These standards cover the preparation of external financial reports.

GASB's mission is "to establish and improve standards of state and local governmental accounting and financial reporting that will: (1) Result in useful information for users of financial reports and (2) Guide and educate the public, including issuers, auditors, and users of those financial reports."

When developing a new standard, GASB follows a process that permits input from individuals and groups. A task force studies a topic, seeks advice of experts, and may write a Discussion Memorandum. This Discussion Memorandum defines the problem, discusses the issue, and presents alternative solutions and the arguments and implications of each alternative solution.

A public hearing is then held to allow interested individuals or groups to give input relative to the issue and to suggest alternative solutions. Written input is also accepted. Board members

study the comments made during the open hearing period and discuss the issue until they have reached a conclusion.

An Exposure Draft is written and voted on by the Board. If a majority of the seven-member board approves the Exposure Draft, it is issued. Generally, a period of 60 days or more is allowed for written comments on the draft. After this public comment period is over, the Board will again study the comments received and issue a final Statement.

This Statement, when issued, will explain the new statement, its effective date, background information, and the basis for the Board's decision.

The seven members of the Board are selected from government, public accounting, and accounting education associations. Each member serves on a part-time basis.

Required:
Using your local library or the Internet, find the most recent Statement of Standard that has been issued by GASB. Report your findings in written form. Include the name and the effective date of the new Standard.

Financial Reporting for a Not-for-Profit Organization

Chapter 24　**727**

- Summarize the chapter by reviewing the end-of-period work required for a not-for-profit governmental organization. Also review the purpose of governmental accounting—to control the expenditure of funds.

INDEPENDENT PRACTICE

- Assign Mastery Problem 24-4 to students who need the reinforcement of a problem that combines all end of period work for a governmental organization in one problem; this will be most students.

- Assign Challenge Problem 24-5 to accelerated students who do not require the reinforcement of the Mastery Problem.

- Students can use Peachtree and QuickBooks data files to automate Mastery Problem 24-4.

- Students can use QuickBooks data files to automate Challenge Problem 24-5.

- Assign Study Guide 24.

- Students can access Personal Trainer to work end-of-chapter problems on the computer.

- Students can access the Xtra! Web Site for the Xtra! Review and Quizzing.

- Students can access the Student Companion CD for additional review material.

ONGOING ASSESSMENT

- Review solutions to the assigned problems in class, diagnosing trouble spots.

RETEACH

- Call on students to describe how they avoid the trouble spots diagnosed.

- Use reteaching suggestions from section lesson plans as required.

- Assign Recycling Problem 24-1 if needed.

EXPLORE ACCOUNTING
EXPLORE ACCOUNTING

Answers will vary, according to whether students research the most recent Statement of Standard adopted or the most recent statement of standard proposed. As students write their reports, they should be careful to include the name and the (proposed) effective date of the new standard.

ENRICH

- Assign the Explore Accounting Feature. Ask students to share the information they have gathered in a report to the class.

- Students can access the Xtra! Web Site for the Xtra! Enrichment material.

- Assign Applied Communication.

- Assign the SCANS Workplace Competency.

- Assign Graphing Workshop.

- Assign Analyzing Costco's Financial Statements.

- Assign the Automated Accounting Activity on page 735.

24-1 APPLICATION PROBLEM
Preparing a work sheet for a governmental organization

The town of Winona uses a general fund. The trial balance for December 31 of the current year is recorded on a work sheet in the *Working Papers*. The following adjustment information is available.

Adjustment Information, December 31

Supplies Inventory	$3,534.00
Interest Revenue Due but not Collected	2,900.00

An estimated 20% of the interest revenue due will not be collected.
The reserve for encumbrances for the current year is reclassified to prior year status.

Instructions:
1. Analyze the adjustment information and record the adjustments on the work sheet.
2. Complete the work sheet. Save your work to complete Application Problems 24-2 and 24-3.

24-2 APPLICATION PROBLEM
Preparing financial statements for a governmental organization

Use the work sheet prepared in Application Problem 24-1 to complete this problem.

The town of Winona's general fund operating budget for the current year is shown on page 729.

Instructions:
1. Prepare a statement of revenues, expenditures, and changes in fund balance—budget and actual for the year ended December 31 of the current year. The unreserved fund balance on January 1 was $41,244.00.
2. Prepare a balance sheet for December 31 of the current year.

24-3 APPLICATION PROBLEM (PEACHTREE)
Journalizing adjusting and closing entries for a governmental organization

Use the work sheet prepared in Application Problem 24-1 to complete this problem.

Instructions:
1. Use page 23 of a journal. Journalize the adjusting entries.
2. Continue using page 23 of a journal. Journalize the closing entries.

Town of Winona
Annual Operating Budget—General Fund
For Year Ended December 31, 20--

ESTIMATED REVENUES

Property Tax	$1,459,000.00	
Interest	8,950.00	
Other	9,000.00	
Total Estimated Revenues		$1,476,950.00

ESTIMATED EXPENDITURES AND BUDGETARY FUND BALANCE

General Government:		
Personnel	$ 250,250.00	
Supplies	13,230.00	
Other Charges	124,740.00	
Capital Outlays	14,600.00	
Total General Government		$ 402,820.00
Public Safety:		
Personnel	$ 414,740.00	
Supplies	22,000.00	
Other Charges	168,460.00	
Capital Outlays	81,270.00	
Total Public Safety		686,470.00
Public Works:		
Personnel	$ 157,730.00	
Supplies	6,160.00	
Other Charges	52,250.00	
Capital Outlays	46,350.00	
Total Public Works		262,490.00
Recreation:		
Personnel	$ 55,350.00	
Supplies	22,170.00	
Other Charges	27,780.00	
Capital Outlays	10,460.00	
Total Recreation		115,760.00
Total Estimated Expenditures		$1,467,540.00
Budgetary Fund Balance		9,410.00
Total Estimated Expenditures and Budgetary Fund Balance		$1,476,950.00

24-4 MASTERY PROBLEM

Completing the end-of-fiscal-period work for a governmental organization

The town of Duluth uses a general fund. The trial balance for December 31 of the current year is recorded on a work sheet in the *Working Papers*. The following adjustment information is available.

Adjustment Information, December 31

Supplies Inventory	$2,900.00
Interest Revenue Due but not Collected	2,350.00

An estimated 20% of the interest revenue due will not be collected.
The reserve for encumbrances for the current year is reclassified to prior year status.

Mastery Problem 24-4

2. Work Sheet column totals: Trial Balance, 2,633,500.00; Adjustments, 7,120.00; Revenues/Expenditures, 2,563,550.00; Balance Sheet, 119,070.00; Excess of Revenue Over Expenditures, 43,870.00.

3. Increase in Unreserved Fund Balance for the Year: Budget, 40,000.00; Actual, 42,000.00; Variance, 2,000.00, Favorable. (4) Total Assets, 111,660.00; Unreserved Fund Balance, 77,550.00; Total Fund Equity, 82,320.00.

Instructions:

1. Analyze the adjustment information and record the adjustments on the work sheet.
2. Complete the work sheet.

Duluth's general fund operating budget for the current fiscal year is as follows.

Town of Duluth
Annual Operating Budget—General Fund
For Year Ended December 31, 20--

ESTIMATED REVENUES

Property Tax	$1,265,000.00	
Interest	7,250.00	
Other	7,750.00	
Total Estimated Revenues		$1,280,000.00

ESTIMATED EXPENDITURES AND BUDGETARY FUND BALANCE

General Government:		
Personnel	$ 211,750.00	
Supplies	11,360.00	
Other Charges	106,700.00	
Capital Outlays	12,390.00	
Total General Government		$ 342,200.00
Public Safety:		
Personnel	$ 397,590.00	
Supplies	18,900.00	
Other Charges	144,290.00	
Capital Outlays	72,320.00	
Total Public Safety		633,100.00
Public Works:		
Personnel	$ 92,270.00	
Supplies	5,280.00	
Other Charges	44,770.00	
Capital Outlays	39,680.00	
Total Public Works		182,000.00
Recreation:		
Personnel	$ 48,220.00	
Supplies	1,880.00	
Other Charges	23,690.00	
Capital Outlays	8,910.00	
Total Recreation		82,700.00
Total Estimated Expenditures		$1,240,000.00
Budgetary Fund Balance		40,000.00
Total Estimated Expenditures and Budgetary Fund Balance		$1,280,000.00

3. Prepare a statement of revenues, expenditures, and changes in fund balance—budget and actual for the year ended December 31 of the current year. The unreserved fund balance on January 1 was $35,550.00.
4. Prepare a balance sheet for December 31 of the current year.
5. Use page 42 of a journal. Journalize the adjusting entries.
6. Continue using page 42 of the journal. Journalize the closing entries.

24-5 CHALLENGE PROBLEM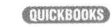

Completing end-of-fiscal-period work for a governmental organization

The town of Plymouth uses a general fund. The trial balance for December 31 of the current year is recorded on a work sheet in the *Working Papers*. The following adjustment information is available.

Adjustment Information, December 31

Supplies Inventory	$3,382.00
Interest Revenue Due but not Collected	6,080.00

An estimated 20% of the interest revenue due will not be collected.
The reserve for encumbrances for the current year is reclassified to prior year status.

Plymouth's general fund operating budget for the current fiscal year is shown as follows.

Town of Plymouth
Annual Operating Budget—General Fund
For Year Ended December 31, 20--

ESTIMATED REVENUES AND BUDGETARY FUND BALANCE		
Property Tax	$1,455,900.00	
Interest	13,360.00	
Other	16,580.00	
Total Estimated Revenues		$1,485,840.00
Budgetary Fund Balance		25,320.00
Estimated Revenues and Budgetary Fund Balance		$1,511,160.00

ESTIMATED EXPENDITURES		
General Government:		
Personnel	$ 260,480.00	
Supplies	14,280.00	
Other Charges	130,240.00	
Capital Outlays	15,130.00	
Total General Government		$ 420,130.00
Public Safety:		
Personnel	$ 484,610.00	
Supplies	23,080.00	
Other Charges	176,920.00	
Capital Outlays	84,920.00	
Total Public Safety		769,530.00
Public Works:		
Personnel	$ 113,300.00	
Supplies	6,660.00	
Other Charges	53,120.00	
Capital Outlays	48,875.00	
Total Public Works		221,955.00
Recreation:		
Personnel	$ 56,855.00	
Supplies	2,790.00	
Other Charges	28,925.00	
Capital Outlays	10,975.00	
Total Recreation		99,545.00
Total Estimated Expenditures		$1,511,160.00

Challenge Problem 24-5

2. Work Sheet column totals: Trial Balance, 3,104,485.00; Adjustments, 10,538.00; Revenues/Expenditures, 3,020,263.00; Balance Sheet, 115,089.00; Excess of Revenue Over Expenditures, 21,405.00.

3. Decrease in Unreserved Fund Balance for the Year: Budget, 25,320.00; Actual, 22,481.00; Variance, 2,839.00, Favorable.

4. Total Assets, 81,243.00; Unreserved Fund Balance, 40,969.00; Total Fund Equity, 45,427.00.

Plymouth's town council permits departmental managers to exceed budgeted amounts for supplies, other charges, and capital outlays. However, total amounts expended for these three types of expenditure must be within the total budget amounts for these three items within each department.

Plymouth is prohibited from deficit spending. However, if sufficient funds are on hand at the beginning of a year, the town council may choose to appropriate more than the estimated revenues. Sufficient funds are on hand when the beginning fund balance plus estimated revenues equals or exceeds appropriations.

Instructions:

1. Analyze the adjustment information and record the adjustments on the work sheet.
2. Complete the work sheet.
3. Prepare a statement of revenues, expenditures, and changes in fund balance—budget and actual for the year ended December 31 of the current year. The unreserved fund balance on January 1 was $63,450.00.
4. Prepare a balance sheet for December 31 of the current year.
5. Use page 40 of a journal. Journalize the adjusting entries.
6. Continue using page 40 of the journal. Journalize the closing entries.

• applied communication

In this course, you have learned a wide variety of facts and concepts about accounting and the business world. Regardless of your future educational and career goals, this knowledge will provide you with a sound foundation to become a productive member of society.

Instructions:

Prepare an essay to discuss how your knowledge of accounting will be useful to you in the future. How will accounting help you to complete your education, obtain a job, start a business, make personal investment decisions, and be succcessful in other facets of your life?

• cases for critical thinking

Case 1

The town of Spearman's statement of revenue, expenditures, and changes in fund balance—budget and actual lists expenditures by type. Expenditures listed are personnel, supplies, other charges, and capital outlays. Charles Lambert, a new accountant, suggested that expenditures be reported on this statement by departmental organization. Do you agree with Mr. Lambert? Explain your response.

Case 2

Vicki Bonilla, a new accounting clerk for the town of Evergreen, recorded the closing entries for the current year. Miss Bonilla questions the necessity of making a closing entry for encumbrance accounts with balances. She suggests not closing the encumbrances. Then when items are received for which the encumbrances were recorded, make the regular journal entries. That is, (1) reverse the encumbrance entry and (2) debit Expenditures and credit Cash. Do you agree with Miss Bonilla? Explain your response.

• SCANS workplace competency

Personal Qualities: Self-Management

Concept: Successful employees are able to assess their own knowledge, skill, and abilities accurately, set well-defined and realistic personal goals, monitor progress toward goal attainment, motivate themselves, exhibit self-control, respond to feedback non-defensively, and initiate action.

Application: Write down three realistic goals that you can achieve in one month. Remember, a long-term goal is attained by accomplishing many short-term goals. Your goals may be related to academics, attendance, tardiness, athletics, nutrition, exercise, homework, relationships, activities, college research, employment, or behavior. Make these goals challenging yet obtainable. Review your progress after two weeks and make needed adjustments. Prepare two copies of your goals; give one to your instructor and post the other in a location where you can review your goals every day.

APPLIED COMMUNICATION

Student answers should be grammatically correct and should make the instructor feel a sense of accomplishment for what students have learned.

CASES FOR CRITICAL THINKING

Case 1

Yes, agree with Charles Lambert. Financial control is a major purpose for governmental accounting since there is no profit motive to encourage good financial management. Control is generally implemented by assigning to each departmental manager of an organization accountability for financial control of the department. By reporting the budgeted and actual amounts expended by each department for an accounting period, statement readers can determine how well each department controlled its expenditures.

Case 2

No, disagree with Vicki Bonilla's suggestion. Encumbrances are recorded when a commitment is made to spend money. However, the expenditure transaction has not yet occurred. Thus the encumbrance account is a budgetary account and the reserve for encumbrances is a balancing account for encumbrances. If Encumbrances is not closed, this budgetary account balance would have to be reported on the only statement with account balances at year end—the balance sheet. A balance sheet reports only assets, liabilities, and fund equity. For Commitments to spend money in the future, encumbrances should not be reported on a balance sheet.

SCANS WORKPLACE COMPETENCY

Stress the importance of realistic and attainable goals. Emphasize goals must be challenging and beyond what the student is already accomplishing. Discuss commitment. Return written goals to students after two weeks and direct them to indicate their progress. Recollect the goal statements and return them again at the end of one month. Direct students to mark each goal as attained or not. Discuss factors that might prevent students from accomplishing their goals and how obstacles might be overcome. Ask students at the beginning of the activity if they would be willing to post their goals in the classroom.

GRAPHING WORKSHOP

1. The general government and recreation departments.

2. The public safety and public works departments.

3. The general government department had the largest budget (approximately $80,000.00) for expenditures.

ANALYZING COSTCO'S FINANCIAL STATEMENTS

1. Consolidated balance sheet, statement of income, statement of stockholders' equity, and statement of cash flows.

2. The 52-week periods ending September 1, 2002 and August 31, 2003.

3. "The accompanying consolidated financial statements of Costco Wholesale Corporation and subsidiaries as of September 2, 2001 were audited by other auditors who have ceased operations."

4. No, "standards require that we plan and perform the audit to obtain *reasonable* assurance about whether the consolidated financial statements are free of material misstatement."

5. No, an audit includes examining evidence on a "test basis," meaning that auditors examine only a sample of transactions.

6. KPMG from its Seattle, Washington office.

• graphing workshop

The town of Riverdale prepared a graph charting the budgeted and actual expenditures for each of its four departments.

Instructions:

Analyze the graph to answer the following questions.

1. Which departments showed favorable variances regarding their expenditures?

2. Which departments showed unfavorable variances regarding their expenditures?

3. Which department had the largest budget for expenditures? Approximately how much?

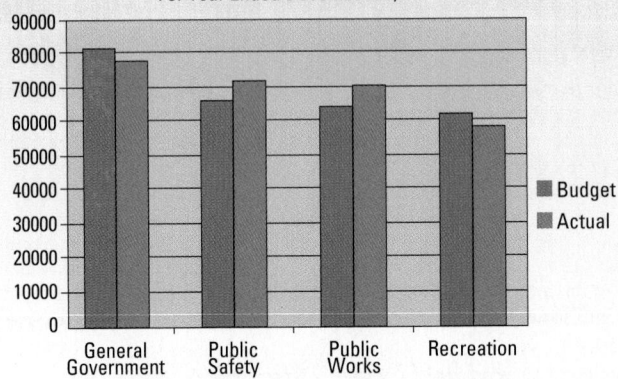

**Town of Riverdale
Statement of Expenditures**
For Year Ended December 21, 20--

• analyzing Costco's financial statements

Every publicly traded company is required to have an annual audit of its financial statements. Independent auditors—accountants from outside the company—examine how a company records transactions and prepares its financial statements. Auditors examine the records that support the financial records of a business to ensure that generally accepted accounting principles are followed. Based on their audit, the auditors issue an opinion that states whether the financial statements "present fairly, in all material respects, the consolidated financial position" of the company. The auditors' opinion gives external users confidence in the financial statement information. With this confidence, individuals and other companies are more likely to enter into business transactions.

Instructions:

Using Appendix B in this textbook, refer to the Independent Auditors' Report on page B-4 to answer the following questions.

1. List the four financial statements that were verified by independent auditors.

2. Identify the two fiscal periods reviewed by independent auditors.

3. State why the auditors' opinion does not cover all of the fiscal periods presented on the financial statements.

4. State whether the independent auditors are required by auditing standards to obtain "total and complete" assurance that the financial statements are free of material misstatement. Explain.

5. Determine if the independent auditors examine every business transaction conducted by Costco. Explain.

6. Name the public accounting firm and which office was responsible for the audit of Costco's financial statements in 2003.

TEACHING STRATEGIES   PORTFOLIO ASSESSMENT

Students should select an example of financial reporting activities for a not-for-profit organization to include in their portfolio. A copy of the Portfolio Assessment form (blackline master in the Teacher's Resource Guide; also on the Student Companion CD) should be completed by the student and the Description section should include any comments regarding how the student mastered these concepts and procedures.

· Automated Accounting

Using the Journal Wizard to Customize the Appearance of Journals

Throughout this text, the column headings in the journals have varied depending on the needs of the business. For example, departmentalized businesses have columns in the purchases journal for purchases made by each department.

Customizing Journals

Automated Accounting 8.0 and higher includes a utility that allows the user to define the amount columns to be included in the various journals. This utility is the Journal Wizard. A wizard is simply a step-by-step guide created by the programmer to help the user easily modify some aspect of the software or to easily complete a complex task.

The Journal Wizard is a tab located on the Customize Accounting System window. Before it can be used, a company must be set up. Modifications to journals should be made before any data are entered into the journals.

The control buttons for the wizard are located at the bottom of the Journal Wizard tab at the left. The buttons direct the user through the process. The user can move to the next screen, back a screen, finish the process, close the wizard without completing the task, or get help.

For each screen of the wizard, the user must carefully read the screen and make the appropriate choice. The screens contained in the wizard are described in the following paragraphs.

Select Journal

Only one journal at a time may be modified. If General Journal is selected, the next two screens do not appear.

Establish Offsetting Account

In most cases, the default account that appears with this screen will be the correct choice. However, the user may modify the account, the column type, and the column heading.

General Debit and Credit

This screen allows the user to include a General Debit and General Credit column in the journal. The default choice of the software is generally correct.

Special Journal Columns

This screen is used to identify all special columns in the journal. The user enters the account title, the header, and checks whether the account will be debited or credited. The header may have two lines. Each line is limited to 7 to 9 characters depending upon the font and the letters used.

After all items have been specified, click the Finish button. The Journal Wizard will complete the process. The modified journal will be available each time the company and problem are used. This journal is associated with the open company and problem. No other companies or problems are affected.

USING THE JOURNAL WIZARD
(Note: This template does not use data from a problem in the text.)

Instructions:

1. Load *Automated Accounting 8.0* or higher software.

2. Select database ARA-2 from the accounting template disk.

3. Select File from the menu bar and choose the Save As menu command. Key the path to the drive and directory that contains your data files. Save the database with a filename of XXX241 (where XXX are your initials).

4. Access Problem Instructions by clicking the Browser tool bar button.

5. Click the Custom tool and change the Company Info. to two departments.

6. Change the chart of accounts so that there are two purchase accounts: Purchases—Dept. 1 and Purchases—Dept. 2.

7. Use the Journal Wizard to change the purchases journal. Replace the Purch. Debit column with a Debit column for each of the two new purchases accounts.

8. Create a purchase on account transaction for each department and enter each in the purchases journal to test whether the journal has been changed properly.

9. Repeat the process for the sales journal and the cash receipts journal if time permits. Note that you will first need to change the chart of accounts so that there is a Sales account for each department. Note: To be a complete departmentalized accounting system, it would also be necessary to departmentalize the purchases and sales discount and returns and allowances account. However the purpose of this problem is to experiment with the Journal Wizard.

10. Exit the Automated Accounting software.

Financial Reporting for a Not-for-Profit Organization

Chapter 24   **735**

Accounting Concepts

Accountants follow concepts commonly accepted by the profession as guides for reporting and interpreting accounting information. The accounting procedures described in this textbook are based on the application of accepted concepts. Eleven commonly accepted concepts are described in this appendix and referenced throughout the textbook.

ACCOUNTING CONCEPTS

Accounting Period Cycle

Changes in financial information are reported for a specific period of time in the form of financial statements.

Financial statements summarize the financial information that a business records. The time period for which financial statements are prepared depends on the needs of the business. An accounting period may be one month, three months, six months, or one year. For tax purposes, every business prepares financial statements at the end of each year.

Adequate Disclosure

Financial statements contain all information necessary to understand a business' financial condition.

Owners, managers, lenders, and investors rely on financial statements to make informed decisions. All relevant financial information must be adequately and completely disclosed on financial statements.

A business reports only the total liabilities of $200,000.00 on its balance sheet. However, the total liabilities include $75,000.00 in current liabilities and $125,000.00 in long-term liabilities. Therefore, the balance sheet does not adequately disclose the nature of the liabilities. The critical information not disclosed is that $75,000.00 is current and due within a few months.

Business Entity

Financial information is recorded and reported separately from the owner's personal financial information.

A business's records must not be mixed with an owner's personal records and reports. For example, a business owner may buy insurance to protect the business and insurance to protect the owner's home. Only the insurance obtained for the business is recorded in the business' financial records. The insurance purchased for the owner's personal home is recorded in the owner's personal financial records. One bank account is used for the business and another for the owner. A business exists separately from its owners.

Consistent Reporting

The same accounting procedures must be followed in the same way in each accounting period.

Business decisions are based on the financial information reported on financial statements. Some decisions require a comparison of current financial statements with previous financial statements. If accounting information is recorded and reported differently each accounting period, comparisons from one accounting period to another may not be possible. For example, in one period a business reports $170,000.00 for total operating expenses and in the next period it reports $120,000 as cost of merchandise sold and $50,000 as operating expenses. A user of this information cannot adequately compare the two accounting periods. Therefore, unless a change is necessary to make information more easily understood, accounting information is reported in a consistent way for each accounting period.

Going Concern

Financial statements are prepared with the expectation that a business will remain in operation indefinitely.

New businesses are started with the expectation that they will be successful. Accounting records and financial statements are designed as though businesses will continue indefinitely. A business bought store equipment for $30,000.00. The store equipment is expected to last 10 years. Yearly depreciation, therefore, is recorded and reported based on the expected life of the equipment. After six years of the expected 10-year life, the equipment's book value (cost less accumulated depreciation) is $13,200.00. If the business ended operations and the equipment had to be sold, the amount received may be less than the $13,200.00. However, accounting records are maintained with the expectation that the business will remain in operation indefinitely and that the cost will be allocated over the useful life of the equipment. The equipment value, therefore, remains $13,200.00 on the records regardless of what the equipment may be worth when sold.

Historical Cost

The actual amount paid for merchandise or other items bought is recorded.

The actual amount paid for an item in a business transaction may be different from the value. For example, OfficeMart purchased a delivery truck valued at $20,000.00 and advertised at a sale price of $18,000.00. OfficeMart negotiated to purchase the delivery truck for $17,000.00 The amount recorded in accounting records for the delivery truck is the historical cost, $17,000.00—the actual amount paid.

Six months later, OfficeMart sells the delivery truck to Flowers by Giverney for $15,000.00. For Flowers by Giverney, the historical cost of the delivery truck is $15,000.00.

Matching Expenses with Revenue

The revenue from business activities and the expenses associated with earning that revenue are recorded in the same accounting period.

Business activities for an accounting period are summarized in financial statements. To adequately report how a business performed during an accounting period, all revenue earned as a result of business operations must be reported. Likewise, all expenses incurred in producing the revenue during the same accounting period must be reported. Matching expenses with revenue gives a true picture of business operations for an accounting period.

For example, a business had sales of $100,000.00 in December. Expenses before adjustment were $80,000.00. Adjustments for items such as uncollectible accounts expense, supplies expense, and depreciation expense totaled $5,000.00. Therefore, total expenses for December should be reported as $85,000.00. The matching of expenses with revenues results in an accurate report of net income of $15,000.00. By including all expenses, readers of the financial statements have a more complete picture of the financial condition of the business.

Materiality

Business activities creating dollar amounts large enough to affect business decisions should be recorded and reported as separate items in accounting items in accounting records and financial statements.

Business transactions are recorded in accounting records and reported in financial statements in dollar amounts. How the amounts are recorded and reported depends on the amount involved and the relative importance of the item in making business decisions. Dollar amounts that are large will generally be considered in making decisions about future operations. A separate accounting record is kept for items with dollar amounts large enough to be considered in making decisions about future operations. Dollar amounts that are small and not considered important in decision making may be combined with other amounts in the accounting records and financial statements.

For example, modems and print motors used to manufacture fax machines are considered direct materials and accounted for separately. Connectors and gears used in the manufacture of fax machines are parts with a small enough dollar value that they are grouped together and their total value is recorded in the accounting records as indirect material.

Objective Evidence

A source document is prepared for each transaction.

The source document is the original business paper indicating that the transaction did occur and that the amounts recorded in the accounting records are accurate and true. For example, a check is the original business paper for cash payments. The original business paper for purchases on account is the purchase invoice. When accounting information reported on the financial statements needs to be verified, an accountant will first check the accounting record. If the details of an entry need further checking, an accountant will then check the business papers as objective evidence that the transaction did occur.

Realization of Revenue

Revenue is recorded at the time goods or services are sold.

A business may sell either goods or services. Cash may be received at the time of sale or an agreement may be made to receive payment at a later date. Regardless of when cash is actually received, the sale amount is recorded in the accounting records at the time of sale. For example, a business sells office furniture for $2,000.00. The business agrees to an initial payment of $400.00 with the remaining balance to be divided in four monthly payments of $400.00 each. The full $2,000.00 of revenue is recorded at the time of sale even though $1,600.00 will be paid later.

Unit Of Measurement

Business transactions are reported in numbers that have common values—that is, using a common unit of measurement.

All transactions are recorded in accounting records in terms of money. Useful nonfinancial information may also be recorded to describe the nature of a business transaction. If part of the information in the accounting records is financial and part is nonfinancial, the financial statements will not be clear. For example, if Zytech states its sales in number of units sold (nonfinancial) and its expenses in dollars (financial), net profit cannot be calculated. Instead, total expenses (financial) subtracted from money taken in through sales (financial) equals profit.

Annual Report 2003

YEAR ENDED AUGUST 31, 2003

2003

TEN YEAR OPERATING AND FINANCIAL HIGHLIGHTS
(dollars in millions, except per share data)

WAREHOUSES IN OPERATIONS	2003		2002		2001		2000	
Beginning of year	374		345		313		292	
Openings	29		35		39		25	
Closings	(6)		(6)		(7)		(4)	
End of year	397		374		345		313	
OPERATING RESULTS								
Revenue								
Net Sales	$41,693	100.0%	$37,993	100.0%	$34,137	100.0%	$31,621	100.0%
Membership fees and other	853	2.0	769	2.0	660	1.9	543	1.7
Total revenue	42,546	102.0	38,762	102.0	34,797	101.9	32,164	101.7
Operating expenses								
Merchandise costs	37,235	89.3	33,983	89.4	30,598	89.6	28,322	89.6
Selling, general and administrative expenses	4,097	9.8	3,576	9.4	3,129	9.2	2,756	8.7
Preopening expenses	37	0.1	51	0.1	60	0.2	42	0.1
Provision for impaired assets and closing costs	20	0.0	21	0.1	18	—	7	—
Operating expenses	41,389	99.2	37,631	99.0	33,805	99.0	31,127	98.4
Operating income	1,157	2.8	1,131	3.0	992	2.9	1,037	3.3
Other income (expenses)								
Interest expense	(37)	(0.1)	(29)	(0.1)	(32)	(0.1)	(39)	(0.1)
Interest income and other	38	0.1	36	0.1	43	0.1	54	0.2
Provision for merger and restructuring expenses	—	—	—	—	—	—	—	—
Income from continuing operations before income taxes and cumulative effect of accounting change	1,158	2.8	1,138	3.0	1,003	2.9	1,052	3.3
Provision for income taxes	437	1.1	438	1.2	401	1.1	421	1.3
Income from continuing operations before cumulative effect of accounting change	721	1.7	700	1.8	602	1.8	631	2.0
Cumulative effect of accounting change, net of tax	—	—	—	—	—	—	—	—
Income from continuing operations	721	1.7	700	1.8	602	1.8	631	2.0
Discontinued operations:								
Income (loss), net of tax	—	—	—	—	—	—	—	—
Loss on disposal	—	—	—	—	—	—	—	—
Net income (loss)	$ 721	1.7%	$ 700	1.8%	$ 602	1.8%	$ 631	2.0%
Per Share Data—Diluted								
Income from continuing operations before cumulative effect of accounting change	$ 1.53		$ 1.48		$ 1.29		$ 1.35	
Cumulative effect of accounting change, net of tax	—		—		—		—	
Income from continuing operations	1.53		1.48		1.29		1.35	
Discontinued operations:								
Income (loss), net of tax	—		—		—		—	
Loss on disposal	—		—		—		—	
Net income (loss)	$ 1.53		$ 1.48		$ 1.29		$ 1.35	
Shares used in calculation (000's)	479,326		479,262		475,827		475,737	
Balance Sheet Data								
Working capital (deficit)	$ 700		$ 181		$ (230)		$ 66	
Property and equipment, net	6,960		6,524		5,827		4,834	
Total assets	13,192		11,620		10,090		8,634	
Short-term debt	47		104		195		10	
Long-term debt and capital lease obligations	1,290		1,211		859		790	
Stockholders' equity	6,555		5,694		4,883		4,240	
SALES INCREASE (DECREASE) FROM PRIOR YEAR								
Total	10%		11%		8%		17%	
Comparable units	5%		6%		4%		11%	
MEMBERS AT YEAR END (000'S)								
Business (primary cardholders)	4,636		4,476		4,358		4,170	
Gold Star	14,984		14,597		12,737		10,521	

	1999		1998		1997		1996		1995		1994	
	278		261		252		240		221		200	
	21		18		17		20		24		29	
	(7)		(1)		(8)		(8)		(5)		(8)	
	292		278		261		252		240		221	
	$26,976	100.0%	$23,830	100.0%	$21,484	100.0%	$19,214	100.0%	$17,906	100.0%	$16,161	100.0%
	480	1.8	440	1.8	390	1.8	352	1.8	341	1.9	320	2.0
	27,456	101.8	24,270	101.8	21,874	101.8	19,566	101.8	18,247	101.9	16,481	102.0
	24,170	89.6	21,380	89.7	19,314	89.9	17,345	90.3	16,226	90.6	14,663	90.7
	2,338	8.7	2,070	8.7	1,877	8.7	1,691	8.8	1,556	8.7	1,426	8.8
	31	0.1	27	0.1	27	0.1	29	0.1	25	0.1	25	0.2
	57	0.2	6	—	75	0.4	10	—	7	—	7	—
	26,596	98.6	23,483	98.5	21,293	99.1	19,075	99.2	17,814	99.5	16,121	99.8
	860	3.2	787	3.3	581	2.7	491	2.6	433	2.4	360	2.2
	(45)	(0.2)	(48)	(0.2)	(76)	(0.4)	(78)	(0.4)	(68)	(0.4)	(50)	(0.3)
	44	0.2	27	0.1	15	0.1	11	—	3	—	14	0.1
	—	—	—	—	—	—	—	—	—	—	(120)	(0.7)
	859	3.2	766	3.2	520	2.4	424	2.2	368	2.0	204	1.3
	344	1.3	306	1.3	208	0.9	175	0.9	151	0.8	93	0.6
	515	1.9	460	1.9	312	1.5	249	1.3	217	1.2	111	0.7
	(118)	(0.4)	—	—	—	—	—	—	—	—	—	—
	397	1.5	460	1.9	312	1.5	249	1.3	217	1.2	111	0.7
	—	—	—	—	—	—	—	—	—	—	(41)	(0.3)
	—	—	—	—	—	—	—	—	(83)	(0.5)	(182)	(1.1)
	$ 397	1.5%	$ 460	1.9%	$ 312	1.5%	$ 249	1.3%	$ 134	0.7%	$ (112)	(0.7%)
	$ 1.11		$ 1.01		$ 0.73		$ 0.61		$ 0.53		$ 0.25	
	(0.25)		—		—		—		—		—	
	0.86		1.01		0.73		0.61		0.53		0.25	
	—		—		—		—		—		(0.09)	
	—		—		—		—		(0.19)		(0.42)	
	$ 0.86		$ 1.01		$ 0.73		$ 0.61		$ 0.34		$ (0.26)	
	471,120		463,371		449,336		435,781		447,219		438,664	
	$ 450		$ 431		$ 146		$ 57		$ 9		$ (113)	
	3,907		3,395		3,155		2,888		2,535		2,146	
	7,505		6,260		5,476		4,912		4,437		4,236	
	—		—		25		60		76		149	
	919		930		917		1,229		1,095		795	
	3,532		2,966		2468		1,778		1,531		1,685	
	13%		11%		12%		7%		11%		7%	
	10%		8%		9%		5%		2%		(3%)	
	3,887		3,676		3,537		3,435		3,318		3,228	
	9,555		8,654		7,845		7,076		6,683		6,088	

INDEPENDENT AUDITORS' REPORT

To the Board of Directors and Shareholders:

We have audited the accompanying consolidated balance sheets of Costco Wholesale Corporation and subsidiaries as of August 31, 2003 and September 1, 2002 and the related consolidated statements of income, stockholders' equity and cash flows for the 52 weeks then ended. These consolidated financial statements are the responsibility of the Company's management. Our responsibility is to express an opinion on these consolidated financial statements based on our audits. The accompanying consolidated financial statements of Costco Wholesale Corporation and subsidiaries as of September 2, 2001 were audited by other auditors who have ceased operations. Those auditors expressed an unqualified opinion on those consolidated financial statements in their report dated October 8, 2001.

We conducted our audits in accordance with auditing standards generally accepted in the United States of America. Those standards require that we plan and perform the audit to obtain reasonable assurance about whether the consolidated financial statements are free of material misstatement. An audit includes examining, on a test basis, evidence supporting the amounts and disclosures in the consolidated financial statements. An audit also includes assessing the accounting principles used and significant estimates made by management, as well as evaluating the overall consolidated financial statement presentation. We believe that our audits provide a reasonable basis for our opinion.

In our opinion, the consolidated financial statements referred to above present fairly, in all material respects, the consolidated financial position of Costco Wholesale Corporation and subsidiaries as of August 31, 2003 and September 1, 2002, and the results of their operations and their cash flows for the 52 weeks then ended in conformity with accounting principles generally accepted in the United States of America.

As discussed in Note 1 to the consolidated financial statements, the Company changed its method of accounting for stock-based compensation effective September 3, 2002.

KPMG LLP

Seattle, Washington
October 6, 2003

COSTCO WHOLESALE CORPORATION
CONSOLIDATED BALANCE SHEETS
(dollars in thousands except par value)

	August 31, 2003	September 1, 2002
ASSETS		
CURRENT ASSETS		
Cash and cash equivalents	$ 1,545,439	$ 805,518
Receivables, net	556,090	474,861
Merchandise inventories	3,339,428	3,127,221
Other current assets	270,581	222,939
Total current assets	5,711,538	4,630,539
PROPERTY AND EQUIPMENT		
Land	2,173,685	2,017,184
Buildings, leaseholds and land improvements	4,831,236	4,367,395
Equipment and fixtures	1,846,324	1,733,979
Construction in progress	154,181	198,744
	9,005,426	8,317,302
Less accumulated depreciation and amortization	(2,045,418)	(1,793,683)
Net property and equipment	6,960,008	6,523,619
OTHER ASSETS	520,142	466,105
	$13,191,688	$11,620,263
LIABILITIES AND STOCKHOLDERS' EQUITY		
CURRENT LIABILITIES		
Short-term borrowings	$ 47,421	$ 103,774
Accounts payable	3,131,320	2,884,269
Accrued salaries and benefits	734,261	589,927
Accrued sales and other taxes	207,392	163,273
Deferred membership income	401,357	360,515
Other current liabilities	489,356	347,975
Total current liabilities	5,011,107	4,449,733
LONG-TERM DEBT	1,289,649	1,210,638
DEFERRED INCOME TAXES AND OTHER LIABILITIES	209,835	145,925
Total liabilities	6,510,591	5,806,296
COMMITMENTS AND CONTINGENCIES		
MINORITY INTEREST	126,117	119,730
STOCKHOLDERS' EQUITY		
Preferred stock $.005 par value; 100,000,000 shares authorized; no shares issued and outstanding	—	—
Common stock $.005 par value; 900,000,000 shares authorized; 457,479,000 and 455,325,000 shares issued and outstanding	2,287	2,277
Additional paid-in capital	1,280,942	1,220,954
Other accumulated comprehensive loss	(77,980)	(157,725)
Retained earnings	5,349,731	4,628,731
Total stockholders' equity	6,554,980	5,694,237
	$13,191,688	$11,620,263

The accompanying notes are an integral part of these consolidated financial statements.

COSTCO WHOLESALE CORPORATION

CONSOLIDATED STATEMENTS OF INCOME
(dollars in thousands, except per share data)

	52 Weeks Ended August 31, 2003	52 Weeks Ended September 1, 2002	52 Weeks Ended September 2, 2001
REVENUE			
Net sales	$41,692,699	$37,993,093	$34,137,021
Membership fees and other	852,853	769,406	660,016
Total revenue	42,545,552	38,762,499	34,797,037
OPERATING EXPENSES			
Merchandise costs	37,235,383	33,983,121	30,598,140
Selling, general and administrative	4,097,398	3,575,536	3,129,059
Preopening expenses	36,643	51,257	59,571
Provision for impaired assets and closing costs	19,500	21,050	18,000
Operating income	1,156,628	1,131,535	992,267
OTHER INCOME (EXPENSE)			
Interest expense	(36,920)	(29,096)	(32,024)
Interest income and other	38,525	35,745	43,238
INCOME BEFORE INCOME TAXES	1,158,233	1,138,184	1,003,481
Provision for income taxes	437,233	438,201	401,392
NET INCOME	$ 721,000	$ 699,983	$ 602,089
NET INCOME PER COMMON SHARE:			
Basic	$ 1.58	$ 1.54	$ 1.34
Diluted	$ 1.53	$ 1.48	$ 1.29
Shares used in calculation (000's)			
Basic	456,335	453,650	449,631
Diluted	479,326	479,262	475,827

The accompanying notes are an integral part of these consolidated financial statements.

COSTCO WHOLESALE CORPORATION

CONSOLIDATED STATEMENTS OF STOCKHOLDERS' EQUITY

For the 52 weeks ended August 31, 2003, the 52 weeks ended September 1, 2002
and the 52 weeks ended September 2, 2001
(in thousands)

	Common Stock		Additional Paid-In Capital	Other Accumulated Comprehensive Income/(Loss)	Retained Earnings	Total
	Shares	Amount				
BALANCE AT SEPTEMBER 3, 2000	447,297	$2,236	$1,028,414	$(117,029)	$3,326,659	$4,240,280
Comprehensive Income						
Net Income	—	—	—	—	602,089	602,089
Other accumulated comprehensive loss						
Foreign currency translation						
adjustment	—	—	—	(56,581)	—	(56,581)
Total comprehensive income	—	—	—	(56,581)	602,089	545,508
Stock options exercised including income tax						
benefits and other	4,457	23	97,129	—	—	97,152
BALANCE AT SEPTEMBER 2, 2001	451,754	2,259	1,125,543	(173,610)	3,928,748	4,882,940
Comprehensive Income						
Net Income	—	—	—	—	699,983	699,983
Other accumulated comprehensive income						
Foreign currency translation						
adjustment	—	—	—	15,885	—	15,885
Total comprehensive income	—	—	—	15,885	699,983	715,868
Stock options exercised including income tax						
benefits and other	3,571	18	95,402	—	—	95,420
Conversion of convertible debentures	—	—	9	—	—	9
BALANCE AT SEPTEMBER 1, 2002	455,325	2,277	1,220,954	(157,725)	4,628,731	5,694,237
Comprehensive Income						
Net Income	—	—	—	—	721,000	721,000
Other accumulated comprehensive income						
Foreign currency translation						
adjustment	—	—	—	79,745	—	79,745
Total comprehensive income	—	—	—	79,745	721,000	800,745
Stock options exercised including income tax						
benefits and other	2,154	10	47,919	—	—	47,929
Stock-based compensation	—	—	12,069	—	—	12,069
BALANCE AT AUGUST 31, 2003	457,479	$2,287	$1,280,942	$ (77,980)	$5,349,731	$6,554,980

The accompanying notes are an integral part of these consolidated financial statements.

COSTCO WHOLESALE CORPORATION

CONSOLIDATED STATEMENTS OF CASH FLOWS
(dollars in thousands)

	52 Weeks Ended August 31, 2003	52 Weeks Ended September 1, 2002	52 Weeks Ended September 2, 2001
CASH FLOWS FROM OPERATING ACTIVITIES			
Net income	$ 721,000	$ 699,983	$ 602,089
Adjustments to reconcile net income to net cash provided by operating activities:			
Depreciation and amortization	391,302	341,781	301,297
Accretion of discount on zero coupon notes	17,852	17,233	16,654
Stock-based compensation	12,069	—	—
Undistributed equity earnings in affiliates	(21,612)	(21,485)	(17,719)
Net loss/(gain) on sale of property and equipment and other	4,907	4,001	(15,934)
Provision for impaired assets	4,697	—	15,231
Change in deferred income taxes	68,693	12,179	40,797
Tax benefit from exercise of stock options	12,348	27,171	32,552
Change in receivables, other current assets, deferred income, accrued and other current liabilities	232,167	129,883	(6,159)
Increase in merchandise inventories	(162,759)	(380,158)	(271,355)
Increase in accounts payable	226,544	187,655	335,110
Total adjustments	786,208	318,260	430,474
Net cash provided by operating activities	1,507,208	1,018,243	1,032,563
CASH FLOWS FROM INVESTING ACTIVITIES			
Additions to property and equipment	(810,665)	(1,038,605)	(1,447,549)
Proceeds from the sale of property and equipment	51,829	32,849	110,002
Investment in unconsolidated joint venture	—	(1,000)	(28,500)
Decrease in short-term investments	—	4,928	41,599
Increase in other assets and other, net	(31,752)	(31,987)	(15,395)
Net cash used in investing activities	(790,588)	(1,033,815)	(1,339,843)
CASH FLOWS FROM FINANCING ACTIVITIES			
(Repayments)/proceeds from short-term borrowings, net	(58,144)	(99,175)	185,942
Net proceeds from issuance of long-term debt	59,424	300,000	81,951
Repayments of long-term debt	(11,823)	(18,540)	(159,328)
Changes in bank checks outstanding	(31,639)	(35,136)	216,661
Proceeds from minority interests	6,087	3,908	7,119
Exercise of stock options	34,667	66,771	62,000
Net cash (used in)/provided by financing activities	(1,428)	217,828	394,345
EFFECT OF EXCHANGE RATE CHANGES ON CASH	24,729	677	(8,985)
Increase in cash and cash equivalents	739,921	202,933	78,080
CASH AND CASH EQUIVALENTS BEGINNING OF YEAR	805,518	602,585	524,505
CASH AND CASH EQUIVALENTS END OF YEAR	$1,545,439	$ 805,518	$ 602,585
SUPPLEMENTAL DISCLOSURE OF CASH FLOW INFORMATION:			
Cash paid during the year for:			
Interest (excludes amounts capitalized)	$ 20,861	$ 9,511	$ 14,761
Income taxes	$ 320,546	$ 351,003	$ 363,649

The accompanying notes are an integral part of these consolidated financial statements.

COSTCO WHOLESALE CORPORATION

NOTES TO CONSOLIDATED FINANCIAL STATEMENTS
(dollars in thousands, except per share data)

Note 1—Summary of Significant Accounting Policies

Basis of Presentation

The consolidated financial statements include the accounts of Costco Wholesale Corporation, a Washington corporation, and its subsidiaries ("Costco" or the "Company"). All material inter-company transactions between the Company and its subsidiaries have been eliminated in consolidation. Costco primarily operates membership warehouses under the Costco Wholesale name.

Costco operates membership warehouses that offer low prices on a limited selection of nationally branded and selected private label products in a wide range of merchandise categories in no-frills, self-service warehouse facilities. At August 31, 2003, Costco operated 418 warehouse clubs: 309 in the United States; 61 in Canada; 15 in the United Kingdom; five in Korea; three in Taiwan; four in Japan; and 21 warehouses in Mexico with a joint venture partner.

The Company's investment in the Costco Mexico joint venture and in other unconsolidated joint ventures that are less than majority owned are accounted for under the equity method. The investment in Costco Mexico is included in other assets and was $167,293 at August 31, 2003 and $157,312 at September 1, 2002. The equity in earnings of Costco Mexico is included in interest income and other and for fiscal 2003, 2002 and 2001, was $21,400, $21,028 and $17,378, respectively. The amount of retained earnings that represents undistributed earnings of Costco Mexico was $86,074 and $64,674 at August 31, 2003 and September 1, 2002, respectively.

Fiscal Years

The Company reports on a 52/53-week fiscal year basis, which ends on the Sunday nearest August 31st. Fiscal years 2003, 2002 and 2001, were 52-week years.

Cash Equivalents

The Company considers all highly liquid investments with a maturity of three months or less at the date of purchase and proceeds due from credit and debit card transactions with settlement terms of less than five days to be cash equivalents. Of the total cash and cash equivalents of $1,545,439 at August 31, 2003 and $805,518 at September 1, 2002, credit and debit card receivables were $412,861 and $351,788, respectively.

Receivables, net

Receivables consist primarily of vendor rebates and promotional allowances, receivables from government tax authorities and other miscellaneous amounts due to the Company, and are net of allowance for doubtful accounts of $1,529 at August 31, 2003 and $2,224 at September 1, 2002. Management determines the allowance for doubtful accounts based on known troubled accounts and historical experience applied to an aging of accounts.

Vendor Rebates and Allowances

Periodic payments from vendors in the form of buy downs, volume or other purchase discounts that are evidenced by signed agreements are reflected in the carrying value of the inventory when earned and as a component of cost of sales as the merchandise is sold. Other consideration received from vendors is generally recorded as a reduction of merchandise costs upon completion of contractual milestones, terms of the related agreement, or by other systematic and rational approach.

NOTES TO CONSOLIDATED FINANCIAL STATEMENTS
(dollars in thousands, except per share data) (Continued)

Note 1—Summary of Significant Accounting Policies (Continued)

Merchandise Inventories

Merchandise inventories are valued at the lower of cost or market as determined primarily by the retail inventory method, and are stated using the last-in, first-out (LIFO) method for substantially all U.S. merchandise inventories. Merchandise inventories for all foreign operations are primarily valued by the retail method of accounting, and are stated using the first-in, first-out (FIFO) method. The Company believes the LIFO method more fairly presents the results of operations by more closely matching current costs with current revenues. The Company records an adjustment each quarter for the expected annual effect of inflation and these estimates are adjusted to actual results determined at year-end. The Company considers in its calculation of the LIFO cost the estimated net realizable value of inventory in those inventory pools where deflation exists and records a write down of inventory where estimated net realizable value is less than LIFO inventory. The LIFO inventory adjustment for the fourth quarter of fiscal 2003 increased gross margin by approximately $14,650 as compared to $21,000 in the fourth quarter of fiscal 2002. If all merchandise inventories had been valued using the first-in, first-out (FIFO) method, inventories would have been lower by $19,500 at August 31, 2003 and higher by $150 at September 1, 2002.

	August 31, 2003	September 1, 2002
Merchandise inventories consist of:		
United States (primarily LIFO)	$2,668,342	$2,552,820
Foreign (FIFO)	671,086	574,401
Total	$3,339,428	$3,127,221

The Company provides for estimated inventory losses between physical inventory counts on the basis of a standard percentage of sales. This provision is adjusted periodically to reflect the actual shrinkage results of the physical inventory counts, which generally occur in the second and fourth quarters of the Company's fiscal year.

Property and Equipment

Property and equipment are stated at cost. Depreciation and amortization expenses are computed using the straight-line method for financial reporting purposes. Buildings are generally depreciated over twenty-five to thirty-five years; equipment and fixtures are depreciated over three to ten years; and leasehold improvements are amortized over the initial term of the lease.

Interest costs incurred on property and equipment during the construction period are capitalized. The amount of interest costs capitalized was $3,272 in fiscal 2003, $13,480 in fiscal 2002, and $19,157 in fiscal 2001.

Impairment of Long-Lived Assets

The Company periodically evaluates the realizability of long-lived assets for impairment when events or changes in circumstances occur, which may indicate the carrying amount of the asset may not be recoverable. The Company evaluates the carrying value of the asset by comparing the estimated future undiscounted cash flows generated from the use of the asset and its eventual disposition with the asset's reported net book value. In accordance with Statement of Financial Accounting Standards (SFAS) No. 144, the Company recorded a pre-tax, non-cash charge of $4,697 in fiscal 2003 and $0 and $15,231 in fiscal 2002 and 2001, respectively, reflecting its estimate of impairment relating to scheduled warehouse closings. The charge reflects the difference between the carrying value and fair value, which was based on estimated market valuations for those assets whose carrying value is not currently anticipated to be recoverable through future cash flows.

Note 1—Summary of Significant Accounting Policies (Continued)

Goodwill

Goodwill, net of accumulated amortization, resulting from certain business combinations is included in other assets, and totaled $46,549 at August 31, 2003 and $43,920 at September 1, 2002. On September 3, 2001, the Company adopted SFAS No. 142, "Accounting for Goodwill and Other Intangibles," which specifies that goodwill and some intangible assets will no longer be amortized, but instead will be subject to periodic impairment testing. Accordingly, the Company reviews previously reported goodwill for impairment on an annual basis, or more frequently if circumstances dictate. In fiscal 2001 goodwill was amortized on a straight-line basis over lives ranging from two to forty years and was periodically evaluated for impairment as circumstances dictated. The effects on net income and net income per share data would not be significant if the Company had followed the provisions of SFAS No. 142 in the year ended September 2, 2001.

Accounts Payable

The Company's banking system provides for the daily replenishment of major bank accounts as checks are presented. Accordingly, included in accounts payable at August 31, 2003 and September 1, 2002 are $216,980 and $235,458 respectively, representing the excess of outstanding checks over cash on deposit at the banks on which the checks were drawn.

Insurance/Self Insurance Liabilities

The Company uses a combination of insurance and self-insurance mechanisms to provide for the potential liabilities for workers' compensation, general liability, property insurance, director and officers' liability, vehicle liability and employee health care benefits. Liabilities associated with the risks that are retained by the Company are estimated, in part, by considering historical claims experience and outside expertise, demographic factors, severity factors and other actuarial assumptions. The estimated accruals for these liabilities could be significantly affected if future occurrences and claims differ from these assumptions and historical trends.

Derivatives

The Company has limited involvement with derivative financial instruments and uses them only to manage well-defined interest rate and foreign exchange risks. Forward foreign exchange contracts are used to hedge the impact of fluctuations of foreign exchange on inventory purchases. The only significant derivative instruments the Company holds are interest rate swaps, which the Company uses to manage the interest rate risk associated with its borrowings and to manage the Company's mix of fixed and variable-rate debt. As of August 31, 2003, the Company had "fixed-to-floating" interest rate swaps with an aggregate notional amount of $600,000 and an aggregate fair value of $34,204, which is recorded in other assets. These swaps were entered into effective November 13, 2001, and March 25, 2002, and are designated and qualify as fair value hedges of the Company's $300,000 7⅛% Senior Notes and the Company's $300,000 5½% Senior Notes, respectively. As the terms of the swaps match those of the underlying hedged debt, the changes in the fair value of these swaps are offset by corresponding changes in the fair value recorded on the hedged debt, and result in no net earnings impact.

Foreign Currency Translations

The functional currencies of the Company's international subsidiaries are the local currency of the country in which the subsidiary is located. Assets and liabilities recorded in foreign currencies, as well as the Company's investment in the Costco Mexico joint venture, are translated at the exchange rate on the balance sheet date. Translation adjustments resulting from this process are charged or credited to other comprehensive income (loss). Revenue and expenses of the Company's consolidated foreign operations are translated at average rates of exchange prevailing during the year. Gains and losses on foreign currency transactions are included in expenses and were not significant in either fiscal 2003 or 2002.

Note 1—Summary of Significant Accounting Policies (Continued)

Revenue Recognition

The Company recognizes sales, net of estimated returns, at the time the member takes possession of merchandise or receives services. When the Company collects payment from customers prior to the transfer of ownership of merchandise or the performance of services, the amount received is recorded as deferred revenue. The Company provides for estimated sales returns based on historical returns levels. The reserve for sales returns (sales returns net of cost of goods sold) was $4,869 and $3,507 at August 31, 2003 and September 1, 2002, respectively.

Membership fee revenue represents annual membership fees paid by substantially all of the Company's members. The Company accounts for membership fee revenue on a "deferred basis," whereby membership fee revenue is recognized ratably over the one-year life of the membership. The Company's Executive members qualify for a 2% reward (which can be redeemed at Costco warehouses), up to a maximum of $500 per year, on all qualified purchases made at Costco. The Company accounts for this 2% reward as a reduction in sales, with the related liability being classified within other current liabilities. The sales reduction and corresponding liability are computed after giving effect to the estimated impact of non-redemptions based on historical data. The reduction in sales for the fiscal years ended August 31, 2003, September 1, 2002 and September 2, 2001, and the related liability as of those dates were as follows:

	Fiscal Year Ended		
	August 31, 2003	September 1, 2002	September 2, 2001
Two-percent reward sales reduction	$169,612	$143,637	$84,243
Two-percent unredeemed reward liability	$114,681	$ 94,448	$57,840

Merchandise Costs

Merchandise costs consist of the purchase price of inventory sold, inbound shipping charges and all costs related to our depot operations, including freight from depots to selling warehouses. Merchandise costs also include salaries, benefits, depreciation on production equipment, and other related expenses incurred in certain fresh foods and ancillary departments.

Selling, General and Administrative Expenses

Selling, general and administrative expenses consist primarily of salaries, benefits and workers' compensation costs for warehouse employees, other than fresh foods and certain ancillary businesses, as well as all regional and home office employees, including buying personnel. Selling, general and administrative expenses also include utilities, bank charges and substantially all building and equipment depreciation, as well as other operating costs incurred to support warehouse operations.

Marketing and Promotional Expenses

Costco's policy is generally to limit marketing and promotional expenses to new warehouse openings, occasional direct mail marketing to prospective new members and annual direct mail marketing programs to existing members promoting selected merchandise. Marketing and promotional costs are expensed as incurred.

Preopening Expenses

Preopening expenses related to new warehouses, major remodels/expansions, regional offices and other startup operations are expensed as incurred.

Note 1—Summary of Significant Accounting Policies (Continued)

Stock-Based Compensation

The Company adopted the fair value based method of recording stock options consistent with SFAS No. 123 "Accounting for Stock-Based Compensation," for all employee stock options granted subsequent to fiscal year end 2002. Specifically, the Company adopted SFAS No. 123 using the "prospective method" with guidance provided from SFAS No. 148 "Accounting for Stock-Based Compensation—Transition and Disclosure." All employee stock option grants made in fiscal 2003 and in future years will be expensed over the stock option vesting period based on the fair value at the date the options are granted. Prior to fiscal 2003 the Company applied Accounting Principles Board Opinion (APB) No. 25 and related interpretations in accounting for stock options. Because the Company granted stock options to employees at exercise prices equal to fair market value on the date of grant, accordingly, no compensation cost was recognized for option grants.

Had compensation costs for the Company's stock-based compensation plans been determined based on the fair value at the grant dates for awards made prior to fiscal 2003, under those plans and consistent with SFAS No. 123, the Company's net income and net income per share would have been reduced to the pro forma amounts indicated below:

	Fiscal Year Ended		
	August 31, 2003	September 1, 2002	September 2, 2001
Net income, as reported	$721,000	$699,983	$602,089
Add: Stock-based employee compensation expense included in reported net income, net of related tax effects	7,513	—	—
Deduct: Total stock-based employee compensation expense determined under fair value based methods for all awards, net of related tax effects	(70,257)	(75,743)	(65,077)
Pro-forma net income	$658,256	$624,240	$537,012
Earnings per share:			
Basic—as reported	$ 1.58	$ 1.54	$ 1.34
Basic—pro-forma	$ 1.44	$ 1.38	$ 1.19
Diluted—as reported	$ 1.53	$ 1.48	$ 1.29
Diluted—pro-forma	$ 1.40	$ 1.32	$ 1.15

Fair Value of Financial Instruments

The carrying value of the Company's financial instruments, including cash and cash equivalents, short-term investments and receivables approximate fair value due to their short-term nature or variable interest rates. The fair value of fixed rate debt at August 31, 2003 and September 1, 2002 was $1,415,252 and $1,382,569, respectively.

Reorganization of Canadian Administrative Operations

On January 17, 2001, the Company announced plans to reorganize and consolidate the administration of its operations in Canada. Total costs related to the reorganization were $26,765 pre-tax, of which $7,765 pre-tax ($4,775 after-tax, or $.01 per diluted share) was expensed in fiscal 2002 and $19,000 pre-tax ($11,400 after-tax, or $.02 per diluted share) was expensed in fiscal 2001 and reported as part of the provision for impaired assets and closing costs. These costs consisted primarily of employee severance, implementation and consolidation of support systems and employee relocation. The reorganization was completed in the first quarter of fiscal 2002.

NOTES TO CONSOLIDATED FINANCIAL STATEMENTS
(dollars in thousands, except per share data) (Continued)

Note 1—Summary of Significant Accounting Policies (Continued)

Closing Costs

Warehouse closing costs incurred relate principally to the Company's efforts to relocate certain warehouses that were not otherwise impaired to larger and better-located facilities. The provision for fiscal 2003 included charges of $11,836 for warehouse closing expenses and $2,967 for losses on the sale of real property. The fiscal 2002 provision included charges of $13,683 for warehouse closing expenses and $7,765 for Canadian administrative reorganization, which were offset by $398 of net gains on the sale of real property. As of August 31, 2003, the Company's reserve for warehouse closing costs was $8,609, of which $7,833 related to lease obligations. This compares to a reserve for warehouse closing costs of $11,845 at September 1, 2002, of which $10,395 related to lease obligations.

Interest Income and Other

Interest income and other includes:

	Fiscal Year Ended		
	August 31, 2003	September 1, 2002	September 2, 2001
Interest income	$21,200	$16,005	$25,908
Minority interest/earnings of affiliates and other	17,325	19,740	17,330
Total	$38,525	$35,745	$43,238

Income Taxes

The Company accounts for income taxes under the provisions of SFAS No. 109, "Accounting for Income Taxes." That standard requires companies to account for deferred income taxes using the asset and liability method.

Under the asset and liability method of SFAS No. 109, deferred tax assets and liabilities are recognized for the future tax consequences attributed to differences between the financial statement carrying amounts of existing assets and liabilities and their respective tax bases and tax credits and loss carry-forwards. Deferred tax assets and liabilities are measured using enacted tax rates expected to apply to taxable income in the years in which those temporary differences and carry-forwards are expected to be recovered or settled. The effect on deferred tax assets and liabilities of a change in tax rates is recognized in income in the period that includes the enactment date. A valuation allowance is established when necessary to reduce deferred tax assets to amounts expected to be realized.

Note 1—Summary of Significant Accounting Policies (Continued)

Net Income Per Common and Common Equivalent Share

The following data show the amounts used in computing earnings per share and the effect on income and the weighted average number of shares of dilutive potential common stock.

	52 Weeks Ended August 31, 2003	52 Weeks Ended September 1, 2002	52 Weeks Ended September 2, 2001
Net income available to common stockholders used in basic EPS	$721,000	$699,983	$602,089
Interest on convertible bonds, net of tax	11,109	10,602	9,992
Net income available to common stockholders after assumed conversions of dilutive securities	$732,109	$710,585	$612,081
Weighted average number of common shares used in basic EPS (000's)	456,335	453,650	449,631
Stock options (000's)	3,646	6,267	6,851
Conversion of convertible bonds (000's)	19,345	19,345	19,345
Weighted number of common shares and dilutive potential common stock used in diluted EPS (000's)	479,326	479,262	475,827

The diluted share base calculation for fiscal years ended August 31, 2003, September 1, 2002 and September 2, 2001, excludes 33,362,000, 6,908,000 and 7,108,000 stock options outstanding, respectively. These options are excluded due to their anti-dilutive effect.

On November 30, 2001, the Company's Board of Directors approved a stock repurchase program authorizing the repurchase of up to $500,000 of Costco Common Stock through November 30, 2004. Under the program, the Company can repurchase shares at any time in the open market or in private transactions as market conditions warrant. The repurchased shares would constitute authorized, but non-issued shares and would be used for general corporate purposes, including stock option grants under stock option programs. To date, no shares have been repurchased under this program.

Recent Accounting Pronouncements

In June 2001, the Financial Accounting Standards Board (FASB) issued SFAS No. 143, "Accounting for Asset Retirement Obligations," which provides the accounting requirements for retirement obligations associated with tangible long-lived assets. SFAS No. 143 requires entities to record the fair value of a liability for an asset retirement obligation in the period in which it is incurred. SFAS No. 143 was effective for the Company's 2003 fiscal year. The adoption of SFAS No. 143 did not have a material impact on the Company's consolidated results of operations, financial position or cash flows.

In August 2001, the FASB issued SFAS No. 144, "Accounting for the Impairment or Disposal of Long-Lived Assets," effective for the Company's 2003 fiscal year. This Statement supersedes FASB Statement No. 121, "Accounting for the Impairment of Long-Lived Assets and for Long-Lived Assets to Be Disposed Of," and other related accounting guidance. The adoption of SFAS No. 144 did not have a material impact on the Company's consolidated results of operations, financial position, or cash flows.

In June 2002, the FASB issued SFAS No. 146, "Accounting for Costs Associated with Exit or Disposal Activities." This statement addresses financial accounting and reporting for costs associated with exit or disposal activities and nullifies Emerging Issues Task Force (EITF) Issue No. 94-3, "Liability Recognition for Certain Employee Termination Benefits and Other Costs to Exit an Activity (including Certain Costs Incurred in a Restructuring)." This statement requires that a liability for a cost associated with an exit or disposal activity should be recognized at fair value when the liability is incurred. SFAS No. 146 was effective for the Company's

NOTES TO CONSOLIDATED FINANCIAL STATEMENTS
(dollars in thousands, except per share data) (Continued)

Note 1—Summary of Significant Accounting Policies (Continued)

2003 fiscal year. The adoption of SFAS No. 146 did not have a material impact on the Company's consolidated results of operations, financial position or cash flows, other than to impact the timing of charges related to future warehouse relocations.

In December 2002, the FASB issued SFAS No. 148, "Accounting for Stock-Based Compensation—Transition and Disclosure," which provides guidance for transition to the fair value based method of accounting for stock-based employee compensation and the required financial statement disclosure. Effective September 3, 2002 the Company adopted the fair value based method of accounting for stock-based compensation. See Note (1) and Note (5) of the Company's consolidated financial statements.

In November 2002, the FASB issued FASB Interpretation No. 45, "Guarantor's Accounting and Disclosure Requirements for Guarantees, Including Indirect Guarantees of Indebtedness of Others." This standard established financial statement disclosure requirements for companies that enter into or modify certain types of guarantees subsequent to December 31, 2002. Beginning in calendar 2003, the standard requires that companies record the fair value of certain types of guarantees as a liability in the financial statements. The adoption of this interpretation did not have a material impact on the Company's consolidated results of operations, financial position or cash flows.

In January 2003, the FASB issued FASB Interpretation No. 46 "Consolidation of Variable Interest Entities." In general, a variable interest entity is a corporation, partnership, trust, or any other legal structure used for business purposes that either does not have equity investors with voting rights or has equity investors that do not provide sufficient financial resources for the entity to support its activities. Interpretation No. 46 requires a variable interest entity to be consolidated by a company if that company is subject to a majority of the risk of loss from the variable interest entity's activities or entitled to receive a majority of the entity's residual returns or both. The consolidation requirements of Interpretation No. 46 apply immediately to variable interest entities created after January 31, 2003. The consolidation requirements apply to older entities in the first fiscal year or interim period beginning after June 15, 2003. Certain of the disclosure requirements apply in all financial statements issued after January 31, 2003, regardless of when the variable interest entity was established. The adoption of the Interpretation did not have a material impact on the Company's consolidated results of operation, financial position or cash flows.

In November 2002, the EITF reached a consensus on EITF 00-21, "Revenue Arrangements with Multiple Deliverables," with respect to determining when and how to allocate revenue from sales with multiple deliverables. The EITF 00-21 consensus provides a framework for determining when and how to allocate revenue from sales with multiple deliverables based on a determination of whether the multiple deliverables qualify to be accounted for as separate units of accounting. The consensus is effective prospectively for arrangements entered into in fiscal periods beginning after June 15, 2003. The adoption of this consensus did not have a material impact on the Company's consolidated results of operations, financial position or cash flows.

In November 2002, the EITF reached consensus on certain issues discussed in EITF 02-16, "Accounting by a Customer (Including a Reseller) for Certain Consideration Received from a Vendor," with respect to determining how a reseller should characterize consideration received from a vendor and when to recognize and how to measure that consideration in its income statement. Requirements for recognizing volume-based rebates are effective for arrangements entered into or modified after November 21, 2002 and resellers with other supplier payments should generally apply the new rules prospectively for agreements entered into or modified after December 31, 2002. The adoption of this consensus did not have a material impact on the Company's consolidated results of operations, financial position or cash flows in fiscal 2003 and is not expected to have a significant impact in the future on an annual basis. However, the Company does expect the adoption of this consensus to impact interim quarterly financial information, commencing with the first quarter of fiscal 2004, as the applica-

Note 1—Summary of Significant Accounting Policies (Continued)

tion of the consensus will result in a change in the timing for the recognition of some vendor allowances for certain agreements entered into subsequent to December 31, 2002.

Use of Estimates

The preparation of financial statements in conformity with accounting principles generally accepted in the United States requires management to make estimates and assumptions that affect the reported amounts of assets and liabilities at the date of the financial statements and the reported amounts of revenues and expenses during the reporting period. Actual results could differ from those estimates.

Note 2—Comprehensive Income

Comprehensive income is net income, plus certain other items that are recorded directly to stockholders' equity. Comprehensive income was $800,745 for fiscal 2003 and $715,868 for fiscal 2002. Foreign currency translation adjustments are the predominant components applied to net income to calculate the Company's comprehensive income.

Note 3—Debt

Bank Lines of Credit and Commercial Paper Programs

The Company has in place a $500,000 commercial paper program supported by a $300,000 bank credit facility with a group of 10 banks, of which $150,000 expires on November 9, 2004 and $150,000 expires on November 15, 2005. At August 31, 2003, no amounts were outstanding under the commercial paper program and no amounts were outstanding under the credit facility.

In addition, a wholly owned Canadian subsidiary has a $144,000 commercial paper program supported by a $43,000 bank credit facility with a Canadian bank, which expires in March 2004. At August 31, 2003, no amounts were outstanding under the Canadian commercial paper program or the bank credit facility.

The Company has agreed to limit the combined amount outstanding under the U.S. and Canadian commercial paper programs to the $343,000 combined amounts of the respective supporting bank credit facilities.

The Company's wholly-owned Japanese subsidiary has a short-term ¥3 billion ($25,782) bank line of credit, which expires in November 2004. At August 31, 2003, no amounts were outstanding under the line of credit.

The Company's UK subsidiary has a £60 million ($94,842) bank revolving credit facility and a £20 million ($31,614) bank overdraft facility, both expiring in February 2007. At August 31, 2003, $47,421 was outstanding under the revolving credit facility with an applicable interest rate of 4.413% and no amounts were outstanding under the bank overdraft facility.

Letters of Credit

The Company has letter of credit facilities (for commercial and standby letters of credit), totaling approximately $369,000. The outstanding commitments under these facilities at August 31, 2003 totaled approximately $125,000, including approximately $44,000 in standby letters of credit.

Using a Calculator and Computer Keypad

KINDS OF CALCULATORS

Many different models of calculators, both desktop and handheld, are available. All calculators have their own features and particular placement of operating keys. Therefore, it is necessary to refer to the operator's manual for specific instructions and locations of the operating keys for the calculator being used. A typical keyboard of a desktop calculator is shown in the illustration.

DESKTOP CALCULATOR SETTINGS

Several operating switches on a desktop calculator must be engaged before the calculator will produce the desired results.

The *decimal selector* sets the appropriate decimal places necessary for the numbers that will be entered. For example, if the decimal selector is set at 2, both the numbers entered and the answer will have two decimal places. If the decimal selector is set at F, the calculator automatically sets the decimal places. The F setting allows the answer to be unrounded and carried out to the maximum number of decimal places possible.

The *decimal rounding selector* rounds the answers. The down arrow position will drop any digits beyond the last digit desired. The up arrow position will drop any digits beyond the last digit desired and round the last digit up. In the 5/4 position, the calculator rounds the last desired digit up only when the following digit is 5 or greater. If the following digit is less than 5, the last desired digit remains unchanged.

The *GT* or *grand total switch* in the on position accumulates totals.

KINDS OF COMPUTER KEYBOARDS

The computer has a keypad on the right side of the keyboard, called the *numeric keypad*. Even though several styles of keyboards are found, there are two basic layouts for the numeric keypad. The standard layout and enhanced layout are shown in the illustration. On the standard keyboard, the directional arrow keys are found on the number keys. To use the numbers, press the key called *Num Lock*. (This key is found above the "7" key.) When the Num Lock is turned on, numbers are entered when the keys on the keypad are pressed. When the Num Lock is off, the arrow, Home, Page Up, Page Down, End, Insert, and Delete keys can be used.

The enhanced keyboards have the arrow keys and the other directional keys mentioned above to the left of the numeric keypad. When using the keypad on an enhanced keyboard, Num Lock can remain on.

The asterisk (*) performs a different function on the computer than the calculator. The asterisk on the calculator is used for the total while the computer uses it for multiplication.

Another difference is the division key. The computer key is the forward slash key (/). The calculator key uses the division key (÷).

Standard
Keyboard Layout

Enhanced
Keyboard Layout

TEN-KEY TOUCH SYSTEM

Striking the numbers 0 to 9 on a calculator or numeric keypad without looking at the keyboard is called the *touch system*. Using the touch system develops both speed and accuracy.

The 4, 5, and 6 keys are called the *home row*. If the right hand is used for the keyboard, the index finger is placed on the 4 key, the middle finger on the 5 key, and the ring finger on the 6 key. If the left hand is used, the ring finger is placed on the 4 key, the middle finger on the 5 key, and the index finger on the 6 key.

Place the fingers on the home row keys. Curve the fingers and keep the wrist straight. These keys may feel slightly concaved or the 5 key may have a raised dot. The differences in the home row allow the operator to recognize the home row by touch rather than by sight.

Maintain the position of the fingers on the home row. The finger used to strike the 4 key will also strike the 7 key and the 1 key. Stretch the finger up to reach the 7 key; then stretch the finger down to reach the 1 key. Visualize the position of these keys.

Again, place the fingers on the home row. Stretch the finger that strikes the 5 key up to reach the 8 key, then down to reach the 2 key. Likewise, stretch the finger that strikes the 6 key up to strike the 9 key and down to strike the 3 key. This same finger will stretch down again to hit the decimal point.

If the right hand is used, the thumb will be used to strike the 0 and 00 keys and the little finger to strike the addition key. If the left hand is used, the little finger will be used to strike the 0 and 00 keys and the thumb to strike the addition key.

HANDHELD CALCULATORS

Handheld calculators are slightly different from desktop calculators, not only in their size and features but also in their operation. Refer to the operator's manual for specific instructions for the calculator being used.

On a handheld calculator, the numeric keys are usually very close together. In addition, the keys do not respond to touch as easily as on a desktop calculator. Therefore, the touch system is usually not used on a handheld calculator.

PERFORMING MATHEMATICAL OPERATIONS ON DESKTOP CALCULATORS

Mathematical operations can be performed on a calculator both quickly and efficiently. The basic operations of addition, subtraction, multiplication, and division are used frequently on a calculator.

Addition
Each number to be added is called an *addend*. The answer to an addition problem is called the *sum*.

Addition is performed by entering an addend and striking the addition key (+). All numbers are entered on a calculator in the exact order they are given. To enter the number 4,455.65, strike the 4, 4, 5, 5, decimal, 6, and 5 keys in that order, and then strike the addition key. Commas are not entered. Continue in this manner until all addends have been entered. To obtain the sum, strike the total key on the calculator.

Subtraction
The top number or first number of a subtraction problem is called the *minuend*. The number to be subtracted from the minuend is called the *subtrahend*. The answer to a subtraction problem is called the *difference*.

Subtraction is performed by first entering the minuend and striking the addition key (+). The subtrahend is then entered, followed by the minus key (−), followed by the total key.

Multiplication
The number to be multiplied is called the *multiplicand*. The number of times the multiplicand will be multiplied is called the *multiplier*. The answer to a multiplication problem is called the *product*.

Multiplication is performed by entering the multiplicand and striking the multiplication key (×). The multiplier is then entered, followed by the equals key (=). The calculator will automatically multiply and give the product.

Division
The number to be divided is called the *dividend*. The number the dividend will be divided by is called the *divisor*. The answer to a division problem is called the *quotient*.

Division is performed by entering the dividend and striking the division key (÷). The divisor is then entered, followed by the equals key (=). The calculator will automatically divide and give the quotient.

Correcting Errors
If an error is made while using a calculator, several methods of correction may be used. If an incorrect number has been entered and the addition key or equals key has not yet been struck, strike the clear entry (CE) key one time.

This key will clear only the last number that was entered. However, if the clear entry key is depressed more than one time, the entire problem will be cleared on some calculators. If an incorrect number has been entered and the addition key has been struck, strike the minus key one time only. This will automatically subtract the last number added, thus removing it from the total.

PERFORMING MATHEMATICAL OPERATIONS ON COMPUTERS AND HANDHELD CALCULATORS

On a computer keypad or a handheld calculator, addition is performed in much the same way as on a desktop calculator. However, after the + key is depressed, the display usually shows the accumulated total. Therefore, the total key is not found. Some computer programs will not calculate the total until Enter is pressed.

Subtraction is performed differently on many computer keypads and handheld calculators. The minuend is usually entered, followed by the minus (−) key. Then the subtrahend is entered. Pressing either the + key or the = key will display the difference. Some computer programs will not calculate the difference until Enter is pressed.

Multiplication and division are performed the same way on a computer keypad and handheld calculator as on a desktop calculator. Keep in mind that computers use the * for multiplication and / for division.

SAFETY CONCERNS

Whenever electrical equipment such as a calculator or computer is being operated in a classroom or office, several safety rules apply. These rules protect the operator of the equipment, other persons in the environment, and the equipment itself.

1. Do not unplug equipment by pulling on the electrical cord. Instead, grasp the plug at the outlet and remove it.
2. Do not stretch electrical cords across an aisle where someone might trip over them.

3. Avoid food and beverages near the equipment where a spill might result in an electrical short.
4. Do not attempt to remove the cover of a calculator, computer, or keyboard for any reason while the power is turned on.
5. Do not attempt to repair equipment while it is plugged in.
6. Always turn the power off or unplug equipment when finished using it.

CALCULATION DRILLS

Instructions for Desktop Calculators
Complete each drill using the touch method. Set the decimal selector at the setting indicated in each drill. Compare the answer on the calculator to the answer in the book. If the two are the same, progress to the next problem. It is not necessary to enter 00 in the cents column if the decimal selector is set at 0-F. However, digits other than zeros in the cents column must be entered preceded by a decimal point.

Instructions for Computer Keypads
Complete each drill using the touch method. There is no decimal selector on computer keypads. Set the number of decimal places as directed in the instructions for the computer program. In spreadsheets, for example, use the formatting options to set the number of decimal places. When the drill indicates "F" for floating, leave the computer application in its default format. Compare the answer on the computer

monitor to the answer in the book. If the two are the same, progress to the next problem. It is not necessary to enter 00 in the cents column. However, digits other than zeros in the cents column must be entered preceded by a decimal point.

DRILL C-1 Performing addition using the home row keys
Decimal Selector—2

4.00	44.00	444.00	4,444.00	44,444.00
5.00	55.00	555.00	5,555.00	55,555.00
6.00	66.00	666.00	6,666.00	66,666.00
5.00	45.00	455.00	4,455.00	44,556.00
4.00	46.00	466.00	4,466.00	44,565.00
5.00	54.00	544.00	5,544.00	55,446.00
6.00	56.00	566.00	5,566.00	55,664.00
5.00	65.00	655.00	6,655.00	66,554.00
4.00	64.00	644.00	6,644.00	66,555.00
5.00	66.00	654.00	6,545.00	65,465.00
49.00	561.00	5,649.00	56,540.00	565,470.00

DRILL C-2 Performing addition using the 0, 1, 4, and 7 keys
Decimal Selector—2

4.00	11.00	444.00	4,440.00	44,000.00
7.00	44.00	777.00	7,770.00	77,000.00
4.00	74.00	111.00	1,110.00	11,000.00
1.00	71.00	741.00	4,400.00	41,000.00
4.00	70.00	740.00	1,100.00	71,000.00
7.00	10.00	101.00	4,007.00	10,000.00
4.00	14.00	140.00	7,001.00	10,100.00
1.00	17.00	701.00	1,007.00	40,100.00
4.00	40.00	700.00	1,004.00	70,100.00
7.00	77.00	407.00	7,700.00	74,100.00
43.00	428.00	4,862.00	39,539.00	448,400.00

DRILL C-3 Performing addition using the 2, 5, and 8 keys
Decimal Selector—2

5.00	58.00	588.00	8,888.00	88,855.00
8.00	52.00	522.00	5,555.00	88,822.00
5.00	85.00	888.00	2,222.00	88,852.00
2.00	52.00	222.00	8,525.00	88,222.00
5.00	25.00	258.00	2,585.00	85,258.00
8.00	58.00	852.00	8,258.00	22,255.00
5.00	82.00	225.00	8,585.00	22,288.00
2.00	28.00	885.00	5,258.00	22,258.00
5.00	88.00	882.00	2,852.00	22,888.00
8.00	22.00	228.00	2,288.00	25,852.00
53.00	550.00	5,550.00	55,016.00	555,550.00

DRILL C-4 Performing addition using the 3, 6, 9, and decimal point keys
Decimal Selector—2

6.00	66.66	666.66	6,666.99	66,699.33
9.00	99.99	999.99	9,999.66	99,966.66
6.00	33.33	333.33	3,333.99	33,366.33
3.00	33.66	666.99	3,366.99	36,963.36
6.36	33.99	999.66	6,699.33	69,636.36
3.36	99.66	333.66	9,966.33	33,333.66
9.36	99.33	696.36	9,636.69	66,666.99
9.63	33.36	369.63	3,696.36	99,999.33
6.33	33.69	336.69	6,963.99	96,369.63
9.93	69.63	963.36	6,699.33	36,963.36
68.97	603.30	6,366.33	67,029.66	639,965.01

DRILL C-5 Performing subtraction using all number keys
Decimal Selector—F

456.73	789.01	741.00	852.55	987.98
−123.21	−456.00	−258.10	−369.88	−102.55
333.52	333.01	482.90	482.67	885.43

DRILL C-6 Performing multiplication using all number keys
Decimal Selector—F

654.05	975.01	487.10	123.56	803.75
× 12.66	× 27.19	× 30.21	× 50.09	× 1.45
8,280.273	26,510.5219	14,715.291	6,189.1204	1,165.4375

DRILL C-7 Performing division using all number keys
Decimal Selector—F

900.56	÷	450.28	=	2.
500.25	÷	100.05	=	5.
135.66	÷	6.65	=	20.4
269.155	÷	105.55	=	2.550023685*
985.66	÷	22.66	=	43.49779346*

*Number of decimal places may vary, due to machine capacity.

Recycling Problems

RECYCLING PROBLEM 1-1

Journalizing departmental purchases and cash payments

ShowRoom Floors has two departments: Carpeting and Linoleum. All of the vendors from which merchandise is purchased on account offer terms of 2/10, n/30. Source documents are abbreviated as follows: check, C; debit memorandum, DM; purchase invoice, P.

Transactions:

Nov.
  1. Paid cash for administrative supplies, $62.50. C301.
  2. Paid cash for rent, $1,000.00. C302.
  4. Paid cash on account to Lyndale Linoleum, $2,763.60, covering P176 for linoleum for $2,820.00, less discount, $56.40. C303.
  5. Purchased carpeting on account from King Carpets, $3,740.00. P178.
  7. Paid cash on account to Floors and More, $1,651.30, covering P177 for linoleum for $1,685.00, less discount, $33.70. C304.
  8. Returned carpeting to King Carpets, $186.00, from P178. DM19.
  10. Purchased linoleum on account from Mercury Floors, $2,680.00. P179.
  12. Paid cash on account to King Carpets, $3,482.92, covering P178 for carpeting for $3,740.00, less DM19 for $186.00, and less discount, $71.08. C305.
  14. Purchased carpeting on account from Carpet Distributors, $2,670.00. P180.
  14. Paid cash for advertising, $82.50. C306.
  15. Returned linoleum to Floors and More, $212.40, from P177. DM20.
  15. Returned carpeting to Carpet Distributors, $450.00, from P180. DM21.
  17. Paid cash on account to Mercury Floors, $2,626.40, covering P179 for linoleum for $2,680.00, less discount, $53.60. C307.
  18. Purchased linoleum on account from Mercury Floors, $1,360.00. P181.
  19. Paid cash for administrative supplies, $62.75. C308.
  21. Paid cash on account to Carpet Distributors, $2,175.60, covering P180 for carpeting for $2,670.00, less DM21 for $450.00, and less discount, $44.40. C309.
  24. Purchased carpeting on account from King Carpets, $1,925.00. P182.
  25. Paid cash on account to Mercury Floors, $1,332.80, covering P181 for linoleum for $1,360.00, less discount, $27.20. C310.
  28. Purchased linoleum on account from Lyndale Linoleum, $4,340.00. P183.
  30. Paid cash to replenish the petty cash fund, $214.00: administrative supplies, $65.50; advertising, $87.30; miscellaneous, $61.20. C311.

Instructions:

1. Journalize the transactions completed during November of the current year. Page 11 of a purchases journal, page 8 of a general journal, and page 21 of a cash payments journal are provided in the *Recycling Problem Working Papers*.
2. Prove and rule the special journals.

Recycling Problem 1-1
Purchases journal totals: 16,715.00, 8,335.00, 8,380.00.
General journal: Three entries dated Nov. 8, 15, and 15.
Cash payments journal totals: 1,421.75, 14,319.00, 115.48, 170.90, 15,454.37.

Journalizing department sales, sales returns and allowances, and cash receipts

Phoenix Computing, Inc., has two departments: Hardware and Software.

Instructions:

1. Journalize the transactions completed during April of the current year. Calculate and record sales tax on all sales and sales returns and allowances as described in this chapter. Page 4 of a sales journal and a general journal and page 7 of a cash receipts journal are provided in the *Recycling Problem Working Papers*. Phoenix Computing offers its customers terms of 2/10, n/30. The sales tax rate is 5%. Source documents are abbreviated as follows: credit memorandum, CM; receipt, R; sales invoice, S; terminal summary, TS.

Transactions:

Apr.	1.	Sold hardware on account to Davis Design Co., $1,640.00, plus sales tax. S119.
	2.	Recorded cash and credit card sales: hardware, $3,170.00; software, $2,690.00; plus sales tax. TS22.
	5.	Received cash on account from Western Co., for software purchased on S116 for $176.40, less discount. R72.
	5.	Granted credit to Odum Personnel Agency for software returned, $30.00, plus sales tax, from S118. CM21.
	8.	Sold software on account to Geig Enterprises, $680.00, plus sales tax. S120.
	8.	Received cash on account from O'Leary Management Co., for hardware purchased on S117 for $892.50, less discount. R73.
	9.	Received cash on account from Odum Personnel Agency for software purchased on S118 for $176.40, less CM21 for $31.50, less discount. R74.
	9.	Recorded cash and credit card sales: hardware, $5,780.00; software, $4,620.00; plus sales tax. TS23.
	11.	Received cash on account from Davis Design Co. for hardware purchased on S119 for $1,722.00, less discount. R75.
	13.	Sold software on account to Newman Data Co., $75.00, plus sales tax. S121.
	15.	Sold hardware on account to O'Leary Management Co., $480.00, plus sales tax. S122.
	16.	Recorded cash and credit card sales: hardware, $6,210.00; software, $5,030.00; plus sales tax. TS24.
	18.	Received cash on account from Geig Enterprises, for software purchased on S120 for $714.00, less discount. R76.
	19.	Granted credit to Newman Data Co. for software returned, $18.00, plus sales tax, from S121. CM22.
	22.	Sold hardware on account to Melrose Schools, $1,640.00; no sales tax. S123.
	23.	Received cash on account from Newman Data Co. for software purchased on S121 for $78.75, less CM22 ($18.00 plus sales tax), less discount. R77.
	23.	Recorded cash and credit card sales: hardware, $6,630.00; software, $4,720.00; plus sales tax. TS25.
	25.	Received cash on account from O'Leary Management Co. for hardware purchased on S122 for $504.00, less discount. R78.
	27.	Sold software on account to Odum Personnel Agency, $100.00; plus sales tax. S124.
	30.	Recorded cash and credit card sales: hardware, $3,890.00; software, $3,930.00; plus sales tax. TS26.

2. Prove and rule the sales journal.
3. Prove and rule the cash receipts journal.

Recycling Problem 2-1

Sales journal totals: 4,763.75, 148.75, 3,760.00, 855.00.

General journal: Two entries dated April 5 and 19.

Cash receipts journal totals: 4,213.65, 2,333.50, 25,680.00, 20,990.00, 62.37, 21.91, 53,132.87.

Completing payroll records, journalizing payment of a payroll, and journalizing payroll taxes

Sheridan Shoes has two departments: Men's Shoes and Women's Shoes. A biweekly payroll system of 26 pay periods per year is used. Salesclerks and employees in the accounting department are paid on an hourly basis and receive 1½ times the regular hourly rate for all hours worked over 80 each pay period. Departmental supervisors are paid a biweekly salary and receive monthly commissions of 1% of net sales. Commissions are paid in the first pay period of the following month.

Instructions:

1. In the *Recycling Problem Working Papers*, prepare the commissions record for each departmental supervisor for the month ended January 31 of the current year. Use the basic payroll information provided in the problem table. The following additional information is needed to complete the commission records.
   a. Men's Shoes department: sales on account, $5,143.77; cash and credit card sales, $9,656.04; sales discount, $115.17; sales returns and allowances, $389.94.
   b. Women's Shoes department: sales on account, $6,712.50; cash and credit card sales, $9,320.40; sales discount, $124.30; sales returns and allowances, $517.60.

Employee		Position	Dept.	Marital Status	Allow.	Total Hours	Regular Pay	Overtime Pay
No.	Name							
1	Aldrich, Joan J.	Salesclerk	W	M	2	83	$520.00	$29.25
2	Bryant, Mark K.	Supervisor	M	S	1	—	525.00	
3	Colfax, Mary D.	Clerk	A	S	2	82	520.00	19.50
4	Emerson, Theodore A.	Salesclerk	M	M	3	80	525.00	—
5	James, Kelly A.	Salesclerk	W	M	2	84	600.00	45.00
6	Newton, Loretta M.	Supervisor	W	M	4	—	610.00	—
7	Penn, Joseph P.	Clerk	A	M	3	82	648.00	24.30
8	Russell, Eileen R.	Salesclerk	M	S	1	84	440.00	33.00
9	Thomas, Emily R.	Salesclerk	M	S	1	83	456.00	25.65
10	Washburn, Mark S.	Salesclerk	W	S	2	83	448.00	25.20

Departments: Men's Shoes, M; Women's Shoes, W; Administrative, A

2. Prepare Sheridan Shoes' payroll register for the biweekly pay period ended February 13 and paid February 20 of the current year. The following additional data are needed to complete the payroll register.
   a. A deduction for federal tax is to be made from each employee's total earnings. Use the appropriate income tax withholding tables shown in Chapter 3.
   b. A deduction of 4.5% for state income tax is to be made from each employee's total earnings.
   c. A deduction of 6.2% for social security tax and 1.45% for Medicare tax is to be made from each employee's total earnings.
   d. All employees have dental insurance, $9.10, and health insurance, $13.40, deducted from their pay each biweekly pay period. Write the letter *D* in front of the dental insurance deduction and the letter *H* in front of the health insurance deduction.
3. Complete Joan Aldrich's employee earnings record for the third pay period ended February 13 of the current year. The following data about Joan Aldrich are needed to complete the record.
   a. Hourly rate, $6.50.
   b. Social security number, 514-30-2258.
4. Journalize the February 20 payroll payment, using page 4 of a cash payments journal. The source document is Check No. 125.
5. Use a grid similar to the one in Chapter 3 to calculate departmental payroll taxes. Employer tax rates are social security, 6.2%; Medicare, 1.45%; federal unemployment, 0.8%; and state unemployment, 5.4%.
6. Journalize the employer payroll taxes using page 4 of a general journal. Use February 20 of the current year as the date. The source document is Memorandum No. 10.

Recycling Problem 3-1
Total payroll, 5,790.76.
Total deductions, 1,089.58.
Net pay, 4,701.18.

RECYCLING PROBLEM 4-1

Completing end-of-fiscal-period work for a merchandising business using departmental margins

Lawn Care is a merchandising business that specializes in lawn mowers and mower parts. The trial balance on December 31 of the current year is provided in the Trial Balance columns of the work sheet in the *Recycling Problem Working Papers*.

Instructions:

1. Complete the 12-column work sheet for the year ended December 31 of the current year. The following adjusting information is available. Extend amounts to the proper debit and credit columns for Departmental Margin Statement—Mowers, Departmental Margin Statement—Parts, Income Statement, and Balance Sheet. Accounts on trial balance lines 55–63 are classified as indirect expenses.

Adjustment Information, December 31

Uncollectible accounts expense—mowers estimated as 1.0% of sales on account.

Sales on account for year	$78,000.00
Merchandise Inventory—Mowers	$74,220.30
Merchandise Inventory—Parts	54,853.00
Supplies Used—Administrative	1,609.00
Supplies Used—Mowers	2,413.00
Supplies Used—Parts	4,023.00
Insurance Expired	5,550.00
Depreciation Expense—Office Equipment	359.00
Depreciation Expense—Store Equipment, Mowers	896.00
Depreciation Expense—Store Equipment, Parts	582.00
Federal Income Tax Expense for the Year	6,566.64

2. Prepare a departmental margin statement for each department. Calculate and record the component percentages for each item on the statements. Round percentage calculations to the nearest 0.1%.
3. Prepare an income statement. Calculate and record the component percentages for each item on the statements. Round percentage calculations to the nearest 0.1%.

Recycling Problem 4-1
Departmental margin—Mowers, 63,804.60.
Departmental margin—Parts, 93,710.00.
Net income after federal income tax, 37,210.96.

RECYCLING PROBLEM 5-1

Journalizing transactions in a voucher system

Walston Company uses a voucher system, including a voucher register and a check register, similar to those described in Chapter 5.

Transactions:

May
1. Purchased merchandise on account from Moraska Company, $790.00. V30.
2. Bought sales supplies on account from Waldoch Supplies, $159.78. V31.
4. Bought store equipment on account from Murphy Equipment, $1,449.77. V32.
8. Purchased merchandise on account from Westhaven Company, $1,278.00. V33.
8. Paid cash to Moraska Company, $774.20, covering V30 for $790.00, less 2% discount, $15.80. C19.
10. Made a deposit in the checking account, $2,957.50.
14. Received invoice for delivery service from Davis Delivery, $29.50. V34.
14. Paid cash to Davis Delivery, $29.50, covering V34. C20.
14. Issued DM5 to Westhaven Company for return of merchandise purchased, $170.00. Cancel V33. V35.
15. Paid cash to Westhaven Company, $1,085.84, covering V35 for $1,108.00, less 2% discount, $22.16. C21.

16. Recorded voucher for semimonthly payroll for period ended May 15, $1,396.47 (total payroll: sales, $1,116.00; administrative, $744.00; less deductions: employee income tax payable—federal, $280.50; employee income tax payable—state, $34.23; social security tax payable, $120.90; Medicare tax payable, $27.90). V36.

16. Paid cash for semimonthly payroll, $1,396.47, covering V36. C22.

22. Paid cash to Waldoch Supplies, $159.78, covering V31. C23.

25. Bought office equipment on account from Yurik Company, $1,979.99. V37.

29. Made a deposit in the checking account, $1,279.51.

30. Purchased merchandise on account from Moraska Company, $1,875.95. V38.

Instructions:

1. Page 7 of a check register is provided in the *Recycling Problem Working Papers*. Record the bank balance brought forward on May 1 of the current year, $6,597.66.

2. Journalize the transactions completed during May of the current year. Use page 8 of a voucher register and page 7 of a check register. When a voucher is paid or canceled, make appropriate notations in the voucher register. Source documents are abbreviated as follows: check, C; debit memorandum, DM; voucher, V.

3. Prove and rule both the voucher register and the check register.

RECYCLING PROBLEM 6-1

Determining cost of merchandise inventory; estimating cost of merchandise using estimating methods; calculating merchandise inventory turnover ratio and average number of days' sales in merchandise inventory

On December 31 of the current year, Rackley, Inc., took a periodic inventory. Selected information about the inventory is provided in the *Recycling Problem Working Papers*.

Instructions:

1. Calculate the total inventory costs using the fifo, lifo, and weighted-average inventory costing methods, using the form provided in the *Recycling Problems Working Papers*.

2. Rackley uses the weighted-average costing method to determine the cost of inventory. Use the market price to determine the cost of inventory using the lower of cost or market method. Total the Lower of Cost or Market column.

3. Calculate the corporation's estimated ending inventory using the gross profit method of estimating inventory. The gross profit percentage is 40%. The following information is obtained from the corporation's records on December 31 of the current year:

Item	Cost	Retail
Beginning merchandise inventory	$ 400.00	$ 670.00
Net purchases to date	3,000.00	5,080.00
Net sales to date	—	4,600.00

4. Calculate the corporation's estimated ending inventory using the retail method of estimating inventory. Round the percentage to the nearest 0.1%.

5. Use the information and the estimated inventory calculated in Instruction 4. Calculate the corporation's merchandise inventory turnover ratio. Round the ratio to the nearest 0.1%.

6. Calculate the corporation's average number of days' sales in merchandise inventory. Round the amount to the nearest day.

Recycling Problem 5-1
Voucher register, Vouchers Payable, 10,067.46.
Check register, Vouchers Payable, 3,483.75.
Nov. 30 bank balance, 7,388.88.

Recycling Problem 6-1
1. Total cost, 603.00, 604.00, 605.24.
2. Total, 550.46.
3. 640.00.
4. 679.65.
5. 5.3.
6. 69 days.

RECYCLING PROBLEM 7-1

Estimating and journalizing uncollectible accounts using a percentage of net sales—allowance method; calculating and journalizing the adjusting entry for uncollectible accounts expense

Motion, Inc., uses the allowance method of recording uncollectible accounts expense.

Transactions:

Jan.   18.   Wrote off Judith Tessman's past-due account as uncollectible, $43.96. M25.
Mar.   4.   Wrote off James York's past-due account as uncollectible, $80.85. M34.
Mar.   28.   Received cash in full payment of Judith Tessman's account, previously written off as uncollectible, $43.96. M45 and R83.
June   20.   Wrote off Beverly Axel's past-due account as uncollectible, $17.16. M63.
Oct.   7.   Wrote off Tanya Wadsworth's past-due account as uncollectible, $108.15. M79.
Dec.   11.   Received cash in full payment of James York's account, previously written off as uncollectible, $80.85. M87 and R97.

Instructions:

1. Journalize the transactions completed during the current year. Page 1 of a general journal and page 1 of a cash receipts journal are provided in the *Recycling Problem Working Papers*.
2. Journalize the adjusting entry for uncollectible accounts expense on December 31 of the current year. Motion, Inc., has the following account balances on December 31 before adjusting entries are recorded.

Accounts Receivable	$ 19,768.25
Sales	104,463.79
Sales Discount	1,573.58
Sales Returns and Allowances	901.42

Motion, Inc., estimates that the amount of uncollectible accounts expense is equal to 0.5% of net sales.
3. If all the entries recorded in the general journal and cash receipts journal were posted, including the adjusting entry, what would be the new balance of Allowance for Uncollectible Accounts? The January 1 balance of Allowance for Uncollectible Accounts, before the transactions for the year were recorded, was $1,434.61.

Recycling Problem 7-1
Adjusting entry, debit Uncollectible Accounts Expense, 509.94.
New balance of Allowance for Uncollectible Accounts, 1,819.24.

RECYCLING PROBLEM 8-1

Journalizing transactions for plant assets

Ludden, Inc., uses the straight-line method of calculating depreciation expense. Ludden uses one plant asset account, Office Equipment.

Transactions:

Jan. 5, 20X1.   Paid cash for chair, $200.00: estimated salvage value, none; estimated useful life, 2 years; Serial No., none. C30.
Mar. 3, 20X1.   Paid cash for desk, $650.00: estimated salvage value, $150.00; estimated useful life, 4 years; Serial No., D125. C45.
Jan. 5, 20X2.   Paid cash for file cabinet, $300.00: estimated salvage value, $75.00; estimated useful life, 5 years; Serial No., F325. C115.
July 3, 20X2.   Paid cash for table, $270.00: estimated salvage value, $20.00; estimated useful life, 10 years; Serial No., none. C170.
Jan. 3, 20X3.   Discarded chair bought in 20X1. M50.
Mar. 5, 20X3.   Received cash for sale of desk, Serial No., D125, $300.00. M55 and R50.
June 29, 20X3.   Paid cash, $200.00, plus old file cabinet, Serial No. F325, for new file cabinet: estimated salvage value of new cabinet, $80.00; estimated useful life of new cabinet, 5 years; Serial No. of new cabinet, F915. M70 and C200.
July 1, 20X3.   Paid cash for typewriter, $1,000.00: estimated salvage value, $200.00; estimated useful life, 5 years; Serial No., A6501M341. C230.

Instructions:

Journalize the transactions. Journalize an entry for additional depreciation expense if needed. Page 1 of a general journal, page 5 of a cash receipts journal, and page 5 of a cash payments journal are provided in the *Recycling Problem Working Papers*.

Recycling Problem 8-1
No check figure provided.

RECYCLING PROBLEM 8-2

Calculating depreciation expense

On January 5 of the current year, Burdick, Inc., paid cash for a new company car, $15,000.00: estimated salvage value, $1,500.00; estimated useful life, 5 years. Forms used to prepare the depreciation tables are provided in the *Recycling Problem Working Papers*.

Instructions:
1. Prepare a depreciation table, similar to one in Chapter 8, showing depreciation expense calculated using the straight-line, declining-balance, and sum-of-the-years'-digits methods.
2. Assume that Burdick's car has an estimated useful life of 100,000 miles. Also assume that the car is driven the following number of miles: 1st year, 27,000; 2d year, 23,000; 3d year, 15,000; 4th year, 20,000; 5th year, 15,000. Prepare a depreciation table, similar to one in Chapter 8, using the production-unit method of calculating depreciation expense.

Recycling Problem 8-2
Book value, 1,500.00 for each.

RECYCLING PROBLEM 8-3

Calculating and journalizing property tax

Amluxson, Inc., has real property with an assessed value of $400,000.00. The tax rate in the city where the property is located is 5% of assessed value. Property tax is paid in two installments.

Instructions:
1. Calculate Amluxson's total annual property tax for the current year.
2. Journalize the payment of the first installment of property tax on May 1. Page 9 of a cash payments journal is provided in the *Recycling Problem Working Papers*. Check No. 142.

Recycling Problem 8-3
20,000.00 for year.

RECYCLING PROBLEM 9-1

Journalizing adjusting and reversing entries for prepaid expenses initially recorded as expenses and for accrued expenses

Sutton, Inc., completed the following transactions during the current year. Sutton initially records prepaid expenses as expenses. Source documents are abbreviated as follows: check, C; note payable, NP.

Transactions:

Aug.	1.	Issued a 1-month, 10% note, $700.00. NP1.
Sept.	1.	Paid cash for the maturity value of NP1: principal, $700.00, plus interest, $5.83; total, $705.83. C95.
Sept.	1.	Issued a 150-day, 10% note, $1,300.00. NP2.
Oct.	1.	Issued a 120-day, 12% note, $1,500.00. NP3.
Dec.	1.	Discounted at 12% a 60-day non-interest-bearing note, $800.00; proceeds, $784.00, interest, $16.00. NP4.

Instructions:

1. Calculate the maturity dates for Notes Payable Nos. 2, 3, and 4.
2. Journalize the transactions. Page 15 of a cash receipts journal and page 17 of a cash payments journal are provided in the *Recycling Problem Working Papers*.
3. Sutton, Inc., has the following general ledger balances on December 31 of the current year before adjusting entries are recorded.

Supplies Expense—Administrative	$600.00
Supplies Expense—Sales	900.00
Insurance Expense	800.00

Using the following adjustment information, journalize the adjusting entries for prepaid and accrued expenses on December 31. Use page 13 of a general journal.

Adjustment Information, December 31

Administrative Supplies Inventory	$300.00
Sales Supplies Inventory	350.00
Value of Prepaid Insurance	400.00
Remaining Prepaid Interest	8.00
Accrued Interest on Notes Payable	89.19
Accrued Salaries—Administrative	250.00
Accrued Salaries—Sales	215.00
Accrued Payroll Taxes—Social Security Tax	30.23
Accrued Payroll Taxes—Medicare Tax	6.97
Accrued Payroll Taxes—Federal Unemployment Tax	3.72
Accrued Payroll Taxes—State Unemployment Tax	25.11
Accrued Federal Income Tax	400.00

4. Journalize the reversing entries on January 1 of the next year. Use page 1 of a general journal.

Recycling Problem 9-1
Maturity dates: Jan. 29, Jan. 29, Jan. 30.

RECYCLING PROBLEM 10-1

Journalizing notes receivable, unearned revenue, and accrued revenue initially recorded as revenue transactions

Marastreet, Inc., completed the following transactions during the current year. Marastreet initially records unearned items as revenue.

Transactions:

July   1.   Received a 60-day, 10% note from Juan Beldoza for an extension of time on his account, $200.00. NR20.

July   5.   Received a 2-month, 12% note from David Symanski for an extension of time on his account, $400.00. NR21.

Aug.   30.   Juan Beldoza dishonored NR20, a 60-day, 10% note, maturity value due today: principal, $200.00; interest $3.33; total, $203.33. M39.

Sept.   5.   Received cash for the maturity value of NR21: principal, $400.00, plus interest, $8.00; total, $408.00. R70.

Nov.   1.   Received cash for three months' rent in advance from Clarkson, Inc., $1,800.00. R75.

Nov.   29.   Received cash from Juan Beldoza for dishonored NR20: maturity value, $203.33, plus additional interest, $5.14; total, $208.47. R90.

Instructions:

1. Journalize the transactions. Page 7 of a general journal and page 17 of a cash receipts journal are provided in the *Recycling Problem Working Papers*. Source documents are abbreviated as follows: memorandum, M; note receivable, NR; receipt, R.
2. Continue using page 7 of the general journal. Journalize the adjusting entries using the following information.

Adjustment Information, December 31

Accrued Interest on Notes Receivable	$ 17.57
Rent Received in Advance and Still Unearned	600.00

3. Journalize the reversing entries on January 1 of the next year. Use page 8 of a general journal.

RECYCLING PROBLEM 11-1

Journalizing transactions for starting a corporation, paying dividends, and preparing a balance sheet

Hillcrest, Inc., received its charter on July 1 of the current year. The corporation is authorized to issue 500,000 shares of $1.00 stated-value common stock and 1,000 shares of 8%, $50.00 par-value preferred stock.

Transactions:

July 5. Received cash from five incorporators for 300,000 shares of $1.00 stated-value common stock, $300,000.00. R1-5.

July 8. Paid cash to George Quitman as reimbursement for organization costs, $4,000.00. C1.

July 12. Received a subscription from Angela Smith for 50,000 shares of $1.00 stated-value common stock, $50,000.00. M1.

July 25. Received a subscription from Dayne Wilson for 5,000 shares of $1.00 stated-value common stock, $5,000.00. M2.

Aug. 10. Received cash from Dayne Wilson in payment of stock subscription, $5,000.00. R6.

Aug. 10. Issued Stock Certificate No. 6 to Dayne Wilson for 5,000 shares of $1.00 stated-value common stock, $5,000.00. M3.

Oct. 1. Received cash from Angela Smith in partial payment of stock subscription, $25,000.00. R7.

Oct. 15. Received a subscription from Lance Mosier for 30,000 shares of $1.00 stated-value common stock, $30,000.00. M4.

Nov. 1. Received cash from Angela Smith in final payment of stock subscription, $25,000.00. R8.

Nov. 1. Issued Stock Certificate No. 7 to Angela Smith for 50,000 shares of $1.00 stated-value common stock, $50,000.00. M5.

Instructions:

1. Journalize the transactions. Page 1 of a cash receipts journal, a cash payments journal, and a general journal are provided in the *Recycling Problem Working Papers*.
2. Prepare a balance sheet for Hillcrest, Inc., as of November 2 of the current year.
3. Journalize the following transactions completed during the following two years to record the declaration and payment of the dividends. Continue using page 1 of the general journal and the cash payments journal.

Nov. 24. Hillcrest's board of directors declared an annual dividend of $50,000.00. Preferred stock issued is $250,000.00 of 8%, $50.00 par-value preferred stock. Common stock issued is $400,000.00 of $1.00 stated-value common stock. Date of payment is January 15. M106.

Jan. 15. Paid cash for annual dividend declared November 24, $50,000.00. C257.

Journalizing stocks and bonds transactions

Fleming, Inc., is authorized to issue 200,000 shares of $20.00 stated-value common stock and 50,000 shares of 12%, $200.00 par-value preferred stock.

Transactions:

Jan. 1, 20X1. Received cash for the face value of a 5-year, 10%, $1,000.00 par-value bond issue, $100,000.00. R104.

Jan. 8, 20X1. Received cash from Mary Brooker for 800 shares of $20.00 stated-value common stock at $20.00 per share, $16,000.00. R110.

Feb. 15, 20X1. Paid cash to Alfred Clark for 800 shares of $20.00 stated-value common stock at $21.00 per share, $16,800.00. C124.

Feb. 27, 20X1. Received cash from Connie Boyle for 300 shares of $200.00 par-value preferred stock at $198.00 per share, $59,400.00. R127.

Mar. 13, 20X1. Received cash from Edward Timmell for 100 shares of $20.00 stated-value common stock at $21.00 per share, $2,100.00. R143.

Mar. 22, 20X1. Received cash from Carol Petre for 200 shares of treasury stock at $21.00 per share, $4,200.00. Treasury stock was bought on February 15 at $21.00 per share. R149.

Apr. 15, 20X1. Received cash from Dennis Cochran for 100 shares of treasury stock at $22.00 per share, $2,200.00. Treasury stock was bought on February 15 at $21.00 per share. R155.

Apr. 21, 20X1. Received cash from David Vassel for 300 shares of $200.00 par-value preferred stock at $202.00 per share, $60,600.00. R156.

July 1, 20X1. Paid cash to bond trustee for semiannual interest on bond issue, $5,000.00. C308.

July 1, 20X1. Paid cash to bond trustee for semiannual deposit to bond sinking fund, $10,000.00. C309.

July 12, 20X1. Received store equipment from Jake Smith at an agreed value of $50,000.00 for 250 shares of $200.00 par-value preferred stock. M361.

July 30, 20X1. Received cash from Lester Branch for 100 shares of treasury stock at $20.50 per share, $2,050.00. Treasury stock was bought on February 15 at $21.00 per share. R215.

Jan. 1, 20X2. Paid cash to bond trustee for semiannual interest on bond issue, $5,000.00. C519.

Jan. 1, 20X2. Paid cash to bond trustee for semiannual deposit to bond sinking fund, $9,700.00, and recorded interest earned on bond sinking fund, $300.00. C520.

Jan. 5, 20X6. Received notice from bond trustee that bond issue was retired using bond sinking fund, $100,000.00. M491.

Instructions:

Journalize the following transactions. Page 1 of a cash receipts journal, page 2 of a cash payments journal, and page 7 of a general journal are provided in the *Recycling Problem Working Papers*.

Recycling Problem 12-1
No check figure provided.

End-of-fiscal-period work for a corporation

The trial balance of Nichol, Inc., on December 31 of the current year is provided in the Trial Balance columns of the work sheet in the *Recycling Problem Working Papers*. Statement paper is also provided in the *Recycling Problem Working Papers*.

Instructions:

1. Complete the work sheet. Use the following information to prepare the adjustments.

Adjustment Information, December 31

Accrued Interest Income	$ 122.33
Uncollectible accounts expense estimated as 1.0% of sales on account.	
Sales on account for year,	$277,474.00
Merchandise Inventory	110,939.29
Sales Supplies Inventory	4,951.42
Administrative Supplies Inventory	6,106.97
Value of Prepaid Insurance	3,153.46
Prepaid Interest	4.06
Annual Depreciation Expense—Store Equipment	6,626.28
Annual Depreciation Expense—Office Equipment	8,965.31
Organization Expense	100.00
Accrued Interest Expense	9,005.64
Accrued Salaries—Sales	488.36
Accrued Salaries—Administrative	1,302.77
Accrued Payroll Taxes—Social Security Tax	116.42
Accrued Payroll Taxes—Medicare Tax	26.87
Accrued Payroll Taxes—Federal Unemployment Tax	1.69
Accrued Payroll Taxes—State Unemployment Tax	11.39

Use the tax rates listed on page 351 in Chapter 13 to calculate the federal income tax for the year.

2. Prepare an income statement. Calculate and record the following component percentages. (a) Cost of merchandise sold. (b) Gross profit on operations. (c) Total selling expenses. (d) Total administrative expenses. (e) Total operating expenses. (f) Income from operations. (g) Net addition or deduction resulting from other revenue and expenses. (h) Net income before federal income tax. (i) Federal income tax expense. (j) Net income after federal income tax. Round percentage calculations to the nearest 0.1%.

3. Analyze Nichol's income statement by determining if component percentages are within acceptable levels. If any component percentage is not within an acceptable level, suggest steps that the company should take. Nichol considers the following component percentages acceptable.

Cost of merchandise sold	Not more than 43.0%
Gross profit on operations	Not less than 57.0%
Total administrative expenses	Not more than 18.0%
Total operating expenses	Not more than 31.0%
Income from operations	Not less than 26.0%
Net deduction from other revenue and expenses	Not more than 8.0%
Net income before federal income tax	Not less than 18.0%

4. Calculate earnings per share. Nichol's has 24,000 shares of $4.00 stated-value common stock issued and 940 shares of $100.00 par-value preferred stock issued. Treasury stock consists of 160 shares of common stock. The dividend rate on preferred stock is 10.0%.

5. Prepare a statement of stockholders' equity for the year ended December 31 of the current year. Use the following additional information.

	January 1 Balance	Issued During the Year	December 31 Balance
Common stock:			
No. of shares	20,000	4,000	24,000
Amount	$100,000.00	$20,000.00	$120,000.00
Preferred stock:			
No. of shares	900	40	940
Amount	$90,000.00	$4,000.00	$94,000.00

The January 1 balance of Retained Earnings was $29,439.29.

6. Calculate the following items based on information from the statement of stockholders' equity. (a) Equity per share of stock. (b) Price-earnings ratio. The market price of common stock on December 31 is $24.25.

Recycling Problem 13-1

Federal Income Tax, 31,833.28.

2. (a) 41.2
   (b) 58.8
   (c) 13.7
   (d) 16.8
   (e) 30.5
   (f) 28.3
   (g) 2.9
   (h) 25.4
   (i) 6.5
   (j) 18.9

4. Preferred, 10.00.
   Common, 3.50.

6. a. Preferred, 100.00.
      Common, 9.77.
   b. PE Ratio, 6.9.

8. a. 63,600.32, 4.4.
   b. 271,768.91, 34.1.
   c. 439,458.72, 21.1.

---

7. Prepare a balance sheet for December 31 of the current year.
8. Calculate the following items based on information from the balance sheet. Net sales on account are $277,474.00. (a) Accounts receivable turnover ratio. Accounts receivable and allowance for uncollectible accounts on January 1 were $64,984.46 and $2,482.57, respectively. (b) Rate earned on average stockholders' equity. Total stockholders' equity on January 1 was $216,559.29. (c) Rate earned on average total assets. Total assets on January 1 were $421,689.57.
9. Journalize the adjusting entries. Use page 13 of a general journal.
10. Journalize the closing entries. Use page 14 of a general journal.
11. Journalize the reversing entries. Use page 15 of a general journal. Use January 1 of the following year as the date.

RECYCLING PROBLEM 14-1

Preparing a budgeted income statement and a cash budget with supporting budget schedules

On December 31, 20X2, the accounting records of Reilly Corporation show the following unit sales for 20X2.

1st quarter	20,600 units	3d quarter	22,800 units
2d quarter	21,500 units	4th quarter	35,100 units

The following are additional actual amounts for the 4th quarter of 20X2.

Sales (35,100 units @ $5.00)	$175,500
Purchases (29,400 units @ $2.60)	76,440
Ending inventory	11,500 units

Management has established a unit sales goal of 120,000 units for 20X3 and 25,000 units for the first quarter of 20X4. The sales manager, after reviewing price trends and checking with the company's merchandise suppliers, projects the unit cost of merchandise will increase from $2.60 to $2.80 in the first quarter of 20X3. Because of the increase in costs, the company will need to increase its unit sales price from $5.00 to $5.20 in the first quarter of 20X3. After considering the time required to reorder merchandise, the sales manager requests that 50.0% of each quarter's unit sales be available in the prior quarter's ending inventory. Expenses are projected as follows. Except where noted, percentages are based on quarterly projected net sales. For these items, calculate each quarter's amount by multiplying the percentage times that quarter's net sales. Calculate the annual total by adding the four quarterly amounts. When a dollar amount is given, the total amount should be divided equally among the four quarters.

Selling Expenses

Advertising Expense	1.2%
Delivery Expense	0.7%
Depreciation Expense—Delivery Equipment	$4,200
Depreciation Expense—Store Equipment	$1,800
Miscellaneous Expense—Sales	0.2%
Salary Expense—Sales	5.4%
Supplies Expense—Sales	0.8%

Administrative Expenses

Depreciation Expense—Office Equipment	$1,440
Insurance Expense	$3,640
Miscellaneous Expense—Administrative	$2,400
Payroll Taxes Expense	12.0% of salaries
Rent Expense	$6,640
Salary Expense—Administrative	$26,000
Supplies Expense—Administrative	$1,800
Uncollectible Accounts Expense	0.5%
Utilities Expense	1.5%

Interest expense for each quarter is projected to be $450.

Federal income taxes are calculated using the tax rates listed on page 372 in Chapter 13. Equal quarterly income tax payments are based on the projected annual federal income tax expense.

Additional information is listed as follows.
a. The balance of cash on hand on January 1, 20X3 is $22,540.
b. In each quarter, cash sales are 20.0% and collections of accounts receivable are 25.0% of the projected net sales for the current quarter. Collections from the preceding quarter's net sales are 54.5% of that quarter. Uncollectible accounts expense is 0.5% of net sales.
c. In each quarter, cash payments for cash purchases are 10.0% and for accounts payable 50.0% of the purchases for the current quarter. Cash payments for purchases of the preceding quarter are 40.0% of that quarter.
d. In the first quarter, $12,000 will be borrowed on a promissory note, and equipment costing $17,500 will be purchased for cash. In each quarter, dividends of $15,000 will be paid in cash. In the fourth quarter, the promissory note plus interest will be paid in cash, $13,800.

Instructions:

Prepare the following budget schedules for the year ended December 31, 20X3. Use the forms provided in the *Recycling Problem Working Papers*. Round percentage amounts to the nearest 0.1%, unit amounts to the nearest 100 units, and dollar amounts to the nearest $10.
1. Prepare a sales budget schedule (Schedule 1).
2. Prepare a purchases budget schedule (Schedule 2).
3. Prepare a selling expenses budget schedule (Schedule 3).
4. Prepare an administrative expenses budget schedule (Schedule 4).
5. Prepare another revenue and expenses budget schedule (Schedule 5).
6. Prepare a budgeted income statement.
7. Prepare a cash receipts budget schedule (Schedule A).
8. Prepare a cash payments budget schedule (Schedule B).
9. Prepare a cash budget.

RECYCLING PROBLEM 15-1

Calculating contribution margin and breakeven point; calculating sales dollars and unit sales for planned net income

NewWave Cycle, Inc., manufactures and sells racing bicycles. The company's income statement for January of the current year appears in the *Recycling Problem Working Papers*.

Instructions:
1. Prepare NewWave Cycle's January income statement reporting contribution margin using the form provided in the *Recycling Problems Working Papers*.
2. Calculate the contribution margin rate.
3. Calculate the sales dollar breakeven point.
4. Calculate the unit sales breakeven point.
5. If an $18,000.00 monthly net income is planned, calculate the required (a) sales dollars and (b) number of cycles to be sold.
6. NewWave Cycle currently produces one of the components of its cycles. However, the company can also purchase the component from another company, reducing fixed costs by $5,000.00 per month, but increasing variable costs by $25.00 per cycle. Calculate the projected net income assuming NewWave Cycle sells 180 cycles per month. Should NewWave Cycle purchase the component from another company? Explain your answer.

Recycling Problem 14-1
1. 624,000, 128,440, 134,160, 142,480, 218,920.
2. 73,080, 74,480, 97,440, 93,800.
3. 57,790, 12,170, 12,630, 13,320, 19,670.
4. 61,550, 14,660, 14,810, 15,030, 17,050.
7. 165,450, 130,370, 137,240, 176,160.
8. 143,570, 126,140, 141,340, 170,120.
9. 44,420, 48,650, 44,550, 50,590.

Recycling Problem 15-1
2. $40,500 \div 135,000 = 30\%$.
3. $27,000 \div 30\% = 90,000$.
4. $90,000 \div 750 = 120$ units.
5. (a) $45,000 \div 30\% = 150,000$.
    (b) $150,000 \div 750 = 200$ units.

Calculating net present values

ReTrax Company is evaluating the purchase of equipment from two vendors. Differences in the technology and labor requirements to operate the equipment of each vendor affect the projected net cash flows. The equipment purchased from Lione Industries would cost $115,000.00 and is projected to generate total net cash flows of $177,000.00. The equipment from Timco Manufacturing would cost $157,800.00 and is projected to generate net cash flows totaling $251,000.00. The net cash flows for each year follow.

Year	Lione Industries	Timco Manufacturing
1	$32,000.00	$15,000.00
2	29,000.00	24,000.00
3	31,000.00	35,000.00
4	27,000.00	42,000.00
5	24,000.00	48,000.00
6	19,000.00	58,000.00
7	15,000.00	29,000.00

Instructions:

1. Assuming that ReTrax Company wants to earn a 15% rate of return, calculate the net present value of each equipment purchase.
2. Would you purchase the equipment and, if so, from which vendor?

Preparing and analyzing comparative financial statements

Information taken from the financial records of Reardon Corporation for two fiscal years ended December 31 are provided in the *Recycling Problem Working Papers*.

The following additional information is known:

Dividends Declared	$25,000.00	$25,000.00
Shares of Capital Stock Outstanding	3,000	3,000
Accounts Receivable (Book Value), January 1	62,430.00	59,480.00
Merchandise Inventory, January 1	$229,690.00	$120,830.00
Total Assets, January 1	493,180.00	421,200.00
Capital Stock, January 1	300,000.00	300,000.00
Retained Earnings, January 1	49,860.00	43,220.00
Market Price per Share of Stock, December 31	112.50	123.00

Instructions:

1. Prepare the following comparative financial statements using trend analysis. Use the forms provided in the *Recycling Problem Working Papers*. Round percentage calculations to the nearest 0.1%.
   a. Comparative income statement
   b. Comparative stockholders' equity statement
   c. Comparative balance sheet
2. Use the financial statements' trend analysis to determine if the trend from the prior to current year for each of the following items appears to be favorable or unfavorable. Give reasons for these trends.
   a. Net sales
   b. Net income
   c. Total stockholders' equity
   d. Total assets
3. Prepare a comparative income statement using component percentage analysis. Round percentage calculations to the nearest 0.1%.

Recycling Problem 16-1
Lione Industries: Net present value, $(3,618.00).
Timco Manufacturing: Net present value, $2,864.00.

4. Record from the statement prepared in Instruction 3 or calculate the component percentages for each of the following. Determine if the current year's results, compared with the prior year, appear to be favorable or unfavorable. Give reasons for your responses.

    a. As a percentage of net sales:
       1. Cost of merchandise sold
       2. Gross profit on operations
       3. Total operating expenses
       4. Net income after federal income tax
    b. As a percentage of total stockholders' equity:
       1. Retained earnings
       2. Capital stock
    c. As a percentage of total assets or total liabilities and stockholders' equity:
       1. Current assets
       2. Current liabilities

5. Based on Reardon's comparative financial statements, calculate the following ratios for each year.

    a. Profitability ratios:
       1. Rate earned on average total assets
       2. Rate earned on average stockholders' equity
       3. Rate earned on net sales
       4. Earnings per share
       5. Price-earnings ratio
    b. Efficiency ratios:
       1. Accounts receivable turnover ratio
       2. Merchandise inventory turnover
    c. Short-term financial strength ratios:
       1. Working capital
       2. Current ratio
       3. Acid-test ratio
    d. Long-term financial strength ratios:
       1. Debt ratio
       2. Equity ratio
       3. Equity per share

6. For each of the items in Instruction 5, indicate if there appears to be a favorable or an unfavorable trend from the prior to current year. Give reasons for these trends.

RECYCLING PROBLEM 18-1

Preparing a statement of cash flows

An analysis of the annual income statement and comparative balance sheet of Cascade Trucking Supply, Inc., reveals the following net income, depreciation expense, amortization costs, and changes in current assets and current liabilities:

Net Income	$122,370.00
Amortized Organization Costs	10,000.00
Depreciation Expense	51,500.00
Increase in Notes Receivable	5,100.00
Decrease in Accounts Receivable	35,600.00
Increase in Supplies	3,300.00
Increase in Merchandise Inventory	68,200.00
Decrease in Notes Payable	8,700.00
Increase in Accounts Payable	14,000.00
Decrease in Salaries Payable	1,200.00

Recycling Problem 17-1
2. (a) 10.1%
   (b) −0.9%
   (c) 1.8%
   (d) 30.6%
4. a. (1) 77.4%, 76.3%
     (2) 22.6%, 23.7%
     (3) 16.3%, 17.4%
     (4) 3.6%, 4.1%
   b. (1) 15.8%, 14.3%
     (2) 84.2%, 85.7%
   c. (1) 78.8%, 70.1%
     (2) 33.2%, 12.2%
5. a. (1) 5.5%, 6.9%
     (2) 8.9%, 9.1%
     (3) 3.6%, 4.1%
     (4) 10.45, 10.55
     (5) 10.8, 11.7
   b. (1) 11.7, 12.8
     (2) 2.3, 3.4
   c. (1) 2.4, 5.7
     (2) 0.7, 1.8
   d. (1) 44.7%, 29.1%
     (2) 55.3%, 70.9%
     (3) 118.74, 116.62

Instructions:

1. Prepare the cash flows from operating activities section of the statement of cash flows for the current year ending December 31. Use the form provided in the *Recycling Problem Working Papers*.

   An analysis of the current comparative balance sheet of Cascade Trucking Supply, Inc., shows the following changes in long-term assets:

Increase in Office Equipment	$30,200.00	Increase in Building	$154,000.00
Increase in Office Furniture	12,340.00	Decrease in Land Due to Sale	75,000.00

2. Prepare the cash flows from investing activities section.

   An examination of the comparative balance sheet and statement of stockholders' equity of Cascade Trucking Supply, Inc., reveals the following changes in long-term liabilities and stockholders' equity:

Increase in Mortgage Payable	$40,000.00
Sale of Common Stock	20,000.00
Payment of Cash Dividend	25,500.00

3. Prepare the cash flows from financing activities section.
4. Compute the net increase or decrease in cash resulting from the operating, investing, and financing activities of the business.
5. Enter a beginning cash balance of $98,700.00 on the statement of cash flows.
6. Complete the statement of cash flows for Cascade Trucking Supply, Inc., by computing the ending cash balance for the fiscal year ending December 31.
7. Verify the accuracy of the statement of cash flows by comparing its ending cash balance with the cash balance of $158,630.00 listed for the current year on Cascade Trucking Supply's comparative balance sheet.

RECYCLING PROBLEM 19-1

Preparing cost records

Air Wave, Inc., manufactures CB (citizen band) radios. The company records manufacturing costs by job number and uses a factory overhead applied rate to charge overhead costs to its products. The company estimates it will manufacture 5,000 radios next year. For this amount of production, total factory overhead is estimated to be $198,000.00. Estimated direct labor costs for next year are $220,000.00. On November 6, Air Wave began work on Job No. 753. The order is for 30 No. LR75 CB radios for stock, date wanted November 21.

Transactions:

Nov.	6.	Direct materials, $762.00. Materials Requisition No. 524.
	6.	Direct labor, $120.00. Daily summary of job-time records.
	7.	Direct labor, $180.00. Daily summary of job-time records.
	8.	Direct materials, $230.00. Materials Requisition No. 535.
	8.	Direct labor, $136.00. Daily summary of job-time records.
	9.	Direct labor, $126.00. Daily summary of job-time records.
	10.	Direct materials, $185.00. Materials Requisition No. 542.
	10.	Direct labor, $210.00. Daily summary of job-time records.
	13.	Direct materials, $156.00. Materials Requisition No. 548.
	13.	Direct labor, $198.00. Daily summary of job-time records.
	14.	Direct materials, $112.00. Materials Requisition No. 556.
	14.	Direct labor, $186.00. Daily summary of job-time records.
	15.	Direct materials, $145.00. Materials Requisition No. 563.
	15.	Direct labor, $112.00. Daily summary of job-time records.
	16.	Direct labor, $52.00. Daily summary of job-time records.

Recycling Problem 18-1

Cash provided by operating activities, 146,970.00.

Cash used for investing activities, (121,540.00).

Cash provided by financing activities, 34,500.00.

Instructions:

1. Calculate Air Wave's factory overhead applied rate for next year as a percentage of direct labor cost.
2. Open a cost sheet for job No. 753 and record the transactions. Use the job cost sheet provided in the *Recycling Problem Working Papers.*
3. Complete the cost sheet, recording factory overhead at the rate calculated in Instruction 1.
4. Prepare a finished goods ledger card for Stock No. LR75 CB radio. Minimum quantity is set at 10. Inventory location is Area B-11.
5. Record on the finished goods ledger card the beginning balance on November 1. The November 1 balance of LR75 CB radios is 20 units at a unit cost of $133.50. Air Wave uses the first-in, first-out method to record inventory costs.
6. Record the following transactions on the finished goods ledger card for LR75 CB radios.

Nov. 10. Sold 8 LR75 CB radios. Sales Invoice No. 743.
  16. Received 30 LR75 CB radios. Record cost from cost sheet for Job No. 753.
  21. Sold 20 LR75 CB radios. Sales Invoice No. 757.

Recycling Problem 19-1
30 units finished, 136.60 each.
Finished goods final total, 3,005.20.

RECYCLING PROBLEM 20-1

Journalizing entries that summarize cost records at the end of a fiscal period; preparing statement of cost of goods manufactured

The following information is taken from the records of Bartley Company on January 31 of the current year.

a. The various general ledger accounts used in recording actual factory overhead expenses during the month have the following balances on January 31.

5510	Depreciation Expense—Factory Equipment	$ 2,885.12
5515	Depreciation Expense—Building	1,411.20
5520	Heat, Light, and Power Expense	4,527.60
5525	Insurance Expense—Factory	752.64
5530	Miscellaneous Expense—Factory	6,890.24
5535	Payroll Taxes Expense—Factory	21,868.00
5540	Property Tax Expense—Factory	3,044.16
5545	Supplies Expense—Factory	9,031.68

b. Inventory accounts have the following balances on January 1.

Account No. 1125 Materials	$272,244.00
Account No. 1130 Work in Process	95,961.60
Account No. 1135 Finished Goods	71,442.00

c. The following accounts are needed for completing the posting. No beginning balances are needed.

2110	Employee Income Tax Payable		3120	Income Summary
2120	Social Security Tax Payable		5105	Cost of Goods Sold
2125	Medicare Tax Payable		5505	Factory Overhead

d. The total factory payroll for the month according to the payroll register is $154,000.00, distributed as follows.

Work in Process	$114,520.00	Employee Income Tax Payable	$16,940.00
Factory Overhead	39,480.00	Social Security Tax Payable	10,010.00
Cash	124,740.00	Medicare Tax Payable	2,310.00

e. The total of all requisitions of direct materials issued during the month is $126,115.00. The total of all requisitions of indirect materials issued during the month is $10,085.00.

f. The factory overhead to be charged to Work in Process is 87% of the direct labor cost.

g. The total of all cost sheets completed during the month is $314,440.00.

h. The total of costs recorded on all sales invoices for January is $327,026.00.

Instructions:

1. Open ledger accounts and record balances for information items in (a), (b), and (c). Use the accounts provided in the *Recycling Problem Working Papers*.
2. Journalize the factory payroll entry on page 2 of a cash payments journal. C1012. Post the general debit and general credit amounts.
3. Journalize the following entries on page 1 of a general journal. Post the entries.
    a. An entry to transfer the total of all direct materials requisitions to Work in Process and indirect materials to Factory Overhead. M844.
    b. An entry to close all individual manufacturing expense accounts to Factory Overhead. M845.
    c. An entry to record applied factory overhead to Work in Process. M846.
4. Continue using page 1 of the general journal. Journalize and post the entry to close the balance of the factory overhead account to Income Summary. M847.
5. Journalize and post the entry to transfer the total of all cost sheets completed from Work in Process to Finished Goods. M848.
6. Journalize and post the entry to transfer the cost of products sold from Finished Goods to Cost of Goods Sold. M849.
7. Prepare for Bartley Company a statement of cost of goods manufactured for the month ended January 31 of the current year.

RECYCLING PROBLEM 21-1

Forming and expanding a partnership

On January 1 of the current year, Richard Meyer and Susan Rusk form a partnership. The partnership accepts the assets and liabilities of Mr. Meyer's existing business. Miss Rusk invests cash equal to Mr. Meyers' investment. The partners share equally in all changes in equity. The January 1 balance sheet for Mr. Meyer's existing business is provided in the *Recycling Problem Working Papers*.

Transactions:

Jan. 1. Received cash from partner, Susan Rusk, as an initial investment, $6,000.00. R1.
      1. Accepted assets and liabilities of Richard Meyer's existing business as an initial investment, $6,000.00. R2.
Mar. 1. Journalized personal sale of equity to new partner, Luke Chin, $4,000.00, distributed as follows: from Richard Meyer, $2,000.00; from Susan Rusk, $2,000.00. M18.
Aug. 1. Received cash from new partner, Penney Cory, for a one-fourth equity in the business, $4,000.00. R92.
Sept. 2. Received cash from new partner, Chad Breslau, for a one-fifth equity in the business, $3,600.00. Existing equity is redistributed as follows: from Richard Meyer, $80.00; from Susan Rusk, $80.00; from Luke Chin, $80.00; from Penney Cory, $80.00. R121 and M32.
Nov. 1. Received cash from new partner, Sharon Logan, for a one-sixth equity in the business, $4,200.00. Goodwill, $1,400.00, is distributed as follows: Richard Meyer, $280.00; Susan Rusk, $280.00; Luke Chin, $280.00; Penney Cory, $280.00; Chad Breslau, $280.00. R181 and M42.

Instructions:

Journalize the transactions. Page 1 of a cash receipts journal and page 1 of a general journal are provided in the *Recycling Problem Working Papers*. Source documents are abbreviated as follows: memorandum, M; receipt, R.

Recycling Problem 20-1
Cost of goods manufactured, 314,440.00.

Recycling Problem 21-1
No check figure provided.

RECYCLING PROBLEM 22-1

Completing end-of-fiscal-period work for a partnership

James Dyson and Gerald Nickle are partners in a partnership called Fast Service Plumbing. The partnership's work sheet for the year ended December 31 of the current year is provided in the *Recycling Problem Working Papers*. Statement paper is also provided in the *Recycling Problem Working Papers*.

Instructions:

1. Prepare an income statement. Calculate and record the component percentages for total operating expenses and for net income. Round percentage calculations to the nearest 0.1%.
2. Prepare a distribution of net income statement. Each partner is to receive 8% interest on January 1 equity. The January 1 equity is: Mr. Dyson, $22,000.00; Mr. Nickle, $20,000.00. Also, the partners' salaries are: Mr. Dyson, $10,000.00; Mr. Nickle, $8,000.00. The partners share remaining net income, net loss, or deficit equally.
3. Prepare an owners' equity statement.
4. Prepare a balance sheet.
5. Journalize the adjusting entries. Use page 12 of a general journal.
6. Continue using page 12 of the general journal. Journalize the closing entries.

Recycling Problem 22-1
3. Dyson, 28,647.23; Nickle, 24,487.23.

RECYCLING PROBLEM 23-1

Journalizing governmental transactions

The town of Osage uses a general fund for all financial transactions. Expenditures are recorded by type of expenditure and by department. The four categories of expenditures are: personnel, supplies, other charges, and capital outlays. Departments are: General Government, Public Safety, Public Works, and Recreation.

Transactions:

Jan. 2. Recorded current year's approved operating budget: estimated revenues, $1,148,500.00; appropriations, $1,113,000.00; budgetary fund balance, $35,500.00. M35.

2. Recorded current year's property tax levy: taxes receivable—current, $1,033,000.00; allowance for uncollectible taxes—current, $15,500.00; property tax revenue, $1,017,500.00. M36.

9. Paid cash for gas utility service in recreation department, $182.00. C134.

15. Issued a 1-month, 9% note, $100,000.00. NP7.

16. Received cash for current taxes receivable, $61,200.00. R85.

19. Encumbered estimated amount for supplies in general government department, $120.00. M52.

31. Received cash from traffic fines, $490.00. R100. (Other Revenue)

Feb. 3. Paid cash for general government department supplies, $117.00, encumbered January 19 per M52. M61 and C155.

15. Paid cash for the maturity value of NP7: principal, $100,000.00, plus interest, $750.00; total, $100,750.00. C189.

22. Paid cash for library books for recreation department, $450.00. C192. (Capital Outlays)

Mar. 1. Recorded reclassification of current taxes receivable to delinquent status, $72,000.00, and the accompanying allowance for uncollectible accounts, $15,500.00. M73.

15. Paid cash for a 4-month, 8% certificate of deposit, $300,000.00. C209.

Apr. 5. Encumbered estimated amount for supplies in public safety department, $250.00. M94.

18. Received cash for delinquent taxes receivable, $34,500.00. R255.

26. Paid cash for public safety department supplies, $254.00, encumbered April 5 per M94. M102 and C244.

May   8. Paid cash for consultant's services in general government department, $500.00. C265. (Personnel)

July 15. Received cash for the maturity value of certificate of deposit due today: principal, $300,000.00, plus interest, $8,000.00; total $308,000.00. R314.

D-20

Instructions:

Journalize the transactions completed during the current year. Page 1 of a journal is provided in the *Recycling Problem Working Papers*.

RECYCLING PROBLEM 24-1

Completing end-of-fiscal-period work for a governmental organization

The town of Weston uses a general fund. The trial balance on December 31 of the current year is provided in the Trial Balance columns of the work sheet in the *Recycling Problem Working Papers*. Statement paper is also provided in the *Recycling Problem Working Papers*.

Instructions:

1. Analyze the following adjustment information and record the adjustments on the work sheet.

Adjustment Information, December 31

Supplies inventory	$3,380.00
Interest revenue due but not collected	3,650.00

An estimated 20% of the interest revenue due will not be collected.
The reserve for encumbrances for the current year is reclassified to prior year status.

2. Complete the work sheet.

   Weston's general fund operating budget for the current fiscal year is provided in the *Recycling Problem Working Papers*.

3. Prepare a statement of revenues, expenditures, and changes in fund balance—budget and actual for the year ended December 31 of the current year. The unreserved fund balance on January 1 was $47,610.00.

4. Prepare a balance sheet for December 31 of the current year.

5. Journalize the adjusting and closing entries. Use page 48 of a journal.

Answers to Audit Your Understanding

Chapter 1, Page 11
1. Assets = Liabilities + Owner's Equity.
2. An asset account has a normal debit balance; a revenue account has a normal credit balance.
3. (1) A separate numeric listing is provided for each ledger division. (2) A predesigned arrangement of numbers is provided within each ledger division. (3) Account number digits are spaced to allow the addition of new accounts.

Chapter 1, Page 17
1. Purchases—Video is debited; Accounts Payable is credited.
2. Accounts Payable is debited; Purchases Returns and Allowances—Video is credited.

Chapter 1, Page 24
1. Accounts Payable is debited; Cash and Purchases Discount—Video are credited.
2. In the General Debit and Credit columns of the cash payments journal.
3. To assure that all expenses are recorded during the fiscal period in which they occurred.

Chapter 2, Page 43
1. A tax-exempt customer is not required to pay sales tax. Examples include federal, state, and local government agencies; nonprofit educational institutions; and certain religious and charitable organizations.
2. A credit memorandum is issued by a vendor to show the amount deducted from the customer's account for returns and allowances.

Chapter 2, Page 50
1. A 2% sales discount may be deducted if sales on account are paid within 10 days of the invoice date. All sales on account must be paid within 30 days of the invoice date.
2. Both cash sales and credit card sales result in an immediate increase in the bank account balance.

Chapter 3, Page 68
1. Federal income tax, social security tax, and Medicare tax.
2. By consulting withholding tax tables provided by the Internal Revenue Service.
3. Total Earnings − Total Deductions = Net Pay.
4. Total earnings for the pay period.

Chapter 3, Page 76
1. Cash.
2. a. Employer social security tax.
   b. Employer Medicare tax.
   c. Federal unemployment tax.
   d. State unemployment tax.

Chapter 4, Page 91
1. a. Each manager is assigned responsibility for those revenues, costs, and expenses for which the manager can make decisions and affect the outcome.
   b. The revenues, costs, and expenses must be readily identifiable with the manager's unit.
2. Revenue, cost of merchandise sold, and direct expenses.
3. The amount of the invoice that applies to each department should be recorded separately.

Chapter 4, Page 97
1. Interim departmental statement of gross profit, departmental statement of gross profit, estimated merchandise inventory sheet.
2. Periodic inventory and perpetual inventory.
3. Operating Revenue, Cost of Merchandise Sold, and Gross Profit on Operations.

Chapter 4, Page 110
1. Schedule of accounts receivable and schedule of accounts payable.
2. To bring certain general ledger accounts up to date.

3. Asset, liability, and stockholders' equity accounts.

Chapter 4, Page 117

1. Totals are obtained from the departmental margin statements.
2. By dividing the amount on each line by the amount of departmental net sales.
3. (1) Current period's departmental margin component percentage compared with the company-assigned departmental margin goal and (2) current period's departmental margin component percentage compared with previous periods' departmental margin component percentages.
4. Account titles and balances are obtained from the Income Statement columns of the work sheet.

Chapter 4, Page 124

1. To update general ledger accounts at the end of a fiscal period.
2. All temporary accounts or all income statement accounts and the dividends account.
3. To prove that debits equal credits in the general ledger after closing entries have been prepared.
4. a. Prepare schedules of accounts receivable and accounts payable.
   b. Prepare a trial balance on the work sheet and complete the work sheet.
   c. Prepare financial statements.
   d. Journalize and post adjusting and closing entries.
   e. Prepare a post-closing trial balance.

Chapter 5, Page 149

1. Vouchers Payable.
2. To serve as an additional control: all vouchers can be accounted for.
3. Purchases journal.

Chapter 5, Page 153

1. Cash payments journal.
2. According to the name of the vendor.
3. Vouchers Payable.

Chapter 5, Page 159

1. Vouchers Payable is debited; Purchases Returns and Allowances is credited.

2. Remove the voucher from the unpaid voucher file and write Canceled across Section 5.
3. A payroll register.

Chapter 6, Page 175

1. a. Cost of beginning merchandise inventory.
   b. Cost of the net purchases added to the inventory during the fiscal period.
2. Understated.
3. a. By physically counting the items.
   b. By keeping a continuous record showing the number purchased and sold for each item.

Chapter 6, Page 181

1. A method that best matches the revenue and costs for that business during the fiscal period.
2. The last-in, first-out (lifo) method.
3. The first-in, first-out (fifo) method.
4. a. The cost of the inventory using the fifo, lifo, or weighted-average method.
   b. The current market price of the inventory.

Chapter 6, Page 186

1. That a continuing relationship exists between gross profit and net sales.
2. Separate records of both cost and retail prices for net purchases, net sales, and beginning merchandise inventory.
3. That the business sold the average merchandise inventory five times during the current year.
4. Days in year (365) divided by merchandise inventory turnover ratio equals average number of days' sales in merchandise inventory.

Chapter 7, Page 203

1. When a customer's account is believed to be uncollectible, it should be written off because it is no longer an asset of the business.
2. Uncollectible Accounts Expense is debited; Accounts Receivable is credited. The customer's account in the accounts receivable ledger is also credited.
3. To provide a complete history of a customer's credit activities.

Chapter 7, Page 210

1. a. Percentage of sales method.
   b. Percentage of accounts receivable method.
2. Net sales times the percentage expected to be uncollectible equals the estimated uncollectible accounts expense.
3. a. Compute an estimate for each age group.
   b. Compute the total estimate.
   c. Subtract the current balance of Allowance for Uncollectible Accounts.
   d. Compute the addition to the allowance account.

Chapter 7, Page 213

1. Net sales on account divided by average book value of accounts receivable equals accounts receivable turnover ratio.
2. Customers are taking about 60 days to pay their accounts. The business needs to encourage more prompt payment in order to reduce the number of days to receive payment to 30 days.
3. Business can be lost as some customers may buy from competitors with less restrictive credit terms.

Chapter 8, Page 228

1. a. General information completed when the asset is bought.
   b. Disposal section completed when the asset is discarded, sold, or traded.
   c. Section to record annual depreciation expense.
2. The entry does not involve the purchase of merchandise.
3. Property Tax Expense is debited; Cash is credited.

Chapter 8, Page 234

1. Over the useful life of the plant asset.
2. Matching Expenses with Revenue.
3. Because of its permanent nature, depreciation is not recorded for land.
4. Original cost, estimated salvage value, and estimated useful life.
5. A calendar month.

Chapter 8, Page 241

1. The date, type, and amount of disposal.
2. Depreciation Expense will be debited; Accumulated Depreciation will be credited to bring the accounts up to date before disposal.
3. Cash received minus the book value of the asset sold.
4. Cash plus the book value of the store equipment traded equals the book value of the new store equipment.

Chapter 8, Page 248

1. Declining balance.
2. The amount of use the asset receives.
3. Tons of mineral mined times the depletion rate equals the annual depletion expense. The depletion rate is calculated by dividing the estimated total value of the mineral resource by the estimated number of tons of the mineral to be recovered.

Chapter 9, Page 265

1. Principal times interest rate times fraction of a year equals the interest to be paid on a note.
2. As an annual rate.
3. Principal and interest expense.

Chapter 9, Page 271

1. Matching Expenses with Revenue.
2. To record the amount of supplies used during the period as an expense.
3. If an adjusting entry creates a balance in an asset or a liability account, the adjusting entry is reversed.

Chapter 9, Page 279

1. a. Accrued interest expense.
   b. Accrued salary expense.
   c. Accrued employer payroll taxes expense.
   d. Accrued federal income tax.
2. Interest Expense is debited; Interest Payable is credited.
3. Salaries Payable, Employee Income Tax Payable, Social Security Tax Payable, and Medicare Tax Payable are debited; Salary Expense (for each department) is credited.

Chapter 10, Page 296

1. To provide an extension of time to pay on account.
2. Accounts Receivable is debited; Notes Receivable and Interest Income are credited.
3. The additional interest is charged from maturity date to payment date.

Chapter 10, Page 302

1. Cash is debited; Rent Income is credited.
2. If the adjusting entry creates a balance in an asset or liability account.
3. Unearned Rent is debited; Rent Income is credited.
4. Interest Receivable is debited; Interest Income is credited.
5. Interest Income is debited; Interest Receivable is credited.

Chapter 11, Page 322

1. Determine corporate policies and select corporate officers to supervise the day-to-day management of the corporation.
2. a. The right to vote at stockholders' meetings.
   b. The right to share in the corporation's earnings.
   c. The right to share in the distribution of a corporation's assets if a corporation ceases operations and sells its assets.
3. Common stock and preferred stock.
4. A single summary general ledger capital account is used for each kind of stock issued.
5. Cash is debited; Capital Stock—Common is credited.
6. a. An incorporation fee paid to the state when the articles of incorporation are submitted.
   b. Attorney fees for legal services during the process of incorporation.
   c. Other incidental expenses incurred prior to receiving a charter.

Chapter 11, Page 327

1. Stock Subscribed is debited; Capital Stock is credited. (The kind of stock issued will be included in the account title.)
2. Under the heading Intangible Assets, as the last subdivision of the Assets section.

Chapter 11, Page 332

1. The board of directors.
2. The corporation is obligated to pay the dividend.
3. a. To avoid a large number of entries in the corporation's cash payments journal.
   b. To reserve cash specifically for paying dividends.

Chapter 12, Page 348

1. Selling stock to investors and borrowing money.
2. Cash is debited; Capital Stock—Preferred is credited.
3. Cash is debited; Capital Stock—Preferred and Paid-in Capital in Excess of Par Value—Preferred are credited.
4. Cash and Discount on Sale of Preferred Stock are debited; Capital Stock—Preferred is credited.
5. May be assigned to no-par value stock and it serves the same function as par value.

Chapter 12, Page 354

1. Stock that has been issued and reacquired by a corporation.
2. Cash is debited; Treasury Stock and Paid-in Capital from Sale of Treasury Stock are credited.
3. Historical Cost.

Chapter 12, Page 360

1. a. Additional capital becomes part of a corporation's permanent capital.
   b. Dividends do not have to be paid unless earnings are sufficient.
2. Stockholders' equity is not spread over additional shares of stock.
3. Interest must be paid on the loan, which decreases net income.
4. Bond Sinking Fund is debited; Cash and Interest Income are credited.

Chapter 13, Page 376

1. Recognizing a portion of an intangible expense over a period of years.
2. Quarterly.

Chapter 13, Page 385

1. The amount of net income belonging to a single share of stock.

E-4

2. The relationship between the market value per share and earnings per share.
3. Total assets at the beginning and end of the fiscal period and net income after federal income tax.

Chapter 13, Page 392

1. a. Closing entry for income statement accounts with credit balances.
   b. Closing entry for income statement accounts with debit balances.
   c. Closing entry to record net income or net loss in the retained earnings account and close the income summary account.
   d. Closing entry for the dividends account.
2. Form 1120.
3. The gains and losses on the sale of non-cash assets are subject to taxation. Thus, additional tax reports for the corporation must be filed.

Chapter 14, Page 417

1. A business can control expenses by comparing actual expenses with projected expenses. The comparison identifies differences where costs are higher than projected. The business can then take action to correct the differences.
2. One year.
3. Net income will increase. If net sales increase at a higher percentage than cost and expense items, net income will be favorably affected.

Chapter 14, Page 426

1. Establish targets to work toward in the coming year; help coordinate the efforts of all areas toward a common direction.
2. Previous net sales and the trend in net sales for a period of several years, general economic conditions, consumer buying trends, competition, new products on the market, and such activities as planned special sales.

Chapter 14, Page 433

1. Good cash management requires the planning and controlling of cash so that cash will be available to meet obligations when due.
2. Projected beginning cash balance, cash receipts, cash payments, and ending cash balance.

3. A performance report compares actual amounts with projected amounts for the same fiscal period. A comparative income statement compares actual amounts of one fiscal period with actual amounts of a prior fiscal period.

Chapter 15, Page 450

1. The line would be straight, parallel to the base. The line is straight because fixed costs are exactly the same for each month.
2. Gross profit is determined by subtracting only the cost of merchandise sold from net sales. Contribution margin is determined by subtracting all variable costs from net sales.

Chapter 15, Page 454

1. In sales dollars or unit sales.
2. As an alternative method to calculate the breakeven point when no financial statements exist.
3. Prepare an income statement using the breakeven point numbers. If the breakeven point is accurate, net income will be zero.

Chapter 15, Page 462

1. Fixed costs and variable costs.
2. Total fixed costs plus planned net income.

Chapter 16, Page 478

1. Compounding interest causes the annual interest earned to increase each year.
2. The present value factor is determined by finding the intersection of the interest rate in the columns and the number of years in the rows in a present value table.
3. As percentages.

Chapter 16, Page 483

1. The annual payment is multiplied by the present value factor to calculate the present value of the annuity.
2. They can determine the amount of money they need to have saved before their retirement.
3. Effective managers will not purchase equipment that does not yield a positive net present value. Rather, they will search for alternative uses of an investment that will achieve the desired rate of return.

Chapter 17, Page 502

1. To assist in decision making. For managers: to identify areas for improving profitability. For lenders: to decide whether to loan money to a business. For owners and potential owners: to decide whether to buy, sell, or keep their investment.
2. Determine (a) profitability, (b) efficiency, (c) short-term financial strength, and (d) long-term financial strength.
3. Adequate disclosure.
4. Prior company performance and comparison with published trade performance standards.

Chapter 17, Page 511

1. How well a business is using its assets to earn net income.
2. How much net income stockholders' investment is earning.
3. Accounts are being collected 9.1 times a year.

Chapter 17, Page 517

1. a. Owners' investments and retained earnings.
   b. Loans.
2. a. Working capital.
   b. Current ratio.
   c. Acid-test ratio.
3. Quick assets include all current assets except merchandise inventory and prepaid expenses.
4. Total quick assets divided by total current liabilities equals the acid-test ratio.
5. The debt ratio, equity ratio, and equity per share.
6. Total liabilities divided by total assets equals the debt ratio.
7. Total stockholders' equity divided by shares of capital stock outstanding equals equity per share.

Chapter 18, Page 536

1. The accrual basis of accounting recognizes revenue when it is earned and expenses when they are incurred.
2. The cash basis of accounting recognizes revenue when cash is received and expenses when cash is paid out.
3. a. Operating activities.
   b. Investing activities.
   c. Financing activities.

Chapter 18, Page 542

1. The actual cash outflow occurred in a prior fiscal period when the asset was bought.
2. A company made more credit sales than it collected during the year.
3. A company owes more to its vendors at the end of the year than at the beginning of the year.
4. Net income (net loss).

Chapter 18, Page 548

1. By analyzing the changes in long-term assets (plant assets) on the comparative balance sheet.
2. The increase in accumulated depreciation matches the depreciation expense that was recorded on the income statement. The effect on cash flows due to depreciation expense was already accounted for under operating activities.
3. By examining the changes in long-term liabilities on the balance sheet and reviewing the statement of stockholders' equity.
4. If the Cash Balance, End of Period shown on the statement of cash flows equals the current year's cash balance reported on the comparative balance sheet.

Chapter 19, Page 564

1. a. Direct materials.
   b. Direct labor.
   c. Factory overhead.
2. Work in process.
3. To keep a record of all charges for direct materials, direct labor, and factory overhead for each specific job.

Chapter 19, Page 572

1. Ordered, received, issued, and balance.
2. Purchase order.
3. To authorize transfer of items from the storeroom to the factory.
4. Estimated factory overhead divided by estimated direct labor cost equals factory overhead applied rate.
5. Because the unit costs of each job frequently are different.

Chapter 20, Page 592

1. On cost sheets.
2. Overapplied overhead.

3. Applied factory overhead is only an estimate used to assign factory overhead to jobs. The amount of actual factory overhead is determined at the end of the period; it consists of the actual costs for indirect labor, indirect materials, and other factory expenses.

Chapter 20, Page 601

1. Income Statement Debit column.
2. Underapplied overhead is added to the cost of goods sold.
3. Current Assets.

Chapter 21, Page 627

1. To avoid misunderstandings. Some states require that partnership agreements be in writing.
2. The existing partnership is terminated.
3. The right of all partners to contract for a partnership.

Chapter 21, Page 634

1. The existing partnership is terminated.
2. Total equity (including investment by new partner) multiplied by new partner's share of equity equals the new partner's equity.
3. Goodwill is debited; existing partners' capital accounts are credited.

Chapter 22, Page 654

1. In the partnership agreement.
2. a. Fixed percentage.
   b. Percentage of total equity.
   c. Interest on equity.
   d. Salaries.
   e. Combination of methods.
3. The partner's drawing account.
4. The partner's drawing account.

Chapter 22, Page 664

1. Because a partnership does not pay federal income tax.
2. When the allowances to partners exceed net income.
3. To summarize the changes in owners' equity during the fiscal period.

Chapter 22, Page 669

1. Cash received from the sale of assets during liquidation of a partnership.
2. The partners' capital accounts.

Chapter 23, Page 689

1. a. No profit motive exists.
   b. Leadership is subject to frequent change.
   c. Users of services do not necessarily pay for the services.
   d. Conflicting pressures for differing objectives exist.
2. a. The accounting equation is applied.
   b. An appropriate chart of accounts is prepared.
   c. Transactions are analyzed into debit and credit elements.
   d. Transactions are journalized and posted to ledgers.
   e. Financial statements are prepared for each fiscal period.
   f. Most of the same accounting concepts are applied.
3. A governmental accounting entity with a set of accounts in which assets always equal liabilities plus equities.
4. To authorize and provide the basis for control of financial operations during a fiscal year.
5. Estimated Revenues is debited; Appropriations and Budgetary Fund Balance are credited.

Chapter 23, Page 694

1. When property taxes are levied.
2. Cash is debited; Taxes Receivable—Current is credited.
3. Cash is debited; Taxes Receivable—Delinquent is credited.

Chapter 23, Page 701

1. A commitment to pay for goods or services that have been ordered but not yet provided.
2. a. The encumbrance entry is reversed to remove the estimated amount from the encumbrance and reserve for encumbrance accounts.
   b. The expenditure is recorded.
3. Because the organization does not earn a net income and therefore has no need for expense information.
4. A document issued by a bank as evidence of money invested with the bank.

Chapter 24, Page 718

1. Revenues/Expenditures.
2. Interest Receivable is debited; Allowance for Uncollectible Interest and Interest Revenue are credited.

3. Revenues/Expenditures Credit column.
4. Revenues/Expenditures Credit column total less Revenues/Expenditures Debit column total equals excess of revenues over expenditures.

Chapter 24, Page 723
1. a. Revenues.
   b. Expenditures.
   c. Changes in unreserved fund balance.
2. The work sheet.
3. Favorable.

4. Total assets must equal total liabilities and fund equity.

Chapter 24, Page 726
1. Work sheet's Adjustments columns.
2. Unreserved Fund Balance.
3. Appropriations and Budgetary Fund Balance are debited; Estimated Revenues is credited.
4. Reserve for Encumbrances—Prior Year; Taxes Receivable—Delinquent; Unreserved Fund Balance.

GLOSSARY

A

Acid-test ratio. A ratio that shows the numeric relationship of quick assets to current liabilities. (p. 513)

Account. A record summarizing all the information pertaining to a single item in the accounting equation. (p. 9)

Accounting cycle. The series of accounting activities included in recording financial information for a fiscal period. (p. 123)

Accounting equation. An equation showing the relationship among assets, liabilities, and owner's equity. (p. 7)

Accounts receivable turnover ratio. The number of times the average amount of accounts receivable is collected during a specified period. (p. 211)

Accrual basis of accounting. The accounting method that records revenues when they are earned and expenses when they are incurred. (p. 530)

Accrued expenses. Expenses incurred in one fiscal period but not paid until a later fiscal period. (p. 272)

Accrued revenue. Revenue earned in one fiscal period but not received until a later fiscal period. (p. 299)

Adjusting entries. Journal entries recorded to update general ledger accounts at the end of a fiscal period. (p. 118)

Administrative expenses budget schedule. A statement that shows the projected expenses for all operating expenses not directly related to selling operations. (p. 423)

Aging accounts receivable. Analyzing accounts receivable according to when they are due. (p. 206)

Allowance method of recording losses from uncollectible accounts. Crediting the estimated value of uncollectible accounts to a contra account. (p. 204)

Amortization. Recognizing a portion of an expense in each of several years. (p. 371)

Annuity. A series of equal cash flows. (p. 479)

Applied overhead. The estimated amount of factory overhead recorded on cost sheets. (p. 569)

Appropriations. Authorizations to make expenditures for specified purposes. (p. 687)

B

Articles of incorporation. A written application requesting permission to form a corporation. (p. 315)

Assessed value. The value of an asset determined by tax authorities for the purpose of calculating taxes. (p. 227)

Asset. Anything of value that is owned. (p. 7)

Automatic check deposit. Depositing payroll checks directly to an employee's checking or savings account in a specified bank. (p. 70)

Average number of days' sales in merchandise inventory. The period of time needed to sell an average amount of merchandise inventory. (p. 184)

Balance sheet. A financial statement that reports assets, liabilities, and owners' equity on a specific date. (p. 116)

Board of directors. A group of persons elected by the stockholders to manage a corporation. (p. 315)

Bond. A printed, long-term promise to pay a specified amount on a specified date and to pay interest at stated intervals. (p. 355)

Bond issue. All bonds representing the total amount of a loan. (p. 355)

Bond sinking fund. An amount set aside to pay a bond issue when due. (p. 357)

Book value of a plant asset. The original cost of a plant asset minus accumulated depreciation. (p. 231)

Book value of accounts receivable. The difference between the balance of Accounts Receivable and its contra account, Allowance for Uncollectible Accounts. (p. 211)

Breakeven point. The amount of sales at which net sales is equal to total costs. (p. 451)

Budget. A written financial plan of a business for a specific period of time, expressed in dollars. (p. 412)

Budget period. The length of time covered by a budget. (p. 413)

Budgeted income statement. A statement that shows a company's projected sales, costs, expenses, and net income. (p. 425)

Budgeting. Planning the financial operations of a business. (p. 412)

C

Capital stock. Total shares of ownership in a corporation. (p. 115)

Cash basis. The accounting method that records revenues when they are received and expenses when they are paid. (p. 530)

Cash budget. A statement that shows for each month or quarter a projection of a company's beginning cash balance, cash receipts, cash payments, and ending cash balance. (p. 430)

Cash discount. A deduction that a vendor allows on the invoice amount to encourage prompt payment. (p. 18)

Cash flows. The cash receipts and cash payments of a company. (pp. 477, 532)

Cash payments budget schedule. A statement that reports projected cash payments for a budget period. (p. 429)

Cash receipts budget schedule. A statement that reports projected cash receipts for a budget period. (p. 427)

Certificate of deposit. A document issued by a bank as evidence of money invested with the bank. (p. 699)

Charter. The approved articles of incorporation. (p. 315)

Check register. A journal used in a voucher system to record cash payments. (p. 151)

Closing entries. Journal entries used to prepare temporary accounts for a new fiscal period. (p. 119)

Common stock. Stock that does not give stockholders any special preferences. (p. 316)

Comparative income statement. An income statement containing sales, cost, and expense information for two or more years. (p. 415)

Component percentage. The percentage relationship between one financial statement item and the total that includes that item. (p. 95)

Compounding. Earning interest on previously earned interest. (p. 475)

Consignee. The person or business that receives goods on consignment. (p. 172)

Consignment. Goods that are given to a business to sell but for which title remains with the vendor. (p. 172)

Consignor. The person or business that gives goods on consignment. (p. 172)

Contra account. An account that reduces a related account on a financial statement. (p. 16)

Contribution margin. Income determined by subtracting all variable costs from net sales. (p. 447)

Controlling account. An account in a general ledger that summarizes all accounts in a subsidiary ledger. (p. 10)

Corporation. An organization with the legal rights of a person and that may be owned by many persons. (p. 314)

Cost ledger. A ledger containing all cost sheets for products in the process of being manufactured. (p. 562)

Credit memorandum. The source document prepared by the vendor showing the amount deducted for returns and allowances. (p. 40)

Current ratio. A ratio that shows the numeric relationship of current assets to current liabilities. (p. 513)

D

Date of a note. The day a note is issued. (p. 261)

Date of declaration. The date on which a board of directors votes to distribute a dividend. (p. 328)

Date of payment. The date on which dividends are actually to be paid to stockholders. (p. 328)

Date of record. The date that determines which stockholders are to receive dividends. (p. 328)

Debit memorandum. A form prepared by the customer showing the price deduction for purchase returns and allowances. (p. 16)

Debt ratio. The ratio found by dividing total liabilities by total assets. (p. 514)

Declaring a dividend. Action by a board of directors to distribute corporate earnings to stockholder. (p. 328)

Declining-balance method of depreciation. Multiplying the book value at the end of each fiscal period by a constant depreciation rate. (p. 242)

Deficit. The amount by which allowances to partners exceed net income. (p. 659)

Departmental accounting system. An accounting system showing accounting information for two or more departments. (p. 12)

Departmental margin. The revenue earned by a department less its cost of merchandise sold and less its direct expenses. (p. 89)

Departmental margin statement. A statement that reports departmental margin for a specific department. (p. 89)

Departmental statement of gross profit. A statement showing gross profit for each department. (p. 93)

Depletion. The decrease in the value of a plant asset because of the removal of a natural resource. (p. 247)

Depreciation expense. The portion of a plant asset's cost that is transferred to an expense account in each fiscal period during a plant asset's useful life. (p. 106)

Direct expense. An operating expense identifiable with and chargeable to the operation of a specific department. (p. 89)

Direct labor. Salaries of factory workers who make a product. (p. 561)

Direct materials. Materials that are of significant value in the cost of a finished product and that become an identifiable part of the product. (p. 561)

Direct write-off method of recording losses from uncollectible accounts. Recording uncollectible accounts expense only when an amount is actually known to be uncollectible. (p. 201)

Discount on capital stock. An amount less than par or stated value at which capital stock is sold. (p. 345)

Dishonored note. A note that is not paid when due. (p. 293)

Distribution of net income statement. A partnership financial statement showing distribution of net income or net loss to partners. (p. 658)

Dividends. Earnings distributed to stockholders. (p. 115)

Double-entry accounting. The recording of debit and credit parts of a transaction. (p. 8)

E

Earnings per share. The amount of net income belonging to a single share of stock. (p. 379)

Electronic funds transfer (EFT). A computerized cash payments system that transfers funds without the use of checks, currency, or other paper documents. (p. 70)

Employee earnings record. A business form used to record details affecting payments made to an employee. (p. 67)

Encumbrance. A commitment to pay for goods or services that have been ordered but not yet provided. (p. 695)

Equities. Financial rights to the assets of a business. (p. 7)

Equity per share. The amount of total stockholders' equity belonging to a single share of stock. (p. 379)

Equity ratio. The ratio found by dividing stockholders' equity by total assets. (p. 515)

Expenditures. Cash disbursements and liabilities incurred for the cost of goods delivered or services rendered. (p. 684)

F

Factory overhead. All expenses other than direct materials and direct labor that apply to making products. (p. 561)

File maintenance. The procedure for arranging accounts in a general ledger, assigning account numbers, and keeping records current. (p. 10)

Financing activities. Cash receipts and payments involving debt or equity transactions. (p. 535)

Finished goods. Manufactured products that are fully completed. (p. 561)

Finished goods ledger. A ledger containing records of all finished goods on hand. (p. 562)

First-in, first-out inventory costing method. Using the price of merchandise purchased first to calculate the cost of merchandise sold first. (p. 176)

Fiscal period. The length of time for which a business summarizes and reports financial information. (p. 88)

Fixed costs. Total costs that remain constant regardless of change in business activity. (p. 446)

Fund. A governmental accounting entity with a set of accounts in which assets always equal liabilities plus equities. (p. 683)

Future value. The value of money invested today at some point in the future. (p. 475)

G

General fixed assets. Governmental properties that benefit future periods. (p. 698)

General ledger. A ledger that contains all accounts needed to prepare financial statements. (p. 10)

Goodwill. The value of a business in excess of the total investment of owners. (p. 631)

Gross profit. The amount of revenue from sales less the cost of goods sold. (p. 93)

Gross profit method of estimating an inventory. Estimating inventory by using the previous year's percentage of gross profit on operations. (p. 93)

I

Income statement. A financial statement showing the revenue and expenses for a fiscal period. (p. 114)

Indirect expense. An operating expense chargeable to overall business operations and not identifiable with a specific department. (p. 89)

Indirect labor. Salaries paid to factory workers who are not actually making products. (p. 561)

Indirect materials. Materials used in the completion of a product that are of insignificant value to justify accounting for separately. (p. 561)

Intangible assets. Assets of a non-physical nature that have value for a business. (p. 326)

Interest. An amount paid for the use of money for a period of time. (p. 261)

Interest expense. The interest accrued on money borrowed. (p. 263)

Interest rate of a note. The percentage of the principal that is paid for use of the money. (p. 261)

Inventory record. A form used during a periodic inventory to record information about each item of merchandise on hand. (p. 174)

Investing activities. Cash receipts and cash payments involving the sale or purchase of assets used to earn revenue over a period of time. (p. 534)

J

Journal. A form for recording transactions in chronological order. (p. 8)

L

Last-in, first-out inventory costing method. Using the price of merchandise purchased last to calculate the cost of merchandise sold first. (p. 177)

Ledger. A group of accounts. (p. 10)

Liability. An amount owed by a business. (p. 7)

Liquidation of a partnership. The process of paying a partnership's liabilities and distributing remaining assets to the partners. (p. 665)

Lower of cost or market inventory costing method. Using the lower of cost or market price to calculate the cost of ending merchandise inventory. (p. 180)

M

Market value. The price at which a share of stock may be sold on the stock market. (p. 380)

Materials ledger. A ledger containing all records of materials. (p. 562)

Maturity date of a note. The date a note is due. (p. 261)

Maturity value. The amount that is due on the maturity date of a note. (p. 263)

Merchandise inventory turnover ratio. The number of times the average amount of merchandise inventory is sold during a specific period of time. (p. 184)

Merchandising business. A business that purchases and sells goods. (p. 12)

Modified Accelerated Cost Recovery System (MACRS). A depreciation method required by the Internal Revenue Service to be used for income tax calculation purposes for most plant assets placed in service after 1986. (p. 246)

Mutual agency. The right of all partners to contract for a partnership. (p. 624)

N

Net cash flow. The difference between cash receipts and cash payments. (p. 477)

Net present value. The difference between the discounted cash flows and the investment. (p. 477)

No-par-value stock. A share of stock that has no authorized value printed on the stock certificate. (p. 317)

Not-for-profit organization. An organization providing goods or services with neither a conscious motive nor expectation of earning a profit. (p. 680)

Notes payable. Promissory notes signed by a business and given to a creditor. (p. 261)

Notes receivable. Promissory notes that a business accepts from customers. (p. 291)

O

Operating activities. The cash receipts and payments necessary to operate a business on a day-to-day basis. (p. 534)

Operating budget. A plan of current expenditures and the proposed means of financing those expenditures. (p. 686)

Organization costs. Fees and other expenses of organizing a corporation. (p. 320)

Other revenue and expenses budget schedule. A statement showing budgeted revenue and expenses from activities other than normal operations. (p. 424)

Overapplied overhead. The amount by which applied factory overhead is more than actual factory overhead. (p. 589)

Owner's equity. The amount remaining after the value of all liabilities is subtracted from the value of all assets. (p. 7)

Owners' equity statement. A financial statement that summarizes the changes in owners' equity during a fiscal period. (p. 660)

P

Par value. A value assigned to a share of stock and printed on the stock certificate. (p. 317)

Par-value stock. A share of stock that has an authorized value printed on the stock certificate. (p. 317)

Partnership agreement. A written agreement setting forth the conditions under which a partnership is to operate. (p. 624)

Pay period. The period covered by a salary payment. (p. 60)

Payroll. The total amount earned by all employees for a pay period. (p. 60)

Payroll register. A business form used to record payroll information. (p. 64)

Payroll taxes. Taxes based on the payroll of a business. (p. 60)

Performance report. A report showing a comparison of projected and actual amounts for a specific period of time. (p. 432)

Periodic inventory. A merchandise inventory determined by counting, weighing, or measuring items of merchandise on hand. (p. 93)

Perpetual inventory. A merchandise inventory determined by keeping a continuous record of increases, decreases, and balance on hand. (p. 93)

Personal property. All property not classified as real property. (p. 227)

Petty cash. An amount of cash kept on hand and used for making small payments. (p. 22)

Plant asset record. An accounting form on which a business records information about each plant asset. (p. 225)

Plant assets. Assets that will be used for a number of years in the operation of a business. (p. 106)

Point-of-sale (POS) terminal. A computer used to collect, store, and report all the information of a sales transaction. (p. 47)

Post-closing trial balance. A trial balance prepared after the closing entries are posted. (p. 122)

Posting. Transferring transaction information from a journal entry to a ledger account. (p. 14)

Preferred stock. Stock that gives stockholders preference in earnings and other rights. (p. 316)

Prepaid expenses. Expenses paid in one fiscal period but not reported as expenses until a later fiscal period. (p. 266)

Present value. The current value of a future cash payment or receipt. (p. 476)

Present value of an annuity. An amount invested at a given interest rate that supports the payments of an annuity. (p. 479)

Price-earnings ratio. The relationship between the market value per share and earnings per share of a stock. (p. 380)

Principal of a note. The original amount of a note. (p. 261)

Production-unit method of depreciation. Calculating estimated annual depreciation expense based on the amount of production expected from a plant asset. (p. 245)

Promissory note. A written and signed promise to pay a sum of money at a specified time. (p. 261)

Purchase order. A completed form authorizing a seller to deliver goods with payment to be made later. (p. 173)

Purchases budget schedule. A statement prepared to show the projected amount of purchases that will be required during a budget period. (p. 420)

Purchases discount. A cash discount on purchases taken by a customer. (p. 18)

Q

Quick assets. Those current assets that are cash or that can be quickly turned into cash. (p. 513)

R

Rate earned on average stockholders' equity. The relationship between net income and average stockholders' equity. (p. 383)

Rate earned on average total assets. The relationship between net income and average total assets. (p. 383)

Rate earned on net sales. The rate found by dividing net income after federal income tax by net sales. (p. 506)

Rate of return. The relationship of money earned compared to the money invested. (p. 477)

Ratio. A comparison between two numbers showing how many times one number exceeds the other. (p. 495)

Real property. Land and anything attached to it. (p. 227)

Realization. Cash received from the sale of assets during liquidation of a partnership. (p. 665)

Responsibility accounting. Assigning control of business revenues, costs, and expenses as a responsibility of a specific manager. (p. 89)

Responsibility statements. Financial statements reporting revenue, costs, and direct expenses under a specific department's control. (p. 111)

Retail method of estimating inventory. Estimating inventory by using a percentage based on both cost and retail prices. (p. 183)

Retained earnings. An amount earned by a corporation and not yet distributed to stockholders. (p. 115)

Retiring a bond issue. Paying the amounts owed to bondholders for a bond issue. (p. 358)

Reversing entry. An entry made at the beginning of one fiscal period to reverse an adjusting entry made in the previous fiscal period. (p. 269)

S

Salary. The money paid for employee services. (p. 60)

Sales budget schedule. A statement that shows the projected net sales for a budget period. (p. 419)

Sales discount. A cash discount on sales. (p. 44)

Sales mix. Relative distribution of sales among various products. (p. 460)

Schedule of accounts payable. A list of vendor accounts, account balances, and total amount due all vendors. (p. 99)

Schedule of accounts receivable. A list of customer accounts, account balances, and total amount due from all customers. (p. 99)

Selling expenses budget schedule. A statement prepared to show projected expenditures related directly to the selling operations. (p. 421)

Serial bonds. Portions of a bond issue that mature on different dates. (p. 358)

Source documents. Original business papers from which information about business transactions is obtained. (p. 7)

Special journal. A journal used to record only one kind of transaction. (p. 8)

Stated-value stock. No-par-value stock that is assigned a value by the corporation. (p. 317)

Statement of cash flows. A statement that summarizes cash receipts and cash payments resulting from business activities during a fiscal period. (p. 532)

Statement of cost of goods manufactured. A statement showing details about the cost of finished goods. (p. 598)

Statement of stockholders' equity. A financial statement that shows changes in a corporation's ownership for a fiscal period. (p. 115)

Stock certificate. Written evidence of the number of shares that each stockholder owns in a corporation. (p. 317)

Stock ledger. A file of stock records for all merchandise on hand. (p. 173)

Stock record. A form used to show the type of merchandise, quantity received, quantity sold, and balance on hand. (p. 173)

Stockholders' equity. The owner's equity in a corporation. (p. 7)

Straight-line method of depreciation. Charging an equal amount of depreciation expense for a plant asset in each year of useful life. (p. 230)

Subscribing for capital stock. Entering into an agreement with a corporation to buy capital stock and pay at a later date. (p. 324)

Subsidiary ledger. A ledger that is summarized in a single general ledger account. (p. 10)

Sum-of-the-years'-digits method of depreciation. Using fractions based on the number of years of a plant asset's useful life to calculate depreciation. (p. 243)

T

Tax base. The maximum amount of earnings on which a tax is calculated. (p. 61)

Tax levy. Authorized action taken by a governmental organization to collect taxes by legal authority. (p. 690)

Term bonds. Bonds that all mature on the same date. (p. 358)

Terminal summary. The report that summarizes the cash and credit card sales of a point-of-sale terminal. (p. 47)

Time value of money. The expectation that invested money will increase over time. (p. 474)

Total costs. All costs for a specific period of time. (p. 445)

Treasury stock. A corporation's own stock that has been issued and reacquired. (p. 350)

Trend analysis. A comparison of the relationship between one item on a financial statement and the same item on a previous fiscal period's financial statement. (p. 496)

Trial balance. A proof of the equality of debits and credits in a general ledger. (p. 100)

Trustee. A person or institution, usually a bank, given legal authorization to administer property for the benefit of property owners. (p. 356)

U

Uncollectible accounts. Accounts receivable that cannot be collected. (p. 200)

Underapplied overhead. The amount by which applied factory overhead is less than actual factory overhead. (p. 589)

Unearned revenue. Revenue received in one fiscal period but not earned until the next fiscal period. (p. 297)

Unit cost. An amount spent for one unit of a specific product or service. (p. 445)

V

Variable costs. Total costs that change in direct proportion to a change in the number of units. (p. 446)

Voucher. A business form used to show an authorized person's approval for a cash payment. (p. 144)

Voucher check. A check with space for writing details about a cash payment. (p. 150)

Voucher register. A journal used to record vouchers. (p. 144)

Voucher system. A set of procedures for controlling cash payments by preparing and approving vouchers before payments are made. (p. 144)

W

Weighted-average inventory costing method. Using the average cost of beginning inventory plus merchandise purchased during a fiscal period to calculate the cost of merchandise sold. (p. 178)

Withholding allowance. A deduction from total earnings for each person legally supported by a taxpayer. (p. 61)

Work in process. Products that are being manufactured but are not yet complete. (p. 561)

Work sheet. A columnar accounting form used to summarize the general ledger information needed to prepare financial statements. (p. 100)

Working capital. The amount of total current assets less total current liabilities. (p. 512)

Writing off an account. Canceling the balance of a customer account because the customer is not expected to pay. (p. 200)

INDEX